DRAMA:

The Major Genres

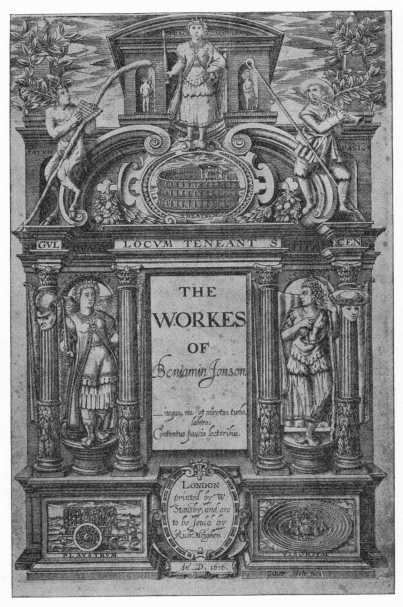

The title page of the 1616 Folio of the Works of Ben Jonson. For a complete description of the details of the design, see pages 340–342. (*Reproduced by courtesy of the Elizabethan Club, Yale University.*)

DRAMA:
The Major Genres

AN INTRODUCTORY CRITICAL ANTHOLOGY

ROBERT HOGAN

UNIVERSITY OF CALIFORNIA, DAVIS

SVEN ERIC MOLIN

RANDOLPH-MACON WOMAN'S COLLEGE

Dodd, Mead & Company

NEW YORK   TORONTO   1970

CAUTION: Professionals and amateurs are hereby warned that *Tartuffe* and *The Silent Woman*, being fully protected by copyright, are subject to royalty. All rights to any kind of performance, including professional, amateur, motion picture, recitation, lecturing, public reading, radio, and television broadcasting, are strictly reserved, and inquiries concerning performances should be addressed to Sven Eric Molin, Randolph-Macon Woman's College, Lynchburg, Virginia.

ACKNOWLEDGMENTS

Grateful acknowledgment is made to the following for permission to use copyrighted material:

GEORGE BRAZILLER, INC. for an extract from *The Green Crow*. Reprinted by permission of George Braziller, Inc. from *The Green Crow* by Sean O'Casey. Copyright 1956 by Sean O'Casey.

CAMBRIDGE UNIVERSITY PRESS for an extract from *The Origin of Attic Comedy* by F. M. Cornford and extracts from *Prolegomena to the Study of Greek Religion* by Jane Ellen Harrison. Reprinted by permission of the Cambridge University Press.

THE CLARENDON PRESS, Oxford, England, for extracts from Gilbert Murray's Preface to *Aristotle on the Art of Poetry* translated by Ingram Bywater. Used with the permission of the Clarendon Press.

DODD, MEAD & COMPANY and THE SOCIETY OF AUTHORS for *The Six of Calais* by George Bernard Shaw. Copyright 1934, 1936, George Bernard Shaw. Copyright 1961, The Public Trustee as Executor of the Estate of George Bernard Shaw. For an excerpt from *Mrs Warren's Profession* by George Bernard Shaw. Copyright 1898, 1913, 1926, 1930, 1933, 1941, George Bernard Shaw. Copyright 1905, Brentano's. Copyright 1957, The Public Trustee as Executor of the Estate of George Bernard Shaw. Reprinted by permission of Dodd, Mead & Company and the Society of Authors.

E. P. DUTTON & CO., INC. for "Pan" from the book *Lemprière's Classical Dictionary* by Dr. J. Lemprière, revised by F. A. Wright. Published by E. P. Dutton & Co., Inc. and reprinted with their permission.

HARCOURT, BRACE & WORLD, INC. for *The Antigone of Sophocles: An English Version* by Dudley Fitts and Robert Fitzgerald, copyright, 1939, by Harcourt, Brace & World, Inc. For extracts from *The Modern Temper* by Joseph Wood Krutch, copyright, 1929, by Harcourt, Brace & World, Inc.; renewed, 1956, by Joseph Wood Krutch. Reprinted

Sᴛ Mᴀʀᴛɪɴ's Pʀᴇss, Iɴᴄ. for *The Plough and the Stars* by Sean O'Casey. Reprinted by permission of Macmillan & Company Ltd. and St Martin's Press, Inc. For extracts from *The Experiments of Sean O'Casey* by Robert Hogan; reprinted by permission of St Martin's Press, Inc. For an extract from *Shakesperian Tragedy* by A. C. Bradley; reprinted by permission of Macmillan & Company Ltd. and St Martin's Press, Inc.

Tʜᴇ Vɪᴋɪɴɢ Pʀᴇss, Iɴᴄ. for an extract from *A View from the Bridge* by Arthur Miller. Copyright © 1955 by Arthur Miller. Reprinted by permission of The Viking Press, Inc.

Yᴀʟᴇ Uɴɪᴠᴇʀsɪᴛʏ Pʀᴇss for Alexander Bakshy's translation of *Yegor Bulychov and the Others* from *Seven Plays of Maxim Gorky*. Copyright, 1945, by Yale University Press and used with their permission. For extracts from *The Pattern of Tragicomedy in Beaumont and Fletcher* by Eugene M. Waith. Copyright, 1952, by Yale University Press and used with their permission.

CONTENTS

PART TWO. COMEDY

PART THREE. TRAGICOMEDY

APPENDIX: TWO PLAYS FOR STUDY

TO THE STUDENT

The pupose of this book is to help you make your own judgments about that form of literature called drama.

What is drama? If you have read a lot of plays and criticism and drama reviews, you may well feel that it is all things to all men, that it is extremely subtle, and that it gives clever men a chance to say whatever they want to say.

The situation is really not that complicated. Although thousands of sophisticated books have been written about it, the drama itself is usually not very sophisticated. It is, in the genuine meaning of the word, "play." It is make-believe, and, like all good make-believe, it fully engages the imagination and deeply appeals to the emotions. In other words, drama is first of all the imitation by actors of people doing something.

When children play "house" or "cowboys and Indians," they imitate actions, but they do not usually tell a coherent story. The drama differs from this kind of imitation because the incidents in a play cling together, cause each other, and add up to some meaningful point that touches the emotions of the audience. In other words, drama second of all has an ordered story, or plot, that is meaningful and moving.

A plot has certain necessities, and the chief of these is a conflict that begins, is developed to a climax, and ends. Probably these two qualities—imitation and plot—are the most important for drama. Without them you don't have drama. Even the complex modern plays of Samuel Becket and Eugene Ionesco, which sometimes claim to be "anti-plays," have imitation and plot.

Further, the dramatist knows that people have all sorts of emotions, and dramatists write all sorts of dramas to appeal to our different emotions. A drama which frightens and appalls at the same time that it draws forth our compassion is usually considered a tragedy. A drama which draws forth our laughter by showing us how ridiculous people frequently are is a comedy. A drama which ambitiously tries to make us weep and laugh at the same time is a tragicomedy, and if it is successful it probably leaves its audience torn between a need to laugh at man's stupidity and a compulsion to weep for his plight.

The emotion a play attempts to arouse determines what kind of play it is, its genre or type. The genres of tragedy, comedy, and tragicomedy are not the only kinds of plays that can be written, but they are probably the kinds that move people the most deeply. They are the major genres. At their best they are high art.

These three genres are the only ones that we shall study in this book, because while it is most difficult to learn to judge well a tragedy, a comedy, or a tragicomedy, these types are the more important. For your own pleasure, after you have worked your way though this book, you can try your critical wings on the easier genres of, say, melodrama, which tries to excite you, or farce, which tries to move you to wild, almost thoughtless laughter. The difference between the major and the minor genres is probably that the minor ones do not attempt to say or do as much. There are excellent, even brilliant, plays in these genres, but plays with a smaller scope. After studying the necessities of the major genres, you will be pretty well prepared to relish the minor ones on your own.

As we said in the beginning, this book is to help you make judgments, to decide how and in what ways a play is good or bad. To do this we present you with a diversity of material. At the core of the book are the texts of eleven plays. Reading them will give you a fair introductory acquaintance with many kinds and styles of plays. You will see eleven concrete answers to the question, What is drama? Although the book is more critical than historical, you will also get a fair survey of the history of the drama in its greatest periods. The plays range in time from an ancient Greek tragedy to a modern Broadway hit, and they range in nationality from the Greek and American through French, Russian, Irish, and English.

These plays are arranged in three sections, plus an Appendix containing two plays on which we ask you to try out the notions you develop in the main part of the book. Each section begins with an essay on the history of the genre followed by a generous selection of quotations from critics who have talked about the genre. These quotations are useful in several ways. They explain the nature of the genre in enough detail to give you a working idea of it. We have arranged them under headings so that you will see the principal points that commentators have made about each genre. They will show you how critics talk about the drama. They amount, in short, to a brief introduction to dramatic criticism.

Almost all of these quotations are by critics who are considered great because of their grasp of and penetration into their subject. We begin with the greatest, Aristotle, because he was the first critic to consider drama in detail and to regard it as the most respected form of literature. As you will come to see, he has provided all subsequent critics with their basic vocabulary for discussing, analyzing, and judging plays. If you have ever talked about something being a "tragedy," for instance, or if you have ever discussed the "plot" and "character" of a work of art, you have probably been an Aristotelian critic, even though you didn't know you were. His criticism is pre-eminent because everyone who thinks seriously about the drama must sooner or later reckon with his pronouncements. During the immense changes of cultural climate that have occurred since Aristotle, every age has felt some applicability of what he said to its own art and has had to reinterpret him for itself. Its own tragedies may be very unlike the Greek, but it feels also a persistent general likeness in the nature of the form of tragedy.

Occasionally in reading the critics, you will see that they disagree among themselves, if not outright, at least in matters of emphasis. Occasionally you will find them wrong or puzzling. While we do not deliberately want to confuse you, we do want to give you a sense of critical variety. You will have to learn to judge the experts, choosing from among their different viewpoints the ones you consider right or more useful or more interesting. In doing this, you will be in the position of the layman trying to judge the experts, and at first you may find yourself uneasy in the process. But with a little reflection, you will see that in drama as in all other fields where expert knowledge is involved you can, by learning more yourself, come to have some sense of how expert the experts are.

From reading the critics, then, you should develop a general idea of each genre that complements your particular knowledge of the plays. Following each play, we give you a brief, informative analysis of it, and after this, we ask you a great many questions about the play. As teachers, we think these questions are the most useful part of the book. You are asked to do three things—to read each play imaginatively with close attention to its details, to compare it with other plays you read, and to compare it with the ideas you have developed from reading the critics. In other words, you are asked to draw together your intellectual knowledge of the genre and your emotional response to the play and to judge each play in the light of your developing range of experience in the drama.

Why do we ask you to do all this? Three statements will begin to answer the question. First, the drama is flourishing in America today, if not especially on Broadway, then off Broadway, in community theatres, and on college and university campuses. The audiences that fill the theatres, however, are not especially informed ones, in the best sense of that word. That is, they do not share a common experience of the theatre that is informed by a knowledge of what drama can do and of what it has done in the past. As a rule (although not without exceptions), community theatres satisfy local taste by presenting warmed-over Broadway hits of several seasons past, while the university theatres present an uneasy program of the avant-garde and the classics, with an occasional nod to Broadway when they want to draw an audience.

Allied to this situation is a critical cleavage that reflects the absence of a theatrical heritage and experience. On the one hand, the popular reviewers approach every play as if it had no real connection with any other plays ever written; for the most part they approach it only as potential "box office," as entertainment whose only problem is the competition of television and the movies. On the other hand, academic writers who do have a sense of the theatrical past tend to approach every play as if it were in direct competition with Shakespeare's highest moment. They write for each other and for the reader capable of understanding a contemplative novel or a lyric poem at its subtlest.

Third, the ideas of genre today are confused and confusing. For instance, Broadway's biggest money-makers are musical comedies, yet the musical comedy is the most formless of genres. Its only necessity is that it contain music, usually adorning some more-or-less slight story line. This formlessness makes critical judgment almost impossible, so the customary judgments are either quantitative ("It's a hit!") or subjective ("I liked it"). For another instance, movie and television dramas so consistently aim at the excitement of melodrama and the glamor of romance that the audience's sense of high art, the most deeply moving art, simply atrophies from disuse.

Because the modern cultural heritage has become so heterogeneous, some commentators say that an idea of genres is misleading or dead beyond revival. As you will see, Joseph Wood Krutch argues that tragedy is impossible in the age of democracy and the common man; *The Death of Tragedy* is the title of a current critical work. We don't think these views are right, or else they are right only if you think of the genres as fixed and definite things, incapable of change. Often in the past, Aristotle has been approached as if he were a rule maker who laid down infallible laws about the drama or as if he were a dry-as-dust philosopher interested only in definitions. We think, by contrast, that his laws and definitions are better understood as hints, insights, suggestions, and probings into the nature of the drama. As we suggested at the beginning, drama is not child's play, but its elements are directly perceived and simple. Like all simplicity in a time of confusion, it has to be worked for, and we think an Aristotelian notion of genres provides a key to understanding and judgment. With some hesitation, we hope, too, that in doing what we ask you to do you find whatever fun comes from looking at something closely and deciding how you feel about it.

Robert Hogan
Sven Eric Molin

February, 1962

ACKNOWLEDGMENTS

We wish to thank the following people for various kinds of assistance: Professors Catherine Nicholson and Abraham Kreusler of Randolph-Macon Woman's College; Professor Albert Kitzhaber of the University of Oregon; Mrs. Genia Graves of Dodd, Mead, & Company; Mr. Robert Watkins of Lynchburg, Virginia; and Betty Hogan and Ann Molin, on whose reserves of toleration and encouragement we drew pretty considerably.

R. H.
S. E. M.

PART ONE

Tragedy

Tragedy

Sometimes from the very furnace of affliction a conviction seems borne to us that somehow, if we could see it, this agony counts as nothing against the heroism and love which appear in it and thrill our hearts. Sometimes we are driven to cry out that these mighty or heavenly spirits who perish are too great for the little space in which they move, and that they vanish not into nothingness but into freedom. Sometimes from these sources and from others comes a presentiment, formless but haunting and even profound, that all the fury of conflict, with its waste and woe, is less than half the truth, even an illusion, "such stuff as dreams are made on." But these faint and scattered intimations that our tragic world, being but a fragment of a whole beyond our vision, must needs be a contradiction and no ultimate truth, avail nothing to interpret the mystery. We remain confronted with the inexplicable fact, or the no less inexplicable appearance, of a world travailing for perfection, but bringing to birth, together with glorious good, an evil which it is able to overcome only by self-torture and self-waste. And this fact or appearance is tragedy.

A. C. BRADLEY

Tragedy, by common consent, is the most magnificent and profound mode of literary expression. Its definition and essence have been of central importance to those people who, over the centuries, have believed that literature was important. You are about to read three of the world's great tragedies, one from ancient Greece, one from Renaissance England, and one from modern Spain. Although two of the plays were written centuries ago and the third pictures a remote village in a foreign country, each has much to tell man in the modern world. Sophocles' play is ultimately about more than Antigone, Shakespeare's about more than Lear, and Lorca's about more than a remote Spanish family. Each dramatist presents to us intuitively and with great force almost inexpressible qualities of humanity. Each play is ultimately about us. The ability to move people shatteringly, to make them feel afresh old and highly poignant emotions, to make an audience tremble on the verge of greatness, is what is common to them and what is common to great tragedy.

The origins of tragedy are buried deeply in pre-history, and we shall leave those origins and their implications to be discussed below by one of our critics, Gilbert Murray. Literary tragedy that was written out and that has passed down to us appears first in the work of the three great Greek tragic writers—Aeschylus, Sophocles, and Euripides—in the fifth century B.C. These writers set a standard for tragedy that has seldom been equaled and scarcely surpassed.

About the plays of these men the philosopher Aristotle (384–322 B.C.) wrote his *Poetics*, which, although it has come to us in fragmentary fashion, is perhaps the best and certainly the most influential piece of literary criticism that the world has ever seen. For centuries Aristotle, reinterpreted and sometimes misinterpreted by Ancient, Renaissance, and Neo-classic critics, sternly dictated the form and the boundaries of tragedy. This stern strictness, this insistence upon Aristotelian "rules" was not quite fair to Aristotle himself, for he was tentative and logical rather than dogmatic.

Although Rome had the gory tragedies of Seneca (c. 4 B.C.–A.D. 65), it was not really until the Renaissance that tragedy regained its vitality. In Elizabethan England, Christopher Marlowe, Thomas Kyd, and Shakespeare mingled the Senecan tragedy with such romantic exuberance that they burst out from the confines of traditional tragic form. In France, Pierre Corneille (1606–84) and Jean Racine (1639–99) generally adhered to what critics considered classic form and the three pseudo-Aristotelian unities of time, place, and action.[1] Germany had to wait until the advent of Goethe (1749–1832) and Schiller (1759–1805) for any great tragic drama.

Among the offshoots of tragedy that deserve note is the revenge tragedy or blood tragedy of such Elizabethans as Kyd, John Webster, and Cyril Tourneur. *Hamlet* is in part a revenge tragedy. These plays by their gory excesses seem frequently more truly melodramatic than tragic.

Another offshoot of tragedy is the eighteenth-century bourgeois or domestic tragedy like *George Barnwell* by the Englishman George Lillo, or *Miss Sarah Sampson* by the German critic and dramatist Gotthold Ephraim Lessing. The domestic tragedy was an attempt to make the tragic hero a common man. Compared to the grandeur of the great tragedies, most of the domestic tragedies seem narrow and flat.

Tragedy in a domestic setting is the scene of many of the plays written by the great Norwegian, Henrik Ibsen (1828–1906). Because of his realistic prose dramas and his tremendous influence, Ibsen deserves more than anyone else the title of the father of the modern drama. Many, perhaps most, critics would deny that Ibsen wrote tragedies; his plays were so different in manner and form from what was usually considered tragedy that any comparison is difficult. We

---

[1] The unities are stage conventions that seem rather arbitrary today. Not all of them were practiced in every Greek play, and not all of them were mentioned by Aristotle. The unity of action means that a play must be a coherent and complete story. The unity of time means that the action should take place within twenty-four hours, and if possible within twelve. The unity of place means that the action should occur in one spot—one building, one street, one room.

The thought behind the unities was the commonsensical one of making the representation of an action seem logical, plausible, and real. However, as we have in this book some plays which are logical, plausible, and real, and which break all of the unities, we have not thought them important enough to use as meaningful keys to understanding the drama.

have the feeling that it is not so much a dramatist's subject or his method that determines a tragedy as it is his intensity of effect. And certainly many critics who deny that Ibsen wrote tragedies would be willing to admit that *Miss Julie* by the Swedish dramatist August Strindberg (1849–1912) and *Riders to the Sea* by the Irishman John Millington Synge (1871–1909), although similarly lacking the outward form, are possibly the best short tragedies ever written.

This battle has carried over into our time, and the critic Joseph Wood Krutch, quoted below, well states the case against tragedy being written in the twentieth century. However, dramatists still make the attempt and plays like *The House of Bernarda Alba* by the Spaniard Federico García Lorca, *Murder in the Cathedral* by the Anglo-American T. S. Eliot (1888–), *Mourning Becomes Electra* and *Long Day's Journey Into Night* by the American Eugene O'Neill (1888–1953), and *Death of a Salesman* by Arthur Miller continue to add fuel to the controversy. This chapter will give you the chance to evaluate one modern tragedy, Lorca's *Bernarda Alba,* by the standards of the past.

One final word about tragedy before you pass into the hands of our critics. The word "tragedy" implies something intensely sad and terrible, but tragedies do not usually end upon a blackly pessimistic note. (Lorca's *Bernarda Alba* is somewhat exceptional in this respect.) If they did, the effect upon the audience would be one of almost intolerable depression. The evil forces in a tragedy most frequently destroy the tragic hero, but the tragedy rarely ends with evil triumphant.

As tragedy is probably the most revealing comment upon humanity, it seems to show us that the downfall of the human individual is perhaps inescapable. The individual inevitably has some flaw or makes some error in judgment. The hero, like any man, is human. He deviates from morality or from a full knowledge of his situation, and his deviation destroys him. Yet perhaps you remember the story of Pandora's box which contained all the evil qualities that have since bedeviled mankind and which Pandora let loose upon the world. In the box remained one more quality to be let loose—hope. Or, to take another example, the story of Adam and Eve who sinned in the garden of Eden and were fiercely punished. Yet before they were sent out into the world to work out their punishment, they were also given hope.

The quality of hope is affirmative. It is necessary to morality and to a striving for a reasoned understanding of life and, therefore, necessary to tragedy. If there were no hope, there would be no consciousness of the moral and intellectual life; and if there were no such consciousness a tragic downfall would not only be untragic, it would also be meaningless. After every tragic action must come, at the end of the play, a reaffirmation of morality and a hope that tomorrow the world will be better.

And, of course, perhaps it will.

The Critics

THE CLASSIC STATEMENT

ARISTOTLE, from *The Poetics:*

VI. . . . Let us now discuss Tragedy, resuming its formal definition, as resulting from what has been already said.

Tragedy, then, is an imitation of an action that is serious, complete, and of a certain magnitude; in language embellished with each kind of artistic ornament, the several kinds being found in separate parts of the play; in the form of action, not of narrative; through pity and fear effecting the proper purgation of these emotions. By "language embellished," I mean language into which rhythm, "harmony," and song enter. By "the several kinds in separate parts," I mean that some parts are rendered through the medium of verse alone, others again with the aid of song.

Now as tragic imitation implies persons acting, it necessarily follows, in the first place, that Spectacular equipment will be a part of Tragedy. Next, Song and Diction, for these are the medium of imitation. By "Diction" I mean the mere metrical arrangement of the words: as for "Song," it is a term whose sense everyone understands.

Again, Tragedy is the imitation of an action; and an action implies personal agents, who necessarily possess certain distinctive qualities both of character and thought; for it is by these that we qualify actions themselves, and these—thought and character—are the two natural causes from which actions spring, and on actions again all success or failure depends. Hence, the Plot is the imitation of the action: for by plot I here mean the arrangement of the incidents. By Character I mean that in virtue of which we ascribe certain qualities to the agents. Thought is required wherever a statement is proved, or, it may be, a general truth enunciated. Every Tragedy, therefore, must have six parts, which parts determine its quality—namely, Plot, Character, Diction, Thought, Spectacle, Song. Two of the parts constitute the medium of imitation, one the manner, and three the objects of imitation. And these complete the list. These elements have been employed, we may say, by the poets to a man; in fact, every play contains Spectacular elements as well as Character, Plot, Diction, Song, and Thought.

But most important of all is the structure of the incidents. For Tragedy is an imitation, not of men, but of an action and of life, and life consists in action, and its end is a mode of action, not a quality. Now character determines men's qualities, but it is by their actions that they are happy or the reverse. Dramatic action, therefore, is not with a view to the representation of character: character comes in as subsidiary to the actions. Hence the incidents and the plot are the end of a tragedy; and the end is the chief thing of all. Again, without action there cannot be a tragedy; there may be without character. The tragedies of most of our modern poets fail in the rendering of character; and of poets in general this is often true. It is the same in painting; and here lies the difference between Zeuxis and Polygnotus. Polygnotus delineates character well: the style of Zeuxis is devoid of ethical quality. Again, if you string together a set of speeches expressive of character, and well finished in point of diction and thought, you will not produce the essential tragic effect nearly so well as with a play which, however deficient in these respects, yet has a plot and artistically constructed incidents. Besides which, the most powerful elements of emotional interest in Tragedy—Peripeteia or Reversal of the Situation, and Recognition scenes—are parts of the plot. A further proof is that novices in the art attain to finish of diction and precision of portraiture before they can construct the plot. It is the same with almost all the early poets.

The Plot, then, is the first principle, and, as it were, the soul of a tragedy: Character holds the second place. A similar fact is seen in painting. The most beautiful colors, laid on confusedly, will not give as much pleasure as the chalk outline of a portrait. Thus Tragedy is the imitation of an action, and of the agents mainly with a view to the action.

Third in order is Thought—that is, the faculty of saying what is possible and pertinent in given circumstances. In the case of oratory, this is the function of the political art and of the art of rhetoric: and so indeed the older poets make their characters speak the language of civic life; the poets of our time, the language of the rhetoricians. Character is that which reveals moral purpose, showing what kind of things a man chooses or avoids. Speeches, therefore, which do not make this manifest, or in which the speaker does not choose or avoid anything whatever, are not expressive of character. Thought, on the other hand, is found where something is proved to be or not to be, or a general maxim is enunciated.

Fourth among the elements enumerated comes Diction; by which I mean, as has been already said, the expression of the meaning in words; and its essence is the same both in verse and prose.

Of the remaining elements Song holds the chief place among the embellishments.

The Spectacle has, indeed, an emotional attraction of its own, but, of all the parts, it is the least artistic, and connected least with the art of poetry. For the power of Tragedy, we may be sure, is felt even apart from representation and actors. Besides, the production of spectacular effects depends more on the art of the stage machinist than on that of the poet.

VII. These principles being established, let us now discuss the proper structure of the Plot, since this is the first and most important thing in Tragedy.

Now, according to our definition, Tragedy is an imitation of an action that is complete, and whole, and of a certain magnitude; for there may be a whole that is wanting in magnitude.

A whole is that which has a beginning, a middle, and an end. A beginning is that which does not itself follow anything by causal necessity, but after which something naturally is or comes to be. An end, on the contrary, is that which itself naturally follows some other thing, either by necessity, or as a rule, but has nothing following it. A middle is that which follows something as some other thing follows it. A well-constructed plot, therefore, must neither begin nor end at haphazard, but conform to these principles.

Again, a beautiful object, whether it be a living organism or any whole composed of parts, must not only have an orderly arrangement of parts, but must also be of a certain magnitude; for beauty depends on magnitude and order. Hence a very small animal organism cannot be beautiful; for the view of it is confused, the object being seen in an almost imperceptible moment of time. Nor, again, can one of vast size be beautiful; for as the eye cannot take it all in at once, the unity and sense of the whole is lost for the spectator; as for instance if there were one a thousand miles long. As, therefore, in the case of animate bodies and organisms a certain magnitude is necessary, and a magnitude which may be easily embraced in one view; so in the plot, a certain length is necessary, and a length which can be easily embraced by the memory. The limit of length in relation to dramatic competition and sensuous presentment is no part of artistic theory. For had it been the rule for a hundred tragedies to compete together, the performance would have been regulated by the water clock—as indeed we are told was formerly done. But the limit as fixed by the nature of the drama itself is this: the greater the length, the more beautiful will the piece be by reason of its size, provided that the whole be perspicuous. And to define the matter roughly, we may say that the proper magnitude is comprised within such limits that the sequence of events, according to the law of probability or necessity, will admit of a change from bad fortune to good, or from good fortune to bad.

VIII. Unity of plot does not, as some persons think, consist in the unity of the hero. For infinitely various are the incidents in one man's life which cannot be reduced to unity; and so, too, there are many actions of one man out of which we cannot make one action. Hence the error, as it appears, of all poets who have composed a *Heracleid,* a *Theseid,* or other poems of the kind. They imagine that as Heracles was one man, the story of Heracles must also be a unity. But Homer, as in all else he is of surpassing merit, here too—whether from art or natural genius—seems to have happily discerned the truth. In composing the *Odyssey* he did not include all the adventures of Odysseus—such as his wound on Parnassus, or his feigned madness at the mustering of the host—incidents between which there was no necessary or probable connection: but he made the *Odyssey,* and likewise the *Iliad,* to center round an action that in our sense of the word is one. As, therefore, in the other imitative arts, the imitation is one when the object imitated is one, so the plot, being an imitation of an action, must imitate one action and that a whole, the structural union of the parts being such that, if any one of them is displaced or removed, the whole will be disjointed and disturbed. For a thing whose presence or absence makes no visible difference is not an organic part of the whole.

IX. It is, moreover, evident from what has been said that it is not the function of the poet to relate what has happened, but what may happen —what is possible according to the law of probability or necessity. The poet and the historian differ not by writing in verse or in prose. The work of Herodotus might be put into verse, and it would still be a species of history, with meter no less than without it. The true difference is that one relates what has happened, the other what may happen. Poetry, therefore, is a more philosophical and a higher thing than history: for poetry tends to express the universal, history the particular. By the universal I mean how a person of a certain type will on occasion speak or act, according to the law of probability or necessity; and it is this universality at which poetry aims in the names she attaches to the personages. The particular is— for example—what Alcibiades did or suffered. In Comedy this is already apparent: for here the poet first constructs the plot on the lines of probability, and then inserts characteristic names—unlike the lampooners who write about particular individuals. But tragedians still keep to real names, the reason being that what is possible is credible: what has not happened we do not at once feel sure to be possible, but what has happened is manifestly possible: otherwise it would not have happened. Still there are even some tragedies in

which there are only one or two well-known names, the rest being fictitious. In others, none are well known—as in Agathon's *Antheus,* where incidents and names alike are fictitious, and yet they give none the less pleasure. We must not, therefore, at all costs keep to the received legends, which are the usual subjects of Tragedy. Indeed, it would be absurd to attempt it; for even subjects that are known are known only to a few, and yet give pleasure to all. It clearly follows that the poet or "maker" should be the maker of plots rather than of verses, since he is a poet because he imitates, and what he imitates are actions. And even if he chances to take an historical subject, he is none the less a poet; for there is no reason why some events that have actually happened should not conform to the law of the probable and possible, and in virtue of that quality in them he is their poet or maker.

Of all plots and actions the epeisodic are the worst. I call a plot "epeisodic" in which the episodes or acts succeed one another without probable or necessary sequence. Bad poets compose such pieces by their own fault, good poets, to please the players; for, as they write show pieces for competition, they stretch the plot beyond its capacity and are often forced to break the natural continuity.

But again, Tragedy is an imitation not only of a complete action, but of events inspiring fear or pity. Such an effect is best produced when the events come on us by surprise; and the effect is heightened when, at the same time, they follow as cause and effect. The tragic wonder will then be greater than if they happened of themselves or by accident, for even coincidences are most striking when they have an air of design. We may instance the statue of Mitys at Argos, which fell upon his murderer while he was a spectator at a festival, and killed him. Such events seem not to be due to mere chance. Plots, therefore, constructed on these principles are necessarily the best.

X. Plots are either Simple or Complex, for the actions in real life, of which the plots are an imitation, obviously show a similar distinction. An action which is one and continuous in the sense above defined, I call Simple, when the change of fortune takes place without Reversal of the Situation and without Recognition.

A Complex action is one in which the change is accompanied by such Reversal, or by Recognition, or by both. These last should arise from the internal structure of the plot, so that what follows should be the necessary or probable result of the preceding action. It makes all the difference whether any given event is a case of *propter hoc* or *post hoc*.

XI. Reversal of the Situation is a change by which the action veers round to its opposite, subject always to our rule of probability or necessity. Thus in the *Oedipus*, the messenger comes to cheer Oedipus and free him from his alarms about his mother, but by revealing who he is, he produces the opposite effect. Again in the *Lynceus*, Lynceus is being led away to his death, and Danaus goes with him, meaning to slay him; but the outcome of the preceding incidents is that Danaus is killed and Lynceus saved.

Recognition, as the name indicates, is a change from ignorance to knowledge, producing love or hate between the persons destined by the poet for good or bad fortune. The best form of recognition is coincident with a Reversal of the Situation, as in the *Oedipus*. There are indeed other forms. Even inanimate things of the most trivial kind may in a sense be objects of recognition. Again, we may recognize or discover whether a person has done a thing or not. But the recognition which is most intimately connected with the plot and action is, as we have said, the recognition of persons. This recognition, combined with Reversal, will produce either pity or fear; and actions producing these effects are those which, by our definition, Tragedy represents. Moreover, it is upon such situations that the issues of good or bad fortune will depend. Recognition, then, being between persons, it may happen that one person only is recognized by the other—when the latter is already known—or it may be necessary that the recognition should be on both sides. Thus Iphigenia is revealed to Orestes by the sending of the letter; but another act of recognition is required to make Orestes known to Iphigenia.

Two parts, then, of the Plot—Reversal of the Situation and Recognition—turn upon surprises. A third part is the Scene of Suffering. The Scene of Suffering is a destructive or painful action, such as death on the stage, bodily agony, wounds and the like. . . .

XIII. As the sequel to what has already been said, we must proceed to consider what the poet should aim at, and what he should avoid, in constructing his plots; and by what means the specific effect of Tragedy will be produced.

A perfect tragedy should, as we have seen, be arranged not on the simple but on the complex plan. It should, moreover, imitate actions which excite pity and fear, this being the distinctive mark of tragic imitation. It follows plainly, in the first place, that the change of fortune presented must not be the spectacle of a virtuous man brought from prosperity to adversity: for this moves neither pity nor fear; it merely shocks us. Nor, again, that of a bad man passing from adversity to prosperity, for nothing can be more alien to the spirit of Tragedy: it possesses no single tragic quality; it neither satisfies the moral sense nor calls forth pity or fear. Nor, again, should the downfall of the utter villain be exhibited. A plot of this kind would, doubtless, satisfy the moral sense, but it would inspire neither pity nor fear; for pity is aroused by unmerited misfortune, fear by the misfortune of a man like ourselves. Such an event, therefore, will be neither pitiful nor terrible. There remains, then, the character between these two extremes— that of a man who is not eminently good and just, yet whose misfortune is brought about not by vice or depravity, but by some error or frailty. He must be one who is highly renowned and prosperous—a personage like Oedipus, Thyestes, or other illustrious men of such families.

A well-constructed plot should, therefore, be single in its issue, rather than double as some maintain. The change of fortune should be not from bad to good, but, reversely, from good to bad. It should come about as the result not of vice, but of some great error or frailty, in a character either such as we have described, or better rather than worse. The practice of the stage bears out our view. At first the poets recounted any legend that came in their way. Now, the best tragedies are founded on the story of a few houses—on the fortunes of Alcmaeon, Oedipus, Orestes, Meleager, Thyestes, Telephus, and those others who have done or suffered something terrible. A tragedy, then, to be perfect according to the rules of art should be of this construction. Hence they are in error who censure Euripides just because he follows this principle in his plays, many of which end unhappily. It is, as we have said, the right ending. The best proof is that, on the stage and in dramatic competition, such plays, if well worked out, are the most tragic in effect; and Euripides, faulty though he may be in the general management of his subject, yet is felt to be the most tragic of the poets.

In the second rank comes the kind of tragedy which some place first. Like the *Odyssey*, it has a double thread of plot, and also an opposite catastrophe for the good and for the bad. It is accounted the best because of the weakness of the spectators; for the poet is guided in what he writes by the wishes of his audience. The pleasure, however, thence derived is not the true tragic pleasure. It is proper rather to Comedy, where those who, in the piece, are the deadliest enemies —like Orestes and Aegisthus—quit the stage as friends at the close, and no one slays or is slain.

XIV. Fear and pity may be aroused by spectacular means; but they may also result from the inner structure of the piece, which is the better way, and indicates a superior poet. For the plot ought to be so constructed that, even without the aid of the eye, he who hears the tale told will thrill with horror and melt to pity at what takes place. This is the impression we should receive from hearing the story of the *Oedipus*. But to produce this effect by the mere spectacle is a less artistic method, and dependent on extraneous aids. Those who employ spectacular means to create a sense not of the terrible but only the monstrous, are strangers to the purpose of Tragedy; for we must not demand of Tragedy any and every kind of pleasure, but only that which is proper to it. And since the pleasure which the poet should afford is that which comes from pity and fear through imitation, it is evident that this quality must be impressed upon the incidents.

Let us then determine what are the circumstances which strike us as terrible or pitiful.

Actions capable of this effect must happen between persons who are either friends or enemies or indifferent to one another. If an enemy kills an enemy, there is nothing to excite pity either in the act or the intention —except so far as the suffering in itself is pitiful. So again with indifferent persons. But when the tragic incident occurs between those who are near or dear to one another—if, for example, a brother kills, or intends to kill, a brother, a son his father, a mother her son, a son his mother, or any other deed of the kind is done— these are the situations to be looked for by the poet. He may not indeed destroy the framework of the received legends—the fact for instance, that

Clytemnestra was slain by Orestes and Eriphyle by Alcmaeon—but he ought to show invention of his own, and skillfully handle the traditional material. Let us explain more clearly what is meant by skillful handling.

The action may be done consciously and with knowledge of the persons, in the manner of the older poets. It is thus too that Euripides makes Medea slay her children. Or, again, the deed of horror may be done, but done in ignorance, and the tie of kinship or friendship be discovered afterwards. The *Oedipus* of Sophocles is an example. Here, indeed, the incident is outside the drama proper; but cases occur where it falls within the action of the play: one may cite the *Alcmaeon* of Astydamas, or Telegonus in the *Wounded Odysseus*. Again, there is a third case—<to be about to act with knowledge of the persons and then not to act. The fourth case is> when someone is about to do an irreparable deed through ignorance, and makes the discovery before it is done. These are the only possible ways. For the deed must either be done or not done—and that wittingly or unwittingly. But of all these ways, to be about to act knowing the persons, and then not to act, is the worst. It is shocking without being tragic, for no disaster follows. It is, therefore, never, or very rarely, found in poetry. One instance, however, is in the *Antigone*, where Haemon threatens to kill Creon. The next and better way is that the deed should be perpetrated. Still better, that it should be perpetrated in ignorance, and the discovery made afterwards. There is then nothing to shock us, while the discovery produces a startling effect. The last case is the best, as when in the *Cresphontes* Merope is about to slay her son, but, recognizing who he is, spares his life. So in the *Iphigenia,* the sister recognizes the brother just in time. Again in the *Helle,* the son recognizes the mother when on the point of giving her up. This, then, is why a few families only, as has been already observed, furnish the subjects of tragedy. It was not art, but happy chance, that led the poets in search of subjects to impress the tragic quality upon their plots. They are compelled, therefore, to have recourse to those houses whose history contains moving incidents like these.

Enough has now been said concerning the structure of the incidents, and the right kind of plot.

XV. In respect of Character there are four things to be aimed at. First, and most important, it must be good. Now any speech or action that manifests moral purpose of any kind will be expressive of character: the character will be good if the purpose is good. This rule is relative to each class. Even a woman may be good, and also a slave; though the woman may be said to be an inferior being, and the slave quite worthless. The second thing to aim at is propriety. There is a type of manly valor; but valor in a woman, or unscrupulous cleverness, is inappropriate. Thirdly, character must be true to life: for this is a distinct thing from goodness and propriety, as here described. The fourth point is consistency, for though the subject of the imitation, who suggested the type, be inconsistent, still he must be consistently inconsistent. As an example of motiveless degradation of character we have Menelaus in

the *Orestes;* of character indecorous and inappropriate, the lament of Odysseus in the *Scylla,* and the speech of Melanippe; of inconsistency, the *Iphigenia at Aulis*—for Iphigenia the suppliant in no way resembles her later self.

As in the structure of the plot, so too in the portraiture of character, the poet should always aim either at the necessary or the probable. Thus a person of a given character should speak or act in a given way, by the rule either of necessity or of probability, just as this event should follow that by necessary or probable sequence. It is therefore evident that the unraveling of the plot, no less than the complication, must arise out of the plot itself, it must not be brought about by the *Deus ex Machina* —as in the *Medea,* or in the Return of the Greeks in the *Iliad.* The *Deus ex Machina* should be employed only for events external to the drama— for antecedent or subsequent events, which lie beyond the range of human knowledge, and which require to be reported or foretold; for to the gods we ascribe the power of seeing all things. Within the action there must be nothing irrational. If the irrational cannot be excluded, it should be outside the scope of the tragedy. Such is the irrational element in the *Oedipus* of Sophocles.

Again, since Tragedy is an imitation of persons who are above the common level, the example of good portrait painters should be followed. They, while reproducing the distinctive form of the original, make a likeness which is true to life and yet more beautiful. So too the poet, in representing men who are irascible or indolent, or have other defects of character, should preserve the type and yet ennoble it. In this way Achilles is portrayed by Agathon and Homer.

These then are rules the poet should observe. Nor should he neglect those appeals to the senses, which, though not among the essentials, are the concomitants of poetry; for here too there is much room for error. But of this enough has been said in our published treatises.

XVI. What Recognition is has been already explained. We will now enumerate its kinds.

First, the least artistic form, which, from poverty of wit, is most commonly employed—recognition by signs. Of these some are congenital—such as "the spear which the earth-born race bear on their bodies," or the stars introduced by Carcinus in his *Thyestes*. Others are acquired after birth, and of these some are bodily marks, as scars; some external tokens, as necklaces, or the little ark in the *Tyro* by which the discovery is effected. Even these admit of more or less skillful treatment. Thus in the recognition of Odysseus by his scar, the discovery is made in one way by the nurse, in another by the swineherds. The use of tokens for the express purpose of proof—and, indeed, any formal proof with or without tokens—is a less artistic mode of recognition. A better kind is that which comes about by a turn of incident, as in the Bath Scene in the *Odyssey*.

Next come the recognitions invented at will by the poet, and on that account wanting in art. For example, Orestes in the *Iphigenia* reveals the fact that he is Orestes. She, indeed, makes herself known by the letter; but he, by speaking himself and saying what the poet, not what the plot, requires. This, therefore, is nearly allied to the fault above mentioned, for Orestes might as well have brought tokens with him. Another similar instance is the "voice of the shuttle" in the *Tereus* of Sophocles.

The third kind depends on memory when the sight of some object awakens a feeling: as in the *Cyprians* of Dicaeogenes, where the hero breaks into tears on seeing the picture; or again in the *Lay of Alcinous*, where Odysseus, hearing the minstrel play the lyre, recalls the past and weeps, and hence the recognition.

The fourth kind is by process of reasoning. Thus in the *Choëphori:* "Someone resembling me has come: no one resembles me but Orestes: therefore Orestes has come." Such too is the discovery made by Iphigenia in the play of Polyidus the Sophist. It was a natural reflection for Orestes to make, "So I too must die at the altar like my sister." So, again, in the *Tydeus* of Theodectes, the father says, "I came to find my son, and I lose my own life." So too in the *Phineidae:* the women, on seeing the place, inferred their fate—"Here we are doomed to die, for here we were cast forth." Again, there is a composite kind of recognition involving false inference on the part of one of the characters, as in the Odysseus Disguised as a Messenger. A said <that no one else was able to bend the bow; . . . hence B (the disguised Odysseus) imagined that A would> recognize the bow which, in fact, he had not seen; and to bring about a recognition by this means—the expectation that A would recognize the bow—is false inference.

But, of all recognitions, the best is that which arises from the incidents themselves, where the startling discovery is made by natural means. Such is that in the *Oedipus* of Sophocles, and in the *Iphigenia;* for it was natural that Iphigenia should wish to dispatch a letter. These recognitions alone dispense with the artificial aid of tokens or amulets. Next come the recognitions by process of reasoning. . . .

XVIII. Every tragedy falls into two parts—Complication and Unraveling or Denouement. Incidents extraneous to the action are frequently combined with a portion of the action proper, to form the Complication; the rest is the Unraveling. By the Complication I mean all that extends from the beginning of the action to the part which marks the turning point to good or bad fortune. The Unraveling is that which extends from the beginning of the change to the end. Thus, in the *Lynceus* of Theodectes the Complication consists of the incidents presupposed in the drama, the seizure of the child, and then again * * <The Unraveling> extends from the accusation of murder to the end.

There are four kinds of Tragedy: the Complex, depending entirely on Reversal of the Situation and Recognition; the Pathetic (where the motive is passion)—such as the tragedies on Ajax and Ixion; the Ethical (where the motives are ethical)—such as the *Phthiotides* and the *Peleus.* The fourth kind is the Simple. <We here exclude the purely spectacular element>, exemplified by the *Phorcides,* the *Prometheus,* and scenes laid in Hades.

The poet should endeavor, if possible, to combine all poetic elements; or, failing that, the greatest number and those the most important; the more so, in face of the caviling criticism of the day. For whereas there have hitherto been good poets, each in his own branch, the critics now expect one man to surpass all others in their several lines of excellence.

In speaking of a tragedy as the same or different, the best test to take is the plot. Identity exists where the Complication and Unraveling are the same. Many poets tie the knot well, but unravel it ill. Both arts, however, should always be mastered.

Again, the poet should remember what has been often said, and not make an Epic structure into a Tragedy—by an Epic structure I mean one with a multiplicity of plots—as if, for instance, you were to make a tragedy out of the entire story of the *Iliad.* In the Epic poem, owing to its length, each part assumes its proper magnitude. In the drama the result is far from answering to the poet's expectation. The proof is that the poets who have dramatized the whole story of the Fall of Troy, instead of selecting portions, like Euripides, or who have taken the whole tale of Niobe, and not a part of her story, like Aeschylus, either fail utterly or meet with poor success on the stage. Even Agathon has been known to fail from this one defect. In his Reversals of the Situation, however, he shows a marvelous skill in the effort to hit the popular taste—to produce a tragic effect that satisfies the moral sense. This effect is produced when the clever rogue, like Sisyphus, is outwitted, or the brave

villain defeated. Such an event is probable in Agathon's sense of the word:
"it is probable," he says, "that many
things should happen contrary to probability."

The Chorus too should be regarded
as one of the actors; it should be an
integral part of the whole, and share
in the action, in the manner not of
Euripides but of Sophocles. As for
the later poets, their choral songs per-
tain as little to the subject of the piece
as to that of any other tragedy. They
are, therefore, sung as mere interludes
—a practice first begun by Agathon.
Yet what difference is there between
introducing such choral interludes and
transferring a speech, or even a whole
act, from one play to another? . . .

XXII. The perfection of style is to
be clear without being mean. The
clearest style is that which uses only
current or proper words; at the same
time it is mean—witness the poetry of
Cleophon and of Sthenelus. That diction, on the other hand, is lofty and
raised above the commonplace which
employs unusual words. By unusual, I
mean strange (or rare) words, metaphorical, lengthened—anything, in
short, that differs from the normal
idiom. Yet a style wholly composed of
such words is either a riddle or a
jargon; a riddle, if it consists of metaphors; a jargon, if it consists of strange
(or rare) words. For the essence of
a riddle is to express true facts under
impossible combinations. Now this
cannot be done by any arrangement
of ordinary words, but by the use of
metaphor it can. Such is the riddle:
"A man I saw who on another man
had glued the bronze by aid of fire,"
and others of the same kind. A diction that is made up of strange (or

rare) terms is a jargon. A certain in-
fusion, therefore, of these elements is
necessary to style; for the strange (or
rare) word, the metaphorical, the ornamental, and the other kinds above
mentioned, will raise it above the commonplace and mean, while the use of
proper words will make it perspicuous.
But nothing contributes more to produce a clearness of diction that is remote from commonness than the
lengthening, contraction, and alteration of words. For by deviating in
exceptional cases from the normal
idiom, the language will gain distinction; while, at the same time, the partial conformity with usage will give
perspicuity. . . . To employ such
license at all obtrusively is, no doubt,
grotesque; but in any mode of poetic
diction there must be moderation.
Even metaphors, strange (or rare)
words, or any similar forms of speech,
would produce the like effect if used
without propriety and with the express
purpose of being ludicrous. How great
a difference is made by the appropriate use of lengthening, may be seen in
Epic poetry by the insertion of ordinary forms in the verse. So, again, if
we take a strange (or rare) word, a
metaphor, or any similar mode of expression, and replace it by the current
or proper term, the truth of our observation will be manifest. . . .

Again, Ariphrades ridiculed the
tragedians for using phrases which no
one would employ in ordinary speech.
. . . It is precisely because such
phrases are not part of the current
idiom that they give distinction to the
style. This, however, he failed to see.

It is a great matter to observe propriety in these several modes of expression, as also in compound words,

strange (or rare) words, and so forth. But the greatest thing by far is to have a command of metaphor. This alone cannot be imparted by another; it is the mark of genius, for to make good metaphors implies an eye for resemblances.

Of the various kinds of words, the compound are best adapted to dithyrambs, rare words to heroic poetry, metaphors to iambic. In heroic poetry, indeed, all these varieties are serviceable. But in iambic verse, which reproduces, as far as may be, familiar speech, the most appropriate words are those which are found even in prose. These are—the current or proper, the metaphorical, the ornamental.

Concerning Tragedy and imitation by means of action this may suffice.

SOME MODERN APPROACHES

DRAMA, RITUAL, AND SOCIETY

GILBERT MURRAY, from *The Classical Tradition in Poetry:*

Drama was held by Aristotle to spring spontaneously from the needs of human nature, which loves imitating and loves rhythm and therefore is pretty sure to indulge in rhythmic imitations. And it seems to be found, in one form or another, among most peoples in the world who are not debarred from it by some religious scruple. Yet it is well to remember that all the things that we habitually do seem to us to spring from human nature, while a great many of them in reality owe their present form to a quite complicated and fortuitous historical process. The drama that we know in Europe is his-

torically derived from Greek sources; and the same may perhaps be true of Indian and Chinese drama as well. The dates at any rate permit of it.

Now the peculiar characteristic of classical Greek drama is the sharp and untransgressed division between tragedy and comedy. The two styles are separate and never combined. No classical author is known to have written in both. At the end of a rather voluminous literature which has appeared recently about the origin of the Greek drama, I think we may accept the general conclusions reached in the preceding chapter: that both forms of drama have their origin in ritual; that the ritual was connected with the cult of what is sometimes called a Year-Daemon, or a Vegetation God, or a Life Spirit, which everywhere forms the heart of Mediterranean religion; and, lastly, that we can find a sort of degraded survival of the original form of drama in the Mummers' Play, which still survives among the peasantry of Europe. In that play there are two main elements. The hero, like the typical Year-Daemon, appears as a child who grows tall and strong with surpassing swiftness and is married amid a revel or *Comos* of rejoicing. Secondly, he fights various enemies and eventually meets some dark antagonist, by whom he is killed, though he shows a tendency to come to life afterwards. We know from Herodotus that tragedy represented the sufferings of Dionysus, and that these were, except for certain details, identical with those of Osiris. And Osiris, we know, was slain by his enemy, the burning Set; torn in pieces as a corn-sheaf is torn and scattered over the fields; bewailed and sought for in vain during many months, and rediscovered in fresh life when the new corn began to shoot in spring. Tragedy is the enactment of the death of the Year-Spirit; and comedy is the enactment of his marriage, or rather of the *Comos* which accompanies his marriage. The centre of tragedy is a death; the centre of comedy is a union of lovers.

Thus Greek drama starts, not as a mere picture of ordinary life, or even of ordinary adventure, but as a recreation, or *mimesis*, of the two most intense experiences that life affords; a re-creation of life at its highest power. The purpose of the drama was —it is generally agreed—originally magical. The marriage *Comos* was intended actually to produce fertility; the death-celebration was the expulsion of evil from the community, the casting-out of the Old Year with its burden of decay, of the polluted, the Scapegoat, the Sin-Bearer. It is well to remember that dramatic performances were introduced into Rome *inter alia caelestis irae placamina* in order to cure a pestilence.[1] This occurred actually during the lifetime of Aristotle. But Aristotle himself has forgotten as completely as we have that tragedy was ever a magical rite: he treats it simply as an artistic performance, and judges it, not for any concrete effect it may have on the public health, but simply on aesthetic grounds. And this shows us that, for whatever reason it was created, drama persisted and increased because it answered to some constant need in human nature. . . .

First, let us remember how Greek

[1] With other things to appease the anger of heaven. Livy, VII, 2.

tragedy dwells on the danger of greatness and the envy of the gods. Sometimes the poets are at pains to explain that it is not greatness in itself that brings on disaster, but only the pride or cruelty that is often associated with greatness. But in the main popular conception there is no such subtlety: life is seen in the tragic pattern. As the Sun every year and every morning begins weak and lovely, then grows strong and fierce, then excessive and intolerable, and then, by reason of that excess, is doomed to die, so runs the story with trees, beasts, and men, with kings and heroes and cities. Herodotus sees the history of the Persian War in the same tragic pattern: Xerxes, tall, strong, beautiful, lord of a vast empire, became proud and desired too much, was led into Atê and stricken down. Thucydides sees the history of Athens in the same pattern: incredible achievements, beauty, splendour; then pride, battle, determination to win at all costs; crime, brutality, dishonour, and defeat after all. That is the essential tragic idea, however we translate it into modern language, climax followed by decline, or pride by judgement. . . .

JOSEPH WOOD KRUTCH, from *The Tragic Fallacy:*

An age which could really "appreciate" Shakespeare or Sophocles would have something comparable to put beside them—something like them, not necessarily in form, or spirit, but at least in magnitude—some vision of life which would be, however different, equally ample and passionate. But when we move to put a modern masterpiece beside them, when we seek to compare them with, let us say, a *Ghosts* or a *Weavers,* we shrink as from the impulse to commit some folly and we feel as though we were about to superimpose Bowling Green upon the Great Prairies in order to ascertain which is the larger. The question, we see, is not primarily one of art but of the two worlds which two minds inhabited. No increased powers of expression, no greater gift for words, could have transformed Ibsen into Shakespeare. The materials out of which the latter created his works— his conception of human dignity, his sense of the importance of human passions, his vision of the amplitude of human life—simply did not and could not exist for Ibsen, as they did not and could not exist for his contemporaries. God and Man and Nature had all somehow dwindled in the course of the intervening centuries, not because the realistic creed of modern art led us to seek out mean people, but because this meanness of human life was somehow thrust upon us by the operation of that same process which led to the development of realistic theories of art by which our vision could be justified.

Hence, though we still apply, sometimes, the adjective "tragic" to one or another of those modern works of literature which describe human misery and which end more sadly even than they begin, the term is a misnomer since it is obvious that the works in question have nothing in common with the classical examples of the genre and produce in the reader a sense of depression which is the exact opposite of that elation generated when the spirit of a Shakespeare rises joyously superior to the outward calamities which he recounts and celebrates the greatness of the human spirit whose travail he describes. Tragedies, in that only sense of the word which has any distinctive meaning, are no longer written in either the dramatic or any other form, and the fact is not to be accounted for in any merely literary terms. It is not the result of any fashion in literature or of any deliberation to write about human nature or character under different aspects, any more than it is of either any greater sensitiveness of feeling which would make us shrink from the contemplation of the suffering of Medea or Othello or of any greater optimism which would make us more likely to see life in more cheerful terms. It is, on the contrary, the result of one of those enfeeblements of the human spirit not unlike that described in the previous chapter of this essay, and a further illustration of that gradual weakening of man's confidence in his ability to impose upon the phenomenon of life an interpretation acceptable to his desires which is the subject of the whole of the present discussion. . . .

And yet, nevertheless, the idea of nobility is inseparable from the idea of tragedy, which cannot exist without it. If tragedy is not the imitation or even the modified representation of noble actions it is certainly a representation of actions *considered* as noble, and herein lies its essential nature, since no man can conceive it unless he is capable of believing in the greatness and importance of man. Its action is usually, if not always, calamitous, because it is only in calamity that the human spirit has the opportunity to reveal itself triumphant over the outward universe which fails to conquer it; but this calamity in tragedy is only a means to an end and the essential thing which distinguishes real tragedy from those distressing modern works sometimes called by its name is the fact that it is in the former alone that the artist has found himself capable of considering and of making us consider that his people and his actions have that amplitude and importance which make them noble. Tragedy arises then when, as in Periclean Greece or Elizabethan England, a people fully aware of the calamities of life is nevertheless serenely confident of the greatness of man, whose mighty passions and supreme fortitude are revealed when one of these calamities overtakes him.

. . . A too sophisticated society on the other hand—one which, like ours, has outgrown not merely the simple optimism of the child but also that vigorous, one might almost say adolescent, faith in the nobility of man which marks a Sophocles or a Shakespeare, has neither fairy tales to assure it that all is always right in the end nor tragedies to make it believe that it rises superior in soul to the outward calamities which befall it.

Distrusting its thought, despising its passions, realizing its impotent unimportance in the universe, it can tell itself no stories except those which make it still more acutely aware of its trivial miseries. When its heroes (sad misnomer for the pitiful creatures who people contemporary fiction) are struck down it is not, like Oedipus, by the gods that they are struck but only, like Oswald Alving, by syphilis, for they know that the gods, even if they existed, would not trouble with them and they cannot attribute to themselves in art an im-

portance in which they do not believe. Their so-called tragedies do not and cannot end with one of those splendid calamities which in Shakespeare seem to reverberate through the universe, because they cannot believe that the universe trembles when their love is, like Romeo's, cut off or when the place where they (small as they are) have gathered up their trivial treasure is, like Othello's sanctuary, defiled. Instead, mean misery piles on mean misery, petty misfortune follows petty misfortune, and despair becomes intolerable because it is no longer even significant or important.

ARTHUR MILLER, from *On Social Plays:*

Time is moving; there is a world to make, a civilization to create that will move toward the only goal the humanistic, democratic mind can ever accept with honor. It is a world in which the human being can live as a naturally political, naturally private, naturally engaged person, a world in which once again a true tragic victory may be scored.

But that victory is not really possible unless the individual is more than theoretically capable of being recognized by the powers that lead society. Specifically, when men live, as they do under any industrialized system, as integers who have no weight, no *person*, excepting as customers, draftees, machine tenders, ideologists, or whatever, it is unlikely (and in my opinion impossible) that a dramatic picture of them can really overcome the public knowledge of their nature in real life. In such a society, be it communistic or capitalistic, man is not tragic, he is pathetic. The tragic figure must have certain innate powers which he uses to pass over the boundaries of the known social law—the accepted mores of his people—in order to test and discover necessity. Such a quest implies that the individual who has moved onto that course must be somehow recognized by the law, by the mores, by the powers that design—be they anthropomorphic gods or economic and political laws—as having the worth, the innate value, of a whole people asking a basic question and demanding its answer. We are so atomized socially that no character in a play can conceivably stand as our vanguard, as our heroic questioner. Our society—and I am speaking of every industrialized society in the world—is so complex, each person being so specialized an integer, that the moment any individual is dramatically characterized and set forth as a hero, our common sense reduces him to the size of a complainer, a misfit. For deep down we no longer believe in the rules of the tragic contest; we no longer believe that some ultimate sense can in fact be made of social causation, or in the possibility that any individual can, by a heroic effort, make sense of it. Thus the man that is driven to question the moral chaos in which we live ends up in our estimate as a possibly commendable but definitely odd fellow, and probably as a compulsively driven neurotic. In place of a social aim which called an all-around excellence—physical, intellectual, and moral—the ultimate good, we have set up a goal which can best be characterized as "happiness"—namely, staying out of trouble. This concept is the end result of the truce which all of us have made with society. And a truce implies two enemies. When the truce is broken it means either that the individual has broken out of his ordained place as an integer, or that the society has broken the law by harming him unjustly—that is, it has not left him alone to be a peaceful integer. In the heroic and tragic time the act of questioning the-way-things-are implied that a quest was being carried on to discover an ultimate law or way of life which would yield excellence; in the present time the quest is that of a man made unhappy by rootlessness and, in every important modern play, by a man who is essentially a victim. We have abstracted from the Greek drama its air of doom, its physical destruction of the hero, but its victory escapes us. Thus it has even become difficult to separate in our minds the ideas of the pathetic and of the tragic. And behind this melting of the two lies the overwhelming power of the modern industrial state, the ignorance of each person in it of anything but his own technique as an economic integer, and the elevation of that state to a holy, quite religious sphere.

THE TRAGIC STRUCTURE

JOHN DRYDEN, from *An Essay of Dramatic Poesy:*

Aristotle indeed divides the integral parts of a play into four. First, the *Protasis,* or entrance, which gives light only to the characters of the persons, and proceeds very little into any part of the action. Secondly, the *Epitasis,* or working up of the plot; where the play grows warmer, the design or action of it is drawing on, and you see something promising that it will come to pass. Thirdly, the *Catastasis*, called by the Romans, *Status*, the height and full growth of the play: we may call it properly the counter-turn, which destroys that expectation, imbroils the action in new difficulties, and leaves you far distant from that hope in which it found you; as you may have observed in a violent stream resisted by a narrow passage,—it runs round to an eddy, and carries back the waters with more swiftness than it brought them on. Lastly, the *Catastrophe*, which the Grecians called λύσις, the French *le dénouement,* and we the discovery, or unravelling of the plot: there you see all things settling again upon their first foundations; and, the obstacles which hindered the design or action of the play once removed, it ends with that resemblance of truth and nature, that the audience are satisfied with the conduct of it.

SCOTT BUCHANAN, from *Poetry and Mathematics:*

The fundamental notions in tragedy are called *hybris* and *nemesis.* The first is the attitude of arrogance or insolence that arises from blindness in human nature. The second is the eventual consequence of that blindness and arrogance, the vengeance that the ignored factor in a situation takes on man and his virtues. These are moralistic terms but the intellectualistic transformation is easy. It can be performed on the terms of Aristotle's analysis of tragedy.

A tragic character must have besides hybris, the virtue of irony. This quality is the exercise of the capacity to discover and systematize clear ideas. It appears at first as a naïve idealism

that makes it impossible to take circumstances at their face value, and expresses itself in a kind of satirical questioning, such as that of Socrates. Accompanying it is a sense of humor which condenses and dispels intervening fogs. At bottom it is a faith that there are ideas to be discovered and a conviction that the task is not easy. St. Francis and Don Quixote are additional good examples in literature. Dramatic tragedy usually discloses such a character in some advanced stage when the idea is in sight, so that action is understood as aiming to achieve its clarification. This is the situation presented in the prologue.

Action moves on exemplifying and expanding the idea. Even at this point there are at least two possible interpretations of the events. One is held by the audience who usually know the outcome already. The other is that held by the hero who is possessed of the idea to such an extent that he builds up a separate story or interpretation for himself in conformity with his ideal. Events pile up and are turned to his account by the alchemy of his own rationality. The situation becomes complicated and each event is charged with dramatic foreshadowing. The hero sees dilemmas in everything and sticks to his course in spite of the oppositions. His determination finally reaches desperation. This is the complication of the situation and the advent of hybris.

At length he is faced with some crucial and unavoidable predicament. He must decide. Using all his intellectual powers he makes the only decision possible on his interpretation of the situation. This is the crisis. In terms of mathematics and poetry, he has developed a system of relations, his idea; and the events have supplied a corresponding set of qualities. The situation is a full-rounded sphere.

Events come faster and pile themselves high on either side of his chosen path. They now have a threatening aspect for him, but there is no turning back. There is a dull inevitability about them. Finally they break and all is ruin with no compensating circumstance. This is the reversal of circumstance and catastrophe. The rounded sphere of apparent success is in a thousand pieces.

Then if he has the true quality of irony there is a recognition of what he had ignored. There comes the still small voice in the calm following the thunder and the earthquake, the voice of a god speaking not words of pity or revenge, but the decrees of necessity on his situation and his idea. Both are thrown upon a vaster background than he had envisaged, the doings of fate. In these decrees there is light and the hero recognizes himself, his idea, and his plight in terms of laws that are not for yesterday, today or tomorrow, but for always. This is the purgation.

But this may be only one episode, the first of a trilogy. The same hero, or another implicated character goes on into the new sphere with the new version of the eternal verities. No man should be judged happy until he is dead.

This pattern is the Greek view of life. It is the method of their and our science, history, and philosophy. In it poetry becomes criticism of life. It is, I believe, the final metaphysical conclusion of Greek philosophy in Plato and Aristotle.

KENNETH BURKE, from *A Grammar of Motives:*

. . . Stated broadly the dialectical (agonistic) approach to knowledge is through the *act* of assertion, whereby one "suffers" the kind of knowledge that is the reciprocal of his act.

This is the process embodied in tragedy, where the agent's action involves a corresponding passion, and from the sufferance of the passion there arises an understanding of the act, an understanding that transcends the act. The act, in being an assertion, has called forth a counter-assertion in the elements that compose its context. And when the agent is enabled to see in terms of this counter-assertion, he has transcended the state that characterized him at the start. In this final state of tragic vision, intrinsic and extrinsic motivations are merged. That is, although purely circumstantial factors participate in his tragic destiny, these are not felt as exclusively external, or scenic; for they bring about a representative kind of accident, the kind of accident that belongs with the agent's particular kind of character.

It is deplorable, but not tragic, simply to be a victim of circumstance, for there is an important distinction between destiny and sheer victimization. Sheer victimization is not an assertion —and it naturally makes not for vision but for frustration. The victimizing circumstances, or accidents, seem arbitrary and exorbitant, even "silly." But at the moment of tragic vision, the fatal accidents are felt to bear fully upon the act, while the act itself is felt to have summed up the character of the agent. Nor is this vision a sense of cosmic persecution; for in seeing the self in terms of the situation which the act has brought about, the agent transcends the self. And whereas the finality and solemnity of death often leads to the assumption that the tragic vision is possible only at the point of death, we must recognize that dialectically one may die many times (in fact, each time an assertion leads beyond itself to a new birth) and that tragedy is but a special case of the dialectical process in general. . . .

We can discern something of the "tragic" grammar behind the Greek proverb's way of saying "one learns by experience"; "*ta pathemata mathemata*," the suffered is the learned. We can also catch glimpses of a relation between dialectic and mathematics . . . in the fact that *mathemata* means both things learned in general, and the mathematical sciences (arithmetic, geometry, astronomy) in particular. A *pathema* (of the same root as our word, "passive") is the opposite of a *poiema* (a deed, doing, action, act; anything done; a poem). A *pathema* can refer variously to a suffering, misfortune, passive condition, situation, state of mind. The initial requirement for a tragedy, however, is an *action*. Hence, by our interpretation, if the proverb were to be complete at the risk of redundance, it would have three terms: *poiemata* [the act], *pathemata* [the sufferance or state], *mathemata* [the thing learned], suggesting that the act organizes the opposition (brings to the fore whatever factors resist or modify the act), that the agent thus "suffers" this opposition, and as he learns to take the oppositional motives into account, widening his terminology accordingly, he has arrived at a higher order of understanding.

THE TRAGIC HERO

GILBERT MURRAY, from *The Classical Tradition in Poetry:*

Put briefly, it seems that historically the tragic hero is derived both from the Life Spirit—call him Dionysus or what you will—who comes to save the community with the fruits of the New Year, and from the polluted Old Year, the *Pharmakos* or Scapegoat, who is cast out to die or to wander in the wilderness, bearing with him the sins of the community. Every Year-Spirit is first new and then old, first pure and then polluted; and both phases tend to be combined in the tragic hero. Oedipus is the saviour of Thebes, the being whose advent delivered Thebes from death; Oedipus is also the abomination, the polluter of Thebes, the thing which must be cast out, if Thebes is to live and be clean. Orestes is the saviour who comes to redeem the House of Atreus from the rule of murderers; Orestes is also the murderer, the matricide, whose polluting presence must be removed from all human society. Pentheus, the stricken blasphemer, is, as we have seen, identical with Dionysus, the sacrificed god. The conflict between two rights or two commands of conscience, which is said by Hegel to be the essence of tragedy, is already present in the tragic hero himself.

The emotion which the striving and the death of such a hero rouses in the normal man must be far from simple. We feel love for him because he is a saviour and a champion, a brave man fighting and suffering to redeem those who without him would be lost; we feel horror toward him because of his sins and pollutions, and their awful expiation. And both feelings must have been intensified in ancient tragedy by the subconscious memory that the sins he expiates are really ours. The Greek hero, when he suffers, almost always suffers in order to save others.[1] And the artist knows how to make us feel that such suffering is a better thing than success.

It is only through sacrifice and suffering that courage and greatness of soul can be made visible, and the dramatist who knows his business knows how to make the beauty of such sacrifice resplendent while hiding away the ugliness of the mere pain and humiliation. He shows the beauty of human character fighting against fate and circumstance; he conceals the heavy toll of defeats and weaknesses and infidelities which fate and circumstance generally levy on the way.

If this analysis is historically correct, and I believe it is, it goes far toward answering our whole problem about "the pleasure of tragedy." . . .

S. H. BUTCHER, from *Aristotle's Theory of Poetry and Fine Art:*

The tragic sufferer is a man like ourselves . . . ; and on this inner likeness the effect of tragedy, as described in the *Poetics,* mainly hinges. Without it our complete sympathy would not be enlisted. The resemblance on which

Aristotle insists is one of moral character. His hero (*Poet.* ch. xiii) is not a man of flawless perfection, nor yet one of consummate villainy; by which we must not understand that he has merely average or mediocre qualities. He rises, indeed, above the common level in moral elevation and dignity, but he is not free from frailties and imperfections. His must be a rich and full humanity, composed of elements which other men possess, but blended more harmoniously or of more potent quality. So much human nature must there be in him that we are able in some sense to identify ourselves with him, to make his misfortunes our own. At the same time he is raised above us in external dignity and station. He is a prince or famous man who falls from a height of greatness. Apart from the impressive effect of the contrast so presented, there is a gain in the hero being placed at an ideal distance from the spectator. We are not confronted with outward conditions of life too like our own. The pressure of immediate reality is removed; we are not painfully reminded of the cares of our own material existence. We have here part of the refining process which the tragic emotions undergo within the region of art. They are disengaged from the petty interests of self, and are on the way to being universalised.

The tragic fear, though modified in passing under the conditions of art, is not any languid emotion. It differs, indeed, from the crushing apprehension of personal disaster. In reading or witnessing the *Oedipus Tyrannus* we are not possessed with a fear that we may be placed in circumstances similar to those of Oedipus, or be overtaken by the same calamities. Yet a thrill

---

[1] This point has not been sufficiently realized. Thus Oedipus suffers for Thebes, Orestes for his father, Alcestis for her husband, Prometheus for mankind, Eteocles for Thebes, Menoikeus for Thebes, Antigone for her brother, Iphigenia in Aulis for Hellas, Macaria for her brethren, etc. Some suffer for the Gods or for duty, but nearly all suffer for somebody or something. The tragic hero is thus affiliated to the Suffering God and the Babylonian "Faithful Son."

runs through us, a shudder of horror or of vague foreboding. The feeling is immediate and unreflective. The tension of mind, the agonised expectation with which we await the impending catastrophe, springs from our sympathy with the hero in whose existence we have for the time merged our own. The events as they pass before us seem almost as if we were directly concerned. We are brought into a mood in which we feel that we too are liable to suffering. Yet the object of dread is not a definite evil threatening us at close quarters. In the spectacle of another's errors or misfortunes, in the shocks and blows of circumstance, we read the "doubtful doom of human kind." The vividness with which the imagination pictures unrealised calamity produces the same intensity of impression as if the danger were at hand. The true tragic fear becomes an almost impersonal emotion, attaching itself not so much to this or that particular incident, as to the general course of the action which is for us an image of human destiny. We are thrilled with awe at the greatness of the issues thus unfolded, and with the moral inevitableness of the result. In this sense of awe the emotions of fear and pity are blended. . . .

With the exception of the definition of tragedy itself, probably no passage in the *Poetics* has given rise to so much criticism as the description of the ideal tragic hero in ch. xiii. The qualities requisite to such a character are here deduced from the primary fact that the function of tragedy is to produce the *katharsis* of pity and fear; pity being felt for a person who, if not wholly innocent, meets with suffering beyond his deserts; fear being awakened when the sufferer is a man of like nature with ourselves. Tragic character must be exhibited through the medium of a plot which has the capacity of giving full satisfaction to these emotions. Certain types, therefore, of character and certain forms of catastrophe are at once excluded, as failing either in whole or in part to produce the tragic effect. . . .

We now come to the ideal protagonist of tragedy. . . . He is composed of mixed elements, by no means supremely good, but a man "like ourselves". . . . The expression, if taken alone, might seem to describe a person of mediocre virtue and average powers. But Aristotle must not be read in detached sections; and the comparison of ch. ii and ch. xv with our passage shows us that this character, while it has its basis in reality, transcends it by a certain moral elevation. We could wish that Aristotle had gone farther and said explicitly that in power, even more than in virtue, the tragic hero must be raised above the ordinary level; that he must possess a deeper vein of feeling, or heightened powers of intellect or will; that the morally trivial, rather than the morally bad, is fatal to tragic effect. As it is, we arrive at the result that the tragic hero is a man of noble nature, like ourselves in elemental feelings and emotions; idealised, indeed, but with so large a share of our common humanity as to enlist our eager interest and sympathy. He falls from a position of lofty eminence; and the disaster that wrecks his life may be traced not to deliberate wickedness, but to some great error or frailty.

This last expression is not free from difficulty, and has been variously in-

terpreted. . . . In either case, however, the error is unintentional; it
arises from want of knowledge; and its
moral quality will depend on whether
the individual is himself responsible
for his ignorance.

Distinct from this, but still limited
in its reference to a single act, is the
. . . fault or error where the act is
conscious and intentional, but not deliberate. Such are acts committed in
anger or passion.

Lastly, the word may denote a defect of character, distinct on the one
hand from an isolated error or fault,
and, on the other, from the vice which
has its seat in a depraved will. This
use, though rarer, is still Aristotelian.
Under this head would be included
any human frailty or moral weakness,
a flaw of character that is not tainted
by a vicious purpose. In our passage
there is much to be said in favour of
the last sense, as it is here brought
into relation with other words of
purely moral significance, words moreover which describe not an isolated
act, but a more permanent state.

Francis MacDonald Cornford, from
The Origin of Attic Comedy:

Turning from plot to character, we
find again that Comedy alike enjoys
a greater freedom than Tragedy, and,
as a consequence, departs less from
the old tradition. In Tragedy, as Aristotle says, "the persons in the play do
not go through their action (or 'experience') in order to give a representation of their characters; they include
a representation of character for the
sake of the action." The tragic poet
starts with a given action, the experience of a certain group of legendary
persons. These persons generally have

only that one context, in which their
whole being moves: they are the
people who went through just that
great and significant experience. . . .
Their very names—Agamemnon, Cly-
taemnestra, Aegisthus, Cassandra—
bring that action at once before us,
and nothing else. They come (so to
say) as supporting this action, which
is itself the primary thing. It dictates
their characters, demanding that these
shall be moulded to fit the experience
they must carry through to its traditional end. Hence, the tragedians were
forced to create characters capable of
doing and suffering what the story relates. The action requires certain motives; the characters must be such as
can have those motives, and, further,
such that those motives will be the
characteristic motives. So the tragic
poet must work from action to motive,
and from motive to character. These
causes led to the creation of types
which had never before appeared in
literature, and could not have been
conceived except by a man of genius
working under these stern necessities.
We may instance the heroic maiden,
Antigone, and a whole gallery of
women in Euripides. These are not
taken from the Epic, still less from
ordinary Athenian life; for we know
from Aristophanes how they startled
and scandalised Athenian society.
Once invented, these characters, of
course, became types for the imitation of inferior artists. But originally
they were imaginative creations. The
effect was to enlarge and deepen
knowledge of human nature, by dis-
covering possibilities of character and
motive that lie within its compass, but
are rarely shown in common life, and
are beyond the power of observation

of ordinary men, who, indeed, not seldom remain unable to conceive them, even when the artist has put them before their eyes.

SAMUEL JOHNSON, from *Preface to Shakespeare:*

His [Shakespeare's] adherence to general nature has exposed him to the censure of criticks, who form their judgments upon narrow principles. *Dennis* [1] and *Rhymer* [2] think his Romans not sufficiently *Roman;* and *Voltaire* [3] censures his kings as not completely royal. *Dennis* is offended, that *Menenius,* a senator of *Rome,* should play the buffoon; and *Voltaire* perhaps thinks decency violated when the *Danish* Usurper is represented as a drunkard. But *Shakespeare* always makes nature predominate over accident; and if he preserves the essential character, is not very careful of distinctions superinduced and adventitious. His story requires Romans or kings, but he thinks only on men. He knew that *Rome,* like every other city, had men of all dispositions; and wanting a buffoon, he went into the senate-house for that which the senate-house would certainly have afforded him. He was inclined to shew an usurper and a murderer not only odious but despicable, he therefore added drunkenness to his other qualities, knowing that kings love wine like other men, and that wine exerts its natural power upon kings. These are the petty cavils of petty minds; a poet overlooks the casual distinction of country and condition, as a painter, satisfied with the figure, neglects the drapery.

THE TRAGIC STYLE

WILLIAM G. MCCOLLOM, from *Tragedy:*

The words these actors speak will tell the playwright's story, define the characters, elaborate their conflicts; the spoken word will be his chief means of showing how well or badly the characters reason and his only medium for that "sententious excitation to virtue" which until recently seemed an important part of the dramatist's concern; and as David Hume once wrote, "the force of expression and beauty of oratorial numbers" will serve to make a terrible action bearable, to raise "a pleasure from the bosom of uneasiness." Moreover, the language of tragedy is beautiful in itself. Although we have been warned by modern critics not to experience that *ekstasis* which Longinus held to be the effect of great literature, we do make judgments based on the "density" of a given passage, its "levels of meaning," and so on. And critics trained to assess the value of a lyrical poem according to the complexity of its internal relations have sought to show that the image patterns in a tragedy may constitute the chief organizing principle of the work. Whether or not we accept this position, we can agree that the imagery of tragedy enormously enriches its aesthetic quality.

In tragedy the language plays many parts. In the great writers, however, it has a purpose not so far mentioned. For it acts as the medium not only of plot and character but of character-in-action; and in so doing it communi-

---

[1] John Dennis, English critic.
[2] Thomas Rhymer, English critic.
[3] Pseudonym of François-Marie Arouet, French satirist (1694–1778).

cates a profound sense of human consciousness and purpose, of the ways in which these interact, and of their confrontation with the outside world. In so far as tragedy attains the universality of great art, it does so by representing the human situation through words that audiences can almost imagine as their own. We smile at Coleridge's remark that he had a touch of Hamlet about his nature. We are not so frank in this.

In asking what a dramatist is "saying" in his play, we mean: How does this action apply to the society which produced it or, better, to the actions of men in all times and all places? In the best tragedies, the writer usually communicates his meaning by implication, and so we are driven to assert that on the whole he indicates certain attitudes toward pride, egotism, and other ethical traits. Yet his words are the fullest objectification of these attitudes, whether subtle, confused, profound, obscurantist, or whatever. The plays of Marlowe obviously suggest conflicting judgments in the poet himself as to the proper limits of individual assertiveness. Marlowe was drawn to the ruthlessness his heroes represent, and his words, glittering like precious stones, are the best evidence for our belief. Since his plays insufficiently criticize—through words —the folly of his Tamburlaines and Guises, he betrays his immaturity as a writer.

Though customarily speaking by implication, great tragedy does not always avoid explicit statement. Aeschylus, Sophocles, and Shakespeare do not allow aesthetic scruples to keep them from praise or blame or from recording in specific and general terms

the interaction of character and fate. In Sophocles' *Antigone*, for example, the words clearly tell us (1) that this is *not* a tragedy of pure fate, (2) that Antigone's catastrophe is the product of fate *and* her self-willed temper, and (3) that Creon's downfall is the result of his own wrongdoing. Although the characters often testify to the power of Fate, Fortune, Love (Aphrodite), and the gods, these references are balanced against clear assertions of human responsibility. As Antigone begins her journey to the rocky vault which will be her tomb, the Chorus declares that she had "rushed forward to the utmost verge of daring; and against that throne where Justice sits on high thou hast fallen, my daughter, with a grievous fall." A few lines later, after Antigone laments that Polyneices' death has "undone" her life, the Chorus continues: "Reverent action claims a certain praise for reverence; but an offence against power cannot be brooked by him who hath power in his keeping. Thy self-willed temper hath wrought thy ruin." With characteristic timidity, the Chorus is avoiding a blunt statement of the merits of the dispute. But while absolving Antigone of serious moral guilt and implying a mysterious intervention of the supernatural, the elders are none the less asserting that Antigone's reverence has expressed itself in provocative actions which have inevitably destroyed her. If the choral speeches in *Antigone* are frequently equivocal (and this is owing not to Sophocles' fear of explicit statement but to the character of the speakers), the dénouement clearly emphasizes the faults of the human actors, particularly Creon. The results of Creon's autocracy are now apparent. When the Chorus concludes by praising wisdom (*to phronein*) and piety (*sebas*) and condemning pride (*auchê*), there is no ambiguity. And there is no doubt that the words are rightly applied.

Tragedy speaks to audiences about themselves and their problems. It is no accident that the most famous line in *Hamlet* touches an ontological question. While serving other and possibly more refined purposes, *Hamlet* will continue to furnish audiences with popular and practical philosophy and to stimulate their metaphysical impulses. . . .

Before proceeding further, we may distinguish three situations in which character functions in the theatre:

1. Character speaks to character, thereby tending to create dramatic illusion.

2. Character speaks to the audience but retains its histrionic consciousness, thereby breaking full dramatic illusion but preserving aesthetic distance. This is the situation during the choral odes in Greek tragedy.

3. Character speaks to the audience not as a character but as a prologue, surrogate for the dramatist, and so on, thereby breaking dramatic illusion and reducing aesthetic distance. This is the situation obtaining when a playwright, deprived of his Chorus or *nuntius,* wishes to speak quite directly to his audience. He may or may not be aware of the extent to which he has deprived his character of dramatic quality. . . .

Greek tragedy could fuse the dramatic and the extra-dramatic in a form unavoidable to the Elizabethan playwright. If read superficially, the choral odes of Sophocles occasionally seem unconnected with the dramatic action and even with the emotion that the Chorus is presumably experiencing at the moment. Actually the Chorus may be expressing both a conscious and a subconscious response to the action, and through playing one against the other, the playwright may be introducing his evaluation of the tragic issues. In the second Episode of *Antigone,* the Chorus listens to the debate between the heroine and Creon and makes only two comments indicating its attitude. It calls Antigone passionate and unbending . . . and later asks Creon: "Wilt thou indeed rob thy son of this maiden?" . . . Antigone is placed under guard. In the following Stasimon,[1] the Chorus begins by lamenting the fate of the house of Labdacus. It then asserts that hope has been destroyed "by the blood-stained dust due to the gods infernal, and by folly in speech and frenzy at the heart." The Chorus is referring to the dust Antigone has thrown over Polyneices' body despite Creon's decree. Since the elders have already called Antigone "passionate," one will probably assume that they are now charging *her* with folly and frenzy. But as one studies the ode as a whole, one sees that, consciously or unconsciously, the Chorus is making an oblique criticism of Creon, although the words just given more obviously refer to Antigone. As Mr. Goheen notices: ". . . in its full context, . . . [this] strophe suggests that Antigone, who was concerned about divine laws and their transgression, may be more right than Creon who accused her of

---

[1] In tragedy, a choral ode.

folly." [2] The Chorus, more expressive than it knows, does not fully grasp the implications of its own words. Sophocles, we conclude, is voicing his own sense of the complexity of the tragic issue. . . .

Profound understanding of human nature and sensitive response to its dilemmas will not in themselves yield tragic poetry of a high order, but without these qualifications the most gifted writer can hardly produce tragic art. Tragedy embodies artistic insight into the intrinsication of sense, passion, reason, will, and necessity; and the tone of the tragic diction accords with this insight. Attending to the dramatic action, we are continually aware of the tension between what is willed and what is beyond will (sensation, passion, fate). Attending to the style, we are continually impressed by its controlled intensity.

In such writers as Aeschylus, Sophocles, Shakespeare, and Racine, however they may differ in other ways, this tone will be sounded and resounded. In Sophocles and Racine the element of control is relatively prominent; in Aeschylus and Shakespeare the intensity may seem to dominate; but the tonal differences among these four are differences of degree. . . .

ALLARDYCE NICOLL, from *The Theory of Drama:*

. . . we find that, whereas many plays popular in their own time have irretrievably perished . . . there are plays, such as *Oedipus Rex, Hamlet,*

[2] Robert F. Goheen, *The Imagery of Sophocles' "Antigone"* (Princeton, New Jersey: Princeton University Press, 1951), pp. 61–62.

and *Othello,* which remain permanent masterpieces, inspiring the theatre to ever new efforts as decade follows decade. Unquestionably the greater part of their strength lies in their poetry— to use that word in a general sense so as to apply to all writing of creative order; it is this which has preserved them as living things over the long stretch of years from the time they were written up till to-day. It would be wrong, however, to speak merely of their poetical power, for the 'poetry' of a *Hamlet* or an *Othello* is not as the poetry of a *Paradise Lost* or a *Divina Commedia.* It is poetry applied to, and ever kept subservient to, dramatic necessity. . . . What Shakespeare has done is to put himself, as it were, in the place of the finest, most gifted, and most inspired actor . . . and to write down for him the most delicate and subtle dialogue he could possibly have imagined. This, we may say, is what is meant by perfect dramatic poetry; it is simply inspired improvisation captured by the artist as it is extemporized and made permanent. When an actor speaks of a 'good' part he does not always mean merely a 'fat' part; more often he means a part with such dialogue that every line, every word, rings true. Similarly 'good dialogue' does not by any means invariably signify poetic dialogue; it is dramatic language subordinated to character and eminently suitable for histrionic enunciation. The perfect dramatist is he who is able to put himself in the place, not of a series of living characters, but of a company of actors each of whom is taking a certain part in his play, and who at the same time has the ability to prevent his own personality from intruding into what should be the dialogue of another's. There may be as much poetry, as much sheer lyricism, as you like in a drama; only, that poetry must not seem the poetic speech of one man, and it must be subordinate to the essential requirements of stage performance.

. . . In general, it may be said, it would appear that the Elizabethan dramatists were right in employing verse in their tragedies, and that the more modern prose development is uninformed, an experiment dangerous and antagonistic to the spirit of high tragedy.

That which is appealed to most in a tragedy is the emotions. Tragedy does not often direct itself to the intellect as such; it deals always with the deepest moments of human feeling. There are few tragedies of pure thought; even *Hamlet*, which is more philosophical than the majority of the Elizabethan dramas, has emotion constantly threading the intellectual framework of Hamlet's character. It has been proved, however, by the practice of long ages and of diverse races, that the emotions invariably find their fittest literary expression in rhythmical form. There is a certain natural melody in passion of any kind, and tragedy, in dealing with the passions, will therefore find its true utterance in rhythmical words. It is possible here, perhaps, to make an exception for some modern plays in which the emotional element seems to be continually and consistently repressed, and where consequently prose might be considered a more fitting medium. . . .

Poetic Prose. Modern playwrights, however, are faced by a serious diffi-culty, for the blank verse which was natural, right, and creative in the Elizabethan age seems now to have grown stale and outworn. The nineteenth- and twentieth-century tradition in the 'poetic play' has yielded hardly anything of worth, and it appears unlikely that there will be any recrudescence of a vital dramatic expression by means of this form in the future. Already, on the other hand, there are signs that some dramatists, unconsciously feeling the want of that medium which so greatly served Shakespeare and his contemporaries, are striving toward a dramatic language which contains in itself something of the poetic quality. . . . None of these is the result of an unconscious lapse from prose rhythm into the movement of blank verse; in each there is a deliberate evolving of a special kind of prose music, with a form harmonious and proper to itself. Herein, perhaps, lies a hope for the tragic drama of the future. Blank verse has served its day; the rhythmic prose may, in the future, take the place that it occupied in the seventeenth century.

The Universality of Rhythm. In speaking, then, of 'verse' in tragic drama, this new 'poetic prose' may be put alongside of the special form of dialogue used by the Elizabethans; and, thus broadening the significance of the term, we may well say that, as a means of raising the events of a drama above the levels of real life and as the natural expression for emotion, verse claims the close attention of every tragic dramatist. Before he casts off verse, possibly because of some hastily conceived critical theory, he must consider well whether verse be not one of the necessary and integral parts of true drama, or at least whether in abandoning verse he will not be forced to give to his drama something else as a recompense for its loss. Verse, too, has other forces. The figment of the music of the spheres has at least a symbolic truth about it. Through rhythm and melody we seem to reach some universal chords of human feeling. By mere rhythm alone we certainly touch vibrations otherwise impossible of realization. A foreign prose work may be unintelligible to us, but a foreign symphony will be interpreted by us as easily as by a native of the land that gave it birth; and even a foreign poem, well recited, may awaken feelings and emotions in our hearts beyond the unintelligibility of the words. Rhythm, after all, is a common heritage; it strikes deep at primeval and general instincts of mankind. It is, moreover, not confined to man; it is universal to the whole of nature. The songs of the birds possess a melody pleasurable not only to themselves but to humanity. There are symphonies of sounds and of colours appreciated by the entirety of the natural world. Such a consideration of the force of verse obviously leads us back to our primal consideration of universality. Herein lies one other main means of securing the broader atmosphere demanded by tragedy. Verse will aid not only in removing tragedy from the levels of actual life, but in giving to it that universality demanded by the highest art. . . .

In dispensing with verse, therefore, the adherents of the realistic prose drama appear to be abandoning a legitimate method of securing atmosphere and of giving pleasure. Verse is seen to be not merely a traditional remnant of choral song or cathedral chant; it is something closely connected with the inner spirit of tragedy itself. If verse and the opportunity for securing lyricism be neglected then other qualities must be deeply stressed in an endeavour to atone for the loss. Occasionally it is not possible so to stress these other qualities; often their introduction seems unnatural and strained. The ordinary prose tragedy fails partly because of a lack of melody, partly because prose, by its very nature, prohibits the introduction of many of those features which in the poetic drama seem but natural and just.

Eric Bentley, from *The Playwright as Thinker:*

. . . Ibsen pretends to write flat dialogue, but the opaque, uninviting sentences carry rich meanings which are enforced only by their context. An Ibsenite sentence often performs four or five functions at once. It sheds light on the character speaking, on the character spoken to, on the character spoken about; it furthers the plot; it functions ironically in conveying to the audience a meaning different from that conveyed to the characters (and it is not merely that the characters say things which mean more to the audience than to them, but that they also say things which, as one senses, mean more to the characters than to the audience); finally, an Ibsenite sentence is part of the rhythmic pattern which constitutes the whole act. The naturalistic prose, then, is not there for its own sake. It is not there to display Ibsen's ability to write "natural" conversation. It is as rich in artifice as the verse of *Peer Gynt*. Its very naturalness is the final artifice, the art that conceals art. It is—above all—a way of giving concreteness and immediacy to themes that might have led a lesser artist into grandiosity and abstraction. It is anti-Wagnerite. . . . Ibsen did not reject poetry when he rejected verse.

THE TRAGIC CHORUS

FRANCIS FERGUSSON, from *The Idea of a Theater:*

According to Aristotle, a Sophoclean chorus is a character that takes an important role in the action of the play, instead of merely making incidental music between the scenes, as in the plays of Euripides. The chorus may be described as a group personality, like an old Parliament. It has its own traditions, habits of thought and feeling, and mode of being. It exists, in a sense, as a living entity, but not with the sharp actuality of an individual. It perceives; but its perception is at once wider and vaguer than that of a single man. It shares, in its way, the seeking action of the play as a whole; but it cannot act in all the modes; it depends upon the chief agonists to invent and try out the detail of policy, just as a rather helpless but critical Parliament depends upon the Prime Minister to act but, in its less specific form of life, survives his destruction.

. . . It is the function of the chorus to mark the stages of this action, and to perform the suffering and perceiving part of the tragic rhythm. The protagonist and his antagonists develop the "purpose" with which the tragic sequence begins; the chorus, with its less than individual being,

broods over the agons, marks their stages with a word . . . , and (expressing its emotions and visions in song and dance) suffers the results, and the new perception at the end. . . .

The choral odes are lyrics but they are not to be understood as poetry, the art of words, only, for they are intended also to be danced and sung. And though each chorus has its own shape, like that of a discrete lyric—its beginning, middle, and end—it represents also one passion or pathos in the changing action of the whole. This passion, like the other moments in the tragic rhythm, is felt at so general or, rather, so deep a level that it seems to contain both the mob ferocity that Nietzsche felt in it and, at the other extreme, the patience of prayer. It is informed by faith in the unseen order of nature and the gods, and moves through a sequence of modes of suffering. . . .

It is also to be noted that the chorus changes the scene which we, as audience, are to imagine. . . . Mr. Burke has expounded the fertile notion that human action may be understood in terms of the scene in which it occurs, and vice versa: the scene is defined by the mode of action. The chorus's action is not limited by the sharp, rationalized purposes of the protagonist; its mode of action, more patient, less sharply realized, is cognate with a wider, if less accurate, awareness of the scene of human life. But the chorus's action . . . is not that of passion itself . . . but suffering informed by the faith of the tribe in a human and a divinely sanctioned natural order. . . . Thus it is one of the most important functions of the chorus to reveal, in its widest and most mysterious extent, the theater of human life which the play, and indeed the whole Festival of Dionysos, assumed. Even when the chorus does not speak, but only watches, it maintains this theme and this perspective—ready to take the whole stage when the fighters depart.

If one thinks of the movement of the play, it appears that the tragic rhythm analyzes human action temporally into successive modes, as a crystal analyzes a white beam of light spatially into the colored bands of the spectrum. The chorus, always present, represents one of these modes, and at the recurrent moments when reasoned purpose is gone, it takes the stage with its faith-informed passion, moving through an ordered succession of modes of suffering, to a new perception of the immediate situation.

ALLARDYCE NICOLL, from *The Theory of Drama:*

. . . There is much that is permanent in the tragedies of Aeschylus, Sophocles, and Euripides, but there is also much that has a purely temporary value. The chorus, for example, is essentially an incidental feature. It is part of the traditional origin of the Greek stage, and in the hands of Euripides it was . . . relegated to a subordinate position. That it was not necessary for the expression of true tragic emotion has been proved not only by the romantic genius of Shakespeare, but by the classical genius of Racine. On the other hand, the chorus marked that lyrical quality in tragedy which later iconoclasts were inclined too recklessly to neglect. The spirit of the chorus, that of which it was the expression, is a permanent thing, wellnigh necessary in all high tragedy, but the form of the chorus is purely temporary and topical. Quite apart from this lyrical element, too, the chorus presents features of a kind essential to tragic expression. Countless commentators have noted the chorus-like words of Enobarbus in *Antony and Cleopatra,* and perhaps such figures as the Fool in *Lear* and Horatio in *Hamlet* bear a similar quality. In other words, the fundamental comments made by the chanting crowds which appeared on the Athenian stage have been passed over in Elizabethan and modern drama to individual characters who sometimes, like Lear's Fool and Horatio, have an integral part in the working out of the tragic theme and sometimes, like Enobarbus, remain apart.

The Plays

ANTIGONE

BY SOPHOCLES

TRANSLATED BY DUDLEY FITTS AND ROBERT FITZGERALD

CHARACTERS

ANTIGONE	CREON	A SENTRY
ISMENE	HAIMON	A MESSENGER
EURYDICE	TEIRESIAS	CHORUS

[SCENE: *Before the palace of Creon, King of Thebes. A central double door, and two lateral doors. A platform extends the length of the façade, and from this platform three steps lead down into the orchestra, or chorus-ground. Time: dawn of the day after the repulse of the Argive army from the assault on Thebes.*]

PROLOGUE

[*Antigonê and Ismenê enter from the central door of the Palace.*]

ANTIG. Ismenê, dear sister,
You would think that we had already suffered enough
For the curse on Oedipus:
I cannot imagine any grief
That you and I have not gone through. And now—
Have they told you the new decree of our King Creon?
ISMENE. I have heard nothing: I know
That two sisters lost two brothers, a double death
In a single hour; and I know that the Argive army
Fled in the night; but beyond this, nothing.
ANTIG. I thought so. And that is why I wanted you
To come out here with me. There is something we must do.
ISMENE. Why do you speak so strangely?
ANTIG. Listen, Ismenê:
Creon buried our brother Eteoclês
With military honours, gave him a soldier's funeral,
And it was right that he should; but Polyneicês,
Who fought as bravely and died as miserably,—
They say that Creon has sworn
No one shall bury him, no one mourn for him,
But his body must lie in the fields, a sweet treasure
For carrion birds to find as they search for food.
That is what they say, and our good Creon is coming here
To announce it publicly; and the penalty—
Stoning to death in the public square!
                                        There it is,

And now you can prove what you are:
A true sister, or a traitor to your family.

ISMENE. Antigonê, you are mad!
What could I possibly do?

ANTIG. You must decide whether you will help me or not.

ISMENE. I do not understand you.
Help you in what?

ANTIG. Ismenê, I am going to bury him. Will you come?

ISMENE. Bury him! You have just said the new law forbids it.

ANTIG. He is my brother. And he is your brother, too.

ISMENE. But think of the danger! Think what Creon will do!

ANTIG. Creon is not strong enough to stand in my way.

ISMENE. Ah sister!
Oedipus died, everyone hating him
For what his own search brought to light, his eyes
Ripped out by his own hand; and Iocastê died,
His mother and wife at once: she twisted the cords
That strangled her life; and our two brothers died,
Each killed by the other's sword. And we are left:
But oh, Antigonê,
Think how much more terrible than these
Our own death would be if we should go against Creon
And do what he has forbidden! We are only women,
We cannot fight with men, Antigonê!
The law is strong, we must give in to the law
In this thing, and in worse. I beg the Dead
To forgive me, but I am helpless: I must yield

To those in authority. And I think it is dangerous business
To be always meddling.

ANTIG. If that is what you think,
I should not want you, even if you asked to come.
You have made your choice, you can be what you want to be.
But I will bury him; and if I must die,
I say that this crime is holy: I shall lie down
With him in death, and I shall be as dear
To him as he to me.
It is the dead,
Not the living, who make the longest demands:
We die for ever . . .
You may do as you like,
Since apparently the laws of the gods mean nothing to you.

ISMENE. They mean a great deal to me; but I have no strength
To break laws that were made for the public good.

ANTIG. That must be your excuse, I suppose. But as for me,
I will bury the brother I love.

ISMENE.   Antigonê,
I am so afraid for you!

ANTIG.   You need not be:
You have yourself to consider, after all.

ISMENE. But no one must hear of this, you must tell no one!
I will keep it a secret, I promise!

ANTIG.   Oh tell it! Tell everyone!
Think how they'll hate you when it all comes out
If they learn that you knew about it all the time!

ISMENE. So fiery! You should be cold with fear.

ANTIG. Perhaps. But I am doing only what I must.

ISMENE. But can you do it? I say
that you cannot.

ANTIG. Very well: when my strength
gives out, I shall do no more.

ISMENE. Impossible things should
not be tried at all.

ANTIG. Go away, Ismenê:
I shall be hating you soon, and the
dead will too,
For your words are hateful. Leave me
my foolish plan:
I am not afraid of the danger; if it
means death,
It will not be the worst of deaths—
death without honour.

ISMENE. Go then, if you feel that
you must.
You are unwise,
But a loyal friend indeed to those who
love you.

[*Exit into the Palace. Antigonê goes
off, L. Enters the Chorus.*]

PARODOS

[STROPHE 1
CHORUS. Now the long blade of the
sun, lying
Level east to west, touches with glory
Thebes of the Seven Gates. Open, un-
lidded
Eye of golden day! O marching light
Across the eddy and rush of Dircê's
stream,
Striking the white shields of the enemy
Thrown headlong backward from the
blaze of morning!

CHORAG. Polyneicês their com-
mander
Roused them with windy phrases,
He the wild eagle screaming
Insults above our land,
His wings their shields of snow,
His crest their marshalled helms.

[ANTISTROPHE 1
CHORUS. Against our seven gates in
a yawning ring
The famished spears came onward in
the night;
But before his jaws were sated with
our blood,
Or pinefire took the garland of our
towers,
He was thrown back; and as he
turned, great Thebes—
No tender victim for his noisy power—
Rose like a dragon behind him, shout-
ing war.

CHORAG. For God hates utterly
The bray of bragging tongues;
And when he beheld their smiling,
Their swagger of golden helms,
The frown of his thunder blasted
Their first man from our walls.

[STROPHE 2
CHORUS. We heard his shout of triumph high in the air
Turn to a scream; far out in a flaming arc
He fell with his windy torch, and the
earth struck him.
And others storming in fury no less
than his
Found shock of death in the dusty joy
of battle.

CHORAG. Seven captains at seven
gates
Yielded their clanging arms to the god
That bends the battle-line and breaks
it.
These two only, brothers in blood,
Face to face in matchless rage,
Mirroring each the other's death,
Clashed in long combat.

[ANTISTROPHE 2
CHORUS. But now in the beautiful
morning of victory
Let Thebes of the many chariots sing
for joy!

With hearts for dancing we'll take
    leave of war:
Our temples shall be sweet with
    hymns of praise,
And the long night shall echo with
    our chorus.

SCENE ONE

CHORAG. But now at last our new
    King is coming:
Creon of Thebes, Menoiceus' son.
In this auspicious dawn of his reign
What are the new complexities
That shifting Fate has woven for him?
What is his counsel? Why has he sum-
    moned
The old men to hear him?
    [*Enter Creon from the Palace. He
addresses the Chorus from the top
step.*]
    CREON. Gentlemen: I have the
honour to inform you that our Ship
of State, which recent storms have
threatened to destroy, has come safely
to harbour at last, guided by the merciful wisdom of Heaven. I have summoned you here this morning because
I know that I can depend upon you:
your devotion to King Laïos was absolute; you never hesitated in your
duty to our late ruler Oedipus; and
when Oedipus died, your loyalty was
transferred to his children. Unfortunately, as you know, his two sons, the
princes Eteoclês and Polyneicês, have
killed each other in battle; and I, as
the next in blood, have succeeded to
the full power of the throne.

    I am aware, of course, that no Ruler
can expect complete loyalty from his
subjects until he has been tested in
office. Nevertheless, I say to you at
the very outset that I have nothing
but contempt for the kind of Governor
who is afraid, for whatever reason, to
follow the course that he knows is best
for the State; and as for the man who
sets private friendship above the public welfare,—I have no use for him,
either. I call God to witness that if I
saw my country headed for ruin, I
should not be afraid to speak out
plainly; and I need hardly remind you
that I would never have any dealings
with an enemy of the people. No one
values friendship more highly than I;
but we must remember that friends
made at the risk of wrecking our Ship
are not real friends at all.

    These are my principles, at any
rate, and that is why I have made
the following decision concerning the
sons of Oedipus: Eteoclês, who died
as a man should die, fighting for his
country, is to be buried with full military honours, with all the ceremony
that is usual when the greatest heroes
die; but his brother Polyneicês, who
broke his exile to come back with fire
and sword against his native city and
the shrines of his fathers' gods, whose
one idea was to spill the blood of his
blood and sell his own people into
slavery—Polyneicês, I say, is to have
no burial: no man is to touch him or
say the least prayer for him; he shall
lie on the plain, unburied; and the
birds and the scavenging dogs can do
with him whatever they like.

    This is my command, and you can
see the wisdom behind it. As long as I
am King, no traitor is going to be honoured with the loyal man. But whoever shows by word and deed that he
is on the side of the State,—he shall
have my respect while he is living,
and my reverence when he is dead.

    CHORAG. If that is your will, Creon
    son of Menoiceus,
You have the right to enforce it: we

CREON. That is my will. Take care that you do your part.

CHORAG. We are old men: let the younger ones carry it out.

CREON. I do not mean that: the sentries have been appointed.

CHORAG. Then what is it that you would have us do?

CREON. You will give no support to whoever breaks this law.

CHORAG. Only a crazy man is in love with death!

CREON. And death it is; yet money talks, and the wisest
Have sometimes been known to count a few coins too many.

[*Enter Sentry.*]

SENTRY. I'll not say that I'm out of breath from running, King, because every time I stopped to think about what I have to tell you, I felt like going back. And all the time a voice kept saying, 'You fool, don't you know you're walking straight into trouble?'; and then another voice: 'Yes, but if you let somebody else get the news to Creon first, it will be even worse than that for you!' But good sense won out, at least I hope it was good sense, and here I am with a story that makes no sense at all; but I'll tell it anyhow, because, as they say, what's going to happen's going to happen, and—

CREON. Come to the point. What have you to say?

SENTRY. I did not do it. I did not see who did it. You must not punish me for what someone else has done.

CREON. A comprehensive defence! More effective, perhaps,
If I knew its purpose. Come: what is it?

SENTRY. A dreadful thing . . . I don't know how to put it—

CREON. Out with it!

SENTRY.   Well, then;
The dead man—
               Polyneicês—

[*Pause. The Sentry is overcome, fumbles for words. Creon waits impassively.*]
               out there—
               someone,—
New dust on the slimy flesh!

[*Pause. No sign from Creon.*]

Someone has given it burial that way, and
Gone . . .

[*Long pause. Creon finally speaks with deadly control:*]

CREON. And the man who dared do this?

SENTRY.   I swear I
Do not know! You must believe me!
               Listen:
The ground was dry, not a sign of digging, no,
Not a wheeltrack in the dust, no trace of anyone.
It was when they relieved us this morning: and one of them,
The corporal, pointed to it.
               There it was,
The strangest—
               Look:
The body, just mounded over with light dust: you see?
Not buried really, but as if they'd covered it
Just enough for the ghost's peace. And no sign
Of dogs or any wild animal that had been there.

And then what a scene there was! Every man of us
Accusing the other: we all proved the other man did it,
We all had proof that we could not

have done it.
We were ready to take hot iron in our hands,
Walk through fire, swear by all the gods,
It was not I!
I do not know who it was, but it was not I!

[*Creon's rage has been mounting steadily, but the Sentry is too intent upon his story to notice it.*]
And then, when this came to nothing, someone said
A thing that silenced us and made us stare
Down at the ground: you had to be told the news,
And one of us had to do it! We threw the dice,
And the bad luck fell to me. So here I am,
No happier to be here than you are to have me:
Nobody likes the man who brings bad news.

CHORAG. I have been wondering, King: can it be that the gods have done this?

CREON. [*Furiously.*] Stop!
Must you doddering wrecks
Go out of your heads entirely? 'The gods!'
Intolerable!
The gods favour this corpse? Why? How had he served them?
Tried to loot their temples, burn their images,
Yes, and the whole State, and its laws with it!
Is it your senile opinion that the gods love to honour bad men?
A pious thought!—
            No, from the very beginning
There have been those who have whispered together,
Stiff-necked anarchists, putting their heads together,
Scheming against me in alleys. These are the men,
And they have bribed my own guard to do this thing.
[*Sententiously.*]
Money!
There's nothing in the world so demoralising as money.
Down go your cities,
Homes gone, men gone, honest hearts corrupted,
Crookedness of all kinds, and all for money!
[*To Sentry:*] But you—!
I swear by God and by the throne of God,
The man who has done this thing shall pay for it!
Find that man, bring him here to me, or your death
Will be the least of your problems: I'll string you up
Alive, and there will be certain ways to make you
Discover your employer before you die;
And the process may teach you a lesson you seem to have missed:
The dearest profit is sometimes all too dear.
That depends on the source. Do you understand me?
A fortune won is often misfortune.

SENTRY. King, may I speak?

CREON. Your very voice distresses me.

SENTRY. Are you sure that it is my voice, and not your conscience?

CREON. By God, he wants to analyse me now!

SENTRY. It is not what I say, but what has been done, that hurts you.

CREON. You talk too much.

SENTRY.   Maybe; but I've done nothing.

CREON. Sold your soul for some silver: that's all you've done.

SENTRY. How dreadful it is when the right judge judges wrong!

CREON. Your figures of speech
May entertain you now; but unless you bring me the man,
You will get little profit from them in the end.

          [*Exit Creon into the Palace.*]

SENTRY. 'Bring me the man'—!
I'd like nothing better than bringing him the man!
But bring him or not, you have seen the last of me here.
At any rate, I am safe!

          [*Exit Sentry.*]

ODE I

[STROPHE 1

CHORUS. Numberless are the world's wonders, but none
More wonderful than man; the storm-grey sea
Yields to his prows, the huge crests bear him high;
Earth, holy and inexhaustible, is graven
With shining furrows where his plows have gone
Year after year, the timeless labour of stallions.

[ANTISTROPHE 1

The lightboned birds and beasts that cling to cover,
The lithe fish lighting their reaches of dim water,
All are taken, tamed in the net of his mind;
The lion on the hill, the wild horse windy-maned,

Resign to him; and his blunt yoke has broken
The sultry shoulders of the mountain bull.

[STROPHE 2

Words also, and thought as rapid as air,
He fashions to his good use; statecraft is his,
And his the skill that deflects the arrows of snow,
The spears of winter rain: from every wind
He has made himself secure—from all but one:
In the late wind of death he cannot stand.

[ANTISTROPHE 2

O clear intelligence, force beyond all measure!
O fate of man, working both good and evil!
When the laws are kept, how proudly his city stands!
When the laws are broken, what of his city then?
Never may the anarchic man find rest at my hearth,
Never be it said that my thoughts are his thoughts.

SCENE TWO

[*Re-enter Sentry leading Antigonê.*]

CHORAG. What does this mean? Surely this captive woman
Is the Princess, Antigonê. Why should she be taken?

SENTRY. Here is the one who did it! We caught her
In the very act of burying him.— Where is Creon?

CHORAG. Just coming from the house.

[*Enter Creon, C.*]

CREON.   What has happened?
Why have you come back so soon?
[*Expansively.*]
SENTRY.   O King,
A man should never be too sure of
    anything:
I would have sworn
That you'd not see me here again:
    your anger
Frightened me so, and the things you
    threatened me with;
But how could I tell then
That I'd be able to solve the case so
    soon?

No dice-throwing this time: I was
    only too glad to come!

Here is this woman. She is the guilty
    one:
We found her trying to bury him.

Take her, then; question her; judge
    her as you will.
I am through with the whole thing
    now, and glad of it.
CREON. But this is Antigonê! Why
    have you brought her here?
SENTRY. She was burying him, I tell
    you!
CREON. [*Severely.*] Is this the truth?
SENTRY. I saw her with my own
    eyes. Can I say more?
CREON. The details: come, tell me
    quickly!
SENTRY.   It was like this:
After those terrible threats of yours,
    King,
We went back and brushed the dust
    away from the body.
The flesh was soft by now, and stink-
    ing,
So we sat on a hill to windward and
    kept guard.
No napping this time! We kept each
    other awake.

But nothing happened until the white
    round sun
Whirled in the centre of the round
    sky over us:
Then, suddenly,
A storm of dust roared up from the
    earth, and the sky
Went out, the plain vanished with all
    its trees
In the stinging dark. We closed our
    eyes and endured it.
The whirlwind lasted a long time, but
    it passed;
And then we looked, and there was
    Antigonê!
I have seen
A mother bird come back to a stripped
    nest, heard
Her crying bitterly a broken note or
    two
For the young ones stolen. Just so,
    when this girl
Found the bare corpse, and all her
    love's work wasted,
She wept, and cried on heaven to
    damn the hands
That had done this thing
        And then she brought more dust
And sprinkled wine three times for
    her brother's ghost.

We ran and took her at once. She was
    not afraid,
Not even when we charged her with
    what she had done.
She denied nothing.
        And this was a comfort to me,
And some uneasiness: for it is a good
    thing
To escape from death, but it is no
    great pleasure
To bring death to a friend.
                Yet I always say
There is nothing so comfortable as
    your own safe skin!

CREON. [*Slowly, dangerously.*] And you, Antigonê,
You with your head hanging,—do you confess this thing?
ANTIG. I do. I deny nothing.
CREON. [*To Sentry:*] You may go.
                                    [*Exit Sentry.*]
[*To Antigonê:*] Tell me, tell me briefly:
Had you heard my proclamation touching this matter?
ANTIG. It was public. Could I help hearing it?
CREON. And yet you dared defy the law.
ANTIG.   I dared.
It was not God's proclamation. That final Justice
That rules the world below makes no such laws.

Your edict, King, was strong,
But all your strength is weakness itself against
The immortal unrecorded laws of God.
They are not merely now: they were, and shall be,
Operative for ever, beyond man utterly.

I knew I must die, even without your decree:
I am only mortal. And if I must die
Now, before it is my time to die,
Surely this is no hardship: can anyone
Living, as I live, with evil all about me,
Think Death less than a friend? This death of mine
Is of no importance; but if I had left my brother
Lying in death unburied, I should have suffered.
Now I do not.
                    You smile at me. Ah Creon,
Think me a fool, if you like; but it may

well be
That a fool convicts me of folly.
CHORAG. Like father, like daughter: both headstrong, deaf to reason!
She has never learned to yield.
CREON.   She has much to learn.
The inflexible heart breaks first, the toughest iron
Cracks first, and the wildest horses bend their necks
At the pull of the smallest curb.
                                    Pride? In a slave?
This girl is guilty of a double insolence,
Breaking the given laws and boasting of it.
Who is the man here,
She or I, if this crime goes unpunished?
Sister's child, or more than sister's child,
Or closer yet in blood—she and her sister
Win bitter death for this!
    [*To Servants:*]   Go, some of you,
Arrest Ismenê. I accuse her equally.
Bring her: you will find her sniffling in the house there.

Her mind's a traitor: crimes kept in the dark
Cry for light, and the guardian brain shudders;
But how much worse than this
Is brazen boasting of barefaced anarchy!
ANTIG. Creon, what more do you want than my death?
CREON.   Nothing.
That gives me everything.
ANTIG.   Then I beg you: kill me.
This talking is a great weariness: your words
Are distasteful to me, and I am sure that mine

Seem so to you. And yet they should
not seem so:
I should have praise and honour for
what I have done.
All these men here would praise me
Were their lips not frozen shut with
fear of you.
[*Bitterly.*]
Ah the good fortune of kings,
Licensed to say and do whatever they
please!
CREON. You are alone here in that
opinion.
ANTIG. No, they are with me. But
they keep their tongues in leash.
CREON. Maybe. But you are guilty,
and they are not.
ANTIG. There is no guilt in reverence
for the dead.
CREON. But Eteoclês—was he not
your brother too?
ANTIG. My brother too.
CREON. And you insult his memory?
ANTIG. [*Softly.*] The dead man
would not say that I insult it.
CREON. He would: for you honour
a traitor as much as him.
ANTIG. His own brother, traitor or
not, and equal in blood.
CREON. He made war on his coun-
try. Eteoclês defended it.
ANTIG. Nevertheless, there are hon-
ours due all the dead.
CREON. But not the same for the
wicked as for the just.
ANTIG. Ah Creon, Creon,
Which of us can say what the gods
hold wicked?
CREON. An enemy is an enemy, even
dead.
ANTIG. It is my nature to join in
love, not hate.
CREON. [*Finally losing patience.*]
Go join them, then; if you must have
your love,

Find it in hell!
CHORAG. But see, Ismenê comes:
[*Enter Ismenê, guarded.*]
Those tears are sisterly, the cloud
That shadows her eyes rains down
gentle sorrow.
CREON. You too, Ismenê,
Snake in my ordered house, sucking
my blood
Stealthily—and all the time I never
knew
That these two sisters were aiming at
my throne!
                              Ismenê,
Do you confess your share in this
crime, or deny it?
Answer me.
ISMENE. Yes, if she will let me say
so. I am guilty.
ANTIG. [*Coldly.*] No, Ismenê. You
have no right to say so.
You would not help me, and I will not
have you help me.
ISMENE. But now I know what you
meant; and I am here
To join you, to take my share of pun-
ishment.
ANTIG. The dead man and the gods
who rule the dead
Know whose act this was. Words are
not friends.
ISMENE. Do you refuse me, Antig-
onê? I want to die with you:
I too have a duty that I must dis-
charge to the dead.
ANTIG. You shall not lessen my
death by sharing it.
ISMENE. What do I care for life
when you are dead?
ANTIG. Ask Creon. You're always
hanging on his opinions.
ISMENE. You are laughing at me.
Why, Antigonê?
ANTIG. It's a joyless laughter, Is-
menê.

ISMENE.   But can I do nothing?

ANTIG. Yes. Save yourself. I shall not envy you.

There are those who will praise you;
    I shall have honour, too.

ISMENE. But we are equally guilty!

ANTIG.   No, more, Ismenê.

You are alive, but I belong to Death.

CREON. [*To the Chorus:*] Gentlemen, I beg you to observe these girls:

One has just now lost her mind; the other,

It seems, has never had a mind at all.

ISMENE. Grief teaches the steadiest minds to waver, King.

CREON. Yours certainly did, when you assumed guilt with the guilty!

ISMENE. But how could I go on living without her?

CREON.   You are.

She is already dead.

ISMENE. But your own son's bride!

CREON. There are places enough for him to push his plow.

I want no wicked women for my sons!

ISMENE. O dearest Haimon, how your father wrongs you!

CREON. I've had enough of your childish talk of marriage!

CHORAG. Do you really intend to steal this girl from your son?

CREON. No; Death will do that for me.

CHORAG.   Then she must die?

CREON. You dazzle me.

            —But enough of this talk!

[*To Guards:*]

You, there, take them away and guard them well:

For they are but women, and even brave men run

When they see Death coming.

[*Exeunt Ismenê, Antigonê, and Guards.*]

ODE II

[STROPHE 1

CHORUS. Fortunate is the man who has never tasted God's vengeance!

Where once the anger of heaven has struck, that house is shaken

For ever: damnation rises behind each child

Like a wave cresting out of the black northeast,

When the long darkness under sea roars up

And bursts drumming death upon the windwhipped sand.

[ANTISTROPHE 1

I have seen this gathering sorrow from time long past

Loom upon Oedipus' children: generation from generation

Take the compulsive rage of the enemy god.

So lately this last flower of Oedipus' line

Drank the sunlight! but now a passionate word

And a handful of dust have closed up all its beauty.

[STROPHE 2

What mortal arrogance
Transcends the wrath of Zeus?

Sleep cannot lull him, nor the effortless long months

Of the timeless gods: but he is young for ever,

And his house is the shining day of high Olympos.

All that is and shall be,
And all the past, is his.

No pride on earth is free of the curse
of heaven.

[ANTISTROPHE 2

The straying dreams of men
May bring them ghosts of joy:
But as they drowse, the waking em-
bers burn them;
Or they walk with fixed eyes, as blind
men walk.
But the ancient wisdom speaks for our
own time:
Fate works most for woe
With Folly's fairest show.
Man's little pleasure is the spring of
sorrow.

SCENE THREE

CHORAG. But here is Haimon, King,
the last of all your sons.
Is it grief for Antigonê that brings him
here,
And bitterness at being robbed of his
bride?
[*Enter Haimon.*]
CREON. We shall soon see, and no
need of diviners.

—Son,

You have heard my final judgment on
that girl:
Have you come here hating me, or
have you come
With deference and with love, whatever I do?
HAIMON. I am your son, father. You
are my guide.
You make things clear for me, and I
obey you.
No marriage means more to me than
your continuing wisdom.
CREON. Good. That is the way to
behave: subordinate
Everything else, my son, to your
father's will.
This is what a man prays for, that he

may get
Sons attentive and dutiful in his house,
Each one hating his father's enemies,
Honouring his father's friends. But if
his sons
Fail him, if they turn out unprofitably,
What has he fathered but trouble for
himself
And amusement for the malicious?

So you are right

Not to lose your head over this woman.
Your pleasure with her would soon
grow cold, Haimon,
And then you'd have a hellcat in bed
and elsewhere.
Let her find her husband in Hell!
Of all the people in this city, only she
Has had contempt for my law and
broken it.

Do you want me to show myself weak
before the people?
Or to break my sworn word? No, and
I will not.
The woman dies.

I suppose she'll plead 'family ties.'
Well, let her.
If I permit my own family to rebel,
How shall I earn the world's obedi-
ence?
Show me the man who keeps his house
in hand,
He's fit for public authority.

I'll have no dealings

With law-breakers, critics of the gov-
ernment:
Whoever is chosen to govern should
be obeyed—
Must be obeyed, in all things, great
and small,
Just and unjust! O Haimon,
The man who knows how to obey,
and that man only,
Knows how to give commands when

the time comes.
You can depend on him, no matter how fast
The spears come: he's a good soldier, he'll stick it out.

Anarchy, anarchy! Show me a greater evil!
This is why cities tumble and the great houses rain down,
This is what scatters armies!

No, no: good lives are made so by discipline.
We keep the laws then, and the lawmakers,
And no woman shall seduce us. If we must lose,
Let's lose to a man, at least! Is a woman stronger than we?

CHORAG. Unless time has rusted my wits,
What you say, King, is said with point and dignity.

HAIMON. [*Boyishly earnest.*] Father:
Reason is God's crowning gift to man, and you are right
To warn me against losing mine. I cannot say—
I hope that I shall never want to say!—that you
Have reasoned badly. Yet there are other men
Who can reason, too; and their opinions might be helpful.
You are not in a position to know everything
That people say or do, or what they feel:
Your temper terrifies them—everyone
Will tell you only what you like to hear.
But I, at any rate, can listen; and I have heard them
Muttering and whispering in the dark about this girl.

They say no woman has ever, so unreasonably,
Died so shameful a death for a generous act:
'She covered her brother's body. Is this indecent?
'She kept him from dogs and vultures. Is this a crime?
'Death?—She should have all the honour that we can give her!'

This is the way they talk out there in the city.

You must believe me:
Nothing is closer to me than your happiness.
What could be closer? Must not any son
Value his father's fortune as his father does his?
I beg you, do not be unchangeable:
Do not believe that you alone can be right.
The man who thinks that,
The man who maintains that only he has the power
To reason correctly, the gift to speak, the soul—
A man like that, when you know him, turns out empty.

It is not reason never to yield to reason!

In flood time you can see how some trees bend,
And because they bend, even their twigs are safe,
While stubborn trees are torn up, roots and all.
And the same thing happens in sailing:
Make your sheet fast, never slacken,—and over you go,
Head over heels and under: and

there's your voyage.
Forget you are angry! Let yourself be
moved!
I know I am young; but please let me
say this:
The ideal condition
Would be, I admit, that men should
be right by instinct;
But since we are all too likely to go
astray,
The reasonable thing is to learn from
those who can teach.

CHORAG. You will do well to listen to
him, King,
If what he says is sensible. And you,
Haimon,
Must listen to your father.—Both
speak well.

CREON. You consider it right for a
man of my years and experience
To go to school to a boy?

HAIMON.   It is not right
If I am wrong. But if I am young, and
right,
What does my age matter?

CREON. You think it right to stand
up for an anarchist?

HAIMON. Not at all. I pay no respect
to criminals.

CREON. Then she is not a criminal?

HAIMON. The City would deny it,
to a man.

CREON. And the City proposes to
teach me how to rule?

HAIMON. Ah. Who is it that's talking
like a boy now?

CREON. My voice is the one voice
giving orders in this City!

HAIMON. It is no City if it takes orders from one voice.

CREON. The State is the King!

HAIMON. Yes, if the State is a desert.
[Pause.]

CREON. This boy, it seems, has sold
out to a woman.

HAIMON. If you are a woman: my
concern is only for you.

CREON. So? Your 'concern'! In a
public brawl with your father!

HAIMON. How about you, in a public brawl with justice?

CREON. With justice, when all that
I do is within my rights?

HAIMON. You have no right to trample on God's right.

CREON. [Completely out of control.]
Fool, adolescent fool! Taken in by a
woman!

HAIMON. You'll never see me taken
in by anything vile.

CREON. Every word you say is for
her!

HAIMON. [Quietly, darkly.] And for
you.
And for me. And for the gods under
the earth.

CREON. You'll never marry her
while she lives.

HAIMON. Then she must die.—But
her death will cause another.

CREON. Another?
Have you lost your senses? Is this an
open threat?

HAIMON. There is no threat in
speaking to emptiness.

CREON. I swear you'll regret this
superior tone of yours!
You are the empty one!

HAIMON. If you were not my father,
I'd say you were perverse.

CREON. You girlstruck fool, don't
play at words with me!

HAIMON. I am sorry. You prefer
silence.

CREON.   Now, by God—!
I swear, by all the gods in heaven
above us,
You'll watch it, I swear you shall!
[To the Servants.]   Bring her out!
Bring the woman out! Let her die

before his eyes,
Here, this instant, with her bride-
groom beside her!
HAIMON. Not here, no; she will not
die here, King.
And you will never see my face again.
Go on raving as long as you've a friend
to endure you.
[*Exit Haimon.*]
CHORAG. Gone, gone.
Creon, a young man in a rage is dan-
gerous!
CREON. Let him do, or dream to do,
more than a man can.
He shall not save these girls from
death.
CHORAG.   These girls?
You have sentenced them both?
CREON.   No, you are right.
I will not kill the one whose hands are
clean.
CHORAG. But Antigonê?
CREON. [*Sombrely.*] I will carry her
far away
Out there in the wilderness, and lock
her
Living in a vault of stone. She shall
have food,
As the custom is, to absolve the State
of her death.
And there let her pray to the gods of
Hell:
They are her only gods:
Perhaps they will show her an escape
from death,
Or she may learn,
                    though late,
That piety shown the dead is pity in
vain.
[*Exit Creon.*]

ODE III

[STROPHE
CHORUS. Love, unconquerable

Waster of rich men, keeper
Of warm lights and all-night vigil
In the soft face of a girl:
Sea-wanderer, forest-visitor!
Even the pure Immortals cannot es-
cape you,
And mortal man, in his one day's
dusk,
Trembles before your glory.
[ANTISTROPHE
Surely you swerve upon ruin
The just man's consenting heart,
As here you have made bright anger
Strike between father and son—
And none has conquered but Love!
A girl's glance working the will of
heaven:
Pleasure to her alone who mocks us,
Merciless Aphroditê.

SCENE FOUR

[*As Antigonê enters guarded.*]
CHORAG. But I can no longer stand
in awe of this,
Nor, seeing what I see, keep back my
tears.
Here is Antigonê, passing to that
chamber
Where all find sleep at last.
[STROPHE 1
ANTIG. Look upon me, friends, and
pity me
Turning back at the night's edge to
say
Good-bye to the sun that shines for
me no longer;
Now sleepy Death
Summons me down to Acheron, that
cold shore:
There is no bridesong there, nor any
music.
CHORUS. Yet not unpraised, not
without a kind of honour,
You walk at last into the underworld;

Untouched by sickness, broken by no
     sword.
What woman has ever found your way
     to death?

[ANTISTROPHE 1

ANTIG. How often I have heard the
     story of Niobê,
Tantalos' wretched daughter, how the
     stone
Clung fast about her, ivy-close: and
     they say
The rain falls endlessly
And sifting soft snow; her tears are
     never done.
I feel the loneliness of her death in
     mine.
     CHORUS. But she was born of
          heaven, and you
Are woman, woman-born. If her death
     is yours,
A mortal woman's, is this not for you
Glory in our world and in the world
     beyond?

[STROPHE 2

     ANTIG. You laugh at me. Ah,
          friends, friends,
Can you not wait until I am dead? O
     Thebes,
O men many-charioted, in love with
     Fortune,
Dear springs of Dircê, sacred Theban
     grove,
Be witnesses for me, denied all pity,
Unjustly judged! and think a word of
     love
For her whose path turns
Under dark earth, where there are no
     more tears.
     CHORUS. You have passed beyond
          human daring and come at last
Into a place of stone where Justice
     sits.
I cannot tell
What shape of your father's guilt ap-
     pears in this.

[ANTISTROPHE 2

ANTIG. You have touched it at last:
     that bridal bed
Unspeakable, horror of son and mother
     mingling:
Their crime, infection of all our fam-
     ily!
O Oedipus, father and brother!
Your marriage strikes from the grave
     to murder mine.
I have been a stranger here in my own
     land:
All my life
The blasphemy of my birth has fol-
     lowed me.
     CHORUS. Reverence is a virtue, but
          strength
Lives in established law: that must
     prevail.
You have made your choice,
Your death is the doing of your con-
     scious hand.

[EPODE

ANTIG. Then let me go, since all
     your words are bitter,
And the very light of the sun is cold
     to me.
Lead me to my vigil, where I must
     have
Neither love nor lamentation; no song,
     but silence.
[Creon interrupts impatiently.]
     CREON. If dirges and planned lamen-
          tations could put off death,
Men would be singing for ever.
[To the Servants.]   Take her, go!
You know your orders: take her to the
     vault
And leave her alone there. And if she
     lives or dies,
That's her affair, not ours: our hands
     are clean.
     ANTIG. O tomb, vaulted bride-bed
          in eternal rock,
Soon I shall be with my own again

Where Persephonê welcomes the thin
ghosts underground:
And I shall see my father again, and
you, mother,
And dearest Polyneicês—
dearest indeed
To me, since it was my hand
That washed him clean and poured
the ritual wine:
And my reward is death before my
time!

And yet, as men's hearts know, I have
done no wrong,
I have not sinned before God. Or if I
have,
I shall know the truth in death. But if
the guilt
Lies upon Creon who judged me,
then, I pray,
May his punishment equal my own.
CHORAG.   O passionate heart,
Unyielding, tormented still by the
same winds!
CREON. Her guards shall have good
cause to regret their delaying.
ANTIG. Ah! That voice is like the
voice of death!
CREON. I can give you no reason to
think you are mistaken.
ANTIG. Thebes, and you my fathers'
gods,
And rulers of Thebes, you see me now,
the last
Unhappy daughter of a line of kings,
Your kings, led away to death. You
will remember
What things I suffer, and at what
men's hands,
Because I would not transgress the
laws of heaven.
[*To the Guards, simply.*] Come: let us
wait no longer.
[*Exit Antigonê, L., guarded.*]

ODE IV

[STROPHE 1
CHORUS. All Danaê's beauty was
locked away
In a brazen cell where the sunlight
could not come:
A small room, still as any grave, en-
closed her.
Yet she was a princess too,
And Zeus in a rain of gold poured
love upon her.
O child, child,
No power in wealth or war
Or tough sea-blackened ships
Can prevail against untiring Destiny!
[ANTISTROPHE 1
And Dryas' son also, that furious king,
Bore the god's prisoning anger for his
pride:
Sealed up by Dionysos in deaf stone,
His madness died among echoes.
So at the last he learned what dread-
ful power
His tongue had mocked:
For he had profaned the revels,
And fired the wrath of the nine
Implacable Sisters that love the sound
of the flute.
[STROPHE 2
And old men tell a half-remembered
tale
Of horror done where a dark ledge
splits the sea
And a double surf beats on the grey
shores:
How a king's new woman, sick
With hatred for the queen he had im-
prisoned,
Ripped out his two sons' eyes with her
bloody hands
While grinning Arês watched the
shuttle plunge

Four times: four blind wounds crying
    for revenge,
                [ANTISTROPHE 2
Crying, tears and blood mingled.—
    Piteously born,
Those sons whose mother was of heav-
    enly birth!
Her father was the god of the North
    Wind
And she was cradled by gales,
She raced with young colts on the
    glittering hills
And walked untrammeled in the open
    light:
But in her marriage deathless Fate
    found means
To build a tomb like yours for all her
    joy.

SCENE FIVE

[*Enter blind Teiresias, led by a boy.
The opening speeches of Teiresias
should be in singsong contrast to the
realistic lines of Creon.*]

    TEIRES. This is the way the blind
    man comes, Princes, Princes,
Lock-step, two heads lit by the eyes
    of one.
    CREON. What new thing have you
    to tell us, old Teiresias?
    TEIRES. I have much to tell you:
    listen to the prophet, Creon.
    CREON. I am not aware that I have
    ever failed to listen.
    TEIRES. Then you have done wisely,
    King, and ruled well.
    CREON. I admit my debt to you. But
    what have you to say?
    TEIRES. This, Creon: you stand once
    more on the edge of fate.
    CREON. What do you mean? Your
    words are a kind of dread.
    TEIRES. Listen, Creon:

I was sitting in my chair of augury, at
    the place
Where the birds gather about me.
    They were all a-chatter,
As is their habit, when suddenly I
    heard
A strange note in their jangling, a
    scream, a
Whirring fury; I knew that they were
    fighting,
Tearing each other, dying
In a whirlwind of wings clashing. And
    I was afraid.
I began the rites of burnt-offering at
    the altar,
But Hephaistos failed me: instead of
    bright flame,
There was only the sputtering slime
    of the fat thigh-flesh
Melting: the entrails dissolved in grey
    smoke,
The bare bone burst from the welter.
    And no blaze!

This was a sign from heaven. My boy
    described it,
Seeing for me as I see for others.

I tell you, Creon, you yourself have
    brought
This new calamity upon us. Our
    hearths and altars
Are stained with the corruption of
    dogs and carrion birds
That glut themselves on the corpse of
    Oedipus' son.
The gods are deaf when we pray to
    them, their fire
Recoils from our offering, their birds
    of omen
Have no cry of comfort, for they are
    gorged
With the thick blood of the dead.
                O my son,
These are no trifles! Think: all men

make mistakes,
But a good man yields when he knows
his course is wrong,
And repairs the evil. The only crime
is pride.

Give in to the dead man, then: do not
fight with a corpse—
What glory is it to kill a man who is
dead?
Think, I beg you:
It is for your own good that I speak
as I do.
You should be able to yield for your
own good.

CREON. It seems that prophets have
made me their especial province.
All my life long
I have been a kind of butt for the dull
arrows
Of doddering fortune-tellers!
                    No, Teiresias:
If your birds—if the great eagles of
God himself
Should carry him stinking bit by bit
to heaven,
I would not yield. I am not afraid of
pollution:
No man can defile the gods.
                    Do what you will,
Go into business, make money, spec-
ulate
In India gold or that synthetic gold
from Sardis,
Get rich otherwise than by my consent
to bury him.
Teiresias, it is a sorry thing when a
wise man
Sells his wisdom, lets out his words
for hire!

TEIRES. Ah Creon! Is there no man
left in the world—

CREON. To do what?—Come, let's
have the aphorism!

TEIRES. No man who knows that
wisdom outweighs any wealth?

CREON. As surely as bribes are baser
than any baseness.

TEIRES. You are sick, Creon! You are
deathly sick!

CREON. As you say: it is not my
place to challenge a prophet.

TEIRES. Yet you have said my prophecy is for sale.

CREON. The generation of prophets
has always loved gold.

TEIRES. The generation of kings has
always loved brass.

CREON. You forget yourself! You are
speaking to your King.

TEIRES. I know it. You are a king
because of me.

CREON. You have a certain skill; but
you have sold out.

TEIRES. King, you will drive me to
words that—

CREON.   Say them, say them!
Only remember: I will not pay you for
them.

TEIRES. No, you will find them too
costly.

CREON.   No doubt. Speak:
Whatever you say, you will not change
my will.

TEIRES. Then take this, and take it
to heart!
The time is not far off when you shall
pay back
Corpse for corpse, flesh of your own
flesh.
You have thrust the child of this world
into living night,
You have kept from the gods below
the child that is theirs:
The one in a grave before her death,
the other,
Dead, denied the grave. This is your
crime:

And the Furies and the dark gods of
Hell
Are swift with terrible punishment for
you.

Do you want to buy me now, Creon?

Not many days,
And your house will be full of men
and women weeping,
And curses will be hurled at you from
far
Cities grieving for sons unburied, left
to rot before the walls of Thebes.

These are my arrows, Creon: they are
all for you.
[*To Boy:*]
But come, child: lead me home.
Let him waste his fine anger upon
younger men.
Maybe he will learn at last
To control a wiser tongue in a better
head.
[*Exit Teiresias.*]
CHORAG. The old man has gone,
King, but his words
Remain to plague us. I am old, too,
But I can not remember that he was
ever false.
CREON. That is true. . . . It trou-
bles me.
Oh it is hard to give in! but it is
worse
To risk everything for stubborn pride.
CHORAG. Creon: take my advice.
CREON.   What shall I do?
CHORAG. Go quickly: free Antigonê
from her vault
And build a tomb for the body of
Polyneicês.
CREON. You would have me do this?
CHORAG.   Creon, yes!
And it must be done at once: God
moves

Swiftly to cancel the folly of stubborn
men.
CREON. It is hard to deny the heart!
But I
Will do it: I will not fight with des-
tiny.
CHORAG. You must go yourself, you
cannot leave it to others.
CREON. I will go.
                —Bring axes, servants:
Come with me to the tomb. I buried
her, I
Will set her free.
                Oh quickly!
My mind misgives—
The laws of the gods are mighty, and
a man must serve them
To the last day of his life!
[*Exit Creon.*]

PÆAN

[STROPHE 1
CHORAG. God of many names
CHORUS.   O Iacchos
                son
of Cadmeian Sémelê
                O born of the Thunder!
Guardian of the West
                Regent
of Eleusis' plain
                O Prince of mænad Thebes
and the Dragon Field by rippling
Ismenos:
[ANTISTROPHE 1
CHORAG. God of many names
CHORUS.   the flame of torches
flares on our hills
                the nymphs of Iacchos
dance at the spring of Castalia:

from the vine-close mountain
                come ah come in ivy:
Evohé evohé! sings through the streets
of Thebes

[STROPHE 2

CHORAG. God of many names

CHORUS.   Iacchos of Thebes
heavenly Child
     of Sémelê bride of the Thunderer!
The shadow of plague is upon us:
                              come
with clement feet
              oh come from Parnasos
down the long slopes
          across the lamenting water.
                         [ANTISTROPHE 2
CHORAG. Iô Fire! Chorister of the
     throbbing stars!
O purest among the voices of the
     night!
Thou son of God, blaze for us!
     CHORUS. Come with choric rapture
     of circling Mænads
Who cry *Iô Iacche!*

               God of many names!

EXODOS

[*Enter Messenger.*]

MESS. Men of the line of Cadmos,
     you who live
Near Amphion's citadel:
                    I cannot say
Of any condition of human life 'This
     is fixed,
This is clearly good, or bad.' Fate
     raises up,
And Fate casts down the happy and
     unhappy alike:
No man can foretell his Fate.
              Take the case of Creon:
Creon was happy once, as I count
     happiness:
Victorious in battle, sole governor of
     the land,
Fortunate father of children nobly
     born.

And now it has all gone from him!
     Who can say
That a man is still alive when his life's
     joy fails?
He is a walking dead man. Grant him
     rich,
Let him live like a king in his great
     house:
If his pleasure is gone, I would not
     give
So much as the shadow of smoke for
     all he owns.
     CHORAG. Your words hint at sorrow:
     what is your news for us?
MESS. They are dead. The living are
     guilty of their death.
CHORAG. Who is guilty? Who is
     dead? Speak!
MESS.   Haimon.
Haimon is dead; and the hand that
     killed him
Is his own hand.
     CHORAG. His father's? or his own?
MESS. His own, driven mad by the
     murder his father had done.
CHORAG. Teiresias, Teiresias, how
     clearly you saw it all!
MESS. This is my news: you must
     draw what conclusions you can
     from it.
CHORAG. But look: Eurydicê, our
     Queen:
Has she overheard us?
     [*Enter Eurydicê from the Palace,
     C.*]
EURYD. I have heard something,
     friends:
As I was unlocking the gate of Pallas'
     shrine,
For I needed her help today, I heard
     a voice
Telling of some new sorrow. And I
     fainted
There at the temple with all my maid-
     ens about me.

But speak again: whatever it is, I can
    bear it:
Grief and I are no strangers.
    MESS.   Dearest Lady,
I will tell you plainly all that I have
    seen.
I shall not try to comfort you: what is
    the use,
Since comfort could lie only in what is
    not true?
The truth is always best.
                   I went with Creon
To the outer plain where Polyneicês
    was lying,
No friend to pity him, his body shred-
    ded by dogs.
We made our prayers in that place to
    Hecatê
And Pluto, that they would be merci-
    ful. And we bathed
The corpse with holy water, and we
    brought
Fresh-broken branches to burn what
    was left of it,
And upon the urn we heaped up a
    towering barrow
Of the earth of his own land.
          When we were done, we ran
To the vault where Antigonê lay on
    her couch of stone.
One of the servants had gone ahead,
And while he was yet far off he heard
    a voice
Grieving within the chamber, and he
    came back
And told Creon. And as the King went
    closer,
The air was full of wailing, the words
    lost,
And he begged us to make all haste.
    'Am I a prophet?'
He said, weeping, 'And must I walk
    this road,
'The saddest of all that I have gone
    before?

'My son's voice calls me on. Oh
    quickly, quickly!
'Look through the crevice there, and
    tell me
'If it is Haimon, or some deception of
    the gods!'

We obeyed; and in the cavern's far-
    thest corner
We saw her lying:
She had made a noose of her fine linen
    veil
And hanged herself. Haimon lay be-
    side her,
His arms about her waist, lamenting
    her,
His love lost under ground, crying out
That his father had stolen her away
    from him.
When Creon saw him the tears rushed
    to his eyes
And he called to him: 'What have you
    done, child? Speak to me.
'What are you thinking that makes
    your eyes so strange?
'O my son, my son, I come to you on
    my knees!'
But Haimon spat in his face. He said
    not a word,
Staring—
          And suddenly drew his sword
And lunged. Creon shrank back, the
    blade missed; and the boy,
Desperate against himself, drove it
    half its length
Into his own side, and fell. And as he
    died
He gathered Antigonê close in his
    arms again,
Choking, his blood bright red on her
    white cheek.
And now he lies dead with the dead,
    and she is his
At last, his bride in the houses of the
    dead.

[*Exit Eurydicê into the Palace.*]

CHORAG. She has left us without a word. What can this mean?

MESS. It troubles me, too; yet she knows what is best,

Her grief is too great for public lamentation,

And doubtless she has gone to her chamber to weep

For her dead son, leading her maidens in his dirge.

CHORAG. It may be so: but I fear this deep silence.

[*Pause.*]

MESS. I will see what she is doing. I will go in.

[*Exit Messenger into the Palace.*]

[*Enter Creon with attendants, bearing Haimon's body.*]

CHORAG. But here is the King himself: oh look at him,

Bearing his own damnation in his arms.

CREON. Nothing you say can touch me any more.

My own blind heart has brought me

From darkness to final darkness. Here you see

The father murdering, the murdered son—

And all my civic wisdom!

Haimon my son, so young, so young to die,

I was the fool, not you; and you died for me.

CHORAG. That is the truth; but you were late in learning it.

CREON. This truth is hard to bear. Surely a god

Has crushed me beneath the hugest weight of heaven,

And driven me headlong a barbaric way

To trample out the thing I held most dear.

The pains that men will take to come to pain!

[*Enter Messenger from the Palace.*]

MESS. The burden you carry in your hands is heavy,

But it is not all: you will find more in your house.

CREON. What burden worse than this shall I find there?

MESS. The Queen is dead.

CREON. O port of death, deaf world,

Is there no pity for me? And you, Angel of evil,

I was dead, and your words are death again.

Is it true, boy? Can it be true?

Is my wife dead? Has death bred death?

MESS. You can see for yourself.

[*The doors are opened, and the body of Eurydicê is disclosed within.*]

CREON. Oh pity!

All true, all true, and more than I can bear!

O my wife, my son!

MESS. She stood before the altar, and her heart

Welcomed the knife her own hand guided,

And a great cry burst from her lips for Megareus dead,

And for Haimon dead, her sons; and her last breath

Was a curse for their father, the murderer of her sons.

And she fell, and the dark flowed in through her closing eyes.

CREON. O God, I am sick with fear.

Are there no swords here? Has no one a blow for me?

MESS. Her curse is upon you for the deaths of both.

CREON. It is right that it should be. I alone am guilty.

I know it, and I say it. Lead me in,

Quickly, friends.
I have neither life nor substance. Lead
  me in.
CHORAG. You are right, if there can
  be right in so much wrong.
The briefest way is best in a world of
  sorrow.
CREON. Let it come,
Let death come quickly, and be kind
  to me.
I would not ever see the sun again.
CHORAG. All that will come when it
  will; but we, meanwhile,
Have much to do. Leave the future to
  itself.
CREON. All my heart was in that
  prayer!
CHORAG. Then do not pray any
  more: the sky is deaf.

CREON. Lead me away. I have been
  rash and foolish.
I have killed my son and my wife.
I look for comfort; my comfort lies
  here dead.
Whatever my hands have touched has
  come to nothing.
Fate has brought all my pride to a
  thought of dust.
[As Creon is being led into the
house, the Choragos advances and
speaks directly to the audience.]
  CHORAG. There is no happiness
  where there is no wisdom;
No wisdom but in submission to the
  gods.
Big words are always punished,
And proud men in old age learn to be
  wise.

DISCUSSION OF ANTIGONE

Antigone, like all Greek tragedies, is a retelling of a well-known story. Antigone
is a princess of the royal house of Thebes which was founded by Cadmus. The
third of Theban kings was Laius, who married Jocasta. When the Delphic
Oracle prophesied to Laius that his son should kill him and marry Jocasta, Laius
had the infant abandoned on a mountainside. However, the child did not die
but came to be raised as the son of King Polybus of Corinth. When the boy,
named Oedipus, grew older, he also heard of the prophecy that he would kill
his father and marry his mother.

Accordingly, he left Corinth and became a homeless wanderer. In his travels,
he became involved in a fight at a crossroads and killed a man. Presently he
came to Thebes, which was in a state of desolation and famine because of the
depredations of a terrible monster, part lion and part woman, named the
Sphinx. By answering a riddle of the Sphinx, Oedipus was able to deliver
Thebes, and in gratitude, he was made king, and he married Jocasta, the former
king's wife, not knowing that she was his mother.

For some years Thebes was at peace, and Oedipus and Jocasta had four
children: two boys, Polyneices and Eteocles, and two girls, Antigone and
Ismene. But then a new plague ravaged Thebes, and the Oracle prophesied that
only when the man who had killed Laius was cast out would the state again

become healthy. After a search for this man, Oedipus discovered that he himself had killed his father and married his mother. Now Jocasta kills herself, and Oedipus blinds himself. He is led out from Thebes by his daughter, Antigone, and finally makes his way to Athens, where he is received by the king, Theseus the hero, and where he dies.

After Oedipus' death his sons, Polyneices and Eteocles, go to war over Thebes, and in a great battle both are killed. Jocasta's brother Creon becomes king, and at this point our play opens.

Antigone was played before a huge audience whose theatre was greatly different from ours. Instead of a darkened theatre in which rows of people sit gazing at an illuminated box, a make-believe room with one of its walls cut away, you should think of the Greek theatre as a large outdoor arena, rather like a modern football field, in which thousands of people gathered to gaze down at the tiny figures in the center.

To make themselves larger, the chief actors wore some sort of elevated shoe, a padded costume, and a high headdress. They were hence more noticeable and more stately. To make themselves heard to their vast audience, as well as for purposes of ritualistic rather than realistic acting, they wore large masks whose mouths acted as a trumpet to project their voices. The chorus did not merely declaim its lines but also danced, thus providing a needed action and spectacle which is less necessary in our smaller, more intimate theatres.

As our convention of realistic staging in usually three acts informs the audience more or less what to expect, so also did the Greek theatre have its own convention or theatrical form. Each scene between the principal actors was followed by a choral ode. There were usually five such scenes, and these were preceded by a prologue and followed by an "exodus," or epilogue. The choral ode was customarily divided into three parts called the strophe, the antistrophe, and the epode, and these three parts corresponded to the dancing of the chorus.

The plays were usually put on in threes as a trilogy, in which each play was part of a longer story, as in Aeschylus' trilogy of the House of Atreus, *The Oresteia*. The trilogy was then followed by a burlesque skit called a satyr play. At their best the plays evidently generated an excitement probably less noisy but considerably more intense than that madness which assails spectators at a college football game. The plays were a sort of civic function that was all the more moving because of its religious overtones. As Gilbert Murray comments, the origin of the drama has its roots sunk deeply in the mother loam of both religion and the national welfare. The drama dated back to the almost forgotten religious practices of sacrifice to the god for a prosperous harvest.

We can see the shadow of the old religion lurking in the background of *Antigone*. The state is out of joint; Thebes has been torn by dissension and war. For the state to be rejuvenated, a sacrifice must be made of the god or king. In this case the sacrificial figure is the princess Antigone. With Antigone's death come also the deaths of Haimon and Eurydice. The old order dies off, and by its dying the state is born anew. The deaths of Antigone, Haimon, and Eurydice gave to Creon, the leader of the state, a revelation, an understanding. With this understanding, the state can now flourish anew in another cycle.

The Antigone story repeats the form of the ancient myth in more sophisticated, modern terms, but the form that Gilbert Murray analyzes (uncovered first by Sir James Frazer in *The Golden Bough*), the form of the ancient harvest sacrifice, gives meaning and purpose to the modern version.

This story is contained in two formal molds: one of them demanded by the nature of Greek theatrical convention and one by the nature of tragedy itself. The form of the theatrical convention—whether it be the Greek prologue, choral interludes, and dramatic episodes, or the modern realistic staging, in usually three acts—changes from age to age. The interior form of the tragic action rarely changes.

Scott Buchanan in his essay well outlines the tragic pattern, and we may apply it to the action of *Antigone*. Antigone, besides her overweening pride, has the capacity to systematize clear ideas. She, better than Ismene, sees the necessary action to which Creon's edict must drive her; that is, she sees the consequences of not defying Creon. "Dramatic tragedy," writes Mr. Buchanan, "usually discloses such a character in some advanced stage when the idea is in sight, so that action is understood as aiming to achieve its clarification." *Antigone* opens at such an advanced stage, with the "background" explained in the prologue between Antigone and Ismene, and with Antigone already convinced of the rightness and determined about the necessity of her coming action. (Later plays, particularly Elizabethan ones like *King Lear* and *Macbeth,* often show us more of the preceding action that determined the hero, but Sophocles, like Ibsen later, starts his action at the crisis.) Antigone, already made desperate, has already decided upon her course. "There is no turning back." She buries her brother and is discovered. "This is the reversal of circumstance and catastrophe."

There is one more necessity of the action—the recognition. Here the structure of *Antigone* shows its complexity, for the character of the hero is actually split in two. Antigone is the sacrificial victim, but Creon gets the recognition. (Oedipus and King Lear are characters who contain both qualities.) This division of the qualities of the hero, however, does not mean that Sophocles was wrenching the tragic pattern, but that he was using a sophisticated version of it appropriate for his own time. In the old religion that is an emotional backdrop to this play, it had become usual for the king himself not to die, but for an image or a totem to be destroyed in his place. Antigone is the destroyed image, for she embodies many "kingly" attributes—her royal blood, her nobility of purpose. Creon is the rejuvenated king. Although it seems on the level of plot that Antigone and Creon are antagonists, more deeply they are alike in their pride that knows no moderation and recognizes no counsel. While the play is thus somewhat unusual in having a dual hero, its structure is typical of tragedy. You may, to understand it better, apply John Dryden's terms or Kenneth Burke's, but whatever structural terms you use, the parts are, of course, always the same, in the same place and in the same proportion.

It is practically impossible even in an excellent translation to appreciate the language of Greek tragedy. But, although one doesn't know the original Greek, and the translation isn't as intensely moving as a Shakespearian sonnet or the Gettysburg Address, it does tell us something of the nature of the original words. We can see where Sophocles' language was grand, where it was lyrical, where it was—between Creon and Haimon—dramatically argumentative, where it was —between Creon and Teiresias—querulous and sharp, where it was pathetic, and where it was ironic. And even if we cannot appreciate how pathetic or grand or lyrical, we can still see that the language did not play merely in one key. It utilized all the resources of rhetoric to wring the human emotions.

The function of the chorus is well explained by Fergusson and Nicoll, but one word might be added. The student whose main experiences of drama have been through the movies and television often finds the chorus of Greek plays strange. Because of the technical devices of films and television, the transition from scene to scene can be effected immediately. One gets accustomed to shifting from scene to scene with no lapse in time. In the live theatre, such changes are made by dropping the curtain or by lowering the lights. In these ways, which the audience easily understands, the playwright can indicate a change of even years of dramatic time or of continents of dramatic space.

In the open-air, day-lit Greek theatre, the chorus was a practical necessity. It made the transitions between scenes, giving actors the chance to enter and leave the playing area and even announcing what characters those actors portrayed. But the function of the chorus, as Fergusson and Nicoll point out, goes beyond this. The choral odes, accompanied by dancing and music, were part of the entertainment itself. The chorus both commented on the events and participated in them, so that it was both involved in the action and detached from it. In this way, Sophocles and his contemporaries made a dramatic virtue of a stage necessity.

DISCUSSION QUESTIONS ON *ANTIGONE*

Antigone has long posed some perplexing problems, and the chief of these is whose play is it, Antigone's or Creon's? The first four questions below suggest some answers to this central problem.

1. Jean Racine, the great French dramatist, in his first preface to his tragedy *Britannicus* wrote that it is Antigone's play, and that the later action is mere unraveling of the plot. He wrote:

I myself have always thought that Tragedy is the imitation of a complete action in which several characters take part, and that the action is not really complete until the audience knows what happened to all of the characters. Sophocles always shows us this. In *Antigone* he writes many lines to show us Haemon's rage and Creon's punishment after the death of the princess.

How sound does this interpretation seem? If it is correct, how much of the play would the unraveling be? Too much?

2. John Dryden in his "Preface to *Troilus and Cressida*" wrote that, "Antigone herself is the heroine of the tragedy." And Goethe in his conversations with Eckermann not only asserted that Antigone is the heroine and Creon the villain, but gave the following reason:

> Everything noble is in itself quiet, and appears to slumber until it is awakened and brought forth by contrast. Creon is such a contrast. He is introduced partly to emphasize Antigone's noble nature and the right which is on her side, and partly to make his unhappy error appear hateful to us.

How plausible is this interpretation? What do you find in the play to substantiate it? If it is correct, then has not Sophocles given too much importance to his villain at the end of the play?

3. On behalf of Creon, H. D. F. Kitto says in his *Greek Tragedy:*

> The most satisfactory proof is performance. Creon can dominate the play; in the Glasgow production he did, easily and naturally. But even without performance, we may note that Creon's part is half as long again as Antigone's, a point which is less mechanical than it sounds, and that it is the more dynamic part. Hers is impressive and affecting enough, but his has the wider range and is the more elaborate. Her fate is decided in the first few verses and she can but go to meet it; most of the dramatic forces used in the play are deployed against Creon—the slight reserve with which the chorus receives his edict . . . , the news that he has been defied, and that too by a woman, the opposition of Haemon, the disapproval of the city . . . , the supernatural machinery of Teiresias, the desertion of the chorus . . . , the death of Haemon (foreshadowed), the death of Eurydice (unforeshadowed). Creon truly says
>
> > "Old sir, ye all like bowmen at a mark
> > Let fly your shafts at me."
>
> Antigone is indeed opposed, but not like this. Her tragedy is terrible, but it is foreseen and swift; Creon's grows before our eyes.

Arguing as specifically as you can from the play, how sound would you say this theory is when compared with Racine's? With Goethe's?

4. To tie the last questions together, let us pose some more:

a. Would the play have been more dramatic if it were differently structured? Antigone does not appear in the last third of the play. Would it have been better for Sophocles to have resolved the play in terms of Antigone's tragedy and death?

b. Since the play is resolved in terms of the devastating effect of the action on Creon, would it have been even more forceful to play down Antigone's role early in the play and to stress Creon's? Should the play have been called *Creon?*

c. When he wrote this play, Sophocles was a mature dramatist at the height of his powers. Since he is one of the great playwrights of all time, we may assume that he was superbly in control of his medium. Is it not possible that he wrote precisely the play that he wanted, that his structure is the most effective for what he wanted to say, and that it could not have been said any better? Can you defend the play as it is, with the hero split into the scapegoat Antigone and the sufferer Creon?

5. Goethe made one of the most telling criticisms of the play when he commented to Eckermann that:

> After the heroine has in the play explained the noble reasons for her deed, and shown the high purity of her soul, she finally, when she is led to her death, mentions another reason which is utterly unworthy and almost borders upon the ridiculous.
>
> She says that, if she had been a mother, she would not do either for her dead children or dead husband what she has done for her dead brother. For, says she, if my husband died, I could marry again, and if my children died I could have more by my new husband. But the situation is different with my brother. I cannot have another brother, for my mother and father are dead, and there is no one to beget another brother.
>
> This is, at any rate, the basic sense of the passage, which to my mind, when placed in the mouth of a heroine about to die, harms the tragic tone and seems awfully farfetched. . . . I should like a philologist to prove that the passage is spurious.

By ordinary human standards of love, does Antigone's comment seem silly or reasonable? Her reasoning, incidentally, is borrowed from the Greek historian Herodotus; and H. D. F. Kitto attempts to explain it by asking, "A frigid sophism borrowed from Herodotus? Yes, the finest borrowing in literature. This is the final tragedy of Antigone . . . she can cling to nothing but a frigid sophism."

Do you think that Goethe or Kitto is right? If Kitto, how successful do you think this speech would be on the modern stage? Would a modern audience understand it? Would it alienate them from Antigone? Is it meant to?

6. Ismene is in Sophocles' play because she was in the original story that Sophocles used. However, Sophocles was too proficient a writer to make no dramatic use of her. To hark back to Goethe again, we find him giving to Eckermann this reason for Ismene:

> But, since Sophocles meant to show the noble nature of his heroine even before her deed, another contrast was needed to develop her character; and this contrast is with her sister Ismene. In this character, the poet has

painted an excellent picture of the ordinary, so that Antigone's surpassing greatness is all the more strikingly visible.

How sound a reading is this? Does Ismene only act in an ordinary fashion? What of her willingness to share Antigone's guilt? What other function than that mentioned by Goethe does Ismene perform in the play?

7. Is Eurydice's death a mere piling up of corpses? Would it have been better for Sophocles to have introduced her earlier? Or could he count on his audience already knowing about Eurydice, and could he, therefore, allow himself a dramatic shortcut?

8. Much of the later action is related by messengers. How much of this narration is necessitated by the dramatic form itself and how much by the stage tradition of the Greeks? Would a modern dramatist find this method undramatic? Is it undramatic?

9. The chorus in Greek plays is no mere disembodied voice of the author. It does not really correspond to a modern *raisonneur* like Enobarbus in *Antony and Cleopatra* or the Stage Manager in *Our Town*. The chorus had a distinct character that differed from play to play according to the people it was portraying. Therefore, it becomes something of a problem to determine whether we should believe and how much we should believe the chorus. For instance, the chorus ends this play by praising wisdom and piety and by condemning overweening boasting. "Taught by adversity," it says, "old age learns, too late, to be wise." Are we to take these sentiments as the theme and essence of the play, or are we to take them as the in-character comments of a weak and vacillating public morality?

To answer this, you should work out a notion of the attitudes of the chorus earlier in the play. How does it respond to Antigone and to Creon at first? Do its responses change? Is the chorus given to platitudes? Are these mere platitudes that are awkwardly intruded, or do they have an integral dramatic function? Why does the chorus apostrophize the gods and talk about nature?

The Tragedy of King Lear

BY WILLIAM SHAKESPEARE

EDITED BY ALFRED HARBAGE

CHARACTERS

LEAR, King of Britain	EARL OF KENT
KING OF FRANCE	EARL OF GLOUCESTER
DUKE OF BURGUNDY	EDGAR, son to Gloucester
DUKE OF CORNWALL	EDMUND, bastard son to Gloucester
DUKE OF ALBANY	CURAN, a courtier

OLD MAN, tenant to Gloucester
DOCTOR
LEAR'S FOOL
OSWALD, steward to Goneril
A CAPTAIN under Edmund's command
GENTLEMEN
A HERALD

SERVANTS to Cornwall
GONERIL ⎫
REGAN ⎬ daughters to Lear
CORDELIA ⎭
KNIGHTS attending on Lear, OFFICERS,
MESSENGERS, SOLDIERS, ATTENDANTS

Scene: Britain

ACT I

SCENE ONE

Enter Kent, Gloucester, and Edmund.

KENT. I thought the King had more affected [1] the Duke of Albany [2] than Cornwall.

GLOUCESTER. It did always seem so to us; but now, in the division of the kingdom, it appears not which of the dukes he values most, for equalities are so weighed [3] that curiosity in neither can make choice of either's moiety.[4]

KENT. Is not this your son, my lord?

GLOUCESTER. His breeding,[5] sir, hath been at my charge. I have so often blushed to acknowledge him that now I am brazed [6] to't.

KENT. I cannot conceive [7] you.

GLOUCESTER. Sir, this young fellow's mother could; whereupon she grew round-wombed, and had indeed, sir, a son for her cradle ere she had a husband for her bed. Do you smell a fault?

KENT. I cannot wish the fault undone, the issue of it being so proper.[8]

GLOUCESTER. But I have a son, sir, by order of law, some year elder than this who yet is no dearer in my account: [9] though this knave came something saucily [10] to the world before he was sent for, yet was his mother fair, there was good sport at his making, and the whoreson [11] must be acknowledged. Do you know this noble gentleman, Edmund?

EDMUND. No, my lord.

GLOUCESTER. My Lord of Kent. Remember him hereafter as my honorable friend.

EDMUND. My services to your lordship.

KENT. I must love you, and sue to

Note on the text. The text and notes used here are from Alfred Harbage's Pelican Shakespeare edition (Penguin Books, 1958), which is based mainly on the First Folio. Passages in square brackets indicate earlier, fuller Quarto readings, the Globe edition divisions of Acts and Scenes, and some explanatory material. For details, see The Pelican Shakespeare *King Lear*, p. 29.

I, i [1] *affected* warmly regarded
[2] *Albany* i.e. Scotland (once ruled by 'Albanacte')
[3] *equalities . . . weighed* i.e. the portions weigh so equally

[4] *curiosity . . . moiety* careful analysis by neither can make him prefer the other's portion
[5] *breeding* rearing
[6] *brazed* brazened
[7] *conceive* understand (with pun following)

[8] *proper* handsome
[9] *account* estimation
[10] *saucily* (1) impertinently (2) bawdily
[11] *whoreson* (affectionate abuse, but literally applicable, like 'knave' above)

know you better.

EDMUND. Sir, I shall study deserving.

GLOUCESTER. He hath been out [12] nine years, and away he shall again. [*Sound a*] *sennet.*[13] The King is coming.

Enter [one bearing a coronet, then] King Lear, [then the Dukes of] Cornwall [and] Albany, [next] Goneril, Regan, Cordelia, and Attendants.

LEAR. Attend the lords of France and Burgundy, Gloucester.

GLOUSTER. I shall, my lord. *Exit [with Edmund].*

LEAR. Meantime we shall express our darker purpose.[14] Give me the map there. Know that we have divided In three our kingdom; and 'tis our fast [15] intent To shake all cares and business from our age, Conferring them on younger strengths while we Unburdened crawl toward death. Our son of Cornwall, And you our no less loving son of Albany, We have this hour a constant will to publish [16] Our daughters' several dowers,[17] that future strife May be prevented now. The princes, France and Burgundy, Great rivals in our youngest daughter's love,

Long in our court have made their amorous sojourn,[18] And here are to be answered. Tell me, my daughters (Since now we will divest us both of rule, Interest [19] of territory, cares of state), Which of you shall we say doth love us most, That we our largest bounty may extend Where nature doth with merit challenge.[20] Goneril, Our eldest-born, speak first.

GONERIL. Sir, I love you more than word can wield [21] the matter; Dearer than eyesight, space,[22] and liberty; Beyond what can be valuèd, rich or rare; No less than life, with grace, health, beauty, honor; As much as child e'er loved, or father found; A love that makes breath [23] poor, and speech unable.[24] Beyond all manner of so much I love you.

CORDELIA. [*Aside*] What shall Cordelia speak? Love, and be silent.

LEAR. Of all these bounds, even from this line to this, With shadowy forests and with champains riched,[25] With plenteous rivers and wide-skirted [26] meads, We make thee lady. To thine and Al-

---

[12] *out* away (for training, or in military service)
[13] *sennet* trumpet flourish (heralding a procession)
[14] *darker purpose* more secret intention (to require declarations of affection)
[15] *fast* firm
[16] *constant . . . publish* fixed intention to announce
[17] *several* individual
[18] *amorous sojourn* i.e. visit of courtship
[19] *Interest* legal possession
[20] *nature . . . challenge* natural affection matches other merits
[21] *wield* handle
[22] *space* scope (for the exercise of 'liberty')
[23] *breath* voice
[24] *unable* inadequate
[25] *champains riched* plains enriched
[26] *wide-skirted* far-spreading

bany's issues [27]
Be this perpetual.[28]—What says our
second daughter,
Our dearest Regan, wife of Cornwall?
    REGAN. I am made of that self met-
tle as my sister,
And prize me at her worth.[29] In my
true heart
I find she names my very deed of [30]
love;
Only she comes too short, that I pro-
fess
Myself an enemy to all other joys
Which the most precious square of
sense possesses,[31]
And find I am alone felicitate [32]
In your dear Highness' love.
    CORDELIA. [*Aside*] Then poor Cor-
delia;
And yet not so, since I am sure my
love's
More ponderous [33] than my tongue.
    LEAR. To thee and thine hereditary
ever
Remain this ample third of our fair
kingdom,
No less in space, validity,[34] and pleas-
ure [35]
Than that conferred on Goneril.—
Now, our joy,
Although our last and least; [36] to
whose young love
The vines [37] of France and milk [38] of
Burgundy
Strive to be interest; [39] what can you
say to draw
A third more opulent than your sis-

ters? Speak.
    CORDELIA. Nothing, my lord.
    LEAR. Nothing?
    CORDELIA. Nothing.
    LEAR. Nothing will come of noth-
ing. Speak again.
    CORDELIA. Unhappy that I am, I
cannot heave
My heart into my mouth. I love your
Majesty
According to my bond,[40] no more nor
less.
    LEAR. How, how, Cordelia? Mend
your speech a little,
Lest you may mar your fortunes.
    CORDELIA.   Good my lord,
You have begot me, bred me, loved
me. I
Return those duties back as are right
fit,[41]
Obey you, love you, and most honor
you.
Why have my sisters husbands if they
say
They love you all? Haply, when I shall
wed,
That lord whose hand must take my
plight [42] shall carry
Half my love with him, half my care
and duty.
Sure I shall never marry like my sisters,
[To love my father all.]
    LEAR.   But goes thy heart with
this?
    CORDELIA.   Ay, my good lord.
    LEAR. So young, and so untender?

---

[27] *issues* descendants
[28] *perpetual* in perpetuity
[29] *prize . . . worth* value
me at her value
[30] *my very deed of* the
true fact of my
[31] *Which . . . possesses*
which the most precise
measurement   by   the

senses holds to be most
precious
[32] *felicitate* made happy
[33] *ponderous* weighty
[34] *validity* value
[35] *pleasure* pleasing qualities
[36] *least* smallest, youngest
[37] *vines* vineyards

[38] *milk* pasture-lands (?)
[39] *interest* concerned as interested parties
[40] *bond* obligation
[41] *Return . . . fit* i.e. am
fittingly dutiful in return
[42] *plight* pledge, troth-
plight

CORDELIA. So young, my lord, and true.

LEAR. Let it be so, thy truth then be thy dower!
For, by the sacred radiance of the sun,
The mysteries of Hecate [43] and the night,
By all the operation of the orbs [44]
From whom we do exist and cease to be,
Here I disclaim all my paternal care,
Propinquity [45] and property [46] of blood,
And as a stranger to my heart and me
Hold thee from this for ever. The barbarous Scythian,[47]
Or he that makes his generation messes [48]
To gorge his appetite, shall to my bosom
Be as well neighbored, pitied, and relieved,
As thou my sometime [49] daughter.

KENT. Good my liege—

LEAR. Peace, Kent!
Come not between the dragon and his [50] wrath.
I loved her most, and thought to set my rest [51]
On her kind nursery.[52]—Hence and avoid my sight!—
So be my grave my peace as [53] here I give
Her father's heart from her! Call France. Who stirs!
Call Burgundy. Cornwall and Albany,
With my two daughters' dowers digest the third;
Let pride, which she calls plainness, marry her.
I do invest you jointly with my power,
Preeminence, and all the large effects [54]
That troop with majesty. Ourself,[55] by monthly course,
With reservation of an hundred knights,
By you to be sustained, shall our abode
Make with you by due turn. Only we shall retain
The name, and all th' addition [56] to a king. The sway,
Revenue, execution of the rest,
Belovèd sons, be yours; which to confirm,
This coronet [57] part between you.

KENT. Royal Lear,
Whom I have ever honored as my king,
Loved as my father, as my master followed,
As my great patron thought on in my prayers—

LEAR. The bow is bent and drawn; make [58] from the shaft.

KENT. Let it fall [59] rather, though the fork [60] invade
The region of my heart. Be Kent unmannerly

[43] *Hecate* infernal goddess, patroness of witches
[44] *operation . . . orbs* astrological influences
[45] *Propinquity* relationship
[46] *property* i.e. common property, something shared
[47] *Scythian* (proverbially barbarous)
[48] *makes . . . messes* makes meals of his offspring
[49] *sometime* former
[50] *his* its
[51] *set my rest* (1) risk my stake (a term in the card game primero) (2) rely for my repose
[52] *nursery* nursing, care
[53] *So . . . peace as* let me rest peacefully in my grave only as
[54] *effects* tokens
[55] *Ourself* I (royal plural)
[56] *th' addition* honors and prerogatives
[57] *coronet* (symbol of rule, not necessarily the royal crown)
[58] *make* make away
[59] *fall* strike
[60] *fork* two-pronged head

When Lear is mad. What wouldst
thou do, old man?
Think'st thou that duty shall have
dread to speak
When power to flattery bows? To
plainness honor's bound
When majesty falls to folly. Reserve
thy state,[61]
And in thy best consideration [62] check
This hideous rashness. Answer my
life [63] my judgment,
Thy youngest daughter does not love
thee least,
Nor are those empty-hearted whose
low sounds
Reverb no hollowness.[64]

LEAR.   Kent, on thy life, no more!

KENT. My life I never held but as a
pawn [65]
To wage [66] against thine enemies;
ne'er fear to lose it,
Thy safety being motive.[67]

LEAR.   Out of my sight!

KENT. See better, Lear, and let me
still [68] remain
The true blank [69] of thine eye.

LEAR. Now by Apollo—

KENT.   Now by Apollo, King,
Thou swear'st thy gods in vain.

LEAR.   O vassal! Miscreant! [70]
          [*Grasping his sword.*]

ALBANY, CORNWALL. Dear sir, forbear!

KENT. Kill thy physician, and thy
fee bestow

Upon the foul disease. Revoke thy
gift,
Or, whilst I can vent clamor from my
throat,
I'll tell thee thou dost evil.

LEAR.   Hear me, recreant,[71]
On thine allegiance, hear me!
That [72] thou hast sought to make us
break our vows,
Which we durst never yet, and with
strained [73] pride
To come betwixt our sentence and our
power,[74]
Which nor our nature nor our place
can bear,
Our potency made good,[75] take thy
reward.
Five days we do allot thee for provi-
sion
To shield thee from disasters [76] of the
world,
And on the sixth to turn thy hated
back
Upon our kingdom. If, on the tenth
day following,
Thy banished trunk [77] be found in our
dominions,
The moment is thy death. Away. By
Jupiter,
This shall not be revoked.

KENT. Fare thee well, King. Sith [78]
thus thou wilt appear,
Freedom lives hence, and banishment
is here.
[*To Cordelia*] The gods to their dear

---

[61] *Reserve thy state* retain
your kingly authority
[62] *best consideration* most
careful deliberation
[63] *Answer my life* i.e. I'll
stake my life on
[64] *Reverb no hollowness*
i.e. do not reverberate
(like a drum) as a result
of hollowness
[65] *pawn* stake

[66] *wage* wager, pit
[67] *motive* the moving
cause
[68] *still* always
[69] *blank* center of the tar-
get (to guide your aim
truly)
[70] *Miscreant* (1) rascal
(2) infidel
[71] *recreant* traitor
[72] *That* in that, since

[73] *strained* excessive
[74] *To come . . . power* i.e.
to oppose my power to
sentence
[75] *Our . . . good* if my
power is to be demon-
strated as real
[76] *disasters* accidents
[77] *trunk* body
[78] *Sith* since

shelter take thee, maid,
That justly think'st and hast most
    rightly said.
[*To Regan and Goneril*] And your
    large speeches may your deeds
    approve,[79]
That good effects [80] may spring from
    words of love.
Thus Kent, O princes, bids you all
    adieu;
He'll shape his old course [81] in a coun-
    try new.   *Exit.*
    Flourish. Enter Gloucester, with
France and Burgundy; Attendants.
    GLOUCESTER. Here's France and
    Burgundy, my noble lord.
    LEAR. My Lord of Burgundy,
We first address toward you, who with
    this king
Hath rivalled for our daughter. What
    in the least
Will you require in present dower
    with her,
Or cease your quest of love?
    BURGUNDY.   Most royal Maj-
    esty.
I crave no more than hath your High-
    ness offered,
Nor will you tender less.
    LEAR.   Right noble Burgundy,
When she was dear to us, we did hold
    her so;
But now her price is fallen. Sir, there
    she stands.
If aught within that little seeming sub-
    stance,[82]
Or all of it, with our displeasure
    pieced [83]

And nothing more, may fitly like your
    Grace,
She's there, and she is yours.
    BURGUNDY.   I know no answer.
    LEAR. Will you, with those infirmi-
    ties she owes,[84]
Unfriended, new adopted to our hate,
Dow'red with our curse, and stran-
    gered with [85] our oath,
Take her, or leave her?
    BURGUNDY.   Pardon me, royal sir.
Election makes not up on such condi-
    tions.[86]
    LEAR. Then leave her, sir, for by the
    pow'r that made me
I tell you all her wealth. [*To France*]
    For you, great King,
I would not from your love make such
    a stray [87]
To match you where I hate; therefore
    beseech you
T' avert [88] your liking a more worthier
    way
Than on a wretch whom nature is
    ashamed
Almost t' acknowledge hers.
    FRANCE.   This is most strange,
That she whom even but now was
    your best [89] object,
The argument [90] of your praise, balm
    of your age,
The best, the dearest, should in this
    trice of time
Commit a thing so monstrous to dis-
    mantle [91]
So many folds of favor. Sure her of-
    fense
Must be of such unnatural degree

---

[79] *approve* confirm
[80] *effects* consequences
[81] *shape . . . course* keep
to his customary ways (of
honesty)
[82] *seeming substance* i.e.
nothing, mere shell

[83] *pieced* joined
[84] *owes* owns
[85] *strangered with* made
alien by
[86] *Election . . . conditions*
no choice is possible on
such terms

[87] *make . . . stray* stray
so far as
[88] *avert* turn
[89] *best* favorite
[90] *argument* theme
[91] *to dismantle* so to strip
off

That monsters it,[92] or your fore-
vouched [93] affection
Fall'n into taint; [94] which to believe
of her
Must be a faith that reason without
miracle [95]
Should never plant in me.
    CORDELIA. I yet beseech your Maj-
esty,
If for I want that glib and oily art
To speak and purpose not [96] since
what I well intend
I'll do't before I speak, that you make
known
It is no vicious blot, murder, or foul-
ness,
No unchaste action or dishonorèd
step,
That hath deprived me of your grace
and favor;
But even for want of that for which I
am richer—
A still-soliciting [97] eye, and such a
tongue
That I am glad I have not, though not
to have it
Hath lost me in your liking.
    LEAR.   Better thou
Hadst not been born than not t' have
pleased me better.
    FRANCE. Is it but this? A tardiness
in nature [98]
Which often leaves the history unspoke [99]
That it intends to do. My Lord of Burgundy,

What say you to the lady? Love's not
love
When it is mingled with regards that
stands
Aloof from th' entire point.[100] Will
you have her?
She is herself a dowry.
    BURGUNDY.   Royal King,
Give but that portion which yourself
proposed,
And here I take Cordelia by the hand,
Duchess of Burgundy.
    LEAR. Nothing. I have sworn. I am
firm.
    BURGUNDY. I am sorry then you
have so lost a father
That you must lose a husband.
    CORDELIA.   Peace be with Bur-
gundy.
Since that respects [101] of fortune are
his love,
I shall not be his wife.
    FRANCE. Fairest Cordelia, that art
most rich being poor,
Most choice forsaken, and most loved
despised,
Thee and thy virtues here I seize
upon.
Be it lawful I take up what's cast
away.
Gods, gods! 'Tis strange that from
their cold'st neglect
My love should kindle to inflamed respect.[102]
Thy dow'rless daughter, King, thrown
to my chance,

[92] *That monsters it* as
makes it monstrous (i.e.
abnormal, freakish)
[93] *fore-vouched* previously
sworn
[94] *taint* decay (with the
implication that the af-
fection, and the oath at-
testing it, were tainted
in the first place)

[95] *reason . . . miracle* i.e.
rational, unaided by mi-
raculous, means of per-
suasion
[96] *purpose not* i.e. without intending to act in
accordance with my
words
[97] *still-soliciting* always-
begging

[98] *tardiness in nature* natural reticence
[99] *history unspoke* actions
unannounced
[100] *mingled . . . point* i.e.
mixed with irrelevant
considerations
[101] *respects* considerations
[102] *inflamed respect* ardent
regard

Is queen of us, of ours, and our fair
France.
Not all the dukes of wat'rish [103] Bur-
gundy
Can buy this unprized [104] precious
maid of me.
Bid them farewell, Cordelia, though
unkind.
Thou losest here,[105] a better where [106]
to find.
LEAR. Thou hast her, France; let her
be thine, for we
Have no such daughter, nor shall ever
see
That face of hers again. Therefore be
gone
Without our grace, our love, our beni-
son.[107]
Come, noble Burgundy.
*Flourish. Exeunt [Lear, Burgundy,
Cornwall, Albany, Gloucester, and
Attendants].*
FRANCE.   Bid farewell to your sis-
ters.
CORDELIA. The jewels [108] of our
father, with washed [109] eyes
Cordelia leaves you. I know you what
you are;
And, like a sister,[110] am most loath
to call
Your faults as they are named.[111] Love
well our father.
To your professèd [112] bosoms I commit
him;
But yet, alas, stood I within his grace,

I would prefer [113] him to a better
place.
So farewell to you both.
REGAN. Prescribe not us our duty.
GONERIL.   Let your study
Be to content your lord, who hath re-
ceived you
At fortune's alms.[114] You have obedi-
ence scanted,
And well are worth the want that you
have wanted.[115]
CORDELIA. Time shall unfold what
plighted [116] cunning hides,
Who covers faults, at last with shame
derides.[117]
Well may you prosper.
FRANCE. Come, my fair Cordelia.
Exit France and Cordelia.
GONERIL. Sister, it is not little I have
to say of what most nearly appertains
to us both. I think our father will
hence to-night.
REGAN. That's most certain, and
with you; next month with us.
GONERIL. You see how full of
changes his age is. The observation
we have made of it hath not been little. He always loved our sister most,
and with what poor judgment he hath
now cast her off appears too grossly.[118]
REGAN. 'Tis the infirmity of his age;
yet he hath ever but slenderly known
himself.[119]
GONERIL. The best and soundest of

---

[103] *wat'rish* (1) watery, weak (2) watered, diluted
[104] *unprized* unvalued
[105] *here* this place
[106] *where* other place
[107] *benison* blessing
[108] *jewels* i.e. things held precious
[109] *washed* tear-washed
[110] *like a sister* i.e. with

sisterly loyalty
[111] *as . . . named* by their true names
[112] *professèd* i.e. love-professing
[113] *prefer* promote
[114] *alms* small offerings
[115] *worth . . . wanted* i.e. deserving no affection since you have shown no affection

[116] *plighted* pleated, enfolded
[117] *Who . . . derides* i.e. time at first conceals faults, then exposes them to shame
[118] *grossly* crudely conspicuous
[119] *known himself* i.e. been aware of what he truly is

his time [120] hath been but rash; then must we look from his age to receive not alone the imperfections of long-ingraffed [121] condition, but therewithal [122] the unruly waywardness that infirm and choleric years bring with them.

REGAN. Such unconstant starts [123] are we like to have from him as this of Kent's banishment.

GONERIL. There is further compliment [124] of leave-taking between France and him. Pray you let us hit [125] together; if our father carry authority with such disposition as he bears, this last surrender [126] of his will but offend [127] us.

REGAN. We shall further think of it.

GONERIL. We must do something, and i' th' heat.[128] *Exeunt.*

SCENE TWO

Enter Bastard [Edmund, solus, with a letter].

EDMUND. Thou, Nature,[1] art my goddess; to thy law
My services are bound. Wherefore should I
Stand in the plague of custom,[2] and permit
The curiosity [3] of nations to deprive me,

For that [4] I am some twelve or four-teen moonshines [5]
Lag of [6] a brother? Why bastard? Wherefore base,
When my dimensions are as well compact,[7]
My mind as generous,[8] and my shape as true,
As honest [9] madam's issue? Why brand they us
With base? with baseness? Bastardy base? Base?
Who, in the lusty stealth of nature,[10] take
More composition [11] and fierce [12] quality
Than doth, within a dull, stale, tirèd bed,
Go to th' creating a whole tribe of fops [13]
Got [14] 'tween asleep and wake? Well then,
Legitimate Edgar, I must have your land.
Our father's love is to the bastard Edmund
As to th' legitimate. Fine word, 'legitimate.'
Well, my legitimate, if this letter speed,
And my invention thrive,[15] Edmund the base
Shall top th' legitimate. I grow, I

[120] *of his time* period of his past life
[121] *long-ingraffed* ingrown, chronic
[122] *therewithal* along with that
[123] *unconstant starts* impulsive moves
[124] *compliment* formality
[125] *hit* agree
[126] *surrender* i.e. yielding up of authority
[127] *offend* harm
[128] *i' th' heat* i.e. while

the iron is hot
I, ii [1] *Nature* i.e. the material and mechanistic as distinct from the spiritual and heaven-ordained
[2] *Stand . . . custom* submit to the affliction of convention
[3] *curiosity* nice distinctions
[4] *For that* because
[5] *moonshines* months
[6] *Lag of* behind (in age)
[7] *compact* fitted, matched

[8] *generous* befitting the high-born
[9] *honest* chaste
[10] *lusty . . . nature* secrecy of natural lust
[11] *composition* completeness of constitution, robustness
[12] *fierce* mettlesome, thoroughbred
[13] *fops* fools
[14] *Got* begotten
[15] *invention thrive* plot succeed

prosper.
Now, gods, stand up for bastards.
Enter Gloucester.

GLOUCESTER. Kent banished thus?
and France in choler parted?
And the King gone to-night? pre-
scribed [16] his pow'r?
Confined to exhibition? [17] All this
done
Upon the gad? [18] Edmund, how now?
What news?

EDMUND. So please your lordship,
none.

GLOUCESTER. Why so earnestly seek
you to put up [19] that letter?

EDMUND. I know no news, my lord.

GLOUCESTER. What paper were you
reading?

EDMUND. Nothing, my lord.

GLOUCESTER. No? What needed
then that terrible dispatch of it into
your pocket? The quality of nothing
hath not such need to hide itself. Let's
see. Come, if it be nothing, I shall not
need spectacles.

EDMUND. I beseech you, sir, pardon
me. It is a letter from my brother that
I have not all o'er-read; and for so
much as I have perused, I find it not
fit for your o'erlooking.[20]

GLOUCESTER. Give me the letter, sir.

EDMUND. I shall offend, either to
detain or give it. The contents, as in
part I understand them, are to
blame.[21]

GLOUCESTER. Let's see, let's see.

EDMUND. I hope, for my brother's

justification, he wrote this but as an
essay [22] or taste [23] of my virtue.

GLOUCESTER. (*Reads*) 'This policy
and reverence [24] of age makes the
world bitter to the best of our times; [25]
keeps our fortunes from us till our
oldness cannot relish them. I begin to
find an idle and fond [26] bondage in the
oppression of aged tyranny, who
sways,[27] not as it hath power, but as
it is suffered.[28] Come to me, that of
this I may speak more. If our father
would sleep till I waked him, you
should enjoy half his revenue [29] for
ever, and live the beloved of your
brother,
                                          EDGAR.'

Hum! Conspiracy? 'Sleep till I waked
him, you should enjoy half his revenue.' My son Edgar! Had he a hand
to write this? A heart and brain to
breed it in? When came you to this? [30]
Who brought it?

EDMUND. It was not brought me, my
lord; there's the cunning of it. I found
it thrown in at the casement [31] of my
closet.[32]

GLOUCESTER. You know the character [33] to be your brother's?

EDMUND. If the matter [34] were
good, my lord, I durst swear it were
his; but in respect of that,[35] I would
fain [36] think it were not.

GLOUCESTER. It is his.

EDMUND. It is his hand, my lord;
but I hope his heart is not in the contents.

---

[16] *prescribed* limited
[17] *exhibition* an allowance,
a pension
[18] *gad* spur
[19] *put up* put away
[20] *o'erlooking* examination
[21] *to blame* blameworthy
[22] *essay* trial
[23] *taste* test

[24] *policy and reverence*
policy of reverencing
[25] *the best of our times*
our best years
[26] *idle, fond* foolish (syno-
nyms)
[27] *who sways* which rules
[28] *suffered* allowed
[29] *revenue* income

[30] *to this* upon this
[31] *casement* window
[32] *closet* room
[33] *character* handwriting
[34] *matter* contents
[35] *in respect of that* i.e.
considering what those
contents are
[36] *fain* prefer to

GLOUCESTER. Has he never before sounded you [37] in this business?

EDMUND. Never, my lord. But I have heard him oft maintain it to be fit that, sons at perfect age,[38] and fathers declined, the father should be as ward to the son, and the son manage his revenue.

GLOUCESTER. O villain, villain! His very opinion in the letter. Abhorred villain, unnatural, detested, brutish villain; worse than brutish! Go, sirrah,[39] seek him. I'll apprehend him. Abominable villain! Where is he?

EDMUND. I do not well know, my lord. If it shall please you to suspend your indignation against my brother till you can derive from him better testimony of his intent, you should run a certain course; [40] where, if you violently proceed against him, mistaking his purpose, it would make a great gap in your own honor and shake in pieces the heart of his obedience. I dare pawn down my life for him that he hath writ this to feel [41] my affection [42] to your honor, and to no other pretense of danger.[43]

GLOUCESTER. Think you so?

EDMUND. If your honor judge it meet,[44] I will place you where you shall hear us confer of this and by an auricular assurance [45] have your satisfaction, and that without any further delay than this very evening.

GLOUCESTER. He cannot be such a monster.

[EDMUND. Nor is not, sure.

GLOUCESTER. To his father, that so tenderly and entirely loves him. Heaven and earth!] Edmund, seek him out; wind me [46] into him, I pray you; frame [47] the business after your own wisdom. I would unstate myself to be in a due resolution.[48]

EDMUND. I will seek him, sir, presently; [49] convey [50] the business as I shall find means, and acquaint you withal.[51]

GLOUCESTER. These late [52] eclipses in the sun and moon portend no good to us. Though the wisdom of nature [53] can reason it thus and thus, yet nature finds itself scourged [54] by the sequent [55] effects.[56] Love cools, friendship falls off, brothers divide. In cities, mutinies; [57] in countries, discord; in palaces, treason; and the bond cracked 'twixt son and father. This villain of mine comes under the prediction,[58] there's son against father; the King falls from bias of nature,[59] there's father against child. We have seen the best of our time. Machinations, hollowness, treachery, and all ruinous disorders follow us disquietly to our

---

[37] *sounded you* sounded you out
[38] *perfect age* prime of life
[39] *sirrah* sir (familiar, or contemptuous, form)
[40] *run . . . course* i.e. know where you are going
[41] *feel* feel out, test
[42] *affection* attachment, loyalty
[43] *pretense of danger* dangerous intention
[44] *judge it meet* consider it fitting

[45] *by . . . assurance* i.e. by the proof of your own ears
[46] *wind me* worm
[47] *frame* plan
[48] *unstate . . . resolution* i.e. give everything to know for certain
[49] *presently* at once
[50] *convey* conduct
[51] *withal* therewith
[52] *late* recent
[53] *wisdom of nature* natural lore, science

[54] *scourged* whipped
[55] *sequent* following
[56] *can . . . effects* i.e. can supply explanations, yet punitive upheavals in nature (such as earthquakes) follow
[57] *mutinies* rebellions
[58] *comes . . . prediction* i.e. is included among these ill-omened things
[59] *bias of nature* natural tendency

graves. Find out this villain, Edmund, it shall lose thee nothing; [60] do it carefully. And the noble and true-hearted Kent banished; his offense, honesty. 'Tis strange.   *Exit.*

EDMUND. This is the excellent foppery [61] of the world, that when we are sick in fortune, often the surfeits [62] of our own behavior, we make guilty of our disasters the sun, the moon, and stars; as if we were villains on necessity; fools by heavenly compulsion; knaves, thieves, and treachers [63] by spherical predominance;[64] drunkards, liars, and adulterers by an enforced obedience of planetary influence; and all that we are evil in, by a divine thrusting on. An admirable evasion of whoremaster man, to lay his goatish [65] disposition on the charge of a star. My father compounded [66] with my mother under the Dragon's Tail, and my nativity [67] was under Ursa Major,[68] so that it follows I am rough and lecherous. Fut! I should have been that I am, had the maidenliest star in the firmament twinkled on my bastardizing. Edgar—

Enter Edgar.

and pat he comes, like the catastrophe [69] of the old comedy. My cue is villainous melancholy, with a sigh like Tom o' Bedlam.[70]—O, these eclipses do portend these divisions. Fa, sol, la, mi.

EDGAR. How now, brother Edmund; what serious contemplation are you in?

EDMUND. I am thinking, brother, of a prediction I read this other day, what should follow these eclipses.

EDGAR. Do you busy yourself with that?

EDMUND. I promise you, the effects he writes of succeed unhappily: [71] [as of unnaturalness [72] between the child and the parent; death, dearth, dissolutions of ancient amities; divisions in state, menaces and maledictions against king and nobles; needless diffidences,[73] banishment of friends, dissipation of cohorts,[74] nuptial breaches, and I know not what.

EDGAR. How long have you been a sectary astronomical? [75]

EDMUND. Come, come,] when saw you my father last?

EDGAR. The night gone by.

EDMUND. Spake you with him?

EDGAR. Ay, two hours together.

EDMUND. Parted you in good terms? Found you no displeasure in him by word nor countenance? [76]

EDGAR. None at all.

EDMUND. Bethink yourself wherein you may have offended him; and at

[60] *lose thee nothing* i.e. you will not lose by it
[61] *foppery* foolishness
[62] *we are sick . . . surfeits* i.e. our fortunes grow sickly, often from the excesses
[63] *treachers* traitors
[64] *spherical predominance* i.e. ascendancy, or rule, of a particular sphere
[65] *goatish* lecherous
[66] *compounded* (1) came

to terms (2) created
[67] *nativity* birthday
[68] *Dragon's Tail, Ursa Major* (constellations, cited because of the suggestiveness of their names)
[69] *catastrophe* conclusion
[70] *Tom o' Bedlam* (a type of beggar, mad or pretending to be, so named from the London madhouse, Bethlehem or 'Bedlam' Hospital)

[71] *succeed unhappily* unluckily follow
[72] *unnaturalness* unkindness, enmity
[73] *diffidences* instances of distrust
[74] *dissipation of cohorts* melting away of supporters
[75] *sectary astronomical* of the astrological sect
[76] *countenance* expression, look

my entreaty forbear his presence until some little time hath qualified [77] the heat of his displeasure, which at this instant so rageth in him that with the mischief [78] of your person it would scarcely allay.[79]

EDGAR. Some villain hath done me wrong.

EDMUND. That's my fear. I pray you have a continent forbearance [80] till the speed of his rage goes slower; and, as I say, retire with me to my lodging, from whence I will fitly [81] bring you to hear my lord speak. Pray ye, go; there's my key. If you do stir abroad, go armed.

EDGAR. Armed, brother?

EDMUND. Brother, I advise you to the best. Go armed. I am no honest man if there be any good meaning toward you. I have told you what I have seen and heard; but faintly, nothing like the image and horror [82] of it. Pray you, away.

EDGAR. Shall I hear from you anon? [83]

EDMUND. I do serve you in this business.   Exit [Edgar].

A credulous father, and a brother noble,
Whose nature is so far from doing harms
That he suspects none; on whose foolish honesty
My practices [84] ride easy. I see the business.

Let me, if not by birth, have lands by wit; [85]
All with me's meet [86] that I can fashion fit.[87]   Exit.

SCENE THREE

Enter Goneril and Steward [Oswald].

GONERIL. Did my father strike my gentleman for chiding of his fool?

OSWALD. Ay, madam.

GONERIL. By day and night,[1] he wrongs me! Every hour
He flashes into one gross crime [2] or other
That sets us all at odds. I'll not endure it.
His knights grow riotous,[3] and himself upbraids us
On every trifle. When he returns from hunting,
I will not speak with him. Say I am sick.
If you come slack of former services,[4]
You shall do well; the fault of it I'll answer.[5]   [Horns within.]

OSWALD. He's coming, madam; I hear him.

GONERIL. Put on what weary negligence you please,
You and your fellows. I'd have it come to question.[6]
If he distaste [7] it, let him to my sister,
Whose mind and mine I know in that are one,
[Not to be overruled. Idle [8] old man,

[77] qualified moderated
[78] mischief injury
[79] allay be appeased
[80] continent forbearance cautious inaccessibility
[81] fitly conveniently
[82] image and horror horrible true picture
[83] anon soon

[84] practices plots
[85] wit intelligence
[86] meet proper, acceptable
[87] fashion fit i.e. rig up, shape to the purpose
I, iii [1] day and night (an oath)
[2] crime offense
[3] riotous boisterous

[4] come . . . services i.e. serve him less well than formerly
[5] answer answer for
[6] question i.e. open issue, a thing discussed
[7] distaste dislike
[8] Idle foolish

That still would manage those authorities
That he hath given away. Now, by
my life,
Old fools are babes again, and must
be used
With checks as flatteries, when they
are seen abused.⁹]
Remember what I have said.

OSWALD.   Well, madam.

GONERIL. And let his knights have
colder looks among you.
What grows of it, no matter; advise
your fellows so.
[I would breed from hence occasions,
and I shall,
That I may speak.] ¹⁰ I'll write straight
to my sister
To hold my course. Prepare for dinner.
                                        Exeunt.

SCENE FOUR

Enter Kent [disguised].

KENT. If but as well I other accents
borrow
That can my speech defuse,¹ my good
intent
May carry through itself to that full
issue ²
For which I razed my likeness.³ Now,
banished Kent,
If thou canst serve where thou dost
stand condemned,

So may it come, thy master whom thou
lov'st
Shall find thee full of labors.
     Horns within. Enter Lear, [Knight,]
and Attendants.

LEAR. Let me not stay ⁴ a jot for
dinner; go get it ready. [Exit an Attendant.] How now, what art thou?

KENT. A man, sir.

LEAR. What dost thou profess? ⁵
What wouldst thou with us?

KENT. I do profess ⁶ to be no less
than I seem, to serve him truly that
will put me in trust, to love him that
is honest, to converse ⁷ with him that
is wise and says little, to fear judgment,⁸ to fight when I cannot choose,
and to eat no fish.⁹

LEAR. What art thou?

KENT. A very honest-hearted fellow,
and as poor as the King.

LEAR. If thou be'st as poor for a
subject as he's for a king, thou art
poor enough. What wouldst thou?

KENT. Service.

LEAR. Who wouldst thou serve?

KENT. You.

LEAR. Dost thou know me, fellow?

KENT. No, sir, but you have that in
your countenance which I would
fain ¹⁰ call master.

LEAR. What's that?

KENT. Authority.

LEAR. What services canst thou do?

KENT. I can keep honest counsel,¹¹

⁹ checks . . . abused re-
straints in place of cajol-
ery when they (the old
men) are seen to be de-
ceived (about their true
state)
¹⁰ breed . . . speak   i.e.
make an issue of it so that
I may speak
I, iv ¹ defuse disorder,

disguise
² full issue perfect result
³ razed my likeness erased
my natural appearance
⁴ stay wait
⁵ profess do, work at (with
pun following)
⁶ profess claim
⁷ converse associate

⁸ judgment   i.e.   God's
judgment
⁹ eat no fish be a Protes-
tant (anachronism), or
avoid unmanly diet (?)
¹⁰ fain like to
¹¹ keep honest counsel
keep counsel honestly,
i.e. respect confidences

ride, run, mar a curious [11a] tale in telling it and deliver a plain message bluntly. That which ordinary men are fit for I am qualified in, and the best of me is diligence.

LEAR. How old art thou?

KENT. Not so young, sir, to love a woman for singing, nor so old to dote on her for anything. I have years on my back forty-eight.

LEAR. Follow me; thou shalt serve me. If I like thee no worse after dinner, I will not part from thee yet. Dinner, ho, dinner! Where's my knave? [12] my fool? Go you and call my fool hither. [*Exit an Attendant.*]
Enter Steward [Oswald].
You, you, sirrah, where's my daughter?

OSWALD. So please you— *Exit.*

LEAR. What says the fellow there? Call the clotpoll [13] back. [*Exit Knight.*] Where's my fool? Ho, I think the world's asleep.
[*Enter Knight.*]
How now? Where's that mongrel?

KNIGHT. He says, my lord, your daughter is not well.

LEAR. Why came not the slave back to me when I called him?

KNIGHT. Sir, he answered me in the roundest manner, he would not.

LEAR. He would not?

KNIGHT. My lord, I know not what the matter is; but to my judgment your Highness is not entertained [14] with that ceremonious affection as you were wont. There's a great abatement

of kindness appears as well in the general dependants as in the Duke himself also and your daughter.

LEAR. Ha? Say'st thou so?

KNIGHT. I beseech you pardon me, my lord, if I be mistaken; for my duty cannot be silent when I think your Highness wronged.

LEAR. Thou but rememb'rest [15] me of mine own conception. I have perceived a most faint neglect [16] of late, which I have rather blamed as mine own jealous curiosity [17] than as a very pretense [18] and purpose of unkindness. I will look further into't. But where's my fool? I have not seen him this two days.

KNIGHT. Since my young lady's going into France, sir, the fool hath much pined away.

LEAR. No more of that; I have noted it well. Go you and tell my daughter I would speak with her. [*Exit Knight.*] Go you, call hither my fool.
[*Exit an Attendant.*]
Enter Steward [Oswald].
O, you, sir, you! Come you hither, sir. Who am I, sir?

OSWALD. My lady's father.

LEAR. 'My lady's father'? My lord's knave, you whoreson dog, you slave, you cur!

OSWALD. I am none of these, my lord; I beseech your pardon.

LEAR. Do you bandy [19] looks with me, you rascal? [*Strikes him.*]

OSWALD. I'll not be strucken,[20] my lord.

[11a] *curious* elaborate, embroidered (as contrasted with 'plain')
[12] *knave* boy
[13] *clotpoll* clodpoll, dolt
[14] *entertained* rendered hospitality

[15] *rememb'rest* remind
[16] *faint neglect* i.e. the 'weary negligence' of Goneril's speech in Sc. iii
[17] *jealous curiosity* i.e.

suspicious concern about trifles
[18] *very pretense* true intention
[19] *bandy* volley, exchange
[20] *strucken* struck

KENT. Nor tripped neither, you base football [21] player. [*Trips up his heels.*]

LEAR. I thank thee, fellow. Thou serv'st me, and I'll love thee.

KENT. Come, sir, arise, away. I'll teach you differences.[22] Away, away. If you will measure your lubber's length again, tarry; but away. Go to! Have you wisdom? [23] So.

[*Pushes him out.*]

LEAR. Now, my friendly knave, I thank thee. There's earnest [24] of thy service.   [*Gives money.*]

Enter Fool.

FOOL. Let me hire him too. Here's my coxcomb.[25] [*Offers Kent his cap.*]

LEAR. How now, my pretty knave? How dost thou?

FOOL. Sirrah, you were best take my coxcomb.

KENT. Why, fool?

FOOL. Why? For taking one's part that's out of favor. Nay, an thou canst not smile as the wind sits,[26] thou'lt catch cold shortly. There, take my coxcomb. Why, this fellow has banished [27] two on's daughters, and did the third a blessing against his will. If thou follow him, thou must needs wear my coxcomb.—How now, nuncle? [28] Would I had two coxcombs and two daughters.

LEAR. Why, my boy?

FOOL. If I gave them all my living, I'd keep my coxcombs myself. There's mine; beg another of thy daughters.

LEAR. Take heed, sirrah—the whip.

FOOL. Truth's a dog must to kennel; he must be whipped out, when the Lady Brach [29] may stand by th' fire and stink.

LEAR. A pestilent gall [30] to me.

FOOL. Sirrah, I'll teach thee a speech.

LEAR. Do.

FOOL. Mark it, nuncle.
Have more than thou showest,
Speak less than thou knowest,
Lend less than thou owest,[31]
Ride more than thou goest,[32]
Learn [33] more than thou trowest,[33a]
Set less than thou throwest; [34]
Leave thy drink and thy whore,
And keep in-a-door,
And thou shalt have more
Than two tens to a score.[35]

KENT. This is nothing, fool.

FOOL. Then 'tis like the breath [36] of an unfee'd lawyer—you gave me nothing for't. Can you make no use of nothing, nuncle?

LEAR. Why, no, boy. Nothing can be made out of nothing.

FOOL. [*To Kent*] Prithee tell him, so much the rent of his land [37] comes to; he will not believe a fool.

---

[21] *football* (an impromptu street and field game, held in low esteem)
[22] *differences* distinctions in rank
[23] *Go to! . . . wisdom* i.e. Get along! Do you know what's good for you?
[24] *earnest* part payment
[25] *coxcomb* (cap of the professional fool, topped with an imitation comb)
[26] *smile . . . sits* i.e. adapt yourself to prevailing forces
[27] *banished* i.e. provided the means for them to become alien to him
[28] *nuncle* mine uncle
[29] *Brach* hound bitch
[30] *gall* sore, source of irritation
[31] *owest* borrow (?) own, keep (?)
[32] *goest* walk
[33] *Learn* hear, listen to
[33a] *trowest* believe
[34] *Set . . . throwest* stake less than you throw for (i.e. play for odds)
[35] *have . . . score* i.e. do better than break even
[36] *breath* voice, counsel (reliable only when paid for)
[37] *rent . . . land* (nothing, since he has no land)

LEAR. A bitter fool.

FOOL. Dost thou know the difference, my boy, between a bitter fool and a sweet [38] one?

LEAR. No, lad; teach me.

FOOL.

[That lord that counselled thee
　　To give away thy land,
Come place him here by me—
　　Do thou for him stand.[39]
The sweet and bitter fool
　　Will presently appear;
The one in motley here,
　　The other found out [40] there.

LEAR. Dost thou call me fool, boy?

FOOL. All thy other titles thou hast given away; that thou wast born with.

KENT. This is not altogether fool, my lord.

FOOL. No, faith; lords and great men will not let me.[41] If I had a monopoly out, they would have part on't. And ladies too, they will not let me have all the fool to myself; they'll be snatching.[42]] Nuncle, give me an egg, and I'll give thee two crowns.

LEAR. What two crowns shall they be?

FOOL. Why, after I have cut the egg i' th' middle and eat up the meat, the two crowns of the egg. When thou clovest thy crown i' th' middle and gav'st away both parts, thou bor'st thine ass on thy back o'er the dirt.[43]

Thou hadst little wit in thy bald crown when thou gav'st thy golden one away. If I speak like myself [44] in this, let him be whipped that first finds it so.[45]

[Sings]

Fools had ne'er less grace in a year,[46]
　　For wise men are grown foppish,[47]
And know not how their wits to wear,[48]
　　Their manners are so apish.

LEAR. When were you wont to be so full of songs, sirrah?

FOOL. I have used [49] it, nuncle, e'er since thou mad'st thy daughters thy mothers; for when thou gav'st them the rod, and put'st down thine own breeches,

[Sings]

Then they for sudden joy did weep,
　　And I for sorrow sung,
That such a king should play bo-
　　peep [50]
　　And go the fools among.

Prithee, nuncle, keep a schoolmaster that can teach thy fool to lie. I would fain learn to lie.

LEAR. An [51] you lie, sirrah, we'll have you whipped.

FOOL. I marvel what kin thou and thy daughters are. They'll have me whipped for speaking true; thou'lt have me whipped for lying; and sometimes I am whipped for holding my peace. I had rather be any kind o' thing than a fool, and yet I would

---

[38] bitter, sweet satirical, non-satirical
[39] Do . . . stand (the Fool thus identifying Lear as his own foolish counsellor)
[40] found out revealed (since Lear is the 'born' fool as distinct from himself, the fool in motley, professionally satirical)
[41] let me (i.e. be all fool, since they seek a share of folly)
[42] snatching (like greedy courtiers seeking shares in royal patents of monopoly)
[43] bor'st . . . dirt (thus foolishly reversing normal behavior)
[44] like myself i.e. like a fool
[45] let . . . so i.e. let him

be whipped (as a fool) who mistakes this truth as my typical folly
[46] grace . . . year favor at any time
[47] foppish foolish
[48] their wits to wear i.e. to use their intelligence
[49] used practiced
[50] play bo-peep i.e. act like a child
[51] An if

not be thee, nuncle: thou hast pared thy wit o' both sides and left nothing i' th' middle.⁵² Here comes one o' the parings.

Enter Goneril.

LEAR. How now, daughter? What makes that frontlet ⁵³ on? You are too much of late i' th' frown.

FOOL. Thou wast a pretty fellow when thou hadst no need to care for her frowning. Now thou art an O without a figure.⁵⁴ I am better than thou art now: I am a fool, thou art nothing. [*To Goneril*] Yes, forsooth, I will hold my tongue. So your face bids me, though you say nothing. Mum, mum,

He that keeps nor crust nor crum,⁵⁵
Weary of all, shall want ⁵⁶ some.—
[*Points at Lear.*] That's a shealed peascod.⁵⁷

GONERIL. Not only, sir, this your all-licensed ⁵⁸ fool,
But other of your insolent retinue
Do hourly carp ⁵⁹ and quarrel, breaking forth
In rank and not-to-be-endurèd riots. Sir,
I had thought by making this well known unto you
To have found a safe ⁶⁰ redress, but now grow fearful,

By what yourself too late have spoke and done,
That you protect this course, and put it on ⁶¹
By your allowance; ⁶² which if you should, the fault
Would not 'scape censure, nor the redresses sleep,⁶³
Which, in the tender of ⁶⁴ a wholesome weal,⁶⁵
Might in their working do you that offense,
Which else were shame, that then necessity
Will call discreet proceeding.⁶⁶

FOOL. For you know, nuncle,
The hedge-sparrow fed the cuckoo ⁶⁷ so long
That it's had it ⁶⁸ head bit off by it young.
So out went the candle, and we were left darkling.⁶⁹

LEAR. Are you our daughter?

GONERIL. I would you would make use of your good wisdom (Whereof I know you are fraught) ⁷⁰ and put away
These dispositions ⁷¹ which of late transport you
From what you rightly are.

FOOL. May not an ass know when the cart draws the horse?

⁵²*pared . . . middle* i.e. completely disposed of your wits (in disposing of your power)
⁵³*frontlet* band worn across the brow; hence, frown
⁵⁴*O . . . figure* cipher without a digit to give it value
⁵⁵*crum* soft bread within the crust
⁵⁶*want* need
⁵⁷*shealed peascod* shelled (empty) pea-pod

⁵⁸*all-licensed* all-privileged
⁵⁹*carp* complain
⁶⁰*safe* sure
⁶¹*put it on* instigate it
⁶²*allowance* approval
⁶³*redresses sleep* correction lie dormant
⁶⁴*tender of* care for
⁶⁵*weal* state
⁶⁶*Might . . . proceeding* in their operation might be considered humiliating to you but, under the circumstances, are merely prudent

⁶⁷*cuckoo* (an image suggesting illegitimacy as well as voraciousness, since the cuckoo lays its eggs in the nests of other birds)
⁶⁸*it* its
⁶⁹*darkling* in the dark (like the dead hedge-sparrow and the threatened Lear)
⁷⁰*fraught* freighted, laden
⁷¹*dispositions* moods

Whoop, Jug,[72] I love thee!

LEAR. Does any here know me?
This is not Lear.
Does Lear walk thus? speak thus?
Where are his eyes?
Either his notion [73] weakens, his discernings
Are lethargied—Ha! Waking? [74] 'Tis not so.
Who is it that can tell me who I am?

FOOL. Lear's shadow.

[LEAR. I would learn that; for, by the marks of sovereignty,[75]
Knowledge, and reason, I should be false persuaded
I had daughters.

FOOL. Which they will make an obedient father.]

LEAR. Your name, fair gentlewoman?

GONERIL. This admiration,[76] sir, is much o' th' savor
Of other your new pranks. I do beseech you
To understand my purposes aright.
As you are old and reverend, should be wise.
Here do you keep a hundred knights and squires,
Men so disordered, so deboshed,[77] and bold
That this our court, infected with their manners,
Shows like a riotous inn. Epicurism [78] and lust

Makes it more like a tavern or a brothel
Than a graced [79] palace. The shame [80] itself doth speak
For instant remedy. Be then desired
By her that else will take the thing she begs
A little to disquantity your train,[81]
And the remainders that shall still depend [82]
To be such men as may besort [83] your age,
Which know [84] themselves, and you.

LEAR.   Darkness and devils!
Saddle my horses; call my train together.
Degenerate [85] bastard, I'll not trouble thee:
Yet have I left a daughter.

GONERIL. You strike my people, and your disordered rabble
Make servants of their betters.

Enter Albany.

LEAR. Woe that too late repents.—
[O, sir, are you come?]
Is it your will? Speak, sir.—Prepare my horses.
Ingratitude! thou marble-hearted fiend,
More hideous when thou show'st thee in a child
Than the sea-monster.

ALBANY.   Pray, sir, be patient.

LEAR. Detested kite,[86] thou liest.
My train are men of choice and rarest parts,[87]

---

[72] *Jug* Joan (evidently part of some catchphrase)
[73] *notion* understanding
[74] *Ha! Waking* i.e. so I am really awake (presumably accompanied by the 'business' of pinching himself)
[75] *marks of sovereignty* evidences that I am King

(and hence the father of the princesses)
[76] *admiration* air of wonderment
[77] *deboshed* debauched
[78] *Epicurism* loose living
[79] *graced* honored
[80] *shame* disgrace
[81] *disquantity your train* reduce the size of your retinue

[82] *depend* be attached
[83] *besort* befit
[84] *Which know* i.e. who are aware of the status of
[85] *Degenerate* unnatural, fallen away from kind
[86] *Detested kite* detestable bird of prey
[87] *parts* accomplishments

That all particulars of duty know
And in the most exact regard [88] sup-
port
The worships [89] of their name. O most
small fault,
How ugly didst thou in Cordelia
show!
Which, like an engine,[90] wrenched my
frame of nature
From the fixed place; [91] drew from my
heart all love
And added to the gall.[92] O Lear, Lear,
Lear!
Beat at this gate that let thy folly in
                              [Strikes his head.]
And thy dear judgment out. Go, go,
my people.
  ALBANY. My lord, I am guiltless, as
    I am ignorant
Of what hath moved you.
  LEAR.   It may be so, my lord.
Hear, Nature, hear; dear goddess,
hear:
Suspend thy purpose if thou didst in-
tend
To make this creature fruitful.
Into her womb convey sterility,
Dry up in her the organs of increase,
And from her derogate [93] body never
spring
A babe to honor her. If she must
teem,[94]
Create her child of spleen,[95] that it
may live
And be a thwart disnatured [96] tor-
ment to her.

Let it stamp wrinkles in her brow of
youth,
With cadent [97] tears fret [98] channels
in her cheeks,
Turn all her mother's pains and bene-
fits [99]
To laughter and contempt, that she
may feel
How sharper than a serpent's tooth it
is
To have a thankless child. Away,
away!   Exit.
  ALBANY. Now, gods that we adore,
    whereof comes this?
  GONERIL. Never afflict yourself to
    know more of it,
But let his disposition [100] have that
scope
As dotage gives it.
  Enter Lear.
  LEAR. What, fifty of my followers
    at a clap?
Within a fortnight?
  ALBANY.   What's the matter, sir?
  LEAR. I'll tell thee. [To Goneril]
    Life and death, I am ashamed
That thou hast power to shake my
manhood thus!
That these hot tears, which break from
me perforce,[101]
Should make thee worth them. Blasts
and fogs upon thee!
Th' untented [102] woundings of a fa-
ther's curse
Pierce every sense about [103] thee! Old
fond [103a] eyes,

[88] exact regard careful attention, punctiliousness
[89] worships honor
[90] engine destructive contrivance of war
[91] wrenched . . . place
set askew my natural
structure, distorted my
normal self
[92] gall bitterness

[93] derogate degraded
[94] teem increase
[95] spleen ill-humor, spite-
fulness
[96] thwart disnatured perverse unnatural
[97] cadent falling
[98] fret wear
[99] pains and benefits care
and offerings

[100] disposition mood
[101] perforce by force,
against my will
[102] untented untentable,
too deep for treatment
by a probe
[103] sense about faculty
possessed by
[103a] fond foolish

Beweep this cause [104] again I'll pluck ye out
And cast you, with the waters that you loose,[105]
To temper [106] clay. [Yea, is it come to this?]
Ha! Let it be so. I have another daughter,
Who I am sure is kind and comfortable.[107]
When she shall hear this of thee, with her nails
She'll flay thy wolvish visage. Thou shalt find
That I'll resume the shape [108] which thou dost think
I have cast off for ever.
Exit [Lear with Kent and Attendants].
GONERIL.   Do you mark that?
ALBANY. I cannot be so partial, Goneril,
To [109] the great love I bear you—
GONERIL. Pray you, content.—What, Oswald, ho!
[*To Fool*] You, sir, more knave than fool, after your master!
FOOL. Nuncle Lear, nuncle Lear, tarry. Take the fool [110] with thee.
A fox, when one has caught her,
And such a daughter,
Should sure to the slaughter,[111]
If my cap would buy a halter.[112]
So the fool follows after.[113]   *Exit.*
GONERIL. This man hath had good counsel [114]—a hundred knights!
'Tis politic [115] and safe to let him keep
At point [116] a hundred knights—yes, that on every dream,
Each buzz,[117] each fancy, each complaint, dislike,
He may enguard his dotage with their pow'rs
And hold our lives in mercy.[118]—Oswald, I say!
ALBANY. Well, you may fear too far.
GONERIL.   Safer than trust too far.
Let me still take away the harms [119] I fear,
Not fear still to be taken.[120] I know his heart.
What he hath uttered I have writ my sister.
If she sustain him and his hundred knights,
When I have showed th' unfitness—
Enter Steward [Oswald].
                    How now, Oswald?
What, have you writ that letter to my sister?
OSWALD. Ay, madam.
GONERIL. Take you some company,[121] and away to horse.
Inform her full of my particular [122] fear,
And thereto add such reasons of your own
As may compact it more.[123] Get you

[104] *Beweep this cause* if you weep over this matter
[105] *loose* let loose
[106] *temper* soften
[107] *comfortable* ready to comfort
[108] *shape* i.e. rôle of authority
[109] *partial . . . To* made partial . . . by
[110] *the fool* i.e. both your fool and your folly
[111] *slaughter* hanging and quartering
[112,113] *halter, after* (pronounced 'hauter,' 'auter')
[114] *good counsel* i.e. from such company (ironic)
[115] *politic* prudent
[116] *At point* in arms
[117] *buzz* murmur
[118] *in mercy* at his mercy
[119] *still . . . harms* always eliminate the sources of injury
[120] *still . . . taken* always to be overtaken (by them)
[121] *some company* an escort
[122] *particular* own
[123] *compact it more* substantiate it further

gone,
And hasten your return. [*Exit Oswald.*] No, no, my lord,
This milky gentleness and course [124] of yours,
Though I condemn not, yet under pardon,
You are much more atasked [125] for want of wisdom
Than praised for harmful mildness.[126]

ALBANY. How far your eyes may pierce I cannot tell;
Striving to better, oft we mar what's well.

GONERIL. Nay then—

ALBANY. Well, well; th' event.[127]

Exeunt.

SCENE FIVE

Enter Lear, Kent, and Fool.

LEAR. Go you before to Gloucester with these letters. Acquaint my daughter no further with anything you know than comes from her demand out of [1] the letter. If your diligence be not speedy, I shall be there afore you.

KENT. I will not sleep, my lord, till I have delivered your letter.   *Exit.*

FOOL. If a man's brains were in's heels, were't not in danger of kibes? [2]

LEAR. Ay, boy.

FOOL. Then I prithee be merry. Thy wit shall not go slipshod.[3]

LEAR. Ha, ha, ha.

FOOL. Shalt [4] see thy other daughter will use thee kindly;[5] for though she's as like this as a crab's [6] like an apple, yet I can tell what I can tell.

LEAR. What canst tell, boy?

FOOL. She will taste as like this as a crab does to a crab. Thou canst tell why one's nose stands i' th' middle on's face?

LEAR. No.

FOOL. Why, to keep one's eyes of either side 's nose, that what a man cannot smell out he may spy into.

LEAR. I did her [7] wrong.

FOOL. Canst tell how an oyster makes his shell?

LEAR. No.

FOOL. Nor I neither; but I can tell why a snail has a house.

LEAR. Why?

FOOL. Why, to put 's head in; not to give it away to his daughters, and leave his horns [8] without a case.[9]

LEAR. I will forget my nature.[10] So kind a father!—Be my horses ready?

FOOL. Thy asses are gone about 'em. The reason why the seven stars are no moe [11] than seven is a pretty reason.

LEAR. Because they are not eight.

---

[124] *milky . . . course* mildly gentle way
[125] *atasked* censured, taken to task
[126] *harmful mildness* mildness that proves harmful
[127] *th' event* the outcome, i.e. we shall see what happens
I, v [1] *demand out of* i.e. questioning provoked by reading
[2] *kibes* chilblains

[3] *wit . . . slipshod* intelligence (brain) shall not go slippered (because of 'kibes')
[4] *Shalt* thou shalt
[5] *kindly* after her kind, i.e. in the same way as this daughter
[6] *crab* crabapple
[7] *her* i.e. Cordelia (the first of the remarkable intimations of Lear's in-

ner thoughts in this scene)
[8] *horns* i.e. snail's horns (with pun on cuckold's horns; the legitimacy of Goneril and Regan being, figuratively, suspect throughout)
[9] *case* covering
[10] *nature* i.e. fatherly instincts
[11] *moe* more

FOOL. Yes indeed. Thou wouldst make a good fool.

LEAR. To take 't again perforce [12]— Monster ingratitude!

FOOL. If thou wert my fool, nuncle, I'ld have thee beaten for being old before thy time.

LEAR. How's that?

FOOL. Thou shouldst not have been old till thou hadst been wise.

LEAR. O, let me not be mad, not mad, sweet heaven! Keep me in temper; [13] I would not be mad!

[Enter a Gentleman.]

How now, are the horses ready?

GENTLEMAN. Ready, my lord.

LEAR. Come, boy.

FOOL. She that's a maid now, and laughs at my departure, Shall not be a maid long, unless things be cut shorter.[14]   Exeunt.

ACT II

SCENE ONE

Enter Bastard [Edmund] and Curan severally.

EDMUND. Save [1] thee, Curan.

CURAN. And you, sir. I have been with your father, and given him notice that the Duke of Cornwall and Regan his Duchess will be here with him this night.

EDMUND. How comes that?

CURAN. Nay, I know not. You have heard of the news abroad—I mean the whispered ones, for they are yet but ear-kissing arguments? [2]

EDMUND. Not I. Pray you, what are they?

CURAN. Have you heard of no likely [3] wars toward,[4] 'twixt the Dukes of Cornwall and Albany?

EDMUND. Not a word.

CURAN. You may do, then, in time. Fare you well, sir.   Exit.

EDMUND. The Duke be here tonight? The better best! [5] This weaves itself perforce [6] into my business. My father hath set guard to take my brother, And I have one thing of a queasy question [7] Which I must act. Briefness and fortune,[8] work! Brother, a word: descend. Brother, I say!

Enter Edgar.

My father watches. O sir, fly this place. Intelligence is given where you are hid. You have now the good advantage of the night. Have you not spoken 'gainst the Duke of Cornwall? He's coming hither; now i' th' night, i' th' haste, And Regan with him. Have you nothing said Upon his party 'gainst [9] the Duke of

---

[12] perforce by force
[13] in temper properly balanced
[14] She . . . shorter (an indecent gag addressed to the audience, calculated to embarrass the maids who joined in the laughter)

II, i [1] Save God save
[2] ear-kissing arguments whispered topics
[3] likely probable
[4] toward impending
[5] better best (hyperbole)
[6] perforce of necessity (?) of its own accord (?)
[7] of . . . question deli-

cately balanced as to outcome, touch-and-go
[8] Briefness and fortune decisive speed and good luck
[9] Upon his party 'gainst i.e. reflecting upon his feud against

Albany?

Advise yourself.[10]

EDGAR. I am sure on't,[10a] not a word.

EDMUND. I hear my father coming.

Pardon me:

In cunning [11] I must draw my sword
upon you.

Draw, seem to defend yourself; now
quit you [12] well.—

Yield! Come before my father! Light
ho, here!—

Fly, brother.—Torches, torches!—So
farewell.   *Exit Edgar.*

Some blood drawn on me would beget opinion

Of my more fierce endeavor. [*Wounds
his arm.*] I have seen drunkards

Do more than this in sport.—Father,
father!

Stop, stop! No help?

*Enter Gloucester, and Servants with
torches.*

GLOUCESTER.   Now, Edmund,
where's the villain?

EDMUND. Here stood he in the dark,
his sharp sword out,

Mumbling of wicked charms, conjur-
ing the moon

To stand auspicious mistress.

GLOUCESTER.   But where is he?

EDMUND. Look, sir, I bleed.

GLOUCESTER. Where is the villain,
Edmund?

EDMUND. Fled this way, sir, when
by no means he could—

GLOUCESTER. Pursue him, ho! Go
after. [*Exeunt some Servants.*]

By no means what?

EDMUND. Persuade me to the murder of your lordship;

But that I told him the revenging gods

'Gainst parricides did all the thunder
bend; [13]

Spoke with how manifold and strong
a bond

The child was bound to th' father—
sir, in fine,[14]

Seeing how loathly opposite [15] I stood

To his unnatural purpose, in fell [16]
motion

With his preparèd sword he charges
home

My unprovided [17] body, latched [17a]
mine arm;

And when he saw my best alarumed [18]
spirits

Bold in the quarrel's right,[19] roused to
th' encounter,

Or whether gasted [20] by the noise I
made,

Full suddenly he fled.

GLOUCESTER.   Let him fly far.

Not in this land shall he remain un-
caught;

And found—dispatch.[21] The noble
Duke my master,

My worthy arch [22] and patron, comes
to-night:

By his authority I will proclaim it

That he which finds him shall deserve
our thanks,

Bringing the murderous coward to the
stake;

He that conceals him, death.

EDMUND. When I dissuaded him
from his intent

[10] *Advise yourself* take thought

[10a] *on't* of it

[11] *In cunning* i.e. as a ruse

[12] *quit you* acquit yourself

[13] *bend* aim

[14] *in fine* finally

[15] *loathly opposite* in loathing opposition

[16] *fell* deadly

[17] *unprovided* undefended

[17a] *latched* lanced, pierced

[18] *best alarumed* fully aroused

[19] *Bold . . . right* confident in the justice of the cause

[20] *gasted* struck aghast

[21] *dispatch* (equivalent to 'death' or 'finis')

[22] *arch* superior

And found him pight [23] to do it, with
curst [24] speech
I threatened to discover [25] him. He re-
plied,
'Thou unpossessing [26] bastard; dost
thou think,
If I would stand against thee, would
the reposal [27]
Of any trust, virtue, or worth in thee
Make thy words faithed? [28] No. What
I should deny
(As this I would, ay, though thou
didst produce
My very character) [29] I'ld turn it all
To thy suggestion,[30] plot, and damnèd
practice; [31]
And thou must make a dullard of the
world,[32]
If they not thought [33] the profits of my
death
Were very pregnant and potential
spirits [34]
To make thee seek it.'
  GLOUCESTER. O strange and fast'-
ned [35] villain!
Would he deny his letter, said he? [I
never got [36] him.]
                    Tucket [37] *within.*
Hark, the Duke's trumpets. I know
not why he comes.
All ports I'll bar; the villain shall not
'scape;
The Duke must grant me that. Besides, his picture
I will send far and near, that all the
kingdom

May have due note of him; and of my
land,
Loyal and natural boy, I'll work the
means
To make thee capable.[38]
  *Enter Cornwall, Regan, and At-
tendants.*
  CORNWALL. How now, my noble
friend? Since I came hither
(Which I can call [39] but now) I have
heard strange news.
  REGAN. If it be true, all vengeance
comes too short
Which can pursue th' offender. How
dost, my lord?
  GLOUCESTER. O madam, my old
heart is cracked, it's cracked.
  REGAN. What, did my father's god-
son seek your life?
He whom my father named, your Ed-
gar?
  GLOUCESTER. O lady, lady, shame
would have it hid.
  REGAN. Was he not companion with
the riotous knights
That tended upon my father?
  GLOUCESTER. I know not, madam.
'Tis too bad, too bad.
  EDMUND. Yes, madam, he was of
that consort.[40]
  REGAN. No marvel then though he
were ill affected.[41]
'Tis they have put [42] him on the old
man's death,
To have th' expense and waste [43] of his
revenues.

---

[23] *pight* determined, set
[24] *curst* angry
[25] *discover* expose
[26] *unpossessing* having no
claim, landless
[27] *reposal* placing
[28] *faithed* believed
[29] *character* written testimony
[30] *suggestion* instigation
[31] *practice* devices

[32] *make . . . world* i.e.
consider everyone stupid
[33] *not thought* did not
think
[34] *pregnant . . . spirits*
teeming and powerful
spirits, i.e. the devils
which 'possess' him
[35] *fast'ned* confirmed
[36] *got* begot
[37] *Tucket* personal signa-

ture in trumpet notes
[38] *capable* i.e. legitimate,
able to inherit
[39] *call* i.e. say was
[40] *consort* company, set
[41] *affected* disposed
[42] *put* set
[43] *expense and waste*
wasteful expenditure

I have this present evening from my
 sister
Been well informed of them, and with
 such cautions
That, if they come to sojourn at my
 house,
I'll not be there.

CORNWALL. Nor I, assure thee, Regan.

Edmund, I hear that you have shown
 your father
A childlike [44] office.

EDMUND.   It was my duty, sir.

GLOUCESTER. He did bewray his
 practice,[45] and received
This hurt you see, striving to apprehend him.

CORNWALL. Is he pursued?

GLOUCESTER.   Ay, my good lord.

CORNWALL. If he be taken, he shall
 never more
Be feared of doing [46] harm. Make your
 own purpose,
How in my strength you please.[47] For
 you, Edmund,
Whose virtue and obedience [48] doth
 this instant
So much commend itself, you shall be
 ours.
Natures of such deep trust we shall
 much need;
You we first seize on.

EDMUND.   I shall serve you, sir,
Truly, however else.

GLOUCESTER. For him I thank your
 Grace.

CORNWALL. You know not why we
 came to visit you?

REGAN. Thus out of season, threading dark-eyed night.
Occasions, noble Gloucester, of some
 prize,[49]
Wherein we must have use of your
 advice.
Our father he hath writ, so hath our
 sister,
Of   differences,[50] which [51] I best
 thought it fit
To answer from our home.[52] The several messengers
From hence attend dispatch.[53] Our
 good old friend,
Lay comforts to your bosom,[54] and
 bestow
Your needful [55] counsel to our busi-
 nesses,
Which craves the instant use.[56]

GLOUCESTER.   I serve you, madam.
Your Graces are right welcome.
                    Exeunt. Flourish.

SCENE TWO

*Enter Kent and Steward [Oswald],
severally.*

OSWALD. Good dawning [1] to thee,
friend. Art of this house? [2]

KENT. Ay.

OSWALD. Where may we set our
horses?

[44] *childlike* filial
[45] *bewray his practice* expose his plot
[46] *of doing* lest he do
[47] *Make . . . please* i.e.
accomplish your purpose,
making free use of my
powers
[48] *virtue and obedience*
virtuous obedience
[49] *prize* price, importance
[50] *differences* quarrels

[51] *which* (refers, indefi-
nitely, to the whole situation)
[52] *answer . . . home* cope
with away from home
(where she need not re-
ceive Lear)
[53] *attend   dispatch* i.e.
await settlement of the
business
[54] *Lay . . . bosom* be
consoled (about your

own trouble)
[55] *needful* needed
[56] *craves . . . use* requires immediate trans-
action (?) or use of your
counsel (?)
II, ii [1] *dawning* (perhaps
indicating that it is too
early for 'good morning')
[2] *Art . . . house* i.e. do
you belong to this house-
hold

KENT. I' th' mire.

OSWALD. Prithee, if thou lov'st me, tell me.

KENT. I love thee not.

OSWALD. Why then, I care not for thee.

KENT. If I had thee in Lipsbury Pinfold,[3] I would make thee care for me.

OSWALD. Why dost thou use me thus? I know thee not.

KENT. Fellow, I know thee.

OSWALD. What dost thou know me for?

KENT. A knave, a rascal, an eater of broken meats;[4] a base, proud, shallow, beggarly, three-suited,[5] hundred-pound,[6] filthy worsted-stocking[7] knave; a lily-livered, action-taking,[8] whoreson, glass-gazing, superserviceable, finical[9] rogue; one-trunk-inheriting[10] slave; one that wouldst be a bawd in way of good service,[11] and art nothing but the composition[12] of a knave, beggar, coward, pander, and the son and heir of a mongrel bitch; one whom I will beat into clamorous whining if thou deny'st the least syllable of thy addition.[13]

OSWALD. Why, what a monstrous fellow art thou, thus to rail on one that is neither known of thee nor knows thee!

KENT. What a brazen-faced varlet art thou to deny thou knowest me! Is it two days ago since I tripped up thy heels and beat thee before the King? [Draws his sword.] Draw, you rogue, for though it be night, yet the moon shines. I'll make a sop o' th' moonshine[14] of you. You whoreson cullionly barbermonger,[15] draw!

OSWALD. Away, I have nothing to do with thee.

KENT. Draw, you rascal. You come with letters against the King, and take Vanity the puppet's[16] part against the royalty of her father. Draw, you rogue, or I'll so carbonado[17] your shanks. Draw, you rascal. Come your ways![18]

OSWALD. Help, ho! Murder! Help!

KENT. Strike, you slave! Stand, rogue! Stand, you neat[19] slave! Strike!
                              [Beats him.]

OSWALD. Help, ho! Murder, murder!

Enter Bastard [Edmund, with his rapier drawn], Cornwall, Regan, Gloucester, Servants.

EDMUND. How now? What's the matter? Part!

KENT. With you, goodman boy,[20] if you please! Come, I'll flesh ye;[21] come on, young master.

---

[3] Lipsbury Pinfold i.e. between the teeth (cant term: 'pen in the region of the lips')
[4] broken meats scraps
[5] three-suited with three suits (the wardrobe allowed serving-men)
[6] hundred-pound (the minimal estate for anyone aspiring to gentility)
[7] worsted-stocking (serving-men's attire)
[8] action-taking i.e. cowardly (resorting to law instead of fighting)
[9] glass-gazing, superserv-

iceable, finical i.e. conceited, toadying, foppish
[10] inheriting possessing
[11] a bawd . . . service i.e. a pander, if pleasing your employer required it
[12] composition composite
[13] addition titles
[14] sop o' th' moonshine i.e. something that sops up moonshine through its perforations
[15] cullionly barbermonger vile fop (i.e. always dealing with hairdressers)

[16] Vanity the puppet i.e. Goneril (here equated with a stock figure in morality plays, now dwindled into puppet shows)
[17] carbonado dice (like a steak)
[18] your ways get along
[19] neat priming
[20] goodman boy (doubly contemptuous, since peasants were addressed as 'goodmen')
[21] flesh ye give you your first taste of blood

GLOUCESTER. Weapons? Arms? What's the matter here?

CORNWALL. Keep peace, upon your lives.

He dies that strikes again. What is the matter?

REGAN. The messengers from our sister and the King.

CORNWALL. What is your difference? Speak.

OSWALD. I am scarce in breath, my lord.

KENT. No marvel, you have so bestirred [22] your valor. You cowardly rascal, nature disclaims [23] in thee. A tailor made thee.

CORNWALL. Thou art a strange fellow. A tailor make a man?

KENT. A tailor, sir. A stonecutter [24] or a painter could not have made him so ill, though they had been but two years o' th' trade.

CORNWALL. Speak yet, how grew your quarrel?

OSWALD. This ancient ruffian, sir, whose life I have spared at suit of [25] his gray beard—

KENT. Thou whoreson zed,[26] thou unnecessary letter! My lord, if you will give me leave, I will tread this unbolted [27] villain into mortar and daub the wall of a jakes [28] with him. Spare my gray beard? you wagtail.[29]

CORNWALL. Peace, sirrah!

You beastly [30] knave, know you no reverence?

KENT. Yes, sir, but anger hath a privilege.

CORNWALL. Why art thou angry?

KENT. That such a slave as this should wear a sword,

Who wears no honesty. Such smiling rogues as these

Like rats oft bite the holy cords [31] atwain

Which are too intrinse [32] t' unloose; smooth [33] every passion

That in the natures of their lords rebel,[34]

Being oil to fire, snow to the colder moods; [35]

Renege,[36] affirm, and turn their halcyon beaks [37]

With every gale and vary [38] of their masters,

Knowing naught, like dogs, but following.

A plague upon your epileptic [39] visage!

Smile you [40] my speeches, as I were a fool?

Goose, if I had you upon Sarum Plain,[41]

---

[22] *bestirred* exercised
[23] *disclaims* claims no part
[24] *stonecutter* sculptor
[25] *at suit of* on the plea of, moved to mercy by
[26] *zed* z (last and least useful of letters)
[27] *unbolted* unsifted, crude
[28] *jakes* privy
[29] *wagtail* (any of several birds whose tail-feathers wag or bob, suggesting obsequiousness or effeminacy)

[30] *beastly* beast-like, irrational
[31] *holy cords* sacred bonds (between parents and children, husbands and wives, man and God)
[32] *intrinse* intrinsic, inextricable
[33] *smooth* flatter, cater to
[34] *rebel* (i.e. against reason and moral restraint)
[35] *Being . . . moods* (i.e. feeders of intemperance)
[36] *Renege* deny
[37] *halcyon beaks* king-

fisher beaks (supposedly serving as weathervanes when the birds were hung up by their necks)
[38] *gale and vary* varying wind
[39] *epileptic* contorted in a grin (?)
[40] *Smile you* smile you at, mock you
[41] *Sarum Plain* Salisbury Plain (said to have been associated with geese, but the allusion remains cryptic)

I'ld drive ye cackling home to Camelot.[42]

CORNWALL. What, art thou mad,
old fellow?

GLOUCESTER. How fell you out? Say
that.

KENT. No contraries [43] hold more
antipathy
Than I and such a knave.

CORNWALL. Why dost thou call him
knave? What is his fault?

KENT. His countenance likes me not.

CORNWALL. No more perchance
does mine, nor his, nor hers.

KENT. Sir, 'tis my occupation to be
plain:
I have seen better faces in my time
Than stands on any shoulder that I
see
Before me at this instant.

CORNWALL.   This is some fellow
Who, having been praised for blunt-
ness, doth affect
A saucy roughness, and constrains the
garb
Quite from his nature.[44] He cannot
flatter, he;
An honest mind and plain—he must
speak truth.
An they will take it, so; if not, he's
plain.
These kind of knaves I know which
in this plainness

Harbor more craft and more corrupter
ends
Than twenty silly-ducking observants [45]
That stretch their duties nicely.[46]

KENT. Sir, in good faith, in sincere
verity,
Under th' allowance [47] of your great
aspect,[48]
Whose influence,[49] like the wreath of
radiant fire
On flick'ring Phoebus' front [50]—

CORNWALL. What mean'st by this?

KENT. To go out of my dialect,[51]
which you discommend so much. I
know, sir, I am no flatterer. He [52] that
beguiled you in a plain accent was a
plain knave, which, for my part, I will
not be, though I should win your displeasure to entreat me to't.[53]

CORNWALL. What was th' offense
you gave him?

OSWALD. I never gave him any.
It pleased the King his master very
late [54]
To strike at me, upon his misconstruction; [55]
When he, compact,[56] and flattering his
displeasure,
Tripped me behind; being down, insulted, railed,
And put upon him such a deal of
man [57]

[42] Camelot legendary seat
of King Arthur, variously
sited at Winchester, near
Cadbury, in Wales, etc.
[43] contraries opposites
[44] constrains . . . nature
distorts the plain fash-
ion from its true nature,
caricatures it
[45] silly-ducking observants
ludicrously bowing form-
servers
[46] nicely fussily

[47] allowance approval
[48] aspect (1) appearance
(2) heavenly position
[49] influence astrological
force
[50] Phoebus' front sun's
forehead (i.e. face)
[51] go . . . dialect depart
from my way of speak-
ing
[52] He (the type of plain-
speaker Cornwall has
condemned)

[53] though . . . to't though
I should persuade your
disapproving self to beg
me to do so (? with 'dis-
pleasure'   sarcastically
substituted for 'grace')
[54] very late quite recently
[55] misconstruction misun-
derstanding
[56] compact in league with
[57] And put . . . man i.e.
affected such excessive
manliness

That worthied [58] him, got praises of the King
For him attempting who was self-subdued; [59]
And, in the fleshment of [60] this dread exploit,
Drew on me here again.

KENT. None of these rogues and cowards
But Ajax is their fool.[61]

CORNWALL. Fetch forth the stocks!
You stubborn [62] ancient knave, you reverent [63] braggart,
We'll teach you.

KENT.   Sir, I am too old to learn.
Call not your stocks for me, I serve the King—
On whose employment I was sent to you;
You shall do small respect, show too bold malice [64]
Against the grace [65] and person of my master,
Stocking his messenger.

CORNWALL. Fetch forth the stocks.
As I have life and honor,
There shall he sit till noon.

REGAN. Till noon? Till night, my lord, and all night too.

KENT. Why, madam, if I were your father's dog,
You should not use me so.

REGAN.   Sir, being his knave, I will.

CORNWALL. This is a fellow of the selfsame color [66]

Our sister speaks of. Come, bring away [67] the stocks.
                    Stocks brought out.
GLOUCESTER. Let me beseech your Grace not to do so.
[His fault is much, and the good King his master
Will check [68] him for't. Your purposed [69] low correction
Is such as basest and contemnèd'st [70] wretches
For pilf'rings and most common trespasses
Are punished with.]
The King his master needs must take it ill
That he, so slightly valued in [71] his messenger,
Should have him thus restrained.

CORNWALL.   I'll answer [72] that.

REGAN. My sister may receive it much more worse,
To have her gentleman abused, assaulted,
[For following her affairs. Put in his legs.] [Kent is put in the stocks.]
CORNWALL. Come, my lord, away!
Exit [with all but Gloucester and Kent.]

GLOUCESTER. I am sorry for thee, friend. 'Tis the Duke's pleasure,
Whose disposition [73] all the world well knows
Will not be rubbed [74] nor stopped. I'll entreat for thee.

KENT. Pray do not, sir. I have

---

[58] *worthied* enhanced his worth
[59] *For him . . . self-subdued* for assailing him (Oswald) who chose not to resist
[60] *fleshment of* bloodthirstiness induced by
[61] *None . . . fool* i.e. the Ajax type, stupidly bel-

ligerent, is the favorite butt of cowardly rogues like Oswald
[62] *stubborn* rude
[63] *reverent* aged
[64] *malice* ill will
[65] *grace* royal honor
[66] *color* kind
[67] *away* along
[68] *check* rebuke

[69] *purposed* intended
[70] *contemnèd'st* most harshly sentenced
[71] *slightly valued in* i.e. little respected in the person of
[72] *answer* answer for
[73] *disposition* inclination
[74] *rubbed* deflected (bowling term)

watched [75] and travelled hard.
Some time I shall sleep out, the rest
　I'll whistle.
A good man's fortune may grow out
　at heels. [76]
Give [77] you good morrow.

GLOUCESTER. The Duke 's to blame
　in this. 'Twill be ill taken. [78]

　　　　　　　　　　　　　　Exit.

KENT. Good King, that must ap-
　prove [79] the common saw, [80]
Thou out of heaven's benediction
　com'st
To the warm sun. [81]
Approach, thou beacon to this under
　globe, [82]
That by thy comfortable beams I may
Peruse this letter. Nothing almost sees
　miracles
But misery. [83] I know 'tis from Cor-
　delia,
Who hath most fortunately been in-
　formed
Of my obscurèd [84] course. And shall
　find time
From this enormous state, [85] seeking to
　give
Losses [86] their remedies. [87]—All weary
　and o'erwatched,
Take vantage, [88] heavy eyes, not to be-
　hold

This shameful lodging. [89] Fortune,
　good night;
Smile once more, turn thy wheel. [90]
　　　　　　　　　　　　　[*Sleeps.*]

SCENE THREE

Enter Edgar.

EDGAR. I heard myself proclaimed,
And by the happy hollow [1] of a tree
Escaped the hunt. No port is free, no
　place
That guard and most unusual vigi-
　lance
Does not attend my taking. [2] Whiles I
　may 'scape,
I will preserve myself; and am be-
　thought [3]
To take the basest and most poorest
　shape
That ever penury, in contempt of
　man,
Brought near to beast: my face I'll
　grime with filth,
Blanket my loins, elf [4] all my hairs in
　knots,
And with presented [5] nakedness out-
　face
The winds and persecutions of the sky.
The country gives me proof [6] and
　precedent

[75] *watched* gone sleep-
less
[76] *A good . . . heels* i.e.
it is no disgrace to de-
cline in fortune
[77] *Give* God give
[78] *taken* received
[79] *approve* demonstrate
the truth of
[80] *saw* saying, proverb
[81] *Thou . . . sun* (proverb, meaning from better
to worse, i.e. from heav-
enly shelter to earthly exposure—'the heat of the
day')

[82] *beacon . . . globe* i.e.
the sun (here viewed as
benign)
[83] *Nothing . . . misery*
i.e. miraculous aid is
seldom seen (or searched
for?) except by the mis-
erable
[84] *obscurèd* disguised
[85] *enormous state* monstrous situation
[86] *Losses* reverses
[87] *And . . . remedies* (in-
coherent: perhaps cor-
rupt, or perhaps snatches
read from the letter)

[88] *vantage* i.e. advantage
of sleep
[89] *lodging* (in the stocks)
[90] *wheel* (Fortune's wheel
was represented as verti-
cal. Kent is at its bot-
tom.)
II, iii [1] *happy hollow* i.e.
lucky hiding-place
[2] *attend my taking* contemplate my capture
[3] *bethought* in mind
[4] *elf* tangle (into 'elf-
locks')
[5] *presented* a show of
[6] *proof* example

Of Bedlam [7] beggars, who, with roaring voices,
Strike [8] in their numbed and mortified [9] bare arms
Pins, wooden pricks,[10] nails, sprigs of rosemary;
And with this horrible object,[11] from low farms,
Poor pelting [12] villages, sheepcotes, and mills,
Sometimes with lunatic bans,[13] sometime with prayers,
Enforce their charity. Poor Turlygod,[14] poor Tom,
That's something yet: Edgar [15] I nothing am.   *Exit.*

SCENE FOUR

Enter Lear, Fool, and Gentleman.

LEAR. 'Tis strange that they should so depart from home,
And not send back my messenger.
GENTLEMAN.   As I learned,
The night before there was no purpose [1] in them
Of this remove.[2]
KENT. Hail to thee, noble master.
LEAR. Ha!
Mak'st thou this shame thy pastime?
KENT.   No, my lord.
FOOL. Ha, ha, he wears cruel [3] garters. Horses are tied by the heads, dogs and bears by th' neck, monkeys by th' loins, and men by th' legs.

When a man's over-lusty at legs,[4]
then he wears wooden nether-stocks.[5]
LEAR. What's he that hath so much thy place mistook
To set thee here?
KENT.   It is both he and she,
Your son and daughter.
LEAR. No.
KENT. Yes.
LEAR. No, I say.
KENT. I say yea.
[LEAR. No, no, they would not.
KENT. Yes, they have.]
LEAR. By Jupiter, I swear no!
KENT. By Juno, I swear ay!
LEAR.   They durst not do't;
They could not, would not do't. 'Tis worse than murder
To do upon respect such violent outrage.[6]
Resolve [7] me with all modest [8] haste which way
Thou mightst deserve or they impose this usage,
Coming from us.
KENT. My lord, when at their home
I did commend [9] your Highness' letters to them,
Ere I was risen from the place that showed
My duty kneeling, came there a reeking post,
Stewed [10] in his haste, half breathless, panting forth
From Goneril his mistress salutations;

---

[7] *Bedlam* (see I, ii)
[8] *Strike* stick
[9] *mortified* deadened to pain
[10] *pricks* skewers
[11] *object* picture
[12] *pelting* paltry
[13] *bans* curses
[14] *Turlygod* (unidentified, but evidently another

name for a Tom o' Bedlam)
[15] *Edgar* i.e. as Edgar
II, iv [1] *purpose* intention
[2] *remove* removal
[3] *cruel* painful (with pun on 'crewel,' a yarn used in garters)
[4] *over-lusty at legs* i.e. too much on the go (?) or too much given to

kicking (?)
[5] *nether-stocks* stockings (as distinct from 'upper-stocks' or breeches)
[6] *To . . . outrage* i.e. to show such outrageous disrespect
[7] *Resolve* enlighten
[8] *modest* seemly
[9] *commend* entrust
[10] *Stewed* steaming

Delivered letters, spite of intermission,[11]
Which presently[12] they read; on[13] whose contents
They summoned up their meiny,[14] straight took horse,
Commanded me to follow and attend
The leisure of their answer, gave me cold looks;
And meeting here the other messenger,
Whose welcome I perceived had poisoned mine,
Being the very fellow which of late
Displayed[15] so saucily against your Highness,
Having more man[16] than wit[17] about me, drew;
He raised[18] the house with loud and coward cries.
Your son and daughter found this trespass worth
The shame which here it suffers.

FOOL. Winter's not gone yet, if the wild geese fly that way.[19]
Fathers that wear rags
　Do make their children blind,[20]
But fathers that bear bags[21]
　Shall see their children kind.
Fortune, that arrant whore,[22]
Ne'er turns the key[23] to th' poor.
But for all this, thou shalt have as many dolors[24] for thy daughters as thou canst tell[25] in a year.

LEAR. O, how this mother[26] swells up toward my heart!
Hysterica passio,[27] down, thou climbing sorrow;
Thy element's[28] below. Where is this daughter?

KENT. With the Earl, sir, here within.

LEAR. Follow me not; Stay here.　　　　　　*Exit.*

GENTLEMAN. Made you no more offense but what you speak of?

KENT. None.
How chance the King comes with so small a number?

FOOL. An thou hadst been set i' th' stocks for that question, thou'dst well deserved it.

KENT. Why, fool?

FOOL. We'll set thee to school to an ant, to teach thee there's no laboring i' th' winter.[29] All that follow their noses are led by their eyes but blind men, and there's not a nose among twenty but can smell him that's stinking.[30] Let go thy hold when a great wheel runs down a hill, lest it break thy neck with following. But the great one that goes upward, let him draw thee after. When a wise man gives thee better counsel, give me mine

[11] *spite of intermission* in disregard of its being an interruption
[12] *presently* immediately
[13] *on* on the strength of
[14] *meiny* attendants
[15] *Displayed* showed off
[16] *man* manhood
[17] *wit* sense
[18] *raised* aroused
[19] *Winter's . . . way* i.e. the ill season continues according to these signs (with Cornwall and Regan equated with 'wild geese,' proverbially evasive)
[20] *blind* (to their fathers' needs)
[21] *bags* (of gold)
[22] *Fortune . . . whore* (because so fickle and callous)
[23] *turns the key* i.e. opens the door
[24] *dolors* sorrows (with pun on 'dollars,' continental coins)
[25] *tell* count
[26,27] *mother, Hysterica passio* hysteria (the popular and the medical terms)
[28] *element* proper place
[29] *no laboring . . . winter* (Lear, accompanied by 'so small a number,' is equated with winter bereft of workers, such as ants.)
[30] *All . . . stinking* i.e. almost anyone can smell out a person decayed in fortune

again. I would have none but knaves [31]
follow it since a fool gives it.
That sir which serves and seeks for
    gain,
    And follows but for form,[32]
Will pack [33] when it begins to rain
    And leave thee in the storm.
But I will tarry; the fool will stay,
    And let the wise man fly.
The knave turns fool that runs
        away; [34]
    The fool no knave, perdy.[35]
    KENT. Where learned you this, fool?
    FOOL. Not i' th' stocks, fool.[36]
Enter Lear and Gloucester.
    LEAR. Deny to speak with me?
        They are sick, they are weary,
They have travelled all the night?
        Mere fetches,[37]
The images [38] of revolt and flying
    off! [39]
Fetch me a better answer.
    GLOUCESTER.   My dear lord,
You know the fiery quality [40] of the
    Duke,
How unremovable and fixed he is
In his own course.
    LEAR. Vengeance, plague, death,
        confusion!
Fiery? What quality? Why, Glouces-
    ter, Gloucester,
I'ld speak with the Duke of Cornwall
    and his wife.
GLOUCESTER. Well, my good lord, I
    have informed them so.

LEAR. Informed them? Dost thou
    understand me, man?
GLOUCESTER. Ay, my good lord.
LEAR. The King would speak with
    Cornwall. The dear father
Would with his daughter speak, com-
    mands—tends [41]—service.
Are they informed of this? My breath
    and blood!
Fiery? The fiery Duke, tell the hot
    Duke that—
No, but not yet. May be he is not well.
Infirmity doth still neglect all office [42]
Whereto our health is bound.[43] We
    are not ourselves
When nature, being oppressed, com-
    mands the mind
To suffer with the body. I'll forbear;
And am fallen out with my more head-
    ier [44] will
To take the indisposed and sickly fit
For the sound man.—Death on my
    state! Wherefore
Should he [45] sit here? This act per-
    suades me
That this remotion [46] of the Duke and
    her
Is practice [47] only. Give me my serv-
    ant forth.
Go tell the Duke and's wife I'ld speak
    with them!
Now, presently! [48] Bid them come
    forth and hear me,
Or at their chamber door I'll beat the
    drum

---

[31] *none but knaves* (Here
and in what follows the
Fool repudiates his ad-
vice to abandon Lear.)
[32] *form* show
[33] *pack* be off
[34] *The knave . . . away*
i.e. faithlessness is the
true folly
[35] *perdy* I swear (from
par dieu)

[36] *fool* (persiflage, but
also a term of honor; cf.
V, iii)
[37] *fetches* counterfeit reasons, false likenesses of
truth
[38] *images* true likenesses
[39] *flying off* revolt
[40] *quality* disposition
[41] *tends* attends, awaits (?)
or tenders, offers (?)

[42] *all office* duties
[43] *Whereto . . . bound*
to which, in health, we
are bound
[44] *headier* headstrong
[45] *he* i.e. Kent
[46] *remotion* remaining remote, inaccessible
[47] *practice* trickery
[48] *presently* immediately

Till it cry [49] sleep to death.

GLOUCESTER. I would have all well betwixt you.   *Exit.*

LEAR. O me, my heart, my rising heart! But down!

FOOL. Cry to it, nuncle, as the cockney [50] did to the eels when she put 'em i' th' paste [51] alive. She knapped [52] 'em o' th' coxcombs with a stick and cried, 'Down, wantons,[53] down!' 'Twas her brother that, in pure kindness to his horse, buttered his hay.[54]

Enter Cornwall, Regan, Gloucester, Servants.

LEAR. Good morrow to you both.

CORNWALL.   Hail to your Grace.

Kent here set at liberty.

REGAN. I am glad to see your Highness.

LEAR. Regan, I think you are. I know what reason
I have to think so. If thou shouldst not be glad,
I would divorce me from thy mother's tomb,
Sepulchring an adultress.[55] [*to Kent*]
O, are you free?
Some other time for that.—Beloved Regan,
Thy sister 's naught. O Regan, she hath tied
Sharp-toothed unkindness, like a vulture, here.
I can scarce speak to thee. Thou'lt not believe

With how depraved a quality [56]—O Regan!

REGAN. I pray you, sir, take patience. I have hope [57]
You less know how to value her desert
Than she to scant [58] her duty.

LEAR.   Say? how is that?

REGAN. I cannot think my sister in the least
Would fail her obligation. If, sir, perchance
She have restrained the riots of your followers,
'Tis on such ground, and to such wholesome end,
As clears her from all blame.

LEAR. My curses on her!

REGAN.   O, sir, you are old;
Nature in you stands on the very verge
Of his confine.[59] You should be ruled, and led
By some discretion that discerns your state [60]
Better than you yourself. Therefore I pray you
That to our sister you do make return;
Say you have wronged her.

LEAR.   Ask her forgiveness?
Do you but mark how this becomes the house: [61]
'Dear daughter, I confess that I am old.   [*Kneels.*]
Age is unnecessary. On my knees I beg

[49] *cry* pursue with noise (like a pack or 'cry' of hounds)
[50] *cockney* city-dweller
[51] *paste* pastry pie
[52] *knapped* rapped
[53] *wantons* i.e. frisky things
[54] *buttered his hay* (another example of rustic humor at the expense of cockney inexperience)

[55] *divorce . . . adultress* i.e. refuse to be buried with your mother since such a child as you must have been conceived in adultery
[56] *how . . . quality* i.e. what innate depravity
[57] *have hope* i.e. suspect
[58] *scant* (in effect, a double negative; 'do' would

be more logical though less emphatic)
[59] *Nature . . . confine* i.e. your life nears the limit of its tenure
[60] *some discretion . . . state* someone discerning enough to recognize your condition
[61] *the house* household or family decorum

That you'll vouchsafe me raiment, bed, and food.'

REGAN. Good sir, no more. These are unsightly tricks.
Return you to my sister.

LEAR.   [Rises] Never, Regan.
She hath abated[62] me of half my train,
Looked black upon me, struck me with her tongue
Most serpent-like upon the very heart.
All the stored vengeances of heaven fall
On her ingrateful top![63] Strike her young bones,
You taking[64] airs, with lameness.

CORNWALL.   Fie, sir, fie!

LEAR. You nimble lightnings, dart your blinding flames
Into her scornful eyes! Infect her beauty,
You fen-sucked[65] fogs drawn by the pow'rful sun
To fall and blister.[66]

REGAN.   O the blest gods!
So will you wish on me when the rash mood is on.

LEAR. No, Regan, thou shalt never have my curse.
Thy tender-hefted[67] nature shall not give
Thee o'er to harshness. Her eyes are fierce, but thine
Do comfort, and not burn. 'Tis not in thee
To grudge my pleasures, to cut off my train,

To bandy[68] hasty words, to scant my sizes,[69]
And, in conclusion, to oppose the bolt[70]
Against my coming in. Thou better know'st
The offices of nature,[71] bond of childhood,
Effects[72] of courtesy, dues of gratitude.
Thy half o' th' kingdom hast thou not forgot,
Wherein I thee endowed.

REGAN.   Good sir, to th' purpose.[73]
                    Tucket within.

LEAR. Who put my man i' th' stocks?

CORNWALL.   What trumpet's that?

REGAN. I know't—my sister's. This approves[74] her letter,
That she would soon be here.
    Enter Steward [Oswald].
                Is your lady come?

LEAR. This is a slave, whose easy-borrowèd[75] pride
Dwells in the fickle grace[76] of her he follows.
Out, varlet,[77] from my sight.

CORNWALL.   What means your Grace?

LEAR. Who stocked my servant?
Regan, I have good hope
Thou didst not know on't.
    Enter Goneril.
            Who comes here? O heavens!
If you do love old men, if your sweet sway

---

[62] abated curtailed
[63] ingrateful top ungrateful head
[64] taking infectious
[65] fen-sucked drawn up from swamps
[66] fall and blister strike and raise blisters (such as those of smallpox)
[67] tender-hefted swayed by tenderness, gently disposed
[68] bandy volley
[69] sizes allowances
[70] oppose the bolt i.e. bar the door
[71] offices of nature natural duties
[72] Effects actions
[73] purpose point
[74] approves confirms
[75] easy-borrowèd acquired on small security
[76] grace favor
[77] varlet low fellow

Allow [78] obedience, if you yourselves
    are old,
Make it your cause.[79] Send down, and
    take my part.
[*To Goneril*] Art not ashamed to look
    upon this beard?
O Regan, will you take her by the
    hand?
  GONERIL. Why not by th' hand, sir?
    How have I offended?
All's not offense that indiscretion
    finds [80]
And dotage terms so.
    LEAR. O sides,[81] you are too tough!
Will you yet hold? How came my man
    i' th' stocks?
  CORNWALL. I set him there, sir; but
    his own disorders
Deserved much less advancement.[82]
    LEAR.   You? Did you?
  REGAN. I pray you, father, being
    weak, seem so.[83]
If till the expiration of your month
You will return and sojourn with my
    sister,
Dismissing half your train, come then
    to me.
I am now from home, and out of
    that provision
Which shall be needful for your enter-
    tainment.[84]
    LEAR. Return to her, and fifty men
    dismissed?
No, rather I abjure all roofs, and
    choose

To wage [85] against the enmity o' th'
    air,
To be a comrade with the wolf and
    owl,
Necessity's sharp pinch.[86] Return with
    her?
Why, the hot-blooded [87] France, that
    dowerless took
Our youngest born, I could as well be
    brought
To knee [88] his throne, and, squire-
    like,[89] pension beg
To keep base life afoot. Return with
    her?
Persuade me rather to be slave and
    sumpter [90]
To this detested groom.[91]
    GONERIL.   At your choice, sir.
  LEAR. I prithee, daughter, do not
    make me mad.
I will not trouble thee, my child; fare-
    well.
We'll no more meet, no more see one
    another.
But yet thou art my flesh, my blood,
    my daughter;
Or rather a disease that's in my flesh,
Which I must needs call mine. Thou
    art a boil,
A plague-sore, or embossèd [92] car-
    buncle
In my corrupted blood. But I'll not
    chide thee.
Let shame come when it will, I do not
    call it.

---

[78] *Allow* approve
[79] *Make . . . cause* i.e. make my cause yours
[80] *indiscretion finds* ill judgment detects as such
[81] *sides* breast (which should burst with grief)

[82] *less advancement* i.e. more abasement
[83] *seem so* i.e. act the part
[84] *entertainment* lodging
[85] *wage* fight
[86] *Necessity's sharp pinch* (a summing up of the hardships previously listed)

[87] *hot-blooded* choleric (cf. I, ii)
[88] *knee* kneel at
[89] *squire-like* like an attendant
[90] *sumpter* packhorse
[91] *groom* i.e. Oswald
[92] *embossèd* risen to a head

I do not bid the thunder-bearer [93]
shoot,
Nor tell tales of thee to high-judg-
ing [94] Jove.
Mend when thou canst, be better at
thy leisure;
I can be patient, I can stay with Re-
gan,
I and my hundred knights.
    REGAN.   Not altogether so.
I looked not for you yet, nor am pro-
vided
For your fit welcome. Give ear, sir, to
my sister;
For those that mingle reason with
your passion [95]
Must be content to think you old,
and so—
But she knows what she does.
    LEAR.   Is this well spoken?
    REGAN. I dare avouch [96] it, sir.
What, fifty followers?
Is it not well? What should you need
of more?
Yea, or so many, sith that [97] both
charge [98] and danger
Speak 'gainst so great a number? How
in one house
Should many people, under two commands,
Hold amity? 'Tis hard, almost impossible.
    GONERIL. Why might not you, my
lord, receive attendance
From those that she calls servants, or
from mine?
    REGAN. Why not, my lord? If then
they chanced to slack [99] ye,

We could control them. If you will
come to me
(For now I spy a danger), I entreat
you
To bring but five-and-twenty. To no
more
Will I give place or notice.[100]
    LEAR. I gave you all.
    REGAN. And in good time you gave
it.
    LEAR. Made you my guardians, my
depositaries,[101]
But kept a reservation to be[102] fol-
lowèd
With such a number. What, must I
come to you
With five-and-twenty? Regan, said
you so?
    REGAN. And speak't again, my lord.
No more with me.
    LEAR. Those wicked creatures yet
do look well-favored [103]
When others are more wicked; not
being the worst
Stands in some rank of praise.[104] [To
Goneril] I'll go with thee.
Thy fifty yet doth double five-and-
twenty,
And thou art twice her love.[105]
    GONERIL.   Hear me, my lord.
What need you five-and-twenty? ten?
or five?
To follow in a house where twice so
many
Have a command to tend you?
    REGAN.   What need one?
    LEAR. O reason [106] not the need!
    Our basest beggars

---

[93] thunder-bearer Jupiter
[94] high-judging judging from on high
[95] mingle . . . passion interpret your passion in the light of reason
[96] avouch swear by

[97] sith that since
[98] charge expense
[99] slack neglect
[100] notice recognition
[101] depositaries trustees
[102] kept . . . to be stipulated that I be

[103] well-favored comely
[104] Stands . . . praise i.e. is at least relatively praiseworthy
[105] her love i.e. as loving as she
[106] reason analyze

Are in the poorest thing superflu-
ous.[107]
Allow not nature more than nature
needs,[108]
Man's life is cheap as beast's. Thou art
a lady:
If only to go warm were gorgeous,
Why, nature needs not what thou gor-
geous wear'st,
Which scarcely keeps thee warm.[109]
But, for true need—
You heavens, give me that patience,
patience I need.
You see me here, you gods, a poor old
man,
As full of grief as age, wretched in
both.
If it be you that stirs these daughters'
hearts
Against their father, fool [110] me not
so much
To bear it tamely; touch me with no-
ble anger,
And let not women's weapons, water
drops,
Stain my man's cheeks. No, you unnat-
ural hags!
I will have such revenges on you both
That all the world shall—I will do
such things—
What they are, yet I know not; but
they shall be
The terrors of the earth. You think
I'll weep.
No, I'll not weep. *Storm and tempest.*
I have full cause of weeping, but this
heart

Shall break into a hundred thousand
flaws [111]
Or ere [112] I'll weep. O fool, I shall go
mad!
    Exeunt [Lear, Fool, Kent, and
        Gloucester].
CORNWALL. Let us withdraw; 'twill
be a storm.
REGAN. This house is little; the old
man and 's people
Cannot be well bestowed.
GONERIL. 'Tis his own blame; hath
put himself from rest [113]
And must needs taste his folly.
REGAN. For his particular,[114] I'll re-
ceive him gladly,
But not one follower.
GONERIL.   So am I purposed.[115]
Where is my Lord of Gloucester?
CORNWALL. Followèd the old man
forth.
Enter Gloucester.
    He is returned.
GLOUCESTER. The King is in high
rage.
CORNWALL.   Whither is he going?
GLOUCESTER. He calls to horse, but
will I know not whither.
CORNWALL. 'Tis best to give him
way; he leads himself.
GONERIL. My lord, entreat him by
no means to stay.
GLOUCESTER. Alack, the night comes
on, and the high winds
Do sorely ruffle.[116] For many miles
about
There's scarce a bush.

---

[107] *Are . . . superfluous*
i.e. have some poor pos-
session not utterly indispensable
[108] *than nature needs* i.e.
than life needs for mere
survival
[109] *If . . . warm* i.e. if to
be dressed warmly (i.e.

for need) were consid-
ered sufficiently gor-
geous, you would not
need your present attire,
which is gorgeous rather
than warm
[110] *fool* play with, hu-
miliate
[111] *flaws* fragments

[112] *Or ere* before
[113] *hath . . . rest* i.e. he
himself is responsible for
leaving his resting place
with her (?) or, he is
self-afflicted (?)
[114] *particular* own person
[115] *purposed* determined
[116] *ruffle* rage

REGAN. O, sir, to willful men
The injuries that they themselves pro-
 cure
Must be their schoolmasters. Shut up
 your doors.
He is attended with a desperate train,
And what they may incense him to,
 being apt
To have his ear abused,[117] wisdom
 bids fear.
 CORNWALL. Shut up your doors, my
 lord; 'tis a wild night.
My Regan counsels well. Come out o'
 th' storm.   *Exeunt.*

ACT III

SCENE ONE

*Storm still. Enter Kent and a Gentle-
man severally.*

 KENT. Who's there besides foul
 weather?
 GENTLEMAN. One minded like the
 weather, most unquietly.[1]
 KENT. I know you. Where's the
 King?
 GENTLEMAN. Contending [2] with the
 fretful elements;
Bids the wind blow the earth into the
 sea,
Or swell the curlèd waters 'bove the
 main,[3]
That things might change [4] or cease;
 [tears his white hair,

Which the impetuous blasts, with eye-
 less [5] rage,
Catch in their fury and make nothing
 of;
Strives in his little world [6] of man to
 outscorn
The to-and-fro-conflicting wind and
 rain.
This night, wherein the cub-drawn [7]
 bear would couch,
The lion and the belly-pinchèd [8] wolf
Keep their fur dry, unbonneted he
 runs,
And bids what will take all.[9]]
 KENT. But who is with him?
 GENTLEMAN. None but the fool,
 who labors to outjest
His heart-struck injuries.
 KENT.   Sir, I do know you,
And dare upon the warrant of my
 note [10]
Commend a dear thing [11] to you.
 There is division,
Although as yet the face of it is
 covered
With mutual cunning, 'twixt Albany
 and Cornwall;
Who have—as who have not, that [12]
 their great stars [13]
Throned [14] and set high?—servants,
 who seem no less,[15]
Which are to France the spies and
 speculations [16]
Intelligent [17] of our state. What hath
 been seen,

---

[117] *apt . . . abused* i.e.
predisposed to listen to
ill counsel
III, i [1] *minded . . . unquietly* i.e. in disturbed
mood
[2] *Contending* quarrelling
[3] *main* mainland
[4] *change* revert to chaos
(?) or, improve (?)
[5] *eyeless* (1) blind (2)

invisible
[6] *little world* (the 'microcosm,' which is dis-
turbed like the great
world or 'macrocosm')
[7] *cub-drawn* cub-sucked
(and hence ravenous)
[8] *belly-pinchèd* famished
[9] *take all* (the cry of the
desperate gambler in
staking his last)

[10] *warrant . . . note* assurance of my knowledge
[11] *Commend . . . thing*
entrust a precious matter
[12] *that* whom
[13] *stars* destinies
[14] *Throned* have throned
[15] *no less* i.e. truly so
[16] *speculations* spies
[17] *Intelligent* supplying intelligence

Either in snuffs [18] and packings [19] of
the Dukes,
Or the hard rein which both of them
have borne [20]
Against the old kind King, or something deeper,
Whereof, perchance, these are but
furnishings [21]—
[But, true it is, from France there
comes a power [22]
Into this scatterèd [23] kingdom, who
already,
Wise in our negligence, have secret
feet
In some of our best ports and are at
point
To show their open banner. Now to
you:
If on my credit [24] you dare build [25] so
far
To make your speed to Dover, you
shall find
Some that will thank you, making just
report
Of how unnatural and bemadding
sorrow [26]
The King hath cause to plain.[27]
I am a gentleman of blood and breed-
ing,
And from some knowledge and as-
surance offer
This office [28] to you.]
    GENTLEMAN. I will talk further with
you.
    KENT. No, do not.
For confirmation that I am much more

Than my out-wall,[29] open this purse
and take
What it contains. If you shall see
Cordelia,
As fear not but you shall, show her
this ring,
And she will tell you who that fellow
is
That yet you do not know. Fie on this
storm!
I will go seek the King.
    GENTLEMAN. Give me your hand.
Have you no more to say?
    KENT. Few words, but, to effect,[30]
more than all yet:
That when we have found the King—
in which your pain [31]
That way, I'll this—he that first lights
on him
Holla the other.   Exeunt [severally].

SCENE TWO

Storm still. Enter Lear and Fool.

    LEAR. Blow, winds, and crack your
cheeks. Rage, blow.
You cataracts and hurricanoes,[1] spout
Till you have drenched our steeples,
drowned the cocks.[2]
You sulph'rous and thought-executing
fires,[3]
Vaunt-couriers [4] to oak-cleaving thun-
derbolts,
Singe my white head. And thou, all-
shaking thunder,

[18] snuffs quarrels
[19] packings intrigues
[20] hard rein . . . borne
i.e. harsh curbs . . .
exercised
[21] furnishings pretexts
[22] power army
[23] scatterèd divided
[24] my credit trust in me

[25] build take constructive
action
[26] bemadding   sorrow
maddening grievances
[27] plain lament
[28] office service
[29] out-wall surface ap-
pearance
[30] to effect in their import

[31] pain pains, care
III, ii [1] hurricanoes water-
spouts
[2] cocks weathercocks
[3] thought-executing fires
i.e. flashes of lightning
swift as thought (?) or,
dazing, benumbing the
mind (?)
[4] Vaunt-couriers heralds

Strike flat the thick rotundity o' th'
    world,
Crack Nature's moulds,[5] all germains [5a]
    spill at once,
That makes ingrateful man.

FOOL. O nuncle, court holy-water [6]
in a dry house is better than this rain
water out o' door. Good nuncle, in; ask
thy daughters' blessing. Here's a night
pities neither wise men nor fools.

LEAR. Rumble thy bellyful. Spit, fire.
    Spout, rain.
Nor rain, wind, thunder, fire are my
    daughters.
I tax [7] not you, you elements, with un-
    kindness.
I never gave you kingdom, called you
    children;
You owe me no subscription.[8] Then let
    fall
Your horrible pleasure.[9] Here I stand
    your slave,
A poor, infirm, weak, and despised
    old man.
But yet I call you servile minis-
    ters,[10]
That will with two pernicious daugh-
    ters join
Your high-engendered battles [11] 'gainst
    a head
So old and white as this. O, ho! 'tis
    foul.

FOOL. He that has a house to put 's
head in has a good head-piece.

The codpiece [12] that will house
    Before the head has any,
The head and he [13] shall louse:
    So beggars marry many.[14,15]
The man that makes his toe
    What he his heart should make
Shall of a corn cry woe,
    And turn his sleep to wake.[16]

For there was never yet fair woman
but she made mouths in a glass.[17]
    Enter Kent.

LEAR. No, I will be the pattern of
    all patience;
I will say nothing.

KENT. Who's there?

FOOL. Marry, here's grace and a
codpiece; that's a wise man and a fool.

KENT. Alas, sir, are you here?
    Things that love night
Love not such nights as these. The
    wrathful skies
Gallow [18] the very wanderers of the
    dark
And make them keep their caves.[19]
    Since I was man,
Such sheets of fire, such bursts of hor-
    rid [20] thunder,
Such groans of roaring wind and rain,
    I never

---

[5] *moulds* (in which Nature's creations are formed)
[5a] *germains* seeds
[6] *court holy-water* flattery (slang)
[7] *tax* charge
[8] *subscription* deference
[9] *pleasure* will
[10] *ministers* agents
[11] *high-engendered battles* heavenly battalions
[12] *codpiece* padded gusset at the crotch of the

trunks (slang for 'phallus')
[13] *he* it
[14] *The codpiece . . . many* (The moral of the rime is that improvident cohabitation spells penury.)
[15] *many* (head-lice and body-lice, accompanying poverty)
[16] *The man . . . wake* (a parallel instance of misery deriving from reckless impulse: to transpose the

tender and precious heart and the tough and base toe is to invite injury; with 'heart' also suggesting Cordelia)
[17] *made . . . glass* i.e. posed before a mirror (irrelevant, except as vanity is a form of folly, the Fool's general theme)
[18] *Gallow* frighten
[19] *keep their caves* i.e. keep under cover
[20] *horrid* horrible

Remember to have heard. Man's na-
ture cannot carry [21]
Th' affliction nor the fear.
LEAR.   Let the great gods
That keep this dreadful pudder [22] o'er
our heads
Find out their enemies [23] now. Trem-
ble, thou wretch,
That hast within thee undivulgèd
crimes
Unwhipped of justice. Hide thee, thou
bloody hand,
Thou perjured, and thou simular [24] of
virtue
That art incestuous. Caitiff, to pieces
shake,
That under covert and convenient
seeming [25]
Has practiced on [26] man's life. Close [27]
pent-up guilts,
Rive [28] your concealing continents [29]
and cry
These dreadful summoners [30] grace.[31]
I am a man
More sinned against than sinning.
KENT.   Alack, bareheaded?
Gracious my lord,[32] hard by here is a
hovel;
Some friendship will it lend you 'gainst
the tempest.
Repose you there, while I to this hard
house [33]
(More harder than the stones whereof

'tis raised,
Which even but now, demanding
after [34] you,
Denied me to come in) return, and
force
Their scanted [35] courtesy.
LEAR.   My wits begin to turn.
Come on, my boy. How dost, my boy?
Art cold?
I am cold myself. Where is this straw,
my fellow?
The art [36] of our necessities is strange,
And can make vile things precious.
Come, your hovel.
Poor fool and knave, I have one part
in my heart
That's sorry yet for thee.
FOOL. [Sings]
He that has and a little tiny wit,
With, heigh-ho, the wind and the
rain,
Must make content with his fortunes
fit [37]
Though the rain it raineth every
day.
LEAR. True, boy. Come, bring us to
this hovel.
        Exit [with Kent].
FOOL. This is a brave [38] night to cool
a courtesan. I'll speak a prophecy ere
I go:
When priests are more in word than
matter; [39]

[21] carry bear
[22] pudder turmoil
[23] Find . . . enemies i.e.
discover sinners (by their
show of fear)
[24] simular counterfeit
[25] seeming hypocrisy
[26] practiced on plotted
against
[27] Close secret
[28] Rive split, break
through

[29] continents containers,
covers
[30] summoners arresting officers of ecclesiastical
courts
[31] grace mercy
[32] Gracious my lord my
gracious lord
[33] house household (both
building and occupants)
[34] demanding after inquiring for

[35] scanted stinted
[36] art magic skill (as in
alchemy)
[37] make . . . fit i.e. reconcile himself to his fortunes
[38] brave fine
[39] are . . . matter i.e. can
outshine the gospel mes-
sage (At present their
ability to speak is quite
unworthy of their theme.)

When brewers mar [40] their malt with water;
When nobles are their tailors' tutors,[41]
No heretics burned,[42] but wenches' suitors; [43]
When every case in law is right,
No squire in debt nor no poor knight;
When slanders do not live in tongues,
Nor cutpurses come not to throngs;
When usurers tell [44] their gold i' th' field,[45]
And bawds and whores do churches build—
Then shall the realm of Albion [46]
Come to great confusion.[47]
Then comes the time, who lives to see't,
That going shall be used with feet.[48]
This prophecy Merlin [49] shall make, for I live before his time. *Exit.*

Scene Three

Enter Gloucester and Edmund.

GLOUCESTER. Alack, alack, Edmund, I like not this unnatural dealing. When I desired their leave that I might pity [1] him, they took from me the use of mine own house, charged me on pain of perpetual displeasure neither to speak of him, entreat [2] for him, or any way sustain him.

EDMUND. Most savage and unnatural.

GLOUCESTER. Go to; say you nothing. There is division [3] between the Dukes, and a worse [4] matter than that. I have received a letter this night—'tis dangerous to be spoken—I have locked the letter in my closet.[5] These injuries the King now bears will be revenged home; [6] there is part of a power [7] already footed; [8] we must incline to [9] the King. I will look [10] him and privily [11] relieve him. Go you and maintain talk with the Duke, that my charity be not of him perceived. If he ask for me, I am ill and gone to bed. If I die for it, as no less is threatened me, the King my old master must be relieved. There is strange things toward,[12] Edmund; pray you be careful.
  Exit.

EDMUND. This courtesy [13] forbid thee shall the Duke
Instantly know, and of that letter too.
This seems a fair deserving,[14] and must draw me
That which my father loses—no less than all.

---

[40] *mar* i.e. dilute (At present they dilute water with malt, producing very small beer.)
[41] *are . . . tutors* i.e. are no longer subservient to fashion (Each subsequent line also reverses the present state of affairs.)
[42] *burned* (pun on contracting venereal disease)
[43] *wenches' suitors* i.e. libertines
[44] *tell* count
[45] *i' th' field* (instead of in secret places)

[46] *Albion* England
[47] *confusion* ruin (ironic: an edifice of abuses is 'ruined' by reform)
[48] *going . . . feet* walking will be done with feet (the humor of anticlimax, but suggesting a return to normality)
[49] *Merlin* (a legendary magician associated with King Arthur, who reigned later than King Lear)
III, iii [1] *pity* have mercy upon

[2] *entreat* plead
[3] *division* contention
[4] *worse* more serious
[5] *closet* chamber
[6] *home* thoroughly
[7] *power* army
[8] *footed* landed
[9] *incline to* side with
[10] *look* search for
[11] *privily* secretly
[12] *toward* imminent
[13] *courtesy* kind attention (to Lear)
[14] *fair deserving* i.e. action that should win favor

The younger rises when the old doth fall.   *Exit.*

SCENE FOUR

Enter Lear, Kent, and Fool.

KENT. Here is the place, my lord. Good my lord,[1] enter.
The tyranny of the open night's too rough
For nature to endure.   *Storm still.*
    LEAR.   Let me alone.
    KENT. Good my lord, enter here.
    LEAR.   Wilt break my heart?[2]
    KENT. I had rather break mine own. Good my lord, enter.
    LEAR. Thou think'st 'tis much that this contentious storm
Invades us to the skin. So 'tis to thee,
But where the greater malady is fixed[3]
The lesser is scarce felt. Thou'dst shun a bear;
But if thy flight lay toward the roaring sea,
Thou'dst meet the bear i' th' mouth.[4]
When the mind's free,[5]
The body's delicate. The tempest in my mind
Doth from my senses take all feeling else
Save what beats there. Filial ingratitude,
Is it not as this mouth should tear this hand
For lifting food to't? But I will punish home.[6]
No, I will weep no more. In such a night

To shut me out! Pour on; I will endure.
In such a night as this! O Regan, Goneril,
Your old kind father, whose frank[7] heart gave all—
O, that way madness lies; let me shun that.
No more of that.
    KENT.   Good my lord, enter here.
    LEAR. Prithee go in thyself; seek thine own ease.
This tempest will not give me leave to ponder
On things would hurt me more, but I'll go in.
[*To the Fool*] In, boy; go first. You houseless[8] poverty—
Nay, get thee in. I'll pray, and then I'll sleep.   *Exit* [*Fool*].
Poor naked wretches, wheresoe'er you are,
That bide the pelting of this pitiless storm,
How shall your houseless heads and unfed sides,
Your looped[9] and windowed raggedness, defend you
From seasons such as these? O, I have ta'en
Too little care of this! Take physic, pomp;[10]
Expose thyself to feel what wretches feel,
That thou mayst shake the superflux[11] to them
And show the heavens more just.
    EDGAR. [*Within*] Fathom and half,[12] fathom and half! Poor Tom!

III, iv [1] *Good my lord* my good lord
[2] *break my heart* i.e. by removing the distraction of mere physical distress
[3] *fixed* lodged
[4] *i' th' mouth* i.e. in the teeth
[5] *free* free of care
[6] *home* i.e. to the hilt
[7] *frank* liberal
[8] *houseless* unsheltered
[9] *looped* loopholed
[10] *Take physic, pomp* i.e. cure yourself, you vainglorious ones
[11] *superflux* superfluities
[12] *Fathom and half* (nautical cry in taking soundings, perhaps suggested by the deluge)

Enter Fool.

FOOL. Come not in here, nuncle; here's a spirit. Help me, help me!

KENT. Give me thy hand. Who's there?

FOOL. A spirit, a spirit. He says his name's poor Tom.

KENT. What art thou that dost grumble there i' th' straw? Come forth.

Enter Edgar [as Tom o' Bedlam].

EDGAR. Away! the foul fiend follows me. Through the sharp hawthorn blow the winds.[13] Humh! go to thy bed, and warm thee.[14]

LEAR. Didst thou give all to thy daughters? And art thou come to this?

EDGAR. Who gives anything to poor Tom? whom the foul fiend hath led through fire and through flame, through ford and whirlpool, o'er bog and quagmire; that hath laid knives under his pillow and halters in his pew,[15] set ratsbane [16] by his porridge, made him proud of heart, to ride on a bay trotting horse over four-inched bridges,[17] to course his own shadow for a traitor.[18] Bless thy five wits, Tom's acold. O, do, de, do, de, do, de. Bless thee from whirlwinds, star-blasting,[19] and taking.[20] Do poor Tom some charity, whom the foul fiend

vexes. There could I have him now— and there—and there again—and there—   *Storm still.*

LEAR. Has his daughters brought him to this pass? [21] Couldst thou save nothing? Wouldst thou give 'em all?

FOOL. Nay, he reserved a blanket,[22] else we had been all shamed.

LEAR. Now all the plagues that in the pendulous [23] air Hang fated o'er men's faults [24] light on thy daughters!

KENT. He hath no daughters, sir.

LEAR. Death, traitor; nothing could have subdued nature To such a lowness but his unkind daughters. Is it the fashion that discarded fathers Should have thus little mercy on their flesh? [25] Judicious punishment—'twas this flesh begot Those pelican [26] daughters.

EDGAR. Pillicock sat on Pillicock Hill.[27] Alow, alow, loo, loo! [28]

FOOL. This cold night will turn us all to fools and madmen.

EDGAR. Take heed o' th' foul fiend; obey thy parents; keep thy words' justice; [29] swear not; commit not [30] with man's sworn spouse; set not thy

---

[13] *Through . . . winds* (cf. p. 112, col. 1, l. 24; a line from a ballad)
[14] *go . . . thee* (evidently a popular retort; cf. *Taming of the Shrew,* Induction, I)
[15] *pew* a gallery or balcony
[16] *knives, halters, ratsbane* (temptations to suicide)
[17] *ride . . . bridges* i.e. take mad risks
[18] *course . . . traitor* chase his own shadow as an

enemy
[19] *star-blasting* i.e. becoming the victim of malignant stars
[20] *taking* pestilence
[21] *pass* evil condition
[22] *blanket* (to cover his nakedness)
[23] *pendulous* ominously suspended
[24] *Hang . . . faults* i.e. destined to chastise sins
[25] *have . . . flesh* i.e. torture themselves

[26] *pelican* i.e. feeding upon the parent's blood (a supposed habit of this species of bird)
[27] *Pillicock . . . Hill* (probably from a nursery rime; 'Pillicock' is a pet-name for a child)
[28] *Alow . . . loo* (hunting cry ?)
[29] *justice* i.e. dependability
[30] *commit not* (i.e. adultery)

sweet heart on proud array. Tom's acold.

LEAR. What hast thou been?

EDGAR. A servingman, proud in heart and mind; that curled my hair, wore gloves in my cap;[31] served the lust of my mistress' heart, and did the act of darkness with her; swore as many oaths as I spake words, and broke them in the sweet face of heaven. One that slept in the contriving of lust, and waked to do it. Wine loved I deeply, dice dearly; and in woman out-paramoured the Turk.[32] False of heart, light of ear,[33] bloody of hand; hog in sloth, fox in stealth, wolf in greediness, dog in madness, lion in prey. Let not the creaking of shoes nor the rustling[34] of silks betray thy poor heart to woman. Keep thy foot out of brothels, thy hand out of plackets,[35] thy pen from lenders' books,[36] and defy the foul fiend. Still through the hawthorn blows the cold wind; says suum, mun, nonny.[37] Dolphin my boy, boy, sessa! let him trot by.[38]   Storm still.

LEAR. Thou wert better in a grave than to answer[39] with thy uncovered body this extremity of the skies. Is man no more than this? Consider him well. Thou ow'st[40] the worm no silk, the beast no hide, the sheep no wool, the cat[41] no perfume. Ha! here's three on's are sophisticated.[42] Thou art the thing itself; unaccommodated[43] man is no more but such a poor, bare, forked[44] animal as thou art. Off, off, you lendings![45] Come, unbutton here.

[Begins to disrobe.]

FOOL. Prithee, nuncle, be contented; 'tis a naughty[46] night to swim in. Now a little fire in a wild[47] field were like an old lecher's heart—a small spark, all the rest on's body cold. Look, here comes a walking fire.

Enter Gloucester with a torch.

EDGAR. This is the foul Flibbertigibbet.[48] He begins at curfew,[49] and walks till the first cock.[50] He gives the web and the pin,[51] squints[52] the eye, and makes the harelip; mildews the white[53] wheat, and hurts the poor creature of earth.

Swithold[54] footed[55] thrice the 'old;[56]
He met the nightmare,[57] and her nine fold;[58]
Bid her alight[59]

---

[31] gloves . . . cap (a fashion with Elizabethan gallants)
[32] out-paramoured the Turk outdid the Sultan in mistress-keeping
[33] light of ear i.e. attentive to flattery and slander
[34] creaking, rustling (both considered seductively fashionable sounds)
[35] plackets slits in skirts
[36] pen . . . books (in signing for loans)
[37] suum . . . nonny (the refrain of the wind ?)
[38] Dolphin . . . trot by (variously explained as

cant phrases or ballad refrain, equivalent to 'Let it go')
[39] answer bear the brunt of
[40] ow'st have borrowed from
[41] cat civet cat
[42] sophisticated altered by artifice
[43] unaccommodated unpampered
[44] forked two-legged
[45] lendings borrowed coverings
[46] naughty evil
[47] wild barren

[48] Flibbertigibbet (a dancing devil)
[49] curfew (9 p.m.)
[50] first cock (midnight)
[51] web . . . pin cataract of the eye
[52] squints crosses
[53] white ripening
[54] Swithold St. Withold (Anglo-Saxon exorcist)
[55] footed walked over
[56] 'old wold, uplands
[57] nightmare incubus, demon
[58] fold offspring
[59] alight i.e. from the horse she was afflicting

And her troth plight,[60]
And aroint thee,[61] witch, aroint thee!

KENT. How fares your Grace?

LEAR. What's he?

KENT. Who's there? What is't you seek?

GLOUCESTER. What are you there? Your names?

EDGAR. Poor Tom, that eats the swimming frog, the toad, the tod-pole,[62] the wall-newt and the water; [63] that in the fury of his heart, when the foul fiend rages, eats cow-dung for sallets,[64] swallows the old rat and the ditch-dog,[65] drinks the green mantle [66] of the standing [67] pool; who is whipped from tithing [68] to tithing, and stock-punished [69] and imprisoned; who hath had three suits to his back, six shirts to his body,
Horse to ride, and weapon to wear,
But mice and rats, and such small deer,[70]
Have been Tom's food for seven long year.
Beware my follower! Peace, Smul-kin,[71] peace, thou fiend!

GLOUCESTER. What, hath your Grace no better company?

EDGAR. The prince of darkness is a gentleman.
Modo [72] he's called, and Mahu.[73]

GLOUCESTER. Our flesh and blood, my lord, is grown so vile
That it doth hate what gets [74] it.

EDGAR. Poor Tom's acold.

GLOUCESTER. Go in with me. My duty cannot suffer [75]
T' obey in all your daughters' hard commands.
Though their injunction be to bar my doors
And let this tyrannous night take hold upon you,
Yet have I ventured to come seek you out
And bring you where both fire and food is ready.

LEAR. First let me talk with this philosopher.
What is the cause of thunder?

KENT. Good my lord, take his offer; go into th' house.

LEAR. I'll talk a word with this same learnèd Theban.[76]
What is your study? [77]

EDGAR. How to prevent [78] the fiend, and to kill vermin.

LEAR. Let me ask you one word in private.

KENT. Importune him once more to go, my lord.
His wits begin t' unsettle.

GLOUCESTER. Canst thou blame him?
Storm still.
His daughters seek his death. Ah, that good Kent,
He said it would be thus, poor banished man!
Thou say'st the King grows mad—I'll

---

[60] *her troth plight* plight her troth, pledge her good intentions
[61] *aroint thee* be gone (a direct command, concluding the charm)
[62] *todpole* tadpole
[63] *water* water-newt
[64] *sallets* salads
[65] *ditch-dog* (carcass)
[66] *mantle* scum

[67] *standing* stagnant
[68] *tithing* a ten-family district within a parish
[69] *stock-punished* placed in the stocks
[70] *deer* game (adapted from lines in the romance *Bevis of Hampton*)
[71-3] *Smulkin, Modo, Mahu* (devils described in Harsnett's *Declaration,* 1603)

[74] *gets* begets (a reference to Edgar, Goneril, and Regan)
[75] *suffer* permit
[76] *Theban* (an unexplained association of Thebes with philosophy, i.e. science)
[77] *study* i.e. scientific specialty
[78] *prevent* thwart

tell thee, friend,
I am almost mad myself. I had a son,
Now outlawed from my blood; [79] he
  sought my life
But lately, very late. I loved him,
  friend,
No father his son dearer. True to tell
  thee,
The grief hath crazed my wits. What
  a night's this!
I do beseech your Grace—
    LEAR.   O, cry you mercy,[80] sir.
Noble philosopher, your company.
    EDGAR. Tom's acold.
    GLOUCESTER. In, fellow, there, into
th' hovel; keep thee warm.
    LEAR. Come, let's in all.
    KENT.   This way, my lord.
    LEAR.   With him!
I will keep still with my philosopher.
    KENT. Good my lord, soothe [81] him;
  let him take the fellow.
    GLOUCESTER. Take him you on.[82]
    KENT. Sirrah, come on; go along
  with us.
    LEAR. Come, good Athenian.[83]
    GLOUCESTER. No words, no words!
  Hush.
    EDGAR. Child Rowland [84] to the dark
  tower came;
His word was still,[85] 'Fie, foh, and
  fum,
I smell the blood of a British man.' [86]
                              Exeunt.

SCENE FIVE

Enter Cornwall and Edmund.

    CORNWALL. I will have my revenge
ere I depart his house.
    EDMUND. How, my lord, I may be
censured,[1] that nature thus gives way
to loyalty, something fears me [2] to
think of.
    CORNWALL. I now perceive it was
not altogether your brother's evil disposition made him seek his death; but
a provoking merit, set awork by a
reproveable badness in himself.[3]
    EDMUND. How malicious is my for-
tune that I must repent to be just! This
is the letter which he spoke of, which
approves [4] him an intelligent party to
the advantages [5] of France. O heavens,
that this treason were not! or not I
the detector!
    CORNWALL. Go with me to the
Duchess.
    EDMUND. If the matter of this paper
be certain, you have mighty business
in hand.
    CORNWALL. True or false, it hath
made thee Earl of Gloucester. Seek
out where thy father is, that he may be
ready for our apprehension.
    EDMUND. [*Aside*] If I find him com-
forting [6] the King, it will stuff his
suspicion more fully.—I will persever [7]

---

[79] *outlawed . . . blood*
proscribed as no child
of mine
[80] *cry you mercy* I beg
your pardon
[81] *soothe* humor
[82] *you on* along with you
[83] *Athenian* i.e. philosopher
[84] *Child* (i.e. a candidate
for knighthood) *Rowland*
Roland of the Charle-

magne legends (the line
perhaps from a lost bal-
lad)
[85] *His word was still* i.e.
his repeated word, his
motto, was always
[86] *Fie . . . man* (absurdly
heroic)
III, v [1] *censured* judged
[2] *something fears me*
frightens me somewhat

[3] *a provoking . . . himself* i.e. evil justice in-
cited by evil (a case of
poison driving out poi-
son)
[4] *approves* proves
[5] *intelligent . . . advantages* spying partisan on
behalf of
[6] *comforting* aiding
[7] *persever* persevere

in my course of loyalty, though the conflict be sore between that and my blood.[8]

CORNWALL. I will lay trust upon thee,[9] and thou shalt find a dearer father in my love.   *Exeunt.*

SCENE SIX

Enter Kent and Gloucester.

GLOUCESTER. Here is better than the open air; take it thankfully. I will piece out the comfort with what addition I can. I will not be long from you.

KENT. All the power of his wits have given way to his impatience.[1] The gods reward your kindness.

     Exit [Gloucester].

Enter Lear, Edgar, and Fool.

EDGAR. Frateretto [2] calls me, and tells me Nero [3] is an angler in the lake of darkness. Pray, innocent,[4] and beware the foul fiend.

FOOL. Prithee, nuncle, tell me whether a madman be a gentleman or a yeoman.[5]

LEAR. A king, a king.

FOOL. No, he's a yeoman that has a gentleman to his son; for he's a mad yeoman that sees [6] his son a gentleman before him.

LEAR. To have a thousand with red burning spits

Come hizzing [7] in upon 'em—

[EDGAR. The foul fiend bites my back.

FOOL. He's mad that trusts in the tameness of a wolf, a horse's health, a boy's love, or a whore's oath.

LEAR. It shall be done; I will arraign [8] them straight.

[*To Edgar*] Come, sit thou here, most learned justice.

[*To the Fool*] Thou, sapient sir, sit here. Now, you she-foxes—

EDGAR. Look, where he [9] stands and glares. Want'st thou eyes [10] at trial, madam?

    Come o'er the bourn,[11] Bessy,
      to me.

FOOL.   Her boat hath a leak,
     And she must not speak
    Why she dares not come over
      to thee.

EDGAR. The foul fiend haunts poor Tom in the voice of a nightingale.[12] Hoppedance [13] cries in Tom's belly for two white [14] herring. Croak not, black angel; I have no food for thee.

KENT. How do you, sir? Stand you not so amazed.[15] Will you lie down and rest upon the cushions?

LEAR. I'll see their trial first. Bring in their evidence.

[*To Edgar*] Thou, robèd man of jus-

[8] *blood* natural feelings
[9] *lay . . . thee* trust you(?) reward you with a place of trust(?)
III, vi [1] *impatience* rage
[2] *Frateretto* (a devil mentioned in Harsnett's *Declaration*)
[3] *Nero* (In Rabelais, Trajan was the angler, Nero a fiddler, in Hades.)
[4] *innocent* hapless victim, plaything
[5] *yeoman* a property

owner, next in rank to a gentleman (The allusion is to self-penalizing indulgence of one's children.)
[6] *sees* i.e. sees to it
[7] *hizzing* hissing (Lear is musing on vicious military retaliation.)
[8] *arraign* bring to trial
[9] *he* Lear (?) or one of Edgar's 'devils' (?)
[10] *eyes* such eyes (?) or spectators (?)

[11] *bourn* brook (Edgar's line is from a popular song; the Fool's are a ribald improvisation.)
[12] *nightingale* i.e. the fool
[13] *Hoppedance* (a devil mentioned in Harsnett's *Declaration* as 'Hobberdidance')
[14] *white* unsmoked (in contrast with 'black angel,' i.e. smoked devil)
[15] *amazed* bewildered

tice, take thy place.
[*To the Fool*] And thou, his yokefel-
low of equity,
Bench by his side. [*To Kent*] You are
o' th' commission; [16]
Sit you too.

EDGAR. Let us deal justly.
Sleepest or wakest thou, jolly shepherd?
Thy sheep be in the corn; [17]
And for one blast of thy minikin
mouth [18]
Thy sheep shall take no harm.
Purr, the cat is gray.[19]

LEAR. Arraign her first. 'Tis Goneril,
I here take my oath before this honorable assembly, kicked the poor King
her father.

FOOL. Come hither, mistress. Is your
name Goneril?

LEAR. She cannot deny it.

FOOL. Cry you mercy, I took you for
a joint-stool.[20]

LEAR. And here's another, whose
warped looks proclaim
What store her heart is made on. Stop
her there!
Arms, arms, sword, fire! Corruption in
the place! [21]
False justicer, why hast thou let her
'scape?]

EDGAR. Bless thy five wits!

KENT. O pity! Sir, where is the
patience now
That you so oft have boasted to retain?

EDGAR. [*Aside*] My tears begin to
take his part [22] so much
They mar my counterfeiting.[23]

LEAR. The little dogs and all,
Tray, Blanch, and Sweetheart—see,
they bark at me.

EDGAR. Tom will throw his head at
them. Avaunt, you curs.
Be thy mouth or black or white,
Tooth that poisons if it bite;
Mastiff, greyhound, mongrel grim,
Hound or spaniel, brach [24] or lym,[25]
Or bobtail tike, or trundle-tail [26]—
Tom will make him weep and wail;
For, with throwing thus my head,
Dogs leaped the hatch,[27] and all are
fled.
Do, de, de, de. Sessa! [28] Come, march
to wakes [29] and fairs and market
towns. Poor Tom, thy horn is dry.[30]

LEAR. Then let them anatomize
Regan. See what breeds about her
heart. Is there any cause in nature
that makes these hard hearts? [*To
Edgar*] You, sir, I entertain for one of
my hundred; only I do not like the
fashion of your garments. You will say
they are Persian; [31] but let them be

---

[16] *commission* those com-
missioned as King's jus-
tices
[17] *corn* wheatfield
[18] *one . . . mouth* one
strain on your delicate
shepherd's pipe (?)
[19] *gray* (Gray cats were
among the forms suppos-
edly assumed by devils.)
[20] *Cry . . . joint-stool* (a
cant expression for 'Par-
don me for failing to no-
tice you,' but two joint-
stools—cf. 'warped,' line
below—were probably

the actual stage objects
arraigned as Goneril and
Regan)
[21] *Corruption . . . place*
i.e. bribery in the court
[22] *take his part* i.e. fall on
his behalf
[23] *counterfeiting* i.e. sim-
ulating madness
[24] *brach* hound bitch
[25] *lym* bloodhound
[26] *bobtail . . . trundle-tail*
short-tailed cur or long-
tailed
[27] *hatch* lower half of a
'Dutch door'

[28] *Sessa* (interjection,
equivalent to 'Away!')
[29] *wakes* parish feasts
[30] *Poor . . . dry* (Edgar
expresses his exhaustion
in his rôle, by an allusion
to the horns proffered by
Tom o' Bedlams in beg-
ging drink.)
[31] *Persian* (Persian costume was reputedly gor-
geous. Ironically, or in
actual delusion, Lear re-
fers thus to Edgar's rags,
as he refers to bed cur-
tains in his next speech.)

changed.

KENT. Now, good my lord, lie here and rest awhile.

LEAR. Make no noise, make no noise; draw the curtains. So, so. We'll go to supper i' th' morning.

FOOL. And I'll go to bed at noon.

Enter Gloucester.

GLOUCESTER. Come hither, friend. Where is the King my master?

KENT. Here, sir, but trouble him not; his wits are gone.

GLOUCESTER. Good friend, I prithee take him in thy arms. I have o'erheard a plot of death upon him. There is a litter ready; lay him in't And drive toward Dover, friend, where thou shalt meet Both welcome and protection. Take up thy master. If thou shouldst dally half an hour, his life, With thine and all that offer to defend him, Stand in assurèd loss. Take up, take up, And follow me, that will to some provision [32] Give thee quick conduct. [33]

[KENT.   Oppressèd nature sleeps. This rest might yet have balmed [34] thy broken sinews, [35] Which, if convenience [36] will not allow,

Stand in hard cure. [37] [*To the Fool*] Come, help to bear thy master. Thou must not stay behind.]

GLOUCESTER.   Come, come, away!
    Exeunt [*all but Edgar*].

[EDGAR. When we our betters see bearing our woes, [38] We scarcely think our miseries our foes. [39] Who alone suffers suffers most i' th' mind, Leaving free [40] things and happy shows [41] behind; But then the mind much sufferance [42] doth o'erskip When grief hath mates, and bearing fellowship. [43] How light and portable [44] my pain seems now, When that which makes me bend makes the King bow. He childed as I fatherèd. Tom, away. Mark the high noises, [45] and thyself bewray [46] When false opinion, whose wrong thoughts [47] defile thee, In thy just proof repeals and reconciles thee. [48] What will hap more [49] to-night, safe 'scape the King! Lurk, [50] lurk.]   [*Exit.*]

SCENE SEVEN

Enter Cornwall, Regan, Goneril, Bastard [*Edmund*], *and Servants.*

[32] *provision* supplies
[33] *conduct* guidance
[34] *balmed* healed
[35] *sinews* nerves
[36] *convenience* propitious circumstances
[37] *Stand . . . cure* will be hard to cure
[38] *our woes* woes like ours
[39] *our foes* i.e. our peculiar foes (They seem rather a part of universal misery.)
[40] *free* carefree
[41] *shows* scenes
[42] *sufferance* suffering
[43] *bearing fellowship* enduring has company
[44] *portable* bearable
[45] *Mark . . . noises* i.e. heed the rumors concerning those in power (?)
[46] *bewray* reveal
[47] *wrong thoughts* misconceptions
[48] *In . . . reconciles thee* i.e. upon your vindication recalls you and makes peace with you
[49] *What . . . more* whatever more happens
[50] *Lurk* i.e. keep covered

CORNWALL. [*To Goneril*] Post speedily to my lord your husband; show him this letter. The army of France is landed. [*To Servants*] Seek out the traitor Gloucester.

[*Exeunt some Servants.*]

REGAN. Hang him instantly.

GONERIL. Pluck out his eyes.

CORNWALL. Leave him to my displeasure. Edmund, keep you our sister company. The revenges we are bound [1] to take upon your traitorous father are not fit for your beholding. Advise the Duke where you are going, to a most festinate [2] preparation. We are bound to the like. Our posts shall be swift and intelligent [3] betwixt us. Farewell, dear sister; farewell, my Lord of Gloucester.[4]

Enter Steward [Oswald].

How now? Where's the King?

OSWALD. My Lord of Gloucester hath conveyed him hence.
Some five or six and thirty of his knights,
Hot questrists [5] after him, met him at gate;
Who, with some other of the lord's dependants,
Are gone with him toward Dover, where they boast
To have well-armèd friends.

CORNWALL. Get horses for your mistress.   *Exit [Oswald].*

GONERIL. Farewell, sweet lord, and sister.

CORNWALL. Edmund, farewell.

[*Exeunt Goneril and Edmund.*]

Go seek the traitor Gloucester,
Pinion him like a thief, bring him before us. [*Exeunt other Servants.*]
Though well we may not pass upon [6] his life
Without the form of justice, yet our power
Shall do a court'sy to [7] our wrath, which men
May blame, but not control.

Enter Gloucester and Servants.

Who's there, the traitor?

REGAN. Ingrateful fox, 'tis he.

CORNWALL. Bind fast his corky [8] arms.

GLOUCESTER. What means your Graces? Good my friends, consider
You are my guests. Do me no foul play, friends.

CORNWALL. Bind him, I say.

[*Servants bind him.*]

REGAN. Hard, hard! O filthy traitor.

GLOUCESTER. Unmerciful lady as you are, I'm none.

CORNWALL. To this chair bind him. Villain, thou shalt find—

[*Regan plucks his beard.*]

GLOUCESTER. By the kind gods, 'tis most ignobly done
To pluck me by the beard.

REGAN. So white, and such a traitor?

GLOUCESTER.   Naughty [9] lady,
These hairs which thou dost ravish from my chin
Will quicken [10] and accuse thee. I am your host.
With robber's hands my hospitable favors [11]
You should not ruffle [12] thus. What will you do?

III, vii ¹ *bound* required
² *festinate* speedy
³ *intelligent* informative
⁴ *Lord of Gloucester* (as now endowed with his father's title and estates)

⁵ *questrists* seekers
⁶ *pass upon* issue a sentence against
⁷ *do a court'sy to* i.e. defer to, act in conformity with

⁸ *corky* (because aged)
⁹ *Naughty* evil
¹⁰ *quicken* come to life
¹¹ *favors* features
¹² *ruffle* tear at

CORNWALL. Come, sir, what letters had you late [13] from France?

REGAN. Be simple-answered,[14] for we know the truth.

CORNWALL. And what confederacy have you with the traitors Late footed [15] in the kingdom?

REGAN. To whose hands you have sent the lunatic King. Speak.

GLOUCESTER. I have a letter guessingly [16] set down, Which came from one that's of a neutral heart, And not from one opposed.

CORNWALL.   Cunning.

REGAN.   And false.

CORNWALL. Where hast thou sent the king?

GLOUCESTER. To Dover.

REGAN. Wherefore to Dover? Wast thou not charged at peril [17]—

CORNWALL. Wherefore to Dover? Let him answer that.

GLOUCESTER. I am tied to th' stake, and I must stand the course.[18]

REGAN. Wherefore to Dover?

GLOUCESTER. Because I would not see thy cruel nails Pluck out his poor old eyes; nor thy fierce sister In his anointed [19] flesh stick boarish fangs. The sea, with such a storm as his bare head

In hell-black night endured, would have buoyed [20] up And quenched the stellèd [21] fires. Yet, poor old heart, he holp [22] the heavens to rain. If wolves had at thy gate howled that stern time, Thou shouldst have said, 'Good porter, turn the key.' [23] All cruels else subscribe.[24] But I shall see The wingèd [25] vengeance overtake such children.

CORNWALL. See't shalt thou never. Fellows, hold the chair. Upon these eyes of thine I'll set my foot.

GLOUCESTER. He that will think [26] to live till he be old, Give me some help.—O cruel! O ye gods!

REGAN. One side will mock [27] another. Th' other too.

CORNWALL. If you see vengeance—

1. SERVANT. Hold your hand, my lord! I have served you ever since I was a child; But better service have I never done you Than now to bid you hold.

REGAN.   How now, you dog?

1. SERVANT. If you did wear a beard upon your chin, I'ld shake it [28] on this quarrel.[29] What

[13] *late* of late
[14] *Be simple-answered* i.e. give plain answers
[15] *footed* landed
[16] *guessingly* i.e. tentatively, not stated as an assured fact
[17] *charged at peril* ordered on peril of your life
[18] *course* coursing (as by a string of dogs baiting a bear or bull tied in the pit)

[19] *anointed* (as king)
[20] *buoyed* surged
[21] *stellèd* starry
[22] *holp* helped
[23] *turn the key* i.e. let them come in to shelter
[24] *All . . . subscribe* i.e. at such times all other cruel creatures give way, agree to renounce their cruelty (?)
[25] *wingèd* heavenly (?)

or swift (?)
[26] *will think* hopes, expects
[27] *mock* i.e. subject to ridicule (because of the contrast)
[28] *shake it* (as Regan has done with Gloucester's—an act of extreme defiance)
[29] *on this quarrel* in this cause

do you mean! [30]

CORNWALL. My villain! [31]

[*Draw and fight.*]

1. SERVANT. Nay, then, come on, and take the chance of anger.

REGAN. Give me thy sword. A peasant stand up thus?

[*She takes a sword and runs at him behind,*] *kills him.*

1. SERVANT. O, I am slain! My lord, you have one eye left

To see some mischief [32] on him. O!

CORNWALL. Lest it see more, prevent it. Out, vile jelly.

Where is thy lustre now?

GLOUCESTER. All dark and comfortless. Where's my son Edmund?

Edmund, enkindle all the sparks of nature [33]

To quit [34] this horrid [35] act.

REGAN.   Out, treacherous villain;

Thou call'st on him that hates thee. It was he

That made the overture [36] of thy treasons to us;

Who is too good to pity thee.

GLOUCESTER. O my follies! Then Edgar was abused.[37]

Kind gods, forgive me that, and prosper him.

REGAN. Go thrust him out at gates, and let him smell

His way to Dover.

Exit [one] *with Gloucester.*

How is't, my Lord? How look you? [38]

CORNWALL. I have received a hurt.

Follow me, lady.

Turn out that eyeless villain. Throw this slave

Upon the dunghill. Regan, I bleed apace.

Untimely comes this hurt. Give me your arm.   *Exeunt.*

[2. SERVANT. I'll never care what wickedness I do,

If this man come to good.

3. SERVANT.   If she live long,

And in the end meet the old course of death,[39]

Women will all turn monsters.

2. SERVANT. Let's follow the old Earl, and get the bedlam

To lead him where he would. His roguish madness

Allows itself to anything.[40]   [*Exit.*]

3. SERVANT. Go thou. I'll fetch some flax and whites of eggs

To apply to his bleeding face. Now heaven help him.   *Exit.*]

ACT IV

SCENE ONE

Enter Edgar.

EDGAR. Yet better thus, and known to be contemned,[1]

Than still contemned and flattered. To be worst,

The lowest and most dejected [2] thing of fortune,

Stands still in esperance,[3] lives not in

---

[30] *What . . . mean* i.e. how dare you (The words are given to Regan by most editors, but they are no more 'unservantlike' than those that precede them.)

[31] *My villain* i.e. my serf (with play on its more modern meaning)

[32] *mischief* injury
[33] *nature* natural feeling
[34] *quit* requite, avenge
[35] *horrid* horrible
[36] *overture* disclosure
[37] *abused* wronged
[38] *How look you* i.e. how looks it with you, what is your condition
[39] *meet . . . death* i.e.

die a natural death
[40] *His roguish . . . anything* i.e. his being an irresponsible wanderer allows him to do anything

IV, i   [1] *contemned* despised
[2] *dejected* cast down, abased
[3] *esperance* hope

fear.
The lamentable change is from the best;
The worst returns to laughter.[4] Welcome then,
Thou unsubstantial air that I embrace:
The wretch that thou hast blown unto the worst
Owes nothing [5] to thy blasts.

Enter Gloucester and an Old Man.
                            But who comes here?
My father, poorly [6] led? World, world, O world!
But that thy strange mutations make us hate thee,
Life would not yield to age.[7]

OLD MAN.   O my good lord,
I have been your tenant, and your father's tenant,
These fourscore years.

GLOUCESTER. Away, get thee away. Good friend, be gone.
Thy comforts [8] can do me no good at all;
Thee they may hurt.[9]

OLD MAN. You cannot see your way.

GLOUCESTER. I have no way, and therefore want [10] no eyes;
I stumbled when I saw. Full oft 'tis seen
Our means secure us, and our mere defects
Prove our commodities.[11] O dear son Edgar,
The food [12] of thy abusèd [13] father's wrath,
Might I but live to see thee in [14] my touch
I'ld say I had eyes again!

OLD MAN.   How now? Who's there?

EDGAR. [*Aside*] O gods! Who is't can say 'I am at the worst'?
I am worse than e'er I was.

OLD MAN.   'Tis poor mad Tom.

EDGAR. [*Aside*] And worse I may be yet. The worst is not
So long as we can say 'This is the worst.' [15]

OLD MAN. Fellow, where goest?

GLOUCESTER.   Is it a beggarman?

OLD MAN. Madman and beggar too.

GLOUCESTER. He has some reason,[16] else he could not beg.
I' th' last night's storm I such a fellow saw,
Which made me think a man a worm. My son
Came then into my mind,[17] and yet my mind
Was then scarce friends with him. I have heard more since.
As flies to wanton [18] boys are we to th' gods;
They kill us for their sport.

EDGAR. [*Aside*] How should this be?
Bad is the trade that must play fool

---

[4] *The worst . . . laughter* i.e. the worst extreme is the point of return to happiness
[5] *nothing* i.e. nothing good (and hence he is free of debt)
[6] *poorly* poor-like, i.e. like a blind beggar (?)
[7] *But . . . age* i.e. were it not for your hateful mutability, we would never be reconciled to old age and death
[8] *comforts* ministrations
[9] *hurt* do injury (since they are forbidden)
[10] *want* need
[11] *Our means . . . commodities* i.e. prosperity makes us rash, and sheer affliction proves a boon
[12] *food* i.e. the object fed upon
[13] *abusèd* deceived
[14] *in* i.e. by means of
[15] *The worst . . . worst* (because at the very worst there will be no such comforting thought)
[16] *reason* powers of reason
[17] *My son . . . mind* (because it was actually he —a natural touch)
[18] *wanton* irresponsibly playful

to sorrow,
Ang'ring [19] itself and others.—Bless thee, master.

GLOUCESTER. Is that the naked fellow?

OLD MAN. Ay, my lord.

GLOUCESTER. Get thee away. If for my sake
Thou wilt o'ertake us hence a mile or twain
I' th' way toward Dover, do it for ancient love; [20]
And bring some covering for this naked soul,
Which I'll entreat to lead me.

OLD MAN. Alack, sir, he is mad.

GLOUCESTER. 'Tis the time's plague [21] when madmen lead the blind.
Do as I bid thee, or rather do thy pleasure.[22]
Above the rest, be gone.

OLD MAN. I'll bring him the best 'parel [23] that I have,
Come on't what will. *Exit.*

GLOUCESTER. Sirrah naked fellow—

EDGAR. Poor Tom's acold. [*Aside*] I cannot daub it [24] further.

GLOUCESTER. Come hither, fellow.

EDGAR. [*Aside*] And yet I must.—
Bless thy sweet eyes, they bleed.

GLOUCESTER. Know'st thou the way to Dover?

EDGAR. Both stile and gate, horseway and footpath. Poor Tom hath been scared out of his good wits. Bless thee, good man's son, from the foul fiend. [Five fiends have been in poor Tom at once: of lust, as Obidicut; [25] Hobbididence, prince of dumbness; [26] Mahu, of stealing; Modo, of murder; Flibbertigibbet, of mopping and mowing,[27] who since possesses chambermaids and waiting women. So, bless thee, master.]

GLOUCESTER. Here, take this purse, thou whom the heavens' plagues
Have humbled to [28] all strokes. That I am wretched
Makes thee the happier.[29] Heavens, deal so still!
Let the superfluous [30] and lust-dieted [31] man,
That slaves your ordinance,[32] that will not see
Because he does not feel, feel your pow'r quickly;
So distribution should undo excess,
And each man have enough. Dost thou know Dover?

EDGAR. Ay, master.

GLOUCESTER. There is a cliff, whose high and bending [33] head
Looks fearfully in the confinèd deep.[34]
Bring me but to the very brim of it,

[19] *Ang'ring* offending
[20] *ancient love* i.e. such love as formerly bound master and man (nostalgic)
[21] *time's plague* i.e. malady characteristic of these times
[22] *thy pleasure* as you please
[23] *'parel* apparel
[24] *daub it* lay it on, act the part

[25] *Obidicut* Hoberdicut (a devil mentioned in Harsnett's *Declaration,* as are the four following)
[26] *dumbness* muteness (Shakespeare identifies each devil with some form of possession.)
[27] *mopping and mowing* grimaces, affected facial expressions
[28] *humbled to* reduced to bearing humbly

[29] *happier* i.e. less wretched
[30] *superfluous* possessed of superfluities
[31] *lust-dieted* i.e. whose desires are feasted
[32] *slaves your ordinance* subordinates your injunction (to share)
[33] *bending* overhanging
[34] *in . . . deep* i.e. to the sea hemmed in below

And I'll repair the misery thou dost
bear
With something rich about me. From
that place
I shall no leading need.
    EDGAR.   Give me thy arm.
Poor Tom shall lead thee.   *Exeunt.*

SCENE TWO

*Enter Goneril, Bastard [Edmund], and
Steward [Oswald].*

    GONERIL. Welcome, my lord. I mar-
vel our mild husband
Not met [1] us on the way. [*To Oswald*]
Now, where's your master?
    OSWALD. Madam, within, but never
man so changed.
I told him of the army that was
landed:
He smiled at it. I told him you were
coming:
His answer was, 'The worse.' Of
Gloucester's treachery
And of the loyal service of his son
When I informed him, then he called
me sot [2]
And told me I had turned the wrong
side out.
What most he should dislike seems
pleasant to him;
What like,[3] offensive.
    GONERIL. [*To Edmund*] Then shall

you go no further.
It is the cowish [4] terror of his spirit,
That dares not undertake.[5] He'll not
feel wrongs
Which tie him to an answer.[6] Our
wishes on the way
May prove effects.[7] Back, Edmund, to
my brother.
Hasten his musters [8] and conduct his
pow'rs.[9]
I must change names [10] at home, and
give the distaff [11]
Into my husband's hands. This trusty
servant
Shall pass between us. Ere long you
are like to hear
(If you dare venture in your own be-
half)
A mistress's [12] command. Wear this.
Spare speech.   [*Gives a favor.*]
Decline your head. This kiss, if it durst
speak,
Would stretch thy spirits up into the
air.
Conceive,[13] and fare thee well.
    EDMUND. Yours in the ranks of
death.   *Exit.*
    GONERIL. My most dear Glouces-
ter.
O, the difference of man and man:
To thee a woman's services are
due;
My fool usurps [14] my body.

IV, ii [1] *Not met* has not
met
[2] *sot* fool
[3] *What like* what he
should like
[4] *cowish* cowardly
[5] *undertake* engage
[6] *an answer* retaliation
[7] *Our wishes . . . effects*
i.e. our wishes, that you
might supplant Albany,

may materialize
[8] *musters* enlistments
[9] *conduct his pow'rs* lead
his army
[10] *change names* i.e. exchange the name of 'mis-
tress' for 'master'
[11] *distaff* spinning-staff
(symbol of the house-
wife)
[12] *mistress's* (At present

she plays the rôle of
master, but, mated with
Edmund, she would again
'change names.')
[13] *Conceive* (1) understand (2) quicken (with
the seed I have planted
in you)
[14] *usurps* wrongfully occupies

OSWALD. Madam, here comes my lord. [*Exit.*]

Enter Albany.

GONERIL. I have been worth the whistle.[15]

ALBANY. O Goneril, You are not worth the dust which the rude wind Blows in your face. [I fear your disposition: [16] That nature which contemns its origin Cannot be bordered certain [17] in itself. She that herself will sliver and disbranch [18] From her material sap,[19] perforce must wither And come to deadly use.

GONERIL. No more; the text is foolish.

ALBANY. Wisdom and goodness to the vile seem vile; Filths savor [20] but themselves. What have you done? Tigers not daughters, what have you performed? A father, and a gracious agèd man, Whose reverence even the headlugged [21] bear would lick,[22] Most barbarous, most degenerate,[23] have you madded.[24] Could my good brother suffer you to do it?

A man, a prince, by him so benefited! If that the heavens do not their visible [25] spirits Send quickly down to tame these vile offenses, It [26] will come, Humanity must perforce prey on itself, Like monsters of the deep.]

GONERIL. Milk-livered [27] man, That bear'st a cheek for blows, a head for wrongs; Who hast not in thy brows an eye discerning Thine honor from thy suffering; [28] [that not know'st Fools [29] do those villains pity who are punished Ere they have done their mischief. Where's thy drum? [30] France spreads his banners in our noiseless [31] land, With plumèd helm [32] thy state begins to threat, Whilst thou, a moral [33] fool, sits still and cries 'Alack, why does he so?']

ALBANY. See thyself, devil: Proper [34] deformity seems not in the fiend So horrid as in woman.

GONERIL. O vain fool!

[ALBANY. Thou changèd [35] and self-

[15] *worth the whistle* i.e. valued enough to be welcomed home ('not worth the whistle' applying proverbially to a 'poor dog')
[16] *fear your disposition* distrust your nature
[17] *bordered certain* safely contained (It will be unpredictably licentious.)
[18] *sliver, disbranch* cut off
[19] *material sap* sustaining stock, nourishing trunk
[20] *savor* relish

[21] *head-lugged* dragged with a head-chain (hence, surly)
[22] *lick* i.e. treat with affection
[23] *degenerate* unnatural
[24] *madded* maddened
[25] *visible* made visible, material
[26] *It* i.e. chaos
[27] *Milk-livered* i.e. spiritless
[28] *discerning . . . suffer-*

ing distinguishing between dishonor and tolerance
[29] *Fools* i.e. only fools
[30] *drum* i.e. military preparation
[31] *noiseless* i.e. unaroused
[32] *helm* war-helmet
[33] *moral* moralizing
[34] *Proper* i.e. fair-surfaced
[35] *changèd* transformed (diabolically, as in witchcraft)

covered thing,[36] for shame
Bemonster not thy feature.[37] Were't my fitness [38]
To let these hands obey my blood,[39]
They are apt enough to dislocate and tear
Thy flesh and bones. Howe'er thou art a fiend,
A woman's shape doth shield thee.

GONERIL. Marry,[40] your manhood —mew! [41]]

Enter a Messenger.

[ALBANY. What news?]

MESSENGER. O, my good lord, the Duke of Cornwall's dead,
Slain by his servant, going to [42] put out
The other eye of Gloucester.

ALBANY.   Gloucester's eyes?

MESSENGER. A servant that he bred,[43] thrilled with remorse,[44]
Opposed against the act, bending his sword
To his great master; who, thereat enraged,
Flew on him, and amongst them [45] felled him dead;
But not without that harmful stroke which since
Hath plucked him after.[46]

ALBANY. This shows you are above,
You justicers,[47] that these our nether

crimes [48]
So speedily can venge.[49] But, O poor Gloucester,
Lost he his other eye?

MESSENGER. Both, both, my lord.
This letter, madam, craves [50] a speedy answer.
'Tis from your sister.

GONERIL. [*Aside*] One way I like this well;
But being widow, and my Gloucester with her,
May all the building in my fancy pluck
Upon my hateful life.[51] Another way [52]
The news is not so tart.[53]—I'll read, and answer.   [*Exit.*]

ALBANY. Where was his son when they did take his eyes?

MESSENGER. Come with my lady hither.

ALBANY. He is not here.

MESSENGER. No, my good lord; I met him back [54] again.

ALBANY. Knows he the wickedness?

MESSENGER. Ay, my good lord.
'Twas he informed against him,
And quit the house on purpose, that their punishment
Might have the freer course.

ALBANY.   Gloucester, I live
To thank thee for the love thou

---

[36] *self-covered* i.e. your natural self overwhelmed by evil (?) or devil disguised as woman (?)
[37] *Bemonster . . . feature* i.e. do not exchange your human features for a monster's
[38] *my fitness* fit for me
[39] *blood* passion
[40] *Marry* (oath, derived from 'By Mary')
[41] *your manhood—mew* i.e. 'What a man!' followed by a contemptuous

interjection (?) or mew up (contain) this display of manliness
[42] *going to* about to
[43] *bred* reared
[44] *thrilled with remorse* in the throes of pity
[45] *amongst them* i.e. aided by the others
[46] *plucked him after* drawn him along (to death)
[47] *justicers* dispensers of justice
[48] *nether crimes* sins com-

mitted here below
[49] *venge* avenge
[50] *craves* requires
[51] *May . . . life* i.e. may make my life hateful by destroying my dream-castles
[52] *Another way* the other way (alluded to in sentence above, probably the removal of Cornwall as an obstacle to sole reign with Edmund)
[53] *tart* distasteful
[54] *back* going back

showed'st the King,
And to revenge thine eyes. Come
hither, friend.
Tell me what more thou know'st.

Exeunt.

SCENE THREE

[*Enter Kent and a Gentleman.*

KENT. Why the King of France is
so suddenly gone back know you no
reason?

GENTLEMAN. Something he left imperfect in the state,[1] which since his
coming forth is thought of, which imports [2] to the kingdom so much fear [3]
and danger that his personal return
was most [4] required and necessary.

KENT. Who hath he left behind him
general?

GENTLEMAN. The Marshal of
France, Monsieur La Far.

KENT. Did your letters pierce [5] the
Queen to any demonstration of grief?

GENTLEMAN. Ay, sir. She took them,
read them in my presence,
And now and then an ample tear
trilled [6] down
Her delicate cheek. It seemed she was
a queen
Over her passion, who,[7] most rebel-
like,
Sought to be king o'er her.

KENT.   O, then it movèd her?

GENTLEMAN. Not to a rage. Patience
and sorrow strove
Who should express her goodliest.[8]

You have seen
Sunshine and rain at once—her smiles
and tears
Were like, a better way: [9] those happy
smilets
That played on her ripe lip seem not
to know
What guests were in her eyes, which
parted thence
As pearls from diamonds dropped. In
brief,
Sorrow would be a rarity [10] most be-
lovèd,
If all could so become it.

KENT. Made she no verbal question?

GENTLEMAN. Faith, once or twice
she heaved the name of father
Pantingly forth,[11] as if it pressed her
heart;
Cried 'Sisters, sisters, shame of ladies,
sisters!
Kent, father, sisters? What, i' th' storm
i' th' night?
Let pity [12] not be believed!' There
she shook
The holy water from her heavenly
eyes,
And clamor moistened; [13] then away
she started
To deal with grief alone.

KENT.   It is the stars,
The stars above us govern our conditions; [14]
Else one self mate and make [15] could
not beget
Such different issues.[16] You spoke not
with her since?

IV, iii [1] *imperfect . . .
state* i.e. rift in affairs of
state
[2] *imports* means
[3] *fear* uneasiness
[4] *most* most urgently
[5] *pierce* goad
[6] *trilled* trickled
[7] *who* which
[8] *goodliest* i.e. most be-
comingly
[9] *Were . . . way* i.e. improved upon that spec-
tacle
[10] *rarity* gem
[11] *heaved . . . forth* uttered . . . chokingly
[12] *Let pity* let it for
pity (?)
[13] *clamor moistened* i.e.
mixed, and thus muted,
lamentation with tears
[14] *govern our conditions*
determine our characters
[15] *Else . . . make* otherwise the same husband
and wife
[16] *issues* children

GENTLEMAN. No.

KENT. Was this before the King returned?

GENTLEMAN.   No, since.

KENT. Well, sir, the poor distressèd Lear's i' th' town;

Who sometime, in his better tune,[17] remembers

What we are come about, and by no means

Will yield to see his daughter.

GENTLEMAN.   Why, good sir?

KENT. A sovereign [18] shame so elbows [19] him; his own unkindness,

That stripped [20] her from his benediction,[21] turned her

To foreign casualties,[22] gave her dear rights

To his dog-hearted daughters—these things sting

His mind so venomously that burning shame

Detains him from Cordelia.

GENTLEMAN. Alack, poor gentleman.

KENT. Of Albany's and Cornwall's powers you heard not?

GENTLEMAN. 'Tis so; [23] they are afoot.

KENT. Well, sir, I'll bring you to our master Lear

And leave you to attend him. Some dear cause [24]

Will in concealment wrap me up awhile.

When I am known aright, you shall not grieve

Lending me this acquaintance. I pray you go

Along with me.   Exeunt.]

SCENE FOUR

Enter, with Drum and Colors, Cordelia, Gentleman [Doctor], and Soldiers.

CORDELIA. Alack, 'tis he! Why, he was met even now

As mad as the vexed sea, singing aloud,

Crowned with rank fumiter [1] and furrow weeds,[2]

With hardocks,[3] hemlock, nettles, cuckoo flow'rs,

Darnel,[4] and all the idle [5] weeds that grow

In our sustaining corn.[6] A century [7] send forth!

Search every acre in the high-grown field

And bring him to our eye. [*Exit an Officer.*] What can [8] man's wisdom

In the restoring his bereavèd [9] sense?

He that helps him take all my outward worth.[10]

DOCTOR. There is means, madam.

Our foster [11] nurse of nature is repose,

The which he lacks. That to provoke [12] in him

Are many simples operative,[13] whose power

---

[17] *better tune* i.e. more rational state, less jangled
[18] *sovereign* overruling
[19] *elbows* jogs
[20] *stripped* cut off (cf. 'disbranch,' IV, ii, footnote 18)
[21] *benediction* blessing
[22] *casualties* chances
[23] *'Tis so* i.e. I have to this extent
[24] *dear cause* important

IV, iv [1] *fumiter* fumitory
[2] *furrow weeds* (those that appear after ploughing?)
[3] *hardocks* (variously identified as burdock, 'hoar dock,' 'harlock,' etc.)
[4] *Darnel* tares
[5] *idle* useless
[6] *sustaining corn* life-giving wheat

[7] *century* troop of a hundred men
[8] *can* i.e. can accomplish
[9] *bereavèd* bereft
[10] *outward worth* material possessions
[11] *foster* fostering
[12] *provoke* induce
[13] *simples operative* medicinal herbs, sedatives

Will close the eye of anguish.

CORDELIA.   All blest secrets,
All you unpublished virtues [14] of the
    earth,
Spring [15] with my tears; be aidant and
    remediate [16]
In the good man's distress. Seek, seek
    for him,
Lest his ungoverned rage dissolve the
    life
That wants [17] the means [18] to lead
    it. [19]

Enter Messenger.

MESSENGER.   News, madam.
The British pow'rs are marching hith-
    erward.

CORDELIA. 'Tis known before. Our
    preparation stands
In expectation of them. O dear father,
It is thy business that I go about.
Therefore [20] great France
My mourning, and importuned [21] tears
    hath pitied.
No blown [22] ambition doth our arms
    incite,
But love, dear love, and our aged
    father's right.
Soon may I hear and see him!
                              Exeunt.

SCENE FIVE

Enter Regan and Steward [Oswald].

REGAN. But are my brother's pow'rs
set forth?
OSWALD.   Ay, madam.
REGAN. Himself in person there?

OSWALD. Madam, with much ado. [1]
Your sister is the better soldier.
REGAN. Lord Edmund spake not
    with your lord at home?
OSWALD. No, madam.
REGAN. What might import [2] my
    sister's letter to him?
OSWALD. I know not, lady.
REGAN. Faith, he is posted [3] hence
    on serious matter.
It was great ignorance, [4] Gloucester's
    eyes being out,
To let him live. Where he arrives he
    moves
All hearts against us. Edmund, I think,
    is gone,
In pity of his misery, to dispatch
His nighted [5] life; moreover, to descry
The strength o' th' enemy.
OSWALD. I must needs after him,
    madam, with my letter.
REGAN. Our troops set forth to-
    morrow. Stay with us.
The ways are dangerous.
OSWALD.   I may not, madam.
My lady charged [6] my duty in this
    business.
REGAN. Why should she write to Ed-
    mund? Might not you
Transport her purposes [7] by word?
    Belike, [8]
Some things—I know not what. I'll
    love thee much,
Let me unseal the letter.
OSWALD.   Madam, I had rather—
REGAN. I know your lady does not
    love her husband,

[14] *unpublished virtues* i.e.
little-known benign herbs
[15] *Spring* grow
[16] *remediate* remedial
[17] *wants* lacks
[18] *means* i.e. power of
reason
[19] *lead it* govern it (the
rage)

[20] *Therefore* therefor, because of that
[21] *importuned* importu-
nate
[22] *blown* swollen
IV, v [1] *much ado* great
bother
[2] *import* bear as its message

[3] *is posted* has sped
[4] *ignorance* error
[5] *nighted* benighted,
blinded
[6] *charged* strictly ordered
[7] *Transport her purposes*
convey her intentions
[8] *Belike* probably

I am sure of that; and at her late [9] being here

She gave strange eliads [10] and most speaking looks

To noble Edmund. I know you are of her bosom.[11]

OSWALD. I, madam?

REGAN. I speak in understanding— y'are, I know't—

Therefore I do advise you take this note: [12]

My lord is dead; Edmund and I have talked,

And more convenient [13] is he for my hand

Than for your lady's. You may gather more.[14]

If you do find him, pray you give him this; [15]

And when your mistress hears thus much from you,

I pray desire her call [16] her wisdom to her.

So fare you well.

If you do chance to hear of that blind traitor,

Preferment [17] falls on him that cuts him off.

OSWALD. Would I could meet him, madam! I should show

What party I do follow.

REGAN.   Fare thee well.

Exeunt.

SCENE SIX

Enter Gloucester and Edgar.

GLOUCESTER. When shall I come to

th' top of that same hill?

EDGAR. You do climb up it now. Look how we labor.

GLOUCESTER. Methinks the ground is even.

EDGAR.   Horrible steep. Hark, do you hear the sea?

GLOUCESTER.   No, truly.

EDGAR. Why, then, your other senses grow imperfect

By your eyes' anguish.[1]

GLOUCESTER. So may it be indeed.

Methinks thy voice is altered, and thou speak'st

In better phrase and matter than thou didst.

EDGAR. Y'are much deceived. In nothing am I changed

But in my garments.

GLOUCESTER. Methinks y'are better spoken.

EDGAR.   Come on, sir; here's the place. Stand still. How fearful

And dizzy 'tis to cast one's eyes so low!

The crows and choughs [2] that wing the midway [3] air

Show scare so gross [4] as beetles. Halfway down

Hangs one that gathers sampire [5]— dreadful trade;

Methinks he seems no bigger than his head.

The fishermen that walk upon the beach

Appear like mice; and yond tall anchoring [6] bark,

[9] *late* recently
[10] *eliads* amorous glances
[11] *of her bosom* in her confidence
[12] *take this note* note this
[13] *convenient* appropriate
[14] *gather more* i.e. draw your own conclusions

[15] *this* this word, this reminder
[16] *call* recall
[17] *Preferment* advancement

IV, vi [1] *anguish* affliction
[2] *choughs* jackdaws

[3] *midway* i.e. halfway down
[4] *gross* large
[5] *sampire* samphire (aromatic herb used in relishes)
[6] *anchoring* anchored

Diminished to her cock; [7] her cock, a buoy
Almost too small for sight. The murmuring surge
That on th' unnumb'red idle pebble [8] chafes
Cannot be heard so high. I'll look no more,
Lest my brain turn, and the deficient sight [9]
Topple [10] down headlong.

GLOUCESTER. Set me where you stand.

EDGAR. Give me your hand. You are now within a foot
Of th' extreme verge. For all beneath the moon
Would I not leap upright.[11]

GLOUCESTER. Let go my hand.
Here, friend, 's another purse; in it a jewel
Well worth a poor man's taking. Fairies [12] and gods
Prosper it with thee. Go thou further off;
Bid me farewell, and let me hear thee going.

EDGAR. Now fare ye well, good sir.

GLOUCESTER.   With all my heart.

EDGAR. [Aside] Why I do trifle [13] thus with his despair
Is done to cure it.

GLOUCESTER.   O you mighty gods!
[He kneels.]
This world I do renounce, and in your sights
Shake patiently my great affliction off.

If I could bear it longer and not fall
To quarrel with [14] your great opposeless [15] wills,
My snuff and loathèd part of nature [16] should
Burn itself out. If Edgar live, O bless him!
Now, fellow, fare thee well.
[He falls forward and swoons.]

EDGAR.   Gone, sir—farewell.
And yet I know not how conceit [17] may rob
The treasury of life when life itself
Yields to [18] the theft. Had he been where he thought,
By this had thought been past. Alive or dead?
Ho you, sir! Friend! Hear you, sir? Speak!
Thus might he pass indeed. Yet he revives.
What are you, sir?

GLOUCESTER. Away, and let me die.

EDGAR. Hadst thou been aught but gossamer, feathers, air,
So many fathom down precipitating,[19]
Thou'dst shivered like an egg; but thou dost breathe,
Hast heavy substance, bleed'st not, speak'st, art sound.
Ten masts at each [20] make not the altitude
Which thou hast perpendicularly fell.
Thy life's [21] a miracle. Speak yet again.

[7] *Diminished . . . cock* reduced to the size of her cockboat
[8] *unnumb'red idle pebble* i.e. barren reach of countless pebbles
[9] *the deficient sight* i.e. my dizziness
[10] *Topple* topple me
[11] *upright* i.e. even upright, let alone forward
[12] *Fairies* (the usual wardens of treasure)
[13] *Why . . . trifle* i.e. the reason I toy with ('done' in l. below being redundant)
[14] *fall . . . with* i.e. rebel against (irreligiously)
[15] *opposeless* not to be opposed
[16] *My snuff . . . nature* i.e. the guttering and hateful tag end of my life
[17] *conceit* imagination
[18] *Yields to* i.e. welcomes
[19] *precipitating* falling
[20] *at each* end to end
[21] *life* survival

GLOUCESTER. But have I fall'n, or no?

EDGAR. From the dread summit of this chalky bourn.[22]
Look up a-height.[23] The shrill-gorged [24] lark so far
Cannot be seen or heard. Do but look up.

GLOUCESTER. Alack, I have no eyes.
Is wretchedness deprived that benefit
To end itself by death? 'Twas yet some comfort
When misery could beguile [25] the tyrant's rage
And frustrate his proud will.

EDGAR.   Give me your arm.
Up—so. How is't? Feel [26] you your legs? You stand.

GLOUCESTER. Too well, too well.

EDGAR. This is above all strangeness.
Upon the crown o' th' cliff what thing was that
Which parted from you?

GLOUCESTER.   A poor unfortunate beggar.

EDGAR. As I stood here below, me-thought his eyes
Were two full moons; he had a thou-sand noses,
Horns whelked [27] and waved like the enridgèd [28] sea.
It was some fiend. Therefore, thou

happy father,[29]
Think that the clearest [30] gods, who make them honors
Of men's impossibilities,[31] have pre-servèd thee.

GLOUCESTER. I do remember now.
Henceforth I'll bear
Affliction till it do cry out itself
'Enough, enough, and die.' That thing you speak of,
I took it for a man. Often 'twould say
'The fiend, the fiend'—he led me to that place.

EDGAR. Bear free [32] and patient thoughts.

Enter Lear [mad, bedecked with weeds].

                    But who comes here?
The safer [33] sense will ne'er accom-modate [34]
His [35] master thus.

LEAR. No, they cannot touch [36] me for coining; [36a]
I am the King himself.

EDGAR. O thou side-piercing sight!

LEAR. Nature's above art in that respect.[37] There's your press money.[38]
That fellow handles his bow like a crow-keeper.[39] Draw me a clothier's yard.[40] Look, look, a mouse! Peace, peace; this piece of toasted cheese will do't. There's my gauntlet; [41] I'll prove

---

[22] *bourn* boundary, head-land
[23] *a-height* on high
[24] *gorged* throated
[25] *beguile* outwit
[26] *Feel* test
[27] *whelked* corrugated
[28] *enridgèd* blown into ridges
[29] *happy father* lucky old man
[30] *clearest* purest
[31] *who . . . impossibilities* i.e. whose glory it is to do for man what he can-

not do for himself
[32] *free* (of despair)
[33] *safer* saner
[34] *accommodate* accoutre
[35] *His* its
[36] *touch* i.e. interfere with
[36a] *coining* minting coins (a royal prerogative)
[37] *Nature . . . respect* i.e. a born king is above a made king in legal im-munity (cf. the coeval debate on the relative merits of poets of nature,

i.e. born, and poets of art, i.e. made by self-ef-fort)
[38] *press money* i.e. the 'king's shilling' (token payment on military im-pressment or enlistment)
[39] *crow-keeper* i.e. farm-hand warding off crows
[40] *clothier's yard* i.e. ar-row (normally a yard long)
[41] *gauntlet* armored glove (hurled as challenge)

it on [42] a giant. Bring up the brown bills.[43] O, well flown,[44] bird. I' th' clout,[45] i' th' clout—hewgh! Give the word.[46]

EDGAR. Sweet marjoram.[47]

LEAR. Pass.

GLOUCESTER. I know that voice.

LEAR. Ha! Goneril with a white beard? They flattered me like a dog,[48] and told me I had the white hairs in my beard [49] ere the black ones were there. To say 'ay' and 'no' [50] to everything that I said! 'Ay' and 'no' too was no good divinity.[51] When the rain came to wet me once, and the wind to make me chatter; when the thunder would not peace at my bidding; there I found 'em, there I smelt 'em out. Go to, they are not men o' their words. They told me I was everything. 'Tis a lie—I am not ague-proof.[52]

GLOUCESTER. The trick [53] of that voice I do well remember.
Is't not the King?

LEAR.   Ay, every inch a king.
When I do stare, see how the subject quakes.
I pardon that man's life. What was thy cause? [54]

Adultery?
Thou shalt not die. Die for adultery? No.
The wren goes to't, and the small gilded fly
Does lecher [55] in my sight.
Let copulation thrive; for Gloucester's bastard son
Was kinder to his father than my daughters
Got [56] 'tween the lawful sheets.
To't, luxury,[57] pell-mell, for I lack soldiers.[58]
Behold yond simp'ring dame,
Whose face between her forks [59] presages snow,[60]
That minces [61] virtue, and does shake the head
To hear of pleasure's name.[62]
The fitchew [63] nor the soilèd [64] horse goes to't
With a more riotous appetite.
Down from the waist they are Centaurs,[65]
Though women all above.
But to the girdle [66] do the gods inherit,[67]
Beneath is all the fiend's.
There's hell, there's darkness, there is

[42] *prove it on* maintain it against
[43] *brown bills* varnished halberds
[44] *well flown* (hawking cry)
[45] *clout* bull's-eye (archery term)
[46] *word* password
[47] *Sweet marjoram* (herb, associated with treating madness?)
[48] *like a dog* i.e. fawningly
[49] *I . . . beard* i.e. I was wise
[50] *To say . . . 'no'* i.e. to agree
[51] *no good divinity* i.e.

bad theology (For 'good divinity' cf. 2 Corinthians 1:18: 'But as God is true, our word to you was not yea and nay'; also Matthew 5:36–37, James 5:12.)
[52] *ague-proof* proof against chills and fever
[53] *trick* peculiarity
[54] *cause* case
[55] *lecher* copulate
[56] *Got* begotten
[57] *luxury* lechery
[58] *for . . . soldiers* (and therefore a higher birth rate)
[59] *face . . . forks* i.e.

loins (?)
[60] *presages snow* i.e. shows signs of advancing years (?) (cf. *Hamlet* III, iv, 82–88)
[61] *minces* mincingly affects
[62] *pleasure's name* i.e. the very name of sexual indulgence
[63] *fitchew* polecat, prostitute
[64] *soilèd* pastured
[65] *Centaurs* (lustful creatures of mythology, half-human and half-beast)
[66] *girdle* waist
[67] *inherit* possess

the sulphurous pit; burning, scalding, stench, consumption. Fie, fie, fie! pah, pah! Give me an ounce of civet,[68] good apothecary, sweeten my imagination! There's money for thee.

GLOUCESTER. O, let me kiss that hand.

LEAR. Let me wipe it first; it smells of mortality.[69]

GLOUCESTER. O ruined piece of nature; this great world
Shall so wear out to naught.[70] Dost thou know me?

LEAR. I remember thine eyes well enough. Dost thou squiny at me? No, do thy worst, blind Cupid; I'll not love. Read thou this challenge; mark but the penning of it.

GLOUCESTER. Were all thy letters suns, I could not see.

EDGAR. [*Aside*] I would not take [71] this from report—it is,
And my heart breaks at it.

LEAR. Read.

GLOUCESTER. What, with the case [72] of eyes?

LEAR. O, ho, are you there with me? [73] No eyes in your head, nor no money in your purse? Your eyes are in a heavy case,[74] your purse in a light; yet you see how this world goes.

GLOUCESTER. I see it feelingly.[75]

LEAR. What, art mad? A man may see how this world goes with no eyes. Look with thine ears. See how yond justice rails upon yond simple [76] thief. Hark in thine ear. Change places and, handy-dandy,[77] which is the justice, which is the thief? Thou hast seen a farmer's dog bark at a beggar?

GLOUCESTER. Ay, sir.

LEAR. And the creature run from the cur. There thou mightst behold the great image [78] of authority—a dog's obeyed in office.[79]
Thou rascal beadle,[80] hold thy bloody hand!
Why dost thou lash that whore? Strip thy own back.
Thou hotly lusts [81] to use her in that kind [82]
For which thou whip'st her. The usurer hangs the cozener.[83]
Through tattered clothes small vices do appear; [84]
Robes and furred gowns hide all. Plate sin with gold,
And the strong lance of justice hurtless [85] breaks;
Arm it in rags,[86] a pygmy's straw does pierce it.
None does offend, none—I say none! I'll able [87] 'em.
Take that [88] of me, my friend, who

---

[68] *civet* musk perfume
[69] *mortality* death
[70] *this . . . naught* i.e. the universe (macrocosm) will decay like this man (microcosm; cf. III, i, footnote 6)
[71] *take* accept
[72] *case* sockets
[73] *are . . . me* is that the situation
[74] *case* plight (pun)
[75] *feelingly* (1) only by touch (2) by feeling pain

[76] *simple* mere
[77] *handy-dandy* (old formula used in the child's game of choosing which hand)
[78] *great image* universal symbol
[79] *a dog's . . . office* i.e. man bows to authority regardless of who exercises it
[80] *beadle* parish constable
[81] *lusts* wish (suggestive form of 'lists')
[82] *kind* i.e. same act

[83] *The usurer . . . cozener* i.e. the great cheat, some money-lending judge, sentences to death the little cheat
[84] *appear* show plainly
[85] *hurtless* without hurting
[86] *Arm . . . rags* i.e. armored (cf. "Plate sin with gold," above) only in rags
[87] *able* authorize
[88] *that* (i.e. the assurance of immunity)

have the power
To seal th' accuser's lips. Get thee
  glass eyes
And, like a scurvy politician,[89] seem
To see the things thou dost not. Now,
  now, now, now!
Pull off my boots. Harder, harder! So.

EDGAR. O, matter and impertinency[90] mixed;
Reason in madness.

LEAR. If thou wilt weep my fortunes, take my eyes.
I know thee well enough; thy name is
  Gloucester.
Thou must be patient. We came crying
  hither;
Thou know'st, the first time that we
  smell the air
We wawl and cry. I will preach to
  thee. Mark.

GLOUCESTER. Alack, alack the day.

LEAR. When we are born, we cry
  that we are come
To this great stage of fools.—This' a
  good block.[91]
It were a delicate[92] stratagem to shoe
A troop of horse with felt. I'll put't in
  proof,[93]
And when I have stol'n upon these
  son-in-laws,
Then kill, kill, kill, kill, kill, kill!

Enter a Gentleman [with Attendants].

GENTLEMAN. O, here he is! Lay hand
  upon him.—Sir,
Your most dear daughter—

LEAR. No rescue? What, a prisoner?
  I am even
The natural fool[94] of fortune. Use me
  well;
You shall have ransom. Let me have
  surgeons;
I am cut[95] to th' brains.

GENTLEMAN. You shall have anything.

LEAR. No seconds? All myself?
Why, this would make a man a man
  of salt,[96]
To use his eyes for garden waterpots,
[Ay, and laying autumn's dust.] I will
  die bravely,
Like a smug bridegroom.[97] What, I
  will be jovial!
Come, come, I am a king; masters,
  know you that?

GENTLEMAN. You are a royal one,
and we obey you.

LEAR. Then there's life[98] in't. Come,
an you get it, you shall get it by running. Sa, sa, sa, sa![99]

Exit [running, followed by Attendants].

GENTLEMAN. A sight most pitiful in
  the meanest wretch,
Past speaking of in a king. Thou hast
  one daughter
Who redeems nature from the general
  curse[100]
Which twain[101] have brought her to.

EDGAR. Hail, gentle sir.

GENTLEMAN.   Sir, speed[102] you.
  What's your will?

---

[89] *scurvy politician* vile opportunist
[90] *matter and impertinency* sense and nonsense
[91] *block* felt hat (?)
[92] *delicate* subtle
[93] *in proof* to the test
[94] *natural fool* born plaything

[95] *cut* wounded
[96] *salt* i.e. all tears
[97] *smug bridegroom* spruce bridegroom (the image suggested by the secondary meaning of 'bravely,' i.e. handsomely, and the sexual suggestion of 'will die')

[98] *life* (and therefore 'hope')
[99] *Sa . . . sa* (hunting and rallying cry)
[100] *general curse* universal condemnation
[101] *twain* i.e. the other two
[102] *speed* God speed

EDGAR. Do you hear aught, sir, of a battle toward? [103]

GENTLEMAN. Most sure and vulgar.[104] Every one hears that Which can distinguish sound.

EDGAR.   But, by your favor, How near's the other army?

GENTLEMAN. Near and on speedy foot.[105] The main descry Stands on the hourly thought.[106]

EDGAR. I thank you, sir. That's all.

GENTLEMAN. Though that the Queen on special cause is here, Her army is moved on.

EDGAR.   I thank you, sir.
             Exit [Gentleman].

GLOUCESTER. You ever-gentle gods, take my breath from me; Let not my worser spirit [107] tempt me again To die before you please.

EDGAR.   Well pray you, father.

GLOUCESTER. Now, good sir, what are you?

EDGAR. A most poor man, made tame [108] to fortune's blows, Who, by the art of known and feeling sorrows,[109] Am pregnant [110] to good pity. Give me your hand; I'll lead you to some biding.[111]

GLOUCESTER.   Hearty thanks. The bounty and the benison [112] of heaven To boot, and boot.

Enter Steward [Oswald].

OSWALD. A proclaimed prize! [113] Most happy; [114] That eyeless head of thine was first framed flesh [115] To raise my fortunes. Thou old unhappy traitor, Briefly thyself remember.[116] The sword is out That must destroy thee.

GLOUCESTER. Now let thy friendly [117] hand Put strength enough to't.
           [Edgar interposes.]

OSWALD.   Wherefore, bold peasant, Dar'st thou support a published [118] traitor? Hence, Lest that th' infection of his fortune take Like hold on thee. Let go his arm.

EDGAR. Chill [119] not let go, zir, without vurther 'casion.[120]

OSWALD. Let go, slave, or thou diest.

EDGAR. Good gentleman, go your gait,[121] and let poor voke [122] pass. An chud [123] ha' bin zwaggered [124] out of my life, 'twould not ha' bin zo long as 'tis by a vortnight. Nay, come not near th' old man. Keep out, che vore [125] ye, or Ise [126] try whether your costard [127] or my ballow [128] be the harder. Chill

---

[103] *toward* impending
[104] *sure and vulgar* commonly known certainty
[105] *on speedy foot* rapidly marching
[106] *main . . . thought* sight of the main body is expected hourly
[107] *worser spirit* i.e. bad angel
[108] *tame* submissive
[109] *art . . . sorrows* i.e. lesson of sorrows painfully experienced

[110] *pregnant* prone
[111] *biding* biding place
[112] *benison* blessing
[113] *proclaimed prize* i.e. one with a price on his head
[114] *happy* lucky
[115] *framed flesh* born, created
[116] *thyself remember* i.e. pray, think of your soul
[117] *friendly* i.e. unconsciously befriending
[118] *published* proclaimed

[119] *Chill* I'll (rustic dialect)
[120] *vurther 'casion* further occasion
[121] *gait* way
[122] *voke* folk
[123] *An chud* if I could
[124] *zwaggered* swaggered, bluffed
[125] *che vore* I warrant, assure
[126] *Ise* I shall
[127] *costard* head
[128] *ballow* cudgel

be plain with you.

OSWALD.   Out, dunghill! [*They fight.*]

EDGAR. Chill pick [129] your teeth, zir. Come. No matter vor your foins.[130] [*Oswald falls.*]

OSWALD. Slave, thou hast slain me. Villain,[131] take my purse. If ever thou wilt thrive, bury my body, And give the letters [132] which thou find'st about [133] me To Edmund Earl of Gloucester. Seek him out Upon the English party.[134] O, untimely death! Death!   [*He dies.*]

EDGAR. I know thee well. A serviceable [135] villain, As duteous [136] to the vices of thy mistress As badness would desire.

GLOUCESTER.   What, is he dead?

EDGAR. Sit you down, father; rest you. Let's see these pockets; the letters that he speaks of May be my friends. He's dead; I am only sorry He had no other deathsman.[137] Let us see. Leave, gentle wax; [138] and, manners, blame us not To know [139] our enemies' minds. We rip their hearts;

Their papers [140] is more lawful.

      Reads the letter.

'Let our reciprocal vows be remembered. You have many opportunities to cut him off. If your will want not,[141] time and place will be fruitfully offered. There is nothing done, if he return the conqueror. Then am I the prisoner, and his bed my gaol; [142] from the loathed warmth whereof deliver me, and supply the place for your labor.

    'Your (wife, so I would [143] say)   affectionate servant,   'GONERIL.'

O indistinguished [144] space of woman's will [145]—
A plot upon her virtuous husband's life,
And the exchange [146] my brother! Here in the sands
Thee I'll rake up,[147] the post unsanctified
Of murderous lechers; and in the mature [148] time
With this ungracious paper strike [149] the sight
Of the death-practiced [150] Duke. For him 'tis well
That of thy death and business I can tell.

GLOUCESTER. The King is mad. How stiff [151] is my vile sense,[152] That I stand up, and have ingenious

---

[129] *Chill pick* i.e. I'll knock out
[130] *foins* thrusts
[131] *Villain* serf
[132] *letters* letter
[133] *about* upon
[134] *party* side
[135] *serviceable* usable
[136] *duteous* ready to serve
[137] *deathsman* executioner
[138] *Leave, gentle wax* by your leave, kind seal

(formula used in opening sealed documents)
[139] *To know* i.e. for growing intimate with
[140] *Their papers* i.e. to rip their papers
[141] *want not* is not lacking
[142] *gaol* jail
[143] *would* wish to
[144] *indistinguished* unlimited

[145] *will* desire
[146] *exchange* substitute
[147] *rake up* cover, bury
[148] *in the mature* at the ripe
[149] *strike* blast
[150] *death-practiced* whose death is plotted
[151] *stiff* obstinate
[152] *vile sense* i.e. hateful consciousness

feeling [153]
Of my huge sorrows! Better I were
    distract; [154]
So should my thoughts be severed
    from my griefs,
And woes by wrong imaginations [155]
    lose
The knowledge of themselves.
                    Drum afar off.
    EDGAR.   Give me your hand.
Far off methinks I hear the beaten
    drum.
Come, father, I'll bestow [156] you with
    a friend.   *Exeunt.*

SCENE SEVEN

*Enter Cordelia, Kent, [Doctor,] and
Gentleman.*

    CORDELIA. O thou good Kent, how
        shall I live and work
To match thy goodness? My life will
    be too short
And every measure fail me.
    KENT. To be acknowledged, madam,
        is o'erpaid.
All my reports go [1] with the modest
    truth;
Nor more nor clipped,[2] but so.
    CORDELIA.   Be better suited.[3]
These weeds [4] are memories [5] of those
    worser hours.
I prithee put them off.
    KENT.   Pardon, dear madam.

Yet to be known shortens my made
    intent.[6]
My boon I make it [7] that you know
    me not
Till time and I think meet.[8]
    CORDELIA. Then be't so, my good
        lord. [*To the Doctor*] How does
        the King?
    DOCTOR. Madam, sleeps still.
    CORDELIA. O you kind gods,
Cure this great breach in his abusèd [9]
    nature!
Th' untuned and jarring [10] senses, O,
    wind up [11]
Of this child-changèd [12] father!
    DOCTOR.   So please your Majesty
That we may wake the King? He hath
    slept long.
    CORDELIA. Be governed by your
        knowledge, and proceed
I' th' sway of [13] your own will. Is he
    arrayed?
*Enter Lear in a chair carried by
Servants.*
    GENTLEMAN. Ay, madam. In the
        heaviness of sleep
We put fresh garments on him.
    DOCTOR. Be by, good madam, when
        we do awake him.
I doubt not of his temperance.
    [CORDELIA.   Very well. [*Music.*]
    DOCTOR. Please you draw near.
        Louder the music there.]
    CORDELIA. O my dear father, resto-
        ration hang

---

[153] *ingenious feeling* i.e.
awareness
[154] *distract* distracted
[155] *wrong   imaginations*
i.e. delusions
[156] *bestow* lodge
IV, vii [1] *go* conform
[2] *clipped* i.e. less (curtailed)
[3] *suited* attired
[4] *weeds* clothes

[5] *memories* reminders
[6] *Yet . . . intent* i.e. to
reveal myself just yet
would mar my plan
[7] *My   boon . . . it*   the
reward I ask is
[8] *meet* proper
[9] *abusèd* confused, disturbed
[10] *jarring* discordant

[11] *wind up* tune
[12] *child-changèd . .*   (1)
changed to a child (2)
changed by his children
(suggesting 'changeling,'
wherein mental defect is
associated with the ma-
lignance of witches)
[13] *I' th' sway of* according to

Thy medicine on my lips, and let this kiss
Repair those violent harms [14] that my two sisters
Have in thy reverence [15] made.

KENT.   Kind and dear princess.

CORDELIA. Had you not been their father, these white flakes [16]
Did challenge [17] pity of them. Was this a face
To be opposed against the jarring winds?
[To stand against the deep dread-bolted [18] thunder?
In the most terrible and nimble stroke
Of quick cross lightning to watch, poor perdu,[19]
With this thin helm? [20]] Mine enemy's dog,
Though he had bit me, should have stood that night
Against my fire; and wast thou fain,[21] poor father,
To hovel thee with swine and rogues forlorn
In short [22] and musty straw? Alack, alack,
'Tis wonder that thy life and wits at once
Had not concluded all.—He wakes. Speak to him.

DOCTOR. Madam, do you; 'tis fittest.

CORDELIA. How does my royal lord? How fares your Majesty?

LEAR. You do me wrong to take me out o' th' grave.
Thou art a soul in bliss; but I am bound
Upon a wheel of fire,[23] that mine own tears
Do scald like molten lead.

CORDELIA.   Sir, do you know me?

LEAR. You are a spirit, I know. Where did you die?

CORDELIA. Still, still, far wide! [24]

DOCTOR. He's scarce awake. Let him alone awhile.

LEAR. Where have I been? Where am I? Fair daylight?
I am mightily abused.[25] I should e'en die with pity
To see another thus. I know not what to say.
I will not swear these are my hands. Let's see—
I feel this pin prick. Would I were assured
Of my condition.

CORDELIA.   O look upon me, sir,
And hold your hand in benediction o'er me.
You must not kneel.

LEAR.   Pray, do not mock me.
I am a very foolish fond old man,
Fourscore and upward, not an hour more nor less;
And, to deal plainly,
I fear I am not in my perfect mind.
Methinks I should know you, and know this man;
Yet I am doubtful, for I am mainly ignorant
What place this is; and all the skill I have
Remembers not these garments; nor I know not

---

[14] *harms* wounds
[15] *reverence* reverend person
[16] *flakes* strands of hair
[17] *challenge* demand
[18] *deep dread-bolted* deep-voiced and full of dreadful bolts
[19] *perdu* (1) expendable outpost (military term) (2) lost one
[20] *helm* military helmet; here, thin hair
[21] *fain* glad
[22] *short* scanty (?) tramped to fragments (?)
[23] *wheel of fire* (implement combining the tortures of breaking and burning, figuring in medieval visions of hell)
[24] *wide* off the mark
[25] *abused* confused

Where I did lodge last night. Do not
    laugh at me;
For, as I am a man, I think this lady
To be my child Cordelia.
    CORDELIA.   And so I am! I am!
    LEAR. Be your tears wet? Yes, faith.
    I pray weep not.
If you have poison for me, I will drink
    it.
I know you do not love me; for your
    sisters
Have, as I do remember, done me
    wrong.
You have some cause, they have not.
    CORDELIA.   No cause, no cause.
    LEAR. Am I in France?
    KENT.   In your own kingdom, sir.
    LEAR. Do not abuse [26] me.
    DOCTOR. Be comforted, good madam.
    The great rage
You see is killed in him; [and yet it is
    danger
To make him even o'er [27] the time he
    has lost.]
Desire him to go in. Trouble him no
    more
Till further settling.[28]
    CORDELIA. Will't please your High-
ness walk?
    LEAR.   You must bear with me.
Pray you now, forget and forgive. I
    am old and foolish.
*Exeunt. [Manent Kent and Gentle-
man.]*
    [GENTLEMAN. Holds it true, sir, that
the Duke of Cornwall was so slain?
    KENT. Most certain, sir.
    GENTLEMAN. Who is conductor of
his people?
    KENT. As 'tis said, the bastard son
of Gloucester.
    GENTLEMAN. They say Edgar, his
banished son, is with the Earl of Kent
in Germany.
    KENT. Report is changeable. 'Tis
time to look about; the powers [29] of
the kingdom approach apace.
    GENTLEMAN. The arbitrement [30] is
like to be bloody. Fare you well, sir.
                          [Exit.]
    KENT. My point and period will be
    throughly wrought,[31]
Or [32] well or ill, as this day's battle 's
    fought.   *Exit.]*

ACT V

SCENE ONE

*Enter, with Drum and Colors,[1] Ed-
mund, Regan, Gentleman, and Soldiers.*

    EDMUND. Know [2] of the Duke if his
    last purpose hold,[3]
Or whether since he is advised [4] by
    aught
To change the course. He's full of
    alteration
And self-reproving. Bring his con-
    stant [5] pleasure.
              [Exit an Officer.]
    REGAN. Our sister's man is certainly
    miscarried.[6]
    EDMUND. 'Tis to be doubted,[7]
    madam.
    REGAN.   Now, sweet lord,

[26] *abuse* deceive
[27] *even o'er* fill in
[28] *settling* calming
[29] *powers* armies
[30] *arbitrement* decisive
action
[31] *My point . . . wrought*
i.e. my destiny will be
completely worked out
[32] *Or* either
V, i [1] *Drum and Colors*
drummer and standard-
bearers
[2] *Know* learn
[3] *last purpose hold* most
recent intention (i.e. to
fight) holds good
[4] *advised* induced
[5] *constant pleasure* firm
decision
[6] *miscarried* met with
mishap
[7] *doubted* feared

You know the goodness I intend [8]
upon you.
Tell me, but truly—but then speak the
truth—
Do you not love my sister?

EDMUND.　　　　In honored [9] love.

REGAN. But have you never found
my brother's way
To the forfended [10] place?

[EDMUND. That thought abuses [11]
you.

REGAN. I am doubtful that you have
been conjunct
And bosomed with her, as far as we
call hers.[12]]

EDMUND. No, by mine honor,
madam.

REGAN. I never shall endure her.
Dear my lord,
Be not familiar with her.

EDMUND.　　　　Fear me not.
She and the Duke her husband!

Enter, with Drum and Colors, Albany, Goneril, Soldiers.

[GONERIL. *[Aside]* I had rather lose
the battle than that sister
Should loosen [13] him and me.]

ALBANY. Our very loving sister, well
bemet.[14]
Sir, this I heard: the King is come to
his daughter,
With others whom the rigor [15] of our
state
Forced to cry out. [Where I could not

be honest,[16]
I never yet was valiant. For this business,
It touches us as [17] France invades our
land,
Not bolds the King with others, whom
I fear
Most just and heavy causes make oppose.[18]

EDMUND. Sir, you speak nobly.]

REGAN.　　Why is this reasoned? [19]

GONERIL. Combine together 'gainst
the enemy;
For these domestic and particular
broils [20]
Are not the question [21] here.

ALBANY.　　　　Let's then determine
With th' ancient of war [22] on our proceeding.

[EDMUND. I shall attend you presently [23] at your tent.]

REGAN. Sister, you'll go with us?

GONERIL. No.

REGAN. 'Tis most convenient.[24] Pray
go with us.[25]

GONERIL. O ho, I know the riddle.[26]
—I will go.

　　　　　Exeunt both the Armies.

Enter Edgar.

EDGAR. *[To Albany]* If e'er your
Grace had speech [27] with man
so poor,
Hear me one word.

ALBANY. *[To those departing]* I'll

---

[8] *goodness I intend* boon
I plan to confer
[9] *honored* honorable
[10] *forfended* forbidden
[11] *abuses* deceives
[12] *doubtful . . . hers* i.e.
fearful you have been intimately linked with her
both in mind and body
[13] *loosen* separate
[14] *bemet* met
[15] *rigor* tyranny
[16] *honest* honorable

[17] *touches us as* concerns
me because
[18] *Not bolds . . . oppose*
i.e. but not because he
supports the King and
others whose truly great
grievances arouse them
to arms
[19] *reasoned* argued
[20] *particular broils* private
quarrels
[21] *question* issue
[22] *th' ancient of war* i.e.

seasoned officers
[23] *presently* immediately
[24] *convenient* fitting
[25] *with us* (i.e. with her
rather than Edmund as
each leads an 'army'
from the stage)
[26] *riddle* (i.e. the reason
for Regan's strange demand)
[27] *had speech* i.e. has condescended to speak

overtake you. [*To Edgar*] Speak.

EDGAR. Before you fight the battle,
ope this letter.
If you have victory, let the trumpet
sound [28]
For him that brought it. Wretched
though I seem,
I can produce a champion that will
prove [29]
What is avouchèd [30] there. If you miscarry,
Your business of the world hath so an
end,
And machination [31] ceases. Fortune
love you.

ALBANY. Stay till I have read the
letter.

EDGAR. I was forbid it.
When time shall serve, let but the
herald cry,
And I'll appear again.

ALBANY. Why, fare thee well. I will
o'erlook [32] thy paper.
Exit [Edgar].
Enter Edmund.

EDMUND. The enemy's in view; draw
up your powers.[33]
Here is the guess [34] of their true
strength and forces
By diligent discovery; [35] but your haste
Is now urged on you.

ALBANY. We will greet [36] the time.
Exit.

EDMUND. To both these sisters have
I sworn my love;
Each jealous [37] of the other, as the
stung

Are of the adder. Which of them shall
I take?
Both? One? Or neither? Neither can
be enjoyed,
If both remain alive. To take the
widow
Exasperates, makes mad her sister
Goneril;
And hardly [38] shall I carry out my side,
Her husband being alive. Now then,
we'll use
His countenance [39] for the battle,
which being done,
Let her who would be rid of him
devise
His speedy taking off. As for the
mercy
Which he intends to Lear and to Cor-
delia—
The battle done, and they within our
power,
Shall never see his pardon; for my
state
Stands on me to defend, not to de-
bate.[40]   *Exit*.

SCENE TWO

*Alarum within. Enter, with Drum and
Colors, Lear [held by the hand by]
Cordelia; and Soldiers [of France],
over the stage and exeunt.*

Enter Edgar and Gloucester.

EDGAR. Here, father, take the
shadow of this tree
For your good host. Pray that the
right may thrive.

[28] *sound* sound a sum-mons
[29] *prove* (in trial by com-bat)
[30] *avouchèd* charged
[31] *machination* i.e. all plots and counterplots
[32] *o'erlook* look over
[33] *powers* troops

[34] *guess* estimate
[35] *discovery* reconnoiter-ing
[36] *greet* i.e. meet the de-mands of
[37] *jealous* suspicious
[38] *hardly . . . side* with difficulty shall I play my

part (as Goneril's lover, or as a great power in England?)
[39] *countenance* backing
[40] *my state . . . debate* i.e. my status depends upon my strength, not my arguments

If ever I return to you again,
I'll bring you comfort.

GLOUCESTER. Grace go with you, sir.

Exit [Edgar].

Alarum and retreat [1] *within. Enter Edgar.*

EDGAR. Away, old man! Give me thy hand. Away!

King Lear hath lost, he and his daughter ta'en.[2]

Give me thy hand. Come on.

GLOUCESTER. No further, sir. A man may rot [3] even here.

EDGAR. What, in ill [4] thoughts again? Men must endure [5]

Their going hence, even as their coming hither;

Ripeness [6] is all. Come on.

GLOUCESTER.   And that's true too.

Exeunt.

SCENE THREE

Enter, in conquest, with Drum and Colors, Edmund; Lear and Cordelia as prisoners; Soldiers, Captain.

EDMUND. Some officers take them away. Good guard

Until their greater pleasures [1] first be known

That are to censure [2] them.

CORDELIA.   We are not the first

Who with best meaning [3] have incurred the worst.

For thee, oppressèd king, I am cast down;

Myself could else outfrown false Fortune's frown.

Shall we not see these daughters and these sisters?

LEAR. No, no, no, no! Come, let's away to prison.

We two alone will sing like birds i' th' cage.

When thou dost ask me blessing, I'll kneel down

And ask of thee forgiveness.[4] So we'll live,

And pray, and sing, and tell old tales, and laugh

At gilded butterflies, and hear poor rogues

Talk of court news; [5] and we'll talk with them too—

Who loses and who wins; who's in, who's out—

And take upon 's the mystery of things

As if we were God's spies; [6] and we'll wear out,[7]

In a walled prison, packs and sects of great ones

That ebb and flow by th' moon.[8]

EDMUND.   Take them away.

LEAR. Upon such sacrifices, my Cordelia,

V, ii [1] *Alarum and retreat* (trumpet sounds, signalling the beginning and the ending of a battle)
[2] *ta'en* captured
[3] *rot* i.e. die
[4] *ill* i.e. suicidal
[5] *endure* put up with, suffer through
[6] *Ripeness* i.e. the time decreed by the gods for the fruit to fall from the branch

V, iii [1] *greater pleasures* i.e. the desires of those in higher command
[2] *censure* judge
[3] *meaning* intentions
[4] *When . . . forgiveness* (cf. IV, vii; p. 138, col. 2, "O look upon me, sir, . . . kneel.")
[5] *laugh . . . news* view with amusement bright ephemera, such as gallants preoccupied with

court gossip
[6] *take . . . spies* i.e. contemplate the wonder of existence as if with divine insight, seek eternal rather than temporal truths
[7] *wear out* outlast
[8] *packs . . . moon* i.e. partisan and intriguing clusters of 'great ones' who gain and lose power monthly

The gods themselves throw incense.[9]
Have I caught thee?
He that parts us shall bring a brand
from heaven
And fire us hence like foxes.[10] Wipe
thine eyes.
The goodyears [11] shall devour them,
flesh and fell,[12]
Ere they shall make us weep! We'll
see 'em starved first.
Come.
Exeunt [Lear and Cordelia, guarded].
    EDMUND. Come hither, captain;
hark.
Take thou this note. [*Gives a paper.*]
Go follow them to prison.
One step I have advanced thee. If
thou dost
As this instructs thee, thou dost make
thy way
To noble fortunes. Know thou this,
that men
Are as the time is.[13] To be tender-
minded
Does not become [14] a sword. Thy great
employment
Will not bear question.[15] Either say
thou'lt do't,
Or thrive by other means.
    CAPTAIN.   I'll do't, my lord.
    EDMUND. About it; and write
happy [16] when th' hast done.
Mark, I say instantly, and carry it so
As I have set it down.
    [CAPTAIN. I cannot draw a cart, nor

eat dried oats—
If it be man's work, I'll do't.]   *Exit.*
    *Flourish. Enter Albany, Goneril,
Regan, Soldiers.*
    ALBANY. Sir, you have showed to-
day your valiant strain,
And fortune led you well. You have
the captives
Who were the opposites of [17] this
day's strife.
I do require them of you, so to use
them
As we shall find their merits [18] and
our safety
May equally determine.
    EDMUND.   Sir, I thought it fit
To send the old and miserable King
To some retention [and appointed
guard]; [19]
Whose age had charms in it, whose
title more,
To pluck the common bosom [20] on his
side
And turn our impressed lances in our
eyes [21]
Which do command them. With him I
sent the Queen,
My reason all the same; and they are
ready
To-morrow, or at further space,[22] t'
appear
Where you shall hold your session.[23]
[At this time
We sweat and bleed, the friend hath
lost his friend,

---

[9] *Upon . . . incense* i.e.
the gods themselves are
the celebrants at such
sacrificial offerings to
love as we are
[10] *He . . . foxes* i.e. to
separate us, as foxes are
smoked out and scat-
tered, would require not
a human but a heavenly
torch

[11] *goodyears* (undefined
forces of evil)
[12] *fell* hide
[13] *as the time is* (i.e.
ruthless in war)
[14] *become* befit
[15] *bear question* admit
discussion
[16] *write happy* consider
yourself fortunate
[17] *opposites of* enemies in

[18] *merits* deserts
[19] *some . . . guard* de-
tention under duly ap-
pointed guards
[20] *pluck . . . bosom* draw
popular sympathy
[21] *turn . . . eyes* i.e.
make our conscripted
lancers turn on us
[22] *space* interval
[23] *session* trials

And the best quarrels,[24] in the heat, are cursed
By those that feel their sharpness.[25]
The question of Cordelia and her father
Requires a fitter place.]

ALBANY.   Sir, by your patience,
I hold you but a subject of [26] this war,
Not as a brother.

REGAN. That's as we list to grace [27] him.
Methinks our pleasure might have been demanded
Ere you had spoke so far. He led our powers,
Bore the commission of my place and person,
The which immediacy [28] may well stand up
And call itself your brother.

GONERIL.   Not so hot!
In his own grace he doth exalt himself
More than in your addition.[29]

REGAN.   In my rights
By me invested, he compeers [30] the best.

ALBANY. That were the most [31] if he should husband [31a] you.

REGAN. Jesters do oft prove prophets.

GONERIL.   Holla, holla!

That eye that told you so looked but asquint.[32]

REGAN. Lady, I am not well; else I should answer
From a full-flowing stomach.[33] General,
Take thou my soldiers, prisoners, patrimony; [34]
Dispose of them, of me; the walls is thine.[35]
Witness the world that I create thee here
My lord and master.

GONERIL.   Mean you to enjoy him?

ALBANY. The let-alone [36] lies not in your good will.

EDMUND. Nor in thine, lord.

ALBANY. Half-blooded [37] fellow, yes.

REGAN. [To Edmund] Let the drum strike, and prove my title thine.[38]

ALBANY. Stay yet; hear reason. Edmund, I arrest thee
On capital treason; and, in thy attaint,[39]
This gilded serpent. [Points to Goneril.] For your claim, fair sister,
I bar it in the interest of my wife.
'Tis she is subcontracted [40] to this lord,
And I, her husband, contradict your banes.[41]
If you will marry, make your loves [42]

---

[24] best quarrels worthiest causes
[25] sharpness i.e. painful effects
[26] subject of subordinate in
[27] list to grace please to honor
[28] immediacy i.e. present status (as my deputy)
[29] your addition honors conferred by you
[30] compeers equals
[31] most i.e. most complete investiture in your rights
[31a] husband wed

[32] asquint   cross-eyed, crookedly
[33] stomach anger
[34] patrimony inheritance.
[35] walls is thine i.e. you have stormed the citadel (myself)
[36] let-alone permission
[37] Half-blooded i.e. by birth only half noble
[38] Let . . . thine i.e. fight and win for yourself my rights in the kingdom
[39] in thy attaint i.e. as party to your corruption

(cf. the 'serpent' of Eden)
[40] subcontracted i.e. engaged, though previously married (sarcastic play on 'precontracted,' a legal term applied to one facing an impediment to marriage because previously engaged to another)
[41] contradict your banes forbid your banns, i.e. declare an impediment
[42] loves love-suits

to me;
My lady is bespoke.
GONERIL. An interlude! [43]
ALBANY. Thou art armed, Glouces-
ter. Let the trumpet sound.
If none appear to prove upon thy
person
Thy heinous, manifest, and many
treasons,
There is my pledge. [*Throws down
a glove.*] I'll make [44] it on thy
heart,
Ere I taste bread, thou art in nothing
less [45]
Than I have here proclaimed thee.
REGAN. Sick, O, sick!
GONERIL. [*Aside*] If not, I'll ne'er
trust medicine.[46]
EDMUND. There's my exchange.
[*Throws down a glove.*] What
in the world he is
That names me traitor, villain-like he
lies.
Call by the trumpet.[47] He that dares
approach,
On him, on you, who not? I will main-
tain
My truth and honor firmly.
ALBANY. A herald, ho!
[EDMUND. A herald, ho, a herald!]
ALBANY. Trust to thy single virtue; [48]
for thy soldiers,
All levied in my name, have in my
name
Took their discharge.
REGAN. My sickness grows upon me.
ALBANY. She is not well. Convey
her to my tent.
[*Exit Regan, attended.*]
Enter a Herald.

Come hither, herald. Let the trumpet
sound,
And read out this.
[CAPTAIN. Sound, trumpet!]
A trumpet sounds.
HERALD. (*Reads*) 'If any man of
quality or degree [49] within the lists [50]
of the army will maintain upon Ed-
mund, supposed Earl of Gloucester,
that he is a manifold traitor, let him
appear by the third sound of the
trumpet. He is bold in his defense.'
[EDMUND. Sound!] *First trumpet.*
HERALD. Again! *Second trumpet.*
Again! *Third trumpet.*
Trumpet answers within.
*Enter Edgar, armed, [at the third
sound, a Trumpet before him].*
ALBANY. Ask him his purposes, why
he appears
Upon this call o' th' trumpet.
HERALD. What are you?
Your name, your quality, and why you
answer
This present summons?
EDGAR. Know my name is lost,
By treason's tooth bare-gnawn and
canker-bit; [51]
Yet am I noble as the adversary
I come to cope.
ALBANY. Which is that adversary?
EDGAR. What's he that speaks for
Edmund Earl of Gloucester?
EDMUND. Himself. What say'st thou
to him?
EDGAR. Draw thy sword.
That, if my speech offend a noble
heart,
Thy arm may do thee justice. Here is
mine.

[43] *An interlude* a quaint
playlet (equivalent to
saying 'How dramatic!'
or 'How comical!')
[44] *make* prove

[45] *nothing less* i.e. no respect less guilty
[46] *medicine* i.e. poison
[47] *trumpet* trumpeter
[48] *single virtue* unaided

prowess
[49] *degree* rank
[50] *lists* muster
[51] *canker-bit* eaten, as by
the rose-caterpillar

Behold it is my privilege,
The privilege of mine honors,
My oath, and my profession.[52] I protest—
Maugre [53] thy strength, place, youth,
and eminence,
Despite thy victor sword and fire-
new [54] fortune,
Thy valor and thy heart [55]—thou art
a traitor,
False to thy gods, thy brother, and
thy father,
Conspirant [56] 'gainst this high illustri-
ous prince,
And from th' extremest upward [57] of
thy head
To the descent and dust [58] below thy
foot
A most toad-spotted [59] traitor. Say
thou 'no,'
This sword, this arm, and my best
spirits are bent [60]
To prove upon thy heart, whereto I
speak,
Thou liest.

EDMUND. In wisdom [61] I should ask
thy name,
But since thy outside looks so fair and
warlike,
And that thy tongue some say [62] of
breeding breathes,

What safe and nicely [63] I might well
delay
By rule of knighthood I disdain and
spurn.
Back do I toss these treasons [64] to
thy head,
With the hell-hated [65] lie o'erwhelm
thy heart,
Which—for they yet glance by and
scarcely bruise—
This sword of mine shall give them
instant way
Where they shall rest for ever.[66]
Trumpets, speak!
Alarums. Fight. [Edmund falls.]
ALBANY. Save him,[67] save him.
GONERIL. This is practice,[68]
Gloucester.
By th' law of war thou wast not bound
to answer
An unknown opposite. Thou art not
vanquished,
But cozened [69] and beguiled.
ALBANY. Shut your mouth, dame,
Or with this paper shall I stop it.—
Hold,[70] sir.—
[*To Goneril*] Thou worse than any
name, read thine own evil.
No tearing, lady! I perceive you know
it.
GONERIL. Say if I do—the laws are

---

[52] *it . . . profession* i.e. wielding this sword is the privilege of my knightly honor, oath, and function
[53] *Maugre* in spite of
[54] *fire-new* brand-new
[55] *heart* courage
[56] *Conspirant* in conspiracy
[57] *extremest upward* uppermost extreme
[58] *descent and dust* i.e. all that intervenes from the head to the dust

[59] *toad-spotted* i.e. exuding venom like a toad
[60] *bent* directed
[61] *wisdom* prudence
[62] *some say* some assay, i.e. proof (?) or, one might say (?)
[63] *safe and nicely* cautiously and punctiliously
[64] *treasons* accusations of treason
[65] *hell-hated* hateful as hell
[66] *Which . . . ever* i.e. the accusations of trea-

son, now flying about harmlessly, will be routed into you with my sword-thrust and lodge there permanently
[67] *Save him* spare him (cf. Albany's l. below)
[68] *practice* trickery
[69] *cozened* cheated
[70] *Hold* wait (If addressed to Edmund, this suggests a motive for the 'Save him' of Albany's l. above: i.e. Albany hopes to obtain a confession.)

mine,[71] not thine.
Who can arraign me for't?

ALBANY.   Most monstrous! O,
Know'st thou this paper?

GONERIL. Ask me not what I know.
                    Exit.

ALBANY. Go after her. She's desperate; govern [72] her.
            [*Exit an Officer.*]

EDMUND. What you have charged
me with, that have I done,
And more, much more. The time will
bring it out.
'Tis past, and so am I.—But what art
thou
That hast this fortune on [73] me? If
thou'rt noble,
I do forgive thee.

EDGAR.   Let's exchange charity.[74]
I am no less in blood than thou art,
Edmund;
If more,[75] the more th' hast wronged
me.
My name is Edgar and thy father's
son.
The gods are just, and of our pleas-
ant [76] vices
Make instruments to plague us.
The dark and vicious place [77] where
thee he got [78]
Cost him his eyes.

EDMUND. Th' hast spoken right; 'tis
true.
The wheel [79] is come full circle; I am
here.[80]

ALBANY. Methought thy very gait
did prophesy [81]

A royal nobleness. I must embrace
thee.
Let sorrow split my heart if ever I
Did hate thee, or thy father.

EDGAR.   Worthy prince, I
know't.

ALBANY. Where have you hid yourself?
How have you known the miseries of
your father?

EDGAR. By nursing them, my lord.
List a brief tale;
And when 'tis told, O that my heart
would burst!
The bloody proclamation to escape
That followed me so near (O, our
lives' sweetness!
That we the pain of death would
hourly die [82]
Rather than die at once) taught me
to shift
Into a madman's rags, t' assume a
semblance
That very dogs disdained; and in this
habit [83]
Met I my father with his bleeding
rings,[84]
Their precious stones new lost; became
his guide,
Led him, begged for him, saved him
from despair;
Never—O fault!—revealed myself unto
him
Until some half hour past, when I was
armed,[85]
Not sure, though hoping of this good
success,

[71] *mine* (i.e. as ruler)
[72] *govern* control
[73] *fortune on* i.e. victory over
[74] *charity* forgiveness and love
[75] *If more* if greater (since legitimate)
[76] *of our pleasant* out of our pleasurable
[77] *place* i.e. the bed of adultery
[78] *got* begot
[79] *wheel* (of fortune)
[80] *here* (at its bottom)
[81] *prophesy* promise
[82] *O . . . die* i.e. how sweet is life that we would prefer to suffer death-pangs hourly
[83] *habit* attire
[84] *rings* sockets
[85] *armed* in armor

I asked his blessing, and from first to last
Told him our pilgrimage.[86] But his flawed [87] heart—
Alack, too weak the conflict to support—
'Twixt two extremes of passion, joy and grief,
Burst smilingly.

EDMUND. This speech of yours hath moved me,
And shall perchance do good; but speak you on—
You look as you had something more to say.

ALBANY. If there be more, more woeful, hold it in,
For I am almost ready to dissolve,[88]
Hearing of this.

[EDGAR. This would have seemed a period [89]
To such as love not sorrow; but another,
To amplify too much, would make much more,
And top extremity.[90]
Whilst I was big in clamor,[91] came there in a man,
Who, having seen me in my worst estate,[92]
Shunned my abhorred society; but then, finding
Who 'twas that so endured, with his strong arms
He fastenèd on my neck, and bellowèd out
As he'd burst heaven, threw him on my father,

Told the most piteous tale of Lear and him
That ever ear received; which in recounting
His grief grew puissant,[93] and the strings of life
Began to crack. Twice then the trumpets sounded,
And there I left him tranced.[94]

ALBANY.   But who was this?

EDGAR. Kent, sir, the banished Kent; who in disguise
Followèd his enemy [95] king and did him service
Improper for a slave.]

Enter a Gentleman [with a bloody knife].

GENTLEMAN. Help, help! O, help!

EDGAR.   What kind of help?

ALBANY.   Speak, man.

EDGAR. What means this bloody knife?

GENTLEMAN.   'Tis hot, it smokes.[96]
It came even from the heart of—O, she's dead.

ALBANY. Who dead? Speak, man.

GENTLEMAN. Your lady, sir, your lady; and her sister
By her is poisonèd; she confesses it.

EDMUND. I was contracted [97] to them both. All three
Now marry [98] in an instant.

EDGAR.   Here comes Kent.

Enter Kent.

ALBANY. Produce the bodies, be they alive or dead. [*Exit Gentleman.*]
This judgment of the heavens, that makes us tremble,

---

[86] *our pilgrimage* of our journey
[87] *flawed* cracked
[88] *dissolve* melt into tears
[89] *a period* the limit
[90] *another . . . extremity*

i.e. another sorrow, too fully described, would exceed the limit
[91] *big in clamor* loud in lamentation
[92] *estate* state

[93] *puissant* powerful
[94] *tranced* insensible
[95] *enemy* inimical
[96] *smokes* steams
[97] *contracted* engaged
[98] *marry* (i.e. in death)

Touches us not with pity.—O, is this
  he?
The time will not allow the compli-
  ment [99]
Which very manners [100] urges.
  KENT.   I am come
To bid my king and master aye good
  night.
Is he not here?
  ALBANY. Great thing [101] of [102] us
  forgot!
Speak, Edmund, where's the King?
  and where's Cordelia?
*Goneril and Regan's bodies brought
out.*
Seest thou this object,[103] Kent?
  KENT. Alack, why thus?
  EDMUND. Yet [104] Edmund was be-
  loved.
The one the other poisoned for my
  sake,
And after slew herself.
  ALBANY. Even so. Cover their faces.
  EDMUND. I pant for life.[105] Some
  good I mean to do,
Despite of mine own nature. Quickly
  send—
Be brief in it—to the castle, for my
  writ [106]
Is on the life of Lear and on Cordelia.
Nay, send in time.
  ALBANY.   Run, run, O, run!
  EDGAR. To who, my lord? Who has
  the office? [107] Send
Thy token of reprieve.
  EDMUND. Well thought on. Take my
  sword;

Give it the captain.
  EDGAR.   Haste thee for thy life.
                    [*Exit Officer.*]
  EDMUND. He hath commission from
  thy wife and me
To hang Cordelia in the prison and
To lay the blame upon her own despair
That she fordid [108] herself.
  ALBANY. The gods defend her! Bear
  him hence awhile.
                [*Edmund is borne off.*]
  *Enter Lear, with Cordelia in his
arms, [Gentleman, and others follow-
ing].*
  LEAR. Howl, howl, howl! O, you are
  men of stones.
Had I your tongues and eyes, I'ld use
  them so
That heaven's vault should crack. She's
  gone for ever.
I know when one is dead, and when
  one lives.
She's dead as earth. Lend me a look-
  ing glass.
If that her breath will mist or stain
  the stone,[109]
Why then she lives.
  KENT. Is this the promised end? [110]
  EDGAR. Or image [111] of that horror?
  ALBANY.   Fall and cease.[112]
  LEAR. This feather stirs; she lives! If
  it be so,
It is a chance which does redeem [113]
  all sorrows
That ever I have felt.
  KENT.   O my good master.
  LEAR. Prithee away.

---

[99] *compliment* ceremony
[100] *very manners* i.e. sheer decency
[101] *thing* matter
[102] *of* by
[103] *object* sight
[104] *Yet* despite all

[105] *pant for life* i.e. gasp for life's breath
[106] *writ* i.e. order of execution
[107] *office* commission
[108] *fordid* destroyed
[109] *stone* i.e. glass

[110] *promised end* i.e. doomsday
[111] *image* duplicate
[112] *Fall and cease* i.e. strike once and for all, make an end of things
[113] *redeem* atone for

EDGAR. 'Tis noble Kent, your friend.

LEAR. A plague upon you murderers, traitors all;
I might have saved her; now she's gone for ever.
Cordelia, Cordelia, stay a little. Ha,
What is't thou say'st? Her voice was ever soft,
Gentle, and low—an excellent thing in woman.
I killed the slave that was a-hanging thee.

GENTLEMAN. 'Tis true, my lords, he did.

LEAR.   Did I not, fellow?
I have seen the day, with my good biting falchion [114]
I would have made them skip. I am old now,
And these same crosses [115] spoil me.[116] Who are you?
Mine eyes are not o' th' best. I'll tell you straight.[117]

KENT. If fortune brag of two [118] she loved and hated,[119]
One of them we behold.

LEAR. This is a dull sight.[120] Are you not Kent?

KENT.   The same:
Your servant Kent; where is your servant Caius? [121]

LEAR. He's a good fellow, I can tell you that.

He'll strike, and quickly too. He's dead and rotten.

KENT. No, my good lord; I am the very man.

LEAR. I'll see that straight.[122]

KENT. That from your first of difference and decay [123]
Have followed your sad steps.

LEAR.   You are welcome hither.

KENT. Nor no man else.[124] All's cheerless, dark, and deadly.
Your eldest daughters have fordone [125] themselves,
And desperately [126] are dead.

LEAR.   Ay, so I think.

ALBANY. He knows not what he says; and vain is it
That we present us to him.

EDGAR.   Very bootless.[127]

Enter a Messenger.

MESSENGER. Edmund is dead, my lord.

ALBANY.   That's but a trifle here.
You lords and noble friends, know our intent.
What comfort to this great decay may come [128]
Shall be applied. For us, we will resign,
During the life of this old Majesty,
To him our absolute power; [*To Edgar and Kent*] you to your rights,
With boot [129] and such addition [130] as

---

[114] *falchion* small sword slightly hooked
[115] *crosses* adversities
[116] *spoil me* i.e. sap my strength
[117] *tell you straight* i.e. recognize you in a moment
[118] *two* (i.e. Lear, and a hypothetical second extreme example of Fortune's cruelty with whom he may be equated)

[119] *loved and hated* i.e. favored, then victimized
[120] *sight* eyesight (Instinctively Lear shuns the admission that he is dazed and weeping.)
[121] *Caius* (Kent's alias)
[122] *see that straight* understand that in a moment
[123] *difference and decay* change and decline in fortune

[124] *Nor no man else* i.e. no, nor anyone else
[125] *fordone* destroyed
[126] *desperately* in a state of despair
[127] *bootless* useless
[128] *What . . . come* i.e. whatever means of aiding this ruined great one presents itself
[129] *boot* good measure
[130] *addition* titles, advancement in rank

your honors
Have more than merited. All friends
     shall taste
The wages of their virtue, and all foes
The cup of their deservings.—O, see,
     see!
     LEAR. And my poor fool [131] is
     hanged: no, no, no life?
Why should a dog, a horse, a rat,
     have life,
And thou no breath at all? Thou'lt
     come no more,
Never, never, never, never, never.
Pray you undo this button. Thank you,
     sir.
Do you see this? Look on her! Look
     her lips,
Look there, look there—   *He dies.*
     EDGAR. He faints. My lord, my
     lord—
     KENT. Break, heart, I prithee break!
     EDGAR.   Look up, my lord.
     KENT. Vex not his ghost.[132] O, let
     him pass! He hates him
That would upon the rack [133] of this

tough world
Stretch him out longer.
     EDGAR.   He is gone indeed.
     KENT. The wonder is, he hath en-
     dured so long.
He but usurped [134] his life.
     ALBANY. Bear them from hence. Our
     present business
Is general woe. [*To Kent and Edgar*]
     Friends of my soul, you twain
Rule in this realm, and the gored state
     sustain.
     KENT. I have a journey, sir, shortly
     to go.
My master calls me; I must not say
     no.
     EDGAR. The weight of this sad time
     we must obey,[135]
Speak what we feel, not what we
     ought to say.
The oldest hath borne most; we that
     are young
Shall never see so much, nor live so
     long.
          Exeunt with a dead march.

[131] *fool* i.e. Cordelia ('Fool' was often a term of affection, and sometimes, as in Erasmus and elsewhere in Shakespeare, of praise—as ironic commentary upon self-seeking 'worldly wisdom.')

[132] *Vex . . . ghost* do not trouble his departing spirit

[133] *rack* instrument of torture
[134] *usurped* possessed contrary to (natural) law
[135] *obey* i.e. accept

DISCUSSION OF *KING LEAR*

You have read two of the best tragedies from the world's two periods of great tragic drama, the Greek and the Elizabethan. At first, the plays may seem to be more different than they are alike, but a closer consideration of their ritual elements, of the character of their heroes, of their structure, and of their language will probably indicate that the similarities are crucial and that the differences are unimportant.

You might note that both plays begin with a domestic tragedy that has political implications so that the characters become involved in war and chaos in the state. Further, by Creon's persecution of Antigone and by Regan and

Goneril's persecution of Lear, a natural order is disturbed, and morality and religion are crucially involved.

Both plays are primarily about the effects of evil, and the power of the plays probably stems largely from the terrible inevitability with which the forces of evil grow until they seem to swamp and engulf the world. These are times in which, in W. B. Yeats' words, "Things fall apart" and "the center will not hold," times in which the best of men are ineffectual and the worst are "full of passionate intensity." In both plays, the foundations of society, in the family, crumble. Father is pitted against child, brother against brother, sister against sister. And the family is only the microcosm, the symbol of the state which is itself sick. The actions and speeches of both Antigone and Lear are indictments of the unnatural enormities of a sick state. Both plays seem the passionate evocations of the nature and essence of an evil which it seems that man can scarcely avert and which, perhaps, it is his tragic destiny to suffer.

Perhaps one of the most fearful facets of *King Lear* is the nature of Goneril and Regan. Although they relentlessly and with clear-eyed reason increasingly persecute Lear, they never become unbelievable monsters. If they were monsters, the play would probably become either allegorical, like *Pilgrim's Progress,* or melodramatic, like *Uncle Tom's Cabin.* But never for a moment do we cease to believe in them as chillingly plausible and perhaps even inevitable human beings.

Certainly it is a further tribute to the dramatist's genius that his evocation of evil did not stop with the sisters, but that other characters in the play—Edmund, Cornwall, Oswald—in their own ways not only suggest that evil takes many forms, but also that it permeates every level of society. When Goneril and Regan triumph over Lear and Cordelia, when Edmund and Cornwall triumph over Gloucester and Edgar, and even when Oswald triumphs over Kent by having him put ignominiously in the stocks, a terrible feeling of pessimism and dread begins to overtake us. Against the ever-triumphant reason of the evil characters, those irrational emotional qualities of love and loyalty cannot stand. Lear and his Fool are driven onto the heath. Cordelia is exiled. Kent is forced into a humble disguise. Edgar is metamorphosed into a mad beggar. Everywhere is chaos, degradation, and horror.

Aristotle commented upon the necessity of one complete action, and in *Antigone* we certainly have one complete action. In *Lear* we have in one sense a complete action of the progress and eventual defeat of evil; but we also seem to have at least one important minor plot, the story of Gloucester and his sons. In the Elizabethan drama, this minor action is called a sub-plot or, in Ben Jonson's term, an under-plot. We discuss its function at length in Part Three, on tragicomedy. Frequently the sub-plot was not particularly or even at all necessary to the main plot. In *King Lear,* however, it has an integral and necessary function. We commented earlier that in *Lear* much of our depression arises from our growing feeling that evil is beginning to permeate every stratum of society. This feeling is greatly strengthened when we see the action of Lear's story repeated in the story of Gloucester. As Lear's daughters turn against him, so does one of Gloucester's sons betray him. Shakespeare, then, uses his sub-plot in a most effective and necessary fashion. We might almost say that there actually is only one action in the play—the action of the progress of evil—and that this action consists of two parallel strands. Sophocles, although he does not use a sub-plot, creates in his own way this feeling of universal involvement in the action, and perhaps Sophocles' chief method is his chorus which in its awe and terror and inability to act finally conveys the sense of frightened and ineffectual mankind.

The characters of the villains of the sub-plot, by being individual and not stereotypes or little Gonerils and Regans, further enhance the sense of evil in the play. Edmund is particularly interesting because of his change of heart late in the last act. However, a modern reader must be wary of a feeling of sympathy for Edmund as an underdog. His speech at the beginning of Act I, Scene ii, for instance, is a speech that might well be calculated to appeal to the modern temper. We must, of course, remember to stay within the morality of the play, and within that morality Edmund, through no fault of his own, is a tainted and unnatural character. His motives and his actions are unnatural and outside the boundary of law and morality.

Cornwall, who is attached to both the main and the sub-plot, is probably the most ferocious character in the play. In the last scene of Act III, in which he puts Gloucester's eyes out, he seems one of the most vivid embodiments of insane malevolence in all of Shakespeare. After the First Servant says to Gloucester, "My lord, you have one eye left to see some mischief on him," Cornwall is able to make that grim wisecrack: "Lest it see more, prevent it. Out, vile jelly! Where is thy lustre now?"

Oswald has none of the force of the other villains, but in his own way he is superbly loathsome. By his cowardice and clever lying and by his juxtaposition to the brave and honest Kent, he becomes possibly the most contemptible character in the play.

The many forms of evil and the complete impotence and degradation of good make this one of the blackest and most pessimistic works in our literature. If the play had ended on this note, the effect would have been one of almost intolerable depression. But in *Lear* a re-affirmation of morality comes at the end when Albany and Edgar pick up the reins of state.

Both *Antigone* and *King Lear* are about characters who grow to morality, who learn something, who have a moment of revelation, as Creon does. It is not difficult to trace Lear's growth to awareness. In Act I he makes his mistake, and the mistake is caused by his pride, selfishness, and spiritual blindness. In Act II the actions of Goneril and Regan slowly draw him to the realization that he has acted foolishly and unnaturally. This dawning realization is as hard for Lear to accept as was Creon's for him. All his life Lear has never questioned his essential rightness. As Regan says in Act I, Scene i, " 'Tis the infirmity of his age. Yet he hath ever but slenderly known himself." And perhaps we may take "of his age" to mean not only Lear's years, but Lear's time, his era. Shakespeare has chosen his words most carefully throughout the play to inform the reader by many small ironies of his meaning. Most of the Fool's speeches and songs are ironic commentaries on Lear's action, commentaries which Lear cannot or will not recognize, but which have a cumulatively devastating effect upon the audience. Here we have an example of one of the chief weapons of the tragic writer, dramatic irony.

Perhaps like mankind in general, Lear is stubbornly engrained in error and his moral education will be a slow and emotionally wrenching process, so wrenching that he will be unable at first to face the consequences of his actions and to condemn his former nature. The process will be as painful as Gloucester's blinding. Incidentally, the Gloucester story may well indicate the use Shakespeare constantly makes in this play of ironic symbolism. A careful reader might note that while Gloucester can physically see, he is spiritually blind. In Act II, Scene i, Edmund calls for light and Gloucester enters with torches. Perhaps it is not pushing the matter too far to say that Gloucester is convinced by the false light of reason that Edgar is a traitor, and only when Gloucester is physically blinded does he become mentally clearheaded.

In Act I, Lear committed his crime while in his full kingly regalia. He begins by this action to divest himself of the trappings of kingship. His pride and spiritual blindness are symbolically connected to his full kingly accouterments, and through the rest of the play Lear is shorn not only of the symbols of his rank, such as his retinue of knights, but also of lodging and finally even of most of his clothes. You may find this clothing imagery well traced in Robert B. Heilman's book *The Great Stage*. Clothing is symbolic of covering, and when Lear is most fully clothed, he is most fully blind. When he begins in his madness to tear his clothes off, he grows in humility and insight. He grows out of his selfishness. He makes the Fool enter the hovel first. He cries pityingly of "Poor naked wretches, wheresoe'er you are/That bide the pelting of this pitiless storm. . . ." In the last scene of the play, Lear has emerged a much chastened and humbled old man. After the wild mourning cry for Cordelia, "Never, never, never, never, never," the next line, "Pray you, undo this button," stands in brilliant juxtaposition and takes on a most meaningful symbolic value. Lear, in divesting himself of this last shard of symbolic clothing, is dying and attaining pure spiritual nakedness. Through suffering and anguish, he has recognized and atoned for his human frailty. In other words, the play can be seen as the story of an approach to spiritual clarity or, indeed, to saintliness.

After reading *Antigone* and *King Lear*, we might phrase the fable common to all tragedies like this: Man is flawed. He must sin. He must atone and suffer for his sin. Some critics have wished for some alleviation of the almost unbearable pain of the last act of *Lear*. They have wished that Cordelia might not have died, and that she and Lear might have lived out their days together in peace. The message of tragedy, however, is a hard and angry one, and the true tragic writer must see clearly that man's capacity to envision the good also demands that man suffer to the ends of his strength to attain that good.

Perhaps it is now becoming clear that, although the trappings of Shakespearian tragedy are much different from Sophoclean tragedy, the essence is the same.

DISCUSSION QUESTIONS ON *KING LEAR*

1. To what exent does Lear fulfill Murray's theory of the tragic hero as scapegoat and saviour? How well does Lear fit Aristotle's definition of the tragic hero? How well does he fit Butcher's interpretation of Aristotle?

2. Samuel Johnson might consider Cornford's discussion of the heroic character as a judgment formed "upon narrow principles." Does Lear seem to fit in more with Cornford's view of an austere tragic type or Johnson's of a full natural man?

3. Both Creon and Lear are foolish and headstrong. By the end of the play, both have been fully punished for their folly. Yet it is hard to push this comparison further, for Lear is a much more individualized character than Creon. The difference between them is really the difference between two traditions of the drama. Is *King Lear* a better play for having a more memorable character? Or, conversely, is *Lear* a poorer play because its hero is, as Cornford would say, too individualized and specific for tragedy?

4. Much has been written of Lear's grandeur, force, and magnificence. Is he ever presented, however, as a comic figure? How do we regard him in Act I, Scene iv, when he asks the Fool, "Dost thou call me fool, boy?" and the Fool answers, "All thy other titles thou hast given away; that thou wast born with"? How do we regard him in Act III, Scene iv, when he says to the Fool, "In, boy; go first"? Find other examples of such responses by the Fool and of such reversals of decorum by Lear. In Greek satyr plays, it was usual to make fun of gods and kings, but rare to find such sport in tragedy. Do these scenes weaken or strengthen the tragedy? Does this presentation of Lear's character jibe more with Butcher's or Johnson's conception of the tragic hero?

5. Kenneth Burke makes the proverb "One learns by experience" stand at the center of the tragic action. This notion is similar to Aristotle's about revelation, and it is a good way to understand the central structure of tragedy. Chart Lear's tragic progression by using Burke's three terms, the act, the sufferance, and the thing learned.

6. Many people have said that the Fool functions in *King Lear* as the Chorus does in Greek tragedy. How much is this so? For instance, how much does he participate in the action and how much does he comment on it? What sort of comments does he make? Is he the voice of the audience and of common sense? Is he sometimes this and sometimes not? Look at several of his songs and explain why he sings them. How much is he given to platitudes? Are there any other characters who sometimes function as the Chorus?

7. What is the function of Oswald in the play? of Kent? What is the point of their meeting in Act II, Scene ii, where Kent abuses Oswald? Is this scene functional in the play or an excrescence? What are the functions of Curan and

the Old Man? Could Shakespeare have omitted them? Compare Shakespeare's use of minor characters with Sophocles'.

8. Much recent criticism of Shakespeare has focused on his use of imagery. An image is a verbal suggestion of a concrete sensation or thing; it is usually but not necessarily visual. In her book *Shakespeare's Imagery and What It Tells Us* (New York: Macmillan, 1936), Caroline F. E. Spurgeon points out the great number of images in *King Lear* that suggest "a human body in anguished movement." Throughout the play there are also many images associated with the following ideas: animals, seeing and blindness, health and disease, the stars and the solar system, clothing and nakedness, weather and storms, and royal ceremonies and pageantry. Generally, an image does one or more of these things: clarifies, intensifies, or extends an emotion, an action, or a meaning. Choose any one or two images and note their recurrence through the play. Then describe the connection between the images you choose and the action or characterization.

9. In Act III, Scene vi, Lear in his madness convenes a court to try his daughters for their crimes against him. This scene is a travesty of a real courtroom scene, and a travesty is a form of humor. While some actual humor may reside in the Fool's ironies of Act I, Scene vi, there is no humor here. Nor does the scene advance the plot. What effect, then, is Shakespeare striving for? What does he want the scene to do? What is its effect?

10. If you pay close attention to the realistic details of the play, you will find many inconsistencies. A. C. Bradley notes that "The improbabilities in *King Lear* surely far surpass those of the other great tragedies in number and in grossness." For example, Gloucester does not recognize his son's handwriting, and Gloucester and Edgar react quickly and rashly to Edmund's reports about each other; many characters fail to recognize others they have known for a long time; the geography and time scheme are confusing. These inconsistencies led Leo Tolstoy to say that *Lear* "does not satisfy the most elementary demands of art." Do you think that the following statement by Samuel Johnson is an adequate refutation of Tolstoy's?

> There is perhaps no play which keeps the attention so strongly fixed; which so much agitates our passions and interests our curiosity. The artful involutions of distinct interests, the striking opposition of contrary characters, the sudden changes of fortune, and the quick succession of events, fill the mind with a perpetual tumult of indignation, pity, and hope. There is no scene which does not contribute to the aggravation of the distress or conduct of the action, and scarce a line which does not conduce to the progress of the scene. So powerful is the current of the poet's imagination, that the mind, which once ventures within it, is hurried irresistibly along.

11. Shakespeare had several sources for the story of King Lear, who in Shakespeare's time was thought to be a real historical person. Shakespeare's major alteration of the story is to make it end unhappily; in all the other

versions, Lear and Cordelia live and are reconciled and Lear regains his throne. In the late 17th century a writer named Nahum Tate rewrote the ending of Shakespeare's version and made it end happily. Throughout the 18th century Tate's revision was very popular. It is printed below. The scene picks up at Act IV, Scene vii.

Scene, A Prison

[*Lear asleep, with his Head on Cordelia's Lap.*]

CORD. What Toils, thou wretched King, hast thou endur'd
To make thee draw, in Chains, a Sleep so sound?
Thy better Angel charm thy ravish'd Mind
With fancy'd Freedom; Peace is us'd to lodge
On Cottage Straw. Thou hast the Beggar's Bed,
Therefore should'st have the Beggar's careless Thought.
And now, my Edgar, I remember thee:
What Fate has seiz'd thee in this general Wreck
I know not, but I know thou must be wretched,
Because Cordelia holds thee dear.
O Gods! A sudden Gloom o'erwhelms me, and the Image
Of Death o'erspreads the Place.—Ha! Who are there?

[*Enter Captain and Officers with Cords.*]

CAPT. Now, Sirs, dispatch; already you are paid
In Part, the Best of your Reward's to come.
LEAR. Charge, charge upon their Flank, their last Wing halts.
Push, push the Battle, and the Day's our own.
Their Ranks are broke, down with Albany.
Who holds my Hands? O thou deceiving Sleep,
I was this very Minute on the Chace;
And now a Prisoner here.—What mean the Slaves?
You will not murder me?
CORD. Help, Earth and Heaven!
For your Souls sake, dear Sirs, and for the Gods.
OFF. No Tears, good Lady; no pleading against Gold and Preferment.
Come, Sirs, make ready your Cords.
CORD. You, Sir, I'll seize,
You have a human Form, and if no Prayers
Can touch your Soul to spare a poor King's Life,
If there be any thing that you hold dear,
By that I beg you to dispatch me first.
CAPT. Comply with her Request; dispatch her first.
LEAR. Off Hell-Hounds, by the Gods I charge you spare her;
'Tis my Cordelia, my true pious Daughter;
No pity?—Nay, then take an old Man's Vengeance.

[*Snatches a Partisan, and strikes down two of them; the rest quit Cordelia, and turn upon him.*]

[*Enter Edgar and Albany.*]

EDG. Death! Hell! Ye Vultures, hold your impious Hands,
Or take a speedier Death than you wou'd give.
CAPT. By whose Command?

EDG. Behold the Duke, your Lord.

ALB. Guards, seize those Instruments of Cruelty.

CORD. My Edgar, Oh!

EDG. My dear Cordelia! Lucky was the Minute

Of our Approach; the Gods have weigh'd our Suff'rings;

W'are past the Fire, and now must shine to Ages.

GENT. Look here, my Lord, see where the generous King

Has slain two of 'em.

LEAR. Did I not, Fellow?

I've seen the Day, with my good biting Faulchion

I cou'd have made 'em skip: I am Old now,

And these vile Crosses spoil me; out of Breath,

Fie, oh! quite out of Breath, and spent.

ALB. Bring in old Kent; and, Edgar, guide you hither

Your Father, whom you said was near;

[*Exit Edgar.*]

He may be an Ear-Witness at the least

Of our Proceedings.

[*Kent brought in here.*]

LEAR. Who are you?

My Eyes are none o'th'best, I'll tell you streight;

Oh Albany! Well, Sir, we are your Captives,

And you are come to see Death pass upon us.

Why this Delay?—Or is't your Highness's Pleasure

To give us first the Torture? Say ye so?

Why here's old Kent and I, as tough a Pair

As e'er bore Tyrant's Stroke.—But my Cordelia,

My poor Cordelia here, O pity—

ALB. Take off their Chains.—Thou injur'd Majesty,

The Wheel of Fortune now has made her Circle,

And Blessings yet stand 'twixt thy Grave and thee.

LEAR. Com'st thou, inhuman Lord, to sooth us back

To a Fool's Paradise of Hope, to make

Our Doom more wretched? Go to, we are too well

Acquainted with Misfortune, to be gull'd

With lying Hope; no, we will hope no more.

ALB. I have a Tale t'unfold, so full of Wonder

As cannot meet an easy Faith;

But by that Royal injur'd head 'tis true.

KENT. What wou'd your Highness?

ALB. Know, the noble Edgar

Impeach'd Lord Edmund, since the Fight, of Treason

And dar'd him for the Proof to single Combat,

In which the Gods confirm'd his Charge by Conquest;

I left ev'n now the Traitor wounded mortally!

LEAR. And whither tends this Story?

ALB. 'Ere they fought,

Lord Edgar gave into my Hands this Paper;

A blacker Scroll of Treason and of Lust,

Than can be found in the Records of Hell;

There, Sacred Sir, behold the Character

Of Goneril, the worst of Daughters, but

More vicious Wife.

CORD. Cou'd there be yet Addition to their Guilt!

What will not they that wrong a Father do?

ALB. Since then my Injuries, Lear, fall in with thine,

I have resolv'd the same Redress for both.

KENT. What says my Lord?

CORD. Speak, for methought I heard The charming Voice of a descending God.

ALB. The Troops, by Edmund rais'd, I have disbanded;

Those that remain are under my Command.

What Comfort may be brought to chear your Age,

And heal your savage Wrongs, shall be apply'd;

For to your Majesty we do resign Your Kingdom, save what Part yourself confer'd

On us in Marriage.

KENT. Hear you that, my Liege?

CORD. Then they are Gods, and Virtue is their Care.

LEAR. Is't possible?

Let the Spheres stop their Course, the Sun make halt,

The Winds be hush'd, the Seas and Fountains rest;

All Nature pause, and listen to the Change.

Where is my Kent, my Cajus?

KENT. Here, my Liege.

LEAR. Why I have News that will recall thy Youth:

Ha! Didst thou hear't, or did th'inspiring Gods

Whisper to me alone? Old Lear shall be

A King again.

KENT. The Prince, that like a God has Pow'r, has said it.

LEAR. Cordelia then shall be a Queen, mark that:

Cordelia shall be a Queen; Winds catch the Sound,

And bear it on your rosy Wings to Heav'n—

Cordelia is a Queen.

[Re-enter Edgar with Gloster.]

ALB. Look, Sir, where pious Edgar comes,

Leading his Eyeless Father. O my Liege!

His wond'rous Story well deserves your Leisure;

What he has done and suffer'd for your Sake,

What for the fair Cordelia's.

GLOST. Where's my Liege? Conduct me to his Knees, to hail

His second Birth of Empire: My dear Edgar

Has, with himself, reveal'd the King's blest Restauration.

LEAR. My poor dark Gloster.

GLOST. O let me kiss that once more scepter'd Hand!

LEAR. Hold, thou mistak'st the Majesty, kneel here;

Cordelia has our Pow'r, Cordelia's Queen.

Speak, is not that the noble suff'ring Edgar?

GLOST. My pious Son, more dear than my lost Eyes.

LEAR. I wrong'd him too, but here's the fair Amends.

EDG. Your Leave, my Liege, for an unwelcome Message.

Edmund (but that's a Trifle) is expired.

What more will touch you, your imperious Daughters,

Goneril and haughty Regan, both are dead,

Each by the other poison'd at a Banquet:

This, dying, they confess'd.

CORD. O fatal Period of ill-govern'd Lives!

LEAR. Ingrateful as they were, my Heart feels yet
A pang of Nature for their wretched Fall.—
But Edgar, I defer thy Joys too long:
Thou serv'dst distress'd Cordelia; take her crown'd,
Th' imperial Grace fresh blooming on her Brow;
Nay, Gloster, thou hast here a Father's Right,
Thy helping Hand t'heap Blessings on their Heads.

KENT. Old Kent throws in his hearty Wishes too.

EDG. The Gods and you too largely recompence
What I have done; the Gift strikes Merit dumb.

CORD. Nor do I blush to own myself o'er-paid
For all my Suff'rings past.

GLOST. Now, gentle Gods, give Gloster his Discharge.

LEAR. No, Gloster, thou hast Business yet for Life;
Thou, Kent, and I, retir'd to some close Cell,
Will gently pass our short Reserves of Time
In calm Reflections on our Fortunes past,
Cheer'd with Relation of the prosperous Reign
Of this celestial Pair; thus our Remains
Shall in an even Course of Thoughts be past,
Enjoy the present Hour, nor fear the last.

EDG. Our drooping Country now erects her Head,
Peace spreads her balmy Wings, and Plenty blooms.
Divine Cordelia, all the Gods can witness
How much thy Love to Empire I prefer!
Thy bright Example shall convince the World
(Whatever Storms of Fortune are decreed)
That Truth and Virtue shall at last succeed.

[Ex. Omnes.]

Tate's audacity in changing Shakespeare has caused much comment. Yet at least one highly respected critic, Samuel Johnson, approved of the change. Here is what he said:

. . . Shakespeare has suffered the virtue of Cordelia to perish in a just cause, contrary to the natural ideas of justice, to the hope of the reader, and, what is yet more strange, to the faith of chronicles. . . . A play in which the wicked prosper, and the virtuous miscarry, may doubtless be good, because it is a just representation of the common events of life: but since all reasonable beings naturally love justice, I cannot easily be persuaded, that the observation of justice makes a play worse; or, that if other excellencies are equal, the audience will not always rise better pleased from the final triumph of persecuted virtue.

In the present case the publick has decided. Cordelia, from the time of Tate, has always retired with victory and felicity. And, if my sensations could add any thing to the general sufferage, I might relate, that I was many years ago so shocked by Cordelia's death, that I know not whether I ever endured to read again the last scenes of the play till I undertook to revise them as an editor.

a. Work out an argument defending or attacking Tate's change. Notice that Johnson refers to the public's having its desires fulfilled. In our own day people who go to movies or read novels often ask for happy endings. Judging by what Tate did to Shakespeare, is this a reasonable request? Is Tate's *King Lear* still a tragedy? Is it now a melodrama? What effect does this change have on the earlier portions of the play? For example, what is the point of Act III, Scene vi, if the play ends happily? How is this point different if the play ends as Shakespeare ended it? Are the last lines of Tate's version a statement of the point of tragedy?

b. Find in Tate's version some verbal echoes of Shakespeare's. For example, compare Cordelia's opening speech with her speech in Act IV, scene vii (p. 138, col. 1), or Lear's "Ingrateful as they were, my Heart feels yet/A pang . . ." with his speech in Act V, scene iii (p. 149, col. 2), beginning "Howl, howl, howl! O, you are men of stones." What are the major differences in language? Which is more compact? More elevated? Simpler? Clearer? Richer? Abstract?

c. Shakespeare's Act V is difficult to manage on the stage because it is so full of action. How does Tate simplify this? Does Tate adequately tie up or unravel all the strands of the plot and dispose of all the characters? What are the major stage actions in Tate's version? Johnson says that a play may end happily rather than sadly "if other excellencies are equal." Are Tate's language and action equal in excellency to Shakespeare's? Could you argue that Tate is superior to Shakespeare at least in being clearer?

12. Trace out those portions of the play that embody the sub-plot of Edmund scheming against Edgar. What portion of the whole are they? How does Shakespeare join the sub-plot to the main plot? Where, for instance, do they come together? Here is what Samuel Johnson said about the sub-plot:

> The injury done by Edmund to the simplicity of the action is abundantly recompensed by the addition of variety, by the art with which he is made to co-operate with the chief design, and the opportunity which he gives the poet of combining perfidy with perfidy, and connecting the wicked son with the wicked daughters, to impress this important moral, that villany is never at a stop, that crimes lead to crimes, and at last terminate in ruin.

What kinds of "variety" does the sub-plot add to the main plot? If the play were simpler, might it be better for being more consistent and easier to follow? Or do you think Johnson is right when he says "the simplicity of the action is abundantly recompensed"?

THE HOUSE OF BERNARDA ALBA

BY FEDERICO GARCÍA LORCA

A DRAMA ABOUT WOMEN IN THE VILLAGES OF SPAIN

TRANSLATED BY JAMES GRAHAM-LUJÁN AND RICHARD L. O'CONNELL

CHARACTERS

BERNARDA (age: 60)
MARIA JOSEFA, Bernarda's Mother (age: 80)
ANGUSTIAS, Bernarda's Daughter (age: 39)
MAGDALENA, Bernarda's Daughter (age: 30)
AMELIA, Bernarda's Daughter (age: 27)

MARTIRIO, Bernarda's Daughter (age: 24)
ADELA, Bernarda's Daughter (age: 20)
A MAID (age: 50)
LA PONCIA, A Maid (age: 60)
PRUDENCIA (age: 50)
WOMEN IN MOURNING

The writer states that these Three Acts are intended as a photographic document.

ACT ONE

[*A very white room in Bernarda Alba's house. The walls are white. There are arched doorways with jute curtains tied back with tassels and ruffles. Wicker chairs. On the walls, pictures of unlikely landscapes full of nymphs or legendary kings.*

It is summer. A great brooding silence fills the stage. It is empty when the curtain rises. Bells can be heard tolling outside.]

FIRST SERVANT. [*Entering.*] The tolling of those bells hits me right between the eyes.

PONCIA. [*She enters, eating bread and sausage.*] More than two hours of mumbo jumbo. Priests are here from all the towns. The church looks beautiful. At the first responsory for the dead, Magdalena fainted.

FIRST SERVANT. She's the one who's left most alone.

PONCIA. She's the only one who loved her father. Ay! Thank God we're alone for a little. I came over to eat.

FIRST SERVANT. If Bernarda sees you . . . !

PONCIA. She's not eating today so she'd just as soon we'd all die of hunger! Domineering old tyrant! But she'll be fooled! I opened the sausage crock.

FIRST SERVANT. [*With an anxious sadness.*] Couldn't you give me some for my little girl, Poncia?

PONCIA. Go ahead! And take a fistful of peas too. She won't know the difference today.

VOICE. [*Within.*] Bernarda!

PONCIA. There's the grandmother!

Isn't she locked up tight?

FIRST SERVANT. Two turns of the key.

PONCIA. You'd better put the crossbar up too. She's got the fingers of a lock-picker!

VOICE. [*Within.*] Bernarda!

PONCIA. [*Shouting.*] She's coming! [*To The Servant.*] Clean everything up good. If Bernarda doesn't find things shining, she'll pull out the few hairs I have left.

SERVANT. What a woman!

PONCIA. Tyrant over everyone around her. She's perfectly capable of sitting on your heart and watching you die for a whole year without turning off that cold little smile she wears on her wicked face. Scrub, scrub those dishes!

SERVANT. I've got blood on my hands from so much polishing of everything.

PONCIA. She's the cleanest, she's the decentest, she's the highest everything! A good rest her poor husband's earned!

[*The bells stop.*]

SERVANT. Did all the relatives come?

PONCIA. Just hers. His people hate her. They came to see him dead and make the sign of the cross over him; that's all.

SERVANT. Are there enough chairs?

PONCIA. More than enough. Let them sit on the floor. When Bernarda's father died people stopped coming under this roof. She doesn't want them to see her in her "domain." Curse her!

SERVANT. She's been good to you.

PONCIA. Thirty years washing her sheets. Thirty years eating her leftovers. Nights of watching when she had a cough. Whole days peeking through a crack in the shutters to spy on the neighbors and carry her the tale. Life without secrets one from the other. But in spite of that—curse her! May the "pain of the piercing nail" strike her in the eyes.

SERVANT. Poncia!

PONCIA. But I'm a good watchdog! I bark when I'm told and bite beggars' heels when she sics me on 'em. My sons work in her fields—both of them already married, but one of these days I'll have enough.

SERVANT. And then . . . ?

PONCIA. Then I'll lock myself up in a room with her and spit in her face —a whole year. "Bernarda, here's for this, that and the other!" Till I leave her—just like a lizard the boys have squashed. For that's what she is—she and her whole family! Not that I envy her her life. Five girls are left her, five ugly daughters—not counting Angustias the eldest, by her first husband, who has money—the rest of them, plenty of eyelets to embroider, plenty of linen petticoats, but bread and grapes when it comes to inheritance.

SERVANT. Well, I'd like to have what they've got!

PONCIA. All we have is our hands and a hole in God's earth.

SERVANT. And that's the only earth they'll ever leave to us—to us who have nothing!

PONCIA. [*At the cupboard.*] This glass has some specks.

SERVANT. Neither soap nor rag will take them off.

[*The bells toll.*]

PONCIA. The last prayer! I'm going over and listen. I certainly like the way our priest sings. In the Pater Noster his voice went up, and up— like a pitcher filling with water little by little. Of course, at the end his voice cracked, but it's glorious to hear it. No, there never was anybody like the old Sacristan—Tronchapinos. At my mother's Mass, may she rest in peace, he sang. The walls shook—and when he said "Amen," it was as if a wolf had come into the church. [*Imitating him.*] A-a-a-a-men! [*She starts coughing.*]

SERVANT. Watch out—you'll strain your windpipe!

PONCIA. I'd rather strain something else! [*Goes out laughing.*]

[*The Servant scrubs. The bells toll.*]

SERVANT. [*Imitating the bells.*] Dong, dong, dong. Dong, dong, dong. May God forgive him!

BEGGAR WOMAN. [*At the door, with a little girl.*] Blesséd be God!

SERVANT. Dong, dong, dong. I hope he waits many years for us! Dong, dong, dong.

BEGGAR. [*Loudly, a little annoyed.*] Blesséd be God!

SERVANT. [*Annoyed.*] Forever and ever!

BEGGAR. I came for the scraps.

[*The bells stop tolling.*]

SERVANT. You can go right out the way you came in. Today's scraps are for me.

BEGGAR. But you have somebody to take care of you—and my little girl and I are all alone!

SERVANT. Dogs are alone too, and they live.

BEGGAR. They always give them to me.

SERVANT. Get out of here! Who let you in anyway? You've already tracked up the place. [*The Beggar Woman and Little Girl leave. The Servant goes on scrubbing.*] Floors finished with oil, cupboards, pedestals, iron beds—but us servants, we can suffer in silence—and live in mud huts with a plate and a spoon. I hope someday not a one will be left to tell it. [*The bells sound again.*] Yes, yes—ring away. Let them put you in a coffin with gold inlay and brocade to carry it on—you're no less dead than I'll be, so take what's coming to you, Antonio María Benavides—stiff in your broadcloth suit and your high boots—take what's coming to you! You'll never again lift my skirts behind the corral door!

[*From the rear door, two by two, women in mourning with large shawls and black skirts and fans, begin to enter. They come in slowly until the stage is full.*]

SERVANT. [*Breaking into a wail.*] Oh, Antonio María Benavides, now you'll never see these walls, nor break bread in this house again! I'm the one who loved you most of all your servants. [*Pulling her hair.*] Must I live on after you've gone? Must I go on living?

[*The two hundred women finish coming in, and Bernarda and her five daughters enter. Bernarda leans on a cane.*]

BERNARDA. [*To The Servant.*] Silence!

SERVANT. [*Weeping.*] Bernarda!

BERNARDA. Less shrieking and more work. You should have had all this cleaner for the wake. Get out. This isn't your place. [*The Servant goes off crying.*] The poor are like animals—they seem to be made of different stuff.

FIRST WOMAN. The poor feel their sorrows too.

BERNARDA. But they forget them in front of a plateful of peas.

FIRST GIRL. [*Timidly.*] Eating is necessary for living.

BERNARDA. At your age one doesn't talk in front of older people.

WOMAN. Be quiet, child.

BERNARDA. I've never taken lessons from anyone. Sit down. [*They sit down. Pause. Loudly:*] Magdalena, don't cry. If you want to cry, get under your bed. Do you hear me?

SECOND WOMAN. [*To Bernarda.*] Have you started to work the fields?

BERNARDA. Yesterday.

THIRD WOMAN. The sun comes down like lead.

FIRST WOMAN. I haven't known heat like this for years. [*Pause. They all fan themselves.*]

BERNARDA. Is the lemonade ready?

PONCIA. Yes, Bernarda. [*She brings in a large tray full of little white jars which she distributes.*]

BERNARDA. Give the men some.

PONCIA. They're already drinking in the patio.

BERNARDA. Let them get out the way they came in. I don't want them walking through here.

A GIRL. [*To Angustias.*] Pepe el Romano was with the men during the service.

ANGUSTIAS. There he was.

BERNARDA. His mother was there. She saw his mother. Neither she nor I saw Pepe . . .

GIRL. I thought . . .

BERNARDA. The one who *was* there was Darajalí, the widower. Very close to your Aunt. We all of us saw him.

SECOND WOMAN. [*Aside, in a low voice.*] Wicked, worse than wicked woman!

THIRD WOMAN. A tongue like a knife!

BERNARDA. Women in church shouldn't look at any man but the priest—and him only because he wears skirts. To turn your head is to be looking for the warmth of corduroy.

FIRST WOMAN. Sanctimonious old snake!

PONCIA. [*Between her teeth.*] Itching for a man's warmth.

BERNARDA. [*Beating with her cane on the floor.*] Bléssed be God!

ALL. [*Crossing themselves.*] Forever blesséd and praised.

BERNARDA. Rest in peace with holy company at your head.

ALL. Rest in peace!

BERNARDA. With the Angel Saint Michael, and his sword of justice.

ALL. Rest in peace!

BERNARDA. With the key that opens, and the hand that locks.

ALL. Rest in peace!

BERNARDA. With the most blesséd, and the little lights of the field.

ALL. Rest in peace!

BERNARDA. With our holy charity, and all souls on land and sea.

ALL. Rest in peace!

BERNARDA. Grant rest to your servant, Antonio María Benavides, and give him the crown of your blesséd glory.

ALL. Amen.

BERNARDA. [*She rises and chants.*] Requiem aeternam donat eis domine.

ALL. [*Standing and chanting in the Gregorian fashion.*] Et lux perpetua luce ab eis. [*They cross themselves.*]

FIRST WOMAN. May you have health to pray for his soul. [*They start filing out.*]

THIRD WOMAN. You won't lack loaves of hot bread.

SECOND WOMAN. Nor a roof for your daughters.

[*They are all filing in front of Bernarda and going out. Angustias leaves by the door to the patio.*]

FOURTH WOMAN. May you go on enjoying your wedding wheat.

PONCIA. [*She enters, carrying a money bag.*] From the men—this bag of money for Masses.

BERNARDA. Thank them—and let them have a glass of brandy.

GIRL. [*To Magdalena.*] Magdalena . . .

BERNARDA. [*To Magdalena, who is starting to cry.*] Sh-h-h-h! [*She beats with her cane on the floor. All the women have gone out. To the women who have just left.*] Go back to your houses and criticize everything you've seen! I hope it'll be many years before you pass under the archway of my door again.

PONCIA. You've nothing to complain about. The whole town came.

BERNARDA. Yes, to fill my house with the sweat from their wraps and the poison of their tongues.

AMELIA. Mother, don't talk like that.

BERNARDA. What other way is there to talk about this curséd village with no river—this village full of wells where you drink water always fearful it's been poisoned?

PONCIA. Look what they've done to the floor!

BERNARDA. As though a herd of goats had passed through. [*Poncia cleans the floor.*] Adela, give me a fan.

ADELA. Take this one. [*She gives her a round fan with green and red flowers.*]

BERNARDA. [*Throwing the fan on the floor.*] Is that the fan to give to a widow? Give me a black one and learn to respect your father's memory.

MARTIRIO. Take mine.

BERNARDA. And you?

MARTIRIO. I'm not hot.

BERNARDA. Well, look for another, because you'll need it. For the eight years of mourning, not a breath of air will get in this house from the street. We'll act as if we'd sealed up doors and windows with bricks. That's what happened in my father's house—and in my grandfather's house. Meantime, you can all start embroidering your hope-chest linens. I have twenty bolts of linen in the chest from which to cut sheets and coverlets. Magdalena can embroider them.

MAGDALENA. It's all the same to me.

ADELA. [*Sourly.*] If you don't want to embroider them—they can go without. That way yours will look better.

MAGDALENA. Neither mine nor yours. I know I'm not going to marry. I'd rather carry sacks to the mill. Anything except sit here day after day in this dark room.

BERNARDA. That's what a woman is for.

MAGDALENA. Cursed be all women.

BERNARDA. In this house you'll do what I order. You can't run with the story to your father any more. Needle and thread for women. Whiplash and mules for men. That's the way it has to be for people who have certain obligations. [*Adela goes out.*]

VOICE. Bernarda! Let me out!

BERNARDA. [*Calling.*] Let her out now!

[*The First Servant enters.*]

FIRST SERVANT. I had a hard time holding her. In spite of her eighty years, your mother's strong as an oak.

BERNARDA. It runs in the family. My grandfather was the same way.

SERVANT. Several times during the wake I had to cover her mouth with an empty sack because she wanted to shout out to you to give her dishwater to drink at least, and some dogmeat, which is what she says you feed her.

MARTIRIO. She's mean!

BERNARDA. [*To Servant.*] Let her get some fresh air in the patio.

SERVANT. She took her rings and the amethyst earrings out of the box, put them on, and told me she wants to get married. [*The daughters laugh.*]

BERNARDA. Go with her and be careful she doesn't get near the well.

SERVANT. You don't need to be afraid she'll jump in.

BERNARDA. It's not that—but the neighbors can see her there from their windows. [*The Servant leaves.*]

MARTIRIO. We'll go change our clothes.

BERNARDA. Yes, but don't take the 'kerchiefs from your heads. [*Adela enters.*] And Angustias?

ADELA. [*Meaningfully.*] I saw her looking out through the cracks of the back door. The men had just gone.

BERNARDA. And you, what were *you* doing at the door?

ADELA. I went there to see if the hens had laid.

BERNARDA. But the men had already gone!

ADELA. [*Meaningfully.*] A group of them were still standing outside.

BERNARDA. [*Furiously.*] Angustias! Angustias!

ANGUSTIAS. [*Entering.*] Did you want something?

BERNARDA. For what—and at whom —were you looking?

ANGUSTIAS. Nobody.

BERNARDA. Is it decent for a woman of your class to be running after a man the day of her father's funeral? Answer me! Whom were you looking at? [*Pause.*]

ANGUSTIAS. I . . .

BERNARDA. Yes, you!

ANGUSTIAS. Nobody.

BERNARDA. Soft! Honeytongue! [*She strikes her.*]

PONCIA. [*Running to her.*] Bernarda, calm down! [*She holds her. Angustias weeps.*]

BERNARDA. Get out of here, all of you! [*They all go out.*]

PONCIA. She did it not realizing what she was doing—although it's bad, of course. It really disgusted me to see her sneak along to the patio. Then she stood at the window listening to the men's talk which, as usual, was not the sort one should listen to.

BERNARDA. That's what they come to funerals for. [*With curiosity.*] What were they talking about?

PONCIA. They were talking about Paca la Roseta. Last night they tied her husband up in a stall, stuck her on a horse behind the saddle, and carried her away to the depths of the olive grove.

BERNARDA. And what did she do?

PONCIA. She? She was just as happy —they say her breasts were exposed and Maximiliano held on to her as if he were playing a guitar. Terrible!

BERNARDA. And what happened?

PONCIA. What had to happen. They came back almost at daybreak. Paca la Roseta with her hair loose and a wreath of flowers on her head.

BERNARDA. She's the only bad woman we have in the village.

PONCIA. Because she's not from here. She's from far away. And those who went with her are the sons of outsiders too. The men from here aren't up to a thing like that.

BERNARDA. No, but they like to see it, and talk about it, and suck their fingers over it.

PONCIA. They were saying a lot more things.

BERNARDA. [*Looking from side to side with a certain fear.*] What things?

PONCIA. I'm ashamed to talk about them.

BERNARDA. And my daughter heard them?

PONCIA. Of course!

BERNARDA. That one takes after her Aunts: white and mealy-mouthed and casting sheep's eyes at any little barber's compliment. Oh, what one has to go through and put up with so people will be decent and not too wild!

PONCIA. It's just that your daughters are of an age when they ought to have husbands. Mighty little trouble they give you. Angustias must be much more than thirty now.

BERNARDA. Exactly thirty-nine.

PONCIA. Imagine. And she's never had a beau . . .

BERNARDA. [*Furiously.*] None of them has ever had a beau and they've never needed one! They get along very well.

PONCIA. I didn't mean to offend you.

BERNARDA. For a hundred miles around there's no one good enough to come near them. The men in this town are not of their class. Do you want me to turn them over to the first shepherd?

PONCIA. You should have moved to another town.

BERNARDA. That's it. To sell them!

PONCIA. No, Bernarda, to change. . . . Of course, any place else, they'd be the poor ones.

BERNARDA. Hold your tormenting tongue!

PONCIA. One can't even talk to you. Do we, or do we not share secrets?

BERNARDA. We do not. You're a servant and I pay you. Nothing more.

PONCIA. But . . .

FIRST SERVANT. [*Entering.*] Don Arturo's here. He's come to see about dividing the inheritance.

BERNARDA. Let's go [*To The Servant.*] You start whitewashing the patio. [*To La Poncia.*] And you start putting all the dead man's clothes away in the chest.

PONCIA. We could give away some of the things.

BERNARDA. Nothing—not a button even! Not even the cloth we covered his face with. [*She goes out slowly, leaning on her cane. At the door she turns to look at the two servants. They go out. She leaves.*]

[*Amelia and Martirio enter.*]

AMELIA. Did you take the medicine?

MARTIRIO. For all the good it'll do me.

AMELIA. But you took it?

MARTIRIO. I do things without any faith, but like clockwork.

AMELIA. Since the new doctor came you look livelier.

MARTIRIO. I feel the same.

AMELIA. Did you notice? Adelaida wasn't at the funeral.

MARTIRIO. I know. Her sweetheart doesn't let her go out even to the front doorstep. Before, she was gay. Now, not even powder on her face.

AMELIA. These days a girl doesn't know whether to have a beau or not.

MARTIRIO. It's all the same.

AMELIA. The whole trouble is all these wagging tongues that won't let us live. Adelaida has probably had a bad time.

MARTIRIO. She's afraid of our mother. Mother is the only one who knows the story of Adelaida's father and where he got his lands. Everytime she comes here, Mother twists the knife in the wound. Her father killed his first wife's husband in Cuba so he could marry her himself. Then he left her there and went off with another woman who already had one daughter, and then he took up with this other girl, Adelaida's mother, and married her after his second wife died insane.

AMELIA. But why isn't a man like that put in jail?

MARTIRIO. Because men help each other cover up things like that and no one's able to tell on them.

AMELIA. But Adelaida's not to blame for any of that.

MARTIRIO. No. But history repeats itself. I can see that everything is a terrible repetition. And she'll have the same fate as her mother and grandmother—both of them wife to the man who fathered her.

AMELIA. What an awful thing!

MARTIRIO. It's better never to look at a man. I've been afraid of them since I was a little girl. I'd see them in the yard, yoking the oxen and lifting grain sacks, shouting and stamping, and I was always afraid to grow up for fear one of them would suddenly take me in his arms. God has made me weak and ugly and has definitely put such things away from me.

AMELIA. Don't say that! Enrique Humanas was after you and he liked you.

MARTIRIO. That was just people's ideas! One time I stood in my nightgown at the window until daybreak because he let me know through his shepherd's little girl that he was going to come, and he didn't. It was all just talk. Then he married someone else who had more money than I.

AMELIA. And ugly as the devil.

MARTIRIO. What do men care about ugliness? All they care about is lands, yokes of oxen, and a submissive bitch who'll feed them.

AMELIA. Ay!

[*Magdalena enters.*]

MAGDALENA. What are you doing?

MARTIRIO. Just here.

AMELIA. And you?

MAGDALENA. I've been going through all the rooms. Just to walk a little, and look at Grandmother's needlepoint pictures—the little woolen dog, and the black man wrestling with the lion—which we liked so much when we were children. Those were happier times. A wedding lasted ten days and evil tongues weren't in style. Today people are more refined. Brides wear white veils, just as in the cities, and we drink bottled wine, but we rot inside because of what people might say.

MARTIRIO. Lord knows what went on then!

AMELIA. [*To Magdalena.*] One of your shoelaces has come untied.

AMELIA. You'll step on it and fall.

MAGDALENA. One less!

MARTIRIO. And Adela?

MAGDALENA. Ah! She put on the green dress she made to wear for her birthday, went out to the yard, and began shouting: "Chickens! Chickens, look at me!" I had to laugh.

AMELIA. If Mother had only seen her!

MAGDALENA. Poor little thing! She's the youngest one of us and still has her illusions. I'd give something to see her happy.

[*Pause. Angustias crosses the stage, carrying some towels.*]

ANGUSTIAS. What time is it?

MAGDALENA. It must be twelve.

ANGUSTIAS. So late?

AMELIA. It's about to strike. [*Angustias goes out.*]

MAGDALENA. [*Meaningfully.*] Do you know what? [*Pointing after Angustias.*]

AMELIA. No.

MAGDALENA. Come on!

MARTIRIO. I don't know what you're talking about!

MAGDALENA. Both of you know it better than I do, always with your heads together, like two little sheep, but not letting anybody else in on it. I mean about Pepe el Romano!

MARTIRIO. Ah!

MAGDALENA. [*Mocking her.*] Ah! The whole town's talking about it. Pepe el Romano is coming to marry Angustias. Last night he was walking around the house and I think he's going to send a declaration soon.

MARTIRIO. I'm glad. He's a good man.

AMELIA. Me too. Angustias is well off.

MAGDALENA. Neither one of you is glad.

MARTIRIO. Magdalena! What do you mean?

MAGDALENA. If he were coming because of Angustias' looks, for Angustias as a woman, I'd be glad too, but he's coming for her money. Even though Angustias is our sister, we're her family here and we know she's old and sickly, and always has been the least attractive one of us! Because if she looked like a dressed-up stick at twenty, what can she look like now, now that she's forty?

MARTIRIO. Don't talk like that. Luck comes to the one who least expects it.

AMELIA. But Magdalena's right after all! Angustias has all her father's money; she's the only rich one in the house and that's why, now that Father's dead and the money will be divided, they're coming for her.

MAGDALENA. Pepe el Romano is twenty-five years old and the best looking man around here. The natural thing would be for him to be after you, Amelia, or our Adela, who's twenty—not looking for the least likely one in this house, a woman who, like her father, talks through her nose.

MARTIRIO. Maybe he likes that!

MAGDALENA. I've never been able to bear your hypocrisy.

MARTIRIO. Heavens!

[*Adela enters.*]

MAGDALENA. Did the chickens see you?

ADELA. What did you want me to do?

AMELIA. If Mother sees you, she'll drag you by your hair!

ADELA. I had a lot of illusions about this dress. I'd planned to put it on the day we were going to eat watermelons at the well. There wouldn't have been another like it.

MARTIRIO. It's a lovely dress.

ADELA. And one that looks very good on me. It's the best thing Magdalena's ever cut.

MAGDALENA. And the chickens, what did they say to you?

ADELA. They presented me with a few fleas that riddled my legs. [*They laugh.*]

MARTIRIO. What you can do is dye it black.

MAGDALENA. The best thing you can do is give it to Angustias for her wedding with Pepe el Romano.

ADELA. [*With hidden emotion.*] But

Pepe el Romano . . .

AMELIA. Haven't you heard about it?

ADELA. No.

MAGDALENA. Well, now you know!

ADELA. But it can't be!

MAGDALENA. Money can do anything.

ADELA. Is that why she went out after the funeral and stood looking through the door? [*Pause.*] And that man would . . .

MAGDALENA. Would do anything. [*Pause.*]

MARTIRIO. What are you thinking, Adela?

ADELA. I'm thinking that this mourning has caught me at the worst moment of my life for me to bear it.

MAGDALENA. You'll get used to it.

ADELA. [*Bursting out, crying with rage.*] I will not get used to it! I can't be locked up. I don't want my skin to look like yours. I don't want my skin's whiteness lost in these rooms. Tomorrow I'm going to put on my green dress and go walking in the streets. I want to go out!

[*The First Servant enters.*]

MAGDALENA. [*In a tone of authority.*] Adela!

SERVANT. The poor thing! How she misses her father. . . . [*She goes out.*]

MARTIRIO. Hush!

AMELIA. What happens to one will happen to all of us.

[*Adela grows calm.*]

MAGDALENA. The servant almost heard you.

SERVANT. [*Entering.*] Pepe el Romano is coming along at the end of the street. [*Amelia, Martirio and Magdalena run hurriedly.*]

MAGDALENA. Let's go see him!

[*They leave rapidly.*]

SERVANT. [*To Adela.*] Aren't you going?

ADELA. It's nothing to me.

SERVANT. Since he has to turn the corner, you'll see him better from the window of your room.

[*The Servant goes out. Adela is left on the stage, standing doubtfully; after a moment, she also leaves rapidly, going toward her room. Bernarda and La Poncia come in.*]

BERNARDA. Damned portions and shares.

PONCIA. What a lot of money is left to Angustias!

BERNARDA. Yes.

PONCIA. And for the others, considerably less.

BERNARDA. You've told me that three times now, when you know I don't want it mentioned! Considerably less; a lot less! Don't remind me any more. [*Angustias comes in, her face heavily made up.*] Angustias!

ANGUSTIAS. Mother.

BERNARDA. Have you dared to powder your face? Have you dared to wash your face on the day of your father's death?

ANGUSTIAS. He wasn't my father. Mine died a long time ago. Have you forgotten that already?

BERNARDA. You owe more to this man, father of your sisters, than to your own. Thanks to him, your fortune is intact.

ANGUSTIAS. We'll have to see about that first!

BERNARDA. Even out of decency! Out of respect!

ANGUSTIAS. Let me go out, Mother!

BERNARDA. Let you go out? After I've taken that powder off your face, I will. Spineless! Painted hussy! Just like your aunts! [*She removes the powder violently with her handkerchief.*] Now get out!

PONCIA. Bernarda, don't be so hateful!

BERNARDA. Even though my mother is crazy, I still have my five senses and I know what I'm doing.

[*They all enter.*]

MAGDALENA. What's going on here?

BERNARDA. Nothing's 'going on here'!

MAGDALENA. [*To Angustias.*] If you're fighting over the inheritance, you're the richest one and can hang on to it all.

ANGUSTIAS. Keep your tongue in your pocketbook!

BERNARDA. [*Beating on the floor.*] Don't fool yourselves into thinking you'll sway me. Until I go out of this house feet first I'll give the orders for myself and for you!

[*Voices are heard and María Josefa, Bernarda's mother, enters. She is very old and has decked out her head and breast with flowers.*]

MARIA JOSEFA. Bernarda, where is my mantilla? Nothing, nothing of what I own will be for any of you. Not my rings nor my black moiré dress. Because not a one of you is going to marry—not a one. Bernarda, give me my necklace of pearls.

BERNARDA. [*To The Servant.*] Why did you let her get in here?

SERVANT. [*Trembling.*] She got away from me!

MARIA JOSEFA. I ran away because I want to marry—I want to get married to a beautiful manly man from the shore of the sea. Because here the men run from women.

BERNARDA. Hush, hush, Mother!

MARIA JOSEFA. No, no—I won't hush. I don't want to see these single women, longing for marriage, turning their hearts to dust; and I want to go to my home town. Bernarda, I want a man to get married to and be happy with!

BERNARDA. Lock her up!

MARIA JOSEFA. Let me go out, Bernarda! [*The Servant seizes María Josefa.*]

BERNARDA. Help her, all of you! [*They all grab the old woman.*]

MARIA JOSEFA. I want to get away from here! Bernarda! To get married by the shore of the sea—by the shore of the sea!

QUICK CURTAIN

ACT TWO

[*A white room in Bernarda's house. The doors on the left lead to the bedrooms.*

Bernarda's Daughters are seated on low chairs, sewing. Magdalena is embroidering. La Poncia is with them.]

ANGUSTIAS. I've cut the third sheet.

MARTIRIO. That one goes to Amelia.

MAGDALENA. Angustias, shall I put Pepe's initials here too?

ANGUSTIAS. [*Dryly.*] No.

MAGDALENA. [*Calling, from off stage to Adela.*] Adela, aren't you coming?

AMELIA. She's probably stretched out on the bed.

PONCIA. Something's wrong with that one. I find her restless, trembling, frightened—as if a lizard were between her breasts.

MARTIRIO. There's nothing, more or less, wrong with her than there is with all of us.

MAGDALENA. All of us except

Angustias.

ANGUSTIAS. I feel fine, and anybody who doesn't like it can pop.

MAGDALENA. We all have to admit the nicest things about you are your figure and your tact.

ANGUSTIAS. Fortunately, I'll soon be out of this hell.

MAGDALENA. Maybe you won't get out!

MARTIRIO. Stop this talk!

ANGUSTIAS. Besides, a good dowry is better than dark eyes in one's face!

MAGDALENA. All you say just goes in one ear and out the other.

AMELIA. [To La Poncia.] Open the patio door and see if we can get a bit of a breeze. [La Poncia opens the door.]

MARTIRIO. Last night I couldn't sleep because of the heat.

AMELIA. Neither could I.

MAGDALENA. I got up for a bit of air. There was a black storm cloud and a few drops even fell.

PONCIA. It was one in the morning and the earth seemed to give off fire. I got up too. Angustias was still at the window with Pepe.

MAGDALENA. [With irony.] That late? What time did he leave?

ANGUSTIAS. Why do you ask, if you saw him?

AMELIA. He must have left about one-thirty.

ANGUSTIAS. Yes. How did you know?

AMELIA. I heard him cough and heard his mare's hoofbeats.

PONCIA. But I heard him leave around four.

ANGUSTIAS. It must have been someone else!

PONCIA. No, I'm sure of it!

AMELIA. That's what it seemed to me, too.

MAGDALENA. That's very strange!
[Pause.]

PONCIA. Listen, Angustias, what did he say to you the first time he came by your window?

ANGUSTIAS. Nothing. What should he say? Just talked.

MARTIRIO. It's certainly strange that two people who never knew each other should suddenly meet at a window and be engaged.

ANGUSTIAS. Well, I didn't mind.

AMELIA. I'd have felt very strange about it.

ANGUSTIAS. No, because when a man comes to a window he knows, from all the busybodies who come and go and fetch and carry, that he's going to be told "yes."

MARTIRIO. All right, but he'd have to ask you.

ANGUSTIAS. Of course!

AMELIA. [Inquisitively.] And how did he ask you?

ANGUSTIAS. Why, no way:—"You know I'm after you. I need a good, well brought up woman, and that's you—if it's agreeable."

AMELIA. These things embarrass me!

ANGUSTIAS. They embarrass me too, but one has to go through it!

PONCIA. And did he say anything more?

ANGUSTIAS. Yes, he did all the talking.

MARTIRIO. And you?

ANGUSTIAS. I couldn't have said a word. My heart was almost coming out of my mouth. It was the first time I'd ever been alone at night with a man.

MAGDALENA. And such a handsome man.

ANGUSTIAS. He's not bad looking!

PONCIA. Those things happen among

people who have an idea how to do things, who talk and say and move their hand. The first time my husband, Evaristo the Short-tailed, came to my window . . . Ha! Ha! Ha!

AMELIA. What happened?

PONCIA. It was very dark. I saw him coming along and as he went by he said, "Good evening." "Good evening," I said. Then we were both silent for more than half an hour. The sweat poured down my body. Then Evaristo got nearer and nearer as if he wanted to squeeze in through the bars and said in a very low voice—"Come here and let me feel you!"

[*They all laugh. Amelia gets up, runs, and looks through the door.*]

AMELIA. Ay, I thought mother was coming!

MAGDALENA. What she'd have done to us! [*They go on laughing.*]

AMELIA. Sh-h-h! She'll hear us.

PONCIA. Then he acted very decently. Instead of getting some other idea, he went to raising birds, until he died. You aren't married but it's good for you to know, anyway, that two weeks after the wedding a man gives up the bed for the table, then the table for the tavern, and the woman who doesn't like it can just rot, weeping in a corner.

AMELIA. You liked it.

PONCIA. I learned how to handle him!

MARTIRIO. Is it true that you sometimes hit him?

PONCIA. Yes, and once I almost poked out one of his eyes!

MAGDALENA. All women ought to be like that!

PONCIA. I'm one of your mother's school. One time I don't know what he

said to me, and then I killed all his birds—with the pestle!

[*They laugh.*]

MAGDALENA. Adela, child! Don't miss this.

AMELIA. Adela! [*Pause.*]

MAGDALENA. I'll go see! [*She goes out.*]

PONCIA. That child is sick!

MARTIRIO. Of course. She hardly sleeps!

PONCIA. What *does* she do, then?

MARTIRIO. How do I know what she does?

PONCIA. You probably know better than we do, since you sleep with just a wall between you.

ANGUSTIAS. Envy gnaws on people.

AMELIA. Don't exaggerate.

ANGUSTIAS. I can tell it in her eyes. She's getting the look of a crazy woman.

MARTIRIO. Don't talk about crazy women. This is one place you're not allowed to say that word.

[*Magdalena and Adela enter.*]

MAGDALENA. Didn't you say she was asleep?

ADELA. My body aches.

MARTIRIO. [*With a hidden meaning.*] Didn't you sleep well last night?

ADELA. Yes.

MARTIRIO. Then?

ADELA. [*Loudly.*] Leave me alone. Awake or asleep, it's no affair of yours. I'll do whatever I want to with my body.

MARTIRIO. I was just concerned about you!

ADELA.   Concerned?—curious! Weren't you sewing? Well, continue! I wish I were invisible so I could pass through a room without being asked where I was going!

SERVANT. [*Entering.*] Bernarda is calling you. The man with the laces is here.

[*All but Adela and La Poncia go out, and as Martirio leaves, she looks fixedly at Adela.*]

ADELA. Don't look at me like that! If you want, I'll give you my eyes, for they're younger, and my back to improve that hump you have, but look the other way when I go by.

PONCIA. Adela, she's your sister, and the one who most loves you besides!

ADELA. She follows me everywhere. Sometimes she looks in my room to see if I'm sleeping. She won't let me breathe, and always, "Too bad about that face!" "Too bad about that body! It's going to waste!" But I won't let that happen. My body will be for whomever I choose.

PONCIA. [*Insinuatingly, in a low voice.*] For Pepe el Romano, no?

ADELA. [*Frightened.*] What do you mean?

PONCIA. What I said, Adela!

ADELA. Shut up!

PONCIA. [*Loudly.*] Don't you think I've noticed?

ADELA. Lower your voice!

PONCIA. Then forget what you're thinking about!

ADELA. What do you know?

PONCIA. We old ones can see through walls. Where do you go when you get up at night?

ADELA. I wish you were blind!

PONCIA. But my head and hands are full of eyes, where something like this is concerned. I couldn't possibly guess your intentions. Why did you sit almost naked at your window, and with the light on and the window open, when Pepe passed by the second night he came to talk with your sister?

ADELA. That's not true!

PONCIA. Don't be a child! Leave your sister alone. And if you like Pepe el Romano, keep it to yourself. [*Adela weeps.*] Besides, who says you can't marry him? Your sister Angustias is sickly. She'll die with her first child. Narrow waisted, old—and out of my experience I can tell you she'll die. Then Pepe will do what all widowers do in these parts: he'll marry the youngest and most beautiful, and that's you. Live on that hope, forget him, anything; but don't go against God's law.

ADELA. Hush!

PONCIA. I won't hush!

ADELA. Mind your own business. Snooper, traitor!

PONCIA. I'm going to stick to you like a shadow!

ADELA. Instead of cleaning the house and then going to bed and praying for the dead, you root around like an old sow about goings on between men and women—so you can drool over them.

PONCIA. I keep watch; so people won't spit when they pass our door.

ADELA. What a tremendous affection you've suddenly conceived for my sister.

PONCIA. I don't have any affection for any of you. I want to live in a decent house. I don't want to be dirtied in my old age!

ADELA. Save your advice. It's already too late. For I'd leap not over you, just a servant, but over my mother to put out this fire I feel in my legs and my mouth. What can you possibly say about me? That I lock myself in my room and will not open the door? That I don't sleep? I'm smarter than you! See if you can catch the hare with your hands.

PONCIA. Don't defy me, Adela, don't defy me! Because I can shout, light lamps, and make bells ring.

ADELA. Bring four thousand yellow flares and set them about the walls of the yard. No one can stop what has to happen.

PONCIA. You like him that much?

ADELA. That much! Looking in his eyes I seem to drink his blood in slowly.

PONCIA. I won't listen to you.

ADELA. Well, you'll have to! I've been afraid of you. But now I'm stronger than you!

[Angustias enters.]

ANGUSTIAS. Always arguing!

PONCIA. Certainly. She insists that in all this heat I have to go bring her I don't know what from the store.

ANGUSTIAS. Did you buy me the bottle of perfume?

PONCIA. The most expensive one. And the face powder. I put them on the table in your room. [Angustias goes out.]

ADELA. And be quiet!

PONCIA. We'll see!

[Martirio and Amelia enter.]

MARTIRIO. [To Adela.] Did you see the laces?

AMELIA. Angustias', for her wedding sheets, are beautiful.

ADELA. [To Martirio, who is carrying some lace.] And these?

MARTIRIO. They're for me. For a nightgown.

ADELA. [With sarcasm.] One needs a sense of humor around here!

MARTIRIO. [Meaningfully.] But only for me to look at. I don't have to exhibit myself before anybody.

PONCIA. No one ever sees us in our nightgowns.

MARTIRIO. [Meaningfully, looking at Adela.] Sometimes they don't! But I love nice underwear. If I were rich, I'd have it made of Holland Cloth. It's one of the few tastes I've left.

PONCIA. These laces are beautiful for babies' caps and christening gowns. I could never afford them for my own. Now let's see if Angustias will use them for hers. Once she starts having children, they'll keep her running night and day.

MAGDALENA. I don't intend to sew a stitch on them.

AMELIA. And much less bring up some stranger's children. Look how our neighbors across the road are—making sacrifices for four brats.

PONCIA. They're better off than you. There at least they laugh and you can hear them fight.

MARTIRIO. Well, you go work for them, then.

PONCIA. No, fate has sent me to this nunnery!

[Tiny bells are heard distantly as though through several thicknesses of wall.]

MAGDALENA. It's the men going back to work.

PONCIA. It was three o'clock a minute ago.

MARTIRIO. With this sun!

ADELA. [Sitting down.] Ay! If only we could go out in the fields too!

MAGDALENA. [Sitting down.] Each class does what it has to!

MARTIRIO. [Sitting down.] That's it!

AMELIA. [Sitting down.] Ay!

PONCIA. There's no happiness like that in the fields right at this time of year. Yesterday morning the reapers arrived. Forty or fifty handsome young men.

MAGDALENA. Where are they from this year?

PONCIA. From far, far away. They came from the mountains! Happy! Like weathered trees! Shouting and throwing stones! Last night a woman who dresses in sequins and dances, with an accordion, arrived, and fifteen of them made a deal with her to take her to the olive grove. I saw them from far away. The one who talked with her was a boy with green eyes—tight knit as a sheaf of wheat.

AMELIA. Really?

ADELA. Are you sure?

PONCIA. Years ago another one of those women came here, and I myself gave my eldest son some money so he could go. Men need things like that.

ADELA. Everything's forgiven *them*.

AMELIA. To be born a woman's the worst possible punishment.

MAGDALENA. Even our eyes aren't our own.

[*A distant song is heard, coming nearer.*]

PONCIA. There they are. They have a beautiful song.

AMELIA. They're going out to reap now.

CHORUS.
   The reapers have set out
   Looking for ripe wheat;
   They'll carry off the hearts
   Of any girls they meet.

[*Tambourines and carrañacas are heard. Pause. They all listen in the silence cut by the sun.*]

AMELIA. And they don't mind the sun!

MARTIRIO. They reap through flames.

ADELA. How I'd like to be a reaper so I could come and go as I pleased. Then we could forget what's eating us all.

MARTIRIO. What do you have to forget?

ADELA. Each one of us has something.

MARTIRIO. [*Intensely.*] Each one!

PONCIA. Quiet! Quiet!

CHORUS. [*Very distantly.*]
Throw wide your doors and windows,
You girls who live in the town
The reaper asks you for roses
With which to deck his crown.

PONCIA. What a song!

MARTIRIO. [*With nostalgia.*]
Throw wide your doors and windows,
You girls who live in the town.

ADELA. [*Passionately.*]
The reaper asks you for roses
With which to deck his crown.

[*The song grows more distant.*]

PONCIA. Now they're turning the corner.

ADELA. Let's watch them from the window of my room.

PONCIA. Be careful not to open the shutters too much because they're likely to give them a push to see who's looking.

[*The three leave. Martirio is left sitting on the low chair with her head between her hands.*]

AMELIA. [*Drawing near her.*] What's wrong with you?

MARTIRIO. The heat makes me feel ill.

AMELIA. And it's no more than that?

MARTIRIO. I was wishing it were November, the rainy days, the frost— anything except this unending summertime.

AMELIA. It'll pass and come again.

MARTIRIO. Naturally. [*Pause.*] What time did you go to sleep last night?

AMELIA. I don't know. I sleep like a log. Why?

MARTIRIO. Nothing. Only I thought I heard someone in the yard.

AMELIA. Yes?

MARTIRIO. Very late.

AMELIA. And weren't you afraid?

MARTIRIO. No. I've heard it other nights.

AMELIA. We'd better watch out! Couldn't it have been the shepherds?

MARTIRIO. The shepherds come at six.

AMELIA. Maybe a young, unbroken mule?

MARTIRIO. [*To herself, with double meaning.*] That's it! That's it. An unbroken little mule.

AMELIA. We'll have to set a watch.

MARTIRIO. No. No. Don't say anything. It may be I've just imagined it.

AMELIA. Maybe. [*Pause. Amelia starts to go.*]

MARTIRIO. Amelia!

AMELIA. [*At the door.*] What? [*Pause.*]

MARTIRIO. Nothing. [*Pause.*]

AMELIA. Why did you call me? [*Pause.*]

MARTIRIO. It just came out. I didn't mean to. [*Pause.*]

AMELIA. Lie down for a little.

ANGUSTIAS. [*She bursts in furiously, in a manner that makes a great contrast with previous silence.*] Where's that picture of Pepe I had under my pillow? Which one of you has it?

MARTIRIO. No one.

AMELIA. You'd think he was a silver St. Bartholomew.

ANGUSTIAS. Where's the picture? [*Poncia, Magdalena and Adela enter.*]

ADELA. What picture?

ANGUSTIAS. One of you has hidden it on me.

MAGDALENA. Do you have the effrontery to say that?

ANGUSTIAS. I had it in my room, and now it isn't there.

MARTIRIO. But couldn't it have jumped out into the yard at midnight? Pepe likes to walk around in the moonlight.

ANGUSTIAS. Don't joke with me! When he comes I'll tell him.

PONCIA. Don't do that! Because it'll turn up. [*Looking at Adela.*]

ANGUSTIAS. I'd like to know which one of you has it.

ADELA. [*Looking at Martirio.*] Somebody has it! But not me!

MARTIRIO. [*With meaning.*] Of course not you!

BERNARDA. [*Entering, with her cane.*] What scandal is this in my house in the heat's heavy silence? The neighbors must have their ears glued to the walls.

ANGUSTIAS. They've stolen my sweetheart's picture!

BERNARDA. [*Fiercely.*] Who? Who?

ANGUSTIAS. They have!

BERNARDA. Which one of you? [*Silence.*] Answer me! [*Silence. To La Poncia.*] Search their rooms! Look in their beds. This comes of not tying you up with shorter leashes. But I'll teach you now! [*To Angustias.*] Are you sure?

ANGUSTIAS. Yes.

BERNARDA. Did you look every-where?

ANGUSTIAS. Yes, Mother.

[*They all stand in an embarrassed silence.*]

BERNARDA. At the end of my life— to make me drink the bitterest poison a mother knows. [*To Poncia.*] Did you find it?

PONCIA. Here it is.

BERNARDA. Where did you find it?

PONCIA. It was . . .

BERNARDA. Say it! Don't be afraid.

PONCIA. [*Wonderingly.*] Between the sheets in Martirio's bed.

BERNARDA. [*To Martirio.*] Is that true?

MARTIRIO. It's true.

BERNARDA. [*Advancing on her, beating her with her cane.*] You'll come to a bad end yet, you hypocrite! Trouble maker!

MARTIRIO. [*Fiercely.*] Don't hit me, Mother!

BERNARDA. All I want to!

MARTIRIO. If I let you! You hear me? Get back!

PONCIA. Don't be disrespectful to your mother!

ANGUSTIAS. [*Holding Bernarda.*] Let her go, please!

BERNARDA. Not even tears in your eyes.

MARTIRIO. I'm not going to cry just to please you.

BERNARDA. Why did you take the picture?

MARTIRIO. Can't I play a joke on my sister? What else would I want it for?

ADELA. [*Leaping forward, full of jealousy.*] It wasn't a joke! You never liked to play jokes. It was something else bursting in her breast—trying to come out. Admit it openly now.

MARTIRIO. Hush, and don't make me speak; for if I should speak the walls would close together one against the other with shame.

ADELA. An evil tongue never stops inventing lies.

BERNARDA. Adela!

MAGDALENA. You're crazy.

AMELIA. And you stone us all with your evil suspicions.

MARTIRIO. But some others do things more wicked!

ADELA. Until all at once they stand forth stark naked and the river carries them along.

BERNARDA. Spiteful!

ANGUSTIAS. It's not my fault Pepe el Romano chose me!

ADELA. For your money.

ANGUSTIAS. Mother!

BERNARDA. Silence!

MARTIRIO. For your fields and your orchards.

MAGDALENA. That's only fair.

BERNARDA. Silence, I say! I saw the storm coming but I didn't think it'd burst so soon. Oh, what an avalanche of hate you've thrown on my heart! But I'm not old yet—I have five chains for you, and this house my father built, so not even the weeds will know of my desolation. Out of here! [*They go out. Bernarda sits down desolately. La Poncia is standing close to the wall. Bernarda recovers herself, and beats on the floor.*] I'll have to let them feel the weight of my hand! Bernarda, remember your duty!

PONCIA. May I speak?

BERNARDA. Speak. I'm sorry you heard. A stranger is always out of place in a family.

PONCIA. What I've seen, I've seen.

BERNARDA. Angustias must get married right away.

PONCIA. Certainly. We'll have to get her away from here.

BERNARDA. Not her, him!

PONCIA. Of course. He's the one to get away from here. You've thought it all out.

BERNARDA. I'm not thinking. There

are things that shouldn't and can't be thought out. I give orders.

PONCIA. And you think he'll be satisfied to go away?

BERNARDA. [*Rising.*] What are you imagining now?

PONCIA. He will, of course, marry Angustias.

BERNARDA. Speak up! I know you well enough to see that your knife's out for me.

PONCIA. I never knew a warning could be called murder.

BERNARDA. Have you some "warning" for me?

PONCIA. I'm not making any accusations, Bernarda. I'm only telling you to open your eyes and you'll see.

BERNARDA. See what?

PONCIA. You've always been smart, Bernarda. You've seen other people's sins a hundred miles away. Many times I've thought you could read minds. But, your children are your children, and now you're blind.

BERNARDA. Are you talking about Martirio?

PONCIA. Well, yes—about Martirio . . . [*With curiosity.*] I wonder why she hid the picture?

BERNARDA. [*Shielding her daughter.*] After all, she says it was a joke. What else could it be?

PONCIA. [*Scornfully.*] Do you believe that?

BERNARDA. [*Sternly.*] I don't merely believe it. It's so!

PONCIA. Enough of this. We're talking about your family. But if we were talking about your neighbor across the way, what would it be?

BERNARDA. Now you're beginning to pull the point of the knife out.

PONCIA. [*Always cruelly.*] No, Bernarda. Something very grave is happening here. I don't want to put the blame on your shoulders, but you've never given your daughters any freedom. Martirio is lovesick, I don't care what you say. Why didn't you let her marry Enrique Humanas? Why, on the very day he was coming to her window did you send him a message not to come?

BERNARDA. [*Loudly.*] I'd do it a thousand times over! My blood won't mingle with the Humanas' while I live! His father was a shepherd.

PONCIA. And you see now what's happening to you with these airs!

BERNARDA. I have them because I can afford to. And you don't have them because you know where you came from!

PONCIA. [*With hate.*] Don't remind me! I'm old now. I've always been grateful for your protection.

BERNARDA. [*Emboldened.*] You don't seem so!

PONCIA. [*With hate, behind softness.*] Martirio will forget this.

BERNARDA. And if she doesn't—the worse for her. I don't believe this is that "very grave thing" that's happening here. Nothing's happening here. It's just that you wish it would! And if it should happen one day, you can be sure it won't go beyond these walls.

PONCIA. I'm not so sure of that! There are people in town who can also read hidden thoughts, from afar.

BERNARDA. How you'd like to see me and my daughters on our way to a whorehouse!

PONCIA. No one knows her own destiny!

BERNARDA. I know my destiny! And my daughters! The whorehouse was for a certain woman, already dead. . . .

PONCIA. [*Fiercely.*] Bernarda, respect the memory of my mother!

BERNARDA. Then don't plague me with your evil thoughts!

[*Pause.*]

PONCIA. I'd better stay out of everything.

BERNARDA. That's what you ought to do. Work and keep your mouth shut. The duty of all who work for a living.

PONCIA. But we can't do that. Don't you think it'd be better for Pepe to marry Martirio or . . . yes! . . . Adela?

BERNARDA. No, I *don't* think so.

PONCIA. [*With meaning.*] Adela! She's Romano's real sweetheart!

BERNARDA. Things are never the way we want them!

PONCIA. But it's hard work to turn them from their destined course. For Pepe to be with Angustias seems wrong to me—and to other people— and even to the wind. Who knows if they'll get what they want?

BERNARDA. There you go again! Sneaking up on me—giving me bad dreams. But I won't listen to you, because if all you say should come to pass—I'd scratch your face.

PONCIA. Frighten someone else with that.

BERNARDA. Fortunately, my daughters respect me and have never gone against my will!

PONCIA. That's right! But, as soon as they break loose they'll fly to the rooftops!

BERNARDA. And I'll bring them down with stones!

PONCIA. Oh, yes! You were always the bravest one!

BERNARDA. I've always enjoyed a good fight!

PONCIA. But aren't people strange. You should see Angustias' enthusiasm for her lover, at her age! And he seems very smitten too. Yesterday my oldest son told me that when he passed by with the oxen at four-thirty in the morning they were still talking.

BERNARDA. At four-thirty?

ANGUSTIAS. [*Entering.*] That's a lie!

PONCIA. That's what he told me.

BERNARDA. [*To Angustias.*] Speak up!

ANGUSTIAS. For more than a week Pepe has been leaving at one. May God strike me dead if I'm lying.

MARTIRIO. [*Entering.*] I heard him leave at four too.

BERNARDA. But did you see him with your eyes?

MARTIRIO. I didn't want to look out. Don't you talk now through the side window?

ANGUSTIAS. We talk through my bedroom window.

[*Adela appears at the door.*]

MARTIRIO. Then . . .

BERNARDA. What's going on here?

PONCIA. If you're not careful, you'll find out! At least Pepe was at *one* of your windows—and at four in the morning too!

BERNARDA. Are you sure of that?

PONCIA. You can't be sure of anything in this life!

ADELA. Mother, don't listen to someone who wants us to lose everything we have.

BERNARDA. I know how to take care of myself! If the townspeople want to come bearing false witness against me, they'll run into a stone wall! Don't any of you talk about this! Sometimes other people try to stir up a wave of filth to drown us.

MARTIRIO. I don't like to lie.

PONCIA. So there must be something.

BERNARDA. There won't be anything. I was born to have my eyes always open. Now I'll watch without closing them 'til I die.

ANGUSTIAS. I have the right to know.

BERNARDA. You don't have any right except to obey. No one's going to fetch and carry for me. [*To La Poncia.*] And don't meddle in our affairs. No one will take a step without my knowing it.

SERVANT. [*Entering.*] There's a big crowd at the top of the street, and all the neighbors are at their doors!

BERNARDA. [*To Poncia.*] Run see what's happening! [*The Girls are about to run out.*] Where are you going? I always knew you for window-watching women and breakers of your mourning. All of you, to the patio! [*They go out. Bernarda leaves. Distant shouts are heard.*]

[*Martirio and Adela enter and listen, not daring to step farther than the front door.*]

MARTIRIO. You can be thankful I didn't happen to open my mouth.

ADELA. I would have spoken too.

MARTIRIO. And what were you going to say? Wanting isn't doing!

ADELA. I do what I can and what happens to suit me. You've wanted to, but haven't been able.

MARTIRIO. You won't go on very long.

ADELA. I'll have everything!

MARTIRIO. I'll tear you out of his arms!

ADELA. [*Pleadingly.*] Martirio, let me be!

MARTIRIO. None of us will have him!

ADELA. He wants me for his house!

MARTIRIO. I saw how he embraced you!

ADELA. I didn't want him to. It's as if I were dragged by a rope.

MARTIRIO. I'll see you dead first!

[*Magdalena and Angustias look in. The tumult is increasing. A Servant enters with Bernarda. Poncia also enters from another door.*]

PONCIA. Bernarda!

BERNARDA. What's happening?

PONCIA. Librada's daughter, the unmarried one, had a child and no one knows whose it is!

ADELA. A child?

PONCIA. And to hide her shame she killed it and hid it under the rocks, but the dogs, with more heart than most Christians, dug it out and, as though directed by the hand of God, left it at her door. Now they want to kill her. They're dragging her through the streets—and down the paths and across the olive groves the men are coming, shouting so the fields shake.

BERNARDA. Yes, let them all come with olive whips and hoe handles— let them all come and kill her!

ADELA. No, not to kill her!

MARTIRIO. Yes—and let us go out too!

BERNARDA. And let whoever loses her decency pay for it!

[*Outside a woman's shriek and a great clamor is heard.*]

ADELA. Let her escape! Don't you go out!

MARTIRIO. [*Looking at Adela.*] Let her pay what she owes!

BERNARDA. [*At the archway.*] Finish her before the guards come! Hot coals in the place where she sinned!

ADELA. [*Holding her belly.*] No! No!

BERNARDA. Kill her! Kill her!

CURTAIN

ACT THREE

[*Four white walls, lightly washed in blue, of the interior patio of Bernarda Alba's house. The doorways, illumined by the lights inside the rooms, give a tenuous glow to the stage.*

At the center there is a table with a shaded oil lamp about which Bernarda and her Daughters are eating. La Poncia serves them. Prudencia sits apart. When the curtain rises, there is a great silence interrupted only by the noise of plates and silverware.]

PRUDENCIA. I'm going. I've made you a long visit. [*She rises.*]

BERNARDA. But wait, Prudencia. We never see one another.

PRUDENCIA. Have they sounded the last call to rosary?

PONCIA. Not yet. [*Prudencia sits down again.*]

BERNARDA. And your husband, how's he getting on?

PRUDENCIA. The same.

BERNARDA. We never see him either.

PRUDENCIA. You know how he is. Since he quarrelled with his brothers over the inheritance, he hasn't used the front door. He takes a ladder and climbs over the back wall.

BERNARDA. He's a real man! And your daughter?

PRUDENCIA. He's never forgiven her.

BERNARDA. He's right.

PRUDENCIA. I don't know what he told you. I suffer because of it.

BERNARDA. A daughter who's disobedient stops being a daughter and becomes an enemy.

PRUDENCIA. I let water run. The only consolation I've left is to take refuge in the church, but, since I'm losing my sight, I'll have to stop coming so the children won't make fun of me. [*A heavy blow is heard against the walls.*] What's that?

BERNARDA. The stallion. He's locked in the stall and he kicks against the wall of the house. [*Shouting.*] Tether him and take him out in the yard! [*In a lower voice.*] He must be too hot.

PRUDENCIA. Are you going to put the new mares to him?

BERNARDA. At daybreak.

PRUDENCIA. You've known how to increase your stock.

BERNARDA. By dint of money and struggling.

PONCIA. [*Interrupting.*] And she has the best herd in these parts. It's a shame that prices are low.

BERNARDA. Do you want a little cheese and honey?

PRUDENCIA. I have no appetite.

[*The blow is heard again.*]

PONCIA. My God!

PRUDENCIA. It quivered in my chest!

BERNARDA. [*Rising, furiously.*] Do I have to say things twice? Let him out to roll on the straw. [*Pause. Then, as though speaking to The Stableman.*] Well then, lock the mares in the corral, but let him run free or he may kick down the walls. [*She returns to the table and sits again.*] Ay, what a life!

PRUDENCIA. You have to fight like a man.

BERNARDA. That's it. [*Adela gets up from the table.*] Where are you going?

ADELA. For a drink of water.

BERNARDA. [*Raising her voice.*] Bring a pitcher of cool water. [*To Adela.*] You can sit down. [*Adela sits down.*]

PRUDENCIA. And Angustias, when will she get married?

BERNARDA. They're coming to ask for her within three days.

PRUDENCIA. You must be happy.

ANGUSTIAS. Naturally!

AMELIA. [*To Magdalena.*] You've spilled the salt!

MAGDALENA. You can't possibly have worse luck than you're having.

AMELIA. It always brings bad luck.

BERNARDA. That's enough!

PRUDENCIA. [*To Angustias.*] Has he given you the ring yet?

ANGUSTIAS. Look at it. [*She holds it out.*]

PRUDENCIA. It's beautiful. Three pearls. In my day, pearls signified tears.

ANGUSTIAS. But things have changed now.

ADELA. I don't think so. Things go on meaning the same. Engagement rings should be diamonds.

PONCIA. The most appropriate.

BERNARDA. With pearls or without them, things are as one proposes.

MARTIRIO. Or as God disposes.

PRUDENCIA. I've been told your furniture is beautiful.

BERNARDA. It cost sixteen thousand *reales.*

PONCIA. [*Interrupting.*] The best is the wardrobe with the mirror.

PRUDENCIA. I never saw a piece like that.

BERNARDA. We had chests.

PRUDENCIA. The important thing is that everything be for the best.

ADELA. And that you never know.

BERNARDA. There's no reason why it shouldn't be.

[*Bells are heard very distantly.*]

PRUDENCIA. The last call. [*To Angustias.*] I'll be coming back to have you show me your clothes.

ANGUSTIAS. Whenever you like.

PRUDENCIA. Good evening—God bless you!

BERNARDA. Good-bye, Prudencia.

ALL FIVE DAUGHTERS. [*At the same time.*] God go with you! [*Pause. Prudencia goes out.*]

BERNARDA. Well, we've eaten. [*They rise.*]

ADELA. I'm going to walk as far as the gate to stretch my legs and get a bit of fresh air.

[*Magdalena sits down in a low chair and leans against the wall.*]

AMELIA. I'll go with you.

MARTIRIO. I too.

ADELA. [*With contained hate.*] I'm not going to get lost!

AMELIA. One needs company at night. [*They go out. Bernarda sits down. Angustias is clearing the table.*]

BERNARDA. I've told you once already! I want you to talk to your sister Martirio. What happened about the picture was a joke and you must forget it.

ANGUSTIAS. You know she doesn't like me.

BERNARDA. Each one knows what she thinks inside. I don't pry into anyone's heart, but I want to put up a good front and have family harmony. You understand?

ANGUSTIAS. Yes.

BERNARDA. Then that's settled.

MAGDALENA. [*She is almost asleep.*] Besides, you'll be gone in no time. [*She falls asleep.*]

ANGUSTIAS. Not soon enough for me.

BERNARDA. What time did you stop talking last night?

ANGUSTIAS. Twelve-thirty.

BERNARDA. What does Pepe talk about?

ANGUSTIAS. I find him absent-minded. He always talks to me as though he were thinking of something else. If I ask him what's the matter, he answers—"We men have our worries."

BERNARDA. You shouldn't ask him. And when you're married, even less. Speak if he speaks, and look at him when he looks at you. That way you'll get along.

ANGUSTIAS. But, Mother, I think he's hiding things from me.

BERNARDA. Don't try to find out. Don't ask him, and above all, never let him see you cry.

ANGUSTIAS. I should be happy, but I'm not.

BERNARDA. It's all the same.

ANGUSTIAS. Many nights I watch Pepe very closely through the window bars and he seems to fade away—as though he were hidden in a cloud of dust like those raised by the flocks.

BERNARDA. That's just because you're not strong.

ANGUSTIAS. I hope so!

BERNARDA. Is he coming tonight?

ANGUSTIAS. No, he went into town with his mother.

BERNARDA. Good, we'll get to bed early. Magdalena!

ANGUSTIAS. She's asleep.

[Adela, Martirio and Amelia enter.]

AMELIA. What a dark night!

ADELA. You can't see two steps in front of you.

MARTIRIO. A good night for robbers, for anyone who needs to hide.

ADELA. The stallion was in the middle of the corral. White. Twice as large. Filling all the darkness.

AMELIA. It's true. It was frightening. Like a ghost.

ADELA. The sky has stars as big as fists.

MARTIRIO. This one stared at them till she almost cracked her neck.

ADELA. Don't you like them up there?

MARTIRIO. What goes on over the roof doesn't mean a thing to me. I have my hands full with what happens under it.

ADELA. Well, that's the way it goes with you!

BERNARDA. And it goes the same for you as for her.

ANGUSTIAS. Good night.

ADELA. Are you going to bed now?

ANGUSTIAS. Yes, Pepe isn't coming tonight. [She goes out.]

ADELA. Mother, why, when a star falls or lightning flashes, does one say:

Holy Barbara, blessed on high
May your name be in the sky
With holy water written high?

BERNARDA. The old people know many things we've forgotten.

AMELIA. I close my eyes so I won't see them.

ADELA. Not I. I like to see what's quiet and been quiet for years on end, running with fire.

MARTIRIO. But all that has nothing to do with us.

BERNARDA. And it's better not to think about it.

ADELA. What a beautiful night! I'd like to stay up till very late and enjoy the breeze from the fields.

BERNARDA. But we have to go to bed. Magdalena!

AMELIA. She's just dropped off.

BERNARDA. Magdalena!

MAGDALENA. [Annoyed.] Leave me alone!

BERNARDA. To bed!

MAGDALENA. [Rising, in a bad humor.] You don't give anyone a moment's peace! [She goes off grumbling.]

AMELIA. Good night! [*She goes out.*]

BERNARDA. You two get along, too.

MARTIRIO. How is it Angustias' sweetheart isn't coming tonight?

BERNARDA. He went on a trip.

MARTIRIO. [*Looking at Adela.*] Ah!

ADELA. I'll see you in the morning! [*She goes out. Martirio drinks some water and goes out slowly, looking at the door to the yard. La Poncia enters.*]

PONCIA. Are you still here?

BERNARDA. Enjoying this quiet and not seeing anywhere the "very grave thing" that's happening here—according to you.

PONCIA. Bernarda, let's not go any further with this.

BERNARDA. In this house there's no question of a yes or a no. My watchfulness can take care of anything.

PONCIA. Nothing's happening outside. That's true, all right. Your daughters act and are as though stuck in a cupboard. But neither you nor anyone else can keep watch inside a person's heart.

BERNARDA. My daughters breathe calmly enough.

PONCIA. That's your business, since you're their mother. I have enough to do just with serving you.

BERNARDA. Yes, you've turned quiet now.

PONCIA. I keep my place—that's all.

BERNARDA. The trouble is you've nothing to talk about. If there were grass in this house, you'd make it your business to put the neighbors' sheep to pasture here.

PONCIA. I hide more than you think.

BERNARDA. Do your sons still see Pepe at four in the morning? Are they still repeating this house's evil litany?

PONCIA. They say nothing.

BERNARDA. Because they can't. Because there's nothing for them to sink their teeth in. And all because my eyes keep constant watch!

PONCIA. Bernarda, I don't want to talk about this because I'm afraid of what you'll do. But don't you feel so safe.

BERNARDA. Very safe!

PONCIA. Who knows, lightning might strike suddenly. Who knows but what all of a sudden, in a rush of blood, your heart might stop.

BERNARDA. Nothing will happen here. I'm on guard now against all your suspicions.

PONCIA. All the better for you.

BERNARDA. Certainly, all the better!

SERVANT. [*Entering.*] I've just finished with the dishes. Is there anything else, Bernarda?

BERNARDA. [*Rising.*] Nothing. I'm going to get some rest.

PONCIA. What time do you want me to call you?

BERNARDA. No time. Tonight I intend to sleep well. [*She goes out.*]

PONCIA. When you're powerless against the sea, it's easier to turn your back on it and not look at it.

SERVANT. She's so proud! She herself pulls the blindfold over her eyes.

PONCIA. I can do nothing. I tried to head things off, but now they frighten me too much. You feel this silence?—in each room there's a thunderstorm—and the day it breaks, it'll sweep all of us along with it. But I've said what I had to say.

SERVANT. Bernarda thinks nothing can stand against her, yet she doesn't know the strength a man has among women alone.

PONCIA. It's not all the fault of Pepe el Romano. It's true last year he was running after Adela; and she was crazy about him—but she ought to keep her place and not lead him on. A man's a man.

SERVANT. And some there are who believe he didn't have to talk many times with Adela.

PONCIA. That's true. [*In a low voice.*] And some other things.

SERVANT. I don't know what's going to happen here.

PONCIA. How I'd like to sail across the sea and leave this house, this battleground, behind!

SERVANT. Bernarda's hurrying the wedding and it's possible nothing will happen.

PONCIA. Things have gone much too far already. Adela is set no matter what comes, and the rest of them watch without rest.

SERVANT. Martirio too . . . ?

PONCIA. That one's the worst. She's a pool of poison. She sees El Romano is not for her, and she'd sink the world if it were in her hand to do so.

SERVANT. How bad they all are!

PONCIA. They're women without men, that's all. And in such matters even blood is forgotten. Sh-h-h-h! [*She listens.*]

SERVANT. What's the matter?

PONCIA. [*She rises.*] The dogs are barking.

SERVANT. Someone must have passed by the back door.

[*Adela enters wearing a white petticoat and corselet.*]

PONCIA. Aren't you in bed yet?

ADELA. I want a drink of water. [*She drinks from a glass on the table.*]

PONCIA. I imagined you were asleep.

ADELA. I got thirsty and woke up. Aren't you two going to get some rest?

SERVANT. Soon now.

[*Adela goes out.*]

PONCIA. Let's go.

SERVANT. We've certainly earned some sleep. Bernarda doesn't let me rest the whole day.

PONCIA. Take the light.

SERVANT. The dogs are going mad.

PONCIA. They're not going to let us sleep.

[*They go out. The stage is left almost dark. María Josefa enters with a lamb in her arms.*]

MARIA JOSEFA. [*Singing.*]
Little lamb, child of mine,
Let's go to the shore of the sea,
The tiny ant will be at his doorway,
I'll nurse you and give you your bread.
Bernarda, old leopard-face,
And Magdalena, hyena-face,
Little lamb . . .
Rock, rock-a-bye,
Let's go to the palms at Bethlehem's gate.

[*She laughs.*]
Neither you nor I would want to sleep
The door will open by itself
And on the beach we'll go and hide
In a little coral cabin.
Bernarda, old leopard-face,
And Magdalena, hyena-face,
Little lamb . . .
Rock, rock-a-bye,
Let's go to the palms at Bethlehem's gate.

[*She goes off singing.*]

[*Adela enters. She looks about cautiously and disappears out the door leading to the corral. Martirio enters by another door and stands in anguished watchfulness near the center of the stage. She also is in petticoats. She covers herself with a small black scarf. María Josefa crosses before her.*]

MARTIRIO. Grandmother, where are you going?

MARIA JOSEFA. You are going to open the door for me? Who are you?

MARTIRIO. How did you get out here?

MARIA JOSEFA. I escaped. You, who are you?

MARTIRIO. Go back to bed.

MARIA JOSEFA. You're Martirio. Now I see you. Martirio, face of a martyr. And when are you going to have a baby? I've had this one.

MARTIRIO. Where did you get that lamb?

MARIA JOSEFA. I know it's a lamb. But can't a lamb be a baby? It's better to have a lamb than not to have anything. Old Bernarda, leopard-face, and Magdalena, hyena-face!

MARTIRIO. Don't shout.

MARIA JOSEFA. It's true. Everything's very dark. Just because I have white hair you think I can't have babies, but I can—babies and babies and babies. This baby will have white hair, and I'd have *this* baby, and another, and this *one* other; and with all of us with snow white hair we'll be like the waves—one, then another, and another. Then we'll all sit down and all of us will have white heads, and we'll be seafoam. Why isn't there any seafoam here? Nothing but mourning shrouds here.

MARTIRIO. Hush, hush.

MARIA JOSEFA. When my neighbor had a baby, I'd carry her some chocolate and later she'd bring me some, and so on—always and always and always. You'll have white hair, but your neighbors won't come. Now I have to go away, but I'm afraid the dogs will bite me. Won't you come with me as far as the fields? I don't like fields. I like houses, but open houses, and the neighbor women asleep in their beds with their little tiny tots, and the men outside sitting in their chairs. Pepe el Romano is a giant. All of you love him. But he's going to devour you because you're grains of wheat. No, not grains of wheat. Frogs with no tongues!

MARTIRIO. [*Angrily.*] Come, off to bed with you. [*She pushes her.*]

MARIA JOSEFA. Yes, but then you'll open the door for me, won't you?

MARTIRIO. Of course.

MARIA JOSEFA. [*Weeping.*]
Little lamb, child of mine,
Let's go to the shore of the sea,
The tiny ant will be at his doorway,
I'll nurse you and give you your bread.

[*Martirio locks the door through which María Josefa came out and goes to the yard door. There she hesitates, but goes two steps farther.*]

MARTIRIO. [*In a low voice.*] Adela! [*Pause. She advances to the door. Then, calling:*] Adela!

[*Adela enters. Her hair is disarranged.*]

ADELA. And what are you looking for me for?

MARTIRIO. Keep away from him.

ADELA. Who are you to tell me that?

MARTIRIO. That's no place for a decent woman.

ADELA. How you wish *you'd* been there!

MARTIRIO. [*Shouting.*] This is the moment for me to speak. This can't go on.

ADELA. This is just the beginning. I've had strength enough to push myself forward—the spirit and looks you lack. I've seen death under this roof, and gone out to look for what was mine, what belonged to me.

MARTIRIO. That soulless man came for another woman. You pushed yourself in front of him.

ADELA. He came for the money, but

his eyes were always on me.

MARTIRIO. I won't allow you to snatch him away. He'll marry Angustias.

ADELA. You know better than I he doesn't love her.

MARTIRIO. I know.

ADELA. You know because you've seen—he loves me, me!

MARTIRIO. [Desperately.] Yes.

ADELA. [Close before her.] He loves me, *me!* He loves me, *me!*

MARTIRIO. Stick me with a knife if you like, but don't tell me that again.

ADELA. That's why you're trying to fix it so I won't go away with him. It makes no difference to you if he puts his arms around a woman he doesn't love. Nor does it to me. He could be a hundred years with Angustias, but for him to have his arms around me seems terrible to you— because you too love him! You love him!

MARTIRIO. [Dramatically.] Yes! Let me say it without hiding my head. Yes! My breast's bitter, bursting like a pomegranate. I love him!

ADELA. [Impulsively, hugging her.] Martirio, Martirio, I'm not to blame!

MARTIRIO. Don't put your arms around me! Don't try to smooth it over. My blood's no longer yours, and even though I try to think of you as a sister, I see you as just another woman. [She pushes her away.]

ADELA. There's no way out here. Whoever has to drown—let her drown. Pepe is mine. He'll carry me to the rushes along the river bank. . . .

MARTIRIO. He won't!

ADELA. I can't stand this horrible house after the taste of his mouth. I'll be what he wants me to be. Everybody in the village against me, burning me with their fiery fingers; pursued by those who claim they're decent, and I'll wear, before them all, the crown of thorns that belongs to the mistress of a married man.

MARTIRIO. Hush!

ADELA. Yes, yes. [In a low voice.] Let's go to bed. Let's let him marry Angustias. I don't care any more, but I'll go off alone to a little house where he'll come to see me whenever he wants, whenever he feels like it.

MARTIRIO. That'll never happen! Not while I have a drop of blood left in my body.

ADELA. Not just weak you, but a wild horse I could force to his knees with just the strength of my little finger.

MARTIRIO. Don't raise that voice of yours to me. It irritates me. I have a heart full of a force so evil that, without my wanting to be, I'm drowned by it.

ADELA. You show us the way to love our sisters. God must have meant to leave me alone in the midst of darkness, because I can see you as I've never seen you before.

[A whistle is heard and Adela runs toward the door, but Martirio gets in front of her.]

MARTIRIO. Where are you going?

ADELA. Get away from that door!

MARTIRIO. Get by me if you can!

ADELA. Get away! [They struggle.]

MARTIRIO. [Shouts.] Mother! Mother!

ADELA. Let me go!

[Bernarda enters. She wears petticoats and a black shawl.]

BERNARDA. Quiet! Quiet! How poor I am without even a man to help me!

MARTIRIO. [Pointing to Adela.] She was with him. Look at those skirts covered with straw!

BERNARDA. [Going furiously toward

Adela.] That's the bed of a bad woman!

ADELA. [*Facing her.*] There'll be an end to prison voices here! [*Adela snatches away her mother's cane and breaks it in two.*] This is what I do with the tyrant's cane. Not another step. No one but Pepe commands me! [*Magdalena enters.*]

MAGDALENA. Adela!

[*La Poncia and Angustias enter.*]

ADELA. I'm his. [*To Angustias.*] Know that—and go out in the yard and tell him. He'll be master in this house.

ANGUSTIAS. My God!

BERNARDA. The gun! Where's the gun? [*She rushes out. La Poncia runs ahead of her. Amelia enters and looks on frightened, leaning her head against the wall. Behind her comes Martirio.*]

ADELA. No one can hold me back! [*She tries to go out.*]

ANGUSTIAS. [*Holding her.*] You're not getting out of here with your body's triumph! Thief! Disgrace of this house!

MAGDALENA. Let her go where we'll never see her again!

[*A shot is heard.*]

BERNARDA. [*Entering.*] Just try looking for him now!

MARTIRIO. [*Entering.*] That does away with Pepe el Romano.

ADELA. Pepe! My God! Pepe! [*She runs out.*]

PONCIA. Did you kill him?

MARTIRIO. No. He raced away on his mare!

BERNARDA. It was my fault. A woman can't aim.

MAGDALENA. Then, why did you say . . . ?

MARTIRIO. For her! I'd like to pour a river of blood over her head!

PONCIA. Curse you!

MAGDALENA. Devil!

BERNARDA. Although it's better this way! [*A thud is heard.*] Adela! Adela!

PONCIA. [*At her door.*] Open this door!

BERNARDA. Open! Don't think the walls will hide your shame!

SERVANT. [*Entering.*] All the neighbors are up!

BERNARDA. [*In a low voice, but like a roar.*] Open! Or I'll knock the door down! [*Pause. Everything is silent.*] Adela! [*She walks away from the door.*] A hammer! [*La Poncia throws herself against the door. It opens and she goes in. As she enters, she screams and backs out.*] What is it?

PONCIA. [*She puts her hands to her throat.*] May we never die like that! [*The Sisters fall back. The Servant crosses herself. Bernarda screams and goes forward.*] Don't go in!

BERNARDA. No, not I! Pepe, you're running now, alive, in the darkness, under the trees, but another day you'll fall. Cut her down! My daughter died a virgin. Take her to another room and dress her as though she were a virgin. No one will say anything about this! She died a virgin. Tell them, so that at dawn, the bells will ring twice.

MARTIRIO. A thousand times happy she, who had him.

BERNARDA. And I want no weeping. Death must be looked at face to face. Silence! [*To one daughter.*] Be still, I said! [*To another daughter.*] Tears when you're alone! We'll drown ourselves in a sea of mourning. She, the youngest daughter of Bernarda Alba, died a virgin. Did you hear me? Silence, silence, I said. Silence!

CURTAIN

DISCUSSION OF *THE HOUSE OF BERNARDA ALBA*

Perhaps the easiest thing to notice about *The House of Bernarda Alba* is its impact. Partly its impact comes from three strong curtains, the last stronger than the second, and the second stronger than the first. Partly its impact comes from its economy. Omitting nothing essential, Lorca has written a play short enough to be played in an hour. Briefly and cleanly it rises to its increasingly important climaxes. One can imagine an Aristotelian commentator admiring its tight construction as well as its adherence to two of the unities, place and time. In its bare and unencumbered way, *Bernarda Alba* is stark, strong, and effective. However, the impact of the play probably chiefly derives, as we shall see, from the grimness of its theme and its untraditional negation of hope.

Short, tight, and simple in technique, the play offers some provocative problems for the student of tragedy. It differs not only in theme, but also in other curious ways from traditional tragedy. Hence, it may be a good idea to glance at some of the differences so that you do not get the idea, as commentators have before, that there is a strait-jacket of tragic form into which plays must be properly fitted before they can be considered really legitimate.

First of all, the plot of the play is unusual. Despite *Antigone,* a simple Aristotelian tragic plot has only one hero or protagonist, and only one villain or antagonist. *Bernarda Alba* has really two plots and two sets of heroes and villains. Unlike *King Lear,* in which the sub-plot of Gloucester runs parallel to the main plot of Lear, Lorca's two plots are like two locomotives on the same track. One is going east and one west, and both go faster and faster until an inevitable crash and a mutual destruction. The main character of one plot is Bernarda; the main character of the other plot is Adela. Both plots have antagonists that try to avert the disaster. Bernarda is opposed by Poncia who clearly sees what is going to happen, and who tries repeatedly to warn Bernarda. With equal clarity, if more dubious motives, Martirio sees what Adela is planning and tries with equal force to avert it.

The other sisters, as members of the little society in the house of Bernarda Alba, are a kind of chorus. They are more passively but just as deeply involved as the four principals. Their fate is inextricably bound up with their younger sisters, and they are carried along. Adela's failure to break outside the bounds of the house is also their failure, and the play ends with all of the household weeping, stricken, and doomed.

A plot that most clearly fits Aristotle's definition is the plot of Sophocles' *Oedipus Rex,* the example which Aristotle, incidentally, uses. The three tragedies which you have read all vary in some way from this classic definition of one single, coherent action with a beginning, a middle, and an end. In their different ways, the plots of *Antigone, King Lear,* and *The House of Bernarda Alba* are all more complex. It would be difficult to prove that they are more satisfying than the plot of *Oedipus Rex,* just as it would be more difficult to prove that complexity is more satisfying than simplicity. They are different, they are trying to do different things, and they are each satisfying in their own way. They are each tragedies in their own way.

Allied to the somewhat complex plot of *Bernarda Alba* is a greater thickness of character. Most plays, even very good ones, tend to depict character rather simply. Even in *King Lear,* Cordelia is a wholly sympathetic character. So is Kent, and so is the Fool. Regan, Goneril, Edmund, Cornwall, and Oswald are, in their different fashions, almost wholly reprehensible. Few, if any, of the characters in Lorca's play can be regarded in such black and white terms.

Adela, whom many regard as the most sympathetic, sometimes acts with a hard, cold, and unsympathetic selfishness. For instance, her impulsive sympathy when she discovers Martirio's love for Pepe is quickly countered by a succession of heartless brutalities. "Not just weak you," she says, "but a wild horse I could force to his knees with just the strength of my little finger."

Martirio, who acts as venomously as anyone in the play, is never as unadulteratedly black as Goneril or Regan. She may say, "I have a heart full of a force so evil that, without my wanting to be, I'm drowned by it." But she is also an anguished and pathetic figure, who may wincingly gasp, "Stick me with a knife if you like, but don't tell me that again . . . Yes! My breast's bitter, bursting like a pomegranate." Even the irritable Angustias is not wholly intolerable. We glimpse her vulnerability when she speaks to her mother about Pepe at the beginning of Act III. Magdalena, despite her self-pity and lumpish hopelessness, shows her affection for Adela in Act I. The vapid and catty Amelia has a naive and appealing timidity. You may even trace this thickness in the casual characters. The long-suffering Prudencia has an indulgent self-pity. The sympathetic mourners are viciously catty. Even the pitiable Beggar Woman shows her irritability.

Most characters in most plays are conceived in simpler terms. We are able to regard them without such ambivalence. Of course, our experience of reality tells us that we seldom meet a real person whom we can rationally regard with a wholehearted approval. We are used to going to plays, however, and condemning or approving wholeheartedly. We usually apply to plays a simpler morality than we apply to life. Lorca refuses to let us regard his characters so simply, and that fact brings us to the real complexity of the play, its unusual theme and its hard and hopeless ending.

The daughters are all straining against the kind of life that their mother has imposed upon them. Such a life seems to them and to us unnatural, oppressive, and deadening. It has warped each of them. It brings out the worst in their characters. Although they have, like most real people, genuinely kind and warm spots in their characters, these qualities are negated by the life they lead. These qualities do not set the tone of the play, and the play does not really leave a pleasant aftertaste. Its general tone is of querulous bickering, catty recrimination, vicious hypocrisy, and dull resignation.

As readers and viewers, we condemn this negation of life and tend immediately to side with the daughters. Particularly so in the pathetic little scene in Act II when the reapers pass outside, swinging along to work and singing joyously, as the women embroidering for their hope chests are all transfixed by a glimpse of the life that Bernarda has denied them. However, to understand the full meaning of the play, we must realize that our one-sided sympathy is dangerous. We must realize that something is to be said for Bernarda's point of view, unpalatable as it may seem.

Why has Bernarda enforced this hateful and unnatural life upon her family? The simplest, if not the fairest, answer is that she is moved entirely by the force of social decorum. It is easy to see Bernarda as a narrow, middle-class woman supremely conscious of what the neighbours will say. It is easy to think that she merely wants to appear above reproach and that she does not care how individuals feel, so long as they present an acceptable appearance to the world. It is a little too easy to think this.

If Bernarda were merely a narrow prude, she would be a figure more fitting for comedy than tragedy. If she derived her power merely from a narrow fanaticism, she probably would not have the human weight and worth needed to support tragedy. And if the world she wanted to placate were only the world that Lorca describes, hers would be a hollow and meaningless task indeed.

Consider the picture that Lorca paints of the world outside the house of Bernarda Alba. All of the stories that we hear of Bernarda's village are in some way scandalous, shocking, licentious, petty, or immoral. To this world Bernarda wishes to present an upright front, but of this world she is supremely contemptuous. She recognizes the hypocrisy of the mourners as clearly as she recognizes the more obvious sins of Paca la Roseta. Time after time, Lorca stresses that, in presenting a picture of righteousness, Bernarda is not imitating or approving what she sees around her. Quite the contrary. She is trying to maintain a haven of morality in the midst of it.

Although we tend to be on the side of life and youth and Adela, each specific instance of that life—even the dead father's flirtation with the servant—is painted in deplorable terms. Even Adela's liaison with Pepe, we must realize, is only a deplorable solution.

Often the choice that initiates a tragedy is fairly clear-cut. If Oedipus knew he was killing his father, there would have been no argument at all. If Lear and Othello had been wiser, they would have seen what choice they must make. In these plays, the choice may not be apparent to the characters, but it is to us. Here, however, is a situation in which the choice is not clear-cut to us. If Adela's choice is on the side of life, it is also on the side of immorality. If Bernarda's choice is on the side of a life which has little to recommend it over death, it is also a choice on the side of morality.

With such an irresolvable thematic dilemma, the play cannot end on the traditional note of hope and reaffirmation. This grim ending is the way in which the play chiefly differs from *Antigone* and from *Lear*.

Perhaps Lorca here has hit on the truly tragic choice, the dilemma, when one is faced with an unsolvable problem and two awful alternatives. This is, indeed, a grim theme, but it would take a buoyant optimist to say that life does not sometimes pose such choices.

Perhaps it is too much to say that the greatest tragedies are not really those that pose simple choices, but the ones that pose dilemmas. But certainly we can say that the dilemma posed by *The House of Bernarda Alba* has, just as much as *Oedipus Rex* or *Antigone* or *Lear*, the wrenching and agonizing quality of reality.

DISCUSSION QUESTIONS ON *THE HOUSE OF BERNARDA ALBA*

1. Francisco García Lorca, the dramatist's brother, wrote of *The House of Bernarda Alba*:

> And the play's dramatic tension is born precisely out of the clash of these wills. Of the domineering will of the mother, upheld by the forces of tradition, of custom, of social values—and of the deaf and invincible wills of the daughters, dragged by their thirst for living and by impulses and instincts which clash with each other in their turn. And over all of them, a tragic sense of life against which nothing avails. That is why it is curious and why it underscores the attitude of the central character that, when she is faced with the death of the daughter who has hanged herself with the cord with which the mother symbolically would have bound all of them, Bernarda finishes the drama with a shout of triumph, an illusory triumph. . . .

The crucial word seems to be "curious." The theme and the ending, as we pointed out in the discussion, are indeed curious. But would it be even more curious if Bernarda's last speech were a "shout of triumph"? What precisely is Bernarda feeling at the end of the play? Does Lorca tell us enough so that we can be sure? What clues does he give us? Is Bernarda saying less than she feels? And what is the effect of her speech against the choral background of weeping?

2. Lorca prefaces *Bernarda Alba* with a note that tells us the play is intended as a photographic document. And in his book, *Lorca: The Poet and His People*, Arturo Barea relates that, "Lorca, reading his play aloud, proudly exclaimed after each scene, 'Not a drop of poetry! Reality! Realism!' "

These two comments clearly indicate what Lorca was after, and certainly *Bernarda Alba* seems much more a transcription of reality than either *Antigone* or *Lear*. Does Lorca's realism help his tragic effect in any ways that are different from or better than the nonrealistic manners of *Antigone* and *Lear*? If you were to write a tragedy, which manner would you choose as likely to aid you most: the very formal arrangement of *Antigone*, the loose and lyrical freedom of *Lear*, or the photographic realism of *Bernarda Alba*?

3. Actually, how close to realism is *Bernarda Alba*? How much of a photographic document is it? Is there anything in the play which is unrealistic?

4. John van Druten once wrote a play called *I Am a Camera*. His title implied, as does Lorca's prefatory note, that the dramatist merely records what he

sees, that he merely transcribes an unarranged slice of life. One might push this camera analogy further, however. Cameras do not take pictures willy-nilly; their subjects are chosen. In fact, the more thoughtful the choice, the better the picture. Also, by focusing a camera, one decides what to include and what to eliminate in the picture. The best photographers even go further and make an artistic arrangement of what is to be in the picture. Does "photographic realism" imply, therefore, formlessness? Is Lorca's play formless? How much has he arranged his picture and controlled his structure?

5. Allardyce Nicoll points out that the language of realism tends to be flat, repetitive, and unevocative. Therefore, he says, the language of realistic tragedy surrenders many of the tragic dramatist's most effective tools. Does Lorca ever diverge from the language of realism? Does he ever attempt to reach a lyrical pitch? Can you cite instances? Are they, as much as you can tell in translation, successful instances?

6. In defending Ibsen's realistic prose, Eric Bentley points out how really subtle and effective it is in accomplishing several tasks at the same time. Apply Bentley's analysis of Ibsen's language to a passage from Lorca. Does Lorca's language do as much as Ibsen's?

7. What use of irony, in situation and in language, does Lorca make? For instance, are María Josefa's scenes ironic? Does Lorca's irony flow naturally out of the situation or does it seem imposed by the author?

8. What is the function of the grandmother, María Josefa? of Prudencia? of the mourners? of the Beggar Woman?

9. How many symbols of life and fruitfulness can you find in the play? Can symbols be successfully used by a realistic author?

10. A big difference between *Antigone* and *Lear* on the one hand and *Bernarda Alba* on the other is that Creon and Lear grow into wisdom and that nobody in *Bernarda Alba* has such a growth and revelation. Does Adela learn by suffering? Does Bernarda? Does this lack make Lorca's play anti-tragic?

11. Imagine the same series of events as seen by Pepe el Romano. Would they seem to him tragic, comic, or something else? Why does Lorca make Martirio lie about having killed Pepe?

12. Lorca's setting is remote from modern America, and the Spanish customs are somewhat different from American ones. Do these facts harm the effectiveness of the play by making it too local and limited? Do you think that modern tragedies can be written only about people that, like Lorca's or Shakespeare's or Sophocles' people, are in some way remote? Do you think that tragedy can be written only about people who live in a strictly authoritarian society with marked social classes?

13. Allied to the last question, do you think that Bernarda and Adela are too modern, in Joseph Wood Krutch's and Arthur Miller's sense, to be tragic? Are they, in other words, too little? Are Bernarda and Adela littler than Creon and Antigone?

PART TWO

Comedy

Comedy

Comedy has been particularly unpropitious to definers.

JOHNSON

The origins of comedy are as obscure as those of tragedy. Like tragedy, comedy seems to have evolved from a primitive ritual connected with the cult of a Vegetation Deity or Life Spirit. But while tragedy was concerned with the expulsion of death and decay, in the person of the Scapegoat or Dying God, comedy celebrated fruition and life by a Comus or ritual marriage of the Young God. As Gilbert Murray put it, "Tragedy is the enactment of his marriage, or rather of the *Comus* which accompanies his marriage. The centre of tragedy is a death; the centre of comedy is a union of lovers."

Comedy as an art form developed separately from tragedy, and somewhat later. There seems to have been no civic contest for comedy until about 486 B.C., or about fifty years after the first tragic contests. This Greek Old Comedy is known to us through the highly topical and satirical plays of Aristophanes. From these plays we can deduce that Old Comedy fiercely satirized prominent individuals like Socrates, that it contained both the bawdiest jokes and the loveliest poetry, and that the singing and dancing of its Chorus played an important part.

Greek New Comedy appeared in the third and fourth centuries B.C., and is known to us by one play and several fragments of Menander. In New Comedy the fiercely personal satire of real individuals disappeared and so also, to a large extent, did the Chorus. The characters of New Comedy were types rather than individuals, and the plots tended to follow a certain narrow formula. New Comedy is important, however, because of its great influence on the Roman dramatists Plautus and Terence and, through them, on our entire comic tradition.

Like New Comedy, the plays of Plautus and Terence used a few stock situations and stock characters. A young man is in love with a beautiful young girl, frequently a slave girl who has been separated from respectable parents. Many obstacles stand in the young man's way, and the chief of these is frequently a miserly, lecherous, and testy old man, his father. The young man is aided by his clever servant; and after many intrigues, mistaken identities, and twistings of the plot, the true identity of the girl is revealed, and the young couple live happily ever after.

After the fall of the Roman Empire and during the Middle Ages, the drama fell on evil days, and it would be tedious to enumerate the many forms of near-drama and sub-drama with which people amused themselves during these long centuries. With the Renaissance of Learning, however, and especially in the early seventeenth century of Queen Elizabeth's England, there suddenly and luxuriantly bloomed one of the great periods of the drama.

Of all those talented men who wrote scripts to fill Philip Henslowe's playhouse, by far the greatest comic writers were, of course, Shakespeare and Ben Jonson. Of Shakespeare enough has been said; and of Jonson, John Dryden's words, in his "Essay of Dramatic Poesy," are still the freshest and the best.

> . . . I think him the most learned and judicious writer which any theatre ever had. He was a most severe judge of himself, as well as others. One cannot say he wanted wit, but rather that he was frugal of it. In his works you find little to retrench or alter. Wit, and language, and humour also in some measure, we had before him; but something of art was wanting to the Drama till he came. He managed his strength to more advantage than any who preceded him. You seldom find him making love in any of his scenes, or endeavouring to move the passions; his genius was too sullen and saturnine to do it gracefully, especially when he knew he came after those who had performed both to such an height. Humour was his proper sphere; and in that he delighted most to represent mechanic people. He was deeply conversant in the Ancients, both Greek and Latin, and he borrowed boldly from them: there is scarce a poet or historian among the Roman authors of those times whom he has not translated in *Sejanus* and *Catiline*.[1] But he has done his robberies so openly, that one may see he fears not to be taxed by any law. He invades authors like a monarch; and what would be theft in other poets is only victory in him. With the spoils of these writers he so represents old Rome to us, in its rites, ceremonies, and customs, that if one of their poets had written either of his tragedies, we had seen less of it than in him. If there was any fault in his language, 'twas that he weaved it too closely and laboriously, in his comedies especially: perhaps, too, he did a little too much Romanise our tongue, leaving the words which he translated almost as much Latin as he found them: wherein, though he learnedly followed their language, he did not comply with the idiom of ours. If I would compare him with Shakespeare, I must acknowledge him the more correct poet, but Shakespeare the greater wit. Shakespeare was the Homer, or father of our dramatic poets; Jonson was the Vergil, the pattern of elaborate writing; I admire him, but I love Shakespeare. To conclude of him; as he has given us the most correct plays, so in the precepts which he has laid down in his Discoveries, we have as many and profitable rules for perfecting the stage, as any wherewith the French can furnish us.

[1] Jonson's two tragedies. While proper and correct, where Shakespeare's are sprawling and untidy, Jonson's tragedies pale by comparison, and have seemed cold and dull to many people.

To this we need only add that Jonson was the great innovator of dramatic comedy. He firmly set the comic scene down in the London of his time; he took comedy out of the Roman forum and out of the Forest of Arden. Further, he rephrased in his doctrine of the Humours [2] the necessities of comic characterization; he rephrased it for his time and solidified it for ours.

The next great master of comedy, Jean-Baptiste Poquelin, was born in France in 1622. Under his stage name of Molière, he traveled through France for many years with his troupe of players, learning every facet of the dramatic art. Before his death he became a successful producer, a brilliant comic actor, and the greatest comic dramatist of his time. He has been called by the French critic Sainte-Beuve, "the fullest and most complete poetic genius we have had in France," and by Tolstoy, "the most universal and, hence, most excellent artist of modern times." Goethe told his friend Eckermann that "Molière is so great that he astonishes us anew each time we read him. He is unique; his plays border on tragedy . . . and no one has the strength to imitate him." He has probably been the most influential of modern comic writers. To Molière, Morris Bishop attributes the formula for Hollywood farce and comedy, and that statement might be broadened to include Broadway and television.

Although, in their best plays, Molière and Jonson are very similar, the influences upon Molière were not, like those upon Jonson, mainly classical. Much of his inspiration came from French farce and Italian *commedia dell' arte.* These forms were, of course, the living embodiments of Plautus and Terence (they relied much upon the stock character and the stock plot), but the difference is that they *were* living. The comic tradition had not on the continent yet so solidified into rules, and, consequently, Molière is far more careless about his plots than Ben Jonson sometimes was. Burlesque, farce, the gag, the comic pratfall—all of these exist in wild abandon in Molière's plays. But for many years the well-made play structure of *Volpone* or *The Misanthrope* was the admired comic pattern; it was forgotten that Jonson and Molière had written wild conglomerations like *The Alchemist* or *The Would-Be Gentleman,* plays whose structures seemed either grotesquely askew or utterly submerged under a welter of joyful incident.

The Italian *commedia dell' arte,* which so influenced Molière, did not have completely written down playscripts. Rather, actors, who had worked together for years perfecting one particular stock part, would decide upon a certain stock plot as a skeleton and then launch into the production. Because of their familiarity with each other, much of the dialogue and action was predictable, but much also was improvised. In the eighteenth century, Carlo Goldoni, the father of modern Italian comedy, attempted to substitute written comedies for the now debased *commedia,* which shortly died, and of which there are few modern remnants unless they be the lingering Harlequinade, the Punch and Judy show, or the fading films of Mack Sennett's improvised Keystone comedies.

[2] For Jonson's definition of a "Humour," see the Induction to *Everyman Out of His Humour* below.

In England after the Restoration of Charles II in 1660, the theatres which had been closed under the Puritan Commonwealth reopened, and for a few years an extremely witty, if perhaps too ingrown, group of comic writers flourished. These Restoration comic writers—Congreve, Wycherley, Vanbrugh, Etherege—wrote almost exclusively to and about a small segment of society, the highest. The plots of Restoration comedies are not particularly important, for they resemble each other almost as much as the plots of Roman comedy. A new group of stock characters, including the fop and the beau, evolved, but these characters reflected their own time and society so well that they were not particularly fertile for later times. However, the glory of Restoration comedy is in its beguiling and delightful language and wit. That language and wit may be seen at its rarest in *The Way of the World*, the best play of the best of the Restoration comic writers, William Congreve. In that play, Congreve dispensed with plot as much as did Jonson and Molière at their best.

The great English middle class was growing hugely in power and influence, and the down-to-earth burgher both resented and deplored what he called, with some justice, the amorality of Restoration comedy. Consequently, a debased kind of comedy, the sentimental drama, in which romantic love was predominant and virtue was rewarded, came to the fore. In the plays of the only later comic dramatists of any importance in the eighteenth century—Farquhar, Steele, Goldsmith, and Sheridan—Restoration wit exists side by side with middle-class sentimentality.

From Sheridan's death until the end of the nineteenth century, there were no really important plays written in England. There were a lot of poor plays, and prominent individuals like Shelley, Tennyson, and Browning tried their hands at the stage without much success. Only at the end of the century appeared some wise and witty Irishmen, whose work could compare with the best of preceding centuries. Oscar Wilde's masterpiece, *The Importance of Being Earnest*, with an unimportant plot, well-etched character types, and witty dialogue of remarkable excellence, seems a direct throwback to Restoration comedy.

After Wilde comes Bernard Shaw, the first modern man of the English drama, and undoubtedly the most prolific, witty, and influential comic dramatist that England had seen in two hundred years. Of him, his friend Sean O'Casey wrote:

> He set down a lamp in the theatre that has ever since been a light to our feet and a guide to our path . . . Let those who write plays today throw a wider chest than Shaw's, in either poetry or prose— if they can! . . . He was a great playwright . . . This silvery thread of laughter runs through all of Shaw's plays, and most of his writing, weaving a delightful decoration into his keen thought and thrusting satire. This joking sage has been a godsend to England (and to Ireland, too) for his wisdom, his love of truth and freedom, his gay spirit and fearless conduct have been a banner before us, a banner

and a bugle band leading the slow, the certain, the glorious ascent of man.[3]

Shaw's work is so much with us that it scarcely needs to be described. Into his plays he poured great doses of melodrama, farce, preaching, prophecy, and, above all, high spirits and wit. He is able to construct the tightest well-made plot, the most dazzling comic mélange, or the most complicated Chekhovian structure. But perhaps even more typically Shavian are the sting of his dialogue and the freshness and topsy-turvy unpredictability of his characters.

Quite different and much less prolific than Shaw was John Millington Synge, whom W. B. Yeats persuaded to return home to Ireland from France and to devote himself to Irish subjects. Synge moved to the far west of Ireland and diligently studied the customs, the manners, and the rich speech of the people. His study is brilliantly reflected in the superb lyric dialogue of his six plays. Of these, the most important are *Riders to the Sea,* perhaps the best one-act tragedy ever written, and *The Playboy of the Western World,* his comic masterpiece. Like most great comedy, *The Playboy* is basically concerned with appearance and reality. It seems equally suffused with grotesque satire and genial detail, but the grotesquerie was enough to cause a riot at the Abbey Theatre in 1907, and the play yet retains its dramatic bite.

In the early 1920's, the financially tottering Abbey Theatre presented three plays of a Dublin day laborer, Sean O'Casey, and found itself rejuvenated both financially and artistically. O'Casey's first three long plays, although containing thick slabs of the most exciting and rich comedy of the modern drama, are primarily tragicomedies. It was not until the plays of his old age that O'Casey began a demonstration of his ability to write almost formally classic but deeply original comedies that integrally fused such disparate elements as whimsy, fantasy, satire, the song, and the dance. Perhaps the best of these later plays are *Cock-a-Doodle Dandy, Purple Dust,* and *The Drums of Father Ned.*

For what it is worth, the seven or eight chief comic writers of the last two hundred and fifty years have been Irishmen. And for that matter, perhaps the two most promising younger comic writers, Samuel Beckett and Brendan Behan, are also Irishmen.

Dramatic comedy in America has had several craftsmanlike practitioners, but so far no writer of brilliance has turned his hand to it. Despite his love for the theatre, Charles Dickens, the comic genius of the Victorian age, wrote novels; Mark Twain, the only authentic American comic genius, wrote one play in collaboration with William Dean Howells, but his great work was done in the novel and the essay.

[3] "A Whisper About Bernard Shaw," *The Green Crow* (New York: George Braziller, Inc., 1956), pp. 200–204.

The Critics

THE COMIC SUBJECT AND THE COMIC MANNER

MOLIÈRE, from *The Critique of the School for Wives:*

DORANTE. How amusing you are, with all your talk of rules to embarrass the ignorant and dazzle us daily. To hear you talk, it would seem that these rules of art are the greatest mysteries in the world. But they're only convenient observations which good sense has made about whatever diminishes the pleasure of this sort of art. And the same good sense which made these observations before can easily make them now, without the help of Horace and Aristotle. I'd like to know if the great rule of rules isn't to please, and if a dramatic performance which has reached this goal hasn't followed the right path. Do you think the whole public is misguided about this sort of thing, and that each person can't judge his own pleasure?

EDITORS' TRANSLATION.

CARLO GOLDONI, from *The Comic Theatre:*

Comedy was invented to correct vices and to hold folly up to ridicule; and when the comedy of the ancients did this, the audience was pleased, because each person saw in himself or in others the original of the character represented on the stage. But when comedy strayed away from its original purpose and began to stoop to any fantastic nonsense to cause laughter,

it became merely ridiculous and people lost interest in it. Now that we are again fishing comedies from the *Mare Magnum* [1] of nature, men can once more look inward and identify themselves with the character or emotion represented; and they can tell whether an emotion is well sustained or a character is natural.

. . . A single character is enough to sustain a French comedy. Around a single well-conceived and well-executed passion, a great number of speeches will cluster, which by their verbal brilliance give an air of novelty. We Italians want more. We want the principal character to be strong, original, and natural, and most of the lesser characters to be distinctly realized, and the plot to be rather complex, and novel. We want morals mixed with witticisms. We want the end to be unexpected and yet to derive naturally from the previous action. We want an infinity of things, too many to relate here, and only with time and practice will we be able to know and attain them.

TRANSLATED BY ROBERT WATKINS.

GEORGE MEREDITH, from *An Essay on Comedy:*

If you believe that our civilization is founded in common-sense (and it is the first condition of sanity to believe it), you will, when contemplating men, discern a Spirit overhead; not more heavenly than the light flashed up-

[1] Great Sea.

ward from glassy surfaces, but luminous and watchful; never shooting beyond them, nor lagging in the rear; so closely attached to them that it may be taken for a slavish reflex, until its features are studied. It has the sage's brows, and the sunny malice of a faun lurks at the corners of the half-closed lips drawn in an idle wariness of half-tension. That slim feasting smile, shaped like the long-bow, was once a big round satyr's laugh, that flung up the brows like a fortress lifted by gunpowder. The laugh will come again, but it will be of the order of the smile, finely tempered, showing sunlight of the mind, mental richness rather than noisy enormity. Its common aspect is one of unsolicitous observation, as if surveying a full field and having leisure to dart on its chosen morsels, without any fluttering eagerness. Men's future upon earth does not attract it; their honesty and shapeliness in the present does; and whenever they wax out of proportion, overblown, affected, pretentious, bombastical, hypocritical, pedantic, fantastically delicate; whenever it sees them self-deceived or hoodwinked, given to run riot in idolatries, drifting into vanities, congregating in absurdities, planning short-sightedly, plotting dementedly; whenever they are at variance with their professions, and violate the unwritten but perceptible laws binding them in consideration one to another; whenever they offend sound reason, fair justice; are false in humility or mined with conceit, individually, or in the bulk—the Spirit overhead will look humanely malign and cast an oblique light on them, followed by volleys of silvery laughter. That is the Comic Spirit.

JOHN MILLINGTON SYNGE, the Preface to *The Tinker's Wedding:*

The drama is made serious—in the French sense of the word—not by the degree in which it is taken up with problems that are serious in themselves, but by the degree in which it gives the nourishment, not very easy to define, on which our imaginations live. We should not go to the theatre as we go to a chemist's, or a dramshop, but as we go to a dinner, where the food we need is taken with pleasure and excitement. This was nearly always so in Spain and England and France when the drama was at its richest— the infancy and decay of the drama tend to be didactic—but in these days the playhouse is too often stocked with the drugs of many seedy problems, or with the absinthe or vermouth of the last musical comedy.

The drama, like the symphony, does not teach or prove anything. Analysts with their problems, and teachers with their systems, are soon as old-fashioned as the pharmacopœia of Galen,—look at Ibsen and the Germans—but the best plays of Ben Jonson and Molière can no more go out of fashion than the blackberries on the hedges.

Of the things which nourish the imagination humour is one of the most needful, and it is dangerous to limit or destroy it. Baudelaire calls laughter the greatest sign of the Satanic element in man; and where a country loses its humour, as some towns in Ireland are doing, there will be morbidity of mind, as Baudelaire's mind was morbid.

In the greater part of Ireland, however, the whole people, from the tinkers to the clergy, have still a life, and view of life, that are rich and genial and humorous. I do not think that these country people, who have so much humour themselves, will mind being laughed at without malice, as the people in every country have been laughed at in their own comedies.

L. J. Potts, from *Comedy:*

He [the comic writer] is trying to present a social point of view; to measure human conduct against a norm rather than an ideal. He is, or should be, actuated always by a sense of proportion. What he depicts—his subject matter—may therefore be defined as the abnormal. He may include some normal characters in his work, to serve as a kind of yard-stick; but for the most part he will leave his public to deduce his norm from the way he depicts the clash and contrast of varied abnormalities. In any case, far the greater part of his matter must inevitably be abnormal. . . .

It may be said that whereas tragedy deals with the unusual but normal, comedy deals with the abnormal but not unusual. The abnormality of comic characters is not absolute; we should feel that they are capable of behaving normally if they would. But it is the main concern of the comic writer to discriminate between what is normal and abnormal in human behaviour; he is detached from his subject-matter in a sense in which other artists are not. He needs not merely a strong feeling for normality, but also a clear notion of it. It is therefore necessary for him to be in some measure a moral philosopher; for the norm is a philosophical concept. The usual, or average,

is not; it can be calculated statistically from observed facts. But normality, like the cognate concepts of health and sanity, is not a fact, nor a complex of facts, nor even a simplification of facts; it is an idea, and exists only in the mind that has brought itself to bear on all the relevant facts. There is not one norm of human behaviour, but many: some of them widely divergent and even contradictory. Jane Austen's norm differs drastically in some respects from Chaucer's or Fielding's. But all comic writers must have a norm in view. To detect eccentricity you must have a centre: that is to say a consistent, if not consciously worked out, standard of character and conduct.

From these considerations it might be deduced that the world of comedy would be a realistically depicted world peopled by eccentric characters. This formula fits some comic writers: Fielding and Jane Austen in particular. It was also the formula laid down by Ben Jonson and in the main followed by him. But as a general definition it is too narrow, and also radically misleading. Meredith puts his finger on the error contained in it, in the passage I have quoted . . . [see p. 205]: comedy *may be taken for* a slavish reflex of real life, *until its features are closely studied.* There is always an element of caricature in comedy, the caricature being so designed as to stress the eccentricity of the individual. Everyone, however nearly normal, has his foibles, however slight. But this, perhaps, is obvious.

A more serious objection to this formula is that comedy is not necessarily at all realistic in technique. None of Shakespeare's comedies are:

even *Measure for Measure*, which is often classed as a realistic play, is strange and remote—suffused in "the light that never was on sea or land". The Fable (as used by Aesop, for example) is one of the earliest and most efficient vehicles for comedy, and it is quite unrealistic. Even allegory,[1] which is more unrealistic still, adapts itself well and easily to comic purposes: the vice in the late medieval morality plays was a comic figure, and probably the literary ancestor of Shakespeare's Falstaff. Even in so tedious an allegory as the *Roman de la Rose*[2] the character of Fals-Semblant is fully developed comedy; it provided Chaucer with the outline of the character of his Pardoner. Chaucer himself took his first exercises in comedy in *The House of Fame* and *The Parliament of Fowls* (an allegory and a fable). . . . The best plays of the first great European comic writer, Aristophanes, are all fantasies, although the central character in an Aristophanic comedy is usually a realistically conceived middle-aged and middle-class Athenian citizen. There is a similar blend of realism and fantasy in the greatest of all European comedies, *Don Quixote*: and there is comedy, both realistic and unrealistic, in Bunyan's *Pilgrim's Progress*, the general structure of which is allegorical.

Even this cursory survey shows that comedy demands the utmost latitude in its choice of setting and in the form of its subject matter; and that its

[1] An allegory is a sort of prolonged metaphor in which every action and every character have usually a clear symbolic meaning.—Ed.
[2] A French satirical and allegorical poem of the 13th century.—Ed.

bias is away from rather than towards, a close imitation, or as Meredith put it, a slavish reflection, of real life.

THE COMIC STRUCTURE

JOHN DRYDEN, from *An Essay of Dramatic Poesy:*

Another thing in which the French differ from us and from the Spaniards, is that they do not embarrass, or cumber themselves with too much plot; they only represent so much of a story as will constitute one whole and great action sufficient for a play; we, who undertake more, do but multiply adventures which, not being produced from one another, as effects from causes, but rarely following, constitute many actions in the drama, and consequently make it many plays.

But by pursuing closely one argument, which is not cloyed with many turns, the French have gained more liberty for verse, in which they write; they have leisure to dwell on a subject which deserves it; and to represent the passions (which we have acknowledged to be the poet's work), without being hurried from one thing to another, as we are in the plays of Calderon, which we have seen lately upon our theatres under the name of Spanish plots.

L. J. POTTS, from *Comedy:*

. . . the concept of plot must not be a rigid one: there are other ways of synthesising the elements of a story than to fit them into a logical sequence leading by a chain of cause and effect to an inevitable conclusion. Indeed, in many well-constructed comedies (for example, *As You Like It*, or *Tom*

Jones) the conclusion is far from inevitable. It may be appropriate; but that is quite another matter.

In his Preface to Shakespeare, Dr Johnson remarked that "Shakespeare's plays are not in the rigorous or critical sense either tragedies or comedies". In saying that, Dr Johnson did not intend to find fault with Shakespeare, as his namesake Ben Jonson had done, for "wanting art". He was following a later tradition, begun by Dryden; he was praising Shakespeare as an irregular genius, a poet of nature, who understood life so profoundly that he could afford to defy the narrower proprieties of art. Dryden and Johnson were right in refusing to throw Shakespeare overboard because he did not satisfy the rigid notions of characterisation and plot that prevailed in the dramatic theory of their time. But it is no longer necessary to defend Shakespeare against that particular charge. Even Dryden (in his bolder moments), and Johnson (more consistently), suggested that it was the theory rather than Shakespeare that was wide of the mark. The fact is that the wholesale censure of Shakespeare's comic plots was not only "rigorous" but *un*critical, since it was based on an unscientific application to comedy of Aristotle's theory of tragic drama. At least three of Shakespeare's comedies—*A Midsummer Night's Dream, As You Like It,* and *The Tempest*—are admirably plotted: because their structure or form follows a pattern appropriate to comedy, and *therefore* different from the Aristotelian pattern for tragedy. . . .

It might be better if we put the word "plot" out of commission, and

spoke on the one hand of *structure* or *design* (which is what plot really means) and on the other hand of the *story* (which is something quite different). When people speak of plot, they usually have in mind a logical sequence of significant events, like the events that lead from the return of Oedipus to his native country up to the death of his wife and his own blindness, or from Macbeth's military successes to his murder of Duncan and on to his own death. With this notion in mind, critics find fault with a large proportion of our comedies: Shakespeare's comic plots are careless, Jane Austen's are trivial, Congreve's are improbable, Sterne's are non-existent. That is based on a fallacy: that the plot of a comedy ought to be of the same kind as that of a tragedy. But the end of comedy is not the same as the end of tragedy; and this not only justifies but demands a difference of structure.

One of Aristotle's most profound principles is his principle of "probability or necessity" in a work of fiction. By this he does not mean that the writer must give us a picture of what has often happened and is therefore probable in a merely statistical sense; but rather that he must depict "what would happen". Unfortunately he does not finish the sentence by giving the "if" clause. From what he says elsewhere in the *Poetics* we may conclude that he meant "what would happen given the hypotheses on which the story is based"; or "what is the right sort of thing to happen in a really consistent world". In writing of tragedy he stresses chiefly the need for probability in the sequence of events. In this he was quite right. A feeling that the hero is doomed from the very beginning of the play stresses his loneliness and importance, throws the other characters into the shade, and so gives us a sense of the significance of the individual and his particular environment. Unless there is a logical sequence of cause and effect in the events from beginning to end, the tragic atmosphere is lost; and if chance or accident interferes with this sequence at a single point, the tragic atmosphere is so far disturbed. But this is not the effect at which comedy is aiming. For in comedy we must feel that man is free, not fated; if anything goes wrong with him, the remedy is in his own hands. Shakespeare and Jane Austen and the rest of them were therefore quite right not to do in comedy what Aristotle (also quite rightly) had said that the tragic dramatist should do. For to show the free interplay of character, you must release your men and women from the pressure of circumstance: you must therefore make your story either fantastic (as Shakespeare does) or commonplace (as Jane Austen does). A comedy may even fail in its effect simply because the author has taken pains to make the plot conform strictly to the law of cause and effect; because he has insisted too ruthlessly on fate, and especially retribution.

The pattern we want in comedy is of a different kind: a grouping of characters rather than a march of events. In comedy it is in the contrast and balance of characters that probability is concentrated and the imagination and originality of the writer is displayed. The finest comic plot I

know is that of *Don Quixote*, where the whole significance of the story lies in the contrast between Quixote and Sancho Panza, and in two subordinate contrasts within this dominant one: between Quixote's nobility of mind and his absurdity of behaviour, and between Sancho's cynical peasant selfishness and his irrational loyalty to his master. Not only does this book contain two of the most famous characters in the literature of the world; but in conceiving them Cervantes almost divided the whole of human nature in two, with the neatness of a surgeon's knife. Yet in *Don Quixote* it does not matter whether the events have any particular connexion with each other; it does not even matter in what order they come in; and they are all trivial and mostly fantastic. What matters is that the characters become increasingly clear, both in their relationship to each other and as representatives of human nature. . . .

In these sometimes rather lengthy analyses I have tried to illustrate the nature of plot in comedy. I have argued that a lack of logic in the sequence of events so far from being a weakness in the art of the writer, is proper in comedy; though provided the events are not in themselves out of the ordinary . . . they may be made to follow a logical sequence. What is essential to a good comic plot is an exact balance and proportion between the characters, and a progressive revelation of their true nature by means of contrast, interplay, and mutual influence. Partly because of Aristotle, but without his authority (for he was writing of tragedy) the only kind of plot we are accustomed to recognise is

a pattern in time. But there is no justification for this narrow view. There
are at least two kinds of plot: the
tragic plot, in *time,* and the comic plot,
in *space.*

THE COMIC HERO

BEN JONSON, from the Induction to
Everyman Out of His Humour:

Why, humour . . . we thus define it:
To be a quality of air or water,
And in itself holds these two prop-
   erties,
Moisture and fluxure: as, for demon-
   stration,
Pour water on this floor, 'twill wet and
   run;
Likewise the air, forced through a horn
   or trumpet,
Flows instantly away and leaves be-
   hind
A kind of dew; and hence we do con-
   clude
That whatsoe'er hath fluxure and hu-
   midity
As wanting power to contain itself
Is humour. So in every human body
The choler, melancholy, phlegm, and
   blood,
By reason that they flow continually
In some one part, and are not con-
   tinent,
Receive the name of humours. *Now
   thus far*
It may by metaphor apply itself
Unto the general disposition:
As when some one peculiar quality
*Doth so possess a man that it doth
   draw*
*All his affects, his spirits, and his
   powers,*
*In their confluxions, all to run one
   way,*
This may be truly said to be a humour.

WILLIAM CONGREVE, from *Concerning Humor in Comedy:*

But if I tell you my thoughts of
humor, I must at the same time confess that which I take for true humor
has not been so often written by them
as is generally believed; and some who
have valued themselves and have been
esteemed by others for that kind of
writing, have seldom touched upon
it. . . .

   To define humor perhaps were as
difficult as to define wit; for, like that,
it is of infinite variety. To enumerate
the several humors of men were a
work as endless as to sum up their
several opinions. . . . But though we
cannot certainly tell what wit is, or
what humor is, yet we may go near
to show something which is not wit
or not humor, and yet often mistaken
for both. And since I have mentioned
wit and humor together, let me make
the first distinction between them, and
observe to you that *wit is often mistaken for humor.*

   . . . For my part, I am as willing to
laugh as anybody, and as easily diverted with an object truly ridiculous;
but at the same time, I can never care
for seeing things that force me to
entertain low thoughts of any nature.
Sometimes *personal defects are mis-
represented for humors.*

   I mean, sometimes characters are
barbarously exposed on the stage, ridiculing natural deformities, casual defects in the senses, and infirmities of
age. Sure the poet must be very ill-
natured himself, and think his audience so, when he proposes by showing
a man deformed, or deaf, or blind, to
give them an agreeable entertainment, and hopes to raise their mirth

by what is truly an object of compassion. But much need not be said upon this head to anybody, especially to you, who, in one of your Letters to me concerning Mr. Jonson's *Fox,* have justly expected against this immortal part of ridicule in Corbaccio's character; and there I must agree with you to blame him whom otherwise I cannot enough admire for his great mastery of true humor in comedy.

External habit of body is often mistaken for humor.

By *external habit* I do not mean the ridiculous dress or clothing of a character, though that goes a good way in some received characters. (But undoubtedly, a man's humor may incline him to dress differently from other people.) But I mean a singularity of manners, speech, and behavior, peculiar to all or most of the same country, trade, profession, or education. I cannot think that a humor which is only a habit or disposition contracted by use or custom; for by a disuse, or compliance with other customs, it may be worn off or diversified.

Affectation is generally mistaken for humor.

These are indeed so much alike that at a distance they may be mistaken one for the other. For what is humor in one may be affectation in another; and nothing is more common than for some to affect particular ways of saying and doing things, peculiar to others whom they admire and would imitate. Humor is the life, affectation the picture. He that draws a character of affectation shows humor at the second hand; he at best but publishes a translation, and his pictures are but copies.

But as these two last distinctions are the nicest, so it may be most proper to explain them by particular instances from some author of reputation. Humor I take either to be born with us, and so of a natural growth, or else to be grafted into us by some accidental change in the constitution, or revolution of the internal habit of body, by which it becomes, if I may so call it, naturalized.

Humor is from nature, habit from custom, and affectation from industry.

Humor shows us as we are.

Habit shows us as we appear under a forcible impression.

Affectation shows what we would be under a voluntary disguise.

Though here I would observe by the way that a continued affectation may in time become a habit.

The character of Morose in *The Silent Woman* I take to be a character of Humor. And I choose to instance this character to you from many others of the same author, because I know it has been condemned by many as unnatural and farce; and you have yourself hinted some dislike of it for the same reason, in a Letter to me concerning some of Jonson's plays.

Let us suppose Morose to be a man naturally splenetic and melancholy; is there anything more offensive to one of such a disposition than noise and clamor? Let any man that has a spleen (and there are enough in England) be judge. We see common examples of this humor, in little, every day. 'Tis ten to one but three parts in four of the company that you dine with are discomposed and startled at the cutting of a fork or scratching a plate with a knife. It is a proportion of the same humor that makes such or any other noise offensive to the person that hears it; for there are others who will not be disturbed at all by it. Well, but Morose, you will say, is so extravagant, he cannot hear any discourse or conversation above a whisper. Why, it is his excess of this humor that makes him become ridiculous, and qualifies his character for comedy. If the poet had given him but a moderate proportion of that humor, 'tis odds but half the audience would have sided with the character and have condemned the author for exposing a humor which was neither remarkable nor ridiculous. Besides, the distance of the stage requires the figure represented to be something larger than the life; and such a picture may have figures larger in proportion, and yet be very like the original. If this exactness of quantity were to be observed in wit, as some would have it in humor, what would become of those comedies that are designed for men of wit? I believe that if a poet should steal a dialogue of any length from the extempore discourse of the two wittiest men upon earth, he would find the scene but coldly received by the town. But to the purpose.

The character of Sir John Daw in the same play is a character of affectation. He everywhere discovers an affectation of learning, when he is not only conscious to himself, but the audience also plainly perceives that he is ignorant. Of this kind are the characters of Thraso in *The Eunuch* of Terence, and Pyrgopolinices in the *Miles Gloriosus* of Plautus. They affect to be thought valiant, when both themselves and the audience know they are not. Now, such a boasting of valor in men who were really valiant would

undoubtedly be a humor; for a fiery disposition might naturally throw a man into the same extravagance, which is only affected in the characters I have mentioned.

The character of Cob in *Every Man in His Humour* and most of the under characters in *Bartholomew Fair*, discover only a singularity of manners, appropriate to the several educations and professions of the persons represented. They are not humors, but habits contracted by custom. Under this head may be ranged all country-clowns, sailors, tradesmen, jockeys, gamesters, and such-like, who make use of *cants* or peculiar dialects in their several arts and vocations. One may almost give a receipt for the composition of such a character: for the poet has nothing to do but to collect a few proper phrases and terms of art, and to make the person apply them by ridiculous metaphors in his conversation with characters of different natures. Some late characters of this kind have been very successful; but in my mind they may be painted without much art or labor, since they require little more than a good memory and superficial observation. But true humor cannot be shown without a dissection of nature, and a narrow search to discover the first seeds from whence it has its root and growth.

If I were to write to the world, I should be obliged to dwell longer upon each of these distinctions and examples, for I know that they would not be plain enough to all readers. But a bare hint is sufficient to inform you of the notions which I have on this subject: and I hope by this time you are of my opinion, that humor is neither wit, nor folly, nor personal defect, nor affectation, nor habit, and yet that each and all of these have been both written and received for humor.

I should be unwilling to venture even on a bare description of humor, much more to make a definition of it, but now my hand is in, I'll tell you what serves one instead of either. I take it to be *A singular and unavoidable manner of doing or saying anything, peculiar and natural to one man only, by which his speech and actions are distinguished from those of other men.* . . .

A man may change his opinion but I believe he will find it a difficulty to part with his humor, and there is nothing more provoking than the being made sensible of that difference. Sometimes one shall meet with those who perhaps innocently enough, but at the same time impertinently, will ask the question, *Why are you not merry? Why are you not gay, pleasant, and cheerful?* then, instead of answering, could I ask such a one, *Why are you not handsome? Why have you not black eyes and a better complexion?* Nature abhors to be forced. . . .

I don't say but that very entertaining and useful characters, and proper to comedy, may be drawn from affectation and those other qualities which I have endeavored to distinguish from humor; but I would not have such imposed on the world for humor, nor esteemed with equal value with it. It were perhaps the work of a long life to make one comedy true in all its parts, and to give every character in it a true and distinct humor. Therefore every poet must be beholding to other helps to make out his number of ridiculous characters. But I think such

a one deserves to be broke, who makes all false monsters; who does not show one true humor in a comedy, but entertains his audience to the end of the play with everything out of nature.

HENRY FIELDING, from the Preface to *Joseph Andrews:*

The only source of the true Ridiculous (as it appears to me) is affectation. But though it arises from one spring only, when we consider the infinite streams into which this one branches, we shall presently cease to admire at the copious field it affords to an observer. Now, affectation proceeds from one of these two causes, vanity or hypocrisy: for as vanity puts us on affecting false characters, in order to purchase applause; so hypocrisy sets us on an endeavour to avoid censure, by concealing our vices under an appearance of their opposite virtues. And though these two causes are often confounded (for there is some difficulty in distinguishing them), yet, as they proceed from very different motives, so they are as clearly distinct in their operations: for indeed, the affectation which arises from vanity is nearer to truth than the other, as it hath not that violent repugnancy of nature to struggle with, which that of the hypocrite hath. It may be likewise noted, that affectation doth not imply an absolute negation of those qualities which are affected; and, therefore, though, when it proceeds from hypocrisy, it be nearly allied to deceit; yet when it comes from vanity only, it partakes of the nature of ostentation: for instance, the affectation of liberality in a vain man differs visibly from the same affectation in the avaricious;

for though the vain man is not what he would appear, or hath not the virtue he affects, to the degree he would be thought to have it; yet it sits less awkwardly on him than on the avaricious man, who is the very reverse of what he would seem to be.

From the discovery of this affectation arises the Ridiculous, which always strikes the reader with surprise and pleasure; and that in a higher and stronger degree when the affectation arises from hypocrisy, than when from vanity; for to discover any one to be the exact reverse of what he affects, is more surprising, and consequently more ridiculous, than to find him a little deficient in the quality he desires the reputation of. I might observe that our Ben Jonson, who of all men understood the Ridiculous the best, hath chiefly used the hypocritical affectation.

Now, from affectation only, the misfortunes and calamities of life, or the imperfections of nature, may become the objects of ridicule. Surely he hath a very ill-framed mind who can look on ugliness, infirmity, or poverty, as ridiculous in themselves: nor do I believe any man living, who meets a dirty fellow riding through the streets in a cart, is struck with an idea of the Ridiculous from it; but if he should see the same figure descend from his coach and six, or bolt from his chair with his hat under his arm, he would then begin to laugh, and with justice. In the same manner, were we to enter a poor house and behold a wretched family shivering with cold and languishing with hunger, it would not incline us to laughter (at least we must have very diabolical natures if it would); but should we

discover there a grate, instead of coals, adorned with flowers, empty plate or china dishes on the sideboard, or any other affectation of riches and finery, either on their persons or in their furniture, we might then indeed be excused for ridiculing so fantastical an appearance. Much less are natural imperfections the object of derision; but when ugliness aims at the applause of beauty, or lameness endeavours to display agility, it is then that these unfortunate circumstances, which at first moved our compassion, tend only to raise our mirth.

The poet carries this very far:

None are for being what they are in
    fault,
But for not being what they would be
    thought.

Where if the metre would suffer the word Ridiculous to close the first line, the thought would be rather more proper. Great vices are the proper objects of our detestation, smaller faults, of our pity; but affectation appears to me the only true source of the Ridiculous.

THE COMIC LANGUAGE

Lope de Vega, from *The New Art of Writing Comedies in Our Time:*

Begin then, and with well-chosen simplicity; waste no wit or fancy on casual family conversation where only the talk of two or three people is to be represented. But when a character is introduced to persuade, advise, or dissuade, then aphorisms and wit are needed; for it is doubtless true that a man speaks differently than he ordinarily does when he is advising, persuading, or refuting something. Aristides, the rhetorician, is our source for this. He wants the language of Comedy to be clean, clear, and fluent; he adds that it should imitate the way that people normally speak, rather than the niceties of polite discourse which would be polished, solemn, and eloquent. The language should not offend by a far-fetched diction, but should be appropriate to the speaker.

When the King speaks, imitate as well as you can his regal gravity. When a wise old man speaks, imitate his sententious modesty. Lovers should speak passionately to carry away the listener. Soliloquies should be handled so that they transform the speaker and, consequently, also transform the listener. Let the speaker question and reply to himself. . . . Be careful to guard against the impossible, for it is a maxim of the greatest importance that only the probable should be represented. Do not allow a lackey to speak of lofty matters or to speak with the elaborate fancifulness, such as we have seen in certain foreign plays. He should certainly not contradict what he has already said. . . . End the scenes with some epigram, mot, or elegant verse, so that when the speaker quits the stage he leaves the audience pleased. . . . Always fit your language with great care to your subject. . . . Use such rhetorical devices as repetition and tying the sentences together with key words at the end or at the beginning. Use also irony, questions, apostrophes, and exclamations.

To trick the audience by telling the truth slantingly or ironically is always an effective device. . . . Equivocal speeches and ambiguities have always been favored by the public, because each person thinks that he alone understands what has been said. . . . These matters you may regard as maxims.

EDITORS' TRANSLATION.

JONATHAN SWIFT, from *Verses on the Death of Dr. Swift:*

Perhaps I may allow, the Dean
Had too much Satyr in his Vein;
And seem'd determin'd not to starve it,
Because no Age could more deserve it.
Yet, Malice never was his Aim;
He lash'd the Vice but spar'd the Name.
No Individual could resent,
Where Thousands equally were meant.
His Satyr points at no Defect,
But what all Mortals may correct;
For he abhorr'd that senseless Tribe,
Who call it Humour when they jibe:
He spar'd a Hump or crooked Nose,
Whose Owners set not up for Beaux.
True genuine Dulness mov'd his Pity,
Unless it offer'd to be witty.
Those, who their Ignorance confess'd,
He ne'er offended with a Jest;
But laugh'd to hear an Idiot quote,
A Verse from *Horace,* learn'd by Rote.

WILLIAM CONGREVE, from *Concerning Humor in Comedy:*

I have observed that when a few things have been wittily and pleasantly spoken by any character in a comedy, it has been very usual for those who make their remarks on a play while it is acting, to say, *Such a thing is very humorously spoken; There is a great deal of humor in that part.* Thus the character of the person speaking, may be, surprisingly and pleasantly is mistaken for a character of humor, which indeed is a character of wit. But there is a great difference between a comedy wherein there are many things *hu-*

morously, as they call it, which is *pleasantly*, spoken, and one where there are several characters of humor, distinguished by the particular and different humors appropriated to the several persons represented, and which naturally arise from the different constitutions, complexions, and dispositions of men. The saying of humorous things does not distinguish characters; for every person in a comedy may be allowed to speak them. From a witty man they are expected; and even a fool may be permitted to stumble on 'em by chance. Though I make a difference betwixt wit and humor, yet I do think that humorous characters exclude wit: no, but the manner of wit should be adapted to the humor. As, for instance, a character of a splenetic and peevish humor should have a satirical wit. A jolly and sanguine humor should have a facetious wit. The former should speak positively; the latter, carelessly: for the former observes and shows things as they are; the latter rather overlooks nature, and speaks things as he would have them, and wit and humor have both of them less alloy of judgment than the others.

As wit, so its opposite, *folly, is sometimes mistaken for humor.*

When a poet brings a character on the stage committing a thousand absurdities, and talking impertinencies, roaring aloud, and laughing immoderately on every or rather upon no occasion, this is a character of humor.

Is anything more common than to have a pretended comedy stuffed with such grotesques, figures and farce fools? Things that either are not in nature, or, if they are, are monsters and births of mischance, and consequently, as such, should be stifled and huddled out of the way. . . .

The Plays

THE SILENT WOMAN

BY BEN JONSON

AN ADAPTATION FOR THE MODERN STAGE IN TWO ACTS

BY ROBERT HOGAN AND SVEN ERIC MOLIN

PREFACE

Since Nahum Tate supplied a ridiculously inappropriate happy ending for *King Lear*, and since Colley Cibber with equal clumsiness tinkered with Shakespeare, the role of him who attempts to modernize a classic play written in his own language has been one of derision if not of contumely. The actual fact is, however, that since Ben Jonson wrote *The Silent Woman* the language has greatly changed. Many of his best jokes, witticisms, and allusions are hidden behind a curtain of language which is often obsolete or archaic.

Since we believe that nothing is

more destructive to comedy than the footnote, and since we believe that most of *The Silent Woman* is as alive and funny today as it was when Jonson wrote it, we have not hesitated to brave the anger of scholars by consistently translating Jonson's more obscure allusions and more archaic words into ones which the contemporary playgoer and playreader can appreciate.

Though we have translated Jonson's decoration, we have always attempted to remain faithful to his tone and to his sense. When he is able, as he is most of the time, to speak entirely in his own voice, we have allowed him to do so.

Our other liberties have been limited to a very occasional shortening of some few passages that both required and defied adaptation, and to changing Jonson's five-act structure into the two acts which are more appropriate for the modern stage.

We plead for our model the best modern translations of classic plays from other languages, such as Benjamin Bickley Rogers' Aristophanes or Lady Gregory's Kiltartan Molière. Such translations attempt above all to find the most contemporary equivalents for the classic phrasing. We have done nothing more.

R. H.

S. E. M.

A NOTE ON THE STAGING: *Because Act I requires several quick changes of scene, the play should be staged simply. Actually, two or three easily movable pieces of furniture—a chair, a table, a couch—would serve both for variety and for indicating a change of scene. To specify the scene more precisely, some simple device, such as the old vaudeville placard that announced the name of a new turn, would suffice: "A Room in Morose's House", "A Street", etc.*

Costumes are a matter for the director's judgment and for his pocketbook. The modernized diction would allow the play to be played without incongruity by actors in modern dress. Our own experience with relatively bare staging is that some more flamboyant or colorful period costume makes the audience more at ease with a comedy.

However, the play's story, characters and jokes remain its strength, and they will still carry the play, no matter whether it is staged elaborately or upon a bare stage. And that strength is one reason for crying "Amen" to the poet's epitaph: O rare Ben Jonson!

CHARACTERS

MOROSE, A Gentleman who loves no noise

SIR DAUPHINE EUGENIE, A Knight, his nephew

NED CLERIMONT, A Gentleman, his friend

TRUEWIT, another friend

SIR JOHN DAW, A Knight

SIR AMOROUS LA-FOOLE, A Knight

THOMAS OTTER, A land and sea Captain

CUTBEARD, A Barber

A SERVANT of Morose

A PARSON

A PAGE to Clerimont

PAGES, SERVANTS, etc.

EPICENE, The Silent Woman

LADY HAUGHTY

LADY CENTAURE

MISTRESS DOLL MAVIS

MISTRESS OTTER, The Captain's Wife

MISTRESS TRUSTY, Lady Haughty's Woman

The Scene: London

ACT ONE

SCENE ONE

[*A Room in Clerimont's House. Clerimont enters getting dressed, and followed by his Page.*]

CLERIMONT. Have you memorized the song I gave you, boy?

PAGE. Yes, sir.

CLERIMONT. Let's hear it.

PAGE. Well—you can, sir, but nobody else.

CLERIMONT. Oh—why not?

PAGE. You'd get a bad name in town, sir. They'd call you a poet. Besides, the song would do me a lot of harm at the house of the lady whom it's about. Now, I'm the welcomest creature below a man that goes there.

CLERIMONT. Hmm, and above a woman too, I imagine.

PAGE. Oh no, sir. The gentlewomen just kid around with me and throw me on the bed and carry me in to my lady. And she just kisses me with her oily face and puts a wig on my head and asks me if I won't wear her gown. And I just say no and she boxes me on the ear and calls me innocent and lets me go. And—that's all.

CLERIMONT. Small wonder I can't get inside when they're having such a pleasant time with you. Get on with your song.

PAGE. [*Singing.*] Still to be neat, still to be dressed—

[*Truewit enters.*]

TRUEWIT. Ah, here's the fellow who can fribble away his time and not know it! Between your mistress abroad and your fireplace at home, between your good food and your soft lodging, your fine clothes and your fiddle, you think the hours have no wings. Well, sir gallant, if you were struck with the plague this minute or condemned to death tomorrow, you'd begin to value every minute of your time.

CLERIMONT. Why, what would you have me doing then?

TRUEWIT. Oh, nothing! Nothing at all. Just keep following the next horse-race and the next hunting-match. Keep on laying wagers, visiting the ladies at night and discussing the merits of every bowler on the green in the day. That's the life for you men about town—and me too.

CLERIMONT. Come now, when we have grey heads and weak hams, moist eyes and shrunk limbs, we can begin to pray and fast.

TRUEWIT. You mean, leave off doing good to our old age when we haven't the ability to do evil?

CLERIMONT. Isn't that the time for good?

TRUEWIT. Oh yes, if a man wants to sleep all day and try and do all his business in the last hour before closing. Oh, Clerimont, we waste away our time in vanity and misery indeed, not finding an end to our wretchedness but only changing its contents.

CLERIMONT. Nonsense! You've been reading Plutarch or some such fusty old moralizer, and it makes you damned dull to listen to. Talk about pins and feathers and ladies, and leave this sad Stoicism for sermons.

TRUEWIT. All right. I'll certainly reform nobody against his will. When were you at the college?

CLERIMONT. What college?

TRUEWIT. Ah, as if you didn't know!

CLERIMONT. No, I just came from court yesterday.

TRUEWIT. Hasn't the news arrived there yet? Why, sir, it's a new organization of ladies here in town. They call themselves the collegiates, and live away from their husbands, and entertain all the wits and bloods. They talk down, or up, whatever fashions they please, and every day they gain new members.

CLERIMONT. Who's the president?

TRUEWIT. The Lady Haughty.

CLERIMONT. She's as ancient as autumn, a pox on her fall's face. She won't even see a man nowadays until she's painted and perfumed and washed and scoured. Oh, she'll see the boy here. She'll wipe her oily lips on him like a sponge. Boy, sing the song I made about her.

PAGE. [Singing.]
Still to be neat, still to be dressed,
As you were going to a feast;
Still to be powdered, still perfumed:
Lady, it is to be presumed,
Though art's hid causes are not found,
All is not sweet, all is not sound.

Give me a look, give me a face
That makes simplicity a grace:
Robes loosely flowing, hair as free:
Such sweet neglect more taketh me
Than all the adulteries of art;

They strike mine eyes, but not my heart.

TRUEWIT. I don't agree. A woman should dress herself up as much as she can. There's more variety in it: she can be a different person every hour. Let her consult her mirror, and play up her best. If she has good ears, show them; good hair, display it; good legs, wear short dresses; a good hand, gesture with it. Let her mend her breath, clean her teeth and touch up her eyebrows. She shouldn't be ashamed to admit she uses cosmetics.

CLERIMONT. Publicly?

TRUEWIT. Well, she can say that she does it, but not how she does it. A lot that seems repulsive in the doing seems attractive when it's done. A lady should study her face when we think she's asleep. And when her doors are shut, we shouldn't be nosing about, because what goes on inside is sacred and secret. Why should we see them put their wigs on, their false teeth, their false complexions, their eyebrows and their fingernails? Does the artist unveil his statue before it's finished?

CLERIMONT. Well said, Truewit.

TRUEWIT. A wise lady'll guard against being discovered in the act. I once followed a clod who burst into a lady's room so hastily that the poor woman snatched at her wig to cover her baldness and clapped it on backwards. And then the lout stood complimenting her reversed face for an hour.

CLERIMONT. You should have rescued her.

TRUEWIT. No, I let her alone, as we'll let this subject, if you please, and pass to another. When did you last see Dauphine Eugenie?

CLERIMONT. Not for three days. Like to go see him this morning? I hear he's pretty depressed.

TRUEWIT. Sick of his uncle, probably. I met that stiff piece of formality yesterday, with a huge turban of nightcaps buckled over his ears.

CLERIMONT. He always does that when he leaves home. He can't endure noise.

TRUEWIT. I heard he paid the fishwives and orange-sellers not to howl around his house.

CLERIMONT. He can't stand costardmongers either. He faints if he hears one.

TRUEWIT. What if he heard a blacksmith?

CLERIMONT. He won't let one live in the parish.

TRUEWIT. I'd bet a trumpet would make him jump.

CLERIMONT. Clear out of his senses.

PAGE. And, sir, he lives in a street too narrow for coaches and carts to rumble down it. But some of us manage to entertain him now and then, so his virtue won't rust with inaction. I persuaded a bear-keeper to cry his games under Master Morose's window one day—poor fellow, he got an awfully bloody head.

TRUEWIT. How can he stand the bells?

CLERIMONT. He used to leave town on holidays. Now, he's so sick and old that he's fixed up a room with double walls, triple ceilings and caulked windows. He lives in it by candlelight. Why, last week he turned away a man for having a pair of new shoes that squeaked. His new servant has to wear stockings or slippers soled with wool.

[*Sir Dauphine Eugenie enters.*]

DAUPHINE. Hallo there! Well, what ails you? Struck dumb?

TRUEWIT. Almost struck into stone, I'm so amazed at these stories about your uncle.

DAUPHINE. I wish you'd drop that subject. It's my friends who've gotten me into the predicament I am with him.

TRUEWIT. What's that?

DAUPHINE. He wants to disinherit me. He thinks my friends and I have cooked up all of these ridiculous stories about him.

TRUEWIT. I'd do more than that to irk a fellow like him. I'll tell you what I'd do. I'd have a false calendar printed for him, and then lure him outside on Coronation Day, and kill him with the noise of the cannon. Disinherit you! He can't do that, man! Aren't you his next of kin, his nephew?

DAUPHINE. Yes, but he intends to get married.

TRUEWIT. He can't stand noise, and he intends to get married!

CLERIMONT. Oh, you haven't heard his latest trick. For the last half a year, he's hired a fellow to search all over England and find him a dumb wife. He doesn't care whether she's rich or pretty—just so she's fertile. Her silence is enough dowry for him.

TRUEWIT. I hope to God he's found nobody.

CLERIMONT. He's heard of one who lives in the very next street. She's said to speak only six words a day, and he's vowed to have her.

TRUEWIT. Who's handling the business for him?

CLERIMONT. Cutbeard, the barber. He's an honest fellow who betrays all Morose's plans to Dauphine.

TRUEWIT. You dazzle me. A silent woman *and* a whispering barber! Let's go and see these two wonders.

DAUPHINE. I can't. I have some other business.

TRUEWIT. You can't neglect this business. We'll make that silent woman talk. Or, if we can't, we'll say we have. It's your duty, when he accuses you without cause, to torment him.

DAUPHINE. No, I won't have it. He'll never be able to say I opposed his least wish.

TRUEWIT. Would you like to be a beggar? Do you want this barber or one of the old fool's grooms to get him an heir? Ned, where does she live?

CLERIMONT. Right next to the barber's. In the same house where Sir John Daw lives.

TRUEWIT. Does Morose know that? That would ruin her reputation for silence.

CLERIMONT. Why?

TRUEWIT. Why? She lives in the same house with the greatest chatterer in town. Jack Daw!—Well, I must be off. I've just remembered a little business I have.

CLERIMONT. You're not going to see her, then?

TRUEWIT. I'm too prone to earaches to expose myself to Daw.

CLERIMONT. I thought you two were on good terms.

TRUEWIT. Yes, of keeping apart.

CLERIMONT. They say's he's an excellent scholar.

TRUEWIT. But he says it first.

CLERIMONT. No, really, I've heard him say some very good things.

TRUEWIT. Would they were his own. Good day, gentlemen. [*He goes out hastily.*]

DAUPHINE. I wish you wouldn't tell everybody about my uncle.

CLERIMONT. Why, Dauphine, Truewit's an honest fellow.

DAUPHINE. He can't keep a secret.

CLERIMONT. Oh, that's not so! I know—

DAUPHINE. I won't argue with you, Ned, but the fewer who know about this business, the better we'll carry it off. Do you want to go and see the silent woman with me?

CLERIMONT. Yes, certainly. When were you there last?

DAUPHINE. Last night, and good sport it was. Daw does nothing but court her, and he's utterly inept. He wants to seduce her, and he praises her modesty. He wants her to talk to him freely, and he writes verses praising her silence. The verses, incidentally, he reads himself and swears are the best ever made by man.

CLERIMONT. I've got to see this— bring me some water, boy.

[*The Page goes out.*]

DAUPHINE. Sir La-Foole has invited Daw and me to dinner tonight.

CLERIMONT. That booby.

DAUPHINE. Do you know him?

CLERIMONT. Who could help it? If he meets you just once, he'll know you, too. Even if he should spot you in church in the middle of your prayers. He'd greet a judge on the bench, a bishop in the pulpit, a lawyer in court, and a lady dancing with someone else. Why, he invites guests to his suppers by leaning out of his window and hailing them as they ride past.

DAUPHINE. Gad. What's his Christian name?

[*The Page comes in.*]

CLERIMONT. Sir Amorous La-Foole.

PAGE. That gentleman is here now, sir.

CLERIMONT. Ten to one he's come to invite me to dinner.

DAUPHINE. Probably. Let's have him up.

CLERIMONT. Hurry him along, boy.

PAGE. With a club, sir?

CLERIMONT. Get along with you! [*The Page goes out.*] I'll bet you he tells us: one, his pedigree; two, what he's going to have for dinner; three, who his guests are; and, four, the whole course of his fortunes—and all in one breath.

[*Sir Amorous enters.*]

LA-FOOLE. Dear Master Clerimont! And Dear Sir Dauphine!

CLERIMONT. Sir Amorous, your visit honors my poor lodgings.

LA-FOOLE. Oh, pooh, sir, it's a fine lodging, almost as delicate as mine.

CLERIMONT. Oh, no, no, nonsense.

LA-FOOLE. Really, it is!—if it were only in the Strand, of course. But I've come to ask you to wait upon two or three ladies at dinner today, Master Clerimont.

CLERIMONT. Wait on them! Did you ever see me carry dishes!

LA-FOOLE. No, no, sir. I meant to keep them company.

CLERIMONT. Glad to, sir. But that phrase you used might cause you a quarrel with some people.

LA-FOOLE. I-I shouldn't like to quarrel with anybody, sir.

CLERIMONT. I can well believe it. Where is your feast?

LA-FOOLE. At Tom Otter's, sir.

DAUPHINE. Tom Otter? Who's he?

LA-FOOLE. Captain Otter, sir. He's a kind of gambler, but he's had commands both by sea and land. His wife is my kinswoman, a La-Foole by my mother's side. She'll invite any great ladies to her house for me.

DAUPHINE. Not the La-Fooles of Essex?

LA-FOOLE. No, sir. The La-Fooles of London.

CLERIMONT. [*Whispering to Dauphine.*] One!

LA-FOOLE. Of course, there are La-Fooles everywhere. The La-Fooles of the north, the La-Fooles of the west, the La-Fooles of the east and south. We're as old a family as any in Europe. But, never mind; nobody respects tradition now. I had a brace of fat does sent me, gentlemen, and half a dozen pheasants—

CLERIMONT. Two!

LA-FOOLE. —and some other fowl, and I want to eat them in good company. And I'll have good company, too. There'll be some great ladies like Lady Haughty, Lady Centaure—

CLERIMONT. Three!

LA-FOOLE. —Mistress Doll Mavis. All of them are coming specially to see Mistress Epicene, the famous silent woman whom Sir John Daw's promised to bring along. Then Mistress Trusty, my lady's woman, will be there, and, of course, you two gentlemen. Oh, we'll have a merry time, yes, we will. We'll have fiddlers and dancing. Dancing, you know, I have been a mad wag in my time. Yes, I've kicked up my wild oats and sown my heels, but that's all over. All over. I've reformed, and spent a good deal to acquire my knighthood in

Ireland—

CLERIMONT. Four!

LA-FOOLE. The day I was knighted I wore as handsome a gold suit as you'd see anywhere. I came right over to London in it and showed it to all my friends. Then I went down to my tenants in the country, looked over my lands, let new leases, took their money, spent it here upon the ladies, and now I do whatever I please. I'm my own master.

DAUPHINE. Do you—

CLERIMONT. Let him get his breath. He'll strangle.

LA-FOOLE. Now, sir, excuse me. I have another guest or two to invite and chat with. Good day, gentlemen. [He goes out.]

CLERIMONT. Did you ever hear such a wind-sucker as this?

DAUPHINE. Or such a rook as Daw who'll betray his mistress to the sneers and snickers of the college? Come, it's time we put a stop to that. [They both go out.]

SCENE TWO

[A Room in Morose's House. Morose enters followed by a servant.]

MOROSE. There must be some easy way to save my servants the labor of speech and me the pain of listening. All voices but my own drive me wild, wild! They're harsh, impertinent, grating and irksome. Can't you answer me by signs, fellow? Have you taken the doorbell off, as I told you? Don't speak unless the answer's no! [The Servant bows.] Very good. And have you fastened a thick quilt outside the door, so that if they pound on it with their daggers and brickbats, they can make no noise? Bow your answer un-

less it's no. [The Servant bows.] Very good. And have you told Cutbeard the barber to come here? [The Servant bows.] Good. And will he be here shortly? Bow if yes, and—hmm—shake your head if no. [The Servant bows.] How long will it be till he gets here? Wait! If it's an hour, hold up your hand. Half an hour, hold up two fingers. Fifteen minutes, one finger. [The Servant holds up a finger bent.] Good. Seven and a half minutes, eh? [The Servant bows.] Did you give him a key so he can get in without knocking? [The Servant bows.] And did you oil the lock and the hinges today? [The Servant bows.] Very good! [A horn blows offstage.] Oh! Oh! What villain is that? Look and see! Look and see! [The horn blows again, as the Servant goes out.] Oh, cut his throat, cut his throat! What murderer, hell-hound and devil can it be!

[The Servant returns.]

SERVANT. It's a post from the court—

MOROSE. Get out of here, you rogue! Do you have to blow your own horn, too?

SERVANT. But it's a post from the court, sir, who says he must speak to you on a matter of life and death.

MOROSE. On your own life and death, be quiet!

[Truewit comes in, carrying a post-horn and a halter.]

TRUEWIT. Pardon me, sir. I'm a stranger here. Is your name Master Morose?—I say, is your name Master Morose?—Cat got your tongue? Hmm. Well, I guess you're probably him, so I'll just give you the message. Your friends at court greet you, sir—

MOROSE. O men! O manners! Was

there ever such impudence!

TRUEWIT. Your friends at court are quite worried about you, sir.

MOROSE. FETCH ME MY SWORD!

TRUEWIT. You'll taste half of my dagger if you do, groom. And you the other half if you stir, sir. Now, be patient in the King's name, and listen. Your friends hear that you are about to marry—to marry! Do you understand, sir?

MOROSE. Yes! What of it?

TRUEWIT. Your friends wonder why you want to marry, sir, when you live so near the Thames where you can drown handsomely. Or when a fine leap off London Bridge would hurry you nicely down the stream. Or when you have such a lovely steeple in town as the Bow to jump off of. Or an even braver tower like St. Paul's. Or, if you wanted to do it nearer home, when you have an excellent garret window leading to the street. Or a stout beam in said garret for this noose which they sent hoping you would commit your grave head to it rather than the noose of matrimony. Or, if it's a matter of convenience, you could take a little rat poison. Anything but embrace this goblin matrimony. Why, my poor sir, do you think you'll find a chaste wife in these times? *Now?* When there are so many masques, plays, Puritan preachers, madmen, and other strange sights. If you'd lived in King Arthur's time you might have found one in some cold country hamlet—some dull, frosty wench would have been contented with one man. Nowadays, they'd as soon be pleased with one leg or one eye. I tell you, sir, you don't realize the monstrous hazards you run with a wife.

MOROSE. Good sir, have I ever cheated any friends of yours out of their land? Foreclosed on their mortgages? Bastarded their issue? What have I done to deserve this?

TRUEWIT. Nothing, sir, that I know, except your itch for marriage.

MOROSE. Why, if I'd assassinated your father, used up your mother, ravished your sisters—

TRUEWIT. I'd kill you, sir, I'd kill you if you had.

MOROSE. YOU'RE DOING IT ANYHOW!

TRUEWIT. Sorry, sir. I'm only a messenger. I'm just telling you what you ought to know for your own good. Your friends are worried about your peace of mind, sir.

MOROSE. So am I.

TRUEWIT. They want you to realize the danger you face. If, after you're married, your wife runs away with an athlete or a French tightrope walker or a fencing master, why, it won't be their fault. They'll have done their duty. Now, suffer valiantly, sir, for I must tell you all the obnoxious perils of marriage. If your wife is fair, young and lusty, you'll find that no candy ever drew more flies. All the yellow doublets in town'll swarm around. If she's foul and crooked, she'll swarm around them and buy them doublets, sir. If she's rich, she'll rule your house like a widow. If she's noble, all her kinfolks will lord it over you. If she's fertile, she'll be as proud as May and as humorous as April. She'll have to have her doctors, midwives, nurses and special fancies every hour. If she's learned, you'll never know such a chatterbox. You'll go bankrupt entertaining the guests she invites to hear her speak Latin and Greek. If she's religious, you'll have to feast the Ministers every three days, entertain the brethren just as often, hear long-winded sermonds, psalms, singings and catechisms. She'll preach to you and pray over you and—ahh! beginning to sweat I see! But this isn't the half of it. Of course, you can do whatever you want. As I said before, I didn't come to persuade you.

MOROSE. What, what, WHAT have I done to deserve this?!!!

TRUEWIT. And if you love her, if you dote on her, oho, sir, how she'll torture you. And how she'll enjoy it! You'll lie with her only when she feels like it. She'll put you off, saying she doesn't want to hurt her complexion. And when she does allow you, you'll have to bribe her first with a jewel or pearl. Every half-hour's pleasure you'll have to buy anew, with all the pain and trouble you used to court her at the first. Also, you'll have to keep what servants she likes, and what company. She'll determine who comes to the house and who doesn't. And, of course, her friends at the college will teach her all the wiles of writing letters, corrupting servants, and taming spies. They'll tell her she must have a certain rich gown for a certain day, a new one for the next, and a more expensive one yet for the third. She'll have to be served in silver plates, and have the room filled with grooms, footmen, ushers, lackeys, pages, and other messengers. Not to mention her embroiderers, jewellers, dressmakers, hairdressers, and perfumers. Oh, it won't bother her how your land drops away, how your acres melt, how the mercer has your woods for her velvets.

MOROSE. Oh, oh, oh!

TRUEWIT. All this is very true, sir. And then she'll have her eccentricities and superstitions, like going to the fortune teller. And the first question she'll ask him is, how soon shall you die? And the next question, does her present servant love her? And the next, when shall she have a new servant, and how many? And she'll write down all the answers and take more stock in them than Scripture.

MOROSE. Kind sir, isn't that all? Haven't you told me everything? Believe me, I think about all these things.

TRUEWIT. Yes, sir. God be with you, sir.—Oh, one thing more. I'd almost forgot it. She may already have presented her virginity to some friend, sir. Who knows? Or, if she hasn't done it yet, she probably will on the wedding-day, or the night before. Oh, yes, it's been heard of. It's not impossible, sir. Well, God be with you. I'll just leave this rope with you, sir, as a memento. [*Truewit goes out.*]

MOROSE. Oh, take me to my room —but first shut the door! [*Truewit blows his horn offstage.*] Oh, shut the door, shut the door! He's come back!

[*Cutbeard comes in.*]

CUTBEARD. It's just me, sir, your barber.

MOROSE. Oh, Cutbeard, Cutbeard, Cutbeard, there's been a cut-throat with me. Help me into bed. [*They go out.*]

SCENE THREE

[*A Room in Sir John Daw's House. Daw, Clerimont, Dauphine, and Epicene enter.*]

DAW. Let her decide whether she wants to go. It's nothing to me, gentlemen. Nothing to me. Nothing at all.

I don't care. Of course, she won't be invited to such a feast every day.

CLERIMONT. Oh, she can't possibly refuse—[*Whispers to Epicene.*]—to stay at home. This trumpeter's already blown your praises. He's taking you there to be laughed at.

DAUPHINE. [*Whispers to Epicene.*] Don't go. Let him be laughed at for not bringing you.

CLERIMONT. He'll suspect us. Talk outloud.—Er, Mistress Epicene, let's see the verses Sir John has written you. Don't hide your servant's merit and your own praises.

DAW. Show them, show them, by all means, mistress. I'll read them myself. An author should recite his more accomplished works, don't you think? Now, this one is a Madrigal to Modesty. Harumph. "Modesty".

Be modest and fair, not bright and
    clever,
However.

CLERIMONT. "However"?

DAUPHINE. Very good!

CLERIMONT. —Yes, isn't it!

DAW. Admirable qualities of char-
    acter were never single;
They mingle.

To praise, consequently, one virtue
    alone I'd abhor;
Therefore,
It is your modesty and beauty inter-
    twined together I bless,
I guess.

DAUPHINE. Admirable.

CLERIMONT. Just like Seneca.

DAUPHINE. No, it has more the flavor of Euclid I think.

DAW. Seneca, Euclid, those scribblers. Bah, scribblers, I say!

CLERIMONT. They're very respected authors.

DAW. Respected asses! Asses! Mere essayists, hacks, tragedians, and journalists. A few loose sentences strung higgledy-piggledy together, and that's all. Why, I say things just as good every hour, if only someone would have the wit to take them down.

DAUPHINE. Really!

DAW. Yes, yes, indeed! Why, what's your Arrowstootle, but a commonplace fellow? And that babbler Pluto, not a bit better. Or Thudydices and Levy, dry as dust both of them.

CLERIMONT. What do you think of the poets, Sir John?

DAW. Poets! Poets! Bah! Not worthy of the name, sir, not worthy of the name. Take Homer, that old, tedious, prolix ass, always talking about sides of beef. Take Vergil, always talking about manure and bees, manure and bees. And Horace, I don't know what on earth he talks about.

CLERIMONT. I can believe that. Er, I'm surprised that this lady can remain so silent in the face of such an eloquent lover.

DAW. As a matter of fact, I've written a piece about her silence, and I may just possibly have it with me. Ahh yes, here it is.

CLERIMONT. Let's hear it, by all means, Sir John.

DAW. Well, if you insist. Harumph. "Silence."

Shall I wasting in old hair,
    Nearly bald and nearly bare,
While on my pate the filmy fuzz
    Wanders where the tresses was?

DAUPHINE. "Silence"?

CLERIMONT. Silence!

DAW. Your silence, love, is like my
    curls,

More appropriate for girls;
Who could think this conceit poor,
To compare my hair and whore?

DAUPHINE. Hair, Hair!

EPICENE. [*Quietly.*] Please give me my verses back.

DAW. You'll have to ask for them aloud. Aloud, I say. [*Daw and Epicene go out.*]

CLERIMONT. Here's Truewit again. [*Truewit enters with his horn.*] Where in the name of madness have you been with that horn?

TRUEWIT. Where the sound of it should have pierced your ears with gladness. Dauphine, fall down and worship me. I've been with your virtuous uncle and broken off the match.

DAUPHINE. You haven't!

TRUEWIT. I have! This horn got me into the house, kiss it! I pretended to be a post, but once inside I turned him to a post by thundering out the inconveniences of a wife and the miseries of a marriage. If ever Gorgon was seen in the shape of a woman, he's seen her in my description. I've put him off the scent forever. Well, why don't you applaud, gentlemen?— What are you looking at me like that for?—Say something, Dauphine.—I did it for your own good.

DAUPHINE. Didn't I tell you? Mischief!

CLERIMONT. I wish you'd taken this good somewhere else.

TRUEWIT. What!

CLERIMONT. You've done the most inconsiderate, rash thing a man ever did to his friend.

DAUPHINE. Friend! My worst enemy couldn't have done anything worse.

TRUEWIT. For God's sake, tell me what I've done.

DAUPHINE. I warned you, Clerimont.

CLERIMONT. I wish my lips had been soldered. What in Heaven's name made you be so meddling?

TRUEWIT. I was just trying to do you—

DAUPHINE. Do me! By God, you've undone me. Four months' planning you've blasted in a minute. Well, I might as well tell you now. This gentlewoman was lodged here by me on purpose. I wanted my uncle to hear of her. She's kept this obstinate silence for my sake. If I'd helped her to marry my uncle and come into his fortune, she'd have made me a handsome allowance. But now everything's ruined by this miserable accident.

CLERIMONT. This is always what happens when some ignorant busybody tries to help. What courteous itch possessed you? You never did a sillier thing in your life.

[*Cutbeard enters.*]

DAUPHINE. Well, Cutbeard, anything new?

CUTBEARD. The best that ever was, sir. There was a wild madman with your uncle this morning—[*He sees Truewit.*]—this is the gentleman. And he almost talked him out of his wits threatening him away from marriage—

DAUPHINE. Ohhh.

CUTBEARD. And your uncle, sir, he thinks you sent the madman.

DAUPHINE. Ohhhhh.

CUTBEARD. Therefore, he wants to see the lady immediately. And, by my razor strop, if she's as silent as I've told him, he swears he'll marry her today. Instantly!

DAUPHINE. No! Oh, excellent! Better than I'd hoped.

TRUEWIT. And just what I expected.

DAUPHINE. Oh, Truewit, forgive me.

TRUEWIT. No, I was inconsiderate, meddling, ignorant. Hah! I knew it would turn out like this. My genius is never false to me in these matters.

DAUPHINE. Well, anyway, it turned out all right. [*Speaking to them, he leads Epicene on.*] You two find Sir John while I send the lady off with her instructions. Madam—

TRUEWIT. Introduce me to the lady first.

CLERIMONT. Master Truewit, madam, a dear and trusted friend of ours.

TRUEWIT. I'm sorry not to have known you sooner, madam, to have celebrated this rare virtue of your silence.

[*Epicene curtsies. Dauphine leads Epicene out, and Cutbeard follows them. Daw enters.*]

TRUEWIT. Jack Daw, hello there! When's the last time you saw La-Foole?

DAW. Not since last night, Master Truewit. Not since last night.

TRUEWIT. That's a miracle. I thought you two were inseparable.

DAW. He's gone to invite his guests.

TRUEWIT. By God, that's right. And I'm one of them. What a poor memory I have about that man. I met him just now dashing about with his horse all in a lather to remind every one.

DAW. Where's Mistress Epicene?

CLERIMONT. She went ahead to the feast with Sir Dauphine.

DAW. Gone? Without me? Without me? Well, let her! Let her, I say, let her. She can sit alone silent in her room for a week, sit alone in her room for a whole week without me to chat with.

TRUEWIT. If I were you, I wouldn't speak a word to her today for that.

DAW. By George, I won't.

TRUEWIT. Nor to anybody else.

DAW. Well, I wouldn't go so far as to say that. No, I shouldn't go quite that far. Well, shall we be off too, gentlemen?

CLERIMONT. You'd better walk ahead by yourself, Sir John. You'll look sadder that way, and ladies are always impressed by melancholy.

TRUEWIT. We'll follow right behind you.

[*Daw goes out.*]

CLERIMONT. It would have been better for us all if you had convinced him to be silent. Was there ever such a two yards of knighthood made to be laughed at?

TRUEWIT. A mere talking mole, a fellow so utterly nothing that he doesn't know what he would be if he could.

CLERIMONT. Before we follow him, let's find Dauphine. He'll be hovering about his uncle's house to hear any news.

SCENE FOUR

[*A Room in Morose's House. Morose and his Servant enter, followed by Cutbeard and Epicene.*]

MOROSE. Welcome, Cutbeard. Bring your fair charge over here. So!—Is the door locked? [*The Servant bows.*] Good! Now, Cutbeard, answer me the same way he does. Is this the lady who you think might make me a proper wife? [*Cutbeard bows.*] I presume you're acquainted with her birth, education, and character? [*Cutbeard bows.*] That's right. Bow if the answer's yes. [*Cutbeard bows.*] Well now, let's examine her. Humph. Hmmm. Yesss. I say, let's examine her aptitude for my affection. Hmmm, a well-favored wench, having a—hmm—sweet composition or—hmm—harmony of limbs, as it were. Come here, young lady. Don't be frightened by my seemingly gruff behaviour. [*Epicene curtseys.*] No, madam, you may speak, though Cutbeard and my man may not, for the one sound which doesn't grate on my ears is the sweet voice of a lovely lady. Hmm, I wonder if this could be love at first sight. Do you feel any such sudden emotion shoot through you, as you look at me, eh? [*Epicene curtseys.*] Come now, these silent gestures are too rustic and simple. My wife will have to be accomplished and courtly. Can't you speak?

EPICENE. [*Almost inaudibly.*] Yes.

MOROSE. What did you say? Come, speak up.

EPICENE. Yes.

MOROSE. What a divine softness! But will you really be able to give up woman's chief pleasure of chattering? Will you be able to answer me chiefly with gestures? [*Epicene curtseys.*] Oh, excellent! Superb! If it's only true! Cutbeard, if she can pass my tests, your fortune's made. Let me try her again.—Lady, my wife must be able to feast my ears with merry pleasantries, japes, sallies, quips, and witticisms. The ladies of the court are all adept at such amorous discourse and pretty nothings. But you're not, eh? Do you really differ so much from other women? Can you really bury yourself in silence?

EPICENE. [*Almost inaudibly.*] I'd be sorry if I couldn't.

MOROSE. What was that? Good lady, speak out.

EPICENE. I'd be sorry if I couldn't.

MOROSE. What happy sorrow; it fills me with gladness. Oh, Morose, you're the happiest of men! Egad, contain yourself. I'll try her just once more with the stiffest test of all.—Ahem, young lady, I want to see my wife dress in the height of fashion. In fact, I want her to set the fashion. So she'll have to confer constantly with dress designers, tailors, lace-women, seamstresses, and embroiderers. She'll probably have to meet with them twice a day to judge the last French fashions. Now, with all this silence of yours, how could you give all of the hundreds of necessary instructions about this embroidery, that lace, those skirts, this cut, that stitch, those roses, this girdle, that fan, the other scarf, these gloves? How could you do that?

EPICENE. [*Almost inaudibly.*] I'll leave it to you, sir.

MOROSE. I didn't quite catch that. What did you say?

EPICENE. I'll leave it to your judgment, sir.

MOROSE. Oh, admirable creature! I'll trouble you no more. What a shame to sin against so sweet a simplicity. Just let me boldly print on those divine lips the seal of being mine. Oh, by the way, Cutbeard, I give you the lease of your house free. No! Just thank me by a bow. [*Cutbeard bows.*] I know what you'd tell me—she's poor and her friends are dead. But she's brought a wealthy dowry in her silence, Cutbeard. The poorer she is, the more obedient she'll be anyway. So, go fetch a minister, Cutbeard, right away—one with a soft, low voice. [*Cutbeard goes out, and Morose turns to the Servant.*]

Conduct your new mistress to the dining-room. [*The Servant goes out, followed by Epicene.*] Oh, joy! How I'll be revenged on my insolent nephew for all his plots to frighten me from marrying. This night I'll get me an heir, ah-hah! And cut Dauphine off without a cent! [*He goes out, chortling gleefully.*]

SCENE FIVE

[*A Lane near Morose's House. Truewit, Dauphine, and Clerimont enter.*]

TRUEWIT. Are you sure he hasn't gone by already?

DAUPHINE. No, I've been watching in that shop over there ever since he left me.

CLERIMONT. He could leave by the other end of the lane.

DAUPHINE. I told him I'd be at this —here he comes.

[*Cutbeard comes in.*]

DAUPHINE. Cutbeard! Did it work?

CUTBEARD. Past imagination, sir. By my soapdish, you couldn't have prayed for it to turn out better. He's so happy he's given me the lease free to my house. I'm running now for a silent minister to marry him.

DAUPHINE. For God's sake, get along with you then. I wouldn't stop you for anything.

[*Cutbeard goes out.*]

TRUEWIT. I've thought of a rare joke to celebrate this marriage, gentlemen.

DAUPHINE. What is it?

TRUEWIT. Let's transport all La-Foole's company and his feast to your uncle's house.

DAUPHINE. [*Laughing.*] But how could we do it?

TRUEWIT. Simple. I'll send all the lady-guests there, and then the meal must follow.

CLERIMONT. What a comedy of noises that would be. Jack Daw, La-Foole, and that college of chattering magpies. Who knows where Captain Otter's house is?

TRUEWIT. I'll lead you. Weren't you ever there?

DAUPHINE. Not I.

CLERIMONT. Nor I.

TRUEWIT. Where've you lived then, don't you know Tom Otter?

CLERIMONT. No, for God's sake, who is he?

TRUEWIT. An excellent animal, just like Daw or La-Foole, if not better. He babbles Latin as much as the barber. He's utterly henpecked. He calls his wife "princess" and follows her around the house like a page, with his hat off, partly for heat, partly for reverence. Right now he's getting his bull, bear, and horse ready.

DAUPHINE. What in the name of Sphinx are those?

TRUEWIT. Why, sir, he was a great man at the Bear-garden in his time, and from that subtle sport has taken the witty names of his drinking cups. One he calls his bull, another his bear, the third his horse. He's never at ease or thinks any party a success until he has brought these out and shown them to everybody.

CLERIMONT. For God's sake! We can't miss this.

TRUEWIT. He has a thousand tricks just like that to keep him talking all day. He'll rage against his wife behind her back, and to her face—

DAUPHINE. Nothing more about him, let's go see him to his face. [*They go out.*]

SCENE SIX

[*A Room in Otter's House. Captain Otter enters carrying three drinking mugs, one shaped like a bull, another like a bear, and the third like a horse. Mistress Otter follows at his heels.*]

MRS. OTTER. I'll chain you up with your bulls and your bears if you don't keep a civil tongue. I'll put you out to live in the kennel if you pester me with your bull, bear, and horse again. Can't the courtiers or the collegiates ever come to this house without you dragging those miserable drinking mugs out?

OTTER. Now princess, now princess, they expect to see my drinking cups. My drinking cups are famous all over England.

[*Truewit, Clerimont and Dauphine come in at the rear.*]

MRS. OTTER. Not one syllable more! I won't have my house polluted with bears and bulls when it's perfumed for great ladies. When I married you, didn't you say I would be treated like a princess? Didn't you say I would reign in my own house? Didn't you say that you would obey me? Don't I allow you a half-crown a day to spend with your nasty gambling friends? Then why do you torment me like this? Why? Who gives you your keep? Tell me that? Who puts the meat on the table? Who buys your three suits of clothes a year? And your four pair of stockings, one silk and three worsted? Who buys your clean linen, your nice ruffs and cuffs— not that you could be persuaded to wear clean linen. Who brings courtiers and famous people to this house? Did any Lord or Lady ever pay a bit, one bit of attention to you before I married you? Did they? Did they?

TRUEWIT. For God's sake, let's go pull her off him.

MRS. OTTER. Answer me that. Didn't I take you up when all you had on your back was an old greasy buff doublet? Are you forgetting that? [*The three men come forward.*] Oh, here are some of the gallants! [*To Otter.*] You behave yourself, or I'll cut off your allowance.

TRUEWIT. Good day, Mistress Otter. May I introduce these gentlemen?

MRS. OTTER. I shan't be obnoxious to that honor, sir.

TRUEWIT. How do you do, Captain? Are your bear, bull, and horse to be seen today?

MRS. OTTER. No, and he's going to intimate them. Off to the kitchen, and get the toast and butter ready for the woodcocks; that's the job for you. [*She drives him out.*]

CLERIMONT. What a tyrant this poor fellow's married to.

DAUPHINE. Does he ever speak out?

TRUEWIT. Oh, the sport will be when we get him alone. Then no demagogue, confirmed bachelor, misanthrope or parson ever railed and ranted so fiercely.

MRS. OTTER. [*Returning.*] Gentlemen, you are very ineptly come. My cousin, Sir Amorous, will be here shortly.

TRUEWIT. Has Sir John Daw arrived yet?

MRS. OTTER. I cannot insure you for certain, Master Truewit. I did glimpse some melonchilly knight—

DAUPHINE. What excellent phrases this lady expresses herself with.

TRUEWIT. Oh, sir, she's the most authentic courtier in the city.

MRS. OTTER. I'm only the servant of the court and the courtiers, sir.

TRUEWIT. Rather, they are your idolaters.

[Cutbeard enters.]

DAUPHINE. Cutbeard! Is anything wrong?

CUTBEARD. Oh no, sir, omnia bene. It's going as smoothly as a new-shaven jaw. He's delighted with the curate I found. It's a fellow with a cold who can hardly be heard six inches away. He's a fine, quick fellow, sir, an excellent barber of prayers.

DAUPHINE. A barber?

CUTBEARD. He cuts them off short.

DAUPHINE. Thanks, honest Cutbeard. Now, go and watch for us with a key to let us in.

CUTBEARD. I won't fail you, sir. [He goes out.]

TRUEWIT. And I'll go and watch for Daw's coach.

CLERIMONT. Do, and we'll send him to you, if you miss him. [Truewit goes out.]

MRS. OTTER. Won't you step inside, gentlemen?

DAUPHINE. Thank you, no, madam. We're waiting to speak with a knight, Sir John Daw, who is to come here. We'll follow you in shortly.

[Daw enters and is taken aside by Clerimont.]

MRS. OTTER. Whatever you say, sir. After all, it's my cousin's feast, not mine.

DAUPHINE. I know, madam.

MRS. OTTER. Of course, it's mine too. But it's for his honor, so naturally I take no credit for it, except for it being at my house.

DAUPHINE. You're very generous.

MRS. OTTER. [Simpering as she goes out.] Your servant, sir.

CLERIMONT. Why, don't you know, Sir John?

DAW. No, I'm a rook if I do.

CLERIMONT. And rooked if you don't. Well, I'll tell you. She's married by this time. I know that she left with Sir Dauphine, but he's been the noblest and honestest friend to you that a man could boast of. Why, he discovered the whole plot, and made your mistress admit it. In fact, he made her so ashamed of injuring you, that she wants you to forgive her and grace her wedding with your presence. She's to be married to a good fortune, to Dauphine's uncle, old Morose. And she told me to say—in confidence, you understand—that she'll be able to do more for you now and with more safety than before.

DAW. Did she really say that? Did she really? My word!

CLERIMONT. Why, what do you take me for, Sir John? Ask Sir Dauphine.

DAW. No, no, no. I believe you. Good Sir Dauphine, did she want me to forgive her?

DAUPHINE. Yes, Sir John, she did indeed.

DAW. Well, then, I do with all my heart.

CLERIMONT. And listen, sir. La-Foole intended this feast to honor her wedding day. He was going to invite her and give you the gate. But now that Sir Dauphine has made her see the light, she wants you to bring all the ladies to Morose's house, and there she'll have a dinner which shall be in your name and which will utterly confound La-Foole.

DAW. By my knighthood, I honor her and forgive her heartily! Heartily!

CLERIMONT. Truewit's already gone for your coach. Go find him and— [*Sir Amorous enters.*] Here comes your antagonist. Don't pay any attention to him. Keep smiling.

LA-FOOLE. Ah, Sir John Daw, are the ladies and your mistress here yet? [*Daw goes out.*] Sir Dauphine, you're welcome, indeed. And you too, honest Master Clerimont. Where's my cousin? Haven't you seen any of the collegiates, gentlemen?

DAUPHINE. Collegiates! Haven't you heard, Sir Amorous, how you've been insulted?

LA-FOOLE. Sir?

CLERIMONT. Are you still on such good terms with Sir John Daw after what he's done?

LA-FOOLE. What has he done, gentlemen? Tell me.

CLERIMONT. Why, sir, his mistress married Sir Dauphine's uncle today, and Daw has diverted all your company over there to disgrace you. He was just now trying to entice us away, too. But we told him off.

LA-FOOLE. Has he really treated me like this?

DAUPHINE. He has, Sir Amorous, most maliciously and treacherously, but I can tell you how to get even with him.

LA-FOOLE. What is it, gentlemen? I'll do anything, anything!

DAUPHINE. Well, sir, get your pheasants and your best meat and put them in your cousin's best silver dishes. Then clap a clean towel around you like a waiter, and march bareheaded before the dinner right over to her house. It's quite close by, and we'll back you up when you set it on the table and tell them they're welcome to it. That'll show it's yours,

and completely disgrace his preparations. And for your cousin, she shan't have to go to all of the trouble here at home, but she'll transfer it all there, and be a guest herself. She'll sit with the college ladies and have her health drunk as often and as loud as the best of them.

LA-FOOLE. I'll tell her right away. I'll do it, and that's that! [*He hurries out.*]

CLERIMONT. I thought that would catch him.

DAUPHINE. Well, now we have guests and food; what shall we do for music?

CLERIMONT. The smell of venison going through the street will attract plenty of fiddlers, you can depend on it.

DAUPHINE. I wish it would attract a few trumpet players too. At any rate, it's going to be a ghastly day for my uncle and a delightful one for us.

CLERIMONT. Yes, if we can keep up the quarrel between Foole and Daw.

DAUPHINE. Just flatter them both like Truewit says, and they'll believe anything.

[*La-Foole enters, dressed like a waiter.*]

CLERIMONT. Look, Sir Amorous has his towel on already. Have you persuaded your cousin?

LA-FOOLE. Yes, she says she'll do anything rather than have the La-Fooles made foolish.

DAUPHINE. Fine! Oh, this will pound all your enemy's plans to powder, Sir Amorous, and utterly annihilate him.

LA-FOOLE. I'll fight fire with fire!

CLERIMONT. But you mustn't give it away. Don't show anyone you're angry.

[*Captain Otter enters.*]

OTTER. Gentlemen, my princess says you shall have all her silver dishes immediately. She's gone to change her clothes, and then she'll be right with you.

CLERIMONT. Well, you're coming too, Captain Otter.

DAUPHINE. By all means, sir!

OTTER. Yes sir, I am. But would you gentlemen ask my princess if I could carry my bear and bull and horse along?

CLERIMONT. Take them, Captain.

LA-FOOLE. My cousin won't like it, gentlemen.

DAUPHINE. She must listen to reason, Sir Amorous.

LA-FOOLE. She'd say the ladies couldn't bear the nasty scent of those cups.

CLERIMONT. Sir, all ladies are con-cup-iscent.

DAUPHINE. Where is your princess, Captain? Lead us on.

OTTER. Follow me, sir!

CLERIMONT. Hurry up, Sir Amorous! [*They all go out.*]

Scene Seven

[*A Room in Morose's House. Morose, Epicene, the Parson and Cutbeard enter.*]

MOROSE. [*Giving the Parson some money.*] Take this for yourself, sir. Here, take two more for having a cold. Your good nose is my good news.

PARSON. [*Speaks as if he had a bad cold.*] I thank your worship.

MOROSE. What did he say, Cutbeard?

CUTBEARD. He says, sir, he'll be glad to catch a cold whenever you need him.

MOROSE. I thank him, but no more talk.

PARSON. God bless your worship, and give you much happiness with your new bride! [*Coughs.*] Uh! Uh! Uh!

MOROSE. Oh, oh, stop him, Cutbeard! Make him give me five shillings of my money back. If it's fair to reward benefits, it's fair to be compensated for injuries. I'll have five shillings back.

CUTBEARD. He says he hasn't the right change, sir.

MOROSE. Then he's got to get it.

CUTBEARD. [*Whispers to the Parson.*] Cough again.

MOROSE. What did he say?

CUTBEARD. He said he'll cough out the difference, sir.

PARSON. Uh, uh, uh!

MOROSE. Take him away, take him away! Keep him quiet! I forgive him! [*Cutbeard leaves, pushing the Parson before him.*]

EPICENE. Shame on you, Master Morose, for using such violence to a man of the church.

MOROSE. Eh, what's this?

EPICENE. This outrage certainly doesn't become a man of your gravity and breeding. Especially to a man of the cloth.

MOROSE. You can speak?

EPICENE. Of course, I can.

MOROSE. You can speak out loud?

EPICENE. Certainly. Did you think you'd married some statue or mario-nette or pure-born idiot who would just stand and gawk at you?

MOROSE. Oh, treachery! Just like a woman! CUTBEARD!

EPICENE. Don't quarrel with Cutbeard. It's too late now. My modesty is somewhat less as a wife than it was as a maiden, I admit, but I hope it will still be suitable to your position in life.

MOROSE. She can talk!

EPICENE. Fluently.

[*Morose's Servant comes in.*]

MOROSE. Where is that rascal Cut-beard?

[*The Servant gestures.*]

EPICENE. Speak to him, fellow, speak to him! I'll have none of this absurd and unnatural dumbness in my house, not in the family that I govern!

[*The Servant goes out.*]

MOROSE. Govern? Good God, I married an Amazon.

[*Truewit comes in.*]

TRUEWIT. Where's Master Morose?

MOROSE. Him again! God have mercy on me!

TRUEWIT. I wish you the best of happiness, Mistress Epicene, in your marriage.

EPICENE. And I thank you, Master Truewit, for your friendly wish.

MOROSE. She's got friends!

TRUEWIT. And my best wishes to you, sir, for happiness with your beautiful bride. Before I was the messenger of night to you, the owl. But now I am the messenger of peace, the dove, and bring you the glad wishes of many friends in celebration of this good hour.

MOROSE. What good hour?

TRUEWIT. Your marriage hour, sir. I congratulate you on your resolution and your fortitude. Notwithstanding all the dangers I told you of, you went right ahead. That's real heroism, sir.

MOROSE. How did you know I was married?

TRUEWIT. Why, sir, after telling your secret to a barber, surely you didn't hope that anybody less than the whole town would know about it? You might have told the newspapers with greater secrecy. But, sir, forgive yourself the fault, now, and be sociable with your friends. Why, soon three or four fashionable ladies from the college are coming to congratulate you, bringing with them their train of minions and followers.

MOROSE. Bar the doors! Bar the doors! Where are all my servants? [*The Servant enters.*] Bar the doors, you varlet!

EPICENE. He's a varlet who takes one step to do it. Let those doors stand open. Just let me see you dare move your eye to those doors! Shall I barricade myself against my friends? Shall I deprive myself of the pleasure of their visit?

[*The Servant goes out.*]

MOROSE. Amazonian impudence!

TRUEWIT. She's only being reasonable, sir. And, incidentally, more modest than you. Do you want to leap off to bed before noon, sir? A mature gentleman like you should owe more respect to the marriage ceremony, and not mount the marriage bed like the town bull or a mountain goat. Wait till the proper time, sir, and approach it with reverence and fear. Those delights are to be tasted in the silence of the night. Give the day over to open pleasures—feasting, music, revels, conversation. We'll have everything to make your wedding hilarious.

MOROSE. Oh torment, torment!

TRUEWIT. Now, sir, if you're going to be so petulant and fussy in the first half-hour of your marriage, what hope can this lovely lady have for all the years to come?

MOROSE. Years of affliction! Leave me alone! Go away! Hush!

TRUEWIT. Not another word, sir.

MOROSE. Oh, that damned barber!

TRUEWIT. Yes, indeed, a damned wretch, sir.

MOROSE. Blast him!

TRUEWIT. Curse him a few times, sir. It'll make you feel better. May he get the pox he tries to cure his customers of. When he's curling somebody's hair, may all his own drop off. May he burn some pimp's locks and get all his brains beat out with the curling iron.

MOROSE. No, let the wretch live wretched! May he get the itch. May his shop be so lousy nobody will come near it. May his warming-pan always be cold.

TRUEWIT. Perpetual frost underneath it, sir.

MOROSE. May he never hope to see fire again.

TRUEWIT. Except in hell, sir.

MOROSE. May his chairs be always empty, may his scissors rust, may his combs mould in their cases.

TRUEWIT. Dreadful, dreadful!

MOROSE. May he be so poor, he'll be glad to eat his sponge for bread.

TRUEWIT. May he have to drink his hair lotion.

MOROSE. And when he's eaten all his sponges—

TRUEWIT. May he have to eat earwax, sir.

MOROSE. May all the botches and burns that he's cured on others break out on him.

TRUEWIT. May he forget how to cure them on himself.

MOROSE. May he never be able to

open up his shop again. May he get gout in his hands for ever. Now, no more, sir.

TRUEWIT. Oh, that last was too strong, sir. You could be easier on him and still be revenged. Wish instead that he'd never be able to re-paint his barber pole.

MOROSE. Please, no more. I forgot myself for a moment.

TRUEWIT. May he have no credit at the comb-makers.

MOROSE. No more, sir.

TRUEWIT. May he break his mirror and not be able to afford a new one.

MOROSE. Please, I beg you, no more.

TRUEWIT. May he never trim anybody but chimney-sweepers.

MOROSE. Sir, sir—

TRUEWIT. May he cut a collier's throat with his razor and be hanged for it.

MOROSE. Please, sir, I'd rather forgive him than hear any more.

[*Daw, Lady Haughty, Centaure, Mavis, and Trusty come in.*]

DAW. This way, ladies.

MOROSE. Oh, the dikes have broken. A flood! A deluge! An inundation! I'll be overwhelmed with noise.

DAW. Your servant, Mistress Epicene.

MOROSE. Has she servants too!

DAW. I've brought some ladies here to meet you. My Lady Haughty. [*As he presents each one, Epicene kisses them.*] My Lady Centaure. Mistress Doll Mavis. Mistress Trusty, my Lady Haughty's woman. Where's your husband? Let's see the old fellow. I hear he can't endure noise. Har, Har! Just let me meet him, just let me meet him!

MOROSE. What sort of names are these?

TRUEWIT. Sir John Daw, sir, and your wife's servant.

MOROSE. If her servant's a daw, her maid must be a parrot and her page a hyena. [*He starts to leave.*]

TRUEWIT. You mustn't leave now, sir. First you must kiss the ladies. They've come especially to meet you.

HAUGHTY. Shame on you, Master Morose, trying to sneak into marriage without telling your friends. Well, I'll forgive you this time, and kiss you anyhow. You won't mind a little lady-like familiarity with your husband, will you, mistress?

EPICENE. Certainly not. He's entirely at your disposal. Your ladyship honors me by your interest in him, as you have complimented me by your visit.

MOROSE. [*Escaping from Haughty.*] Compliment! Compliment!

HAUGHTY. Is *this* the Silent Woman?

CENTAURE. Truewit says she found her tongue after she got married.

HAUGHTY. Master Truewit, what kind of creature is this bride here? She speaks! Jack Daw told us she couldn't.

TRUEWIT. Ah, it was all a plot, Madam, that Sir Dauphine and a few of us hatched to marry her off to this old fellow. But she's a woman of excellent poise and wit. You'll see her make rare sport with Daw before the day's over.

HAUGHTY. And *he* brought us to laugh at *her!*

TRUEWIT. Madam, he who thinks himself a master-wit often turns out to be a master-fool. You won't have a laugh at her expense.

HAUGHTY. We'll have to have her in our college. If she's really witty, we'll make her a collegiate, eh Centaure?

CENTAURE. Certainly, madam. Let's have Mavis turn her celebrated judgment on her.

TRUEWIT. Believe me, ladies, Mistress Epicene will hold her own.

MAVIS. I'll tell you that after I've talked with her. [*Mavis whispers something to Lady Haughty.*]

MOROSE. Blessed moment! Why can't they always talk like that?

TRUEWIT. In the meantime, madam, help me vex the old gentleman. You know his crotchet, so talk to him about your gloves or the wedding or something.

HAUGHTY. Leave it to me. Master bridegroom, where are you?

MOROSE. I knew it was too good to last.

HAUGHTY. I don't see any signs of a wedding here—no flowers, no champagne, no veils, no gloves, no garters. Shame on you, sir. You've been brought up a courtier. Why, it's terrible to be so casual about such an important event. You should have had a great reception. Why, just think of all the wedding gifts you're losing.

MOROSE. Madam—

HAUGHTY. Please don't interrupt when I'm criticizing. It's very poor manners. You haven't even arranged for an epithalamium or a masque to entertain us.

DAW. Ah, madam, it just so happens that I've composed a little epithalamium. Hmm, hmm. Would you care to hear it?

HAUGHTY. Certainly. How delightful. But you'll have to speak very loudly so I can hear it.

MOROSE. Wouldn't your ladyship prefer a private room for your friend's poem? Take any room in the house. And then any other room if you'd like to be even more private afterwards. Since you've been unhappily diverted here I wouldn't want to break any of your honorable customs.

EPICENE. Well, that's certainly a rude way to speak to ladies of honor.

CENTAURE. He's a rude lout, indeed.

TRUEWIT. Why, sir, for such a comment you deserve to be cuckolded by every poxy beggar in the city. Oh, don't mistake me, sir. I said that to make the ladies feel at ease, not for any malice to you.

MOROSE. Is this one of your gallants too, ladies?

TRUEWIT. God help me, another word like that, and I'll seek out one of your private rooms for me and your bride. Ah, what am I saying? We're all friends here, and a joke's a joke.

[*Clerimont comes in, followed by a band of musicians.*]

CLERIMONT. Pardon me, ladies. Do you want any music? Play, gentlemen!

[*The musicians strike up in horrible discord.*]

MOROSE. Oh, a plot, a plot, a wicked plot! They're trying to grate me apart. Ugh, it's worse than the rasp of a saw.

TRUEWIT. Stop, stop, you fellows!

CLERIMONT. Play! Play, I say!

TRUEWIT. Stop, you rascals! [*The musicians stop.*] See who's your friend now, sir. Take courage. Take heart. Bear it like a martyr. It's only for a day. You can suffer heroically that long. Should a jackass exceed you in fortitude? No, I say! No! [*La-Foole passes across the stage, dressed as a waiter and followed by servants carrying dishes, and Mistress Otter.*] Look here, sir, what an unexpected honor your nephew's done you. Here's a wedding dinner and a knight to serve it, and fine Mistress Otter bringing up the tail or rump of the procession, as it were.

MOROSE. Mistress Otter, that Gorgon! That Medusa! Hide me! Hide me!

TRUEWIT. She won't turn you to stone, sir. Take heart. Entertain her. Lead your guests into the feast. No! —Mistress bride, ask the ladies if they won't go in. Your bridegroom is too shy.

EPICENE. Ladies, won't you come in to dinner?

HAUGHTY. With the benefit of your company, mistress.

EPICENE. Servant, please perform your duties.

DAW. Glad to be commanded, mistress.

CENTAURE. How do you like her wit, Mavis?

MAVIS. Very well, indeed.

MRS. OTTER. Pardon me, isn't this my place here?

MAVIS. Pardon *me*, Mistress Otter, but it's not.

MRS. OTTER. Oh, but I'm in the college now.

MAVIS. Hmm, we'll discuss that inside.

[*The ladies go out. Captain Otter comes in.*]

TRUEWIT. Captain Otter, glad to see you!

OTTER. I've brought my bull, bear and horse, and the trumpeters and the drummers are just outside, gentlemen.

[*The drum and trumpets sound off-*

stage. The musicians onstage strike up too.]

MOROSE. Oh, oh, oh, oh!

OTTER. Sound out again, men! [*The musicians strike up again.*]

MOROSE. OH, OH, OH, OHHHH! [*Throwing his hands up to his ears, he dashes out.*]

EVERYBODY. After him! Follow him! Don't let him get away!

[*Musicians pour across the stage, beating their drums and blowing their trumpets.*]

[THE END OF ACT I]

ACT TWO

SCENE ONE

[*A Room in Morose's House. Truewit and Clerimont come in.*]

TRUEWIT. Was ever a bridegroom so tormented?

CLERIMONT. Was ever a man so tormented?

TRUEWIT. He'll surely go straight to Heaven after all this Purgatory—all this spitting, coughing, laughing, sneezing, dancing, and singing. And Mistress Epicene!—she's so masculine and loud in urging the party on that he must think he's married a fury.

CLERIMONT. She's carrying it off beautifully.

TRUEWIT. Yes, she speaks constantly.

CLERIMONT. And what a poker face Dauphine has.

TRUEWIT. I think he's almost convinced his uncle he had nothing to do with this. Here he comes. [*Dauphine comes in.*] What's become of your uncle, Dauphine?

DAUPHINE. Oh, hold me up, or I'll die laughing. He's got on his whole nest of nightcaps, and has locked himself up in the top of the house, as high as he can climb away from the noise. I peeped in at a cranny, and saw him sitting over a cross-beam of the roof.

CLERIMONT. And where's the college?

DAUPHINE. They're talking alone with the bride.

TRUEWIT. If they like her, they'll tell her all their secrets.

CLERIMONT. Lady Haughty looks rather handsome today—despite what I said about her this morning. I think I'm coming round to your opinion, Truewit.

TRUEWIT. Believe me, it's right. Women ought to repair the losses time and the years make. If an intelligent woman knows she has a fault, she'll try and hide it, or even turn it to advantage. If she's short, let her sit a great deal. That way nobody'll think she's sitting when she's standing. If she has ugly feet, let her wear a longer gown. If fat hands and chewed nails, wear gloves. If a sour breath, let her stand off to talk. If black and rugged teeth, let her not laugh so much, especially if she throws her mouth wide open.

CLERIMONT. Some women laugh like they were braying.

TRUEWIT. And others stalk along in huge strides like an ostrich. Ugh, I love a graceful walk as well as a melodious voice. These are charms just as attractive as a pretty face.

DAUPHINE. How did you come to study the creatures so closely? I wish you could make me as clever about them.

TRUEWIT. Quite simple, really. First, you must stay in your room for a month reading romances. Then when you're steeped to the gills in such frivolous stuff, you're prepared to meet the ladies. Then you should go to court, and tiltings, and public shows, and feasts, and plays, and—yes, even to church. They frequently go to church; it's a superb spot to show off new clothes. You must go out and look around, Dauphine. After all, a pleasant wench won't come dropping down from the ceiling while you're lying on your backside puffing away at a pipe. Go where they go.

DAUPHINE. I wouldn't be any nearer than I am now.

TRUEWIT. Nonsense. But you'll never succeed by being bashful.

CLERIMONT. He's right, Dauphine.

TRUEWIT. A man should never doubt his ability to captivate a woman. Think you can vanquish them and you can. Seducers are made, not born.

CLERIMONT. No, ladies are made; seducers are—

TRUEWIT. They just say they don't want to be tempted. Really, they do. Penelope herself couldn't hold out forever. Persevere, lad. Why, they'd come begging us if they weren't so timid. In their hearts, they want us to chase them. So, praise them, flatter them. The thicker you lay it on, the better. They delight in it. Of course, you'll have to mix a few kisses in with the praises. And remember, if they take one kiss, they'll take two hundred.

CLERIMONT. But you have to be careful about using too much force.

TRUEWIT. Force! They don't mind force. Half the time it works twice as well as courtesy. The lass who could have been forced, and whom you let go free, will seem to thank you, but really she'll hate you ever afterwards.

CLERIMONT. But some gambits will work better on some women than others.

TRUEWIT. That's right. If you appear too witty to an ignorant wench, or too merry to a sad one, why she'll begin to be leery. You have to approach them on their own terms. Many a girl's been frightened off by the inept tactics of a noble fellow into the arms of a clever rascal. If she loves wit, send her verses; they don't have to be your own. If she loves bravery, boast of your swordsmanship and your quarrels; it won't sound like boasting to her. If she's fond of athletics, charge around on horseback and leap over stools. If she likes clothes, consult your tailor and your barber; let your mirror and your comb be your dearest friends. In fact, wish that the nation be troubled rather than a hair on your head. That'll snag her. If she's greedy, promise her everything, but don't give her too much. That'll keep her appetite keen. Seem to be always about to give, but be like a barren field that yields little, or unlucky dice to foolish gamblers. Let your gifts be slight and dainty, rather than precious. Give her cherries or apricots in season, and tell her they were sent to you from France, even though you bought them in Cheapside. Admire her clothes. Invent dreams to flatter her. Like what she likes, praise whom she praises. And, above all, make friends with her servants. In fact, with her whole family. Call them by their first names. It's a cheap price for their friendship. Get her doctor in your debt, and also her maid. It's a good idea to make love to the maid, too; that'll keep her from blabbing later.

DAUPHINE. Whew! On whose lovely lap have you been sleeping to have discovered so much?

TRUEWIT. I'd rather ask why you're so interested in these mysteries. Are you in love? Come on; out with it.

DAUPHINE. I guess I can't hide it. I am.

TRUEWIT. With which one of them?

DAUPHINE. With all the collegiates.

CLERIMONT. All of them! We'll have to lock you up in the stable if you're such a stallion.

TRUEWIT. No, I approve his taste. If a man loves wisely, he must love all women: some for their faces, some for their figures, some for their voices; when their qualities mingle, let his emotions mingle too. What would you say if I should make them all fall in love with you before the night's over?

DAUPHINE. I'd say you had the best love potion in the world.

TRUEWIT. If I can't do it, let me spend the rest of my life paying for my dinner by playing the clown, and for my drink by playing the pimp.

[*Otter enters with his three cups, followed by Daw and La-Foole, the drummer and two trumpet players.*]

OTTER. Gentlemen, we've been looking for you everywhere.

CLERIMONT. What can we do for you, captain?

OTTER. Watch me have a bout with my bull, bear, and horse.

TRUEWIT. Have at it, captain.

LA-FOOLE. My cousin won't like it.

OTTER. Tush, don't bother about her. Here's my bull for myself, my bear for Sir John—

TRUEWIT. I wouldn't have thought him bearable.

OTTER. —and my horse for Sir Amorous. Now, set your foot to mine, and yours to his, and—

LA-FOOLE. I hope my cousin doesn't look in.

OTTER. For St. George and St. Andrew, and the devil with all cousins! Trumpets, sound, sound!

[*The drum and trumpets sound, and the three chug-a-lug.*]

TRUEWIT. Well said, captain. Well fought at the bull.

CLERIMONT. And well held at the bear.

DAUPHINE. Oh, oh, the horse has kicked off his rider already.

LA-FOOLE. By my knighthood, I can't drink it down.

TRUEWIT. Off with his spurs, somebody.

LA-FOOLE. It goes against my conscience. My cousin won't like it.

DAW. I've downed mine.

TRUEWIT. You fought high and fair, Sir John.

CLERIMONT. [*To Daw.*] You're not paying any attention to this business of La-Foole's, I hope?

DAW. Not a bit, sir, not a bit. Keep smiling, keep smiling.

OTTER. Sir Amorous, don't dally. Drink it down, and the devil take your cousin.

CLERIMONT. [*To La-Foole.*] If you don't drink it, they'll think you're angry. You'll give it all away by being surly.

LA-FOOLE. I-I'll try and drink it then.

OTTER. Pull the horse to his knees, Sir Amorous. Fear no cousins. Down the hatch!

TRUEWIT. Now he's off. The least hint of his wife now will make him foam at the mouth.

CLERIMONT. Mention her, mention her.

TRUEWIT. You do it, and I'll go fetch her. [*He goes out.*]

DAUPHINE. Captain He-Otter, your She-Otter is coming. Your wife is here!

OTTER. Wife! I never heard the word. I don't know what you're talking about. No such creature ever existed. Oh, I admit, gentlemen, I have an old cook, a laundress, a house-drudge that sometimes calls herself my wife. But he's an ass that ties his affections down to one spot. Why, the very name of wife dulls my appetite. Here, fill them up again. Another bout! Wives are nasty, sluttish animals. Where's Master Truewit?

DAW. I saw him leave a minute ago.

CLERIMONT. Never mind that. Drink up, and keep smiling.

DAW. Give it to me.

LA-FOOLE. And me too!

DAW. Let's all keep smiling!

LA-FOOLE. As much as you like!

OTTER. Agreed! Now, you shall have the bear, cousin, and Sir John the horse, and I'll have the bull still. Sound, you Tritons of the Thames! [*The drum and trumpets sound again.*]

MOROSE. [*Above.*] Villains, murderers, traitors, what are you doing down there?

CLERIMONT. Ah, the trumpets have waked him up. He'll be down in a minute.

OTTER. I tell you, a wife is a scurvy clogdogdo, a bad penny, yesterday's dirty socks, a bear-whelp without any breeding.

[*Truewit and Mistress Otter enter behind.*]

DAUPHINE. Why did you marry one then, captain?

OTTER. Hellsbells, I married six thousand pounds. That was what I was in love with. I haven't kissed the old Fury in the last forty weeks.

TRUEWIT. Wait, Mistress Otter, hear what he says first.

OTTER. Her breath stinks worse than an alligator's armpit.

MRS. OTTER. Oh! Treacherous liar! Kiss me, Master Truewit, and I'll prove he's wrong.

TRUEWIT. Uh, ah, I'll take your word for it, madam.

OTTER. She's got a head of hair like a pound of hemp made up into shoelaces.

MRS. OTTER. Oh, viper!

OTTER. She spends forty pounds a year on make-up, but her face would still stop a clock. Why, it would wither weeds. All her teeth were made in Blackfriars, both her eyebrows in the Strand, and her hair in Silver street. Every part of the town owns a piece of her.

MRS. OTTER. [*Coming forward.*] I can't stand it!

OTTER. When she goes to bed at night, she has to dismantle herself and put the pieces away in twenty boxes. About noon the next day, she manages to get reassembled like some great German clock, and spends the rest of the day crying "Cuckoo."

MRS. OTTER. [*Falls upon him and beats him.*] Cuckoo, is it! I'll cuckoo you, you cuckold you!

OTTER. Oh, princess, stop it, stop it, good princess! Ouch, Ow, Oooo

TRUEWIT. Sound!

[*The drum and trumpets sound.*]

CLERIMONT. A battle, a battle!

MRS. OTTER. You notorious stinkardly bearkeeper, does my breath smell? Does it?

OTTER. No, dear; no, darling; no, princess; no, love! It's like a lily, like a rose. Watch out for my bear and horse, gentlemen! Ouch! Ooooof!

MRS. OTTER. I need teeth and eyebrows, eh? You miserable wretch!

TRUEWIT. Sound, sound again!

[*The drum and trumpets sound.*]

OTTER. Oh, don't, don't! I won't say it anymore! Oooo!

MRS. OTTER. I'll say you won't! Betray your princess, will you, you Judas Iscarrion! I'll make an example out of you!

[*Morose comes in brandishing a long sword.*]

MOROSE. You'll make no such examples in my house, Lady Otter.

MRS. OTTER. Oh! [*She, Daw, and La-Foole run out.*]

MOROSE. Now, you rogues, hellhounds, and stentors! Out of my house! Out, you sons of noise and tumult. Out, out, out! [*He drives the musicians out.*]

DAUPHINE. Something wrong, sir?

MOROSE. [*Going out after the musicians and waving his sword horribly.*] They've rent my roof, walls, and all my windows apart with their brazen throats!

TRUEWIT. Better follow him, Dauphine.

DAUPHINE. I will. [*He goes out.*]

CLERIMONT. Where's Daw and La-Foole?

OTTER. They both ran away, sir. Oh, please, gentlemen, help me pacify my princess. I'll have to sleep in the stable for a fortnight and stay out of her way till I've smoothed things over. Did you see my bull-head, gentlemen?

CLERIMONT. Isn't it on, Captain?

OTTER. Oh, here it is. Well, if you ever get down to Ratcliff, gentlemen, look me up. Just ask for Tom Otter, and we'll have another bout. There is bona spes—that is to say, good hope—left yet.

TRUEWIT. You'd better get off, Captain, while you can.

[*Otter leaves.*]

CLERIMONT. Thank God he's gone.

TRUEWIT. He'd still be here if we hadn't sicked his wife on him. His humor is as tedious at last as it was ridiculous at first. [*They go out.*]

SCENE TWO

[*A Long Gallery in Morose's House. Lady Haughty, Mistress Otter, Mavis, Daw, La-Foole, Centaure, and Epicene enter.*]

HAUGHTY. We wondered why you shrieked so, Mistress Otter.

MRS. OTTER. Oh lord, madam, he came at me with a high long naked weapon in his hand, and he looked so dreadful I'm sure he must be out of his mind.

MAVIS. What were you doing, Mistress Otter?

MRS. OTTER. Just chastising my husband, Mistress Mavis. Not bothering anybody.

DAW. You can learn something from Mistress Otter there, ladies. She's trained her husband to speak to her with respect, with respect!

LA-FOOLE. And with his hat off, too. It would do you good to see it.

HAUGHTY. That's good. You should treat your husband that way, Morose. I'll call you Morose now as I call the others Centaure and Mavis.

CENTAURE. You must come to the college and live with us.

HAUGHTY. We'll teach you how to

handle your husband.

MAVIS. Train him carefully at first, and he'll do whatever you want afterwards.

CENTAURE. Make him give you your own coach and four horses, your maid, your chambermaid, your page, your gentleman-usher, your French cook, and four grooms.

HAUGHTY. And you must let us take you to Bedlam with us, and to the chinahouses, the theatres, and the Exchange.

CENTAURE. To establish your reputation.

[*Clerimont and Truewit come in.*]

EPICENE. But, ladies, is it in good taste to have so many servants, and to be familiar with them all?

HAUGHTY. Why not? Why should women deny their favors to men? Are we any the poorer for our generosity?

DAW. Is the Thames the less for pouring itself into the sea?

LA-FOOLE. Or a torch for lighting other torches?

CENTAURE. The gift of love is an empty loss to a woman. She has always more to spare.

HAUGHTY. Besides we won't be young forever. The best of our days pass first.

MAVIS. We are rivers that cannot be called back, madam. She who excludes her loves now may live to lie a forsaken hag in a frozen bed.

CENTAURE. True, Mavis. And who'll hold the doors of our coaches then? Who'll write and tell us the news then? Who'll make anagrams of our names, invite us to the Cockpit, kiss our hands, and draw weapons for our honors then?

HAUGHTY. Not a one.

DAW. Now, now, my mistress is not altogether unaware of these things. There may—harumph, harumph—be someone here who has tasted her favors.

CLERIMONT. What a loudmouth.

EPICENE. But no one here who would boast of it, servant. Have you any good prescriptions, madam, to keep from bearing children?

HAUGHTY. Oh yes, Morose. How should we stay young and lovely if we didn't? Many births age a woman just as many crops age the soil.

[*Morose and Dauphine enter.*]

MOROSE. Oh, what evil star led me into this fate!

DAUPHINE. Fate, sir?

MOROSE. That I should be clipped by so foolish a devil as that barber.

DAUPHINE. I wish I'd known your plans, sir. I would never have allowed you to trust him.

MOROSE. I'd trade an eye, nephew, or a hand, or any other member, if I could take it all back.

DAUPHINE. God forbid, sir, that you should geld yourself to spite your wife.

MOROSE. At least it would rid me of her! I'd do penance in a belfry to get rid of her. At London Bridge, Paris Garden, Billingsgate—wherever the noises are loudest. I'd even sit out a play filled with sea battles, drums, trumpets, and explosions.

DAUPHINE. I hope you won't need to, sir. Have patience. This party will only last for the day.

MOROSE. No, no, forever, nephew. I foresee it, forever. Strife and tumult are the dowry that come with a wife.

TRUEWIT. I told you so, sir, but you wouldn't believe me.

MOROSE. Don't rub salt in my wounds, Master Truewit. Don't add affliction to affliction. Mistress Otter's example has shown me what's in store for me.

EPICENE. How do you do, sir?

MOROSE. Did you ever hear a more unnecessary question? As if she couldn't see for herself. Why, I do as you see, princess. No—empress, empress!

EPICENE. Ah, you're not well, sir. You look very ill. Something must have put you out of sorts.

MOROSE. Oh horrible, monstrous impertinences! Wouldn't one of those sentences have served? Sir, wouldn't one of them have done the job alone?

TRUEWIT. Yes, sir, but they are just signs of female kindness, sir. Just little indications that she has a voice.

MOROSE. Really? Does she? That had escaped me.

EPICENE. How are you feeling now, sir?

MOROSE. Awooo, again!

EPICENE. They tell me you're going crazy, sir.

MOROSE. Not for love of you, I assure you. See, gentlemen—chatter, chatter, chatter! Blab, blab, blab! [*He rushes at her in a frenzy, and Dauphine and Truewit restrain him.*]

EPICENE. Oh, lord, gentlemen! Seize him, for God's sake. What shall I do? Who's his doctor? Where can I send for him? Good sir, tell me. Otherwise I'll send for one of my doctors.

MOROSE. What for? To poison me? If you think I'm going to die and leave you everything, you're—

EPICENE. Lord, how madly he babbles. How his eyes glitter. How green he is about the temples! Do you see what strange blue spots he has?

CLERIMONT. It's not strange he's a little blue; I'm surprised he's not crying.

EPICENE. Gentlemen, for Heaven's sake, tell me what to do. Shall we tie him up and put him in the cellar? Ladies—servant, haven't you read Pliny and Paracelsus? Have none of you a word to comfort a poor gentlewoman? Ah me, what bad luck to marry a madman.

TRUEWIT. [*To Clerimont.*] Isn't she superb?

DAW. I'll tell you, mistress. His disease is called technically, in Latin, insania or sometimes furor.

MOROSE. Will you dissect me before I'm dead?

DAW. He may only be phreneticus yet, and phrenetis is only delirium.

EPICENE. Yes, yes, that's the disease, servant, but what's the cure? We know he's crazy.

MOROSE. Turn me loose!

TRUEWIT. We'll ask her to be quiet, sir.

MOROSE. No, don't try to shut her off. She's like a faucet that will gush out with more force when she opens up again.

HAUGHTY. [*To Epicene.*] Read him some theology or some novels, Morose. They're dull enough to calm anybody.

DAW. Tut, he must have Sinaked read to him, or Patriarch and the other ancients.

CLERIMONT. Why, you called them worthless earlier, Sir John.

DAW. Eh? Ah, hum, well, in some cases, they're the best. Quite the best. Especially Arrowstootle's Ithacas.

HAUGHTY. Where's my woman, Trusty? I'll end this quarrel. Call her,

OTTER. Her father and mother were both mad when they gave her to me.

MOROSE. I believe it. Gentlemen, I'm sane, I tell you. This is only a test, I know, a trial, a marriage ceremony that I must go through.

[*Trusty comes in.*]

MRS. OTTER. My lady just called you, Mistress Trusty. You must decide a controversy.

HAUGHTY. Trusty, what was it cured your father and mother, reading ancient authors or modern novels?

TRUSTY. Something else, madam. We had a preacher that would preach folks asleep. So the old crone who was my parents' doctor prescribed they should go to church three times a week. And every night they were supposed to read themselves to sleep with sermons.

LA-FOOLE. I'll be glad to read a few sermons to Master Morose.

EPICENE. No, I must do that, sir. That's my job. You'll be all right, sir, if you can only sleep.

MOROSE. I'd be all right if you could only sleep. Haven't I got any friend who'll get her drunk or give her a little opium?

TRUEWIT. Why, sir, she talks ten times worse in her sleep.

CLERIMONT. Didn't you know, sir? She doesn't stop all night.

TRUEWIT. And she snores like a porpoise.

MOROSE. Oh, God save me, God save me. Quick, tell me, nephew, what are the grounds for divorce?

DAUPHINE. I don't know, sir.

TRUEWIT. You'll have to ask a clergyman, sir.

MOROSE. I won't rest, I won't rest till I know. [*He exits distractedly with Dauphine.*]

CLERIMONT. Ah, the poor man.

TRUEWIT. If you keep on, ladies, you'll really drive him mad.

HAUGHTY. Well, we'll give him a breather for fifteen minutes or so. Who's that fellow with him—his keeper?

DAW. His nephew, madam.

LA-FOOLE. Sir Dauphine Eugenie.

CENTAURE. He's a pitiful-looking figure of a knight.

DAW. A sorry fellow, indeed, madam. This marriage has cut him out of his uncle's will.

LA-FOOLE. He hasn't a penny in his purse, madam.

DAW. He's been moaning and mooning about all day.

LA-FOOLE. An insignificant fellow. Ignore him, ladies, ignore him.

TRUEWIT. How they babble on.

CLERIMONT. Otter's wine has set them off.

HAUGHTY. Morose, let's go into the salon. I like your couches there. We'll lie down and have a nice chat.

[*Haughty, Centaure, Mavis, Trusty, La-Foole, and Daw go out.*]

EPICENE. [*Following them.*] After you, madam.

TRUEWIT. [*Stopping her.*] Listen, if you're a good-hearted girl and want to do Dauphine a favor, talk to the ladies about him. Praise him all you can. I've a good reason for it. And try and chase those two boobs, Daw and La-Foole, out here. Do it, and I'll honor you forever.

EPICENE. It'll be a pleasure. It irked me to hear them talk so pertly about me.

TRUEWIT. I'll wait for them here. Get rid of them as soon as you can.

EPICENE. Expect one of them shortly.

[*She goes out.*]

CLERIMONT. What a couple of flies those two are, always hovering about the honey.

[*Dauphine enters.*]

CLERIMONT. Oh, Dauphine.

TRUEWIT. Where's your uncle?

DAUPHINE. He dashed outside in his nightcaps to talk to a lawyer about his divorce. The plan's working admirably.

TRUEWIT. Ha, you'd have said so if you'd been here and heard the ladies snickering at you as you went out, Dauphine.

CLERIMONT. And asking if you were your uncle's keeper.

TRUEWIT. And that brace of baboons, Daw and La-Foole answered, Yes, and you were a poor pitiful fellow who had only three suits of clothes and lived on handouts.

DAUPHINE. Oh, they did, did they? I'll fix them! I'll—

TRUEWIT. You leave it to me. I've a little plot in store for those birds.

DAUPHINE. Oh, you have a lot of plots. You had one to make all the wenches fall in love with me.

TRUEWIT. And if I don't manage it before night, I'll eat the biggest dunce cap in the kingdom.

CLERIMONT. I heard that. I'm your witness, Dauphine.

TRUEWIT. Agreed. Now, see these two doors leading off this room? Each leads into a little study. I have a special use for them in the little tragicomedy I mean to stage between Daw and La-Foole. You two keep out of sight behind those curtains. Oh, if I don't make them keep the peace for the rest of the day—Oh, oh, one of them's coming. Quick, hide! [*They hide behind the curtain.*] And

don't laugh, for God's sake.

[*Daw enters.*]

DAW. Which way is the garden?

TRUEWIT. Oh, Jack Daw! Glad I met you. Now, this can't go any further between you two. It's got to stop before someone gets hurt.

DAW. What? What's this? Between whom? What are you talking about?

TRUEWIT. Come off it. Between Sir Amorous and you. Now, be a good fellow, Jack, and give me your sword. [*Takes his sword.*] The bride's begged me to stop any bloodshed on her wedding day. You saw her whispering to me.

DAW. As I hope to finish Tackytus, I intended no murder.

TRUEWIT. You're not laying for Sir Amorous?

DAW. No, no, certainly not! I swear it by my knighthood.

TRUEWIT. And your scholarship too?

DAW. Yes, yes and my scholarship. Cross my heart.

TRUEWIT. All right then. Here's your sword back, and I beg your pardon. But you'd better keep a sharp eye peeled in case he tries something. Why, I thought you knew that, and just came over here to dare him. I thought you held your life higher than your honor.

DAW. No, no. No such thing, I assure you. Why, he and I parted just now as good friends as ever. Good friends, the best of friends.

TRUEWIT. Don't trust that two-faced rascal. You should have seen how mean he looked at dinner. Oh, I've known a lot of angry fellows in my time, but never anyone as wild as Sir Amorous. Why, you stole his guests away today, sir; that's the reason. You should have heard him telling

Dauphine that you were the biggest jackass that—

DAW. Oh, well, sticks and stones may break my bones—

TRUEWIT. They may, indeed. He says you're too much a coward to stand up to him, but he's going to corner you like a rat anyway.

DAW. Cowardice, why it's not a matter of cowardice, sir. Not a matter of cowardice at all. I'm willing to give him any satisfaction he desires, any satisfaction.—Of course, fighting is something else again.

TRUEWIT. He's so enraged that I don't know what would satisfy him. It's blood he thirsts for, and blood he will have.

DAW. B-blood?

TRUEWIT. He hasn't been able to decide yet what part of your body he wants to extract it from.

DAW. Master Truewit, you must help me. Speak to him. Reason with him. Beg him.

TRUEWIT. Well, sir, I'll try. You hide in this study till I return. [*He puts Daw into the study.*] I'd better lock you in for your own protection. Good Lord, here he comes. Don't make a sound. Maybe you'd better hold your breath.—Believe me, Sir Amorous, he isn't here. He isn't here. Please be merciful. Don't murder him. Remember, he's a poor Christian like you. Dauphine! Pull him away. Pull him away! Good Lord, I never knew a man in such a rage before. He won't even listen to reason.—Jack Daw! Jack!

DAW. [*Within.*] Is he gone, Master Truewit?

TRUEWIT. Yes, did you hear him?

DAW. Oh, Lord, yes!

TRUEWIT. What a sharp ear fear has! Come on out.

DAW. [*Peeping out the door.*] Is he —armed?

TRUEWIT. Armed! He's a walking arsenal. He's got somebody's old two-hand sword to mow you off at the knees. And he's gripping a dagger in the other hand, and he's hung with pikes, halberds, maces, calivers, petronels, and muskets. You'd think he meant to murder all the parish. Why, if he could stuff six months' rations in his breeches, he's armed well enough to over-run the country.

DAW. Good Lord! H-h-help, help, help, help me, Master Truewit. I say, help me!

TRUEWIT. Well, I'll ask him if he'll be satisfied with a leg or an arm. If he won't—well—[*Drawing his finger across his throat.*] kiiiiiiiit!

DAW. I shouldn't like to lose my right arm; it's the one I write madrigals with.

TRUEWIT. Well, I'll ask if he'll be satisfied with a thumb or a little finger. Believe me, I'll do my best. [*Shuts him up again.*]

DAW. Do, do, please do!

[*Clerimont and Dauphine come forward.*]

CLERIMONT. How did you work it?

TRUEWIT. He did all the work himself. He's offered me his left arm.

DAUPHINE. Take it, by all means!

TRUEWIT. What! Maim a man forever for a joke? What kind of a conscience have you?

DAUPHINE. It's no loss to him. He hasn't a use for it, but sopping up food. Besides, that's no worse than maiming his reputation.

TRUEWIT. His reputation as a scholar and a wit isn't maimed because we long ago decided he was an ass. Here comes the other one. Back to your places now.

[*Dauphine and Clerimont withdraw as before La-Foole comes in.*]

TRUEWIT. Sir Amorous!

LA-FOOLE. Master Truewit.

TRUEWIT. Where are you going?

LA-FOOLE. Just down to the court to make water.

TRUEWIT. Don't you dare, sir.

LA-FOOLE. Why not?

TRUEWIT. It's better to endanger your breeches than your life. [*He opens the door of the other study.*] Quick, hide in here.

LA-FOOLE. Why? Why?

TRUEWIT. Just stand there asking questions until your throat's cut. Just dally around till that madman finds you.

LA-FOOLE. What madman?

TRUEWIT. Daw; who else? Now, will you get inside?

LA-FOOLE. Yes, yes, certainly. But what's wrong?

TRUEWIT. If he'd been calm enough to tell us, there might have been some hope of reconciliation. But he's implacable. What have you done to provoke him so? Have you made some joke about him before the ladies?

LA-FOOLE. Not I. I've never made a joke about anybody. The bride was praising Sir Dauphine, and Daw went out in a huff, so I followed him. Maybe he took offence when I couldn't drink my horse dry.

TRUEWIT. That may be it. At any rate, he's searching the house for you, carrying a towel in his hand and crying, "Where's La-Foole? Who saw La-Foole?" And when Dauphine and I asked why, all he'd do was gnash his teeth and snarl, "Oh, revenge, how sweet you are. I'll strangle him in his

towel." So probably he's maddened by your bringing the dinner today and discrediting him.

LA-FOOLE. If he's angry for that, I'll just stay in here till he cools off.

TRUEWIT. That's a good idea.

LA-FOOLE. And at the first chance, I'll sneak away into the country.

TRUEWIT. How'll you get out of the house? He knows you're here, and he'll be watching like a hawk. He won't move.

LA-FOOLE. Well, then, I'll stay here.

TRUEWIT. You'll have to eat.

LA-FOOLE. Then, Master Truewit, can't you ask my cousin Otter to send me a cold venison pasty, a bottle or two of wine, and a chamber pot. If you could see her about the chamber pot immediately—. And, oh yes, a pallet to lie on.

TRUEWIT. I wouldn't advise you to sleep.

LA-FOOLE. You wouldn't? Well, then, I won't.

TRUEWIT. Of course, there's another danger.

LA-FOOLE. Is there? What is it, what is it?

TRUEWIT. No, surely he can't break this door down with his foot.

LA-FOOLE. I'll set my back against it. I have a good back.

TRUEWIT. But if he batters it—

LA-FOOLE. I'll sue him for battery.

TRUEWIT. He's already sent for the dynamite. God knows what he plans to do with it. Perhaps blow up this corner of the house. Oh, here he comes. In, quickly! [*Pushes La-Foole in, and shuts the door.*] No, no, no, Sir John, he's not been this way. No, I won't let you put that bomb there, no. I'll die first. Won't you take my word? He's not here.—Sir Amorous, he's made a bomb to blow the door down. Think of something to satisfy him.

LA-FOOLE. [*Within.*] Whatever he wants, whatever he wants!

TRUEWIT. Will you leave it to me?

LA-FOOLE. Yes, sir, any terms, any terms at all.

TRUEWIT. [*Beckoning Clerimont and Dauphine out.*] Well now, what do you think, gentlemen? Wouldn't it be a job to decide which is the more frightened?

CLERIMONT. I'll fetch the ladies to see their heroes.

TRUEWIT. By all means.

DAUPHINE. Certainly not. Let them go on thinking them wits and fine fellows. Serve those women right.

TRUEWIT. No, fetch them, Clerimont. I've a good reason. Tell them what's happened, and bring them in.

DAUPHINE. This is just vanity, Truewit. You have to advertise all your jokes.

TRUEWIT. You'll see how unjust that is shortly. Clerimont, tell them it was Dauphine's plot. [*Clerimont goes out.*] Just see if I'm not doing you a good turn. Now, I want you to go into the next room and wrap a table-cloth around you, and this scarf over your face, and put a cushion on your head, and be ready when I call Amorous. Off with you, now. [*Dauphine goes out.*] John Daw! [*He goes to Daw's door and brings him out.*]

DAW. What did he say? Wh-what did he say?

TRUEWIT. Well, I argued your case with him. I said you were a knight and a scholar and a cultivated and philosophic gentleman.

DAW. Yes, yes, yes.

TRUEWIT. And that you would bear the punishment bravely. At first, I thought he demanded too much.

DAW. What was that, sir?

TRUEWIT. Your upper lip and six of your front teeth.

DAW. Oh, that was unreasonable.

TRUEWIT. That was what I said. So after some haggling, I worked him down to two molars.

DAW. Oh, good work, good work. He shall have them.

TRUEWIT. Oh, no, he shan't. I talked some more. Now, because you're to be good friends afterwards, and so that there's no painful reminder of this quarrel, I've persuaded him to come here in disguise—

DAW. In disguise?

TRUEWIT. Certainly. A friend shouldn't be able to boast that he's submitted to such an indignity in his own person. He's coming in disguise to give you five kicks in private, take your sword away, and lock you up in that study till he's ready to let you go. That won't be long. We'll get him to relent shortly.

DAW. Five kicks. He'll have six, sir, to be friends.

TRUEWIT. It might not be a bad idea to mention that to him.

DAW. Do! Do mention it. What's a kick more or less between friends? Oh, lord, sir, it's nothing. Nothing at all.

TRUEWIT. Good, good. Keep smiling, and I'll call him. Sir Amorous! [*Dauphine enters disguised.*] Now, no speaking to each other, or hashing over old quarrels. Bend over, Sir John. Fire when ready, Sir Amorous.

DAW. [*As Dauphine kicks him.*] One, ouch! Two, oooo! Three, awwkk! Four, ugghh! Five, yeowww! Please, Sir Amorous, have another. On me.

TRUEWIT. Now, I told you to keep quiet. Come, then, Sir Amorous, take advantage of his, ah, largesse. [*Dauphine kicks him again.*] Your sword, Sir John. Now, back to the study. Soon you'll meet each other before the ladies and be the best of friends. [*Puts Daw back inside.*] Give me the scarf. You can beat the other one barefaced. Stand by. [*Dauphine retires, and Truewit releases La-Foole.*] Sir Amorous!

LA-FOOLE. What's this? A sword!

TRUEWIT. He sent it to you.

LA-FOOLE. No, no, I don't want it. Take it away.

TRUEWIT. He just wants you to fasten it against the wall and break your head in a few places against the hilt.

LA-FOOLE. I won't do it. You can tell him that. I can't stand the sight of blood. Especially my own. Tell him I'll beat it against a flat wall if he likes.

TRUEWIT. This is a strange way to act after all I've done for you. Well, I offered him an alternative.

LA-FOOLE. What's that?

TRUEWIT. Will you be beaten in private?

LA-FOOLE. Only with the flat side of the sword.

[*Haughty, Centaure, Mavis, Mrs. Otter, Epicene, and Trusty enter at the rear.*]

TRUEWIT. Then let me blindfold you and take you to him. He'll take your sword away, and give you a blow in the mouth and a few strong tweaks on the nose.

LA-FOOLE. Well, I'll agree to that. But why must I be blindfolded?

TRUEWIT. That's for your own good, sir. If he should grow insolent later

and tell people about this—I hope he won't—but if he should, then you could swear that you never saw him beat you.

LA-FOOLE. Oh, I understand.

TRUEWIT. Really, though, I expect you'll be perfectly good friends afterwards.

LA-FOOLE. Naturally, naturally. I've always said he was a charming man.

TRUEWIT. [*Binding his eyes.*] Come along then. [*Leads him forward.*] All ready, Sir John.

[*Dauphine enters and tweaks him by the nose.*]

LA-FOOLE. Oh, Sir John, Sir John! Ohhhhhh!

TRUEWIT. Sir John, Sir John, stop it. You'll pull it off! There, that's enough. Now, Sir Amorous, Sir John insists that I lock you back up for a bit. [*He puts Amorous back in the study.*] I imagine they'll be a little tamer in their language now. Dauphine, you were superb. Oh! the ladies have surprised us.

[*Haughty and the others come forward.*]

HAUGHTY. Oh, Centaure, how badly we've judged those wretched knights.

CENTAURE. Well, madam, Mavis was more taken in than we were. She recommended them.

HAUGHTY. How valiant and witty Sir Dauphine is. Was this his idea?

MRS. OTTER. Master Clerimont says so.

HAUGHTY. Morose, when you come to the college, bring him with you. He seems a charming gentleman.

EPICENE. He is, madam. Utterly delightful.

CENTAURE. And when will you visit us, Morose?

EPICENE. In three or four days,

madam. Just as soon as I have a coach and horses.

HAUGHTY. No, tomorrow, Morose. Centaure will send her coach for you.

MAVIS. Yes, do come, and bring Sir Dauphine along.

HAUGHTY. She's promised to, Mavis.

MAVIS. He's really a handsome man.

HAUGHTY. And he has excellent taste in clothes.

CENTAURE. Yet he's not a fashion-plate, like some of these fops.

HAUGHTY. Who have every hair in place.

MAVIS. And wear cleaner linen than we do.

HAUGHTY. Sir Dauphine's casualness is very becoming.

CENTAURE. I could fancy a man with a nose like that.

MAVIS. Or a leg like that.

CENTAURE. And what eyes!

MAVIS. And what hair!

CENTAURE. Morose, bring him to my rooms first.

TRUEWIT. See how they eye you, man. They're snared, I tell you.

[*Haughty comes forward.*]

HAUGHTY. So you've unhorsed our knights, Master Truewit.

TRUEWIT. Not I, madam. It was Dauphine's scheme. But I'm sure if he's frightened off your knights-errant, he'd be delighted to serve in their places.

HAUGHTY. Really? He doesn't seem to suggest it.

CENTAURE. My God, Mavis, Haughty's about to kiss him.

MAVIS. Let's get in line.

[*They come forward.*]

HAUGHTY. How fortunate we met, Sir Dauphine.

CENTAURE. We'd be delighted to see you at the college.

MAVIS. Often!

[*Truewit nudges Dauphine and flashes an I-told-you-so smirk.*]

HAUGHTY. Now shall we go back in, Morose?

EPICENE. Yes, madam.

CENTAURE. But Sir Dauphine must come with us.

TRUEWIT. Wait, ladies. You'll want to see us bring Alphonse and Gaston together. I'll fetch them out.

DAUPHINE. And don't let them see you're onto the joke, ladies.

HAUGHTY. We won't, dear Sir Dauphine.

CENTAURE & MAVIS. On our honor, Sir Dauphine.

TRUEWIT. [*Going to the first door.*] Sir Amorous, Sir Amorous! The ladies are here.

LA-FOOLE. Are they?

TRUEWIT. Yes. When I call you, slip out casually while their backs are turned, and meet Sir John here as if by accident. [*He goes to the other door.*] Jack Daw!

DAW. Yes, sir?

TRUEWIT. Whip out behind me suddenly when I give the word. And remember, no surly looks toward your adversary. Now, now!

[*La-Foole and Daw pop out and salute each other.*]

LA-FOOLE. Noble Sir John Daw! Where have you been?

DAW. Looking for you, good Sir Amorous.

LA-FOOLE. Me! How kind of you.

DAW. No, no, how kind of you.

CLERIMONT. They've lost their swords.

DAUPHINE. Where's your sword, Sir John?

CLERIMONT. And yours, Sir Amorous?

DAW. Uh, mine? Uh, I just now sent my boy off to have the handle mended.

LA-FOOLE. Yes! My gold handle was broken too, and my boy just took it away.

DAUPHINE. Indeed, sir? What a curious coincidence.

[*Morose comes in, with the two swords in his hands.*]

MRS. OTTER. Oh, me! Here he comes again, the madman! Run, ladies! Run for your lives!

[*The ladies, Daw, and La-Foole run off.*]

MOROSE. Who's dropping swords all around the house?

TRUEWIT. Oh, sir, there was almost a murder here. Two knights had a falling-out about your bride's favors, and we had to take their weapons away.

MOROSE. Fighting for her favors!

TRUEWIT. They were. But it's all smoothed over. Clerimont, you can give them their swords back. They probably won't bother anybody now.

[*Clerimont goes out with the two swords.*]

DAUPHINE. Did you speak with the lawyer, sir?

MOROSE. No. There's so much noise in court that I was frightened home faster than I left. Such speaking and refuting. Everybody raving at once about writs, torts, citations, appellations, allegations, certifications, attachments, interrogations, references, convictions, and afflictions. The babble here is silence compared to it.

TRUEWIT. Well, sir, if you have your mind made up about the matter, I can fetch you an excellent lawyer and a learned clergyman who will investigate your case.

MOROSE. Can you really, Master Truewit?

TRUEWIT. Oh, yes, sir. Very quiet, sober men both of them. They'll wrap it all up with a whisper or two.

MOROSE. Should I trust you?

TRUEWIT. Oh, sir, your nephew and I have been absolutely enraged about how you're abused. Go and lock yourself in your room, sir, till we call you. Let us take care of everything.

MOROSE. I'm in your hands, gentlemen. [*He goes out.*]

DAUPHINE. What do you have up your sleeve now, wit?

TRUEWIT. Run out, and see if you can find Otter and the barber.

DAUPHINE. What for?

TRUEWIT. Oh, I'll make the deepest divine and the learnedest lawyer out of them that ever you—

DAUPHINE. Out of *them*?

TRUEWIT. Dress them in the proper clothes and put a little Latin in their mouths, and they'll drive him as mad as any proper preacher or lawyer could. Come on, now.

[*They go out one side, as La-Foole, Clerimont, and Daw enter the other.*]

LA-FOOLE. Where did you find our swords, Master Clerimont?

CLERIMONT. Why, Dauphine must have taken them from the madman.

LA-FOOLE. And he must have snatched them away from our boys.

CLERIMONT. Very likely, sir.

LA-FOOLE. Thank you, good Master Clerimont. Sir John and I are both beholden to you.

DAW. Sir Amorous and I are your servants, sir. Your servants.

CLERIMONT. Well, now that we're alone, we can talk more easily. Sir John, I was just about to tell Sir Amorous that you two bowl over the ladies wherever you go. You carry the whole sex before you.

DAW. Oh, they can carry us, sir, wherever they'd like. Ha-ha. Wherever they'd like.

CLERIMONT. You're the greatest ladies' men in the city.

DAW. Not I. Sir Amorous is.

LA-FOOLE. Oh, no, no. Sir John is.

DAW. Certainly not. Sir Amorous is far better looking.

LA-FOOLE. No, Sir John, you're better looking and infinitely wittier.

DAW. Not I, sir. I have no wit. Besides I'm not nearly as athletic as you.

LA-FOOLE. I protest, Sir John. Compared to you, I'm an invalid.

CLERIMONT. Well, don't quarrel over it. Whatever you say, knights, between you you divide the kingdom of the ladies' affections. I can see how they look at you adoringly, how they hang on your words. Oh, you could tell me strange stories if you wanted to, couldn't you?

DAW. Well—ha-ha—we have seen a thing or two.

LA-FOOLE. That we have. A few velvet petticoats and lace smocks. Heh-heh.

DAW. Ha-Ha!

CLERIMONT. Now, out with it, Sir John. Don't begrudge me the pleasure of hearing what you've had the pleasure of tasting.

DAW. Why, ah—uh—well, you tell him, Sir Amorous.

LA-FOOLE. No, you tell him, Sir John.

DAW. No, you sir, I insist.

LA-FOOLE. And I insist too.

DAW. Well—we've lain in some strange places.

CLERIMONT. And these ladies with you, gentlemen?

LA-FOOLE. No, certainly not, sir.

DAW. We mustn't blacken reputations.

CLERIMONT. Well, tell me one thing, Sir John. Honestly now.

DAW. If I can, sir.

CLERIMONT. You live in the same house as the bride here?

DAW. Yes, and talked with her hourly, sir.

CLERIMONT. What's she really like? Open, free?

DAW. Oh, exceedingly open, sir. I was her servant, and Sir Amorous was to have been.

CLERIMONT. Come on now, you've both had favors from her. Admit it.

DAW. Oh no, sir. No, no, certainly not.

LA-FOOLE. We mustn't blacken reputation.

CLERIMONT. Why, she's married; you can't hurt her reputation now. So speak up. How many times? And which of you was first?

LA-FOOLE. Sir John, of course, had her maidenhead.

DAW. Oh, that's what he says, sir. But he knows what really happened.

CLERIMONT. Do you, Sir Amorous?

LA-FOOLE. Well—in a manner of speaking, sir.

CLERIMONT. Well, I congratulate you, lads. Ha! If the bridegroom only knew about this! Oh, don't worry; I won't tell him.

DAW. The devil with him, the old goat.

CLERIMONT. Shhh. Here comes his nephew with Lady Haughty. He'll steal the ladies away from you, sirs, if you don't watch him.

LA-FOOLE. Why, if he does, we'll just fetch them right back.

[*He goes out with Daw. Clerimont*

follows them part way. Dauphine and Haughty enter.]

HAUGHTY. Believe me, Sir Dauphine, it's only your great merit that's overcome my resistance.

DAUPHINE. Your ladyship sets too high a price on my merit.

HAUGHTY. Sir, I can distinguish gems from pebbles. I hope that I don't suffer in your judgment by my friendship with Centaure and Mavis.

DAUPHINE. Not at all, madam. I can see they're only your foils.

HAUGHTY. Ah, that makes me love you the more. It's the inner man, the real you, I love. Centaure and Mavis can't see that; they love flatly and dully.

CENTAURE. [*Offstage.*] Where are you, Lady Haughty?

HAUGHTY. I'm coming, Centaure.— My page shall show you my room, sir. And Trusty, my woman, shall be watching for you. Don't be afraid of her, she's close-mouthed as can be. Now, wear this jewel for my sake. [*Centaure enters.*] Where's Mavis, Centaure?

CENTAURE. In there, madam, writing. I'll be right with you. I just want a word with Sir Dauphine.

[*Haughty goes out.*]

DAUPHINE. With me, Madam?

CENTAURE. Sir Dauphine, don't trust Haughty. Whatever you do, don't trust her. You can't believe a thing she says. She's the perfect courtier, only interested in making use of people for her own ends. Besides, her physician's told me that she's not—ah—quite healthy, if you know what I mean. She's fifty if she's a day, and what could you expect after the wild life she's led? You ought to see her in the morning be-fore she's put her face together. Oh, here comes Mavis. She looks even ghastlier then than Haughty. In fact, you couldn't stand her face by candle-light. [*Mavis enters.*] Come to my room one of these mornings early, or late in the evening, and I'll tell you more.—Where's Haughty, Mavis dear?

MAVIS. In there, Centaure dear.

CENTAURE. What's that you have?

MAVIS. Just a riddle for Sir Dauphine.—No, you shan't see it, Centaure. [*Centaure stalks out.*] Good Sir Dauphine, solve this riddle for me. I'll call for the answer shortly. [*She goes out.*]

CLERIMONT. [*Coming forward.*] Well, Dauphine! How did you manage to get rid of them all?

DAUPHINE. Good Lord, they haunt me. They give me jewels. I can't get rid of them. I was never so assaulted in my life. One loves me for my virtue and bribes me with this jewel. Another loves me with caution. A third woos me with riddles. And all of them are jealous of each other.

CLERIMONT. A riddle. Let's see it. [*Reads.*] "Sir Dauphine, please for-give this subtle ruse. The ladies here, although you may not realize it, have designs upon you. I know how re-pugnant this must be to so sensitive a nature, dear sir, and if you would care to visit me privately, I might find some method of giving you solace. Mavis." If this is their sublety, I'd hate to see their plain-dealing.

DAUPHINE. We'd need Truewit to riddle us that.

CLERIMONT. We need him anyway. His knights are as insolent as ever.

DAUPHINE. No, not really.

CLERIMONT. No drunken braggart

ever confessed such stories as they did. I wouldn't bet a fly's leg against all the women's reputations here, if they're telling the truth. Both of them admit seducing the bride.

DAUPHINE. I don't believe it.

CLERIMONT. They tell the time and the place and the whys and wherefores. I almost had them admitting they'd done it today.

DAUPHINE. Both of them?

CLERIMONT. Yes! If I'd been with them a minute more, they'd have put it in writing.

DAUPHINE. Evidently they intend to amuse us whether we want it or not.

[*Truewit enters.*]

TRUEWIT. Oh, here you are. Dauphine, call your uncle. I've costumed my preacher and my lawyer, dyed beards and all. The knaves hardly recognize themselves. When we get your uncle here, you'd better watch one door, and I'll watch the other, so he shan't escape when they get going strong. Then in the middle of it I've instructed the bride to herd the ladies in. Oh, it will be full and twanging. Get along now. Fetch him. [*Dauphine goes out. Otter enters disguised as a preacher, and Cutbeard as a canon lawyer.*] All right, master doctor and master parson, remember your lines. If you flub one, don't give it away by standing and hemming and hawing, or gaping at each other. Just go on, and talk loudly and eagerly. Use a lot of gestures, and you'll be all right. Start off solemnly, and then you can cut loose later. Here he comes. Look pompous.

[*Dauphine enters with Morose.*]

MOROSE. Are these two learned men?

TRUEWIT. Yes, sir. Make them welcome, won't you?

MOROSE. Make them welcome! I'd rather do anything than waste time so foolishly. I wonder how these absurd phrases like "Good day" and "How do you do" came to be such a habit. Or "I'm glad to see you." I don't give a damn whether they're glad to see me. Their happiness won't increase mine.

OTTER. Good day, sir.

CUTBEARD. How do you do, sir.

TRUEWIT. Well, to the business at hand. Gentlemen, I've told you enough to acquaint you with the case. This is the gentleman who wants your help. So, begin when you're ready.

OTTER. After you, master doctor.

CUTBEARD. No, no, after you, good master parson.

OTTER. I think that canon law should speak first.

CUTBEARD. The law must always give way to morality, sir.

MOROSE. Gentlemen! Be swift. I don't care for all this disputation. My father educated me to collect and contain my mind, and not allow it to flow loosely; to discover what was necessary and what superfluous; to embrace the one and to avoid the other; in short, to endear myself to calm and to avoid turmoil. So I stay away from your public pleadings, your places of noise, your babbling orators that never know when to be still. Now, it's because of noise that I sent for you. You don't know what misery I've been in today, what a torrent of evil. My house spins round like a windmill in a thunderstorm. It's Bedlam, the tower of Babel, the cave of Aeolus.

TRUEWIT. Well, doctor, will you

break the ice? The parson can wade in after.

CUTBEARD. Sir, though unworthy and weak, I will presume to commence to begin.

OTTER. No presumption, no presumption whatsoever, domine.

MOROSE. They're at it again.

CUTBEARD. Your question is, For how many causes may a man have divortium legititatatum? First, you must understand the nature of the word "divorce."

MOROSE. No semantics, good doctor; to the question.

CUTBEARD. Hem. I answer, then, that the canon law allows divorce only in a few cases. The principal case is the common case; that is to say, the adulterous case. Inasmuch as wherein therefore—

OTTER. He can't be too clear, sir.

MOROSE. Aowwww!

CUTBEARD. —moreover, there are twelve impedimentatatum to, as we say in Latin, matrimonium. In other words, matrimony, marriage, or wedlock.

MOROSE. Just skip the translating.

OTTER. He can't be too clear, sir.

CUTBEARD. First is impedimentatum erroris.

OTTER. That is, if you contract yourself to a party of the first part, thinking her to be a party of another part.

CUTBEARD. If, for instance, to take an example, if she be poor and you thought her rich, or possibly wealthy.

OTTER. Or if she prove stubborn, headstrong, and intractable, and you thought her obedient and meek.

MOROSE. What? Is that legal? Say that again.

OTTER. It's legal ante copulam, but not post copulam. After marriage, obstinacy is legal.

CUTBEARD. In fact, normal.

OTTER. Very sapientia, very sapientia.

CUTBEARD. Gratia tabu. Now, if either party, of the first part or the second part or any other parts, has made a vow of chastity.

OTTER. That's rare. You can pass that by.

CUTBEARD. I always have. Now, if you were her cousin. That is to say, if her mother were your mother's sister, or if her father were your mother's—

MOROSE. Pass on.

CUTBEARD. But he might be spiritually related. If you were her godfather, sir, then the marriage is incestuous.

OTTER. But, in a broader sense, master doctor, we are all brothers and sisters, and as much akin as godfathers and god-daughters.

MOROSE. I was never a godfather in my life, sir. Pass on to the next.

CUTBEARD. The next is adulterii. And the sixth, cultus desperado.

TRUEWIT. Disparitas!

CUTBEARD. That is to say, difference of religion. Have you ever examined her about her religion?

MOROSE. I'd rather she had none than have to ask her. On to the rest. Shan't you ever get done?

TRUEWIT. He's half through, sir. Be patient.

CUTBEARD. The next is vice.

TRUEWIT. Vis!

CUTBEARD. That is to say, compulsion, or force.

MOROSE. It was hideously voluntary.

CUTBEARD. The eighth is ordo. That

is to say, wherein or whereinunder, she has taken holy orders.

MOROSE. Would she were in a nunnery.

CUTBEARD. The ninth is ligament; that is to say, if you were affianced to anybody else before.

MOROSE. I thrust myself into these chains all too soon.

CUTBEARD. The tenth is—

MOROSE. Just skip over to the last.

OTTER. The last is impedimentatatum gravissimum. That is to say, if you are frigiditatatem.

TRUEWIT. There's some hope there, sir. Confess yourself impotent, and she'll beg for a divorce.

OTTER. Yes, or you might have some scrofulous disease like paralysis, elephantiasis, or halitosis.

CUTBEARD. Or neurosis, pleurosis, or metempsychosis.

DAUPHINE. I think impotence is the best way, gentlemen.

MOROSE. I conceive you, sir.

OTTER. Oh, no, sir. You don't conceive at all. Just as a boy or child under years isn't fit for marriage because he is omnipotentes.

TRUEWIT. Impotentes, you whoreson lobster.

MOROSE. Let me out of here! I'm strangling.

DAUPHINE. They dispute very learnedly.

MOROSE. Good sir, let me escape.

OTTER. And, therefore, post ergo hook, if he be manifeste frigidus—

CUTBEARD. Ah, if he be manifeste frigidus, I grant you that—

OTTER. Precisely my conclusion.

CUTBEARD. And mine too.

MOROSE. Oh, my ears!! I'll do anything you say!

[*Epicene rushes in, followed by Haughty, Centaure, Mavis, Mistress Otter, Daw, and La-Foole.*]

EPICENE. I won't stand it any longer. Ladies, help me! A bride was never treated like this before. On her marriage day to have her husband plot against her, to drag in a couple of hired logic choppers to plot a separation. Oh, gentlemen, if you had blood or virtue in you, you wouldn't allow such scorpions to creep between man and wife.

MOROSE. Oh, the endless variety of my torment.

HAUGHTY. Let's sic our grooms on them.

CENTAURE. I'll lend you my footman.

MAVIS. We'll have our men toss them in a blanket. The bridegroom first.

DAUPHINE. Ladies, please, for my sake.

HAUGHTY. Yes, for Sir Dauphine's sake.

CENTAURE. He shall command us.

LA-FOOLE. He's as fine a gentleman as any in the town, ladies.

TRUEWIT. Now, sir, confess your infirmity, and she'll be afire to be rid of you. You couldn't beg her to stay.

MOROSE. Ladies, I must crave all of your pardons—

TRUEWIT. Silence, ladies.

MOROSE. —for a wrong I've done to your whole sex in marrying this fair and virtuous gentlewoman—

CLERIMONT. Hear him out, ladies.

MOROSE. —being guilty of an infirmity which, before I conferred with these learned men, I had thought to conceal.

TRUEWIT. But which now, being better informed in his conscience, he wants to make a clean breast of, and ask your public forgiveness.

MOROSE. I am no man, ladies.

ALL. What?

MOROSE. Utterly unable in nature to perform any of the duties of a husband.

MAVIS. Monster!

CENTAURE. Beast!

HAUGHTY. Loathsome toad!

EPICENE. Tut, it's a trick, a trick. He made it up himself.

TRUEWIT. Why, if you suspect him, ladies, you may have him searched.

DAW. By a jury of physicians.

MOROSE. Must I undergo that?

MRS. OTTER. No, let the women search him, madam. We can do it ourselves.

MOROSE. Worse yet!

EPICENE. Don't bother, ladies. I'll take him with all his faults.

MOROSE. Worst of all!

CLERIMONT. Then it's no divorce, doctor, if she doesn't consent, is it?

CUTBEARD. No, the wife must demand it.

MOROSE. Worse, worse than worst.

TRUEWIT. Don't give up, sir. We still have a glimmer of hope. Clerimont, where are your two knights? What was that you said, Master Parson, about adultery?—Dauphine, tell the bride to look guilty and ashamed.

OTTER. Well, sir, if the bride is corrupta, that is to say, vitiated or broken up, but was espoused for a maid.

MOROSE. What then, sir?

OTTER. It dirimere contractum and irritum reddere and uh, ah, that is to say, it dissolvere the whole business.

TRUEWIT. If that's the case, you're in luck, sir. Here are an honorable pair of knights that can prove it.

DAW. Pardon me, good Master Clerimont. I just remembered an engagement.

LA-FOOLE. Excuse me too, Master Clerimont. I just remembered a pressing appointment.

CLERIMONT. Oh, no, you're not going to make me eat my words for you. You know what you told me.

DAW. Is this gentlemanly, sir?

TRUEWIT. [Whispers to Daw.] Jack Daw, this fellow's much fiercer than Sir Amorous. [Whispers to La-Foole.] Sir Amorous, watch out. It would take ten wild Daws to make one Clerimont.

LA-FOOLE. I confess!

DAW. Sir Amorous, will you wound reputation?

LA-FOOLE. If something's going to be wounded, I'd prefer it to be reputation.

TRUEWIT. Why hold back, Jack Daw? She's only a disgraced woman. Morose will be glad to hear of it.

DAW. Will he? I'd have thought he'd be angry.

CLERIMONT. Well, knights?

TRUEWIT. Don't tempt his patience.

DAW. It's true, sir. True. True.

LA-FOOLE. Yes, yes, it is, sir.

MOROSE. What is true, gentlemen? What are you telling me?

DAW. That we have known your bride, sir—as it were—

LA-FOOLE. That is to say, she was our mistress, in a manner of speaking—

CLERIMONT. Try a plain manner of speaking, knights.

OTTER. Yes, the question is, did you have carmel knowledge?

TRUEWIT. A sticky question.

LA-FOOLE. Yes, sir, that was it.

OTTER. Well, then, wherein consequently, the marriage is plainly void.

EPICENE. [Weeping.] Oh, I am undone.

MOROSE. Gentlemen, let me worship and adore you. Give me your hands, knights. And Master Parson, let me thank you another way. [*He gives the Parson money.*]

CENTAURE. So, they confessed, the wretches.

MAVIS. The miserable informers.

TRUEWIT. See what creatures you bestow your favors on, ladies.

MRS. OTTER. Poor girl, how she takes it.

HAUGHTY. Now, now, Morose, I love you the better for it.

CENTAURE. So do I.

CUTBEARD. But, gentlemen, have you known her since matrimonium?

DAW. Not today, master doctor.

LA-FOOLE. No, sir, not today.

CUTBEARD. Well, then, I say that any act before matrimonium is allowable unless the bridegroom precisely before witnesses asked if she were virago ante nuptias.

TRUEWIT. Virgo before; virago afterwards.

EPICENE. He didn't ask me, master doctor.

CUTBEARD. Then naturally there is no causus divortium.

MOROSE. Oh, my heart, will you break! This is the worst of all worse worsts that hell could have devised. Marry a whore and so much noise too.

DAUPHINE. I suspect that this doctor and parson are purposely abusing this gentleman. And I think you knights put them up to it. Listen to me, uncle—

MOROSE. Oh, don't talk to me, nephew. Don't take away the pleasure of dying in silence.

DAUPHINE. Sir, I must speak. I know I'm just a poor relation, and that you've never really approved of me. But now I'll prove that my affection is really sincere. If I free you

from this unhappy match absolutely and instantly—

MOROSE. Impossible.

DAUPHINE. So that you'll never again be troubled with a murmur of it, what shall I hope for from you?

MOROSE. What? Why, whatever you want, nephew. Anything. Everything!

DAUPHINE. You won't toss me aside and forget?

MOROSE. Make your own conditions. My whole estate is yours. Manage it, and I'll be your ward.

DAUPHINE. I shouldn't be so unreasonable, sir.

EPICENE. Are you turning against me too, Dauphine?

DAUPHINE. You know, uncle, how long I've begged you to sign this paper allowing me a mere five hundred pounds out of your revenue, and settling the rest upon me at your death.

MOROSE. You'll have it, nephew! That and more!

DAUPHINE. If I can't rid you of this marriage immediately, you'll have the power before all these witnesses to revoke your act and leave me penniless. Is that fair?

MOROSE. Give me the document. I'll sign it, or anything else. Even a blank sheet of paper, and let you write in your own conditions afterwards. Just *help* me!

EPICENE. Oh, dear.

HAUGHTY. Will Sir Dauphine really do this to her?

EPICENE. Good sir, have some pity on me.

MOROSE. Get away, you crocodile. My nephew's probably slept with you himself.

DAUPHINE. Here, sir. Sign this. [*Gives him the document.*]

MOROSE. Give me the pen, nephew. I'll sign anything, if you'll just get me out of this ghastly mess.—Here it is. And if the document's not in proper legal form, I promise I won't take advantage of that. [*Gives Dauphine the document.*]

DAUPHINE. Here's your release, sir. [*He snatches off Epicene's wig.*] You've married a boy, a gentleman's son I trained for this purpose. What do you say now, Master Doctor? Is this justum impedimentum or not?

OTTER. Oh, yes sir, in primo gradu.

CUTBEARD. In primo gradu.

DAUPHINE. I thank you, good doctor Cutbeard and parson Otter. [*He pulls their false beards and gowns off.*] Thank them for their pains, uncle. And thank my friend Truewit for costuming them. Now, you may go in and rest as quietly as you like. You won't be disturbed. [*Morose staggers out.*] I'll not trouble you till you trouble me with your funeral— but don't worry about that. Anytime will do. Cutbeard, I'll make your lease good. No, not a word. Thank me by bowing, Cutbeard. And Tom Otter, your princess shall forgive you. Well, gentlemen, what are you staring for?

CLERIMONT. A boy!

TRUEWIT. Well, Dauphine, you've tricked us all. So good luck to you; you well deserve it. And Clerimont, you deserve a wreath for wringing a confession out of these two. Well, Sir Daw and Sir La-Foole, you see the gentlewoman who's given you her favors. Womankind should thank you for lying about her and not with her. The next time we'll all know whether to believe the common slanders ladies receive from cuckoos like you. Get out of here both of you, and dream up some new nonsense for us to laugh at. [*Daw and La-Foole slink shamefacedly out.*] And ladies, why so silent? Mistress Epicene has vindicated your honor. But beware of insects like those knights after this. And don't worry about any secrets you may have told this young gentleman. He's almost of age, and will make a good swain in twelve months. In the meantime, we promise you he'll be as secret as he has been silent. [*Comes forward and speaks to the audience.*] Spectators, if you like this comedy, rise cheerfully and clap loudly enough for Morose to hear you. Even if the noise won't cure him, I'm sure it'll please him.

———

JOHN DRYDEN, "An Examination of *The Silent Woman*," from *An Essay of Dramatic Poesy*:

To begin first with the length of the action; it is so far from exceeding the compass of a natural day, that it takes not up an artificial one. 'Tis all included in the limits of three hours and a half, which is no more than is required for the presentment on the stage: a beauty perhaps not much observed; if it had, we should not have looked on the Spanish translation of *Five Hours* with so much wonder. The scene of it is laid in London; the latitude of place is almost as little as you can imagine; for it lies all within the compass of two houses, and after the first act, in one. The continuity of scenes is observed more than in any of our plays, except his own *Fox* and *Alchemist*. They are not broken above twice or thrice at most in the whole comedy; and in the two best of Corneille's plays, the *Cid* and *Cinna,* they are interrupted once. The action of the play is entirely one; the end or aim of which is the settling Morose's estate on Dauphine. The intrigue of it is the greatest and most noble of any pure unmixed comedy in any language; you see in it many persons of various characters and humours, and all delightful. As first, Morose, or an old man, to whom all noise but his own talking is offensive. Some who would be thought critics, say this humour of his is forced: but to remove that objection, we may consider him first to be naturally of a delicate hearing, as many are, to whom all sharp sounds are unpleasant; and secondly, we may attribute much of it to the peevishness of his age, or the wayward authority of an old man in his own house, where he may make himself obeyed; and to this the poet seems to allude in his name Morose. Besides this, I am assured from divers persons, that Ben Jonson was actually acquainted with such a man, one altogether as ridiculous as he is here represented. Others say, it is not enough to find one man of such an humour; it must be common to more, and the more common the more natural. To prove this, they instance in the best of comical characters, Falstaff. There are many men resembling him; old, fat, merry, cowardly, drunken, amorous, vain, and lying. But to convince these people, I need but tell them that humour is the ridiculous extravagance of conversation, wherein one man differs from all others. If then it be common, or communicated to many, how differs it from other men's? or what indeed causes it to be ridiculous so much as the singularity of it?

As for Falstaff, he is not properly one humour, but a miscellany of humours or images, drawn from so many several men: that wherein he is singular is his wit, or those things he says *præter expectatum,* unexpected by the audience; his quick evasions, when you imagine him surprised, which, as they are extremely diverting of themselves, so receive a great addition from his person; for the very sight of such an unwieldy old debauched fellow is a comedy alone. And here, having a place so proper for it, I cannot but enlarge somewhat upon this subject of humour into which I am fallen. The ancients had little of it in their comedies; for the τὸ γελοῖον [1] of the old comedy, of which Aristophanes was chief, was not so much to imitate a man, as to make the people laugh at some odd conceit, which had commonly somewhat of unnatural or obscene in it. Thus, when you see Socrates brought upon the stage, you are not to imagine him made ridiculous by the imitation of his actions, but rather by making him perform something very unlike himself; something so childish and absurd, as by comparing it with the gravity of the true Socrates, makes a ridiculous object for the spectators. In their New Comedy which succeeded, the poets sought indeed to express the ἦθος, as in their tragedies the πάθος [2] of mankind. But this ἦθος contained only the general characters of men and manners; as old men, lovers, serving-men, courtezans, parasites, and such other persons as we see in their comedies; all which they made alike: that is, one old man or father, one lover, one

---

[1] "The laughable."

[2] ἦθος, "character"; πάθος, "emotion."

courtezan, so like another, as if the first of them had begot the rest of every sort: *Ex homine hunc natum dicas.*[3] The same custom they observed likewise in their tragedies. As for the French, though they have the word *humeur* among them, yet they have small use of it in their comedies or farces; they being but ill imitations of the *ridiculum*, or that which stirred up laughter in the Old Comedy. But among the English 'tis otherwise: where by humour is meant some extravagant habit, passion, or affection, particular (as I said before) to some one person, by the oddness of which, he is immediately distinguished from the rest of men; which being lively and naturally represented, most frequently begets that malicious pleasure in the audience which is testified by laughter; as all things which are deviations from customs are ever the aptest to produce it: though by the way this laughter is only accidental, as the person represented is fantastic or bizarre; but pleasure is essential to it, as the imitation of what is natural. The description of these humours, drawn from the knowledge and observation of particular persons, was the peculiar genius and talent of Ben Jonson; to whose play I now return.

Besides Morose, there are at least nine or ten different characters and humours in *The Silent Woman;* all which persons have several concernments of their own, yet are all used by the poet to the conducting of the main design to perfection. I shall not waste time in commending the writing of this play; but I will give you

my opinion, that there is more wit and acuteness of fancy in it than in any of Ben Jonson's. Besides that he has here described the conversation of gentlemen in the persons of True-Wit, and his friends, with more gaiety, air, and freedom, than in the rest of his comedies. For the contrivance of the plot, 'tis extreme, elaborate, and yet withal easy; for the . . . untying of it, 'tis so admirable, that when it is done, no one of the audience would think the poet could have missed it; and yet it was concealed so much before the last scene, that any other way would sooner have entered into your thoughts. But I dare not take upon me to commend the fabric of it, because it is altogether so full of art, that I must unravel every scene in it to commend it as I ought. And this excellent contrivance is still the more to be admired, because 'tis comedy, where the persons are only of common rank, and their business private, not elevated by passions or high concernments, as in serious plays. Here every one is a proper judge of all he sees, nothing is represented but that with which he daily converses: so that by consequence all faults lie open to discovery, and few are pardonable. 'Tis this which Horace has judiciously observed:

Creditur, ex medio quia res arcessit, habere
Sudoris minimum; sed habet Comedia tanto
Plus oneris, quanto veniae minus.[4]

---

[3] "You would say that this fellow was born from that man." Terence: *Eunuchus* III. 2, 7.

[4] "Comedy is believed to require the least pains, because it fetches its subjects from common life; but the less indulgence it meets with, the more labor it requires." Horace: *Epist.* II, i, 168. Smart trans.

But our poet who was not ignorant of these difficulties has made use of all advantages; as he who designs a large leap takes his rise from the highest ground. One of these advantages is that which Corneille has laid down as the greatest which can arrive to any poem, and which he himself could never compass above thrice in all his plays; viz., the making choice of some signal and long-expected day, whereon the action of the play is to depend. This day was that designed by Dauphine for the settling of his uncle's estate upon him; which to compass, he contrives to marry him. That the marriage had been plotted by him long beforehand, is made evident by what he tells True-Wit in the second act, that in one moment he had destroyed what he had been raising many months.

There is another artifice of the poet, which I cannot here omit, because by the frequent practice of it in his comedies he has left it to us almost as a rule; that is, when he has any character or humour wherein he would show a *coup de Maistre*, or his highest skill, he recommends it to your observation by a pleasant description of it before the person first appears. Thus, in *Bartholomew-Fair* he gives you the pictures of Numps and Cokes, and in this those of Daw, Lafoole, Morose, and the Collegiate Ladies; all which you hear described before you see them. So that before they come upon the stage, you have a longing expectation of them, which prepares you to receive them favourably; and when they are there, even from their first appearance you are so far acquainted with them, that nothing of their humour is lost to you.

I will observe yet one thing further of this admirable plot; the business of it rises in every act. The second is greater than the first; the third than the second; and so forward to the fifth. There too you see, till the very last scene, new difficulties arising to obstruct the action of the play; and when the audience is brought into despair that the business can naturally be effected, then, and not before, the discovery is made. But that the poet might entertain you with more variety all this while, he reserves some new characters to show you, which he opens not till the second and third act; in the second Morose, Daw, the Barber, and Otter; in the third the Collegiate Ladies: all which he moves afterwards in by-walks, or under-plots, as diversions to the main design, lest it should grow tedious, though they are still naturally joined with it, and somewhere or other subservient to it. Thus, like a skilful chessplayer, by little and little he draws out his men, and makes his pawns of use to his greater persons.

If this comedy and some others of his were translated into French prose (which would now be no wonder to them, since Molière has lately given them plays out of verse, which have not displeased them), I believe the controversy would soon be decided betwixt the two nations, even making them the judges.

DISCUSSION OF *THE SILENT WOMAN*

John Dryden's examination of *The Silent Woman* is the classic comment on Jonson's play. It is difficult to improve it, but it is no presumption to try; for one of the nicest things about criticism is that it takes a little courage and it depends upon freedom.

First of all, then, Dryden talks about most of the things in Jonson's play that are worth talking about. He discusses the play's subject and manner, the play's structure, the play's characterization, and the play's language. He makes some of his points more important than others, perhaps even too important.

For instance, the play's unity of place and time does not seem really as important as he suggests, and the play's unity of action is not really as neat as he thinks it is. The commentators who built upon Aristotle's theory of the drama thought that the three unities were of great importance in determining the value of a play, particularly of a tragedy. We have already seen, in *Antigone*, a play which holds pretty well to the three unities. However, we have also seen, in *King Lear*, a play which dispenses with all three of them. *Lear* is no worse a play than *Antigone* because it takes place over several weeks, over half of England, and has two parallel plots. It merely has a different manner.

The unities may, of course, impart a certain virtue of dramatic compression to a play. They may even heighten the intensity of a particular story. Playwrights from Sophocles to Ibsen and Arthur Miller have found that they have. But other playwrights have other ways of attaining intensity, and there are other dramatic virtues than intensity. To force the unities on *King Lear* would be to squash the play, to squeeze all the life out of it. The unities are a dramatic virtue, but they are not the only one.

So we would say, then, that it does not really matter whether or not Ben Jonson approached a unity of time and place, and that it is strongly to his credit that he did not approach a conventional unity of action. Viewed as a dramatic virtue in themselves, the unities are only a kind of trick of craftsmanship; and other plays, including some of Jonson's, observe them more closely. Dryden, incidentally, did not have the play freshly in his mind when he wrote his examination, for he thinks that it is more unified than it actually is. For instance, he says that the action occurs in two houses, but if you will glance back over the play, you will notice that it really occurs in four houses and a street.

Little can, we think, be added to Dryden's appreciation of the play's characterization. He quite correctly spends his time dissecting Morose, who is the central comic figure of the play. To this, we can only add, as he does, that the minor comic characters, particularly Daw and La-Foole, are just as excellently executed. We mention this rather obvious fact because, in being excellently ridiculous, Daw, La-Foole, the Collegiate Ladies, Captain and Mrs. Otter, and the rest have an importance for the play that Dryden missed. They may destroy a unity of action, but they create a unity of excellence. More of this presently.

Dryden's analysis of the kinds of characters that you get in comedy is sound and perceptive, and deserves a lot more attention than it has ever gotten. He distinguishes three kinds of comic characterization: first, the kind of Greek Old Comedy which has come down to us only in the plays of Aristophanes; second, the kind of the Roman comic writers like Plautus and Terence and of the French comic writers like Molière; and, finally, the kind of the English comic writers, the kind best exemplified by Ben Jonson.

By the first kind, Dryden means the characterization of slapstick and farce. When an eminently dignified person like Socrates, in Aristophanes' *The Clouds,* is put into an utterly undignified situation, you have the same kind of farcical, stereotyped humor that you get when a portly and dignified society matron is hit in the face by a very messy custard pie. Dryden is not quite fair to Aristophanes when he says that this is the only kind of characterization you see in Greek comedy, but he is pretty exact in defining one type of characterization that you see in the Keystone Kops, in Laurel and Hardy, and in the Three Stooges as well as in Aristophanes. An intelligent person must probably have a soft spot in his head for such "low" humor, but it is, nevertheless, the characterization of comic entertainment, not of comic art. It can be enjoyed as much by the ignorant person and the child as by the intelligent person. Dryden is quite right in suggesting that the great writers and the great comedians have, like Jonson in this play, given us more.

The second type of comic characterization is the kind found in Roman comedy. It is the characterization of types. In Plautus and Terence you find the same kinds of characters recurring. You find the crotchety old man who—just like Morose—wants to marry the beautiful young girl, or who—just, as you shall see, like Orgon in *Tartuffe*—wants to force the beautiful young girl into an absurd marriage. You find the young lovers. You find the clever servant who aids them—just as Truewit aids Dauphine in *The Silent Woman,* and, even more closely, just as the actual servant Dorine aids the young lovers in *Tartuffe.* In our time you will find this second kind of comic characterization in television's situation comedies. You will find it in comic comic-strips like *Blondie.* In such comedies, Father is always a befuddled boob, Mother is always his wise and beautiful savior, and their children are always mischievous, lovable, and cute in a way one hopes exists more in imagination than in reality.

We would go along with Dryden in suggesting that all comic characterization is based upon such types, and that the best, the third kind of characterization, transcends them. Dryden's example is perhaps the greatest comic character of them all, Shakespeare's Falstaff. Falstaff is an example of what Jonson and Dryden call a "humor." That is, Falstaff springs from a type, but he is much more than a type. In Roman comedy, you find a type called the braggart soldier, a loudmouthed, boastful, and utterly cowardly bully. After bragging about his tremendous exploits and frightening all of the timid souls in sight, he is suddenly called upon to show his bravery. Then he runs off in the most ludicrous, abject, and humiliating manner. Jonson has a superb braggart soldier called Captain Bobadill in *Everyman in His Humour,* and Daw and La-Foole are descendants of the type.

This third type of comic characterization differs from the second in its individuality. Falstaff is a braggart soldier, but he is so unique that he magnificently transcends the type to become probably the most memorably etched individual in our comic literature. This is what Dryden means, then, when he refers to the humor. Morose is a crotchety old man, but he is a much more individualized crotchety old man than any you will find in Plautus and Terence. It is this third type of comic characterization that you will find, and that you should look for, in art.

We are not saying that the society matron who gets the custard pie in the face is not funny. We are not even saying that Dagwood Bumstead is not funny. But to prefer either figure to Falstaff or even to Morose is to prefer hotdogs and hamburgers to a filet mignon.

Dryden says that he "shall not waste time in commending the writing of this play," but we cannot but wish that he had, because little has been written that is really first-rate about the language of comedy. However, Dryden gives us the hint of what to look for when he mentions "wit and acuteness of fancy," and also when he says that Jonson "has here described the conversation of gentlemen in the persons of True-Wit and his friends, with more gaiety, air, and freedom than in the rest of his comedies."

In talking about characterization, we were really talking about three kinds of comedy—slapstick farce, stereotyped entertainment, and art. Just as there is a kind of characterization appropriate to each, so is there a kind of language appropriate to each.

Slapstick farce does not require much dialogue. In fact, the more it can depend upon action and the less upon dialogue, the better. When our society matron receives her custard pie, it isn't necessary for her to say more than "Ooof!" Entertainment requires more dialogue, but not a great deal more. Dagwood Bumstead talks, but he is a stereotype talking about a stereotyped situation in a stereotyped way. When he gets the equivalent of a custard pie in the face—that is, when he is outsmarted by his wife, his boss, or his children —he will say something rather more intellectual than "Ooof!" but not much more mentally arresting than "Gee Whizz!" or "I'll be doggoned!" As Dagwood's character doesn't offer an intelligent person food for more than passing contemplation, so also is his dialogue pretty vapid after more than a moment's consideration.

What kind of dialogue, then, is appropriate for comic art? Dryden says the "conversation of gentlemen." Don't be put off by the word "gentlemen." What Dryden means is the language of civilization. He means the language men speak when they are educated and perceptive. He means the language that reflects thought and engaging personality. And when we speak of the language of comedy, we would then mean something like the playful language of perceptive minds.

What, more specifically, would such minds talk about, and how would they talk? Truewit, Jonson's best example of a gentleman, regards the world with true wit. He sees that certain people such as Daw and La-Foole and the

Collegiate Ladies behave absurdly, and as a civilized man he enjoys the absurdities. He is entertained by pointing them out and by talking about them. Truewit's language is, like all great comic language, based on the perception of a difference between how some people act and how a reasonable person would act. This perception is, in essence, wit. To make it is to have wit, and to be witty.

Because Truewit is educated as well as perceptive, he describes absurdities playfully. That is, he has the vocabulary and the mental fluency to make puns, spoonerisms, comparisons, similes, metaphors, and images which are unique, fresh, and appropriate. His wit consists first in seeing that something is absurd, and then in commenting artistically and imaginatively upon it.

Morose is almost as perceptive as Truewit, and his view of the world in many ways coincides with Truewit's. But, while Truewit's attitude toward absurdity is genial, Morose's is—morose. Truewit prevents Dauphine from maiming Daw, but Morose approaches his tormentors with a sword. Thus, Truewit really exemplifies some of the sunny geniality of Meredith's comic spirit, while Morose, viewing the same human foibles, only becomes querulous, crotchety, eccentric, and misanthropic.

Actually, Ben Jonson is here showing us the civilized and the uncivilized view of the world. Truewit's benevolent amusement and playful tolerance are the moral standard against which Jonson tosses all the absurdities of the play.

To return to language for a moment, just as there is a truly witty language in the conversation of Truewit and his friends, there is the falsely witty language of Daw and La-Foole, who attempt to imitate wit without being witty, and who try to be civilized without being bright. The dialogue of Daw and La-Foole is from first to last a caricature of comic wit. It is funny because it is such a bad caricature, just as they are funny because they are such bad caricatures of true gentlemen like Truewit.

Dryden compliments the well-made structure of the play, and here we have to diverge pretty widely from him. We think that he is quite correct when he admiringly notices how well Jonson plants his information about characters who have not yet entered, but we think that he is quite wrong in discussing the play's structure as if it were the same as the structure of *Antigone*. He discusses it as if it were Aristotle's well-made plot, which has no extraneous incident, and which has one incident causing the next, more exciting one.

This kind of plot structure, perhaps because of the prestige that Aristotle gave it, has, as you have seen in the chapter on tragedy, long been considered the proper structure for plays. To recapitulate, it is what we prefer to call, somewhat misleadingly, the tragic structure. In other words, the traditionally appropriate, the archetypical structure, for the serious or the tragic play. That is not to say that all tragedies use it, for some, like *King Lear,* transcend it.

But we would now add that this structure is traditionally inappropriate for comedy. You find it used in many comedies, but it is most successful in farce or other comic entertainment. When someone tries to weld it to art, he very frequently creates a botched job. We would say, then, that it is not the archetypical structure of comic art, and it is not the structure of *The Silent Woman.*

What, then, is the comic structure? And what is the structure of Ben Jonson's play? Our quotation from L. J. Potts gives a plausible and persuasive theory of comic structure. That structure is the freer, looser kind of plot that you find in Cervantes' *Don Quixote,* in Mark Twain's *Huckleberry Finn,* in Fielding's *Tom Jones,* in J. D. Salinger's *Catcher in the Rye,* and in the great comedies of Shakespeare.

Dryden suggests that there is one tightly-knit plot in *The Silent Woman.* We think this is a mistake. Daw and La-Foole and the Collegiate Ladies have little to do with the tricking of Morose. Captain and Mrs. Otter have practically nothing to do with it. However, the incidents involving these characters take up at least half of the play. If Ben Jonson were interested only in the plot of Morose and Dauphine, he could have shortened and tightened up his play by half. We doubt, however, that the play would have been half as good.

What do these other incidents, then, do for the play? Why are they there? For one thing, they provide other examples of absurdity. They provide examples of a different manner of absurdity. The story of Morose is absurd, but it has an undercurrent of dark seriousness about it. It would not take much to turn it into a kind of tragedy. Apparently, the greatest comedy always runs this danger. It yearns toward the tragic. The reason is probably the simple one that comic art takes morality seriously, while comic entertainment is hardly concerned with morality at all. Something is needed to alleviate the serious undercurrent, and that is why these other, airier, less serious examples are needed.

It is not merely Morose who is mad in Ben Jonson's comedy, as it is not merely Goneril and Regan who are wicked in Shakespeare's tragedy. The comic artist sees a mad world, and he wants to give it to us in some of its fulness as well as in some of its depth. If Morose is in the play to give us some of Jonson's depth of vision, Daw and La-Foole and the rest are there to give us some of his fulness of experience.

So we should say, then, that when you see a rather simple comedy concerned wholly with one story that has no digressions in it, you are not seeing comic art. But when you see a comedy that has a strong serious plot, fully embellished with other attached and more extravagant examples, then you are seeing the comic structure at its best, and the comic art at its best. If you demand that *The Silent Woman* have a plot like *Antigone,* then you are probably also asking that the play be poorer than it is.

One of the best qualities of a serious discussion is that it proceeds on a straight line. One of the beauties of a humorous discussion is that it playfully twists and unexpectedly turns back upon itself. Those twists and turns may stand as a kind of symbol for the plot structure of comic art. This is what we meant when we said that the play has a unity of excellence, if not a narrow unity of plot.

One word of caution. This theory of structure is a useful tool, a helpful key. There are some plays, however, that it will not unlock, for there are some plays that break rules superbly. It would be a great mistake for you to beat such plays over the head with this narrow notion of structure. Critics and appreciative readers have to be concerned with rules, but pedagogues and pedants become more concerned with rules than with real values.

And one last word. At the end of his discussion, Dryden suggests a comparison between English comedy and French. In other words, a comparison between Jonson and Molière. As there was probably more resemblance between *Antigone* and *Lear* than there was difference, so there is probably more resemblance than difference between Jonson and Molière. In this instance, Dryden is doing Molière something of an injustice.

At least, that is the way it seems to us. You may decide the point differently for yourself.

DISCUSSION QUESTIONS ON *THE SILENT WOMAN*

1. Like most great comedies, *The Silent Woman* is difficult to define. If you ask what it is about, you might answer that it is about noise. However, it is also about marriage, social climbing, greed, lust, misanthropy, woman's dress, and a host of other topics. Could you answer, then, what it is mainly about? Does such a diversity of subjects hurt the play or help it? Does the diversity grow out of the comic plot? In other words, how necessary, how intrinsic is this diversity to comedy?

2. *The Silent Woman* has the stamp of Jonson's personality throughout. It is thoroughly individual. However, many of the incidents and some of the dialogue are either copied, borrowed, or traditional. Some of the dialogue closely imitates the classic poets Juvenal and Horace. The comic duel between Daw and La-Foole seems to come from *Twelfth Night*. The trick of concealed sex is in *Twelfth Night*, in Aretino's [1] comedy *Il Marescalco*, and in many other places. The comic old man who cannot bear noise comes from a declamation by Libanius,[2] which has a similar old man also called Morosus. The situation between Captain and Mrs. Otter is the traditional overbearing wife and henpecked husband routine, and doubtless you can find other hackneyed situations in the play.

With all of this debt to tradition and to previous writers, then, in just what do Jonson's individuality and originality in this play consist?

3. Why does Jonson have three heroes? Wouldn't two or even one suffice?

4. Similarly, are all of the Collegians necessary? Could Jonson have used fewer?

5. In *King Lear* we saw that clothing was a unifying symbol and that imagery concerned with clothing pervaded the play. There are several discussions about dress in *The Silent Woman*. Can you find any shorter, casual references to dress throughout the play? In *Lear* clothing and nakedness symbolized, to put it

---

[1] Pietro Aretino (1492–1556), Renaissance Italian author of bawdy sonnets, dialogues, and comedies.
[2] Libanius (A.D. 314–393), curmudgeonish Greek sophist and rhetorician.

baldly, delusion and insight, appearance and reality. What does clothing symbolize in *The Silent Woman?*

6. Jonson well disguises his central plot secret, that Epicene is really a boy. However, just as a good detective story writer does, he plants plenty of clues and hints throughout the play. The first and most obvious, of course, is the name of Epicene. Scan the play closely, and see if there are many other references to hermaphrodites, amphibians, Amazons, and other ambiguous creatures.

7. Do these clusters of images that center around clothing and ambiguous sexuality suggest anything about Jonson's comic language? Could you make a case for it being comparable in subtlety to the language of a Shakespearian tragedy like *King Lear?*

8. In the world of romance, women are quiet and demure, but in the world of comedy, they are loud and brassy. In comedy, a "silent woman" is an impossibility and a contradiction in terms. Can you find other instances in Jonson's comic language of such traditional paradox and irony?

9. The formula of boy meets girl—boy loses girl—boy gets girl would seem a reasonable artistic translation of comedy's ritual origin. Does Jonson dismiss this formula entirely, or can you find any inverted trace of it in *The Silent Woman?* If it is there, Jonson has considerably refined it. Does this suggest anything about the relative sophistication of the play? Is simple and traditional comedy necessarily poorer than sophisticated and original comedy?

10. Are there many places in the play where nothing exciting is happening or about to happen? Are there more of these places toward the beginning or the end of the play? Does your conclusion suggest anything about Jonson's plotting and his general comic technique?

11. Would a modern audience admire Dauphine's desire to love all of the Collegians? Does their foolish credulity and willingness to be taken in soften or harden our feelings toward Dauphine? Toward them?

12. Would a modern audience occasionally feel that Morose is persecuted too much? Are we ever in danger of feeling for him some of the sympathy we feel for Shylock in *The Merchant of Venice,* or for Edmund when he gives his famous soliloquy early in *King Lear?*

13. Allied to both previous questions, does the comic spirit of the playwright seem genial like Meredith's or harsh like Swift's?

14. What would happen to the play if it were harsher? If, for instance, Truewit allowed Dauphine to break La-Foole's arm?

15. What would happen to the play if it were softer? If, for instance, Epicene were really a girl, if her marriage to Morose were only a joke thought up by Dauphine and performed by the false parson Cutbeard, and if the play ended with the marriage of Epicene and Dauphine?

TARTUFFE

BY MOLIÈRE

TRANSLATED BY SVEN ERIC MOLIN AND ROBERT HOGAN

CHARACTERS

MADAM PERNELLE, mother of Orgon
ORGON, husband of Elmire
ELMIRE, wife of Orgon
DAMIS, son of Orgon
MARIANE, daughter of Orgon and in love with Valere
VALERE, in love with Mariane

CLEANTE, brother-in-law of Orgon
TARTUFFE, a hypocrite
DORINE, companion of Mariane
MR. LOYAL, a process server
POLICE OFFICER
FLIPOTE, servant of Madam Pernelle

The scene throughout is the well-to-do middle-class home of Orgon, in Paris.

ACT I

[*Madam Pernelle, Flipote her servant, Elmire, Mariane, Dorine, Damis, and Cleante enter.*]

MADAM PERNELLE. Hurry up, Flipote, hurry up so I can get away from them.

ELMIRE. You rush about so quickly that I can't keep up with you.

MADAM PERNELLE. Then don't, daughter-in-law. Don't bother to see me out. I don't need all these formalities.

ELMIRE. We're only doing what we should for you, mother. But why are you rushing off from us so quickly?

MADAM PERNELLE. Because I can't stand to watch the goings-on here. Nobody tries to please me at all. Oh, I'm going away from you having learned my lesson. I'm opposed in everything I try to tell you. Nobody respects anything here. Everybody talks down to me. It's Pandemonium, a madhouse.

DORINE. If—

MADAM PERNELLE. You, my friend, are just a little too saucy. You're always butting in with your advice and your opinions.

DAMIS. But—

MADAM PERNELLE. And you, my son, are, in one word, a fool, f-o-o-l. I, your grandmother, tell you so. I've told your father a thousand times that you're a rascal. You bring him nothing but pain.

MARIANE. I think—

MADAM PERNELLE. Good heavens, how cautious you are. Butter wouldn't melt in your mouth. Ah, but they say still waters run deep. You go about things in that sly way I detest.

ELMIRE. But, Mother—

MADAM PERNELLE. Daughter, with all due respect, your behaviour in everything is completely bad. A fine example you put before them. Their poor dead mother behaved much better. You're extravagant. A spendthrift. Oh, it pains me how you dress yourself like a princess. Whoever wants to please only her husband doesn't need to dress herself up so much.

CLEANTE. But, Madam, after all—

MADAM PERNELLE. As for you, her brother, I think well of you. I like you and I respect you. But if I were my son and Elmire's husband, I'd ask you very strongly not to come to my house. All you do is preach rules of conduct that are impossible for respectable people to follow. Perhaps I speak a little too frankly, but that's my way. I don't hide what I have on my mind.

DAMIS. Your Mr. Tartuffe was no doubt very happy—

MADAM PERNELLE. He's an honest man. You ought to pay attention to him. I can't stand to see him opposed by a fool like you without getting very angry.

DAMIS. What! Why must I put up with this super-critic who's come here to be a dictator? Why can't we do anything to amuse ourselves unless this Mr. Tartuffe deigns to let us?

DORINE. If we have to listen to him and believe his rules, we can't do anything that's not a crime. He criticizes everything, that snoop!

MADAM PERNELLE. Everything he criticizes deserves to be criticized. He promises to lead you on the path to heaven. And my son's aim is to lead you all to follow him.

DAMIS. No, no, Madam. Neither my father nor anyone else could make me want to follow that fellow to heaven. I'd be lying to myself if I said anything else. His way of doing things enrages me. I warn you, something's going to happen. With such a scoundrel around, I'll have to explode.

DORINE. It's scandalous to see a perfect unknown set himself up as ruler here. Why, when he was a wandering beggar, he didn't have any shoes and his clothes weren't worth even five francs. Since coming here, he forgets what he was, opposing everyone and making himself master.

MADAM PERNELLE. Good heavens! Things would be much better here if everyone would be governed by his pious rules.

DORINE. He passes for a saint in your dreams. But, believe me, what he does is nothing but hypocrisy.

MADAM PERNELLE. Watch what you say!

DORINE. I'd no more trust him than I would a banker. Nor his servant Laurent either.

MADAM PERNELLE. I don't know what the servant's character may be, but I guarantee the master's a good man. The only reason you don't like him and ignore what he says is that he tells you all your faults. He hates sin. The interest of heaven is all that moves him.

DORINE. Well, but why, then, hasn't he let anyone visit this house any more? How can a simple visit enrage heaven, and make him stir up a fuss and snap off our heads? Do you want me to tell you, just between us, what's at the bottom of it? I think—heaven help us—that he's jealous of Madam.

MADAM PERNELLE. Hush! Think what you're saying. He's not the only one who disapproves of these visits. All this fracas that your visitors make, their carriages parked all around the door, their footmen milling about—it makes a noise that disturbs the whole neighborhood. I'm sure it doesn't mean anything, but people talk about it, and that's not good.

CLEANTE. Ah, Madam, how do you stop the unstoppable? It would be a fine thing in life if we had to give up our best friends because of the foolish talk of our neighbors. And even if we wanted to, do you think we could get everyone to stop talking? There's no defense against gossip. Don't pay any attention to such tale-telling. Let's try to live innocently and let the gossips do what they please.

DORINE. It's our neighbor Daphne and her little husband who speak badly of us, isn't it? The absurdest people are always the first to spread tales. They never fail to snap up the least spark of a possible scandal. And then gleefully sow the news everywhere, twisting it any way they can to make people believe it. They think the exaggerated faults of others justify their own faults. Either they hope wrongly that some similarity between their intrigues and other people's will make their own seem innocent, or else they want to scatter their own faults everywhere.

MADAM PERNELLE. All these rationalizations are nothing to the point. Everyone knows that Orante leads an exemplary life. Her attention is directed entirely to heaven. And I've heard that she strongly condemns the crowd which comes here.

DORINE. Orante! Oh, admirable example, that virtuous lady! Yes, she's very austere, but it's her age that makes her so. She's a prude because she can't help it. She did as much as she could to attract hearts. She played her advantages for all they were worth. Now, seeing the brilliance of her eyes start to dim, she renounces the world that ignores her. And under a heavy veil of great wisdom disguises the feebleness of her worn-out beauty. These are the ways

of old coquettes. It's hard for them to see themselves deserted by the gallants. When they're left like that, their dull uneasiness can find no other occupation but a prude's. The severity of these good women censures everything, pardons nothing. They boldly blame everyone else's life, not out of charity, only out of envy. They can't stand to see other people have a good time when the decline of old age has cut off their own.

MADAM PERNELLE. So this is the kind of nonsense you amuse yourself with. Daughter-in-law, at your house one has to be quiet because young miss here is babbling all the time. But at last it's my turn. I tell you that my son has done nothing wiser than to receive into his house this devout person, whom heaven sent here out of necessity to redress all of your corrupted spirits. For your own salvation you ought to pay attention to him. He reprehends nothing but the reprehensible. These visits, these balls, these tête-à-têtes are all the invention of the devil. Here no one ever listens to pious words, but only idle chatter, nonsense, chit-chat. Often enough our neighbors come in for their share of your detraction. You gossip about everyone. In fact, sensible people are upset by the confusion of your crowd. A thousand geese gather here, and just as a learned professor said the other day, it's really the tower of Babylon—everybody babbles on and on and on. And to tell you where this all started—[She glances at Cleante.] Hah! He's snickering already! Go find your foolish friends to make you laugh, and don't— Goodby, daughter-in-law, I no longer have anything to say. This place has lowered itself by half in my estimation, and it will be a long time before I set foot here again. [*She slaps Flipote.*] Come on, let's go. You're dreaming, you empty-headed cow. Good heavens, I'd better warm your ears. Come on, slut, get going!

[*Madam Pernelle, Flipote, Elmire, Mariane, and Damis go out.*]

CLEANTE. I'm not going down with her. She might start to lecture me again. The old woman—

DORINE. Ah! It certainly is a pity that she doesn't hear how you talk about her. She'd be sure to tell you off for calling her old before she thinks she is.

CLEANTE. How angry she got at us over nothing! And how enchanted she is with her Tartuffe!

DORINE. Oh, that's nothing compared to her son. When you see him, you'll say, "He's much worse." During the recent troubles he was highly esteemed and showed his courage in serving our Prince, but now, since Tartuffe has bewitched him, he's become a complete fool. He calls Tartuffe "brother," and loves him a hundred times more than his mother, son, daughter, or wife. Tartuffe's the only confidant of all his secrets and the advisor of all his actions. He embraces Tartuffe and pets him. He couldn't show any more fondness for a sweetheart. At dinner Tartuffe has to be seated at the top of the table. He eats more than six others, and the master makes us give him the best of everything. When he belches, the master says, "God bless you." He worships him. Tartuffe's his everything, his hero. The master admires everything he does. He quotes him everywhere. Tartuffe's least actions seem miracles to him, and his least words

oracles. Tartuffe makes the most of the master's foolishness and gulls him in a hundred different ways. The hypocrite works him for money all the time, and leaps to comment on everything we do. He's only an oaf who should be a servant, but he doesn't hesitate to give us his advice. He sermonizes us with wild eyes, and throws our ribbons and rouge and beauty spots away. The other day the big ox tore up right in front of us a handkerchief he found pressed into *The Lives of the Saints.* He said we'd committed the unpardonable crime of mixing the devil's finery with holiness.

[*Elmire, Damis, and Mariane come in.*]

ELMIRE. You're lucky you didn't come to hear her parting speech at the door. But I saw my husband coming. I'm going up to wait for him. [*Elmire and Mariane go out.*]

CLEANTE. Not to waste time, I'll wait for him here. I just want to say hello.

DAMIS. You might casually mention my sister's marriage. I think Tartuffe opposes it, and is making my father change his mind. You know how interested I am in it. If a great love unites my sister and Valere, Valere's sister is just as dear to me. And if it should happen that—

DORINE. Here he comes.

[*Damis leaves through one door as Orgon enters through another.*]

ORGON. Ah! Good morning, brother.

CLEANTE. I was just going, but I'm happy to see you. It's not very pleasant in the country yet, is it?

ORGON. Dorine—wait just a minute please, Cleante—tell me the news here and relieve my worries. Did everything go well these last two days?

What did you all do here? How is everyone?

DORINE. Two days ago Madam had a fever in the evening and a headache beyond imagination.

ORGON. And Tartuffe?

DORINE. Tartuffe? Marvelous. Big, fat, red-faced, and healthy.

ORGON. [*Affectionately.*] Poor man.

DORINE. In the afternoon she was nauseated, and at dinner couldn't touch anything at all because her headache was so bad.

ORGON. And Tartuffe?

DORINE. He ate right in front of her, all by himself, and managed to gobble up two partridges topped off with half a leg of mutton hash.

ORGON. Ah, the poor fellow.

DORINE. She didn't get a minute's sleep all night. Her fever kept her awake, and we had to sit up with her until daybreak.

ORGON. And Tartuffe?

DORINE. Comfortably drowsy, he went to his bedroom on leaving the table and plopped himself into his warm bed, where he slept soundly through till morning.

ORGON. Ah, the poor chap.

DORINE. Finally we persuaded her to be bled, and relief came immediately.

ORGON. And Tartuffe?

DORINE. He recovered nicely and fortified his soul against all evils. To make up for the blood which Madam had lost, he drank four large bowls of wine at breakfast.

ORGON. Ah, poor man!

DORINE. Finally, both of them got well. And I'm just now going to Madam to tell her how much interest you showed in her convalescence. [*Dorine flounces out.*]

CLEANTE. Brother, she laughs in your face. And, in all frankness, I must say, though I don't want to make you mad, that she's right. Who ever heard of such foolishness? How can this man have such power to make you forget everything for him? Especially when, after you've taken him into your house and helped him out of his distress, he—

ORGON. Stop right there, brother. You don't know the man you're talking about.

CLEANTE. All right, I don't know him, if that's what you want. But in order to know him, perhaps you—

ORGON. Dear brother, you'd be charmed to know him. You'd be overcome by him. He's a man who—who —oh!—a man who—in other words— a man! Whoever follows his example knows perfect peace, and finds the world a dungheap. With his teaching I've become a different man. He leads me to have affection for nothing. He draws my heart away from all friendships. I could see my brother, my children, my mother, my wife all die without caring as much as that. [*He snaps his fingers dismissively.*]

CLEANTE. Such human sentiments, my brother, such feeling!

ORGON. Oh, if you'd seen him as I first saw him you'd think as well of him as I do. Every day he came to church and fell on his knees opposite me in such a sweet way. Everyone in the congregation noticed how ardently he prayed to heaven. With great sighs and sudden outbursts he humbly kissed the ground. And when I left, he hurried ahead of me to offer me holy water at the door. I learned from his servant, who imitates him in everything, who he was and how poor he was, and I gave him gifts. He always modestly wanted to return part of them. "It's too much," he said, "too much by half. I don't deserve your pity." And when I'd refuse to take any back, he'd divide it among the poor, right in front of me. Finally, heaven saw fit to send him to live with me, and since then everything here seems to go well. He disapproves of everything, and he takes an interest, for my honor's sake, in my wife. He tells me who looks tenderly at her, and he shows six times as much jealousy as I do. You'd never believe how far he'd go to show his zeal. He calls his least trifling a sin. Almost nothing is too small to scandalize him. Why, just the other day he blamed himself for interrupting his prayers to kill a flea with too much anger.

CLEANTE. My God, Orgon, I think you're mad. Are you joshing me? What do you mean by all this ranting?

ORGON. Cleante, this sounds to me like atheism. Your soul, dear brother, is a little tainted. As I've told you a dozen times, you're leading yourself into trouble.

CLEANTE. People like you always talk like that. They want everyone to be as blind as they are. It's atheism and heresy to show good sense. And whoever fails to worship their own brand of vain foolishness has neither respect nor regard for sacred things. Away with you. All your talk can't make me afraid. I know what I say, and heaven can see my heart. We're not slaves to people like you. There's such a thing as false devotion, just as there's false bravery. You don't learn who the truly brave are because they make a lot of noise about their honor, and you don't learn who the truly

good and devout are because they talk about it and fall on their knees all the time. Why, don't you make any distinction between piety and religiosity? You want to deal with both in the same terms, give the same honor to the false face as to the true one, equate pretense with sincerity, confuse appearance with reality, think as well of a shadow as of a real person, and make the counterfeit equal the true. Oh, men are strange! One never sees them leading a moderate life. The limits of reason are too narrow for them. In everything they do, they go beyond its bounds. They spoil the most noble things by pushing them too far.—All this is by-the-by, dear Orgon.

ORGON. Yes, you're no doubt a respected theologian. All the world's wisdom's retired into your head. You're the only sage, the only enlightened one, the oracle, the Cato of our time. Next to you, all men are fools.

CLEANTE. I'm not a respected theologian, Orgon, and all the world's wisdom hasn't retired into my head. But, in a word, I know, though it be all I know, that there's a difference between the false and the true. And just as I know of no kind of hero more estimable than those who are perfectly devout—nothing in the world's more admirable than a saint who is moved by true religious zeal—so I know of nothing more odious than the false face of a hypocritical zealot. Those bare-faced humbugs, those hirelings of religion who flaunt sacrilege and false piety with impunity, who play at will with what's most sacred and holy to men. Those people whose souls have been bought, who make a market place out of devotion because they want to buy credit and dignity at once, without effort, by raising their eyes and sighing affectedly. Those people, I say, who want a fortune not found on the path to heaven; who, burning and full of prayer, are always making absurd demands like preaching solitude in the middle of court. Those people who know how to adapt their zeal to their vices; who are quick to anger, vindictive, untrustworthy, deceitful; who cloak their own proud resentment under the cover of heavenly interest in order most insolently to ruin an enemy; who are all the more dangerous in their rabid hatred because they use as arms against us the things we revere; and who, because they are well thought of, try to kill us with the sword of sanctity. One sees lots of these scoundrels, but the sincerely religious are still easy to recognize. Our century, Orgon, has shown us many who can serve as glorious examples. Think of Ariston, Periandre, Orante, Alcidamas, Polydore, Clitandre. Nobody denies their right to the title. They don't have about them all this boasting of virtue. They aren't unbearable show-offs. Their devotion is human and reasonable. They don't disapprove of everything we do. To such constant reprimanding shows too much pride. They leave haughty words to others, and convert us by their actions. They don't believe everything evil that might be, and their hearts lead them to judge well of others. Their aim, without cabals or cliques or intrigues, is to lead a good life. They're implacable against sin, but their wrath doesn't attack the sinner, and they don't zealously call down heaven on their own behalf any more than heaven appears of its own accord. These are my kind of people, people worth following, people whose example needs to be put forward. Your Tartuffe isn't one of them. Oh, you're sincere in your belief, but I think you're misled by false appearances.

ORGON. Cleante, have you had your say?

CLEANTE. Yes.

ORGON. Then goodby. [*He starts to leave.*]

CLEANTE. Please, one more word, on a different subject. You know you've promised Valere that he may marry Mariane?

ORGON. Yes.

CLEANTE. You've already set the day.

ORGON. That's right.

CLEANTE. Why, then, has it been postponed?

ORGON. I don't know.

CLEANTE. Do you have other ideas?

ORGON. Perhaps.

CLEANTE. Are you going to go back on your word?

ORGON. I didn't say that.

CLEANTE. Then there's nothing to stop you from keeping your promise.

ORGON. That depends.

CLEANTE. Is it necessary to be so crafty over one word? Valere sent me to ask about it.

ORGON. [*Sarcastically.*] Heaven be praised.

CLEANTE. What should I tell him?

ORGON. Anything you like.

CLEANTE. But we need to know your plans. What are they?

ORGON. To do what heaven wishes.

CLEANTE. Let's talk seriously. Valere has your word. Will you keep it or not?

ORGON. Goodby. [*Orgon goes out.*]

CLEANTE. Poor Valere. I'd better tell him what's going on here.

ACT II

[*Orgon and Mariane enter from different sides of the stage.*]

ORGON. Mariane.

MARIANE. Yes, Father.

ORGON. Come here. I have something to say to you in private. [*He peers suspiciously into a little closet.*]

MARIANE. What are you looking for?

ORGON. To see if anyone is here who could eavesdrop on us. This closet is just the place for someone to hide.—Mariane, I've always found you a dutiful daughter, and you've always been close to me.

MARIANE. I'm grateful for your love, father.

ORGON. Well said, my dear. And to deserve it, you need do nothing except please me.

MARIANE. I've always been proud to do that.

ORGON. Excellent. What do you think of Tartuffe?

MARIANE. Who, me?

ORGON. You! Be careful how you answer.

MARIANE. Oh my!—I'll say whatever you like.

ORGON. Well spoken. Now, then, daughter, tell me that great merit shines through all of his character, that you're fond of him, and that you'd be happy to see him my choice for your husband.

MARIANE. [*Falling back in surprise.*] Oh!

ORGON. What?

MARIANE. What did you say?

ORGON. What do you mean, "What did I say"?

MARIANE. Did I misunderstand you?

ORGON. How?

MARIANE. Whom did you want me to say touches my heart and would make me happy to see your choice as my husband?

ORGON. Tartuffe.

MARIANE. But, Father, it's not true. Not at all. Why do you want to make me lie?

ORGON. Because I want it to become true. It's enough for you that I've decided upon it.

MARIANE. What? You, Father, want—?

ORGON. Yes, Mariane, I want to unite Tartuffe to my family by marriage. He will be your husband. I've decided it. And since your wishes are determ—[*Dorine comes in.*] What are you doing here? Your curiosity is very strong, my girl, to make you eavesdrop on us this way.

DORINE. Really, I don't know whether this rumor got started by guesswork or by sheer luck. But when someone told me about this marriage, I thought it was only so much hot air.

ORGON. What! What! Do you mean it's unbelievable?

DORINE. So much so that I don't even believe you yourself.

ORGON. I know how to make you believe me.

DORINE. Ah, you're telling us a fairy tale.

ORGON. I'm telling you exactly what will soon happen.

DORINE. Pooh!

ORGON. I tell you, my dear girl, it's not a joke.

DORINE. [*To Mariane.*] Come, don't believe a word your father says. He's raving.

ORGON. I tell you—

DORINE. No, no, you've done well. No one will believe you at all.

ORGON. I'll—I'll—!

DORINE. Hold on! I believe you—and so much the worse for you. Can a man like you, with all this air of wisdom and a face covered by a beard, be crazy enough to want—

ORGON. Listen! I tell you plainly, my girl, you've taken certain familiarities in this house that don't please me at all.

DORINE. Please, let's talk without getting angry, sir. Are you trying to make fun of people with this scheme? Your daughter wasn't made to be a bigot's match. He has his holy affairs to think about. Besides, how will such a match help you? How could you, with all your money, choose a beggar as a son-in-law?

ORGON. Be quiet. If he has absolutely nothing, you should for that very reason respect him. His poverty is honest poverty. It should raise him above the grandeur of the world because he let all his goods be taken from him by too little care for worldly things and his great love for eternal ones. But my help may give him the way to escape from his embarrassments and recover his property—a well-known country estate which is rightfully his. He's a true gentleman, a squire.

DORINE. Yes, so he tells us himself, and this vanity doesn't sit well with his piety. Someone who adopts the holy life shouldn't boast about his name and birth. The humble ways of devotion suffer from the show of earthly ambition. Why all this pride? —But this conversation pains you. Let's talk about his character, and leave his nobility alone. Can you, without a twinge, make a girl like that the possession of a man like him? Haven't you thought of decency, of what might come of this marriage? Don't you know that a young woman's virtue is strained by a marriage she doesn't want? That her intention to be honest depends on the qualities of the man you give her to? That those men who are deceived by their wives often drive them to be what they are? It's hard enough to be faithful to certain men. A father who gives his daughter to a man she hates is responsible to heaven for her faults. Think of the dangers your plan exposes you to.

ORGON. I tell you I don't have to learn about life from you.

DORINE. You could do worse than listen to me.

ORGON. Mariane, we won't waste our time with such nonsense. I know what you must do, and I'm your father. I've given my promise to Valere, but I've heard that he gambles and is inclined to be irreligious. I haven't noticed him at church often.

DORINE. Do you expect him to go there at exactly the same hours you do? Only people who want to be noticed go then.

ORGON. I'm not asking for your advice.—In short, Tartuffe is in heaven's best graces, and that is richness beyond compare. This marriage will exceed all expectation. It will overflow with sweetness and pleasure. Wrapped up in each other, faithful in your love, you'll be true children, true turtledoves. No anger, no quarrelling will ever disturb you, and you can make him whatever you please.

DORINE. She can't make him anything but a cuckold, I tell you.

ORGON. Scandalous! Such talk!

DORINE. He's built for it, I tell you. He was born to be a cuckold. His fate can overcome every bit of virtue your daughter has.

ORGON. Stop interrupting me. Shut up! You do nothing but stick your nose into our conversation.

DORINE. I only speak for your own good, sir. [*She interrupts him every time he turns to speak to Mariane.*]

ORGON. You're too considerate. Please be quiet.

DORINE. It's for love of you—

ORGON. I don't want your love.

DORINE. I love you in spite of yourself, sir.

ORGON. Oh!!

DORINE. Your honor, sir. I can't stand to think of everybody making jokes about you.

ORGON. Will you be quiet!

DORINE. My conscience won't let me see you make this match.

ORGON. Snake! Serpent! Shut up! Your impudence—

DORINE. So holy! And yet you explode in anger!

ORGON. Yes, your twaddle drives me mad. I want you to be QUIET!

DORINE. All right. Not another word. But I can't stop thinking.

ORGON. Think if you want to. But be careful. Don't say a word to me or—enough! [*Turns back to Mariane.*] I've wisely and maturely considered everything.

DORINE. How maddening not to be able to speak! [*She stops the moment he turns his head.*]

ORGON. Although he's not handsome, Tartuffe is the kind of—

DORINE. Ye-ess, not handsome.

ORGON. —person whose best qualities you might have overlooked.

DORINE. Lucky girl! If I were in her place, surely no man would marry me without suffering for it. He'd know soon enough after the ceremony that a woman can get her revenge.

ORGON. [*Turns to Dorine and stands with folded arms.*] So nothing I say has any force?

DORINE. What's wrong? I wasn't talking to you.

ORGON. What were you doing then?

DORINE. Talking to myself.

ORGON. Excellent. What she needs for her insolence is a good slap in the face. [*He stands ready to slap her, and Dorine, each time he whirls about and glares at her, stands silent.*] Mariane, you must approve of my plan— think of this husband—I've chosen for you. [*To Dorine.*] Why don't you say something?

DORINE. I've nothing to say to myself.

ORGON. Just one little word more.

DORINE. No thanks, not now.

ORGON. Because I was waiting for you!

DORINE. I'm no fool.

ORGON. So, Mariane, you must be obedient and show complete respect for my choice.

DORINE. [*Running off.*] You'd never catch me with such a man!

ORGON. [*Trying to slap her.*] Mariane, that girl of yours is such a pest that I can't live with her anymore without falling into the sin of anger. I'm too upset to cope with her. Her insolence infuriates me. I'm going outside to calm down a bit. [*Orgon leaves by one door, and Dorine pops back in by another.*]

DORINE. What's wrong with you? Have you lost your tongue? Do I have to play your part for you? How can you stand to hear the stupidest plan put before you without answering a single word?

MARIANE. What do you want me to do against so positive a father?

DORINE. Whatever you have to do to stop such a threat.

MARIANE. But what?

DORINE. Tell him that the heart doesn't fall in love by command. You're marrying for yourself, not for him. It's you the whole affair is arranged for. It's you, not him, the husband has to please. Tell him that if his Tartuffe is so charming, he can marry him. No one will stop him.

MARIANE. But, Dorine, a father has such complete control over his daughter that I've never been able to speak back to him.

DORINE. Let's figure this out. Valere has committed himself. I ask you: do you love him or don't you?

MARIANE. Dorine! How can you doubt my love like that? Why do you ask me such a question? Haven't I confided in you a hundred times? Don't you know how much I love him?

DORINE. How do I know if your lips speak for your heart? How do I know if you really love him?

MARIANE. You do me wrong to doubt it, Dorine. I've shown my true feelings all too clearly.

DORINE. So you love him, then?

MARIANE. Yes, yes, very much.

DORINE. And he seems to love you too?

MARIANE. I think so.

DORINE. And both of you want very much to be married?

MARIANE. Yes, yes!

DORINE. What do you plan to do about this other marriage?

MARIANE. If I have to—kill myself.

DORINE. Good! That's a remedy I hadn't thought of. All you have to do is kill yourself to get out of it. Marvelous! Oh, it infuriates me to hear such talk.

MARIANE. Dorine, Dorine, don't get mad. You don't understand other people's troubles.

DORINE. I don't understand when people talk nonsense and give way when the going gets rough.

MARIANE. But what can I do? I'm timid.

DORINE. Love's supposed to make you strong.

MARIANE. Haven't I remained true to Valere? Isn't it his job to win me from my father?

DORINE. But how? If your father is a perfect crank who's totally bewitched by his Tartuffe? If he breaks his word over an already settled marriage? How can your lover be blamed for all that?

MARIANE. But what should I do? Show that my heart is already captured by making a scornful outburst in public? For his sake, do you want me to cause a scandal and outrage my parents? Should I show my love to the whole world?

DORINE. Oh, no, I don't want you to do anything. I can see you want to be Mrs. Tartuffe. I was wrong, come to think of it, to turn you from this marriage. Why should I go against your wishes? It's a very advantageous marriage! Mr. Tartuffe—oh, he's not a nobody! Surely Mr. Tartuffe can get what he wants without jumping through hoops for it. Already everybody admires him. He's noble, he's handsome. He's got red ears and a red face. You'll live happily ever after with such a husband.

MARIANE. Oh dear!

DORINE. What gaiety! What joy in your heart when you're the bride of such a fine husband.

MARIANE. Stop, please stop talking like that and help do something to stop this marriage. I give in. I'm ready to do anything.

DORINE. No, a girl has to do what her father wants. Even if he wants to give her a monkey for a husband. Besides, you're lucky. Why complain? You'll go in a coach to his village where you'll find plenty of interesting cousins and uncles and aunts. You'll be presented to local society. You can call on Mrs. Grocer and Mrs. Police Chief who'll honor you by bringing out some canvas chairs to sit on. Once a year at carnival time, you can hope for a grand ball with a fine orchestra—two fiddles—and a trained monkey, perhaps even some marionettes. Though maybe your husband—

MARIANE. Oh, you want to hurt me. Why don't you help me with your advice, instead.

DORINE. You'll have to excuse me.

MARIANE. Oh, Dorine, please!

DORINE. It'll serve you right to have this marriage go through.

MARIANE. Help me.

DORINE. No.

MARIANE. If I say what I want—

DORINE. First point: Tartuffe is yours, and you can have your fill of him.

MARIANE. You know that I've always confided in you. Tell me—

DORINE. No, my dear, you shall be Tartuffified!

MARIANE. Well, since you're not moved by my situation, I'll get consolation from despair. I know one cer-tain remedy for my anguish. [*She starts to go.*]

DORINE. Stop, stop, come back! I can't be angry with you. I have to pity you, no matter what.

MARIANE. Don't you see, Dorine, that if they force me to face this man I'll die.

DORINE. Don't worry so much. We'll find some way to get you out of this—look, here comes Valere.

[*Valere comes in.*]

VALERE. They were just talking about a bit of news that I didn't know before. It's very good.

MARIANE. What's that?

VALERE. You're going to marry Tartuffe!

MARIANE. This is something my father started.

VALERE. Your father—

MARIANE. He's changed his mind. He just now told me about it.

VALERE. What? Seriously?

MARIANE. Yes, seriously. He came right out and said it.

VALERE. And what do you think about it?

MARIANE. I don't know.

VALERE. That's an honest answer. You don't know?

MARIANE. No.

VALERE. No?

MARIANE. What do you think I should do?

VALERE. Do? Why, marry him, make him your husband.

MARIANE. You think I should do that?

VALERE. Yes!

MARIANE. Do you mean it?

VALERE. By all means. The choice is glorious, well worth taking.

MARIANE. All right. I'll just take your advice, then.

VALERE. You won't have any great difficulty in taking it, I'm sure.

MARIANE. No more difficulty than you had in giving it.

VALERE. Me? I gave it to you to please you.

MARIANE. And I'll follow it to please *you*.

DORINE. [*Withdrawing to the back of the stage.*] Let's see what will come of this.

VALERE. So that's what your love amounts to? And it was just a joke when you—

MARIANE. Let's not mention that, if you please. You told me as frankly as you could that I should accept as a husband whoever father wants to give me. And I tell you that, since you give me such very good advice, I intend to take it.

VALERE. Don't get out of it by blaming what I said. You'd already made up your mind, and now you grab the slightest straw to let yourself break your word.

MARIANE. That's right. You put it very well.

VALERE. I'm sure I do. You never loved me at all.

MARIANE. Oh, you can think so if you want to.

VALERE. Yes, yes, I *can* think so. Well, you may think you've hurt me, but I know somewhere else to offer my love and my hand.

MARIANE. Oh, I don't doubt it at all. Your merits excite so much love—

VALERE. Good Lord, leave my merits out of it. I have all too few, no doubt. You've proved that. But I hope a certain other person will receive me more kindly. I think I know someone who's willing not to stand on pride in helping me recover from my loss.

MARIANE. Your loss isn't great. You can console yourself easily enough over the change.

VALERE. I'll do my best, you can believe that. A woman who forgets us brings out all our pride. We men have to forget too. And if that's impossible, we have to pretend we have. The worst thing a man can do is show love for a woman who's left him.

MARIANE. No doubt that's a fine, noble feeling.

VALERE. Noble enough, and one every man agrees with. What do you want? Me to go around carrying a torch for you while I see you, right in front of my eyes, in somebody else's arms? Can't I give someone else the love you rejected?

MARIANE. Go ahead! I just wish it were done already.

VALERE. That's what you wish, eh?

MARIANE. Yes.

VALERE. You've insulted me enough. I'll make your wish come true right now.

MARIANE. Good!

VALERE. [*Starts to leave and then comes back.*] Just remember at least that it was you who drove me to it.

MARIANE. Certainly.

VALERE. I'm just following your example.

MARIANE. If you say so.

VALERE. You're going to be faithfully copied.

MARIANE. All the better.

VALERE. You're now seeing me for the last time.

MARIANE. Happy moment!

VALERE. Hah! [*He starts to leave, but when he's near the door he comes back.*]

MARIANE. Well?

VALERE. Didn't you call me?

MARIANE. Me? You're dreaming.

VALERE. All right! Then I'm going to meet my fate! Goodby!

MARIANE. Goodby.

DORINE. I must say, you two have lost your minds if you ever had them. I let this foolish quarrel go on just to see how far you two would go. Hey, Mister Valere. [*She grabs him by the arm, and he makes a great show of resisting.*]

VALERE. What do you want? Let me go!

DORINE. Come here, come here.

VALERE. No, no, she's made me furious. Don't try to stop me from doing what she wants.

DORINE. Stop!

VALERE. No, my mind's made up. I'm determined.

DORINE. Oh, pooh!

MARIANE. It hurts him to see me. My being here pains him. It would be much better if I left. [*She starts to leave.*]

DORINE. [*Leaving Valere and going to Mariane.*] Now the other one! Where are *you* going?

MARIANE. Leave me alone.

DORINE. You have to come back.

MARIANE. No, no, Dorine. Don't waste your time trying to make me.

VALERE. I see that the sight of me is torture to her. It would be much better if I released her from it. [*He starts to leave.*]

DORINE. [*Leaving Mariane and going to Valere.*] What, again? Oh, the devil with both of you. Stop this foolishness and come here, you two. [*She pulls them both together.*]

VALERE. What do you want?

MARIANE. What are you doing to us?

DORINE. Bringing you both together and stopping this nonsense. You must be mad to carry on so.

VALERE. Didn't you hear how she spoke to me?

DORINE. What a fool to get so mad.

MARIANE. Didn't you see how he acted, how he treated me?

DORINE. You're a couple of idiots. [*To Valere.*] She doesn't care about anything except being with you, I tell you. [*To Mariane.*] You're the only one he loves. He only wants to be married to you. Cross my heart.

MARIANE. Then why did he give me such advice?

VALERE. Why did she have to ask for advice on such a question?

DORINE. What dumbbells, both of you! Here, give me your hands. Come on now.

VALERE. [*Giving Dorine his hand.*] What good's my hand?

DORINE. Fine. Now yours.

MARIANE. [*Giving Dorine her hand.*] Oh, what's the use?

DORINE. Good heavens! Now come here. You both love each other more than you know.

[*They hold hands without looking at each other.*]

VALERE. [*Glancing at Mariane.*] Don't hold it as if it might burn you. Come, look at me as if you didn't hate me.

[*Mariane glances at Valere and smiles sheepishly.*]

DORINE. To tell you the truth, lovers are mad.

VALERE. Admit it, don't I have some reason to complain? Wasn't it unkind to enjoy hurting me so?

MARIANE. You! Aren't you the one who was ungrateful?

DORINE. Let's leave all this for another time and try to think how to get you out of this awful marriage.

MARIANE. Tell us what we should do.

DORINE. All sorts of tricks. Your father is out of his mind. [*To Valere.*] His plans are wild. [*To Mariane.*] For you, the best thing is to go along with his proposals, pretending sweetly that you agree with everything. Then, if he wants to rush the marriage, it will be easy to make up excuses. You can put it off by any means at all. Just now, you are sick—something that came all of a sudden, so a delay is necessary. Just then, you had a bad omen—you met a funeral in the street, you broke a mirror, you dreamed of muddy water. Remember, best of all, that they can't make you marry unless you say, "Yes." But I think that the best thing for both of you is not to be seen talking together at all. [*To Valere.*] You, go at once to your friends and get them to remind him of his promise to you. We'll get his brother to do the same thing, and we'll try to get the step-mother on our side too.

VALERE. [*To Mariane.*] Whatever we do, my greatest hope is in you.

MARIANE. [*To Valere.*] I can't answer for my father's whims, but I'll never be anyone's but Valere's.

VALERE. How happy you make me. Whatever happens—

DORINE. Talk! Talk! You can't stop lovers from talking. Go on now, I tell you.

VALERE. [*Starting out and then returning.*] Then—

DORINE. Talk, talk, talk, talk, talk. You go out that way, and you go out this way. [*She takes each one by the shoulders and pushes them firmly out on opposite sides of the stage.*]

ACT III

[*Damis strides in, followed by Dorine.*]

DAMIS. May lightning strike me on the spot! Let everyone call me the greatest scoundrel alive! Nothing on heaven or earth can stop me from doing something drastic right now.

DORINE. Easy, easy! Don't get so angry. Your father hasn't done anything yet but talk. Everything doesn't happen that is supposed to. It's a long road from talking to doing.

DAMIS. I have to do something to stop this idiot's scheming. What he needs to hear is a couple of home truths.

DORINE. Go slow, now. Take it easy. Leave him—and your father too—in the hands of your step-mother. She has some power over Tartuffe. He pays attention to what she says, and I think he even has a soft spot for her. I hope to heaven it's true! That would be fine. Besides, she sent for him because of you. She wants to sound him out on your marriage, and find out what he thinks about it. She's going to point out to him how much trouble he can cause if he keeps pushing this stupid proposal. His valet says he's at prayers and I can't see him now. But he also says he'll be down shortly. So, please, go away and let me wait for him.

DAMIS. I can be here while you talk.

DORINE. No, not at all. They have to be alone.

DAMIS. I won't say anything to him.

DORINE. You're fooling yourself. You're too hot-headed, and that's the best way to ruin everything. Get out.

DAMIS. No, I want to see him. I

won't get angry.

DORINE. What a nuisance you're being. Here he comes. Get out.

[*Damis leaves, and Tartuffe comes in. When he sees Dorine, he calls off-stage to his servant Laurent.*]

TARTUFFE. Put my hair shirt away with my scourge, Laurent. And pray always that heaven lead you right. If anyone comes to see me, say that I've gone to the prison to distribute the alms I've collected.

DORINE. What hooey.

TARTUFFE. What do you want?

DORINE. To talk to you.

TARTUFFE. [*Taking a handkerchief from his pocket.*] Ah! Good heavens! Please, before you say anything, take this handkerchief.

DORINE. What for?

TARTUFFE. To cover your bosom. I can't bear to look at it. Our souls are offended by such sights. They lead us to guilty thoughts.

DORINE. You must be awfully sensitive to temptation. I don't understand where all this heat comes from. I'm not that lustful. In fact, I could see you naked from head to toe and all that hide wouldn't excite me in the least.

TARTUFFE. Show a little more modesty in your speech, or I must leave you at once.

DORINE. No, no, I'm going to leave you peacefully enough. I have only two words to say to you. Madam is soon coming down, and would like to talk to you.

TARTUFFE. Indeed! Very willingly!

DORINE. [*To herself.*] How soft he gets! I'm sure I've hit on it!

TARTUFFE. Is she coming soon?

DORINE. I think I hear her now. Yes, here she comes. I'll leave you to your-

selves. [*Dorine goes out, and Elmire comes in.*]

TARTUFFE. May heaven's overwhelming bounty bring good health to your body and to your soul, and bless your days as much as the desires of its most humble worshipers could want.

ELMIRE. Thank you very much for your pious thoughts. But let's sit down so we can be a little more at ease.

TARTUFFE. Have you recovered from your illness?

ELMIRE. Very nicely, thank you. The fever has quite gone away.

TARTUFFE. It was not my all too unworthy prayers, I'm afraid, that were adequate to bring this blessing to you from above. But I have not petitioned once to heaven without mentioning your recovery as a worthy object.

ELMIRE. You are too solicitous for me.

TARTUFFE. One cannot value your valuable health too highly. To bring it back, I would give my own.

ELMIRE. That's pushing Christian charity too far, but I am greatly indebted for all your good wishes.

TARTUFFE. I do much too little for what you deserve.

ELMIRE. I wanted to speak privately with you about something. I'm glad that nobody can listen to us here.

[*Damis steals silently in and pops into the closet.*]

TARTUFFE. Madam, I am enchanted. You don't know how sweet it is for me to be alone with you. It is something I often asked for from heaven, but not until now has it happened.

ELMIRE. What I hope for is a conversation in which you open your heart to me, hiding nothing.

TARTUFFE. I could wish for no more special favor than to bare before your eyes my whole soul, and swear solemnly to you that all the bother I made over those visits attracted here by your charms are not directed towards you as the result of any dislike. Quite the opposite. It is my ardent zeal that leads me, my purest motives—

ELMIRE. I understand. My health worries you.

TARTUFFE. [*Squeezing her fingertips.*] Oh, it does, Madam. My devotion is—

ELMIRE. Ouch. You're squeezing me.

TARTUFFE. From too much zeal, Madam. I would never mean to hurt you, and I'd as soon— [*He puts his hand on her knee.*]

ELMIRE. What's your hand doing there?

TARTUFFE. Just feeling your dress. How soft it is!

ELMIRE. Please let go. I'm very ticklish. [*She moves her chair away, and Tartuffe moves his closer.*]

TARTUFFE. My, my, how wonderfully made this lace is. They work miracles nowadays. I've never before seen such well-made things.

ELMIRE. True, very true. But let's get to our business. They say that my husband intends to break his word and give our daughter to you. Tell me, is that right?

TARTUFFE. He's hinted at it. But, to tell the truth, Madam, that's not the happiness I'm seeking. I see somewhere else the marvelous charms and attractions that are the real object of my desires.

ELMIRE. That's because you love nothing on this earth.

TARTUFFE. The heart within my bosom is not a stone.

ELMIRE. I'm sure that all your sighs are directed to heaven. Nothing less could hold your attention.

TARTUFFE. The love that leads us to eternal beauty doesn't put out the spark of temporal love. Our senses are easily charmed by the perfect works of heaven, which are brilliantly reflected in people like you. In you heaven displays its rarest miracle. In your face are collected such beauties as surprise the eyes and make the heart jump. I cannot look on you, my dearest, without admiring the author of nature, my heart inflamed by the ardent love with which He created the most beautiful image of Himself. At first I was afraid that my hidden love was the secret trap of the Devil. I resolved even to avoid looking at you, thinking you an obstacle to my salvation. But at last I knew, my loved one, my beautiful, that this passion was not at all sinful, that I could reconcile it with modesty. It was this that made me lose my heart entirely. I know it's a very great presumption to dare to offer my heart to you. But I depend entirely on your goodness, not at all on the vain attempts of my own weakness. In you are my hope, my joy, my peace. On you my happiness or pain depend. I will be whatever you decide—happy if you like, wretched if you like.

ELMIRE. A gallantly phrased declaration, but, to tell the truth, a little surprising. You should have armed your heart a little better and thought a little more about what you are doing. A religious man like you, a man known everywhere—

TARTUFFE. Oh, even though I am

religious, I am no less a man. When I see your heavenly charms, my heart surrenders. It doesn't reason. I know that such words seem strange from me, but I'm not an angel, Madam. And if you condemn the avowal I just made, you have only your own charms to blame for it. Since I first saw your more than earthly beauty, you've become sovereign of my soul. Your heavenly looks overcame my still-resisting heart. They conquered everything—fasts, prayers, tears. They turned my worship entirely to you. My eyes and my sighing spoke to you a thousand times, and only to explain myself better do I now use my voice. If you could just look with some favor on the sufferings of your wretched slave, if you could just in your goodness console me, if you could deign to lower yourself to my nothingness, then I would show you such a devotion, my lovely miracle, as the world has never seen. Your honor runs no risks with me. You need not fear any disgrace. These court gallants with foolish wives are noisy in their affairs and vain in their talk. They boast endlessly of their triumphs. No sooner do they make a conquest than they tell about it. By their indiscreet language, they defile the altar at which their hearts have sacrificed. But men like me burn with a secret fire. You can be sure your secret will be kept. The care we take for our reputation answers everything the loved one could want. If you accept our heart, you find in us a love without scandal and a pleasure without fear.

ELMIRE. You've made yourself quite clear, but aren't you afraid that I'll tell my husband of this impassioned flirting? Aren't you afraid of the change in his friendship that such a prompt report might bring about?

TARTUFFE. I know that you're too compassionate to do that, and that you'll forgive my boldness. You must excuse the human weakness of my passion, which so offends you, and think, when you look in your mirror, that man isn't blind, that he is made of flesh.

ELMIRE. Perhaps other women would do something else, but I'm willing to be discreet about this. I won't tell my husband. But I want something from you in return. I want you to support frankly and without reservations or double dealing the marriage of Valere and Mariane. I want you to stop using your influence to enrich yourself with what belongs to someone else, and—

DAMIS. [*Coming out of the closet.*] No, no, stop! This must be made public. I heard everything you said in the closet. It seems that heaven's goodness led me there so I could overthrow the pride of this scoundrel. So I could get revenge for his hypocrisy and insolence. So I could open my father's eyes and show him in plain daylight the soul of a wretch who would make love to you.

ELMIRE. No, Damis, no. It's enough for him to be wiser from this and to learn to deserve the forgiveness I show him. When I've promised something, don't make me go back on my word. It's not my nature to make a fuss. A woman can laugh to herself about such things without troubling her husband's ears over them.

DAMIS. You have your reasons for doing what you want, and I have my own for doing otherwise. To spare him would be a mockery. His insolent pride has lorded it too long over my righteous anger, and stirred up too much trouble around here. This vermin has influenced father too long, and ruined both Valere's and my own love affairs. Father should be shown his double-dealing, and heaven has given me the perfect way to do it. I'm much indebted for this chance, and it's too good to let go. If I miss it, I don't deserve another one like it.

ELMIRE. Damis—

DAMIS. No, please, I have to trust myself in this. Oh, I'm delighted! You won't get me to renounce the pleasure of revenge. I'll finish this business off right now. Here comes just the person I'm looking for. [*Orgon enters.*] Father, we're going to welcome you with a surprising bit of news. All your tender care has been well worth it, and Tartuffe here is now paying you back for the attention you've given him. His great love for you was just declaring itself—by the very means that would dishonor you most. I caught him making great vows of his love to mother. She's in a forgiving mood, and her all-too-discreet heart wanted to keep this secret from you, but I don't have it in me to flatter this impudence. I think it would hurt you not to know about it.

ELMIRE. I've always thought that a wife shouldn't bother her husband about such foolish propositions. Her honor doesn't depend on them, but on her knowing herself that they've been rejected. These are my feelings about it, and you shouldn't have said anything, Damis, if you wanted me to respect you. [*She goes out.*]

ORGON. What am I hearing? Good heavens, should I believe it?

TARTUFFE. Yes, dear brother, I am evil. I am guilty, an unhappy sinner full of iniquity, the worst scoundrel ever born. Every instant of my life is stained with filth. It is nothing but a pile of dung and sordidness. Heaven is punishing me now by humbling me. Whatever crimes people want to accuse me of are true. I won't be proud and defend myself. Believe whatever they say, get ready to be angry, kick me out of your house like a common thief. No matter how shamefully I'm treated, it's not shameful enough.

ORGON. [*To Damis.*] You scoundrel, you wretch, you villain, how dare you cast doubt on his virtue and stain his honor?

DAMIS. What? Are you taken in by this fake hypocritical humility—?

ORGON. Shut up, you damned liar!

TARTUFFE. Let him speak. You accuse him wrongly. You'd do much better to believe what he says. Why be on my side? After all, do you know what I'm guilty of? Why do you believe in my saintly exterior? Why judge me favorably just from what you see? No, no, you're letting yourself be deceived by appearances. Oh dear, I'm not at all what people think I am. Everyone takes me for a holy man, but the simple truth is that I'm worthless. [*To Damis.*] Speak, my dear boy, speak. Call me a traitor, a lost soul, a thief, a notorious wretch, a murderer. Throw worse insults than that at me. I won't say a word. I deserve them. I'll suffer such debasement on my knees as penance for the crimes of my life.

ORGON. [*To Tartuffe.*] Dear brother, that's too much. [*To Damis.*] Doesn't this move you, you dog?

DAMIS. What do you mean? His babbling has misled you so—

ORGON. Shut up, you rascal! [*To Tartuffe.*] Stand up, stand up, brother. I beg you.

DAMIS. He can—

ORGON. SILENCE!

DAMIS. Who do you think—?

ORGON. Another word and I'll break every bone in your body.

TARTUFFE. Brother, brother, in the name of God, don't get so angry. I'd rather be tortured than have him suffer the least scratch for me.

ORGON. [*To Damis.*] Ungrateful monster!

TARTUFFE. Leave him alone. On both knees I beg you—

ORGON. [*To Tartuffe.*] You're joking. [*To Damis.*] Traitor! See how good he is.

DAMIS. But—

ORGON. Silence!

DAMIS. What! I—

ORGON. SILENCE, I say! I know very well why you're attacking him. You hate him, all of you. This very day I've seen my wife, my children, and my servants all unleashed on him. You use every trick to make this fine, devout person leave my house. But the more you do to get rid of him, the more I'm determined to keep him. I'm going to hurry up this wedding with my daughter. That will humble all of you.

DAMIS. Are you going to force her to accept him?

ORGON. Yes, you false son, and this very evening too, just to enrage you. I defy every one of you. I'll make you know you have to obey me. I'm the master here. Now, on your knees, at once, and take back everything you've said. Beg his pardon.

DAMIS. Who, me? To this scoundrel, this fraud who's pulled the wool—

ORGON. Ah! You resist, you beggar! You insult him again? [*To Tartuffe.*] A stick! A stick! Don't stop me. [*To Damis.*] Get out of here! Get out of my house! Don't you ever dare come back!

DAMIS. All right. I'm going, but—

ORGON. Quick, get out at once! I cut you off right now, and my curses, too, into the bargain! [*Damis goes out.*]

ORGON. Such outrages to a holy person!

TARTUFFE. Oh heaven, forgive him the pain he gives me. [*To Orgon.*] If you could know how unpleasant it is for me to see them try to blacken my reputation with you, brother—

ORGON. Oh dear!

TARTUFFE. Just to think of this ingratitude makes my soul suffer torture—how horrible. My heart is crushed more than I can tell. I'll die of it.

ORGON. [*Running to the door with tears in his eyes and calling after Damis.*] You wretch! I'm sorry I was kind enough to let you go, and didn't kill you on the spot. [*To Tartuffe.*] Brother, pull yourself together. Don't be too angry.

TARTUFFE. Oh, let us stop, let us stop these terrible, bitter fights. I see all around me the great trouble I've brought here. I think it would be better, brother, if I went away.

ORGON. What? No, you're joking.

TARTUFFE. Everyone hates me here. I can tell that they look around for ways to make you doubt my holiness.

ORGON. What does that matter? Do you see my heart listening to them?

TARTUFFE. They won't fail to follow this up, and maybe the same reports that you reject now, you might listen to some other time.

ORGON. No, brother, never!

TARTUFFE. Ah, brother, a wife may easily move her husband.

ORGON. No, no!

TARTUFFE. Let me leave at once, and get far away from here. That will remove all cause for such attacks.

ORGON. No, stay here. My life depends on it.

TARTUFFE. If I do that, I must mortify myself. However, if you want—

ORGON. Ah!

TARTUFFE. It's done. Say no more. But I know how I have to behave now. Honor is delicate, and friendship requires that I forestall any scandal or even suspicion of it. I shall avoid your wife, and you shall never see me even—

ORGON. No. Just to spite them all, see her often. My greatest pleasure is to make everyone angry. I want them to see you with her constantly. And that's not all. The better to outrage them, I want you to be my only heir. To make it legal, I'm going to give you all my possessions, everything I own. A kind and honest friend, my son-in-law to be, is dearer to me than son, than wife, than any relatives. Please, please accept what I offer.

TARTUFFE. Heaven's will be done in all things.

ORGON. Poor man! Let's go quickly and draw up the document. Then, let envy burst itself in spite!

ACT IV

[*Cleante and Tartuffe come in.*]

CLEANTE. Oh, yes, everyone's talking about it, and, believe me, the rumors aren't exactly to your credit either. I'm glad I ran across you. I wanted to tell you quite clearly what I think about it. Without weighing all the evidence, let me assume the worst is true. Let me assume that Damis acted badly and you've been falsely accused. Even so, shouldn't you as a Christian forgive him? Shouldn't you forget this desire for revenge? Should you let the son be driven from his father's house just because he's quarrelled with you? I tell you frankly that everybody's scandalized by this. If you take my advice, you won't push matters too far. Offer up your anger to God, and let the son come back into his father's good graces.

TARTUFFE. Alas! That's exactly what I want, with all my heart. I don't bear him any grudge. I pardon him. I don't blame him for anything. I'm more than willing to help him. Unfortunately, however, God's will isn't my own, and if he returns, I must go. After his impossible behaviour it would be scandalous for us to live under the same roof. Why, imagine how people would talk. Everybody would say that it was pure guile on my part, that I knew I was guilty and wanted to placate him to keep him quiet.

CLEANTE. These are all far-fetched, sham excuses, sir. Why are you taking the interests of heaven upon yourself? Does heaven need our help to punish the guilty? Vengeance is mine, saith the Lord. Judge not, lest you be judged. Would you let an absurd concern for what people would say keep you from a good and noble action? No, no, let's just do what heaven commands and not bother our heads about anything else.

TARTUFFE. Sir, I've already told you that I forgive him, and that's what heaven commands. But, after the scandal, the affront of today, heaven certainly doesn't command me to live with him.

CLEANTE. Does heaven command you to take advantage of the father's whim and accept a gift of property you've no claim to?

TARTUFFE. Nobody who knows me could think I'd be motivated by self-interest. This world's riches have no attraction for me. I'm not dazzled by their false glamor. And, if I decide to accept this gift which the father insists on thrusting on me, it's only so it won't fall into wicked hands and be put to criminal uses, instead of being employed for the greater glory of God and the welfare of mankind. As I will employ it.

CLEANTE. Ah, sir, don't be so delicately scrupulous and give the rightful heir cause for complaint. Let him, without bothering your head about the matter, enjoy his possessions at his own risk. After all, it's better he should misuse them than you be accused of cheating him. I'm amazed that you could even have listened to such an offer without being embarrassed. Has true piety any maxim which teaches you to rob legitimate heirs? And if heaven's put in your heart an invincible obstacle to living with Damis, wouldn't it be better for a discreet person like yourself to beat an honorable retreat? Wouldn't that be better than utterly unreasonably driving the son away from his own house? Believe me, sir, this would prove your good intentions—

TARTUFFE. Sir, it's half-past three. My religious duties call me upstairs. Please excuse me for leaving you so soon. [He goes out.]

CLEANTE. Ah-hah!

[Elmire, Mariane and Dorine enter.]

DORINE. Please, sir, help us with her. She's suffering cruelly. The marriage contract which her father insists on signing tonight drives her to distraction. Oh, let's work together to defeat however we can this wretched plan that's caused us all so much trouble.

[Orgon comes in.]

ORGON. Ah, I'm glad to have caught you all together. [To Mariane.] There's something in this contract here which'll make you smile. You know what I mean, eh?

MARIANE. [Sinking to her knees.] Oh, Father, in heaven's name, in the name of all that can move your heart, relax a little my duty to you. Don't make me obey you in this. Don't make me complain to heaven of my duty to you. Alas, don't make the life which you gave me miserable. If you forbid me, in spite of all the sweet hopes which I cherished, to marry the man I love, at least be kind enough to save me from the torment of a man I hate. On my knees I beg you. Don't drive me to despair by exerting your authority over me.

ORGON. [To himself.] Come, come, I must be firm. No human weakness.

MARIANE. Your tenderness for him doesn't grieve me. Give him your wealth. If that's not enough, give him mine too. I consent to that with all my heart. I abandon it to you. But at least don't give me to him too. Let me use up the last sad days which heaven has allotted to me in the austerities of a convent.

ORGON. Oh! So that's it! When your father crosses you in love, you'd fly to a convent. Get up! The more repulsive he is to you, the better it'll be for you to accept him. Mortify your senses by this marriage, and don't bother me about it any more.

DORINE. But what—

ORGON. Shut up! Speak when you're spoken to. I forbid you to speak another word.

CLEANTE. If you'll permit a word of advice—

ORGON. My brother, your advice is the best in the world. It's also the most reasonable, and I esteem it tremendously. But allow me to ignore it.

ELMIRE. [To Orgon.] I really don't know what to say. But I have to admire your blindness. You must be utterly hypnotized to ignore today's little incident.

ORGON. My sweet, I judge by appearances, and you're so indulgent to my rascally son that you were afraid to disown the trick he tried to play on that poor fellow. You were entirely too calm and composed to be convincing. You'd have been more distraught if you really cared.

ELMIRE. Oh, must our honor bluster so vehemently at a simple declaration of love? Can't one answer it without fire flashing from one's eyes and abuse from one's mouth? I'm merely amused by such chatter, and I'd much prefer to ignore it. I'd rather show my discretion quietly. I can't respect those savage prudes who defend their honor with tooth and claw, and who would scratch people's eyes out at the merest hint. God save me from such goodness. I like a less angry virtue that can effectively discourage an admirer by a discreet and cold rebuff.

ORGON. Bah! I know all about it. My mind's made up.

ELMIRE. Again I'm amazed by your weird gullibility. But what would you say if I could show you we've told the truth?

ORGON. Show me?

ELMIRE. Show you.

ORGON. Bah!

ELMIRE. What if I found a way to show it to you plainly?

ORGON. You're day-dreaming.

ELMIRE. Oh, what a man! Answer me anyhow. I don't ask you to believe us. But suppose we could find a place where you could see and hear everything, what would you say then about your worthy friend?

ORGON. In that case I'd say that—I wouldn't say anything. It's impossible.

ELMIRE. You've been deluded entirely too long, and you've accused me of lying just once too often. So, here and now, for my own satisfaction, I'm going to make you see I've been telling the truth.

ORGON. All right. I'll take you up on that. Let's see how cleverly you're able to keep your promise.

ELMIRE. [To Dorine.] Tell Tartuffe I want to see him.

DORINE. He's tricky. Maybe it'll be hard to catch him out.

ELMIRE. No, we're easily tricked by those we love. Besides his conceit will trip him up. Send him to me. [To Cleante and Mariane.] You two go on out for awhile.

[Dorine, Cleante, and Mariane leave.]

ELMIRE. Now, crawl under the table.

ORGON. Do what?

ELMIRE. You have to be hidden.

ORGON. Why under the table?

ELMIRE. Oh, for heaven's sake, do as you're told. I've a plan, and you'll see how it works out. Get under there,

I tell you, and be sure he doesn't see or hear you.

ORGON. I'll humor you. But I can't wait to see how it backfires on you.

ELMIRE. Oh, you won't be able to reproach *me*. [*Orgon crawls under the table which is covered by a large cloth that hangs almost to the floor.*] Mind, I'm going to talk about a touchy subject, so don't be shocked. I must be allowed to say what I like since it's all to convince you, as I promised. I'm going to make this hypocrite doff his mask by sweet words, by flattering his insolent passion, by giving him a free field for his boldness. Since it's all for you and the better to expose him, I'll pretend to return his love. I'll stop as soon as you're convinced, so things needn't go any farther than you want. You can stop his advances when you think they've gone far enough. As soon as you've heard sufficient, you'll have to spare me and not expose me any more than you think necessary. It's entirely up to you how far it goes—shhh, he's coming. Be quiet, and don't let him see you. [*Tartuffe comes in.*]

TARTUFFE. Someone said you wanted to see me.

ELMIRE. Yes. I've something confidential to say. But close the door first and look around to see if anyone can hear us. We certainly don't want another scene like this morning's. I was never so startled in my life. Damis put me in a terrible fright for you. You saw how I tried to stop him and calm him down. Of course, I was so confused that I never thought to deny what he said, but, thank heaven, everything turned out all right. Your reputation smoothed things over, and now my husband can't possibly suspect you. In fact, he wants us to be together as much as possible in order to squelch any gossip. So that's why I can be alone with you without being blamed, why I feel I can tell you how I really feel—but perhaps I'm too forward.

TARTUFFE. I don't quite understand you, Madam. A little while ago you spoke quite differently.

ELMIRE. Ah! If such a refusal has put you off, how little you know of a woman's heart! How little you know what we really mean when we defend ourselves so weakly! Our modesty always struggles with the tender feelings we really have. However we rationalize the love that overwhelms us, we always feel a certain shame in admitting it. At first we deny it, but in such a way that you can see our heart surrenders. Simply for the sake of honor we don't say all that we feel, but such refusals promise everything. No doubt, this is too frank and immodest, but since I've already said it —do you think I'd have tried to restrain Damis, or have listened to you so long or so calmly, if what you said didn't please me? When I tried to make you refuse the marriage, shouldn't that have told you how vexed I was at a marriage which would divide a heart I wanted all my own?

TARTUFFE. It's delightful, Madam, to hear such words from such beloved lips. Their honey sends through all my senses a sweetness that I never tasted before. My highest aim is to please you, and my heart finds all its bliss in your love. Yet, forgive me for thinking your words a trick to make me break off the approaching marriage. Frankly, I won't trust these tender words until some of those favors I sigh for have assured me of your sincerity, and have planted in my heart a conviction of the enchanting kindness you have for me.

ELMIRE. [*Coughing to warn her husband.*] What! You'd move so quickly and exhaust all the tenderness of my heart at once? I've forced myself to declare my fond feelings for you. Isn't that enough for now? Must you have the ultimate favors at the very first?

TARTUFFE. The less one deserves a blessing, the more one dares hope for it. Love can scarcely rely on words alone. We may easily suspect a future happiness, but we wish to enjoy it before we really believe in it. For me, who deserves your favors so little and who doubts his boldness so much, nothing could convince me, Madam, but fact.

ELMIRE. My God, what a tyrant your love is. How confused it makes me. How fiercely it rules my heart. How violently it demands its desires. Can't I find shelter from your pursuit? Won't you give me time to breathe? Is it decent to be so exacting? Should you insist on being satisfied immediately? Should your impetuosity take advantage of my weakness for you?

TARTUFFE. Well, if you're so kindly disposed toward me, why not?

ELMIRE. How can I consent without offending the heaven you're always talking about?

TARTUFFE. Oh, if it's only heaven you're worrying about, I can remove that obstacle. That needn't restrain your desire.

ELMIRE. But the judgments of heaven are so very frightening.

TARTUFFE. I can dispel these ridiculous fears, Madam. I know the art of allaying scruples. Heaven forbids certain gratifications, it's true, but one can find ways of getting around that. There is a plausible theory which makes our conscience depend upon our desires, so that the immorality of our action is negated by the purity of our intention. I shall have to instruct you in these secrets, Madam. Just let yourself be advised by me. Satisfy my desires, and don't be afraid. I'll answer for everything and take the sin upon myself. [*Elmire coughs loudly.*] You're coughing a great deal, Madam.

ELMIRE. Yes, I'm in considerable torment.

TARTUFFE. Care for a piece of licorice?

ELMIRE. No, it's very obstinate. All the licorice in the world won't help it.

TARTUFFE. It must be very trying.

ELMIRE. More than you know.

TARTUFFE. Well, Madam, see how easily your scruples are removed. Rest assured that your secret will be kept. The only evil is in being found out. To scandalize the world is the only crime. Sinning in secret isn't sinning at all.

ELMIRE. [*Coughing again.*] I see that I must yield, that I must grant everything, that otherwise I couldn't hope to convince a man asking for such absolute proof. It's hard for me to go that far, and it's very much against my will, but if a certain individual obstinately drives me to it, if a certain individual obstinately won't believe me without proof, then I must make up my mind to satisfy his doubts. If my consent carries with it any offense, so much the worse for the one who forces me to it. The fault certainly isn't mine.

TARTUFFE. Yes, Madam, I take it entirely upon myself.

ELMIRE. Open the door a little and see that my husband's not in the gallery. Please!

TARTUFFE. Why bother so much about him? Just between you and me, he's a fellow I can lead by the nose. Why, he'd probably be proud to find us together. I've got him to the point where he sees everything but believes nothing.

ELMIRE. All the same, please go and take a good look.

[*Tartuffe goes out, and Orgon emerges from under the table.*]

ORGON. So! What an abominable scoundrel! I can't get over it! I'm stunned!

ELMIRE. What! Coming out already? You must be joking. Get back under the table. It's not time yet. Aren't you going to wait till it's *all* over so you can be absolutely sure?

ORGON. NO! Nothing wickeder ever slithered out of hell!

ELMIRE. Heavens, you shouldn't believe so easily. Be sure you're convinced. Take your time, or you may be mistaken. [*Hearing Tartuffe approach, she hides Orgon behind her.*]

TARTUFFE. [*Entering.*] The coast's clear, Madam. I've looked all over, and no one's around. Ah, my delighted soul—! [*Tartuffe advances toward her with open arms and pursed lips, and walks right into Orgon.*]

ORGON. Hold on. You're a bit too eager and impetuous. Oh, oh, you wanted to trick me, did you, you saintly man? How your soul leaps toward temptation! Marry my daughter and covet my wife, eh! I've had my doubts about you for a long time. I thought you'd show your true colors. But this is pushing proof far enough.

I'm satisfied. I don't need any more evidence.

ELMIRE. [*To Tartuffe.*] I didn't want to do all this, but I was forced to by necessity.

TARTUFFE. Why, sir, you can't really think that—

ORGON. Come now, no more noise please. Just take yourself out of here at once.

TARTUFFE. I only meant to—

ORGON. Speeches won't help you now. Just pack up and get out.

TARTUFFE. You're the one who'll have to get out, my smug and confident fellow. This is my house, and you'd better realize it now. I tell you plainly it's useless to try and trick me. I have ways of avenging offended heaven and making those who talk of turning me out regret it. [*Tartuffe stalks out.*]

ELMIRE. What's this he said? What does he mean?

ORGON. Good Lord, I'm all mixed up. This isn't funny at all.

ELMIRE. What is it?

ORGON. What he says frightens me. I'm worried about that deed of gift.

ELMIRE. Deed—?

ORGON. Yes, the thing's done. But there's something else that frightens me too.

ELMIRE. What's that?

ORGON. I'll tell you all about it, but first let's see if a certain strongbox is still upstairs.

ACT V

[*Orgon and Cleante enter from opposite sides of the stage.*]

CLEANTE. Where are you running off to?

ORGON. How the devil do I know?

CLEANTE. We'd better talk things

over to see what we can do about this emergency.

ORGON. The strongbox worries me terribly. More than anything else.

CLEANTE. Does it contain some important secret?

ORGON. My poor friend Argas left it with me in greatest confidence. He picked me for the trust when he fled, and from what he told me I think it must contain papers on which his life and fortune depend.

CLEANTE. Then how could you trust them to somebody else?

ORGON. I wanted to salve my conscience. So I went straight to that rascal Tartuffe and told him all about it. And he slyly persuaded me to give him the strongbox to keep, so that in case of inquiry I could say I didn't have it, and ease my conscience by staying just inside the bounds of truth.

CLEANTE. This looks bad. Both the deed of gift and this confidence are, to my mind, rash steps. He can entangle you nicely now. As long as the fellow has these advantages over you, it would be imprudent to push him too far. You'd better try some softer way.

ORGON. What? Oh, to hide such a wicked, double-crossing heart under such a show of zeal and piety! And I, who took him into my house as a poor beggar—! Oh, this is enough for me! All these pious people can go to the devil. From now on, I'll detest them worse than the devil himself.

CLEANTE. Oh, come now! You're exaggerating again. Can't you ever steer down the middle of the road? You never keep within sensible limits. You're always hurtling from one extreme to another. You see your mistake, and you admit you were tricked

by hypocritical piety. But to reform, must you fall into a still greater error, and say that all pious people are like this scoundrel? Leave such silly conclusions to atheists, and distinguish between virtue and its mere appearances. Don't be too hasty in admiring. Keep in the middle of the road. Guard yourself if you can from charlatans, but at the same time don't attack true virtue. If you must lean to an extreme, better to be too lenient than too strict.

[Damis comes in.]

DAMIS. Father, is it true that this cowardly, contemptible rascal is threatening you? Has he forgotten all your favors?

ORGON. Yes, my boy, and it causes me unspeakable grief.

DAMIS. Leave him to me. I'll crop his ears for him. Such insolence is intolerable. I'll get rid of him and end this business. I'll squash him.

CLEANTE. Spoken like a stout fellow, but just take it easy if you please. Nowadays violence only makes matters worse.

[Madam Pernelle, Mariane, Elmire, and Dorine enter.]

MADAM PERNELLE. What's going on here? What's happened?

ORGON. I've seen some strange sights today. Oh, you see how I'm repaid for my kindness. I take care of a man in his misery. I take him into my own house and treat him like a brother. I heap favors on him every day. I give him my daughter, everything I have. And at the same time, the perfidious, infamous wretch foully plots to seduce my wife. And not content with that, he schemes and plots and threatens me with my own gifts. He's trying to ruin me by using the advantages which my own idiotic good nature gave him. He's trying to drive me out of my property which I've transferred to him, and to reduce me to the same poverty I rescued him from.

DORINE. Poor fellow!

MADAM PERNELLE. Oh, my son, I can't believe he'd do such a black deed.

ORGON. What!

MADAM PERNELLE. Saints are always envied.

ORGON. What are you saying, Mother!

MADAM PERNELLE. I told you a hundred times when you were a child that the virtuous were always persecuted. The envious may die, but envy never does.

ORGON. What's all this got to do with what happened today?

MADAM PERNELLE. They've made up a hundred foolish stories against him.

ORGON. I tell you, I saw it myself!

MADAM PERNELLE. Slanderers are always malicious.

ORGON. You'll drive me mad, Mother. I tell you I saw his criminal attempt with my own eyes.

MADAM PERNELLE. Evil tongues have always a little venom to pour out. There's no way on earth to guard against them.

ORGON. That's senseless! I saw it, I tell you, saw it, saw it with my own eyes. S-A-W, *saw!* Do I have to scream it out a hundred times?!

MADAM PERNELLE. Heavens, appearances are often deceiving. You can't believe everything you see.

ORGON. I'm going mad.

MADAM PERNELLE. Human nature is subject to false suspicions, and the good often is mistaken for evil.

ORGON. So his attempt to kiss my wife is good?

MADAM PERNELLE. You ought to have good reasons before you accuse people. You ought to have waited till you were quite certain.

ORGON. How the devil could I have been more certain? Should I have waited, Mother, till he did it right before my eyes? Oh, you'll make me say something idiotic!

MADAM PERNELLE. No, his soul burns with too pure a flame. I can't imagine him attempting what you accuse him of.

ORGON. I'm going mad! If you weren't my mother, I don't know what I'd say to you.

CLEANTE. We're wasting time on mere trifles when we should be deciding what to do. You can't sleep while this rascal threatens you.

DAMIS. What? Has his impudence gone that far?

ELMIRE. I don't think he'd go to court. His ingratitude would be too obvious.

CLEANTE. Don't be too sure. He'll find some way to justify his actions against you. Powerful organizations have gotten people into nastier messes than this for less reason. I tell you again, armed with what he knows, he shouldn't have been pushed so far.

ORGON. Yes, yes, but what could I do? I couldn't keep my temper in the face of that scoundrel's impertinence.

CLEANTE. If we could just patch up a shadow of peace between the two of you.

ELMIRE. If I'd only known he was so well armed, I wouldn't have brought things to such a head. I—

[*Mister Loyal appears at the door, and Dorine goes over to him.*]

ORGON. What does that fellow want? Go and see. What a state I'm in to receive visitors.

LOYAL. Good day, dear sister in God. Please tell your master I must speak with him.

DORINE. He's busy. I doubt if he'll be able to see anyone.

LOYAL. I don't want to intrude. However, I don't think he'll find my visit unpleasant. In fact, I come about a matter he'll be glad to know of.

DORINE. What's your name?

LOYAL. Just tell him that I come for his own good from Mister Tartuffe.

DORINE. It's a polite gentleman who comes from Tartuffe with, so he says, some good news.

CLEANTE. Better see what he wants.

ORGON. Maybe he's coming to patch things up. How should I act?

CLEANTE. Hide your resentment, and if he speaks of some agreement hear him out.

LOYAL. Good day, sir. May heaven punish your enemies and shower its blessings upon you.

ORGON. [Whispers to Cleante.] I told you so. This diplomatic beginning hints at some reconciliation.

LOYAL. Your whole family is very dear to me. I served your father.

ORGON. Sir, I'm ashamed to say I don't remember either you or your name.

LOYAL. My name is Loyal. I'm a process server. For forty years, by the grace of heaven, I've had the good fortune to exercise that office with considerable honor. I've come, sir, with your permission, to present you this legal document.

ORGON. WHAT? You came to—

LOYAL. Gently, sir, gently. This is only a summons, just a little eviction

notice to inform you and your family to take your furniture and put it somewhere else, without delay or deferment, as is herein decreed.

ORGON. Me? Leave?

LOYAL. Yes sir, if you don't mind. The house now, as you well know, belongs incontestably to the good Mister Tartuffe. According to this deed I have here, he is now lord and master of all your estates. The deed is in proper form, and cannot be contested.

DAMIS. Enormous impudence!

LOYAL. Sir, my business isn't with you, but with this gentleman, who is sweetly reasonable and knows better than to attempt to oppose the law.

ORGON. But—

LOYAL. Ah, sir, I know you wouldn't disobey the law, even for a million dollars. You'll allow me, like a good honest man then, to execute here the orders given me.

DAMIS. You're about to get the dust beaten out of your black gown, Mister Process Server.

LOYAL. Make your son keep quiet or leave, sir. I'd regret having to put your name down on my official report.

DORINE. This Loyal doesn't look very loyal to me.

LOYAL. Because I sympathize with honest people, sir, I undertook this business myself in order to oblige and please you. In that way I prevented the choice from falling upon others who might not have been so considerate and gentle.

ORGON. What can be worse than ordering people to leave their own home?

LOYAL. Well, I intend to give you a little time, sir. I won't execute the writ until tomorrow. I just came to pass the night here quietly with ten of my men. For form's sake, do you mind bringing me, before you go to bed, your door keys? I won't trouble your rest or permit anything unseemly. But the first thing in the morning you must clear the house completely, down to the last spoon. My men will help you. They're strong fellows. They can carry it all outside. Oh, I don't think you'll find many more considerate than I am. And, since I'm treating you with the greatest indulgence, sir, I trust that you'll do as well by me and not hinder the execution of my duty.

ORGON. [*To himself.*] I'd give my last hundred gold pieces to lay a Sunday punch on his ugly snout.

CLEANTE. [*To Orgon.*] Take it easy. Don't make things worse.

DAMIS. Oh, I can hardly restrain myself. Oh, my fingers are itching!

DORINE. You know, Mister Loyal, a good broad back like yours just seems to beg for a beating.

LOYAL. Wicked words like that, my dear, can be punished. The law is for women too.

CLEANTE. [*To Loyal.*] Enough of this, sir. Finish up. Just give us your paper and let us alone.

LOYAL. I'll see you soon. Till then, heaven bless you all. [*He goes out.*]

ORGON. And may it confound you and the fellow who sent you! Well, Mother, was I right? Can you judge the rest of it by this writ? Do you believe he's a rascal now?

MADAM PERNELLE. I'm dumbfounded, flabbergasted.

DORINE. [*To Orgon.*] You're wrong to complain and blame him, sir. This just confirms his pious intentions. It shows he loves his neighbour. He knows that often goods corrupt, so

in pure disinterested charity, he wants to relieve you of any such obstacle to your salvation.

ORGON. Oh, shut up. How often do I have to tell you?

CLEANTE. Come now. Let's decide what we must do.

ELMIRE. Expose the ingratitude of the wretch. Surely it will invalidate the deed. His treachery will look too black for him to succeed.

[*Valere comes in.*]

VALERE. I'm very sorry to bother you, sir, but I'm forced to by a grave danger. A dear friend who knows how interested I am in your concerns risked violating state secrecy and hinted to me that you should fly immediately. The villain who's imposed on you so long has just now accused you to the king of, among other things, giving him an important strongbox which you'd received from a state criminal, and which you'd illegally kept secret. I don't know the details of the crime, but there's a warrant out for you. And so it may be properly executed, your accuser himself is accompanying the arresting officer.

CLEANTE. Now he gets armed support to help him take over your property.

ORGON. The man's a beast, I tell you, a monster!

VALERE. The least delay may be fatal. My coach is at the door to whisk you away, and I've brought you a thousand louis. Let's don't lose any time. The only way to parry such a blow is to run. I'll take you to a safe place. I'm in this with you till the end.

ORGON. Alas! What don't I owe to your kindness! I'll have to thank you another time. Heaven help me one day to repay your generosity as I ought.

Goodby. Be careful, all of you—

CLEANTE. Go quickly. We'll do all we can, brother. [*Orgon and Valere hurry to the door, but they are stopped there by Tartuffe and a police officer.*]

TARTUFFE. Gently, sir, gently. Don't hurry off so fast. You don't have to hurry out to look for a lodging. We're here to give you one of the king's.

ORGON. Wretch! You saved the worst blow for last. This is the coup de grâce. This tops all your other villainies.

TARTUFFE. Your abuse doesn't disturb me. Heaven has taught me to suffer everything in silence.

CLEANTE. What admirable moderation.

DAMIS. How impudently the villain flaunts heaven!

TARTUFFE. All these outbursts won't faze me. I'm only doing my duty.

MARIANE. A lot of honor and glory you'll get from this business!

TARTUFFE. A task must be glorious when it comes from the power that sent me here.

ORGON. Don't you remember, you ingrate, how my hand lifted you out of your wretched poverty?

TARTUFFE. Yes, you helped me somewhat, but my first duty is to the king. The just obligation of that sacred duty stifles all the gratitude in my heart. To that powerful consideration I would sacrifice friends, wife, relatives, even myself.

ELMIRE. Faker!

DORINE. How cunningly he cloaks himself in everything we hold sacred.

CLEANTE. But if this zeal which inspires you and which you're so proud of is as perfect as you say, why didn't it show itself until Orgon caught you making love to his wife? Why didn't you denounce him before his honor made him drive you out of his house? I'm not saying that his gift of his whole estate should have turned you from your duty, but if you meant to treat him as a criminal today, why did you allow yourself to take anything from him?

TARTUFFE. [*To the Officer.*] Sir, deliver me from all this babble. Do your duty.

THE OFFICER. Yes, doubtless I've dallied too long. You very properly reminded me. Will you please come along with me to prison where we have a room reserved for you?

TARTUFFE. —Who? Me?

THE OFFICER. Yes, you.

TARTUFFE. Prison?

THE OFFICER. I don't owe you an explanation. [*To Orgon.*] Compose yourself, sir, after this frightening alarm. We live under a prince who is an enemy of fraud, a prince who sees into men's hearts, who is not taken in by impostors. His great and discerning soul sees things clearly. He is not tricked by exaggeration. His sound reason does not fall into excess. To good men he gives lasting glory, but his zeal is not blind, and his love of sincerity doesn't close his heart to the horror which falsehood inspires. Even this fellow couldn't hoodwink him, for he's seen through more puzzling ruses. He soon saw, by his canny insight, all the vileness in this fellow's heart. In coming to accuse you, the rascal only trapped himself. And by a bit of poetic justice, he betrayed himself as a notorious rogue already wanted under another name. It would take a long book to tell all his black deeds. Our monarch, in short, loathed his vile ingratitude and disloyalty to you, and added this crime to all his others. The king ordered me to allow the impertinence to be played out to the end, and to make him give you full satisfaction. Yes, he wants me to take all of your documents from him. By his sovereign power he annuls this contract by which you made over your property. And finally he pardons you for the secret offense in which the flight of your friend involved you. This is the reward for your previous zeal in upholding his rights, to show that he knows how to reward good actions when least expected. He never forgets merit, and he remembers good better than evil.

DORINE. Heaven be praised.

MADAM PERNELLE. Now I can breathe again.

ELMIRE. Everything's all right!

MARIANE. Who could have guessed it!

ORGON. [*To Tartuffe.*] Ah-hah, now, you wretch!

CLEANTE. Ah, brother, don't. Don't descend to abuse. Leave him to his miserable fate. Don't add to his remorse. Instead, hope that from this day he may be converted to virtue, reform his life, despise his crimes, and in this way soften the king's justice. Better that you should throw yourself on your knees and thank the king for his goodness and leniency.

ORGON. Yes, well said. Joyfully throw ourself at his feet and praise his kindness! Then, after that first duty, let's remember another, and by a happy marriage crown Valere's generous and sincere love.

MOLIÈRE, the Preface to *Tartuffe.*

Here is a comedy about which there has been considerable noise: it has been persecuted for a long time, and the people it represents have shown

themselves to be the most powerful I have portrayed in France. The Marquises, the Pedants, and the Doctors have quietly suffered themselves to be represented, and they have appeared to be diverted, like everyone else, with the pictures I painted of them. But the Hypocrites were not amused. They were at first amazed, for they found it strange that I should have the gall to hit off their absurdities and to criticize a profession in which so many honest people are occupied. That is a crime which they cannot pardon, and they are all up in arms against my comedy with a terrible wrath. They were careful not to attack it where it wounded them. They are too cunning for that, and they are too clever to show what they really think. Following their laudable custom, they have camouflaged their own interests by the interest of God. According to them, *Tartuffe* is a play which offends piety. All the way through, it is full of abominations. There is nothing in it that doesn't deserve to be burnt. Every syllable is impious. Even the gestures are criminal. The least batting of an eyelash, the least shake of the head, the least step to the right or the left, all contain mysteries which they are able to twist to my disadvantage. I had submitted it in vain to the criticism of my friends and to the public. The corrections which I had made, the judgment of the King and the Queen who had seen it, the approbation of great princes and ministers who had publicly honored it by their presence, the testimony of worthy men who had found it profitable, all this was not enough. They didn't hold off at all, and every day they are still sicking on me in public their indiscreet zealots, who load me with pious abuse and charitably damn me to hell.

I would care very little for what they say were it not for their stratagem of making people whom I respect my enemies, and of enlisting on their side genuinely worthy men whose good faith they take advantage of and whose warmth for the interests of heaven they may easily impress. Therefore, I must defend myself. I wish to justify the conduct of my comedy to the truly devout, and I conjure these people with all my heart not to condemn things before they have seen them, not to be biased, and not to serve the passion of disgraceful humbugs.

If one takes the pain to examine my comedy in good faith, he will find without a doubt that my intentions throughout are entirely innocent, that it does not tend to treat flippantly things which ought to be revered, that I have treated them with all the precautions which the delicacy of the matter demanded, and that I have taken all the art and care in my power to distinguish clearly between the Hypocrite and the truly pious. For that purpose I have used two entire acts to prepare for the entrance of my rascal. He does not make the spectator hesitate a single minute. One immediately knows him by the marks I have given him. From the first to the last he doesn't say a word or commit an act which does not depict the character of an evil man and which is not in strong contrast to the good man whom I have opposed to him.

I know well that those gentlemen have attempted to hint that the theatre should not speak of these matters. But I ask them, with their permission, on what is this lovely maxim based? It is only a theory which they are in no way able to prove. And doubtless it would not be difficult to make them see that comedy among the ancient writers originated in religion and was a part of its mysteries; that the Spaniards, our neighbours, never celebrate a holy day which is not mixed up with comedy, and that, even among us, comedy owes its birth to the cares of a brotherhood which still owns the Hotel de Bourgogne [1] today. That place was given so that the most important mysteries of our faith might be represented there. One can still see there comedies printed in Gothic letters written by a doctor of the Sorbonne. Without searching so far away, the holy pieces of M. de Corneille, which have been admired by all France, have been played there in our time.

If the purpose of comedy is to correct men's vices, then I see no reason for any privileged class. Such a class would be in a position much more dangerous than any other, and we have seen that the theatre has the great virtue of correction. The most beautiful passages of a serious fable are often less powerful than those of a satire, and nothing reprimands most men better than painting their faults. It is a great blow to vice to expose it to everybody's laughter. We easily endure reprimands, but we cannot

[1] The Hotel de Bourgogne was the first permanent theatre in Paris. It was built by the Confrèrie de la Passion et Resurrection de Notre Seigneur, a company of actors who intended to perform mystery plays there. In 1584 the performance of mysteries was forbidden in Paris, and the Confrèrie rented the theatre to various companies of actors.

stand being laughed at. We do not mind being wicked, but no one wants to be ridiculed.

I have been reproached for putting pious terms in the mouth of my Hypocrite. But if I am to draw the character of a Hypocrite accurately, how could I avoid it? It seems to me that it is enough to show the criminal motives which made him say those things and to avoid using the sacred terms which might have caused pain if used badly. "But in Act IV he utters a pernicious moral." Hasn't this moral already been dinned into everybody's ears? Does my comedy say anything new? Could there be any fear that things so generally detested could make any impression on people's minds? Could I make them dangerous by showing them in the theatre, and could they receive any authority coming from the mouth of a scoundrel? There is no indication that they could. No, one must either approve the comedy of *Tartuffe* or condemn all comedies in general.

It is comedy in general which has been attacked so furiously recently. In fact, never has there been such a strong outburst against the theatre. I cannot deny that there have been some Fathers of the Church who have condemned comedy, but one cannot deny either that there have been some others who have treated it a little more easily. Therefore, the authority on which people would found a censorship is destroyed by this division of opinion. The only thing of consequence which equally enlightened minds are able to deduce from this diversity of opinion is that comedy has been differently regarded, and that while some have considered it in its purity, others have regarded it in its corruption and confused all comedy with those villainous spectacles which they correctly called sinful.

And, in effect, since we have to argue about things and not about words, and since most contradictions cannot be reconciled, and since the same word often contains two opposite meanings, we must lift the veil of the equivocal and look at what comedy really is, if we are to see whether it should be condemned. Obviously, being only an ingenious poem which tries to reform men's faults by agreeable lessons, it could not justly be censured. And on that point if we listen to the testimony of antiquity, it will tell us that the most celebrated philosophers, those who made a profession of austere wisdom and who carped without ceasing at the vices of their century, have praised comedy. It will tell us that Aristotle spent his nights at the theatre and took the trouble to reduce the making of comedy to precepts of art. It will tell us that the greatest men, the first in dignity, have gloried in composing comedies themselves, and that others have not disdained to recite in public comedies they had composed, and that Greece proclaimed her esteem for that art by the glorious prizes and the superb theatres she gave to honor it, and that, finally, in Rome that same art received extraordinary honors. I am not speaking of a Rome debauched and under the licentiousness of the emperors, but a Rome disciplined and under the wisdom of the consuls, in the time of vigor and true Roman virtue.

I admit that there have been times when comedy was corrupt. But what is there in the world that does not become corrupt every day? There is nothing so innocent that men cannot use it criminally, no art so salutary that its intentions cannot be reversed, nothing so good that it cannot be turned to bad uses. Medicine is a profitable art, and everyone esteems it as one of the most excellent things that we have; however, there was a time when it made itself odious, and often it has used its art to poison people. Philosophy is a gift of heaven. It has been given to us to carry our spirits to a knowledge of God by the contemplation of the marvels of nature. However, one cannot forget that often it has been turned from its proper use and has publicly occupied itself with supporting impiety. Even the most sacred things are not hidden from men's corruption, and we see scoundrels who, every day, abuse piety and wickedly make it serve the greatest crimes. But, nevertheless, we make those distinctions which we must. We do not confuse by a false deduction the goodness of things which might corrupt with the malice of the corrupters. We always separate the bad use from the good intention of the art; and, as we would not dream of defending medicine for having been banished from Rome, or philosophy for having been publicly condemned in Athens, neither would we prohibit comedy for having been, at certain times, censured. That censure had reasons which have no pertinence here. It confined itself to what it saw, and we ought not to stretch it beyond its own application, extend it further than necessary, and make it class the innocent with the guilty. The comedy which it intended to attack is not at all the comedy which we would de-

fend. It is necessary to avoid confusing that comedy with this. They are two entirely different things. They have utterly no resemblance other than the name, and it would be a wicked injustice to condemn Olympia the good woman because she has the same name as an Olympia who is debauched. Such verdicts without a doubt cause great disorder in the world. Nothing could escape condemnation, so since we are not so rigorous about other things which are abused every day, we ought to extend the same grace to comedy, and approve honest and instructive plays.

I know that there are certain delicate souls who cannot tolerate any comedy, who say that the most honest comedies are the most dangerous, that the passions which they depict are more stirring because they are full of virtue, and that people are too affected by such representations. I don't see any great crime in being moved by watching an honest passion, or that that high plane of insensibility to which they would elevate our souls is a high plane of virtue. I doubt that such great perfection is possible for human nature, and I wonder if it would not be better to work to rectify and mollify men's passions than to eliminate them entirely. I admit that there are better places to go than the theatre. And if we want to condemn everything which doesn't directly concern God and our salvation, certainly comedy should be one of them, and I would not mind its being condemned with the rest. But suppose, as is the case, that there must be intervals to pious devotions and that men need diversion. Then I say that nothing more innocent than comedy can be found. I have digressed too long. Let me conclude with a remark of a great prince about the comedy *Tartuffe*.

Eight days after it had been forbidden, there was performed before the court a play called *Scaramouche, a Hermit,* and the King, leaving the theatre, said to the great prince whom I have just mentioned, "I should greatly like to know why the people who were so scandalized by Molière's comedy do not say a word about this *Scaramouche*." To that the prince answered, "The reason is this—that *Scaramouche* makes a joke out of heaven and religion, and the gentlemen don't mind that. But Molière's play makes a joke out of them, and that they can't stand."

EDITORS' TRANSLATION.

DISCUSSION OF *TARTUFFE*

Because *Tartuffe* was not only attacked, but for several years actually prohibited from public performance, Molière took special pains in rewriting it. The events behind that attack need not detain us, except as they indicate something of the play's quality. Molière first produced it in May 1664, for Louis XIV at Versailles, in a three-act version of which we have no copy. From contemporary reports, scholars speculate that it was more or less close to the present first three acts. Opposition arose from powerful religious authorities, against whose vehemently personal attacks Molière argues in his Preface. Not until 1669, after several petitions to the King, was it legally produced again, this time, after much revising, in its present form. Its fame had already spread far, and "Tartuffe" had become a byword for the religious hypocrite. It has been Molière's most frequently staged play. As you can tell from Molière's Preface, the Puritanical opposition was part of a much broader attack on the stage in general, and especially on comedy. That is why Molière in his defense traces the history of comedy and argues for its legitimacy on several different grounds—its connection with religion, its moral purpose as a corrector of men's vices, and its comparative innocence as a means of amusement.

Tartuffe is a darker and deeper play than *The Silent Woman*. Its comedy contains a more condemnatory satire, and its subject is broader than a criticism of individual religious hypocrisy. It reviews the entire religious response to life. But before stressing these aspects, we might well consider it as a stage performance.

Molière himself was an accomplished actor and the director of his own theatrical troup, for which he wrote his plays. In *Tartuffe* we can see the work of, first of all, a canny practicing man of the theatre. From the actors' viewpoints, each part has something notably attractive about it: each character has at least one good scene and one notable speech. Even the extremely minor ones, Mr. Loyal and the Police Officer, capture our attention while on-stage. In terms of stage-business, too, each act has at least one notably diverting comic incident, as well as a striking opening and ending. Act I opens with Madam Pernelle's curmudgeonish blustering and closes with Orgon's equivocation. Within the act, Orgon's interest in Tartuffe's health rather than his wife's illness is exceptionally good although it is handled with a standard comic device of repetition ("Poor fellow").

Several acts have more than one brilliant scene. In Act II, there are Orgon's impotent fury at Dorine and the love quarrel; in Act III, Tartuffe's prudishness over Dorine's clothing and his making love to Elmire. In Act IV, the most hilarious comic business comes at the high point of the plot, when Orgon is hidden under the table listening to Tartuffe make love to his wife. Such incidents are both diverting at the moment and part of a larger structural development. There is much more to the play, but this is worth noticing as a starting point because it indicates Molière's practical inventive richness.

You might note next Molière's great range of language, a range that comes through even in translation. Orgon and Tartuffe between them share a kind of mystic and ecstatic language of extremism that Molière is satirizing. This language contrasts markedly with the flippancy of Dorine in her scenes with each of them. It contrasts also with Cleante, who is not flippant but impassionedly serious in his defense of reason, restraint, honor, consistency, and the middle path. This range has its counterpart in the number of diverse characters who are lined up against Orgon and Tartuffe and in the diversity of emotions the play elicits. Act II, for instance, ends with a tenderness that is kept from being maudlin by Dorine's presence, but throughout the play there are also all sorts of anger, spleen, protestation, invective, foolishness, guffawing, and ranting, as well as understatement and overstatement. One of the few speeches we might criticize as being extrinsic to the plot is Cleante's in Act I when he lectures Orgon about his infatuation with Tartuffe. Fine as this speech is, it perhaps could be briefer and arises partly out of Molière's desire to lecture his audience directly.

We might briefly contrast Molière's language with Jonson's. Most notable is the difference between Jonson's use of puns and similes and repartee, and Molière's avoidance of them. Molière has very few purely verbal witticisms; for example, Madam Pernelle's confusion between the Tower of Babel and Babylon, the invented verb "Tartuffified," and Loyal's hidden pun, "I *served* your father, too." [1]

Molière's verbal fluency arises more strongly from his sense of the situation. For example, Tartuffe's declaration of love in Act III would not by itself be funny. It is funny in context because of Elmire's response and because Damis is hiding in the closet. Damis is given to inarticulate outbursts, like Morose, but he has none of Morose's verbal cleverness. Dorine, like Truewit, elicits a variety of responses from people—tenderness and pain from Mariane, hypocritical prudery from Tartuffe, rage and frustration from Orgon. But unlike Truewit she

[1] There is also an untranslatable one in a speech by Dorine, where she picks up Orgon's remark about Tartuffe's not being good-looking, as well as a 17th-century vulgarism by Dorine which we have omitted.

has little range of high humor or *joie de vivre.* For example, contrast her sympathetic and effective yet satirical response to the lovers in Act II with Truewit's explanation of courtship procedure to Clerimont. These differences arise mainly from a difference of character, but they lead to a further point about comic language.

Often the wit or irony of a given speech depends on its context. Such a speech as Truewit's magnificent attack on marriage, which piles up so many details on a central theme, sustains its own wit. Cleante's attack on enthusiastic religious cant has no such wit, but is much closer to impassioned seriousness. Molière runs more to set-pieces, longer speeches that have one force in themselves and another as seen in their situations. Molière uses the device of the character who is hidden on-stage more than does Jonson, and the presence of this character makes the audience see an additional irony to the speeches.

The differences in language go back to the characters and to the writer's involvement in or distance from his theme and plot. In *The Silent Woman,* Truewit obviously embodies Jonson's highest good humor. He also is the most effective mover of the plot. He arranges almost everything that happens. In *Tartuffe,* Molière's spokesman is Cleante, who is of the type known as the *raisonneur,* the man who embodies good sense and states the author's viewpoint. Compared to Truewit, Cleante is an ineffective intellectual. He has several impassioned speeches that the audience recognizes to be sensible and that form the moral center of the play. However, no one heeds what he says, he comes up with no practical plans, and he is twice rather stingingly rebuked. Both Madam Pernelle and Orgon acknowledge his wisdom, but forcefully reject it. One must be wary of speculating about Molière's intentions, but it is not hard to see Cleante as a somewhat pitiful stage character. Admirable as what he says is, he has nothing to do.

The doer, by contrast, is Dorine, who descends from the comic type of the crafty and powerful servant. Act II has her best scenes. She effectively makes her point to Orgon about his foolishness, and she unites the lovers after their quarrel. Like Truewit, she is full of practical inventiveness, notably when she tells Mariane how to delay the wedding. After the beginning of Act III, however, Molière seems to lose interest in her, and he drops her as an effective character. While in Act III she is quite capable of standing up to Tartuffe, in the denouement she is no longer his equal in power or cleverness. The resolution of the plot, which might well have taken place through her canniness, depends on characters quite outside the play.

In comparison, then, Cleante and Dorine embody two aspects that Jonson combines in the single character of Truewit. Similarly, where Jonson has the single Morose, Molière has a double comic villain in Tartuffe and Orgon. This needs some explanation, which will lead us to the greatest problem of the play, Molière's resolution of the plot.

Although the play is called *Tartuffe,* and although its portrait of the religious hypocrite is its most notable quality, there is good reason to think that Orgon occupied as much of Molière's attention as Tartuffe and that the portrait of

Orgon really caused the religious attacks on the play. To give external evidence, Molière, who presumably had the choice of parts in the original production, played Orgon, not Tartuffe. Internally, it is Orgon who is more complicated and even more despicable than Tartuffe. In Act I both Dorine and Cleante show him up or tell him off. In Act II Dorine shows him up again, and he appears brutally insensitive to Mariane. In Act III he is more wildly unreasonable than even Tartuffe can understand. In Act IV he is made to witness his own gulling and duping. In Act V a greater catastrophe threatens him than anyone else. Here too, although he now has presumably been brought to good sense by the events of Act IV, Orgon still needs reprimanding. Cleante tells him, "Oh, come now! You're exaggerating again. Can't you ever steer down the middle of the road?" Further, as Ramon Fernandez points out in his excellent book *Molière, the Man as Seen Through His Plays*, Molière seems to be as much interested in the problem of the response to religion by the truly ardent as he was by the problem of hypocrisy. Molière, Fernandez says, was condemning the extremity to which Orgon would sincerely go, the complete rejection of earthly things to which he was led by Tartuffe. In Act I, for example, Cleante is repelled by Orgon's indifference to all his relatives and by his finding this world a dung heap. But these sentiments lie at the heart of religion, for Orgon's attitude is necessary to the achievement of Christian sainthood. Indifference to this world is basic to Christianity. Molière, Fernandez speculates, was more involved in Orgon's problems than in the relatively simpler ones of Tartuffe, whom he could outrightly condemn.

This is not to say that Molière, a highly conscious and skilled artist, lost control of his characters, but that extremely deep concerns are at work in this play. Consider for a moment the resolution of the plot, which has always elicited comment from Molière's audiences. The plot joins together two subjects, the love triangle that is traditional to comedy and the satire on religious hypocrisy. Both are fully established in the first two acts, the exposition of which Goethe admired so much. The hindrance to the marriage of the lovers is the counter-proposal by Orgon that Mariane marry Tartuffe. This obstacle presumably is resolved by Act IV, when Orgon discovers Tartuffe's hypocrisy. The announcement of its resolution comes in Act V, after Valere has proven himself worthy to Orgon and after Orgon's affairs are again in order. (Notice, by the way, that Orgon is Tartuffe's agent in this plot. Tartuffe himself is never seen as Mariane's suitor but as Elmire's. Orgon originates the idea of his marriage to Mariane and speaks for him.)

This plot is fairly slender compared to the complications of the religious satire. Between Act II and Act V, the principal stage-time is taken up with Tartuffe's involvement with Elmire. When Orgon gives Tartuffe his whole fortune, we have what Dryden in his analysis of dramatic structure calls the counter-turn or further complication. Orgon's realization that Tartuffe is indeed a hypocrite leads to the entirely new intrigue of Act V, when Tartuffe's possession of the strongbox leaves Orgon completely in his power. This further twist is presumably the most comic, the ultimate working out of the situation. It is the equivalent of the Parson-Lawyer-Morose scene in *The Silent Woman*. But here in *Tartuffe* a curious thing happens. Molière brings Tartuffe on stage in full triumph, but then resolves the plot by a device equivalent to the Greek tragic *deus ex machina*, in this case a *rex ex machina*, the police officer of the King. The officer's speech, which announces the King's awareness of Tartuffe's scheming and the King's goodness in restoring Orgon, has often been criticized. Some have seen in it merely Molière's flattery of a king whose protection he needed.

In terms of comic structure one might make the following points about that speech. The way it shows Tartuffe up is extraneous to the earlier parts of the play. It does not rise logically out of the action but comes as a complete and rather arbitrary surprise. It doesn't really show Tartuffe up by outsmarting him or by watching him stumble. A usual comic ending is to have the trickster tricked, a dupe to his own cleverness. This is what happens to Morose, for instance, when he is tricked into making Dauphine his heir in order to get out of the marriage that he undertook for the opposite reason in the first place. It happens to the fox in Chaucer's Nun's Priest's Tale, it happens in Jonson's *Volpone*, it happens to Fainall in Congreve's *Way of the World*, to Joseph Surface in Sheridan's *School for Scandal*, and even to Orgon in Act V of *Tartuffe*, when he is victimized by his earlier foolish generosity.

In *Tartuffe* Molière has established several good and clever characters who are Tartuffe's equal in wits. One can imagine a resolution of the plot in which Tartuffe is outwitted by Dorine or Elmire, rather than simply overwhelmed by the outside power of the King. If Molière did not choose to do this, he could still have done something else. He could have omitted the last act entirely by cutting also the very end of Act III. If he had not made Orgon sign over his fortune to Tartuffe in Act III, Act V would be unnecessary. The lovers' obstacles would have been resolved at the end of Act IV.

This *ex machina* ending is a much less clever one than Ben Jonson's, and one that is much more frequently used. It is the equivalent of the arrival of the cavalry in the last reel of the melodrama. It should not simply be scorned, however, for while it often reveals incompetent plotting, it also reveals something about the nature of comedy. If the comic plot depends much more on illustrative incidents than on Aristotelian cause-and-effect, the ending may be relatively unimportant. Many instances can be found where a great comic writer falters in his ending. Congreve's *Way of the World*, for instance, depends on a hidden strongbox in somewhat the same way as does *Tartuffe*. *Huckleberry Finn* gets into marked trouble in its denouement, as do Fielding's *Tom Jones* and Kingsley Amis's *Lucky Jim*. In all of these the author tends to drop his comedy momentarily in order to arrive by non-comic means at the traditional happy ending, where vice is punished and virtue rewarded. In *Tartuffe* the audience cannot laugh at the Police Officer's praise of the King. Presumably the proper reaction is a sense of relief at finding out that everything will be all right for the good characters. Fernandez makes the point that at this stage in his career Molière was finding it increasingly difficult to reconcile his sense of comedy with his employment as an entertainer of the aristocratic court. This point is probably right. But it only reinforces the point that the denouement of Tartuffe has moved outside of the comic for a moment. If this is a fault, however, it is not an ultimately damning one. In a tapestry as rich as *Tartuffe*, a few strands may go awry without impairing the superb effect of the whole.

DISCUSSION QUESTIONS ON *TARTUFFE*

1. In his discussion of *The Silent Woman*, John Dryden mentions three levels of comic characterization. Examine the characters in *Tartuffe* according to their comic types. Which of these characters go beyond the merely typical? How?

2. In his Preface to *Tartuffe*, Molière points out his careful preparation for Tartuffe's first entrance in Act III. We have suggested in our discussion that the real problem character of the play is not Tartuffe, but Orgon. Contrast Molière's handling of these two characters. How are they presented differently? Which is presented most fully onstage? Which undergoes the greater change? How is that change effected? If, as Molière says, Tartuffe is consistently odious and Orgon is not always odious, then how do their characterizations fit with Molière's comment that there is no class of people exempt from comedy?

3. How are Dorine, Elmire, and Cleante similar in function? How are they different in character? For example, compare the interchange between Dorine and Tartuffe in Act III with the interchange between Cleante and Tartuffe in Act IV. Now add to the comparison a discussion of the functions of Damis and Valere. Roughly, all of these characters are unified in their opposition to Orgon and Tartuffe, but they are all different. What, for a further example, does Molière accomplish by Orgon's dismissal of Damis in Act III, and why does he have Valere come on to rescue Orgon in Act V?

4. Madam Pernelle has usually been considered one of the best comic characters in the play. Why? What part does comic exaggeration play in her character? How, in her two scenes, does Madam Pernelle help the plot?

5. In our discussion we pointed out that each act has one or two highly comic incidents. Goethe, in his conversations with Eckermann, said on July 26, 1826:

Each incident [in a play] must be meaningful and lead to another more important. The *Tartuffe* of Molière is in this respect a superb example. Just think about the first scene—what exposition you have there! From the very beginning, everything is meaningful and leads to something more important to come. The exposition of Lessing's *Minna von Barnhelm* is also excellent; however, this of *Tartuffe* is unique. It is the greatest and best of its kind.

To discover how and why Molière's interlocked incidents are so frequently excellent, make a list of them by scenes. Consider what the comic point of each one is. How much is the audience involved in each, or, in other words, what is the audience's distance from the comedy in each case?

6. Even the most modern movie or television comedy is related to the ritual origins of comedy in that it is concerned with young lovers overcoming obstacles to their union, and living happily ever after. In *Tartuffe*, the lovers' union, which could be the material for a light-hearted and gay play, is considerably darkened by the incidents involving Orgon and Tartuffe. Sort out the parts of the play that are strictly related to the love plot and the parts that are bitterly satirical or somberly serious. Are these latter parts an intrusion on the love story? Are they the strength or the weakness of the play?

7. Although you are reading a translation and thus cannot tell exactly what Molière's language was like, you can probably see that it differs from the comic language of Jonson. For instance, Molière uses several long speeches that are not witty in their diction or turns of language, but that are impassioned and strongly persuasive. Some instances are Orgon's description of Tartuffe in Act I, Cleante's rebuke of Orgon in Act I, and the Police Officer's eulogy of the King in Act V. Compare these speeches with Truewit's speeches to Clerimont about the nature of women and women's dress. What are the differences in tone? The differences in comic devices? Find on your own speeches in *Tartuffe* that are equivalent in tone and technique to ones in *The Silent Woman*.

8. The comic writer frequently has trouble with his endings. In Dryden's terms, "the audience must be satisfied with the outcome." Here are some questions on the ending of *Tartuffe*. Before you answer any, you might look them all over to see their drift.

a. In discussing the ending of *Tartuffe,* we speculated on two possible alternatives. Choose either one, and compare it with the actual ending. Work out an argument justifying what Molière did or speculating on why, in comparison with these other possibilities, he did it.

b. Suppose Molière had decided to shorten the play and make it less complicated. Suppose he cut the last part of Act III, where Orgon signs over his fortune to Tartuffe. That would allow Act V to be almost entirely eliminated then. With slight revision, Act IV could end the play; and Orgon, recognizing Tartuffe's hypocrisy, would permit the marriage of Valere and Mariane. This would certainly tighten up the plot, but would it, in terms of comic effect, be an improvement?

c. Suppose Molière made the end of the play arise out of his already established characters. As Cleante, Elmire, and Dorine have been presented as clever people, Molière could allow them to outwit Tartuffe at his own game. Dorine seems especially appropriate for this, because she is cleverer than Cleante and because Elmire in Act IV has already outwitted Tartuffe once.

Suppose that in Act V Dorine reveals that she has the important papers from the strongbox and also the deed to Orgon's estate, that she got them by leading Tartuffe on and playing on his vanity and greed. Suppose, then, that Tartuffe enters and discovers that he has been tricked. In terms of comic effect, would this be an improvement over Molière's ending?

9. The great French critic Sainte-Beuve wrote in his *Portraits Littéraires,* "To love Molière—and I mean by that to love him sincerely and with all your heart—is really to have a protection within yourself against many faults, caprices, and vices of the mind." Sainte-Beuve seems to be suggesting that Molière's plays can have a practical effect on the way that a man regards the world and conducts his life. Would *Tartuffe* be an effective guard against contemporary hypocrisy? Also, if you agree with Sainte-Beuve, could you then make out a case for comedy having an effect comparable to the catharsis of tragedy?

THE SIX OF CALAIS

BY BERNARD SHAW

CHARACTERS

EDWARD III, King of England, age 35
PHILIPPA OF HAINAULT, Queen, age 33

EDWARD, the Black Prince, age 17
JOHN OF GAUNT, age 7

EUSTACHE DE ST PIERRE
PIERS DE WISSANT
JACQUES DE WISSANT
JEAN D'AIRE
GILLES D'OUDEBOLLE
PIERS DE ROSTY (HARDMOUTH)

> the Six of Calais

A GROOM
LADIES ATTENDANT ON THE QUEEN

SIR WALTER MANNY, LORDS DERBY, NORTHAMPTON, ARUNDEL, NOBLEMEN ATTENDANT ON THE KING

A.D. 4th August 1347. Before the walls of Calais on the last day of the siege. The pavilion of Edward III, King of England, is on your left as you face the walls. The pavilion of his consort Philippa of Hainault is on your right. Between them, near the King's pavilion, is a two-seated chair of state for public audiences. Crowds of tents cover the background; but there is a clear way in the middle through the camp to the great gate of the city with its drawbridge still up and its flag still flying.

The Black Prince, aged 17, arrives impetuously past the Queen's tent, a groom running after him.

THE PRINCE. Here is the King's pavilion without a single attendant to announce me. What can the matter be?

A child's scream is heard from the royal pavilion; and John of Gaunt, aged 7, dashes out and is making for his mother's tent when the Prince seizes him.

THE PRINCE. How now, Johnny? Whats the matter?

JOHN [*struggling*] Let me go. Father is in a frightful wax.

THE PRINCE. I shall be in a wax myself presently. [*Releasing him*] Off with you to mother. [*The child takes refuge in the Queen's pavilion*].

THE KING'S VOICE. Grrr! Yah! Why was I not told? Gogswoons, why was I not told? [*Edward III, aged 35, dashes from his pavilion, foaming*]. Out! [*The groom flies for his life*]. How long have you been here? They never tell me anything. I might be a dog instead of a king.

THE PRINCE [*about to kneel*] Majesty—

THE KING. No no: enough of that. Your news. Anything from Scotland? Anything from Wales?

THE PRINCE. I—

THE KING [*not waiting for the answer*] The state of things here is past words. The wrath of God and all his saints is upon this expedition.

THE PRINCE. I hope not, sir. I—

THE KING [*raging on*] May God wither and blast this accursed town! You would have thought that these dogs would have come out of their kennels and grovelled for mercy at my summons. Am I not their lawful king, ha?

THE PRINCE. Undoubtedly, sir. They—

THE KING. They have held me up for twelve months! A whole year! ! My business ruined! My plans upset! My money exhausted! Death, disease, mutiny, a dog's life here in the field winter and summer. The bitch's bastard who is in command of their walls came to demand terms from me! to demand terms! ! ! looked me straight in the eyes with his head up as if I— I, his king! were dirt beneath his feet. By God, I will have that head: I will kick it to my dogs to eat. I will chop his insolent herald into four quarters—

THE PRINCE [*shocked*] Oh no, sir: not a herald: you cannot do that.

THE KING. They have driven me to such extremity that I am capable of cutting all the heralds in Christendom into their quarterings. [*He sits down in his chair of state and suddenly becomes ridiculously sentimental*]. I have not told you the worst. Your mother, the Queen, my Philippa, is here: here! Edward, in her delicate state of health. Even that did not move them. They want her to die: they are trying to murder her and our innocent unborn child. Think of that, boy: oh, think of that [*he almost weeps*].

THE PRINCE. Softly, father: that is not their fault: it is yours.

THE KING. Would you make a jest of this? If it is not their fault it shall be their misfortune; for I will have every man, woman, and child torn to pieces with red hot pincers for it.

THE PRINCE. Truly, dear Sir, you have great cause to be annoyed; but in sober earnest how does the matter stand? They must be suffering the last extremity of famine. Their walls may hold out; but their stomachs cannot. Cannot you offer them some sort of terms to end the business? Money is running short. Time is running short. You only make them more desperate by threatening them. Remember: it is good policy to build a bridge of silver for a flying foe.

THE KING. Do I not know it? Have I not been kind, magnanimous? Have I not done all that Christian chivalry could require of me? And they abuse my kindness: it only encourages them: they despise me for it.

THE PRINCE. What terms have you offered them?

THE KING. I have not threatened the life of a single knight. I have said that no man of gentle condition and noble blood shall be denied quarter and ransom. It was their knightly duty to make a show of arms against me. But [rising wrathfully] these base rascals of burgesses: these huckstering hounds of merchants who have made this port of Calais a nest of pirates: these usurers and tradesmen: these rebel curs who have dared to take up arms against their betters: am I to pardon their presumption? I should be false to our order, to Christendom, if I did not make a signal example.

THE PRINCE. By all means, sir. But what have you demanded?

THE KING. Six of the most purse-proud of their burgesses, as they call themselves—by God, they begin to give themselves the airs of barons—six of them are to come in their shirts with halters round their necks for me to hang in the sight of all their people. [Raising his voice again and storming] They shall die the dog's death they deserve. They shall—

A court lady comes in.

THE COURT LADY. Sir: the Queen. Sssh!

THE KING [subsiding to a whisper] The Queen! Boy: not a word here. Her condition: she must not be upset: she takes these things so amiss: be discreet, for heaven's sake.

Queen Philippa, aged 33, comes from her pavilion, attended.

THE QUEEN. Dear child: welcome.

THE PRINCE. How do you, lady mother? [He kisses her hand].

THE KING [solicitously] Madam: are you well wrapped up? Is it wise to come into the cold air here? Had they better not bring a brazier and some cushions, and a hot drink—a posset—

THE QUEEN [curtseying] Sir: beloved: dont fuss. I am very well; and the air does me good. [To the Prince] You must cheer up your father, my precious. He will fret about my health when it is his own that needs care. I have borne him eleven children; and St Anne be my witness they have cost less looking after than this one big soldier, the greatest baby of them all. [To the King] Have you put on your flannel belly band, dearest?

THE KING. Yes, yes, yes, my love: do not bother about me. Think of yourself and our child—

THE QUEEN. Oh, leave me to take care of myself and the child. I am no maternal malingreuse I promise you. And now, sir sonny, tell me all your news. I—

She is interrupted by a shrill trumpet call.

THE KING. What is that? What now?

John of Gaunt, who has been up to the town gates to see the fun, runs in excitedly.

JOHN OF GAUNT [bending his knee very perfunctorily] Sire: they have surrendered: the drawbridge is down. The six old men have come out in their shirts with ropes round their necks.

THE KING [*clouting him*] Sssh! Hold your tongue, you young devil.

THE QUEEN. Old men in their shirts in this weather! ! They will catch cold.

THE KING. It is nothing, madam my love: only the ceremony of surrender. You must go in: it is not fitting that these half naked men should be in your presence. I will deal with them.

THE QUEEN. Do not keep them too long in the cold, dearest sir.

THE KING [*uxoriously waving her a kiss*] My love!

The Queen goes into her pavilion; and a group of noblemen attendant on the King, including Sir Walter Manny and the Lords Derby, Northampton, and Arundel, issue from their tents and assemble behind the chair of state, where they are joined by the Black Prince, who stands at the King's right hand and takes charge of John of Gaunt.

THE KING. Now for these swine, these bloodsuckers. They shall learn —[*shouting*] Fetch me these fellows in here. Drag them in. I'll teach them to hold me up here for twelve months. I'll—

The six burgesses, hustled by men-at-arms, enter in their shirts and halters, each carrying a bunch of massive iron keys. Their leader, Eustache de St Pierre, kneels at the King's feet. Four of his fellow victims, Piers de Wissant, Jacques de Wissant, Jean d'Aire, and Gilles d'Oudebolle, kneel in pairs behind him, and, following his example, lay their keys on the ground. They are deeply cast down, bearing themselves like condemned men, yet maintaining a melancholy dignity. Not so the sixth, Piers de

Rosty (nicknamed Hardmouth), the only one without a grey or white beard. He has an extraordinarily dogged chin with a few bristles on it. He deliberately separates himself from the rest by passing behind the royal chair to the King's right and planting himself stiffly erect in an attitude of intense recalcitrance. The King, scowling fiercely at St Pierre and the rest, does not notice this until Peter flings down his keys with a violence which suggests that he would very willingly have brained Edward with them.

THE KING. On your knees, hound.

PETER. I am a good dog, but not of your kennel, Neddy.

THE KING. Neddy! ! ! !

PETER. Order your own curs: I am a free burgess and take commands from nobody.

Before the amazed monarch can retort, Eustache appeals to Peter.

EUSTACHE. Master Peter: if you have no regard for yourself, remember that our people, our wives and children, are at the mercy of this great king.

PETER. You mistake him for his grandfather. Great! [*He spits*].

EUSTACHE. Is this your promise to be patient?

PETER. Why waste civilities on him, Master Mayor? He can do no worse than hang us; and as to the town, I would have burnt it to the last brick, and every man, woman and child along with it, sooner than surrender. I came here to make up the tale of six to be hanged. Well, he can hang me; but he shall not outface me. I am as good a dog as he, any day in the week.

THE PRINCE. Fie, fellow! is this a way for one of thy degree to speak to an anointed king? Bear thyself as befits one of thy degree in the royal presence, or by Holy Paul—

PETER. You know how we have borne ourselves in his royal presence these twelve months. We have made some of you skip. Famine and not you, has beaten us. Give me a square meal and a good sword and stake all on a fair single combat with this big bully, or his black whelp here if he is afraid of me; and we shall see which is the better dog of the two.

THE KING. Drag him to his knees. Hamstring him if he resists.

Three men-at-arms dash at Peter and drag him to his knees. They take his halter and tie his ankles and wrists with it. Then they fling him on his side, where he lies helpless.

THE KING. And so, Master Burgess—

PETER. Bow-wow-wow!

THE KING [*furious*] Gag him. Gogswoons, gag him.

They tear a piece of linen from the back of his shirt, and bind his mouth with it. He barks to the last moment. John of Gaunt laughs ecstatically at this performance, and sets off some of the soldiers.

THE KING. If a man laughs I will have him flayed alive.

Dead silence.

THE KING. And now, fellows, what have ye to say to excuse your hardy and stubborn resistance for all these months to me, your king?

EUSTACHE. Sir, we are not fellows. We are free burgesses of this great city.

THE KING. Free burgesses! Are you still singing that song? Well, I will bend the necks of your burgesses when the hangman has broken yours. Am I not your overlord? Am I not your anointed king?

EUSTACHE. That is your claim, sir; and you have made it good by force of arms. We must submit to you and to God.

THE KING. Leave God out of this! What hast thou or thy like to do with God?

EUSTACHE. Nothing, sir: we would not so far presume. But with due respect to your greatness I would humbly submit to your Majesty that God may have something to do with us, seeing that he created us all alike and redeemed us by the blood of his beloved son.

THE KING [*to the Prince*] Can you make head or tail of this, boy? Is he accusing me of impiety? If he is, by God—

EUSTACHE. Sir, is it for me to accuse you of anything? Here we kneel in the dust before you, naked and with the ropes on our necks with which you will presently send us into the presence of our maker and yours. [*His teeth chatter*].

THE KING. Ay: you may well tremble. You have cause.

EUSTACHE. Yes: I tremble; and my teeth chatter: the few I have left. But you gentlemen that see our miserable plight, I call on your generosity as noblemen, on your chivalry as good knights, to bear witness for us that it is the cold of the morning and our naked condition that shakes us. We kneel to implore your King's mercy for our wretched and starving townsfolk, not for ourselves.

THE KING. Whose fault is it that they are starving? They have themselves to thank. Why did they not open their gates to me? Why did they take arms against their anointed king? Why should I have mercy on them or on you?

EUSTACHE. Sir: one is merciful not for reasons, but for the love of God, at whose hand we must all sue for mercy at the end of our days.

THE KING. You shall not save yourself by preaching. What right have you to preach? It is for churchmen and learned divines to speak of these mysteries, not for tradesmen and usurers. I'll teach you to rebel against your betters, whom God has appointed to keep you in obedience and loyalty. You are traitors; and as traitors you shall die. Thank my mercy that you are spared the torments that traitors and rebels suffer in England. [*Rising*] Away with them to the hangman; and let our trumpeters summon the townspeople to the walls to take warning from their dangling corpses.

The three men-at-arms begin to lift Peter. The others lay hands on his five colleagues.

THE KING. No: let that hound lie. Hanging is too good for him.

The Queen hurries in with her ladies in great concern. The men-at-arms release the burgesses irresolutely. It is evident that the Queen's arrival washes out all the King's orders.

THE QUEEN. Sir, what is this they tell me?

THE KING [*hurrying across to intercept her*] Madam: this is no place for you. I pray you, retire. The business is one in which it becomes you not to meddle.

THE QUEEN [*evading him and passing on to inspect the burgesses*] But these gentlemen. They are almost naked. It is neither seemly nor sufficient. They are old: they are half frozen: they should be in their beds.

THE KING. They soon will be. Leave us, madam. This is business of State. They are suffering no more than they deserve. I beg and pray you—I command you—

THE QUEEN. Dear sir, your wishes are my law and your commands my duty. But these gentlemen are very cold.

THE KING. They will be colder presently; so you need not trouble about that. Will it please you, madam, to withdraw at once?

THE QUEEN. Instantly, my dear lord. [*To Eustache*] Sir: when his Majesty has ended his business with you, will you and your friends partake of some cups of hot wine in my pavilion? You shall be furnished with gowns.

THE KING [*choking with wrath*] Hot w—!

EUSTACHE. Alas, madam, when the King has ended his business with us we shall need nothing but our coffins. I also beg you to withdraw and hasten our despatch to that court where we shall not be held guilty for defending our hearths and homes to the last extremity. The King will not be baulked of his revenge; and we are shriven and ready.

THE QUEEN. Oh, you mistake, sir: the King is incapable of revenge: my husband is the flower of chivalry.

EUSTACHE. You little know your husband, madam. We know better what to expect from Edward Plantagenet.

THE KING [*coming to him threateningly past his consort*] Ha! do you, Master Merchant? You know better than the Queen! You and your like know what to expect from your lords and rulers! Well, this time you shall not be disappointed. You have guessed aright. You shall hang, every man of you, in your shirts, to make mirth for my horseboys and their trulls.

THE QUEEN. Oh no—

THE KING [*thundering*] Madam: I forbid you to speak. I bade you go: you would not; and now you shall see what I would have spared you had you been obedient. By God, I will be master in my own house and king in my own camp. Take these fellows out and hang them in their white beards. *The King takes his place on his chair of state with his arms folded implacably. The Queen follows him slowly and desolately. She takes her place beside him. The dead silence is very trying.*

THE QUEEN [*drooping in tears and covering her face with her hands*] Oh!

THE KING [*flinching*] No no no no NO. Take her away.

THE QUEEN. Sir: I have been always a great trouble to you. I have asked you for a thousand favors and graces and presents. I am impatient and ungrateful, ever asking, asking, asking. Have you ever refused me even once?

THE KING. Well, is that a reason why I should give and grant, grant and give, for ever? Am I never to have my own way?

THE QUEEN. Oh, dearest sir, when next I ask you for a great thing, refuse me: teach me a lesson. But this is such a little thing. [*Heartbroken*] I cannot bear your refusing me a little thing.

THE KING. A little thing! You call this a little thing!

THE QUEEN. A very very little thing, sir. You are the King: you have at your disposal thousands of lives: all our lives from the noblest to the meanest. All the lives in that city are in

your hand to do as you will with in this your hour of victory: it is as if you were God himself. You said once that you would lead ten kings captive to my feet. Much as I have begged from you I have never asked for my ten kings. I ask only for six old merchants, men beneath your royal notice, as my share of the spoils of your conquest. Their ransom will hardly buy me a new girdle; and oh, dear sir, you know that my old one is becoming too strait for me. Will you keep me begging so?

THE KING. I see very well that I shall not be allowed my own way. [*He begins to cry*].

THE QUEEN [*throwing her arms round him*] Oh, dear sir, you know I would die to spare you a moment's distress. There, there, dearest! [*She pets him*].

THE KING [*blubbering*] I am never allowed to do anything I want. I might as well be a dog as a king. You treat me like a baby.

THE QUEEN. Ah no: you are the greatest of kings to me, the noblest of men, my dearest lord and my dearest dearest love. [*Throwing herself on her knees*] Listen: do as you will: I will not say another word: I ask nothing.

THE KING. No: you ask nothing because you know you will get everything. [*He rises, shouting*] Take those men out of my sight.

THE PRINCE. What shall we do with them, sir?

THE KING [*flinging himself back into his seat*] Ask the Queen. Banquet them: feast them: give them my crown, my kingdom. Give them the clothes off my back, the bread out of my mouth, only take them away. Will you go, curses on you.

The five burgesses kneel gratefully to the Queen.

EUSTACHE [*kissing her hand*] Madam: our ransom shall buy you a threefold girdle of gold and a cradle of silver.

THE KING. Aye, well, see that it does: see that it does.

The burgesses retire, bowing to the Queen, who, still on her knees, waves her hand graciously to them.

THE QUEEN. Will you not help me up, dear sir?

THE KING. Oh yes, yes [*raising her*]: you should be more careful: who knows what harm you may have done yourself flopping on your knees like that?

THE QUEEN. I have done myself no harm, dear sir; but you have done me a world of good. I have never been better nor happier in my life. Look at me. Do I not look radiant?

THE KING. And how do I look? Like a fool.

JOHN OF GAUNT. Sir: the men-at-arms want to know what they are to do with this fellow?

THE KING. Aye, I forgot him. Fetch him here.

The three men-at-arms carry Peter to the King, and fling him down. The King is now grinning. His paroxysm of tears has completely discharged his ill temper. It dawns on him that through Peter he may get even with Philippa for his recent domestic defeat.

THE QUEEN. Oh, the poor man has not even a proper shirt to wear. It is all torn: it is hardly decent.

THE KING. Look well at this man, madam. He defied me. He spat at me. There is no insult that he did not

heap on me. He looked me in the face and spoke to me as if I were a scullion. I swear to you by the Holy Rood, he called me Neddy! Donkeys are called Neddy. What have you to say now? Is he, too, to be spared and petted and fed and have a gown from you?

THE QUEEN [*going to Peter*] But he is blue with cold. I fear he is dying. Untie him. Lift him up. Take that bandage off his mouth. Fie fie! I believe it is the tail of his shirt.

THE KING. It is cleaner than his tongue.

The men-at-arms release Peter from his bonds and his gag. He is too stiff to rise. They pull him to his feet.

PETER [*as they lift him groaning and swearing*] Ah-ooh-oh-ow!

THE KING. Well? Have you learnt your lesson? Are you ready to sue for the Queen's mercy?

PETER. Yah! Henpecked! Kiss mammy!

THE KING [*chuckles*]! !

THE QUEEN [*severely*] Are you mad, Master Burgess? Do you not know that your life is in the King's hand? Do you expect me to recommend you to his mercy if you forget yourself in this unseemly fashion?

PETER. Let me tell you, madam, that I came here in no ragged shirt. I have a dozen shirts of as fine a web as ever went on your back. Is it likely that I, a master mercer, would wear aught but the best of the best to go to my grave in?

THE QUEEN. Mend your manners first, sir; and then mend your linen; or you shall have no countenance from me.

PETER. I have naught to do with you, madam, though I well see who wears the breeches in this royal household. I am not skilled in dealing with fine handsome ladies. Leave me to settle my business with your henpecked husband.

THE QUEEN. You shall suffer for this insolence. [*To the King*] Will you, my lord, stand by and hear me spoken to in this tone by a haberdasher?

THE KING [*grinning*] Nay: I am in a merciful mood this morning. The poor man is to be pitied, shivering there in his shirt with his tail torn off.

PETER. Shivering! You lie in your teeth, though you were fifty kings. No man alive shall pity Peter Hardmouth, a dog of lousy Champagne.

THE KING [*going to him*] Ha! A dog of Champagne! Oh, you must pardon this man, madam; for my grandmother hailed from that lousy province; so I also am a dog of Champagne. We know one another's bark. [*Turning on him with bristling teeth*] Eh?

PETER [*growling in his face like a dog*] Grrrr!!!

THE KING [*returning the growl chin to chin*] Grrrr!!!!!!

They repeat this performance, to the great scandal of the Queen, until it develops into a startling imitation of a dog fight.

THE QUEEN [*tearing the two dogs asunder*] Oh, for shame, sir! And you, fellow: I will have you muzzled and led through the streets on a chain and lodged in a kennel.

THE KING. Be merciful, lady. I have asked you for many favors, and had them granted me too, as the world, please God, will soon have proof. Will you deny me this?

THE QUEEN. Will you mock my condition before this insolent man and before the world? I will not endure it.

THE KING. Faith, no, dearest: no mockery. But you have no skill in dealing with the dogs of lousy Champagne. We must pity this poor trembling fellow.

THE QUEEN [*angrily*] He is not trembling.

PETER. No, by all the saints in heaven and devils in hell. Well said, lass.

He nudges her, to her extreme indignation.

THE KING. Hear that, dearest: he calls thee lass. Be kind to him. He is only a poor old cur who has lost half his teeth. His condition would move a heart of stone.

PETER. I may be an old cur; but if I had sworn to hang the six of us as he swore, no shrew should scold me out of it, nor any softbosomed beauty wheedle me out of it. Yah, cry baby! Give her your sword and sit in the corner with her distaff. The grey mare is the better horse here. Do your worst, dame: I like your spunk better than his snivel.

THE QUEEN [*raging*] Send him away, sir. He is too ugly; and his words are disgusting. Such objects should be kept out of my sight: would you have me bear you a monster? Take him away.

THE KING. Away with him. Hurt him not; but let him not come into the Queen's presence. Quick there. Off with him.

The men-at-arms lay hands on Peter who struggles violently.

PETER. Hands off me, spaniels. Arrr! Grrr! [*As they drag him out overpowered*] Gee-up, Neddy. [*He finishes with a spirited imitation of a donkey's bray*].

THE KING. That is how they build

men in Champagne. By the Holy Rood I care not if a bit of him gets into our baby.

THE QUEEN. Oh, for shame! for shame! Have men no decency?

The King snatches her into his arms, laughing boisterously. The laugh spreads to all the soldiers and courtiers. The whole camp seems in a hilarious uproar.

THE QUEEN. No no: for shame! for shame!

The King stops her mouth with a kiss. Peter brays melodiously in the distance.

SHAW, Prefatory to *The Six of Calais*

The most amusing thing about the first performance of this little play was the exposure it elicited of the quaint illiteracy of our modern London journalists. Their only notion of a king was a pleasant and highly respectable gentleman in a bowler hat and Victorian beard, shaking hands affably with a blushing football team. To them a queen was a dignified lady, also Victorian as to her coiffure, graciously receiving bouquets from excessively washed children in beautiful new clothes. Such were their mental pictures of Great Edward's grandson and his queen Philippa. They were hurt, shocked, scandalized at the spectacle of a medieval soldier-monarch publicly raging and cursing, crying and laughing, asserting his authority with thrasonic ferocity and the next moment blubbering like a child in his wife's lap or snarling like a savage dog at a dauntless and defiant tradesman: in short, behaving himself like an unrestrained human being in a very trying situation instead of like a modern constitutional monarch on parade keeping up an elaborate fiction of living in a political vacuum and moving only when his ministers pull his strings. Edward Plantagenet the Third had to pull everybody else's strings and pull them pretty hard, his father having been miserably killed for taking his job too lightly. But the journalist critics knew nothing of this. A King Edward who did not behave like the son of King Edward the Seventh seemed unnatural and indecent to them, and they rent their garments accordingly.

They were perhaps puzzled by the fact that the play has no moral whatever. Every year or so I hurl at them a long play full of insidious propaganda, with a moral in every line. They never discover what I am driving at: it is always too plainly and domestically stated to be grasped by their subtle and far flung minds; but they feel that I am driving at something: probably something they had better not agree with if they value their livelihoods. A play of mine in which I am not driving at anything more than a playwright's direct business is as inconceivable by them as a medieval king.

Now a playwright's direct business is simply to provide the theatre with a play. When I write one with the additional attraction of providing the twentieth century with an up-to-date religion or the like, that luxury is thrown in gratuitously; and the play, simply as a play, is not necessarily either the better or the worse for it. What, then, is a play simply as a play?

Well, it is a lot of things. Life as we see it is so haphazard that it is only by picking out its key situations and arranging them in their significant order (which is never how they actually occur) that it can be made intelligible. The highbrowed dramatic poet wants to make it intelligible and sublime. The farce writer wants to make it funny. The melodrama merchant wants to make it as exciting as some people find the police news. The pornographer wants to make it salacious. All interpreters of life in action, noble or ignoble, find their instrument in the theatre; and all the academic definitions of a play are variations of this basic function.

Yet there is one function hardly ever alluded to now, though it was made much too much of from Shakespear's time to the middle of the nineteenth century. As I write my plays it is continually in my mind and very much to my taste. This function is to provide an exhibition of the art of acting. A good play with bad parts is not an impossibility; but it is a monstrosity. A bad play with good parts will hold the stage and be kept alive by the actors for centuries after the obsolescence of its mentality would have condemned it to death without

them. A great deal of the British Drama, from Shakespear to Bulwer Lytton, is as dead as mutton, and quite unbearable except when heroically acted; yet Othello and Richelieu can still draw hard money into the pay boxes; and The School For Scandal revives again and again with unabated vigor. Rosalind can always pull As You Like It through in spite of the sententious futility of the melancholy Jaques; and Millamant, impossible as she is, still produces the usual compliments to the wit and style of Congreve, who thought that syphilis and cuckoldry and concupiscent old women are things to be laughed at.

The Six of Calais is an acting piece and nothing else. As it happened, it was so well acted that in the eighteenth century all the talk would have been about Siddons as Philippa. But the company got no thanks except from the audience: the critics were prostrated with shock, damn their eyes!

I have had to improve considerably on the story as told by that absurd old snob Froissart, who believed that "to rob and pill was a good life" if the robber was at least a baron. He made a very poor job of it in my opinion.

DISCUSSION OF *THE SIX OF CALAIS*

Bernard Shaw's publishers would have performed a valuable public service by warning the great Irishman's readers to be constantly on their guard. Shaw is a tricky person to read. He is not hard to read—far from it. His style has a deceptive clarity and lucidity. In fact, it is so clear, lucid, fluent, witty, engaging, and charmingly persuasive that it often beguiles readers into attitudes that, with a sharp and sudden shock, they recognize they consider absurd and illogical.

Shaw was often accused of being an irreverent and irresponsible prankster, an amusing practical joker who was not to be taken seriously because he practiced his jokes upon his audience rather than upon his characters in the plays. There is a shred of truth in this notion, and it is not hard to imagine the spirit of Shaw hovering over the heads of his audience, the very embodiment of Meredith's comic spirit, casting "an oblique light on them, followed by volleys of silvery laughter."

No more than a shred of truth, however. When Shaw aimed his sights at a tenet of conventional morality, custom, or accepted social practice, when he turned it inside out and showed that the reverse made more sense to a reasonable man, he was not merely being perverse. He was only being more effective than the popular hack who turned out amusing fribbles, which served to pass an evening pleasantly, but which could be as quickly forgotten when one left the theatre as the ticket stub one dropped in the aisle.

Shaw has called himself a classic writer of comedy, who used the manner of Molière and the characterization of Dickens. A classic writer of comedy tries to do more than pass the time for his audience. Indeed, the classic definition of comedy is to correct the foibles and to ridicule the disagreeable habits of the audience itself, by displaying those foibles and habits in their full absurdity on the stage. The hack writer of comedy presents characters whose faults and foibles so mildly touch reality that the audience is not really touched. Shaw presents characters from reality in a context that illuminates their absurdity as persuasively as it does painfully.

Not only in Shaw's great plays like St. Joan, Heartbreak House, and Back to Methuselah, but even in a little jeu d'esprit like The Six of Calais, the reader or viewer must be strongly on guard. He must guard himself against a superficial condemnation of the play as absurd and, in the case of The Six of Calais, as slight. It is only slight in length.

Shaw's comic method closely resembled that of the hack writer. Both were trying to entertain, and both used the same traditional comic devices. The Six of Calais, for example, is full of horseplay and buffoonery. But how Shaw differed from the hack may be seen both in his plays and in the lengthy prefaces he attached to most of them.

The Six of Calais starts from a central witty conception: the irritated injustice of a medieval king, and the childish petulance of a businessman. From these central characteristics, these Humours, all of the absurd incidents derive. However, these characteristics are never stated; they are presented. In the preface, Shaw talks explicitly, although slyly, about characterization. The prefaces, in other words, suggest a difference between what the playwright can do and what the writer of a reasoned and persuasive essay can do. The essay's main purpose is to present a clear, developed, and logical argument. Its secondary purpose is to present the argument amusingly or compellingly. The play's main purpose is to amuse or enrapture. Its secondary purpose or its hidden purpose is to change the character of its audience. The preface works explicitly; the play, like any work of art, works implicitly.

If Shaw had not been amusing and arresting, his plays would never have reached the stage. His triumph is that he got them there and that he made them so amazingly popular despite their strong dose of intellectual content. Probably more than any other modern, Shaw has stretched the intellectual content of a play, and he has done it while writing bedroom farces, melodramas, and historical romances.

A Shaw play, then, can be enormously entertaining even to a confirmed watcher of situation comedies on television. But it can also be intellectually entertaining to one who takes the art of comedy to be one of the noblest indications of man's spirit.

Even a little play like *The Six of Calais* can work in both ways. Shaw speaks of it rather disarmingly in his prefatory note. Here is a spot to be on your guard, for you shouldn't be disarmed. Anybody can be immediately amused by the spectacle of two grown men growling at each other chin to chin. This is amusing in the same way that it is amusing to see someone pompous receive a custard pie in his face. But Shaw's Edward III and Peter Hardmouth are also amusing because they reveal a facet of human character that in reality is frequently important and horrible.

Shaw says that in writing *The Six of Calais* he simply tried to provide the theatre with a play, and that he wanted simply to write good parts for his actors. All good plays do this—Shakespeare's, Jonson's, Molière's, and Wilde's as well as Shaw's. He is saying, however, that you may take the spectacle as a mere joke, that the play is fairly pointless, that it is only fun. It is fun, of course. Very good fun. But in comic art—perhaps not in comic entertainment like the Three Stooges, but certainly in the comic art of Molière, Jonson, and Shaw—there is no such thing as a pointless joke or mere fun. There is always fun with a point. Fun with meaning. Fun with its full baggage of intellectual implications.

A pointless joke is no joke at all. It is merely a shaggy dog story. So when Shaw beckons you on airily to sit back and enjoy his harmless little play, beware. The fun has a hidden stinger.

What, then, is the fun in this play about? Shaw gives us a good hint in his preface when he talks about the superb characters of Shakespeare's Rosalind and Congreve's Millamant. In the preface to *The Millionairess,* a play he published in the same volume with *The Six of Calais,* there is a sentence which we might take as a further hint:

> Though this play of The Millionairess does not pretend to be anything more than a comedy of humorous and curious contemporary characters such as Ben Jonson might write were he alive now, yet it raises a question that has troubled human life and moulded human society since the creation.

Substitute *The Six of Calais* for *The Millionairess,* and eliminate the word "contemporary," and you have a good notion of what Shaw did in this little one-act.

In the same way that Ben Jonson dissected the extravagant humor of

Morose and that Molière probed the equally wild abnormality of Orgon, Shaw here dissected and probed the extravagance of Edward, Philippa, and Peter Hardmouth. What a good actor's part really is is an incisive revelation of human nature. In Shaw's Edward, Philippa, and Peter we see a beautifully etched cameo of the unreasoning passion and unrestrained emotion that so often disguise themselves as reason and justice and that are so embedded in human nature.

DISCUSSION QUESTIONS ON *THE SIX OF CALAIS*

1. As a King dispensing justice, Edward should act in a certain way. How? What are the traditional qualities we expect from a King? How do Edward's real actions contrast with how he should act? How does this contrast make him a humorous character?

2. Why does Shaw introduce the Black Prince and John of Gaunt?

3. When the Prince says to John of Gaunt, "How now, Johnny? Whats the matter?" and John of Gaunt replies, "Let me go. Father is in a frightful wax," Shaw's language is poles apart from the language of Shakespeare's John of Gaunt. How? And why? And why is it, therefore, comic language?

4. Comedy, perhaps revealing its ritual origins, has traditionally contained a battle of the sexes that resulted finally in a Comus or marriage. Is there, in embryo, any trace of that pattern in *The Six of Calais?*

5. Because Shaw's play is short, its plot does not really resemble Jonson's or Molière's plots or Potts' theory of the typical comic plot. But Shaw's play is thoroughly delightful, so it would seem to follow that his plot is good and effective. So, arguing from the analogy that a short story is to a novel as a playlet is to a play, can you defend Shaw's plot?

6. In both Philippa and Edward we see a reversal of attitude. Explain the nature of the reversals. Are they different? How important are they to the plot? Why does Philippa's come last?

7. The theme of the play might be called the triumph of unreason or the triumph of emotion over reason. Such a theme would seem to push the play more toward Swiftean satire than Meredithean geniality. Yet the tone of the play is never bitter or satirical. How does Shaw keep the tone genial? How, in other words, does he sugar-coat his pill?

PART THREE

Tragicomedy

Tragicomedy

> He who writes a tragicomedy does not intend to compose separately
> either a tragedy or a comedy, but from the two a third thing that
> will be perfect of its kind.
>
> GIAMBATTISTA GUARINI

"Their mongrel tragicomedy," said Sir Philip Sidney. "That linsie-woolsie inter-
mixture," said Edward Phillips. "The bastard muse," said David Krause. Such
are the comments that have usually described the third major genre, tragicomedy.

From the beginnings of the drama, tragicomedy has had a furtive and sur-
reptitious history. Even today the "ignominious" form does not warrant a
separate listing in *The Oxford Companion to the Theatre*, but is limited to
a short paragraph under the topic of "Tragedy." Perhaps the chief reason for
the ambiguous status of tragicomedy is that the commentators on Aristotle
solidified his thoughts on tragedy and comedy into such hardbound rules that
any infringement seemed sacrilegious. When the boundaries of tragedy were
made firmly distinct from those of comedy, a fusion of the two "opposed"
genres seemed the unforgivable dramatic sin.

Yet the greatest dramatists from Aeschylus to O'Casey have never let themselves be hampered by so-called rules. To work within a set of rules is, of
course, excellent and necessary for any artist, but one man's rules may be
another man's poison. So ever since Aeschylus introduced the second actor,
the form of the drama has always in its great periods been fluid and changing.

Even in those periods when many people thought the form of the drama
firmly fixed and permanently established, the great dramatists were chafing
and fighting against the confines of rigid form. The Greek scholar H. D. F.
Kitto finds that he has to regard some of Euripides' plays as tragicomedies.
Even Corneille, the strictly traditional French dramatist, was accused of not
adhering to the tragic form. Dryden, Dr. Johnson, Coleridge, and Shelley all
had to defend Shakespeare's plays against the attacks of purists in their own
day. And in our time, the plays of Anton Chekhov, Sean O'Casey, Maxim
Gorky, Clifford Odets, and William Saroyan have all been attacked as a formless mishmash, so that, for instance, O'Casey finds himself defending his
tragicomedies in the same terms that Dryden, Johnson, Coleridge, and Shelley
used to defend Shakespeare.

Certainly at this late date with testimonials of such men to illuminate the
achievements of these plays for us, we cannot doubt that tragicomedy is a

unique and definite genre. Yet very little close examination of the form has been made, and its history and development have seldom been studied.

"Development" seems the appropriate word; for tragicomedy, lacking the impressive body of criticism that attached to tragedy and even to comedy, seems through the years to have changed more in its essentials, while tragedy and comedy have remained relatively static. Modern tragicomedies are subtler, more refined in technique, and more ambitious in intention than their ancient or Elizabethan counterparts.

But this is jumping ahead. How did tragicomedy get its start? What are its origins? Immediately we run into difficulty, for no one actually knows. So many people through the centuries have denied that there is such a genre as tragicomedy that its beginnings are even more shrouded in mystery than the beginnings of tragedy and comedy.

However, the more closely we look at even the most modern tragicomedies, the more clearly do we begin to see the dim traces and shadowy outlines of its distant ancestors. And if we look long enough, we will begin to see the faint lines of a horned and bearded face. We will begin to see the curve of a broad and sensual mouth that seems twisted almost as much in wild, sardonic glee as it does in terrible agony. We will begin to see the Great God Pan.

Pan is a curious figure in ancient mythology. He is both a god and a goat, both a saint and a satyr, both more than human and less. He is a link with the best in man and with the worst. He is a god of fertility, of riot and carousing, and of shepherds and the fields. He is the god who lustily pursues woodnymphs while joyously dancing and playing on his pipes. But he is also a god of pain and death. He is the god who strikes terror into man. He is the god of panic, the god who is beaten as a scapegoat, and the god who died at the birth of Christianity. And, finally, as his name tells us, he is the god of All, of fusion and union.

We have seen that the ancient Greek dramatists refined tragedy and comedy into civilized arts, but they also played on the pipes of Pan. The Greek tragic writers who entered their trilogies in the civic contests had to write also a satyr play to follow the main performance and to offer some relief from the tragic tension. "Hee too," writes Horace,[1] "that did in Tragick Verse contend/ . . . soone after, forth did send/The rough rude Satyres naked. . . ." These satyr plays treated the gods and heroes who had just figured in the most somber and serious tragedies with ridicule and even indecency. As Horace put it:

> And so the scoffing Satyres . . . turne all earnest into jest,
> As neither any God, were brought in there,
> Or Semi-god, that late was seene to weare
> A royall Crowne, and purple . . . [but was] made to hop,
> With poore base termes, through every baser shop. . . .

[1] *The Art of Poetry*, Ben Jonson's translation.

The plays were burlesque in nature and licentious in manner. Sheldon Cheney calls them a strange mixture "of heroics and buffoonery."

This first dramatic mingling of tragedy and comedy was not long allowed to remain in such a simple and rudimentary state. Euripides, the third of the great Greek tragic writers, began to break away from the rigid tragic form and to include some startling juxtapositions of tragedy and comedy in his plays. H. D. F. Kitto, in his fine book *Greek Tragedy*, finds that *Alcestis*, *Iphigeneia in Tauris*, *Ion*, and *Helen* deviate so far from the tragic mold that they can best be labeled tragicomedies. He lists these ways in which these plays significantly differ from tragedy:

> absence of a tragic theme, avoidance even of an intellectual theme such as would demand serious advocacy, the adoption of a new standard of reality which, by reducing the tragic to the pathetic, made it possible to combine harmoniously into one theatrical whole a wide range of emotional effects.

In other words, when the story is not taken with a somber high seriousness, other elements—such as satire and comic relief—can be harmoniously introduced. In effect, Professor Kitto is saying that these plays with their exciting stories and their happy endings are superbly written entertainments. They are brilliant, highly theatrical, delightfully varied, and among the finest of their kind. But, to our minds, they are not art in the important sense of the term, in the sense that art is a representation that touches us in the most meaningful, moving, and profound way.

To find tragicomedy that is the highest art, we shall have to look further than Euripides.

Although little has come down to us of Greek New Comedy except a few scraps from Menander, there is reason to think that the comic writers also were beginning to stray from their strict, formal boundaries. For instance, the Roman comic writer Plautus is thought to have based his *Amphitryon* on a lost play of the Greek comic writer Philemon. And Plautus' *Amphitryon* is quite distinctly leaning toward tragicomedy. The play is about the comic subject of adultery, but two of the chief characters are the gods Jupiter and Mercury. Mercury, who in some stories is supposed to be the father of Pan, says in the Prologue to the play:

> What? Are you frowning because I said this play was to be a tragedy? I'm a god, so I'll change it if you like from tragedy to comedy, without altering a line. Do you want me to or not? But there! How dense I am not to know what you want when I'm a god. I understand exactly what you want. I'll make the play mixed; let it be a tragicomedy. Naturally it wouldn't do for me to make it utterly comic with kings and gods on the stage. Well, then? Since there's a slave part in it, I'll make it just what I said—a tragicomedy! [1]

[1] Editors' translation.

Despite these brave words, however, *Amphitryon* is only a tragicomedy in the narrow and artificial sense of having both kings and slaves on the stage. A further development would have to wait a few hundred years. After the downfall of Rome, the drama not merely languished; it almost expired. But during the Middle Ages, it received a slow and timid rebirth in the religious and biblical plays, the mysteries and moralities. Some of these plays quickly became secular in tone and spirit. In fact, some of them became licentious and joyously bawdy. Actually a situation developed rather like that which gave rise to the satyr play. After the rigorous reverence of Church, there was a deeply pleasant relief in treating the serious and frightening liturgical figures with irreverent abandon. For example, the many anti-Christ plays on the continent treated the sinister and awful figure of the anti-Christ with rustic familiarity and rowdy, low buffoonery. And even in this naive drama we may see the rudiments of tragicomedy: freedom, contrast, and irony.

Some of the writers of the Renaissance tried to explain and defend tragicomedy by alluding to the satyr plays. Among them were the sixteenth century Italians, Giraldi Cinthio and Giambattista Guarini. According to Cinthio, the effect of a satyr play was a fusion of the emotional effects of a tragedy and a comedy. Probably the best full-scale defense of tragicomedy was Guarini's *The Compendium of Tragicomic Poetry*. In it Guarini wrote:

> Really if men today knew how to compose a good tragicomedy (and it is a difficult thing to do), no other drama would be staged, for tragicomedy can include all the good and reject all the bad qualities of dramatic poetry. It can delight every disposition, every age, and every taste—which is certainly not true of tragedy and comedy.[2]

Of Guarini's view, Eugene M. Waith wrote, "Thus tragicomedy is the ultimate refinement of drama, the one form for truly civilized and well-bred men."[3]

Guarini's *Compendium* is still a remarkable document in the history of criticism. It is a lucid, closely reasoned, painstaking, and moderately successful attempt to deduce from *The Poetics* an Aristotelian basis for tragicomedy. It is an adequate defense for his own play *Il Pastor Fido*, but his thesis falls short of explaining a modern tragicomedy like Chekhov's *The Three Sisters* or O'Casey's *The Plough and the Stars*.

The reason is that Guarini will not allow tragicomedy either the extremes of tragedy or the extremes of comedy. He feels that these extremes of emotion are mutually incompatible. They will not mix. But he feels that if the terror and the horror are removed from tragedy, and the absurd and the ridiculous from comedy, then what remains may be compatibly mixed. The most admired modern tragicomedies have refused to restrict themselves so narrowly, and the glory of an O'Casey tragicomedy is that it is able to blend the most opposite emotions to produce a unique and compelling experience.

---

[2] Editors' translation.
[3] Eugene M. Waith, *The Pattern of Tragicomedy in Beaumont and Fletcher*. (New Haven: Yale University Press, 1952), p. 48.

Guarini's theory was fine as far as it went, and its influence went very far. Waith points out that the Elizabethan playwright John Fletcher was influenced by the *Compendium* and indebted to *Il Pastor Fido* for the rationale and the plot of his own early play *The Faithful Shepherdess*. In the Preface to that play Fletcher defines tragicomedy in terms reminiscent of Guarini:

> A tragi-comedie is not so called in respect of mirth and killing, but in respect it wants deaths, which is inough to make it no tragedie, yet brings some neere it, which is inough to make it no comedie: which must be a representation of familiar people with such kinde of trouble as no life be questioned, so that a God is as lawfull in this as in a tragedie, and meane people as in a comedie.

The tragicomic plays of Francis Beaumont and John Fletcher were quite as popular as the plays of Shakespeare or Jonson, and some of them continue to be staged. Their popularity helped to re-establish tragicomedy, although the plays did not notably advance the form beyond what Euripides had already done. We find in Beaumont and Fletcher's plays perhaps darker overtones of tragedy mingled with the comedy, but we also find that the plot is happily resolved. As Waith put it, in discussing Fletcher's *The Mad Lover,* "Through his half-comic, half-serious adventures Fletcher achieves a beautifully articulated piece of fooling." In other words, here, as in Euripides, we have the artistry of entertainment.

Frequently Shakespeare, as we have seen in *King Lear,* interwove comic elements into a predominantly tragic play. The Porter's scene in *Macbeth* is also a good example. Sometimes he would include more serious themes and incidents in a comedy—the Shylock scenes in *The Merchant of Venice,* for example. And in the *Henry IV* plays the heroic scenes are mixed in about equal proportions with the great comic scenes of Falstaff. "Shakespeare," said W. B. Yeats, "is always a writer of tragicomedy."

Strictly, Shakespeare was not really a writer of tragicomedies, for the comedy and the tragedy, even when they are approximately equal in weight, usually existed in distinct and separate compartments. They are not fused in the same scene to produce a unique and single emotion.

There is one exception. In one play, *The Two Noble Kinsmen,* which Shakespeare and Fletcher wrote together, we find the closest approach yet to modern tragicomedy. Not only is there more diversity of plot, but also there is a conclusion which is not entirely happy. The final scene contains, like comedy, preparations for a wedding. But it also contains, like tragedy, a death.

Nevertheless, it is not really until modern times that tragicomedy fused its disparate elements into one organic whole. In the plays of Anton Chekhov, in Bernard Shaw's masterpiece *Heartbreak House,* in Maxim Gorky's *The Lower Depths,* and in the early plays of Sean O'Casey, we find that tragicomedy has taken a further step. In these plays, which are among the finest of the modern repertoire, we find, if not the perfection of the form that was more simply practiced by Euripides and his successors, the perfection of art.

And now a few brief suggestions about what the modern art of tragicomedy consists of.

The "old quarrel about tragicomedy," as William Empson calls it below, raises not only questions about the mixture of genres, but also about dramatic structure. You remember that in the chapter on tragedy, John Dryden suggested a plot structure, based ultimately upon Aristotle's notion that a plot should be a series of connected and causal incidents, with a beginning and a middle and an end; and that this was the structure that seemed most appropriate for tragedy. Remember also that, in the chapter on comedy, L. J. Potts suggested a looser plot structure composed of illustrative incidents in the manner of the picaresque novel, and that this structure seemed most appropriate for comedy. At least one play in each chapter was selected to suggest that another plot structure than the tragic and another structure than the comic *can* be used effectively in those genres. The tragic structure and the comic structure seem most appropriate, seem prototypical, but others will work.

In a tragicomedy that is a work of art it appears that only one kind of structure, one particularly appropriate for the juxtaposition of the terrible and the ridiculous, can be used.

Dryden, Dr. Johnson, Coleridge, and Shelley have felt a little uncomfortable about tragicomedy, even though they have praised it. When they alluded disparagingly to the mixture, they referred to an Elizabethan variety which sometimes deserves the censure. Frequently in serious Elizabethan plays, the dramatist would include a comic under-plot which had little connection with the main plot. This inclusion was for the benefit of the groundlings who, it was thought, could take only so much seriousness without becoming bored and boisterous. This under-plot can often be almost lifted from the play without particularly damaging the main action. In such cases, we do not have a true or successful tragicomedy, for the under-plot is not integral, not really necessary. In Aristotle's words, it is not "so arranged that . . . being transposed, or taken away, the whole would become different and changed." These plays were only tragedies plus comedies. Their parts were merely mixed in the same way that cartoons on a movie bill or advertisements in a television show simply come between, but have no connection with, the main business.

But we have noticed in *King Lear* how an under-plot may be integral, and how the character of a clown in a tragedy may actually enhance the play's tragic nature. In *Lear* the under-plot of Gloucester contributed to the sense of range and comprehension, as if the whole world were included in the evil of the main action. At the same time the Fool with his ironically appropriate remarks served to define the madness of the supposedly sane characters.

Under-plot in *Lear* works the same way that extra plots work in tragicomedy. *Lear* itself is not a tragicomedy because the tragic action far outweighs the comic. The tragic action overpowers the comic incidents. Tragicomedy requires a balance among its tragic and comic elements that *Lear* does not have.

It requires a blending of comedy and tragedy in its ending, and such an ending *Lear* certainly does not have. Far from being "loose" like the Elizabethan "double-plot," tragicomedy must produce a precarious balance in its structure. The incidents of a tragicomic plot must be as tightly connected in their particular way as the closest knit Aristotelian plot is in its.

To understand tragicomedy's subtle effect, we must be especially alive to interconnections of characters and juxtapositions of scenes. Tragicomedy will have no "under-plot" or "double-plot," but several equal plots. And just as the Fool was an ironic device in *Lear,* so will one scene in tragicomedy ironically modify the effect of another by showing a different viewpoint of the same situation. Often one action, while causally unconnected to another which occurs at about the same time, will actually be a commentary on it. Often verbal echoes of a character on one side of the stage will comment upon what an unconnected character on the other side is doing. The effect of tragicomedy is mixed, alternating, and ironic. A good way to think of it is by Sean O'Casey's image of the varied colors and intensities of light as it is reflected from the prisms of a moving kaleidoscope.

As you can see, this is a fairly subtle effect, and this ironic plot structure is the most sophisticated that we have discussed. If a tragic plot might be pictured as a straight, ascending line, this plot may be pictured as perhaps a half a dozen lines which are connected at the beginning, which intersect and overlap bewilderingly in the middle, and which are again tied together at the end.

But don't be put off by the complexity of the form. Tragicomedy offers an abundance of successive delights. Its effect does not emerge from the ironic plot alone. The characterization, the language, and the delight and the horror of the unexpected, all of which you have met in tragedy and comedy, play their vital roles. If tragicomedy demands a special kind of attention, it repays you in a special kind of way. It merges the goat song of tragedy with the silvery laughter of comedy, while presiding over all is the sardonic smile of the goat-god Pan.

The Critics

THE TRAGICOMIC VISION

JOHN DRYDEN, from *An Essay of Dramatic Poesy:*

. . . As for their new way of mingling mirth with serious plot, I do not, with Lisideius, condemn the thing, though I cannot approve their manner of doing it. He tells us, we cannot so speedily recollect ourselves after a scene of great passion and concernment, as to pass to another of mirth and humour, and to enjoy it with any relish: but why should he imagine the soul of man more heavy than his senses? Does not the eye pass from an unpleasant object to a pleasant in a much shorter time than is required to this? and does not the unpleasantness of the first commend the beauty of the latter? The old rule of logic might have convinced him, that contraries, when placed near, set off each other. A continued gravity keeps the spirit too much bent; we must refresh it sometimes, as we bait in a journey that we may go on with greater ease. A scene of mirth, mixed with tragedy, has the same effect upon us which our music has betwixt the acts; which we find a relief to us from the best plots and language of the stage, if the discourses have been long. I must therefore have stronger arguments, ere I am convinced that compassion and mirth in the same subject destroy each other; and in the meantime cannot but conclude, to the honour of our nation, that we have invented, increased, and perfected a more pleasant way of writing for the stage, than was ever known to the ancients or moderns of any nation, which is tragicomedy.

SAMUEL JOHNSON, from *The Rambler*, No. 156:

I know not whether he who professes to regard no other laws than those of nature, will not be inclined to receive tragi-comedy to his protection, whom, however generally condemned, her own laurels have hitherto shaded from the fulminations of criticism. For what is there in the mingled drama which impartial reason can condemn? The connection of important with trivial incidents, since it is not only common but perpetual in the world, may surely be allowed on the stage, which pretends only to be the mirror of life. The impropriety of suppressing passions before we have raised them to the intended agitation, and of diverting the expectation from an event which we keep suspended only to raise it, may be speciously urged. But will not experience show this objection to be rather subtle than just? Is it not certain that the tragic and comic affections have been moved alternately with equal force, and that no plays have oftener filled the eye with tears, and the heart with palpitation, than those which are variegated with interludes of mirth?

I do not, however, think it safe to judge of works of genius merely by the event. The resistless vicissitudes of the heart, this alternate prevalence of merriment and solemnity, may sometimes be more properly ascribed to the vigor of the writer than the justness of the design; and, instead of vindicating tragi-comedy by the success of Shakespeare, we ought, perhaps, to pay new honors to that transcendent and unbounded genius that could preside over the passions in sport; who, to actuate the affections, needed not the slow gradation of common means, but could fill the heart with instantaneous jollity or sorrow, and vary our disposition as he changed his scenes. Perhaps the effects even of Shakespeare's poetry might have been yet greater, had he not counteracted himself; and we might even have been more interested in the distresses of his heroes, had we not been so frequently diverted by the jokes of his buffoons.

SAMUEL JOHNSON, from *Preface to Shakespeare:*

The censure which he has incurred by mixing comick and tragick scenes, as it extends to all his works, deserves more consideration. Let the fact be first stated, and then examined.

Shakespeare's plays are not in the rigorous and critical sense either tragedies or comedies, but compositions of a distinct kind; exhibiting the real state of sublunary nature, which partakes of good and evil, joy and sorrow, mingled with endless variety of proportion and innumerable modes of combination; and expressing the course of the world, in which the loss of one is the gain of another; in which, at the same time, the reveller is hasting to his wine, and the mourner burying his friend; in which the malignity of one is sometimes defeated by the frolick of another; and many mischiefs and many benefits are done and hindered without design.

Out of this chaos of mingled purposes and casualties the ancient poets, according to the laws which custom had prescribed, selected some the crimes of men, and some their absurdities; some the momentous vicissitudes of life, and some the lighter occurrences; some the terrours of distress, and some the gayeties of prosperity. Thus rose the two modes of imitation, known by the names of *tragedy* and *comedy,* compositions intended to promote different ends by contrary means, and considered as so little allied, that I do not recollect among the *Greeks* or *Romans* a single writer who attempted both.

Shakespeare has united the powers of exciting laughter and sorrow not only in one mind, but in one composition. Almost all his plays are divided between serious and ludicrous characters, and, in the successive evolutions of the design, sometimes produce seriousness and sorrow, and sometimes levity and laughter.

That this is a practice contrary to the rules of criticism will be readily allowed; but there is always an appeal open from criticism to nature. The end of writing is to instruct; the end of poetry is to instruct by pleasing. That the mingled drama may convey all the instruction of tragedy or comedy cannot be denied, because it includes both in its alterations of exhibition and approaches nearer than either to the appearance of life, by shewing how great machinations and slender designs may promote or obviate one another, and the high and the low co-operate in the general system by unavoidable concatenation.

It is objected, that by this change of scenes the passions are interrupted in their progression, and that the principal event, being not advanced by a due gradation of preparatory incidents, wants at last the power to move, which constitutes the perfection of dramatick poetry. This reasoning is so specious, that it is received as true even by those who in daily experience feel it to be false. The interchanges of mingled scenes seldom fail to produce the intended vicissitudes of passion. Fiction cannot move so much, but that the attention may be easily transferred; and though it must be allowed that pleasing melancholy be sometimes interrupted by unwelcome levity, yet let it be considered likewise, that melancholy is often not pleasing, and that the disturbance of one man may be the relief of another; that different auditors have different habitudes; and that, upon the whole, all pleasure consists in variety.

SEAN O'CASEY, from *Letters to a Randolph-Macon Senior:*

As for blending "Comedy with Tragedy," it's no new practice—hundreds have done it, including Shakespeare up to Dion Boucicault in, for instance, "Colleen Bawn" and "Conn, the Shaughraun." And, indeed, Life is always doing it, doing it, doing it. Even where one lies dead, laughter is often heard in the next room. There's no tragedy that isn't tinged with humour, no comedy that hasn't its share of tragedy—if one has eyes to see, ears to hear. Sorrow and Joy are sisters, though Joy isn't always Joy or Sorrow Sorrow; they change appearance often and rapidly.

SEAN O'CASEY, from *The Green Crow:*

. . . it isn't the question of the goodness or badness of a play that is the more important thing; it is the going back on the idea that the drama must change and develop a new outlook, a broader scope, and a fresh style, if it is to live as an art alongside the art of architecture, of painting, and of music. In my opinion, the time has passed for a drama to devote its expression to one aspect of life alone, and to consider that aspect of life as dominant for the time the play takes to unfold itself; that in one play one aspect of life must be the beginning, the middle, and the end of it. Consistency of mood and of manner isn't always, indeed, not even often, found in life,

and why should it then be demanded in a play? This new aspect of playwriting which puzzled audiences here in 1929—and some of the critics too —is now puzzling the Dublin critics in 1947, and provoking them to anger and tears. What angers most of them, however, is that it hasn't been altogether a failure. A jewel moved about in the hand shows many flashes of light and color; and the human life moved about by circumstances of tragedy and comedy shows more than many flashes of diversity in the unity of its many-sided nature. Of course, a great play may be written around one aspect of life, but it doesn't follow that this must be the one way forever in which dramatists are to show life on the stage to those interested in the theatre. Not of course that a fine play, or even a great play, may not again be written by a newer dramatist in the "realistic" manner; but it will need to be a fine one to lift itself from the sameness of the tens of thousands of realistic or naturalistic plays that have gone before it. . . . Dramatists cannot go on imitating themselves, and, when they get tired of that, imitating others. They must change, must experiment, must develop their powers, or try to, if the drama is to live.

EUGENE M. WAITH, from *The Pattern of Tragicomedy in Beaumont and Fletcher:*

An iconographical representation of tragicomedy appears on the title page of the 1616 Folio of Ben Jonson's *Workes.* Although there is no tragicomedy among the plays in this volume, the figure of *Tragicomoedia* stands at the top of the page on the highest level of a baroque façade which seems to symbolize the drama. At the base are the *plaustrum,* the cart in which the first actors are said to have traveled, and the *visorium,* where they acted; higher up is the more modern *theatrum.* In niches to the left and right of the title stand *Tragoedia* and *Comoedia,* each attired in her traditional robes, and in much smaller niches above are the diminutive figures of the tutelary gods Bacchus and Apollo. Tragicomoedia, in an incongruous assortment of the clothes of her elder sisters, seems to preside over the entire fabric of the drama, as she faces eagerly forward, poised on a scroll in front of a niche which she has clearly outgrown. Seated below her, to the left and right of the theatrum, are two figures who turn toward her as if in token of some special relationship. One has goat's legs and a long stave and plays on a syrinx; the other, dressed with the rustic elegance of sixteenth-century Arcadia, has a crook and plays on a shepherd's pipe. These attendants of Tragicomoedia would easily be recognized even without their labels of *Satyr* and *Pastor.*

The presence of Tragicomedy on this title page is not so surprising as it seems at first glance. That Jonson was not the rigid classicist he is sometimes thought to be, and did not view with alarm such relatively new forms as tragicomedy, is shown by a familiar passage from the Induction to *Every Man Out of His Humor,* where Cordatus, after referring to the innovations of Menander, Plautus, and others, concludes with these words: "I see not then, but we should enjoy the same licence, or free power, to illustrate and heighten our invention as they

did; and not bee tyed to those strict and regular formes, which the nicenesse of a few (who are nothing but forme) would thrust upon us." (ll. 266–70.) Furthermore, Jonson not only read and criticized Guarini's pastoral tragicomedy *Il Pastor Fido* but commented to Drummond that Fletcher's *The Faithful Shepherdess* was "a Tragicomedie well done." It is possible that Fletcher's play was responsible for Jonson's interest in this form, or that Jonson, following his own critical principles, urged his young friend to experiment. Thus the title page may be one slight indication of the important relationship between the older and the younger dramatist.

From Tragicomedy's lofty position on the title page we may legitimately conclude that for some critics in 1616 this hybrid was the highest achievement of the drama. We see also that a definite relationship is assumed between Tragicomedy and certain other allegorical figures. The clothing, a combination of what Tragedy and Comedy wear, shows—what Fletcher implies—that the nature of Tragicomedy is a blend of the natures of these two; at the same time the figure of Tragicomedy has an expression, a stance, a gesture all her own. As for the serenading Satyr and Shepherd, they are traditional characters in pastoral, whose conventions often enter into tragicomedy, as they do in *Il Pastor Fido* and *The Faithful Shepherdess.* It is obvious that this gaily dressed Shepherd is, as Fletcher says, no more "hireling" but a gentleman-shepherd, such as "all the ancient poets" portray. The Satyr, of whom Fletcher says nothing, belongs not only in pastoral but also in the Greek satyr play. Satyr and shepherd are fully as important as tragedy and comedy in determining the nature of Fletcherian tragicomedy. The significance of the satyr, never properly appreciated, can best be approached through Renaissance critical theory.

THE TRAGICOMIC STRUCTURE

GIRALDI CINTHIO, from *The Composition of Comedies and Tragedies:*

And here it should be realized that, although double Tragedies are little admired by Aristotle—although some critics disagree—a double structure is nevertheless admirable in Comedy and has made Terence's plays wonderfully successful. I define a double plot as one which has different kinds of characters from the same station in life— that is, two young lovers of different character, two old men of diverse dispositions, two servants of opposite morals, and so on. Just as may be seen in the *Andria* and other plays by Terence, where obviously similar individuals of dissimilar habits make the intrigue and the unravelling of the plot very pleasant. I believe that if this structure should be incorporated in a Tragedy by a good poet, and the intricate action arranged so that its solution is not confusing, then the double structure would be as pleasing in Tragedy—*pace* Aristotle—as it is in Comedy. If some have favored this method and disagreed with Aristotle, they are not really to be blamed, especially if the Tragedy has a happy ending; for such an ending is much like Comedy, and such a Tragedy resembles Comedy in its structure.

EDITORS' TRANSLATION.

GIAMBATTISTA GUARINI, from *The Compendium of Tragicomic Poetry:*

There are two ways in which it can be said that my drama of the *Pastor Fido* does not observe the precept of unity: first, that it contains two forms, the tragic and the comic; second, that it has more than one subject like most of the plays of Terence. To make our argument more convenient and clear, let us call the first way "mixed" and the second "grafted." Concerning the first, it must be considered that tragicomedy is not composed of two entire plots, one of which is a perfect tragedy and the other a perfect comedy, linked together so that they can be separated without harming either. Nor should anyone think that it is a tragic story vitiated by comic baseness or a comic fable contaminated by tragic deaths, for neither of these would be a proper component. The tragicomic writer does not intend to compose separately either a Tragedy or a Comedy, but from mingling of the two a third thing perfect of its kind. He will take from the others the parts that can stand together with the greatest verisimilitude. Consequently, in judging it, one need not confound the terms of "mixed" and "double," as do those of little intelligence, who fail to realize that nothing is mixed if it is not one, and if its separate parts are not so mingled that one cannot be recognized alone or separated from another.

EDITORS' TRANSLATION.

JOHN DRYDEN, from *An Essay of Dramatic Poesy:*

. . . 'Tis very true . . . that one character in all plays, even without the poet's care, will have advantage of all the others; and that the design of the whole drama will chiefly depend on it. But this hinders not that there may be more shining characters in the play: many persons of a second magnitude, nay, some so very near, so almost equal to the first, that greatness may be opposed to greatness, and all the persons be made considerable, not only by their quality, but their action. 'Tis evident that the more the persons are, the greater will be the variety of the plot. If then the parts are managed so regularly, that the beauty of the whole be kept entire, and that the variety become not a perplexed and confused mass of accidents, you will find it infinitely pleasing to be led in a labyrinth of design, where you see some of your way before you, yet discern not the end till you arrive at it. And that all this is practicable, I can produce for examples many of our English plays: as *The Maid's Tragedy, The Alchemist, The Silent Woman.* . . .

WILLIAM EMPSON, from *Some Versions of Pastoral:*

It [the double plot] is an easy-going device, often used simply to fill out a play, and has an obvious effect in the Elizabethans of making you feel the play deals with life as a whole, with any one who comes onto the street the scene so often represents; this may be why criticism has not taken it seriously when it deserved to be. Just because of this carelessness much can be put into it; to those who miss the connections the thing still seems sensible, and queer connections can be insinuated powerfully and unobtrusively; especially if they fit in with ideas the audience already has at the back of its mind. The old quarrel about tragicomedy, which deals with part of the question, shows that the drama in England has always at its best had a certain looseness of structure; one might almost say that the English drama did not outlive the double plot. The matter is not only of theoretical interest; it seems likely that the double plot needs to be revived and must first be understood.

Probably the earliest form of double plot is the comic interlude, often in prose between serious verse scenes. Even here the relation between the two is neither obvious nor constant; the comic part relieves boredom and the strain of belief in the serious part, but this need not imply criticism of it. . . .

Usually it provides a sort of parody or parallel in low life to the serious part; Faustus' servant gets dangerously mixed up with the devils, like his master. This gives the impression of dealing with life completely. . . . Also, the play can thus anticipate the parody a hearer might have in mind without losing its dignity, which again has a sort of completeness. . . . A clear case of "foil" is given by the play of heroic swashbuckles which has a comic cowardly swashbuckler . . . , not at all to parody the heroes but to stop you from doing so: "If you want to laugh at this sort of thing laugh now and get it over." I believe the Soviet Government in its early days paid two clowns, Bim and Bom, to say as jokes the things everybody else would have been shot for saying.

THE TRAGICOMIC HERO

PAN, from *Lemprière's Classical Dictionary:*

Pan was the god of shepherds, of huntsmen, and of all the inhabitants of the country. He was the son of Mercury by Dryope, according to Homer. Some give him Jupiter and Callisto for parents, others Jupiter and Ybis or Oneis. Lucian and Hyginus assert that he was the son of Mercury and Penelope, the daughter of Icarius, and that the god under the form of a goat gained the affections of the princess, as she tended her father's flocks on mount Taygetus, before her marriage with the King of Ithaca. Some authors maintain that Penelope became mother of Pan during the absence of Ulysses in the Trojan war, and that he was the offspring of all the suitors that frequented the palace of Penelope, whence he received the name of *Pan,* which signifies *all* or *everything.* Pan was a monster in appearance; he had two small horns on his head, his complexion was ruddy, his nose flat, and his legs, thighs, tail, and feet were those of a goat. The education of Pan was entrusted to a nymph of Arcadia, called Sinoe, but the nurse, according to Homer, terrified at the sight of such a monster, fled away and left him. He was wrapped up in the skins of beasts by his father, and carried to heaven, where Jupiter and the gods long entertained themselves with the oddity of his appearance. Bacchus was greatly pleased with him, and gave him the name of Pan. The god of shepherds chiefly resided in Arcadia, where the woods and the most rugged mountains were his habitation. He invented the flute with seven reeds, which he called *Syrinx,* in honour of a beautiful nymph of the same name, to whom he attempted to offer violence, and who was changed into a reed. He was continually employed in deceiving the neighbouring nymphs, and often with success. Though deformed in his shape and features, yet he had the good fortune to captivate Diana, and of gaining her favour by transforming himself into a beautiful white goat. He was also enamoured of a nymph of the mountains called Echo, by whom he had a son called Lynx. He also paid his addresses to Omphale, queen of Lydia, and it is well known in what manner he was received. . . . The worship of Pan was well established, particularly in Arcadia, where he gave oracles on mount Lycaeus. His festivals, called by the Greeks *Lycaea,* were brought to Italy by Evander, and they were well known at Rome by the name of *Lupercalia.* . . . The worship, and the different functions of Pan, are derived from the mythology of the ancient Egyptians. This god was one of the eight great gods of the Egyptians, who ranked before the other twelve gods, whom the Romans called *Consentes.* He was worshipped with the greatest solemnity over all Egypt. His statues represented him as a goat, not because he was really such, but this was done for mysterious reasons. He was the emblem of fecundity, and they looked upon him as the principle of all things. His horns, as some observe, represented the rays of the sun, and the brightness of the heavens was expressed by the vivacity and the ruddiness of his complexion. The star which he wore on his breast was the symbol of the firmament, and his hairy legs and feet denoted the inferior parts of the earth, such as the woods and plants. Some suppose that he appeared as a goat because, when the gods fled into Egypt, in their war against the giants, Pan transformed himself into a goat, an example which was immediately followed by all the deities. Pan, according to some, is the same as Faunus, and he is the chief of all the Satyrs. Plutarch mentions that, in the reign of Tiberius, an extraordinary voice was heard near the Echinades, in the Ionian sea, which exclaimed that the great Pan was dead. This was readily believed by the emperor, and the astrologers were consulted; but they were unable to explain the meaning of so supernatural a voice, which probably proceeded from the imposition of one of the courtiers who attempted to terrify Tiberius. In Egypt, in the town of Mendes, which word also signifies a *goat*, there was a sacred goat kept with the most ceremonious sanctity. The death of this animal was always attended with the greatest solemnities, and, like that of another Apis, became the cause of universal mourning. As Pan usually terrified the inhabitants of the neighbouring country, that kind of fear which often seizes men, and which is only ideal and imaginary, has received from him the name of *panic fear*. This kind of terror has been exemplified not only in individuals, but in numerous armies, such as that of Brennus, which was thrown into the greatest consternation at Rome, without any cause or plausible reason.

LEWIS RICHARD FARNELL, from *The Cults of the Greek States:*

The ritual of Pan presents some features of interest. A well-known passage in the idylls of Theokritos informs us that in times of dearth, when the meat-supply was scanty, the Arcadian boys were in the habit of whipping the idol of the god with squills. As this plant was supposed to have a quickening and purifying effect, the object of this discipline was not punishment and insult, but stimulative magic whereby the life-giving power of the deity might be restored. Again, we have reason for thinking that the Pan-worship was orgiastic, and therefore specially attractive to women; we have a general statement to this effect, and Aristophanes at the beginning of the *Lysistrata* is sarcastic on the subject. We may suppose that the Attic cult was influenced by the Arcadian tradition, and we can better understand the women's enthusiasm for the herdsmen's god if we assume that Pan had associated himself early with the earth-goddess and the mother of the gods. And this assumption receives some support from the ode of Pindar and one record of Athenian ritual. The herdsmen of Arcadia, clad in goatskins as votaries of Pan, may have danced ritual-dances in spring to commemorate the awakening of the earth-goddess.

JANE ELLEN HARRISON, from *Prolegomena to the Study of Greek Religion:*

The *locus classicus* [1] on beating with leek is of course the beating of the god

[1] Classic instance. Eds.

Pan by his Arcadian worshippers. Theocritus makes Simichidas sing:

"Dear Pan, if this my prayer may granted be
Then never shall the boys of Arcady
Flog thee on back and flank with leeks that sting
When scanty meat is left for offering;
If not, thy skin with nails be flayed and torn
And amid nettles mayst thou couch till morn."

And the scholiast remarks, "they say that a festival was held in Arcadia in which the youths beat Pan with leeks when the officials sacrificed a small victim, and there was not enough to eat for the worshipper; or the Arcadians when they went out hunting if they had good sport paid honour to Pan; if the reverse they maltreated him with leeks because, being a mountain god, he had power over the produce of the chase." The first explanation confuses cause with effect, the second is undoubtedly right. Pan is beaten because, as lord of the chase, he has failed to do his business.

It is sometimes said that Pan is beaten, and the pharmakoi [2] beaten, in order to "stimulate their powers of fertility." In a sense this is ultimately true, but such a statement gives a false and misleading emphasis. The image and the pharmakoi are beaten partly to drive out evil influences, partly, it should not be forgotten, to relieve the feelings of the beaters. When the evil influences are beaten out, the god will undoubtedly do better next time, but it is only in this sense that the powers of fertility are stimulated. The pharmakos has no second

[2] Scapegoats. Eds.

chance. He is utterly impure, so that the more purifying influences, the more good medicine brought to bear upon him, the better; but he is doomed to death, not to reform. In the Lupercalia [3] . . . the women are struck by the *februm* [4] as a fertility charm, but even here the primary notion must have been the expulsion of evil influences. . . .

The Olympians concern themselves as little with the Before as with the Hereafter; they are not the source of life nor are they its goal. Moreover, another characteristic is that they are, with the strictest limitations, *human*. They are not one with the life that is in beasts and streams and woods as well as in man. Eros, "whose feet are on the flowers," who "couches in the folds," is all of life, he is Dionysos, he is Pan. Under Athenian influence Eros secludes himself into purely human form, but the Phanes of Orpheus was polymorphic, a beast-mystery god. . . .

In theology as in ritual, Orphism reverted to the more primitive forms, lending them deeper and intenser significance. These primitive forms, shifting and inchoate, were material more malleable than the articulate accomplished figures of the Olympians.

[3] Pan's festivals at Rome. See Lempriere above. Eds.
[4] Earlier in her book (p. 51), Harrison had cited Ovid's definition of the februm: ". . . he notes that the term was applied to many things, wool, a branch from a pine-tree, grain roasted with salt, and finally concludes that 'any thing by which the soul was purged was called by his rude ancestors *februum*.'" We might note the special connection of the branch from the pine-tree with Pan, for the nymph Pitys, when she fled from Pan, was changed into a pine-tree. Eds.

The conception of Phanes Protog-onos remained always somewhat eso-teric, a thing taught in mysteries, but his content is popularized in the figure of the goat-god who passed from being . . . the feeder, the shep-herd, to be . . . Pan the All-God.

Pan came to Athens after the Per-sian War, came at a time when scepti-cism was busy with the figures of the Olympians and their old prestige was on the wane. Pan of course had to have his reception into Olympus, and a derivation duly Olympian was found for his name. The Homeric Hymn, even if it be of Alexandrian date, is thoroughly Homeric in religious tone: the poet tells how

"Straight to the seats of the gods im-
    mortal did Hermes fare
With his child wrapped warmly up
    in skins of the mountain hare,
And down by the side of Zeus and
    the rest, he made him to sit,
And showed him that boy of his, and
    they all rejoiced at it.
But most of all Dionysos, the god of
    the Bacchanal,
And they called the name of him PAN
    because he delighted them ALL."

Dionysos the Bull-god and Pan the Goat-god both belong to early pre-anthropomorphic days, before man had cut the ties that bound him to the other animals; one and both they were welcomed as saviours by a tired humanity. Pan had no part in Orphic ritual, but in mythology as the All-god he is the popular reflection of Protogonos. He gave a soul of life and reality to a difficult monotheistic dogma, and the last word was not said in Greek religion, until over the mid-night sea a voice was heard crying "Great Pan is dead."

THE TRAGICOMIC STYLE

CICERO, from *The Orator:*

There are in all three styles of oratory, and some men have excelled in each, although very few have reached the ideal of excelling equally in all. The— if I may use the word—grandiloquent orators were full of grave thoughts and majestic words. They were strong, varied, full, and solemn, instructed and prepared to move and persuade men's minds. Some gained their effect by a hard, severe, harsh style, irregu-larly constructed and lacking smooth sentences. Others used an easy, regular sentence structure with a flowing rhythm. Completely opposed to them were the orators who were plain and clear, who fully explained everything and made each point crystal-clear rather than imposing. Some of this class were clever but unpolished, and purposely resembled untrained and maladroit speakers. Others had the same plainness of style, but were more correct and even very slightly ornate. There is a medium between these two styles, a tempered style which does not make the purely mental and logi-cal appeal of the latter or have the fiery and evocative strength of the former. It is similiar to both, but ex-cels in the qualities of neither. This style keeps the proverbial middle of the road, with ease and regularity, or at the most adding a few flowers of rhetoric, and varying the entire speech with simple decorations of thought and diction. . . .

The eloquent man . . . is able . . . to prove, to please, and to persuade.

To prove is a prime necessity, to please is a charm, and to persuade is a victory. . . . For these three oratorical functions there are three styles: the plain style for proof, the middle style for pleasure, and the vigorous style for persuasion. . . . The man who can utilize these three diverse styles altogether requires a rare discrimination and a great talent. . . . He must, moreover, consider what is appropriate in both thought and diction; for the same thoughts and the same diction cannot portray every condition in life, every rank, every social position, or every age. . . . The universal rule in oratory as well as in life is to pick the appropriate.

EDITORS' TRANSLATION.

BEN JONSON, from *Discoveries:* [1]

Some men are tall, and big, so some Language is high and great. Then the words are chosen, their sound ample, the composition full, the absolution plenteous and poured out, all grave, sinewy, and strong. Some are little, and Dwarfs: so of speech it is humble, and low, the words poor and flat; the members and Periods, thin and weak, without knitting, or number. The middle are of a just stature. There the Language is plain, and pleasing: even without stooping, round without swelling; all well-turned, composed, elegant, and accurate. . . . And according to their subject, these styles vary, and lose their names: For that which is high and lofty, declaring excellent matter, becomes vast and tumorous, speaking of petty and inferior things: so that which was even, and apt in a mean and plain subject,

[1] The spelling of this passage has been modernized. Eds.

will appear most poor and humble in a high Argument.

EUGENE M. WAITH, from *The Pattern of Tragicomedy in Beaumont and Fletcher:*

The pattern of tragicomedy which dominates the Beaumont and Fletcher plays imposes upon them a special language whose effect . . . is above all emotional. There are, of course, speeches whose sole purpose is to convey information, and others which define a character or present an idea, but the most memorable and distinctive speeches are the tirades, the laments, the defenses of honor, which contain the very life of Fletcherian tragicomedy. Therefore, a study of the genre culminates logically in an examination of this emotional language. . . .

To discuss poetic style from the point of view of rhetoric is to regard the poem as a means to elicit a certain response rather than to regard it, as we are more apt to do, as almost an end in itself—a living entity whose form gives unique expression to certain thoughts and feelings. Each method has its advantages. The Renaissance method is well suited to the study of dramatic poetry, especially when it is poetry of primarily emotional appeal, for this sort of poetry is good just to the extent that it creates its effect. Rhetorical analysis is singularly appropriate . . . in examining the language of Fletcherian tragicomedy. . . .

Although the style of Fletcherian tragicomedy is typically elaborate there are two reasons why it is not uniformly so. One is that the three styles distinguished by Cicero were thought not only to be conducive to three different effects but to be appropriate to three categories of speakers and of topics—the grand style for gods and princes and what concerns them (and hence for hymns, epics, and tragedies), the middle style for the "civiller and better sort" of citizens and their affairs (and hence for comedy), and the plain style for laborers of all kinds, including shepherds, and for "base and low matters" (and hence for pastoral and satire . . .). The decorum of tragicomedy, which is the inheritor of tragedy, epic (via romance), comedy, pastoral, and satire, properly makes room for every style. . . .

To an age more apt to admire understatement than exaggeration, to an age shy of dramatic poetry, to an age brought up on the notion that it is more artful to express strong emotion on the stage by the smallest visible gesture or the briefest outburst, the exuberant rhetoric of Beaumont and Fletcher has very little appeal. The conventions of realistic tragedy and comedy have led the modern theater audience to expect something totally unlike Fletcherian tragicomedy. In our times the attitudes necessary have become attached exclusively to other arts—to music, for example, and to painting. There the most dramatic contrasts, the boldest designs, the purest abstractions, the most powerful emotional stimuli are frankly acknowledged and admired. Only in ballet, in opera, and in the more recent "musical drama" do such techniques enter the theater. One may speculate that if a modern audience approached Beaumont and Fletcher with the expectations it has on going to the opera, it would find much to enjoy, for

it would accept the contrivance of the play more readily and would await the more declamatory passages as eagerly as the famous arias, duets, or quartets of grand opera.

THE TRAGICOMIC CHORUS

DAVID MAGARSHACK, from *Chekhov the Dramatist:*

The chorus element is another indispensable feature of the play of indirect-action.[1] In Greek drama it was a special actor, or groups of actors, who gave expression to the moral and religious sentiments evoked by the action of the play. In the French pseudo-classical drama it was again a special actor who was entrusted with the task of passing a moral judgment on the characters, known in the Russian early pseudo-classical plays as the *raisonneur,* a somewhat tedious character spouting conventional moral sentiments. But quite often in a modern indirect-action play the rôle of the chorus is divided up between several characters, who stand apart from the main characters and are not directly involved in the action. In a Chekhov play, however, it is the characters themselves who provide the moral judgment on the action, and in it the chorus element therefore becomes an integral part of the whole play, as Aristotle urged the Greek playwrights to make it. His characters, as it were, assume the mantle of the chorus whenever their inner life bursts through the outer shell of their everyday appearance and overflows into a torrent of

---

[1] Instead of Magarshack's term "play of indirect-action," we would say simply a tragicomedy. Eds.

words. It is this spontaneous and almost palpable transmutation into speech of hidden thoughts and deeply buried emotions that is perhaps the most subtle expression of dramatic action in a Chekhov play. If not treated as such, it is liable to transform these flashes of self-revelation into static, isolated and disconnected statements of opinion. It is important to remember that no other great classical Russian playwright has employed this method of revealing the "inner man" of his character and that the notion, which is so common in England and America, that the Chekhov characters express themselves in such a way because they are "Russians" is entirely mistaken. Chekhov himself offered a very clear indication of his use of the chorus element in the opening scene of *The Three Sisters*, a play in which it is predominant. Indeed, the scenery of the first act of the play was conceived by Chekhov in the form of a Greek theatre: he divided the stage into two parts separated by a colonnade, the front part representing a drawing-room and the back part a dining-room. There are six characters in the opening scene, divided into two groups, each keeping to its own part of the stage, the three sisters in front of the columns and Chebutykin, Tusenbach and Solyony behind the columns. Their dialogue, too, is conducted in a sort of strophe and antistrophe manner.

The Plays

THE THREE SISTERS

BY ANTON CHEKHOV

TRANSLATED BY ELISAVETA FEN

CHARACTERS [1]

PROZOROV, Andrey Serghyeevich [PROZ-orov, And-REY Sergh-YE-evich]

NATASHA (Natalia Ivanovna) [Na-TA-sha (Na-TA-lia I-VAN-ovna)], his fiancée, afterwards his wife

OLGA (Olga Serghyeevna, Olia) [O-lga Sergh-YE-evna, O-lia]

MASHA (Maria Serghyeevna) [MA-sha, Mar-I-a]   } his sisters

IRENA (Irena Serghyeevna) [I-RE-na]

KOOLYGHIN, Fiodor Ilyich [Kool-Y-ghin, Fi-O-dor Il-YICH], master at the High School for boys, husband of Masha

---

[1] The proper accentuation of each character's name is indicated in square brackets by capital letters. The editors wish to thank Professor Abraham Kreusler of Randolph-Macon Woman's College for his assistance with the pronunciation of Russian names in *The Three Sisters* and *Yegor Bulychov and the Others*.

VERSHININ, Alexandr Ignatyevich [Ver-SHIN-in, Alex-AN-dr Ig-NAT-yevich], Lieutenant-Colonel, Battery Commander

TOOZENBACH, Nikolai Lvovich [Toozen-BACH, Niko-LAI L-VO-vich], Baron, Lieutenant in the Army

SOLIONY, Vassily Vassilich [Sol-IO-ny, Vas-SI-ly Vas-SI-lich], Captain

CHEBUTYKIN, Ivan Romanych [Chebu-TY-kin, I-VAN Ro-MAN-ych], Army Doctor

FEDOTIK, Aleksey Petrovich [Fe-DO-tik, Alek-SEY Pet-RO-vich], Second Lieutenant

RODÉ, Vladimir Karlovich [RO-dé, Vla-DI-mir KARL-ovich], Second Lieutenant

FERAPONT (Ferapont Spiridonych) [Fera-PONT Spiri-DO-nych], an old porter from the County Office

ANFISA [An-FI-sa], the Prozorovs' former nurse, an old woman of 80

The action takes place in a county town.

ACT ONE

[*A drawing-room in the Prozorovs' house; it is separated from a large ballroom* [1] *at the back by a row of columns. It is midday; there is cheerful sunshine outside. In the ballroom the table is being laid for lunch. Olga, wearing the regulation dark-blue dress of a secondary school mistress, is correcting her pupils' work, standing or walking about as she does so. Masha, in a black dress, is sitting reading a book, her hat on her lap. Irena, in white, stands lost in thought.*]

OLGA. It's exactly a year ago that Father died, isn't it? This very day, the fifth of May—your Saint's day, Irena. I remember it was very cold and it was snowing. I felt then as if I should never survive his death; and you had fainted and were lying quite still, as if you were dead. And now— a year's gone by, and we talk about it so easily. You're wearing white, and your face is positively radiant. . . .

[1] A large room, sparsely furnished, used for receptions and dances in Russian houses.

[*A clock strikes twelve.*] The clock struck twelve then, too. [*A pause.*] I remember when Father was being taken to the cemetery there was a military band, and a salute with rifle fire. That was because he was a general, in command of a brigade. And yet there weren't many people at the funeral. Of course, it was raining hard, raining and snowing.

IRENA. Need we bring up all these memories?

[*Baron Toozenbach, Chebutykin and Soliony appear behind the columns by the table in the ballroom.*]

OLGA. It's so warm to-day that we can keep the windows wide open, and yet there aren't any leaves showing on the birch trees. Father was made a brigadier eleven years ago, and then he left Moscow and took us with him. I remember so well how everything in Moscow was in blossom by now, everything was soaked in sunlight and warmth. Eleven years have gone by, yet I remember everything about it, as if we'd only left yesterday. Oh, Heavens! When I woke up this morning and saw this flood of sunshine, all this spring sunshine, I felt so moved and so happy! I felt such a longing to get back home to Moscow!

CHEBUTYKIN. [To Toozenbach.] The devil you have!

TOOZENBACH. It's nonsense, I agree.

MASHA. [Absorbed in her book, whistles a tune under her breath.]

OLGA. Masha, do stop whistling! How can you? [A pause.] I suppose I must get this continual headache because I have to go to school every day and go on teaching right into the evening. I seem to have the thoughts of someone quite old. Honestly, I've been feeling as if my strength and youth were running out of me drop by drop, day after day. Day after day, all these four years that I've been working at the school. . . . I just have one longing and it seems to grow stronger and stronger. . . .

IRENA. If only we could go back to Moscow! Sell the house, finish with our life here, and go back to Moscow.

OLGA. Yes, Moscow! As soon as we possibly can.

[Chebutykin and Toozenbach laugh.]

IRENA. I suppose Andrey will soon get a professorship. He isn't likely to go on living here. The only problem is our poor Masha.

OLGA. Masha can come and stay the whole summer with us every year in Moscow.

MASHA. [Whistles a tune under her breath.]

IRENA. Everything will settle itself, with God's help. [Looks through the window.] What lovely weather it is to-day! Really, I don't know why there's such joy in my heart. I remembered this morning that it was my Saint's day, and suddenly I felt so happy, and I thought of the time when we were children, and Mother was still alive. And then such wonderful thoughts came to me, such wonderful stirring thoughts!

OLGA. You're so lovely to-day, you really do look most attractive. Masha looks pretty to-day, too. Andrey could be good-looking, but he's grown so stout. It doesn't suit him. As for me, I've just aged and grown a lot thinner. I suppose it's through getting so irritated with the girls at school. But to-day I'm at home, I'm free, and my headache's gone, and I feel much younger than I did yesterday. I'm only twenty-eight, after all. . . . I suppose everything that God wills must be right and good, but I can't help thinking sometimes that if I'd got married and stayed at home, it would have been a better thing for me. [A pause.] I would have been very fond of my husband.

TOOZENBACH. [To Soliony.] Really, you talk such a lot of nonsense, I'm tired of listening to you. [Comes into the drawing-room.] I forgot to tell you: Vershinin, our new battery commander, is going to call on you to-day. [Sits down by the piano.]

OLGA. I'm very glad to hear it.

IRENA. Is he old?

TOOZENBACH. No, not particularly. Forty, forty-five at the most. [Plays quietly.] He seems a nice fellow. Certainly not a fool. His only weakness is that he talks too much.

IRENA. Is he interesting?

TOOZENBACH. He's all right, only he's got a wife, a mother-in-law and two little girls. What's more, she's his second wife. He calls on everybody and tells them that he's got a wife and two little girls. He'll tell you about it, too, I'm sure of that. His wife seems to be a bit soft in the head. She wears a long plait like a girl, she is always philosophizing and talking in high-flown language, and then she often tries to commit suicide, apparently just to annoy her husband. I would have run away from a wife like that years ago, but he puts up with it, and just grumbles about it.

SOLIONY. [*Enters the drawing-room with Chebutykin.*] Now I can only lift sixty pounds with one hand, but with two I can lift two hundred pounds, or even two hundred and forty. So I conclude from that that two men are not just twice as strong as one, but three times as strong, if not more.

CHEBUTYKIN. [*Reads the paper as he comes in.*] Here's a recipe for falling hair . . . two ounces of naphthaline, half-a-bottle of methylated spirit . . . dissolve and apply once a day. . . . [*Writes it down in a notebook.*] Must make a note of it. [*To Soliony.*] Well, as I was trying to explain to you, you cork the bottle and pass a glass tube through the cork. Then you take a pinch of ordinary powdered alum, and . . .

IRENA. Ivan Romanych, dear Ivan Romanych!

CHEBUTYKIN. What is it, my child, what is it?

IRENA. Tell me, why is it I'm so happy to-day? Just as if I were sailing along in a boat with big white sails, and above me the wide, blue sky, and in the sky great white birds floating around?

CHEBUTYKIN. [*Kisses both her hands, tenderly.*] My little white bird!

IRENA. You know, when I woke up this morning, and after I'd got up and washed, I suddenly felt as if every-thing in the world had become clear to me, and I knew the way I ought to live. I know it all now, my dear Ivan Romanych. Man must work by the sweat of his brow whatever his class, and that should make up the whole meaning and purpose of his life and happiness and contentment. Oh, how good it must be to be a workman, getting up with the sun and breaking stones by the roadside—or a shepherd —or a schoolmaster teaching the children—or an engine-driver on the railway. Good Heavens! it's better to be a mere ox or horse, and work, than the sort of young woman who wakes up at twelve, and drinks her coffee in bed, and then takes two hours dressing. . . . How dreadful! You know how you long for a cool drink in hot weather? Well, that's the way I long for work. And if I don't get up early from now on and really work, you can refuse to be friends with me any more, Ivan Romanych.

CHEBUTYKIN. [*Tenderly.*] So I will, so I will. . . .

OLGA. Father taught us to get up at seven o'clock and so Irena always wakes up at seven—but then she stays in bed till at least nine, thinking about something or other. And with such a serious expression on her face, too! [*Laughs.*]

IRENA. You think it's strange when I look serious because you always think of me as a little girl. I'm twenty, you know!

TOOZENBACH. All this longing for work. . . . Heavens! how well I can understand it! I've never done a stroke of work in my life. I was born in Petersburg, an unfriendly, idle city—born into a family where work and worries were simply unknown. I remember a valet pulling off my boots for me when I came home from the cadet school. . . . I grumbled at the way he did it, and my mother looked on in admiration. She was quite surprised when other people looked at me in any other way. I was so carefully protected from work! But I doubt whether they succeeded in protecting me for good and all—yes, I doubt it very much! The time's come: there's a terrific thunder-cloud advancing upon us, a mighty storm is coming to freshen us up! Yes, it's coming all right, it's quite near already, and it's going to blow away all this idleness and indifference, and prejudice against work, this rot of boredom that our society is suffering from. I'm going to work, and in twenty-five or thirty years' time every man and woman will be working. Every one of us!

CHEBUTYKIN. I'm not going to work.

TOOZENBACH. You don't count.

SOLIONY. In twenty-five years' time you won't be alive, thank goodness. In a couple of years you'll die from a stroke—or I'll lose my temper with you and put a bullet in your head, my good fellow. [*Takes a scent bottle from his pocket and sprinkles the scent over his chest and hands.*]

CHEBUTYKIN. [*Laughs.*] It's quite true that I never have done any work. Not a stroke since I left the university. I haven't even read a book, only newspapers. [*Takes another newspaper out of his pocket.*] For instance, here. . . . I know from the paper that there was a person called Dobroliubov, but what he wrote about I've not the faintest idea. . . . God alone knows. . . . [*Someone knocks on the floor from downstairs.*] There! They're calling me to come down: there's someone come

to see me. I'll be back in a moment. . . . [*Goes out hurriedly, stroking his beard.*]

IRENA. He's up to one of his little games.

TOOZENBACH. Yes. He looked very solemn as he left. He's obviously going to give you a present.

IRENA. I do dislike that sort of thing. . . .

OLGA. Yes, isn't it dreadful? He's always doing something silly.

MASHA. "A green oak grows by a curving shore, And round that oak hangs a golden chain" . . . [*Gets up as she sings under her breath.*]

OLGA. You're sad to-day, Masha.

MASHA. [*Puts on her hat, singing.*]

OLGA. Where are you going?

MASHA. Home.

IRENA. What a strange thing to do.

TOOZENBACH. What! Going away from your sister's party?

MASHA. What does it matter? I'll be back this evening. Good-bye, my darling. [*Kisses Irena.*] And once again— I wish you all the happiness in the world. In the old days when Father was alive we used to have thirty or forty officers at our parties. What gay parties we had! And to-day —what have we got to-day? A man and a half, and the place is as quiet as a tomb. I'm going home. I'm depressed to-day, I'm sad, so don't listen to me. [*Laughs through her tears.*] We'll have a talk later, but good-bye for now, my dear. I'll go somewhere or other. . . .

IRENA. [*Displeased.*] Really, you are a . . .

OLGA. [*Tearfully.*] I understand you, Masha.

SOLIONY. If a man starts philosophizing, you call that philosophy, or possibly just sophistry, but if a woman or a couple of women start philosophizing you call that . . . what would you call it, now? Ask me another!

MASHA. What are you talking about? You are a disconcerting person!

SOLIONY. Nothing.
"He had no time to say 'Oh, oh!'
Before that bear had struck him low" . . .

[*A pause.*]

MASHA. [*To Olga, crossly.*] Do stop snivelling!

[*Enter Anfisa and Ferapont, the latter carrying a large cake.*]

ANFISA. Come along, my dear, this way. Come in, your boots are quite clean. [*To Irena.*] A cake from Protopopov, at the Council Office.

IRENA. Thank you. Tell him I'm very grateful to him. [*Takes the cake.*]

FERAPONT. What's that?

IRENA. [*Louder.*] Tell him I sent my thanks.

OLGA. Nanny, will you give him a piece of cake? Go along, Ferapont, they'll give you some cake.

FERAPONT. What's that?

ANFISA. Come along with me, Ferapont Spiridonych, my dear. Come along. [*Goes out with Ferapont.*]

MASHA. I don't like that Protopopov fellow, Mihail Potapych, or Ivanych, or whatever it is. It's best not to invite him here.

IRENA. I haven't invited him.

MASHA. Thank goodness.

[*Enter Chebutykin followed by a soldier carrying a silver samovar. Murmurs of astonishment and displeasure.*]

OLGA. [*Covering her face with her hands.*] A samovar! But this is dreadful! [*Goes through to the ballroom and stands by the table.*]

IRENA. My dear Ivan Romanych,

what are you thinking about?

TOOZENBACH. [*Laughs.*] Didn't I tell you?

MASHA. Ivan Romanych, you really ought to be ashamed of yourself!

CHEBUTYKIN. My dear, sweet girls, I've no one in the world but you. You're dearer to me than anything in the world! I'm nearly sixty, I'm an old man, a lonely, utterly unimportant old man. The only thing that's worth anything in me is my love for you, and if it weren't for you, really I would have been dead long ago. [*To Irena.*] My dear, my sweet little girl, haven't I known you since the very day you were born? Didn't I carry you about in my arms? . . . didn't I love your dear mother?

IRENA. But why do you get such expensive presents?

CHEBUTYKIN. [*Tearfully and crossly.*] Expensive presents! . . . Get along with you! [*To the orderly.*] Put the samovar over there. [*Mimics Irena.*] Expensive presents!

[*The orderly takes the samovar to the ballroom.*]

ANFISA. [*Crosses the drawing-room.*] My dears, there's a strange colonel just arrived. He's taken off his coat and he's coming up now. Irenushka, do be nice and polite to him, won't you? [*In the doorway.*] And it's high time we had lunch, too. . . . Oh, dear! [*Goes out.*]

TOOZENBACH. It's Vershinin, I suppose.

[*Enter Vershinin.*]

TOOZENBACH. Lieutenant-Colonel Vershinin!

VERSHININ. [*To Masha and Irena.*] Allow me to introduce myself—Lieutenant-Colonel Vershinin. I'm so glad, so very glad to be here at last. How you've changed! Dear, dear, how you've changed!

IRENA. Please, do sit down. We're very pleased to see you, I'm sure.

VERSHININ. [Gaily.] I'm so glad to see you, so glad! But there were three of you, weren't there?—three sisters. I remember there were three little girls. I don't remember their faces, but I knew your father, Colonel Prozorov, and I remember he had three little girls. Oh, yes, I saw them myself. I remember them quite well. How time flies! Dear, dear, how it flies!

TOOZENBACH. Alexandr Ignatyevich comes from Moscow.

IRENA. From Moscow? You come from Moscow?

VERSHININ. Yes, from Moscow. Your father was a battery commander there, and I was an officer in the same brigade. [To Masha.] I seem to remember your face a little.

MASHA. I don't remember you at all.

IRENA. Olia, Olia! [Calls towards the ballroom.] Olia, do come!

[Olga enters from the ballroom.]

IRENA. It seems that Lieutenant-Colonel Vershinin comes from Moscow.

VERSHININ. You must be Olga Serghyeevna, the eldest. And you are Maria. . . . And you are Irena, the youngest. . . .

OLGA. You come from Moscow?

VERSHININ. Yes. I studied in Moscow and entered the service there. I stayed there quite a long time, but then I was put in charge of a battery here—so I moved out here, you see. I don't really remember you, you know, I only remember that there were three sisters. I remember your father, though, I remember him very well. All I need to do is close my eyes and I can see him standing there as if he were alive. I used to visit you in Moscow.

OLGA. I thought I remembered everybody, and yet . . .

VERSHININ. My Christian names are Alexandr Ignatyevich.

IRENA. Alexandr Ignatyevich, and you come from Moscow! Well, what a surprise!

OLGA. We're going to live there, you know.

IRENA. We hope to be there by the autumn. It's our home town, we were born there. . . . In Staraya Basmannaya Street. [Both laugh happily.]

MASHA. Fancy meeting a fellow townsman so unexpectedly! [Eagerly.] I remember now. Do you remember, Olga, there was someone they used to call "the lovesick Major"? You were a Lieutenant then, weren't you, and you were in love with someone or other, and everyone used to tease you about it. They called you "Major" for some reason or other.

VERSHININ. [Laughs.] That's it, that's it. . . . "The lovesick Major," that's what they called me.

MASHA. In those days you only had a moustache. . . . Oh, dear, how much older you look! [Tearfully.] How much older!

VERSHININ. Yes, I was still a young man in the days when they called me "the lovesick Major." I was in love then. It's different now.

OLGA. But you haven't got a single grey hair! You've aged, yes, but you're certainly not an old man.

VERSHININ. Nevertheless, I'm turned forty-two. Is it long since you left Moscow?

IRENA. Eleven years. Now what are you crying for, Masha, you funny girl? . . . [Tearfully.] You'll make me cry, too.

MASHA. I'm not crying. What was the street you lived in?

VERSHININ. In the Staraya Basmannaya.

OLGA. We did, too.

VERSHININ. At one time I lived in the Niemietzkaya Street. I used to walk from there to the Krasny Barracks, and I remember there was such a gloomy bridge I had to cross. I used to hear the noise of the water rushing under it. I remember how lonely and sad I felt there. [A pause.] But what a magnificently wide river you have here! It's a marvellous river!

OLGA. Yes, but this is a cold place. It's cold here, and there are too many mosquitoes.

VERSHININ. Really? I should have said you had a really good healthy climate here, a real Russian climate. Forest, river . . . birch-trees, too. The dear, unpretentious birch-trees— I love them more than any of the other trees. It's nice living here. But there's one rather strange thing, the station is fifteen miles from the town. And no one knows why.

SOLIONY. I know why it is. [Everyone looks at him.] Because if the station were nearer, it wouldn't be so far away, and as it is so far away, it can't be nearer. [An awkward silence.]

TOOZENBACH. You like your little joke, Vassily Vassilich.

OLGA. I'm sure I remember you now. I know I do.

VERSHININ. I knew your mother.

CHEBUTYKIN. She was a good woman, God bless her memory!

IRENA. Mamma was buried in Moscow.

OLGA. At the convent of Novo-Dievichye.

MASHA. You know, I'm even beginning to forget what she looked like. I suppose people will lose all memory of us in just the same way. We'll be forgotten.

VERSHININ. Yes, we shall all be forgotten. Such is our fate, and we can't do anything about it. And all the things that seem serious, important and full of meaning to us now will be forgotten one day—or anyway they won't seem important any more. [A pause.] It's strange to think that we're utterly unable to tell what will be regarded as great and important in the future and what will be thought of as just paltry and ridiculous. Didn't the great discoveries of Copernicus—or of Columbus, if you like—appear useless and unimportant to begin with?— whereas some rubbish, written up by an eccentric fool, was regarded as a revelation of great truth? It may well be that in time to come the life we live to-day will seem strange and uncomfortable and stupid and not too clean, either, and perhaps even wicked. . . .

TOOZENBACH. Who can tell? It's just as possible that future generations will think that we lived our lives on a very high plane and remember us with respect. After all, we no longer have tortures and public executions and invasions, though there's still a great deal of suffering!

SOLIONY. [In a high-pitched voice as if calling to chickens.] Cluck, cluck, cluck! There's nothing our good Baron loves as much as a nice bit of philosophizing.

TOOZENBACH. Vassily Vassilich, will you kindly leave me alone? [Moves to another chair.] It's becoming tiresome.

SOLIONY. [As before.] Cluck, cluck, cluck! . . .

TOOZENBACH. [To Vershinin.] The suffering that we see around us—and there's so much of it—itself proves that our society has at least achieved a level of morality which is higher. . . .

VERSHININ. Yes, yes, of course.

CHEBUTYKIN. You said just now, Baron, that our age will be called great; but people are small all the same. . . . [Gets up.] Look how small I am.

[A violin is played off stage.]

MASHA. That's Andrey playing the violin; he's our brother, you know.

IRENA. We've got quite a clever brother. . . . We're expecting him to be a professor. Papa was a military man, but Andrey chose an academic career.

OLGA. We've been teasing him to-day. We think he's in love, just a little.

IRENA. With a girl who lives down here. She'll be calling in to-day most likely.

MASHA. The way she dresses herself is awful! It's not that her clothes are just ugly and old-fashioned, they're simply pathetic. She'll put on some weird-looking, bright yellow skirt with a crude sort of fringe affair, and then a red blouse to go with it. And her cheeks look as though they've been scrubbed, they're so shiny! Andrey's not in love with her—I can't believe it; after all, he has got some taste. I think he's just playing the fool, just to annoy us. I heard yesterday that she's going to get married to Protopopov, the chairman of the local council. I thought it was an excellent idea. [Calls through the side door.] Andrey, come here, will you? Just for a moment, dear.

[Enter Andrey.]

OLGA. This is my brother, Andrey Serghyeevich.

VERSHININ. Vershinin.

ANDREY. Prozorov. [Wipes the perspiration from his face.] I believe you've been appointed battery commander here?

OLGA. What do you think, dear? Alexandr Ignatyevich comes from Moscow.

ANDREY. Do you, really? Congratulations! You'll get no peace from my sisters now.

VERSHININ. I'm afraid your sisters must be getting tired of me already.

IRENA. Just look, Andrey gave me this little picture frame to-day. [Shows him the frame.] He made it himself.

VERSHININ. [Looks at the frame, not knowing what to say.] Yes, it's . . . it's very nice indeed. . . .

IRENA. Do you see that little frame over the piano? He made that one, too.

[Andrey waves his hand impatiently and walks off.]

OLGA. He's awfully clever, and he plays the violin, and he makes all sorts of things, too. In fact, he's very gifted all round. Andrey, please, don't go. He's got such a bad habit—always going off like this. Come here!

[Masha and Irena take him by the arms and lead him back, laughing.]

MASHA. Now just you come here!

ANDREY. Do leave me alone, please do!

MASHA. You are a silly! They used to call Alexandr Ignatyevich "the lovesick Major," and he didn't get annoyed.

VERSHININ. Not in the least.

MASHA. I feel like calling you a "lovesick fiddler."

IRENA. Or a "lovesick professor."

OLGA. He's fallen in love! Our Andriusha's in love!

IRENA. [*Clapping her hands.*] Three cheers for Andriusha! Andriusha's in love!

CHEBUTYKIN. [*Comes up behind Andrey and puts his arms round his waist.*] "Nature created us for love alone." . . . [*Laughs loudly, still holding his paper in his hand.*]

ANDREY. That's enough of it, that's enough. . . . [*Wipes his face.*] I couldn't get to sleep all night, and I'm not feeling too grand just now. I read till four o'clock, and then I went to bed, but nothing happened. I kept thinking about one thing and another . . . and it gets light so early; the sun just pours into my room. I'd like to translate a book from the English while I'm here during the summer.

VERSHININ. You read English, then?

ANDREY. Yes. My father—God bless his memory—used to simply wear us out with learning. It sounds silly, I know, but I must confess that since he died I've begun to grow stout, as if I'd been physically relieved of the strain. I've grown quite stout in a year. Yes, thanks to Father, my sisters and I know French and German and English, and Irena here knows Italian, too. But what an effort it all cost us!

MASHA. Knowing three languages in a town like this is an unnecessary luxury. In fact, not even a luxury, but just a sort of useless encumbrance . . . it's rather like having a sixth finger on your hand. We know a lot of stuff that's just useless.

VERSHININ. Really! [*Laughs.*] You know a lot of stuff that's useless! It seems to me that there's no place on earth, however dull and depressing it may be, where intelligence and edu-

cation can be useless. Let us suppose that among the hundred thousand people in this town, all of them, no doubt, very backward and uncultured, there are just three people like yourselves. Obviously, you can't hope to triumph over all the mass of ignorance around you; as your life goes by, you'll have to keep giving in little by little until you get lost in the crowd, in the hundred thousand. Life will swallow you up, but you'll not quite disappear, you'll make some impression on it. After you've gone, perhaps six more people like you will turn up, then twelve, and so on, until in the end most people will have become like you. So in two or three hundred years life on this old earth of ours will have become marvellously beautiful. Man longs for a life like that, and if it isn't here yet, he must imagine it, wait for it, dream about it, prepare for it, he must know and see more than his father and his grandfather did. [*Laughs.*] And you're complaining because you know a lot of stuff that's useless.

MASHA. [*Takes off her hat.*] I'll be staying to lunch.

IRENA. [*With a sigh.*] Really, someone should have written all that down.

[*Andrey has left the room, unnoticed.*]

TOOZENBACH. You say that in time to come life will be marvellously beautiful. That's probably true. But in order to share in it now, at a distance so to speak, we must prepare for it and work for it.

VERSHININ. [*Gets up.*] Yes. . . . What a lot of flowers you've got here! [*Looks around.*] And what a marvellous house! I do envy you! All my life I seem to have been pigging it in small flats, with two chairs and a sofa and a stove which always smokes. It's the flowers that I've missed in my life, flowers like these! . . . [*Rubs his hands.*] Oh, well, never mind!

TOOZENBACH. Yes, we must work. I suppose you're thinking I'm a sentimental German. But I assure you I'm not—I'm Russian. I don't speak a word of German. My father was brought up in the Greek Orthodox faith. [*A pause.*]

VERSHININ. [*Walks up and down the room.*] You know, I often wonder what it would be like if you could start your life over again—deliberately, I mean, consciously. . . . Suppose you could put aside the life you'd lived already, as though it was just a sort of rough draft, and then start another one like a fair copy. If that happened, I think the thing you'd want most of all would be not to repeat yourself. You'd try at least to create a new environment for yourself, a flat like this one, for instance, with some flowers and plenty of light. . . . I have a wife, you know, and two little girls; and my wife's not very well, and all that. . . . Well, if I had to start my life all over again, I wouldn't marry. . . . No, no!

[*Enter Koolyghin, in the uniform of a teacher.*]

KOOLYGHIN. [*Approaches Irena.*] Congratulations, dear sister—from the bottom of my heart, congratulations on your Saint's day. I wish you good health and everything a girl of your age ought to have! And allow me to present you with this little book. . . . [*Hands her a book.*] It's the history of our school covering the whole fifty years of its existence. I wrote it myself. Quite a trifle, of course—I wrote it in my spare time when I had nothing better to do—but I hope you'll read it nevertheless. Good morning to you all! [*To Vershinin.*] Allow me to introduce myself. Koolyghin's the name; I'm a master at the secondary school here. And a town councillor. [*To Irena.*] You'll find a list in the book of all the pupils who have completed their studies at our school during the last fifty years. *Feci quod potui, faciant meliora potentes.* [*Kisses Masha.*]

IRENA. But you gave me this book last Easter!

KOOLYGHIN. [*Laughs.*] Did I really? In that case, give it me back—or no, better give it to the Colonel. Please do take it, Colonel. Maybe you'll read it some time when you've nothing better to do.

VERSHININ. Thank you very much. [*Prepares to leave.*] I'm so very glad to have made your acquaintance. . . .

OLGA. You aren't going are you? . . . Really, you mustn't.

IRENA. But you'll stay and have lunch with us! Please do.

OLGA. Please do.

VERSHININ. [*Bows.*] I see I've in-truded on your Saint's day party. I didn't know. Forgive me for not offering you my congratulations. [*Goes into the ballroom with Olga.*]

KOOLYGHIN. To-day is Sunday, my friends, a day of rest; let us rest and enjoy it, each according to his age and position in life! We shall have to roll up the carpets and put them away till the winter. . . . We must remember to put some naphthaline on them, or Persian powder. . . . The Romans enjoyed good health because they knew how to work *and* how to rest. They had *mens sana in corpore sano.*

Their life had a definite shape, a form. . . . The director of the school says that the most important thing about life is form. . . . A thing that loses its form is finished—that's just as true of our ordinary, everyday lives. [*Takes Masha by the waist and laughs.*] Masha loves me. My wife loves me. Yes, and the curtains will have to be put away with the carpets, too. . . . I'm cheerful to-day, I'm in quite excellent spirits. . . . Masha, we're invited to the director's at four o'clock to-day. A country walk has been arranged for the teachers and their families.

MASHA. I'm not going.

KOOLYGHIN. [*Distressed.*] Masha, darling, why not?

MASHA. I'll tell you later. . . . [*Crossly.*] All right, I'll come, only leave me alone now. . . . [*Walks off.*]

KOOLYGHIN. And after the walk we shall all spend the evening at the director's house. In spite of weak health, that man is certainly sparing no pains to be sociable. A first-rate, thoroughly enlightened man! A most excellent person! After the conference yesterday he said to me: "I'm tired, Fiodor Ilyich. I'm tired!" [*Looks at the clock, then at his watch.*] Your clock is seven minutes fast. Yes, "I'm tired," he said.

[*The sound of the violin is heard off stage.*]

OLGA. Will you all come and sit down, please! Lunch is ready. There's a pie.

KOOLYGHIN. Ah, Olga, my dear girl! Last night I worked up to eleven o'clock, and I felt tired, but to-day I'm quite happy.

[*Goes to the table in the ballroom.*]

My dear Olga!

CHEBUTYKIN. [*Puts the newspaper in his pocket and combs his beard.*] A pie? Excellent!

MASHA. [*Sternly to Chebutykin.*] Remember, you mustn't take anything to drink to-day. Do you hear? It's bad for you.

CHEBUTYKIN. Never mind. I've got over that weakness long ago! I haven't done any heavy drinking for two years. [*Impatiently.*] Anyway, my dear, what does it matter?

MASHA. All the same, don't you dare drink anything. Mind you don't now! [*Crossly, but taking care that her husband does not hear.*] So now I've got to spend another of these damnably boring evenings at the director's!

TOOZENBACH. I wouldn't go if I were you, and that's that.

CHEBUTYKIN. Don't you go, my dear.

MASHA. Don't go, indeed! Oh, what a damnable life! It's intolerable. . . . [*Goes into the ballroom.*]

CHEBUTYKIN. [*Follows her.*] Well, well! . . .

SOLIONY. [*As he passes Toozenbach on the way to the ballroom.*] Cluck, cluck, cluck!

TOOZENBACH. Do stop it, Vassily Vassilich. I've really had enough of it. . . .

SOLIONY. Cluck, cluck, cluck! . . .

KOOLYGHIN. [*Gaily.*] Your health, Colonel! I'm a schoolmaster . . . and I'm quite one of the family here, as it were. I'm Masha's husband. She's got a sweet nature, such a very sweet nature!

VERSHININ. I think I'll have a little of this dark vodka. [*Drinks.*] Your health! [*To Olga.*] I do feel so happy with you people!

[*Only Irena and Toozenbach re-*

main in the drawing-room.]

IRENA. Masha's a bit out of humour to-day. You know, she got married when she was eighteen, and then her husband seemed the cleverest man in the world to her. It's different now. He's the kindest of men, but not the cleverest.

OLGA. [*Impatiently.*] Andrey, will you please come?

ANDREY. [*Off stage.*] Just coming. [*Enters and goes to the table.*]

TOOZENBACH. What are you thinking about?

IRENA. Oh, nothing special. You know, I don't like this man Soliony, I'm quite afraid of him. Whenever he opens his mouth he says something silly.

TOOZENBACH. He's a strange fellow. I'm sorry for him, even though he irritates me. In fact, I feel more sorry for him than irritated. I think he's shy. When he's alone with me, he can be quite sensible and friendly, but in company he's offensive and bullying. Don't go over there just yet, let them get settled down at the table. Let me stay beside you for a bit. Tell me what you're thinking about. [*A pause.*] You're twenty . . . and I'm not thirty yet myself. What years and years we still have ahead of us, a whole long succession of years, all full of my love for you! . . .

IRENA. Don't talk to me about love, Nikolai Lvovich.

TOOZENBACH. [*Not listening.*] Oh, I long so passionately for life, I long to work and strive so much, and all this longing is somehow mingled with my love for you, Irena. And just because you happen to be beautiful, life appears beautiful to me! What are you thinking about?

IRENA. You say that life is beautiful. Maybe it is—but what if it only seems to be beautiful? Our lives, I mean the lives of us three sisters, haven't been beautiful up to now. The truth is that life has been stifling us, like weeds in a garden. I'm afraid I'm crying. . . . So unnecessary. . . . [*Quickly dries her eyes and smiles.*] We must work, work! The reason we feel depressed and take such a gloomy view of life is that we've never known what it is to make a real effort. We're the children of parents who despised work. . . .

[*Enter Natalia Ivanovna. She is wearing a pink dress with a green belt.*]

NATASHA. They've gone in to lunch already. . . . I'm late. . . . [*Glances at herself in a mirror, adjusts her dress.*] My hair seems to be all right. . . . [*Catches sight of Irena.*] My dear Irena Serghyeevna, congratulations! [*Gives her a vigorous and prolonged kiss.*] You've got such a lot of visitors. . . . I feel quite shy. . . . How do you do, Baron?

OLGA. [*Enters the drawing-room.*] Oh, there you are, Natalia Ivanovna! How are you, my dear? [*They kiss each other.*]

NATASHA. Congratulations! You've such a lot of people here, I feel dreadfully shy. . . .

OLGA. It's all right, they're all old friends. [*Alarmed, dropping her voice.*] You've got a green belt on! My dear, that's surely a mistake!

NATASHA. Why, is it a bad omen, or what?

OLGA. No, but it just doesn't go with your dress . . . it looks so strange. . . .

NATASHA. [*Tearfully.*] Really? But it isn't really green, you know, it's a sort of dull colour. . . . [*Follows Olga to the ballroom.*]

[*All are now seated at the table; the drawing-room is empty.*]

KOOLYGHIN. Irena, you know, I do wish you'd find yourself a good husband. In my view it's high time you got married.

CHEBUTYKIN. You ought to get yourself a nice little husband, too, Natalia Ivanovna.

KOOLYGHIN. Natalia Ivanovna already has a husband in view.

MASHA. [*Strikes her plate with her fork.*] A glass of wine for me, please! Three cheers for our jolly old life! We keep our end up, we do!

KOOLYGHIN. Masha, you won't get more than five out of ten for good conduct!

VERSHININ. I say, this liqueur's very nice. What is it made of?

SOLIONY. Black beetles!

IRENA. Ugh! ugh! How disgusting!

OLGA. We're having roast turkey for dinner to-night, and then apple tart. Thank goodness, I'll be here all day . . . this evening, too. You must all come this evening.

VERSHININ. May I come in the evening, too?

IRENA. Yes, please do.

NATASHA. They don't stand on ceremony here.

CHEBUTYKIN. "Nature created us for love alone." . . . [*Laughs.*]

ANDREY. [*Crossly.*] Will you stop it, please? Aren't you tired of it yet?

[*Fedotik and Rodé come in with a large basket of flowers.*]

FEDOTIK. Just look here, they're having lunch already!

RODÉ. [*In a loud voice.*] Having their lunch? So they are, they're having lunch already.

FEDOTIK. Wait half a minute. [*Takes a snapshot.*] One! Just one minute more! . . . [*Takes another snapshot.*] Two! All over now.

[*They pick up the basket and go into the ballroom where they are greeted uproariously.*]

RODÉ. [*Loudly.*] Congratulations, Irena Serghyeevna! I wish you all the best, everything you'd wish for yourself! Gorgeous weather to-day, absolutely marvellous. I've been out walking the whole morning with the boys. You do know that I teach gym at the high school, don't you? . . .

FEDOTIK. You may move now, Irena Serghyeevna, that is, if you want to. [*Takes a snapshot.*] You do look attractive to-day. [*Takes a top out of his pocket.*] By the way, look at this top. It's got a wonderful hum.

IRENA. What a sweet little thing!

MASHA. "A green oak grows by a curving shore, And round that oak hangs a golden chain." . . . A green chain around that oak. . . . [*Peevishly.*] Why do I keep on saying that? Those lines have been worrying me all day long!

KOOLYGHIN. Do you know, we're thirteen at table?

RODÉ. [*Loudly.*] You don't really believe in these old superstitions, do you? [*Laughter.*]

KOOLYGHIN. When thirteen people sit down to table, it means that some of them are in love. Is it you, by any chance, Ivan Romanych?

CHEBUTYKIN. Oh, I'm just an old sinner. . . . But what I can't make out is why Natalia Ivanovna looks so embarrassed.

[*Loud laughter. Natasha runs out into the drawing-room, Andrey follows her.*]

ANDREY. Please, Natasha, don't take any notice of them! Stop . . . wait a moment. . . . Please!

NATASHA. I feel so ashamed. . . . I don't know what's the matter with me, and they're all laughing at me. It's awful of me to leave the table like that, but I couldn't help it. . . . I just couldn't. . . . [*Covers her face with her hands.*]

ANDREY. My dear girl, please, please don't get upset. Honestly, they don't mean any harm, they're just teasing. My dear, sweet girl, they're really good-natured folks, they all are, and they're fond of us both. Come over to the window, they can't see us there. . . . [*Looks round.*]

NATASHA. You see, I'm not used to being with a lot of people.

ANDREY. Oh, how young you are, Natasha, how wonderfully, beautifully young! My dear, sweet girl, don't get so upset! Do believe me, believe me. . . . I'm so happy, so full of love, of joy. . . . No, they can't see us here! They can't see us! How did I come to love you, when was it? . . . I don't understand anything. My precious, my sweet, my innocent girl, please— I want you to marry me! I love you, I love you as I've never loved anybody. . . . [*Kisses her.*]

[*Enter two officers and, seeing Natasha and Andrey kissing, stand and stare in amazement.*]

ACT TWO

[*The scene is the same as in Act 1. It is eight o'clock in the evening. The faint sound of an accordion is heard coming from the street.*

The stage is unlit. Enter Natalia Ivanovna in a dressing-gown, carrying a candle. She crosses the stage and stops by the door leading to Andrey's room.]

NATASHA. What are you doing, Andriusha? Reading? It's all right, I only wanted to know. . . . [*Goes to another door, opens it, looks inside and shuts it again.*] No one's left a light anywhere. . . .

ANDREY. [*Enters with a book in his hand.*] What is it, Natasha?

NATASHA. I was just going round to see if anyone had left a light anywhere. It's carnival week, and the servants are so excited about it . . . anything might happen! You've got to watch them. Last night about twelve o'clock I happened to go into the dining-room, and—would you believe it?—there was a candle alight on the table. I've not found out who lit it. [*Puts the candle down.*] What time is it?

ANDREY. [*Glances at his watch.*] Quarter past eight.

NATASHA. And Olga and Irena still out. They aren't back from work yet, poor things! Olga's still at some teachers' conference, and Irena's at the post office. [*Sighs.*] This morning I said to Irena: "Do take care of yourself, my dear." But she won't listen. Did you say it was a quarter past eight? I'm afraid Bobik is not at all well. Why does he get so cold? Yesterday he had a temperature, but to-day he feels quite cold when you touch him. . . . I'm so afraid!

ANDREY. It's all right, Natasha. The boy's well enough.

NATASHA. Still, I think he ought to have a special diet. I'm so anxious about him. By the way, they tell me that some carnival party's supposed to be coming here soon after nine. I'd rather they didn't come, Andriusha.

ANDREY. Well, I really don't know what I can do. They've been asked to come.

NATASHA. This morning the dear little fellow woke up and looked at me, and then suddenly he smiled. He recognized me, you see. "Good morning, Bobik," I said, "good morning, darling precious!" And then he laughed. Babies understand everything, you know, they understand us perfectly well. Anyway, Andriusha, I'll tell the servants not to let that carnival party in.

ANDREY. [Irresolutely.] Well . . . it's really for my sisters to decide, isn't it? It's their house, after all.

NATASHA. Yes, it's their house as well. I'll tell them, too. . . . They're so kind. . . . [Walks off.] I've ordered sour milk for supper. The doctor says you ought to eat nothing but sour milk, or you'll never get any thinner. [Stops.] Bobik feels cold. I'm afraid his room is too cold for him. He ought to move into a warmer room, at least until the warm weather comes. Irena's room, for instance—that's just a perfect room for a baby: it's dry, and it gets the sun all day long. We must tell her: perhaps she'd share Olga's room for a bit. . . . In any case, she's never at home during the day, she only sleeps there. . . . [A pause.] Andriusha, why don't you say anything?

ANDREY. I was just day-dreaming. . . . There's nothing to say, anyway. . . .

NATASHA. Well. . . . What was it I was going to tell you? Oh, yes! Ferapont from the Council Office wants to see you about something.

ANDREY. [Yawns.] Tell him to come up.

[Natasha goes out. Andrey, bending over the candle which she has left behind, begins to read his book. Enter Ferapont in an old shabby overcoat, his collar turned up, his ears muffled in a scarf.]

ANDREY. Hullo, old chap! What did you want to see me about?

FERAPONT. The chairman's sent you the register and a letter or something. Here they are. [Hands him the book and the letter.]

ANDREY. Thanks. That's all right. Incidentally, why have you come so late? It's gone eight already.

FERAPONT. What's that?

ANDREY. [Raising his voice.] I said, why have you come so late? It's gone eight already.

FERAPONT. That's right. It was still daylight when I came first, but they wouldn't let me see you. The master's engaged, they said. Well, if you're engaged, you're engaged. I'm not in a hurry. [Thinking that Andrey has said something.] What's that?

ANDREY. Nothing. [Turns over the pages of the register.] Tomorrow's Friday, there's no meeting, but I'll go to the office just the same . . . do some work. I'm so bored at home! . . . [A pause.] Yes, my dear old fellow, how things do change, what a fraud life is! So strange! To-day I picked up this book, just out of boredom, because I hadn't anything to do. It's a copy of some lectures I attended at the University. . . . Good Heavens! Just think—I'm secretary of the local council now, and Protopopov's chairman, and the most I can ever hope for is to become a member of the council myself! I—a member of the local council! I, who dream every night that I'm a professor in Moscow University, a famous academician, the pride of all Russia!

FERAPONT. I'm sorry, I can't tell you. I don't hear very well.

ANDREY. If you could hear properly I don't think I'd be talking to you like this. I must talk to someone, but my wife doesn't seem to understand me, and as for my sisters . . . I'm afraid of them for some reason or other, I'm afraid of them laughing at me and pulling my leg. . . . I don't drink and I don't like going to pubs, but my word! how I'd enjoy an hour or so at Tyestov's, or the Great Moscow Restaurant! Yes, my dear fellow, I would indeed!

FERAPONT. The other day at the office a contractor was telling me about some business men who were eating pancakes in Moscow. One of them ate forty pancakes and died. It was either forty or fifty, I can't remember exactly.

ANDREY. You can sit in some huge restaurant in Moscow without knowing anyone, and no one knowing you; yet somehow you don't feel that you don't belong there. . . . Whereas here you know everybody, and everybody knows you, and yet you don't feel you belong here, you feel you don't belong at all. . . . You're lonely and you feel a stranger.

FERAPONT. What's that? [A pause.] It was the same man that told me— of course, he may have been lying—he said that there's an enormous rope stretched right across Moscow.

ANDREY. Whatever for?

FERAPONT. I'm sorry, I can't tell you. That's what he said.

ANDREY. What nonsense! [Reads the book.] Have you ever been to Moscow?

FERAPONT. [After a pause.] No. It wasn't God's wish. [A pause.] Shall I go now?

ANDREY. Yes, you may go. Good-bye. [Ferapont goes out.] Good-bye. [Reading.] Come in the morning to take some letters. . . . You can go now. [A pause.] He's gone. [A bell rings.] Yes, that's how it is. . . . [Stretches and slowly goes to his room.]

[Singing is heard off stage; a nurse is putting a baby to sleep. Enter Masha and Vershinin. While they talk together, a maid lights a lamp and candles in the ballroom.]

MASHA. I don't know. [A pause.] I don't know. Habit's very important, of course. For instance, after Father died, for a long time we couldn't get accustomed to the idea that we hadn't any orderlies to wait on us. But, habit apart, I think it's quite right what I was saying. Perhaps it's different in other places, but in this town the military certainly do seem to be the nicest and most generous and best-mannered people.

VERSHININ. I'm thirsty. I could do with a nice glass of tea.

MASHA. [Glances at her watch.] They'll bring it in presently. You see, they married me off when I was eighteen. I was afraid of my husband because he was a school-master, and I had only just left school myself. He seemed terribly learned then, very clever and important. Now it's quite different, unfortunately.

VERSHININ. Yes. . . . I see. . . .

MASHA. I don't say anything against my husband—I'm used to him now— but there are such a lot of vulgar and unpleasant and offensive people among the other civilians. Vulgarity upsets me, it makes me feel insulted, I actually suffer when I meet someone who lacks refinement and gentle manners, and courtesy. When I'm with the other teachers, my husband's friends, I just suffer.

VERSHININ. Yes, of course. But I should have thought that in a town like this the civilians and the army people were equally uninteresting. There's nothing to choose between them. If you talk to any educated person here, civilian or military, he'll generally tell you that he's just worn out. It's either his wife, or his house, or his estate, or his horse, or something. . . . We Russians are capable of such elevated thoughts—then why do we have such low ideals in practical life? Why is it, why?

MASHA. Why?

VERSHININ. Yes, why does his wife wear him out, why do his children wear him out? And what about *him* wearing out his wife and children?

MASHA. You're a bit low-spirited today, aren't you?

VERSHININ. Perhaps. I haven't had any dinner to-day. I've had nothing to eat since morning. One of my daughters is a bit off colour, and when the children are ill, I get so worried. I feel utterly conscience-stricken at having given them a mother like theirs. Oh, if only you could have seen her this morning! What a despicable woman! We started quarrelling at seven o'clock, and at nine I just walked out and slammed the door. [*A pause.*] I never talk about these things in the ordinary way. It's a strange thing, but you're the only person I feel I dare complain to. [*Kisses her hand.*] Don't

be angry with me. I've nobody, nobody but you. . . . [*A pause.*]

MASHA. What a noise the wind's making in the stove! Just before Father died the wind howled in the chimney just like that.

VERSHININ. Are you superstitious?

MASHA. Yes.

VERSHININ. How strange. [*Kisses her hand.*] You really are a wonderful creature, a marvellous creature! Wonderful, marvellous! It's quite dark here, but I can see your eyes shining.

MASHA. [*Moves to another chair.*] There's more light over here.

VERSHININ. I love you, I love you, I love you. . . . I love your eyes, I love your movements. . . . I dream about them. A wonderful, marvellous being!

MASHA. [*Laughing softly.*] When you talk to me like that, somehow I can't help laughing, although I'm afraid at the same time. Don't say it again, please. [*Half-audibly.*] Well, no . . . go on. I don't mind. . . . [*Covers her face with her hands.*] I don't mind. . . . Someone's coming. . . . Let's talk about something else. . . .

[*Enter Irena and Toozenbach through the ballroom.*]

TOOZENBACH. I have a triple-barrelled name—Baron Toozenbach-Krone-Alschauer—but actually I'm a Russian. I was baptized in the Greek-Orthodox faith, just like yourself. I haven't really got any German characteristics, except maybe the obstinate patient way I keep on pestering you. Look how I bring you home every evening.

IRENA. How tired I am!

TOOZENBACH. And I'll go on fetching you from the post office and bringing you home every evening for the next twenty years—unless you send me away. . . . [*Noticing Masha and Vershinin, with pleasure.*] Oh, it's you! How are you?

IRENA. Well, here I am, home at last! [*To Masha.*] A woman came into the post office just before I left. She wanted to send a wire to her brother in Saratov to tell him her son had just died, but she couldn't remember the address. So we had to send the wire without an address, just to Saratov. She was crying and I was rude to her, for no reason at all. "I've no time to waste," I told her. So stupid of me. We're having the carnival crowd to-day, aren't we?

MASHA. Yes.

IRENA. [*Sits down.*] How nice it is to rest! I am tired!

TOOZENBACH. [*Smiling.*] When you come back from work, you look so young, so pathetic, somehow. . . . [*A pause.*]

IRENA. I'm tired. No, I don't like working at the post office, I don't like it at all.

MASHA. You've got thinner. . . . [*Whistles.*] You look younger, too, and your face looks quite boyish.

TOOZENBACH. It's the way she does her hair.

IRENA. I must look for another job. This one doesn't suit me. It hasn't got what I always longed for and dreamed about. It's the sort of work you do without inspiration, without even thinking. [*Someone knocks at the floor from below.*] That's the Doctor knocking. [*To Toozenbach.*] Will you answer him, dear? . . . I can't. . . . I'm so tired.

TOOZENBACH. [*Knocks on the floor.*]

IRENA. He'll be up in a moment. We must do something about all this.

Andrey and the Doctor went to the club last night and lost at cards again. They say Andrey lost two hundred roubles.

MASHA. [*With indifference.*] Well, what are we to do about it?

IRENA. He lost a fortnight ago, and he lost in December, too. I wish to goodness he'd lose everything we've got, and soon, too, and then perhaps we'd move out of this place. Good Heavens, I dream of Moscow every night. Sometimes I feel as if I were going mad. [*Laughs.*] We're going to Moscow in June. How many months are there till June? . . . February, March, April, May . . . nearly half-a-year!

MASHA. We must take care that Natasha doesn't get to know about him losing at cards.

IRENA. I don't think she cares.

[*Enter Chebutykin. He has been resting on his bed since dinner and has only just got up. He combs his beard, then sits down at the table and takes out a newspaper.*]

MASHA. There he is. Has he paid his rent yet?

IRENA. [*Laughs.*] No. Not a penny for the last eight months. I suppose he's forgotten.

MASHA. [*Laughs.*] How solemn he looks sitting there!

[*They all laugh. A pause.*]

IRENA. Why don't you say something, Alexandr Ignatyevich?

VERSHININ. I don't know. I'm just longing for some tea. I'd give my life for a glass of tea! I've had nothing to eat since morning. . . .

CHEBUTYKIN. Irena Serghyeevna!

IRENA. What is it?

CHEBUTYKIN. Please come here. *Venez ici!* [*Irena goes over to him and sits down at the table.*] I can't do without you.

[*Irena lays out the cards for a game of patience.*]

VERSHININ. Well, if we can't have any tea, let's do a bit of philosophizing, anyway.

TOOZENBACH.   Yes, let's. What about?

VERSHININ. What about? Well . . . let's try to imagine what life will be like after we're dead, say in two or three hundred years.

TOOZENBACH. All right, then. . . . After we're dead, people will fly about in balloons, the cut of their coats will be different, the sixth sense will be discovered, and possibly even developed and used, for all I know. . . . But I believe life itself will remain the same; it will still be difficult and full of mystery and full of happiness. And in a thousand years' time people will still be sighing and complaining: "How hard this business of living is!" —and yet they'll still be scared of death and unwilling to die, just as they are now.

VERSHININ. [*After a moment's thought.*] Well, you know . . . how shall I put it? I think everything in the world is bound to change gradually —in fact, it's changing before our very eyes. In two or three hundred years, or maybe in a thousand years—it doesn't matter how long exactly—life will be different. It will be happy. Of course, we shan't be able to enjoy that future life, but all the same, what we're living for now is to create it, we work and . . . yes, we suffer in order to create it. That's the goal of our life, and you might say that's the only happiness we shall ever achieve.

MASHA. [*Laughs quietly.*]

TOOZENBACH. Why are you laughing?

MASHA. I don't know. I've been laughing all day to-day.

VERSHININ. [*To Toozenbach.*] I went to the same cadet school as you did but I never went on to the Military Academy. I read a great deal, of course, but I never know what books I ought to choose, and probably I read a lot of stuff that's not worth anything. But the longer I live the more I seem to long for knowledge. My hair's going grey and I'm getting on in years, and yet how little I know, how little! All the same, I think I do know one thing which is not only true but also most important. I'm sure of it. Oh, if only I could convince you that there's not going to be any happiness for our own generation, that there mustn't be and won't be. . . . We've just got to work and work. All the happiness is reserved for our descendants, our remote descendants. [*A pause.*] Anyway, if I'm not to be happy, then at least my children's children will be.

[*Fedotik and Rodé enter the ballroom; they sit down and sing quietly, one of them playing on a guitar.*]

TOOZENBACH. So you won't even allow us to dream of happiness! But what if I *am* happy?

VERSHININ. You're not.

TOOZENBACH. [*Flinging up his hands and laughing.*] We don't understand one another, that's obvious. How can I convince you?

MASHA. [*Laughs quietly.*]

TOOZENBACH. [*Holds up a finger to her.*] Show a finger to her and she'll laugh! [*To Vershinin.*] And life will be just the same as ever not merely in a couple of hundred years' time, but in a million years. Life doesn't change, it always goes on the same; it follows its own laws, which don't concern us, which we can't discover anyway. Think of the birds that migrate in the autumn, the cranes, for instance: they just fly on and on. It doesn't matter what sort of thoughts they've got in their heads, great thoughts or little thoughts, they just fly on and on, not knowing where or why. And they'll go on flying no matter how many philosophers they happen to have flying with them. Let them philosophize as much as they like, as long as they go on flying.

MASHA. Isn't there some meaning?

TOOZENBACH. Meaning? . . . Look out there, it's snowing. What's the meaning of that? [*A pause.*]

MASHA. I think a human being has got to have some faith, or at least he's got to seek faith. Otherwise his life will be empty, empty. . . . How can you live and not know why the cranes fly, why children are born, why the stars shine in the sky! . . . You must either know why you live, or else . . . nothing matters . . . everything's just wild grass. . . . [*A pause.*]

VERSHININ. All the same, I'm sorry my youth's over.

MASHA. "It's a bore to be alive in this world, friends," that's what Gogol says.

TOOZENBACH. And I feel like saying: it's hopeless arguing with you, friends! I give you up.

CHEBUTYKIN. [*Reads out of the paper.*] Balsac's marriage took place at Berdichev.[1]

IRENA. [*Sings softly to herself.*]

[1] A town in Western Russia well known for its almost exclusively Jewish population.

CHEBUTYKIN. Must write this down in my notebook. [*Writes.*] Balsac's marriage took place at Berdichev. [*Reads on.*]

IRENA. [*Playing patience, pensively.*] Balsac's marriage took place at Berdichev.

TOOZENBACH. Well, I've thrown in my hand. Did you know that I'd sent in my resignation, Maria Serghyeevna?

MASHA. Yes, I heard about it. I don't see anything good in it, either. I don't like civilians.

TOOZENBACH. Never mind. [*Gets up.*] What sort of a soldier do I make, anyway? I'm not even good-looking. Well, what does it matter? I'll work. I'd like to do such a hard day's work that when I came home in the evening I'd fall on my bed exhausted and go to sleep at once. [*Goes to the ballroom.*] I should think working men sleep well at nights!

FEDOTIK. [*To Irena.*] I've got you some coloured crayons at Pyzhikov's, in Moscow Street. And this little penknife, too. . . .

IRENA. You still treat me as if I were a little girl. I wish you'd remember I'm grown up now. [*Takes the crayons and the penknife, joyfully.*] They're awfully nice!

FEDOTIK. Look, I bought a knife for myself, too. You see, it's got another blade here, and then another . . . this thing's for cleaning your ears, and these are nail-scissors, and this is for cleaning your nails. . . .

RODÉ. [*In a loud voice.*] Doctor, how old are you?

CHEBUTYKIN. I? Thirty-two. [*Laughter.*]

FEDOTIK. I'll show you another kind of patience. [*Sets out the cards.*]

[*The samovar is brought in, and*

Anfisa attends to it. Shortly afterwards Natasha comes in and begins to fuss around the table. Soliony enters, bows to the company, and sits down at the table.]

VERSHININ. What a wind, though!

MASHA. Yes. I'm tired of winter! I've almost forgotten what summer is like.

IRENA. [*Playing patience.*] I'm going to go out. We'll get to Moscow!

FEDOTIK. No, it's not going out. You see, the eight has to go on the two of spades. [*Laughs.*] That means you won't go to Moscow.

CHEBUTYKIN. [*Reads the paper.*] Tzitzikar. Smallpox is raging. . . .

ANFISA. [*Goes up to Masha.*] Masha, the tea's ready, dear. [*To Vershinin.*] Will you please come to the table, your Excellency? Forgive me, your name's slipped my memory. . . .

MASHA. Bring it here, Nanny. I'm not coming over there.

IRENA. Nanny!

ANFISA. Comi-ing!

NATASHA. [*To Soliony.*] You know, even tiny babies understand what we say perfectly well! "Good morning, Bobik," I said to him only to-day, "Good morning, my precious!"—and then he looked at me in such a special sort of way. You may say it's only a mother's imagination, but it isn't, I do assure you. No, no! He really is an extraordinary child!

SOLIONY. If that child were mine, I'd cook him up in a frying pan and eat him. [*Picks up his glass, goes into the drawing-room and sits down in a corner.*]

NATASHA. [*Covers her face with her hands.*] What a rude, ill-mannered person!

MASHA. People who don't even notice whether it's summer or winter are lucky! I think I'd be indifferent to the weather if I were living in Moscow.

VERSHININ. I've just been reading the diary of some French cabinet minister—he wrote it in prison. He got sent to prison in connection with the Panama affair. He writes with such a passionate delight about the birds he can see through the prison window—the birds he never even noticed when he was a cabinet minister. Of course, now he's released he won't notice them any more. . . . And in the same way, you won't notice Moscow once you live there again. We're not happy and we can't be happy: we only want happiness.

TOOZENBACH. [*Picks up a box from the table.*] I say, where are all the chocolates?

IRENA. Soliony's eaten them.

TOOZENBACH. All of them?

ANFISA. [*Serving Vershinin with tea.*] Here's a letter for you, Sir.

VERSHININ. For me? [*Takes the letter.*] From my daughter. [*Reads it.*] Yes, of course. . . . Forgive me, Maria Serghyeevna, I'll just leave quietly. I won't have any tea. [*Gets up, agitated.*] Always the same thing. . . .

MASHA. What is it? Secret?

VERSHININ. [*In a low voice.*] My wife's taken poison again. I must go. I'll get away without them seeing me. All this is so dreadfully unpleasant. [*Kisses Masha's hand.*] My dear, good, sweet girl. . . . I'll go out this way, quietly. . . . [*Goes out.*]

ANFISA. Where's he off to? And I've just brought him some tea! What a queer fellow!

MASHA. [*Flaring up.*] Leave me alone! Why do you keep worrying me? Why don't you leave me in peace? [*Goes to the table, cup in hand.*] I'm sick and tired of you, silly old woman!

ANFISA. Why. . . . I didn't mean to offend you, dear.

ANDREY'S VOICE. [Off stage.] Anfisa!

ANFISA. [Mimics him.] Anfisa! Sitting there in his den! . . . [Goes out.]

MASHA. [By the table in the ballroom, crossly.] Do let me sit down somewhere! [Jumbles up the cards laid out on the table.] You take up the whole table with your cards! Why don't you get on with your tea?

IRENA. How bad-tempered you are, Mashka!

MASHA. Well, if I'm bad-tempered, don't talk to me, then. Don't touch me.

CHEBUTYKIN. [Laughs.] Don't touch her! . . . Take care you don't touch her!

MASHA. You may be sixty, but you're always gabbling some damn nonsense or other, just like a child. . . .

NATASHA. [Sighs.] My dear Masha, need you use such expressions? You know, with your good looks you'd be thought so charming, even by the best people—yes, I honestly mean it—if only you wouldn't use these expressions of yours! Je vous prie, pardonnez moi, Marie, mais vous avez des manières un peu grossières.

TOOZENBACH. [With suppressed laughter.] Pass me . . . I say, will you please pass me. . . . Is that cognac over there, or what? . . .

NATASHA. Il parait que mon Bobik déjà ne dort pas. . . . I think he's awake. He's not been too well to-day. I must go and see him . . . excuse me. [Goes out.]

IRENA. I say, where has Alexandr Ignatyevich gone to?

MASHA. He's gone home. His wife's done something queer again.

TOOZENBACH. [Goes over to Soliony with a decanter of cognac.] You always sit alone brooding over something or other—though what it's all about nobody knows. Well, let's make it up. Let's have cognac together. [They drink.] I suppose I'll have to play the piano all night to-night—a lot of rubbishy tunes, of course. . . . Never mind!

SOLIONY. Why did you say "let's make it up"? We haven't quarrelled.

TOOZENBACH. You always give me the feeling that there's something wrong between us. You're a strange character, no doubt about it.

SOLIONY. [Recites.] "I am strange, but who's not so? Don't be angry, Aleko!"

TOOZENBACH. What's Aleko got to do with it? . . . [A pause.]

SOLIONY. When I'm alone with somebody I'm all right, I'm just like other people. But in company, I get depressed and shy, and . . . I talk all sorts of nonsense. All the same, I'm a good deal more honest and well-intentioned than plenty of others. I can prove I am.

TOOZENBACH. You often make me angry because you keep on pestering me when we're in company—but all the same, I do like you for some reason. . . . I'm going to get drunk to-night, whatever happens! Let's have another drink!

SOLIONY. Yes, let's. [A pause.] I've never had anything against you personally, Baron. But my temperament's rather like Lermontov's. [In a low voice.] I even look a little like Lermontov, I've been told. . . . [Takes a scent bottle from his pocket and sprinkles some scent on his hands.]

TOOZENBACH. I have sent in my resignation! Finished! I've been considering it for five years, and now I've made up my mind at last. I'm going to work.

SOLIONY. [*Recites.*] "Don't be angry, Aleko. . . . Away, away with all your dreams!"

[*During the conversation Andrey enters quietly with a book in his hand and sits down by the candle.*]

TOOZENBACH. I'm going to work!

CHEBUTYKIN. [*Comes into the drawing-room with Irena.*] And the food they treated me to was the genuine Caucasian stuff: onion soup, followed by chehartma—that's a meat dish, you know.

SOLIONY. Chereshma isn't meat at all; it's a plant, something like an onion.

CHEBUTYKIN. No-o, my dear friend. Chehartma isn't an onion, it's roast mutton.

SOLIONY. I tell you chereshma is a kind of onion.

CHEBUTYKIN. Well, why should I argue about it with you? You've never been to the Caucasus and you've never tasted chehartma.

SOLIONY. I haven't tasted it because I can't stand the smell of it. Chereshma stinks just like garlic.

ANDREY. [*Imploringly.*] Do stop it, friends! Please stop it!

TOOZENBACH. When's the carnival crowd coming along?

IRENA. They promised to be here by nine—that means any moment now.

TOOZENBACH. [*Embraces Andrey and sings.*] "Ah, my beautiful porch, my lovely new porch, my . . ."[1]

ANDREY. [*Dances and sings.*] "My new porch all made of maple-wood. . . ."

CHEBUTYKIN. [*Dances.*] "With fancy

[1] A traditional Russian dance-song.

carving over the door. . . ."

[*Laughter.*]

TOOZENBACH. [*Kisses Andrey.*] Let's have a drink, the devil take it! Andriusha, let's drink to eternal friendship. I'll come with you when you go back to Moscow University.

SOLIONY. Which university? There are two universities in Moscow.

ANDREY. There's only one.

SOLIONY. I tell you there are two.

ANDREY. Never mind, make it three. The more the merrier.

SOLIONY. There are two universities in Moscow. [*Murmurs of protest and cries of "Hush!"*] There are two universities in Moscow, an old one and a new one. But if you don't want to listen to what I'm saying, if my conversation irritates you, I can keep silent. In fact I can go to another room. . . . [*Goes out through one of the doors.*]

TOOZENBACH. Bravo, bravo! [*Laughs.*] Let's get started, my friends, I'll play for you. What a funny creature that Soliony is! . . . [*Sits down at the piano and plays a waltz.*]

MASHA. [*Dances alone.*] The Baron is drunk, the Baron is drunk, the Baron is drunk. . . .

[*Enter Natasha.*]

NATASHA. [*To Chebutykin.*] Ivan Romanych! [*Speaks to him, then goes out quietly. Chebutykin touches Toozenbach on the shoulder and whispers to him.*]

IRENA. What is it?

CHEBUTYKIN. It's time we were going. Good-night.

IRENA. But really. . . . What about the carnival party?

ANDREY. [*Embarrassed.*] The carnival party's not coming. You see, my dear, Natasha says that Bobik isn't very well, and so . . . Anyway, I don't know . . . and I certainly don't care. . . .

IRENA. [*Shrugs her shoulders.*] Bobik's not very well! . . .

MASHA. Never mind, we'll keep our end up! If they turn us out, out we must go! [*To Irena.*] It isn't Bobik who's not well, it's her. . . . There! . . . [*Taps her forehead with her finger.*] Petty little bourgeois housewife! [*Andrey goes to his room on the right. Chebutykin follows him. The guests say good-bye in the ballroom.*]

FEDOTIK. What a pity! I'd been hoping to spend the evening here, but of course, if the baby's ill. . . . I'll bring him some toys to-morrow.

RODÉ. [*In a loud voice.*] I had a good long sleep after lunch today on purpose. I thought I'd be dancing all night. I mean to say, it's only just nine o'clock.

MASHA. Let's go outside and talk it over. We can decide what to do then. [*Voices are heard saying "Good-bye! God bless you!" and Toozenbach is heard laughing gaily. Everyone goes out. Anfisa and a maid clear the table and put out the lights. The nurse sings to the baby off-stage. Enter Andrey, wearing an overcoat and hat, followed by Chebutykin. They move quietly.*]

CHEBUTYKIN. I've never found time to get married, somehow . . . partly because my life's just flashed past me like lightning, and partly because I was always madly in love with your mother and she was married. . . .

ANDREY. One shouldn't marry. One shouldn't marry because it's so boring.

CHEBUTYKIN. That may be so, but what about loneliness? You can philosophize as much as you like, dear boy, but loneliness is a dreadful thing. Al-

though, really . . . well, it doesn't matter a damn, of course! . . .

ANDREY. Let's get along quickly.

CHEBUTYKIN. What's the hurry? There's plenty of time.

ANDREY. I'm afraid my wife may try to stop me.

CHEBUTYKIN. Ah!

ANDREY. I won't play cards to-night, I'll just sit and watch. I'm not feeling too well. . . . What ought I to do for this breathlessness, Ivan Romanych?

CHEBUTYKIN. Why ask me, dear boy? I can't remember—I simply don't know.

ANDREY. Let's go through the kitchen. [*They go out. A bell rings. The ring is repeated, then voices and laughter are heard.*]

IRENA. [*Coming in.*] What's that?

ANFISA. [*In a whisper.*] The carnival party. [*The bell rings again.*]

IRENA. Tell them there's no one at home, Nanny. Apologize to them. [*Anfisa goes out. Irena walks up and down the room, lost in thought. She seems agitated. Enter Soliony.*]

SOLIONY. [*Puzzled.*] There's no one here. . . . Where is everybody?

IRENA. They've gone home.

SOLIONY. How strange! Then you're alone here?

IRENA. Yes, alone. [*A pause.*] Well . . . good-night.

SOLIONY. I know I behaved tactlessly just now, I lost control of myself. But you're different from the others, you stand out high above them—you're pure, you can see where the truth lies. . . . You're the only person in the world who can possibly understand me. I love you. . . . I love you with a deep, infinite . . .

IRENA. Do please go away. Goodnight!

SOLIONY. I can't live without you. [*Follows her.*] Oh, it's such a delight just to look at you! [*With tears.*] Oh, my happiness! Your glorious, marvellous, entrancing eyes—eyes like no other woman's I've ever seen. . . .

IRENA. [*Coldly.*] Please stop it, Vassily Vassilich!

SOLIONY. I've never spoken to you of my love before . . . it makes me feel as if I were living on a different planet. . . . [*Rubs his forehead.*] Never mind! I can't force you to love me, obviously. But I don't intend to have any rivals—successful rivals, I mean. . . . No, no! I swear to you by everything I hold sacred that if there's anyone else, I'll kill him. Oh, how wonderful you are!

[*Enter Natasha carrying a candle.*]

NATASHA. [*Pokes her head into one room, then into another, but passes the door leading to her husband's room.*] Andrey's reading in there. Better let him read. Forgive me, Vassily Vassilich, I didn't know you were here. I'm afraid I'm not properly dressed.

SOLIONY. I don't care. Good-bye. [*Goes out.*]

NATASHA. You must be tired, my poor dear girl. [*Kisses Irena.*] You ought to go to bed earlier.

IRENA. Is Bobik asleep?

NATASHA. Yes, he's asleep. But he's not sleeping peacefully. By the way, my dear, I've been meaning to speak to you for some time but there's always been something . . . either you're not here, or I'm too busy. . . . You see, I think that Bobik's nursery is so cold and damp. . . . And your room is just ideal for a baby. Darling,

do you think you could move into Olga's room?

IRENA. [*Not understanding her.*] Where to?

[*The sound of bells is heard outside, as a "troika" is driven up to the house.*]

NATASHA. You can share a room with Olia for the time being, and Bobik can have your room. He is such a darling! This morning I said to him: "Bobik, you're my very own! My very own!" And he just gazed at me with his dear little eyes. [*The door bell rings.*] That must be Olga. How late she is!

[*A maid comes up to Natasha and whispers in her ear.*]

NATASHA. Protopopov! What a funny fellow! Protopopov's come to ask me to go for a drive with him. In a troika! [*Laughs.*] Aren't these men strange creatures! . . . [*The door bell rings again.*] Someone's ringing. Shall I go for a short drive? Just for a quarter of an hour? [*To the maid.*] Tell him I'll be down in a minute. [*The door bell rings.*] That's the bell again. I suppose it's Olga. [*Goes out.*]

[*The maid runs out; Irena sits lost in thought. Enter Koolyghin and Olga, followed by Vershinin.*]

KOOLYGHIN. Well! What's the meaning of this? You said you were going to have a party.

VERSHININ. It's a strange thing. I left here about half an hour ago, and they were expecting a carnival party then.

IRENA. They've all gone.

KOOLYGHIN. Masha's gone, too? Where has she gone to? And why is Protopopov waiting outside in a troika? Who's he waiting for?

IRENA. Please don't ask me questions. I'm tired.

KOOLYGHIN. You . . . spoilt child!

OLGA. The conference has only just ended. I'm quite worn out. The headmistress is ill and I'm deputizing for her. My head's aching, oh, my head, my head. . . . [*Sits down.*] Andrey lost two hundred roubles at cards last night. The whole town's talking about it. . . .

KOOLYGHIN. Yes, the conference exhausted me, too. [*Sits down.*]

VERSHININ. So now my wife's taken it into her head to try to frighten me. She tried to poison herself. However, everything's all right now, so I can relax, thank goodness. . . . So we've got to go away? Well, good-night to you, all the best. Fiodor Ilyich, would you care to come along with me somewhere or other? I can't stay at home to-night, I really can't. . . . Do come!

KOOLYGHIN. I'm tired. I don't think I'll come. [*Gets up.*] I'm tired. Has my wife gone home?

IRENA. I think so.

KOOLYGHIN. [*Kisses Irena's hand.*] Good-night. We can rest to-morrow and the day after to-morrow, two whole days! Well, I wish you all the best. [*Going out.*] How I long for some tea! I reckoned on spending the evening in congenial company, but— *o, fallacem hominum spem!* Always use the accusative case in exclamations.

VERSHININ. Well, it looks as if I'll have to go somewhere by myself. [*Goes out with Koolyghin, whistling.*]

OLGA. My head aches, oh, my head. . . . Andrey lost at cards . . . the whole town's talking. . . . I'll go and lie down. [*Going out.*] To-morrow I'm free. Heavens, what a joy! To-morrow I'm free, and the day after to-morrow

I'm free. . . . My head's aching, oh, my poor head. . . .

IRENA. [*Alone.*] They've all gone. No one's left.

[*Someone is playing an accordion in the street. The nurse sings in the next room.*]

NATASHA. [*Crosses the ballroom, wearing a fur coat and cap. She is followed by the maid.*] I'll be back in half an hour. I'm just going for a little drive. [*Goes out.*]

IRENA. [*Alone, with intense longing.*] Moscow! Moscow! Moscow!

ACT THREE

[*A bedroom now shared by Olga and Irena. There are two beds, one on the right, the other on the left, each screened off from the centre of the room. It is past two o'clock in the morning. Off-stage the alarm is being sounded on account of a fire which has been raging for some time. The inmates of the house have not yet been to bed. Masha is lying on a couch, dressed, as usual, in black. Olga and Anfisa come in.*]

ANFISA. Now they're sitting down there, under the stairs. . . . I keep telling them to come upstairs, that they shouldn't sit down there, but they just cry. "We don't know where our Papa is," they say, "perhaps he's got burned in the fire." What an idea! And there are people in the yard, too . . . half-dressed. . . .

OLGA. [*Takes a dress out of a wardrobe.*] Take this grey frock, Nanny. . . . And this one. . . . This blouse, too. . . . And this skirt. Oh, Heavens! what is happening! Apparently the whole of the Kirsanovsky Street's been burnt down. . . . Take this . . . and this, too. . . . [*Throws the clothes into Anfisa's arms.*] The poor Vershinins had a fright. Their house only just escaped being burnt down. They'll have to spend the night here . . . we mustn't let them go home. Poor Fedotik's lost everything, he's got nothing left. . . .

ANFISA. I'd better call Ferapont, Oliushka, I can't carry all this.

OLGA. [*Rings.*] No one takes any notice when I ring. [*Calls through the door.*] Is anyone there? Will someone come up, please!

[*A window, red with the glow of the fire, can be seen through the open door. The sound of a passing fire engine is heard.*]

How dreadful it all is! And how tired of it I am! [*Enter Ferapont.*] Take this downstairs please. . . . The Kolotilin girls are sitting under the stairs . . . give it to them. And this, too. . . .

FERAPONT. Very good, Madam. Moscow was burned down in 1812 just the same. Mercy on us! . . . Yes, the French were surprised all right.

OLGA. Go along now, take this down.

FERAPONT. Very good. [*Goes out.*]

OLGA. Give it all away, Nanny, dear. We won't keep anything, give it all away. . . . I'm so tired, I can hardly keep on my feet. We mustn't let the Vershinins go home. The little girls can sleep in the drawing-room, and Alexandr Ignatyevich can share the downstairs room with the Baron. Fedotik can go in with the Baron, too, or maybe he'd better sleep in the ball-room. The doctor's gone and got drunk —you'd think he'd done it on purpose; he's so hopelessly drunk that we can't let anyone go into his room. Vershin-

in's wife will have to go into the drawing-room, too.

ANFISA. [*Wearily.*] Don't send me away, Oliushka, darling! Don't send me away!

OLGA. What nonsense you're talking, Nanny! No one's sending you away.

ANFISA. [*Leans her head against Olga's breast.*] My dearest girl! I do work, you know, I work as hard as I can. . . . I suppose now I'm getting weaker, I'll be told to go. But where can I go? Where? I'm eighty years old. I'm over eighty-one!

OLGA. You sit down for a while, Nanny. . . . You're tired, you poor dear. . . . [*Makes her sit down.*] Just rest a bit. You've turned quite pale.

[*Enter Natasha.*]

NATASHA. They're saying we ought to start a subscription in aid of the victims of the fire. You know—form a society or something for the purpose. Well, why not? It's an excellent idea! In any case it's up to us to help the poor as best we can. Bobik and Sofochka are fast asleep as if nothing had happened. We've got such a crowd of people in the house; the place seems full of people whichever way you turn. There's 'flu about in the town. . . . I'm so afraid the children might catch it.

OLGA. [*Without listening to her.*] You can't see the fire from this room; it's quiet in here.

NATASHA. Yes. . . . I suppose my hair is all over the place. [*Stands in front of the mirror.*] They say I've got stouter, but it's not true! I'm not a bit stouter. Masha's asleep . . . she's tired, poor girl. . . . [*To Anfisa, coldly.*] How dare you sit down in my presence? Get up! Get out of here! [*Anfisa goes out. A pause.*] I can't understand why you keep that old woman in the house.

OLGA. [*Taken aback.*] Forgive me for saying it, but I can't understand how you . . .

NATASHA. She's quite useless here. She's just a peasant woman, her right place is in the country. You're spoiling her. I do like order in the home, I don't like having useless people about. [*Strokes Olga's cheek.*] You're tired, my poor dear! Our headmistress is tired! You know, when my Sofochka grows up and goes to school, I'll be frightened of you.

OLGA. I'm not going to be a headmistress.

NATASHA. You'll be asked to, Olechka. It's settled.

OLGA. I'll refuse. I couldn't do it. . . . I wouldn't be strong enough. [*Drinks water.*] You spoke so harshly to Nanny just now. . . . You must forgive me for saying so, but I just can't stand that sort of thing . . . it made me feel quite faint. . . .

NATASHA. [*Agitated.*] Forgive me, Olia, forgive me. I didn't mean to upset you.

[*Masha gets up, picks up a pillow and goes out in a huff.*]

OLGA. Please try to understand me, dear. . . . It may be that we've been brought up in a peculiar way, but anyway I just can't bear it. When people are treated like that, it gets me down, I feel quite ill. . . . I simply get unnerved. . . .

NATASHA. Forgive me, dear, forgive me! . . . [*Kisses her.*]

OLGA. Any cruel or tactless remark, even the slightest discourtesy, upsets me. . . .

NATASHA. It's quite true, I know I often say things which would be better left unsaid—but you must agree with me, dear, that she'd be better in the country somewhere.

OLGA. She's been with us for thirty years.

NATASHA. But she can't do any work now, can she? Either I don't understand you, or you don't want to understand me. She can't work, she just sleeps or sits about.

OLGA. Well, let her sit about.

NATASHA. [*In surprise.*] What do you mean, let her sit about? Surely she is a servant! [*Tearfully.*] No, I don't understand you, Olia! I have a nurse for the children and a wet nurse and we share a maid and a cook. Whatever do we want this old woman for? What for?

[*The alarm is sounded again.*]

OLGA. I've aged ten years to-night.

NATASHA. We must sort things out, Olia. You're working at your school, and I'm working at home. You're teaching and I'm running the house. And when I say anything about the servants, I know what I'm talking about. . . . That old thief, that old witch must get out of this house to-morrow! . . . [*Stamps her feet.*] How dare you vex me so? How dare you? [*Recovering her self-control.*] Really, if you don't move downstairs, we'll always be quarrelling. This is quite dreadful!

[*Enter Koolyghin.*]

KOOLYGHIN. Where's Masha? It's time we went home. They say the fire's getting less fierce. [*Stretches.*] Only one block got burnt down, but to begin with it looked as if the whole town was going to be set on fire by that wind. [*Sits down.*] I'm so tired, Olechka, my dear. You know, I've often thought that if I hadn't married

Masha, I'd have married you, Olechka. You're so kind. I'm worn out. [*Listens.*]

OLGA. What is it?

KOOLYGHIN. The doctor's got drunk just as if he'd done it on purpose. Hopelessly drunk. . . . As if he'd done it on purpose. [*Gets up.*] I think he's coming up here. . . . Can you hear him? Yes, he's coming up. [*Laughs.*] What a fellow, really! . . . I'm going to hide myself. [*Goes to the wardrobe and stands between it and the wall.*] What a scoundrel!

OLGA. He's been off drinking for two years, and now suddenly he goes and gets drunk. . . . [*Walks with Natasha towards the back of the room.*]

[*Chebutykin enters; walking firmly and soberly he crosses the room, stops, looks round, then goes to the washstand and begins to wash his hands.*]

CHEBUTYKIN. [*Glumly.*] The devil take them all . . . all the lot of them! They think I can treat anything just because I'm a doctor, but I know positively nothing at all. I've forgotten everything I used to know. I remember nothing, positively nothing. . . . [*Olga and Natasha leave the room without his noticing.*] The devil take them! Last Wednesday I attended a woman at Zasyp. She died, and it's all my fault that she did die. Yes. . . . I used to know a thing or two twenty-five years ago, but now I don't remember anything. Not a thing! Perhaps I'm not a man at all, but I just imagine that I've got hands and feet and a head. Perhaps I don't exist at all, and I only imagine that I'm walking about and eating and sleeping. [*Weeps.*] Oh, if only I could simply stop existing! [*Stops crying, glumly.*] God knows. . . . The other day they were talking

about Shakespeare and Voltaire at the club. . . . I haven't read either, never read a single line of either, but I tried to make out by my expression that I had. The others did the same. How petty it all is! How despicable! And then suddenly I thought of the woman I killed on Wednesday. It all came back to me, and I felt such a swine, so sick of myself that I went and got drunk. . . .

[*Enter Irena, Vershinin and Toozenbach. Toozenbach is wearing a fashionable new civilian suit.*]

IRENA. Let's sit down here for a while. No one will come in here.

VERSHININ. The whole town would have been burnt down but for the soldiers. They're a fine lot of fellows! [*Rubs his hands with pleasure.*] Excellent fellows! Yes, they're a fine lot!

KOOLYGHIN. [*Approaches them.*] What's the time?

TOOZENBACH. It's gone three. It's beginning to get light.

IRENA. Everyone's sitting in the ballroom and nobody thinks of leaving. That man Soliony there, too. . . . [*To Chebutykin.*] You ought to go to bed, Doctor.

CHEBUTYKIN. I'm all right. . . . Thanks. . . . [*Combs his beard.*]

KOOLYGHIN. [*Laughs.*] Half seas over, Ivan Romanych! [*Slaps him on the shoulder.*] You're a fine one! *In vino veritas*, as they used to say in Rome.

TOOZENBACH. Everyone keeps asking me to arrange a concert in aid of the victims of the fire.

IRENA. Well, who'd you get to perform in it?

TOOZENBACH. It could be done if we wanted to. Maria Serghyeevna plays the piano wonderfully well, in my opinion.

KOOLYGHIN. Yes, wonderfully well!

IRENA. She's forgotten how to. She hasn't played for three years. . . . or maybe it's four.

TOOZENBACH. Nobody understands music in this town, not a single person. But I do—I really do—and I assure you quite definitely that Maria Serghyeevna plays magnificently. She's almost a genius for it.

KOOLYGHIN. You're right, Baron. I'm very fond of Masha. She's such a nice girl.

TOOZENBACH. Fancy being able to play so exquisitely, and yet having nobody, nobody at all, to appreciate it!

KOOLYGHIN. [Sighs.] Yes. . . . But would it be quite proper for her to play in a concert? [A pause.] I don't know anything about these matters, my friends. Perhaps it'll be perfectly all right. But you know, although our director is a good man, a very good man indeed, and most intelligent, I know that he does hold certain views. . . . Of course, this doesn't really concern him, but I'll have a word with him about it, all the same, if you like.

CHEBUTYKIN. [Picks up a china clock and examines it.]

VERSHININ. I've got my clothes in such a mess helping to put out the fire, I must look like nothing on earth. [A pause.] I believe they were saying yesterday that our brigade might be transferred to somewhere a long way away. Some said it was to be Poland, and some said it was Cheeta, in Siberia.

TOOZENBACH. I heard that, too. Well, the town will seem quite deserted.

IRENA. We'll go away, too!

CHEBUTYKIN. [Drops clock and breaks it.] Smashed to smithereens!

[A pause. Everyone looks upset and embarrassed.]

KOOLYGHIN. [Picks up the pieces.] Fancy breaking such a valuable thing! Ah, Ivan Romanych, Ivan Romanych! You'll get a bad mark for that!

IRENA. It was my mother's clock.

CHEBUTYKIN. Well, supposing it was. If it was your mother's, then it was your mother's. Perhaps I didn't smash it. Perhaps it only appears that I did. Perhaps it only appears to us that we exist, whereas in reality we don't exist at all. I don't know anything, no one knows anything. [Stops at the door.] Why are you staring at me? Natasha's having a nice little affair with Protopopov, and you don't see it. You sit here seeing nothing, and meanwhile Natasha's having a nice little affair with Protopopov. . . . [Sings.] Would you like a date? . . . [Goes out.]

VERSHININ. So. . . . [Laughs.] How odd it all is, really. [A pause.] When the fire started, I ran home as fast as I could. When I got near, I could see that our house was all right and out of danger, but the two little girls were standing there, in the doorway in their night clothes. Their mother wasn't there. People were rushing about, horses, dogs . . . and in the kiddies' faces I saw a frightened, anxious, appealing look, I don't know what! . . . My heart sank when I saw their faces. My God, I thought, what will these children have to go through in the course of their poor lives? And they may live a long time, too! I picked them up and ran back here with them, and all the time I was running, I was thinking the same thing: what will they have to go through? [The alarm *is sounded. A pause.*] When I got here, my wife was here already . . . angry, shouting!

[*Enter Masha carrying a pillow; she sits down on the couch.*]

VERSHININ. And when my little girls were standing in the doorway with nothing on but their night clothes, and the street was red with the glow of the fire and full of terrifying noises, it struck me that the same sort of thing used to happen years ago, when armies used to make sudden raids on towns, and plunder them and set them on fire. . . . Anyway, is there any essential difference between things as they were and as they are now? And before very long, say, in another two or three hundred years, people may be looking at our present life just as we look at the past now, with horror and scorn. Our own times may seem uncouth to them, boring and frightfully uncomfortable and strange. . . . Oh, what a great life it'll be then, what a life! [*Laughs.*] Forgive me, I'm philosophizing my head off again . . . but may I go on, please? I'm bursting to philosophize just at the moment. I'm in the mood for it. [*A pause.*] You seem as if you've all gone to sleep. As I was saying: what a great life it will be in the future! Just try to imagine it. . . . At the present time there are only three people of your intellectual calibre in the whole of this town, but future generations will be more productive of people like you. They'll go on producing more and more of the same sort until at last the time will come when everything will be just as you'd wish it yourselves. People will live their lives in your way, and then even you may be outmoded, and a new lot will come along who will be even

better than you are. . . . [*Laughs.*] I'm in quite a special mood to-day. I feel full of a tremendous urge to live. . . . [*Sings.*]

"To Love all ages are in fee,
The passion's good for you and me." . . . [*Laughs.*]

MASHA. [*Sings.*] Tara-tara-tara. . . .
VERSHININ. Tum-tum. . . .
MASHA. Tara-tara . . .
VERSHININ. Tum-tum, tum-tum. . . . [*Laughs.*]

[*Enter Fedotik.*]

FEDOTIK. [*Dancing about.*] Burnt, burnt! Everything I've got burnt!

[*All laugh.*]

IRENA. It's hardly a joking matter. Has everything really been burnt?

FEDOTIK. [*Laughs.*] Everything, completely. I've got nothing left. My guitar's burnt, my photographs are burnt, all my letters are burnt. Even the little note-book I was going to give you has been burnt.

[*Enter Soliony.*]

IRENA. No, please go away, Vassily Vassilich. You can't come in here.

SOLIONY. Can't I? Why can the Baron come in here if I can't?

VERSHININ. We really must go, all of us. What's the fire doing?

SOLIONY. It's dying down, they say. Well, I must say it's a peculiar thing that the Baron can come in here, and I can't. [*Takes a scent bottle from his pocket and sprinkles himself with scent.*]

VERSHININ. Tara-tara.
MASHA. Tum-tum, tum-tum.
VERSHININ. [*Laughs, to Soliony.*] Let's go to the ballroom.

SOLIONY. Very well, we'll make a note of this. "I hardly need to make my moral yet more clear: That might be teasing geese, I fear!" [1] [*Looks at Toozenbach.*] Cluck, cluck, cluck! [*Goes out with Vershinin and Fedotik.*]

IRENA. That Soliony has smoked the room out. . . . [*Puzzled.*] The Baron's asleep. Baron! Baron!

TOOZENBACH. [*Waking out of his doze.*] I must be tired. The brickworks. . . . No, I'm not talking in my sleep. I really do intend to go to the brick-works and start working there quite soon. I've had a talk with the manager. [*To Irena, tenderly.*] You are so pale, so beautiful, so fascinating. . . . Your pallor seems to light up the darkness around you, as if it were luminous, somehow. . . . You're sad, you're dissatisfied with the life you have to live. . . . Oh, come away with me, let's go away and work together!

MASHA. Nikolai Lvovich, I wish you'd go away.

TOOZENBACH. [*Laughs.*] Oh, you're here, are you? I didn't see you. [*Kisses Irena's hand.*] Good-bye, I'm going. You know as I look at you now, I keep thinking of the day—it was a long time ago, your Saint's day—when you talked to us about the joy of work. . . . You were so gay and high-spirited then. . . . And what a happy life I saw ahead of me! Where is it all now? [*Kisses her hand.*] There are tears in your eyes. You should go to bed, it's beginning to get light . . . it's almost morning. . . . Oh, if only I could give my life for you!

MASHA. Nikolai Lvovich, please go away! Really now. . . .

TOOZENBACH. I'm going. [*Goes out.*]

MASHA. [*Lies down.*] Are you asleep,

Fiodor?

KOOLYGHIN. Eh?

MASHA. Why don't you go home?

KOOLYGHIN. My darling Masha, my sweet, my precious Masha. . . .

IRENA. She's tired. Let her rest a while, Fyedia.

KOOLYGHIN. I'll go in a moment. My wife, my dear, good wife! . . . How I love you! . . . only you!

MASHA. [*Crossly.*] *Amo, amas, amat, amamus, amatis, amant!*

KOOLYGHIN. [*Laughs.*] Really, she's an amazing woman!—I've been married to you for seven years, but I feel as if we were only married yesterday. Yes, on my word of honour, I do! You really are amazing! Oh, I'm so happy, happy, happy!

MASHA. And I'm so bored, bored, bored! [*Sits up.*] I can't get it out of my head. . . . It's simply disgusting. It's like having a nail driven into my head. No, I can't keep silent about it any more. It's about Andrey. . . . He's actually mortgaged this house to a bank, and his wife's got hold of all the money—and yet the house doesn't belong to him, it belongs to all four of us! Surely, he must realize that, if he's got any honesty.

KOOLYGHIN. Why bring all this up, Masha? Why bother about it now? Andriusha owes money all round. . . . Leave him alone.

MASHA. Anyway, it's disgusting. [*Lies down.*]

KOOLYGHIN. Well, we aren't poor, Masha. I've got work, I teach at the county school, I give private lessons in my spare time. . . . I'm just a plain, honest man. . . . *Omnia mea mecum porto*, as they say.

MASHA. I don't ask for anything, but I'm just disgusted by injustice. [*A*

---

[1] From Krylov's fable *Geese* (translated by Bernard Pares).

pause.] Why don't you go home, Fiodor?

KOOLYGHIN. [*Kisses her.*] You're tired. Just rest here for a while. . . . I'll go home and wait for you. . . . Go to sleep. [*Goes to the door.*] I'm happy, happy, happy! [*Goes out.*]

IRENA. The truth is that Andrey is getting to be shallow-minded. He's ageing and since he's been living with that woman he's lost all the inspiration he used to have! Not long ago he was working for a professorship, and yet yesterday he boasted of having at last been elected a member of the County Council. Fancy him a member, with Protopopov as chairman! They say the whole town's laughing at him, he's the only one who doesn't know anything or see anything. And now, you see, everyone's at the fire, while he's just sitting in his room, not taking the slightest notice of it. Just playing his violin. [*Agitated.*] Oh, how dreadful it is, how dreadful, how dreadful! I can't bear it any longer, I can't, I really can't! . . .

[*Enter Olga. She starts arranging things on her bedside table.*]

IRENA. [*Sobs loudly.*] You must turn me out of here! Turn me out; I can't stand it any more!

OLGA. [*Alarmed.*] What is it? What is it, darling?

IRENA. [*Sobbing.*] Where. . . . Where has it all gone to? Where is it? Oh, God! I've forgotten. . . . I've forgotten everything . . . there's nothing but a muddle in my head. . . . I don't remember what the Italian for "window" is, or for "ceiling." . . . Every day I'm forgetting more and more, and life's slipping by, and it will never, never come back. . . . We shall never go to Moscow. . . . I can

see that we shall never go. . . .

OGLA. Don't, my dear, don't. . . .

IRENA. [*Trying to control herself.*] Oh, I'm so miserable! . . . I can't work, I won't work! I've had enough of it, enough! . . . First I worked on the telegraph, now I'm in the County Council office, and I hate and despise everything they give me to do there. . . . I'm twenty-three years old, I've been working all this time, and I feel as if my brain's dried up. I know I've got thinner and uglier and older, and I find no kind of satisfaction in anything, none at all. And the time's passing . . . and I feel as if I'm moving away from any hope of a genuine, fine life, I'm moving further and further away and sinking into a kind of abyss. I feel in despair, and I don't know why I'm still alive, why I haven't killed myself. . . .

OLGA. Don't cry, my dear child, don't cry. . . . It hurts me.

IRENA. I'm not crying any more. That's enough of it. Look, I'm not crying now. Enough of it, enough! . . .

OLGA. Darling, let me tell you something. . . . I just want to speak as your sister, as your friend. . . . That is, if you want my advice. . . . Why don't you marry the Baron?

IRENA. [*Weeps quietly.*]

OLGA. After all, you do respect him, you think a lot of him. . . . It's true, he's not good-looking, but he's such a decent, clean-minded sort of man. . . . After all, one doesn't marry for love, but to fulfil a duty. At least, I think so, and I'd marry even if I weren't in love. I'd marry anyone that proposed to me, as long as he was a decent man. I'd even marry an old man.

IRENA. I've been waiting all this

time, imagining that we'd be moving to Moscow, and I'd meet the man I'm meant for there. I've dreamt about him and I've loved him in my dreams. . . . But it's all turned out to be nonsense . . . nonsense. . . .

OLGA. [*Embracing her.*] My darling sweetheart, I understand everything perfectly. When the Baron resigned his commission and came to see us in his civilian clothes, I thought he looked so plain that I actually started to cry. . . . He asked me why I was crying. . . . How could I tell him? But, of course, if it were God's will that he should marry you, I'd feel perfectly happy about it. That's quite a different matter, quite different!

[*Natasha, carrying a candle, comes out of the door on the right, crosses the stage and goes out through the door on the left without saying anything.*]

MASHA. [*Sits up.*] She goes about looking as if she'd started the fire.

OLGA. You're silly, Masha. You're the stupidest person in our family. Forgive me for saying so.

[*A pause.*]

MASHA. My dear sisters, I've got something to confess to you. I must get some relief, I feel the need of it in my heart. I'll confess it to you two alone, and then never again, never to anybody! I'll tell you in a minute. [*In a low voice.*] It's a secret, but you'll have to know everything. I can't keep silent any more. [*A pause.*] I'm in love, in love. . . . I love that man. . . . You saw him here just now. . . . Well, what's the good? . . . I love Vershinin. . . .

OLGA. [*Goes behind her screen.*] Don't say it. I don't want to hear it.

MASHA. Well, what's to be done? [*Holding her head.*] I thought he was queer at first, then I started to pity him . . . then I began to love him . . . love everything about him—his voice, his talk, his misfortunes, his two little girls. . . .

OLGA. Nevertheless, I don't want to hear it. You can say any nonsense you like, I'm not listening.

MASHA. Oh, you're stupid, Olia! If I love him, well—that's my fate! That's my destiny. . . . He loves me, too. It's all rather frightening, isn't it? Not a good thing, is it? [*Takes Irena by the hand and draws her to her.*] Oh, my dear! . . . How are we going to live through the rest of our lives? What's going to become of us? When you read a novel, everything in it seems so old and obvious, but when you fall in love yourself, you suddenly discover that you don't really know anything, and you've got to make your own decisions. . . . My dear sisters, my dear sisters! . . . I've confessed it all to you, and now I'll keep quiet. . . . I'll be like that madman in the story by Gogol—silence . . . silence! . . .

[*Enter Andrey followed by Ferapont.*]

ANDREY. [*Crossly.*] What do you want? I don't understand you.

FERAPONT. [*Stopping in the doorway, impatiently.*] I've asked you about ten times already, Andrey Serghyeevich.

ANDREY. In the first place, you're not to call me Andrey Serghyeevich —call me "Your Honour."

FERAPONT. The firemen are asking Your Honour if they may drive through your garden to get to the river. They've been going a long way round all this time—it's a terrible business!

ANDREY. All right. Tell them it's all

right. [*Ferapont goes out.*] They keep on plaguing me. Where's Olga? [*Olga comes from behind the screen.*] I wanted to see you. Will you give me the key to the cupboard? I've lost mine. You know the key I mean, the small one you've got. . . .

[*Olga silently hands him the key. Irena goes behind the screen on her side of the room.*]

ANDREY. What a terrific fire! It's going down though. That Ferapont annoyed me, the devil take him! Silly thing he made me say. . . . Telling him to call me "Your Honour"! . . . [*A pause.*] Why don't you say anything, Olia? [*A pause.*] It's about time you stopped this nonsense . . . sulking like this for no reason whatever. . . . You here, Masha? And Irena's here, too. That's excellent! We can talk it over then, frankly and once for all. What have you got against me? What is it?

OLGA. Drop it now, Andriusha. Let's talk it over to-morrow. [*Agitated.*] What a dreadful night!

ANDREY. [*In great embarrassment.*] Don't get upset. I'm asking you quite calmly, what have you got against me? Tell me frankly.

VERSHININ'S VOICE. [*Off stage.*] Tum-tum-tum!

MASHA. [*In a loud voice, getting up.*] Tara-tara-tara! [*To Olga.*] Good-bye, Olia, God bless you! [*Goes behind the screen and kisses Irena.*] Sleep well. . . . Good-bye, Andrey. I should leave them now, they're tired . . . talk it over to-morrow. . . . [*Goes out.*]

OLGA. Really, Andriusha, let's leave it till to-morrow. . . . [*Goes behind the screen on her side of the room.*] It's time to go to bed.

ANDREY. I only want to say one thing, then I'll go. In a moment. . . . First of all, you've got something against my wife, against Natasha. I've always been conscious of it from the day we got married. Natasha is a fine woman, she's honest and straightforward and high-principled. . . . That's my opinion. I love and respect my wife. You understand that I respect her, and I expect others to respect her, too. I repeat: she's an honest, high-principled woman, and all your grievances against her—if you don't mind my saying so—are just imagination, and nothing more. . . . [*A pause.*] Secondly, you seem to be annoyed with me for not making myself a professor, and not doing any academic work. But I'm working in the Council Office, I'm a member of the County Council, and I feel my service there is just as fine and valuable as any academic work I might do. I'm a member of the County Council, and if you want to know, I'm proud of it! [*A pause.*] Thirdly . . . there's something else I must tell you. . . . I know I mortgaged the house without asking your permission. . . . That was wrong, I admit it, and I ask you to forgive me. . . . I was driven to it by my debts. . . . I'm in debt for about thirty-five thousand roubles. I don't play cards any more, I've given it up long ago. . . . The only thing I can say to justify myself is that you girls get an annuity, while I don't get anything . . . no income, I mean. . . . [*A pause.*]

KOOLYGHIN. [*Calling through the door.*] Is Masha there? She's not there? [*Alarmed.*] Where can she be then? It's very strange. . . . [*Goes away.*]

ANDREY. So you won't listen? Natasha is a good, honest woman, I tell you. [*Walks up and down the stage, then stops.*] When I married her, I thought we were going to be happy, I thought we should all be happy. . . . But . . . oh, my God! . . . [*Weeps.*] My dear sisters, my dear, good sisters, don't believe what I've been saying, don't believe it. . . . [*Goes out.*]

KOOLYGHIN. [*Through the door, agitated.*] Where's Masha? Isn't Masha here? Extraordinary! [*Goes away.*]

[*The alarm is heard again. The stage is empty.*]

IRENA. [*Speaking from behind the screen.*] Olia! Who's that knocking on the floor?

OLGA. It's the doctor, Ivan Romanych. He's drunk.

IRENA. It's been one thing after another all night. [*A pause.*] Olia! [*Peeps out from behind the screen.*] Have you heard? The troops are being moved from the district . . . they're being sent somewhere a long way off.

OLGA. That's only a rumour.

IRENA. We'll be left quite alone then. . . . Olia!

OLGA. Well?

IRENA. Olia, darling, I do respect the Baron. . . . I think a lot of him, he's a very good man. . . . I'll marry him, Olia, I'll agree to marry him, if only we can go to Moscow! Let's go, please do let's go! There's nowhere in all the world like Moscow. Let's go, Olia! Let's go!

ACT FOUR

[*The old garden belonging to the Prozorovs' house. A river is seen at the end of a long avenue of fir-trees, and on the far bank of the river a forest. On the right of the stage there is a verandah with a table on which champagne bottles and glasses have been*

left. *It is midday. From time to time people from the street pass through the garden to get to the river. Five or six soldiers march through quickly.*

Chebutykin, radiating a mood of benevolence which does not leave him throughout the act, is sitting in a chair in the garden. He is wearing his army cap and is holding a walking stick, as if ready to be called away at any moment. Koolyghin, with a decoration round his neck and with his moustache shaved off, Toozenbach and Irena are standing on the verandah saying good-bye to Fedotik and Rodé, who are coming down the steps. Both officers are in marching uniform.]

TOOZENBACH. [*Embracing Fedotik.*] You're a good fellow, Fedotik; we've been good friends! [*Embraces Rodé.*] Once more, then. . . . Good-bye, my dear friends!

IRENA. Au revoir!

FEDOTIK. It's not "au revoir." It's good-bye. We shall never meet again!

KOOLYGHIN. Who knows? [*Wipes his eyes, smiling.*] There! you've made me cry.

IRENA. We'll meet some time.

FEDOTIK. Perhaps in ten or fifteen years' time. But then we'll hardly know one another. . . . We shall just meet and say, "How are you?" coldly. . . . [*Takes a snapshot.*] Wait a moment. . . . Just one more, for the last time.

RODÉ. [*Embraces Toozenbach.*] We're not likely to meet again. . . . [*Kisses Irena's hand.*] Thank you for everything . . . everything!

FEDOTIK. [*Annoyed.*] Do just wait a second!

TOOZENBACH. We'll meet again if we're fated to meet. Do write to us.

Be sure to write.

RODÉ. [*Glancing round the garden.*] Good-bye, trees! [*Shouts.*] Heigh-ho! [*A pause.*] Good-bye, echo!

KOOLYGHIN. I wouldn't be surprised if you got married out there, in Poland. . . . You'll get a Polish wife, and she'll put her arms round you and say: Kohane! [1] [*Laughs.*]

FEDOTIK. [*Glances at his watch.*] There's less than an hour to go. Soliony is the only one from our battery who's going down the river on the barge. All the others are marching with the division. Three batteries are leaving to-day by road and three more to-morrow—then the town will be quite peaceful.

TOOZENBACH. Yes, and dreadfully dull, too.

RODÉ. By the way, where's Maria Serghyeevna?

KOOLYGHIN. She's somewhere in the garden.

FEDOTIK. We must say good-bye to her.

RODÉ. Good-bye. I really must go, or I'll burst into tears. [*Quickly embraces Toozenbach and Koolyghin, kisses Irena's hand.*] Life's been very pleasant here. . . .

FEDOTIK. [*To Koolyghin.*] Here's something for a souvenir for you—a note-book with a pencil. . . . We'll go down to the river through here. [*They go off, glancing back.*]

RODÉ. [*Shouts.*] Heigh-ho!

KOOLYGHIN. [*Shouts.*] Good-bye!

[*At the back of the stage Fedotik and Rodé meet Masha, and say good-bye to her; she goes off with them.*]

IRENA. They've gone. . . . [*Sits down on the bottom step of the verandah.*]

[1] A Polish word meaning "beloved."

CHEBUTYKIN. They forgot to say good-bye to me.

IRENA. Well, what about you?

CHEBUTYKIN. That's true, I forgot, too. Never mind, I'll be seeing them again quite soon. I'll be leaving to-morrow. Yes . . . only one more day. And then, in a year's time I'll be retiring. I'll come back here and finish the rest of my life near you. There's just one more year to go and then I get my pension. . . . [*Puts a newspaper in his pocket and takes out another.*] I'll come back here and lead a reformed life. I'll be a nice, quiet, well-behaved little man.

IRENA. Yes, it's really time you reformed, my dear friend. You ought to live a different sort of life, somehow.

CHEBUTYKIN. Yes. . . . I think so, too. [*Sings quietly.*] Tarara-boom-di-ay. . . . I'm sitting on a tomb-di-ay. . . .

KOOLYGHIN. Ivan Romanych is incorrigible! Incorrigible!

CHEBUTYKIN. Yes, you ought to have taken me in hand. You'd have reformed me!

IRENA. Fiodor's shaved his moustache off. I can't bear to look at him.

KOOLYGHIN. Why not?

CHEBUTYKIN. If I could just tell you what your face looks like now—but I daren't.

KOOLYGHIN. Well! Such are the conventions of life! *Modus vivendi,* you know. The director shaved his moustache off, so I shaved mine off when they gave me an inspectorship. No one likes it, but personally I'm quite indifferent. I'm content. Whether I've got a moustache or not, it's all the same to me. [*Sits down.*]

ANDREY. [*Passes across the back of the stage pushing a pram with a child asleep in it.*]

IRENA. Ivan Romanych, my dear friend, I'm awfully worried about something. You were out in the town garden last night—tell me what happened there?

CHEBUTYKIN. What happened? Nothing. Just a trifling thing. [*Reads his paper.*] It doesn't matter anyway.

KOOLYGHIN. They say that Soliony and the Baron met in the town garden outside the theatre last night and . . .

TOOZENBACH. Don't, please! What's the good? . . . [*Waves his hand at him deprecatingly and goes into the house.*]

KOOLYGHIN. It was outside the theatre. . . . Soliony started badgering the Baron, and he lost patience and said something that offended him.

CHEBUTYKIN. I don't know anything about it. It's all nonsense.

KOOLYGHIN. A school-master once wrote "nonsense" in Russian over a pupil's essay, and the pupil puzzled over it, thinking it was a Latin word. [*Laughs.*] Frightfully funny, you know! They say that Soliony's in love with Irena and that he got to hate the Baron more and more. . . . Well, that's understandable. Irena's a very nice girl. She's a bit like Masha, she tends to get wrapped up in her own thoughts. [*To Irena.*] But your disposition is more easy-going than Masha's. And yet Masha has a very nice disposition, too. I love her, I love my Masha.

[*From the back of the stage comes a shout: "Heigh-ho!"*]

IRENA. [*Starts.*] Anything seems to startle me to-day. [*A pause.*] I've got everything ready, too. I'm sending my luggage off after lunch. The Baron and I are going to get married to-morrow, and directly afterwards we're moving to the brick-works, and the day after to-morrow I'm starting work at the school. So our new life will begin, God willing! When I was sitting for my teacher's diploma, I suddenly started crying for sheer joy, with a sort of feeling of blessedness. . . . [*A pause.*] The carrier will be coming for my luggage in a minute. . . .

KOOLYGHIN. That's all very well, but somehow I can't feel that it's meant to be serious. All ideas and theories, but nothing really serious. Anyway, I wish you luck from the bottom of my heart.

CHEBUTYKIN. [*Moved.*] My dearest girl, my precious child! You've gone on so far ahead of me, I'll never catch you up now. I've got left behind like a bird which has grown too old and can't keep up with the rest of the flock. Fly away, my dears, fly away, and God be with you! [*A pause.*] It's a pity you've shaved your moustache off, Fiodor Ilyich.

KOOLYGHIN. Don't keep on about it, please! [*Sighs.*] Well, the soldiers will be leaving to-day, and everything will go back to what it was before. Anyway, whatever they say, Masha is a good, loyal wife. Yes, I love her dearly and I'm thankful for what God has given me. Fate treats people so differently. For instance, there's an excise clerk here called Kozyrev. He was at school with me and he was expelled in his fifth year because he just couldn't grasp the *ut consecutivum*. He's dreadfully hard up now, and in bad health, too, and whenever I meet him, I just say to him: "Hullo, *ut consecutivum!*" "Yes," he replies, "that's just the trouble—*consecutivum*" . . . and he starts coughing. Whereas I—I've been lucky all my life. I'm happy, I've actually been awarded the order of Saint Stanislav, second class —and now I'm teaching the children the same old *ut consecutivum*. Of course, I'm clever, cleverer than plenty of other people, but happiness does not consist of merely being clever. . . .

[*In the house someone plays "The Maiden's Prayer."*]

IRENA. To-morrow night I shan't have to listen to the "Maiden's Prayer." I shan't have to meet Protopopov. . . . [*A pause.*] By the way, he's in the sitting-room. He's come again.

KOOLYGHIN. Hasn't our headmistress arrived yet?

IRENA. No, we've sent for her. If you only knew how difficult it is for me to live here by myself, without Olia! She lives at the school now; she's the headmistress and she's busy the whole day. And I'm here alone, bored, with nothing to do, and I hate the very room I live in. So I've just made up my mind—if I'm really not going to be able to live in Moscow, that's that. It's my fate, that's all. Nothing can be done about it. It's God's will, everything that happens, and that's the truth. Nikolai Lvovich proposed to me. . . . Well, I thought it over, and I made up my mind. He's such a nice man, it's really extraordinary how nice he is. . . . And then suddenly I felt as though my soul had grown wings, I felt more cheerful and so relieved somehow that I wanted to work again. Just to start work! . . . Only something happened yesterday, and now I feel as though something mysterious is hanging over me. . . .

CHEBUTYKIN. Nonsense!

NATASHA. [*Speaking through the window.*] Our headmistress!

KOOLYGHIN. Our headmistress has

arrived! Let's go indoors. [*Goes indoors with Irena.*]

CHEBUTYKIN. [*Reads his paper and sings quietly to himself.*] Tararaboom-di-ay. . . . I'm sitting on a tomb-di-ay. . . .

[*Masha walks up to him; Andrey passes across the back of the stage pushing the pram.*]

MASHA. You look very comfortable sitting here. . . .

CHEBUTYKIN. Well, why not? Anything happening?

MASHA. [*Sits down.*] No, nothing. [*A pause.*] Tell me something. Were you in love with my mother?

CHEBUTYKIN. Yes, very much in love.

MASHA. Did she love you?

CHEBUTYKIN. [*After a pause.*] I can't remember now.

MASHA. Is my man here? Our cook Marfa always used to call her policeman "my man." Is he here?

CHEBUTYKIN. Not yet.

MASHA. When you have to take your happiness in snatches, in little bits, as I do, and then lose it, as I've lost it, you gradually get hardened and bad-tempered. [*Points at her breast.*] Something's boiling over inside me, here. [*Looking at Andrey, who again crosses the stage with the pram.*] There's Andrey, our dear brother. . . . All our hopes are gone. It's the same as when thousands of people haul a huge bell up into a tower. Untold labour and money is spent on it, and then suddenly it falls and gets smashed. Suddenly, without rhyme or reason. It was the same with Andrey. . . .

ANDREY. When are they going to settle down in the house? They're making such a row.

CHEBUTYKIN. They will soon. [*Looks at his watch.*] This is an old-fashioned watch: it strikes. . . . [*Winds his watch which then strikes.*] The first, second and fifth batteries will be leaving punctually at one o'clock. [*A pause.*] And I shall leave to-morrow.

ANDREY. For good?

CHEBUTYKIN. I don't know. I may return in about a year. Although, God knows . . . it's all the same. . . .

[*The sounds of a harp and a violin are heard.*]

ANDREY. The town will seem quite empty. Life will be snuffed out like a candle. [*A pause.*] Something happened yesterday outside the theatre; everybody's talking about it. I'm the only one that doesn't seem to know about it.

CHEBUTYKIN. It was nothing. A lot of nonsense. Soliony started badgering the Baron, or something. The Baron lost his temper and insulted him, and in the end Soliony had to challenge him to a duel. [*Looks at his watch.*] I think it's time to go. . . . At half-past twelve, in the forest over there, on the other side of the river. . . . Bang-bang! [*Laughs.*] Soliony imagines he's like Lermontov. He actually writes poems. But, joking apart, this is his third duel.

MASHA. Whose third duel?

CHEBUTYKIN. Soliony's.

MASHA. What about the Baron?

CHEBUTYKIN. Well, what about him? [*A pause.*]

MASHA. My thoughts are all in a muddle. . . . But what I mean to say is that they shouldn't be allowed to fight. He might wound the Baron or even kill him.

CHEBUTYKIN. The Baron's a good enough fellow, but what does it really matter if there's one Baron more or less in the world? Well, let it be! It's all the same. [*The shouts of "Ah-oo!" and "Heigh-ho!" are heard from beyond the garden.*] That's Skvortsov, the second, shouting from the boat. He can wait.

ANDREY. I think it's simply immoral to fight a duel, or even to be present at one as a doctor.

CHEBUTYKIN. That's only how it seems. . . . We don't exist, nothing exists, it only seems to us that we do. . . . And what difference does it make?

MASHA. Talk, talk, nothing but talk all day long! . . . [*Starts to go.*] Having to live in this awful climate with the snow threatening to fall at any moment, and then on the top of it having to listen to all this sort of talk. . . . [*Stops.*] I won't go into the house, I can't bear going in there. . . . Will you let me know when Vershinin comes? . . . [*Walks off along the avenue.*] Look, the birds are beginning to fly away already! [*Looks up.*] Swans or geese. . . . Dear birds, happy birds. . . . [*Goes off.*]

ANDREY. Our house will seem quite deserted. The officers will go, you'll go, my sister will get married, and I'll be left alone in the house.

CHEBUTYKIN. What about your wife?

[*Enter Ferapont with some papers.*]

ANDREY. My wife is my wife. She's a good, decent sort of woman . . . she's really very kind, too, but there's something about her which pulls her down to the level of an animal . . . a sort of mean, blind, thick-skinned animal—anyway, not a human being. I'm telling you this as a friend, the only person I can talk openly to. I love Natasha, it's true. But at times she appears to me so utterly vulgar, that I feel quite bewildered by it, and then I can't understand why, for what reasons I love her—or, anyway, did love her.

CHEBUTYKIN. [*Gets up.*] Well, dear boy, I'm going away to-morrow and it may be we shall never see each other again. So I'll give you a bit of advice. Put on your hat, take a walking stick, and go away. . . . Go away, and don't ever look back. And the further you go, the better.

[*Soliony passes across the back of the stage accompanied by two officers. Seeing Chebutykin, he turns towards him, while the officers walk on.*]

SOLIONY. It's time, Doctor. Half past twelve already. [*Shakes hands with Andrey.*]

CHEBUTYKIN. In a moment. Oh, I'm tired of you all. [*To Andrey.*] Andriusha, if anyone asks for me, tell them I'll be back presently. [*Sighs.*] Oh-ho-ho!

SOLIONY. "He had no time to say 'Oh, oh!' Before that bear had struck him low." . . .

[*Walks off with him.*] What are you groaning about, old man?

CHEBUTYKIN. Oh, well!

SOLIONY. How do you feel?

CHEBUTYKIN. [*Crossly.*] Like a last year's bird's-nest.

SOLIONY. You needn't be so agitated about it, old boy. I shan't indulge in anything much, I'll just scorch his wings a little, like a woodcock's. [*Takes out a scent bottle and sprinkles scent over his hands.*] I've used up a whole bottle to-day, but my hands still smell. They smell like a corpse. [*A pause.*] Yes. . . . Do you remember that poem of Lermontov's?

"And he, rebellious, seeks a storm, As if in storms there were tranquillity." . . .

CHEBUTYKIN. Yes.

"He had no time to say 'Oh, oh!' Before that bear had struck him low." [*Goes out with Soliony.*]

[*Shouts of "Heigh-ho!" "Ah-oo!" are heard. Enter Andrey and Ferapont.*]

FERAPONT. Will you sign these papers, please?

ANDREY. [*With irritation.*] Leave me alone! Leave me alone, for Heaven's sake. [*Goes off with the pram.*]

FERAPONT. Well, what am I supposed to do with the papers then? They are meant to be signed, aren't they? [*Goes to back of stage.*]

[*Enter Irena and Toozenbach, the latter wearing a straw hat. Koolyghin crosses the stage, calling: "Ah-oo! Masha! Ah-oo!"*]

TOOZENBACH. I think he's the only person in the whole town who's glad that the army is leaving.

IRENA. That's quite understandable, really. [*A pause.*] The town will look quite empty.

TOOZENBACH. My dear, I'll be back in a moment.

IRENA. Where are you going?

TOOZENBACH. I must slip back to the town, and then . . . I want to see some of my colleagues off.

IRENA. It's not true. . . . Nikolai, why are you so absent-minded to-day? [*A pause.*] What happened outside the theatre last night?

TOOZENBACH. [*With a movement of impatience.*] I'll be back in an hour. . . . I'll be back with you again. [*Kisses her hands.*] My treasure! . . . [*Gazes into her eyes.*] It's five years since I first began to love you, and still I can't get used to it, and you seem more beautiful every day. What wonderful, lovely hair! What marvellous eyes! I'll take you away to-morrow. We'll work, we'll be rich, my dreams will come to life again. And you'll be happy! But—there's only one "but," only one—you don't love me!

IRENA. I can't help that! I'll be your wife, I'll be loyal and obedient to you, but I can't love you. . . . What's to be done? [Weeps.] I've never loved anyone in my life. Oh, I've had such dreams about being in love! I've been dreaming about it for ever so long, day and night . . . but somehow my soul seems like an expensive piano which someone has locked up and the key's got lost. [A pause.] Your eyes are so restless.

TOOZENBACH. I was awake all night. Not that there's anything to be afraid of in my life, nothing threatening. . . . Only the thought of that lost key torments me and keeps me awake. Say something to me. . . . [A pause.] Say something!

IRENA. What? What am I to say? What?

TOOZENBACH. Anything.

IRENA. Don't, my dear, don't. . . . [A pause.]

TOOZENBACH. Such trifles, such silly little things sometimes become so important suddenly, for no apparent reason! You laugh at them, just as you always have done, you still regard them as trifles, and yet you suddenly find they're in control, and you haven't the power to stop them. But don't let us talk about all that! Really, I feel quite elated. I feel as if I was seeing those fir-trees and maples and birches for the first time in my life. They all seem to be looking at me with a sort of inquisitive look and waiting for something. What beautiful trees—and how beautiful, when you think of it, life ought to be with trees like these! [Shouts of "Ah-oo! Heigh-ho!" are heard.] I must go, it's time. . . . Look at that dead tree, it's all dried-up, but it's still swaying in the wind along with the others. And in the same way, it seems to me that, if I die, I shall still have a share in life somehow or other. Good-bye, my dear. . . . [Kisses her hands.] Your papers, the ones you gave me, are on my desk, under the calendar.

IRENA. I'm coming with you.

TOOZENBACH. [Alarmed.] No, no! [Goes off quickly, then stops in the avenue.] Irena!

IRENA. What?

TOOZENBACH. [Not knowing what to say.] I didn't have any coffee this morning. Will you tell them to get some ready for me? [Goes off quickly.]

[Irena stands, lost in thought, then goes to the back of the stage and sits down on a swing. Enter Andrey with the pram; Ferapont appears.]

FERAPONT. Andrey Serghyeevich, the papers aren't mine, you know, they're the office papers. I didn't make them up.

ANDREY. Oh, where has all my past life gone to?—the time when I was young and gay and clever, when I used to have fine dreams and great thoughts, and the present and the future were bright with hope? Why do we become so dull and commonplace and uninteresting almost before we've begun to live? Why do we get lazy, indifferent, useless, unhappy? . . . This town's been in existence for two hundred years; a hundred thousand people live in it, but there's not one who's any different from all the others! There's never been a scholar or an artist or a saint in this place, never a single man sufficiently outstanding to make you feel passionately that you wanted to emulate him. People here do nothing but eat, drink and sleep. . . . Then they die and some more take their places, and they eat, drink and sleep, too,—and just to introduce a bit of variety into their lives, so as to avoid getting completely stupid with boredom, they indulge in their disgusting gossip and vodka and gambling and law-suits. The wives deceive their husbands, and the husbands lie to their wives, and pretend they don't see anything and don't hear anything. . . . And all this overwhelming vulgarity and pettiness crushes the children and puts out any spark they might have in them, so that they, too, become miserable, half-dead creatures, just like one another and just like their parents! . . . [*To Ferapont, crossly.*] What do you want?

FERAPONT. What? Here are the papers to sign.

ANDREY. What a nuisance you are!

FERAPONT. [*Hands him the papers.*] The porter at the finance department told me just now . . . he said last winter they had two hundred degrees of frost in Petersburg.

ANDREY. I hate the life I live at present, but oh! the sense of elation when I think of the future! Then I feel so lighthearted, such a sense of release! I seem to see light ahead, light and freedom. I see myself free, and my children, too,—free from idleness, free from *kvass*, free from eternal meals of goose and cabbage, free from

after-dinner naps, free from all this degrading parasitism! . . .

FERAPONT. They say two thousand people were frozen to death. They say everyone was scared stiff. It was either in Petersburg or in Moscow, I can't remember exactly.

ANDREY. [*With sudden emotion, tenderly.*] My dear sisters, my dear good sisters! [*Tearfully.*] Masha, my dear sister! . . .

NATASHA. [*Through the window.*] Who's that talking so loudly there? Is that you, Andriusha? You'll wake Sofochka. *Il ne faut pas faire du bruit, la Sophie est dormie déjà. Vous êtes un ours.* [*Getting angry.*] If you want to talk, give the pram to someone else. Ferapont, take the pram from the master.

FERAPONT. Yes, Madam. [*Takes the pram.*]

ANDREY. [*Shamefacedly.*] I was talking quietly.

NATASHA. [*In the window, caressing her small son.*] Bobik! Naughty Bobik! Aren't you a naughty boy!

ANDREY. [*Glancing through the papers.*] All right, I'll go through them and sign them if they need it. You can take them back to the office later. [*Goes into the house, reading the papers.*]

[*Ferapont wheels the pram into the garden.*]

NATASHA. [*In the window.*] What's Mummy's name, Bobik? You darling! And who's that lady? Auntie Olia. Say: "Hullo, Auntie Olia."

[*Two street musicians, a man and a girl, enter and begin to play on a violin and a harp; Vershinin, Olga and Anfisa come out of the house and listen in silence for a few moments;*

then Irena approaches them.]

OLGA. Our garden's like a public road; everybody goes through it. Nanny, give something to the musicians.

ANFISA. [*Giving them money.*] Go along now, God bless you, good people! [*The musicians bow and go away.*] Poor, homeless folk! Whoever would go dragging round the streets playing tunes if he had enough to eat? [*To Irena.*] How are you, Irenushka? [*Kisses her.*] Ah, my child, what a life I'm having! Such comfort! In a large flat at the school with Oliushka—and no rent to pay, either! The Lord's been kind to me in my old age. I've never had such a comfortable time in my life, old sinner that I am! A big flat, and no rent to pay, and a whole room to myself, with my own bed. All free. Sometimes when I wake up in the night I begin to think, and then— Oh, Lord! Oh, Holy Mother of God!—there's no one happier in the world than me!

VERSHININ. [*Glances at his watch.*] We shall be starting in a moment, Olga Serghyeevna. It's time I went. [*A pause.*] I wish you all the happiness in the world . . . everything. . . . Where's Maria Serghyeevna?

IRENA. She's somewhere in the garden. I'll go and look for her.

VERSHININ. That's kind of you. I really must hurry.

ANFISA. I'll come and help to look for her. [*Calls out.*] Mashenka, ah-oo! [*Goes with Irena towards the far end of the garden.*] Ah-oo! Ah-oo!

VERSHININ. Everything comes to an end. Well, here we are—and now it's going to be "good-bye." [*Looks at his watch.*] The city gave us a sort of farewell lunch. There was champagne,

and the mayor made a speech, and I ate and listened, but in spirit I was with you here. . . . [*Glances round the garden.*] I've grown so . . . so accustomed to you.

OLGA. Shall we meet again some day, I wonder?

VERSHININ. Most likely not! [*A pause.*] My wife and the two little girls will be staying on here for a month or two. Please, if anything happens, if they need anything. . . .

OLGA. Yes, yes, of course. You needn't worry about that. [*A pause.*] To-morrow there won't be a single officer or soldier in the town. . . . All that will be just a memory, and, of course, a new life will begin for us here. . . . [*A pause.*] Nothing ever happens as we'd like it to. I didn't want to be a headmistress, and yet now I am one. It means we shan't be going to live in Moscow. . . .

VERSHININ. Well. . . . Thank you for everything. Forgive me if ever I've done anything. . . . I've talked a lot too much, far too much. . . . Forgive me for that, don't think too unkindly of me.

OLGA. [*Wipes her eyes.*] Now . . . why is Masha so long coming?

VERSHININ. What else can I tell you now it's time to say "good-bye"? What shall I philosophize about now? . . . [*Laughs.*] Yes, life is difficult. It seems quite hopeless for a lot of us, just a kind of impasse. . . . And yet you must admit that it is gradually getting easier and brighter, and it's clear that the time isn't far off when the light will spread everywhere. [*Looks at his watch.*] Time, it's time for me to go. . . . In the old days the human race was always making war, its entire existence was taken up with campaigns, advances, retreats, victories. . . . But now all that's out of date, and in its place there's a huge vacuum, clamouring to be filled. Humanity is passionately seeking something to fill it with and, of course, it will find something some day. Oh! If only it would happen soon! [*A pause.*] If only we could educate the industrious people and make the educated people industrious. . . . [*Looks at his watch.*] I really must go. . . .

OLGA. Here she comes!

[*Enter Masha.*]

VERSHININ. I've come to say good-bye. . . .

[*Olga walks off and stands a little to one side so as not to interfere with their leave-taking.*]

MASHA. [*Looking into his face.*] Good-bye! . . . [*A long kiss.*]

OLGA. That'll do, that'll do.

MASHA. [*Sobs loudly*].

VERSHININ. Write to me. . . . Don't forget me! Let me go . . . it's time. Olga Serghyeevna, please take her away . . . I must go . . . I'm late already. . . . [*Deeply moved, kisses Olga's hands, then embraces Masha once again and goes out quickly.*]

OLGA. That'll do, Masha! Don't, my dear, don't. . . .

[*Enter Koolyghin.*]

KOOLYGHIN. [*Embarrassed.*] Never mind, let her cry, let her. . . . My dear Masha, my dear, sweet Masha. . . . You're my wife, and I'm happy in spite of everything. . . . I'm not complaining, I've no reproach to make —not a single one. . . . Olga here is my witness. . . . We'll start our life over again in the same old way, and you won't hear a word from me . . . not a hint. . . .

MASHA. [*Suppressing her sobs.*] "A green oak grows by a curving shore, And round that oak hangs a golden chain." . . . "A golden chain round that oak." . . . Oh, I'm going mad. . . . By a curving shore . . . a green oak. . . .

OLGA. Calm yourself, Masha, calm yourself. . . . Give her some water.

MASHA. I'm not crying any more. . . .

KOOLYGHIN. She's not crying any more . . . she's a good girl.

[*The hollow sound of a gun-shot is heard in the distance.*]

MASHA. "A green oak grows by a curving shore, And round that oak hangs a golden chain." . . . A green cat . . . a green oak . . . I've got it all mixed up. . . . [*Drinks water.*] My life's messed up. . . . I don't want anything now. . . . I'll calm down in a moment. . . . It doesn't matter. . . . What *is* "the curving shore"? Why does it keep coming into my head all the time? My thoughts are all mixed up.

[*Enter Irena.*]

OLGA. Calm down, Masha. That's right . . . good girl! . . . Let's go indoors.

MASHA. [*Irritably.*] I'm not going in there! [*Sobs, but immediately checks herself.*] I don't go into that house now, and I'm not going to. . . .

IRENA. Let's sit down together for a moment, and not talk about anything. I'm going away to-morrow, you know. . . .

[*A pause.*]

KOOLYGHIN. Yesterday I took away a false beard and a moustache from a boy in the third form. I've got them here. [*Puts them on.*] Do I look like our German teacher? . . . [*Laughs.*] I do, don't I? The boys are funny.

MASHA. It's true, you do look like that German of yours.

OLGA. [*Laughs.*] Yes, he does.

[*Masha cries.*]

IRENA. That's enough, Masha!

KOOLYGHIN. Very much like him, I think!

[*Enter Natasha.*]

NATASHA. [*To the maid.*] What? Oh, yes. Mr. Protopopov is going to keep an eye on Sofochka, and Andrey Serghyeevich is going to take Bobik out in the pram. What a lot of work these children make! . . . [*To Irena.*] Irena, you're really leaving to-morrow? What a pity! Do stay just another week, won't you? [*Catching sight of Koolyghin, shrieks; he laughs and takes off the false beard and moustache.*] Get away with you! How you scared me! [*To Irena.*] I've grown so accustomed to you being here. . . . You mustn't think it's going to be easy for me to be without you. I'll get Andrey and his old violin to move into your room: he can saw away at it as much as he likes there. And then we'll move Sofochka into his room. She's such a wonderful child, really! Such a lovely little girl! This morning she looked at me with such a sweet expression, and then she said: "Mamma!"

KOOLYGHIN. It's quite true, she is a beautiful child.

NATASHA. So to-morrow I'll be alone here. [*Sighs.*] I'll have this fir-tree avenue cut down first, then that maple tree over there. It looks so awful in the evenings. . . . [*To Irena.*] My dear, that belt you're wearing doesn't suit you at all. Not at all in good taste. You want something brighter to go with that dress. . . . I'll tell them to put flowers all round here, lots of flowers, so that we get plenty of scent from them. . . . [*Sternly.*] Why is there a fork lying on this seat? [*Going into the house, to the maid.*] Why is that fork left on the seat there? [*Shouts.*] Don't answer me back!

KOOLYGHIN. There she goes again!

[*A band plays a military march off-stage; all listen.*]

OLGA. They're going.

[*Enter Chebutykin.*]

MASHA. The soldiers are going. Well. . . . Happy journey to them! [*To her husband.*] We must go home. . . . Where's my hat and cape? . . .

KOOLYGHIN. I took them indoors. I'll bring them at once.

OLGA. Yes, we can go home now. It's time.

CHEBUTYKIN. Olga Serghyeevna!

OLGA. What is it? [*A pause.*] What?

CHEBUTYKIN. Nothing. . . . I don't know quite how to tell you. . . . [*Whispers into her ear.*]

OLGA. [*Frightened.*] It can't be true!

CHEBUTYKIN. Yes . . . a bad business. . . . I'm so tired . . . quite worn out. . . . I don't want to say another word. . . . [*With annoyance.*] Anyway, nothing matters! . . .

MASHA. What's happened?

OLGA. [*Puts her arms round Irena.*] What a dreadful day! . . . I don't know how to tell you, dear. . . .

IRENA. What is it? Tell me quickly, what is it? For Heaven's sake! . . . [*Cries.*]

CHEBUTYKIN. The Baron's just been killed in a duel.

IRENA. [*Cries quietly.*] I knew it, I knew it. . . .

CHEBUTYKIN. [*Goes to the back of the stage and sits down.*] I'm tired. . . . [*Takes a newspaper out of his pocket.*] Let them cry for a bit. . . .

[*Sings quietly to himself.*] Tarara-boom-di-ay, I'm sitting on a tomb-di-ay. . . . What difference does it make? . . .

[*The three sisters stand huddled together.*]

MASHA. Oh, listen to that band! They're leaving us . . . one of them's gone for good . . . for ever! We're left alone . . . to start our lives all over again. We must go on living . . . we must go on living. . . .

IRENA. [*Puts her head on Olga's breast.*] Some day people will know why such things happen, and what the purpose of all this suffering is. . . . Then there won't be any more riddles. . . . Meanwhile we must go on living . . . and working. Yes, we must just go on working! To-morrow I'll go away alone and teach in a school somewhere; I'll give my life to people who need it. . . . It's autumn now, winter will soon be here, and the snow will cover everything . . . but I'll go on working and working! . . .

OLGA. [*Puts her arms round both her sisters.*] How cheerfully and jauntily that band's playing—really I feel as if I wanted to live! Merciful God! The years will pass, and we shall all be gone for good and quite forgotten. . . . Our faces and our voices will be forgotten and people won't even know that there were once three of us here. . . . But our sufferings may mean happiness for the people who come after us. . . . There'll be a time when peace and happiness reign in the world, and then we shall be remembered kindly and blessed. No, my dear sisters, life isn't finished for us yet! We're going to live! The band is playing so cheerfully and joyfully—maybe, if we wait a little longer, we shall find out why we live, why we suffer. . . . Oh, if we only knew, if only we knew!

[*The music grows fainter and fainter. Koolyghin, smiling happily, brings out the hat and the cape. Andrey enters; he is pushing the pram with Bobik sitting in it.*]

CHEBUTYKIN. [*Sings quietly to himself.*] Tarara-boom-di-ay. . . . I'm sitting on a tomb-di-ay. . . . [*Reads the paper.*] What does it matter? Nothing matters!

OLGA. If only we knew, if only we knew! . . .

DISCUSSION OF *THE THREE SISTERS*

Probably your first impression of *The Three Sisters* is that it is confusing. Unlike *Antigone* and *King Lear* it has no central figure or single focal action. A cluster of characters seems to come and go at random and seldom engages for long in a consecutive conversation. On the other hand, this conversation, while intense, is not so dazzlingly funny as to distract you from the apparent lack of plot.

Much of the important action happens offstage and is only reported. Andrey loses at gambling, Natasha gains control over the household, Toozenbach proposes to Olga, Chebutykin kills a woman through his medical ignorance, Soliony kills Toozenbach in a duel. These actions in a conventional play might well be the meat of the onstage business. Any one of them or any one of the three love triangles would be enough to fill out a conventional plot.

In *The Three Sisters* we watch instead of action the effect of these actions on the characters. The surface of the dialogue tends to show us their psychological state at the moment, not to advance the action. Chekhov demands that we ourselves make connections between the superficially unrelated events. "When writing," he said of his short stories, "I rely entirely on the reader to add the missing subjective elements in the story." The same is true in *The Three Sisters*. Those missing subjective elements, which are its key, are submerged beneath the banality and foolishness of the surface. "It is necessary," Chekhov said, "that on the stage everything should be as complex and as simple as in life. People are having dinner, and while they're having it, their future happiness may be decided or their lives may be about to be shattered."

An instance of the shattering of lives is Natasha's growing control over the household. In Act II Natasha suggests rather aimlessly, more to herself than to Andrey, that their baby Bobik would be more comfortable in Irena's room. Act III opens in Olga's bedroom, which she now shares with Irena. We have seen no direct confrontation between Natasha and Irena, but Natasha has triumphed. That triumph is shown in a dozen other small ways. Natasha cancels the celebration in Act II. She constantly pries into what people are doing. She scolds and yells out the window. The sisters spend as much time as they can away from the house, and Andrey is reduced to pushing the baby carriage. Yet the triumph is never directly stated. We have to supply the missing subjective element of this part of the story.

Chekhov's oblique presentation has led his best critic, David Magarshack, in his book *Chekhov the Dramatist,* to call the plays "plays of indirect action." Against the position that Chekhov has no plot, Magarshack argues convincingly: "As for plot, it is not its absence but rather its complexity that distinguishes them, and the producer who fails to realize that simply cannot see the wood for the trees." In *The Three Sisters* no one series of causally connected events is sufficiently emphasized to become a main plot. All of the action, as Magarshack attests, is of equal necessity, and most of it is so complex that it seems disconnected. A play like *Antigone* that emphasizes progressive action is highly selective. Only incidents that contribute to the main action are included. A certain amount of extrinsic incident may be allowed, as in *King Lear,* but this incident is sternly limited to throw the main action into bolder relief. In the tragicomic structure of *The Three Sisters,* however, catharsis results from a fusion of all the individual, equally important actions. These offer different points of view on a central problem and converge at the end of the play in a synthesis which embodies the author's intellectual purpose, his theme.

Two structural devices that advance the actions are duets and ensembles. Duets consist of scenes in which a few characters, usually two, are onstage alone and in direct conflict. For a play that gives a dominant impression of many people onstage at once, there are a surprising number of duets. In the ensembles, most or all of the characters are onstage at once. These ensemble scenes ironically comment on the different stories advanced in the duets. Verbose interludes on trivial subjects largely make up these scenes. Such interludes seem pointlessly trivial, but they function like a Greek chorus. Magarshack explains how the opening of the first act, despite its conversational realism, is highly formal and choral. The men's conversation, sporadically emerging from the back room, forms a flippant and mocking antistrophe to the strophic conversation of the sisters. When Olga says, "I felt such a longing to be back home!" [in Moscow], Chebutykin's comment intrudes: "The devil you did!" and Toozenbach replies: "It's all nonsense, of course." When Olga cries, "Yes, to Moscow as soon as possible," Chebutykin and Toozenbach laugh. After Olga's next speech, Toozenbach is heard saying, "Really, you talk such a lot of nonsense, I'm tired of listening to you."

Such choral elements pervade the play. The desire of the three sisters to return to Moscow, for instance, is one of the play's themes. But, inevitably, when one of them plaintively announces such a desire, another character's comments show it is an idle, hopeless daydream. We learn from Ferapont, for example, that life in Moscow is just as tedious and horrible and dreary as in the provincial town. Chebutykin's famous lines about Balsac's marriage and the epidemic in Tzitzikar tell us that life is the same everywhere. The new province where the regiment is going will be the same as where it is now.

These many individual strands of action result from well-individualized characters. In plays involving a closely knit group of people, like a family and its friends, you usually expect stereotyped characters at least in the minor roles. In Hollywood and on television they are called "character actors"—the cowboy's sidekick, the angry boss, the villain, the befuddled husband, the lovable grandma, the boobish cop. Rarely do we ever see anything but the young, the lovable, the healthy, the happy, and the half-witted. Even at the higher level of the drawing-room comedy, while the dialogue and characters may be more glossy and sophisticated, the characters and situations tend to be fixed. An unremarkable boy meets, loses, and wins an unnoticeable girl in an invariable way.

It is just such stereotyping of role and situation that Chekhov opposed and avoided. He once gave his brother the following advice:

Try to be original in your play, and, as far as possible, intelligent, but do not be afraid to appear silly. . . . Incidentally, love declarations, infidelities by husbands and wives, and tears shed by widows, orphans and other people have been described long ago.

And in another letter he gave a list of characters who should be avoided: "Retired captains with red noses, drunken press reporters, starving writers, consumptive and hard-working wives, honest young men without a blot on their characters, lofty-minded young ladies, and dear old nannies." To the playwright Suvorin, Chekhov wrote about one of his characters:

The father seems to have no weakness of any sort. He does not drink, he does not smoke, he does not play cards, and he is not ill. You ought to attach some kind of quality to him to give the actor something to hang on to.

The closest thing to a stock character in *The Three Sisters* is Koolyghin, the boorish, Polonius-like pedant. But even he is given good lines and several funny scenes. One of his lines states the moral heart of the play: "A thing that loses its form is finished—that's just as true of our ordinary, everyday lives." And as a character he has sufficient depth to draw forth our mixed responses. He is funny, and, as he says of himself, happy, but we dislike his insensitivity to Masha and to Olga's suffering.

All the other characters are less simple-minded and undergo some change from beginning to end that makes their stories wry or wrenching. Masha and Vershinin have their delightful love scene in Act III, with a kind of Meredithian lighthearted glee in their spontaneous singing, but their love scene is permeated by the news of the attempted suicide of Vershinin's wife. Chebutykin at the beginning commits the faux pas of giving a too elaborate present to Irena. By the end, our response to this at first comically pitiful old man has changed immensely. We come to sympathize deeply with his tragic withdrawal from the world he sees as chaotic, nonsensical, and cruel.

Even the villains draw forth our deepest responses. Natasha's triumph over the sisters and Andrey is real but hollow. She makes a henpecked cuckold and an ineffective local councilman out of Andrey. But for all of her victory, she is isolated, scorned by the others. Her last gesture is to shriek at the servant's disobedience, thrown into a rage by a misplaced fork.

Soliony too is something more than a villain who is rejected by Olga. He is, as Magarshack points out, "a villain with a soul, and it is the utter emptiness of his soul that provides the key to his character and his actions." Much as he grates on everyone's nerves with his unwanted and ignorant attempts at humor, and much as we sympathize with Olga for telling him off, we have to pity him too. This third dimension of his character is explained to us by Toozenbach himself, who says of Soliony in Act I, "I'm sorry for him, even though he irritates me. In fact, I feel more sorry than irritated." In the end, the irony of this kindhearted defense rebounds on Toozenbach. Just as he is about to start his new life of hard work, Soliony kills him in the duel.

Because so many of the characters' hopes are frustrated, the mood of the play has often been thought somber and depressing. This mood, however, is only half of the play, a half that is easier to see if you think only of those speeches where characters complain about their fates or wonder about the meaning of life. Equal in effect and intensity to these is the sense of comedy. This comedy does not alternate with the seriousness but runs along with it. The two aspects modify and intensify each other and in the end fuse together. Without a sense of this simultaneity and fusion, the play will appear either pointless or exceedingly grim. From Chekhov's time to our own *The Three*

Sisters has often been misunderstood. Even its first director, Stanislavsky, one of the founders of the great Moscow Art Theatre, played it so somberly that Chekhov quarreled with him over it.

The comic elements are many, and they range through the greatest diversity, from Meredith's bright, tinkling laugh to an almost Swiftian intensity of despair. The characters themselves are from the social level traditional to drawing-room comedy. They are the bourgeois with its usual complement of servants, as in *Tartuffe*. But just as they are three-dimensional rather than cardboard cutouts, so is their action mixed in its effects. Every character has some sort of comic business. Toozenbach has a lighthearted drunken scene, and Chebutykin has a bitter one. Soliony goes, "Cluck, cluck, cluck!" Koolyghin, who gives people marks for their behavior, puts on the false beard he has taken from his student and tries to amuse the sisters just after Toozenbach's death. Even Fedotik dances gaily over the burning of everything he owns.

This comedy is above all ironic, and the strength of the irony increases as the play proceeds. The choral commentary, the recurring snatches of music, and the inane remarks seem almost farcical at the beginning, but they are tinged with a growing foreboding. The last scene of the play holds together the greatest contrast and the greatest range of emotions. The sisters stand together, and Olga puts her arms around the other two, saying, "How cheerfully and jauntily that band's playing—really I feel as if I wanted to live! . . . We're going to live!" Then:

> *The music grows fainter and fainter. Koolyghin, smiling happily, brings out the hat and the cape. Andrey enters; he is pushing the pram. . . .*

All of the elements of the play are brought together. The themes of work and of living, the gaiety of the band music, and the determination to triumph, all come together, intensely modified by the happy foolishness of Koolyghin, the failure of Andrey, and the collapse of Chebutykin. The play ends as it began, with a choral comment: "What does it matter? Nothing matters! . . . If only we knew, if only we knew."

This irony permeates the language as well as the characterization and the action. Each character has his own style of speaking. As the play's over-all style is naturalistic, and as each character is held to what he might naturally say, the language would seem theoretically quite limited. Actually, it is not. The main extensions of the middle or natural style occur in several ways.

First, there are many lyric extensions of natural speech. These occur chiefly in the many songs and literary echoes. There are songs and music in every act, including a violin, an accordion, and the military band. The literary echoes also occur throughout. Although Russian commentators point out that many of these echoes get lost in translation, we can still feel the effect of some of them. For example, Soliony's quotation in Act I provides a clue to Chekhov's whole strategy of action:

> He had no time to say "Oh, oh!"
> Before that bear had struck him low. . . .

And Masha's sensitivity is revealed partly by the song which keeps popping into her head: "A green oak grows by a curving shore, And round that oak hangs a golden chain."

Allied to these lyric moments are what might be called "arias," that is, impassioned speeches on noble subjects. Toozenbach, for example, has several on work, and Vershinin has one on the future and another on the self-sustaining quality of culture and education.

In contrast to these lyrical extensions, there are the many instances of sub-speech and noise. Soliony's gaucheness is shown by his "Cluck, cluck, cluck." Chebutykin quotes recipes for quack remedies from the newspaper. Offstage shouts, greetings, bells, the fire noises, and the famous gun shot punctuate the action.

The effect of such contrasts is a complex of interlocking ironies. No series of speeches continues on the same level for any length of time. The noblest and most intense speech will be interrupted by a foolish response, a crash, or a giggle. Any character's statements will be modified by some action occurring elsewhere, either onstage or off. For example, the invisible character Protopopov is kept in our minds by many references: he sends the cake in Act I, Andrey talks frequently of him, Ferapont delivers messages from him, he calls for Natasha in Act III, and Chebutykin forcefully points out to the sisters what everyone has been ignoring, that Protopopov is allied with Natasha. The final ambiguous triumph of Natasha over the sisters is part of Protopopov's conspiracy. For another example, Chebutykin's presence always reminds us of failure. For a third, at the very moment that Vershinin and Masha recognize their love for each other, Vershinin's wife is attempting suicide.

The irony of structure, of characterization, and of language is both Chekhov's greatest success and his greatest failure. Although it is handled brilliantly, it is the irony that makes his plays difficult for a person brought up on conventional plays to understand.

The irony of structure, of characterization, of language, plus the depth of psychological probing, the combination of the most inane foolishness with the grimmest despair, and the simultaneous victory and defeat of life—all of these qualities which make the play confusing at first make it finally, after reflection, Chekhov's greatest triumph.

DISCUSSION QUESTIONS ON *THE THREE SISTERS*

1. There are three love triangles in *The Three Sisters*—the Irena-Toozenbach-Soliony triangle, the Masha-Koolyghin-Vershinin triangle, and the Natasha-Andrey-Protopopov triangle. Which of these is developed by the traditional tragic structure? Which by other structures? How do the other structures differ from the traditional? How does each triangle come out? Why does Chekhov develop three triangles instead of only one, as is usual in comedy?

2. Much of the action is developed by duets. In a duet, two people speak to each other alone, regardless of how many other people are onstage. Find

several examples of duets. Do all of the characters engage equally in duets, or do some more than others? Why? Why are other characters sometimes onstage during the duets?

3. Each major character has at least one aria—that is, one impassioned speech of some length on a lofty subject. In these arias, the characters reveal their central concerns or desires. What are the chief desires of each of the three sisters? Of Toozenbach? Of Vershinin? Of Soliony? Which of these characters are more active? Which passive?

4. In a phrase or two, describe the differences between the sisters. For example, which is the most sensitive? Which wants the most out of life? Which is the most discontented? Which the most resigned? Which changes the most in the course of the play? Does Chekhov make one more sympathetic than the others? If so, why? If not, why not?

5. Chekhov was interested in stage effects, especially in sounds and music. Find as many examples as you can of noises, of music, of shouting, of sub-spoken utterances like crying, laughing, clucking, whistling, humming, coughing. Many of these are functional: they indicate something about the characters or they change the course of the action. Explain the function of several of your examples.

6. Three of Chekhov's most famous stage techniques are the invisible character, the silent character, and the pause in speech. In *The Three Sisters*, Protopopov is never onstage. Why? What is the effect of his absence? How does the audience know about him? What does the audience think of him? In Act III, Natasha walks the full width of the stage carrying a candle, but saying nothing. What is the effect of this? Find an example of a pause in a character's speech. "Fill in" his pause with what he would have said if he had gone on talking. How are these three techniques related? Are they "dramatic"?

7. The setting of the play is limited to the sisters' house and garden. (There is, incidentally, unity of place, but not of time.) We learn quite a bit about public events in their town. Name some of them. Do you think Chekhov has successfully captured the life of a provincial city? Is the town used symbolically or realistically? That is, is this every town or one specific town? If you know Thornton Wilder's *Our Town*, you might fruitfully compare Wilder's town with Chekhov's. Is Chekhov's use of external events outside of the house and garden comparable to Sophocles'? To Lorca's?

8. Four minor characters appear fairly frequently—Anfisa, Ferapont, Fedotik, and Rodé. Are they all equally important? What use does Chekhov put them to? Could any be omitted?

9. Chekhov wrote to the playwright Suvorin about a character in one of Suvorin's plays: "The father seems to have no weakness of any sort. He does not drink, he does not smoke, he does not play cards, and he is not ill. You ought to attach some kind of quality to him to give the actor something to hang on to." This comment looks two ways, toward the actor's business and toward characterization. David Magarshack points out that all the main characters have some symbol attached to them. Soliony, for example, constantly

uses scent, and Chebutykin constantly reads the newspaper. Find other examples. Are these symbols functional in revealing character, or are they mere stage business? Do you imagine that Chekhov first invented his characters and later added symbols to them, or did he see the characters symbolically from the first?

10. *The Three Sisters* could be acted in several different styles. Stanislavsky emphasized its gloominess and the ineffectuality of its characters. Chekhov himself did not want Soliony played as a melodramatic villain. How might you stage or act the following scenes, and what principal emotion would you strive to draw out of each?

In Act II, Soliony's line, "If that child were mine, I'd cook him up in a frying pan and eat him."

In Act III, Chebutykin's dropping the clock.

In Act III, Ferapont's delivering the message to Andrey.

In Act IV, Koolyghin's putting on the false mustache.

In Act IV, the final scene with the three sisters.

11. How many jokes can you find in the play? Are there more at the beginning or at the end? Are the earlier jokes funnier or grimmer than the later ones?

12. Chekhov was very careful in labeling the genres of his plays. He didn't call *The Three Sisters* a tragedy or a comedy, but a "drama." What does this reveal about his intentions in the play? Can the play still be labeled a tragicomedy? What would you say to the argument that it is gloomy, morbid, and depressing? Does it approach both the extremes of tragedy and of comedy, or does it stop short of them as Guarini would have preferred?

13. Modern Russian accounts of Chekhov say that he predicted the end of the old aristocracy and bourgeoisie, whose downfall the Revolution brought about. That is, they use Chekhov as a propagandist and regard his plays as thesis plays. What evidence would you use to support this stand? To attack it?

14. "Pan," whose character we use as an emblem of tragicomedy, means *All*. Is *The Three Sisters* all-inclusive? Does it omit any subjects that you think important, like religion or politics or love? Does it take a stand on any subjects, like liberalism and conservatism, or deism and atheism? Chekhov said that the drama must above all be "humane." Is the myth of Pan "humane"? Is *The Three Sisters*?

THE PLOUGH AND THE STARS

A TRAGEDY IN FOUR ACTS

BY SEAN O'CASEY

To the gay laugh of my mother
at the gate of the grave

CHARACTERS

JACK CLITHEROE (a bricklayer), Commandant in
  the Irish Citizen Army
NORA CLITHEROE, his wife
PETER FLYNN (a labourer), Nora's uncle
THE YOUNG COVEY (a fitter), Clitheroe's cousin
BESSIE BURGESS (a street fruit-vendor)
MRS. GOGAN (a charwoman)
MOLLSER, her consumptive child
FLUTHER GOOD (a carpenter)

Residents in
the Tenement

LIEUT. LANGON (a Civil Servant), of the Irish Volunteers
CAPT. BRENNAN (a chicken butcher), of the Irish Citizen Army
CORPORAL STODDART, of the Wiltshires
SERGEANT TINLEY, of the Wiltshires
ROSIE REDMOND, a daughter of 'the Digs'
A BAR-TENDER
A WOMAN
THE FIGURE IN THE WINDOW

TIME.—*Acts I and II, November 1915; Acts III and IV, Easter Week, 1916.*
A few days elapse between Acts III and IV.

ACT I.—*The living-room of the Clitheroe flat in a Dublin tenement.*
ACT II.—*A public-house, outside of which a meeting is being held.*
ACT III.—*The street outside the Clitheroe tenement.*
ACT IV.—*The room of Bessie Burgess.*

ACT I

[*The home of the Clitheroes. It consists of the front and back drawing-rooms in a fine old Georgian house, struggling for its life against the assaults of time, and the more savage assaults of the tenants. The room shown is the back drawing-room, wide, spacious, and lofty. At back is the entrance to the front drawing-room. The space, originally occupied by folding doors, is now draped with casement cloth of a dark purple, decorated with* a design in reddish-purple and cream. One of the curtains is pulled aside, giving a glimpse of front drawing-room, at the end of which can be seen the wide, lofty windows looking out into the street. The room directly in front of the audience is furnished in a way that suggests an attempt towards a finer expression of domestic life. The large fireplace on right is of wood, painted to look like marble (the original has been taken away by the landlord). On the mantelshelf are two candlesticks of dark carved wood. Between them is a small clock. Over the clock is hanging a calendar which displays a picture of 'The Sleeping Venus'. In the centre of the breast of the chimney hangs a picture of Robert Emmet. On the right of the entrance to the front drawing-room is a copy of 'The Gleaners', on the opposite side a copy of 'The Angelus'. Underneath 'The Gleaners' is a chest of drawers on which stands a green bowl filled with scarlet dahlias and white chrysanthemums. Near to the fireplace is a settee which at night forms a double bed for Clitheroe and Nora. Underneath 'The Angelus' are a number of shelves containing saucepans and a frying-pan. Under these is a table on which are various articles of delf ware. Near the end of the room, opposite to the fireplace, is a gate-legged table, covered with a cloth. On top of the table a huge cavalry sword is lying. To the right is a door which leads to a lobby from which the staircase leads to the hall. The floor is covered with a dark green linoleum. The room is dim except where it is illuminated from the glow of the fire. Through the window of the room at back can be seen the flaring of the flame of a gasolene lamp giving light to workmen repairing the street. Occasionally can be heard the clang of crowbars striking the setts. Fluther Good is repairing the lock of door, Right. A claw-hammer is on a chair beside him, and he has a screw-driver in his hand. He is a man of forty years of age, rarely surrendering to thoughts of anxiety, fond of his 'oil' but determined to conquer the habit before he dies. He is square-jawed and harshly featured; under the left eye is a scar, and his nose is bent from a smashing blow received in a fistic battle long ago. He is bald, save for a few peeping tufts of reddish hair around his ears; and his upper lip is hidden by a scrubby red moustache, embroidered here and there with a grey hair. He is dressed in a seedy black suit, cotton shirt with a soft collar, and wears a very respectable little black bow. On his head is a faded jerry hat, which, when he is excited, he has a habit of knocking farther back on his head, in a series of taps. In an argument he usually fills with sound and fury generally signifying a row. He is in his shirt-sleeves at present, and wears a soiled white apron, from a pocket in which sticks a carpenter's two-foot rule. He has just finished the job of putting on a new lock, and, filled with satisfaction, he is opening and shutting the door, enjoying the completion of a work well done. Sitting at the fire, airing a white shirt, is Peter Flynn. He is a little, thin bit of a man, with a face shaped like a lozenge; on his cheeks and under his chin is a straggling wiry beard of a dirty-white and lemon hue. His face invariably wears a look of animated anguish, mixed with irritated defiance, as if everybody was at war with him, *and he at war with everybody. He is cocking his head in a way that suggests resentment at the presence of Fluther, who pays no attention to him, apparently, but is really furtively watching him. Peter is clad in a singlet, white whipcord knee-breeeches, and is in his stocking-feet.*

A voice is heard speaking outside of door, Left. It is that of Mrs. Gogan.]

MRS. GOGAN. [*Outside.*] Who are you lookin' for, sir? Who? Mrs. Clitheroe? . . . Oh, excuse me. Oh ay, up this way. She's out, I think: I seen her goin'. Oh, you've somethin' for her; oh, excuse me. You're from Arnott's. . . . I see. . . . You've a parcel for her. . . . Righto. . . . I'll take it. . . . I'll give it to her the minute she comes in. . . . It'll be quite safe. . . . Oh, sign that. . . . Excuse me. . . . Where? . . . Here? . . . No, there; righto. Am I to put Maggie or Mrs.? What is it? You dunno? Oh, excuse me.

[*Mrs. Gogan opens the door and comes in. She is a doleful-looking little woman of forty, insinuating manner and sallow complexion. She is fidgety and nervous, terribly talkative, has a habit of taking up things that may be near her and fiddling with them while she is speaking. Her heart is aflame with curiosity, and a fly could not come into nor go out of the house without her knowing. She has a draper's parcel in her hand, the knot of the twine tying it is untied. Peter, more resentful of this intrusion than of Fluther's presence, gets up from the chair, and without looking around, his head carried at an angry cock, marches into the room at back.*]

MRS. GOGAN. [*Removing the paper*

and opening the cardboard box it contains.] I wondher what's this now? A hat! [*She takes out a hat, black, with decorations in red and gold.*] God, she's goin' to th' divil lately for style! That hat, now, cost more than a penny. Such notions of upperosity she's gettin'. [*Putting the hat on her head.*] Oh, swank, what! [*She replaces it in parcel.*]

FLUTHER. She's a pretty little Judy, all the same.

MRS. GOGAN. Ah, she is, an' she isn't. There's prettiness an' prettiness in it. I'm always sayin' that her skirts are a little too short for a married woman. An' to see her, sometimes of an evenin', in her glad-neck gown would make a body's blood run cold. I do be ashamed of me life before her husband. An' th' way she thries to be polite, with her 'Good mornin', Mrs. Gogan', when she's goin' down, an' her 'Good evenin', Mrs. Gogan', when she's comin' up. But there's politeness an' politeness in it.

FLUTHER. They seem to get on well together, all th' same.

MRS. GOGAN. Ah, they do, an' they don't. The pair o' them used to be like two turtle doves always billin' an' cooin'. You couldn't come into th' room but you'd feel, instinctive like, that they'd just been affter kissin' an' cuddlin' each other. . . . It often made me shiver, for, affter all, there's kissin' an' cuddlin' in it. But I'm thinkin' he's beginnin' to take things more quietly; the mystery of havin' a woman's a mystery no longer. . . . She dhresses herself to keep him with her, but it's no use—affter a month or two, th' wondher of a woman wears off.

FLUTHER. I dunno, I dunno. Not

wishin' to say anything derogatory, I think it's all a question of location: when a man finds th' wondher of one woman beginnin' to die, it's usually beginnin' to live in another.

MRS. GOGAN. She's always grumblin' about havin' to live in a tenement house. 'I wouldn't like to spend me last hour in one, let alone live me life in a tenement,' says she. 'Vaults,' says she, 'that are hidin' th' dead, instead of homes that are sheltherin' th' livin'.' 'Many a good one,' says I, 'was reared in a tenement house.' Oh, you know, she's a well-up little lassie, too; able to make a shillin' go where another would have to spend a pound. She's wipin' th' eyes of th' Covey an' poor oul' Pether—everybody knows that—screwin' every penny she can out o' them, in ordher to turn th' place into a babby-house. An' she has th' life frightened out o' them; washin' their face, combin' their hair, wipin' their feet, brushin' their clothes, thrimmin' their nails, cleanin' their teeth—God Almighty, you'd think th' poor men were undhergoin' penal servitude.

FLUTHER. [*With an exclamation of disgust.*] A-a-ah, that's goin' beyond th' beyonds in a tenement house. That's a little bit too derogatory.

[*Peter enters from room, Back, head elevated and resentful fire in his eyes; he is still in his singlet and trousers, but is now wearing a pair of unlaced boots—possibly to be decent in the presence of Mrs. Gogan. He places the white shirt, which he has carried in on his arm, on the back of a chair near the fire, and, going over to the chest of drawers, he opens drawer after drawer, looking for something; as he fails to find it he closes each drawer with a snap; he pulls out*

pieces of linen neatly folded, and bundles them back again any way.]

PETER. [*In accents of anguish.*] Well, God Almighty, give me patience! [*He returns to room, Back, giving the shirt a vicious turn as he passes.*]

MRS. GOGAN. I wondher what he is foostherin' for now?

FLUTHER. He's adornin' himself for th' meeting to-night. [*Pulling a hand-bill from his pocket and reading.*] 'Great Demonstration an' torchlight procession around places in th' city sacred to th' memory of Irish Patriots, to be concluded be a meetin', at which will be taken an oath of fealty to th' Irish Republic. Formation in Parnell Square at eight o'clock.' Well, they can hold it for Fluther. I'm up th' pole; no more dhrink for Fluther. It's three days now since I touched a dhrop, an' I feel a new man already.

MRS. GOGAN. Isn't oul' Peter a funny-lookin' little man? . . . Like somethin' you'd pick off a Christmas Tree. . . . When he's dhressed up in his canonicals, you'd wondher where he'd been got. God forgive me, when I see him in them, I always think he must ha' had a Mormon for a father! He an' th' Covey can't abide each other; th' pair o' them is always at it, thryin' to best each other. There'll be blood dhrawn one o' these days.

FLUTHER. How is it that Clitheroe himself, now, doesn't have anythin' to do with th' Citizen Army? A couple o' months ago, an' you'd hardly ever see him without his gun, an' th' Red Hand o' Liberty Hall in his hat.

MRS. GOGAN. Just because he wasn't made a Captain of. He wasn't goin' to be in anything where he couldn't be conspishuous. He was so cocksure o' being made one that he bought a Sam Browne belt, an' was always puttin' it on an' standin' at th' door showing it off, till th' man came an' put out th' street lamps on him. God, I think he used to bring it to bed with him! But I'm tellin' you herself was delighted that that cock didn't crow, for she's like a clockin' hen if he leaves her sight for a minute.

[*While she is talking, she takes up book after book from the table, looks into each of them in a near-sighted way, and then leaves them back. She now lifts up the sword, and proceeds to examine it.*]

MRS. GOGAN. Be th' look of it, this must ha' been a general's sword. . . . All th' gold lace an' th' fine figaries on it. . . . Sure it's twiced too big for him.

FLUTHER. A-ah; it's a baby's rattle he ought to have, an' he as he is with thoughts tossin' in his head of what may happen to him on th' day o' judgement.

[*Peter has entered, and seeing Mrs. Gogan with the sword, goes over to her, pulls it resentfully out of her hands, and marches into the room, Back, without speaking.*]

MRS. GOGAN. [*As Peter whips the sword.*] Oh, excuse me! . . . [*To Fluther.*] Isn't he th' surly oul' rascal!

FLUTHER. Take no notice of him. . . . You'd think he was dumb, but when you get his goat, or he has a few jars up, he's vice versa. [*He coughs.*]

MRS. GOGAN. [*She has now sidled over as far as the shirt hanging on the chair.*] Oh, you've got a cold on you, Fluther.

FLUTHER. [*Carelessly.*] Ah, it's only a little one.

MRS. GOGAN. You'd want to be careful, all th' same. I knew a woman, a big lump of a woman, red-faced an' round-bodied, a little awkward on her feet; you'd think, to look at her, she could put out her two arms an' lift a two-storied house on th' top of her head; got a ticklin' in her throat, an' a little cough, an' th' next mornin' she had a little catchin' in her chest, an' they had just time to wet her lips with a little rum, an' off she went. [*She begins to look at and handle the shirt.*]

FLUTHER. [*A little nervously.*] It's only a little cold I have; there's nothing derogatory wrong with me.

MRS. GOGAN. I dunno; there's many a man this minute lowerin' a pint, thinkin' of a woman, or pickin' out a winner, or doin' work as you're doin', while th' hearse dhrawn be th' horses with the black plumes is dhrivin' up to his own hall door, an' a voice that he doesn't hear is muttherin' in his ear, 'Earth to earth, an' ashes t' ashes, an' dust to dust.'

FLUTHER. [*Faintly.*] A man in th' pink o' health should have a holy horror of allowin' thoughts o' death to be festerin' in his mind, for [*With a frightened cough*] be God, I think I'm afther gettin 'a little catch in me chest that time—it's a creepy thing to be thinkin' about.

MRS. GOGAN. It is, an' it isn't; it's both bad an' good. . . . It always gives meself a kind o' threspassin' joy to feel meself movin' along in a mournin' coach, an' me thinkin' that, maybe, th' next funeral 'll be me own, an' glad, in a quiet way, that this is somebody else's.

FLUTHER. An' a curious kind of a gaspin' for breath—I hope there's nothin' derogatory wrong with me.

MRS. GOGAN. [*Examining the shirt.*] Frills on it, like a woman's petticoat.

FLUTHER. Suddenly gettin' hot, an' then, just as suddenly, gettin' cold.

MRS. GOGAN. [*Holding out the shirt towards Fluther.*] How would you like to be wearin' this Lord Mayor's nightdhress, Fluther?

FLUTHER. [*Vehemently.*] Blast you an' your nightshirt! Is a man fermentin' with fear to stick th' showin' off to him of a thing that looks like a shinin' shroud?

MRS. GOGAN. Oh, excuse me!

[*Peter has again entered, and he pulls the shirt from the hands of Mrs. Gogan, replacing it on the chair. He returns to room.*]

PETER. [*As he goes out.*] Well, God Almighty, give me patience!

MRS. GOGAN. [*To Peter.*] Oh, excuse me!

[*There is heard a cheer from the men working outside on the street, followed by the clang of tools being thrown down, then silence. The glare of the gasolene light diminishes and finally goes out.*]

MRS. GOGAN. [*Running into the back room to look out of the window.*] What's the men repairin' th' streets cheerin' for?

FLUTHER. [*Sitting down weakly on a chair.*] You can't sneeze but that oul' one wants to know th' why an' th' wherefore. . . . I feel as dizzy as bedamned! I hope I didn't give up th' beer too suddenly.

[*The Covey comes in by the door, Right. He is about twenty-five, tall, thin, with lines on his face that form a perpetual protest against life as he conceives it to be. Heavy seams fall from each side of nose, down around his lips, as if they were suspenders*]

keeping his mouth from falling. He speaks in a slow, wailing drawl; more rapidly when he is excited. He is dressed in dungarees, and is wearing a vividly red tie. He flings his cap with a gesture of disgust on the table, and begins to take off his overalls.]

MRS. GOGAN. [*To the Covey, as she runs back into the room.*] What's after happenin', Covey?

THE COVEY. [*With contempt.*] Th' job's stopped. They've been mobilized to march in th' demonstration to-night undher th' Plough an' th' Stars. Didn't you hear them cheerin', th' mugs! They have to renew their political baptismal vows to be faithful in seculo seculorum.

FLUTHER. [*Forgetting his fear in his indignation.*] There's no reason to bring religion into it. I think we ought to have as great a regard for religion as we can, so as to keep it out of as many things as possible.

THE COVEY. [*Pausing in the taking off of his dungarees.*] Oh, you're one o' the boys that climb into religion as high as a short Mass on Sunday mornin's? I suppose you'll be singin' songs o' Sion an' songs o' Tara at th' meetin', too.

FLUTHER. We're all Irishmen, anyhow; aren't we?

THE COVEY. [*With hand outstretched, and in a professional tone.*] Look here, comrade, there's no such thing as an Irishman, or an Englishman, or a German or a Turk; we're all only human bein's. Scientifically speakin', it's all a question of the accidental gatherin' together of molly-cewels an' atoms.

[*Peter comes in with a collar in his hand. He goes over to mirror, Left, and proceeds to try to put it on.*]

FLUTHER. Mollycewels an' atoms! D'ye think I'm goin' to listen to you thryin' to juggle Fluther's mind with complicated cunundhrums of mollycewels an' atoms?

THE COVEY. [*Rather loudly.*] There's nothin' complicated in it. There's no fear o' the Church tellin' you that mollycewels is a stickin' together of millions of atoms o' sodium, carbon, potassium o' iodide, etcetera, that, accordin' to th' way they're mixed, make a flower, a fish, a star that you see shinin' in th' sky, or a man with a big brain like me, or a man with a little brain like you!

FLUTHER. [*More loudly still.*] There's no necessity to be raisin' your voice; shoutin's no manifestin' forth of a growin' mind.

PETER. [*Struggling with his collar.*] God, give me patience with this thing. . . . She makes these collars as stiff with starch as a shinin' band o' solid steel! She does it purposely to thry an' twart me. If I can't get it on th' singlet, how, in th' Name o' God, am I goin' to get it on th' shirt?

THE COVEY. [*Loudly.*] There's no use o' arguin' with you; it's education you want, comrade.

FLUTHER. The Covey an' God made th' world, I suppose, wha'?

THE COVEY. When I hear some men talkin' I'm inclined to disbelieve that th' world's eight-hundhred million years old, for it's not long since th' fathers o' some o' them crawled out o' th' sheltherin' slime o' the sea.

MRS. GOGAN. [*From room at back.*] There, they're afther formin' fours, an' now they're goin' to march away.

FLUTHER. [*Scornfully.*] Mollycewels! [*He begins to untie his apron.*] What about Adam an' Eve?

THE COVEY. Well, what about them?

FLUTHER. [*Fiercely.*] What about them, you?

THE COVEY. Adam an' Eve! Is that as far as you've got? Are you still thinkin' there was nobody in th' world before Adam and Eve? [*Loudly.*] Did you ever hear, man, of th' skeleton of th' man o' Java?

PETER. [*Casting the collar from him.*] Blast it, blast it, blast it!

FLUTHER. [*Viciously folding his apron.*] Ah, you're not goin' to be let tap your rubbidge o' thoughts into th' mind o' Fluther.

THE COVEY. You're afraid to listen to th' truth!

FLUTHER. Who's afraid?

THE COVEY. You are!

FLUTHER. G'way, you wurum!

THE COVEY. Who's a worum?

FLUTHER. You are, or you wouldn't talk th' way you're talkin'.

THE COVEY. Th' oul', ignorant savage leppin' up in you, when science shows you that th' head of your god is an empty one. Well, I hope you're enjoyin' th' blessin' o' havin' to live be th' sweat of your brow.

FLUTHER. You'll be kickin' an' yellin' for th' priest yet, me boyo. I'm not goin' to stand silent an' simple listenin' to a thick like you makin' a maddenin' mockery o' God Almighty. It 'ud be a nice derogatory thing on me conscience, an' me dyin', to look back in rememberin' shame of talkin' to a word-weavin' little ignorant yahoo of a red flag Socialist!

MRS. GOGAN. [*She has returned to the front room, and has wandered around looking at things in general, and is now in front of the fireplace looking at the picture hanging over it.*] For God's sake, Fluther, dhrop it;

there's always th' makin's of a row in th' mention of religion . . . [*Looking at picture.*] God bless us, it's a naked woman!

FLUTHER. [*Coming over to look at it.*] What's undher it? [*Reading.*] 'Georgina: The Sleepin' Vennis'. Oh, that's a terrible picture; oh, that's a shockin' picture! Oh, th' one that got that taken, she must have been a prime lassie!

PETER. [*Who also has come over to look, laughing, with his body bent at the waist, and his head slightly tilted back.*] Hee, hee, hee, hee, hee!

FLUTHER. [*Indignantly, to Peter.*] What are you hee, hee-in' for? That' a nice thing to be hee, hee-in' at. Where's your morality, man?

MRS. GOGAN. God forgive us, it's not right to be lookin' at it.

FLUTHER. It's nearly a derogatory thing to be in th' room where it is.

MRS. GOGAN. [*Giggling hysterically.*] I couldn't stop any longer in th' same room with three men, afther lookin' at it! [*She goes out.*]

[*The Covey, who has divested himself of his dungarees, throws them with a contemptuous motion on top of Peter's white shirt.*]

PETER. [*Plaintively.*] Where are you throwin' them? Are you thryin' to twart an' torment me again?

THE COVEY. Who's thryin' to twart you?

PETER. [*Flinging the dungarees violently on the floor.*] You're not goin' to make me lose me temper, me young Covey.

THE COVEY. [*Flinging the white shirt on the floor.*] If you're Nora's pet, aself, you're not goin' to get your way in everything.

PETER. [*Plaintively, with his eyes looking up at the ceiling.*] I'll say nothin'. . . . I'll leave you to th' day when th' all-pitiful, all-merciful, all-lovin' God 'll be handin' you to th' angels to be rievin' an' roastin' you, tearin' an' tormentin' you, burnin' an' blastin' you!

THE COVEY. Aren't you th' little malignant oul' bastard, you lemon-whiskered oul' swine!

[*Peter runs to the sword, draws it, and makes for the Covey, who dodges him around the table; Peter has no intention of striking, but the Covey wants to take no chance.*]

THE COVEY. [*Dodging.*] Fluther, hold him, there. It's a nice thing to have a lunatic like this lashin' around with a lethal weapon! [*The Covey darts out of the room, Right, slamming the door in the face of Peter.*]

PETER. [*Battering and pulling at the door.*] Lemme out, lemme out; isn't it a poor thing for a man who wouldn't say a word against his greatest enemy to have to listen to that Covey's twartin' animosities, shovin' poor, patient people into a lashin' out of curses that darken his soul with th' shadow of th' wrath of th' last day!

FLUTHER. Why d'ye take notice of him? If he seen you didn't, he'd say nothin' derogatory.

PETER. I'll make him stop his laughin' an' leerin', jibin' an' jeerin' an' scarifyin' people with his corner-boy insinuations! . . . He's always thryin' to rouse me: if it's not a song, it's a whistle; if it isn't a whistle, it's a cough. But you can taunt an' taunt —I'm laughin' at you; he, hee, hee, hee, hee, heee!

THE COVEY. [*Singing through the keyhole:*]

Dear harp o' me counthry, in darkness
   I found thee,
The dark chain of silence had hung
   o'er thee long—

PETER. [*Frantically.*] Jasus, d'ye hear that? D'ye hear him soundin' forth his divil-souled song o' provocation?

THE COVEY. [*Singing as before:*]

When proudly, me own island harp,
   I unbound thee,
An' gave all thy chords to light, free-
   dom an' song!

PETER. [*Battering at door.*] When I get out I'll do for you, I'll do for you, I'll do for you!

THE COVEY. [*Through the keyhole.*] Cuckoo-oo!

[*Nora enters by door, Right. She is a young woman of twenty-two, alert, swift, full of nervous energy, and a little anxious to get on in the world. The firm lines of her face are considerably opposed by a soft, amorous mouth and gentle eyes. When her firmness fails her, she persuades with her feminine charm. She is dressed in a tailor-made costume, and wears around her neck a silver fox fur.*]

NORA. [*Running in and pushing Peter away from the door.*] Oh, can I not turn me back but th' two o' yous are at it like a pair o' fightin' cocks! Uncle Peter . . . Uncle Peter . . . UNCLE PETER!

PETER. [*Vociferously.*] Oh, Uncle Peter, Uncle Peter be damned! D'ye think I'm goin' to give a free pass to th' young Covey to turn me whole life into a Holy Manual o' penances an' martyrdoms?

THE COVEY. [*Angrily rushing into the room.*] If you won't exercise some sort o' conthrol over that Uncle Peter o' yours, there'll be a funeral, an' it won't be me that'll be in th' hearse!

NORA. [*Between Peter and the Covey, to the Covey.*] Are yous always goin' to be tearin' down th' little bit of respectability that a body's thryin' to build up? Am I always goin' to be havin' to nurse yous into th' hardy habit o' thryin' to keep up a little bit of appearance?

THE COVEY. Why weren't you here to see th' way he run at me with th' sword?

PETER. What did you call me a lemon-whiskered oul' swine for?

NORA. If th' two o' yous don't thry to make a generous altheration in your goin's on, an' keep on thryin' t' inaugurate th' customs o' th' rest o' th' house into this place, yous can flit into other lodgin's where your bowsey battlin' 'ill meet, maybe, with an encore.

PETER. [*To Nora.*] Would you like to be called a lemon-whiskered oul' swine?

NORA. If you attempt to wag that sword of yours at anybody again, it'll have to be taken off you an' put in a safe place away from babies that don't know th' danger o' them things.

PETER. [*At entrance to room, Back.*] Well, I'm not goin' to let anybody call me a lemon-whiskered oul' swine. [*He goes in.*]

FLUTHER. [*Trying the door.*] Openin' an' shuttin' now with a well-mannered motion, like a door of a select bar in a high-class pub.

NORA. [*To the Covey, as she lays table for tea.*] An', once for all, Willie, you'll have to thry to deliver yourself from th' desire of provokin' oul' Pether into a wild forgetfulness of what's proper an' allowable in a respectable home.

THE COVEY. Well, let him mind his own business, then. Yestherday I caught him hee-hee-in' out of him an' he readin' bits out of Jenersky's *Thesis on th' Origin, Development, an' Consolidation of th' Evolutionary Idea of th' Proletariat.*

NORA. Now, let it end at that, for God's sake; Jack'll be in any minute, an' I'm not goin' to have th' quiet of this evenin' tossed about in an everlastin' uproar between you an' Uncle Pether. [*To Fluther.*] Well, did you manage to settle th' lock, yet, Mr. Good?

FLUTHER. [*Opening and shutting door.*] It's betther than a new one, now, Mrs. Clitheroe; it's almost ready to open and shut of its own accord.

NORA. [*Giving him a coin.*] You're a whole man. How many pints will that get you?

FLUTHER. [*Seriously.*] Ne'er a one at all, Mrs. Clitheroe, for Fluther's on th' wather waggon now. You could stan' where you're stannin' chantin', 'Have a glass o' malt, Fluther; Fluther, have a glass o' malt,' till th' bells would be ringin' th' ould year out an' th' New Year in, an' you'd have as much chance o' movin' Fluther as a tune on a tin whistle would move a deaf man an' he dead.

[*As Nora is opening and shutting door, Mrs. Bessie Burgess appears at it. She is a woman of forty, vigorously built. Her face is a dogged one, hardened by toil, and a little coarsened by drink. She looks scornfully and viciously at Nora for a few moments before she speaks.*]

BESSIE. Puttin' a new lock on her door . . . afraid her poor neighbours

ud break through an' steal. . . . [*In a loud tone.*] Maybe, now, they're a damn sight more honest than your ladyship . . . checkin' th' children playin' on th' stairs . . . gettin' on th' nerves of your ladyship. . . . Complainin' about Bessie Burgess singin' her hymns at night, when she has a few up. . . . [*She comes in half-way on the threshold, and screams.*] Bessie Burgess 'll sing whenever she damn well likes!

[*Nora tries to shut the door, but Bessie violently shoves it in, and, gripping Nora by the shoulders, shakes her.*]

BESSIE. You little over-dressed throllop, you, for one pin I'd paste th' white face o' you!

NORA. [*Frightened.*]   Fluther, Fluther!

FLUTHER. [*Running over and breaking the hold of Bessie from Nora.*] Now, now, Bessie, Bessie, leave poor Mrs. Clitheroe alone; she'd do no one any harm, an' minds no one's business but her own.

BESSIE. Why is she always thryin' to speak proud things, an' lookin' like a mighty one in th' congregation o' th' people!

[*Nora sinks frightened on to the couch as Jack Clitheroe enters. He is a tall, well-made fellow of twenty-five. His face has none of the strength of Nora's. It is a face in which is the desire for authority, without the power to attain it.*]

CLITHEROE. [*Excitedly.*] What's up? what's afther happenin'?

FLUTHER. Nothin', Jack. Nothin'. It's all over now. Come on, Bessie, come on.

CLITHEROE. [*To Nora.*] What's wrong, Nora? Did she say anything to you?

NORA. She was bargin' out of her, an' I only told her to g'up ower o' that to her own place; an' before I knew where I was, she flew at me like a tiger, an' thried to guzzle me!

CLITHEROE. [Going to door and speaking to Bessie.] Get up to your own place, Mrs. Burgess, and don't you be interferin' with my wife, or it'll be th' worse for you. . . . Go on, go on!

BESSIE. [As Clitheroe is pushing her out.] Mind who you're pushin', now. . . . I attend me place o' worship, anyhow . . . not like some o' them that go to neither church, chapel nor meetin'-house. . . . If me son was home from th' threnches he'd see me righted.

[Bessie and Fluther depart, and Clitheroe closes the door.]

CLITHEROE. [Going over to Nora, and putting his arm round her.] There, don't mind that old bitch, Nora, darling; I'll soon put a stop to her interferin'.

NORA. Some day or another, when I'm here be meself, she'll come in an' do somethin' desperate.

CLITHEROE. [Kissing her.] Oh, sorra fear of her doin' anythin' desperate. I'll talk to her to-morrow when she's sober. A taste o' me mind that'll shock her into the sensibility of behavin' herself!

[Nora gets up and settles the table. She sees the dungarees on the floor and stands looking at them, then she turns to the Covey, who is reading Jenersky's 'Thesis' at the fire.]

NORA. Willie, is that th' place for your dungarees?

THE COVEY. [Getting up and lifting them from the floor.] Ah, they won't

do th' floor any harm, will they? [He carries them into room, Back.]

NORA. [Calling.] Uncle Peter, now, Uncle Peter; tea's ready. [Peter and the Covey come in from room, Back; they all sit down to tea. Peter is in full dress of the Foresters: green coat, gold braided; white breeches, top boots, frilled shirt. He carries the slouch hat, with the white ostrich plume, and the sword in his hands. They eat for a few moments in silence, the Covey furtively looking at Peter with scorn in his eyes. Peter knows it and is fidgety.]

THE COVEY. [Provokingly.] Another cut o' bread, Uncle Peter? [Peter maintains a dignified silence.]

CLITHEROE. It's sure to be a great meetin' to-night. We ought to go, Nora.

NORA. [Decisively.] I won't go, Jack; you can go if you wish.

THE COVEY. D'ye want th' sugar, Uncle Peter? [A pause.]

PETER. [Explosively.] Now, are you goin' to start your thryin' an' your twartin' again?

NORA. Now, Uncle Peter, you mustn't be so touchy; Willie has only assed you if you wanted th' sugar.

PETER. He doesn't care a damn whether I want th' sugar or no. He's only thryin' to twart me!

NORA. [Angrily, to the Covey.] Can't you let him alone, Willie? If he wants the sugar, let him stretch his hand out an' get it himself!

THE COVEY. [To Peter.] Now, if you want the sugar, you can stretch out your hand and get it yourself!

CLITHEROE. To-night is th' first chance that Brennan has got of showing himself off since they made a Captain of him—why, God only knows. It'll be a treat to see him swankin' it at th' head of the Citizen Army carryin' th' flag of the Plough an' th' Stars. . . . [*Looking roguishly at Nora.*] He was sweet on you, once, Nora?

NORA. He may have been. . . . I never liked him. I always thought he was a bit of a thick.

THE COVEY. They're bringin' nice disgrace on that banner now.

CLITHEROE. [*Remonstratively.*] How are they bringin' disgrace on it?

THE COVEY. [*Snappily.*] Because it's a Labour flag, an' was never meant for politics. . . . What does th' design of th' field plough, bearin' on it th' stars of th' heavenly plough, mean, if it's not Communism? It's a flag that should only be used when we're buildin' th' barricades to fight for a Workers' Republic!

PETER. [*With a puff of derision.*] P-phuh.

THE COVEY. [*Angrily.*] What are you phuhin' out o' you for? Your mind is th' mind of a mummy. [*Rising.*] I betther go an' get a good place to have a look at Ireland's warriors passin' by. [*He goes into room, Left, and returns with his cap.*]

NORA. [*To the Covey.*] Oh, Willie, brush your clothes before you go.

THE COVEY. Oh, they'll do well enough.

NORA. Go an' brush them; th' brush is in th' drawer there.

[*The Covey goes to the drawer, muttering, gets the brush, and starts to brush his clothes.*]

THE COVEY. [*Singing at Peter, as he does so:*]

Oh, where's th' slave so lowly,
Condemn'd to chains unholy,

Who, could he burst his bonds at first,
Would pine beneath them slowly?

We tread th' land that . . . bore us,
Th' green flag glitters . . . o'er us,
Th' friends we've tried are by our side,
An' th' foe we hate . . . before us!

PETER. [*Leaping to his feet in a whirl of rage.*] Now, I'm tellin' you, me young Covey, once for all, that I'll not stick any longer these tittherin' taunts of yours, rovin' around to sing your slights an' slandhers, reddenin' th' mind of a man to th' thinkin' an' sayin' of things that sicken his soul with sin! [*Hysterical; lifting up a cup to fling at the Covey.*] Be God, I'll—

CLITHEROE. [*Catching his arm.*] Now then, none o' that, none o' that!

NORA. Uncle Pether, Uncle Pether, UNCLE PETHER!

THE COVEY. [*At the door, about to go out.*] Isn't that th' malignant oul' varmint! Lookin' like th' illegitimate son of an illegitimate child of a corporal in th' Mexican army! [*He goes out.*]

PETER. [*Plaintively.*] He's afther leavin' me now in such a state of agitation that I won't be able to do meself justice when I'm marchin' to th' meetin'.

NORA. [*Jumping up.*] Oh, for God's sake, here, buckle your sword on, and go to your meetin', so that we'll have at least one hour of peace! [*She proceeds to belt on the sword.*]

CLITHEROE. [*Irritably.*] For God's sake hurry him up ou' o' this, Nora.

PETER. Are yous all goin' to thry to start to twart me now?

NORA. [*Putting on his plumed hat.*] S-s-sh. Now, your hat's on, your house is thatched; off you pop! [*She gently pushes him from her.*]

PETER. [*Going, and turning as he*

reaches the door.] Now, if that young Covey—

NORA. Go on, go on. [*He goes.*]

[*Clitheroe sits down in the lounge, lights a cigarette, and looks thoughtfully into the fire. Nora takes the things from the table, placing them on the chest of drawers. There is a pause, then she swiftly comes over to him and sits beside him.*]

NORA. [*Softly.*] A penny for them, Jack!

CLITHEROE. Me? Oh, I was thinkin' of nothing.

NORA. You were thinkin' of th' . . . meetin' . . . Jack. When we were courtin' an' I wanted you to go, you'd say, 'Oh, to hell with meetin's,' an' that you felt lonely in cheerin' crowds when I was absent. An' we weren't a month married when you began that you couldn't keep away from them.

CLITHEROE. Oh, that's enough about th' meetin'. It looks as if you wanted me to go th' way you're talkin'. You were always at me to give up th' Citizen Army, an' I gave it up; surely that ought to satisfy you.

NORA. Ay, you gave it up—because you got th' sulks when they didn't make a Captain of you. It wasn't for my sake, Jack.

CLITHEROE. For your sake or no, you're benefitin' by it, aren't you? I didn't forget this was your birthday, did I? [*He puts his arms around her.*] And you liked your new hat; didn't you, didn't you? [*He kisses her rapidly several times.*]

NORA. [*Panting.*] Jack, Jack; please, Jack! I thought you were tired of that sort of thing long ago.

CLITHEROE. Well, you're finding out now that I amn't tired of it yet, anyhow. Mrs. Clitheroe doesn't want to be kissed, sure she doesn't? [*He kisses her again.*] Little, little red-lipped Nora!

NORA. [*Coquettishly removing his arm from around her.*] Oh, yes, your little, little red-lipped Nora's a sweet little girl when th' fit seizes you; but your little, little red-lipped Nora has to clean your boots every mornin', all the same.

CLITHEROE. [*With a movement of irritation.*] Oh, well, if we're goin' to be snotty! [*A pause.*]

NORA. It's lookin' like as if it was you that was goin' to be . . . snotty! Bridlin' up with bittherness, th' minute a body attempts t' open her mouth.

CLITHEROE. Is it any wondher, turnin' a tendher sayin' into a meanin' o' malice an' spite!

NORA. It's hard for a body to be always keepin' her mind bent on makin' thoughts that'll be no longer than th' length of your own satisfaction. [*A pause.*]

NORA. [*Standing up.*] If we're goin' to dhribble th' time away sittin' here like a pair o' cranky mummies, I'd be as well sewin' or doin' something about th' place.

[*She looks appealingly at him for a few moments; he doesn't speak. She swiftly sits down beside him, and puts her arm around his neck.*]

NORA. [*Imploringly.*] Ah, Jack, don't be so cross!

CLITHEROE. [*Doggedly.*] Cross? I'm not cross; I'm not a bit cross. It was yourself started it.

NORA. [*Coaxingly.*] I didn't mean to say anything out o' the way. You take a body up too quickly, Jack. [*In an ordinary tone as if nothing of an angry nature had been said.*] You didn't offer me me evenin' allowance yet.

[*Clitheroe silently takes out a cigarette for her and himself and lights both.*]

NORA. [*Trying to make conversation.*] How quiet th' house is now; they must be all out.

CLITHEROE. [*Rather shortly.*] I suppose so.

NORA. [*Rising from the seat.*] I'm longin' to show you me new hat, to see what you think of it. Would you like to see it?

CLITHEROE. Ah, I don't mind.

[*Nora suppresses a sharp reply, hesitates for a moment, then gets the hat, puts it on, and stands before Clitheroe.*]

NORA. Well, how does Mr. Clitheroe like me new hat?

CLITHEROE. It suits you, Nora, it does right enough. [*He stands up, puts his hand beneath her chin, and tilts her head up. She looks at him roguishly. He bends down and kisses her.*]

NORA. Here, sit down, an' don't let me hear another cross word out of you for th' rest o' the night. [*They sit down.*]

CLITHEROE. [*With his arms around her.*] Little, little, red-lipped Nora!

NORA. [*With a coaxing movement of her body towards him.*] Jack!

CLITHEROE. [*Tightening his arms around her.*] Well?

NORA. You haven't sung me a song since our honeymoon. Sing me one now, do . . . please, Jack!

CLITHEROE. What song? 'Since Maggie Went Away'?

NORA. Ah, no, Jack, not that; it's too sad. 'When You said You Loved Me.'

[*Clearing his throat, Clitheroe thinks*

for a moment and then begins to sing. Nora, putting an arm around him, nestles her head on his breast and listens delightedly.*]

CLITHEROE. [*Singing verses following to the air of 'When You and I were Young, Maggie':*]

Th' violets were scenting th' woods,
        Nora,
    Displaying their charm to th' bee,
When I first said I lov'd only you,
        Nora,
    An' you said you lov'd only me!

Th' chestnut blooms gleam'd through
        th' glade, Nora,
    A robin sang loud from a tree,
When I first said I lov'd only you,
        Nora,
    An' you said you lov'd only me!

Th' golden-rob'd daffodils shone, Nora,
    An' danc'd in th' breeze on th' lea,
When I first said I lov'd only you,
        Nora,
    An' you said you lov'd only me!

Th' trees, birds, an' bees sang a song,
        Nora,
    Of happier transports to be,
When I first said I lov'd only you,
        Nora,
    An' you said you lov'd only me!

[*Nora kisses him.*]

[*A knock is heard at the door, Right; a pause as they listen. Nora clings closely to Clitheroe. Another knock, more imperative than the first.*]

CLITHEROE. I wonder who can that be, now?

NORA. [*A little nervous.*] Take no notice of it, Jack; they'll go away in a minute. [*Another knock, followed by a voice.*]

VOICE.   Commandant   Clitheroe,

Commandant Clitheroe, are you there? A message from General Jim Connolly.

CLITHEROE. Damn it, it's Captain Brennan.

NORA. [*Anxiously.*] Don't mind him, don't mind, Jack. Don't break our happiness. . . . Pretend we're not in. Let us forget everything to-night but our two selves!

CLITHEROE. [*Reassuringly.*] Don't be alarmed, darling; I'll just see what he wants, an' send him about his business.

NORA. [*Tremulously.*] No, no. Please, Jack; don't open it. Please, for your own little Nora's sake!

CLITHEROE. [*Rising to open the door.*] Now don't be silly, Nora. [*Clitheroe opens the door, and admits a young man in the full uniform of the Irish Citizen Army—green suit; slouch green hat caught up at one side by a small Red Hand badge; Sam Browne belt, with a revolver in the holster. He carries a letter in his hand. When he comes in he smartly salutes Clitheroe. The young man is Captain Brennan.*]

CAPT. BRENNAN. [*Giving the letter to Clitheroe.*] A dispatch from General Connolly.

CLITHEROE. [*Reading. While he is doing so, Brennan's eyes are fixed on Nora, who droops as she sits on the lounge.*] 'Commandant Clitheroe is to take command of the eighth battalion of the I.C.A. which will assemble to proceed to the meeting at nine o'clock. He is to see that all units are provided with full equipment; two days' rations and fifty rounds of ammunition. At two o'clock A.M. the army will leave Liberty Hall for a reconnaissance attack on Dublin Castle.—Com.-Gen. Connolly.'

CLITHEROE. I don't understand this. Why does General Connolly call me Commandant?

CAPT. BRENNAN. Th' Staff appointed you Commandant, and th' General agreed with their selection.

CLITHEROE. When did this happen?

CAPT. BRENNAN. A fortnight ago.

CLITHEROE. How is it word was never sent to me?

CAPT. BRENNAN. Word was sent to you. . . . I meself brought it.

CLITHEROE. Who did you give it to, then?

CAPT. BRENNAN. [*After a pause.*] I think I gave it to Mrs. Clitheroe, there.

CLITHEROE. Nora, d'ye hear that? [*Nora makes no answer.*]

CLITHEROE. [*There is a note of hardness in his voice.*] Nora . . . Captain Brennan says he brought a letter to me from General Connolly, and that he gave it to you. . . . Where is it? What did you do with it?

NORA. [*Running over to him, and pleadingly putting her arms around him.*] Jack, please, Jack, don't go out to-night an' I'll tell you; I'll explain everything. . . . Send him away, an' stay with your own little red-lipp'd Nora.

CLITHEROE. [*Removing her arms from around him.*] None o' this nonsense, now; I want to know what you did with th' letter?

[*Nora goes slowly to the lounge and sits down.*]

CLITHEROE. [*Angrily.*] Why didn't you give me th' letter? What did you do with it? . . . [*He shakes her by the shoulder.*] What did you do with th' letter?

NORA. [*Flaming up.*] I burned it, I burned it! That's what I did with it! Is General Connolly an' th' Citizen Army goin' to be your only care? Is your home goin' to be only a place to rest in? Am I goin' to be only somethin' to provide merry-makin' at night for you? Your vanity'll be th' ruin of you an' me yet. . . . That's what's movin' you: because they've made an officer of you, you'll make a glorious cause of what you're doin', while your little red-lipp'd Nora can go on sittin' here, makin' a companion of th' loneliness of th' night!

CLITHEROE. [*Fiercely.*] You burned it, did you? [*He grips her arm.*] Well, me good lady—

NORA. Let go—you're hurtin' me!

CLITHEROE. You deserve to be hurt. . . . Any letter that comes to me for th' future, take care that I get it. . . . D'ye hear—take care that I get it!

[*He goes to the chest of drawers and takes out a Sam Browne belt, which he puts on, and then puts a revolver in the holster. He puts on his hat, and looks towards Nora. While this dialogue is proceeding, and while Clitheroe prepares himself, Brennan softly whistles 'The Soldiers' Song'.*]

CLITHEROE. [*At door, about to go out.*] You needn't wait up for me; if I'm in at all, it won't be before six in th' morning.

NORA. [*Bitterly.*] I don't care if you never come back!

CLITHEROE. [*To Capt. Brennan.*] Come along, Ned.

[*They go out; there is a pause. Nora pulls her new hat from her head and with a bitter movement flings it to the other end of the room. There is a gentle knock at door, Right, which opens, and Mollser comes into*

the room. *She is about fifteen, but looks to be only about ten, for the ravages of consumption have shrivelled her up. She is pitifully worn, walks feebly, and frequently coughs. She goes over to Nora.*]

MOLLSER. [*To Nora.*] Mother's gone to th' meetin', an' I was feelin' terrible lonely, so I come down to see if you'd let me sit with you, thinkin' you mightn't be goin' yourself. . . . I do be terrible afraid I'll die sometime when I'm be meself. . . . I often envy you, Mrs. Clitheroe, seein' th' health you have, an' th' lovely place you have here, an' wondherin' if I'll ever be sthrong enough to be keepin' a home together for a man. Oh, this must be some more o' the Dublin Fusiliers flyin' off to the front.

[*Just before Mollser ceases to speak, there is heard in the distance the music of a brass band playing a regiment to the boat on the way to the front. The tune that is being played is 'It's a Long Way to Tipperary'; as the band comes to the chorus, the regiment is swinging into the street by Nora's house, and the voices of the soldiers can be heard lustily singing the chorus of the song:*]

It's a long way to Tipperary, it's a
    long way to go;
It's a long way to Tipperary, to th'
    sweetest girl I know!
Goodbye, Piccadilly; farewell, Leices-
    ter Square.
It's a long, long way to Tipperary,
    but my heart's right there!

[*Nora and Mollser remain silently listening. As the chorus ends and the music is faint in the distance again,*

Bessie Burgess appears at door,
Right, which Mollser has left open.]

BESSIE. [Speaking in towards the
room.] There's th' men marchin' out
into th' dhread dimness o' danger,
while th' lice is crawlin' about feedin'
on th' fatness o' the land! But yous'll
not escape from th' arrow that flieth
be night, or th' sickness that wasteth
be day. . . . An' ladyship an' all, as
some o' them may be, they'll be scattered abroad, like th' dust in th' darkness!

[Bessie goes away; Nora steals over
and quietly shuts the door. She
comes back to the lounge and wearily
throws herself on it beside Mollser.]

MOLLSER. [After a pause and a
cough.] Is there anybody goin', Mrs.
Clitheroe, with a titther o' sense?

CURTAIN

ACT II

[A commodious public-house at the
corner of the street in which the
meeting is being addressed from Platform No. 1. It is the south corner of
the public-house that is visible to the
audience. The counter, beginning at
Back about one-fourth of the width
of the space shown, comes across
two-thirds of the length of the stage,
and, taking a circular sweep, passes
out of sight to Left. On the counter
are beerpulls, glasses, and a carafe.
The other three-fourths of the Back
is occupied by a tall, wide, two-paned
window. Beside this window at the
Right is a small, box-like, panelled
snug. Next to the snug is a double
swing door, the entrance to that particular end of the house. Farther on
is a shelf on which customers may
rest their drinks. Underneath the

windows is a cushioned seat. Behind
the counter at Back can be seen the
shelves running the whole length of
the counter. On these shelves can be
seen the end (or the beginning) of
rows of bottles. The Barman is seen
wiping the part of the counter which
is in view. Rosie is standing at the
counter toying with what remains of
a half of whisky in a wine-glass. She
is a sturdy, well-shaped girl of
twenty; pretty, and pert in manner.
She is wearing a cream blouse, with
an obviously suggestive glad neck; a
grey tweed dress, brown stockings
and shoes. The blouse and most of
the dress are hidden by a black
shawl. She has no hat, and in her
hair is jauntily set a cheap, glittering,
jewelled ornament. It is an hour
later.]

BARMAN. [Wiping counter.] Nothin'
much doin' in your line to-night,
Rosie?

ROSIE. Curse o' God on th' haporth,
hardly, Tom. There isn't much notice taken of a pretty petticoat of a
night like this. . . . They're all in a
holy mood. Th' solemn-lookin' dials
on th' whole o' them an' they marchin'
to th' meetin'. You'd think they were
th' glorious company of th' saints, an'
th' noble army of martyrs thrampin'
through th' sthreets of paradise.
They're all thinkin' of higher things
than a girl's garthers. . . . It's a tremendous meetin'; four platforms they
have—there's one o' them just outside opposite th' window.

BARMAN. Oh, ay; sure when th'
speaker comes [Motioning with his
hand.] to th' near end, here, you can
see him plain, an' hear nearly everythin' he's spoutin' out of him.

ROSIE. It's no joke thryin' to make up fifty-five shillin's a week for your keep an' laundhry, an' then taxin' you a quid for your own room if you bring home a friend for th' night. . . . If I could only put by a couple of quid for a swankier outfit, everythin' in th' garden ud look lovely—

BARMAN. Whisht, till we hear what he's sayin'.

[*Through the window is silhouetted the figure of a tall man who is speaking to the crowd. The Barman and Rosie look out of the window and listen.*]

THE VOICE OF THE MAN. It is a glorious thing to see arms in the hands of Irishmen. We must accustom ourselves to the thought of arms, we must accustom ourselves to the sight of arms, we must accustom ourselves to the use of arms. . . . Bloodshed is a cleansing and sanctifying thing, and the nation that regards it as the final horror has lost its manhood. . . . There are many things more horrible than bloodshed, and slavery is one of them! [*The figure moves away towards the Right, and is lost to sight and hearing.*]

ROSIE. It's th' sacred thruth, mind you, what that man's afther sayin'.

BARMAN. If I was only a little younger, I'd be plungin' mad into th' middle of it!

ROSIE. [*Who is still looking out of the window.*] Oh, here's the two gems runnin' over again for their oil!

[*Peter and Fluther enter tumultuously. They are hot, and full and hasty with the things they have seen and heard. Emotion is bubbling up in them, so that when they drink, and when they speak, they drink and speak with the fullness of emotional*

passion. *Peter leads the way to the counter.*]

PETER. [*Splutteringly to Barman.*] Two halves . . . [*To Fluther.*] A meetin' like this always makes me feel as if I could dhrink Loch Erinn dhry!

FLUTHER. You couldn't feel any way else at a time like this when th' spirit of a man is pulsin' to be out fightin' for th' thruth with his feet thremblin' on th' way, maybe to th' gallows, an' his ears tinglin' with th' faint, far-away sound of burstin' rifleshots that'll maybe whip th' last little shock o' life out of him that's left lingerin' in his body!

PETER. I felt a burnin' lump in me throat when I heard th' band playin' 'The Soldiers' Song', rememberin' last hearin' it marchin' in military formation with th' people starin' on both sides at us, carryin' with us th' pride an' resolution o' Dublin to th' grave of Wolfe Tone.

FLUTHER. Get th' Dublin men goin' an' they'll go on full force for anything that's thryin' to bar them away from what they're wantin', where th' slim thinkin' counthry boyo ud limp away from th' first faintest touch of compromization!

PETER. [*Hurriedly to the Barman.*] Two more, Tom! . . . [*To Fluther.*] Th' memory of all th' things that was done, an' all th' things that was suffered be th' people, was boomin' in me brain. . . . Every nerve in me body was quiverin' to do somethin' desperate!

FLUTHER. Jammed as I was in th' crowd, I listened to th' speeches pattherin' on th' people's head, like rain fallin' on th' corn; every derogatory thought went out o' me mind, an' I said to meself, 'You can die now,

Fluther, for you've seen th' shadow-dhreams of th' past leppin' to life in th' bodies of livin' men that show, if we were without a titther o' courage for centuries, we're vice versa now!' Looka here. [*He stretches out his arm under Peter's face and rolls up his sleeve.*] The blood was BOILIN' in me veins!

[*The silhouette of the tall figure again moves into the frame of the window speaking to the people.*]

PETER. [*Unaware, in his enthusiasm, of the speaker's appearance, to Fluther.*] I was burnin' to dhraw me sword, an' wave an' wave it over me—

FLUTHER. [*Overwhelming Peter.*] Will you stop your blatherin' for a minute, man, an' let us hear what he's sayin'!

VOICE OF THE MAN. Comrade soldiers of the Irish Volunteers and of the Citizen Army, we rejoice in this terrible war. The old heart of the earth needed to be warmed with the red wine of the battlefields. . . . Such august homage was never offered to God as this: the homage of millions of lives given gladly for love of country. And we must be ready to pour out the same red wine in the same glorious sacrifice, for without shedding of blood there is no redemption! [*The figure moves out of sight and hearing.*]

FLUTHER. [*Gulping down the drink that remains in his glass, and rushing out.*] Come on, man; this is too good to be missed!

[*Peter finishes his drink less rapidly, and as he is going out wiping his mouth with the back of his hand he runs into the Covey coming in. He immediately erects his body like a young cock, and with his chin thrust forward, and a look of venomous dignity on his face, he marches out.*]

THE COVEY. [*At counter.*] Give us a glass o' malt, for God's sake, till I stimulate meself from the shock o' seein' th' sight that's afther goin' out!

ROSIE. [*All business, coming over to the counter, and standing near the Covey.*] Another one for me, Tommy; [*To the Barman.*] th' young gentleman's ordherin' it in th' corner of his eye.

[*The Barman brings the drink for the Covey, and leaves it on the counter. Rosie whips it up.*]

BARMAN. Ay, houl' on there, houl' on there, Rosie!

ROSIE. [*To the Barman.*] What are you houldin' on out o' you for? Didn't you hear th' young gentleman say that he couldn't refuse anything to a nice little bird? [*To the Covey.*] Isn't that right, Jiggs? [*The Covey says nothing.*] Didn't I know, Tommy, it would be all right? It takes Rosie to size a young man up, an' tell th' thoughts that are thremblin' in his mind. Isn't that right, Jiggs?

[*The Covey stirs uneasily, moves a little farther away, and pulls his cap over his eyes.*]

ROSIE. [*Moving after him.*] Great meetin' that's gettin' held outside. Well, it's up to us all, anyway, to fight for our freedom.

THE COVEY. [*To Barman.*] Two more, please. [*To Rosie.*] Freedom! What's th' use o' freedom, if it's not economic freedom?

ROSIE. [*Emphasizing with extended arm and moving finger.*] I used them very words just before you come in. 'A lot o' thricksters,' says I, 'that wouldn't know what freedom was if they got it from their mother.' . . . [*To Barman.*] Didn't I, Tommy?

BARMAN. I disremember.

ROSIE. No, you don't disremember. Remember you said, yourself, it was all 'only a flash in th' pan'. Well, 'flash in th' pan, or no flash in th' pan,' says I, 'they're not goin' to get Rosie Redmond,' says I, 'to fight for freedom that wouldn't be worth winnin' in a raffle!'

THE COVEY. There's only one freedom for th' workin' man: conthrol o' th' means o' production, rates of exchange, an' th' means of disthribution. [*Tapping Rosie on the shoulder.*] Look here, comrade, I'll leave here to-morrow night for you a copy of Jenersky's *Thesis on the Origin, Development, an' Consolidation of the Evolutionary Idea of the Proletariat.*

ROSIE. [*Throwing off her shawl on to the counter, and showing an exemplified glad neck, which reveals a good deal of a white bosom.*] If y'ass Rosie, it's heartbreakin' to see a young fella thinkin' of anything, or admirin' anything, but silk transparent stockin's showin' off the shape of a little lassie's legs!

[*The Covey, frightened, moves a little away.*]

ROSIE. [*Following on.*] Out in th' park in th' shade of a warm summery evenin', with your little darlin' bridie to be, kissin' an' cuddlin' [*She tries to put her arm around his neck.*] kissin' an' cuddlin', ay?

THE COVEY. [*Frightened.*] Ay, what are you doin'? None o' that, now; none o' that. I've something else to do besides shinannickin' afther Judies!

[*He turns away, but Rosie follows, keeping face to face with him.*]

ROSIE. Oh, little duckey, oh, shy little duckey! Never held a mot's hand, an' wouldn't know how to tittle a little Judy! [*She clips him under the chin.*] Tittle him undher th' chin, tittle him undher th' chin!

THE COVEY. [*Breaking away and running out.*] Ay, go on, now; I don't want to have any meddlin' with a lassie like you!

ROSIE. [*Enraged.*] Jasus, it's in a monasthery some of us ought to be, spendin' our holidays kneelin' on our adorers, tellin' our beads, an' knockin' hell out of our buzzums!

THE COVEY. [*Outside.*] Cuckoo-oo!

[*Peter and Fluther come in again, followed by Mrs. Gogan, carrying a baby in her arms. They go over to the counter.*]

PETER. [*With plaintive anger.*] It's terrible that young Covey can't let me pass without proddin' at me! Did you hear him murmurin' 'cuckoo' when we were passin'?

FLUTHER. [*Irritably.*] I wouldn't be everlastin' cockin' me ear to hear every little whisper that was floatin' around about me! It's my rule never to lose me temper till it would be dethrimental to keep it. There's nothin' derogatory in th' use o' th' word 'cuckoo', is there?

PETER. [*Tearfully.*] It's not th' word; it's th' way he says it: he never says it straight out, but murmurs it with curious quiverin' ripples, like variations on a flute!

FLUTHER. Ah, what odds if he gave it with variations on a thrombone! [*To Mrs. Gogan.*] What's yours goin' to be, ma'am?

MRS. GOGAN. Ah, a half o' malt,

Fluther.

FLUTHER. [*To Barman.*] Three halves, Tommy.

[*The Barman brings the drinks.*]

MRS. GOGAN. [*Drinking.*] The Foresthers' is a gorgeous dhress! I don't think I've seen nicer, mind you, in a pantomime. . . . Th' loveliest part of th' dhress, I think, is th' osthrichess plume. . . . When yous are goin' along, an' I see them wavin' an' noddin' an' waggin', I seem to be lookin' at each of yous hangin' at th' end of a rope, your eyes bulgin' an' your legs twistin' an' jerkin', gaspin' an' gaspin' for breath while yous are thryin' to die for Ireland!

FLUTHER. If any o' them is hangin' at the end of a rope, it won't be for Ireland!

PETER. Are you goin' to start th' young Covey's game o' proddin' an' twartin' a man? There's not many that's talkin' can say that for twenty-five years he never missed a pilgrimage to Bodenstown!

FLUTHER. You're always blowin' about goin' to Bodenstown. D'ye think no one but yourself ever went to Bodenstown?

PETER. [*Plaintively.*] I'm not blowin' about it; but there's not a year that I go there but I pluck a leaf off Tone's grave, an' this very day me prayer-book is nearly full of them.

FLUTHER. [*Scornfully.*] Then Fluther has a vice versa opinion of them that put ivy leaves into their prayer-books, scabbin' it on th' clergy, an' thryin' to out-do th' haloes o' th' saints be lookin' as if he was wearin' around his head a glitherin' aroree boree allis! [*Fiercely.*] Sure, I don't care a damn if you slep' in Bodenstown! You can take your breakfast, dinner, an' tea on th' grave in Bodenstown, if you like, for Fluther!

MRS. GOGAN. Oh, don't start a fight, boys, for God's sake; I was only sayin' what a nice costume it is—nicer than th' kilts, for, God forgive me, I always think th' kilts is hardly decent.

FLUTHER. Ah, sure, when you'd look at him, you'd wondher whether th' man was makin' fun o' th' costume, or th' costume was makin' fun o' th' man!

BARMAN. Now, then, thry to speak asy, will yous? We don't want no shoutin' here.

[*The Covey followed by Bessie Burgess comes in. They go over to the opposite end of the counter, and direct their gaze on the other group.*]

THE COVEY. [*To Barman.*] Two glasses o' malt.

PETER. There he is, now; I knew he wouldn't be long till he folleyed me in.

BESSIE. [*Speaking to the Covey, but really at the other party.*] I can't for th' life o' me undherstand how they can call themselves Catholics, when they won't lift a finger to help poor little Catholic Belgium.

MRS. GOGAN. [*Raising her voice.*] What about poor little Catholic Ireland?

BESSIE. [*Over to Mrs. Gogan.*] You mind your own business, ma'am, an' stupefy your foolishness be gettin' dhrunk.

PETER. [*Anxiously.*] Take no notice of her; pay no attention to her. She's just tormentin' herself towards havin' a row with somebody.

BESSIE. There's a storm of anger tossin' in me heart, thinkin' of all th' poor Tommies, an' with them me own son, dhrenched in water an' soaked in blood, gropin' their way to a shatterin' death, in a shower o' shells! Young men with th' sunny lust o' life beamin' in them, layin' down their white bodies, shredded into torn an' bloody pieces, on th' althar that God Himself has built for th' sacrifice of heroes!

MRS. GOGAN. Isn't it a nice thing to have to be listenin' to a lassie an' hangin' our heads in a dead silence, knowin' that some persons think more of a ball of malt than they do of th' blessed saints.

FLUTHER. Whisht; she's always dangerous an' derogatory when she's well oiled. Th' safest way to hindher her from havin' any enjoyment out of her spite, is to dip our thoughts into the fact of her bein' a female person that has moved out of th' sight of ordinary sensible people.

BESSIE. To look at some o' th' women that's knockin' about, now, is a thing to make a body sigh. . . . A woman on her own, dhrinkin' with a bevy o' men, is hardly an example to her sex. . . . A woman dhrinkin' with a woman is one thing, an' a woman dhrinkin' with herself is still a woman—flappers may be put in another category altogether—but a middle-aged married woman makin' herself th' centre of a circle of men is as a woman that is loud an' stubborn, whose feet abideth not in her own house.

THE COVEY. [To Bessie.] When I think of all th' problems in front o' th' workers, it makes me sick to be lookin' at oul' codgers goin' about dhressed up like green-accoutred figures gone asthray out of a toyshop!

PETER. Gracious God, give me patience to be listenin' to that blasted young Covey proddin' at me from over at th' other end of th' shop!

MRS. GOGAN. [Dipping her finger in the whisky, and moistening with it the lips of her baby.] Cissie Gogan's a woman livin' for nigh on twenty-five years in her own room, an' beyond biddin' th' time o' day to her neighbours, never yet as much as nodded her head in th' direction of other people's business, while she knows some as are never content unless they're standin' senthry over other people's doin's!

[Bessie is about to reply, when the tall, dark figure is again silhouetted against the window, and the voice of the speaker is heard speaking passionately.]

VOICE OF SPEAKER. The last sixteen months have been the most glorious in the history of Europe. Heroism has come back to the earth. War is a terrible thing, but war is not an evil thing. People in Ireland dread war because they do not know it. Ireland has not known the exhilaration of war for over a hundred years. When war comes to Ireland she must welcome it as she would welcome the Angel of God! [The figure passes out of sight and hearing.]

THE COVEY. [Towards all present.] Dope, dope. There's only one war worth havin': th' war for th' economic emancipation of th' proletariat.

BESSIE. They may crow away out o' them; but it ud be fitther for some o' them to mend their ways, an' cease from havin' scouts out watchin' for th' comin' of th' Saint Vincent de Paul man, for fear they'd be nailed lowerin' a pint of beer, mockin' th' man with an angel face, shinin' with th' glamour of deceit an' lies!

MRS. GOGAN. An' a certain lassie standin' stiff behind her own door with her ears cocked listenin' to what's being said, stuffed till she's sthrained with envy of a neighbour thryin' for a few little things that may be got be hard sthrivin' to keep up to th' letther an' th' law, an' th' practices of th' Church!

PETER. [*To Mrs. Gogan.*] If I was you, Mrs. Gogan, I'd parry her jabbin' remarks be a powerful silence that'll keep her tantalizin' words from penethratin' into your feelin's. It's always betther to leave these people to th' vengeance o' God!

BESSIE. Bessie Burgess doesn't put up to know much, never havin' a swaggerin' mind, thanks be to God, but goin' on packin' up knowledge accordin' to her conscience: precept upon precept, line upon line; here a little, an' there a little. But [*With a passionate swing of her shawl*], thanks be to Christ, she knows when she was got, where she was got, an' how she was got; while there's some she knows, decoratin' their finger with a well-polished weddin' ring, would be hard put to it if they were assed to show their weddin' lines!

MRS. GOGAN. [*Plunging out into the centre of the floor in a wild tempest of hysterical rage.*] Y' oul' rip of a blasted liar, me weddin' ring's been well earned be twenty years be th' side o' me husband, now takin' his rest in heaven, married to me be Father Dempsey, in th' Chapel o' Saint Jude's, in th' Christmas Week of eighteen hundhred an' ninety-five; an' any kid, livin' or dead, that Jinnie Gogan's had since, was got between th' bordhers of th' Ten Commandments! . . . An' that's more than

some o' you can say that are kep' from th' dhread o' desthruction be a few drowsy virtues, that th' first whisper of temptation lulls into a sleep, that'll know one sin from another only on th' day of their last anointin', an' that use th' innocent light o' th' shinin' stars to dip into th' sins of a night's diversion!

BESSIE. [*Jumping out to face Mrs. Gogan, and bringing the palms of her hands together in sharp claps to emphasize her remarks.*] Liar to you, too, ma'am, y' oul' hardened thresspasser on other people's good nature, wizenin' up your soul in th' arts o' dodgeries, till every dhrop of respectability in a female is dhried up in her, lookin' at your ready-made manœuverin' with th' menkind!

BARMAN. Here, there; here, there; speak asy there. No rowin' here, no rowin' here, now.

FLUTHER. [*Trying to calm Mrs. Gogan.*] Now Jinnie, Jinnie, it's a derogatory thing to be smirchin' a night like this with a row; it's rompin' with th' feelin's of hope we ought to be, instead o' bein' vice versa!

PETER. [*Trying to quiet Bessie.*] I'm terrible dawny, Mrs. Burgess, an' a fight leaves me weak for a long time afterwards. . . . Please, Mrs. Burgess, before there's damage done, try to have a little respect for yourself.

BESSIE. [*With a push of her hand that sends Peter tottering to the end of the shop.*] G'way, you little sermonizing, little yella-faced, little consequential, little pudgy, little bum, you!

MRS. GOGAN. [*Screaming.*] Fluther, leggo! I'm not goin' to keep an unresistin' silence, an' her scattherin'

her festherin' words in me face, stir-
rin' up ever dhrop of decency in a
respectable female, with her restless
rally o' lies that would make a saint
say his prayer backwards!

BESSIE. [*Shouting.*] Ah, everybody
knows well that th' best charity that
can be shown to you is to hide th'
thruth as much as our thrue worship
of God Almighty will allow us!

MRS. GOGAN. [*Frantically.*] Here,
houl' th' kid, one o' yous; houl' th'
kid for a minute! There's nothin' for
it but to show this lassie a lesson or
two. . . . [*To Peter.*] Here, houl' th'
kid, you. [*Before Peter is aware of
it, she places the infant in his arms.*]

MRS. GOGAN. [*To Bessie, standing
before her in a fighting attitude.*]
Come on, now, me loyal lassie, dyin'
with grief for little Catholic Belgium!
When Jinnie Gogan's done with you,
you'll have a little leisure lyin' down
to think an' pray for your king an'
counthry!

BARMAN. [*Coming from behind the
counter, getting between the women,
and proceeding to push them towards the door.*] Here, now, since
yous can't have a little friendly argument quietly, you'll get out o' this
place in quick time. Go on, an' settle
your differences somewhere else—I
don't want to have another endorsement on me licence.

PETER. [*Anxiously, over to Mrs.
Gogan.*] Here, take your kid back,
ower this. How nicely I was picked,
now, for it to be plumped into me
arms!

THE COVEY. She knew who she was
givin' it to, maybe.

PETER. [*Hotly to the Covey.*] Now,
I'm givin' you fair warnin', me young
Covey, to quit firin' your jibes an'

jeers at me. . . . For one o' these
days, I'll run out in front o' God Almighty an' take your sacred life!

BARMAN. [*Pushing Bessie out after
Mrs. Gogan.*] Go on, now; out you
go.

BESSIE. [*As she goes out.*] If you
think, me lassie, that Bessie Burgess
has an untidy conscience, she'll soon
show you to th' differ!

PETER. [*Leaving the baby down
on the floor.*] Ay, be Jasus, wait
there, till I give her back her youngster! [*He runs to the door.*] Ay, there,
ay! [*He comes back.*] There, she's
afther goin' without her kid. What
are we goin' to do with it, now?

THE COVEY. What are we goin' to
do with it? Bring it outside an' show
everybody what you're afther findin'!

PETER. [*In a panic to Fluther.*]
Pick it up, you, Fluther, an' run
afther her with it, will you?

FLUTHER. What d'ye take Fluther
for? You must think Fluther's a right
gom. D'ye think Fluther's like yourself, destitute of a tither of undher-
standin'?

BARMAN. [*Imperatively to Peter.*]
Take it up, man, an' run out afther
her with it, before she's gone too far.
You're not goin' to leave th' bloody
thing here, are you?

PETER. [*Plaintively, as he lifts up
the baby.*] Well, God Almighty, give
me patience with all th' scorners, tormentors, an' twarters that are always
an' ever thryin' to goad me into
prayin' for their blindin' an' blastin'
an' burnin' in th' world to come! [*He
goes out.*]

FLUTHER. God, it's a relief to get
rid o' that crowd. Women is terrible
when they start to fight. There's no
holdin' them back. [*To the Covey.*]

Are you goin' to have anything?

THE COVEY. Ah, I don't mind if I have another half.

FLUTHER. [To Barman.] Two more, Tommy, me son.

[The Barman gets the drinks.]

FLUTHER. You know, there's no conthrollin' a woman when she loses her head.

[Rosie enters and goes over to the counter on the side nearest to Fluther.]

ROSIE. [To Barman.] Divil a use i' havin' a thrim little leg on a night like this; things was never worse. . . . Give us a half till to-morrow, Tom, duckey.

BARMAN. [Coldly.] No more to-night, Rosie; you owe me for three already.

ROSIE. [Combatively.] You'll be paid, won't you?

BARMAN. I hope so.

ROSIE. You hope so! Is that th' way with you, now?

FLUTHER. [To Barman.] Give her one; it'll be all right.

ROSIE. [Clapping Fluther on the back.] Oul' sport!

FLUTHER. Th' meetin' should be soon over, now.

THE COVEY. Th' sooner th' betther. It's all a lot o' blasted nonsense, comrade.

FLUTHER. Oh, I wouldn't say it was all nonsense. Afther all, Fluther can remember th' time, an' him only a dawny chiselur, bein' taught at his mother's knee to be faithful to th' Shan Van Vok!

THE COVEY. That's all dope, comrade; th' sort o' thing that workers are fed on be th' Boorzwawzee.

FLUTHER. [A little sharply.] What's all dope? Though I'm sayin' it that shouldn't: [Catching his cheek with his hand, and pulling down the flesh from the eye.] d'ye see that mark there, undher me eye? . . . A sabre slice from a dragoon in O'Connell Street! [Thrusting his head forward towards Rosie.] Feel that dint in th' middle o' me nut!

ROSIE. [Rubbing Fluther's head, and winking at the Covey.] My God, there's a holla!

FLUTHER. [Putting on his hat with quiet pride.] A skelp from a bobby's baton at a Labour meetin' in th' Phœnix Park!

THE COVEY. He must ha' hitten you in mistake. I don't know what you ever done for th' Labour movement.

FLUTHER. [Loudly.] D'ye not? Maybe, then, I done as much, an' know as much about th' Labour movement as th' chancers that are blowin' about it!

BARMAN. Speak easy, Fluther, thry to speak easy.

THE COVEY. There's no necessity to get excited about it, comrade.

FLUTHER. [More loudly.] Excited? Who's gettin' excited? There's no one gettin' excited! It would take something more than a thing like you to flutther a feather o' Fluther. Blatherin', an', when all is said, you know as much as th' rest in th' wind up!

THE COVEY. Well, let us put it to th' test, then, an' see what you know about th' Labour movement: what's the mechanism of exchange?

FLUTHER. [Roaring, because he feels he is beaten.] How th' hell do I know what it is? There's nothin' about that in th' rules of our Thrades Union!

BARMAN. For God's sake, thry to speak easy, Fluther.

THE COVEY. What does Karl Marx say about th' Relation of Value to th' Cost o' Production?

FLUTHER. [Angrily.] What th' hell do I care what he says? I'm Irishman enough not to lose me head be follyin' foreigners!

BARMAN. Speak easy, Fluther.

THE COVEY. It's only waste o' time talkin' to you, comrade.

FLUTHER. Don't be comradin' me, mate. I'd be on me last legs if I wanted you for a comrade.

ROSIE. [To the Covey.] It seems a highly rediculous thing to hear a thing that's only an inch or two away from a kid, swingin' heavy words about he doesn't know th' meanin' of, an' uppishly thryin' to down a man like Misther Fluther here, that's well flavoured in th' knowledge of th' world he's livin' in.

THE COVEY. [Savagely to Rosie.] Nobody's askin' you to be buttin' in with your prate. . . . I have you well taped, me lassie. . . . Just you keep your opinions for your own place. . . . It'll be a long time before th' Covey takes any insthructions or reprimandin' from a prostitute!

ROSIE. [Wild with humiliation.] You louse, you louse, you! . . . You're no man. . . . You're no man . . . I'm a woman, anyhow, an' if I'm a prostitute aself, I have me feelin's. . . . Thryin' to put his arm around me a minute ago, an' givin' me th' glad eye, th' little wrigglin' lump o' desolation turns on me now, because he saw there was nothin' doin'. . . . You louse, you! If I was a man, or you were a woman, I'd bate th' puss o' you!

BARMAN. Ay, Rosie, ay! You'll have to shut your mouth altogether, if you can't learn to speak easy!

FLUTHER. [To Rosie.] Houl' on there, Rosie; houl' on there. There's no necessity to flutther yourself when you're with Fluther. . . . Any lady that's in th' company of Fluther is goin' to get a fair hunt. . . . This is outside your province. . . . I'm not goin' to let you demean yourself be talkin' to a tittherin' chancer. . . . Leave this to Fluther—this is a man's job. [To the Covey.] Now, if you've anything to say, say it to Fluther, an', let me tell you, you're not goin' to be pass-remarkable to any lady in my company.

THE COVEY. Sure I don't care if you were runnin' all night afther your Mary o' th' Curlin' Hair, but, when you start tellin' luscious lies about what you done for th' Labour movement, it's nearly time to show y'up!

FLUTHER. [Fiercely.] Is it you show Fluther up? G'way, man, I'd beat two o' you before me breakfast!

THE COVEY. [Contemptuously.] Tell us where you bury your dead, will you?

FLUTHER. [With his face stuck into the face of the Covey.] Sing a little less on th' high note, or, when I'm done with you, you'll put a Christianable consthruction on things, I'm tellin' you!

THE COVEY. You're a big fella, you are.

FLUTHER. [Tapping the Covey threateningly on the shoulder.] Now, you're temptin' Providence when you're temptin' Fluther!

THE COVEY. [Losing his temper and bawling.] Easy with them hands there, easy with them hands! You're startin' to take a little risk when you commence to paw the Covey!

[*Fluther suddenly springs into the middle of the shop, flings his hat into the corner, whips off his coat, and begins to paw the air.*]

FLUTHER. [*Roaring at the top of his voice.*] Come on, come on, you lowser; put your mits up now, if there's a man's blood in you! Be God, in a few minutes you'll see some snots flyin' around, I'm tellin' you. . . . When Fluther's done with you, you'll have a vice versa opinion of him! Come on, now, come on!

BARMAN. [*Running from behind the counter and catching hold of the Covey.*] Here, out you go, me little bowsey. Because you got a couple o' halves you think you can act as you like. [*He pushes the Covey to the door.*] Fluther's a friend o' mine, an' I'll not have him insulted.

THE COVEY. [*Struggling with the Barman.*] Ay, leggo, leggo there; fair hunt, give a man a fair hunt! One minute with him is all I ask; one minute alone with him, while you're runnin' for th' priest an' th' doctor.

FLUTHER. [*To the Barman.*] Let him go, let him go, Tom! let him open th' door to sudden death if he wants to!

BARMAN. [*To the Covey.*] Go on, out you go an' do th' bowsey somewhere else. [*He pushes the Covey out and comes back.*]

ROSIE. [*Getting Fluther's hat as he is putting on his coat.*] Be God, you put th' fear o' God in his heart that time! I thought you'd have to be dug out of him. . . . Th' way you lepped out without any of your fancy side-steppin'! 'Men like Fluther,' say I to meself, 'is gettin' scarce nowadays.'

FLUTHER. [*With proud complacency.*] I wasn't goin' to let meself be malignified by a chancer. . . . He got a little bit too derogatory for Fluther. . . . Be God, to think of a cur like that comin' to talk to a man like me!

ROSIE. [*Fixing on his hat.*] Did j'ever!

FLUTHER. He's lucky he got off safe. I hit a man last week, Rosie, an' he's fallin' yet!

ROSIE. Sure, you'd ha' broken him in two if you'd ha' hitten him one clatther!

FLUTHER. [*Amorously, putting his arm around Rosie.*] Come on into th' snug, me little darlin', an' we'll have a few dhrinks before I see you home.

ROSIE. Oh, Fluther, I'm afraid you're a terrible man for th' women.

[*They go into the snug as Clitheroe, Captain Brennan, and Lieut. Langon of the Irish Volunteers enter hurriedly. Captain Brennan carries the banner of the The Plough and the Stars, and Lieut. Langon a green, white, and orange Tri-colour. They are in a state of emotional excitement. Their faces are flushed and their eyes sparkle; they speak rapidly, as if unaware of the meaning of what they said. They have been mesmerized by the fervency of the speeches.*]

CLITHEROE. [*Almost pantingly.*] Three glasses o' port!

[*The Barman brings the drinks.*]

CAPT. BRENNAN. We won't have long to wait now.

LIEUT. LANGON. Th' time is rotten ripe for revolution.

CLITHEROE. You have a mother, Langon.

LIEUT. LANGON. Ireland is greater

than a mother.

CAPT. BRENNAN. You have a wife, Clitheroe.

CLITHEROE. Ireland is greater than a wife.

LIEUT. LANGON. Th' time for Ireland's battle is now—th' place for Ireland's battle is here.

[*The tall, dark figure again is silhouetted against the window. The three men pause and listen.*]

VOICE OF THE MAN. Our foes are strong, but strong as they are, they cannot undo the miracles of God, who ripens in the heart of young men the seeds sown by the young men of a former generation. They think they have pacified Ireland; think they have foreseen everything; think they have provided against everything; but the fools, the fools, the fools!—they have left us our Fenian dead, and, while Ireland holds these graves, Ireland, unfree, shall never be at peace!

CAPT. BRENNAN. [*Catching up The Plough and the Stars.*] Imprisonment for th' Independence of Ireland!

LIEUT. LANGON. [*Catching up the Tri-colour.*] Wounds for th' Independence of Ireland!

CLITHEROE. Death for th' Independence of Ireland!

THE THREE. [*Together.*] So help us God!

[*They drink. A bugle blows the Assembly. They hurry out. A pause. Fluther and Rosie come out of the snug; Rosie is linking Fluther, who is a little drunk. Both are in a merry mood.*]

ROSIE. Come on home, ower o' that, man. Are you afraid or what? Are you goin' to come home, or are you not?

FLUTHER. Of course I'm goin' home. What ud ail me that I wouldn't go?

ROSIE. [*Lovingly.*] Come on, then, oul' sport.

OFFICER'S VOICE. [*Giving command outside.*] Irish Volunteers, by th' right, quick march!

ROSIE. [*Putting her arm round Fluther and singing:*]

I once had a lover, a tailor, but he
    could do nothin' for me,
An' then I fell in with a sailor as strong
    an' as wild as th' sea.
We cuddled an' kissed with devotion,
    till th' night from th' mornin' had
    fled;
An' there, to our joy, a bright bouncin'
    boy
Was dancin' a jig in th' bed!

Dancin' a jig in th' bed, an' bawlin'
    for butther an' bread.
An' there, to our joy, a bright bouncin'
    boy
Was dancin' a jig in th' bed!

[*They go out with their arms round each other.*]

CLITHEROE'S VOICE. [*In command outside.*] Dublin Battalion of the Irish Citizen Army, by th' right, quick march!

CURTAIN

ACT III

[*The corner house in a street of tenements: it is the home of the Clitheroes. The house is a long, gaunt, five-story tenement; its brick front is chipped and scarred with age and neglect. The wide and heavy hall door, flanked by two pillars, has a look of having been charred by a fire in the distant past*

The door lurches a little to one side, disjointed by the continual and reckless banging when it is being closed by most of the residents. The diamond-paned fanlight is destitute of a single pane, the framework alone remaining. The windows, except the two looking into the front parlour (Clitheroe's room), are grimy, and are draped with fluttering and soiled fragments of lace curtains. The front parlour windows are hung with rich, comparatively, casement cloth. Five stone steps lead from the door to the path on the street. Branching on each side are railings to prevent people from falling into the area. At the left corner of the house runs a narrow lane, bisecting the street, and connecting it with another of the same kind. At the corner of the lane is a street lamp.

As the house is revealed, Mrs. Gogan is seen helping Mollser to a chair, which stands on the path beside the railings, at the left side of the steps. She then wraps a shawl around Mollser's shoulders. It is some months later.]

MRS. GOGAN. [*Arranging shawl around Mollser.*] Th' sun'll do you all th' good in th' world. A few more weeks o' this weather, an' there's no knowin' how well you'll be. . . . Are you comfy, now?

MOLLSER. [*Weakly and wearily.*] Yis, ma; I'm all right.

MRS. GOGAN. How are you feelin'?

MOLLSER. Betther, ma, betther. If th' horrible sinkin' feelin' ud go, I'd be all right.

MRS. GOGAN. Ah, I wouldn't put much pass on that. Your stomach maybe's out of ordher. . . . Is th' poor breathin' any betther, d'ye think?

MOLLSER. Yis, yis, ma; a lot betther.

MRS. GOGAN. Well, that's somethin' anyhow. . . . With th' help o' God, you'll be on th' mend from this out. . . . D'your legs feel any sthronger undher you, d'ye think!

MOLLSER. [*Irritably.*] I can't tell, ma. I think so. . . . A little.

MRS. GOGAN. Well, a little aself is somethin'. . . . I thought I heard you coughin' a little more than usual last night. . . . D'ye think you were?

MOLLSER. I wasn't, ma, I wasn't.

MRS. GOGAN. I thought I heard you, for I was kep' awake all night with th' shootin'. An' thinkin' o' that madman, Fluther, runnin' about through th' night lookin' for Nora Clitheroe to bring her back when he heard she'd gone to folly her husband, an' in dhread any minute he might come staggerin' in covered with bandages, splashed all over with th' red of his own blood, an' givin' us barely time to bring th' priest to hear th' last whisper of his final confession, as his soul was passin' through th' dark doorway o' death into th' way o' th' wondherin' dead. . . . You don't feel cold, do you?

MOLLSER. No, ma; I'm all right.

MRS. GOGAN. Keep your chest well covered, for that's th' delicate spot in you . . . if there's any danger, I'll whip you in again. . . . [*Looking up the street.*] Oh, here's th' Covey an' oul' Pether hurryin' along. God Almighty, sthrange things is happenin' when them two is pullin' together.

[*The Covey and Peter come in, breathless and excited.*]

MRS. GOGAN. [*To the two men.*] Were yous far up th' town? Did yous see any sign o' Fluther or Nora? How is things lookin'? I hear they're blazin' away out o' th' G.P.O. That th' Tommies is sthretched in heaps around Nelson's Pillar an' th' Parnell Statue, an' that th' pavin' sets in O'Connell Street is nearly covered be pools o' blood.

PETER. We seen no sign o' Nora or Fluther anywhere.

MRS. GOGAN. We should ha' held her back be main force from goin' to look for her husband. . . . God knows what's happened to her—I'm always seein' her sthretched on her back in some hospital, moanin' with th' pain of a bullet in her vitals, an' nuns thryin' to get her to take a last look at th' crucifix!

THE COVEY. We can do nothin'. You can't stick your nose into O'Connell Street, an' Tyler's is on fire.

PETER. An' we seen th' Lancers—

THE COVEY. [Interrupting.] Throttin' along, heads in th' air; spurs an' sabres jinglin', an' lances quiverin', an' lookin' as if they were assin' themselves, 'Where's these blighters, till we get a prod at them?' when there was a volley from th' Post Office that stretched half o' them, an' sent th' rest gallopin' away wondherin' how far they'd have to go before they'd feel safe.

PETER. [Rubbing his hands.] 'Damn it,' says I to meself, 'this looks like business!'

THE COVEY. An' then out comes General Pearse an' his staff, an', standin' in th' middle o' th' street, he reads th' Proclamation.

MRS. GOGAN. What proclamation?

PETER. Declarin' an Irish Republic.

MRS. GOGAN. Go to God!

PETER. The gunboat Helga's shellin' Liberty Hall, an' I hear the people livin' on th' quays had to crawl on their bellies to Mass with th' bullets that were flyin' around from Boland's Mills.

MRS. GOGAN. God bless us, what's goin' to be th' end of it all!

BESSIE. [Looking out of the top window.] Maybe yous are satisfied now; maybe yous are satisfied now. Go on an' get guns if yous are men—Johnny get your gun, get your gun, get your gun! Yous are all nicely shanghaied now; th' boyo hasn't a sword on his thigh now! Oh, yous are all nicely shanghaied now!

MRS. GOGAN. [Warningly to Peter and the Covey.] S-s-sh, don't answer her. She's th' right oul' Orange bitch! She's been chantin' 'Rule, Britannia' all th' mornin'.

PETER. I hope Fluther hasn't met with any accident, he's such a wild card.

MRS. GOGAN. God grant it; but last night I dreamt I seen gettin' carried into th' house a shtretcher with a figure lyin' on it, stiff an' still, dhressed in th' habit of Saint Francis. An' then, I heard th' murmurs of a crowd no one could see sayin' th' litany for th' dead; an' then it got so dark that nothin' was seen but th' white face of th' corpse, gleamin' like a white wather-lily floatin' on th' top of a dark lake. Then a tiny whisper thrickled into me ear, sayin', 'Isn't the face very like th' face o' Fluther?' an' then, with a thremblin' flutther, th' dead lips opened, an' although I couldn't hear, I knew they were sayin', 'Poor oul' Fluther, afther havin' handed in his gun at last, his shakin' soul moored in th' place where th' wicked are at rest an' th' weary cease from throublin'.'

PETER. [Who has put on a pair of

spectacles, and has been looking down the street.] Here they are, be God, here they are; just afther turnin' th' corner—Nora an' Fluther!

THE COVEY. She must be wounded or something—he seems to be carryin' her.

[*Fluther and Nora enter. Fluther has his arm around her and is half leading, half carrying her in. Her eyes are dim and hollow, her face pale and strained-looking; her hair is tossed, and her clothes are dusty.*]

MRS. GOGAN. [*Running over to them.*] God bless us, is it wounded y'are, Mrs. Clitheroe, or what?

FLUTHER. Ah, she's all right, Mrs. Gogan; only worn out from thravellin' an' want o' sleep. A night's rest, now, an' she'll be as fit as a fiddle. Bring her in, an' make her lie down.

MRS. GOGAN. [*To Nora.*] Did you hear e'er a whisper o' Mr. Clitheroe?

NORA. [*Wearily.*] I could find him nowhere, Mrs. Gogan. None o' them would tell me where he was. They told me I shamed my husband an' th' women of Ireland be carryin' on as I was. . . . They said th' women must learn to be brave an' cease to be cowardly. . . . Me who risked more for love than they would risk for hate. . . . [*Raising her voice in hysterical protest.*] My Jack will be killed, my Jack will be killed! . . . He is to be butchered as a sacrifice to th' dead!

BESSIE. [*From upper window.*] Yous are all nicely shanghaied now! Sorra mend th' lasses that have been kissin' an' cuddlin' their boys into th' sheddin' of blood! . . . Fillin' their minds with fairy tales that had no beginnin', but, please God, 'll have a bloody quick endin'! . . . Turnin' bitther

into sweet, an' sweet into bitther. . . . Stabbin' in th' back th' men that are dyin' in th' threnches for them! It's a bad thing for any one that thries to jilt th' Ten Commandments, for judgements are prepared for scorners an' sthripes for th' back o' fools! [*Going away from window as she sings:*]

Rule, Britannia, Britannia rules th' waves,
Britons never, never, never shall be slaves!

FLUTHER. [*With a roar up at the window.*] Y'ignorant oul' throllop, you!

MRS. GOGAN. [*To Nora.*] He'll come home safe enough to you, you'll find, Mrs. Clitheroe; afther all, there's a power o' women that's handed over sons an' husbands to take a runnin' risk in th' fight they're wagin'.

NORA. I can't help thinkin' every shot fired 'll be fired at Jack, an' every shot fired at Jack 'll be fired at me. What do I care for th' others? I can think only of me own self. . . . An' there's no woman gives a son or a husband to be killed—if they say it, they're lyin', lyin', against God, Nature, an' against themselves! . . . One blasted hussy at a barricade told me to go home an' not be thryin' to dishearten th' men. . . . That I wasn't worthy to bear a son to a man that was out fightin' for freedom. . . . I clawed at her, an' smashed her in th' face till we were separated. . . . I was pushed down th' street, an' I cursed them—cursed the rebel ruffians an' Volunteers that had dhragged me ravin' mad into th' sthreets to seek me husband!

PETER. You'll have to have patience,

NORA. We all have to put up with twarthers an' tormentors in this world.

THE COVEY. If they were fightin' for anything worth while, I wouldn't mind.

FLUTHER. [*To Nora.*] Nothin' derogatory 'll happen to Mr. Clitheroe. You'll find, now, in th' finish up it'll be vice versa.

NORA. Oh, I know that wherever he is, he's thinkin' of wantin' to be with me. I know he's longin' to be passin' his hand through me hair, to be caressin' me neck, to fondle me hand an' to feel me kisses clingin' to his mouth. . . . An' he stands wherever he is because he's brave? [*Vehemently.*] No, but because he's a coward, a coward, a coward!

MRS. GOGAN. Oh, they're not cowards anyway.

NORA. [*With denunciatory anger.*] I tell you they're afraid to say they're afraid! . . . Oh, I saw it, I saw it, Mrs. Gogan. . . . At th' barricade in North King Street I saw fear glowin' in all their eyes. . . . An' in th' middle o' th' sthreet was somethin' huddled up in a horrible tangled heap. . . . His face was jammed again th' stones, an' his arm was twisted round his back. . . . An' every twist of his body was a cry against th' terrible thing that had happened to him. . . . An' I saw they were afraid to look at it. . . . An' some o' them laughed at me, but th' laugh was a frightened one. . . . An' some o' them shouted at me, but th' shout had in it th' shiver o' fear. . . . I tell you they were afraid, afraid, afraid!

MRS. GOGAN. [*Leading her towards the house.*] Come on in, dear. If you'd been a little longer together, th' wrench asundher wouldn't have been so sharp.

NORA. Th' agony I'm in since he left me has thrust away every rough thing he done, an' every unkind word he spoke; only th' blossoms that grew out of our lives are before me now; shakin' their colours before me face, an' breathin' their sweet scent on every thought springin' up in me mind, till, sometimes, Mrs. Gogan, sometimes I think I'm goin' mad!

MRS. GOGAN. You'll be a lot betther when you have a little lie down.

NORA. [*Turning towards Fluther as she is going in.*] I don't know what I'd have done, only for Fluther. I'd have been lyin' in th' streets, only for him. . . . [*As she goes in.*] They have dhriven away th' little happiness life had to spare for me. He has gone from me for ever, for ever. . . . Oh, Jack, Jack, Jack!

[*She is led in by Mrs. Gogan, as Bessie comes out with a shawl around her shoulders. She passes by them with her head in the air. When they have gone in, she gives a mug of milk to Mollser silently.*]

FLUTHER. Which of yous has th' tossers?

THE COVEY. I have.

BESSIE. [*As she is passing them to go down the street.*] You an' your Leadhers an' their sham-battle soldiers has landed a body in a nice way, havin' to go an' ferret out a bit o' bread God knows where. . . . Why aren't yous in th' G.P.O. if yous are men? It's paler an' paler yous are gettin'. . . . A lot o' vipers, that's what th' Irish people is! [*She goes out.*]

FLUTHER. Never mind her. . . . [*To the Covey.*] Make a start an' keep us from th' sin o' idleness. [*To*

Mollser.] Well, how are you to-day, Mollser, oul' son? What are you dhrinkin', milk?

MOLLSER. Grand, Fluther, grand, thanks. Yis, milk.

FLUTHER. You couldn't get a better thing down you. . . . This turn-up has done one good thing, anyhow; you can't get dhrink anywhere, an' if it lasts a week, I'll be so used to it that I won't think of a pint.

THE COVEY. [*Who has taken from his pocket two worn coins and a thin strip of wood about four inches long.*] What's th' bettin'?

PETER. Heads, a juice.

FLUTHER. Harps, a tanner.

[*The Covey places the coins on the strip of wood, and flips them up into the air. As they jingle on the ground the distant boom of a big gun is heard. They stand for a moment listening.*]

FLUTHER. What th' hell's that?

THE COVEY. It's like th' boom of a big gun!

FLUTHER. Surely to God they're not goin' to use artillery on us?

THE COVEY. [*Scornfully.*] Not goin'! [*Vehemently.*] Wouldn't they use anything on us, man?

FLUTHER. Aw, holy Christ, that's not playin' th' game!

PETER. [*Plaintively.*] What would happen if a shell landed here now?

THE COVEY. [*Ironically.*] You'd be off to heaven in a fiery chariot.

PETER. In spite of all th' warnin's that's ringin' around us, are you goin' to start your pickin' at me again?

FLUTHER. Go on, toss them again, toss them again. . . . Harps, a tanner.

PETER. Heads, a juice.

[*The Covey tosses the coins.*]

FLUTHER. [*As the coins fall.*] Let them roll, let them roll. Heads, be God!

[*Bessie runs in excitedly. She has a new hat on her head, a fox fur round her neck over her shawl, three umbrellas under her right arm, and a box of biscuits under her left. She speaks rapidly and breathlessly.*]

BESSIE. They're breakin' into th' shops, they're breakin' into th' shops! Smashin' th' windows, battherin' in th' doors, an' whippin' away everything! An' th' Volunteers is firin' on them. I seen two men an' a lassie pushin' a piano down th' sthreet, an' th' sweat rollin' off them thryin' to get it up on th' pavement; an' an oul' wan that must ha' been seventy lookin' as if she'd dhrop every minute with th' dint o' heart beatin', thryin' to pull a big double bed out of a broken shop-window! I was goin' to wait till I dhressed meself from th' skin out.

MOLLSER. [*To Bessie, as she is going in.*] Help me in, Bessie; I'm feelin' curious. [*Bessie leaves the looted things in the house, and, rapidly returning, helps Mollser in.*]

THE COVEY. Th' selfishness of that one—she waited till she got all she could carry before she'd come to tell anyone!

FLUTHER. [*Running over to the door of the house and shouting in to Bessie.*] Ay, Bessie, did you hear of e'er a pub gettin' a shake up?

BESSIE. [*Inside.*] I didn't hear o' none.

FLUTHER. [*In a burst of enthusiasm.*] Well, you're goin' to hear of one soon!

THE COVEY. Come on, man, an' don't be wastin' time.

PETER. [*To them as they are about to run off.*] Ay, ay, are you goin' to leave me here?

FLUTHER. Are you goin' to leave yourself here?

PETER. [*Anxiously.*] Didn't yous hear her sayin' they were firin' on them?

THE COVEY AND FLUTHER. [*Together.*] Well?

PETER. Supposin' I happened to be potted?

FLUTHER. We'd give you a Christian burial, anyhow.

THE COVEY. [*Ironically.*] Dhressed up in your regimentals.

PETER. [*To the Covey, passionately.*] May th' all-lovin' God give you a hot knock one o' these days, me young Covey, tuthorin' Fluther up now to be tiltin' at me, an' crossin' me with his mockeries an' jibin'!

[*A fashionably dressed, middle-aged, stout woman comes hurriedly in, and makes for the group. She is almost fainting with fear.*]

THE WOMAN. For Gawd's sake, will one of you kind men show any safe way for me to get to Wrathmines? . . . I was foolish enough to visit a friend, thinking the howl thing was a joke, and now I cawn't get a car or a tram to take me home—isn't it awful?

FLUTHER. I'm afraid, ma'am, one way is as safe as another.

WOMAN. And what am I gowing to do? Oh, isn't this awful? . . . I'm so different from others. . . . The mowment I hear a shot, my legs give way under me—I cawn't stir, I'm paralysed—isn't it awful?

FLUTHER. [*Moving away.*] It's a derogatory way to be, right enough, ma'am.

WOMAN. [*Catching Fluther's coat.*] Creeping along the street there, with my head down and my eyes half shut, a bullet whizzed past within an inch of my nowse. . . . I had to lean against the wall for a long time, gasping for breath—I nearly passed away —it was awful! . . . I wonder, would you kind men come some of the way and see me safe?

FLUTHER. I have to go away, ma'am, to thry an' save a few things from th' burnin' buildin's.

THE COVEY. Come on, then, or there won't be anything left to save. [*The Covey and Fluther hurry away.*]

WOMAN. [*To Peter.*] Wasn't it an awful thing for me to leave my friend's house? Wasn't it an idiotic thing to do? . . . I haven't the slightest idea where I am. . . . You have a kind face, sir. Could you possibly come and pilot me in the direction of Wrathmines?

PETER. [*Indignantly.*] D'ye think I'm goin' to risk me life throttin' in front of you? An' maybe get a bullet that would gimme a game leg or something that would leave me a jibe an' a jeer to Fluther an' th' young Covey for th' rest o' me days! [*With an indignant toss of his head he walks into the house.*]

THE WOMAN. [*Going out.*] I know I'll fall down in a dead faint if I hear another shot go off anyway near me —isn't it awful!

[*Mrs. Gogan comes out of the house pushing a pram before her. As she enters the street, Bessie rushes out, follows Mrs. Gogan, and catches hold of the pram, stopping Mrs. Gogan's progress.*]

BESSIE. Here, where are you goin' with that? How quick you were, me lady, to clap your eyes on th' pram. . . . Maybe you don't know that Mrs.

Sullivan, before she went to spend Easther with her people in Dunboyne, gave me sthrict injunctions to give an accasional look to see if it was still standin' where it was left in th' corner of th' lobby.

MRS. GOGAN. That remark of yours, Mrs. Bessie Burgess, requires a little considheration, seein' that th' pram was left on our lobby, an' not on yours; a foot or two a little to th' left of th' jamb of me own room door; nor is it needful to mention th' name of th' person that gave a squint to see if it was there th' first thing in th' mornin', an' th' last thing in th' stillness o' th' night; never failin' to realize that her eyes couldn't be goin' wrong, be sthretchin' out her arm an' runnin' her hand over th' pram, to make sure that th' sight was no deception! Moreover, somethin's tellin' me that th' runnin' hurry of an inthrest you're takin' in it now is a sudden ambition to use th' pram for a purpose that a loyal woman of law an' ordher would stagger away from! [She gives the pram a sudden push that pulls Bessie forward.]

BESSIE. [Still holding the pram.] There's not as much as one body in th' house that doesn't know that it wasn't Bessie Burgess that was always shakin' her voice complainin' about people leavin' bassinettes in th' way of them that, week in an' week out, had to pay their rent, an' always had to find a regular accommodation for her own furniture in her own room. . . . An' as for law an' ordher, puttin' aside th' harp an' shamrock, Bessie Burgess 'll have as much respect as she wants for th' lion an' unicorn!

PETER. [Appearing at the door.]

I think I'll go with th' pair of yous an' see th' fun. A fella might as well chance it, anyhow.

MRS. GOGAN. [Taking no notice of Peter, and pushing the pram on another step.] Take your rovin' lumps o' hands from pattin' th' bassinette, if you please, ma'am; an', steppin' from th' threshold of good manners, let me tell you, Mrs. Burgess, that it's a fat wondher to Jennie Gogan that a lady-like singer o' hymns like yourself would lower her thoughts from sky-thinkin' to stretch out her arm in a sly-seekin' way to pinch anything dhriven asthray in th' confusion of th' battle our boys is makin' for th' freedom of their counthry!

PETER. [Laughing and rubbing his hands together.] Hee, hee, hee, hee, hee! I'll go with th' pair o' yous an' give yous a hand.

MRS. GOGAN. [With a rapid turn of her head as she shoves the pram forward.] Get up in th' prambulator an' we'll wheel you down.

BESSIE. [To Mrs. Gogan.] Poverty an' hardship has sent Bessie Burgess to abide with sthrange company, but she always knew them she had to live with from backside to breakfast time; an' she can tell them, always havin' had a Christian kinch on her conscience, that a passion for thievin' an' pinchin' would find her soul a foreign place to live in, an' that her present intention is quite th' lofty-hearted one of pickin' up anything shaken up an' scatthered about in th' loose confusion of a general plundher!

[By this time they have disappeared from view. Peter is following, when the boom of a big gun in the distance brings him to a quick halt.]

PETER. God Almighty, that's th' big

gun again! God forbid any harm would happen to them, but sorra mind I'd mind if they met with a dhrop in their mad endeyvours to plundher an' desthroy. [*He looks down the street for a moment, then runs to the hall door of the house, which is open, and shuts it with a vicious pull; he then goes to the chair in which Mollser had sat, sits down, takes out his pipe, lights it and begins to smoke with his head carried at a haughty angle. The Covey comes staggering in with a ten-stone sack of flour on his back. On the top of the sack is a ham. He goes over to the door, pushes it with his head, and finds he can't open it; he turns slightly in the direction of Peter.*]

THE COVEY. [*To Peter.*] Who shut th' door? . . . [*He kicks at it.*] Here, come on an' open it, will you? This isn't a mot's hand-bag I've got on me back.

PETER. Now, me young Covey, d'ye think I'm goin' to be your lackey?

THE COVEY. [*Angrily.*] Will you open th' door, y'oul'—

PETER. [*Shouting.*] Don't be assin' me to open any door, don't be assin' me to open any door for you. . . . Makin' a shame an' a sin o' th' cause that good men are fightin' for. . . . Oh, God forgive th' people that, instead o' burnishin' th' work th' boys is doin' to-day with quiet honesty an' patience, is revilin' their sacrifices with a riot of lootin' an' roguery!

THE COVEY. Isn't your own eyes leppin' out o' your head with envy that you haven't th' guts to ketch a few o' th' things that God is givin' to His chosen people? . . . Y'oul' hypocrite, if everyone was blind you'd steal a cross off an ass's back!

PETER. [*Very calmly.*] You're not going to make me lose me temper; you can go on with your proddin' as long as you like; goad an' goad an' goad away; hee, hee, heee! I'll not lose me temper. [*Somebody opens door and the Covey goes in.*]

THE COVEY. [*Inside, mockingly.*] Cuckoo-oo!

PETER. [*Running to the door and shouting in a blaze of passion as he follows the Covey in.*] You lean, long, lanky lath of a lowsey bastard. . . . [*Following him in.*] Lowsey bastard, lowsey bastard!

[*Bessie and Mrs. Gogan enter, the pride of a great joy illuminating their faces. Bessie is pushing the pram, which is filled with clothes and boots; on the top of the boots and clothes is a fancy table, which Mrs. Gogan is holding on with her left hand, while with her right hand she holds a chair on the top of her head. They are heard talking to each other before they enter.*]

MRS. GOGAN. [*Outside.*] I don't remember ever havin' seen such lovely pairs as them, [*They appear.*] with th' pointed toes an' th' cuban heels.

BESSIE. They'll go grand with th' dhresses we're after liftin', when we've stitched a sthray bit o' silk to lift th' bodices up a little higher, so as to shake th' shame out o' them, an' make them fit for women that hasn't lost themselves in th' nakedness o' th' times.

[*They fussily carry in the chair, the table, and some of the other goods. They return to bring in the rest.*]

PETER. [*At door, sourly to Mrs. Gogan.*] Ay, you. Mollser looks as if she was goin' to faint, an' your youngster is roarin' in convulsions in her lap.

MRS. GOGAN. [*Snappily.*] She's never any other way but faintin'! [*She goes to go in with some things in her arms, when a shot from a rifle rings out. She and Bessie make a bolt for the door, which Peter, in a panic, tries to shut before they have got inside.*]

MRS. GOGAN. Ay, ay, ay, you cowardly oul' fool, what are you thryin' to shut th' door on us for?

[*They retreat tumultuously inside. A pause; then Captain Brennan comes in supporting Lieutenant Langon, whose arm is around Brennan's neck. Langon's face, which is ghastly white, is momentarily convulsed with spasms of agony. He is in a state of collapse, and Brennan is almost carrying him. After a few moments Clitheroe, pale, and in a state of calm nervousness, follows, looking back in the direction from which he came, a rifle, held at the ready, in his hands.*]

CAPT. BRENNAN. [*Savagely to Clitheroe.*] Why did you fire over their heads? Why didn't you fire to kill?

CLITHEROE. No, no, Bill; bad as they are they're Irish men an' women.

CAPT. BRENNAN. [*Savagely.*] Irish be damned! Attackin' an' mobbin' th' men that are riskin' their lives for them. If these slum lice gather at our heels again, plug one o' them, or I'll soon shock them with a shot or two meself!

LIEUT. LANGON. [*Moaningly.*] My God, is there ne'er an ambulance knockin' around anywhere? . . . Th' stomach is ripped out o' me; I feel it —o-o-oh, Christ!

CAPT. BRENNAN. Keep th' heart up, Jim; we'll soon get help, now.

[*Nora rushes wildly out of the house and flings her arms round the neck of Clitheroe with a fierce and joyous insistence. Her hair is down, her face is haggard, but her eyes are agleam with the light of happy relief.*]

NORA. Jack, Jack, Jack; God be thanked . . . be thanked. . . . He has been kind and merciful to His poor handmaiden. . . . My Jack, my own Jack, that I thought was lost is found, that I thought was dead is alive again! . . . Oh, God be praised for ever, evermore! . . . My poor Jack. . . . Kiss me, kiss me, Jack, kiss your own Nora!

CLITHEROE. [*Kissing her, and speaking brokenly.*] My Nora; my little, beautiful Nora, I wish to God I'd never left you.

NORA. It doesn't matter—not now, not now, Jack. It will make us dearer than ever to each other. . . . Kiss me, kiss me again.

CLITHEROE. Now, for God's sake, Nora, don't make a scene.

NORA. I won't, I won't; I promise, I promise, Jack; honest to God. I'll be silent an' brave to bear th' joy of feelin' you safe in my arms again. . . . It's hard to force away th' tears of happiness at th' end of an awful agony.

BESSIE. [*From the upper window.*] Th' Minsthrel Boys aren't feelin' very comfortable now. Th' big guns has knocked all th' harps out of their hands. General Clitheroe'd rather be unlacin' his wife's bodice than standin' at a barricade. . . . An' th' professor of chicken-butcherin' there, finds he's up against somethin' a little tougher even than his own chickens, an' that's sayin' a lot!

CAPT. BRENNAN. [*Up to Bessie.*] Shut up, y'oul' hag!

BESSIE. [*Down to Brennan.*] Choke th' chicken, choke th' chicken, choke th' chicken!

LIEUT. LANGON. For God's sake, Bill, bring me some place where me wound 'll be looked afther. . . . Am I to die before anything is done to save me?

CAPT. BRENNAN. [*To Clitheroe.*] Come on, Jack. We've got to get help for Jim, here—have you no thought for his pain an' danger?

BESSIE. Choke th' chicken, choke th' chicken, choke th' chicken!

CLITHEROE. [*To Nora.*] Loosen me, darling, let me go.

NORA. [*Clinging to him.*] No, no, no, I'll not let you go! Come on, come up to our home, Jack, my sweetheart, my lover, my husband, an' we'll forget th' last few terrible days! . . . I look tired now, but a few hours of happy rest in your arms will bring back th' bloom of freshness again, an' you will be glad, you will be glad, glad . . . glad!

LIEUT. LANGON. Oh, if I'd kep' down only a little longer, I mightn't ha' been hit! Everyone else escapin', an' me gettin' me belly ripped asundher! . . . I couldn't scream, couldn't even scream. . . . D'ye think I'm really badly wounded, Bill? Me clothes seem to be all soakin' wet. . . . It's blood . . . My God, it must be me own blood!

CAPT. BRENNAN. [*To Clitheroe.*] Go on, Jack, bid her good-bye with another kiss, an' be done with it! D'ye want Langon to die in me arms while you're dallyin' with your Nora?

CLITHEROE. [*To Nora.*] I must go, I must go, Nora. I'm sorry we met at all. . . . It couldn't be helped—all other ways were blocked be th' British. . . . Let me go, can't you, Nora? D'ye want me to be unthrue to me comrades?

NORA. No, I won't let you go. . . . I want you to be thrue to me, Jack. . . . I'm your dearest comrade; I'm your thruest comrade. . . . They only want th' comfort of havin' you in th' same danger as themselves. . . . Oh, Jack, I can't let you go!

CLITHEROE. You must, Nora, you must.

NORA. All last night at th' barricades I sought you, Jack. . . . I didn't think of th' danger—I could only think of you. . . . I asked for you everywhere. . . . Some o' them laughed. . . . I was pushed away, but I shoved back. . . . Some o' them even struck me . . . an' I screamed an' screamed your name!

CLITHEROE. [*In fear her action would give him future shame.*] What possessed you to make a show of yourself, like that? . . . What way d'ye think I'll feel when I'm told my wife was bawlin' for me at th' barricades? What are you more than any other woman?

NORA. No more, maybe; but you are more to me than any other man, Jack. . . . I didn't mean any harm, honestly, Jack. . . . I couldn't help it. . . . I shouldn't have told you. . . . My love for you made me mad with terror.

CLITHEROE. [*Angrily.*] They'll say now that I sent you out th' way I'd have an excuse to bring you home. . . . Are you goin' to turn all th' risks I'm takin' into a laugh?

LIEUT. LANGON. Let me lie down, let me lie down, Bill; th' pain would be easier, maybe, lyin' down. . . . Oh, God, have mercy on me!

CAPT. BRENNAN. [*To Langon.*] A few steps more, Jim, a few steps more;

thry to stick it for a few steps more.

LIEUT. LANGON. Oh, I can't, I can't, I can't!

CAPT. BRENNAN. [*To Clitheroe.*] Are you comin', man, or are you goin' to make an arrangement for another honeymoon? . . . If you want to act th' renegade, say so, an' we'll be off!

BESSIE. [*From above.*] Runnin' from th' Tommies—choke th' chicken. Runnin' from th' Tommies—choke th' chicken!

CLITHEROE. [*Savagely to Brennan.*] Damn you, man, who wants to act th' renegade? [*To Nora.*] Here, let go your hold; let go, I say!

NORA. [*Clinging to Clitheroe, and indicating Brennan.*] Look, Jack, look at th' anger in his face; look at th' fear glintin' in his eyes. . . . He himself's afraid, afraid, afraid! . . . He wants you to go th' way he'll have th' chance of death sthrikin' you an' missin' him! . . . Turn round an' look at him, Jack, look at him, look at him! . . . His very soul is cold . . . shiverin' with th' thought of what may happen to him. . . . It is his fear that is thryin' to frighten you from recognizin' th' same fear that is in your own heart!

CLITHEROE. [*Struggling to release himself from Nora.*] Damn you, woman, will you let me go!

CAPT. BRENNAN. [*Fiercely, to Clitheroe.*] Why are you beggin' her to let you go? Are you afraid of her, or what? Break her hold on you, man, or go up, an' sit on her lap!

[*Clitheroe trying roughly to break her hold.*]

NORA. [*Imploringly.*] Oh, Jack. . . . Jack. . . . Jack!

LIEUT. LANGON. [*Agonizingly.*] Brennan, a priest; I'm dyin', I think, I'm dyin'!

CLITHEROE. [*To Nora.*] If you won't do it quietly, I'll have to make you! [*To Brennan.*] Here, hold this gun, you, for a minute. [*He hands the gun to Brennan.*]

NORA. [*Pitifully.*] Please, Jack. . . . You're hurting me, Jack. . . . Honestly. . . . Oh, you're hurting . . . me! . . . I won't, I won't, I won't! . . . Oh, Jack, I gave you everything you asked of me. . . . Don't fling me from you, now! [*He roughly loosens her grip, and pushes her away from him. Nora sinks to the ground and lies there.*]

NORA. [*Weakly.*] Ah, Jack. . . . Jack. . . . Jack!

CLITHEROE. [*Taking the gun back from Brennan.*] Come on, come on.

[*They go out. Bessie looks at Nora lying on the street, for a few moments, then, leaving the window, she comes out, runs over to Nora, lifts her up in her arms, and carries her swiftly into the house. A short pause, then down the street is heard a wild, drunken yell; it comes nearer, and Fluther enters, frenzied, wild-eyed, mad, roaring drunk. In his arms is an earthen half-gallon jar of whisky; streaming from one of the pockets of his coat is the arm of a new tunic shirt; on his head is a woman's vivid blue hat with gold lacing, all of which he has looted.*]

FLUTHER. [*Singing in a frenzy:*]

Fluther's a jolly good fella! . . .
    Fluther's a jolly good fella!
Up th' rebels! . . . That nobody can
    deny!

[*He beats on the door.*] Get us a mug or a jug, or somethin', some o' yous, one o' yous, will yous, before I lay one o' yous out! . . . [*Looking down the street.*] Bang an' fire away for all Fluther cares. . . . [*Banging at door.*] Come down an' open th' door, some of yous, one of yous, will yous, before I lay some o' yous out! . . . Th' whole city can topple home to hell, for Fluther!

[*Inside the house is heard a scream from Nora, followed by a moan.*]

FLUTHER. [*Singing furiously:*]

That nobody can deny, that nobody
　　can deny,
For Fluther's a jolly good fella, Fluth-
　　er's a jolly good fella,
Fluther's a jolly good fella . . . Up
　　th' rebels! That nobody can deny!

[*His frantic movements cause him to spill some of the whisky out of the jar.*] Blast you, Fluther, don't be spillin' th' precious liquor! [*He kicks at the door.*] Ay, give us a mug or a jug, or somethin', one o' yous, some o' yous, will yous, before I lay one o' yous out!

[*The door suddenly opens, and Bessie, coming out, grips him by the collar.*]

BESSIE. [*Indignantly.*] You bowsey, come in ower o' that. . . . I'll thrim your thricks o' dhrunken dancin' for you, an' none of us knowin' how soon we'll bump into a world we were never in before!

FLUTHER. [*As she is pulling him in.*] Ay, th' jar, th' jar, th' jar!

[*A short pause, then again is heard a scream of pain from Nora. The door opens and Mrs. Gogan and Bessie are seen standing at it.*]

BESSIE. Fluther would go, only he's too dhrunk. . . . Oh, God, isn't it a pity he's so dhrunk! We'll have to thry to get a docthor somewhere.

MRS. GOGAN. I'd be afraid to go. . . . Besides, Mollser's terrible bad. I don't think you'll get a docthor to come. It's hardly any use goin'.

BESSIE. [*Determinedly.*] I'll risk it. . . . Give her a little of Fluther's whisky. . . . It's th' fright that's brought it on her so soon. . . . Go on back to her, you.

[*Mrs. Gogan goes in, and Bessie softly closes the door. She is moving forward, when the sound of some rifle shots, and the tok, tok, tok of a distant machine-gun brings her to a sudden halt. She hesitates for a moment, then she tightens her shawl round her, as if it were a shield, then she firmly and swiftly goes out.*]

BESSIE. [*As she goes out:*] Oh, God, be Thou my help in time o' throuble. An' shelter me safely in th' shadow of Thy wings!

CURTAIN

ACT IV

[*The living-room of Bessie Burgess. It is one of two small attic rooms (the other, used as a bedroom, is to the Left), the ceiling slopes up towards the back, giving to the apartment a look of compressed confinement. In the centre of the ceiling is a small skylight. There is an unmistakable air of poverty bordering on destitution. The paper on the walls is torn and soiled, particularly near the fire where the cooking is done, and near the washstand where the washing is done. The fireplace is to the Left. A small armchair near fire. One small window at Back. A pane of this window is starred by the entrance of a bullet. Under the window to the Right is an oak coffin standing on two kitchen*] *chairs. Near the coffin is a home-manufactured stool, on which are two lighted candles. Beside the window is a worn-out dresser on which is a small quantity of delf. Tattered remains of cheap lace curtains drape the window. Standing near the window on Left is a brass standard-lamp with a fancy shade; hanging on the wall near the same window is a vividly crimson silk dress, both of which have been looted. A door on Left leading to the bedroom. Another opposite giving a way to the rest of the house. To the Left of this door a common washstand. A tin kettle, very black, and an old saucepan inside the fender. There is no light in the room but that given from the two candles and the fire. The dusk has well fallen, and the glare of the burning buildings in the town can be seen through the window, in the distant sky. The Covey and Fluther have been playing cards, sitting on the floor by the light of the candles on the stool near the coffin. When the curtain rises the Covey is shuffling the cards, Peter is sitting in a stiff, dignified way beside him, and Fluther is kneeling beside the window, cautiously looking out. It is a few days later.]*

FLUTHER. [*Furtively peeping out of the window.*] Give them a good shuffling. . . . Th' sky's gettin' reddher an' reddher. . . . You'd think it was afire. . . . Half o' th' city must be burnin'.

THE COVEY. If I was you, Fluther, I'd keep away from that window. . . . It's dangerous, an', besides, if they see you, you'll only bring a nose on th' house.

PETER. Yes; an' he knows we had to leave our own place th' way they were riddlin' it with machine-gun fire. . . . He'll keep on pimpin' an' pimpin' there, till we have to fly out o' this place too.

FLUTHER. [*Ironically.*] If they make any attack here, we'll send you out in your green an' glory uniform, shakin' your sword over your head, an' they'll fly before you as th' Danes flew before Brian Boru!

THE COVEY. [*Placing the cards on the floor, after shuffling them.*] Come on, an' cut.

[*Fluther comes over, sits on floor, and cuts the cards.*]

THE COVEY. [*Having dealt the cards.*] Spuds up again.

[*Nora moans feebly in room on Left.*]

FLUTHER. There, she's at it again. She's been quiet for a long time, all th' same.

THE COVEY. She was quiet before, sure, an' she broke out again worse than ever. . . . What was led that time?

PETER. Thray o' Hearts, Thray o' Hearts, Thray o' Hearts.

FLUTHER. It's damned hard lines to think of her dead-born kiddie lyin' there in th' arms o' poor little Mollser. Mollser snuffed it sudden too, afther all.

THE COVEY. Sure she never got any care. How could she get it, an' th' mother out day an' night lookin' for work, an' her consumptive husband leavin' her with a baby to be born before he died!

VOICES IN A LILTING CHANT TO THE LEFT IN A DISTANT STREET. Red Cr . . . oss, Red Cr . . . oss! . . . Ambu . . . lance, Ambu . . . lance!

THE COVEY. [*To Fluther.*] Your

deal, Fluther.

FLUTHER. [*Shuffling and dealing the cards.*] It'll take a lot out o' Nora —if she'll ever be th' same.

THE COVEY. Th' docthor thinks she'll never be th' same; thinks she'll be a little touched here. [*He touches his forehead.*] She's ramblin' a lot; thinkin' she's out in th' counthry with Jack; or gettin' his dinner ready for him before he comes home; or yellin' for her kiddie. All that, though, might be th' chloroform she got. . . . I don't know what we'd have done only for oul' Bessie; up with her for th' past three nights, hand runnin'.

FLUTHER. I always knew there was never anything really derogatory wrong with poor oul' Bessie. [*To Peter, who is taking a trick.*] Ay, houl' on, there, don't be so damn quick— that's my thrick.

PETER. What's your thrick? It's my thrick, man.

FLUTHER. [*Loudly.*] How is it your thrick?

PETER. [*Answering as loudly.*] Didn't I lead th' deuce!

FLUTHER. You must be gettin' blind, man; don't you see th' ace?

BESSIE. [*Appearing at the door of room, Left; in a tense whisper.*] D'ye want to waken her again on me, when she's just gone asleep? If she wakes will yous come an' mind her? If I hear a whisper out o' one o' yous again, I'll . . . gut yous!

THE COVEY. [*In a whisper.*] S-s-s-h. She can hear anything above a whisper.

PETER. [*Looking up at the ceiling.*] Th' gentle an' merciful God 'll give th' pair o' yous a scawldin' an' a scarifyin' one o' these days!

[*Fluther takes a bottle of whisky from his pocket, and takes a drink.*]

THE COVEY. [*To Fluther.*] Why don't you spread that out, man, an' thry to keep a sup for to-morrow?

FLUTHER. Spread it out? Keep a sup for to-morrow? How th' hell does a fella know there'll be any to-morrow? If I'm goin' to be whipped away, let me be whipped away when it's empty, an' not when it's half full! [*To Bessie, who has seated herself in an armchair at the fire.*] How is she, now, Bessie?

BESSIE. I left her sleeping quietly. When I'm listenin' to her babblin', I think she'll never be much betther than she is. Her eyes have a hauntin' way of lookin' in instead of lookin' out, as if her mind had been lost alive in madly minglin' memories of th' past. . . . [*Sleepily.*] Crushin' her thoughts . . . together . . . in a fierce . . . an' fanciful . . . [*She nods her head and starts wakefully.*] idea that dead things are livin', an' livin' things are dead. . . . [*With a start.*] Was that a scream I heard her give? [*Reassured.*] Blessed God, I think I hear her screamin' every minute! An' it's only there with me that I'm able to keep awake.

THE COVEY. She'll sleep, maybe, for a long time, now. Ten there.

FLUTHER. Ten here. If she gets a long sleep, she might be all right. Peter's th' lone five.

THE COVEY. Whisht! I think I hear somebody movin' below. Whoever it is, he's comin' up.

[*A pause. Then the door opens and Captain Brennan comes into the room. He has changed his uniform for a suit of civvies. His eyes droop with the heaviness of exhaustion; his face is pallid and drawn. His clothes are dusty and stained here and there with mud. He leans heavily on the back of a chair as he stands.*]

CAPT. BRENNAN. Mrs. Clitheroe; where's Mrs. Clitheroe? I was told I'd find her here.

BESSIE. What d'ye want with Mrs. Clitheroe?

CAPT. BRENNAN. I've a message, a last message for her from her husband.

BESSIE. Killed! He's not killed, is he!

CAPT. BRENNAN. [*Sinking stiffly and painfully on to a chair.*] In th' Imperial Hotel; we fought till th' place was in flames. He was shot through th' arm, an' then through th' lung. . . . I could do nothin' for him— only watch his breath comin' an' goin' in quick, jerky gasps, an' a tiny sthream o' blood thricklin' out of his mouth, down over his lower lip. . . . I said a prayer for th' dyin', an' twined his Rosary beads around his fingers. . . . Then I had to leave him to save meself. . . . [*He shows some holes in his coat.*] Look at th' way a machine-gun tore at me coat, as I belted out o' the buildin' an' darted across th' sthreet for shelter. . . . An' then, I seen The Plough an' th' Stars fallin' like a shot as th' roof crashed in, an' where I'd left poor Jack was nothin' but a leppin' spout o' flame!

BESSIE. [*With partly repressed vehemence.*] Ay, you left him! You twined his Rosary beads round his fingers, an' then you run like a hare to get out o' danger!

CAPT. BRENNAN. I took me chance as well as him. . . . He took it like a man. His last whisper was to 'Tell Nora to be brave; that I'm ready to meet my God, an' that I'm proud to die for Ireland.' An' when our General heard it he said that 'Commandant Clitheroe's end was a gleam of glory.'

Mrs. Clitheroe's grief will be a joy when she realizes that she has had a hero for a husband.

BESSIE. If you only seen her, you'd know to th' differ.

[*Nora appears at door, Left. She is clad only in her nightdress; her hair, uncared for some days, is hanging in disorder over her shoulders. Her pale face looks paler still because of a vivid red spot on the tip of each cheek. Her eyes are glimmering with the light of incipient insanity; her hands are nervously fiddling with her nightgown. She halts at the door for a moment, looks vacantly around the room, and then comes slowly in. The rest do not notice her till she speaks.*]

NORA. [*In a quiet and monotonous tone.*] No . . . Not there, Jack. . . . I can feel comfortable only in our own familiar place beneath th' bramble tree. . . . We must be walking for a long time; I feel very, very tired. . . . Have we to go farther, or have we passed it by? [*Passing her hand across her eyes.*] Curious mist on my eyes. . . . Why don't you hold my hand, Jack. . . . [*Excitedly.*] No, no, Jack, it's not. Can't you see it's a goldfinch. Look at th' black-satiny wings with th' gold bars, an' th' splash of crimson on its head. . . . [*Wearily.*] Something ails me, something ails me. . . . Don't kiss me like that; you take my breath away, Jack. . . . Why do you frown at me? . . . You're going away, and [*Frightened.*] I can't follow you. Something's keeping me from moving. . . . [*Crying out.*] Jack, Jack, Jack!

BESSIE. [*Who has gone over and caught Nora's arm.*] Now, Mrs. Clitheroe, you're a terrible woman to get up out of bed. . . . You'll get cold if you stay here in them clothes.

NORA. Cold? I'm feelin' very cold; it's chilly out here in th' counthry. . . . [*Looking around frightened.*] What place is this? Where am I?

BESSIE. [*Coaxingly.*] You're all right, Nora; you're with friends, an' in a safe place. Don't you know your uncle an' your cousin, an' poor oul' Fluther?

PETER. [*About to go over to Nora.*] Nora, darlin', now—

FLUTHER. [*Pulling him back.*] Now, leave her to Bessie, man. A crowd 'll only make her worse.

NORA. [*Thoughtfully.*] There is something I want to remember, an' I can't. [*With agony.*] I can't, I can't, I can't! My head, my head! [*Suddenly breaking from Bessie, and running over to the men, and gripping Fluther by the shoulders.*] Where is it? Where's my baby? Tell me where you've put it, where've you hidden it? My baby, my baby; I want my baby! My head, my poor head. . . . Oh, I can't tell what is wrong with me. [*Screaming.*] Give him to me, give me my husband!

BESSIE. Blessin' o' God on us, isn't this pitiful!

NORA. [*Struggling with Bessie.*] I won't go away for you; I won't. Not till you give me back my husband. [*Screaming.*] Murderers, that's what yous are; murderers, murderers!

BESSIE. S-s-sh. We'll bring Mr. Clitheroe back to you, if you'll only lie down an' stop quiet. . . . [*Trying to lead her in.*] Come on, now, Nora, an' I'll sing something to you.

NORA. I feel as if my life was thryin' to force its way out of my body. . . . I can hardly breathe . . . I'm frightened, I'm frightened, I'm frightened! For God's sake, don't leave me, Bes-

sie. Hold my hand, put your arms around me!

FLUTHER. [*To Brennan.*] Now you can see th' way she is, man.

PETER. An' what way would she be if she heard Jack had gone west?

THE COVEY. [*To Peter.*] Shut up, you, man!

BESSIE. [*To Nora.*] We'll have to be brave, an' let patience clip away th' heaviness of th' slow-movin' hours, rememberin' that sorrow may endure for th' night, but joy cometh in th' mornin'. . . . Come on in, an' I'll sing to you, an' you'll rest quietly.

NORA. [*Stopping suddenly on her way to the room.*] Jack an' me are goin' out somewhere this evenin'. Where I can't tell. Isn't it curious I can't remember. . . . Maura, Maura, Jack, if th' baby's a girl; any name you like, if th' baby's a boy! . . . He's there. [*Screaming.*] He's there, an' they won't give him back to me!

BESSIE. S-ss-s-h, darlin', s-ssh. I won't sing to you, if you're not quiet.

NORA. [*Nervously holding Bessie.*] Hold my hand, hold my hand, an' sing to me, sing to me!

BESSIE. Come in an' lie down, an' I'll sing to you.

NORA. [*Vehemently.*] Sing to me, sing to me; sing, sing!

BESSIE. [*Singing as she leads Nora into room:*]

Lead, kindly light, amid th' encircling
    gloom,
  Lead Thou me on;
Th' night is dark an' I am far from
    home,
  Lead Thou me on.
Keep Thou my feet; I do not ask to
    see

Th' distant scene—one step enough
  for me.
So long that Thou hast blessed me,
  sure Thou still
  Wilt lead me on;

[*They go in.*]
BESSIE. [*Singing in room:*]

O'er moor an' fen, o'er crag an' torrent, till
Th' night is gone.
An' in th' morn those angel faces
  smile
That I have lov'd long since, an' lost
  awhile!

THE COVEY. [*To Brennan.*] Now
that you've seen how bad she is, an'
that we daren't tell her what has happened till she's betther, you'd best be
slippin' back to where you come from.
  CAPT. BRENNAN. There's no chance
o' slippin' back now, for th' military are everywhere: a fly couldn't
get through. I'd never have got here,
only I managed to change me uniform for what I'm wearin'. . . . I'll
have to take me chance, an' thry to
lie low here for a while.
  THE COVEY. [*Frightened.*] There's
no place here to lie low. Th' Tommies
'll be hoppin' in here, any minute!
  PETER. [*Aghast.*] An' then we'd all
be shanghaied!
  THE COVEY. Be God, there's enough
afther happenin' to us!
  FLUTHER. [*Warningly, as he listens.*] Whisht, whisht, th' whole o'
yous. I think I heard th' clang of a
rifle butt on th' floor of th' hall below.
[*All alertness.*] Here, come on with
th' cards again. I'll deal. [*He shuffles
and deals the cards to all.*]
  FLUTHER. Clubs up. [*To Brennan.*]
Thry to keep your hands from shakin',

man. You lead, Peter. [*As Peter
throws out a card.*] Four o' Hearts
led.
  [*The door opens and Corporal
Stoddart of the Wiltshires enters in
full war kit; steel helmet, rifle and
bayonet, and trench tool. He looks
round the room. A pause and a palpable silence.*]
  FLUTHER. [*Breaking the silence.*]
Two tens an' a five.
  CORPORAL STODDART. 'Ello. [*Indicating the coffin.*] This the stiff?
  THE COVEY. Yis.
  CORPORAL STODDART. Who's gowing
with it? Ownly one allowed to gow
with it, you know.
  THE COVEY. I dunno.
  CORPORAL STODDART. You dunnow?
  THE COVEY. I dunno.
  BESSIE. [*Coming into the room.*]
She's afther slippin' off to sleep again,
thanks be to God. I'm hardly able to
keep me own eyes open. [*To the soldier.*] Oh, are yous goin' to take away
poor little Mollser?
  CORPORAL STODDART. Ay; 'oo's
agowing with 'er?
  BESSIE. Oh, th' poor mother, o'
course. God help her, it's a terrible
blow to her!
  FLUTHER. A terrible blow? Sure,
she's in her element now, woman,
mixin' earth to earth, an' ashes t'ashes
an' dust to dust, an' revellin' in plumes
an' hearses, last days an' judgements!
  BESSIE. [*Falling into chair by the
fire.*] God bless us! I'm jaded!
  CORPORAL STODDART. Was she
plugged?
  THE COVEY. Ah, no; died o' consumption.
  CORPORAL STODDART. Ow, is that
all? Thought she moight 'ave been
plugged.

THE COVEY. Is that all? Isn't it enough? D'ye know, comrade, that more die o' consumption than are killed in th' wars? An' it's all because of th' system we're livin' undher?

CORPORAL STODDART. Ow, I know. I'm a Sowcialist moiself, but I 'as to do my dooty.

THE COVEY. [*Ironically.*] Dooty! Th' only dooty of a Socialist is th' emancipation of th' workers.

CORPORAL STODDART. Ow, a man's a man, an 'e 'as to foight for 'is country, 'asn't 'e?

FLUTHER. [*Aggressively.*] You're not fightin' for your counthry here, are you?

PETER. [*Anxiously, to Fluther.*] Ay, ay, Fluther, none o' that, none o' that!

THE COVEY. Fight for your counthry! Did y'ever read, comrade, Jenersky's *Thesis on the Origin, Development, an' Consolidation of th' Evolutionary Idea of the Proletariat?*

CORPORAL STODDART. Ow, cheese it, Paddy, cheese it!

BESSIE. [*Sleepily.*] How is things in th' town, Tommy?

CORPORAL STODDART. Ow, I fink it's nearly hover. We've got 'em surrounded, and we're clowsing in on the bloighters. Ow, it was only a little bit of a dawg-foight.

[*The sharp ping of the sniper's rifle is heard, followed by a squeal of pain.*]

VOICES TO THE LEFT IN A CHANT. Red Cr . . . oss, Red Cr . . . oss! Ambu . . . lance, Ambu . . . lance!

CORPORAL STODDART. [*Excitedly.*] Christ, that's another of our men 'it by that blawsted sniper! 'E's knocking abaht 'ere, somewheres. Gawd, when we get th' bloighter, we'll give 'im the cold steel, we will. We'll jab the belly

aht of 'im, we will!

[*Mrs. Gogan comes in tearfully, and a little proud of the importance of being directly connected with death.*]

MRS. GOGAN. [*To Fluther.*] I'll never forget what you done for me, Fluther, goin' around at th' risk of your life settlin' everything with th' undhertaker an' th' cemetery people. When all me own were afraid to put their noses out, you plunged like a good one through hummin' bullets, an' they knockin' fire out o' th' road, tinklin' through th' frightened windows, an' splashin' themselves to pieces on th' walls! An' you'll find, that Mollser, in th' happy place she's gone to, won't forget to whisper, now an' again, th' name o' Fluther.

CORPORAL STODDART. Git it aht, mother, git it aht.

BESSIE. [*From the chair.*] It's excusin' me you'll be, Mrs. Gogan, for not stannin' up, seein' I'm shaky on me feet for want of a little sleep, an' not desirin' to show any disrespect to poor little Mollser.

FLUTHER. Sure, we all know, Bessie, that it's vice versa with you.

MRS. GOGAN. [*To Bessie.*] Indeed, it's meself that has well chronicled, Mrs. Burgess, all your gentle hurryin's to me little Mollser, when she was alive, bringin' her somethin' to dhrink, or somethin' t'eat, an' never passin' her without liftin' up her heart with a delicate word o' kindness.

CORPORAL STODDART. [*Impatiently, but kindly.*] Git it aht, git it aht, mother.

[*The Covey, Fluther, Brennan, and Peter carry out the coffin, followed by Mrs. Gogan.*]

CORPORAL STODDART. [*To Bessie,*

who is almost asleep.] 'Ow many men is in this 'ere 'ouse? [*No answer. Loudly.*] 'Ow many men is in this 'ere 'ouse?

BESSIE. [*Waking with a start.*] God, I was nearly asleep! . . . How many men? Didn't you see them?

CORPORAL STODDART. Are they all that are in the 'ouse?

BESSIE. Oh, there's none higher up, but there may be more lower down. Why?

CORPORAL STODDART. All men in the district 'as to be rounded up. Somebody's giving 'elp to the snipers, an we 'as to take precautions. If I 'ad my woy, I'd make 'em all join hup, and do their bit! But I suppowse they and you are all Shinners.

BESSIE. [*Who has been sinking into sleep, waking up to a sleepy vehemence.*] Bessie Burgess is no Shinner, an' never had no thruck with anything spotted be th' fingers o' th' Fenians; but always made it her business to harness herself for Church whenever she knew that God Save the King was goin' to be sung at t'end of th' service; whose only son went to th' front in th' first contingent of the Dublin Fusiliers, an' that's on his way home carryin' a shathered arm that he got fightin' for his King an' counthry!

[*Her head sinks slowly forward again. Peter comes into the room; his body is stiffened and his face is wearing a comically indignant look. He walks to and fro at the back of the room, evidently repressing a violent desire to speak angrily. He is followed in by Fluther, the Covey, and Brennan, who slinks into an obscure corner of the room, nervous of notice.*]

FLUTHER. [*After an embarrassing pause.*] Th' air in th' sthreet outside's shakin' with the firin' o' rifles an' machine-guns. It must be a hot shop in th' middle o' th' scrap.

CORPORAL STODDART. We're pumping lead in on 'em from every side, now; they'll soon be shoving up th' white flag.

PETER. [*With a shout.*] I'm tellin' you either o' yous two lowsers 'ud make a betther hearse-man than Peter; proddin' an' pokin' at me an' I helpin' to carry out a corpse!

FLUTHER. It wasn't a very derogatory thing for th' Covey to say that you'd make a fancy hearse-man, was it?

PETER. [*Furiously.*] A pair o' red-jesthered bowseys pondherin' from mornin' till night on how they'll get a chance to break a gap through th' quiet nature of a man that's always endeavourin' to chase out of him any sthray thought of venom against his fella-man!

THE COVEY. Oh, shut it, shut it, shut it!

PETER. As long as I'm a livin' man, responsible for me thoughts, words, an' deeds to th' Man above, I'll feel meself instituted to fight again' th' sliddherin' ways of a pair o' picaroons, whisperin', concurrin', concoctin', an' conspirin' together to rendher me unconscious of th' life I'm thryin' to live!

CORPORAL STODDART. [*Dumbfounded.*] What's wrong, Daddy; wot 'ave they done to you?

PETER. [*Savagely to the Corporal.*] You mind your own business! What's it got to do with you, what's wrong with me?

BESSIE. [*In a sleepy murmur.*] Will yous thry to conthrol yourselves into quietness? Yous'll waken her . . . up

. . . on . . . me . . . again. [*She sleeps.*]

FLUTHER. Come on, boys, to th' cards again, an' never mind him.

CORPORAL STODDART. No use of you gowing to start cawds; you'll be gowing out of 'ere, soon as Sergeant comes.

FLUTHER. Goin' out o' here? An' why're we goin' out o' here?

CORPORAL STODDART. All men in district to be rounded up, and 'eld in till the scrap is hover.

FLUTHER. An' where're we goin' to be held in?

CORPORAL STODDART. They're puttin 'em in a church.

THE COVEY. A church?

FLUTHER. What sort of a church? Is it a Protestan' Church?

CORPORAL STODDART. I dunnow; I suppowse so.

FLUTHER. [*Dismayed.*] Be God, it'll be a nice thing to be stuck all night in a Protestan' Church!

CORPORAL STODDART. Bring the cawds; you moight get a chance of a goime.

FLUTHER. Ah, no, that wouldn't do. . . . I wondher? [*After a moment's thought*] Ah, I don't think we'd be doin' anything derogatory be playin' cards in a Protestan' Church.

CORPORAL STODDART. If I was you I'd bring a little snack with me; you moight be glad of it before the mawning. [*Sings:*]

I do loike a snoice mince poy,
I do loike a snoice mince poy!

[*The snap of the sniper's rifle rings out again, followed simultaneously by a scream of pain. Corporal Stoddart goes pale, and brings his rifle to the ready, listening.*]

VOICES CHANTING TO THE RIGHT. Red Cro . . . ss, Red Cro . . . ss! Ambu . . . lance, Ambu . . . lance!

[*Sergeant Tinley comes rapidly in, pale, agitated, and fiercely angry.*]

CORPORAL STODDART. [*To Sergeant.*] One of hour men 'it, Sergeant?

SERGEANT TINLEY. Private Taylor; got 'it roight through the chest, 'e did; an 'ole in front of 'im as 'ow you could put your fist through, and 'arf 'is back blown awoy! Dum-dum bullets they're using. Gang of Hassassins potting at us from behind roofs. That's not playing the goime: why down't they come into the owpen and foight fair!

FLUTHER. [*Unable to stand the slight.*] Fight fair! A few hundhred scrawls o' chaps with a couple o' guns an' Rosary beads, again' a hundhred thousand thrained men with horse, fut, an' artillery . . . an' he wants us to fight fair! [*To Sergeant.*] D'ye want us to come out in our skins an' throw stones?

SERGEANT TINLEY. [*To Corporal.*] Are these four all that are 'ere?

CORPORAL STODDART. Four; that's all, Sergeant.

SERGEANT TINLEY. [*Vindictively.*] Come on, then; get the blighters aht. [*To the men.*] 'Ere, 'op it aht! Aht into the streets with you, and if a snoiper sends another of our men west, you gow with 'im! [*He catches Fluther by the shoulder.*] Gow on, git aht!

FLUTHER. Eh, who are you chuckin', eh?

SERGEANT TINLEY. [*Roughly.*] Gow on, git aht, you blighter.

FLUTHER. Who are you callin' a blighter to, eh? I'm a Dublin man, born an' bred in th' city, see?

SERGEANT TINLEY. I down't care if you were Broin Buroo; git aht, git aht.

FLUTHER. [*Halting as he is going out.*] Jasus, you an' your guns! Leave them down, an' I'd beat th' two o' yous without sweatin'!

[*Peter, Brennan, the Covey, and Fluther, followed by the soldiers, go out. Bessie is sleeping heavily on the chair by the fire. After a pause, Nora appears at door, Left, in her night-dress. Remaining at door for a few moments she looks vaguely around the room. She then comes in quietly, goes over to the fire, pokes it, and puts the kettle on. She thinks for a few moments, pressing her hand to her forehead. She looks questioningly at the fire, and then at the press at back. She goes to the press, opens it, takes out a soiled cloth and spreads it on the table. She then places things for tea on the table.*]

NORA. I imagine th' room looks very odd somehow. . . . I was nearly forgetting Jack's tea. . . . Ah, I think I'll have everything done before he gets in. . . . [*She lilts gently, as she arranges the table.*]

Th' violets were scenting th' woods,
      Nora,
   Displaying their charms to th' bee,
When I first said I lov'd only you,
      Nora,
   An' you said you lov'd only me.

Th' chestnut blooms gleam'd through
      th' glade, Nora,
   A robin sang loud from a tree,
When I first said I lov'd only you,
      Nora,
   An' you said you lov'd only me.

[*She pauses suddenly, and glances round the room.*]

NORA. [*Doubtfully:*] I can't help feelin' this room very strange. . . . What is it? . . . What is it? . . . I must think. . . . I must thry to remember. . . .

VOICES CHANTING IN A DISTANT STREET. Ambu . . . lance, Ambu . . . lance! Red Cro . . . ss, Red Cro . . . ss!

NORA. [*Startled and listening for a moment, then resuming the arrangement of the table.*]

Trees, birds, an' bees sang a song,
      Nora,
   Of happier transports to be,
When I first said I lov'd only you,
      Nora,
   An' you said you lov'd only me.

[*A burst of rifle fire is heard in a street near by, followed by the rapid rok, tok, tok of a machine-gun.*]

NORA. [*Staring in front of her and screaming.*] Jack, Jack, Jack! My baby, my baby, my baby!

BESSIE. [*Waking with a start.*] You divil, are you afther gettin' out o' bed again! [*She rises and runs towards Nora, who rushes to the window, which she frantically opens.*]

NORA. [*At window, screaming.*] Jack, Jack, for God's sake, come to me!

SOLDIERS. [*Outside, shouting.*] Git away, git away from that window, there!

BESSIE. [*Seizing hold of Nora.*] Come away, come away, woman, from that window!

NORA. [*Struggling with Bessie.*] Where is it; where have you hidden it? Oh, Jack, Jack, where are you?

BESSIE. [*Imploringly.*] Mrs. Clithe-roe, for God's sake, come away!

NORA. [*Fiercely.*] I won't; he's below. Let . . . me . . . go! You're thryin' to keep me from me husband. I'll follow him. Jack, Jack, come to your Nora!

BESSIE. Hus-s-sh, Nora, Nora! He'll be here in a minute. I'll bring him to you, if you'll only be quiet—honest to God, I will.

[*With a great effort Bessie pushes Nora away from the window, the force used causing her to stagger against it herself. Two rifle shots ring out in quick succession. Bessie jerks her body convulsively; stands stiffly for a moment, a look of agonized astonishment on her face, then she staggers forward, leaning heavily on the table with her hands.*]

BESSIE. [*With an arrested scream of fear and pain.*] Merciful God, I'm shot, I'm shot, I'm shot! . . . Th' life's pourin' out o' me! [*To Nora.*] I've got this through . . . through you . . . through you, you bitch, you! . . . O God, have mercy on me! . . . [*To Nora.*] You wouldn't stop quiet, no, you wouldn't, you wouldn't, blast you! Look at what I'm afther gettin', look at what I'm afther gettin' . . . I'm bleedin' to death, an' no one's here to stop th' flowin' blood! [*Calling.*] Mrs. Gogan, Mrs. Gogan! Fluther, Fluther, for God's sake, somebody, a doctor, a doctor!

[*She staggers frightened towards the door, to seek for aid, but, weakening half-way across the room, she sinks to her knees, and bending forward, supports herself with her hands resting on the floor. Nora is standing rigidly with her back to the wall opposite, her trembling hands held out a little from the sides of her body, her lips quivering, her breast heaving, staring wildly at the figure of Bessie.*]

NORA. [*In a breathless whisper.*] Jack, I'm frightened. . . . I'm frightened, Jack. . . . Oh, Jack, where are you?

BESSIE. [*Moaning.*] This is what's afther comin' on me for nursin' you day an' night. . . . I was a fool, a fool, a fool! Get me a dhrink o' wather, you jade, will you? There's a fire burnin' in me blood! [*Pleadingly.*] Nora, Nora, dear, for God's sake, run out an' get Mrs. Gogan, or Fluther, or somebody to bring a doctor, quick, quick, quick! [*As Nora does not stir.*] Blast you, stir yourself, before I'm gone!

NORA. Oh, Jack, Jack, where are you?

BESSIE. [*In a whispered moan.*] Jesus Christ, me sight's goin'! It's all dark, dark! Nora, hold me hand! [*Bessie's body lists over and she sinks into a prostrate position on the floor.*] I'm dyin', I'm dyin' . . . I feel it. . . . Oh God, oh God! [*She feebly sings:*]

I do believe, I will believe
    That Jesus died for me;
That on th' cross He shed His blood,
    From sin to set me free. . . .
I do believe . . . I will believe
    . . . Jesus died . . . me;
. . . th' cross He shed . . . blood,
    From sin . . . free.

[*She ceases singing, and lies stretched out, still and very rigid. A pause. Then Mrs. Gogan runs hastily in.*]

MRS. GOGAN. [*Quivering with fright.*] Blessed be God, what's afther happenin'? [*To Nora.*] What's wrong, child, what's wrong? [*She sees Bessie, runs to her and bends over the body.*] Bessie, Bessie! [*She shakes the body.*] Mrs. Burgess, Mrs. Burgess! [*She feels Bessie's forehead.*] My God, she's as cold as death. They're afther murdherin' th' poor inoffensive woman!

[*Sergeant Tinley and Corporal Stoddart enter agitatedly, their rifles at the ready.*]

SERGEANT TINLEY. [*Excitedly.*] This is the 'ouse. That's the window!

NORA. [*Pressing back against the wall.*] Hide it, hide it; cover it up, cover it up!

SERGEANT TINLEY. [*Going over to the body.*] 'Ere, what's this? Who's this? [*Looking at Bessie.*] Oh Gawd, we've plugged one of the women of the 'ouse.

CORPORAL STODDART. Whoy the 'ell did she gow to the window? Is she dead?

SERGEANT TINLEY. Oh, dead as bedamned. Well, we couldn't afford to toike any chawnces.

NORA. [*Screaming.*] Hide it, hide it; don't let me see it! Take me away, take me away, Mrs. Gogan!

[*Mrs. Gogan runs into room, Left, and runs out again with a sheet which she spreads over the body of Bessie.*]

MRS. GOGAN. [*As she spreads the sheet.*] Oh, God help her, th' poor woman, she's stiffenin' out as hard as she can! Her face has written on it th' shock o' sudden agony, an' her hands is whitenin' into th' smooth shininess of wax.

NORA. [*Whimperingly.*] Take me away, take me away; don't leave me here to be lookin' an' lookin' at it!

MRS. GOGAN. [*Going over to Nora and putting her arm around her.*] Come on with me, dear, an' you can doss in poor Mollser's bed, till we gather some neighbours to come an' give th' last friendly touches to Bessie in th' lonely layin' of her out. [*Mrs. Gogan and Nora go slowly out.*]

CORPORAL STODDART. [*Who has been looking around, to Sergeant Tinley.*] Tea here, Sergeant. Wot abaht a cup of scald?

SERGEANT TINLEY. Pour it aht, Stoddart, pour it aht. I could scoff hanything just now. [*Corporal Stoddart pours out two cups of tea, and the two soldiers begin to drink. In the distance is heard a bitter burst of rifle and machine-gun fire, interspersed with the boom, boom of artillery. The glare in the sky seen through the window flares into a fuller and a deeper red.*]

SERGEANT TINLEY. There gows the general attack on the Powst Office.

VOICES IN A DISTANT STREET. Ambu . . . lance, Ambu . . . lance! Red Cro . . . ss, Red Cro . . . ss!

[*The voices of soldiers at a barricade outside the house are heard singing:*]

They were summoned from the 'illside,
They were called in from the glen,
And the country found 'em ready
At the stirring call for men.
Let not tears add to their 'ardship,
As the soldiers pass along,
And although our 'eart is breaking,
Make it sing this cheery song.

SERGEANT TINLEY AND CORPORAL STODDART. [*Joining in the chorus, as they sip the tea:*]

Keep the 'owme fires burning,
While your 'earts are yearning;
Though your lads are far away
They dream of 'owme;
There's a silver loining
Through the dark cloud shoining,
Turn the dark cloud inside out,
Till the boys come 'owme!

CURTAIN

DISCUSSION OF *THE PLOUGH AND THE STARS*

Although *The Plough and the Stars* is about the basic and broadly human concerns of love and life and war and death, it may help your appreciation of the play to know a little of the historical incidents that occur offstage.

In Easter Week of 1916 there occurred in Dublin what the Irish call the Rising. On Sunday small groups of armed Irishmen deployed themselves around the city. One group attacked Dublin Castle which was the seat and the symbol of British rule in Ireland. Another small band occupied Stephen's Green. Meanwhile, the main force marched into O'Connell street, took possession of the General Post Office, and issued the Proclamation of the Irish Republic. This Proclamation was Ireland's Declaration of Independence from Great Britain.

For months the attack had been brewing. Patrick Pearse and other members of the secret organization called the Irish Republican Brotherhood had taken over key positions in the large civilian military force of the Irish Volunteers. Separately the labor leader James Connolly had been drilling the Irish Citizen Army, a smaller force composed of members of the Irish Transport and General Workers' Union.

The fighting in Dublin raged for a week until the Irish, hopelessly outnumbered in men and equipment, finally capitulated. The leaders of the rebellion were executed and many others were deported to England to serve life imprisonment. Despite its military failure, the Rising proved ultimately to be a crucial step towards Ireland's independence.

Against this background of history, O'Casey set his savage and poignant indictment of the effects of war upon ordinary people. He was well qualified to write such an indictment, for he had been the first secretary of the Citizen Army, but he had subsequently come to believe that armed force exacted a toll of life and human agony that was not worth paying.

Such an attitude is the equivalent of an American's saying that the Revolutionary War was not worth fighting. We must remember, however, that it is easier for us in our time to speak glibly of that war than it was for Washington and for Jefferson. At any rate, O'Casey had hit upon a sore dilemma which has long confounded men, and it was predictable that his outspoken play would ruffle the feelings of patriotic Irishmen. Actually, it caused a riot in the theatre, and it was only after time had begun to heal old wounds that Ireland recognized, as did the rest of the world, that *The Plough* was one of the masterpieces of the modern drama.

But although the rest of the world may have understood the content of the play, it failed to understand it as a work of art, just as thoroughly as it had earlier failed to understand Chekhov. O'Casey's tragicomedies, like Chekhov's, have been treated as plays with a conventional tragic structure onto which occasional comic interludes are awkwardly grafted. When so interpreted, the dramatist's intention is reversed. In actuality, there are two types of action in these plays—the action with a tragic structure that provides a frame of beginning and end; and the central action that ocurs within the frame, of several different plots ironically played off against each other. Mistaking the frame for the central action turns a play of Chekhov's or O'Casey's from a tough and comic objectivity, à la Molière and Jonson, into a bathetic subjectivity.

The central or interior action of *The Plough* consists of eight strands of plot: that of Nora, of Jack, of Bessie, of Fluther, of Peter, of the Covey, of Mrs. Gogan, and of Mollser. These characters find themselves set in circumstances which render them powerless, and each attempts in various ways to adapt himself to the circumstances: to ignore them, to accept them, or to change them.

Jack attempts to change his circumstances by joining the Irish Citizen Army. When this attempt brings on the fierce retaliation of a battle, Jack continues to fight only because he is too afraid and ashamed to give up. His effort results in his death in battle.

Nora attempts to ignore her environment and to escape it, to defeat the tenement world by creating a world of beauty and romance. She goes insane when the world destroys the romance and kills her husband.

Bessie Burgess accepts life in the Irish tenement and is loyal to England, but when she is humanely drawn to help those who do not accept it, she is killed.

The tenement kills the tubercular Mollser, and Mrs. Gogan, her mother, is wounded through Mollser's death.

The Covey and Peter both erect sham defenses against their circumstances: The Covey by his feckless interpretation of Communism, Peter by his important and splendid uniform. The weakness of both defenses is shown by the way the world controls the two men. They hide in a room to avoid being shot; they are herded into a church with a guarded mob. They make no resistance, since their defenses are too fragile to give them the strength to resist.

Fluther is also herded into the church. He is, despite this, a brave man who risks his life to find Nora. He is also a sensible man, and by refusing to join in the battle he implies that one man is not enough to change the world. Rather, he attempts to live as fully as he can within the world. Instead of getting drunk on patriotic eloquence, he merely gets drunk. Instead of joining the army, he joins his female counterpart, Rosie Redmond.

From the defeats shown in these central actions, O'Casey fashions the meaning and the fusion of his play. And paralleling these defeats is the larger social defeat that we see in the frame of the play. The main characters are set in four different situations: the first act shows intimations of war, the second shows the direct overture and incitement to war, the third shows the war itself, and the last shows the effects of defeat. The four-part action of the frame portrays four different stages of growth and decline.

The frame, then, is presented in the form of the traditional tragic structure. Act I is the Exposition, II the Development, and III the Reversal, the critical point of the battle and also the critical point in most of the central actions. In Act IV, the Resolution, Nora has become insane, a messenger arrives with the report of Jack's death, Bessie is killed, Mollser has died, and Brennan, Peter, the Covey, and Fluther are herded off to be guarded. The comic element in this act has nearly disappeared. The tone is subdued. The characters have grown torpid; even the running war between the Covey and Peter is muted. All of them are concerned with the effects of the war and with the working out of their own personal destinies. The comic appeared in earlier acts when the characters seemed to control their destinies; in this act, their destinies are controlled externally, and their individuality and high spirits are muted.

The frame of the play makes itself more felt in this act. We are continually reminded of the offstage action. Voices cry for the Red Cross. There are shots fired, one of which enters the room and kills Bessie. Finally this external action, in the form of Stoddart and Tinley, invades the stage and drives the characters of the play away.

Spatially, the play is an expansion and a retraction. In the Exposition, the characters are confined to the tenement. In the Development, they revolt, emerge from the tenement, and invade the outside world. In the Reversal, they are driven back to the street in front of the tenement. In the Resolution, they have been driven back inside the tenement, and during the act they are driven further, until finally there is no room for them anywhere. Stoddart and Tinley dispossess or kill them and hold the tenement alone.

What remains to complete this tragicomic structure is a final chorus to fuse the central action and the frame together in one comprehensive, witty, and bitter summation. The choral fusion at the end of Act IV, as well as the choruses at the end of the earlier acts, relies on a number of stage devices which we have seen already in Chekhov. It also relies upon an ironic use of language, so it will be best to postpone a discussion of this chorus until we have looked at O'Casey's language.

O'Casey's dialogue has often been described as "exuberant" or "Elizabethan." It has a rare extravagance of images, word play, and wit. It revels in broad alliteration and thick layers of melody. It is, as Shaw described Shakespeare's language, word music. It draws upon echoes from Shakespeare and the Elizabethan dramatists, from Shelley and the Romantic poets, and from Ruskin and the Victorian prose writers. It incorporates snatches of nostalgic popular song from the Irish poet Tom Moore. It uses the malapropisms of Sheridan and the comic repetitions of Dickens. It is a rich and heady style that makes all but the best of realistic dialogue look pale and timid.

Yet despite all of its liveliness, it is not an uncontrolled gush of rhetoric, and it is not all cut from the same cloth. Its real richness lies in its variety. "The decorum of tragicomedy," writes Waith, ". . . makes room for every style." We can find examples of Cicero's three styles of speech—from the grandiloquence of the offstage orator in Act II to the low brawling of Bessie and Mrs. Gogan.

And if we look more closely, we may see that the same characters do not speak in the same way all of the time. Nora's madness in the last act is as far from her poignant inarticulacy in Act III, as that is from her easy colloquialism in Act I. Notice the difference between the eloquent simplicity of Bessie's exit line in Act III and the fine exaggeration and irony of her sardonic taunt to the three soldiers earlier in the act:

Th' Minsthrel Boys aren't feelin' very comfortable now. Th' big guns has knocked all th' harps out of their hands. General Clitheroe'd rather be unlacin' his wife's bodice than standin' at a barricade. . . . An' th' professor of chicken-butcherin' there, finds he's up against somethin' a little tougher even than his own chickens, an' that's sayin' a lot!

Notice further how the style of Bessie's language changes repeatedly within one speech to indicate her swiftly changing emotions:

BESSIE. [*Moaning.*] This is what's afther comin' on me for nursin' you day an' night. . . . I was a fool, a fool, a fool! Get me a dhrink o' wather, you jade, will you? There's a fire burnin' in me blood! [*Pleadingly.*] Nora, Nora, dear, for God's sake, run out an' get Mrs. Gogan, or Fluther, or somebody to bring a doctor, quick, quick, quick! . . . Blast you, stir yourself, before I'm gone!

Such a speech shows us the real reason for the variety of styles in tragicomedy. To be successful, the genre requires an ever-alternating variety of emotions, and it requires an equally wide variety of language to portray such quick changes. The death speech of Bessie, which appears to be an artless transcription from life, is really a succession of different tones, rather than one. Furthermore, it contains at least one strongly ironic echo, which is unrealized by Bessie but which stirs a responsive chord in the audience. When she cries, "I was a fool, a fool, a fool!" she is only berating herself. However, we have heard something very like it earlier. In the conclusion of his last and strongest speech, the offstage orator cried out, "the fools, the fools, the fools!" And he ended his sentence with, "they have left us our Fenian dead, and, while Ireland holds these graves, Ireland, unfree, shall never be at peace!" Bessie's dying echo turns the orator's own words against him. This is, of course, a calculated use of irony by O'Casey, but it is not an artificial or awkward one. Bessie's words rise so naturally out of her feelings in a moment when she is not even thinking of the orator, that our emotional condemnation of the orator's words is raised to an intensity that O'Casey could probably not have achieved by pages of direct argument.

This point suggests a further reason for the variety of styles and tones in tragicomedy. Variety is a pleasure in itself, but if it is controlled it can have a dramatic function. We have seen how, in *The Three Sisters,* Chekhov used the language of one group onstage to puncture the speeches of another. O'Casey uses language similarly. For instance, just as a costume of a tramp in a seedy frock coat, baggy and tattered striped trousers, battered bowler hat, and wispy rattan cane may be in itself the emblem of hopeless poverty, it may also be a mocking parody of grandiloquence attired in a new frock coat, crisply pressed striped trousers, new bowler hat, and expensive gold-headed cane. In the same way, the low style may be both low in itself and a burlesque of a high style.

Consider, for instance, how the real humorous effect of many of the Covey's speeches comes from their being a travesty of real learning. And consider how Rosie's low style in the following passage punctures the Covey's jargon of socialism:

> THE COVEY. There's only one freedom for th' workin' man: conthrol o' th' means o' production, rates of exchange, an' th' means of disthribution. Look here, comrade, I'll leave here to-morrow night for you a copy of Jenersky's *Thesis on the Origin, Development, an' Consolidation of the Evolutionary Idea of the Proletariat.*
>
> ROSIE. If y'ass Rosie, it's heartbreakin' to see a young fella thinkin' of anything, or admirin' anything, but silk thransparent stockin's showin' off the shape of a little lassie's legs!

Or how, when Rosie really gets wound up, her low style so completely defeats the Covey that he breaks away and rushes out of the pub. "Oh, little duckey, oh, shy little duckey!" she coos, ". . . Tittle him undher th' chin, tittle him undher th' chin!"

In the same way the low language trips up the grandiloquence of the orator and of the three soldiers. The orator says:

> Comrade soldiers of the Irish Volunteers and of the Citizen Army, we rejoice in this terrible war. The old heart of the earth needed to be warmed with the red wine of the battlefields. . . . Such august homage was never offered to God as this: the homage of millions of lives given gladly for love of country. And we must be ready to pour out the same red wine in the same glorious sacrifice, for without shedding of blood there is no redemption!

This language, which is a collection of quotations from Patrick Pearse, is the language of idealism and high purpose. Its diction is grander than the diction of reality. Sometimes people are swept away by such rhetoric, and it seems true and moving, but O'Casey's purpose here is to show that this language is nobler than men are. He wants to puncture and deflate it, and he does so in two ways. First, by the language of the other characters, and, second, by their actions. The language and actions onstage are as concerned with fighting as is the language of the offstage orator. But the language and the fighting onstage are much less grand and noble.

"G'way, you little sermonizing, little yella-faced, little consequential, little pudgy, little bum, you!" roars Bessie to Peter, as the flat of her hand sends him spinning across the room. The ignoble triviality of the fighting onstage

and the wild uncouthness of the language effectively show the other side
of the coin to the orator's grandiosity.

In the same way, the language of the soldiers is shown to be artificial and
pompous. They say:

> We won't have long to wait now. . . . Th' time is rotten ripe for revo-
> lution. . . . You have a mother, Langon. . . . Ireland is greater than a
> mother. . . . You have a wife, Clitheroe. . . . Ireland is greater than a
> wife. . . . Th' time for Ireland's battle is now—th' place for Ireland's
> battle is here. . . . Death for th' Independence of Ireland. . . . Wounds
> for th' Independence of Ireland! Death for th' Independence of Ire-
> land. . . . So help us God!

The artificiality of this noble rant is effectively dramatized by the raucous low
song that Rosie sings as she and Fluther go off:

> Dancin' a jig in th' bed, an' bawlin' for butther an' bread.
> An' there, to our joy, a bright bouncin' boy
> Was dancin' a jig in th' bed!

The terms of the song are the aptest contradiction of the terms used by the
orator and the soldiers. The orator and soldiers say that fighting and dying for
Ireland is more important than any other human consideration. Rosie's song
is about matters usually considered equally important as patriotism—love,
"butther an' bread," and children.

Without overt statement, O'Casey has chosen the action and the words
that most ironically contrast, and the harsh reality of the one brilliantly re-
futes the false nobility of the other.

The way that this irony fuses into choral commentary can be seen in another
song, the one that Tinley and Stoddart sing at the end of the play. "Keep
the Home Fires Burning" is a well-known sentimental song that has about
as much literary value as an advertising jingle about toothpaste. At the play's
climactic moment, we would expect that a writer as eloquent as O'Casey
would call upon all the resources of the language that he can command.
Here, however, O'Casey does just the opposite. He borrows a trite, poorly
written, and mawkish popular ballad. Nothing could seem poorer for his
purposes.

However, we must avoid the temptation of a snap judgment. How much
speed and how much irony does O'Casey really get with the tune? First, it is,
though an unexpected choice, the kind of song that Tinley and Stoddart
would plausibly sing. Second, even though it is sentimentally phrased, it is
about a very real emotion, and the melody in conjunction with the words
has a strong power to evoke a melancholy which is most proper for our mood
at the end of the play. Third, the comfort of the soldiers inside the building
contrasts well with the devastation, the shots and the rising flames and the
cries for the ambulance, going on outside. Fourth, the words despite their
conventional sentimentality are used for one of the strongest ironies in the

play. As the soldiers sing, we see through the windows the growing flames of Dublin burning. What could be more savage, then, than their unconsciously appropriate words, "Keep the 'owme fires burning"?

All in all, these various levels of meaning add together to perform a choral function of the highest order. Stoddart and Tinley do not know that they are a chorus. They do not explicitly state, like the chorus in *Antigone*, the theme of the play. But the fact that O'Casey's meaning here is implied rather than stated makes our discovery of it even more powerful. All of the elements here —the sights and sounds offstage, the sights and sounds on, and the memory of the terrible events that have just happened in the room—all of these fuse together in our memory in a multi-leveled, unique, and eminently moving way.

It might have been easier for O'Casey to have ended the play by covering his stage with corpses, tearing passion to tatters, and weltering in gore. This is the temptation of the tragic writer, and it is the ending that has been traditionally effective in the evocation of horror and pity. The tragicomic writer, like O'Casey and Chekhov, seems to want something more than horror and pity. He seems to want something beyond the catharsis of an emotional bloodbath.

For that matter, even the tragic writer has often felt a dissatisfaction with the tragic ending, and has tempered the unbridled emotion that the ending unleashes. The Greeks tried to temper it by having the deaths occur offstage. We know that when death or torture occurs onstage—Gloucester's torture in *King Lear*, for instance—we seem to have reverted almost to the savage ritual origins of the drama.

Another way in which the tragic writer tempers his endings is by the beauty of his language, with its metrical regularity that perhaps acts as a brake upon the flow of emotion. We have seen how Shakespeare in *Lear* put the unbearable death of Cordelia offstage, and how he modulated Lear's own death from the wildness of the earlier raving to a quiet, almost silent drifting away. We have seen how Shakespeare's language helped him put a brake upon the tragic ending—from the terrible roar of Lear's "Never, never, never, never, never!" to the surprising triviality of his "Pray you, undo this button." This modulation and this ironic switch in tone in Shakespeare's greatest tragedy seem somehow much more moving to a civilized audience than the wildest bloody tirades of some of his contemporaries.

And it is in this same direction that Chekhov and O'Casey have proceeded even farther. Their endings contain tragedy, but the tragedy is tempered by an intellectual control, and melded into a kaleidoscopic variety of other emotions to produce an emotion that views the world with more than the partial perspectives of either comedy or tragedy.

DISCUSSION QUESTIONS ON *THE PLOUGH AND THE STARS*

1. Which character most resembles the character of Pan? Which characters least resemble Pan? What do you make of this stage direction?

A short pause, then down the street is heard a wild, drunken yell; it comes nearer, and Fluther enters, frenzied, wild-eyed, mad, roaring drunk.

2. O'Casey uses several traditional devices in characterizing his people. Fluther, for instance, is fond of the word "derogatory." It becomes a kind of key word for him. Is this a comic device? Is it funny? Does Fluther use the word correctly? Is it funnier the more often he repeats it? Are there other key words or tag lines that O'Casey gives to any of the other characters? In Act I Mrs. Gogan is given certain stage mannerisms. What are they? Are they funny or are they serious? Do they add to her characterization? Do any other characters have similar mannerisms or gestures?

3. Are there any of the characters that would fit Ben Jonson's definition of a "humour"?

4. In the first three acts, Bessie Burgess is mainly a comic character. What qualities make her comic? Bessie's death in Act IV is not at all comic. How does O'Casey manage to shift his focus from comedy to tragedy? Is this shift realistic? believable? Are there other characters whom, like Bessie, we regard in more than one way?

5. Jack Clitheroe would usually be considered a hero and a patriot, yet O'Casey never presents him with any of the qualities of a D'Artagnan, a Cyrano, or a Zorro. How does O'Casey keep Clitheroe from attaining heroic stature in Act I? In Act III?

6. Read Act IV, Scene 5, of Shakespeare's *Hamlet*. How are Nora's actions in Act IV of *The Plough* reminiscent of Ophelia's in Act IV of *Hamlet*? Is this resemblance strong or weak? If it is strong, what dramatic effect does this similarity have?

7. Why does O'Casey use Rosie only in Act II? Is this a waste? Would it have been better if he had brought her in again?

8. Mollser dies between Acts III and IV. Why did O'Casey dispose of her so "undramatically"? Couldn't he have made more of her death if he had dramatized it onstage?

9. There is a great deal of quarreling, squabbling, bickering, and fighting among the characters. Practically every one at one time or another is engaged in a wild and bitter quarrel. List the chief quarrels. Are these quarrels static, or do the characters realign their alliances with each other? Are any of the quarrels patched up or forgotten? Why are there so many quarrels? What dramatic function do they have? And, finally, how, when he has so many quarrels, does O'Casey keep the play from being bad-tempered?

10. Find some examples of arias, duets, and ensemble scenes in the play. Does O'Casey use these techniques in the same way that Chekhov does?

11. In the opening scene of Act I, between Fluther and Mrs. Gogan, Peter is an example of Chekhov's silent character. Does Peter's silence add to or detract from the scene? How?

12. The term "melodrama" is derived from two words, *melos* or melody and *drama*. Melodrama was originally a play with sensational or romantic

actions that were interspersed with song. How many scenes of sensational action or romantic action do you find? How many songs? In other words, what proportion of the play is melodramatic, a large bit or a small? Why does the melodrama not take over the play?

13. In the closing line of Act I, Mollser asks, "Is there anybody goin', Mrs. Clitheroe, with a titther o' sense?" Where elsewhere in the play do you find lines that remind us of a standard of sensible behavior? Do any of the characters ever act as Cleante does in *Tartuffe*—that is, as a *raisonneur* or spokesman for good sense and moderation? Or does O'Casey elicit good sense from different characters at various times? Is Mollser's line a part of a choral comment? Do O'Casey's choruses take the place of a *raisonneur*?

14. Comedy usually ends in the Komos, or Comus, the celebration of the union of lovers. Tragedy usually ends in the death of the hero. Are *The Three Sisters* and *The Plough and the Stars* similar or different in their mixture of the two? Is there as much about love in *The Three Sisters* as in *The Plough and the Stars*? How do the love stories vary from the love stories of a traditional comedy? How do the heroes vary from the heroes of a traditional tragedy?

YEGOR BULYCHOV AND THE OTHERS

BY MAXIM GORKY

TRANSLATED BY ALEXANDER BAKSHY

CHARACTERS

KSENIYA YAKOVLEVNA [KSE-niya YA-kovlevna], Yegor Bulychov's wife

SHURA [SHU-ra], Bulychov's illegitimate daughter living in his house

GLASHA [GLA-sha], a maid in the Bulychovs' house

VARVARA (VARYA) YEGOROVNA [Var-VAR-a (VAR-ya) Ye-GOR-ovna], Andrey Zvontsov's wife and Bulychov's daughter

ANDREY PETROVICH ZVONTSOV [An-DREY Pet-RO-vich Zvont-SOV], a lawyer

YEGOR VASSILYEVICH BULYCHOV [Ye-GOR Vas-SIL-yevich Buly-CHOV]

FATHER PAVLIN SAVELYEV [PAV-lin Sa-VEL-yev]

DONAT [DO-nat], a forester

MOKEY PETROVICH BASHKIN [Mo-KEY Pet-RO-vich BASH-kin], Bulychov's manager

NIFONT GRIGORYEVICH [Ni-FONT Gri-GOR-yevich], a doctor

STEPAN TYATIN [Ste-PAN TYA-tin]

VASSILY YEFIMOVICH DOSTIGAYEV [Vas-SI-ly Ye-FIM-ovich Dosti-GAY-ev], Bulychov's partner in business

ELIZAVETA (LIZA) [Eliza-VET-a], Dostigayev's wife
YAKOV (YASHKA) LAPTEV [YA-kov (YA-shka) LAP-tev], Bulychov's godson
ALEXEY [Alex-EY] ⎫
TONYA [TON-ya] ⎬ Dostigayev's children by his first wife
MELANYA [Mel-AN-ya], an abbess; Kseniya's sister
A TUBA PLAYER
TAISYA [Ta-IS-ya], a nun in Melanya's service
MOKROUSOV [Mokro-U-sov], a policeman
ZOBUNOVA [Zobu-NO-va], a village healer
PROPOTEY [Propo-TEY], a village innocent, exorcist, and prophet

ACT I

[*The dining room in Bulychov's house. Heavy, cumbersome furniture. A wide, leather-upholstered couch by the wall, adjacent to a staircase leading to the second floor. In the corner, right, a recess with French windows and a door to the garden. It is a bright winter day.*

Kseniya, sitting at the table, is washing the tea dishes. Glasha, in the recess, is busy arranging flowers. Enter Shura, in a dressing gown, with slippers on her bare feet. Her uncombed hair is red, like that of her father, Yegor Bulychov.]

KSENIYA. Oh, Shura dear, you do stay in bed late—

SHURA. Don't jump on me, it won't help. Coffee, Glasha. Where's the newspaper?

GLASHA. I took it upstairs, to Varvara Yegorovna.

SHURA. Go get it. Subscribing to one paper for the whole house. The cheapskates!

[*Glasha goes off.*]

KSENIYA. Who are the cheapskates?

SHURA. Is Father in?

KSENIYA. He's gone to visit the wounded soldiers. Who are the cheapskates? The Zvontsovs?

SHURA. That's right. [*Speaking on the telephone.*] 17-63.

KSENIYA. I'll tell the Zvontsovs how well you speak of them!

SHURA. Call Tonya.

KSENIYA. What are you coming to?

SHURA. Is that you, Tonya? Want to go out skiing? No? Why not? Going to a show? Chuck it. Oh, you illegitimate widow! All right.

KSENIYA. How can you call an unmarried girl a widow?

SHURA. Hasn't her fiancé died?

KSENIYA. Still, she's just a girl.

SHURA. How do you know?

KSENIYA. You shameless baggage!

[*Glasha returns.*]

GLASHA. [*Handing Shura a cup of coffee.*] Varvara Yegorovna will bring the paper herself.

KSENIYA. You know much too much for your age. Look out. The less one knows, the better one sleeps. When I was your age I didn't know anything.

SHURA. The same as now.

KSENIYA. Oh, you're hopeless!

[*Varvara comes down the stairs.*]

SHURA. Ah, here comes my dear sister under full sail. Bonjour, Madame. Comment ça va?

VARVARA. It's eleven o'clock, and you're still not dressed, your hair isn't up—

SHURA. Here we go—

VARVARA. You're getting more and

more brazen, the way you take advantage of Father's ill health and the fact that you happen to be his pet—

SHURA. Are you set for a long spiel?

KSENIYA. What does she care about Father's health?

VARVARA. I'll have to tell him about your conduct—

SHURA. Thanks in advance. Have you finished?

VARVARA. You're a fool.

SHURA. I don't believe it. You must be thinking of somebody else.

VARVARA. A redheaded fool!

SHURA. Varvara Yegorovna, you're wasting your breath.

KSENIYA. Why even try to teach her anything?

SHURA. Furthermore, your character is deteriorating.

VARVARA. All right, all right, my dear! Mother, we'd better step into the kitchen. The cook seems to be in some kind of a mood.

KSENIYA. He's out of sorts. His son has been killed.

VARVARA. That's no excuse for being moody. Lots of people are getting killed today.

[*Varvara and Kseniya go out.*]

SHURA. She'd be screaming bloody murder, if her handsome Andrey got knocked off.

GLASHA. You're wasting your time teasing them. Drink your coffee quick —I have to clear the table.

[*She picks up the samovar and goes off. Shura throws herself back in her chair, closing her eyes and clasping her hands behind her head. Zvontsov, in slippers, comes down the staircase, sneaks up to her from behind, and puts his arms around her.*]

ZVONTSOV. What are you dreaming about, my red nanny goat?

SHURA. [*Without stirring, her eyes still closed.*] Don't touch me.

ZVONTSOV. Why not? I thought you like it. You do, don't you?

SHURA. I don't.

ZVONTSOV. Why not?

SHURA. Let go. You're only pretending you like me.

ZVONTSOV. You want me to like you, is that it?

[*Varvara comes down the steps.*]

SHURA. If Varvara hears about it—

ZVONTSOV. Quiet— [*Moves away and assumes a lecturing tone.*] Y-yes— You should pull yourself together— see to your education—

VARVARA. She prefers to be impertinent and to blow soap bubbles with Tonya.

SHURA. So I do blow soap bubbles. I like it. Are you sorry for the soap?

VARVARA. I'm sorry for you. I don't know how you're going to live. You've been asked to leave school—

SHURA. That's not true.

VARVARA. You have a crazy girl for your best friend—

ZVONTSOV. She wants to study music.

VARVARA. Who does?

ZVONTSOV. Shura.

SHURA. That's not true. I don't want to study music.

VARVARA. What made you think she did?

ZVONTSOV. Didn't you say yourself you wanted to, Shura?

SHURA. [*Going off.*] I never said anything of the sort.

ZVONTSOV. H'm! That's strange. Surely I haven't thought it up. You're too hard on her, Varya.

VARVARA. And you're too gentle.

ZVONTSOV. What do you mean, too gentle! You know my plan—

VARVARA. A plan is a plan, but I think you're suspiciously pleasant with her.

ZVONTSOV. You have stupid ideas in your head.

VARVARA. Have I?

ZVONTSOV. Think—is this the time, when things are so serious everywhere, to indulge in jealous scenes?

VARVARA. What brought you down here?

ZVONTSOV. Me? There's an advertisement in the paper. And also the forester's come, says the peasants have surrounded a bear—

VARVARA. Donat's in the kitchen. And what's the advertisement about?

ZVONTSOV. This is really outrageous! Talking to me this way! Am I a schoolboy? Damn it—

VARVARA. Don't excite yourself! I think Father has returned—and you in your slippers.

[*Zvontsov hurries off, up the staircase. Varvara turns to meet her father. Shura, wearing a warm green blouse and a green cap, runs in, heading for the telephone. She is caught on the way by Bulychov, who presses her to his breast. Father Pavlin, in a purple cassock, follows Bulychov into the room.*]

BULYCHOV. [*Sits down at the table, with his arm around Shura's waist, as Shura strokes his graying coppery head.*] They've maimed so many people, it's frightening to look at them.

PAVLIN. Blossoming out, aren't you, Shura? Forgive my not shaking hands with you—

SHURA. I'd have shaken your hand, Father Pavlin, but Daddy grabbed me like a bear—

BULYCHOV. Keep still, Shurka. What can those men do with themselves now? And we had plenty of useless people even before the war. We had no call to get into this scrap—

PAVLIN. [*With a sigh.*] The high authorities had their reasons—

BULYCHOV. They didn't reason it out so well with the Japs either—only disgraced the country before the whole world—

PAVLIN. Still, wars not only bring ruin—they also enrich nations with experience as well as—

BULYCHOV. Yes, some take up a rifle, others rifle the treasury.

PAVLIN. Moreover, nothing happens in this world unless it's the will of God—and what can our complaints mean?

BULYCHOV. Leave off preaching, Pavlin Savelyev. Are you going out skiing, Shura?

SHURA. Yes, I'm waiting for Tonya.

BULYCHOV. Very well. If you're still around in five minutes or so, I'll call you.

[*Shura runs off.*]

PAVLIN. The virgin has filled out—

BULYCHOV. She's got a good body, very supple, but she hasn't had much luck with her face. Her mother was a homely woman. Clever as the devil, but homely.

PAVLIN. Your daughter has—an uncommon face, which is not devoid of charm. Where did her maternal parent come from?

BULYCHOV. She came from Siberia. You say the high authorities, the will of God, and all that sort of thing. What about the Duma? Where does that come from?

PAVLIN. The Duma, one might say, is the high authorities' toleration of their own belittlement. Many people believe that this is a fatal error. But it doesn't become a minister of religion to go into consideration of such matters. Moreover, in these days the priesthood bears the duty of inspiring confidence and deepening the love of throne and country—

BULYCHOV. You inspire and bless—and what a hell of a mess!

PAVLIN. You know I've persuaded the warden of my church to enlarge the choir. I've also spoken to General Bettling requesting a donation for a bell to be installed in the church now under construction and dedicated to our heavenly intercessor and your namesake, Saint—

BULYCHOV. He didn't contribute for the bell?

PAVLIN. Refused—and even joked in an unpleasant way. I dislike brass, even in regimental bands, he said. It'd be a good thing if you made a donation for the bell on account of your ill health.

BULYCHOV. [Rising.] You don't cure a disease by bell ringing.

PAVLIN. Who can say? Science is ignorant of the causes of diseases. I've heard in some foreign sanatoriums they treat patients with music. We too have a fireman who plays a horn to cure sick people—

BULYCHOV. What kind of horn?

PAVLIN. A brass horn. They say it's very big.

BULYCHOV. Well, it must be good if it's big. Does it cure?

PAVLIN. They say it does. Everything is possible, my esteemed Yegor Vassilyevich, everything. We live in a world of mysteries, in the darkness of innumerable and insoluble mysteries. We think we see everything clear in the light of our reason, but it's clear only for our bodily vision, whereas our spirit is merely darkened by reason and perhaps is being gradually extinguished.

BULYCHOV. [With a sigh.] You do have a lot of words, my friend.

PAVLIN. [With growing animation.] Take the God-inspired man Propotey, for example. In what great joy does he live, this man whom the ignorant call a fool!

BULYCHOV. There you go again—preaching—Good-by. I'm tired.

PAVLIN. My heartiest wishes for your good health. I'll be praying for you— [Goes off.]

BULYCHOV. [Feeling his right side, walks to the couch muttering to himself.] Fat hog! Has stuffed his belly with Christ's body and blood. Glasha!

[Enter Varvara.]

VARVARA. What is it?

BULYCHOV. Nothing. I called Glasha. My, aren't you all dolled up! Where are you going?

VARVARA. To a benefit performance for convalescents.

BULYCHOV. A lorgnette, too? Don't tell me you can't see well—it's a lie —you just want to be in fashion—

VARVARA. Father, I wish you'd speak to Shura. She behaves atrociously and is becoming utterly impossible.

BULYCHOV. You're all very fine. Run along. [Muttering to himself.] Impossible? Well, one thing is very possible—when I get stronger I'll kick you all out!

GLASHA. Did you call me?

BULYCHOV. I did. Oh, Glasha—you do look lovely. You're so healthy, so firm. Not like Varvara—she's like a weasel.

GLASHA. [Casting a glance at the staircase.] That's her good luck. If she had looks, you'd be dragging her to bed with you.

BULYCHOV. My own daughter? Come to your senses, you fool. Think what you're saying.

GLASHA. I know what I'm saying. You paw Shura the way you would any strange girl—the way a trooper would.

BULYCHOV. [Astounded.] Have you gone raving mad? Are you jealous of my daughter? Don't you dare think of Shura that way. A trooper! Any strange girl! What do you know about troopers? Have you been in their arms? Well?

GLASHA. This is neither the time nor place to talk about such things. What did you call me for?

BULYCHOV. Tell Donat to come here. Wait, give me your hand. You still love me—sick man that I am?

GLASHA. [Pressing herself to him.] Oh, what a heartache you've been to me! Only don't be sick—get better.

[She breaks away and runs off. Bulychov smiles abstractedly, wetting his lips and shaking his head, then walks over to the couch and lies down. Donat comes in.]

DONAT. Wishing you good health, Yegor Vassilyevich.

BULYCHOV. Thank you. What news have you brought?

DONAT. Good news. We've trapped a bear.

BULYCHOV. [With a sigh.] Well, that doesn't fill me with joy, only envy. I can't amuse myself with bears now. Are you cutting timber?

DONAT. Slowly. We're short of men.

[Enter Kseniya, all dressed up, with many rings on her fingers.]

BULYCHOV. What is it?

KSENIYA. Nothing. I don't think, Yegor, you should bother about the bear. You're not fit to go out hunting.

BULYCHOV. Be still. Short of men, you say?

DONAT. Old men and boys are the only ones left. The prince has been able to get half a hundred war prisoners, but they can't work in the woods.

BULYCHOV. They work on women, I suppose.

DONAT. That's a fact.

BULYCHOV. Yes. Women are hungry now.

KSENIYA. They say there's much debauchery going on in the villages.

DONAT. Why debauchery, Kseniya Yakovlevna? The men have been killed, children have to be produced, don't they? So it follows—those who did the killing must do the producing.

BULYCHOV. Looks like it.

KSENIYA. No good children can come from war prisoners. Though, of course, if the man is strong—

BULYCHOV. And the woman is a fool, he'll have no desire to have children by her.

KSENIYA. Our women are no fools. But all the healthy men have been sent to the front—only lawyers are left at home.

BULYCHOV. Yes, a lot of people have been destroyed.

KSENIYA. But then the rest will have more money.

BULYCHOV. You've got it all figured out.

DONAT. Tsars and kings are always hungry for more people.

BULYCHOV. How was that?

DONAT. I say, tsars and kings are always hungry for more people. Our

Tsar hasn't enough to feed his own people, but he must conquer more of them.

BULYCHOV. You're right there.

DONAT. It's impossible to understand otherwise what sense there is in our fighting. Well, we see the result—we're being beaten for our greed.

BULYCHOV. You talk sense, Donat. My godson Yakov also says—greed is the beginning of all sorrow. How's he doing up there?

DONAT. He's all right. He's a clever fellow.

KSENIYA. A clever fellow! He's impertinent, not clever.

DONAT. He's impertinent because he's clever, Kseniya Yakovlevna. He's picked up deserters up there, Yegor Vassilyevich, about a dozen, and put them to work. They work all right—and it keeps them from thieving, which is what they were doing before.

BULYCHOV. Well, I don't know. That policeman, Mokrousov, will make trouble when he hears about it.

DONAT. He knows it—and he's even glad. It makes it easier for him.

BULYCHOV. Well, look out.

[*Zvontsov comes down the stairs.*]

DONAT. So your orders about the bear—

BULYCHOV. The bear is your stroke of luck.

ZVONTSOV. Allow me to offer the bear to General Bettling. You know, he's very useful to us.

BULYCHOV. I know. Offer it to him. Or, for that matter, offer it to the Archbishop.

KSENIYA. [*Chuckling.*] It would be a sight to see the Archbishop shoot-

ing a bear.

BULYCHOV. Well, I feel tired. Goodby, Donat. Things aren't going well though, are they? Since I got sick, it's all begun to go wrong. [*Donat bows silently and exits.*] Send Shura over, Kseniya. [*Kseniya goes out.*] What is it, Andrey? Don't hem and haw, speak out.

ZVONTSOV. It's about Yakov.

BULYCHOV. Well?

ZVONTSOV. I have information that he has close ties with—subversive elements, and made anti-government speeches to the peasants at the Koposov fair.

BULYCHOV. Forget it! Today there are no fairs worth talking about, nor peasants. And why are you all complaining about Yakov?

ZVONTSOV. But he's practically one of the family.

[*Shura runs in.*]

BULYCHOV. Practically. An awful lot of family feeling you show for him! He's even stopped coming to dinner on Sundays. Leave me now, Andrey. You can tell me the rest of it later.

[*Zvontsov goes off.*]

SHURA. Was he tattling on Yakov?

BULYCHOV. That's none of your business. Sit down here. They're all complaining about you too.

SHURA. Who's all?

BULYCHOV. Kseniya, Varvara—

SHURA. They're not all.

BULYCHOV. I'm speaking seriously, Shura dear.

SHURA. When you speak seriously you speak differently.

BULYCHOV. You're too flip with everybody, run around doing nothing—

SHURA. If I'm not doing anything,

how can I be flip?

BULYCHOV. You don't listen to anybody.

SHURA. I listen to everybody. They make me sick, carrot-top.

BULYCHOV. You're a carrot-top yourself—worse than I am. And another thing, you don't talk—the right way to me either. I should really give you a good scolding, but I don't feel like it.

SHURA. If you don't feel like it, you shouldn't.

BULYCHOV. I shouldn't, eh? If one doesn't feel like it, one shouldn't do it. It would be easy to live that way, but one can't.

SHURA. Who's stopping you?

BULYCHOV. Everybody. That's something you can't understand.

SHURA. Then teach me to understand—to know how to keep them from getting in my way.

BULYCHOV. You can't teach that. [Enter Kseniya.] What is it, Kseniya? Why do you keep wandering about? What are you looking for?

KSENIYA. The Doctor's come, and Bashkin is waiting, too. Pull down your skirt, Shura, look how you sit.

BULYCHOV. [Rising.] All right, call in the doctor. [Kseniya goes off.] It's bad for me to lie down, it makes me feel heavy—Ah! Well, run along, Shura. And be careful you don't sprain your ankle.

[Shura leaves the room. Enter the Doctor.]

DOCTOR. Good morning. How are you feeling?

BULYCHOV. Not so well. Your treatment is none too good, Nifont Grigoryevich.

DOCTOR. Well, let's go into your room.

BULYCHOV. [Walking beside the Doctor.] I want you to give me the strongest and most expensive drugs. I positively must get better. If you cure, I'll build a hospital and make you the head doctor there, to do as you please.

[They go off. Enter Kseniya and Bashkin.]

KSENIYA. What did the doctor tell you?

BASHKIN. He says it's cancer—cancer of the liver—

KSENIYA. Goodness gracious! The things they pick up!

BASHKIN. He says it's a dangerous disease.

KSENIYA. So he would. Everybody thinks his is the hardest job.

BASHKIN. This is the wrong time to get sick. Money's falling all around, as if somebody had a hole in his pocket. People who never had a kopeck make fortunes, and he—

KSENIYA. Yes, people are getting terribly rich.

BASHKIN. Dostigayev, for example —he's put on so much weight he can't button his clothes, and he talks only in thousands. While your Yegor Vassilyevich seems to be sinking slowly into a mental eclipse. The other day he said: My life, he said, has passed by the true work. What can he mean by that?

KSENIYA. Oh, I've noticed too—he speaks very strangely.

BASHKIN. And it was you and your sister's capital that put him on his feet. He ought to be multiplying it.

KSENIYA. I made a mistake, Mokey, I've known that for a long time. I married one of my father's store clerks, but the wrong one. If I'd married you, we'd have had such a peaceful life. But he—Oh, God, what a mischievous man he's been! What I've suffered at his hands! He got himself a daughter by another woman and wished her onto me. He picked a husband for my daughter—the worst he could find. I'm afraid, Mokey Petrovich, my son-in-law and Varvara will trick and cheat me, and leave me without a stitch to my name.

BASHKIN. Everything's possible. It's war. In war there's neither shame nor pity.

KSENIYA. You've served our family a long time, Mokey. My father gave you a start in life. Try to think what I ought to do.

BASHKIN. I am thinking.

[Enter Zvontsov.]

ZVONTSOV. Has the Doctor left?

KSENIYA. He's still in there.

ZVONTSOV. How's the cloth, Mokey Petrovich?

BASHKIN. Bettling refuses to accept it.

ZVONTSOV. How much do we have to give him?

BASHKIN. About five thousand, no less.

KSENIYA. What a robber! And he's an old man.

ZVONTSOV. Through Jeanne?

BASHKIN. Such is the arrangement.

KSENIYA. Five thousand! For what?

ZVONTSOV. Money's cheap today.

KSENIYA. In another man's pocket.

ZVONTSOV. Is my father-in-law agreeable?

BASHKIN. That's what I've come to find out.

[The Doctor enters.]

DOCTOR. [Taking Zvontsov by the arm.] Now, my friend—

KSENIYA. I hope it's good news.

DOCTOR. The patient must be on his back as much as possible. Excitement, annoyances, business affairs of any kind are extremely bad for him. Nothing but rest. Then— [He whispers to Zvontsov.]

KSENIYA. Why can't I be told too? I'm his wife.

DOCTOR. There are things about which it's rather difficult to talk to ladies. [Whispers again.] We'll have it this very evening.

KSENIYA. What will you have?

DOCTOR. A consultation, a council of doctors.

KSENIYA. Oh, my God!

DOCTOR. That's nothing to be afraid of. Well, good-by. [Goes.]

KSENIYA. Such a strict gentleman. And what nerve. Five rubles for five minutes—sixty rubles an hour—I tell you!

ZVONTSOV. He says it's necessary to operate.

KSENIYA. To cut? Oh, no! I'll permit no cutting—

ZVONTSOV. See here—surgery is a science—that's pure ignorance.

KSENIYA. I don't give a damn for your science. There—I can be as rude as you are!

ZVONTSOV. I'm not talking about civilities, but about your darkness.

KSENIYA. You're not too bright yourself. [With a wave of his hand, Zvontsov moves off. Glasha runs in.] Where are you rushing to?

GLASHA. The bedroom bell rang. [Kseniya and Glasha go off.]

ZVONTSOV. My father-in-law has chosen the wrong time to get sick.

BASHKIN. Yes—it does make things more difficult. This is the time when clever people, like conjurors, pull money straight out of the air.

ZVONTSOV. True. Besides, revolution is coming.

BASHKIN. That I don't approve. We had it in 1905. Little sense to it.

ZVONTSOV. In 1905 we had mutiny, not a revolution. The peasants and workers were at home then—now they're at the front. Now the revolution will be against officials, governors, cabinet ministers.

BASHKIN. In that case, God grant it. Officials are a terrible lot. Once they get their hooks into you, you can't shake them off.

ZVONTSOV. It's plain the Tsar is incapable of ruling.

BASHKIN. There's talk about that among the business people too. It's said some peasant has got around the Tsarina.

[*Varvara appears on the staircase and stops to listen.*]

ZVONTSOV. That's right, Grigory Rasputin.

BASHKIN. I don't believe in witchcraft somehow—

ZVONTSOV. Do you believe in lovers?

BASHKIN. It seems incredible. She has hundreds of generals.

VARVARA. You're talking silly nonsense.

BASHKIN. Everybody's talking that, Varvara Yegorovna. Still I don't believe we can do without tsars.

ZVONTSOV. It's not in St. Petersburg we need a tsar. It's in one's own head. Is the show over?

VARVARA. It's been put off. Some high inspector has arrived—a trainload of wounded soldiers is expected this evening, but there's no place to put them.

[*Enter Glasha.*]

GLASHA. You're wanted, Mokey Petrovich.

[*Bashkin goes off, leaving his win-*

ter peaked cap on the table.]

VARVARA. Why are you so frank with him? You know as well as I do that he's spying on us for Mother. This cap of his—he's worn it for ten years, the miser. It's oily all over. I can't understand your having anything to do with such a crook—

ZVONTSOV. Oh, stop it, I want to borrow some money from him to bribe Bettling.

VARVARA. But I've told you Liza Dostigayeva will fix that through Jeanne. And it'll cost less, too.

ZVONTSOV. She'll cheat you, that Liza—

KSENIYA. [*From Bulychov's room.*] Come persuade him to lie down. He keeps walking around scolding Mokey —Oh, Lord!

ZVONTSOV. Go on in, Varya.

[*Enter Bulychov, in a dressing gown and felt slippers.*]

BULYCHOV. What else? An unfortunate war?

[*Bashkin follows Bulychov in.*]

BASHKIN. I'm not arguing.

BULYCHOV. For whom is it unfortunate?

BASHKIN. For us.

BULYCHOV. Who are us? You say yourself millions are being made on the war. Well?

BASHKIN. I mean, for the people.

BULYCHOV. The people are the peasants. It's all the same to them whether they live or die. That's the truth.

KSENIYA. Please don't lose your temper. It's bad for you.

BASHKIN. Now really—what sort of truth is that?

BULYCHOV. The very real truth, the only one. I say frankly—my business is to make money, and the peasants' business is to produce bread and buy merchandise. What other truth is there?

BASHKIN. Of course, that's so. But—

BULYCHOV. Well, what's but—? What do you think of when you steal from me?

BASHKIN. There's no call to be insulting.

KSENIYA. Why don't you do something, Varya? Make him lie down. It's the Doctor's orders.

BULYCHOV. Do you think of the people?

BASHKIN. And insult me in front of others, too. I steal. That has to be proved.

BULYCHOV. No proofs are needed. Everybody knows—stealing is lawful. Nor have I anything to gain by insulting you. It won't make an honest man of you, rather the opposite. And it isn't you who steal—the ruble steals—The ruble by itself is the worst thief—

BASHKIN. Only your godson, Yakov, can say such things.

BULYCHOV. He does say them. Well, you may go. And don't pay any graft to Bettling. We've paid him plenty, enough for the old devil to buy himself a coffin and shroud. [Bashkin goes off.] Why are you all here? What are you waiting for?

VARVARA. Nothing.

BULYCHOV. Nothing, really? If that's the case, go attend to your business. You have something to do, haven't you? Kseniya, tell them to air my room. It's stuffy there, smells of stale medicine. And tell Glasha to bring me some cranberry kvass.

KSENIYA. You're not allowed to drink kvass.

BULYCHOV. Go tell her. I know

what I'm allowed and not allowed to drink.

KSENIYA. I wish you did know—

[Kseniya goes off followed by Varvara and Zvontsov. Bulychov, alone, walks around the table, holding on to it with his hand, then looks at himself in the mirror.]

BULYCHOV. [Lowering his voice but slightly.] Things are in a bad way with you, Yegor. And even your face doesn't look like your own.

[Enter Glasha, carrying a glass of milk on a tray.]

GLASHA. Here's your milk.

BULYCHOV. Give it to the cat. I want kvass—cranberry kvass.

GLASHA. I've been ordered not to give you kvass.

BULYCHOV. They've ordered you not to, but you bring it. Wait. What's your opinion—am I going to die?

GLASHA. It can't be.

BULYCHOV. Why not?

GLASHA. I don't believe it.

BULYCHOV. You don't? No, ma'am, things are in a bad way with me. A very bad way, I know.

GLASHA. I don't believe it.

BULYCHOV. You are obstinate. All right, bring me the kvass. [Glasha goes off.] Meanwhile I'll have some orange brandy. It does one good. [Walks to the sideboard.] They've locked it up, those devils. Pigs! Guarding it. Looks as if I'm a prisoner.

ACT II

[The living room in the Bulychov house. In a corner, sitting at a small round table with wine bottles on it, are Zvontsov and Tyatin.]

ZVONTSOV. [*Lighting a cigarette.*] Do you understand?

TYATIN. To be quite honest with you, Andrey, I don't like it.

ZVONTSOV. But you like money?

TYATIN. Money I do like, I'm sorry to say.

ZVONTSOV. Who are you worrying about?

TYATIN. Myself, of course.

ZVONTSOV. I wouldn't be concerned about that.

TYATIN. Still, you know, I'm the only friend I have.

ZVONTSOV. You should think, not philosophize.

TYATIN. I think. Shura's a spoiled young woman—it won't be easy to live with her.

ZVONTSOV. You'll get a divorce.

TYATIN. And she'll keep the money.

ZVONTSOV. We'll see to it that it stays with you. And I take it upon myself to break her in for you—

TYATIN. Honestly—

ZVONTSOV. That'll make them marry her off as quick as possible, and increase the dowry to boot.

TYATIN. That's a clever idea! And what's the dowry?

ZVONTSOV. Fifty.

TYATIN. Thousand?

ZVONTSOV. No. buttons.

TYATIN. Fifty, really?

ZVONTSOV. But you'll sign me a promissory note for ten.

TYATIN. Thousand?

ZVONTSOV. No, ten rubles! You're a funny fellow, Stepan.

TYATIN. Too much.

ZVONTSOV. Then let's forget about it.

TYATIN. Are you really serious?

ZVONTSOV. Only fools aren't serious about money.

TYATIN. [*With a chuckle.*] It's a darn clever idea, I must say.

[*Enter Dostigayev.*]

ZVONTSOV. I'm glad you're showing signs of comprehension. In these fierce times you, as an intellectual of proletarian standing, cannot permit yourself—

TYATIN. Yes—of course. But I think it's time for me to be getting over to the courtroom.

DOSTIGAYEV. What's bothering you, Stepan?

ZVONTSOV. We've been talking about Rasputin.

DOSTIGAYEV. What an end, isn't it? And this common Siberian peasant played checkers with bishops and cabinet ministers—handled huge sums of money—hundreds of thousands—never took less than ten thousand for a bribe—never. I have inside information. What are you drinking? Burgundy? That's a heavy wine, to be drunk with dinner, you uncivilized people!

ZVONTSOV. How did you find my father-in-law?

DOSTIGAYEV. Why should I be trying to find him—he wasn't hiding. Bring me a glass, Stepan. [*Tyatin goes out unhurriedly.*] Bulychov, I must say frankly, is in a bad way. He's in a dangerous state—

ZVONTSOV. It seems to me, too, that he's—

DOSTIGAYEV. That's right. Just that. And he's afraid of death. For that very reason he's sure to die. And you should reckon with this fact right now—for your own good. In these days a man can't stand gaping with his hands in his pockets—He has to go after what he wants. On all sides swine are uprooting the props on which the state rests, and even the governors now realize that revolution is around the corner.

[*Tyatin returns.*]

TYATIN. Yegor Vassilyevich has come out into the dining room.

DOSTIGAYEV. [*Taking a glass from Tyatin.*] Thank you, Stepan. He's come out, you say? Well, we'll go in there too.

ZVONTSOV. The industrialists seem to understand their role—

[*Enter Varvara and Elizaveta.*]

DOSTIGAYEV. The ones in Moscow? I should say they understand it!

ELIZAVETA. Here they're drinking like little sparrows, and in there Bulychov is roaring out things that make you wince.

DOSTIGAYEV. Why is America flourishing? Because the country is run by men of business who constitute the government.

VARVARA. Bettling's Jeanne believes quite seriously that in America cooks go to market in automobiles.

DOSTIGAYEV. That's quite possible. Though I'm sure it's one of those tall stories. And you're still with the military, Varya? Aiming to be under a colonel?

VARVARA. Such a stale joke! What are you dreaming about, Tyatin?

TYATIN. Oh, nothing in particular—

ELIZAVETA. [*In front of a mirror.*] Yesterday Jeanne told me a marvelous story. A real gem!

DOSTIGAYEV. Come on. Tell us.

ELIZAVETA. Not in the presence of men.

DOSTIGAYEV. The gem must be priceless!

[*Varvara whispers to Elizaveta.*]

ELIZAVETA. Husband! Are you going to stay here until you've finished this bottle?

DOSTIGAYEV. I'm not in anybody's way.

ELIZAVETA. [*To Tyatin.*] You know the psalm, Stepan, dear. "Blessed is the man that walketh not in the counsel of the ungodly, nor standeth in the way of sinners"?

TYATIN. Yes, I recall it vaguely.

ELIZAVETA. [*Taking him by the arm.*] Well, these men here—they are the ungodly sinners, and you are a quiet young man made for the moonlight, love, and that sort of thing. Am I wrong? [*She leads him away.*]

DOSTIGAYEV. Isn't she a chatterbox?

VARVARA. Vassily Yefimovich, Mother and Bashkin have sent out a call for Aunt Melanya.

DOSTIGAYEV. The abbess? Oh, she's a tough customer. She'll be against the firm of Dostigayev and Zvontsov —that's certain. She's for the signboard: Kseniya Bulychova and Dostigayev.

ZVONTSOV. She may insist on pulling out of the business.

DOSTIGAYEV. How much does she have in it? Seventy thousand?

ZVONTSOV. Ninety.

VARVARA. How can one tell?

DOSTIGAYEV. One can. One can find out anything. Look at the Germans. They know not only how many men we have at the front but even how many lice there are on each.

VARVARA. I wish you'd be more serious.

DOSTIGAYEV. My darling Varya. Nobody can trade or fight a war, if he can't count the money in his pocket. Here is the way we can find out about Melanya's money. There's a lady, Sekleteya Poluboyarinova, who takes part in Bishop Nikander's night vigils, and Nikander loves counting his money. In addition, there's a certain man in the diocesan council—we'll keep him in reserve. You have a talk with Poluboyarinova, Varya, and if it turns out that the money belongs to the convent—well, I don't have to explain what that means. Where has my beautiful one disappeared to?

[*Enter Glasha.*]

GLASHA. You're asked to come to the dining room.

DOSTIGAYEV. Right away. [*Glasha goes out.*] Well, let's go. [*He goes off.*]

VARVARA. [*Stopping as if her skirt has been caught in the chair.*] Andrey, help me— Do you believe him?

ZVONTSOV. I'm not such a fool.

VARVARA. Oh, what a crook! It worked quite well though, what I thought up about Melanya. How about Tyatin?

ZVONTSOV. He'll come around. I'll see to that.

VARVARA. You should hurry it up.

ZVONTSOV. Why?

VARVARA. Because you can't get them married for a long time after the funeral—and what with Father's weak heart— Besides, I have other reasons.

[*They go off as Glasha enters. She gazes after them with an expression of hatred and proceeds to clear the table. Enter Yakov Laptev.*]

GLASHA. Oh, it's you, Yakov! Yesterday there was a rumor you had been arrested.

LAPTEV. Was there? It was probably wrong.

GLASHA. Joking as usual.

LAPTEV. Well, it's a hungry life, but a merry one.

GLASHA. You'll break your neck with your jokes.

LAPTEV. For good jokes one gets praise, not beatings. If I get it in the neck, it'll be for poor joking.

GLASHA. Go on, wag your tongue. Look. Tonya Dostigayeva is with Shura.

LAPTEV. Brr! I certainly don't want her.

GLASHA. Shall I call Shura?

LAPTEV. A good idea. How's Bulychov?

GLASHA. [*Crossly.*] He's your godfather. He's not Bulychov to you.

LAPTEV. Don't be cross, Aunt Glasha.

GLASHA. He's very poorly.

LAPTEV. Is he? Oh, look, Aunt Glasha. My friends have almost nothing to eat. Can you get me some flour? A sack won't be too much.

GLASHA. Am I to steal from my masters to help you?

LAPTEV. But you won't be doing it for the first time. You've sinned before—and it's my sin. The boys want to eat, honestly. And remember, you own more in this house, because of your work, than your masters.

GLASHA. I've heard your tales before. We'll be sending flour to Donat tomorrow morning. You can get a sack from him. [*She goes off.*]

LAPTEV. That's fine. Thank you.

[*He sits down on the couch, and yawns so heavily that tears come to his eyes. He brushes away the tears and looks around. Enter Kseniya mumbling to herself.*]

KSENIYA. Everybody's running away like the devil from incense—

LAPTEV. Good afternoon.

KSENIYA. Goodness gracious. What

are you sitting here for?

LAPTEV. Must I walk?

KSENIYA. For weeks you can't be found anywhere, then suddenly you turn up—as if you were playing hide-and-seek. Your godfather is ill. But it's nothing to you, it seems.

LAPTEV. Have I got to fall ill, too?

KSENIYA. You've all gone mad, and spread the same madness among others. I hear the Tsar is to be put in a cage as that old rebel Pugachov was. Is that a lie, you know-it-all?

LAPTEV. Everything is possible, everything.

[Glasha appears at the door.]

GLASHA. Kseniya Yakovlevna, one moment, please.

KSENIYA. Now what do you want? Never a minute's peace, oh, God!

[She and Glasha withdraw. Presently Shura rushes in.]

SHURA. Hello, Yakov!

LAPTEV. Shura dear, I'm going to Moscow but I haven't any money. Help me out.

SHURA. I have thirty rubles.

LAPTEV. Could you make it fifty, eh?

SHURA. I'll get it.

LAPTEV. Tonight, before the train leaves—can you?

SHURA. I will. Listen—is revolution coming?

LAPTEV. It's already come. Don't you read the papers?

SHURA. I don't understand papers.

LAPTEV. Ask Tyatin.

SHURA. Tell me honestly, Yakov— what sort of person is Tyatin?

LAPTEV. Imagine asking me that! Why, you've been seeing him every day for nearly six months.

SHURA. Is he honest?

LAPTEV. Well, yes—he is.

SHURA. Why do you say it so hesitantly?

LAPTEV. He's namby-pamby—and foggy-like—as if life's done him dirt—

SHURA. How?

LAPTEV. Well, he was chucked out of the university in his second year— works as a clerk for his cousin, and his cousin—

SHURA. Zvontsov is a cheat, is he?

LAPTEV. He's a liberal, a Constitutional-Democrat, and those gentry are all that, more or less. You give the money to Glasha—she'll see that I get it.

SHURA. Glasha and Tyatin are helping you?

LAPTEV. In what?

SHURA. Don't hedge, Yashka. You understand me. I want to help too, you hear?

LAPTEV. [Surprised.] What's happened, girl? You talk as if you'd just woke up.

SHURA. [In a temper.] Don't dare make fun of me! You're a fool.

LAPTEV. Possibly I am a fool. Still, I'd like to understand—

SHURA. Varvara's coming.

LAPTEV. She's the last person I want to meet.

SHURA. Come—quick!

LAPTEV. [Putting his arm around her shoulders.] Really, what's the matter with you?

[They go off, locking the door behind them. Varvara enters, through another door. She hears the click of the lock, walks over, and tries the handle.]

VARVARA. Is that you, Glasha? [After a pause.] Is anybody there? Mysterious—

[Walks off quickly. Reënter Shura,

pulling Donat by the hand.]

DONAT. Where are you dragging me, Shura?

SHURA. Wait! Tell me, is Father respected in town?

DONAT. A rich man is respected everywhere. You're always up to some prank.

SHURA. Do they respect or fear him?

DONAT. If they didn't fear him, they wouldn't respect him.

SHURA. And what do they love him for?

DONAT. What for? I don't know.

SHURA. But you know they love him?

DONAT. Him? Well, coach drivers seem to love him—he never haggles with them—gives them what they ask. And a driver, of course, will pass the word around, and so—

SHURA. [*Stamping her foot.*] Are you laughing at me?

DONAT. What should I do that for? I'm only explaining the truth.

SHURA. You're spiteful. You've become a different man.

DONAT. Me? A different man? It's too late to change at my age.

SHURA. You used to speak well of my father.

DONAT. I'm not running him down now. Each fish has its own scales.

SHURA. You're all liars.

[*Enter Glasha.*]

DONAT. [*Looking downcast, and sighing.*] Don't get cross, girlie. You can't prove anything by losing your temper.

SHURA. Go away! [*To Glasha.*] Look, Glasha—oh, somebody's coming—

[*She hides behind a drape. Enter Alexey Dostigayev. He is nattily dressed in breeches and a military jacket, with belts and pockets all over him.*]

ALEXEY. You're looking better every day, Glasha.

GLASHA. [*Sullenly.*] Pleased to hear it.

ALEXEY. I'm not. [*Stands in her way.*] I don't like anything that's good, if it isn't mine.

GLASHA. Let me go, please.

ALEXEY. Most willingly.

[*Glasha goes off. Alexey looks at his watch, yawning. Enter Tonya.*]

SHURA. [*Emerging from behind the drape.*] You seem to be after maids too.

TONYA. He doesn't care—he might be after fish just as well.

ALEXEY. Maids, if you undress them, are in no way inferior to ladies.

TONYA. Hear that? Nowadays he always talks as if he's been living in a low dive, not at the front.

SHURA. Yes, he used to be just as lazy, but not nearly as brave with words.

ALEXEY. I'm just as brave with deeds.

TONYA. What a liar! He's a coward. He's terribly afraid our step-mother may seduce him.

[*Enter Tyatin.*]

ALEXEY. What are you talking about? Little fool!

TONYA. And he's disgustingly greedy. You know, I pay him a ruble and twenty kopecks for every day he doesn't tell me something nasty. And he takes it.

ALEXEY. How do you like Tonya, Tyatin?

TYATIN. Very much.

SHURA. And me?

TYATIN. To tell the truth—

SHURA. Of course, only the truth.

TYATIN. Not very much.

SHURA. Really? Is that the truth?

TYATIN. Yes.

TONYA. Don't believe him. He repeated it like an echo.

ALEXEY. Look, Tyatin, you should marry Tonya. I'm sick and tired of her.

TONYA. What an idiot! Get out of here. You look like a pregnant laundry woman.

ALEXEY. [Putting his arm around Tonya's waist.] Oh, such an aristocratic lady! Ne crackez pas les sunflower seeds, c'est mauvais ton.

TONYA. Leave me alone.

ALEXEY. Delighted. [Dances with her.]

SHURA. Perhaps you don't like me at all, Tyatin?

TYATIN. Why do you want to know that?

SHURA. I need to. And it interests me.

ALEXEY. Don't be sluggard. She's as much as asking you to marry her. Today all girls are in a hurry to become the widows of heroes. It brings an extra ration, a halo, and a pension.

TONYA. He's convinced he's being funny.

ALEXEY. Well, I'll be off on my own tack. See me to the door, Tonka.

TONYA. I won't.

ALEXEY. It's something important. Come on, seriously!

TONYA. I'm sure it's something silly. [Alexey and Tonya go off.]

SHURA. Tyatin, are you truthful?

TYATIN. No.

SHURA. Why not?

TYATIN. It doesn't pay.

SHURA. If you speak like that, you must be truthful. Now tell me straight off—are you being advised to propose to me?

TYATIN. [Lighting a cigarette.] I am.

SHURA. And you realize that it's bad advice?

TYATIN. I do.

SHURA. You are—Well, it's a surprise. I thought you—

TYATIN. You must have thought badly of me?

SHURA. No, you're—remarkable. But perhaps you're shy? Perhaps you're playing at truth to pull the wool over my eyes?

TYATIN. That would be beyond my powers. You're clever, vicious, and mischievous, just like your father. Speaking honestly, I'm afraid of you. And you're redheaded too, as Yegor Vassilyevich is—aflame like a torch.

SHURA. Tyatin, you're splendid. Or else you're sly as the devil—

TYATIN. And your face is an extraordinary one—

SHURA. Is that, about my face, to soften the blow? Yes, you are sly.

TYATIN. Think as you will. In my opinion, you're bound to do something—criminal. And I'm accustomed to living with my little paws turned up—you know, like guilty puppies sprawling on their backs.

SHURA. Guilty of what?

TYATIN. I don't know. Of being puppies, perhaps, and not having teeth to bite you with.

[Enter Tonya.]

TONYA. That fool brother of mine gave me such a tug on the ear, it still hurts. And he took away all my money, the crook! You know, he'll turn into a regular drunkard, I'm sure of it. He and I are such good-for-nothing merchant-family offspring. You think that's funny?

SHURA. Tonya, I want you to forget all the bad things I said about him.

TONYA. About Tyatin? What did you say? I don't recall.

SHURA. Well, that he wants to propose to me.

TONYA. What's bad about that?

SHURA. For the sake of money.

TONYA. Oh, yes. That's a dirty thing to do, Tyatin.

SHURA. Pity you didn't hear him answering my questions.

TONYA. You've been Warumming him? Remember Schubert's "Warum"?

TYATIN. Is it Schubert's?

TONYA. Warum makes me think of that bird the marabou—such a solemn bird—in Africa.

SHURA. Where on earth do you get such crazy ideas?

TONYA. I'm getting so I like scary things. When you're frightened you stop being bored. I like to sit in the dark and wait for a huge serpent to crawl in—

TYATIN. [*With a snicker.*] You mean the one that was in the garden of Eden?

TONYA. No, a more frightful one.

SHURA. You're interesting. You always think up something new, while everybody else talks of nothing but war, Rasputin, the Tsarina, the Germans, the war, revolution—

TONYA. You'll be an actress or a nun.

SHURA. A nun? Nonsense!

TONYA. It's hard to be a nun. You have to play the same role all the time.

SHURA. I want to be cocotte, like Zola's Nana.

TYATIN. Is that the way you feel? Shame!

SHURA. I want to debauch people, to revenge myself.

TYATIN. On whom? And for what?

SHURA. For being a redhead—for my father's illness—for everything! As soon as the revolution begins, I'll spread my wings—you'll see.

TONYA. You believe there's going to be a revolution?

SHURA. Oh, yes.

TYATIN. There'll certainly be a revolution.

[*Enter Glasha.*]

GLASHA. Shura, Mother Melanya has arrived. Yegor Vassilyevich wants to see her in here.

SHURA. Oh, that aunt! Let's skip into my room, children. Tyatin, do you have a great respect for your blood-brother Zvontsov?

TYATIN. He's just my cousin.

SHURA. That's no answer.

TYATIN. Relatives, I think, seldom respect one another.

SHURA. Now there's an answer.

TONYA. Stop prattling about dull things.

SHURA. You're very funny, Tyatin.

TYATIN. Can't help it.

SHURA. And you wear funny clothes.

[*Shura, Tonya, and Tyatin go off. Glasha opens the door screened by drapes. Bulychov appears in the door through which the young people have just left. Abbess Melanya, with an important air, and holding a staff, steps in slowly through the other door. Glasha stands by, with bowed head, holding back the drape.*]

MELANYA. You still hanging around, wanton? They haven't driven you out yet? They will, soon.

BULYCHOV. That'll be a chance for

you to take her into your nunnery—she has money.

MELANYA. Oh, so you're here? Oh, Yegor, how you've changed, God have mercy on us.

BULYCHOV. Shut the door, Glasha, and tell them not to peep out. Sit down—your Reverence. What business shall we take up?

MELANYA. The doctors aren't much help, are they? You see, the Lord bides His time a day, a year, or even an age—

BULYCHOV. We'll discuss the Lord later. Let's tackle business first. I know you've come to talk about your money.

MELANYA. The money is not mine, it's the cloister's.

BULYCHOV. It's all the same—cloister, oyster, grab all you can. What's worrying you about the money? Afraid if I die, it'll be lost?

MELANYA. It's impossible for it to get lost, but I don't want it falling into strange hands.

BULYCHOV. Then you want to take it out of the business? Take it out—it's all the same to me. But mind you—you'll lose by it. Today rubles breed like lice on soldiers. And I'm not so sick yet as to die in short order.

MELANYA. We know not the day or the hour when death shall come. Have you made your will?

BULYCHOV. No.

MELANYA. It's time. Make it. The Lord may call you suddenly—

BULYCHOV. What does he want me for?

MELANYA. Leave your impertinences. You know I don't like listening to them, and my position—

BULYCHOV. Oh, chuck it, Melanya. We know each other both by sight and by touch. You can have your money—Bulychov has plenty.

MELANYA. I've no desire to take the capital out of the business, but I want to make out the papers in Kseniya's name. So I'm informing you now.

BULYCHOV. I see. Well, it's your affair. However, if I die, Zvontsov will wipe out Kseniya—and Varvara will help him.

MELANYA. Oh, this is the way you talk now? It sounds new. No spite in it.

BULYCHOV. My spite is turned in another direction. Well, let's now discuss the God-Lord, the soul. "We ruined and robbed in the days of our youth—now that we're old we must look to our souls."

MELANYA. All right. Speak.

BULYCHOV. Well, then. You serve God by day and night, as for example Glasha serves me.

MELANYA. Don't be profane. How does Glasha serve you at night? Are you out of your mind?

BULYCHOV. Want me to tell you?

MELANYA. Don't be profane. Come to your senses.

BULYCHOV. Don't roar. I'm talking to you in plain, human words, not in official prayers. Now, you said to Glasha that she'd soon be fired. You therefore believe that I'll die soon. Why should I? Dostigayev is nine years older than I am, and much more of a swindler too. But he's in good health and will live long. He has a first-class wife. Of course, I'm a sinner—I've wronged people, and in general, in every way, I've sinned. Well, all people wrong one another—it can't be helped—such is life.

MELANYA. Don't confess your sins

before me or anyone else. Do it before God. Men won't forgive, but God is merciful. You know yourself —in the old days highwaymen committed terrible sins, but when they gave unto God what was His they were saved.

BULYCHOV. Oh, yes, of course. If you steal and make a gift to the church, you're not a thief, you're a godly man.

MELANYA. Yegor! You're blaspheming. I won't go on listening to you. You're not stupid—you must understand if the Lord doesn't permit, the devil won't seduce.

BULYCHOV. Thanks.

MELANYA. What do you mean by that?

BULYCHOV. You've reassured me. It turns out that the Lord is quite willing to let the devil seduce us—so when I sin, he's a party to it with the devil and myself.

MELANYA. [Rising.] These words— these words of yours are such that if I report them to Bishop Nikander—

BULYCHOV. But what have I said that's wrong?

MELANYA. Heretic! Do you realize what heathenish ideas have got into your sick brain? Don't you understand that if God lets the devil seduce you, it means he's renounced you?

BULYCHOV. Renounced me, has he? Why? Because I cared for money, love women, married your fool of a sister for her money, was your lover —for all that he's renounced me? Oh, you big-mouthed crow—you just croak—without thinking.

MELANYA. What are you saying, Yegor? Have you gone mad? Merciful God!

BULYCHOV. You pray day and night under the bells, but who you're praying to you don't know yourself.

MELANYA. Yegor! You're hurtling into an abyss, into the jaws of Hell. And at such a time! Everything is being destroyed, the Tsar's throne is tottering before the forces of evil —it's the antichrist's hour, and the Day of Judgment is probably near—

BULYCHOV. Something to worry about, indeed! The Day of Judgment—the Second Advent—You crow! You fly in, set up a croaking. Go back to your den to kiss your choir girls. And as for your money, all you'll get from me is this! [He makes an offensive gesture with his fingers.]

MELANYA. [Astounded, almost falls into her chair.] Oh, you miserable wretch!

BULYCHOV. You said Glasha is a wanton. And you? What are you?

MELANYA. It's a lie! It's a lie! [Jumping to her feet.] You're a crook! You'll die like a dog soon! Worm!

BULYCHOV. Get out—or I don't know what I'll do to you!

MELANYA. Snake! Devil! [Rushes out.]

BULYCHOV. [Rubbing his right side, growls to himself, then shouts.] Glasha! Hey, there!

[Enter Kseniya.]

KSENIYA. What's the matter? Where's Melanya?

BULYCHOV. She's flown away.

KSENIYA. [Sitting down.] Surely you didn't quarrel again?

BULYCHOV. Have you settled down here for long?

KSENIYA. I wish you'd let me say a word, Yegor. You no longer talk to me. I might just as well be a piece of furniture. Why are you looking at me like that?

BULYCHOV. Go on, fire away.

KSENIYA. The things that are going on in our house! As if the world has come to an end. Our dear son-in-law has practically turned his place upstairs into an inn. Visitors mill around there from morning till night, conferences are held. I don't know what about—Yesterday they drank seven bottles of red wine and heaven knows how much vodka. Ismail, the janitor, is complaining—the police are worrying him to death asking him who the people are that come to our house. And they talk upstairs about the Tsar, about the government—And so every day—a regular inn. Why do you hang your head?

BULYCHOV. Talk away! When I was young I loved to sit in an inn, drinking and listening to music.

KSENIYA. What did Melanya come for?

BULYCHOV. You're a bad hand at lying, Kseniya—too stupid to do it well.

KSENIYA. What did I lie about, when?

BULYCHOV. Right now. Melanya called by prearrangement with you to talk about money.

KSENIYA. When did I arrange with her? Where did you get that idea?

BULYCHOV. Well, let's forget it. Shut up.

[*Dostigayev, Zvontsov, and Father Pavlin enter animatedly.*]

DOSTIGAYEV. Yegor, hear the news Father Pavlin has brought from Moscow.

KSENIYA. You should lie down, Yegor.

BULYCHOV. I'm listening—Father.

PAVLIN. There's little good that I can tell you. And even the good, as I see it, is bad, since it's impossible to think up anything better than the way we lived before the war.

DOSTIGAYEV. No, I protest. No and again no!

[*Zvontsov and Kseniya have been whispering to each other.*]

KSENIYA. Is she crying?

DOSTIGAYEV. Is who crying?

KSENIYA. Our Abbess.

DOSTIGAYEV. What's wrong with her?

BULYCHOV. Go see what's frightened her. Sit down, Father, and let's have it.

DOSTIGAYEV. I'd like to know what Melanya finds so touching that it's reduced her to tears.

[*Kseniya, Zvontsov, and Dostigayev go off.*]

PAVLIN. A great confusion is reigning in Moscow. Even people of ripe intelligence assert that the Tsar must be removed because of his incompetence.

BULYCHOV. He was competent enough for over twenty years.

PAVLIN. A man's powers wear off with the passing of time.

BULYCHOV. In 1913, when the Romanovs celebrated their tercentenary, the Tsar shook my hand. The whole nation was filled with joy—the whole of our city.

PAVLIN. So it was. The people were filled with joy.

BULYCHOV. What's happened? We still have the Duma—No, the trouble is not with the Tsar, it lies at the root of things—

PAVLIN. And the root is the autocracy.

BULYCHOV. I understand autocracy

means self-might. Well, everybody keeps himself going by his own might. Only where is this might? There's none in the war, it appears.

PAVLIN. The Duma has contributed to its destruction.

[*Elizaveta appears at the door.*]

ELIZAVETA. Are you having confession, Father Pavlin?

PAVLIN. Certainly not. What a question!

ELIZAVETA. And where's my husband?

PAVLIN. He was here a while ago.

ELIZAVETA. You *are* very stern today, Father Pavlin. [*She disappears.*]

BULYCHOV. Father—

PAVLIN. I'm listening.

BULYCHOV. Everybody's a father. God is a father, the Tsar is a father, you're a father, I'm a father. But we have no power. We all live to die. I'm not speaking of myself. I'm speaking of the war, the great death. It's like seeing a tiger let loose among the people at a circus.

PAVLIN. You should calm yourself, Yegor Vassilyevich.

BULYCHOV. Calm myself with what? Who can calm me? You? Well, try it—Father. Show your powers.

PAVLIN. You should read the Holy Scripture, the Bible. It's a good thing to recall Joshua and Jericho. War is in the Law.

BULYCHOV. Go on. That's no law—that's a fairy tale. Stop the sun? You can't do it. It's a lie.

PAVLIN. Complaining is the worst sin. One has to accept retribution for our sinful life with peace in our hearts, humbly.

BULYCHOV. Did you bear up under it when the warden, Alexey Gubin, wronged you? You took him to court,

asked Zvontsov to be your lawyer, got the Archbishop to speak for you. And to what court shall I complain against my illness? Against my premature death? Do you mean to tell me you'll die humbly, with peace in your heart? No, you'll groan and yell.

PAVLIN. As a priest I refuse to listen to such speeches. Because these are speeches—

BULYCHOV. Cut it out, Pavlin. You're a man. Your vestment is like paint on one's body. Underneath, you're a human being, the same as I am. The Doctor says your heart is bad, a case of fatty degeneration—

PAVLIN. What can such speeches lead to? Ponder it and be afraid. It has been established from time immemorial—

BULYCHOV. Established, but not too firmly, it seems.

PAVLIN. Leo Tolstoy was a heretic and had anathema pronounced on him for his defection, but when he was facing death he ran away into the woods like a wild beast.

[*Enter Kseniya.*]

KSENIYA. Yegor Vassilyevich, Mokey has come—He says the police arrested Yakov last night, and asks—

BULYCHOV. Well, thank you, Father Pavlin—for your sermon! I'll have—to trouble you later. Call in Bashkin, Kseniya. Tell Glasha to bring me some porridge and—orange brandy.

[*Pavlin goes off.*]

KSENIYA. You musn't have brandy.

BULYCHOV. I can have anything. Go. [*Kseniya leaves the room. Bulychov looks around and murmurs to himself, with a snicker.*] Father—Pavlin—what an owl! Yegor, old fellow, you ought to smoke—it's easier with smoke in your eyes—you can't see everything. [*Enter Bashkin.*] Well, how is it, Mokey?

BASHKIN. How are you feeling, Yegor Vassilyevich?

BULYCHOV. Much better. Yakov has been arrested?

BASHKIN. Yes, last night. Hell of a business!

BULYCHOV. Only he?

BASHKIN. I hear they also got some watchmaker, the schoolteacher Kalmykova who used to give lessons to your daughter Shura, the stoker Yerikhonov, a well-known agitator—altogether about a dozen, they say.

BULYCHOV. All of that crowd—Down with the Tsar?

BASHKIN. They're of different kinds. Some want to do away with the Tsar, others—with all the rich people so that the workers should rule the state—

BULYCHOV. Fiddlesticks!

BASHKIN. That's what I say.

BULYCHOV. They'll drink up the wealth of the state.

BASHKIN. Sure they will.

BULYCHOV. Yes. But suppose they don't.

BASHKIN. What can they do without masters?

BULYCHOV. Truly said. How can anybody live without you or Dostigayev?

BASHKIN. You too are a master.

BULYCHOV. So I am, naturally. What is it they sing?

BASHKIN. [*With a sigh.*] Let us renounce the old world—

BULYCHOV. Go on.

BASHKIN. Let us shake its dust from our feet—

BULYCHOV. The words sound like a prayer.

BASHKIN. I wouldn't say that. The song says: We hate the Tsar—the palace—

BULYCHOV. H'm! The scoundrels! [*Pauses.*] Well, what do you want? [*Glasha brings in porridge and vodka.*]

BASHKIN. Me? Nothing.

BULYCHOV. What have you come for then?

BASHKIN. Just to ask who I should put in Yakov's place.

BULYCHOV. Get Potapov.

BASHKIN. He's of the same way of thinking—neither God, nor Tsar—

BULYCHOV. Is he?

BASHKIN. Allow me to suggest Mokrousov. He's been asking for a job with us—He's had some education, knows how to go about things—

GLASHA. Your porridge will get cold.

BULYCHOV. That policeman—that thief? What's the matter with him?

BASHKIN. It's dangerous on the police force nowadays. Many of them are giving up their jobs.

BULYCHOV. I see—it's dangerous. The fleeing rats—all right, send me Potapov—tomorrow morning. You can go now. Has the tuba player come, Glasha?

[*Bashkin goes off.*]

GLASHA. He's waiting in the kitchen.

BULYCHOV. When I finish the porridge, show him in. Why is it so quiet in the house?

GLASHA. Everybody's upstairs.

BULYCHOV. [*Drinking the vodka.*] It's just as well. What makes you look so sad?

GLASHA. Oh, if you'd only stop drinking and injuring yourself! Get better, Yegor! Give up everything and get away from them. They'll eat you up alive—they will, like worms. Let's go to Siberia—

BULYCHOV. Let go—you're hurting me.

GLASHA. In Siberia I'll work. What good is your staying here? Nobody loves you, everybody's waiting for your death—

BULYCHOV. Stop it, Glasha. Don't upset me. I know and see everything. I know what you are to me—You and Shura are my only gain in life, everyone else would rather I weren't alive at all. I may get better yet. Come on, call in the tuba player.

GLASHA. Please eat your porridge.

BULYCHOV. To the devil with it. Call Shura too.

[*Glasha goes off. Bulychov, alone, avidly drinks one glass of vodka after another. Glasha returns, showing in the Tuba Player, a skinny man looking pitiful and funny, carrying a bag with the tuba on a strap over his shoulder.*]

TUBA PLAYER. Wishing you good health, sir.

BULYCHOV. [*Looking at him with surprise.*] What do you know! Well, sit down. Shut the door, Glasha. So this is what you look like.

TUBA PLAYER. Yes, sir.

BULYCHOV. Well, you're hardly a treat. Now, let's hear about your healing methods.

TUBA PLAYER. My method is simple, sir. Only, people are accustomed to taking drugstore medicines and don't believe me—so I have to ask to be paid in advance.

BULYCHOV. That's a good idea. But does your cure work?

TUBA PLAYER. I've cured hundreds.

BULYCHOV. That hasn't made you rich, though.

TUBA PLAYER. One doesn't get rich doing people good.

BULYCHOV. Oh, you've found that out! Well, what diseases do you cure?

TUBA PLAYER. All diseases are the result of bad air in the stomach—so I treat them all.

BULYCHOV. [*With a light laugh.*] A brave man. Come, let's see your horn.

TUBA PLAYER. Will you pay me a ruble?

BULYCHOV. A ruble? All right. Have you a ruble, Glasha? Here you are. You're too cheap.

TUBA PLAYER. That's to start with. [*Unties his bag and brings out his tuba.*]

[*Shura runs in.*]

BULYCHOV. What a samovar of a horn. How do you like the healer, Shura? Well, blow. [*The Tuba Player clears his throat, plays the tuba not too loudly, and coughs again.*] Is that all?

TUBA PLAYER. You do it four times a day for five minutes, and it's all over.

BULYCHOV. The man blows himself out and dies?

TUBA PLAYER. Oh, never. I've cured hundreds.

BULYCHOV. So. Now tell me the truth—what do you regard yourself as—a fool or a crook?

TUBA PLAYER. And you don't believe me either—just like everybody else.

BULYCHOV. [*Chuckling.*] Don't put your horn away. Tell me honestly— are you a fool or a crook? I'll give you money for that.

SHURA. You mustn't offend the poor fellow, Father.

BULYCHOV. I'm not offending him,

Shura. What's your name, healer?

TUBA PLAYER. Gabriel Uvekov.

BULYCHOV. Gabriel? [*Laughs.*] By Jove! Are you really Gabriel?

TUBA PLAYER. It's a very simple name—nobody else laughs at it.

BULYCHOV. Come on then. Are you stupid or are you a cheat?

TUBA PLAYER. Will you give me sixteen rubles?

BULYCHOV. Bring the money, Glasha. It's in the bedroom. But why sixteen, Gabriel?

TUBA PLAYER. I made a mistake. I should have asked for more.

BULYCHOV. Then you are stupid?

TUBA PLAYER. No, I'm not a fool.

BULYCHOV. Then you are a crook?

TUBA PLAYER. Not a crook either. You know yourself—a man can't make a living without cheating.

BULYCHOV. Perfectly right. It's wrong but right, old fellow.

SHURA. Isn't it a shameful thing to do—cheat people?

TUBA PLAYER. Why shameful, if they believe me?

BULYCHOV. [*Excitedly.*] And this too is true. Do you understand, Shura? It's true. That priest of ours won't say that. He won't dare.

TUBA PLAYER. You should give me more for telling the truth. But—I swear to God— [*He crosses himself.*] the horn does help some people.

BULYCHOV. He's right. Give him twenty-five, Glasha. Give more—all you've got.

TUBA PLAYER. Many humble thanks! But perhaps you will try the horn? God knows how it works, but, it helps, honest.

BULYCHOV. No thank you. Oh, Gabriel, Gabriel! [*Laughs.*] You know what? You show me how it works.

Come on, blow it—and lay it on as thick as you can. [*The Tuba Player produces tense and deafening sounds. Glasha looks at Bulychov with alarm. Shura laughs, closing her ears.*] Go all out!

[*The Dostigayevs, the Zvontsovs, Kseniya, and Bashkin burst into the room.*]

VARVARA. What's going on, Father?

KSENIYA. Yegor—what are you up to this time?

ZVONTSOV. [*To the Tuba Player.*] Are you drunk?

BULYCHOV. Don't you dare touch him! Give it to them, Gabriel! Why, this is Archangel Gabriel trumpeting the end of the world!

KSENIYA. Oh, my God, he's lost his reason!

BASHKIN. [*To Zvontsov.*] You see?

SHURA. Do you hear, Father? They say you've gone mad. Go away, trumpeter, go away!

BULYCHOV. Don't go, Gabriel! Give it to them with all you've got. This is the Day of Judgment, the end of the world! Blow, Gabriel!

ACT III

[*The dining room. Everything in it seems to have been moved out of position. On the table are dirty dishes, a samovar, wine bottles, store packages. In the corner stand several traveling cases. One of them is being unpacked by Taisya, Melanya's servant, who wears a pointed cap. Beside her is Glasha holding a tray. A hanging lamp over the table is lit.*]

GLASHA. Is Mother Melanya going to stay here long?

TAISYA. I don't know.

GLASHA. Why didn't she stop at the convent hostelry?

TAISYA. I don't know.

GLASHA. How old are you?

TAISYA. Nineteen.

[*Zvontsov is coming down the stairs.*]

GLASHA. And you don't know a thing. You're growing up sort of wild.

TAISYA. We're not allowed to talk to lay people.

ZVONTSOV. Has the Abbess had tea?

GLASHA. No.

ZVONTSOV. Go heat the samovar in case she wants some. [*Glasha lifts the samovar and carries it out.*] So you were frightened by soldiers?

TAISYA. Yes, sir.

ZVONTSOV. What did they do to frighten you?

TAISYA. They killed a cow and threatened to set fire to the convent. Excuse me.

[*She goes off, carrying a heap of linen. Varvara appears in the hall.*]

VARVARA. [*From the hall.*] What sloppy weather! Are you having a chat with the nun? [*She enters.*]

ZVONTSOV. You know, it's an awkward thing having the Abbess in our house.

VARVARA. The house isn't ours yet. Has Tyatin agreed about Shura?

ZVONTSOV. Tyatin is an ass, or he's shamming being an honest man.

VARVARA. Wait. I seem to hear Father shouting. [*Listens at the door leading to Bulychov's room.*]

ZVONTSOV. I don't know, the doctors say he's perfectly sane, but after that idiotic scene with the tuba player—

VARVARA. He's pulled worse scenes than that. Shura and Tyatin seem to

have become quite friendly, haven't they?

ZVONTSOV. They have. But I see little good in that. Your sister is a sly thing—she's capable of doing something extremely unpleasant.

VARVARA. It's a pity you didn't think of that when she flirted with you. Well, you enjoyed it anyway.

ZVONTSOV. She flirted with me only to tease you.

VARVARA. How annoying for you! Oh, here's Pavlin heading this way. He's making a habit of it.

ZVONTSOV. Yes, the house is full of priesthood.

[*Enter Elizaveta and Pavlin, arguing, to be followed shortly afterward by Bashkin.*]

PAVLIN. The newspapers are lying as usual. Good evening.

ELIZAVETA. And I'm telling you it's true.

PAVLIN. It has been established beyond any doubt—the Emperor abdicated not of his own free will, but yielding to force, having been captured on his way to Petrograd by members of the liberal party. Yes!

ZVONTSOV. Well, what are we to conclude from this?

ELIZAVETA. Father Pavlin is against revolution and in favor of war. I'm against the war. I want to go to Paris. We've had enough fighting. You agree with me, Varvara? Remember what Henry IV said. Paris is better than war. I know he didn't put it in those words, but he was right.

PAVLIN. I don't insist on anything, since everything is tottering.

VARVARA. We need peace, peace, Father Pavlin. You see how the mob is behaving?

PAVLIN. Alas, I do! But how's our

patient? How is he up here? [*He puts his finger to his head.*]

ZVONTSOV. The doctors have found no signs of disorder.

PAVLIN. I'm glad to hear it. Although the only things doctors find without fail is their fees.

ELIZAVETA. A spiteful man! Jeanne has invited us to supper, Varvara.

BASHKIN. They've released political prisoners, and the police are suffering greater losses than ever.

PAVLIN. That's right. It's most extraordinary. Do you expect anything good from these present events, Andrey Petrovich?

ZVONTSOV. The public forces are in the process of steady organization and will soon have their say. By public forces I mean people who have a firm economic—

VARVARA. [*To Zvontsov.*] Listen, Jeanne has asked us up— [*Draws him aside.*]

ZVONTSOV. That puts me in a rather awkward position, you know. An Abbess on one side, a cocotte on the other—

VARVARA. Not so loud!

BASHKIN. Andrey Petrovich, Mokrousov is here, that police sub-inspector, you know him, don't you?

ZVONTSOV. Yes. What does he want?

BASHKIN. He's giving up his job on account of the times being so dangerous and is asking for a job in our forest station.

ZVONTSOV. Would it be the proper thing to do?

VARVARA. Wait, Andrey—

BASHKIN. Certainly. Yakov Laptev will get up on his hind legs now and start stirring up trouble, and Donat, you know yourself, is not a suitable

man for us. Besides he's a sectarian—keeps mumbling about the law of truth, and what use is it talking truth when—well, you can see for yourself—

ZVONTSOV. That's nonsense! What we're witnessing is precisely the beginning of the triumph of truth—

VARVARA. Wait, Andrey, will you?

ZVONTSOV. And justice.

VARVARA. What is it you want, Mokey?

BASHKIN. I say we should hire Mokrousov. I spoke about him to Yegor Vassilyevich.

VARVARA. What did he say? [*Zvontsov moves away, frowning.*]

BASHKIN. Nothing definite.

VARVARA. You hire Mokrousov.

BASHKIN. Maybe you'll have a look at him?

VARVARA. What for?

BASHKIN. To get acquainted. He's here.

VARVARA. Very well.

[*Bashkin goes off into the hall. Varvara jots something down in her notebook. Bashkin returns with Mokrousov, a round-faced man, with eyebrows raised in surprise, and a smile on his lips, yet looking as if he were about to burst out cursing; he is dressed in a policeman's uniform and carries a revolver on his hip; entering, he clicks his heels.*]

MOKROUSOV. How d'you do, ma'am? I'm deeply grateful for the privilege of serving you.

VARVARA. I'm very glad. You're still in uniform, and I've heard they're disarming the police.

MOKROUSOV. So they are. It's dangerous for us to walk about the streets looking as usual so I wear a civil overcoat, though I still carry arms. Today, however, because of the unfounded hopes which have been aroused, the mob has quieted down and so I've dispensed with my sword.

VARVARA. When do you propose to take up your work with us?

MOKROUSOV. In my mind I've been your humble servant for a long time. I'm ready to go to the station as early as tomorrow. I'm a single man—

VARVARA. Do you think the rioting will last long?

MOKROUSOV. I believe all through the summer. Then rains and cold weather will come, and it'll stop people from fooling around in the streets.

VARVARA. Only during the summer? I hardly think revolution depends on the weather.

MOKROUSOV. Good heavens! Of course it does. Winter cools things off.

VARVARA. [Smiling.] You're an optimist.

MOKROUSOV. We of the police are always optimists.

VARVARA. Really?

MOKROUSOV. It's a fact. We realize our strength.

VARVARA. You served in the army?

MOKROUSOV. Yes, ma'am. In the Buzuluk reserve battalion. I hold the rank of sublieutenant.

VARVARA. [Offering her hand.] Well, I wish you luck.

MOKROUSOV. [Kissing her hand.] I am touched. [He backs out of the room with heavy steps.]

VARVARA. [To Bashkin.] He's a fool, wouldn't you say?

BASHKIN. That's no drawback. Look what the clever ones are doing. If you let them have their way they'll turn the earth inside out—like a pocket.

PAVLIN. [To Bashkin and Elizaveta.] The priesthood must be given the right of free preachment, or nothing good will ever come out of it.

[Enter Bulychov supported by Glasha and Shura. Everybody falls silent as they all gaze at him. A frown comes over his face.]

BULYCHOV. Well? Why have you stopped talking? You've been chattering all the time—

PAVLIN. We've been taken aback by the sudden spectacle—

BULYCHOV. Of what?

PAVLIN. Of a man being led—

BULYCHOV. Being led! When a man loses control of his legs he is led. Mokey, has Yakov been released?

BASHKIN. Yes. All prisoners have been released.

ZVONTSOV. The political ones.

BULYCHOV. Yakov Laptev is set free, and the Tsar is put under arrest. There, Father Pavlin. What do you say to that?

PAVLIN. I'm unversed in these matters. But, in my small comprehension of them, I'd first like to inquire what the intentions of these people are both in speech and deeds.

BULYCHOV. They'll elect a new tsar. Without a tsar you'll be fighting like dogs.

PAVLIN. You have an animated face today—evidently you're overcoming your malady?

BULYCHOV. That's it—overcoming it. You husbands and wives, and you, Mokey, please leave me to talk to Pavlin. You stay here, Shura.

[Bashkin goes out into the hall. The rest go upstairs. A minute or two later Varvara comes halfway down the steps and stops to listen.]

SHURA. You'd better lie down.

BULYCHOV. I don't want to. Well, Father Pavlin, is it about the belfry?

PAVLIN. No. I've dropped in in the hope of seeing you feeling better, and I wasn't wrong. But, of course, remembering your liberal and big-hearted deeds in the past, deeds which were directed to the betterment of the city and our church—

BULYCHOV. You don't pray well for me. My health, you see, is getting worse every day, so I don't feel like paying God. Why should I pay him, for what? I've paid plenty, but what good has it done me?

PAVLIN. Your contributions—

BULYCHOV. Wait. I have a question —isn't God ashamed of himself? Why is death?

SHURA. Don't speak of death— please.

BULYCHOV. Keep quiet—and listen. I'm not talking about myself.

PAVLIN. You shouldn't upset yourself with such thoughts. And what can death mean when the soul is immortal?

BULYCHOV. But why is it squeezed into dirty, tight flesh?

PAVLIN. The Church regards this question as not only idle but also—

[*Varvara, on the staircase, tries to smother her laughter with a handkerchief.*]

BULYCHOV. Don't hiccup! Speak right out. Do you remember the tuba player, Shura?

PAVLIN. In the presence of this young lady—

BULYCHOV. Come off it. She has to live—so she has to know. I've lived long enough and now I ask you: What do you live for?

PAVLIN. I serve in a house of God.

BULYCHOV. I know you serve. But one day you'll have to die. What does it mean? What does our death mean, Pavlin?

PAVLIN. Your questioning is illogical and futile. And—forgive me—it's not of earthly things you ought to be thinking now—

SHURA. You mustn't speak like that!

BULYCHOV. I'm earthly through and through.

PAVLIN. [*Rising.*] Earth is dust.

BULYCHOV. Dust, you say? Then you lousy—Then you must remember yourself that earth is dust. Dust, but you wear a silk cassock. Dust, but you have a gilded cross. Dust, but you're greedy for everything—

PAVLIN. You're saying evil and baleful things in the presence of a virgin—

BULYCHOV. A virgin—a burgeon— [*Varvara hastens up the steps.*] They train you fools as dogs are trained to hunt hares. You've grown rich on penniless Christ—

PAVLIN. Your illness has made you bitter, and in your bitterness you roar like a wild boar— [*He goes off.*]

BULYCHOV. You're leaving? Aha!

SHURA. You shouldn't excite yourself, it only makes you feel worse. You're so unmanageable.

BULYCHOV. Never mind. There's nothing to lose. Oh, how I dislike this priest! You keep your eyes and ears open. I have a purpose in all this.

SHURA. I see everything myself— I'm no child, nor a fool.

[*Zvontsov appears on the stairs.*]

BULYCHOV. After that tuba player they've decided I've gone mad. But the doctors say it's a lie! You do believe the doctors, Shura, don't you?

SHURA. I believe you.

BULYCHOV. That's the girl! No sir,

my brain is working all right. The doctors know. It's true, I stumbled on something sharp. But everybody is interested to know: What is death? Or again: What is life? You understand?

SHURA. I don't believe you're dangerously ill. What you need is to go away from here. Glasha's right about that. You must have thorough medical care. But you don't listen to anybody.

BULYCHOV. I listen to everybody. There's that woman healer, for instance—I'll try her too. What if she helps? It's time she was here. Ah, that gnawing pain—it's like anguish in the heart.

SHURA. Please, Father dear. Don't go on like this. Lie down.

BULYCHOV. I feel worse lying. Once you lie down, you give up the fight, you surrender. Besides, I want to talk. I have to tell you something. It's a funny case—I live on the wrong street, so to speak. I fell in with people not of my kind, and for thirty years I've had nobody but strangers around me. I don't want the same thing to happen to you. My father was a poor craftsman. And I—I don't know how to make clear what I mean.

SHURA. Speak more quietly, more calmly. Talk to me as you used to when you told me fairy tales.

BULYCHOV. I never told you fairy tales. I always spoke to you of true things. You see—those priests, tsars, governors—what the hell do I need them for? I don't believe in God either. Where do you find him here? You see yourself. Nor are there good people to be found. Good people are as rare as—counterfeit coins. You see what everybody's like, don't you? Now they've all got themselves into

a mess, into a war—have gone stark, staring mad. What do I care? What good are they to Yegor Bulychov? And to you too—how will you be able to live with them?

SHURA. You shouldn't worry about me.

[Enter Kseniya.]

KSENIYA. Shura, there are visitors to see you—Tonya with her brother, and that other—

SHURA. Let them wait.

KSENIYA. You'd better go. Your father and I have got to have a talk.

BULYCHOV. Are you sure I have to?

SHURA. Don't talk to him too much.

KSENIYA. Teaching me what to do? Yegor Vassilyevich, Zobunova, the healer, has come.

BULYCHOV. Come back later, Shura, and bring the young people along. Well, go get Zobunova.

[Shura goes off.]

KSENIYA. In a minute. I want to tell you about Shura. She's become friendly with that good-for-nothing, Andrey's cousin. You understand he's not the right man for her. We've taken one pauper under our roof—and how he lords it over us now!

BULYCHOV. Really, Kseniya, you're like a bad dream.

KSENIYA. God forgive your insults. You ought to forbid her to play around with Tyatin.

BULYCHOV. Anything else?

KSENIYA. Melanya's here.

BULYCHOV. What for?

KSENIYA. A misfortune has befallen her. Some army deserters attacked her convent, killed a cow, stole two hatchets, a pick ax, some lengths of rope—what's the world coming to! And Donat, our forester, is being hospitable to bad characters—they live in the workers' barracks at the lumber mill.

BULYCHOV. I notice any man I like is disliked by everybody else.

KSENIYA. You ought to make up with her.

BULYCHOV. With Melanya? What for?

KSENIYA. Why, naturally, for the sake of your health—

BULYCHOV. All right, I'll make up with her. I'll say to her: "And forgive us our debts"—

KSENIYA. Be kind to her. [*She goes off.*]

BULYCHOV. [*Muttering to himself.*] And forgive us our debts—as we forgive— Lies everywhere! The devils!

[*Enter Varvara.*]

VARVARA. Father, I heard Mother talking to you about Stepan Tyatin.

BULYCHOV. Yes, you hear everything, know everything.

VARVARA. Tyatin is a modest young man. He won't demand a big dowry with Shura and he'll make a good match for her.

BULYCHOV. You *are* considerate—

VARVARA. I've been taking a good look at him—

BULYCHOV. But considerate of whom? Oh, you family devils! [*Enter Melanya and Kseniya. Taisya stops at the door.*] Well, Melanya. Let's make up, shall we?

MELANYA. Singing another tune! A warrior! You hurt everybody's feelings for no good reason.

BULYCHOV. "And forgive us our debts," Melanya!

MELANYA. Debts have nothing to do with it. Behave yourself. Look what's going on in the country. Our Tsar anointed by God has been dethroned. Do you realize what that

means? Our Lord has thrown the darkness of confusion over his people, and they have all lost their reason, and with their own hands are digging the ground from under their feet. The mob is rioting. The village women in Koposovo shouted to my face, "We are the people! Our husbands, the soldiers, are the people!" Can you imagine that? Since when have soldiers come to be regarded as the people!

KSENIYA. Yakov Laptev is preaching all that—

MELANYA. They've deprived the Governor of his powers, and have put the notary public Osmolovsky in his place—

BULYCHOV. Another fat one.

MELANYA. Yesterday Bishop Nikander was saying: We live on the eve of devastating events. How can there be such a thing as civil authority? It's impossible. Since biblical times peoples have been ruled by a hand armed with a sword and the cross.

BULYCHOV. In biblical times there was no worship of the cross.

MELANYA. Keep quiet, you brainy one. The Gospels are part of the Bible and come in the same binding. And the cross is a sword. A critic! The Bishop knows better than you do what was worshiped and when. You, seekers after glory, you rejoice at the downfall of the throne. Watch out lest your joy turn into bitter tears. Yegor dear, I want to have a private talk with you.

BULYCHOV. Won't we quarrel again that way? Though, of course, we can have a talk, only later. The woman healer is coming presently. I want to get better, Melanya.

MELANYA. Zobunova is a famous healer. She's way ahead of the doctors. Afterward have a talk with the possessed innocent Propotey.

BULYCHOV. They say he's a faker?

MELANYA. No, no. How can you? You must see him—

BULYCHOV. Well, let's have Propotey too. I feel better today somehow—except for my legs. And gayer too. Somehow everything is funny, looks funny. Call in the healer woman, Kseniya.

[*Kseniya goes off.*]

MELANYA. Oh, Yegor—there's still a lot of the old stuff in you.

BULYCHOV. You're right there, and a good thing there is a lot of it.

[*Kseniya returns.*]

KSENIYA. She says everybody must leave the room.

MELANYA. Well, we'd better go.

[*Everybody goes out except Bulychov, who sits smiling and rubbing his chest and side. Enter Zobunova quietly. Acting as if she were alone but actually intent on attracting Bulychov's attention, she twists her mouth, blows out to the right, and pressing her right hand to her heart, moves her left hand like a fish's fin, as if waving somebody away. As she stops, she passes her right hand over her face.*]

BULYCHOV. Are you praying to the devils?

ZOBUNOVA. [*In a singsong voice.*] Oh, you evil ailments, you sufferings of the flesh. Move away, roll away, go away from this servant of the Lord. This day and this hour I drive you away with my strong word for ever and ever. Good evening, kindly man, called Yegor.

BULYCHOV. Good evening, Auntie.

Were you driving away the devils?

ZOBUNOVA. Whatever are you saying? How can one have dealings with them?

BULYCHOV. When one has to, one can. Priests pray to God. You're not a priest, so you must pray to the devils.

ZOBUNOVA. I don't know where you get these frightful notions. Only stupid people spread stories about me being in with the evil ones.

BULYCHOV. In that case, Auntie, you'll be wasting your breath. Priests have prayed to God for me—but he's refused to help me.

ZOBUNOVA. You're just having your joke, kind man. That's only because you don't believe in me.

BULYCHOV. I would believe in you if you came from the devils. You know, of course—you're sure to have heard it—I'm a loose man, a man harsh with people, greedy for money—

ZOBUNOVA. I've heard that, but I don't believe you'll grudge giving me a little gift.

BULYCHOV. I'm a great sinner, Auntie, and God doesn't care about me. God has washed his hands of Yegor Bulychov. So, if you're not in cahoots with the devils, you'd better go and perform your abortions—that's your trade, isn't it?

ZOBUNOVA. My, my! Truly do people say you are a pushing, mischievous man!

BULYCHOV. Well? What lies do you want to tell? Fire away.

ZOBUNOVA. I know nothing of lies. Tell me what hurts you, how it hurts you, where.

BULYCHOV. My belly hurts me, very painfully—right here.

ZOBUNOVA. You see—but don't tell

anybody, no—not a soul!

BULYCHOV. I won't tell—don't worry.

ZOBUNOVA. There are yellow ailments and there are black ones. Even a doctor can cure a yellow ailment. But a black one—no prayers by either a priest or a monk can ever cure that. The black one—that comes from the evil spirits, and there's only one remedy for it.

BULYCHOV. Kill or cure—is that it?

ZOBUNOVA. The remedy is an expensive one.

BULYCHOV. Naturally. I understand.

ZOBUNOVA. Here you really have to deal with the evil spirits.

BULYCHOV. With Satan himself.

ZOBUNOVA. Well, not directly with him, but still—

BULYCHOV. Can you do it?

ZOBUNOVA. Only not a word to anybody.

BULYCHOV. Go to hell, Auntie!

ZOBUNOVA. Wait a moment—

BULYCHOV. Get out—or I'll let you have it—

ZOBUNOVA. Please listen to me—

GLASHA. [From the hall.] You heard him—go! [Glasha enters.]

ZOBUNOVA. Well, I never! Who do you think you are?

BULYCHOV. Put her out!

GLASHA. You have a nerve—making out you're a witch!

ZOBUNOVA. You're a witch yourself —with such a face, too! Oh, what people! May you have neither sleep nor rest!

[Zobunova and Glasha go off. Bulychov looks around and gives a deep sigh. Enter Melanya and Kseniya.]

MELANYA. So you didn't like Zobunova? She didn't please you?

[Bulychov remains silent, gazing at her.]

KSENIYA. She has a hot temper— been overpraised, and it's given her a swelled head.

BULYCHOV. What do you think, Melanya—does God have the bellyache?

MELANYA. Stop clowning!

BULYCHOV. I'm sure Christ had it. He subsisted on fish—

MELANYA. Stop it, Yegor. Don't provoke me.

[Enter Glasha.]

GLASHA. She asks to be paid for having been bothered.

BULYCHOV. Pay her, Kseniya. [Kseniya goes off.] You'll excuse me, Melanya—I'm tired and am going to my room. Fools are the worst when it comes to making you tired. Come on, Glasha, help me—

[Glasha leads Bulychov off. Kseniya returns and gazes questioningly at her sister.]

MELANYA. He's pretending to be mad—I'm sure—

KSENIYA. I doubt it. He's not well enough to play a part—

MELANYA. It's all right. Let him play-act. It'll work against him if we have to go to court to dispute his will. Taisya will be a witness; also Zobunova, Father Pavlin, the tuba player—any number of them. We'll prove that the testator wasn't in his right mind.

KSENIYA. Oh, I don't know what to do—

MELANYA. That's why I'm teaching you. Oh, Kseniya! You would marry him! I told you to marry Bashkin—

KSENIYA. Yes—but that was ages ago. And he was such a fine figure.

You envied me yourself.

MELANYA. I did? Have you gone mad?

KSENIYA. Well, let's not go into the past.

MELANYA. God be merciful! I envied you, I?

KSENIYA. What about Propotey? Perhaps we can do without him?

MELANYA. Why should we? We've called him up, arranged everything, and all of a sudden—to do without him! No, get him ready, and bring him here. Taisya! [*Taisya comes in from the hall.*] Well?

TAISYA. I couldn't find out anything.

MELANYA. Why couldn't you?

TAISYA. She doesn't talk.

MELANYA. What do you mean, she doesn't talk? You should have pumped her.

TAISYA. I tried, but she only spat like a cat—and called everybody names.

MELANYA. What sort of names?

TAISYA. Crooks.

MELANYA. Why that?

TAISYA. She says you want to drive the man insane.

MELANYA. Did she say that to you?

TAISYA. No, to the innocent, to Propotey.

MELANYA. And what did he say?

TAISYA. He talked in funny sayings all the time.

MELANYA. Funny sayings? You ignorant dolt. He's an innocent, a soothsayer, you fool. Go sit in the hall and don't leave the place. Who else was in the kitchen?

TAISYA. Bashkin.

MELANYA. Well, run along. [*Taisya leaves the room, Melanya walks up*

to Bulychov's door and raps on it.] Yegor, the innocent has come.

[*Enter Propotey, accompanied by Kseniya and Bashkin. He wears shoes of plaited bark and a coarse cotton smock reaching down to his ankles. On his chest are a number of crosses and little icons. His appearance is frightening: thick, disheveled hair; a long, narrow, sparse beard; and abrupt, convulsive movements.*]

PROPOTEY. The room reeks of smoke. It chokes my soul.

KSENIYA. Nobody smokes here, Father.

[*Propotey moans in imitation of the wind.*]

MELANYA. [*To Propotey.*] Wait, let him come out first.

[*Enter Bulychov supported by Glasha.*]

BULYCHOV. Well, just look at you!

PROPOTEY. Don't fear. Don't be afraid. [*Moans.*] Everything is dust, everything will pass. Once there lived Grigory, he went up from story to story, then bumped against a roof, and the devil grabbed him and made off!

BULYCHOV. Is that about Rasputin?

PROPOTEY. Behold, the Tsar has been overthrown and ruin is stalking in his realm where sin, death, and stench now reign. The wind is moaning, the slushy roads are groaning. [*He moans. Then points with his stick at Glasha.*] The devil disguised as a woman is standing by your side —drive him away.

BULYCHOV. I'll drive him for you! Wag your tongue, but know your limit. Did you teach him this, Melanya?

MELANYA. What are you talking

about? How can anybody teach a possessed man?

BULYCHOV. Looks as if it can be done.

[*Shura runs down the staircase followed by Tonya and Tyatin. During the ensuing action Zvontsov and Varvara, Dostigayev and Elizaveta also come down. Propotey silently draws figures in the air and on the floor with his stick. He stands with his head bent, as if absorbed in thought.*]

SHURA. [*Running up to Bulychov.*] What's going on here? What kind of a performance is this?

MELANYA. You keep quiet.

PROPOTEY. [*Speaking with assumed difficulty.*] No sleep comes to the heretic and the clock keeps: tick and tick. If God would, and if he could, it would be good. Whose trouble is it? It's Satan's visit. Play, Satan, play, it's your day. Midnight strikes—the cock cries—the heretic dies—

BULYCHOV. They did teach you to speak smoothly.

MELANYA. Don't interrupt, Yegor.

PROPOTEY. What then to do? What can we do?

TONYA. [*In a tone of regret.*] No, he's not frightening—not at all!

PROPOTEY. They've killed an ant and are singing a chant. Maybe, we should make merry. So let's dance a bit while we're still fit. [*Stamping his feet and singing in a voice gradually rising in volume, begins to dance.*] Astarot, Sabatan, Ascaphat, Idumey, Neponey. Go and neigh. Carra tili—knock—knock, hit your head against a rock! Hey, wench, what's the stench? Stakes—stakes! Billowing smoke! Satan's playing him a joke. Gon-gon-gon, he is alone. Zakatama, the old witch, holds him tight, the

dirty bitch. From carnal lust, the deadly sin, you can't escape to save your skin. Here's Yegor, he looks so sore—

SHURA. [*Shouts.*] Make him go.

BULYCHOV. What are you trying to do, the devil take you? Frighten me?

ZVONTSOV. We must put an end to this hideous scene!

[*Glasha runs up to Propotey. Continuing to whirl around, he swings his stick as if to hit her.*]

PROPOTEY. Hee, hi, ho, hum! On the run, you evil one—

[*Tyatin snatches Propotey's stick from his hand.*]

MELANYA. How dare you? Who are you?

SHURA. Tell them to go, Father, the whole lot of them. Why don't you speak?

BULYCHOV. [*Waving both his hands.*] Wait, Shura, wait.

[*Propotey sits down on the floor, and moans and screeches.*]

MELANYA. You mustn't touch him. He's in a trance—in a rapture.

DOSTIGAYEV. For such raptures, Mother Melanya, one gets a swift kick.

ZVONTSOV. Get up and go—quick!

PROPOTEY. And where to? [*He continues to moan. Kseniya cries.*]

ELIZAVETA. Isn't he clever? He does it with two voices.

BULYCHOV. Go away, everybody—off with you! You've seen enough.

SHURA. [*Stamping her foot at Propotey.*] Get out, you freak. Stepan, put him out.

TYATIN. [*Taking Propotey by the scruff of his neck.*] Come on, holy man—get up! [*Tyatin disappears with Propotey.*]

TAISYA. He wasn't very frightful to-

day—he can do it much more frightfully. If you had given him some
vodka—

MELANYA. What are you saying,
fool? [*She slaps the girl's face.*]

ZVONTSOV. Aren't you ashamed?

MELANYA. Of whom? Of you?

VARVARA. Calm yourself, Auntie.

KSENIYA. My God! What am I to
make of all this?

[*Shura and Glasha help Bulychov
lie down on the sofa. Dostigayev
watches him closely. Zvontsov and
Varvara lead Kseniya and Melanya
away. Glasha follows them.*]

DOSTIGAYEV. [*To Elizaveta.*] Let's
go home, Liza. Bulychov looks very
bad to me. And there's the demonstration going on right now—we must
join it.

ELIZAVETA. It's extraordinary how
he moaned. It's beyond anything you
could imagine.

[*Dostigayev and Elizaveta go off.*]

BULYCHOV. [*To Shura.*] It was the
Abbess' idea—she thought it all up.

SHURA. Are you feeling unwell?

BULYCHOV. She held sort of a requiem mass—over a live man.

SHURA. Tell me, do you feel badly?
Shall I call the Doctor?

BULYCHOV. No, don't. That was his
own, what that clown said about the
Tsar. And did you hear him say: If
God would, and if he could—But God
cannot.

SHURA. You should forget all that.

BULYCHOV. Don't worry, I will. Go
see what they're doing in there—I
don't want them to do anything wrong
to Glasha. Why are they singing in
the street?

SHURA. Don't you get up. [*She hurries from the room.*]

BULYCHOV. And the kingdom reeking of stench will go down in ruins. I
can't see anything. [*He rises to his
feet, holding on to a chair, and rubs
his eyes.*] Thy kingdom— what kingdom? Nothing but beasts! Thy kingdom— Our Father which art— No—
it's all wrong. What sort of father are
you to me, if you've condemned me to
death? What have I done? Everybody
has to die? Why? Well, let others die.
Why should I? [*Sways for a moment.*]
Well? How about it, Yegor? [*Shouts
in a hoarse voice.*] Shura! Glasha! Call
the Doctor! Hey, somebody come, you
wretches! Yegor—Bulychov—Yegor—

[*Shura, Glasha, Tyatin, Taisya rush
in. Bulychov almost falls into their
arms. Glasha and Tyatin support him,
while Shura runs to the window and
opens it. Strains of a revolutionary
song, being sung by a crowd, burst
in.*]

BULYCHOV. What's that? A requiem
mass—again a requiem. Shura, who
is it?

SHURA. Come over here—look!

BULYCHOV. Oh, Shura—

DISCUSSION OF *YEGOR BULYCHOV AND THE OTHERS*

Perhaps it is only coincidence, but the best writers of modern tragicomedy
have been Irishmen and Russians and have written about some kind of revolutionary experience. Maxim Gorky's writing career began when Chekhov's was
near its end, and Gorky continued writing until he died in 1936. He lived
through the abortive 1905 revolution and the successful Communist Revolu-

tion and approved of and actively engaged in them both. He served terms in
jail for subversive activities under the czarist government. Throughout his
career he was a politically committed writer, and he concerned himself with
the artistic problems of socialist realism demanded by Communism.

The best criticism Gorky got of his earliest and most famous play, *The
Lower Depths,* was Chekhov's, and it is pertinent to *Yegor Bulychov.* Chekhov
told Gorky that the fourth act of *The Lower Depths* was the weakest act
because Gorky had "removed all the interesting characters" from it, and he
added: "And now beware lest something happen because of that." In a number
of his later plays, Gorky sacrificed character drawing for ideological preaching.
In *Yegor Bulychov,* to its advantage, the reverse has happened. Writing it
late in his career, in 1931, Gorky is more interested here in the interplay
of characters and in his dynamic and vigorous central figure Yegor Bulychov
than in ideological doctrine. The result is that while the play takes place at
the time of the Revolution, the revolutionary events recede into the background and form its frame, while the foreground is a wry and moving tragicomic study in character.

The frame or background has been clearly explained by Alexander Bakshy,
the translator of *Yegor Bulychov:*

> Yegor Bulychov's rebellion against God is pictured in this play against
> the background of the Russian people's rebellion against the Tsarist gov-
> ernment. The events of the latter rebellion are easily dated. In the open-
> ing scene it is the end of 1916. War with Germany continues. Large
> numbers of wounded soldiers keep arriving in Moscow hospitals. High
> government officials still have to be bribed when supplies are sold to the
> army. Early in 1917 Grigory Rasputin, the Tsar's and the Tsarina's
> favorite, is killed. Public protests about the war and the conduct of the
> war grow louder. In March, 1917, the Tsar abdicates. For a short time
> the power passes into the hands of the representatives of trade and landed
> property. Bulychov's associates and friends look forward to new con-
> quests. The Dostigayevs and Zvontsovs attend meetings and join in
> street demonstrations. But there are also revolutionists like Yakov Laptev,
> and it is clear that they have no intention of accepting the Dostigayevs
> and the Zvontsovs as their new masters. The song Yegor Bulychov hears
> drifting in from the street as he fights off death and rebels against his
> doom is the revolutionary song of the demonstrating crowds, a funeral
> dirge for those fallen in the struggle for freedom and a renunciation of the
> old world.

This external frame of revolutionary events and the internal revolt of Yegor
Bulychov against God function in the same way that the Irish Rebellion does
in *The Plough and the Stars* and the ideas of kingship and royalty do in *King
Lear.* That is, they give scope to the personal tragedy of Yegor Bulychov by
involving him in the greater problems of state and of religion. His somewhat
unusual household involves him in problems of morality and of family. In

some of his earlier plays, Gorky handled similar problems differently, bringing their solutions to the foreground in such a way as to make us commit ourselves to an answer to them. Here, however, he is more interested in the tragicomic mixture of vigor and helplessness in his central character. Alexander Bakshy is worth quoting again. In his preface to *Seven Plays of Maxim Gorky,* he explains Gorky's shift of dramatic focus and concern in the group of four plays of which *Yegor Bulychov* is part:

> . . . in four of these plays, "Vassa Zheleznova," "The Zykovs," "The Old Man," and "Yegor Bulychov," he is seen to be primarily interested in the study of character, which in every case is so masterly in its results that it completely overshadows the moral problems around which the plots of these plays were built. The four plays are also bound together by a revealing and significant feature—Gorky's warm, almost loving, interest in the type of self-made and strong-willed men and women who rose from the lower middle class, mostly without benefit of education, to become rich merchants and manufacturers. His semi-admiring attitude toward these low-born capitalists, of whom Antipa Zykov and Yegor Bulychov are such magnificent specimens, stands in striking contrast to the sarcasm and bitterness with which he pictures the more westernized capitalists in "Enemies" [an earlier Gorky play].

As in *The Three Sisters* and *The Plough and the Stars,* *Yegor Bulychov* has an at first bewildering number of characters and an intricate tangle of plots. At the center of them all, however, stands Yegor Bulychov himself. He is dying, and of all the others, only two, his illegitimate daughter Shura and the maid Glasha, stand by him, doing what he wants and trying to ease his feeling of helplessness and waning power. The rest plot in some way or another against him. They plan how to get his money from him, scheme against Shura, try to prove him crazy. But although Yegor is dying, his force of character still dominates the family. His own feckless son-in-law, the children of his business partner Dostigayev, his wife, her sister the Abbess, and the priest all reprimand him, cower before him, scheme behind his back, or think him crazy. He recognizes them for what they are and tells them so. Only he, out of the native vigor of his character, dares face the facts. He confronts Melanya with her own sinfulness and fully acknowledges his own. He brings into the open his knowledge of all the schemes. He sees clearly into everyone's character. Although he is sentimental when he reminisces fondly about the past, and over-simple when he thinks the people will find a new czar, these contrasts to clearheadedness occur only because he sees the people around him as incapable of managing anything important themselves.

Bulychov's vigor and his clear-sighted view of reality provide most of the play's comedy. Only he has enough sympathy and imagination to see the good side of bad things, and only he has enough truth to call down the characters who take refuge in sham or complacency or religiosity or personal scheming for money. He is Pan himself. He has devoted his life to wine, women, and song, and now, even on his deathbed, he is lusty and drunken. He calls for the music of the tuba player and he recognizes the dirge that is being played over his still-living body. Simultaneously, he knows the tuba player is a fraud and successfully makes him admit it. Later, when his family thinks they can dupe him by setting the village simpleton on him, Yegor recognizes what truth there is in the largely sham performance. He succeeds in finding in everyone around him the kernel of his true nature and in making him yield that kernel up for our examination of its truth or falsity.

Yet *Yegor Bulychov and the Others* might be called *The Death of Pan*. It is wry and wrenching exactly because Bulychov, with all his power and vitality, is dying and knows it. More than that, he knows that his life, for all its success, has not amounted to anything. Here it follows the Pan legend exactly, for Pan, you will remember, was the only ancient god whose death we know of, and his life was extraordinarily vigorous. Yegor Bulychov's death is all the bitterer for him because of his vigor and because he sees no continuity between what he has done and what will happen after he dies. He clearly sees the Revolution coming, and he just as clearly sees the weakness and triviality and fecklessness of the wealthy intelligentsia who surround him.

In a more conventional play than *Yegor Bulychov*, we might expect that the central character would undergo a deathbed conversion, especially when he dies conscious of his sins and uselessness. Part of the strength of *Yegor Bulychov* is that it shows us an unusual old man, still full of vinegar, still incapable of being duped, still acting with forceful unconventionality. If at the last minute Yegor were to be converted, the audience would no doubt be more reassured in its conventional morality. Especially because Yegor wants to have his questions answered, the conventional stage-conversion would make a happy ending. It would also make the play a melodrama. Gorky has avoided such easy emotions and such an easy ending. Having begun with a clear-eyed and animated character, he carries him through to the end.

On the other hand, the voices of conventional morality, which Yegor finds hollow, try to drive him insane. If they were to triumph, the audience would again be reassured. But what makes the play at the same time strongly tragic and comic is Yegor's very sanity. His freedom from cant and insanity makes him a moral man, in Aristotelian terms "like ourselves."

The actual ending perhaps seems despairing and negative, and an abstract description of the play could make it sound like either a thesis play about the decline of the Old Order, of a kind that Gorky early in his career as a playwright was quite capable of writing, or a grimly realistic play about the collapse of religion. Of course, it is partly both of these, but it transcends the limits of either by the diversity of its characterization and incident and by the warmth of Yegor Bulychov himself.

The characters represent a cross-section of society of the time. They represent the professions, industry, religion, the managerial class, and the various levels of servants. They range from the extremely stupid, dishonest, muddled, and incompetent to the highly intelligent, truthful, and clear-headed. Under Bulychov's all-covering roof occurs the widest variety of activities, from revolutionary plotting to carousing, praying, genteel do-gooding, backstairs lechery, petty bribery, and marital scheming. At one moment Bulychov is listening to a tuba player explain how much he charges people for a foolish health cure, at another he is denouncing an abbess, at another he is talking about escaping to Siberia with his maid, at still another he is collapsing from the cancer that is killing him.

This wide diversity of incident and characterization raises *Yegor Bulychov* above being a thesis play about religion. In the thesis play, the central character is one-dimensional, a noble figure without vices who is willing to undergo martyrdom for a high social cause. His speech is characterized by high rhetoric. An apt example is Clifford Odets' *Till the Day I Die*, in which the last speech of the hero, Ernst Taussig, rallies the workers to resist the horrors of Nazism. Here is what he says:

> But we live in the joy of a great coming people. The animal kingdom is past. Day must follow night. Now we are ready: we have been steeled in a terrible fire, but soon all the desolate places of the world must flourish with human genius. Brothers will live in the soviets of the world! Yes, a world of security and freedom is waiting for all mankind. . . . Do your work, comrades.

Taussig sounds like the offstage speaker in *The Plough and the Stars*. His speech has simultaneously a highly emotive tone and a kind of abstract and impersonal flatness. Compare it, however, with Yegor Bulychov's last substantial speech:

> And the kingdom reeking of stench will go down in ruins. I can't see anything. [*He rises to his feet, holding on to a chair, and rubs his eyes.*] Thy kingdom— what kingdom? Nothing but beasts! Thy kingdom— Our Father which art— No— it's all wrong. What sort of father are you to me, if you've condemned me to death? What have I done? Everybody has to die? Why? Well, let others die. Why should I? [*Sways for a moment.*] Shura! Glasha! Call the Doctor! Hey, somebody come, you wretches! Yegor—Bulychov—Yegor—

Unlike the robot Ernst Taussig, this man is a mixture of frailty and virtue, at once honest and yet self-pitying. The middle part of the speech ("What have I done?") is repulsively self-centered, but the movement of the whole speech makes us see Yegor Bulychov as still worth our attention, because he still has his vigorous assertiveness. Yegor's quarrel with God may give the play an added tragic significance, but Yegor's "Hey, somebody come, you wretches!" restores the tone of tragicomic suffering to his voice.

DISCUSSION QUESTIONS ON *YEGOR BULYCHOV AND THE OTHERS*

1. What does Yegor Bulychov look like? How do you imagine him? If you were an actor playing the part, how would you make yourself up to reveal his character?

2. Shakespeare's Lear is generally admitted to be one of the greatest characters in the history of the drama. In many ways Lear and Yegor Bulychov resemble each other. What are some of the ways? In what major ways do Lear and Bulychov differ from each other? Whose judgment is firmer, Lear's or Bulychov's?

In what ways do the families of Lear and Bulychov resemble each other? Do the same attitudes toward the fathers exist in both families? Cite some similar strategy that members of both families use to undermine the power of the father.

Lear's trial seems considerably more intense than Bulychov's, because Shakespeare allows Lear to be driven to madness. How intense is Bulychov's predicament in relation to Lear's? One notable quality that Shakespeare's play has and that Gorky's does not is a kind of magnificent violence. Find some scene in *Yegor Bulychov* that attempts to approach the intensity of *Lear* on the storm-tossed heath. How does the difference in setting contribute to the difference in intensity? How much does the difference between poetry and prose have to do with it? What other devices help Shakespeare attain a kind of dramatic grandeur that Gorky doesn't quite get?

Lear's madness parallels a madness in the state. There is also in Bulychov's family a revolt against the discipline of the father. Is there a parallel, in the background of the play, to the state of Russia? Is Bulychov in any sense a symbolic figure?

Does Bulychov go through as significant a moral growth as Lear does? Lear's tragedy is presented in terms of a conflict between persons. Alexander Bakshy, the translator of the play, mentions "Yegor Bulychov's rebellion against God." How does this conflict compare in significance with Lear's? Does this conflict impart to Bulychov any added breadth, significance, or power? In comparison to the magnificent figure of Lear, does Bulychov seem a mere midget, or does he to some extent hold his own?

3. If Bulychov has many characteristics in common with the tragic hero like Lear, he also has some resemblances to the comic hero like Truewit. If comedy is based on discrepancies between appearance and reality, the comic hero would be the character most able to see those discrepancies. Truewit's wit is true because he has a true and clear vision. In what instances does Bulychov show a true and clear vision? Are some of these instances comic?

Why does Gorky include three scenes in which Bulychov confronts quack healers—the tuba player; Zobunova, the village healer; and Propotey, the prophet? How are these scenes similar? Are they developed in the same way? Does the second one require that the first already have occurred? Is the third the climactic one? That is, would it have the same force if the earlier two hadn't already occurred?

Does Bulychov manage people and events as well as Truewit? Does this similarity or difference indicate anything about the different characters of the tragicomic hero and the comic hero?

4. There are many secondary characters in the play. Do you think there

are too many? If so, what ones do you think could be omitted? What effect would omitting them have on the play?

For example, Donat the forester, Bashkin the manager, and Mokrousov the policeman all represent roughly the same social type and class. Are they similar or different in character? Are they all necessary? Father Pavlin and Melanya both represent religion. Do they do it similarly, and is one of them, therefore, unnecessary? Is Taisya, the nun in Melanya's service, of significant help to the play?

Many of the characters belong to two families, Bulychovs and Dostigayevs. Why is the Dostigayev family shown? Isn't it the same kind of family and from the same class as the Bulychovs? Why couldn't the Dostigayevs be simply described? Why does Gorky bring Yakov Laptev onstage? Why couldn't Laptev's activities be simply described?

5. The above questions about characters are partly questions about the play's complexity. Do you think that there is too much plot? How could it be simplified? Would the story be stronger if it were simpler?

For example, do you think that the incident of the bear could be omitted? Could Zvontsov's trying to talk Tyatin into marrying Shura be omitted? Could the hiring of Mokrousov? Could Yakov Laptev's trying to borrow money from Shura? If these incidents were omitted, the play would surely be simpler. Would it be clearer? Would it have more impact?

6. Sort out the individual actions of the chief characters. How are these actions resolved? Does Gorky resolve all of them with equal finality and clarity? The last act is not mainly devoted to untying the knots of the various actions, but leaves the audience with a certain mood or emotion. Is this fact a virtue or weakness of the play? How "well-made" is the play? Is being "well-made" a valid criterion for this play?

7. Find examples of arias, duets, and ensemble scenes. Does Gorky use arias in the same way as Chekhov? Does he use duets in the same way? Does he have more ensemble scenes? Does he use juxtapositions of characters' comments to provide a realistic chorus? Do any of the characters seem to have an especially choral function? Which ones?

Varvara frequently appears on the stairs, where she overhears conversations. Does Gorky use her as a chorus, or does he use her comically to overhear conversations as Molière does Cleante?

8. In *The Three Sisters* there are three love triangles, and in *The Plough and the Stars* there are at least two. How many are there in *Yegor Bulychov*? How many occur in the present, and how many are referred to as having occurred in the past? How are these old love affairs introduced? What bearing do they have upon the theme or meaning of the immediate action? Why is Shura actively involved in a love plot, and why is Varvara not?

9. If you were directing the play, how would you try to get the actors to play the closing scenes, beginning with Propotey's entrance? Should the Propotey scene be comic or terrifying? Or should it shift from comedy to terror? Should we have first the comedy of Propotey's shamming, and then

the awfulness of Bulychov's speech about the requiem mass and his protest against the Lord's Prayer?

10. As in *The Three Sisters* and *The Plough and the Stars*, there are offstage characters in *Yegor Bulychov*. In fact, there are important references to four offstage characters. Who are they? What is their importance to the onstage action? Does Gorky use any of them in as dramatically important a way as Chekhov and O'Casey use their offstage characters?

11. Is Gorky's range of language as great as Chekhov's and O'Casey's? Can you find examples of heightened speech? Of low speech? Of impassioned speech? Of lyric speech? Of puns, jokes, ironies?

Does Gorky's range include sub-lingual noises like shouts and laughter? Does he use offstage sounds and songs in ways comparable to O'Casey's use of "Keep the Home Fires Burning", or to Chekhov's love-duet between Vershinin and Masha? How would you describe the effect of the ending, when Bulychov hears the revolutionary song outside the window? Compare the ending of *Yegor Bulychov* with the ending of *The Plough and the Stars*. Which is the more forceful? The more ironic? Which makes the more comprehensive comment?

12. Like the comedy of *Tartuffe*, the tragicomedy of *Yegor Bulychov* poses as its central theme a question about religion which would doubtless seem sacrilegious if compared to conventional attitudes toward religion. In fact, Gorky's theme is rather stronger than Molière's. Molière attacked the religious hypocrisy of people, but Gorky attacked God.

Molière, as you will remember, had considerable opposition to his comedy. Would Gorky, despite his stronger theme, have had as much? Does the dimension of seriousness in Gorky's tragicomedy make *Yegor Bulychov* less vulnerable to attack than the purely comic *Tartuffe?*

APPENDIX

Two Plays for Study

Two Plays for Study

This Appendix is here to give you two plays to evaluate yourself, and to give you a chance to apply on your own whatever valid criticisms or approaches you have gleaned from your study of the earlier plays. To allow you to do that, we have restricted the critical comments on the plays, and have presented only enough background information to put the plays in the context of their time and their intentions. The questions that follow the essays you may, of course, use or not use. They are questions that hover closely to the critical approaches used earlier in the book. They do not attempt to push any particular conclusions about the plays, but they are the kind of questions that seem important to ask about any play.

The plays themselves are interesting and notable and offer some difficult problems of judgment. *The American* was not especially successful, and it has been seldom, if ever, revived. However, it was written by one of the cleverest and most brilliant of American novelists, who was also devoted to the theatre. *Bus Stop* has been eminently successful, both as a play and a film. Written by one of the most admired of current American dramatists, it continues to be staged every year by little theatres and by college groups.

Your problem is, as always, not to be influenced either by the eminence of the author or by the success of the play, but to investigate the work itself. One of the easiest mistakes to fall into in judging plays is to use the standard of popularity. Because the drama more than most arts depends upon a living audience that pays to see a performance, popular success is often taken to be the highest measure of value. A little thinking will show you the danger of this standard. It is no doubt true that a living theatre depends on popular success, but the next step is not true: individual plays are not good just because they draw an audience. All the conditions of a performance—the play's stars, its sets, or the popularity of its theme—may draw an audience.

When you consider the playwright as an artist, however, these conditions are accidental, not essential. The plays in the main part of the book are alive on the printed page because of what the playwrights did, not because in their first performances they had good casts or good directors or enthusiastic audiences (although many of them did).

Neither would we argue the opposite point that some super-sophisticates fall into, that a popular play can't be good. Instead, we ask you to leave popularity out of account and to judge these two plays, like any more plays you see or read in the future, against the standards you have developed by your reading in the main part of the book. If you can, on your own, discover what kind of plays these are and, more importantly, what merit they have, then you may begin to consider yourself a successful critic of the drama.

THE AMERICAN

BY HENRY JAMES

CHARACTERS

CHRISTOPHER NEWMAN
VALENTIN DE BELLEGARDE
MARQUIS DE BELLEGARDE
LORD DEEPMERE
M. NIOCHE
M. DE MARIGNAC
THE DOCTOR

MADAME DE BELLEGARDE
MADAME DE CINTRÉ
NOÉMIE NIOCHE
MRS. BREAD
A SISTER OF CHARITY
A SERVANT

ACT FIRST

[*A shabby sitting-room on a small Parisian* quatrième, *with double doors at the back, opening into another room where a table is laid for luncheon; a door on right and on left opening respectively upon the vestibule and staircase, and upon Noémie's room. In front, on left, a small easel with a picture in a frame, turned away from the spectator. Enter Noémie Nioche and Lord Deepmere, rapidly down from centre; she has on an apron and carries in her hand a palette and brushes.*]

NOÉMIE. [*Left.*] I declare that if you touch me I'll paint you all over.

DEEPMERE. [*Left centre.*] You'll convert me into a masterpiece.

NOÉMIE. You're a masterpiece of impertinence. [*Crosses to right and sits on chair.*] Nothing would induce me to sell you a picture.

DEEPMERE. My dear young lady, I'm a great collector.

NOÉMIE. A collector of dear young ladies, yes! You had no right whatever to come here.

DEEPMERE. What could I do? I waited an hour in that accursed gallery.

NOÉMIE. Is that the way you speak of the Salon Carré of the Louvre? If you're as fond of the arts as you pretend to be, you would have been thankful for the opportunity.

DEEPMERE. The art I'm fondest of is that of making up to charming girls. [*Crossing to her and leaning over her: on which she rises.*] Your not being at the Louvre, after giving me so definite a hope, seemed to me simply an opportunity to come here.

NOÉMIE. You're very horrid. [*Goes below table to window.*] How did you find out where I live?

DEEPMERE. It was not *your* fault, certainly. Your discretion is perfect—you never looked behind.

NOÉMIE. You followed me yesterday? Dreadful man, good-bye! [*She goes up toward the back room, Deepmere following.*]

DEEPMERE. Where are you going?

NOÉMIE. To prepare our midday meal.

DEEPMERE. [*Drawing her to otto-*

man, on right of doors, where they sit.] You have plenty of time for that. As I approached the house [*With his hand passed into her arm.*] I met your venerable father leaving it. He had a little basket on his arm. I'm sure he was going out to buy a tender chicken.

NOÉMIE. We don't live on tender chickens.

DEEPMERE. [*Stealing his arm round her waist.*] You might easily, if you would!

NOÉMIE. [*Rising.*] I must take refuge from your abominations in my work—there is nothing like that. [*Begins to paint at the easel. Deepmere follows her, going behind her to left.*]

DEEPMERE. [*Watching her a moment.*] What are you doing there?

NOÉMIE. I'm copying—from memory!

DEEPMERE. And for whom are you performing such a *tour de force?* The inspiration must be great, and you're expecting precisely, now, the person who's the source of it. [*Action— Noémie retouches, rubs and stands off from picture.*] That's why you're so feverishly eager to get rid of me! You're afraid of the person's jealousy. It's a person—I won't be more specific! [*There comes a sharp, short ring at the outer door on which Noémie puts down her implements on stool and goes to centre.*] That's a person, too! I suppose it's your father's ring; it *sounds* like a meek little octogenarian!

NOÉMIE. [*Moving to right, aside.*] It sounds like the American—punctual to the minute. [*Returning to centre, aloud.*] You will leave this place as soon as I have let my father in. I will close these doors [*Indicating those at back.*]—and he will come

into that room. As soon as he has done so, the vestibule [*Pointing right.*] will be clear, and you will pass out by *that* door. [*Indicating door on right.*] Don't move till you hear us come out of the vestibule.

DEEPMERE. Where does your father buy his chickens? I didn't notice there was a poulterer so near. [*Another sharp, short ring, on which Noémie goes to centre.*] The person is losing his temper!

NOÉMIE. [*On the threshold between the two rooms.*] If you don't obey me to the letter, I'll never speak to you again. [*Exit, centre, closing doors.*]

DEEPMERE. [*Alone.*] That means, I suppose, that if I do obey her, I may enjoy the sweet spontaneity of her conversation. [*Goes up by the fireplace to centre.*] It's a refuge for hours of discouragement, when I feel the vanity of higher and sweeter hopes. If I were happy I should never look at her. But hang it, I ain't happy, and it may worry Bellegarde! [*Goes nearer to the back room—listens a moment.*] It's very odd—her father has the voice of some young fellow I know. [*Coming down, left centre.*] Whose is it? I can't make it out!

[*Re-enter Noémie, centre.*]

NOÉMIE. [*Coming back quickly, closing the doors behind her, and opening the door on the right.*] Now, sir, as the coast is clear, you'll please to step out!

DEEPMERE. Let me congratulate you first on your wealth of paternity [*Pointing to centre and going to her.*] —you seem to have two papas! *I* haven't even one, to-day; that's why I can do what I like.

NOÉMIE. What you like?

DEEPMERE. I should like to leave

you a little memento. [*Making, while he seizes her hands, as if to kiss her.*]

NOÉMIE. [*Escaping by crossing him, Deepmere retaining her hands.*] You may come back in an hour—not before. Then I'll scold you properly.

DEEPMERE. In an hour to the minute, lovely being. Let me at least have something to be scolded for! [*Successfully snatches a kiss, and exit, right.*]

NOÉMIE. [*Seated on ottoman, reflectively.*] His father's dead: then he must be a Peer of the Realm! I remember that phrase when we were in England—I used to think it so fine! But he's not in earnest, any more than the Count. No one's in earnest—unless, perhaps, the American! [*Commences to put things in order at table, right; then goes on to chair, left, dusting it, and so on to fireplace, finishing at easel.*] It's only our friendly, foolish Count; it's not the unsophisticated Yankee. Yankees are never Counts, I suppose: that's why they're unsophisticated and order pictures. [*Daubs a little, to touch it up, at picture on easel.*] Do what he likes, did his lordship say? So can the American, evidently, and *he* may like something better. [*Calls.*] Now you can come in —everything is straight! [*Looks at the picture on the easel, while she daubs at it.*] Everything is crooked—more's the pity! [*Calling again.*] Come in, Count, come in! [*Enter, from back, Valentin de Bellegarde.*] I've dusted a chair for you to sit on, and I've put out the little Greuze.

VALENTIN. [*On right of Noémie before the picture.*] I shall miss this very much when I go to the Musée.

NOÉMIE. The original will always be there.

VALENTIN. I know your copy better

—it's the more original of the two.

NOÉMIE. You're laughing at me, but I don't care, for I have found someone to take my work seriously. [*Valentin shrugs shoulders, laughs, goes down to fireplace and puts hat on chest of drawers at left.*] I brought it home yesterday to give it the finishing touches, and when you rang at the door I thought it was the purchaser, who had promised to come this morning and approve.

VALENTIN. You *must* have been disappointed! But I approve! I always approve, you know.

NOÉMIE. It's more than I do, when you come at the wrong time.

VALENTIN. There's no wrong time for seeing *you*. And you would understand my coming if you knew the good people I live with at home, my cosy family circle, as sociable as a pyramid and as cheerful as your tailor's bill! [*Yawning.*] Ah, they make me like Bohemia! [*Comes down, right centre, above easel.*]

NOÉMIE. [*Who has crossed to left centre.*] Bohemia? I'm much obliged to you! [*Curtsies.*]

VALENTIN. It's a charming country, and when I'm with you I feel as if I were in the capital! Who is this happy explorer of the delightful region whom you are expecting alone? [*Sits on table.*]

NOÉMIE. He's very different from you—*he* respects my innocence.

VALENTIN. Let us all respect his!

NOÉMIE. [*Coming to him severely.*] I'm not to see him alone—papa is to be here. He's a pupil of papa's. [*Leans on back of chair to talk to Valentin.*]

VALENTIN. Ah, no wonder he's innocent!

NOÉMIE. *You* needn't stay—*you'll*

be of no particular use.

VALENTIN. My right's as good as his —I'm a pupil of *yours*. [*He kisses her hand; she pretends to be offended*.] What does your father teach him?

NOÉMIE. He gives him lessons in French; he's an ambitious, inquiring American.

VALENTIN. Hadn't he better give him lessons in English?

NOÉMIE. I like the way he speaks —it's so distinct.

VALENTIN. Distinct, but not distinguished. I shall certainly stay to see him.

NOÉMIE. You may see him any time at the Grand Hotel. He sits smoking in the court.

VALENTIN. Is that where you found him?

NOÉMIE. Do you suppose I go to such places? Don't you know how papa's employed there, as commissioner and interpreter?

VALENTIN. Oh yes; he interprets his daughter!

NOÉMIE. As a copyist of the old masters, yes; he brought Mr. Newman to see me at the Louvre. Mr. Newman wants to see more of my copies; he wants to buy some, and that's why he is coming this morning. [*Returns to easel, and resumes work*.]

VALENTIN. Your father has taught him very well. [*Rises and comes to centre*.]

NOÉMIE. Ah, but he won't speak French—though he engaged papa on purpose to practice. Papa's English is so good.

VALENTIN. It isn't so good as yours. You haven't a trace of an accent.

NOÉMIE. We were in London, you know, for years, when I was a child.

VALENTIN. Yes, I have never been

able to make out what you did there.

NOÉMIE. Ah, there it was just the contrary; papa was the interpreter for *French* tourists. [*A timid tinkle at the outer bell*.] There's papa. You had better go. [*Indicating door on right*.]

VALENTIN. Oh, *I'm* a French tourist. I'm all in your father's line. [*Goes, in front, to fireplace*.]

NOÉMIE. Well, he *doesn't* mind you, and a Count, in the house, looks well! Americans like them. [*Exit Noémie centre*.]

VALENTIN. Poor Mr. Newman—I'm glad he's going to like me; I take already such a charitable interest in his fate!

[*Re-enter, centre, Noémie, and enter Nioche, who carries a small basket and a parcel done up in a cotton pocket-handkerchief, both of which his daughter takes from him, going with them to table on right. Nioche is a little old man, dressed with studied, though slightly seedy, gentility, in black. He has a wig, gloves and spectacles, and a habit of folding and unfolding his handkerchief. His hat is on at first*.]

NIOCHE. [*Centre*.] Bonjour, M. le Comte. I salute you very low.

VALENTIN. M. Nioche is always saluting low. You'd salute the executioner if he were going to break you on the wheel.

NOÉMIE. [*Looking into the basket while Nioche polishes his hat with his handkerchief*.] Well, you won't be tortured for stealing, at any rate. Three unhappy little cutlets! If the Count stays there won't even be one apiece.

VALENTIN. The Count will certainly stay.

NIOCHE. [*Putting on his hat again.*] Then I'll go and get another cutlet. [*Goes to door, right.*]

NOÉMIE. It doesn't matter. [*Picking up basket and contents and going up centre.*] We've got half a cold pie. Mr. Newman knows the difficulties of our life.

VALENTIN. Assuredly, since he comes to relieve them. [*The bell rings again, pretty loud and sharp.*] There he is, the ministering angel.

NOÉMIE. Coming! [*Exit, centre, with the basket and parcel.*]

NIOCHE. He *is* a philanthropist, M. le Comte. [*Fumbles out snuffbox.*]

VALENTIN. And what am I then?

NIOCHE. [*Taking snuff.*] You're the purest relic of our old noblesse.

VALENTIN. Rather an object for philanthropy!

[*Re-enter Noémie, centre; enter, behind her, Christopher Newman, with hat and stick.*]

NOÉMIE. This way, Mr. Newman! [*Pointing to the picture on the easel.*] There's the little thing you took such a fancy to.

NEWMAN. [*Looking at picture.*] That's just what I want to see! [*Stands before picture.*]

NOÉMIE. I think I've improved it.

NEWMAN. Well, yes, I suppose you've improved it; but I don't know but I liked it better before it was quite so *good!* However, I guess I'll take it. [*Goes to right.*]

NOÉMIE. [*Advancing, centre.*] There are plenty more in the other room. [*Pointing centre.*] The light's better there.

NIOCHE. [*Obsequiously, to Newman, dusting and giving him chair, right centre.*] I feel it a great honour to receive my munificent patron in my humble home.

NEWMAN. [*Seating himself.*] Oh, I was very glad to come round. When I come to a new country I like to see the *private* life.

NOÉMIE. Oh, sir, we haven't always had it so rough as this!

NEWMAN. Do you call this rough? I've seen it rougher, in my time. I've lived on the beaten earth, between the bare logs.

NOÉMIE. Ah, but you're making that up—at the Grand Hotel!

NEWMAN. My dear young lady, ten years ago, when I was your age, my hotel was grander still—it was sometimes the vault of heaven—the starry night!

NIOCHE. But did you ever lose a fortune, sir, from one day to the other?

NEWMAN. Lose a fortune? Why, I've lost about a hundred! [*Rises.*]

NOÉMIE. Ah, but how many have you made? [*Going up, centre.*] You must come and look at my copies before you lose another.

NEWMAN. Oh, I guess I'm safe now! [*Exit, centre; exit Noémie, centre, preceding.*]

VALENTIN. [*To Nioche.*] I like your American, and his ideas of private life! [*Comes down, centre.*]

NIOCHE. We're more than private, sir—we're obscure! But he's a grand man.

VALENTIN. Do you mean a Grand Hotel man?

NIOCHE. You remember the capacity in which I'm attached to that establishment? He had just arrived in Paris and he wanted me to point him out the most remarkable objects.

VALENTIN. [*Pointing with his thumb to back.*] So you're pointing out your daughter!

NIOCHE. It was to the museum of the Louvre that I took him first, M. le Comte; I was thoroughly conscientious.

VALENTIN. Certainly; you knew he would find your daughter *there*.

NIOCHE. We came upon her, in fact, copying a beautiful picture with her usual devotion.

VALENTIN. Yes, *I* know; that's the way *I* came upon her—last year!

NIOCHE. I remember the visit with which you honoured us here in consequence. You gained our confidence —you enjoy it still.

VALENTIN. I enjoy it very much, M. Nioche; it's my principal enjoyment.

NIOCHE. I esteem you for not having abused it.

VALENTIN. That certainly, in Paris, makes me one of the remarkable objects you just spoke of. [*Goes down, left. Re-enter Noémie and Newman, the latter without hat and stick.*] You should point me out to Mr. Newman.

NEWMAN. [*Left centre, to Nioche.*] Well, sir, they seem to me first-rate, and you may put me down for the lot! [*Takes out note-book, in which he makes note.*]

NOÉMIE. [*Right, aside to Nioche.*] Three thousand francs!

NIOCHE. [*Right centre, aside.*] My precious child! [*Aloud to Newman.*] Allow me, sir, to introduce you to our noble friend, the Count Valentin de Bellegarde. [*Goes up to centre.*]

NEWMAN. [*Shaking hands.*] Happy to make your acquaintance, Count Valentine.

VALENTIN. [*Left.*] I'm afraid you've lost *another* fortune.

NEWMAN. Perhaps you can help me

to get it back! [*They go together to fireplace.*]

NOÉMIE. Oh yes, he'll help you, if it's to play *me* a trick! But while you talk that over, papa and I'll look after lunch.

NIOCHE. I'll put on the cutlets. [*Exit centre.*]

NOÉMIE. [*Raising the lid of ottoman and taking out knifeboard and knives, Valentin assisting in the whole movement.*] We must help ourselves!

NEWMAN. [*Coming a little to centre.*] Can't *I* help you?

NOÉMIE. [*Graciously.*] You have already. But M. de Bellegarde has done nothing, so he can clean these knives. [*Exit centre.*]

VALENTIN. [*At chair right of table, right, cleaning a knife.*] Used you to do this when your life was so rough under the vault of heaven?

NEWMAN. [*Half seated on back of chair, left.*] I guess we didn't polish them! And they were sometimes of another kind.

VALENTIN. Bowie-knives—a foot long? Oh, I should like to hear your adventures.

NEWMAN. This is my principal adventure, sir—visiting your beautiful city.

VALENTIN. I'm glad you like our city, and I hope your adventure will turn out well. If I can help *that*, it will give me great pleasure.

NEWMAN. You're very kind! It *would* be rather a comfort to have a pleasant, bright companion to show me around. Someone who's really *acquainted!*

VALENTIN. You seem to me to have made a good beginning.

NEWMAN. Well, I've begun the study of French! I asked for a teacher at the hotel, and they trotted out the old gentleman there. He came in as quick as if he had been behind the door.

VALENTIN. It's where he was, I suppose!

NEWMAN. Well, he seems a regular patriarch—one of the old school.

VALENTIN. Oh, the old school—*I* could show you the old school!

NEWMAN. That's just what I want to see! [*Comes centre; foot on seat of chair left of table.*] I want to see something that will strike me with awe. Only, it's a pity—if I want to learn the language—that you seem all to speak such fine old English.

VALENTIN. I wouldn't, if I could help it; but I can't. My dear mother is English; she has always, from our infancy, addressed us in that tongue.

NEWMAN. Well, if I had had a dear mother—from my infancy—to address me in a tongue—

VALENTIN. You would have learnt it, you may be sure, if she had been anything like mine!

NEWMAN. [*Seated on chair, left, his head on the hand of which the arm is on back of chair.*] Well, I'm afraid I'm rather ignorant—I haven't a relation in the world.

VALENTIN. One certainly learns many things from one's relations.

NEWMAN. I haven't worked round to the *English* yet. I'll see them later.

VALENTIN. Oh, the English'll keep —they won't run away.

NEWMAN. I don't know as they'll keep *me*. I sailed straight for a *French* port—I wanted to see Paris worst of all.

VALENTIN. That shows you're a good American.

NEWMAN. Because the proverb says they come here when they die? Oh, I ain't dead yet; at least, I *think* I ain't—that's just what I want to see! *I* want to have a regular good time. I've been whistling "Yankee-Doodle" all my life, and now I should like to try another tune. [*Rising.*] I want a little change. [*Goes over to table, right.*] As you were so good as to say just now that you're ready to help me, do you know how you can do it? Help me to a little change! [*Sits left of table, right.*]

VALENTIN. [*Finishing his knives.*] I'm afraid I haven't got change for several millions; but I will do what I can for you. Will you have a cigarette? [*Offers case.*]

NEWMAN. Do you think we can smoke here?

VALENTIN. *I* always do. [*Lights up.*]

NEWMAN. Won't the young lady object? [*Takes cigarette and gets light from Valentin.*]

VALENTIN. My dear fellow, she smokes herself! But you can ask her. [*Re-enter Noémie, centre.*]

NOÉMIE. [*To Valentin.*] You *are* lazy! Is that the way you clean my knives? [*Taking the knives up, between the two men.*]

VALENTIN. They're as bright as your eyes and as sharp as your tongue!

NEWMAN. This gentleman assures me we may smoke; may I, therefore, offer you a cigarette—one of mine?

NOÉMIE. [*Smiling and taking the cigarette, which Newman lights for her.*] Anything of yours! [*Action with cigarette.*] The cutlets are almost done. [*Exit, centre, with knife-board.*]

VALENTIN. I might be jealous of you—if I didn't want to like you. I daresay you've got a bowie-knife somewhere?

NEWMAN. Yes, somewhere in a cupboard, in California. If you want to like me I'll show you how, as far as I know. But I don't see what you have to *envy* me—judging from the familiarity with which she treats you.

VALENTIN. Don't say familiarity—say contempt! I'm the cold dish on the sideboard; who wants it when there's a charming *entrée?*

NEWMAN. What do you mean by that foreign expression?

VALENTIN. I mean *you*—for instance!

NEWMAN. Oh, I shan't show *her* how to like me!

VALENTIN. Aren't you paying a good deal for pure aversion?

NEWMAN. A good deal? Why, I thought the whole thing so cheap!

[*Re-enter Noémie, and goes to the chest, left, where she pulls out a drawer.*]

NOÉMIE. There's a clean napkin somewhere for Mr. Newman.

VALENTIN. Ah, if she throws in a clean napkin!

NOÉMIE. The cutlets are almost done—papa is opening the wine. [*Exit, centre, with the napkin.*]

VALENTIN. A fresh bottle! My dear fellow, she *is* throwing you the handkerchief.

NEWMAN. You mean the napkin! Oh, that's no use! [*Snaps fingers, takes knee in hand.*] I want to get *married*.

VALENTIN. I don't see how you escape!

NEWMAN. Oh, the dangers are too small. I want a big one. I've got a sort of preconceived theory of the finest woman on earth.

VALENTIN. And to realise that theory you have left your own country,

where I'm told the women are so charming?

NEWMAN. So they are, but they've all come over here. I want a *first-class* woman, and I don't care what she is, so long as she's only perfect: beautiful, amiable, clever, good, the product of a long civilization and a great cultivation! I shall expect her to have everything the world can give—except a fortune. I don't care a fig for that—I've enough for two. [*Rises and goes above chair. Left hand out.*]

VALENTIN. [*Looking at Newman from head to foot with a smile of mingled impudence and urbanity.*] My dear sir, don't misunderstand me if I say you've enough for a dozen—I mean enough confidence. And also if I ask you what are your titles to the hand of so exalted a being?

NEWMAN. My titles? Oh, I'll show them to *her!* Meanwhile, I stick to my idea that she must be the rarest flower that grows. I've had a hard life, I've had a rough life, I've had rather an ugly life, and I've had, if I may say so, as regards the inner comfort of the thing, a very lonely life. I've come out all right, but it wasn't all roses and cakes. In that roaring big country of mine everything is big, even to the difficulties and disappointments, the temptations and defeats. But I have come out, thank God, without leaving behind too much of my youth, or too many of my illusions. I've had a long working-day, and [*Stretching himself.*] now I want a big treat. [*Goes to easel.*]

VALENTIN. Might I venture to intimate sympathetically that you yourself are a big treat?

NEWMAN. [*At easel.*] What else

have I toiled and struggled for all these years? I've succeeded, and now what am I to do with my success? To make it a big one, some woman I shall love and admire must be perched on the pile like a statue of marble on a pedestal of gold.

VALENTIN. A very becoming position for the woman you love and admire! [*Rises and comes to Newman.*] May I ask if you have yet come across the lady who would serve for your statue?

NEWMAN. No, hang it—have you?

VALENTIN. [*Putting his hand, with cigarette in it, on Newman's sleeve, as if to speak; then withdrawing it and smoking with hands in his pockets.*] I'll tell you when I know you better!

NEWMAN. Well, I mean to look round.

VALENTIN. Why shouldn't we look round together?

NEWMAN. Oh, I'm afraid the lady'll like *you* best!

VALENTIN. She'll like me for liking you.

NEWMAN. Then you *know* one of the kind I mean? [*Takes out notebook.*]

VALENTIN. Oh, thank heaven, I know some charming women.

NEWMAN. [*With his memoranda.*] Will you just give me their addresses?

VALENTIN. [*Laughing.*] I'll take you to see them! [*Goes to right while Newman goes to chair, left, and sits astride.*] Here comes M. Nioche to announce the feast.

[*Re-enter Nioche, with a bottle and a corkscrew.*]

NIOCHE. In a moment, M. le Comte! My daughter begs you will do her the honour to go and make her an omelette.

VALENTIN. Certainly, if I may break enough eggs! [*Exit Valentin, centre, going round up.*]

NIOCHE. [*Struggling unsuccessfully with the cork of his bottle.*] It's a great pleasure to me to observe, sir, that you have established relations of sociability with our distinguished visitor.

NEWMAN. Is he very distinguished?

NIOCHE. One of the purest relics of our old noblesse—brought up in all the traditions.

NEWMAN. The traditions? That's just what I want to see! But your daughter seems to treat him as the family cook.

NIOCHE. He's the only one we have, sir. The traditions of cookery have always been cherished by the French aristocracy. His family is illustrious and historical.

NEWMAN. That's just what I want to see! See here—ask him to show me his family.

NIOCHE. I should think he would do it, sir. [*Aside.*] That will go down in my bill: "Introduction to the Faubourg Saint-Germain, five thousand francs." [*Struggling still with his cork.*]

NEWMAN. I'm afraid it sticks. [*He throws away cigarette into fireplace.*] Let *me* have a try.

NIOCHE. It's not work for your honoured hands, sir.

NEWMAN. Oh, if you'd seen some of the work my honoured hands have done! Does our friend there *live* in Paris?

NIOCHE. In the Faubourg Saint-Germain, in the grand old family mansion. It dates from hundreds of years back.

NEWMAN. Hundreds of years? That's just what I want to see! Been there yourself?

NIOCHE. Respected sir, I've been everywhere, and I know everything!

NEWMAN. I see [*Sits on table, right.*] that's why they have you at the Grand Hotel.

NIOCHE. My profession is to answer questions, and it's to my honour that none has ever been asked me to which I haven't instantly produced a reply. For instance I can go straight through the great house of Bellegarde. [*Puts bottle down by fire.*]

NEWMAN. The great house of Bellegarde?

NIOCHE. The relations of my noble guest. It's true there are very few left today—that makes it easy. Only his mother, his elder brother, and his beautiful sister!

NEWMAN. [*Who has been looking at a book on table, right, here turns quickly, leg up on chair.*] Has he got a beautiful sister?

NIOCHE. As beautiful as an old picture—some delicate pastel—and a saint into the bargain.

NEWMAN. That's just what I want to see! [*Quickly taking out again his memorandum-book.*] Her name, please?

NIOCHE. [*Importantly.*] Madame la Comtesse Claire de Cintré.

NEWMAN. Damn it then—she's *married?*

NIOCHE. She was, sir; but that's all over. She's now an elegant young widow.

NEWMAN. [*Jotting down.*] That's just what I want to see! [*He sits in chair, right, and, with his legs stretched well out, takes notes as Nioche speaks.*]

NIOCHE. Her mother arranged for her, in her tender youth and terribly against her inclination, a marriage that was expected to be brilliant, but that turned out like a lamp that won't burn—all smoke and bad smell. Fortunately, after three or four years, the Comte de Cintré died—died of his disorders and vices. [*Lowering his voice and giving half a dozen backward nods of the head.*] I believe they were something awful, sir.

NEWMAN. Lord, how mean! How could she do it?

NIOCHE. *She* didn't do it, sir—her mother did it.

NEWMAN. And her father—had *he* nothing to say?

NIOCHE. I believe he had a great deal to say, but the old lady shut him up.

NEWMAN. Shut him up—in a lunatic asylum?

NIOCHE. No, no; in his own private room—in his own curtained bed. The poor gentleman turned sick and died there, just when he wanted most to be afoot—and his high and mighty wife could do what she liked.

NEWMAN. She must have curious likings. Was there no one to step right in?

NIOCHE. Two sons, sir, of whom we have the honour of receiving the younger, our accomplished guest; he was only a boy of twenty, and he was got out of the way—he was sent to England for a year. The present Marquis (the eldest son) is simply second fiddle to his mamma.

NEWMAN. Well, between them they seem to play pretty airs! [*Putting away note-book.*] I've seen rough things in my country, but I haven't met that style.

NIOCHE. Oh, they're very remarkable—in the Faubourg Saint-Germain!

NEWMAN. [*Rising.*] See here—I want to go there!

NIOCHE. [*Shrugging his shoulders and pressing his finger-tips together.*] It's very difficult to get the *entrée.* [*Takes up bottle.*]

NEWMAN. Yes; but with our friend who's making the omelette—

NIOCHE. Oh, sir, if you're agreeable to *him!* [*Looking at his watch.*] He takes an extraordinary time to make it.

NEWMAN. I'll get round him—I'll crack up his omelette.

NIOCHE. [*After another vain tussle with his cork.*] I'm ashamed, sir; but we're so dilapidated that my cork-screw doesn't act. We have an accommodating neighbor—I'll borrow a better one. [*Going to door, right.*]

NEWMAN. Just tell me first if she's all right now.

NIOCHE. [*Staring.*] Our accommodating neighbor? I'm afraid she's behind with her rent.

NEWMAN. No, no; I mean the widowed young Countess—in the grand old house.

NIOCHE. Oh, she just lives on there —in great seclusion. She has never married again.

NEWMAN. Do you suppose she *would?*

NIOCHE. [*Staring a moment, then aside.*] Ciel!—what could we get for that? [*Aloud.*] I'm afraid that's a question you must put to the lady herself.

NEWMAN. Then I've invented the first you can't answer.

NIOCHE. At the Grand Hotel, sir, it *isn't* matrimony!

NEWMAN. I've done with the Grand Hotel! I shall take a house. [*Goes down to chair, left, and sits.*]

NIOCHE. [*Eagerly.*] I shall be very glad to help you find one.

NEWMAN. Please look out, then, for a fine big, bright one, a regular old *palace.* Try in the Faubourg Saint-Germain.

NIOCHE. As near it as possible. [*Aside.*] Mercy on us, there *is* a chance! [*Aloud, glancing at the other room, of which the doors are closed.*] I can't fancy what they're doing there —an omelette's so quick!

NEWMAN. Ain't it rather slow when there are two? [*Rising and crossing to window and looking out; then in another tone.*] What do you suppose made her go back?

NIOCHE. My little daughter, sir?

NEWMAN. No, no—the young Countess. Why did she return to the old woman if the old woman sits on her?

NIOCHE. Those are the traditions, sir. She couldn't live alone, and when they can't live alone they have to live with each other—there's no one else grand enough.

NEWMAN. [*Aside.*] I wonder if *I* should be grand enough! [*Aloud.*] Why couldn't she live alone?

NIOCHE. I fear there was very little money, sir: there isn't much, in some of those stately homes.

NEWMAN. Won't that make it easier for you to scare me up one?

NIOCHE. [*Considering a moment.*] It will make them put on their price, sir!

NEWMAN. Oh, give them their price. [*Crosses to fireplace, below table.*] Wasn't he at least rich, then—the old scallawag?

NIOCHE. The Comtesse's husband?

Ah, that was Madame de Bellegarde's fond calculation. But he had run through everything—he left nothing but debts. That's how she was punished. [*Takes up hat from floor.*]

NEWMAN. I should like to punish her a little more!

[*Re-enter Valentin, centre.*]

VALENTIN. The omelette has fallen on its feet, and Monsieur Nioche is served!

NIOCHE. Served by a son of the crusaders! I'll be with you in a moment. [*Exit with his bottle, right.*]

NEWMAN. [*As he goes.*] Don't forget the house!

VALENTIN. Are you going to take a house?

NEWMAN. With the help of that good old man.

VALENTIN. That's capital news if it means that you're to stay with us.

NEWMAN. I'll stay as long as you make it attractive.

VALENTIN. I'll make it as attractive as I can. [*Sits on the table, back to audience.*] To me, here, you know, it's all rather stuffy—and you're so ventilating!

NEWMAN. [*Looking at him a moment and laying a hand on his shoulder.*] Why shouldn't we strike a bargain, you and I—to give and take? If I've got something you want, perhaps you've got something I want.

VALENTIN. The bargain would be very unequal—I've got so very little! But perhaps I can help you to find a house—or help your deputy there.

NEWMAN. Oh, don't go round with him—go round with me! You must come and see me. [*Puts out his hand.*]

VALENTIN. [*Taking Newman's hand.*] Delighted, and you must return my visit. [*Shakes Newman's hand*

and looks out of window.]

NEWMAN. [*Aside, going to left and round to back.*] Good—perhaps I shall see the old pastel. That treatment sticks in my crop! [*Aloud.*] Oh yes, you must show me Paris.

VALENTIN. [*At the window.*] If I do, I shall show you some queer things.

NEWMAN. [*Going to the easel.*] Oh, I want to see only the best.

VALENTIN. The best are the queerest! [*As Newman stands before Noémie's picture.*] Well, what do you think of that?

NEWMAN. I was thinking of something else. But isn't *this* a little queer?

VALENTIN. [*Going left and laughing.*] Decidedly, though it's not the best! [*Re-enter Noémie, briskly, centre.*] Mr. Newman can't take his eyes off that gem.

NOÉMIE. You may well say gem, since he has given it a golden setting! Everything is ready—please go in. I only want to put on a ribbon, in honour of my munificent patron. [*Exit, left. Valentin comes centre, right of Newman, above easel.*]

NEWMAN. I'm much obliged to her, but I wasn't thinking either of her gem or of its setting. I was thinking of something the old man has just told me. [*Going to Valentin.*]

VALENTIN. Oh, I know he deals in wonders.

NEWMAN. He told me about your home.

VALENTIN. Ah, that *is* a wonder! But you must see it for yourself.

NEWMAN. He says you keep it boarded up.

VALENTIN. That's just the reason for you to come in—it wants ventilation!

NEWMAN. Oh, I'll create a draught! [*Takes Valentin's arm and they go up. Exeunt, centre, Valentin and Newman. While they are turning away, re-enter Noémie, left, with a ribbon in her hand, and quickly closes the central doors behind them as soon as they have gone out.*]

NOÉMIE. [*Putting on her ribbon, using powder-puff and arranging her dress before the glass over mantel.*] I'm dreadfully nervous lest the Peer of the Realm should come back before the coast is clear; and yet I don't want to lose him—he's too good for that! He's better than the American, if the American is going to be whirled away by the Frenchman. Papa considers he's so clever to have introduced Mr. Newman to the Count—he can make him a charge for it. It would have been cleverer to keep him for ourselves—we could make him a charge for that too. Well, whatever happens, we'll make him a charge! [*Pulls down back of her dress.*] I don't know what he thought of me, shut up so long there with a young man distinguished for gallantry! The Count chattered and chattered; but I made him chatter to some profit, since I drew him, cunningly, on the subject of Lord Deepmere, who wants —the double-faced wretch!—to make up to the Count's grand sister. The Count, however, doesn't favour him as a brother-in-law. Well, it serves him right! I didn't let on to the Count that I know him and that *I* do favour him a little; that's just what I want to keep dark. It won't be easy, either, if he comes flaming in. [*Re-enter Lord Deepmere, slowly and cautiously, right, peeping in at the door.*] Here he is—flaming enough!

DEEPMERE. Charming creature, isn't my time up?

NOÉMIE. Do you call this an hour? How did you get in?

DEEPMERE. The door on the landing is gaping open.

NOÉMIE. [*Aside.*] Idiotic papa— foraging for his corkscrew! [*Aloud.*] Then it's just right for you to pass out again.

DEEPMERE. [*Coming in.*] Not till you confess that you tricked me just now, turning me out for fear of your stern parent. I heard the voice, I was sure I knew it, and it has come back to me who the person is. He's neither a parent nor stern.

NOÉMIE. [*Coming centre.*] I don't know what you're talking about, and I've no more time to give you.

DEEPMERE. That only clinches my conviction that Count Valentin is on the premises.

NOÉMIE. Count Valentin? How do you know that I know him? He can't have told you!

DEEPMERE. [*Struck.*] Then you know he knows me? He has told you that! [*Goes up to central doors.*]

NOÉMIE. [*Aside.*] Crac! [*Aloud, majestically.*] Considering the extreme shortness of our acquaintance you are wonderfully wise about my affairs.

DEEPMERE. [*Listening to sounds from back.*] Do you still pretend that's your father's voice? [*Goes toward the doors—movement from Noémie, barring the way.*]

NOÉMIE. You'll please to keep away from there—your suspicions are insulting. My father has a pupil—taking a lesson.

DEEPMERE. A lesson in sword-practice? Count Valentin may need it!

NOÉMIE. [*As if struck with this.*] Why on earth do you dislike him so?

DEEPMERE. Why on earth does he dislike me?

NOÉMIE. It's absurd—he doesn't.

DEEPMERE. Does he say so? Then you *have* seen him! Open the doors yourself, and prove to me that he's not there. I deny the existence of your preposterous pupil—produce him!

NOÉMIE. [*Embarrassed and impatient, going back, left, to her glass.*] I can't be bothered with you any longer. Good-bye!

DEEPMERE. [*Rather mock-sentimental.*] You choose to lose me then forever? Don't think that if I go now I shall ever come back! [*Goes to chair, right.*]

NOÉMIE. [*Aside.*] Perhaps he won't! It's a bore, because I like to keep my interests *separate*. [*Aloud, coming to centre.*] I don't care whether you come back or not; but I won't be falsely accused and I *will* produce the pupil. [*Goes back, opens partly one of the leaves of the door and looks in.*] Mr. Newman, will you be so good as to speak to me a moment? [*To Deepmere.*] Now you'll see your folly. [*Re-enter Newman, from back, Noémie closing the door behind him. Coming down, left centre, to Newman.*] Will you do me a great favour? Will you let this gentleman look at you?

NEWMAN. If it gives him any comfort. [*The two men stand, centre, face to face a moment.*] I hope he'll know me again.

DEEPMERE. I shall certainly know you again. I'm much obliged to you [*And to Noémie*] and to *you*. Good day! [*As if confessing his error, he goes quickly to the door on the right; but before leaving the room he stops and exchanges another look with Newman. Exit Lord Deepmere, right. Action from Noémie.*]

NEWMAN. [*As the Curtain falls.*] I *wasn't* what he wanted to see!

ACT SECOND

[*One of the smaller salons at the Hôtel de Bellegarde, arranged and lighted for a reception. Half way to each side, right and left, across the obtuse angles of the room, a double door opening into other and different lighted apartments. In the middle, against the wall, between the two open doors, a buffet, with a white cloth, with refreshments, &c. Enter Mrs. Bread, left upper entrance, followed by a Servant carrying a tray.*]

MRS. BREAD. [*Pointing to the buffet.*] Put the things there. I'll come back, as Madame la Marquise wishes, and serve the tea in case it's wanted. And please bring another lamp for *that* table. [*Indicating table, left.*] It always seems to me there never can be light *enough* in this dark house.

SERVANT. I'm sure it's blazing tonight—with twenty people at dinner and five hundred more expected! [*Exit, to come back presently and place a lamp on the table, left, indicated by Mrs. Bread, who is going off left, when enter Valentin, right.*]

VALENTIN. Wait a moment, my dear old friend—you're the very person I want. I never have a moment's talk with you now. [*They stand at back at buffet, she giving him a cup of tea.*]

MRS. BREAD. You do me great honour, to choose a moment when the house is full of grand people. [*Re-enter Servant with lamp, and places it left.*]

VALENTIN. There's no one in it so grand as you, Catty—especially when you want to snub a fellow!

MRS. BREAD. [*Looking at him affectionately.*] When did I ever snub the creature in the world I love best and have known the longest?

VALENTIN. Since the hour I was born, stern superintendent of my childhood!

MRS. BREAD. And since the hour your sweet sister was born—Heaven help her, poor lady!

VALENTIN. Heaven *is* helping her, by one of its messengers; it looks very much like it.

MRS. BREAD. Do you mean that your showy American friend is a messenger from Heaven?

VALENTIN. I mean, my dear Catty, that the more I've seen of Mr. Christopher Newman, the more I've liked him, and that I want you to like him as I do. [*Brings her down stage.*]

MRS. BREAD. You want *me*, my dear child? You mean you want the Countess! I'll confide to you that I think she's ready to oblige you.

VALENTIN. Is she ready to oblige *him?*—that's the question.

MRS. BREAD. Let him try—let him try. She doesn't turn her back.

VALENTIN. [*Walking about while Mrs. Bread arranges tables.*] She would be perverse if she did, for from the hour I brought him here, five weeks ago, he seemed to fling open the windows of this temple of staleness and stagnation—he laid the irrepressible ghost.

MRS. BREAD. [*Looking round.*] Hush!—don't talk of the ghost!

VALENTIN. There's nobody to hear. [*He forces her to sit right of table, and places himself on arm of her chair.*] The men are still smoking, and the ladies, in the drawing-room, are counting the cost of each other's gowns.

MRS. BREAD. And trying to guess what your mother means this unparalleled entertainment for.

VALENTIN. What can she mean it for but as a sign to Mr. Newman that, like a good American, he may go ahead? She has beaten the drum for our friends and our enemies, as if to say to him: "There they are! Ain't they grand? You may enter the magic circle!"

MRS. BREAD. But what does she say to *them?*

VALENTIN. Only three words: "He has ever so many millions!"

MRS. BREAD. And what does she say to Lord Deepmere?

VALENTIN. There has been no need to say anything—he has gone back to England.

MRS. BREAD. But won't he turn up again?

VALENTIN. A day after the fair.

MRS. BREAD. He won't like being too late, for I've an idea he has received a bit of encouragement.

VALENTIN. From the heads of the family? [*Rises.*] Oh, they've been awfully civil, and if they've hung back a little, it's only because the figure of his income, though high, isn't quite up to their standard. Everything's low compared to *that!*

MRS. BREAD. [*Rising.*] So that if they throw him over now—?

VALENTIN. He'll have a perfect right not to enjoy it!

MRS. BREAD. Oh, if my lady and the

Marquis have given him their word—

VALENTIN. Trust them to take it back!

MRS. BREAD. Gracious, I'm glad he's gone—and I oughtn't to give you a chance to utter such horrors! [*Exit Mrs. Bread, left.*]

VALENTIN. [*Looking after her.*] Poor old Catty, you have helped us before [*Enter Christopher Newman.*], you shall help us again.

NEWMAN. [*Laying his hand on Valentin's shoulder.*] You're not just what I want to see; but you're the next best thing. [*Takes Valentin's arm and brings him over to right.*]

VALENTIN. To appreciate that tribute, I must know whom you *are* looking for.

NEWMAN. [*With his back to fireplace.*] For whom but Madame de Cintré? I want particularly to speak to her. I could scarcely break away from some of your folks.

VALENTIN. [*Seated on the ottoman.*] My dear fellow, you're a great success; but you don't know—you can never know—what a new departure, for *us,* this is to-night!

NEWMAN. Oh, I guess I've guessed!

VALENTIN. You're in a situation in which your national faculty will find plenty of application. But don't shout till you're out of the wood.

NEWMAN. Why ain't I out of it, if Madame de Cintré thinks me a *gentle* savage, as you've told me she does?

VALENTIN. What I've told you is that you've given a good turn to her life.

NEWMAN. Well, one good turn deserves another! [*Crosses up right above ottoman, and over to left centre.*] That's what I want to remind her of, if I can find her, in this laby-

rinth of rooms. [*Going to door on right, as if to continue his search.*]

VALENTIN. [*Who has risen, stops him, centre, at back.*] Stay here, out of the labyrinth. I want to speak to Claire myself, and I'll bring her this way.

NEWMAN. Oh, Count, if you want to speak to her, speak to her of *me!*

VALENTIN. I never do anything else! [*Exit Valentin, right, and at the same moment enter, by the other door, left, Lord Deepmere.*]

NEWMAN. [*Aside.*] Hallo! Is *he* one of the guests?

DEEPMERE. [*Who has stopped short on seeing Newman, so that the two men stand a moment face to face.*] Excuse my recognising you—we met in such a very odd way.

NEWMAN. I should scarcely forget your *not* recognising me, considering that on that occasion I was produced expressly for your benefit.

DEEPMERE. Let me thank you again!

NEWMAN. Having conjured me up, I'm afraid you must bear with me. [*Comes down and sits on ottoman.*] I don't bite!

DEEPMERE. I certainly shall not shirk any of the consequences of my rashness. [*Leaning on chair, right of table.*] I should have been sooner in a position to learn what they may be, if I had not been called over to England for a couple of months. I came back only a few hours ago.

NEWMAN. Let me congratulate you on returning to so pleasant a place— and on having lost so little time in finding out the pleasantest corner in it.

DEEPMERE. My dear sir, I found out the Hôtel de Bellegarde long before I found out—some other things!

NEWMAN. [*Good-humouredly.*] Oh, well, if you're an old friend, we're all jolly old friends together.

[*Re-enter Valentin, right, hearing the last words.*]

VALENTIN. [*Centre, aside.*] Deepmere back? Oh, bother! [*Aloud.*] Ah, you're jolly old friends?

NEWMAN. Oh yes, that goes away back, but I believe I didn't mention it at the time.

VALENTIN. Good evening, *milord:* welcome again to Paris. [*To Newman.*] Do you know the little blue room? My sister's there, and I daresay she'll be free to see you.

NEWMAN. [*Jumping up.*] I'll free her, if she ain't! [*Exit Newman, right centre.*]

DEEPMERE. [*To Valentin.*] Madame de Cintré is just the person I was hoping to come across.

VALENTIN. [*Stopping him.*] Please don't go to her now—I'm sure she's engaged.

DEEPMERE. [*Aside.*] Engaged—with *that* customer? [*Aloud.*] I've seen your mother and your brother, but I had no idea I was to fall on such a brilliant *fête.* I hope I'm not indiscreet if I inquire if there's any extraordinary reason—

VALENTIN. For our lighting so many candles? Yes, at last we have something to show. [*Goes to fireplace and stands with his back to Deepmere, who is at the ottoman, kneeling on it.*]

DEEPMERE. Do you mean a very surprising guest?

VALENTIN. Mr. Newman *is* surprising—to us scions of effete aristocracies!

DEEPMERE. I congratulate you on his want of resemblance to *other* gentlemen, when he's locked up with young ladies you're interested in!

VALENTIN. [*Turning round.*] Locked up—with young ladies? [*Staring.*] Bless my soul, was it *you* that day, when we were at breakfast with a charming person who suddenly called him out?

DEEPMERE. [*Staring in turn.*] Were *you* at breakfast too? [*Rises and goes left centre.*] Then I *was* humbugged!

VALENTIN. [*Moving to centre.*] Did you think Mr. Newman was alone with her?

DEEPMERE. I thought *you* were alone with her! That was why I insisted on seeing the individual—her father's "pupil."

VALENTIN. It was very good of you to insist!

DEEPMERE. I believed *you* were the pupil; and indeed, among you, you seem to form a promising little class!

VALENTIN. I don't recognise your warrant for interrupting our lesson.

DEEPMERE. My warrant, Monsieur de Bellegarde, is simply that, wherever I find you, you stand, and you have the evident intention of standing, in my way! [*Movement.*]

VALENTIN. [*Seeing Mme. de Cintré, left.*] See, after all, then, how little I succeed, and how fortune *favours* you! [*Enter Madame de Cintré, right; greets Lord Deepmere, and moves to centre. To Mme. de Cintré.*] I just told a friend of ours that you were in the blue room. I hope he hasn't missed you.

CLAIRE. Do you mean Mr. Newman? I think he never misses anything. He must have been waylaid and captured by lovely ladies—he's having immense success.

VALENTIN. He's the success of the evening.

DEEPMERE. To say that to *you*, Madam—!

CLAIRE. Oh, I have my eye on a very different sort of triumph. I came this way, by my mother's request, to make sure there are enough teacups and spoons. [*Goes to table, centre, or buffet.*]

DEEPMERE. Let me help you count them. There are about five hundred!

VALENTIN. Be ready, then. I'll send you all the thirsty people. [*Exit Valentin.*]

DEEPMERE. [*At back, with Mme. de Cintré.*] Your brother knows what I want, and he hopes to interfere with it. So before any one comes, let me tell you frankly what I have returned to Paris for.

CLAIRE. [*Abstractedly.*] Have you been away? [*Counting teaspoons.*]

DEEPMERE. [*Looking at her a moment.*] Haven't you observed it? I went back to England, for a few weeks, in consequence of a conversation I had with your mother. I promised her I would make a thorough examination of the state of my property, with which Madame de Bellegarde was unfortunately but half satisfied. She wanted me to dot my *i's.*

CLAIRE. What had my mother to do with it? [*Crosses to table, left.*]

DEEPMERE. What is there, in this house, that your mother has not to do with?

CLAIRE. [*Crossing to top of card-table, left.*] Dear Lord Deepmere, your property is not in this house.

DEEPMERE. The thing I value most in the world is! There are, however, other things—many other things—in England. I have spent more than a month going into everything, riding over everything, turning everything inside out. I've had up all my people, and I've kicked out more than half of them. Madame de Bellegarde ought to be satisfied with *that!*

CLAIRE. [*Turning over cards.*] Poor people, I'm sorry for them.

DEEPMERE. It serves them right. They were cheating me.

CLAIRE. [*Putting down cards going down left.*] Ah, take care you're not worse cheated!

DEEPMERE. [*Following her.*] What do you mean?

CLAIRE. [*Moving from him.*] I mean that what you tell me is very interesting, but that I have no desire whatever to elicit a report from you. [*Waltz music, pianissimo, off right; musicians on stage.*]

DEEPMERE. Oh, but listen, and see if you don't like my report! [*His hand is on the back of a chair; he moves it a little to one side.*] Everything is now in the best hands—every mortgage is paid off. I don't want to swagger, but I've got half a dozen places. I don't want to bore you, but I'll tell you my income like a shot, if you care to hear it.

CLAIRE. [*Moving up centre, Deepmere following her.*] I congratulate you with all my heart on your prosperity, but I can't aspire to contribute to it.

DEEPMERE. [*Pleading; trying to take her hands.*] You won't care for me—never, never?

CLAIRE. It's utterly impossible!

DEEPMERE. And will you give me no reason?

CLAIRE. I thank you humbly. Please excuse me and let me leave you.

[*Re-enter Newman, right, as Mme. de Cintré is turning quickly away. They meet and talk.*]

NEWMAN. You're just what I wanted to see!

DEEPMERE. [*Aside.*] Can that barbarian be her reason? It's inconceivable! The old lady and her prig of an elder son shall tell me! [*Exit Lord Deepmere, left.*]

CLAIRE. Have you come for a cup of tea?

NEWMAN. No, I've come for something much stronger! The Count told me you were here, and it's a joy to be face to face with you at last. [*Claire goes to bottom of ottoman.*] It's as if there had been a conspiracy to baffle me to-night—we have been kept asunder from the moment I arrived.

CLAIRE. [*Seating herself on the ottoman.*] It's your universal success that has kept us asunder.

NEWMAN. [*With his knee on the ottoman.*] It will be time to call my success universal when you have given me the supreme proof of it. [*Claire rising, he makes her sink down again.*] Let me talk to you about that— quietly, tenderly, reasonably—on your own terms. Listen to me, trust me— I'll check you through! I know you've seen me, as yet, comparatively little —so little that there may even be, to your mind, a kind of failure of respect, or at least of ceremony, in my breaking out this way. That's my misfortune; for I could almost have done so the first time I saw you. The fact is, there was no first time. I had seen you before—I had seen you always, in imagination, in secret ambitions; you seemed an old friend! I felt like that dear old boy Columbus (you know I'm named after him: it's a good omen!) when the ascertained fact bore out his general conclusions and he sighted the New World. Like him

I had exercised our national genius (he must have bequeathed it to us!) —I had *calculated*. [*Stands.*]

CLAIRE. [*Laughing.*] Your national genius is very great!

NEWMAN. Of course it is. Otherwise I'm perfectly aware, I shouldn't stand where I do. I had, like Columbus, a theory that *my* new world was here [*Bends over Claire; she rises.*]; so that as soon as you rose, pale and lovely, above my horizon, I said to myself: "Old man, I told you so!" You were the very woman I had figured out— except that you were a far bigger result. [*Movement from Claire.*] You hold your head just as that tantalising creature has always held **hers**. You say just the things that I have listened to on *her* lips. [*Claire moves to centre.*] You walk about the room as I've seen *her* walk. [*She stops.*] You stop as I have seen *her* stop—you wear exactly the garments I have seen *her* wear! In short, you come up to the mark, and [*Taking her hand.*] I tell you, my mark was high!

CLAIRE. [*Smiling.*] I'm glad I come up to the mark!

NEWMAN. I don't *express* it well; but you know what I mean.

CLAIRE. Not a bit, I assure you, when you talk of your secret ambitions. What ambition can *I* possibly gratify?

NEWMAN. Every one I possess—the wildest I ever entertained. No doubt you'll have to renounce your own; but I'll make that up to you.

CLAIRE. I haven't an ambition left [*Takes away her hand and seats herself by table, left.*]—not the dimmest ghost of one—unless it be to pass *un*noticed!

NEWMAN. [*Laughing.*] Well, if it

will help my case to promise it, I'll lock you up in my safe—I'll keep you back awhile. There's nothing to keep back about *me*, you know—the whole thing can come out. I'm all here, and wherever I am, I'm all there! I've no hidden vices nor nasty tricks. I'm kind [*His hand on her left shoulder.*]—kind—[*Takes her hand.*]—kind. [*Carries her hand to his breast.*]

CLAIRE. [*Slowly, after remaining silent a moment.*] It's strange, Mr. Newman—you don't know how strange it is!

NEWMAN. That I should be in love with you? It would be a queer show if I wasn't!

CLAIRE. [*Rising.*] I don't mean that —I mean that I should trust you as I do.

NEWMAN. You *do* trust me? [*Putting both hands out—taking both her hands.*] That's just what I wanted to see!

CLAIRE. [*Going to fireplace.*] There are not many people I trust.

NEWMAN. You have had unhappy days—you have had unhappy years; I know that! But what on earth have you to do with them now? Turn your back on them forever!

CLAIRE. [*With her head on the mantel-shelf.*] I'm *afraid* of happiness —that's what I trust least.

NEWMAN. It will return you good for evil! Is it the cruel failure that met you on the very threshold of life that has made you sceptical?—the fact that, ten years ago, you put your spare cash into a concern that turned out a swindle?

CLAIRE. I was only seventeen. But let that horrible time alone!

NEWMAN. I speak of it only to remind you that it's a reason the more

for your having a better time now. The joys we've missed in youth are like back numbers and lost umbrellas; we mustn't spend the rest of life wondering where they are! [*The music ceases. Claire turns.*] Ah, Claire! [*Movement to embrace her.*]

CLAIRE. [*Stopping him with both hands up.*] Don't ask me why I say it, but please simply believe that I can't listen to you further till you have spoken to those whom I make it my law not to defy. [*Goes up, centre.*]

NEWMAN. [*At the fireplace.*] Do you mean Madame de Bellegarde and the Marquis?

CLAIRE. [*At the ottoman, her hands upon it.*] They are the heads of the family. Speak to *them* first—obtain *their* sanction.

NEWMAN. [*Following her up.*] I'll do anything in life to please you or to win you. [*With his hands on hers, on the ottoman.*] But doesn't it strike you that you and I together make the only "family" we need think of? You have only to say a word to become the head of mine!

CLAIRE. You must leave me my superstitions—they are all I have!

NEWMAN. *All?*—no sympathy with mine?

CLAIRE. [*At the table, left.*] That too would be a superstition!

NEWMAN. Forgive my profanity, but has your family got *two* heads—like some curious animal in a sideshow?

CLAIRE. [*Abruptly, passionately.*] Yes—to make up for having no heart! [*Crosses to ottoman.*]

NEWMAN. You're more profane than I! Isn't this wonderful occasion in it-self a practical sanction?

CLAIRE. [*Going round ottoman up*

to right centre.] I advise you to get something more explicit.

NEWMAN. All right—I'll go and get it now.

CLAIRE. Don't do that—those crowded rooms are not the place to broach the subject. Are you in a great hurry?

NEWMAN. Did you ever see an American who wasn't?

CLAIRE. [*Going right.*] I'll find Urbain—I'll tell him that he'll oblige me by letting you speak to him.

NEWMAN. Oblige *you?* [*Claire turns and smiles.*] Thank you for that! [*Exit Claire, right. At fireplace.*] But how in creation comes it that the thought of her family scares her like a bad dream? What have they done to make her tread the world on tiptoe, as if she were passing and repassing a death-chamber? [*Re-enter Mrs. Bread, left. Seeing her.*] I wonder if I could get it out of this deep old lady!

MRS. BREAD. [*Who has gone straight to the buffet, accompanied by the same Footman who has come in with her before and who again carries a tray, to take cream and sugar from her, with which he immediately goes off.*] May I take the liberty of offering you a cup of tea, sir?

NEWMAN. I'll have one with pleasure. [*Mrs. Bread brings him a cup of tea, and he continues, sociably.*] Won't you take one yourself?

MRS. BREAD. [*Curtseying.*] Thank you, sir—not here!

NEWMAN. I'm so glad you speak English—it rests my muscles.

MRS. BREAD. I don't speak anything else. I'm a plain Wiltshire woman, sir.

NEWMAN. [*Laughing.*] Oh, plain. I've seen plainer! [*Drinking his tea, which he keeps in his hand during*

this dialogue.] And what do you think of Paris?

MRS. BREAD. Oh I don't think of Paris, sir. I've been here more than forty years. I came over with Lady Emmeline. When others began to come—a year or two after—I was promoted to the supervision of the nurseries. I brought up the young people.

NEWMAN. The children? I wish you'd bring up mine!

MRS. BREAD. [*Staring.*] Yours, sir?

NEWMAN. I'll tell you later what I mean—you're such a venerable domestic presence!

MRS. BREAD. Oh, I keep my eye on most things, sir.

NEWMAN. I guess you've kept it on me, then!

MRS. BREAD. I've taken the liberty of observing you, sir.

NEWMAN. Well, I hope you're on my side. [*Giving back his cup.*]

MRS. BREAD. [*Taking cup.*] I think we're all on your side, sir. Even the Marquis must be—he's not often on any one's side!—for here he comes, apparently looking for you. He mustn't find me mixing with the company! [*Exit hastily, left, with teacup, while the Marquis comes in at the other door, right, crossing to left and bowing slightly to Newman.*]

MARQUIS. As my sister tells me that you do me the honour to desire some conversation with me, we had better remain on this spot. I have mentioned the circumstance to my mother, who must have the predominant voice in our conference. She will join us here in a moment.

NEWMAN. My time is *all* at your service; but a moment is enough for what I have to say. [*Seats himself on ottoman.*] I have made a proposal of marriage to Madame de Cintré, and Madame de Cintré has told me she can give me no reply till I have received from your mother and yourself a declaration that won't put a spoke in our wheel. Hadn't we better get ahead? Hadn't you better *give* me that declaration on the spot? Now that you've *seen* my scheme, the great hospitality you have already shown me—especially this evening—leads me to hope *very* much, you'll put down your name.

MARQUIS. Such a name as ours is a good deal to put down! Of course I must mention that the idea that my sister should receive the attentions of a gentleman in trade has been something of a novelty.

NEWMAN. My dear sir, I'm no *longer* in trade. If I were I shouldn't be fooling round here!

MARQUIS. But isn't the origin of your—a—fortune commercial, industrial?

NEWMAN. Isn't the origin of all fortunes commercial, industrial? I have heard of people's losing money in all sorts of ways, but there's only one in which I ever heard of their making it.

MARQUIS. [*Smiling.*] I don't know —we have never made any.

NEWMAN. [*Rising, and with humorous eagerness.*] Do you want to? I'll put you into any damned thing you like!

MARQUIS. You're most refreshing. It may be that the time has come when we should make some judicious concession to the age.

[*Re-enter Valentin, right.*]

VALENTIN. What's that? My brother's making a judicious concession?

That's a great historical event! My mother follows me, but she bids me inform you that nothing is to be concluded till she is on the field.

NEWMAN. Oh, I guess the battle's won!

VALENTIN. It can only be won according to the rules. You'll see them in a moment. [*Enter Mme. de Bellegarde, right, whom the Marquis rises to meet, offering her an armchair, left, in which she sits.*] Here they are: you can see they're pretty straight! [*Goes round to fireplace.*]

NEWMAN. [*Right centre.*] Dear Madam, we just received your commands not to settle anything till you should be able to attend. But I guess we've got ahead of you, and that everything *is* settled. Ain't it, Marquis?

MARQUIS. [*Seating himself.*] My mother has the predominant voice.

MME. DE BELLEGARDE. [*To Marquis.*] Have you arranged with Mr. Newman that his man of business shall meet *our* man of business?

NEWMAN. Why, Marquise, what do you mean? I'm my *own* man of business.

MME. DE BELLEGARDE. Then our solicitor will wait upon you.

NEWMAN. Your solicitor? What has he got to do with it?

VALENTIN. [*With his back to the fire.*] Everything, my candid Californian! I see you'll never divine, unless I drop it gently into your ear, that they want to know what you're prepared to *do.*

NEWMAN. [*Staring.*] To "do"?

VALENTIN. For your portionless bride, as I may say!

NEWMAN. Why, I'm prepared to— *worship* her!

MME. DE BELLEGARDE. [*Smiling coldly.*] There are many ways of worshipping. We should be glad if, without prejudice to the others, you could make one of them consist of an adequate settlement.

NEWMAN. Do you mean put her into possession of my pile? With all my heart: as I told the Count, a month ago, she shall perch on top of it!

MME. DE BELLEGARDE. Excuse me if I remind you that we are without any definite information as to what your "pile" consists of.

NEWMAN. Why, of the principal precious metals, and a lot of other things. Come round and see me, and I'll tell you all about it!

MARQUIS. We shall have the honour of paying you a visit.

NEWMAN. That's all right. [*Seated on ottoman.*] When will you come?

MME. DE BELLEGARDE. The sooner the better—we'll come to-morrow.

NEWMAN. Won't you come round to lunch? I'll show you my new place. I've left that hotel—I've taken a big house.

MME. DE BELLEGARDE. A big house?

NEWMAN. A big house, with a big garden. There's another garden, too, in the rear of it, that I've made arrangements to add on.

MARQUIS. You'll have a great territory.

NEWMAN. Certainly I shall: a kind of virgin forest—the finest, greenest, airiest thing in Paris, with lots of margin and elbow-room.

MME. DE BELLEGARDE. Your margin must remind you of California.

NEWMAN. That's just why I bought it!

MARQUIS. You've *bought* it?

NEWMAN. For Madame de Cintré!

VALENTIN. [*Aside.*] They thought he had only hired it. Oh, he'll do!

NEWMAN. I'm having the whole place rearranged and furnished and decorated. You must tell me, and above all Madame de Cintré must tell me, how I had better have it fixed.

MME. DE BELLEGARDE. My daughter will accompany us.

NEWMAN. [*Turning to Valentin.*] That's just what I wanted to see! I'm fixing up the gardens too, and—just for the first ideas, in the whole thing—some clever *artistic* friends are helping me.

VALENTIN. [*Startled, aside.*] Artistic friends? Papa Nioche and Noémie, I'll be hanged!

NEWMAN. [*To Valentin.*] Of course you'll come too?

VALENTIN. Rather, my dear boy. [*Aside.*] Fancy Noémie let loose in California! I must go, if only to get her out of the way!

MME. DE BELLEGARDE. [*To Newman.*] You may expect us early.

VALENTIN. The early bird takes the worm!

MME. DE BELLEGARDE. [*To Valentin.*] You're incorrigibly profane. Go away this moment and tell your sister to come to me here. [*Exit Valentin, right, while Mme. de Bellegarde continues, to Newman.*] It's only fair I should warn you that I'm very proud —that I hold my head very high. Don't flatter yourself that my daughter isn't proud. The form is different, but the feeling is the same. Even Valentin is proud, if you touch the right spot —or the wrong one. Urbain, there, is proud; that you can see for yourself.

NEWMAN. [*Looking at the Marquis.*] Oh yes, I see! Well, put your pride in keeping your word to me, and you may all be a set of little Lucifers!

MARQUIS. [*Rising.*] Keep yours to *us*, sir.

[*Re-enter Mme. de Cintré, right, and comes right centre.*]

NEWMAN. [*Rising.*] *My* word is to Madame de Cintré. I'll repeat it to her before you.

CLAIRE. [*To Mme. de Bellegarde.*] Valentin tells me you want me, mother.

MME. DE BELLEGARDE. Yes, so that we may hear what Mr. Newman promises.

NEWMAN. [*Taking Mme. de Cintré's hand.*] To make you as rich as I possibly can, and to make you far happier than you're rich. [*Mme. de Bellegarde rises; she and the Marquis go up left centre.*]

CLAIRE. [*After she has held his hand and looked at him gravely and in silence.*] What a pity Valentin couldn't have come back with me to hear you say that!

NEWMAN. What's the matter with him?

CLAIRE. Lord Deepmere pounced on him and walked him away.

MME. DE BELLEGARDE. Poor Lord Deepmere!

MARQUIS. He's *very* unreasonable! [*Exeunt, left, Marquis and Mme. de Bellegarde.*]

NEWMAN. [*Jubilant.*] It's all right—they've caught on! [*Going round the ottoman, he seats himself on it with Claire.*] They're coming to see me tomorrow, to arrange some technicalities.

CLAIRE. Don't speak to me of your technicalities—I care nothing about them.

NEWMAN. They're not *mine*—

they're *theirs!* Won't you give me a foretaste of happiness by coming too?

CLAIRE. I should like to see your house. I'll look at that.

NEWMAN. That ain't mine either—it's already yours.

CLAIRE. Shall you, then, insist on our living in Paris?

NEWMAN. Oh, yes—*insisting* will be quite in my line! The world's all before us—we'll go where you like.

CLAIRE. What then, will you do with the house?

NEWMAN. We'll give it to Valentine.

CLAIRE. I should like to see your great country.

NEWMAN. The land of gold—the blue Pacific? We'll start as soon as we're married.

CLAIRE. You take my breath away.

NEWMAN. Didn't you take mine—the first time I ever saw you?

CLAIRE. You live too fast.

NEWMAN. It's you that make me—I've had to catch up! But after we're once off we shall go slower—to make it last!

CLAIRE. [*As if with vague uneasiness.*] Do you think it *will* last?

NEWMAN. Will the fish last in the sea?—will the stars last in the sky? Don't you feel safe?

CLAIRE. I *shall* [*Hesitating a moment and smiling dimly.*] in the blue Pacific!

NEWMAN. [*Laughing.*] You speak as if you were going to the bottom! [*With both her hands in his, drawing her closer.*] My own darling—we're going to the top!

CLAIRE. [*Closing her eyes an instant.*] You'll make me dizzy!

NEWMAN. You can be as dizzy as you like, with *my* arm round you! We're going up into the light and the sweet, high air, into the fields of flowers and the great places of love, where we shall look down with pity at the desert in which we didn't know each other.

CLAIRE. Ah, we're out of *that*—we *do* know each other!

NEWMAN. We shall have more to learn, but the more we do learn the more we shall like it. I shall find new things and bigger things to do, but it will be all for *you* I shall do them!

CLAIRE. You've done the newest— and [*Smiling.*] I think I may say the biggest!—in winning your victory to-night.

NEWMAN. Oh, I sha'n't rest on my laurels—there are always new worlds to conquer. We'll explore them and annex them together, and find at every turn some use that we can *be*, some good that we can *do*. The good that *you'll* do, dearest—

CLAIRE. [*Longingly, as he pauses from the fulness of his emotion.*] Ah! if you'll show me *that!*

NEWMAN. [*With ardent responsiveness.*] I'll show it to the whole *earth!*

CLAIRE. [*Laying her hand upon his, with a deliberate movement of his* (*her?*) *own, the only one of this particular kind that she makes during the play.*] I'll follow you, I'll help you, I'll cherish you. But [*Withdrawing her hand, and in another tone, half melancholy, half gay.*] I may mention to you that, when I used to think, as a girl, of what I would do if I were to marry freely and by my own choice, I thought of a man different from you.

NEWMAN. That's nothing against me—your taste wasn't formed.

CLAIRE. Have *you* formed it?

NEWMAN. [*Looking at her a moment.*] Do you know there's some-

thing I *should* like to form? It's formed with the lips!

CLAIRE. [*Rising.*] Not now—not here!

NEWMAN. [*Rising.*] To-morrow, then, when you *come?*

CLAIRE. [*Smiling.*] In that case I'm not so sure I shall come!

NEWMAN. [*Delighted with her.*] You *are* what I wanted to see! [*Kisses her hand.*]

[*Re-enter Valentin, right, and goes slowly left at once.*]

VALENTIN. If you've got so far as that, you had better go a little further! Just walk through the rooms together —show yourselves all over the place.

NEWMAN. [*Humourously, to Claire.*] Didn't you tell me awhile ago that you wanted to pass unnoticed?

CLAIRE. [*Proudly.*] What I want is to show *you!*

VALENTIN. You've no time to lose, then.

[*Re-enter Mrs. Bread, left.*]

NEWMAN. We'll begin with Mrs. Bread. Mrs. Bread, give us your blessing.

MRS. BREAD. [*To Mme. de Cintré, who comes to her and kisses her.*] I gave you them all, my sweet lady, when you needed them more! [*Mme. de Cintré remains with her during the next words spoken by Newman and Valentin.*]

NEWMAN. [*At back of armchair.*] What's the hitch?

VALENTIN. It will be a good precaution against hitches for you to go and bid everyone good night and tell as many people as you can. [*Newman goes up.*]

NEWMAN. [*To Mme. de Cintré.*] Please accept my arm. I'll tell every man and woman in the house. [*Ma-*

zurka music, pianissimo, off right. Mme. de Cintré takes his arm. Exeunt Newman and Mme. de Cintré, right.]

MRS. BREAD. [*Coming down and looking a moment at Valentin, who has thrown himself into armchair.*] I don't like my boy's looks. You're flushed and excited.

VALENTIN. Give me something cool to drink—I'm all right!

MRS. BREAD. A little iced lemonade, made by my own hands. [*She goes to the buffet, and comes back with a glass, Valentin meanwhile sitting in thought.*]

VALENTIN. [*After he has drunk the lemonade and given her back the glass.*] Dear old Catty, keep the heads of the family—or rather its feet—in the straight and narrow path!

MRS. BREAD. There's something you don't tell me.

VALENTIN. It's merely that our noble friend Deepmere is raging over the place like a young vindictive archangel, with a crush hat and a white waistcoat; he has cornered them there and is giving them a piece of his mind. But don't let me detain you— you must be wanted in the cloakroom.

MRS. BREAD. [*Looking round her.*] It doesn't matter; almost everyone's gone.

VALENTIN. Go and blow out the candles then.

MRS. BREAD. I'm afraid to leave you. Something's in the air—you're waiting for Lord Deepmere. Don't, don't have words with him. [*Exit, left.*]

VALENTIN. Not a word too much!

[*Re-enter Lord Deepmere, right.*]

DEEPMERE. You referred me to the responsible parties, and I have seen the responsible parties. You told me I should find you here—

VALENTIN. And you find me here!

DEEPMERE. I congratulate myself, because it gives me an opportunity to tell you that I have had the satisfaction of convicting Madame de Bellegarde and your brother of gross and shameless duplicity. They've deceived me, they've outraged me, and I think they won't soon forget the five minutes I've just had the honour of spending with them!

VALENTIN. [*Rising.*] I certainly sha'n't, *milord!*

DEEPMERE. But I've not done with them yet—I've still my reparation to demand.

VALENTIN. [*After an instant.*] May I consider that you demand it of *me?*

DEEPMERE. My complaint's of your brother—it's from *him* the apology should come.

VALENTIN. I'm afraid we don't make apologies. But we embrace each other's quarrels.

DEEPMERE. Oh, the Marquis doesn't quarrel—he gets out of the way!

VALENTIN. You see *I* don't, *milord*.

DEEPMERE. Oh, I don't accuse *you* of double dealing! If you've tried to trip me up from the first, you've done it frankly—you've done it consistently, you've done it elsewhere as well as here!

VALENTIN. The less you say about elsewhere the better. *Here* will do.

DEEPMERE. [*After a moment.*] It will do very well, then—to choose another place.

VALENTIN. A couple of our friends will do it for us. Mine will be instantly ready to meet any gentlemen you may designate.

DEEPMERE. The earlier the better. I shall go straight home. Good night.

VALENTIN. [*Right centre.*] Good

night! [*As Lord Deepmere is going at back to left.*] I may just mention the circumstance that it would be a convenience to me not to go far.

DEEPMERE. The nearer the better.

VALENTIN. There are quiet places in Paris—with a little ingenuity.

DEEPMERE. The quieter the better. Any friends of yours will be sure to be ingenious. Good night.

VALENTIN. Good night. [*They formally bow to each other. Exit Lord Deepmere, left, after which Valentin, alone, remains a moment in thought.*] No, no; I mustn't be out of it. [*Goes to the fireplace.*] Who was it was talking of a big disused garden—a tract of country in the midst of old Louis Quatorze mansions? By Jove, it was Newman himself—the convenience that man is! [*Looking at his watch.*] Hallo—it's nearly to-morrow now. I must put my hand on a couple of the right ones—all the men have gone. It's not a nice thing to have to tell them; for there's no doubt Deepmere has been trifled with. Bah! I'll tell them something else. One has to stand up for one's nearest and dearest, even when one knows what they are! [*The music ceases. As Valentin is going off he is met by the Marquis, who re-enters hastily, right.*]

MARQUIS. [*Breathless.*] Have you seen Lord Deepmere?—do you know where he is?

VALENTIN. [*Aside.*] That's the sort of thing they're up to! Do they want a little more? [*Aloud.*] I haven't the least idea of his lordship's whereabouts.

MARQUIS. Your mother wishes to speak to him—I hope he hasn't gone! [*Exit Marquis, rapidly, left.*]

VALENTIN. [*Alone.*] My mother wishes—? God forgive me, if he's not, they want to catch him again before he has time to cool! He has poured forth rent-rolls and vouchers like scalding water, and, seeing that they dropped him too soon, they want to pick him up again! Poor Newman! [*Goes right, and as he is going off meets Newman coming in. Re-enter Newman, right. They come down, Newman, left; Valentin, right.*]

NEWMAN. Well, we made the grand tour—everyone seemed to like it. [*Seats himself in armchair.*]

VALENTIN. I don't see how they can get out of that. What have you done with Claire?

NEWMAN. Your mother called her off—she must have sent her to bed.

VALENTIN. That's where we all ought to be.

NEWMAN. I want to sit up *all night* —such a grand night as this!

VALENTIN. How much you're in love! You ought to get home to your dreams.

NEWMAN. To my dreams?

VALENTIN. Make the most of them!

NEWMAN. [*Rising and looking at Valentin.*] What's the matter with you? [*Movement from Valentin.*] I'll go as soon as I've seen Claire again— she hasn't bidden me good night. [*Looking about and going up and round to right.*]

VALENTIN. How can she, if she has been sent to bed?

NEWMAN. She ain't a little girl of six! She won't *go* to bed—or else she'll get up again.

VALENTIN. She's in love too, then!

NEWMAN. [*Still looking.*] She'll make me doubt it if she doesn't come back a moment.

VALENTIN. Well, I must go to bed at any rate. [Goes up to left.]

NEWMAN. Good night, then. Take care of yourself.

VALENTIN. [About to go, left, coming down again.] Do you know I've got an idea? I should like to come in when my mother and brother are with you to-morrow—rather on the quiet.

NEWMAN. I'd rather you came with a band of music!

VALENTIN. No; I should like to appear at the crisis—unexpectedly, dramatically!

NEWMAN. Hide under the table, then, and suddenly pop out.

VALENTIN. I've thought of something better—since you've got a garden.

NEWMAN. A garden?

VALENTIN. The "virgin forest," you know—the big place you swaggered about. I'll come in that way—

NEWMAN. You may come down the chimney if you like!

VALENTIN. Is there room there to hide?

NEWMAN. [Staring.] In the chimney?

VALENTIN. No, no; in the virgin forest! How do you get in?

NEWMAN. Why, by the gates on the three back streets. I'll send you the keys. [Moves to centre.]

VALENTIN. [Aside.] Bravo! [Aloud.] I'm going to play a little game.

NEWMAN. Oh, I know your little games!

VALENTIN. So you'll send me the keys early?

NEWMAN. With the peep of dawn.

VALENTIN. God bless you! [They shake hands.] Good night. [Goes up.]

Good night! [Exit Valentin, left.]

NEWMAN. [Alone, looking after him a moment.] What in creation's his little game?—what's his elaborate plan? [Re-enter Mme. de Bellegarde, right.] They are elaborate, over here! [Moves to right.]

MME. DE BELLEGARDE. Mr. Newman? [Coldly.] I had an impression you had taken leave of us.

NEWMAN. Not yet, Madam! I've not yet taken leave of your daughter.

MME. DE BELLEGARDE. Is that ceremony indispensable?

NEWMAN. [After a moment's look at her.] I think that in this house every ceremony is! Will you be so good as to tell me where you left Madame de Cintré?

MME. DE BELLEGARDE. You must find her yourself!

NEWMAN. I'll try! [Exit Newman, right.]

MME. DE BELLEGARDE. [Alone.] Find her if you can! [Seats herself on ottoman.]

[Re-enter the Marquis, left upper entrance.]

MARQUIS. Deepmere has left the house. [Crossing at back.] Damn his manners! [Goes to fireplace.]

MME. DE BELLEGARDE. Do you think his manners would have been better if he had stayed, after that scene? Where's Valentin?

MARQUIS. He has also gone out.

MME. DE BELLEGARDE. At this hour?

MARQUIS. You know his habits! I saw him cross the court with two gentlemen.

MME. DE BELLEGARDE. To begin the evening, I suppose. A merry party!

MARQUIS. Frankly speaking, they must be merrier than we.

MME. DE BELLEGARDE. It was a bad quarter of an hour; but I'm not in despair. Lord Deepmere will come back.

MARQUIS. Very likely—if you send for him. But haven't you had enough?

MME. DE BELLEGARDE. One can never have enough of hearing about such a magnificent property. The whole thing cleared—a beautiful fresh start. Four English seats and a house in Park Lane.

MARQUIS. He's better, after all, than Newman!

MME. DE BELLEGARDE. Yes, and he's a gentleman.

MARQUIS. You felt he was a gentleman when he let you have it? You sent him away, a month ago, to dot his *i*'s, and I hope you felt he was dotting them!

MME. DE BELLEGARDE. He has dotted them with great gold pieces! He has taken the bad taste of your American out of my mouth.

MARQUIS. Ah, we took a bigger bite of the poor American than we *can* swallow! But Mr. Newman, to do him justice, has never insulted us.

MME. DE BELLEGARDE. He will—he will! Give him time.

MARQUIS. Definitely, then, even after to-night you mean to throw him over?

MME. DE BELLEGARDE. How could I do it before I knew what we have missed? But we haven't missed it yet!

MARQUIS. I've known you long, mother; but there are still moments when you frighten me. What do you mean to do?

MME. DE BELLEGARDE. [Rising.] I must think it over. I'll tell you to-morrow.

MARQUIS. But to-morrow we go to the American's.

MME. DE BELLEGARDE. That will be just our opportunity—it's providential.

MARQUIS. The day after our promise? And on what pretext?

MME. DE BELLEGARDE. I'll find a pretext! [After a pause.] We made no promise to Mr. Newman that didn't strictly depend on his conditions.

MARQUIS. He'll make any conditions we like.

MME. DE BELLEGARDE. I defy him to make any *I* like! [Re-enter Mrs. Bread, right. As she sees Mrs. Bread.] Hold your tongue and give me your arm to my room. [To Mrs. Bread, crossing her.] Everything is upside down, but we shall recover ourselves to-morrow.

MRS. BREAD. Yes, my lady: after such an affair!

MME. DE BELLEGARDE. We shall have a grand putting to rights. Is Mr. Newman gone?

MRS. BREAD. I believe he has just left the house.

MME. DE BELLEGARDE. Then see that the lights are out and that everything is closed. [Exeunt Mme. de Bellegarde and Marquis, left.]

MRS. BREAD. [Alone.] I'm afraid nothing will ever be open again! [Re-enter Newman, right. To Newman.] I just told a fib for you, sir—I knew you weren't gone.

NEWMAN. I want no fibs—I only want Madame de Cintré. [Goes to right.]

MRS. BREAD. She's coming—she took refuge with *me*.

NEWMAN. Refuge? [Re-enter Mme. de Cintré, right. Newman opens his arms to her.] Be so good as to understand that your only refuge is in my arms! [Mme. de Cintré throws herself into them as the Curtain falls.]

ACT THIRD

[*A large deep saloon in the fine old house into which Newman has just moved. The whole place handsome, but rather bare; slight disorder, signs of recent arrival. It must be sufficiently visible that the rooms belong to a set of apartments on the ground floor. The main entrance from outside, is to the left, considerably down to the front. Further up, between left and middle, a wide, high window, opening into the great court of the hôtel. In the middle a door, draped in old tapestry, opening on a passage which leads to a bedroom. To the right of this, balancing with the window, a large open door, leading to staircase and rooms above. Quite at the right, near the front, the entrance of a conservatory which communicates with the grounds. Noémie, expensively and showily dressed, as if with the money extracted from Newman, and divested of her jacket and gloves, though wearing a very smart hat, discovered just after she has hung up, in a florid gilt frame, one of her garish "copies."*]

NOÉMIE. [*On a step-ladder.*] With all the rest upstairs, this makes the seventeenth; I *am* working them off! [*Enter, left, hat in hand, Valentin de Bellegarde.*] Good morning; you get up early!

VALENTIN. So do you, if you come to that!

NOÉMIE. Oh, we've been here an hour—hanging pictures! Papa has gone to get more cord.

VALENTIN. [*Who has looked first on table, left, and then looked, in a different manner, out of window.*] You seem indeed to have the place to yourself. I haven't met a soul.

NOÉMIE. The establishment is still very small.

VALENTIN. Does it consist entirely of *you?*

NOÉMIE. I'm not a member of it— I'm only forming it. We want none but the best people, and they're not so easy to meet.

VALENTIN. [*Looking on piano.*] One of the best people was rather easy to meet when you met the master of this house! May I inquire if he's still in bed?

NOÉMIE. For what do you take him? He dashed out half an hour ago.

VALENTIN. [*Aside.*] Confound him! What then shall I do for my keys? [*Looking vaguely about him.*]

NOÉMIE. [*Coming down from her ladder.*] Is there anything particular you want of him?

VALENTIN. [*Moving toward sofa.*] He promised to do something for me —very early; but he hasn't done it. It doesn't matter; I daresay I can get on. [*He continues to look, covertly, for the keys, and suddenly spies them in a silver bowl on the table, left. Aside.*] Bravo!—there they are. If I could only pick them up!

NOÉMIE. [*Who has seated herself at piano, suddenly turns round on stool.*] You must excuse Mr. Newman if he has forgotten—he's so awfully full of something else. Has he told you about his necklace?—the finest pearls that can be found in Paris—half a dozen rows! He has gone out to buy them, but he'll be back to receive his visitors. [*Suddenly arranging her hat and her hair.*] Do I look very badly?

VALENTIN. Charmingly ill! Are *you* going to help to receive them? See for yourself if you're not in the best form to make an impression.

NOÉMIE. For a wonder, there isn't a mirror in the room; but there are fifty upstairs. Excuse me a moment. [*Exit Noémie, right upper entrance.*]

VALENTIN. *Vanitas vanitatum*—now for my keys! [*Snatches them, at the table, out of the silver bowl.*] These must be right—yes, they're labelled. With those good fellows waiting for me at the back gates I must pass through the grounds and admit them from the inside. The very absurdity of such a place is our protection! If we've only not kept the others waiting! [*Just as he has thrust the keys into his pocket and is hurrying off, he finds himself face to face with Nioche. Enter Nioche, left, with big roll of red cord.*]

NIOCHE. Our noble friend all alone?

VALENTIN. Your daughter left me this moment. I won't wait to see her again, but please tell her I left these words for her: "Good-bye—be a good girl!" [*Exit Valentin, rapidly, through the conservatory.*]

NIOCHE. [*Alone, putting cord down on table, right, and staring after him a moment.*] What's the matter with him? She's good enough for *me!*

[*Enter Newman, left.*]

NEWMAN. You're just what I want to see.

NIOCHE. Comte Valentin has this moment gone out, but you won't have met him—he went *that* way.

NEWMAN. [*Who carries a small box, reminded, snapping his fingers.*] Ah, poor dear fellow, he must have come for his keys—why couldn't I remember? But it's all right [*Looking into the silver bowl.*]; *you* gave them to him.

NIOCHE. Begging your pardon, sir

—I gave him nothing.

NEWMAN. Then whom else did he see?

NIOCHE. He appeared to have seen my daughter.

NEWMAN. Oh then, *she* gave them. If he has got them, for some fantastic purpose—some "little *game*"—it doesn't matter how he came by them. [*Opening the flat jewel-case which he carries in his hand and exhibiting its contents to Nioche.*] I could think of nothing but *this* [*Re-enter Noémie without her hat.*] till I had scrambled out and got hold of it. [*As Nioche, clasping his hands, gives signs of wonder and admiration.*] Do you think she'll *like* it?

NIOCHE. Your beautiful bride, sir? Just try her!

NEWMAN. [*Left centre to Noémie, who comes down.*] I'll try *you*, Miss Noémie. [*Showing her the pearls.*] Do you think they're fine?

NOÉMIE. [*Taking the case from him, with an emotion that breaks out as soon as she looks at it.*] Oh, the lovely darlings! It's *you* that are fine, Mr. Newman!

NEWMAN. I shall be finer when I've put on some clothes. [*Crosses her, going up right.*] Look at it well, and tell me if there's anything the matter with it. [*Exit Newman, right upper entrance.*]

NOÉMIE. [*Gazes at the jewels for some minutes; after which she raises her eyes in silence to her father's.*] To think we're going to lose such a man.

NIOCHE. [*Going to sit at top of table.*] It's very dreadful—but there are others besides. I found a letter for you at home. [*Carefully extracting the missive from an ancient pocket-book.*] A letter with a coronet on the paper.

NOÉMIE. [*Taking the letter, after having deposited the jewel-case reverently on table, right.*] Yes, there are others besides. It's from Lord Deepmere, about a copy he wants me to do. I shall have to write three lines of answer—just wait for me. [*Goes up to door, right.*]

NIOCHE. [*Crossing to sofa.*] I should tell you Comte Valentin left a message for you—a solemn injunction to be a good girl.

NOÉMIE. I'll be too good for *him!* [*Exit Noémie, right.*]

NIOCHE. [*Alone, goes to the table, and carefully lifting the pearl necklace out of its case, holds it to the light and looks at it, examines it.*] Does he want me to see if there's anything the matter with it? The only thing that's the matter with it is that it isn't *ours!* [*Enter Mme. de Bellegarde, left, and stands on the threshold a moment with her glass up, watching him before he sees her. As soon as he does so he quickly puts down the necklace, rubbing his hands, and bowing and backing as she advances.*]

MME. DE BELLEGARDE. [*Aside.*] What an extraordinary person—an old pedlar with jewels! [*Aloud.*] If you're a servant, you had better have been at your post. For want of some one to announce me, I've made my way in alone. My son, who accompanies me, is wandering off into the court in quest of assistance.

NIOCHE. [*Obsequiously, apologetically.*] The staff is only half sketched out!

MME. DE BELLEGARDE. Is that the way you sketch it? [*Re-enter Noémie,*

right upper entrance.] Announce Madame de Bellegarde.

NOÉMIE. [*Aside.*] Madame de Bellegarde? I *do* help to receive them! [*Advances and curtsies low to Mme. de Bellegarde.*] Madame! [*Mme. de Bellegarde goes up, left, looking about her. Noémie gives her father a note.*] Here are two words, in answer to the note—to be taken immediately.

NIOCHE. [*With the note.*] I must first let Mr. Newman know—

NOÉMIE. Never mind that—*I'll* let Mr. Newman know.

NIOCHE. [*Crossing to left.*] Just as you direct. [*About to retire, bowing and retreating before Mme. de Bellegarde.*] Madame!

MME. DE BELLEGARDE. [*Having, on Noémie's appearance, gazed at her in amazement, without acknowledging in any manner her salutation, aside.*] A bold young woman—dressed like a mountebank and quite at home! [*Aloud to Nioche.*] Look for Monsieur le Marquis, and tell him where I am.

NIOCHE. [*Left down, obsequious, as before.*] Madame! [*Exit Nioche, left down, with note, while Mme. de Bellegarde scans Noémie from head to foot.*]

NOÉMIE. [*Aside.*] Mercy, how she glowers! [*Aloud, as if going.*] Shall I have the honour of announcing Madame la Marquise?

MME. DE BELLEGARDE. Wait till I've been rejoined by my son. [*Aside, seating herself on sofa.*] I'll go into this. [*Aloud, after another stern survey of Noémie.*] May I inquire if you're a member of the staff?

NOÉMIE. [*Mystified.*] Of the staff?

MME. DE BELLEGARDE. Perhaps you attend to the correspondence.

NOÉMIE. [*With spirit, conscious of*

Mme. de Bellegarde's increasing irony.] I attend to everything that Mr. Newman asks of me—in the way of friendship.

MME. DE BELLEGARDE. [*Aside.*] Friendship? [*Remembering.*] Ah yes, the clever artistic friends; this is one, and the old pedlar with the pearls is another. [*After another look at Noémie.*] I think I can guess what *she* peddles! [*Aloud.*] Mr. Newman is to be congratulated on your valuable services.

NOÉMIE. [*Not at all disconcerted.*] To render such services to Mr. Newman is a great happiness.

MME. DE BELLEGARDE. You certainly look quite peculiarly happy!

NOÉMIE. [*Understanding and stung.*] It's more than I can say of you, Madame!

MME. DE BELLEGARDE. [*Aside.*] The brazen creature! [*Aloud.*] I didn't come here at this hour of the morning [*Enter, on the left, the Marquis de Bellegarde*] to encounter impudence and vice!

NOÉMIE. [*Smarting, outraged.*] *Quelle horreur!* [*She checks herself on seeing the Marquis; then aside.*] Gracious, he's not much like the Count. [*Aloud, with high superiority, while the Marquis moves round to back.*] I'll tell Mr. Newman you're here, Madame, but I shall describe you in my own terms! [*On the threshold she stops and curtsies exclusively to the Marquis.*] Monsieur! [*Exit Noémie by the stairs, right.*]

MARQUIS. [*Up right centre, looking round him after he has put his hat and stick on piano.*] What a wonderful place and what wonderful people! to say nothing [*at table, right*] of wonderful jewels tossed about with wonderful cigars!

MME. DE BELLEGARDE. Be firm—he'll try to corrupt us. The pearls are of course a present for Claire.

MARQUIS. [*Taking a cigar out of the box and sniffing it appreciatively.*] Perhaps the cigars are a present for *me!*

MME. DE BELLEGARDE. Be firm—be firm!

MARQUIS. [*Sniffing still at his cigar.*] I'll be a rock!

MME. DE BELLEGARDE. I told you I would find a pretext. Very well, I *have* found a pretext.

MARQUIS. [*Vague, with his cigar.*] And pray what may it be?

[*Re-enter Christopher Newman, right, very freshly and handsomely dressed, as if to meet his intended; with white flowers in his buttonhole, quite like a bridegroom.*]

MME. DE BELLEGARDE. [*Becoming aware of Newman, who, on the threshold, looks at them a moment, while her son quickly drops his cigar back into the box.*] See for yourself!

NEWMAN. You're just what I wanted to see! [*Coming down.*] Make yourselves at home! Claire has gone straight into the grounds?

MME. DE BELLEGARDE. [*After a short silence, during which she exchanges a look with the Marquis.*] My daughter has not come with us.

NEWMAN. [*Centre.*] Not come with you? But you promised, and *she* promised!

MARQUIS. [*Seating himself at chair, left of table right.*] My sister's promises are her own affair!

NEWMAN. But yours, Marquis, are mine! I'm greatly disappointed.

MME. DE BELLEGARDE. I'm afraid we've more disappointments than that for you!

NEWMAN. [*Looking from one to the other.*] Look here, my good friends, you don't mean to say you're going to back out!

MME. DE BELLEGARDE. Remember what a very little way we've come in. Fortunately—after what we've just seen!

NEWMAN. [*Staring.*] What you've just *seen?*

MME. DE BELLEGARDE. A flaunting young woman, on a footing of familiarity—of authority.

NEWMAN. Little Noémie? Do you object to little Noémie? [*Perplexed.*] Ah yes, she told me you were rather rough with her!

MME. DE BELLEGARDE. Rough with her? Do you expect me to bow down to your [*She stops a moment, checked a little by Newman's look; then in a slightly different tone.*]—your intimate female friends?

MARQUIS. [*Aside, as his mother's tactics dawn upon him.*] I see—magnificent mother!

NEWMAN. I don't know what you're talking about! That young lady's a charming artist—she does odd *jobs* for me.

MARQUIS. [*Aside.*] That's exactly what we suppose!

MME. DE BELLEGARDE. Your defence of her is compromising! It's even more fortunate than I could suspect that Mme. de Cintré remained at home. I don't mean to say for a moment that we could have apprehended such an encounter. She stayed simply as an unmistakable sign to you that she withdraws from her engagement. [*She rises; the Marquis rises.*]

NEWMAN. [*Falling back to chair up right centre.*] An unmistakable

sign? Do you expect me to *take* thàt?

MME. DE BELLEGARDE. You can take it or leave it. It's what we came to tell you. [*Moves over to her son.*]

MARQUIS. We said we would come, and we *have* come! [*Goes to the top of table.*]

NEWMAN. [*Going to table right, and mechanically offering Mme. de Bellegarde a seat.*] She sends me no message [*Raising his hand to his head.*]—no explanation?

MME. DE BELLEGARDE. [*Seated on chair left of table right.*] She gave us no fine phrases to bring with us; she trusted *us* to explain!

NEWMAN. To explain that she throws me over—without pity, without remorse?

MME. DE BELLEGARDE. She recognises to the full that it took but a few hours to let daylight into her delusion, and that the matter has gone such a very short distance as to leave us at liberty to request that it shall go no further.

NEWMAN. No *further?* After we blazed through the rooms and announced our engagement to five hundred people?

MME. DE BELLEGARDE. You made too much noise—you must pay for your advertisement!

NEWMAN. And must *she* pay too? She told me she wanted every one to know.

MME. DE BELLEGARDE. Now she wants them to know something else.

NEWMAN. Something else indeed! That you're incapable of keeping common faith, of being honest for twenty-four hours!

MME. DE BELLEGARDE. [*To her son.*] Didn't I tell you he would insult us? [*To Newman, rising and com-*

ing centre, while the Marquis steps below table.] It's now that we're honest, quite as honest as you, even if we're a good deal less rude! We're honest in telling you thus frankly and promptly that, after all's said and done, we *can't* make you harmonise with our traditions, our associations, our ideals, with our prejudices, if you choose to call them so! Call them even narrow, call them bigoted, if you will—they are, after all, our religion, our faith, the faith of our ancestors. It has come over us, with the wholesome morning light, which restores the true proportions of things and the true perspective of honour, that we shrink from an intensely new responsibility.

MARQUIS. [*His hand in his waistcoat.*] That of breaking the long chain of an inveterate, a sacred observance. The daughters of our house have, for ages, never contracted alliances but with those of our own species.

NEWMAN. [*Left centre.*] Your species, Marquis? [*With his hands behind his back.*] Ain't that rather hard to find?

MME. DE BELLEGARDE. [*Passing her hands into her son's arm.*] We're quite conscious that we're not like all the world; those who cling to lost causes are certainly less in fashion than the representatives of trade! Let me add, before we retire, that we made no promise to you that didn't explicitly depend on your meeting our conditions.

NEWMAN. And what conditions have I failed to meet? You haven't even mentioned one of them.

MME. DE BELLEGARDE. I'll mention one now. Your having a decent house!

NEWMAN. You go back to *that* folly?

It's too *monstrous!* What do you want me to do with the poor girl?

MME. DE BELLEGARDE. Anything in the world you like!

MARQUIS. [*Looking at the stitching of his glove.*] Only wait till we get out of the house! [*He gives his mother his arm to leave the place as they have come in.*]

NEWMAN. I refuse to accept your statement that Madame de Cintré has given her assent to this hideous proceeding. She's not a child—she's not a slave. She's a woman grown—she's her own mistress. What have you done to her—what have you done *with* her?

MME. DE BELLEGARDE. [*Going toward table, right, with Marquis.*] My happy power is in the grateful submission of my family. Filial obedience is the oldest tradition of our race. [*She leaves the Marquis's arm.*]

NEWMAN. Filial obedience be— [*Pulls up short, then with an abrupt change of tone, a visible, successful effort to be heroically reasonable and conciliatory.*] Let me then do all possible justice to your traditions. I understand you've got peculiar ideas —I've noticed that before. I beg your pardon if I've offended you with wild and extravagant words. A man can't smile and bow when you pluck up the fairest flower that ever took root in his life! [*Goes left, and round to centre.*]

MME. DE BELLEGARDE. He can't smile and bow, but when he's face to face with a dead wall he can have the intelligence to see it and turn round. He can be clever enough for that.

MARQUIS. [*Fatuously, repeating.*] He can be clever enough for that!

NEWMAN. He must try and be as

clever as you, Marquis. [Goes up towards right upper entrance.] You can't expect me to let you go without a protest, without a supplication. Pity me enough to think it over once more—not to turn your backs on me yet—to stay a little longer. Be generous, Madame de Bellegarde—just wait ten minutes!

MME. DE BELLEGARDE. What are we to wait for?

NEWMAN. For that clever boy Valentine. He'll be on my side, and the discussion will therefore be fairer. It's past the hour—he'll turn up any minute; and I ask of you but the common charity of this little delay. [The Marquis goes up. Aside, anxiously looking at his watch.] Why in creation doesn't his little game come off? [Takes Mme. de Bellegarde's hand and leads her up.] You said you would look at my house, and you haven't looked at anything, for this is the meanest part. Go through it all, take your time, think the whole thing over!

MME. DE BELLEGARDE. [Smiling.] Don't say we don't make concessions.

NEWMAN. Ah, make them to Valentine! [Escorting them.] That leads to all sorts of fine places, and to the big rooms above. [Exeunt Mme. de Bellegarde and Marquis, right upper entrance. Newman looks after them a moment.] Why, they're regular old serpents! [Snapping his fingers.] Ah! [Seeing Nioche, who re-enters, left down.] You're just what I want to see!

NIOCHE. A lady, in a cab, to speak to you, sir!

NEWMAN. A lady—in a cab? Thank God, it's Claire! [Enter Mrs. Bread, ushered by Nioche, who goes round to right of Newman.] Ah no, but some better news! Delighted to see you, Mrs. Bread. [To Nioche.] Do me this service, quickly: go straight up there and join a lady and a gentleman who have just left me and are going through the house. Show them the whole place—spare them nothing—keep them as long as you can! [Banging down his hand on piano.]

NIOCHE. [Going.] Oh, I know how, sir—I'll put them through! [Exit Nioche, right upper entrance.]

NEWMAN. [To Mrs. Bread, who is dressed for travelling.] Where's Madame de Cintré?

MRS. BREAD. She sent me to tell you, sir—to beg you to forgive her.

NEWMAN. Forgive her? Then she has broken faith?

MRS. BREAD. She has broken her heart—that's what she has broken! We're going to Fleurières. [After a look from Newman.] The grey, grim château of the Bellegardes, far from Paris. We take the midday train.

NEWMAN. Then she flies from me—without an explanation, without a look?

MRS. BREAD. She flies from her mother, sir—my lady has come down on us. My lady can come down!

NEWMAN. I know she can. She's down here!

MRS. BREAD. There has been an awful scene at home.

NEWMAN. And the Countess has yielded?—she has given me up?

MRS. BREAD. She'll write and tell you—as soon as she can turn round.

NEWMAN. [Bitterly.] Oh, don't let her turn round any more—she has turned round enough!

MRS. BREAD. She'll explain everything—she'll write you a beautiful letter.

NEWMAN. Does she expect a beautiful letter to satisfy me? I can't marry a beautiful letter!

MRS. BREAD. No more you can, sir! Only that was my message—and I must go!

NEWMAN. [*Pleading.*] Let me go *with* you—let me see her again!

MRS. BREAD. There isn't a minute, and it would only be a difficulty where there are more than enough already. Be patient! [*Newman goes right.*] The future's dark; but I'll try to help you.

NEWMAN. I shall hold you to that! But [*Smiting his forehead.*] I'm too *distracted!* [*Drops into chair, right.*] Have you seen Count Valentine?

MRS. BREAD. That's just what I wanted to ask *you.* I'm afraid something's in the wind: his valet spoke to me an hour ago—he has noticed things and he's worried.

NEWMAN. What is he worried about?

MRS. BREAD. The danger of a bloody meeting.

NEWMAN. A bloody meeting? Do you mean a duel? [*Rising.*] With *whom?*

MRS. BREAD. With poor Lord Deepmere—God forgive him!

NEWMAN. The young man with a grievance? And what should they fight about?

MRS. BREAD. The honour of the house of Bellegarde.

NEWMAN. O—oh, that's not worth it!

MRS. BREAD. Tell them so, then—prevent it: before the Countess has an idea!

NEWMAN. She shall have *no* idea —if I can stamp it out!

MRS. BREAD. God keep them, then! God keep *you*—God keep us all! [*Exit Mrs. Bread rapidly, left down.*]

NEWMAN. [*Alone, wondering, thinking.*] His valet's worried—he has noticed things? If it comes to that, I've noticed things too! the keys, the grounds, the "virgin forest," his little game! Is *that* damned foolery his little game? [*Strides to conservatory, as if to look out, but turns away quickly.*] Of course they're ever so far away—out of sight and sound! [*Goes to left.*]

[*Re-enter Nioche, right upper entrance.*]

NIOCHE. They're coming back, sir —they made a short job.

NEWMAN. There's another business now—and a job that may be longer! Go straight into the grounds, and look for Count Valentine. There's some blasted thing on.

NIOCHE. [*Startled.*] What blasted thing?

NEWMAN. That's just what I want to *see!* Go *that* way, and go fast! [*Re-enter, right upper entrance, the Marquis and Mme. de Bellegarde. Newman pushes Nioche out by the conservatory. Exit Nioche, right, Newman remains right, while the others cross to left.*] I'd search myself if I didn't want to have another go at *them!* [*To Mme. de Bellegarde.*] Well, have you thought it all over?

MME. DE BELLEGARDE. [*Left centre.*] Do you think we spin round like tops?

NEWMAN. Oh, tops only spin when they're whipped—and that's not your case.

MARQUIS. [*Left, aside.*] Isn't it, though? We were whipped last night!

NEWMAN. Well, all the same, let me make you a supreme appeal. Why should you object to me so?—what's the matter with me, anyhow? I can't hurt you if I would! A representative of trade? Who told you that? I ain't a representative of anything but the passion I feel and the performance I undertake. At any rate, whatever I represent, I don't misrepresent, and this is the first thing I've taken up for ever so long. Think what such a humiliation as this must be to a woman like *her!* I'll take her right off to the other side of the globe, and you shall never see me nor hear of me again! I'll stay over there the rest of my life—I'll sign a paper that I'll never come back! [*The Marquis goes down to left.*]

MME. DE BELLEGARDE. Don't say that! We shall be delighted to see you in France the day you accept your fate. [*She crosses to left down, the Marquis giving her his arm. Exeunt, left down, Mme. de Bellegarde and Marquis.*]

NEWMAN. [*Alone, his hand on the back of sofa.*] My fate?—with *you* for my Providence? Accept an empty frame as my picture? Accept an empty glass as my wine? [*Re-enter Noémie, right upper entrance.*] Come in! That old swindler's gone! What did the Count say to you when he was here?

NOÉMIE. He said nothing in particular—I don't know why he came.

NEWMAN. If he helped himself to the keys without speaking of them, that adds a symptom.

NOÉMIE. A symptom of what?

NEWMAN. Of his fighting a donkey's duel—with Lord Deepmere.

NOÉMIE. With Lord Deepmere? What about?

NEWMAN. [*Crossing to table, right.*] Perhaps about *you!*

NOÉMIE. [*Crossing at back, aside, joyfully, irrepressibly.*] Oh, that'll give me a lift! [*Aloud.*] Bless me, there's another symptom: his queer words

to my father—to tell me particularly to be a good girl. And the worst symptom of all—this letter from Lord Deepmere! [*Pulling out of her pocket and handing to Newman, open, the note brought her by her father.*] Read that!

NEWMAN. [*Running his eyes over the note.*] "I may never see you again —yet there's half a chance of it. If I don't, you mustn't forget me. If I do, I won't forget you!" [*Characteristically.*] Why, it's quite a love-letter!

NOÉMIE. [*Clasping her hands.*] I do hope he won't be killed!

DOCTOR. [*Outside.*] Take care—take care!

MARIGNAC. [*Together.*] [*Outside.*] Here we are at last!

NIOCHE. [*Outside.*] Ah, the poor young man!

DOCTOR. [*Outside.*] Gently—gently!

NEWMAN. [*Turning quickly, at the sound of voices, as Valentin is borne in.*] Much worse than that—damned if he hasn't killed Valentine! [*Moves sofa with Noémie, while re-enter by the conservatory Valentin, pale and wounded, supported, or as far as possible carried, by Nioche and M. de Marignac and preceded by the Doctor.*]

VALENTIN. [*Who has heard Newman's words.*] I'm afraid he has, old boy: it was the best thing he could do with me!

DOCTOR. Easy—easy! [*Nodding at sofa.*] This is the thing! [*Newman and Noémie quickly wheel sofa still further left, to front. Newman then helps the others to lower Valentin into it. Valentin, sinking back with weakness, lies awhile with closed eyes.*] He must have another drop of brandy! [*Administers it from flask and adjusted cup taken from pocket. Newman and Nioche are at back of sofa, the Doctor in front of it, and Marignac at top, having gone round at once.*]

NIOCHE. [*To Newman.*] I met them coming—in the gardens—it was none too soon! [*Goes and kneels with Doctor, but at bottom of sofa.*]

NEWMAN. [*To the Doctor.*] Are *you* one of his bottle-holders?

DOCTOR. No, I'm only the doctor —I'm an Englishman, and I came with Lord Deepmere, who has now less need of me.

NOÉMIE. [*Left, aside.*] Oh, that's good!

NEWMAN. Do you mean he's dead?

DOCTOR. Oh no, he's wounded, but he'll do well enough. His two friends drove him off—he insisted on my attending to the Count. I begged one of the Count's friends to go for his family physician. This is the other, Monsieur de Marignac.

NEWMAN. [*To Marignac, a man of a certain age, grave and decorous, but rather a "masher," who salutes him with formal courtesy.*] Happy to see you, sir; or rather—hanged if I am! [*Indicating Valentin.*] Is he sinking?—is he very *bad?*

MARIGNAC. [*With his hand to his left side.*] A bad place—very deep— just in here!

DOCTOR. I stanched the wound, as far as I could, on the ground; but I can answer for nothing till I get him on a bed.

NEWMAN. [*To Noémie.*] A bed—a bed, quickly! Have everything got ready in *there!* [*Points centre, exit Noémie, centre.*]

DOCTOR. I'm glad there are no stairs.

I was afraid of them, as I was afraid of the movement of a carriage. That's why we judged it best, with your kind permission, to bring him in here.

VALENTIN. [*Beside whom Nioche has been kneeling, to Newman, opening his eyes.*] My dear fellow, I wanted not to be out of the way, but I'm afraid I've put myself a good deal too much *in* it!

NEWMAN. I'll give it to you when you're better! But I'll fix you up first!

VALENTIN. Oh, Deepmere has given it to me—*he* has fixed me up! He was perfect—he made me take the doctor—he didn't think a moment of himself.

MARIGNAC. Yes, *milord* was perfect. A Frenchman couldn't have been better.

VALENTIN. A Frenchman mustn't be worse! [*To Nioche.*] My venerable friend, do go to his place, with my compliments, and find out how he is.

NIOCHE. [*To Valentin.*] I would rather stay with *you*, M. le Comte; but anything for the honour of France! [*Exit Nioche, left down. Marignac goes round at back and takes Nioche's place.*]

NEWMAN. [*To the Doctor, pointing in the direction of the bedroom.*] Will you go and help the young lady? I'm afraid there is a great deal to do. [*The Doctor, assenting eagerly, goes out by the tapestried door.*]

VALENTIN. Don't move me—don't move me, Newman. I want to talk to you.

NEWMAN. And I want to talk to *you*—depend on it!

VALENTIN. Have the heads of the family been to see you?

NEWMAN. [*Cheerfully.*] Oh yes, Madame de Bellegarde and the Marquis paid me quite a solemn visit. *That's* all right!

VALENTIN. [*Lying and looking at him open-eyed.*] And did my sister come with them?

NEWMAN. Well no, Madame de Cintré, to my disappointment, didn't come round.

VALENTIN. Then it's *not* all right! [*To Marignac.*] Marignac, will you go for my sister? Will you tell her I want her?

NEWMAN. [*Aside.*] Thank God, then, *I* shall see her! [*To Marignac, looking at his watch.*] You may just catch her—she's leaving Paris, going to Fleurières—by the midday train.

VALENTIN. [*Repeating.*] Then it isn't all right! [*To Marignac, beseechingly.*] Stop her—catch her! [*Re-enter Doctor, centre.*] Bring her to me!

MARIGNAC. [*Picking up his hat, hastily.*] I'll do my very best! [*Just as he is going he is stopped by the Doctor, while Newman brings chair from piano and sits, behind sofa, beside Valentin.*]

DOCTOR. [*At left down, to Marignac, aside.*] If you're going out, it's indispensable you should send in a nurse from one of the convents.

MARIGNAC. I'll make for the nearest —you shall have one of the nuns. [*Exit Marignac, left down, at a run.*]

DOCTOR. [*To Newman.*] They're putting up a bed; but it takes time!

NEWMAN. Yes, curse it; but my *own* room's upstairs—if he'll go there?

VALENTIN. Ah, no stairs! Don't move me yet—don't move me!

DOCTOR. I'll hurry them, then; it's too important. [*Exit Doctor, centre.*]

VALENTIN. [*To Newman, who is seated close to him.*] Have they

backed out? Did they come to tell you that?

NEWMAN. I'll tell you all about it. But what's the hurry now?

VALENTIN. Why, if Claire is going to Fleurières, and I'm going to—another place, there's no time to lose! [*In a different tone after looking at Newman a moment.*] Tell me the truth before I die?

NEWMAN. [*Gets up a moment and walks away, hesitating, in distress.*] If I don't tell him, *she* will. [*Aloud, coming back.*] You won't die—you'll live to avenge me! They've no use for me, they can't work me in!

VALENTIN. Shame, shame! I'm glad to go! But you must avenge *yourself*. Don't give her up!

NEWMAN. She has given *me* up! Why does she change, when she was so firm, so fair—when she gave me her perfect faith?

VALENTIN. She doesn't change— she'll never change! She's only gaining time. Her spirit was broken— long ago! My *mother* has had that malignant magic—that damnable art. She isn't used to her liberty—to the liberty *you* have brought her. She's surrounded by the spectres, by the horrors, of the past. But she'll come to me now. [*Raising himself.*] Marignac will bring her. I'll clear up her fears—I'll give her back to you. I'll join your hands together here— [*Sinking back again.*] you'll go away together. Only [*With a sudden gasp of pain.*] she must be quick!

NEWMAN. Dear old boy; easy—easy! We've lots of time—we've the whole future. If you give her back to me she'll nurse you, she'll heal you, she'll save you; she'll give *you* back to me!

VALENTIN. She'll be too late—I'm

sinking. It tortures me to lie ebbing away when *you're* in trouble. But I'll tell you who *can* help you—Mrs. Bread can help you. She knows something about my mother.

NEWMAN. About your mother?

VALENTIN. About my father.

NEWMAN. About your father?

VALENTIN. About my brother.

NEWMAN. About your brother?

VALENTIN. She has a secret—she knows what was done when my father died—when Claire was forced. There was some foul play—something took place. Get it out of Mrs. Bread! It was so base that if I mention it now, it's only because I'm going.

NEWMAN. [*Wondering, calculating.*] It was so *base?*

VALENTIN. Oh, now I've spoken I shall *have* to go.

NEWMAN. [*Pleading.*] Stay, stay, my boy, and I'll never, never think of it again!

VALENTIN. Think of it till you find it out. I'll go to give you a chance—because it will bring them down. They'll come down if they know you know it.

NEWMAN. But my knowledge—what difference will *that* make?

VALENTIN. It will shame them—it will shame them. As it shames *me* now! [*Sinks back exhausted, with closed eyes.*]

[*Re-enter, left down, M. de Marignac; and at the same moment Noémie, centre.*]

MARIGNAC. The Countess is coming—she's just behind me! [*Then to Noémie, whom he approaches.*] And a trained nurse—a quiet nun, to relieve *you,* when you're tired.

NOÉMIE. [*Who has resumed her hat and jacket, aside.*] Countesses and

quiet nuns? I'm not much in *their* line!

[*Re-enter Nioche, left down, while Newman and Marignac are on either side of Valentin.*]

NIOCHE. [*At back of sofa, to Valentin.*] I saw *milord,* and he's not at all bad—he's only bad about his gallant adversary.

NOÉMIE. [*Aside, to her father.*] Has he read my note?

NIOCHE. [*Aside.*] He said it was so graceful! [*Goes to window.*]

NOÉMIE. [*Aside.*] It would be more graceful still of me to go to him! [*Moves to conservatory. Re-enter Doctor, centre.*]

DOCTOR. [*To Newman and Marignac.*] You must help me now—we must get him in! [*Goes to front.*]

NEWMAN. [*To Marignac.*] But where *is* Madame de Cintré?

MARIGNAC. I overtook her at the station—she was to follow in a moment. She bade me come on to tell him. [*Goes to Valentin, and lifts him.*]

NIOCHE. [*At the window.*] There's a carriage in the court—she's here! [*Comes to Newman.*]

NOÉMIE. [*Who has flitted round on tip-toe to the door of the conservatory, and stopped a moment listening, aside.*] I'm off—this way! [*Exit Noémie, right.*]

NEWMAN. [*To Nioche.*] Help the Count, old man. I must meet the Countess! [*The Doctor, Marignac and Nioche raise and sustain Valentin, who, at Newman's last words, opens his eyes with an "A-ah!" a gasp of sharp pain.*]

VALENTIN. [*To Newman.*] Thank you—I am past all help. But find it out—find it out! [*He is carried away, centre, by Marignac, the Doctor and*

Nioche. Newman, left alone, comes down to table right, and, as if dazed with what Valentin has said to him, falls into a chair and remains a moment with his head in his hands. Hearing a sound, he turns round, springing up: it is M. de Marignac, who has re-entered, centre. At the same instant enter Mme. de Cintré, left down, and M. de Marignac, who is nearest to her, goes to meet her, stands answering mutely, with a slow headshake, the appeal of her eyes, and then discreetly and quickly exit left down. Newman, on the right, stands looking at them—then Mme. de Cintré and he are left face to face.]

CLAIRE. [*Seizing Newman's hands.*] How is he? Where is he? Can't I see him?

NEWMAN. They've just moved him to a better place than this; they're arranging him—the doctor'll call you.

CLAIRE. Is he dying? Tell me the truth! What does it all mean?

NEWMAN. He's badly wounded, but we shall see. What *does* it all mean? That's what I ask myself!

CLAIRE. Forgive me—forgive me! you will when you understand!

NEWMAN. Ah, but when shall I *understand?* It's terrible cruel.

CLAIRE. It's crueller for me than for you. We must pity each other.

NEWMAN. I pity *you*—for that dear fellow—too much to utter *now* the reproach that burns my tongue!

CLAIRE. Yes, spare me, in this dreadful hour—spare me and save *him!* He was all I had! [*Giving way, weeping prostrate.*]

NEWMAN. You have *me*—you have *me*—and you won't take me!

CLAIRE. I told you last night that I was *afraid* of happiness. See how

right I was, and what a single hour of it has brought! [*Sinks on sofa, with head on back.*]

NEWMAN. Ain't you afraid of something else?—of turning joy to bitterness?—of broken pledges and blighted hopes? Ain't you afraid to go away, as I find you in the inexorable act of doing, and leave me gnashing my teeth and cursing my fate? [*As she makes no answer but to burst into tears he goes on, abruptly, in another tone.*] Where is Mrs. Bread? Has she stayed behind?

CLAIRE. [*Rising.*] I took the carriage, but she follows. Once away, when I can breathe, when I can think, you shall hear from me.

NEWMAN. When you can *think?* Do you mean when you can repent?

CLAIRE. My repentance will be all my future! But I'm *sick* with this delay—am I not to see my brother?

NEWMAN. Come to him now—let me show you! [*He goes with Mme. de Cintré quickly to centre door, where the Doctor meets them very gravely, bows Mme. de Cintré in and follows. Exit Mme. de Cintré, centre door. While this takes place, re-enter Mrs. Bread, left down, whom Newman comes down and meets.*] Have patience—I *see* what you ask me. He's in danger—he must see but one person at a time.

MRS. BREAD. Ah, the fatal folly, that I didn't prevent it last night, when I felt it in the air!

NEWMAN. I didn't feel it, God knows! But you can help us all yet. You know something. [*Movement of Mrs. Bread.*] Something that happened at Fleurières—ten years ago. Something secret—something shameful!

MRS. BREAD. Ah, did the Count tell you? If he told you, God forgive him —he's going! [*Newman goes round to left. Re-enter Mme. de Cintré, centre.*]

CLAIRE. [*In the deepest agitation and anguish.*] He's gone—he's gone! [*Falls on piano, right.*]

MRS. BREAD. [*With a loud wail.*] Oh, my boy—my boy! [*Exit, centre, with a rush.*]

NEWMAN. [*Left of Mme. de Cintré, stopping her as she hurries left, to go out.*] Gone—gone?

CLAIRE. For ever and ever! [*With quick, sombre passion.*] So shall I go too!

NEWMAN. [*Pleading as she struggles to leave him.*] Claire—Claire! Listen to me—stay with me!

CLAIRE. [*Breaking successfully away.*] Don't oppose me!—don't, in pity, or you'll kill me! [*Exit Mme. de Cintré, left down.*]

NEWMAN. [*Alone.*] What in the name of misery does she mean? What strange things does she threaten? [*Re-enter Mrs. Bread, centre, in blank despair. Newman goes up and comes down right of her, seizing her by the wrist.*] She's gone as well as he, and now you *must* help me, for I'm desperate!

MRS. BREAD. Don't keep me—I must follow her!

NEWMAN. What does she want to do? Where does she want to go? *How* does she want to "repent forever"?

MRS. BREAD. Oh, remember that she's a good Catholic! When they're hard pressed they have a refuge.

NEWMAN. A refuge. Do you mean the convent? A convent for *her*—for *that* woman—for my promised wife?

MRS. BREAD. It's too hideous—you must help me to prevent it!

NEWMAN. Trust me—if you'll show me how!

MRS. BREAD. Come then to Fleurières—come to Fleurières!

NEWMAN. [*Eagerly.*] Will you *tell* me, there?

MRS. BREAD. Will I tell you what?

NEWMAN. The great secret—the great shame!

MRS. BREAD. Come quickly, and I'll see! But come before it's too late! [*Exit Mrs. Bread, left down and re-enter Nioche centre; Newman goes right.*]

NIOCHE. [*Gazing mournfully at Newman.*] Lord, sir, what a sad inauguration of your beautiful house!

NEWMAN. My beautiful house be hanged—I've done with my beautiful house! [*Crosses to left.*]

NIOCHE. Done with it? And what's to become of it?

NEWMAN. [*Going up, left.*] I don't care a rap! Keep it for yourself!

NIOCHE. [*Staring.*] For myself? With all the valuable objects?

NEWMAN. [*At back.*] Damn the valuable objects!

NIOCHE. [*At the table on which the pearl necklace, which he lifts up, is still lying.*] The most valuable of all —the priceless pearls.

NEWMAN. Give 'em to your daughter! [*Comes down, right, while Nioche goes centre.*] And I shall want some baggage, some clothes—I leave Paris to-night!

NIOCHE. [*Overwhelmed.*] You shall be obeyed to the letter, sir! [*At this moment his eyes rest on the Sister of Charity, summoned by Marignac, who has entered left down, and stands silently just within the threshold. He bows to her solemnly.*] You come too late to nurse, good Sister—but not too late to pray!

NEWMAN. [*Becoming aware of her.*] Good Sister, pray for me! [*Action from Sister.*] Ah, Valentine, Valentine! [*Flings himself down on the sofa and buries his face on the arm while the Curtain falls.*] Selfish brute that I am!

ACT FOURTH

[*At the old Château de Fleurières; the closing hours of an early spring day. A high, paneled, central drawing-room, with "subjects," little oval or circular pictures, above the doors, let into the white boiserie, and very tall French windows, with small square panes and long, straight, flowered, faded curtains. Nothing but sparse last century furniture, refined and very much worn. On the left, near the front, a door leading to Mme. de Cintré's apartments or "wing"; another on the same side, higher up, quite at back, communicating with the general entrance. On the right, at back, balancing with this principal entrance, a large window, opening, down to the ground, upon the visible, melancholy, moated terrace of the château. Further down, on the same side, the door of the special apartments, or "wing," of Mme. de Bellegarde and the Marquis. During the act the dusk slowly gathers, and at a given moment a pair of candles are lighted. Enter, left upper entrance, a Servant, the same who has appeared in the second act, but who is now in a mourning livery, preceding M. de Marignac. Enter M. de Marignac, in a high hat with a crape band, carrying in his hand a large bunch of early violets.*]

MARIGNAC. [*Crossing Servant, and taking a card from his pocket.*] I have written a word on this card. [*The Servant takes the card on salver and exit left, while Marignac, alone a moment, has taken off his hat and put it down on table right, looking about the place with a certain wonder.*] It fairly smells of the past—I like my violets better! [*Goes right, sniffing them, while re-enter Servant, left, holding the door open for Mme. de Cintré. Enter Mme. de Cintré, left, in the deepest mourning. Exit Servant left upper entrance, and Marignac, advancing to Mme. de Cintré with an expression of the greatest sympathy and consideration, takes her hand and, bowing over it, raises it to his lips.*] It's so like your gracious goodness to make an exception in my favour.

CLAIRE. It's only for once; I shall never see you again.

MARIGNAC. Do you mean as the penalty of my participation? We couldn't do less for him, and we couldn't do more. He died like a Bellegarde of old, with his hand on his sword.

CLAIRE. Yes, thank God; he was a Bellegarde of old, not one of to-day. [*Crosses to right, Marignac goes left.*] But I don't mean anything vindictive; it would become me strangely little at this hour. I accept the fact, I almost rejoice in it, that my brother has done forever with the troubles of this world. [*Leans on window, resting on her arm.*] For the troubles of this world are too heavy to be borne.

MARIGNAC. You speak as if *you* were going to leave it! There's something in your face that I guess the intention of, and it makes my heart sink.

CLAIRE. [*Turning to him.*] Envy me, envy me! [*Turning back to win-*

dow.] Farewell!

MARIGNAC. Is there no comfort I can give you? Is there no service I can render you?

CLAIRE. Think of me as more at peace than you have ever known me; take no more trouble for me than that.

MARIGNAC. I took a very small trouble half an hour ago. I gathered these violets for you [*Claire comes down to him.*], almost the very first of the spring, in the sweet old churchyard on the side of the hill, where we laid him to rest this morning.

CLAIRE. [*Taking the flowers and kissing them.*] Thank you, thank you. Good-bye. [*Crosses to left, and is going.*]

MARIGNAC. A moment more. Your brother, the last hour of his life, charged me to give *this* to you [*Taking from his waistcoat-pocket a small packet.*]: he usually wore it; he took it off before this lamentable affair.

CLAIRE. [*Taking the little packet; after a look.*] It's a blessed relic; a little cross that belonged to my father, he wore it round his neck. [*Falls into chair, at table, left, and kisses it as she has kissed the violets.*] I'm going where they renounce—*renounce,* but I shall carry *this*—beneath!

MARIGNAC. Beneath the rigid folds of the nun? Heaven help me—I should like to prevent that!

CLAIRE. You *can't* prevent it, Monsieur de Marignac.

MARIGNAC. Upon my honour, I can try!

CLAIRE. You can do nothing.

MARIGNAC. I shall see what I can do. Excuse me if I say I warn you.

CLAIRE. Do you mean that you'll communicate [*Rising and nodding across the stage to right down.*] with them?

MARIGNAC. Your mother and the Marquis? Don't they know it?

CLAIRE. They don't dream of it. It's my own affair, and I appeal to your honour not to betray me. [*Goes to left down.*] Farewell!

MARIGNAC. Oh, I shall see you again!

CLAIRE. Never—never! [*Exit Mme. de Cintré, left down.*]

MARIGNAC. If I don't, may charming women never smile at me more! [*Goes right and up to back.*]

[*Re-enter the Servant, left upper entrance, introducing Newman, as he has introduced Marignac. Enter Newman, left upper entrance.*]

NEWMAN. [*To the Servant.*] All right, I'll wait here while you tell her. Mind you tell her it's *me!*

SERVANT. Oh, she'll come to *you,* sir. [*Exit Servant, left upper entrance, Marignac comes down.*]

NEWMAN. [*To Marignac.*] You're just what I want to see! There's a sickly satisfaction in putting my hand on *you.* [*With his hand on Marignac's shoulder.*] I'm going to want *you.* [*They go up to fireplace; Marignac sits on couch. Newman leans on mantelshelf, after putting his hat on table by fireplace.*]

MARIGNAC. Oh, I want to be wanted —if it's for the right thing!

NEWMAN. It's for the right thing *this* time—you may bet your life on that! I saw you this morning—across the churchyard—at those dismal dreadful proceedings; but I was afraid you would have returned to Paris. At what time is your train?

MARIGNAC. I'll take the train that

suits *you*. I'll do anything in fact that suits you—as a friend of the friend we buried to-day.

NEWMAN. We were both the friends of that friend—but there he lies, in spite of us. [*Looking at his watch.*] Ah, if Mrs. Bread would only come! I've an appointment with her.

MARIGNAC. I'm waiting for her too, to put into her hand a little supreme remembrance [*Taking out another little packet.*] that poor Bellegarde committed to me.

NEWMAN. If you don't want to wait, and will give me the object, I'll answer for her receiving it safely.

MARIGNAC. You'll oblige me very much—I'll put the parcel here. [*Coming down and depositing it on table.*] If you've an appointment, it's naturally for a private end, and I give you up the field.

NEWMAN. It's for two private ends, but I don't mind telling you what one of them is. [*Marignac comes back to left.*] It's to ask her to obtain for *me* an interview with Madame de Cintré.

MARIGNAC. [*With his hand on Newman's arm.*] The other night—at the Hôtel de Bellegarde—that didn't seem to depend on Mrs. Bread!

NEWMAN. It depended on more than you know—or than I know, either! I won't pretend to conceal from you—sore and sombre as I am!—that I'm a man with a grievance, and with more than one.

MARIGNAC. I think I've just learned one, at least, from Madame de Cintré's lips.

NEWMAN. [*Eagerly.*] You saw her? She was here, and I missed her? Curse my luck! [*Goes to cabinet and round at back.*]

MARIGNAC. Courage, courage; your luck may come back to you.

NEWMAN. That's just what I want to see! What then did you learn from her lips?

MARIGNAC. [*Looking at him a moment in silence.*] Don't you know? Don't you guess? It's more your business than mine!

NEWMAN. Do you mean that atrocity of the convent? [*Comes to centre.*] Yes, that's my business—that's why I'm here!

MARIGNAC. You're none too soon! But I myself let her know that, meddler as I might seem to her to be, I was capable of attempting to make such a step impossible.

NEWMAN. Well, *that* was good.

MARIGNAC. Yes, but she asked me what I could do.

NEWMAN. And what did you say to *that?*

MARIGNAC. I said I would see. But unfortunately I don't see!

NEWMAN. Then I'll show you! [*Taking him sharply by the arm, and pointing to the long window.*] Go out of that window—go out on that terrace —go out into those grounds—stand there till I call you. Be patient. Do you understand?

MARIGNAC. Not a bit!

NEWMAN. Then you won't do it for me?

MARIGNAC. I'll do anything for you! [*They shake hands.*]

NEWMAN. Be quick, then, here comes Mrs. Bread! [*Marignac, pushed by Newman, who opens it for him, passes out of the window to the terrace. Newman closes the window and turns to meet Mrs. Bread, who has entered left down.*] I've kept my tryst

—I suppose you saw me this morning.

MRS. BREAD. [*In deep mourning, with reddened eyes, shakes her head tragically.*] Oh, this morning, I couldn't see! Nor can I make out what now you're doing at that window.

NEWMAN. I've a confederate.

MRS. BREAD. M. de Marignac?

NEWMAN. He has brought you a sacred offering, which lies there on the table, something the Count gave him for you on that abominable morning.

MRS. BREAD. [*Crossing and taking the little packet, which consists of a small case that she opens; she seats herself with it at table, right.*] The rare old ring that he used to wear on his blessed, beautiful hand! Oh, and he thought of *me?* [*Bursts into tears.*] My boy, my boy!

NEWMAN. [*Who has gone to the fireplace, where he stands, with his back to the audience, waiting an instant, in respectful silence, while she sobs.*] Now you know how *I* feel, and how I want to see *her!*

MRS. BREAD. [*Drying her eyes.*] I've been with her, that's what has kept me. [*Newman turns round. Mrs. Bread rises.*] She bids me tell you she'll come to you. But you'll find it a sorry joy!

NEWMAN. I'll take the worst part of the sorrow out of it, or I'll know the reason why!

MRS. BREAD. You know it already. The reason why is a horrible big house, twenty miles from here, with high grey walls and little cold cells, full of wasting women who are for ever, on the hard stones, on their knees.

NEWMAN. Well, if it's twenty miles from here it ain't here yet. She has got to get there first!

MRS. BREAD. She expects to get there about midnight, to make it more cheerful!

NEWMAN. [*Coming down right centre to table, aghast.*] Do you mean she leaves to-night?

MRS. BREAD. In less than an hour. [*Goes to left centre.*] She has plotted it all, she's going to drive.

NEWMAN. [*Dryly.*] She'll have to drive over me!

MRS. BREAD. Oh, you'll feel the wheels—you'll feel the hoofs!

NEWMAN. I'll stop the horses—I'll knock the coachman down. Do the heads of the family know?

MRS. BREAD. They haven't an idea. She has arranged it, in secret, successfully, and now that the moment of her flight is near she's in a fever lest they should find her out. [*As the door on right opens.*] Here she comes! [*Comes down side of stage, left. Re-enter Mme. de Cintré, left. Exit Mrs. Bread, left. Claire stands looking at Newman, he having given a shocked start at the sight of her rigid black dress, as if taking it at first for the Carmelite garb.*]

CLAIRE. Don't suffer—you're too good to suffer.

NEWMAN. I think it's only those who are too good who do suffer!

CLAIRE. [*Coming to him.*] There are some whose suffering is expiation. I know I've deceived and injured you —I know I've been cowardly and cruel. I see it as vividly as you, and anything you may have said of me in your angriest passion is nothing to what I've said of myself.

NEWMAN. My angriest passion has spared you—it has clung to you as closely as my tenderest. But there are others whom it hasn't spared—and whom it doesn't mean to spare now!

CLAIRE. Ah, let others go—I'm beyond all others!

NEWMAN. [*Bitterly.*] You seem far away indeed—but you're not in heaven quite yet! Even if you were, however, I should ask you to come down to earth, a moment, to give me a reason, a decent reason, the faintest blush of a reason!

CLAIRE. My reason is all the past—the inseparable, irreparable past. It calls for me [*Raising her hands to her head.*]—it closes round me!

NEWMAN. It calls for *me*, too—and do you know what it says to me? That you're the victim of some unimaginable rigour, some coercion so unnatural that you're trying to hide it. You *can't* hide it—you're mere plate-glass! It's not by the dead you're haunted; you're haunted by the living!

CLAIRE. [*Looking at him a moment and crossing him round to right.*] Have it then that I'm haunted—if that will do for a reason! They won't haunt me *there!* [*Pointing to the window.*]

NEWMAN. In your living tomb?—you stick to that? You can speak of it with your own mild lips?

CLAIRE. I go to-night—I go in an hour. Farewell!

NEWMAN. [*Passing quickly between her and the lower door on left.*] Answer me a question first, and answer it in common pity. I've read somewhere that in the old times there was a thing called the Papal interdict—the strongest argument of the old domineering Church. [*Claire, arrested by his words, moves right.*] The old Popes used to screw it down, like a

big iron roof, over the crowns of the old kings, till all their sky was darkened. The thistles grew in their courts, the terror grew in their hearts, and it was not till the interdict was raised that they were restored to light and reason. That's *your* case to-day: [*Claire drops into chair, right.*] the interdict hangs over *you!* The iron roof is on *your* head, the thistles are in *your* court, the dread is in *your* heart! If I sweep these things utterly away, will you listen to me *then?* Will you come back to me?

CLAIRE. [*Moved, her head bowed.*] What are you going to do?

NEWMAN. I'm going to raise the interdict!

CLAIRE. [*Rising.*] You can't—you won't! Don't touch sacred things!

NEWMAN. Have they made you believe they're sacred? They don't play fair! It seems to me you practically acknowledge everything I want!

CLAIRE. I acknowledge nothing—for I *know* nothing. [*Her eyes down, her hands over her ears.*]

NEWMAN. You bandage your eyes, you stuff your ears, for fear of knowing! [*Moves a little left.*] That makes me sure!

CLAIRE. Let me pass—let me pass!

NEWMAN. And *this* makes me strong! [*Catching her in his arms as she tries to pass to left, he holds her for an instant in a close embrace. She breaks away—exits rapidly, left. Enter the Marquis from right.*] The Marquis? *Here's* a nuisance!

MARQUIS. [*Stopping short on seeing Newman.*] *You* here, sir? I hadn't the pleasure of knowing it.

NEWMAN. As my visit is exclusively to Madame de Cintré, I judged it superfluous to ask for you, or for Madame de Bellegarde, considering the terms on which we last parted.

MARQUIS. Permit me to express a doubt as to whether my sister will see you.

NEWMAN. Your sister *has* seen me, and I'm not without the hope that she will graciously see me again.

MARQUIS. [*Staggered a little, but recovering himself.*] Ah! [*Then, swinging his eyeglass.*] You've gained an advantage of us—prostrate as you find us with our dreadful bereavement; but I'm afraid you're in *precarious* possession. I emerged from the appropriate seclusion of my mother's apartments only because I thought I should find M. de Marignac, who seems to have vanished.

NEWMAN. He's on the premises— in case *I* want him. [*Taking his hat from table up at fireplace.*] I'll bring him right in.

MARQUIS. [*Aside, coming down while Newman goes up again.*] What's there between them—between Marignac and him? [*Moving to left. Turns round at table, left, and aloud, in a tone he has not yet used.*] Don't put yourself out—allow me the pleasure of sending a servant for M. de Marignac.

NEWMAN. [*Struck by his tone and staring a moment.*] You're too polite. I've a word to say to him myself. [*Aside.*] I want to tell him our prospect brightens! [*Exit Newman, rapidly, by the window, which he opens.*]

MARQUIS. [*Alone.*] Why should they hang about together? They're as thick as thieves!

[*Enter Mme. de Bellegarde, right.*]

MME. DE BELLEGARDE. [*Going up a little, then coming right centre.*] Ah, if he's not here, I might have spared myself the effort to meet him.

MARQUIS. He *is* here—very much here! [*Confidentially.*] I may mention to you that he strikes me as a trifle less objectionable than last week.

MME. DE BELLEGARDE. When did we ever find Gaston de Marignac objectionable?

MARQUIS. Pardon my confusion—I thought you meant Christopher Newman!

MME. DE BELLEGARDE. Is Christopher Newman here? [*Grandly, seating herself at head of table, right.*] He presumes on our desolation!

MARQUIS. So he does; but mightn't we, perhaps [*Hesitating, stammering a little and swinging his eyeglass, while he seats himself on sofa.*]— mightn't we, perhaps, presume upon it a little even ourselves? [*Watching the effect of these words on his mother.*] Remember the modifications!

MME. DE BELLEGARDE. The modifications?

MARQUIS. Everything has been modified but Christopher Newman's millions. [*Suggestively.*] *They* haven't, you know!

MME. DE BELLEGARDE. And the fact that we loathe him and despise him— has that been modified? [*The Marquis rises and comes down left centre; makes a prompt movement of deprecation and retraction.*] The fact that he's a base-born vulgar shopkeeper and that we were on the point of stooping to him, and to his abysses, and have picked ourselves up in time —has *that* been modified? [*Rises, while the Marquis repeats the gestures expressing that he humbly backs down. With culminating passion.*] Let us at least hold our heads higher than ever, to make up for having bowed them for an hour! [*Goes up.*]

MARQUIS. [*Aside.*] I see—*that's* settled! Well, it's a comfort to settle it— it's the shifting that tells on me!

[*Re-enter Marignac and Newman by the window, a portion of which has remained open.*]

MARIGNAC. [*Right centre.*] Good evening, Madame. I arrived an hour ago, to give two persons two mementoes which your lamented son put into my hand for them in the last hour of his life. One of these touching remembrances was for your daughter, to whom I've delivered it; the other was for Mrs. Bread—

NEWMAN. [*Right, interrupting.*] To whom *I've* delivered it!

MARQUIS. [*To Newman.*] You've made good use of your time!

NEWMAN. I hope to make still better! [*Goes up.*]

MARQUIS. [*Left, to Marignac.*] And my brother handed you [*Hesitating.*] no touching remembrance for *me?*

MARIGNAC. [*Dryly.*] Nothing.

MARQUIS. And none for his mother?

MARIGNAC. [*Putting his hat on table, right.*] Nothing.

MME. DE BELLEGARDE. [*Aside to Marquis.*] Idiot!

MARQUIS. [*Uncertain, aside, to Mme. de Bellegarde.*] Do you mean Valentin?

MME. DE BELLEGARDE. [*Aside.*] I mean *you!* [*Marquis goes up and round to centre. Aloud, to Marignac.*] If your extraordinary association with Mr. Newman permits you to give her a moment, a deeply afflicted mother would be glad to ask you a few questions.

NEWMAN. [*Aside, to Marignac, coming right of Marquis.*] Look out, she wants to square you! [*Aloud.*] I would

offer to retire, Madame, and leave you free to see Monsieur de Marignac on this spot, were it not that just on this spot I presently have a *very* particular appointment. [*Goes up.*]

MARQUIS. [*To Mme. de Bellegarde.*] He indulges the hope of another interview with Claire! [*Goes round to door, right.*]

MME. DE BELLEGARDE. Another? Monsieur de Marignac, will you please to pass into my boudoir? [*Newman comes down centre. Marignac bows somewhat inexpressively, takes up hat and exits right, the Marquis holding open the door. Mme. de Bellegarde crosses to right, then continues, to Newman.*] You've seen her then?

NEWMAN. Yes, and I'm waiting to see her again.

MME. DE BELLEGARDE. [*After an instant.*] I think you'll wait long! [*Exit Mme. de Bellegarde, right.*]

MARQUIS. [*To Newman, looking at his watch.*] We can't allow you all night, you know!

NEWMAN. [*Looking at his own.*] Allow me a quarter of an hour! [*Exit Marquis, right. Alone.*] I told Marignac to work them up, and [*As the door of Mme. de Cintré's apartment opens.*] here's Mrs. Bread at last, at last, to work *me* up!

[*Re-enter Mrs. Bread, left down.*]

MRS. BREAD. The poor child's terribly nervous; she has but one idea in her head—that her flight may be hindered.

NEWMAN. So it will be, thank God!

MRS. BREAD. Ah, but I've told you their ignorance.

NEWMAN. Their ignorance ain't bliss; they feel there's something in the air.

MRS. BREAD. There's always something in the air now. To-night I can scarcely breathe.

NEWMAN. I can't breathe either—I seem to pant in the void. *What* are you going to give me?

MRS. BREAD. I shall give you strange things, sir, and after I've spoken, this house will be no place for me. I shall have to leave it on the instant.

NEWMAN. That's perfect—you'll come right down to me at the inn. You'll stay right on with me now.

MRS. BREAD. I know a decent woman in the village, and I've just sent my clothes there, and some of the Countess's, in case we stop her.

NEWMAN. Oh, we'll stop her!

MRS. BREAD. Then she'll find her refuge ready—at my end of the village; while at the other, at the inn, *you* wait for dawn. And when the blessed dawn comes—

NEWMAN. [*Interrupting.*] Praise be to the Highest—she'll marry me!

MRS. BREAD. It will take longer than that! One sees you're an American.

NEWMAN. One sees *you* ain't! It won't take longer than *you* take, I guess!

MRS. BREAD. Well, then! [*On the point of speaking she stops again and looks round her. She rises, then goes right, and stands listening a moment at the door.*]

NEWMAN. [*Impatient.*] Oh, *they're* all right—Marignac's looking after them!

MRS. BREAD. [*On the same spot, stands for an instant with her eyes on him. Then, while a visible change suddenly takes place in her face and manner, she comes back to him.*] They're murderers—they're murderers!

NEWMAN. [*Excited, with a kind of joy, as if it is even better than he has* hoped; while they sink together on sofa.*] MURDERERS!

MRS. BREAD. My lady put an end to her husband. I have the precious proof —his own declaration, on his death-bed, when, the hour before he passed away in misery, he accused and denounced them. He wrote it down—he signed it!

NEWMAN. [*Incredulous.*] When he was dying?

MRS. BREAD. I held him up on the pillow, and the God of justice gave him strength. The Comte de Cintré had *loved* my lady—he was her lover still. My lady, in her day, went far, and her day was very long.

NEWMAN. Lord, the old hypocrite [*Aside.*] being shocked at poor little Noémie!

MRS. BREAD. That's how he held her —that's how he made her go! [*Coming closer still.*] He knew things of her—more even than I know! She had had money from him, and to the best of her ability she had made it up to him in money's worth! But he taught her that her debt would hang over her head till she had given him her helpless child.

NEWMAN. [*Attentive, horrified.*] Ah, the infamous scoundrels! No wonder Madame de Cintré takes life hard!

MRS. BREAD. Her father tried to save her, but he was beaten—he was ill. My lady spent half a night in his room—a bitter winter's night.

NEWMAN. And what did she do there?

MRS. BREAD. She stood over him and mocked and threatened him, while the Marquis, in the passage, kept the door. She calculated exactly what would do for him and never leave a mark. The particular potion that the doctor had left to soothe him, to save him, to stop his suffering, which without it was unbearable: do you know what she did with the blessed beneficent drug? She poured it away before his eyes, into the cold ashes of the hearth, and she told him, cruelly, why she did so!

NEWMAN. It sounds like some creepy legend!

MRS. BREAD. I found the traces when she left him—I found the empty phial. She had done her work well—but I did mine. My pity warmed him into life an instant—he flickered up into a kind of supernatural flame, and in the very arms of death he was capable of the miracle of writing twenty words. He was like the angel of *judgment!* [*Sinks back to chair, right, falls into it.*]

NEWMAN. [*Who has followed her closely, critically, and yet with a conviction and a horror that at last completely and visibly hold him.*] And those twenty words, where are they? Ain't I to see them?

MRS. BREAD. As soon as I'm out of the house.

NEWMAN. That makes me want you to go, though unfortunately I'm obliged to recognise that in the eye of the law your wonderful document isn't worth *that!* [*Snapping his fingers.*]

MRS. BREAD. The eye that would look through my lady, in the light of that grim paper, would be a very different one. The eye of a certain society!

NEWMAN. *What* society?

MRS. BREAD. The grand particular world that surrounds her—for which she keeps up appearances.

NEWMAN. The grand particular world to which, last week, she made such a grand particular fool of me?

MRS BREAD. The only world she recognises or considers or fears!

NEWMAN. Do you mean it suspects her—that you spoke at the time?

MRS. BREAD. Never, never; I held my tongue for the younger children's sake. The doctors wondered immensely, but my lady brazened them down—there was no blood and no poison. But the wonder has never really died out. You could wake it up again!

NEWMAN. [*Silent a moment, as if sifting and settling the story in his thoughts, so that he accepts it.*] Well, I guess I'll wake it up! You say you spared the younger children; but the Count's charge to me shows they've known something.

MRS. BREAD. They've heard the echo—they've hovered on the edge of the truth.

NEWMAN. The edge?—Tonight Claire has *crossed* it!

MRS. BREAD. Then the great blow has fallen, the blow by the fear of which my lady has always held her—the constant menace of her own version, the revelation that the late Marquis was secretly abominable, that, for instance, he could stoop to an intrigue with such a one as *me!* [*Newman, with his hands in his pockets, more and more stirred by all he has listened to, walks restlessly up and stands looking a moment out of the window to the terrace, where thick dusk has now gathered.*] She feels that's false—she has guessed what's true.

NEWMAN. [*As he comes quickly down.*] Your paper, your paper, your paper! [*At centre.*] You call it precious, and it has the value of being exactly a test. If they're innocent, it won't have the force of *one* of the heart-beats it has given me to hear about it. But if they're guilty, it will make them perspire! [*Re-enter, right, M. de Marignac, who catches these last words.*]

MARIGNAC. If you're talking of our friends in there, they're perspiring pretty freely already. I seem to have administered a Turkish bath!

NEWMAN. Exactly, you're the eye of society! [*To Mrs. Bread, explaining.*] He's the old lady's grand particular world. She recognises and considers and fears *him*, and she has been keeping up appearances! [*To Marignac again.*] Do you remember all those fine people I was laid out for the other night?

MARIGNAC. Remember them? They're mostly my cousins!

NEWMAN. Then you're all the five hundred in one. [*Mrs. Bread lights candles on table, left, with matches that are on table.*] That's why I wanted you.

MARIGNAC. That, perhaps, is also why they've been abusing you to me at such a rate.

NEWMAN. Glory—glory! They're afraid!

MARIGNAC. I took the liberty of defending you, but you'll have them back on top of you—they're coming to turn you out.

NEWMAN. [*To Mrs. Bread.*] My card, my trump card, if I'm going to win the game!

MRS. BREAD. Come with me, M. de Marignac. [*Marignac goes up to left upper entrance with her.*] There's a great service you can render us.

MARIGNAC. [*To Newman.*] Shall I leave you alone, then? Sha'n't I stay to

help you?

NEWMAN. You'll help me best by doing exactly what this lovely old lady asks of you. [*Exeunt left upper entrance, Mrs. Bread and Marignac, and at the same moment, before they disappear, re-enter Mme. de Bellegarde, right. Newman, who has gone up urgently with the others and who, at their exit, has pressed Mrs. Bread's hand jubilantly, as if for a temporary parting, meets her as he comes down, immediately saying:*] Let me anticipate your just curiosity as to the reasons of my continued intrusion by telling you that I'm *still* waiting to see your daughter!

MME. DE BELLEGARDE. Waiting in remarkable company: that of the menial who answers my bell, and of the pretended man of the world who bargained away the safety of my son!

NEWMAN. [*Aside.*] Lord, she *is* pretty bad! [*Aloud, with his hands in his pockets.*] To me they're delightful people—for they've given me a certain confidence.

MME. DE BELLEGARDE. A certain impudence, I judge!

NEWMAN. Madame de Bellegarde, set your daughter this moment at liberty.

MME. DE BELLEGARDE. [*Looking at him a moment, then, as if altering the intention of her tone before she speaks.*] My daughter's at perfect liberty!

NEWMAN. At liberty to let you grind her to powder! I fully recognise the blight you've cast upon her, but I also recognise that you are perfectly able to dissipate it—that you can do so by saying to her in my presence that you repent of the odious way you've used us, and that you utterly renounce and retract all opposition to our marriage.

MME. DE BELLEGARDE. I shall never utter such words.

NEWMAN. I think I can persuade you to utter them—that I hold in my hand the means. Don't wonder too long what they are. [*Goes close to her.*] Simply remember the night your husband died!

MME. DE BELLEGARDE. I'm not likely to forget it!

NEWMAN. There are other people who haven't forgotten it; but even if they had, a reminder exists.

MME. DE BELLEGARDE. A reminder?

NEWMAN. Written by the hand and signed with the name of the dying man, and denouncing you as his torturer and his murderess. [*Mme. de Bellegarde staggers back, catching at chair.*] Your face tells me it isn't waste paper!

MME. DE BELLEGARDE. It's the stupidest of forgeries.

NEWMAN. Oh, not the stupidest! Reflect upon this, that your reputation, however much draped and arranged, can hardly bear a sudden, strong light. If I open a shutter from within, the others will be opened from without!

MME. DE BELLEGARDE. [*Falling back to the door of her apartments.*] Insulter—calumniator—liar!

NEWMAN. The shutter I speak of is still practically closed, but I have my hand upon the bolt. Call back here this instant the woman you've wrenched out of my arms, recant your incantations and reverse your spells, and your congruous darkness may close round you again, never again to be disturbed.

MME. DE BELLEGARDE. [*With her back to her door and her hand upon its latch, immensely affected but still immensely defiant.*] I'll send my son to drive you from the house and hurl your outrage after you!

NEWMAN. Your son ought to have faced me first, but after all you're the tigress, *he's* only the cub! [*Goes centre, while re-enter rapidly, left upper entrance, M. de Marignac, the sight of whom, bearing in his hand a letter with a visible black seal, arrests Mme. de Bellegarde a moment longer on her threshold.*] You're just what I want to see! [*Newman quickly takes the letter from Marignac, and goes on addressing her.*] Send the Marquis to listen to *this!*

MME. DE BELLEGARDE. Is Catherine Bread the forger? [*To Marignac.*] She was my husband's mistress—she was always a monster of deceit.

MARIGNAC. She has left your house, Madame—she has left it forever.

MME. DE BELLEGARDE. Happy for *her!* [*Exit Mme. de Bellegarde, right.*]

NEWMAN. [*To Marignac.*] I'm getting on beautifully, but the Marquis is coming, and we mustn't be two to one.

MARIGNAC. Then I'll go and wait for you at the inn.

NEWMAN. You've been first-rate [*Taking Marignac's hand.*]; and if you want to oblige me further you might order supper.

MARIGNAC. [*With his hand in Newman's, smiling.*] For how many?

NEWMAN. Well, I guess you had better say four! [*Exit Marignac, left upper entrance, and the moment he has done so re-enter Mme. de Cintré left in a long black mantle, with its hood thrown back, adding to her perceptibly nun-like appearance, as if just prepared for her flight.*]

CLAIRE. What are you doing, Mr. Newman—and what have you already done?

NEWMAN. [*With his letter unopened in his hand.*] How do you know I've done anything?

CLAIRE. Mrs. Bread has just been to me, in intense excitement; she tells me she's leaving us forever.

NEWMAN. Oh, you'll see her again!

CLAIRE. When I asked her what had happened she told me you were still here, and that I must come to you and learn it from *your* lips.

NEWMAN. She never gave you happier advice!

CLAIRE. Why then has she gone?

NEWMAN. Because she's a woman of tact. But she has left behind her [*Holding up the letter.*] something that's almost as good as herself.

CLAIRE. What is it? What *is* it?

NEWMAN. A little scrap of paper that frightens your mother.

CLAIRE. And what are you doing with it?

NEWMAN. I'm raising the interdict!

CLAIRE. I don't understand—you torment me!

NEWMAN. I torment your mother —that's more to the purpose. She'll come back here in a moment and entreat you to forgive the life she has always led you and the injury she has tried to do *me*.

CLAIRE. That won't help you, Mr. Newman—for I'm utterly irrecoverable now! I shall never see her again —the carriage that's to take me away is at the door.

NEWMAN. Well, why don't you go down to it?

CLAIRE. [*Looking at him a moment in silence; then suddenly, passionately.*] Mr. Newman—don't be hard!

Be merciful if you're strong!

NEWMAN. *You* plead for mercy for them?—But I *knew* you are an angel!

CLAIRE. [*In the same way.*] You say you torment them. *Don't* torment them!

NEWMAN. What mercy have they had on *you?*

CLAIRE. Me? Oh, I'm safe forever!

NEWMAN. And am *I* safe, please? What mercy have they had on me?

CLAIRE. It's too terrible—and I don't understand. Give me your paper!

NEWMAN. [*Heedless of her request, going somewhat nearer to the door on the right and listening.*] I'm expecting your brother from one moment to another, so that if you wish to escape you have no time to lose.

CLAIRE. Do you mean that you're capable of telling him where I'm going?

NEWMAN. No, not that; I presume that would be mean!

CLAIRE. That's why I appeal to you —because you're generous, because you're loyal! I appeal to you to give me your letter!

NEWMAN. [*With a kind of grim groan, putting the letter behind him.*] Ah, don't ask me that—don't ask me that!

CLAIRE. You speak as if it gave you a power—but *what* power does it give you?

NEWMAN. God forbid I should denounce a mother to her child—however wronged the child may have been, and however iniquitous the mother. I can't tell you what power it gives me, unless I know how much *you* know.

CLAIRE. [*With a wild movement of denial, waving everything away.*] I know nothing—I know nothing!

NEWMAN. Well, *I* know everything, and now they know that I know!

CLAIRE. Isn't that enough, then? Give me your letter—give me your letter!

NEWMAN. To destroy it, to *spare* them, to *save* them, to deprive me of my immense advantage? You say I'm generous, but don't put my generosity on the rack!

CLAIRE. Don't put my terrors and my sorrows—whatever survives of any piety!

NEWMAN. If I keep my advantage we're free, we're strong, we're happy! You're liberated by your mother's hand, you're reprieved from the death you're bent on! The world's all before us again, and we go forth into it again together! Listen to that—*think* of that —and ask for the sacrifice!

CLAIRE. I can't listen and I can't think! You torture me! Only give it to me? [*She presses upon him, round to left and to right, with clasped hands of entreaty.*] Give it to me—give it to me!

NEWMAN. [*Receding before her and holding the letter out of her reach.*] Be mine—be mine—be mine!

CLAIRE. Pity me—how can I choose?

NEWMAN. If I give you this thing, I give up everything forever!

CLAIRE. I hear them coming, and if you keep me till they come you betray me!

NEWMAN. Why, if I don't speak of your intention?

CLAIRE. They'll see me dressed to go—they'll stop the carriage!

NEWMAN. Go, go, then—if you like that better!

CLAIRE. And leave you to destroy them? I can't—it's too horrible! [*Re-enter the Marquis, right, whom Claire sees, giving a cry.*] Urbain, don't come in!

NEWMAN. [*To Claire, while the Marquis, perceptibly pale, stands looking from one of them to the other.*] Now do you see what I mean by my frightening them? But they've frightened each other even more!

MARQUIS. [*Looking from head to foot at Newman, who still has the letter behind him, and then turning to Mme. de Cintré.*] Why are you dressed to go out?

CLAIRE. [*Bewildered a moment.*] Mrs. Bread has gone away—I'm going to overtake her! [*Then, hurriedly, feverishly.*] Mr. Newman has something in his hand—I'm trying to get it from him!

NEWMAN. [*To Mme. de Cintré.*] I'll give it to you if you'll promise me on your sacred honour to give it back to *me* and not to another creature.

CLAIRE. [*With her hand out.*] I promise—I promise!

NEWMAN. Then *take* it! [*He holds it out to her, at the sight of which, before she can take it, the Marquis makes an unexpected desperate spring for it. Newman recovers it and, moving to centre, jerks it behind him, smiling. To Mme. de Cintré.*] You see how badly they want it! [*To the Marquis.*] It *is* a loaded pistol, Marquis— and dangerous to play with! You can easily understand I don't want to waste the charge!

CLAIRE. [*To the Marquis, imploringly.*] Let *me* take it—I beseech you! [*To Newman.*] Give it to me now— he'll let you. *Give* it to me!

MARQUIS. [*To Newman.*] I forbid you—don't, don't!

NEWMAN. [*Compassionately.*] How foolish you are! Do you think she'll read it? [*To Mme. de Cintré.*] How little they know you, after all!

CLAIRE. Give it to *him*, then—give it to him! You've offered me innumerable services—so how can you refuse the only one I ever asked you? [*Falls on her knees before him.*]

NEWMAN. [*Struggling hard—passing his hand over his face.*] Refuse it? [*Taking her hands and raising her.*] I *love* it too much!—Hang it all, Monsieur de Bellegarde, I let you off! I let your mother off. [*Looking at Mme. de Cintré.*] I let every one off.

CLAIRE. [*With her hand to her heart and a long exhalation of relief.*] A-ah! [*Newman hands the letter to the Marquis, who takes it now with a studied absence of eagerness, and Mme. de Cintré continues, to Newman.*] Oh, you're perfect!

MARQUIS. [*To Mme. de Cintré, while, with affected indifference, he puts the letter, without looking at it, into his breastpocket.*] That's more than can be said of you, Madame! [*Moving to door, right.*] Your mother will say a word to you, first, on the subject of your overtaking Mrs. Bread. [*Exit Marquis, right.*]

NEWMAN. [*To Mme. de Cintré.*] He's gone to tell her—on the other side of the door he'll skip! That shows they feel saved from death! [*He goes to take up his hat.*]

CLAIRE. Their satisfaction will last but an instant.

NEWMAN. That's better than to have none—like me!

CLAIRE. [*Right centre, watching him.*] I was right, I was right—you're magnanimous!

NEWMAN. [*With a flicker of returning hope.*] Ah, Claire—don't say such things *now!*

CLAIRE. Now is just the time—as the carriage is there!

NEWMAN. [*Eagerly.*] The carriage? [*Re-enter the Marquis, right.*]

MARQUIS. [*To Newman.*] You had really better leave the family to itself. My mother's coming.

CLAIRE. [*Giving her left hand to Newman.*] Tell her when she comes that I shall marry Mr. Newman.

NEWMAN. Ah, my beloved! [*Kisses her hand.*]

CLAIRE. You've done it—you've brought me back—you've vanquished me!

NEWMAN. That's just what I wanted to see! [*He has caught her with one arm, and gives her a long kiss. He hurries up with her—exeunt rapidly left upper entrance. At the same moment re-enter Mme. de Bellegarde, right, breaking in with the letter that Newman has given the Marquis, open in her hand.*]

MARQUIS. He's gone—but she's gone with him!

MME. DE BELLEGARDE. [*Crossing swiftly to one of the lighted candles that stand on a table at left and thrusting her paper straight into the flame.*] May they never come back—may they never come back!

MARQUIS. [*On the other side of the stage, watching the paper burn while the Curtain falls.*] Any more than that thing, eh?

FRAGMENT OF NEW FOURTH ACT FOR
THE AMERICAN

[*Same scene as Act Third. On the rise of the Curtain enter rapidly, busily, the Doctor, centre. Feeling in his pocket for a pencil, and looking about for paper, he goes, right, to the table, on which he sees a portfolio and on which his hat has already been placed. He takes a bit of paper from the portfolio and, standing and bending over, hastily writes. Enter Noémie, in her hat and jacket, left, with several unopened letters in her hand.*]

DOCTOR. [*Folding the small paper and giving it to Noémie.*] Something to be *sent* for—for the *nurse.*

NOÉMIE. [*Who has laid down her letters, anxious.*] Isn't the Count better?

DOCTOR. [*Taking his hat.*] I can't *say!*

NOÉMIE. [*Disappointed.*] But I thought this morning was to *show!*

DOCTOR. I promised nothing, Mademoiselle. It was a necessary experiment.

NOÉMIE. But surely it has *succeeded!*

DOCTOR. It *may* succeed. It's too soon to *judge.*

NOÉMIE. [*At right, persistent.*] When *can* you judge?

DOCTOR. [*At left, hesitating, looking at his watch.*] He's quiet—I shall come back at *one.* [*Exit Doctor, left.*]

NOÉMIE. [*At centre, unfolding the small paper he has given her; with, while she looks at it, uplifted eyebrows and a slight grimace of anxiety.*] I must *send.* [*Then gathering up the letters she has laid down and reading from the postmarks on the envelopes.*] New York, Boston, Chicago, London, Rome, Bombay! [*While she speaks the last word enter Newman, centre: perceptibly altered, paler, worn and worried. She turns eagerly as she hears him.*] Is he *quiet?*

NEWMAN. [*With a manner different*

from hitherto—rather curt, preoccupied and impatient.] As quiet as if he'd *money* on it! Are those my *letters?*

NOÉMIE. [*Giving him the letters.*] I just brought them *in.*

NEWMAN. [*Looking rapidly at the successive envelopes, then, with impatient disappointment, chucking them toward the table, so that they fall and lie scattered on the floor.*] You might as well have brought a row of pins!—They ain't what I *want!*

NOÉMIE. [*After an instant, reassuringly.*] What you want will *come,* Mr. Newman. [*Then with intenser decision.*] I *know* it will come!

NEWMAN. You talk, Miss Noémie, as if you had a private *wire!*

NOÉMIE. [*Precipitately.*] Well, I *have!* [*Then catching herself up.*] I know more than you *think.*

NEWMAN. [*Turning away, on his side, restlessly, with irritation, an eclipse of his old geniality.*] "Think"? —I've ceased to think. I've ceased almost to *feel.*

NOÉMIE. [*Taking the risk, as he goes nervously, vaguely up, as if wandering and looking about him for something that hasn't come to pass, that still doesn't appear.*] You may be sure that *she* hasn't! She'll take pity on you *yet!*

NEWMAN. [*Struck, then facing her abruptly.*] Whom are you *talking* about?

NOÉMIE. [*Slightly disconcerted by his manner and explaining.*] I thought you alluded—to a certain lady!

NEWMAN. [*With strong emphasis.*] I *never* allude—to a certain lady!

NOÉMIE. [*Apologetic.*] I was misled by your eagerness for [*Vague.*] some communication.

NEWMAN. The communication I'm

eager for is a communication—"answer paid"!

NOÉMIE. There's a quarter, no doubt, from which you're *not* expecting news. But [*After an instant.*] I daresay you'll have some, all the *same!*

NEWMAN. I won't have any if I can *help* it! I've had about enough to *last* me!

NOÉMIE. Of course I'm thinking of some *better* news!

NEWMAN. [*With a certain irritation.*] You think too much, Miss Noémie. [*Knocking over, with his restless motion, and with some violence, a jar, or some object on the table.*] You had better imitate my *repose!*

NOÉMIE. [*Laughing.*] Your repose is bad for the furniture.

NEWMAN. Oh, if I should *really* lie down I guess you'd have to *renew* it! [*Then with a quick revulsion, penitent, with his hand out.*] Forgive my cussedness! There are moments when I don't know what to *do* with myself!

NOÉMIE. [*With sympathy, taking his hand.*] You're awfully *worried!*

NEWMAN. [*Admitting, explaining.*] About the results of the Count's operation. We hoped for an unmistakeable effect.

NOÉMIE. Which doesn't take *place?*

NEWMAN. It's a bad moment to *pass.* I can see the surgeon's *uneasy.*

NOÉMIE. And the *others*—who were *present?*

NEWMAN. If we're not reassured by this afternoon, they're to meet *again.*

NOÉMIE. And if the operation's a *failure*—

NEWMAN. [*Interrupting, sombre, raising his arms and letting them fall.*] The *worst* may happen!

NOÉMIE. [*With feeling, with resolution.*] The worst shan't happen! His

natural strength's immense!

NEWMAN. [*Considering, agreeing.*] Yes, greater, even now, than *mine! I can't* recuperate!

NOÉMIE. [*Smiling at him, soothingly.*] You want a *nurse!*

NEWMAN. I want about *fifty!*

NOÉMIE. If the effect you speak of, for the Count, *does* take place—

NEWMAN. [*Interrupting.*] He'll come up in an hour!

NOÉMIE. [*With surprise.*] In an *hour?*

NEWMAN. [*Confident.*] In a *minute* —in a *day*, in a *week!* [*With a bitter smile.*] Oh, faster than *I!*

NOÉMIE. [*With recurring intention and significance.*] Oh *you*, Mr. Newman—!

NEWMAN. [*Impatient, weary, interrupting.*] Don't speak of *me*—I ain't sure I'm *alive!*

NOÉMIE. [*With spirit.*] Well, some other people are, thank heaven, and *while* there's life, in any quarter, I've always heard there's *hope!* [*Then, as Newman, fidgety, moves away again with a gesture of nervous pessimism.*] We must *pray* for the Count!

NEWMAN. You *can't* pray. [*Then, in a more explanatory tone, as he turns back to Noémie again.*] I've a *double* anxiety, and a deadly *impatience.* The letter I'm looking for is a letter from *Mrs. Bread.*

NOÉMIE. [*Struck.*] Their English housekeeper?

NEWMAN. The plain Wiltshire woman! I wrote to her three days ago—I begged her to *come* to me.

NOÉMIE. [*Thinking, suggesting.*] Perhaps your letter never *reached* her.

NEWMAN. To their country home. That's where they've *gone.*

NOÉMIE. [*Wondering again.*] You

asked her to come up to Paris?

NEWMAN. To render me a service.

NOÉMIE. [*After an instant.*] What service can *she* render you?

NEWMAN. [*At the centre door.*] That's just what I want to *see!* [*Exit Newman, centre.*]

NOÉMIE. [*Alone, picking up the fallen letters and putting them into her pocket while she repeats his words.*] "A double anxiety—a deadly impatience"? And what are *mine*, I should like to know? [*Eagerly, seeing Nioche at the left. Enter Nioche, left.*] Who *is* it?

NIOCHE. [*Announcing.*] Milord Deepmere! [*Enter Lord Deepmere, with his arm in a sling, left.*]

NOÉMIE. [*With relief, as he takes her hand and raises it respectfully to his lips.*] At *last!*

NIOCHE. [*To Noémie.*] Shall I inform Mr. Newman?

NOÉMIE. [*Giving him the little folded paper left by the Doctor and which she has kept in her hand during the scene with Newman.*] No— you'll go out for *this.* [*Exit Nioche, who has taken the paper obediently, left; on which Noémie goes on, warningly, to Deepmere.*] Be very *quiet* —we've reached the *crisis.*

DEEPMERE. [*Disappointed, anxious.*] Isn't he *better?*

NOÉMIE. We shall know at noon. [*Then pressingly.*] Have you been to the *Convent?*

DEEPMERE. I've just *left* it. She'll *come!*

NOÉMIE. *A la bonne heure!* You followed my *instructions?*

DEEPMERE. To the *letter!* I left your note yesterday, with my own card, on which I wrote a few words. This morning I had a gracious line from her asking to see me at an early hour.

NOÉMIE. And she *did* see you?

DEEPMERE. In the parlour, for five minutes. She's free, a *pensionnaire,* she can receive.

NOÉMIE. She has taken no vow?

DEEPMERE. Not so *soon*—in three *weeks!* She has only taken *refuge*— she has only been *waiting.*

NOÉMIE. For Mr. Newman to try *again?*

DEEPMERE. For her brother to come back to *life!* She has a passionate desire to *see* him.

NOÉMIE. Then why hasn't she come before?

DEEPMERE. How could she enter the house of the man she feels she has terribly *injured?*

NOÉMIE. I hope that if she's coming now it isn't because she has *ceased* to feel it.

DEEPMERE. It's because you've appealed to her for poor Bellegarde, from whom it's only her dread of *meeting* Mr. Newman that has separated her.

NOÉMIE. [*Thinking.*] Does she count on me, by chance, to arrange that she shall *not* meet Mr. Newman?

DEEPMERE. She didn't tell me so, but she rather let me see it.

NOÉMIE. [*With decision.*] Then she let you see a great piece of *nonsense!* I've a perfect little plan that the poor things *shall* meet!

DEEPMERE. Your little plans are no business of mine. I performed your errand to render you the service you required, and you may imagine the *courage*—you must do justice to the *heroism,* I needed, to present myself before her while [*With an expression of strong feeling, of repentant bitterness, and a significant nod toward the other room.*] her brother lies there in such a state!

NOÉMIE. I rendered *you* a service, rather, by putting it in your power to entreat her to *forgive* you!

DEEPMERE. How *will* she forgive me—if Bellegarde doesn't pull through?

NOÉMIE. [*After an instant.*] I don't know how *she* will, Milord—but I know very well that *I* won't!

DEEPMERE. [*Nervously, gloomily.*] I worry myself half to *death*, I'm sick and sore with *suspense!*

NOÉMIE. You have your *alleviations*, Milord—your frequent visits to this house.

DEEPMERE. I come to *ask*—I come to *watch*; but it's *not* an alleviation—for you only torment me *more!*

NOÉMIE. Mr. Newman makes it *up* to you—he makes everything up to *everyone!*

DEEPMERE. He's as kind as he's *queer*—I never did him justice. But what comfort is there in a man who's in still worse spirits than myself?

NOÉMIE. He *is*, to-day, I admit. Therefore you had better not *see* him.

DEEPMERE. I don't *want* to see him. When there's a bad report of Bellegarde I don't want to look any one in the *face!*

NOÉMIE. [*Minimising.*] There isn't exactly a *bad* report.

DEEPMERE. [*Objecting.*] But if there isn't exactly a *good* one—? The only good one will be to see him standing *there!*

NOÉMIE. [*After another instant.*] Well, Milord—you *shall* see him!

DEEPMERE. [*Incredulous, with a backward nod of his head.*] If you could only have a little plan for *that!*

NOÉMIE. I *have* a little plan! I'm wiser than the doctors. *Leave* it to me!

DEEPMERE. I don't know what you mean, but I'm ready to say *this* to you—that if he gets *well*— [*Pausing, hesitating.*]

NOÉMIE. [*Waiting.*] If he gets well?

DEEPMERE. [*Continuing.*] By any intervention of *yours*, there's nothing on *earth* you may ask of me that I won't gladly *give* you!

NOÉMIE. Thank you, Milord. As a general thing I don't *have* to "ask"!

DEEPMERE. Don't you sometimes have to *choose*?

NOÉMIE. [*After a moment.*] Do I understand that in the event you speak of I *may*?

DEEPMERE. [*Emphatically.*] *Anything* that's mine!

NOÉMIE. [*After another instant, looking at him.*] I'll *choose!*—Now leave me to receive the Countess! [*Seeing Nioche, left.*] My father will show you out.

[*Re-enter Nioche, left, with a small packet.*]

NIOCHE. [*With the packet, to Noémie.*] I give it to the nurse?

DEEPMERE. [*To Nioche, on a motion of assent from Noémie.*] Don't mind me! [*Nioche bows and exits with packet at centre, and Deepmere goes up, to Noémie.*] You must really let me come *back!*

NOÉMIE. [*Looking at him an instant.*] Did you *mean* what you said just now?

DEEPMERE. Did you mean what *you* said?

NOÉMIE. [*With a nod of decision.*] I *meant* it!

DEEPMERE. Well—*I* meant it!

NOÉMIE. Then shake hands—*à l'anglaise!* [*He gives her his hand and she gives it a vigorous "British" shake, up and down.*] Come back at *one.*

DEEPMERE. At one! [*Exit Lord Deepmere, left. Re-enter Nioche, centre.*]

NOÉMIE. What does she say?

NIOCHE. [*With his finger to his lips.*] Shshsh!

NOÉMIE. [*Imitating him.*] "Shshsh" indeed! We've got hold of the *Countess!*

NIOCHE. [*Astonished.*] Got *hold* of her?

NOÉMIE. She's coming at any moment.

NIOCHE. [*Bewildered.*] Then what shall we do with Mr. Newman?

NOÉMIE. Get hold of *him!*

NIOCHE. [*Alarmed.*] But think of the possible consequences of their meeting!

NOÉMIE. They're just what I *have* thought of! I shall bring them together, and you must *help* me.

NIOCHE. What shall I *do?*

NOÉMIE. See that she comes straight in *here.*

NIOCHE. [*Troubled, incredulous.*] If he knows she's in here he'll go *out!*

NOÉMIE. I'll keep him at home! [*Seeing Newman, centre.*] Here he *is* —watch for *her!*

[*Re-enter Newman, centre. Exit Nioche, left.*]

[Four pages of the manuscript are missing at this point.]

. . . *his hand into Newman's arm— exeunt Newman and Doctor, centre. Re-enter Nioche, left.*]

NIOCHE. [*Announcing.*] Madame la Comtesse de Cintré.

NOÉMIE. [*To herself, with happy emotion.*] Ah!

[*Enter, left, Madame de Cintré.*

Exit Nioche, discreetly, left.]

NOÉMIE. [*Curtseying very respectfully.*] Madame!

CLAIRE. [*Graciously, but very gravely.*] Mademoiselle.—Let me acknowledge instantly my great obligation to you; but let me also say that I have presumed to find in your intervention a pledge that the step I am taking in response to it shall be attended with inconvenience—to *no* one.—May I see my brother *instantly?*

NOÉMIE. You must allow me to prepare him for your visit.

CLAIRE. [*Surprised.*] He doesn't *expect* me?

NOÉMIE. [*Smiling.*] We don't let him *expect!*

CLAIRE. [*Anxious.*] He's very *weak*, then—he's *worse?*

NOÉMIE. He'll be better when he has seen you!

CLAIRE. [*Nervous.*] I shall be very brief.

NOÉMIE. So shall I, Madame. [*Then, indicating a chair.*] Be so good, meanwhile, as to be seated.

CLAIRE. [*Uneasy, standing, looking round the room and recognising it.*] Is there no place in the house in which my intrusion will be less apparent than *here?*

NOÉMIE. [*Smiling.*] Trust me, Madame, to have measured your risk and to have your interests at *heart!*

CLAIRE. It's only because I trust you that I'm here. Shall I see you again before I leave the house?

NOÉMIE. That will depend, Madame, on your own inclination.

CLAIRE. Let me make sure, at any rate, of this opportunity of thanking you for the kindness Lord Deepmere informs me you have shown my brother. [*Hesitating, then with suppressed*

emotion, a kind of painful effort.]
And if there have been *other* ministrations—and *other* charities—[*Hesitating again with her emotion, pausing.*]

NOÉMIE. [*At right, seeing Newman, centre.*] I've done what I *could*, Madame!

[*Re-enter Newman, centre.*]

CLAIRE. [*At left, violently struck, to herself.*] Ah! [*Exit Noémie, rapidly, discreetly, by the staircase. Arrested, at centre, violently, on his side, a moment, by the sight of Madame de Cintré, then controlling himself with a strong effort, Newman comes down on right. They stand an instant on opposite sides of the stage, not looking at each other. At last, sadly, coldly, but without anger, Claire exclaims.*] The work of that young lady!

NEWMAN. [*After an instant, looking straight before him.*] That young lady *means* well!

CLAIRE. I hesitated half the night —but I've *come!*

NEWMAN. I know what it's for. It must have seemed to you hard you *shouldn't!*

CLAIRE. It seemed *impossible!* But I never *dreamed*—of disturbing *you.* [*Newman looks at her, at this, and there is another silence between them while she stands, motionless and expressionless, with her eyes on the ground.*] Mayn't I *go* to him?

NEWMAN. I must say a word to him *first.*

CLAIRE. [*After an instant, as Newman doesn't move.*] I hoped he might *know.*

NEWMAN. I haven't told him.

CLAIRE. [*Struck, vague.*] You *knew* then I was coming?

NEWMAN. I learned it five minutes ago. If I had done so sooner I would have kept out of your way.

CLAIRE. [*As impersonally as possible.*] Let me get out of yours. [*Then, after another instant, as he still doesn't move.*] But before I do so, let me express in one word— [*Pausing, faltering in her effort to efface all emotion, to be utterly passionless.*]

NEWMAN. [*With a sudden faint hope.*] In one word?

CLAIRE. [*As if to say all she means, but at the same time to check him by her manner—to make any outbreak impossible.*] The intensity of my gratitude.

NEWMAN. [*After standing an instant with his eyes on the ground suddenly shaken by irresistible feeling and breaking out into a single abrupt cry of passionate appeal.*] Claire!

CLAIRE. [*Straightening herself and speaking with rapid and colourless formality.*] Be so very good as to *tell* him! [*Newman, who has instantly, at the sight of her manner, controlled himself again, stands one instant more and gives her one long, fixed and intensely searching look. Then, as if satisfied afresh that he has indeed lost her forever and that nothing more can pass between them, he decides, gives a gesture in which he seems to dash away the last shadow of his hope, and goes out rapidly at centre. Mme. de Cintré, left alone, sinks slowly, and as if with the sense of momentary liberation from the worst distress, into the nearest chair, where she sits an instant staring, with infinite sadness, before her. Then slowly, dolorously, hopelessly.*] Ah, miserable me!

[*Re-enter, left, Nioche, at the sound of whose entrance Mme. de Cintré quickly springs up.*]

NIOCHE. [*Announcing.*] Mrs. Bread!
[*Enter Mrs. Bread, while Nioche, always on tiptoe, retires. Exit Nioche, left.*]

CLAIRE. [*Startled at the sight of Mrs. Bread.*] You?

MRS. BREAD. [*Equally startled on her own side.*] Have you come *back* to him?

CLAIRE. [*With a sharp, clear gesture of negation, then, as if to explain everything.*] Valentin's very *ill!*

MRS. BREAD. [*Surprised.*] He told me he was *better!*

CLAIRE. [*Vague.*] *Who* told you?

MRS. BREAD. Mr. Newman—he *wrote* to me.

CLAIRE. [*Still more surprised, wondering.*] To come to Valentin?

MRS. BREAD. To come to *him.*

CLAIRE. [*Struck, wondering.*] To *him?* For what purpose?

MRS. BREAD. To answer some questions.

CLAIRE. [*After an instant, mystified, with dawning anxiety.*] What questions?

MRS. BREAD. That's what I came up to find out. [*Mme. de Cintré stands looking at her an instant, then, as if with an idea, an alarm, goes up nervously to centre, where, as if listening, she remains another instant. Mrs. Bread, who has passed to right, goes on.*] Is the Count *worse?*

CLAIRE. [*Coming quickly and abruptly down to her.*] Catty—what does Mr. Newman *want* of you?

MRS. BREAD. [*Impenetrable.*] Have you *seen* Mr. Newman?

CLAIRE. For a moment. He's coming back!

MRS. BREAD. Then can't you take pity on him?

CLAIRE. [*Alarmed, listening.*] Hush!

MRS. BREAD. [*Persisting, pleading.*] Everything's not over?

CLAIRE. Everything! [*Then, with abrupt decision.*] Catty—you must leave the house with me.

MRS. BREAD. [*Reluctant, vague.*] Now?

CLAIRE. When I've seen my brother.

MRS. BREAD. And before *I've* seen Mr. Newman?

CLAIRE. [*With the climax of her uneasiness and her appeal, repeating her question of a moment before.*] Catty—what does he *want* of you?

MRS. BREAD. [*Seeing Newman, centre.*] Ask him!

[*Re-enter Newman, centre.*]

NEWMAN. [*After stopping an instant, moved, at the sight of Mrs. Bread, says to her formally:*] You shall *see* him. [*Then to Claire.*] Please go in *first.*

CLAIRE. [*Who has given him a long, fixed, searching look, exactly like the one he has given her before his last exit, and who has then transferred her eyes to Mrs. Bread with the same effect until Mrs. Bread uneasily turns away and Newman passes up to hold back the drapery of the door at centre.*] With the understanding, please, that her visit terminates with *mine.*

NEWMAN. [*Surprised.*] That you take her *away?*

CLAIRE. [*Down at the left, after looking again from Newman at centre to Mrs. Bread at right.*] In a very few minutes. [*Exit Claire rapidly, centre.*]

NEWMAN. [*Sombre, still holding the curtain and looking after her.*] She's lost—she's lost! [*Then dropping the curtain, almost dashing it from him with a gesture of sudden anguish; coming down to Mrs. Bread and speaking in a different tone.*] Are you going *away* with her?

MRS. BREAD. She told me she *wishes* it!

NEWMAN. [*Struck, thinking.*] *Why* does she wish it?

MRS. BREAD. My arrival upsets her.

NEWMAN. [*Catching at every ray of hope.*] Upsets her?

MRS. BREAD. Just as my departure upsets her mother.

NEWMAN. [*Struck, cheered.*] The Marquise tried to prevent it?

MRS. BREAD. [*Smiling.*] Almost by force!

NEWMAN. [*Smiling.*] That's just what I want to *see!*

MRS. BREAD. [*More gravely.*] It has cost me my *home.*

NEWMAN. I'll give you another. You've made a great sacrifice for me.

MRS. BREAD. Wasn't that what you *asked* for?

NEWMAN. It was *indeed,* Mrs. Bread! But no one knows better than I that we don't always *get* what we ask for!

MRS. BREAD. Sometimes we get more! [*After an instant.*] The *Marquis* has also come.

NEWMAN. [*Struck.*] He's *here?*

MRS. BREAD. He's in *Paris.* He must have arrived last night.

NEWMAN. [*Greatly interested.*] Will he come to this *house?*

MRS. BREAD. [*After an instant.*] He never was particularly *shy!*

NEWMAN. [*Encouraged, considering.*] Well, I think that's *good.*

MRS. BREAD. What do you think it's good *for?*

NEWMAN. I'll tell you in a moment, but there's something I want you to tell me first. [*She gives a sign of willingness, and he goes on.*] From what

you know of the state of my account should you suppose I had about *one cent* in the bank?

MRS. BREAD. [*Vague.*] In the bank?

NEWMAN. The *Countess,* Mrs. Bread, is the bank—a splendid but deadly institution. Should you say she had been touched for one *instant* by the miserable spectacle I present?

MRS. BREAD. I was struck just now by the way she *looked* at you.

NEWMAN. The way she looked at me [*Thinking, piecing it together.*] seemed to me to show that she's *afraid* of something; and if she's afraid of anything—she ain't indifferent.

MRS. BREAD. I owe you the truth, Mr. Newman. Whatever she may be afraid of she's not afraid of relenting!

NEWMAN. How can you answer for *that?*

MRS. BREAD. I *begged* her, before you came *in,* to relent.

NEWMAN. And what did she say?

MRS. BREAD. She says it's too *late.*

NEWMAN. [*Struck, smitten, with his last hope dashed, and giving a gesture of despair which definitely indicates this.*] Well then—if it's too late for *her,* it's not too late for *me!* I stand before you, Mrs. Bread, as a man with a damnable grievance, and I call upon you to help me to prove that I can give back blow for blow.

MRS. BREAD. [*After an instant, impressed, very gravely.*] *Now* I understand, sir, why you've *sent* for me.

NEWMAN. I can't blow my head, and I can't break my spirit! It may be very rude, it may be a trifle barbarous of him, but the injured man, the *natural* man, in me, cries *out.* He cries to you, Mrs. Bread, and I'm glad you've guessed the *reason!*

MRS. BREAD. You'll make a tremendous *demand* of me.

NEWMAN. [*Anxious.*] You don't mean to say you'll *reject* it?

MRS. BREAD. I can't help thinking a little of the consequences.

NEWMAN. They're just what I want to *see!*

MRS. BREAD. But if I satisfy you— too *late* [*Hesitating.*]—where's the use—

NEWMAN. [*Interrupting.*] It's never too late to feel better, and there's *always* some use in being satisfied!

MRS. BREAD. [*After considering an instant and composing herself.*] Permit me then to ask what it is you already *know.*

NEWMAN. I already know that in that abominable hour, ten years ago, when two French gentlemen lost their lives— [*Pausing.*]

MRS. BREAD. Yes, Mr. Newman.

NEWMAN. The late Marquis, instructed by his daughter, *did* find on the spot a person—suspected, individually or *unsuspected*—who was keeping an appointment with his son-in-law.

MRS. BREAD. And that person—?

NEWMAN. That person, Mrs. Bread —that person, I have been able to ascertain, was M. de Bellegarde's own wife, the mother of his children, the mother of her *lover's* wife! [*Mrs. Bread sinks into a chair and sits an instant with her face covered with her hands, while Newman, pausing with the effect of his words, stands looking at her.*] So that in the miracle of her successful disappearance and the consequent security of her abominable secret, her audacious reproach to her daughter of having, without justice and without mercy, sent a father and a husband to their death—

MRS. BREAD. [*Interrupting, rising, completing, with a different manner.*] Has made the darkness of that daughter's life, has made her seeming ignorance a ground on which the Marquise has always triumphantly appealed.

NEWMAN. Therefore if such an ignorance is turned to knowledge and such a ground is knocked away—

MRS. BREAD. [*Interrupting again, with decision.*] The Countess will only plunge deeper into her convent!

NEWMAN. [*Struck with the painful and plausible force of this, but resolutely throwing it off.*] Then I shan't be worse off than I *am!*

MRS. BREAD. But if you know the truth what more do you *want?*

NEWMAN. I want the evidence.

MRS. BREAD. [*Thinking, with a sad and ominous but affirmative nod.*] Ah, the evidence—!

NEWMAN. The evidence *exists?*

MRS. BREAD. It exists.

NEWMAN. And in your *hands!*

MRS. BREAD. In my hands.

NEWMAN. Then *give* it to me.

MRS. BREAD. I'll give it to you. But you must give me my *time.*

NEWMAN. Certainly—that's why I want you to *stay* with me.

MRS. BREAD. If I stay with you I can't go with the Countess.

NEWMAN. [*With decision.*] Of course you can't go with the Countess!

MRS. BREAD. [*After another instant.*] I'll *stay* with you!—But [*Looking round her.*] *where* shall I stay?

NEWMAN. [*Seeing Noémie at the foot of the stairs, and with a gesture that indicates and introduces her to Mrs. Bread.*] This young lady'll *show* you. [*Re-enter, at the moment Mrs. Bread speaks and so as to encounter Newman's presentation, Noémie from the staircase. She inclines herself graciously to Mrs. Bread, but before she can speak the Doctor breaks joyously in from the centre.*]

DOCTOR. [*Coming down, in high jubilation.*] Great news—great news! He's *better!*

THE THREE OTHERS. [*Eagerly at once.*] *Better!*

[One page of the manuscript is missing at this point.]

. . . *instant; then, uncontrollably, she breaks out.*] Mr. Newman, what do you *want* of her?

NEWMAN. [*After an instant.*] I want her to talk about *you!*

CLAIRE. [*Passionately.*] *Don't* talk about *me!* I can't *leave* her to you.

NEWMAN. [*Bitterly.*] It's little enough indeed you *leave* to me!

CLAIRE. [*After an instant during which she has stood with her eyes on the ground and then raised them, speaking gently, pleadingly.*] Don't I leave you *my brother?*

NEWMAN. [*With a slow headshake.*] He's *my* brother, now.

CLAIRE. Then act as if you were *his!* He'll take *care* of you—as you have taken care of *him.*

NEWMAN. [*Struck, thinking.*] He'll take *care* of me!

CLAIRE. [*Pressingly.*] Then *call* her to me!

NEWMAN. [*After an instant.*] What you ask of me is a terrible *sacrifice.*

CLAIRE. I ask it because you're loyal —because you're generous.

NEWMAN. I want to be generous— but [*After an instant, struggling.*]— don't put my generosity on the *rack!*

CLAIRE. Don't put my terrors and my sorrows, and don't refuse the only service I ever *asked* you!

NEWMAN. [*Passing up and round, struggling, thinking, stops short, arrested, close to Valentin's door; then suddenly, after listening a moment, breaks out to Mme. de Cintré, with irresistible cheer and from where he stands.*] I hear his old *laugh!*

CLAIRE. God be praised!

NEWMAN. [*Coming down.*] God be praised!

CLAIRE. [*At right, suppliant.*] *Call* her to me!

NEWMAN. [*At left, after a moment of intense inward struggle, culminating in a victory, while he again, for an instant, stands looking at her.*] Hanged then if I *care!* [*With a snap of his fingers and a tone of high decision, giving up, as it were all his own cause.*] I'll *call* her to you! [*Exit Newman, rapidly, with all the energy of his renunciation, centre.*]

CLAIRE. [*Alone an instant at right, with the strong emotion of her relief.*] He *is* loyal—he *is* generous!

[*Re-enter Nioche, left.*]

NIOCHE. [*Announcing.*] Milord Deepmere! [*Re-enter Deepmere, left. Exit Nioche, left.*]

DEEPMERE. [*Eagerly, anxiously, to Claire.*] Is your brother *better?*

CLAIRE. He's *better!* [*Then checking a happy demonstration on Deepmere's part, as if she too just hears the laugh that has been heard by Newman.*] Shshsh—you can *hear* him!

[*Re-enter Nioche, left.*]

NIOCHE. [*Announcing.*] Monsieur le Marquis de Bellegarde! [*Enter, left, the Marquis de Bellegarde. Nioche remains.*]

DEEPMERE. [*Grave, formal, to the Marquis.*] Your brother's *better.*

MARQUIS. [*More formal still and*

very superior.] It was in the hope of hearing so that I took this unconventional step! [*Then to Mme. de Cintré, whom he has made some demonstration of surprise at finding, and with whom he has exchanged a fixed, firm look.*] We were under the impression, Madam, that you had retired to a convent.

CLAIRE. [*With a touch of intensely refined and exquisite comedy.*] Your impression, my dear brother, was an impression I've *hitherto* shared!

DEEPMERE. [*Struck by this, eager, appealing to her.*] Ah, you've come back—?

CLAIRE. [*Troubled, struggling with herself and turning away from him.*] Don't *ask* me!

[*Re-enter, rapidly, Mrs. Bread, centre.*]

MRS. BREAD. [*Coming down, excited, joyous.*] The Count's on his *feet* —the Count's coming *in!*

NIOCHE. [*Catching up the good news, jubilant also.*] Perhaps we shall see him at luncheon—which I've just been requested to *announce!*

MARQUIS. Luncheon? I've scarcely come to a *meal!*

MRS. BREAD. [*To Mme. de Cintré.*] I'm at your ladyship's service—I'm ready to *go.*

CLAIRE. [*After an instant, abruptly.*] Then *I'm* not!

MRS. BREAD. [*Astonished.*] You're *not?*

CLAIRE. [*Still with her agitation, abruptly again.*] Stay *with* me! [*Then seeing Valentin, between Newman and Noémie, at the door.*] Here he *is!*

[*Enter, centre, Valentin, supported on either side by Newman and Noémie. In a short silk dressing-jacket and light trousers and slippers, with a bright silk handkerchief round his*

neck, he is pale and weak but smiling and happy; he has an arm in the arm of each of his companions. They stop with him half way down, and he pauses an instant, looking at the others; then he sinks, gently and with relief, into the chair which Nioche has gone quickly round to place in a position to receive him.*]

VALENTIN. [*To Claire.*] My sister— you've worked a *miracle.*

NEWMAN. [*Who has looked, surprised, at the Marquis.*] A miracle!

NOÉMIE. A miracle!

VALENTIN. [*To Deepmere.*] My poor friend, give me your hand. [*He holds out his hand to Deepmere, who rushes forward and grasps it. Deepmere then comes down again, following Noémie, who when Valentin sinks into the chair, behind which Nioche remains standing, has passed to the extreme right.*]

NEWMAN. [*Still at Valentin's left, after a continued fixed look at the Marquis.*] Marquis, I guess you had better give him *yours.* [*The Marquis comes forward, more majestically, for this purpose, and he and Mrs. Bread address themselves together to Valentin while Nioche continues behind his chair and Newman moves further to left. Claire, on the right, after her brother's words to her, has dropped into the chair at the table and sits there, with her eyes on the ground, in intense concentration.*]

NOÉMIE. [*Triumphant, down in front, to Deepmere.*] Don't you see him there before you?

DEEPMERE. [*Grateful, ardent.*] Exquisite woman—how did you *do* it?

NOÉMIE. [*Radiant with the success of her machination, and indicating with a nod Mme. de Cintré, behind them and at their left.*] I made *her* do it!

DEEPMERE. [*Pressing.*] Couldn't you make her do something *else?*

NOÉMIE. [*After a glance back at her.*] She *will* do it!

DEEPMERE. [*Looking too, embracing the situation and thoroughly satisfied with it.*] Well—what shall I *give* you?

NIOCHE. [*Behind Valentin's chair, before Noémie can answer, to Newman.*] I ought to mention, sir, that I've been requested to announce your *luncheon.*

NEWMAN. [*Speaking gaily to Valentin and quitting the position from which he has been watching Mme. de Cintré, to change places with Nioche, who passes to the left.*] My dear fellow, what do you say to *luncheon?*

VALENTIN. [*Leaning back in his chair.*] I am afraid I must have it *here* and that I must ask you to *join* me.

NEWMAN. [*Behind Valentin's chair, while the Marquis, quitting Valentin, comes down on left and Mrs. Bread comes down on right, below Mme. de Cintré and above Noémie and Deepmere.*] With pleasure, Valentin. Marquis, won't *you* join him?—Lord Deepmere, won't *you?*—Miss Noémie, won't *you?*

NOÉMIE. [*To Newman, while the Marquis, down at the left, considering, hesitating, solemnly smooths his hat and Newman and Valentin wait and watch for his answer.*] Thank you very much—I must *go!*

DEEPMERE. [*Eagerly, to Noémie, while Valentin and Newman continue to watch the Marquis, and Mrs. Bread, on the right, rests her eyes expectantly on Mme. de Cintré who, at her table, sits motionless, detached, immersed in repressed agitation.*] Before you

go—what shall I *give* you?

NOÉMIE. Give me [*Hesitating.*]—give me— [*Pausing, smiling.*]

DEEPMERE. [*In the liveliest suspense.*] *What,* Mademoiselle?

NOÉMIE. [*Aloud, so that the others hear her and Newman's invitation to Deepmere is practically answered.*] Give me your arm! [*She takes it while Deepmere, breathing again, offers it with extravagant alacrity, and they stand together at right.*]

MRS. BREAD. [*To Claire.*] I *am* at your ladyship's service to leave the house.

NEWMAN. [*Looking at Claire, who, still seated in her agitation, has made no answer.*] Perhaps *you,* Madame de Cintré, will give us the honour of your company?

MARQUIS. [*Down at left, majestically, during the silence that follows on Claire's part.*] I regret, Mr. Newman, that I am unable to accept your invitation. [*After an instant.*] I must carry to my mother, without delay, this remarkable news of her son.

CLAIRE. [*Rising rapidly, checking him as he is in the act of going, while, as she moves, Newman, quitting Valentin, comes nearer to her, and Mrs. Bread, passing to centre, occupies Newman's place behind Valentin's chair.*] Urbain! [*The Marquis stops, surprised, as with a challenge, and Claire goes on speaking out loud and clear.*] You can carry our mother as well some remarkable news of her daughter—the news that I've determined—and [*Looking about to the others.*] I'm glad you should all *hear* it!—to become Mr. Newman's *wife!*

NEWMAN. [*Springing to her, and as he folds her in his arms.*] That's just what I wanted to *see!*

DISCUSSION OF *THE AMERICAN*

The drama, said Bernard Shaw, is always in a decline. When Henry James wrote *The American* in 1890, however, the drama seemed to be in an ascent. Oscar Wilde's career was near its height. Ibsen was having his first London and Paris productions. The dramatic careers of Chekhov and Shaw were about to begin. Within the decade, the famous Abbey Theatre in Dublin and the Moscow Art Theatre were to be founded.

This ferment of activity and change occurred in a thriving, commercially successful, and singularly unmemorable theatre. The names of Arthur Wing Pinero and Henry Arthur Jones in England, of Eugène Scribe, Victorien Sardou, and Alexandre Dumas *fils* in France were "box office" then. However, they are only remembered now because they were immensely popular and prolific, and because they gave the name to a special kind of play, the "well-made play" or *pièce-bien-faite*.

The well-made play was not a genre in itself; it was only a cluster of dramatic techniques. In genre, it was usually either a drawing-room comedy or a romantic melodrama sometimes placed in an exotic or period setting. It provided an agreeable and undemanding evening's entertainment for an upper-middle-class audience. What made it "well-made" were its techniques of plot construction, its imitativeness of form, and its adherence to a number of rules derived from the mechanics of neo-classical criticism.

The playwright and mystery writer Wilkie Collins announced the formula for the well-made play: "Make 'em laugh; make 'em weep; make 'em wait." The laughing and weeping came easily enough, for the well-made-playwrights depended on stereotyped characterization and the easy emotionalism of the stock response. The characters were types derived from Restoration comedy and Bourgeois tragedy. The reformed rake, the unreformed rake, the consumptive heroine, the noble but wronged young man, the sinister duchess, the mustachioed lawyer, the upright father, and the faithful servant were the chess pieces of the plot. The overwrought emotionalism was easily achieved by references to standard symbols and abstractions like Honor, Purity, Motherhood, Duty, Obedience, Courage, Patriotism, the flag, the fireside, the home, the baby. Or, on the other hand, references to the cigar, the pack of cards, the empty champagne bottle.

Making 'em wait was a little more complicated and it was achieved by a number of devices, most notably the withholding of necessary information from the audience. As in detective stories, one proof of the writer's cleverness was his ingenuity in deferring the unraveling of the plot, and another was the intricacy of the final unraveling.

Holding back the unraveling was accomplished by a carefully constructed plot in the form of a rigid tragic structure of mounting climaxes that came at the end of each act. First came the Exposition, next the First Clash, next the Complication, next the Reversal, and finally the Unraveling. The Reversal found the hero at the greatest possible distance from happiness. Having brought the plot to its ultimate suspenseful snarl, the playwright would then unravel it by some spectacular and presumably startling device—a lost letter, a little black box containing the crucial documents, a key to a locked room, the appearance of the mysterious and not really dead older brother. With such devices the knot was untied, and poetic justice, retribution, and the happy ending assured.

A number of standard scenes could be introduced as climactic moments into such a plot: the Parting, the Renunciation, the Death-Bed, the Unmasking, the Obligatory Scene. We have all seen these familiar scenes many times. The Obligatory Scene, which might require a bit of definition, was the climactic moment towards which the whole action of the play moved. In the Obligatory Scene, the hero confronted the villain, the scoundrel was exposed, the hero and the heroine finally embraced.

Two devices of the well-made play that strike the modern reader as rather antiquated and artificial are the "aside" and what the French call the "tirade." In the aside, a character whispers some necessary bits of information directly to the audience while the other characters onstage pretend not to hear. In the tirade, which is not quite the same as the equivalent English word, the leading actor, usually in the last act, delivers a noble and impassioned speech of considerable length on a lofty subject. The tirade came to be a show-stopper, a *tour de force* for the star. In addition to these devices, the playwright showed his wit and profundity by a glossy style, fluent dialogue, epigrams, and bits of philosophical statement.

None of these techniques is in itself faulty. All of them have been used in the greatest drama, and it was only excessive imitation, overuse, and slavish formularization that made them sterile and empty. Seeing one such play, the audience had seen them all. The aside, which had been appropriate on the formalized Elizabethan, Restoration, and eighteenth-century stages, was out of tune with the realism of the nineteenth century. Ibsen, in the interest of realism against artificiality, was proud of having written a play totally without asides. Chekhov, as you have seen, turned the tirade into the realistic device which we call the aria. Both Ibsen and Chekhov revolted against the artificial techniques of the well-made play and, more importantly, both revolted against the artificial content.

Slavish imitation, the overuse of certain devices, and a triviality of content, then, were the weaknesses of the well-made play. Its strength lay in the clever formula of its plot construction and in its tightness of form. But however much the form of the well-made play became a formula, neither its devices nor its structure were in themselves faulty. Ibsen's early social dramas, like *An Enemy of the People* or *A Doll's House*, filled the well-made formula with serious themes. As Ibsen developed, his characterization, dialogue, thematic depth, and symbolism burst the mold of the well-made play; and his later dramas, like *The Master Builder* and *John Gabriel Borkman*, found a form of their own. Oscar Wilde, in *The Importance of Being*

Earnest, renewed a number of well-made devices, by bringing to them a true epigrammatic wit and a reversal of many of the character types. Shaw's early plays, like *Mrs. Warren's Profession, Arms and the Man,* and *Candida,* are really well-made plays in reverse. Shaw presented the opposite of whatever the well-made play audience expected. Instead of the sweet and dutiful daughter, Shaw showed a flip and realistic daughter with a mind of her own. Instead of the wise and kindly mother, Shaw showed the foolish and irritable one. He showed his audience that the romantic hero was an ineffectual nincompoop, and gave the heroine to the prosaic hotel-keeper who carried chocolate bars instead of cartridges to war. Instead of the humble, deserving poor, he showed the witty, undeserving poor.

Henry James' *The American* is a well-made play, and your problem is to decide whether it is closer to the well-made plays of Ibsen, Chekhov, Wilde, and Shaw or to the well-made plays of Scribe, Sardou, Pinero, and Jones. James, turning to the stage midway in his career as a distinguished novelist, was eager to be a successful playwright. Throughout his life he had been attracted by the glamor of the theatre. He had frequently attended and reviewed plays. He had often gone to rehearsals and visited backstage. The Comédie Française and the influential French critic Francisque Sarcey, who inflexibly preached "the rules," were his models. "À moi, Scribe; à moi, Sardou; à moi, Dennery!" he exclaimed at the beginning of a visit to Paris. "The French stage I have mastered," he later wrote to his brother William, ". . . I have it in my pocket."

Although James admired and accurately reviewed in detail several productions of Ibsen, he was not, like Ibsen, a theatrical experimentalist. He knew that England lacked good dramatists, but his long experience of the theatre, his taste, and his desire for success led him to the well-made play form.

The first act of *The American* is a drawing-room comedy (remembering James' emphasis on Newman's speech, one might almost call it a drawling-room comedy). It establishes the comic situation of the contrast in manners. Newman is the naive American; Valentin, Lord Deepmere, and the Nioches are the experienced Europeans. In the second act the melodramatic complication appears. The suave and villainous Bellegardes bargain with Newman over his marriage to Claire; then later, unknown to him, they decide that Claire shall marry Lord Deepmere. Act III is the Reversal. When Valentin is wounded and the Bellegardes withdraw their permission and Claire decides to enter the convent, Newman's fortunes are at their lowest ebb. Act IV, depending on how you look at it, attempts either to approach serious drama or to provide a minimally happy ending. The device of Mrs. Bread's piece of paper resolves the love plot, but the death of Valentin gives the play a serious or somber overtone.

The second version of the fourth act James wrote at the request of Edward Compton, who produced, directed, and acted the title role in *The American.* According to Leon Edel, in whose book *The Complete Plays of Henry James* you can find a full account of James' career as a dramatist, Compton "complained to James that the last act, one of unmitigated gloom . . . was out of harmony with the rest of the play." James then rewrote the fourth act in, as he said, "a comedy-sense—heaven forgive me." He added that the play now "will basely gratify their [the Comptons'] artless instincts and British thick-wittedness and thanks to it the poor old play will completely save one's honor . . . as a permanent and regular thing." The Comptons kept the revised *American* in their repertory as "a permanent and regular thing" for several years of provincial touring.

James' contempt for the British public, which he alludes to in the quote above, may have been partly a cover for his very real fear of failure. But it arose also from his sense of the difference between the novel and the drama. Three things about the drama seemed especially to bother James: the relative simplicity of the play compared to the subtlety and complexity of the novel, the need to make a direct impression upon a tangible and immediate audience, and the importance of the play's subject.

In a review, James once paid the highest tribute to the drama, and his words are an apt description of the well-made play at its best:

> The dramatic form seems to me of all literary forms the noblest. . . .
> The fine thing in real drama, generally speaking, is that, more than any other work of literary art, it needs a masterly structure. It needs to be shaped and fashioned and laid together, and this process makes a demand upon an artist's rarest gifts. He must combine and arrange, interpolate and eliminate, play the joiner with the most attentive skill; and yet at the end effectually bury his tools and his sawdust, and invest his elaborate skeleton with the smoothest and most polished integument.

Shortly after, he turned from this stress on technical proficiency to discuss the play's subject:

> In a play, certainly, the subject is of more importance than in any other work of art. Infelicity, triviality, vagueness of subject, may be outweighed in a poem, a novel, or a picture, by charm of manner, by ingenuity of execution; but in a drama the subject is of the essence of work—it *is* the work. If it is feeble, the work can have no force; if it is shapeless, the work must be amorphous.

Taken together, these two quotations show James' conception of a play. It should be as perfectly constructed in form as if it were written by Scribe, and it should be as highly serious in subject as if it were written by Ibsen.

Whether *The American* meets these standards, it is now your problem to discover.

DISCUSSION QUESTIONS ON *THE AMERICAN*

One of the most successful and "advanced" dramatists of James' time was Henry Arthur Jones. To give you a clearer idea of what kind of play James used as his model, we print here the conclusion of Jones' play, *The Masqueraders:*

[*Eddie enters dressed ready to start.*]

EDDIE. Davy, old boy, look alive! The men have got everything on the mules. We've not a moment to waste.

DAVID. I'm not going.

EDDIE. Not going? But they are waiting for us. If we don't go, all the expeditions everywhere will be a failure. Davy, you aren't going to sell them all like a—like a— They'll call you a—well, you fill in the word.

DAVID. I'm not going.

EDDIE. But what excuse can we make?

DAVID. Any excuse you like—I've changed my mind.

HELEN. [*With quiet sarcasm.*] Is that a good excuse for a soldier to make just as he's ordered into battle?

DAVID. I'm not a soldier.

HELEN. Yes, you are. We are all soldiers on this earth, bound to be loyal to every one of our comrades, bound to obey the great rules of life, whether they are easy or hard. Yes, and all the more bound when they are hard, when they may cost us our very life. You'll go—you'll go, and leave her to me and Rosy?

DAVID. I love her! I love her!

HELEN. Then save her for her child. Save her to be a good mother to that helpless creature she has brought into the world, so that when her girl grows up and she has to guide her, she'll not have to say to her child, "You can give yourself to this man, and if you don't like him you can give yourself to another, and to another, and so on. It doesn't matter. It was what I did!"

DAVID. [*Same tone.*] I love her! I love her! I love her! You sha'n't reason me out of my happiness!

HELEN. [*Stopping him.*] I can't reason at all. I can only feel, and I know my instinct is right. I know the woman who gives herself to another man while her husband is alive betrays her sex, and is a bad woman.

DAVID. I love her! I love her! [*Going towards door.*]

HELEN. [*Stopping him.*] Then make your love the best thing in her life, and the best thing in yours. You have loved her so well. You have made so many sacrifices for her. Make this one last sacrifice. Keep her pure for her child.

EDDIE. That's God's voice speaking to you now, Davy.

[*Dulcie enters very quietly, looking off.*]

DULCIE. [*To David.*] She's asleep. Go and look at her.

[*Exit David. Dulcie is about to follow. Helen stops her.*]

HELEN. Dulcie.

DULCIE. What?

HELEN. He's given his word to his comrades. Don't make him play the coward.

[*David re-enters, much calmer.*]

DAVID. Miss Larondie, I'll write to you from Marseilles. I have left everything in order for her. If by any chance I should not return—

DULCIE. Ah! [*Goes to him.*]

DAVID. Take care of her while I'm away.

DULCIE. But if you do not return?

DAVID. [*Very calm, very bitter, very tender, with a little smile.*] Then—we shall have played our parts well in this little puppet-show, shall we not? Don't cry, my dear, why should you? If I were a soldier, you would tell me to go. We shall not be absent from each other long. Don't cry, dear. It's my duty to go, Dulcie. Be brave. Tell me to go.

DULCIE. [Bows her head.] Go. Go.

DAVID. [Going from her some steps.] I've played this great game of love like a fool, as men would say. Perhaps I've played the great game of life like a fool, too. If we are sacrificing ourselves for a shadow we are only doing what earth's best creatures have done before us. If duty is reality, we have done right. Right—wrong—duty—they may be all shadows, but my love for you is real. [Dulcie is sobbing, he comes to her.] Hush! Hush, dear! We shall never know satiety. Our love will never grow stale and commonplace, will it? Dulcie, we've only thrown away the husks. We've kept the immortal part of our love—if there is an immortal part. Look! this is my mother's wedding ring. [Taking a very thin gold ring from his little finger.] She gave it to me as she was dying. It has never left my finger since. I give it you in exchange for the one I took from you. Give me your hand.

[Dulcie gives it.] With this ring I thee wed. As she that bore me was pure, so I leave you pure, dear. Kiss me once—I've held you sacred! [She kisses him.] Good-bye. No, stay. [Pours out a glass of wine, gives it to her.] Drink with me. [She takes the glass, drinks some of it. He takes it from her, drains it, dashes the glass on the floor, where it is shivered to atoms; he then turns very brightly and gaily to Eddie.] Now, Eddie—our work!

EDDIE. Ready, big brother!

DAVID. [To Dulcie.] In six months from now, come to meet me, my wife, and bring our child. Or, it may be a little later—but come and meet me— my wife—a little later.

DULCIE. Where?

DAVID. In that little star in Andromeda. All's real there.

[Exeunt Eddie and David through window.]

CURTAIN

[If curtain is called up, show a picture of David outside the window, in the full morning sunlight, the mountains covered with snow behind him; Eddie is beside him drawing him away.]

In fairness, it must be admitted that Jones wrote better plays than The Masqueraders. But at the time when he was popular, his plays were taken as serious representations of life, and many people were as thoroughly moved by the renunciation of Dulcie and David as they are today by the hokum of soap-operas or the romantic entanglements of film stars.

It is easy with the clarity of sixty years between us and Jones to see that The Masqueraders is wretched, but the modern stage has its own share of Henry Arthur Joneses; and the real trick is to sort out the Joneses from the Ibsens, Chekhovs, and Shaws. That is what this book and, in particular, this chapter are about.

We propose to define how good Henry James' play is by comparing it with

Jones' play. We take Jones to be a fair example of the rock-bottom abysmal. Your problem will be to discover how close to or how far from him James is. That problem will take several steps.

1. The most proficient masters of the French well-made play were Eugène Scribe and Victorien Sardou. Sardou relates that he learned plot construction by reading the first act of a Scribe play, and then writing out the next three acts himself to see how close he could come to what Scribe had originally written. Usually Sardou came very close. What this story suggests is that the well-made play had a formula plot that was quite as predictable as the plot of an adult western.

From your knowledge, then, of the conclusion of *The Masqueraders,* reconstruct the rest of the story.

2. Having established that the plot of the well-made play is artificial and formularized, our next problem is to decide how close *The American* is to the formula. Presumably the closer it is, the more artificial a representation of life it is.

James wrote two fourth acts to *The American,* and there was yet another ending to the story in its original version as a novel. In the novel Christopher Newman decides to use Mrs. Bread's paper to discredit Mme. de Bellegarde, and he approaches one of her friends intending to blurt out the story. However, he is so subtly maneuvered that he has no chance to tell his tale. Then he realizes that he has been maneuvered, and he is ashamed of himself for wanting to use scandal to revenge himself for Claire who has gone off to the convent. The novel ends with a friend of Newman saying:

". . . I suppose there is no harm in saying that you probably did not make them so very uncomfortable. My impression would be that since, as you say, they defied you, it was because they believed that, after all, you would never really come to the point. Their confidence, after counsel taken of each other, was not in their innocence, nor in their talent for bluffing things off; it was in your remarkable good nature! You see they were right."

Newman instinctively turned to see if the little paper was in fact consumed [by the fire]; but there was nothing left of it.

In the novel Newman is defeated in every possible way, and he has also considerably less of a vigorous and blatant nature. Which of these three endings seems farthest away from the well-made formula? Why? Which is the most subtle in terms of what it tries to say about human nature? Would Henry Arthur Jones have found it difficult to dramatize the ending of James' novel?

Which of the two endings of the play seems to come least artificially from the rest of the story? That is, which is the most natural? Why? Which is the most dramatically effective? Why? Which is the most complicated? Why? Are the two endings of the play about different subjects? Do they do different things to the tone and theme of the play? If so, how?

3. Even the little that you have read of *The Masqueraders* should indicate that the four characters onstage are conventional stereotypes. In both language and action, they resemble puppets, rather than people. Why?

Are any of the characters in *The American* such one-dimensional figures? If you think so, which ones? Why? Are any of the main characters stereotypes? The London columnist of the New York *Times* thought that Newman was a caricature, and compared him to "the advance agent of a circus." A review in the London *Star*, probably written by the eminent London critic A. B. Walkley, called Newman a "stage American, with the local color laid on with a trowel." Is Newman drawn in broad enough strokes to warrant such criticisms? Does he have any qualities that help individualize him more than David of *The Masqueraders?* How much better, or worse, does he seem than David? You have read just a bit of Jones' play, but you still have some basis for comparing the two characters, for you have seen them both in similar situations. Both are called upon to renounce the woman they love. Based upon your own experience of human nature, which one of them would you say acts more naturally and believably?

4. Is Valentin's recovery in the new fourth act plausible? Why or why not? Was James conscious of its happening fairly rapidly? Is Valentin's entrance theatrically effective or realistically implausible? Why?

5. Noémie has an important connection with Newman's story in Act III. Is her part in Act III important enough, however, to warrant giving her so much space? What else does she do to contribute significantly to the action?

6. Nioche's chief dramatic function is over by the end of Act I. What is that function? How important is Nioche later in the play? What use does James put him to later in the play? How significant a use is it?

7. Marignac is not introduced until Act III. In the first fourth act, he is fairly important, but in the revised fourth act, he is not used at all. Why did James need him in the first version? Should he have introduced Marignac earlier? Did he need Marignac at all in the revised version?

8. Is the revised fourth act better than the original because it tells what happened to Lord Deepmere, Noémie, and Nioche? Is Lord Deepmere equally necessary in both versions? Why or why not?

9. Two of the best critics of the period were William Archer, the translator of Ibsen, and Bernard Shaw. Both men at one time or another made similar comments on James' dialogue. Archer, in a review of *The American*, spoke of the "neat and charming dialogue which is grateful to the ear even when it does not ring dramatically true."

Taking as the nadir of dialogue the banal phrases of *The Masqueraders*, we must decide how closely and how often James' dialogue approaches it. But before we make the comparison, it might be well to have as another line of reference a contemporary example of excellent dialogue. Consider, then, the following dialogue which forms the conclusion of Bernard Shaw's 1898 play, *Mrs. Warren's Profession:*

VIVIE. No: I am my mother's daughter. I am like you: I must have work, and must make more money than I spend. But my work is not your work, and my way not your way. We must part. It will not make much difference to us: instead of meeting one another for perhaps a few months in twenty years, we shall never meet: that's all.

MRS. WARREN [*her voice stifled in tears*]. Vivie: I meant to have been more with you: I did indeed.

VIVIE. It's no use, mother: I am not to be changed by a few cheap tears and entreaties any more than you are, I daresay.

MRS. WARREN [*wildly*]. Oh, you call a mother's tears cheap.

VIVIE. They cost you nothing; and you ask me to give you the peace and quietness of my whole life in exchange for them. What use would my company be to you if you could get it? What have we two in common that could make either of us happy together?

MRS. WARREN [*lapsing recklessly into her dialect*]. We're mother and daughter. I want my daughter. I've a right to you. Who is to care for me when I'm old? Plenty of girls have taken to me like daughters and cried at leaving me; but I let them all go because I had you to look forward to. I kept myself lonely for you. You've no right to turn on me now and refuse to do your duty as a daughter.

VIVIE [*jarred and antagonized by the echo of the slums in her mother's voice*]. My duty as a daughter! I thought we should come to that presently. Now once for all, mother, you want a daughter and Frank wants a wife. I don't want a mother; and I don't want a husband. I have spared neither Frank nor myself in sending him about his business. Do you think I will spare you?

MRS. WARREN [*violently*]. Oh, I know the sort you are: no mercy for yourself or anyone else. *I* know. My experience has done that for me anyhow: I can tell the pious, canting, hard, selfish woman when I meet her. Well, keep yourself to yourself: *I* don't want you. But listen to this. Do you know what I would do with you if you were a baby again? aye, as sure as there's a Heaven above us.

VIVIE. Strangle me, perhaps.

MRS. WARREN. No: I'd bring you up to be a real daughter to me, and not what you are now, with your pride and your prejudices and the college education you stole from me: yes, stole: deny it if you can: what was it but stealing? I'd bring you up in my own house, I would.

VIVIE [*quietly*]. In one of your own houses.

MRS. WARREN [*screaming*]. Listen to her! listen to how she spits on her mother's grey hairs! Oh, may you live to have your own daughter tear and trample on you as you have trampled on me. And you will: you will. No woman ever had luck with a mother's curse on her.

VIVIE. I wish you wouldn't rant, mother. It only hardens me. Come: I suppose I am the only young woman you ever had in your power that you did good to. Don't spoil it all now.

MRS. WARREN. Yes, Heaven forgive me, it's true; and you are the only one that ever turned on me. Oh, the injustice of it! the injustice! the injustice! I always wanted to be a good woman. I tried honest work; and I was slave-driven until I cursed the day I ever heard of honest work. I was a good mother; and because I made my daughter a good woman she turns me out as if I was a leper. Oh, if I only had my life to live over again! I'd talk to that lying clergyman in the school. From this time forth, so help me Heaven in my last hour, I'll do wrong and nothing but wrong. And I'll prosper on it.

VIVIE. Yes: it's better to choose your line and go through with it. If I had been you, mother, I might have done as you did; but I should not have lived one life and believed in another. You are a conventional woman at heart. That is why I am bidding you goodbye now. I am right, am I not?

MRS. WARREN [taken aback]. Right to throw away all my money!

VIVIE. No: right to get rid of you? I should be a fool not to? Isn't that so?

MRS. WARREN [sulkily]. Oh well, yes, if you come to that, I suppose you are. But Lord help the world if everybody took to doing the right thing! And now I'd better go than stay where I'm not wanted. [She turns to the door.]

VIVIE [kindly]. Won't you shake hands?

MRS. WARREN [after looking at her fiercely for a moment with a savage impulse to strike her]. No, thank you. Goodbye.

VIVIE [matter-of-factly]. Goodbye. [Mrs. Warren goes out, slamming the door behind her. The strain on Vivie's face relaxes; her grave expression breaks up into one of joyous content; her breath goes out in a half sob, half laugh of intense relief. She goes buoyantly to her place at the writing-table; pushes the electric lamp out of the way; pulls over a great sheaf of papers; and is in the act of dipping her pen in the ink when she finds Frank's note. She opens it unconcernedly and reads it quickly, giving a little laugh at some quaint turn of expression in it.] And goodbye, Frank. [She tears the note up and tosses the pieces into the wastepaper basket without a second thought. Then she goes at her work with a plunge, and soon becomes absorbed in its figures.]

The difference between Jones' dialogue and Shaw's is all the more noticeable because Shaw puts into Mrs. Warren's mouth the kind of dialogue that Jones used for all of his characters. At the same time that Mrs. Warren speaks Jonesian dialogue, her daughter Vivie speaks the flat and quiet prose of realistic commonsense. Mrs. Warren uses the language of theatrical melodrama, which she mistakes for the language of real emotion. By the contrast of Vivie's "normal" style, Shaw is able to show that the language of the mother is artificial and that her emotions are melodramatic. And, even more importantly, by Vivie's language Shaw is able to place a clearer vision of reality upon the stage.

Our problem now will be to decide whether James' dialogue verges more closely to Jones' or to Shaw's.

10. At the end of Act II, Claire throws herself into Newman's arms, and it would be generally conceded that this action provides an effective curtain. The action is set up by Newman's final speech. He says to Claire, "Be so good as to understand that your only refuge is in my arms!" Characterize this speech.

Is it natural, easy, normal? Is it stiff, stilted, artificial? Is it closer to Jones or to Shaw? Find other speeches in the play that are like it in tone and diction.

11. The following intriguing dialogue occurs in Act III:

MME. DE BELLEGARDE. Do you think we spin round like tops?

NEWMAN. Oh, tops only spin when they're whipped—and that's not your case.

MARQUIS. [*Aside.*] Isn't it, though? We were whipped last night.

Obviously these lines are strongly different in tone and diction from, "Be so good as to understand that your only refuge is in my arms!" Part of the difference stems from the cleverness of these lines. Mme. de Bellegarde opens the exchange with an appropriate, although not unusually striking, simile. Newman then extends the simile by the double meaning of his pun on the word "whipped." Then the Marquis extends the simile even further by repeating the pun and interjecting still another meaning for "whipped."

The pun has been called the lowest form of humor, but that description is often a misnomer. The two puns that you have just read are wit of a rather high order. They are clever and successful because they contain two meanings simultaneously. A semi-clever and semi-successful pun might be the title of the autobiography of Diana Dors, the British movie actress. *Swingin' Dors* contains one real and one pointless meaning. On one level, we understand that the actress is "hep," but her resemblance to doors, either swinging or shut, is too elusive to make sense.

The half-silly or completely silly pun deserves the "lowest form of humor" description, but James' two puns are clever and admirable. In fact, they are doubly clever because one rides piggyback on the other.

Can you find any other examples of witty word play in *The American*? Are they appropriate to their context? Do they clash ineffectively with a predominantly Jonesian style, or do they fuse effectively in a predominantly Shavian style?

Is it in character for the somewhat naive Newman to make a pun? Is it in character for the Marquis to top Newman's pun? Can it be argued that the Marquis does not know that he has made a pun?

Is this language realistic enough for the stage, or is it too literary? Is it more literary than Ben Jonson's use of Latin in the last act of *The Silent Woman*?

12. Consider the following dialogue from Act III:

VALENTIN: She'll be too late—I'm sinking. It tortures me to lie ebbing away when *you're* in trouble. But I'll tell you who *can* help you—Mrs. Bread can help you. She knows something about my mother.

NEWMAN. About your mother?

VALENTIN. About my father.

NEWMAN. About your father?

VALENTIN. About my brother.

NEWMAN. About your brother?

Is this language easy and fluent, or stiff and inept? How would you portray Newman's reactions in each of his lines? Would it be difficult? Would there be any temptation to overact, to stagger about, and to bulge your eyes wide in melodramatic surprise? What did James want this passage to convey? What does it convey? How many similar passages can you find?

13. Examine Acts I and II for dialogue that you would call "exposition." Which characters are the main mouthpieces for exposition? Is the exposition natural and dramatically effective, or is it stilted and dramatically dead?

14. Find several examples of asides. Explain how each is necessary, or why James thought each was necessary. How could James have gotten rid of these asides? How else could he have conveyed the same information? Is all of the information conveyed by the asides really necessary?

15. Find some jokes in the first and second acts. What subjects are these jokes about? Are James' jokes side-splitters, or are they merely mildly amusing? Are they mainly visual or verbal jokes? Do the jokes continue throughout the rest of the play? Do you find them in both versions of Act IV? Do the jokes have a legitimate dramatic function, or are they merely decoration?

16. The revised fourth act has the same setting as the third act. This gain in unity of place obviously makes the play easier to stage, but does it make it a better play? Why, or why not?

17. The end of comedy is the union of lovers, and the end of tragedy is the death of the hero. Probably the end of both farce and melodrama is the punishment of vice and the reward of virtue. Is the first version of *The American* comic or tragic? Is it a fusion of both? If so, is it a fusion like that of tragicomedy? Is the revised ending of the play comic or melodramatic? Explain why you think it is one or the other.

18. The duel is a standard device of the well-made play. Compare James' use of the duel with Chekhov's. Which uses it more effectively? Which duel is more important to the course of the dramatic action? Should a duel in a well-made play come closer to the beginning or to the ending? Which duel, James' or Chekhov's, is presented more fully and directly? Which is more theatrical?

Is the use of the duel in both plays bad because it is a standard device of the time? Could either playwright have done without it? Chekhov wrote about his play *The Cherry Orchard*, which followed *The Three Sisters*, "I have written a play in which not one gun goes off."

19. James was deeply interested in the conflict between the Old World and the New World customs. This conflict lies behind the main conflict of Newman's pursuit of Claire, making the play partly a comment on contemporary manners. Does James use this as a broader social frame for the play? If so, is his frame at all like Ben Jonson's? Like Chekhov's or O'Casey's?

BUS STOP

BY WILLIAM INGE

CHARACTERS

ELMA DUCKWORTH

GRACE

WILL MASTERS

CHERIE

DR. GERALD LYMAN

CARL

VIRGIL BLESSING

BO DECKER

[*The action of the play takes place in a street-corner restaurant in a small town about thirty miles west of Kansas City.*]

Act One: A night in early March. 1:00 A.M.
Act Two: A few minutes later.
Act Three: Early morning. About 5:00 A.M.

ACT ONE

[SCENE: *The entire play is set inside a street-corner restaurant in a small Kansas town about thirty miles west of Kansas City. The restaurant serves also as an occasional rest stop for the bus lines in the area. It is a dingy establishment with few modern improvements: scenic calendars and pretty-girl posters decorate the soiled walls, and illumination comes from two badly shaded light bulbs that hang on dangling cords from the ceiling; in the center are several quartet tables with chairs, for dining; at far left is the counter with six stools before it, running the depth of the setting; behind the counter are the usual restaurant equipment and paraphernalia (coffee percolator, dishes, glasses, electric refrigerator, etc.); on top of the counter are several large plates of doughnuts, sweet rolls, etc., under glass covers. At the far right, close to the outside entrance door, are a magazine stand and a rack of shelves piled with paper-back novels and books. At back center is an old-fashioned Franklin stove. At the back right is a great window that provide* a view of the local scenery. Against the wall, beneath the window, are two long benches meant for waiting passengers. At the back left is the rear door, close to the upper end of the counter. Above this door is a dim hand-painted sign, "Rest Rooms in the Rear."*

It is 1:00 A.M. on a night in early March and a near blizzard is raging outside. Through the windows we can see the sweeping wind and flying snow. Inside, by comparison, the scene is warm and cozy, the Franklin stove radiating all the heat of which it is capable. Two young women, in uniforms that have lost their starched freshness, are employed behind the counter. Elma is a big-eyed girl still in high school. Grace is a more seasoned character in her thirties or early forties. A bus is expected soon and they are checking, somewhat lackadaisically, the supplies. Outside, the powerful, reckless wind comes and goes, blasting against everything in its path, seeming to shake the very foundation of the little restaurant building; then subsiding, leaving a period of uncertain stillness.

When the curtain goes up, Elma stands far right, looking out the large plate-glass window, awed by the fury of the elements. Grace is at the telephone.]

ELMA. Listen to that wind. March is coming in like a lion. [*Grace jiggles the receiver on the telephone with no results.*] Grace, you should come over here and look out, to see the way the wind is blowing things all over town.

GRACE. Now I wonder why I can't get th' operator.

ELMA. I bet the bus'll be late.

GRACE. [*Finally hanging up.*] I bet it won't. The roads are O.K. as far as here. It's *ahead* they're havin' trouble. I can't even get the operator. She must have more calls than she can handle.

ELMA. [*Still looking out the window.*] I bet the bus doesn't *have* many passengers.

GRACE. Prob'ly not. But we gotta stay open even if there's only *one*.

ELMA. I shouldn't think anyone would take a trip tonight unless he absolutely *had* to.

GRACE. Are your folks gonna worry, Elma?

ELMA. No— Daddy said, before I left home, he bet this'd happen.

GRACE. [*Going behind counter.*] Well, you better come back here and help me. The bus'll be here any min-ute and we gotta have things ready.

ELMA. [*Leaving the window, following Grace.*] Nights like this, I'm glad I have a home to go to.

GRACE. Well, I got a home to go to, but there ain't anyone in it.

ELMA. Where's your husband now, Grace?

GRACE. How should I know?

ELMA. Don't you miss him?

GRACE. No!

ELMA. If he came walking in now, wouldn't you be glad to see him?

GRACE. You ask more questions.

ELMA. I'm just curious about things, Grace.

GRACE. Well, kids your age *are*. I don't know. I'd be happy to see him, I guess, if I knew he wasn't gonna stay very long.

ELMA. Don't you get lonesome, Grace, when you're not working down here?

GRACE. Sure I do. If I didn't have this restaurant to keep me busy, I'd prob'ly go nuts. Sometimes, at night, after I empty the garbage and lock the doors and turn out the lights, I get kind of a sick feelin', 'cause I sure don't look forward to walkin' up those stairs and lettin' myself into an empty apartment.

ELMA. Gee, if you feel that way, why don't you write your husband and tell him to come back?

GRACE. [*Thinks a moment.*] 'Cause I got just as lonesome when he was here. He wasn't much company, 'cept when we were makin' love. But makin' love is *one* thing, and bein' lonesome is another. The resta the time, me and Barton was usually fightin'.

ELMA. I guess my folks get along pretty well. I mean . . . they really seem to like each other.

GRACE. Oh, I know *all* married people aren't like Barton and I. Not all! [*Goes to telephone again.*] Now, maybe I can get the operator. [*Jiggles receiver.*] Quiet as a tomb. [*Hangs up.*]

ELMA. I *like* working here with you, Grace.

GRACE. Do you, honey? I'm glad, 'cause I sure don't know what I'd do without ya. Week ends especially.

ELMA. You know, I dreaded the job at first.

GRACE. [*Kidding her.*] Why? Thought you wouldn't have time for all your boy friends? [*Elma looks a little sour.*] Maybe you'd have more boy friends if you didn't make such good grades. Boys feel kind of embarrassed if they feel a girl is smarter than they are.

ELMA. What should I do? Flunk my courses?

GRACE. I should say not. You're a good kid and ya got good sense. I wish someone coulda reasoned with *me* when I was your age. But I was a headstrong brat, had to have my own way. I had my own way all right, and here I am now, a grass widow runnin' a restaurant, and I'll prob'ly die in this little town and they'll bury me out by the backhouse.

[*Will, the sheriff, comes in the front door, wind and snow flying through the door with him. He is a huge, saturnine man, well over six feet, who has a thick black beard and a scar on his forehead. He wears a battered black hat, clumsy overshoes, and a heavy mackinaw. He looks somewhat forbidding.*]

WILL. [*On entering.*] You girls been able to use your phone?

GRACE. No, Will. The operator don't answer.

WILL. That means *all* the lines are down. 'Bout time fer the Topeka bus, ain't it?

GRACE. Due now.

WILL. You're gonna have to hold 'em here, don't know how long. The highway's blocked 'tween here and Topeka. May be all night gettin' it cleared.

GRACE. I was afraid a that.

WILL. They got the highway gang workin' on it now and the telephone company's tryin' to get the lines back up. March is comin' in like a lion, all right.

GRACE. Yah.

WILL. [*Taking off his mackinaw, hanging it, going to the fire to warm his hands.*] The station house's *cold*. Got any fresh coffee?

GRACE. It just went through, Will. Fresh as ya could want it.

WILL. [*Goes to counter.*] A storm like this makes me mad. [*Grace laughs at his remark and gives him a cup of coffee.*] It *does*. It makes me mad. It's just like all the elements had lost their reason.

GRACE. Nothin' you can do about a wind like *that*.

WILL. Maybe it's just 'cause I'm a sheriff, but I like to see things in order.

GRACE. Let the wind blow! I just pray to God to leave a roof over my head. That's about all a person *can* do.

[*The sound of the bus is heard outside, its great motor coming to a stop.*]

WILL. Here it is.

GRACE. Better fill some water glasses, Elma. Remember, the doughnuts are left over from yesterday but it'll be all right to serve 'em. We got everything for sandwiches but *cheese*.

We got no cheese.

WILL. You *never* got cheese, Grace.

GRACE. I guess I'm kinda self-centered, Will. I don't care for cheese m'self, so I never think t'order it for someone else.

ELMA. Gee, I'm glad I'm not traveling on the bus tonight.

GRACE. I wonder who's drivin' tonight. This is Carl's night, isn't it?

ELMA. I think so.

GRACE. Yes it is. [*Obviously the idea of Carl pleases her. She nudges Elma confidentially.*] Remember, honey, *I* always serve Carl.

ELMA. Sure, Grace.

[*The door swings open, some of the snow flying inside, and Cherie, a young blond girl of about twenty, enters as though driven. She wears no hat, and her hair, despite one brilliant bobby pin, blows wild about her face. She is pretty in a fragile, girlish way. She runs immediately to the counter to solicit the attention of Grace and Elma. She lugs along an enormous straw suitcase that is worn and battered. Her clothes, considering her situation, are absurd: a skimpy jacket of tarnished metal cloth edged with not luxuriant fur, a dress of sequins and net, and gilded sandals that expose brightly enameled toes. Also, her make-up has been applied under the influence of having seen too many movies. Her lipstick creates a voluptuous pair of lips that aren't her own, and her eyebrows also form a somewhat arbitrary line. But despite all these defects, her prettiness still is apparent, and she has the appeal of a tender little bird. Her origin is the Ozarks and her speech is Southern.*]

CHERIE. [*Anxious, direct.*] Is there some place I kin hide?

GRACE. [*Taken aback.*] What?

CHERIE. There's a *man* on that bus . . . I wanta *hide*.

GRACE. [*Stumped.*] Well, gee . . . I dunno.

CHERIE. [*Seeing the sign above the rear door, starting for it.*] I'll hide in the powder room. If a tall, lanky cowboy comes in here, you kin just tell him I disappeared.

GRACE. [*Her voice stopping Cherie at the door.*] Hey, you can't hide out there. It's cold. You'll freeze your . . .

CHERIE. [*Having opened the door, seeing it is an outside toilet.*] Oh! It's outside.

GRACE. This is just a country town.

CHERIE. [*Starting again.*] I kin stand anything fer twenty minutes.

GRACE. [*Stopping her again.*] I got news for ya. The bus may be here all night.

CHERIE. [*Turning.*] What?

GRACE. The highway's blocked. You're gonna have to stay here till it's cleared.

CHERIE. [*Shutting the door, coming to counter, lugging her suitcase. She is about to cry.*] Criminey! What am I gonna do?

GRACE. [*Coming from behind counter, going to front door.*] I better go out and tell Carl 'bout the delay.

CHERIE. [*Dropping to a stool at the counter.*] What am I gonna do? What am I ever gonna do?

ELMA. [*In a friendly way.*] There's a little hotel down the street.

CHERIE. What ya take me for? A millionaire?

WILL. [*Coming to Cherie with a professional interest.*] What's the trouble, miss?

CHERIE. [*Looking at Will suspiciously.*] You a p'liceman?

WILL. I'm the local sheriff.

ELMA. [*Feeling some endorsement is called for.*] But everyone likes him. Really!

CHERIE. Well . . . I ain't askin' t'have no one arrested.

WILL. Who says I'm gonna arrest anyone? What's your trouble?

CHERIE. I . . . I need protection.

WILL. What from?

CHERIE. There's a man after me. He's a cowboy.

WILL. [*Looking around.*] Where is he?

CHERIE. He's on the bus, asleep, him and his buddy. I jumped off the bus the very second it stopped, to make my getaway. But there ain't no place to *get* away to. And he'll be in here purty soon. You just *gotta* make him lemme alone.

WILL. Ya meet him on the bus?

CHERIE. No. I met him in Kansas City. I work at the Blue Dragon night club there, down by the stockyards. *He* come there with the annual rodeo, and him and the resta the cowboys was at the night club ev'ry night. Ev'ry night there was a big fight. The boss says he ain't gonna let the cowboys in when they come back next year.

WILL. Then he followed ya on the bus?

CHERIE. He *put* me on the bus. I'm bein' abducted.

WILL. Abducted! But you took time to pack a suitcase!

CHERIE. I was goin' somewhere else, tryin' to get away from him, but he picked me up and carried me to the bus and put me on it. I din have nothin' to say about it at all.

WILL. Where's he plan on takin' ya?

CHERIE. Says he's got a ranch up in Montana. He says we're gonna git married soon as we get there.

WILL. And yor against it?

CHERIE. I don't wanta go up to some God-forsaken ranch in Montana.

WILL. Well, if this cowboy's really takin' ya against yor will, I s'pose I'll have to stop him from it.

CHERIE. You just don't know this cowboy. He's mean.

WILL. I reckon I kin handle him. You relax now. I'll be around mosta the night. If there's any trouble, I'll put a stop to it.

ELMA. You're safe with Will here. Will is very respected around here. He's never lost a fight.

WILL. What're ya talkin' about, Elma? Of course I've lost a fight . . . once.

ELMA. Grace always said you were *invincible*.

WILL. There ain't no one that's . . . *invincible*. A man's gotta learn that, the sooner the better. A good fighter has gotta know what it is to *get* licked. Thass what makes the diff'rence 'tween a fighter and a *bully*.

CHERIE. [*Shuddering.*] There's gonna be trouble. I kin feel it in my bones.

[*Enter Dr. Gerald Lyman, a man of medium height, about fifty, with a ruddy, boyish face that smilingly defies the facts of his rather scholarly glasses and iron-gray hair. He wears an old tweed suit of good quality underneath a worn Burberry. His clothes are mussed, and he wears no hat, probably having left it somewhere; for he has been drinking and is, at present, very jubilant. He looks over the restaurant approvingly.*]

DR. LYMAN. Ah! "This castle hath a pleasant seat."

CHERIE. [*To Elma.*] Could I hide my suitcase behind the counter, so's he won't see it when he comes in? I ain't gonna say anything to him at all 'bout not goin' on to Montana with him. I'm just gonna let 'im think I'm goin' till the bus pulls out and he finds I ain't on it. Thass th' only thing I know t'do.

ELMA. [*Taking the suitcase and putting it behind counter.*] Oh, you needn't worry with Will here.

CHERIE. Think so? [*She studies Will.*] Looks kinda like Moses, don't he?

ELMA. He *is* a very religious man. Would you believe it? He's a deacon in the Congregational Church.

CHERIE. [*Just because she happens to think of it.*] My folks was Holy Rollers. Will ya gimme a cup of coffee, please? Lotsa cream.

[*Elma draws a cup of coffee for her. Then Carl, the bus driver, comes in, followed by Grace. Carl is a hefty man, loud and hearty, who looks very natty in his uniform.*]

WILL. [*Calling to him from across the room.*] Howdy, Carl! You bring this wind?

CARL. [*Hollering back.*] No! It brought *me!*

[*This greeting probably has passed between them a dozen times, but they still relish it as new.*]

GRACE. Aren't you the comedian?

CARL. The wind is doin' ninety miles an hour. The bus is doin' twenty. What's *your* guess about the roads, Will?

WILL. They got the highway gang out. It may take a few hours.

CARL. Telephone lines down, too?

WILL. Yah. But they're workin' on 'em.

[*Dr. Lyman, having got his extremities warmed at the fire, seeks Carl privately to make certain clarifications.*]

DR. LYMAN. Driver, it seems to me we are still in the state of Kansas. Is that right?

CARL. What do ya mean, *still?* You been in the state of Kansas about a half-hour.

DR. LYMAN. But I don't understand. I was told, when I left Kansas City, that I would be across the state line immediately. And now I find . . .

CARL. [*Eying Dr. Lyman suspiciously.*] You was kinda anxious to get across that state line, too, wasn't you, Jack?

DR. LYMAN. [*Startled.*] Why . . . what ever do you mean?

CARL. Nothin'. Anyway, you're across the line now. In case you didn't know it, Kansas City is in *Missouri*.

DR. LYMAN. Are you joking?

CARL. There's a Kansas City, Kansas, too, but *you* got on in Kansas City, Missouri. That's the trouble with you easterners. You don't know anything about any of the country west of the Hudson River.

DR. LYMAN. Come, come now. Don't scold.

GRACE. [*As Carl gets out of his heavy coat.*] Carl, let me hang up your coat fer ya, while you get warm at the stove.

[*Dr. Lyman's eyes brighten when he sees Elma, and he bows before her like a cavalier.*]

DR. LYMAN. "Nymph, in thy orisons be all my sins remembered!"

ELMA. [*Smiling.*] I'm sorry your bus is held up.

DR. LYMAN. Oohh! Is that a nice way to greet me?

ELMA. [*Confused.*] I mean . . .

DR. LYMAN. After my loving greeting, all you can think of to say is, "I'm sorry your bus is held up." Well, I'm not. I would much rather sit here looking into the innocent blue of your eyes than continue riding on that monotonous bus.

ELMA. Don't you have to get somewhere?

DR. LYMAN. I have a ticket in my pocket to Denver, but I don't have to get there. I never have to get *any*where. I travel around from one town to another just to prove to myself that I'm *free*.

ELMA. The bus probably won't get into Denver for another day.

DR. LYMAN. Ah, well! What is our next stop?

ELMA. Topeka.

DR. LYMAN. Topeka? Oh, yes! that's where the famous hospital is, isn't it?

ELMA. The Menninger Clinic? Yes, it's a very famous place. Lots of movie stars go there for nervous breakdowns and things.

DR. LYMAN. [*Wryly.*] Does the town offer anything else in the way of diversion?

ELMA. It's the capital of Kansas. It's almost as big as Kansas City. They have a university and a museum, and sometimes symphony concerts and plays. I go over there every Sunday to visit my married sister.

DR. LYMAN. Aren't there any Indian tribes around here that have war dances?

ELMA. [*Laughing.*] No, silly! We're very civilized.

DR. LYMAN. I'll make my own judgment about that. Meanwhile, you may fix me a double shot of rye whiskey . . . on the rocks.

ELMA. I'm sorry, sir. We don't sell drinks.

DR. LYMAN. You don't sell drinks?

ELMA. Not intoxicating drinks. No, sir.

DR. LYMAN. Alas!

ELMA. We have fresh coffee, homemade pies and cakes, all kinds of sandwiches . . .

DR. LYMAN. No, my girl. You're not going to sober me up with your dainties. I am prepared for such emergencies. [*Draws a pint bottle of whiskey from his overcoat pocket.*] You may give me a bottle of your finest lemon soda.

ELMA. [*Whispering.*] You'd better not let Will see you do that. You're not supposed to.

DR. LYMAN. Who is *he*, the sheriff?

ELMA. Yes. Lots of people do spike their drinks here and we never say anything, but Will would have to make you stop if *he* saw you.

DR. LYMAN. I shall be *most* cautious. I promise.

[*She sets the bottle of soda before him as he smiles at her benignly. He pours some soda in a glass, then some whiskey, and ambles over to a table, far right, sitting down with his drink before him. Will moves over to Carl, who's at the end of the counter, chiding Grace, where the two of them have been standing, talking in very personal voices that can't be overheard.*]

WILL. I sure don't envy ya, Carl, drivin' in weather like this.

CARL. [*Making it sound like a personal observation.*] Yah! March is comin' in like a *lion*.

WILL. This all the passengers ya got?

CARL. There's a coupla crazy cowboys rolled up in the back seat, asleep. I thought I woke 'em, but I guess I didn't.

WILL. Shouldn't you go out and do it now?

CARL. I'd jest as soon they stayed where they're at. One of 'em's a real troublemaker. You know the kind, first time off a ranch and wild as a bronco. He's been on the make fer this li'l blonde down here . . . [*Indicates Cherie.*]

WILL. She was tellin' me.

CARL. I've had a good mind to put him off the bus, the way he's been actin'. I say, there's a time and place for ev'rything.

WILL. That bus may get snow-bound purty soon.

CARL. I'll go wake 'em in a minute, Will. Just lemme have a li'l *time* here. [*Will sizes up the situation as Carl returns his attention to Grace, then Will picks up a copy of the Kansas City* Star, *sitting down close to the fire to read.*] Ya know what, Grace? This is the first time you and I ever had more'n twenty minutes t'gether.

GRACE. [*Coyly.*] So what?

CARL. Oh, I dunno. I'll prob'ly be here mosta the night. It'd sure be nice to have a nice li'l apartment to go to, some place to sit and listen to the radio, with a good-lookin' woman . . . somethin' like you . . . to talk with . . . maybe have a few beers.

GRACE. That wouldn't be a hint or anything, would it?

CARL. [*Faking innocence.*] Why? Do you have an apartment like that, Grace?

GRACE. Yes, I do. But I never told *you* about it. Did that ornery Dobson fella tell you I had an apartment over the restaurant?

CARL. [*In a query.*] Dobson? Dobson? I can't seem to remember anyone named Dobson.

GRACE. You know him better'n *I* do. He comes through twice a week with the Southwest Bus. He told me you and him meet in Topeka sometimes and paint the town.

CARL. Dobson? Oh, yah, I know Dobson. Vern Dobson. A prince of a fella.

GRACE. Well, if he's been gabbin' to you about my apartment, I can tell ya he's oney been up there *once,* when he come in here with his hand cut, and I took him up there to bandage it. Now that's the oney time he was ever up there. On my word of honor.

CARL. Oh, Vern Dobson speaks very highly of you, Grace. Very highly.

GRACE. Well . . . he better. Now, what ya gonna have?

CARL. Make it a ham and cheese on rye.

GRACE. I'm sorry, Carl. We got no cheese.

CARL. What happened? Did the mice get it?

GRACE. None of your wise remarks.

CARL. O.K. Make it a ham on rye, then.

GRACE. [*At breadbox.*] I'm sorry, Carl, but we got no rye, either.

DR. LYMAN. [*Chiming in, from his table.*] I can vouch for that, sir. I just asked for rye, myself, and was refused.

CARL. Look, mister, don't ya think ya oughta lay off that stuff till ya get home and meet the missus?

DR. LYMAN. The *missus,* did you say? [*He laughs.*] I have no missus, sir. I'm *free.* I can travel the universe, with no one to await my arrival anywhere.

CARL. [*To Grace, bidding for a little sympathy.*] That's all I ever get on my bus, drunks and hoodlums.

GRACE. How's fer whole wheat, Carl?

CARL. O.K. Make it whole wheat.

DR. LYMAN. [*To Elma, as she brings him more soda.*] Yes, I am free. My third and last wife deserted me several years ago . . . for a ballplayer. [*He chuckles as though it were all a big absurdity.*]

ELMA. [*A little astounded.*] Your third?

DR. LYMAN. Yes, my third! Getting married is a careless habit I've fallen into. Sometime, really, I *must* give it all up. Oh, but she was pretty! Blonde, like the young lady over there. [*He indicates Cherie.*] And Southern, too, or pretended to be. However, she was kinder than the others when we parted. She didn't care about money. All she wanted was to find new marital bliss with her ballplayer, so I never had to pay her alimony . . . as if I could. [*He chuckles, sighs, and recalls another.*] My second wife was a different type entirely. But she was very pretty, too. I have always exercised the most excellent taste, if not the best judgment. She was a student of mine, when I was teaching at an eastern university. Alas! she sued me for divorce on the grounds that I was incontinent and always drunk. I didn't have a chance to resign from that position. [*Still he manages to chuckle about it.*]

CHERIE. [*From the counter.*] Hey! how much are them doughnuts? [*She is counting the coins in her purse.*]

ELMA. [*Leaving Dr. Lyman, hurrying back to counter.*] I'll make you a special price, two for a nickel.

CHERIE. O.K.

DR. LYMAN. [*Musingly, he begins to recite as though for his own enjoyment:*]

"That time of year thou may'st in me behold

When yellow leaves, or none, or few, do hang

Upon those boughs—"

CHERIE. [*Shivering, she goes to the stove.*] I never was so cold in my life.

ELMA. [*Setting the doughnuts before her.*] Do you honestly work in a night club?

CHERIE. [*Brightening with this recognition.*] Sure! I'm a *chanteuse*. I call m'self *Cherie*.

ELMA. That's French, isn't it?

CHERIE. I dunno. I jest seen the name once and it kinda appealed t'me.

ELMA. It's French. It means "dear one." Is that all the name you use?

CHERIE. Sure. Thass all the name ya need. Like Hildegarde. She's a *chanteuse*, too.

ELMA. *Chanteuse* means singer.

CHERIE. How come *you* know so much?

ELMA. I'm taking French in high school.

CHERIE. Oh! [*A reflective pause.*] I never got as far as high school. See, I was the oldest girl left in the fam'ly after my sister Violet ran away. I had two more sisters, both younger'n me, and five brothers, most of 'em older. Was they mean! Anyway, I had to quit school when I was twelve, to stay home and take care a the house and do the cookin'. I'm a real good cook. Honest!

ELMA. Did you *study* singing?

CHERIE. [*Shaking her head.*] Huh-uh. Jest picked it up listenin' to the radio, seein' movies, tryin' to put over my songs as good as them people did.

ELMA. How did you get started in the night club?

CHERIE. I won a amateur contest. Down in Joplin, Missouri. I won the second prize there . . . a coupla boys won *first* prize . . . they juggled milk bottles . . . I don't think that's fair, do you? To make an artistic performer compete with jugglers and knife-throwers and people like that?

ELMA. No, I don't.

CHERIE. Anyway, second prize was good enough to get me to Kanz City t'enter the contest there. It was a real *big* contest and I didn't win any prize at all, but it got me the job at the Blue Dragon.

ELMA. Is that where you're from, Joplin?

CHERIE. [*With an acceptance of nature's catastrophes.*] No. Joplin's a *big* town. I lived 'bout a hundred miles from there, in River Gulch, a li'l town in the Ozarks. I lived there till the floods come, three years ago this spring, and washed us all away.

ELMA. Gee, that's too bad.

CHERIE. I dunno where any a my folks are now, 'cept my baby sister Nan. We all just separated when the floods come and I took Nan into Joplin with me. She got a job as a waitress and I went to work in Liggett's drug store, till the amateur contest opened.

ELMA. It must be fun working in a night club.

CHERIE. [*A fleeting look of disillusionment comes over her face.*] Well . . . it ain't all roses.

CARL. [*Leaving Grace for the moment.*] You gonna be here a while, Will?

WILL. I reckon.

CARL. I'm gonna send them cowboys in here now, and leave *you* to look after 'em.

WILL. I'll do my best.

CARL. Tell ya somethin' else, Will. [*Carl looks at Dr. Lyman cautiously, as though he didn't want to be overheard by him, then moves very closely to Will and whispers something in his ear. Will looks very surprised.*]

WILL. I'll be jiggered.

CARL. So, ya better keep an eye on *him*, too. [*Starts off.*]

WILL. Ain't you comin' back, Carl?

CARL. [*Obviously he is faking, and a look between him and Grace tells us something is up between them. He winks at her and stretches.*] To tell the truth, Will, I git so darn *stiff*, sittin' at the wheel all day, I thought I'd go out fer a long walk.

WILL. In this blizzard? You gone crazy?

CARL. No. That's just the kinda fella I am, Will. I like to go fer long walks in the rain and snow. Freshens a fella up. Sometimes I walk fer hours.

WILL. Ya do?

CARL. Yah. Fer hours. That's just the kinda fella I am. [*He saunters out now, whistling to show his nonchalance.*]

WILL. [*To Grace.*] Imagine! Goin' out fer a walk, a night like this.

GRACE. Well, it's really very good for one, Will. It really is.

CHERIE. [*Leaning over counter to talk to Elma privately.*] He said he was gonna wake him up. Then he'll be in here pretty soon. You won't let on I said anything 'bout him, will ya?

ELMA. No. Cross my heart.

[*Dr. Lyman is suddenly reminded of another poem, which he begins to recite in full voice:*]

"Shall I compare thee to a sum-
    mer's day?
Thou art more lovely and more
    temperate:
Rough winds do shake the dar-
    ling buds of May,
And summer's lease hath all too
    short a date."

ELMA. [*Still behind counter, she
hears Dr. Lyman, smiles fondly, and
calls to him across room.*] Why, that's
one of my favorite sonnets.

DR. LYMAN. It is? Do *you* read
Shakespeare?

ELMA. I studied him at school, in
English class. I loved the sonnets. I
memorized some of them myself.

DR. LYMAN. [*Leaving table, returning to counter.*] I used to know them
all, by heart. And many of the plays I
could recite in their entirety. I often
did, for the entertainment and the annoyance of my friends.

[*He and Elma laugh together.*]

ELMA. Last fall I memorized the
Balcony Scene from *Romeo and Juliet*.
A boy in class played Romeo and we
presented it for convocation one day.

DR. LYMAN. Ah! I wish I had been
there to see.

[*Cherie feels called upon to explain
her own position in regard to Shakespeare, as Elma resumes work behind
counter.*]

CHERIE. Where I went to school, we
din read no Shakespeare till the ninth
grade. In the ninth grade everyone
read *Julius Caesar*. I oney got as far as
the eighth. I seen Marlon Brando in
the movie, though. I sure do like that
Marlon Brando.

DR. LYMAN. [*Now that Cherie has
called attention to herself.*] Madam,
where is thy Lochinvar?

CHERIE. [*Giggling.*] I don't understand anything you say, but I just love
the way you say it.

DR. LYMAN. And *I* . . . understand
*every*thing I say . . . but privately
despise the way I say it.

CHERIE. [*Giggling.*] That's so cute.
[*A memory returns.*] I had a very nice
friend once that recited poetry.

DR. LYMAN. [*With spoofing seriousness.*] Whatever could have happened
to him?

CHERIE. I dunno. He left town. His
name was Mr. Everett Brubaker. He
sold second-hand cars at the corner
of Eighth and Wyandotte. He had a
lovely Pontiac car-with-the-top-down.
He talked nice, but I guess he really
wasn't any nicer'n any of the others.

DR. LYMAN. The others?

CHERIE. Well . . . ya meet quite
a few men in the place I worked at,
the Blue Dragon night club, out by
the stockyards. Ever hear of it?

DR. LYMAN. No, and I deeply regret
the fact.

CHERIE. You're just sayin' that. An
educated man like you, you wouldn't
have no use fer the Blue Dragon.

DR. LYMAN. [*With a dubious look.*]
I wouldn't?

[*The front door swings open again
and the two cowboys, Bo Decker and
Virgil Blessing, enter. Their appearance now is rumpledly picturesque
and they both could pass, at first
glance, for outlaws. Bo is in his early
twenties, is tall and slim and good-
looking in an outdoors way. Now he
is very unkempt. He wears faded
jeans that cling to his legs like shedding skin; his boots, worn under his
jeans, are scuffed and dusty; and the
Stetson on the back of his head is
worn and tattered. Over a faded*

denim shirt he wears a shiny horse-hide jacket, and around his neck is tied a bandanna. Virgil is a man in his forties who seems to regard Bo in an almost parental way. A big man, corpulent and slow-moving, he seems almost an adjunct of Bo. Dressed similarly to Bo, perhaps a trifle more tidy, he carries a guitar in a case and keeps a bag of Bull Durham in his shirt pocket, out of which he rolls frequent cigarettes. Both men are still trying to wake up from their snooze, but Bo is quick to recognize Cherie. Neither cowboy has thought to shut the door behind them, and the others begin to shiver.]

BO. [*In a full voice, accustomed to speaking in an open field.*] Hey! Why din anyone wake us up? Virg'n I mighta froze out there.

GRACE. Hey! Shut the door.

BO. [*Calling across the room.*] Cherry! how come you get off the bus, 'thout lettin' me know? That any way to treat the man you're gonna marry?

WILL. [*Lifting his eyes from the paper.*] Shut the door, cowboy! [*Bo doesn't even hear Will, but strides across the room to Cherie, who is huddled over the counter as though hoping he might overlook her. Virgil, still rubbing sleep out of his eyes, lingers open-mouthed in the open doorway.*]

BO. Thass no way to treat a fella, Cherry, to slip off the bus like ya wanted to get rid of him, maybe. And come in here and eat by yourself. I thought we'd have a li'l snack t'*gether.* Sometimes, I don't understand you, Cherry.

CHERIE. Fer the hunderth time, my name ain't *Cherry.*

BO. I cain't say it the way you do. What's wrong with Cherry?

CHERIE. It's kinda embarrassin'.

WILL. [*In a firmer, louder voice.*] Cowboy, will you have the decency to shut that door! [*Virgil now responds immediately and quickly closes the door as Bo turns to Will.*]

BO. [*There is nothing to call him for the moment but insolent.*] Why, what's the matter with you, mister? You afraid of a little fresh air? [*Will glowers but Bo is not fazed.*] Why, man, ya oughta breathe real deep and git yor lungs full of it. Thass the trouble with you city people. You git soft.

VIRGIL. [*Whispering.*] He's the sheriff, Bo.

BO. [*In full voice, for Will's benefit.*] S'posin' he *is* the sheriff! What's that matter t'*me?* That don't give him the right t'insult my manners, does it? No man ever had to tell *me* what t'do, did he, Virge? Did he?

VIRGIL. No. No. But there allus comes a time, Bo, when . . .

BO. [*Ignoring Virgil, speaking out for the benefit of all.*] My name's Bo Decker. I'm twenty-one years old and own me m'own ranch up in Timber Hill, Montana, where I got a herd a fine Hereford cattle and a dozen horses, and the finest sheep and hogs and chickens anywhere in the country. And I jest come back from a rodeo where I won 'bout ev'ry prize there *was,* din I, Virge? [*Joshingly, he elbows Virgil in the ribs.*] Yap, I'm the prize bronco-buster, 'n steer-roper, 'n bulldogger, anywhere 'round. I won 'em all. And what's more, had my picture taken by *Life* magazine. [*Confronting Will.*] So I'd appreciate your talkin' to me with a little respect in yor voice, mister, and not go hollerin' orders to me from across the room like I was some no-'count servant. [*Will is flabbergasted.*]

CHERIE. [*Privately to Elma.*] Did ya ever see anybody like him?

WILL. [*Finally finds his voice and uses it, after a struggle with himself to sound just and impartial.*] You was the last one in, cowboy, and you left the door open. You shoulda closed it, I don't care *who* y'are. That's all I'm saying.

BO. Door's closed now. What ya arguin' 'bout? [*Leaving a hushed and somewhat awed audience, Bo strides over to the counter and drops to a stool.*] Seems like we're gonna be here a while, Virge. How's fer some grub?

VIRGIL. [*Remaining by magazine counter.*] Not yet, Bo. I'm chewin' t'backy.

BO. [*Slapping a thigh.*] Thass ole Virge for ya. Allus happy long's he's got a wad a t'backy in his mouth. Wall, I'm gonna have me a li'l snack. [*To Elma.*] Miss, gimme 'bout three hamburgers.

ELMA. Three? How do you want them?

BO. I want 'em *raw*.

[*Cherie makes a sick face. Dr. Lyman quietly withdraws, taking his drink over to the window.*]

ELMA. Honest?

BO. It's the only way t'eat 'em, raw, with a thick slice a onion and some piccalilli.

ELMA. [*Hesitant.*] Well . . . if you're sure you're not joking.

BO. [*His voice holding Elma on her way to refrigerator.*] Jest a minute, miss. That ain't all. I'd also like me some ham and eggs . . . and some potaty salad . . . and a piece a pie. I ain't so pertikler what *kinda*

pie it is, so long as it's got that murang on top of it.

ELMA. We have lemon and choc'-late. They both have meringue.

BO. [*Thinking it over.*] Lemon'n choc'late. I like 'em both. I dunno which I'd ruther have. [*Ponders a moment.*] I'll have 'em *both*, miss. [*Cherie makes another sick face.*]

ELMA. Both?

BO. Yep! 'N set a quart a milk beside me. I'm still a growin' boy. [*Elma starts preparations as Bo turns to Cherie.*] Travelin' allus picks up my appetite. That all you havin', jest a measly doughnut?

CHERIE. I ain't hungry.

BO. Why not?

CHERIE. I jest ain't.

BO. Ya oughta be.

CHERIE. Well—I ain't!

BO. Wait till I get ya up to the Susie-Q. I'll fatten ya up. I bet in two weeks' time, ya won't recognize yorself. [*Now he puts a bearlike arm around her, drawing her close to him for a snuggle, kissing her on the cheek.*] But doggone, I *love* ya, Cherry, jest the way ya are. Yor about the cutest li'l piece I ever did see. And, man! when I walked into that night club place and hear you singin' my favorite song, standin' before that orkester lookin' like a angel, I told myself then and there, she's fer *me*. I ain't gonna leave this place without her. And now I got ya, ain't I, Cherry?

CHERIE. [*Trying to avoid his embrace.*] Bo . . . there's people here . . . they're lookin' . . . [*And she's right. They are.*]

BO. What if they are? It's no crime to show a li'l affection, is it? 'Specially, when we're gonna git married. It's no crime I ever heard of. [*He squeezes*

her harder now and forces a loud,
smacking kiss on the lips. Cherie
twists loose of him and turns away.]

CHERIE. Bo! fer cryin' out loud,
lemme *be!*

BO. Cherry, thass no way to talk to
yor husband.

CHERIE. That's all ya done since we
left Kanz City, is maul me.

BO. Oh, is zat so? [*This is a deep-
cutting insult.*] Wall, I certainly ain't
one to *pester* any woman with my
affections. I never had to *beg* no
woman to make love to me. [*Calling
over his shoulder to Virgil.*] Did I,
Virge? I never had to coax no woman
to make love to me, *did* I?

VIRGIL. [*In a voice that sounds
more and more restrained.*] No . . .
no . . .

BO. [*Still in full voice.*] No! Ev'ry-
where I go, I got all the wimmin I
want, don't I, Virge? I gotta fight 'em
to keep 'em off me, don't I, Virge?

[*Virgil is saved from having to
make a response as Elma presents
Bo with his hamburgers.*]

ELMA. Here are the hamburgers.
The ham and eggs will take a little
longer.

BO. O.K. These'll gimme a start.

[*Grace rubs her forehead with a
feigned expression of pain.*]

GRACE. Elma, honey, I got the
darndest headache.

ELMA. I'm sorry, Grace.

GRACE. Can you look after things
awhile?

ELMA. Sure.

GRACE. 'Cause the only thing for
me to do is go upstairs and lie down
awhile. That's the only thing gonna
do me any good at all.

WILL. [*From his chair.*] What's the
matter, Grace?

GRACE. [*At the rear door.*] I got a
headache, Will, that's just drivin' me
wild.

WILL. That so?

[*Grace goes out.*]

DR. LYMAN. [*To Elma.*] You are
now the Mistress of the Inn.

ELMA. You haven't told me anything about your first wife.

DR. LYMAN. Now, how could I
have omitted her?

ELMA. What was *she* like?

DR. LYMAN. [*Still in the highest of
spirits.*] Oh . . . she was the loveliest of them all. I do believe she was.
We had such an idyllic honeymoon
together, a golden month of sunshine
and romance, in Bermuda. She sued
me for divorce later, on the grounds
of mental cruelty, and persuaded the
judge that she should have my house
and my motorcar, and an alimony
that I still find it difficult to pay, for
she never chose to marry again. She
found that for all she wanted out of
marriage, she didn't have to marry.
[*He chuckles.*] Ah, but perhaps I am
being unkind.

[*Elma is a little mystified by the
humor with which he always tells of
his difficulties. Bo now leans over the
counter and interrupts.*]

BO. Miss, was you waitin' fer me to
lay them eggs?

ELMA. [*Hurrying to stove.*] Oh, I'm
sorry. They're ready now.

[*Bo jumps up, grabs a plate and
glides over the counter for Elma to
serve him from the stove.*]

BO. Them hamburgers was just a
horse d'oovrey. [*He grins with appreciation of this word. Elma fills his
plate.*] Thank ya, miss. [*He starts back
for the stool but trips over Cherie's
suitcase on the way.*] Daggone! [*He*

looks down to see what has stopped him. Cherie holds a rigid silence. Bo brings his face slowly up, looking at Cherie suspiciously.] Cherry! [*She says nothing.*] Cherry, what'd ya wanta bring yor suitcase in here fer? [*She still says nothing.*] Cherry, I'm askin' ya a civil question. What'd ya bring yor suitcase in fer? *Tell* me?

CHERIE. [*Frightened.*] I . . . I . . . now don't you come near me, Bo.

BO. [*Shaking Cherie by the shoulders.*] Tell me! What's yor suitcase doin' there b'hind the counter? What were ya tryin' to do, *fool* me? Was you plannin' to git away from me? That what you been sittin' here plannin' t'do?

CHERIE. [*Finding it hard to speak while he is shaking her.*] Bo . . . lemme be . . . take your hands off me, Bo Decker.

BO. Tell me, Cherry. Tell me.

[*Now Will intercedes, coming up to Bo, laying a hand on his shoulder.*]

WILL. Leave the little lady alone, cowboy.

BO. [*Turning on Will fiercely.*] Mister, ya got no right interferin' 'tween me and my feeancy.

WILL. Mebbe she's yor feeancy and maybe she ain't. Anyway, ya ain't gonna abuse her while *I'm* here. Unnerstand?

BO. *Abuse* her?

WILL. [*To Cherie.*] I think you better tell him now, miss, jest how you feel about things.

[*Bo looks at Cherie with puzzled wonder.*]

CHERIE. [*Finding it impossible to say.*] I . . . I . . .

BO. What's this critter tryin' to say, Cherry?

CHERIE. Well . . . I . . .

WILL. You better tell him, miss.

CHERIE. Now, Bo, don't git mad.

BO. I'll git mad if I feel like it. What you two got planned?

CHERIE. Bo, I don't wanta go up to Montana and marry ya.

BO. Ya do too.

CHERIE. I do not!

BO. Anyways, you'll come to like it in time. I *promised* ya would. Now we been through all that b'fore.

CHERIE. But, Bo . . . I ain't goin'.

BO. [*A loud blast of protest.*] *What?*

CHERIE. I ain't goin'. The sheriff here said he'd help me. He ain't gonna let you take me any farther. I'm stayin' here and take the next bus back to Kanz City.

BO. [*Grabbing her by the shoulders to reassure himself of her.*] You ain't gonna do nothin' of the kind.

CHERIE. Yes, I am, Bo. You gotta b'lieve me. I ain't goin' with ya. That's final.

BO. [*In a most personal voice, baffled.*] But, Cherry . . . we was *familiar* with each other.

CHERIE. That don't mean ya gotta *marry* me.

BO. [*Shocked at her.*] Why . . . I oughta take you across my knee and blister yer li'l bottom.

CHERIE. [*More frightened.*] Don't you touch me.

BO. [*To Will.*] You cain't pay no tension to what she says, mister. Womenfolk don't know their own minds. Never did. [*Back to Cherie.*] CHERIE. Don't you come near me!

BO. Yor gonna follow me back to Timber Hill and marry up. You just think you wouldn't like it now 'cause ya never been there and the whole idea's kinda strange. But you'll get over them feelin's. In no time at all, yor gonna be happy as a mudhen. I ain't takin' *no* fer an answer. By God, yor comin' along.

[*He grabs her forcefully to him, as Will interferes again, pulling the two apart.*]

WILL. You're not takin' her with ya if she don't wanta go. Can't you get that through your skull? Now leave her be. [*Bo stands looking at Will with sullen hatred. Cherie trembles. Virgil stands far right, looking apprehensive.*]

BO. [*Confronts Will threateningly.*] This ain't no biznes of yors.

WILL. It's *my* business when the little lady comes t'me wantin' protection.

BO. Is that right, Cherry? Did you go to the sheriff askin' fer pertection?

CHERIE. [*Meekly.*] . . . yes, I guess I did.

BO. [*Bellowing out again.*] Why? What'd ya need pertection for . . . from a man that wants to *marry* ya?

CHERIE. [*Shuddering.*] . . . 'cause . . .

BO. [*Bellowing angrily.*] 'Cause why? I said I *loved* ya, din I?

CHERIE. [*About to cry.*] I know ya did.

BO. [*Confronting Will with a feeling of angry unjustness.*] See there? I told her I loved her and I wanta marry her. And with a world fulla crazy people goin' 'round killin' each other, *you* ain't got nothin' better t'do than stand here tryin' to keep me from it.

WILL. Yor overlookin' jest one thing, cowboy.

BO. [*With gruff impatience.*] Yor so smart. Tell me what I'm overlookin'.

WILL. Yor overlookin' the simple but important fack that the little lady don't love *you*.

[*Bo now is trapped into silence. He can say nothing, and one can tell that Will has named a fact that Bo did not intend to face. Virgil watches him alertly. He can tell that Bo is angry enough to attack Will and is about to. Virgil hurries to Bo's side, holding his arms as though to restrain him.*]

VIRGIL. [*Pacifyingly.*] Now, Bo. Take it easy, Bo. Don't blow your lid. He's the sheriff, Bo. Hold yor temper.

BO. [*To Virgil.*] That polecat bastard! He said she din love me.

VIRGIL. [*Trying to draw him away from the scene.*] Pay no 'tention, Bo. Come on over here and sit down. Ya gotta think things over, Bo.

BO. [*Twisting loose from Virgil's hold.*] Lemme be, Virge.

WILL. Ask the li'l lady, if ya don't b'lieve *me*. Ask her if she loves ya.

BO. I won't ask her nothin' of the kind.

WILL. All right then, take my word for it.

BO. I wouldn't take yor word for a cloudy day. I'm tellin' ya, she loves me. And *I* oughta know.

[*Cherie flees to the counter, sobbing.*]

WILL. Wall . . . she ain't gettin' back on the bus with ya. We'll leave it at that. So you better take my advice and sit down with yor friend there, and have a quiet game a pinochle till the bus gets on its way and takes you with it.

VIRGIL. Do like he tells ya, Bo. I think mebbe ya got the li'l lady all wrong, anyway.

BO. [*A defender of womanhood.*] Don't you say nothin' against her, Virge.

VIRGIL. I *ain't* sayin' nothin' *against* her. I jest see no reason why you should marry a gal that says she don't love ya. That's all. And I kinda doubt she's as good a gal as you think she is. Now come on over here and sit down.

BO. [*Turns restlessly from Virgil.*] I don't feel like sittin'. [*Instead, he paces up to the big window, standing there looking out, his back to the audience.*]

ELMA. [*From behind counter, to Virgil.*] What shall I do with the ham and eggs?

VIRGIL. Just put 'em on the stove and keep 'em warm, miss. He'll have 'em a li'l later.

WILL. [*To Cherie.*] I don't think you'll be bothered any more, miss. If y'are, my station's right across the road. You kin holler.

CHERIE. [*Dabbing at her eyes.*] Thank you very much, I'm sure.

WILL. Are you gonna be all right, Elma?

ELMA. [*Surprised at the question.*] Why yes, Will!

[*Will just looks at Dr. Lyman, who, we can tell, is made to feel a little uncomfortable.*]

WILL. I'll look in a little later.

ELMA. O.K., Will.

[*Will goes to the door, takes a final look at Bo, then goes out.*]

DR. LYMAN. I don't know why, but . . . I always seem to relax more easily . . . when a sheriff leaves the room.

[*He chuckles bravely.*]

ELMA. I think it's awfully unfair that people dislike Will just because he's a sheriff.

DR. LYMAN. But you see, my dear, he stands as a symbol of authority, the most dreaded figure of our time. Policemen, teachers, lawyers, judges, doctors, and I suppose, even tax collectors . . . we take it for granted that they are going to punish us for something we didn't do . . . or did do.

ELMA. But you said you were a teacher once.

DR. LYMAN. But not a successful one. I could never stay in one place very long at a time. And I hated having anyone *over* me, like deans and presidents and department heads. I never was a man who could take *orders* . . . from *any*one . . . without feeling resentment. Right or wrong, I have always insisted on having my own way.

[*Bo walks slowly down from his corner retreat, seeking Virgil, who is taking his guitar out of its case. Bo speaks hesitantly, in a low voice.*]

BO. What am I gonna do, Virge?

VIRGIL. Bo, ya jest gotta quit dependin' on me so much. I don't know what to tell ya to do, except to sit down and be peaceful.

BO. I—I can't be peaceful.

VIRGIL. All right then, pace around like a panther and be miserable.

BO. [*To himself.*] I—I jest can't believe it!

VIRGIL. *What* can't ya believe?

BO. [*Now he becomes embarrassed.*] Oh . . . nothin'.

VIRGIL. If ya got anything on your chest, Bo, it's best to get it off.

BO. Well, I . . . I just never realized . . . a gal might not . . . love me.

ACT TWO

[SCENE: *Only a few minutes have elapsed since the close of Act One. Our characters now are patiently trying to pass the time as best they can. Virgil has taken out his guitar and, after tuning it, begun to play a soft, melancholy cowboy ballad. He keeps his music an almost unnoticeable part of the background. Bo lingers in the corner up right, a picture of troubled dejection. Cherie has found a movie magazine, which she sets on one of the tables and reads. Dr. Lyman continues sitting at the bar, sipping his drink and courting Elma, although Elma does not realize she is being courted. She is immensely entertained by him.*]

ELMA. . . . And where else did you teach?

DR. LYMAN. My last position was at one of those revolting little progressive colleges in the East, where they offer a curriculum of what they call *functional* education. Educators, I am sure, have despaired of ever teaching students *any*thing, so they have decided the second-best thing to do is to *understand* them. Every day there would be a meeting of everyone on the entire faculty, with whom the students ever came into any contact, from the President down to the chambermaids, and we would put our collective heads together to try to figure out why little Jane or little Mary was not getting out of her classes what she *should*. The suggestion that perhaps she wasn't studying was too simple, and if you implied that she simply did not have the brains for a college education, you were being

undemocratic.

ELMA. You must have disapproved of that college.

DR. LYMAN. My dear girl, I have disapproved of my entire life.

ELMA. Really?

DR. LYMAN. Yes, but I suppose I couldn't resist living it over again.

[*There is a touch of sadness about him now.*]

ELMA. Did you resign from that position?

DR. LYMAN. One day I decided I had had enough. I walked blithely into the Dean's office and said, "Sir! I graduated *magna cum laude* from the University of Chicago, I studied at Oxford on a Rhodes Scholarship, and returned to take my Ph.D. at Harvard, receiving it with highest honors. I think I have the right to expect my students to try to understand *me*."

ELMA. [*Very amused.*] What did he say?

DR. LYMAN. Oh, I didn't wait for a response. I walked out of the door and went to the railroad station, where I got a ticket for the farthest place I could think of, which happened to be Las Vegas. And I have been traveling ever since. It's a merry way to go to pot. [*He chuckles.*]

ELMA. I had thought *I* might teach one day, but you don't make it sound very attractive.

DR. LYMAN. Ah, suit yourself. Don't let me influence you one way or the other. [*Elma smiles and Dr. Lyman gives in to the sudden compulsion of clasping her hand.*] You're a lovely young girl.

ELMA. [*Very surprised.*] Why . . . thank you, Dr. Lyman.

DR. LYMAN. [*Clears his throat and*

makes a fresh approach.] Did you tell me you plan to go to Topeka tomorrow?

ELMA. [*Looking at clock.*] You mean *today.* Yes. I have a ticket to hear the Kansas City Symphony. They come to Topeka every year to give a concert.

DR. LYMAN. [*Feeling his way.*] You say . . . you stay with your sister there?

ELMA. Yes, then I take an early morning bus back here, in time for school Monday. Then after school, I come here to work for Grace.

DR. LYMAN. [*Obviously he is angling for something.*] Didn't you say there was a university in Topeka?

ELMA. Yes. Washburn University.

DR. LYMAN. Washburn University —of course! You know, it just occurs to me that I should stop there to check some references on a piece of research I'm engaged on.

ELMA. Oh, I've been to Washburn library lots of times.

DR. LYMAN. You have? [*He shows some cunning, but obviously Elma does not see it.*] Perhaps you would take me there!

ELMA. [*Hesitant.*] Well, I . . .

DR. LYMAN. I'll arrive in Topeka before you do, then meet your bus . . .

ELMA. If you really want me to.

DR. LYMAN. You can take me to the library, then perhaps we could have dinner together, and perhaps you would permit me to take you to the symphony.

ELMA. [*Overjoyed.*] Are you serious?

DR. LYMAN. Why, of course I'm serious. Why do you ask?

ELMA. I don't know. Usually, older people are too busy to take notice of kids. I'd just love to.

DR. LYMAN. Then I may depend on it that I have an engagement?

ELMA. Yes. Oh, that'll be lots of fun. I can't wait.

DR. LYMAN. But, my dear . . . let's not tell anyone of our plans, shall we?

ELMA. Why not?

DR. LYMAN. You see . . . I have been married, and I am somewhat older than you, though perhaps not quite as old as you might take me to be . . . anyway, people might not understand.

ELMA. Oh!

DR. LYMAN. So let's keep our plans to ourselves. Promise?

ELMA. O.K. If you think best.

DR. LYMAN. I think it best.

[*Virgil has finished playing a ballad and Cherie applauds.*]

CHERIE. That was real purty, Virgil.

VIRGIL. Thank ya, miss.

[*From his corner, Bo has seen the moment's intimacy between them. He winces. Cherie goes over to the counter and speaks to Elma.*]

CHERIE. Isn't there some other way of me gettin' back to Kanz City?

ELMA. I'm sorry. The bus comes through here from Topeka, and it can't get through, either, until the road's cleared.

CHERIE. I was jest gettin' sorta restless.

[*She sits at center table and lights a cigarette. Suddenly, the front door swings open and Will appears, carrying a thermos jug.*]

WILL. [*Crossing to counter.*] Elma, fill this up for me, like a good girl.

ELMA. Sure, Will. [*Takes thermos from him and starts to fill it at urn.*]

WILL. I'm goin' down the highway a bit to see how the men are gettin' on. Thought they'd enjoy some hot coffee.

ELMA. Good idea, Will.

WILL. [*With a look around.*] Everyone behavin'?

ELMA. Of course.

WILL. [*Puzzled.*] Grace not down yet?

ELMA. No.

WILL. I didn't see Carl any place outside. Suppose somethin' coulda happened to him?

ELMA. I wouldn't worry about him, Will.

WILL. I s'pose he can take care of himself. [*Elma hands him thermos.*] Thank you, Elma. [*He pays her, then starts back out, saying for the benefit primarily of Bo and Dr. Lyman.*] Oh, Elma. If anyone should be wantin' me, I won't be gone very long.

[*He looks around to make sure everyone has heard him, then goes out. Bo has heard and seen him, and suddenly turns from his corner and comes angrily down to Virgil.*]

BO. That dang sheriff! If it wasn't fer *him*, I'd git Cherry now and . . . I . . .

VIRGIL. Where would ya take her, Bo?

BO. There's a justice a the peace down the street. You can see his sign from the window.

VIRGIL. Bo, ya cain't *force* a gal to marry ya. Ya jest cain't do it. That sheriff's a stern man and he'd shoot ya in a minute if he saw it was his duty. Now, why don't ya go over to the counter and have yourself a drink . . . like the perfessor?

BO. I never did drink and I ain't gonna let no woman drive me to it.

VIRGIL. Ya don't drink. Ya don't smoke or chew. Ya oughta have *some* bad habits to rely on when things with women go wrong.

[*Bo thinks for a moment then sits opposite Virge.*]

BO. Virge. I hate to sound like some pitiable weaklin' of a man, but there's been times the last few months, I been so lonesome, I . . . I jest didn't know what t'do with m'self.

VIRGIL. It's no disgrace to feel that way, Bo.

BO. How 'bout you, Virge? Don't you ever git lonesome, too?

VIRGIL. A long time ago, I gave up romancin' and decided I was just gonna take bein' lonesome for granted.

BO. I wish I could do that, but I cain't.

[*They now sit in silence. Cherie, at the counter, lifts her damp eyes to Elma, seeking a confidante.*]

CHERIE. Mebbe I'm a sap.

ELMA. Why do you say that?

CHERIE. I dunno why I *don't* go off to Montana and marry him. I might be a lot better off'n I am now.

ELMA. He says he *loves* you.

CHERIE. He dunno what love is.

ELMA. What makes you say that?

CHERIE. All he wants is a girl to throw his arms around and hug and kiss, that's all. The resta the time, he don't even know I exist.

ELMA. What made you decide to marry him in the first place?

CHERIE. [*Giving Elma a wise look.*] Ya ain't very experienced, are ya?

ELMA. I guess not.

CHERIE. I never *did* decide to marry him. Everything was goin' fine till he brought up *that* subjeck. Bo come in one night when I was singin' "That Ole Black Magic." It's one a my best numbers. And he liked it so much, he jumped up on a chair and yelled like a Indian, and put his fingers in his mouth and whistled like a steam engine. Natur'ly, it made me feel good. Most a the customers at the Blue Dragon was too drunk to pay any attention to my songs.

ELMA. And you liked him?

CHERIE. Well . . . I thought he was awful *cute*.

[*She shows a mischievous smile.*]

ELMA. I think he looks a little like Burt Lancaster, don't you?

CHERIE. Mebbe. Anyway . . . I'd never seen a cowboy before. Oh, I'd seen 'em in movies, a course, but never in the *flesh* . . . Anyway, he's so darn healthy-lookin', I don't mind admittin', I was attracted, right from the start.

ELMA. You were?

CHERIE. But it was only what ya might call a *sexual* attraction.

ELMA. Oh!

CHERIE. The very next mornin', he wakes up and hollers, "Yippee! We're gettin' married." I honestly thought he was crazy. But when I tried to reason with him, he wouldn't listen to a word. He stayed by my side all day long, like a shadow. At night, a course, he had to go back to the rodeo, but he was back to the Blue Dragon as soon as the rodeo was over, in time fer the midnight show. If any other fella claimed t'have a date with me, Bo'd beat him up.

ELMA. And you never told him you'd marry him?

CHERIE. No! He kep tellin' me all week, he and Virge'd be by the night the rodeo ended, and they'd pick me up and we'd all start back to Montana t'gether. I knew that if I was around the Blue Dragon that night, that's what'd happen. So I decided to beat it. One a the other girls at the Blue Dragon lived on a farm 'cross the river in Kansas. She said I could stay with her. So I went to the Blue Dragon last night and just sang fer the first show. Then I told 'em I was quittin' . . . I'd been wantin' to find another job anyway . . . and I picked up my share of the kitty . . . but darn it, I had to go and tell 'em I was takin' the midnight bus. They had to go and tell Bo, a course, when he come in a li'l after eleven. He paid 'em five dollars to find out. So I went down to the bus station and hadn't even got my ticket, when here come Bo and Virge. He just steps up to the ticket window and says, "Three tickets to Montana!" I din know what to say. Then he dragged me onto the bus and I been on it ever since. And somewhere deep down inside me, I gotta funny feelin' I'm gonna end up in Montana. [*She sits now in troubled contemplation as Elma resumes her work. On the other side of the stage, Bo, after a period of gestation, begins to question Virgil.*]

BO. Tell me somethin', Virge. We been t'gether since my folks died, and I allus wondered if mebbe I din spoil yer chances a settlin' down.

VIRGIL. [*Laughs.*] No, you never, Bo. I used to tell myself ya did, but I just wanted an excuse.

BO. But you been lookin' after me since I was ten.

VIRGIL. I coulda married up, too.

BO. Was ya ever in love?

VIRGIL. Oncet. B'fore I went to work on your daddy's ranch.

BO. What happened?

VIRGIL. Nuthin'.

BO. Ya ask her to marry ya?

VIRGIL. Nope.

BO. Why not?

VIRGIL. Well . . . there comes a time in every fella's life, Bo, when he's gotta give up his own ways . . .

BO. How ya mean?

VIRGIL. Well, I was allus kinda uncomfortable around this gal, 'cause she was sweet and kinda refined. I was allus scared I'd say or do somethin' wrong.

BO. I know how ya mean.

VIRGIL. It was cowardly of me, I s'pose, but ev'ry time I'd get back from courtin' her, and come back to the bunkhouse where my buddies was sittin' around talkin', or playin' cards, or listenin' to music, I'd jest relax and feel m'self so much at home, I din wanta give it up.

BO. Yah! Gals can scare a fella.

VIRGIL. Now I'm kinda ashamed.

BO. Y'are?

VIRGIL. Yes I am, Bo. A fella can't live his whole life dependin' on buddies.

[*Bo takes another reflective pause, then asks directly.*]

BO. Why don't she like me, Virge?

VIRGIL. [*Hesitant.*] Well . . .

BO. Tell me the truth.

VIRGIL. Mebbe ya don't go about it right.

BO. What do I do wrong?

VIRGIL. Sometimes ya sound a li'l bullheaded and mean.

BO. I do?

VIRGIL. Yah.

BO. How's a fella s'posed to act?

VIRGIL. I'm no authority, Bo, but it seems t'me you should be a little more gallant.

BO. Gall—? Gallant? I'm as gallant as I know how to be. You hear the way Hank and Orville talk at the ranch, when they get back from sojournin' in town, 'bout their women.

VIRGIL. They like to brag, Bo. Ya caint b'lieve ev'rything Hank and Orville say.

BO. Is there any reason a gal wouldn't go fer *me*, soon as she would fer Hank or Orville?

VIRGIL. They're a li'l older'n you. They learned a li'l more. They can be *gallant* with gals . . . when they *wanta* be.

BO. I ain't gonna *pertend*.

VIRGIL. I caint blame ya.

BO. But a gal *oughta* like me. I kin read and write, I'm kinda tidy, and I got good manners, don't I?

VIRGIL. I'm no judge, Bo. I'm used to ya.

BO. And I'm tall and strong. Ain't that what girls like? And if I do say so, m'self, I'm purty good-lookin'.

VIRGIL. Yah.

BO. When I get spruced up, I'm just as good-lookin' a fella as a gal might hope to see.

VIRGIL. I know ya are, Bo.

BO. [*Suddenly seized with anger at the injustice of it all.*] Then hellfire and damnation! Why don't she go back to the ranch with me? [*His hands in his hip pockets, he begins pacing, returning to his corner like a panther, where he stands with his back to the others, watching the snow fly outside the window.*]

ELMA. [*Having observed Bo's disquiet.*] Gee, if you only loved him!

CHERIE. That'd solve ev'rything, wouldn't it? But I don't. So I jest can't see m'self goin' to some God-forsaken ranch in Montana where I'd never see no one but him and a lotta cows.

ELMA. No. If you don't love him, it'd be awfully lonely.

CHERIE. I dunno why I keep expectin' m'self to fall in love with someone, but I do.

ELMA. I know *I* expect to, some day.

CHERIE. I'm beginnin' to seriously wonder if there *is* the kinda love I have in mind.

ELMA. What's that?

CHERIE. Well . . . I dunno. I'm oney nineteen, but I been goin' with guys since I was fourteen.

ELMA. [*Astounded.*] Honest?

CHERIE. Honey, I almost married a cousin a mine when I was fourteen, but Pappy wouldn't have it.

ELMA. I never heard of anyone marrying so young.

CHERIE. Down in the Ozarks, we don't waste much time. Anyway, I'm awful glad I never married my cousin Malcolm, 'cause he turned out real bad, like Pappy predicted. But I sure was crazy 'bout him at the time. And I been losin' my head 'bout some guy ever since. But Bo's the first one wanted to marry me, since Cousin Malcolm. And natur'ly, I'd like to get married and raise a fam'ly and all them things, but . . .

ELMA. But you've *never* been in love?

CHERIE. Mebbe I have and din know it. Thass what I mean. Mebbe I don't know what love is. Mebbe I'm expectin' it t'be somethin' it ain't. I jest feel that, regardless how crazy ya are 'bout some guy, ya gotta feel . . . and it's hard to put into words, but . . . ya gotta feel he *respects* ya. Yah, thass what I means.

ELMA. [*Not impudent.*] I should think so.

CHERIE. I want a guy I can look up to and respect, but I don't want one that'll browbeat me. And I want a guy who can be sweet to me but I don't wanta be treated like a baby. I . . . I just gotta feel that . . . whoever I marry . . . has some real regard for me, apart from all the lovin' and sex. Know what I mean?

ELMA. [*Busily digesting all this.*] I think so. What are you going to do when you get back to Kansas City?

CHERIE. I dunno— There's a hill-billy program on one a the radio stations there. I might git a job on it. If I don't, I'll prob'ly git me a job in Liggett's or Walgreen's. Then after a while, I'll prob'ly marry some guy, whether I think I love him or not. Who'm *I* to keep insistin' I should fall in love? You hear all about love when yor a kid and jest take it for granted that such a thing really exists. Maybe ya have to find out fer yorself it don't. Maybe everyone's afraid to tell ya.

ELMA. [*Glum.*] Maybe you're right . . . but I hope not.

CHERIE. [*After squirming a little on the stool.*] Gee, I hate to go out to that cold powder room, but I guess I better not put it off any longer.

[*Cherie hurries out the rear door as Dr. Lyman sits again at the counter, having returned from the book shelves in time to overhear the last of Cherie's conversation. He muses for a few moments, gloomily, then speaks to Elma out of his unconscious reflections.*]

DR. LYMAN. How defiantly we pursue love, like it was an inheritance due, that we had to wrangle about with angry relatives in order to get our share.

ELMA. You shouldn't complain. You've had three wives.

DR. LYMAN. Don't shame me. I loved them all . . . with passion. [*An afterthought.*] At least I *thought* I did . . . for a while. [*He still chuckles about it as though it were a great irony.*]

ELMA. I'm sorry if I sounded sarcastic, Dr. Lyman. I didn't mean to be.

DR. LYMAN. Don't apologize. I'm too egotistical ever to take offense at anything people *say.*

ELMA. You're not egotistical at all.

DR. LYMAN. Oh, believe me. The greatest egos are those which are too egotistical to show just how egotistical they are.

ELMA. I'm sort of idealistic about things. I like to think that people fall in love and stay that way, forever and ever.

DR. LYMAN. Maybe we have lost the ability. Maybe Man has passed the stage in his evolution wherein love is possible. Maybe life will continue to become so terrifyingly complex that man's anxiety about his mere survival will render him too miserly to give of himself in any true relation.

ELMA. You're talking over my head. *Any*one can fall in love, I always thought . . . and . . .

DR. LYMAN. But two people, *really* in love, must give up something of them*selves.*

ELMA. [*Trying to follow.*] Yes.

DR. LYMAN. That is the gift that men are afraid to make. Sometimes they keep it in their bosoms forever, where it withers and dies. Then they never know love, only its facsimiles, which they seek over and over again

in meaningless repetition.

ELMA. [*A little depressed.*] Gee! How did we get onto this subject?

DR. LYMAN. [*Laughs heartily with sudden release, grabbing Elma's hand.*] Ah, my dear! Pay no attention to me, for whether there is such a thing as love, we can always . . . [*Lifts his drink.*] . . . pretend there is. Let us talk instead of our forthcoming trip to Topeka. Will you wear your prettiest dress?

ELMA. Of course. If it turns out to be a nice day, I'll wear a new dress Mother got me for spring. It's a soft rose color with a little lace collar.

DR. LYMAN. Ah, you'll look lovely, *lovely.* I know you will. I hope it doesn't embarrass you for me to speak these endearments . . .

ELMA. No . . . it doesn't embarrass me.

DR. LYMAN. I'm glad. Just think of me as a fatherly old fool, will you? And not be troubled if I take such rapturous delight in your sweetness, and youth, and innocence? For these are qualities I seek to warm my heart as I seek a fire to warm my hands.

ELMA. Now I *am* kind of embarrassed. I don't know what to say.

DR. LYMAN. Then say nothing, or nudge *me* and I'll talk endlessly about the most trivial matters.

[*They laugh together as Cherie comes back in, shivering.*]

CHERIE. Brrr, it's cold. Virgil, I wish you'd play us another song. I think we all need somethin' to cheer us up.

VIRGIL. I'll make a deal with ya. I'll play if you'll sing.

ELMA. [*A bright idea comes to her.*] Let's have a floor show! [*Her suggestion comes as a surprise and*

there is silence while all consider it.]
Everyone here can do *some*thing!

DR. LYMAN. A brilliant idea, straight from Chaucer. You must read Juliet for me.

ELMA. [*Not hearing Dr. Lyman, running to Virgil.*] Will you play for us, Virgil?

VIRGIL. I don't play opery music or jitterbug.

ELMA. Just play anything you want to play. [*To Bo.*] Will you take part? [*Stubbornly, Bo just turns the other way.*] Please! It won't be fun unless we all do something.

VIRGIL. G'wan, Bo.

BO. I never was no play-actor, miss.

VIRGIL. Ya kin say the Gettysburg Address.

BO. [*Gruffly.*] I ain't gonna say it now.

VIRGIL. Then why don't ya do your rope tricks? Yer rope's out on the bus. I could get it for ya easy enough.

ELMA. Oh, please! Rope tricks would be lots of fun.

BO. [*Emphatically.*] No! I ain't gonna get up before a lotta strangers and make a fool a m'self.

VIRGIL. [*To Elma.*] I guess he means it, miss.

ELMA. Shucks!

VIRGIL. [*Quietly to Bo.*] I don't see why ya couldn't a co-operated a little, Bo.

BO. I got too much on my mind to worry about doin' stunts.

ELMA. [*To Cherie.*] You'll sing a song for us, won't you, Cherie?

CHERIE. I will fer a piece a pie and another cup a coffee.

ELMA. Sure.

[*Cherie hurries to Virgil.*]

CHERIE. Virgil, kin you play "That Ole Black Magic"?

VIRGIL. You start me out and I think I can pick out the chords.

[*Cherie sits by his side as they work out their number together. Elma hurries to Dr. Lyman.*]

ELMA. And you'll read poetry for us, won't you?

DR. LYMAN. [*Already assuming his character.*] Why, I intend to play Romeo opposite your Juliet.

ELMA. Gee, I don't know if I can remember the lines.

DR. LYMAN. [*Handing her a volume he has taken off the shelves.*] Sometimes one can find Shakespeare on these shelves among the many lurid novels of juvenile delinquents. Here it is, *Four Tragedies of Shakespeare*, with my compliments.

[*They begin to go over the scene together as Bo, resentful of the closeness between Cherie and Virgil, goes to them belligerently.*]

BO. [*To Cherie.*] Thass *my* seat.

ELMA. [*Taking book from Dr. Lyman.*] If I read it over a few times, it'll come back. Do you know the Balcony Scene?

CHERIE. [*Jumping to her feet.*] You kin have it. [*Hurries to Elma, at counter.*]

DR. LYMAN. My dear, I know the entire play by heart. I can recite it backwards.

CHERIE. [*To Elma.*] I got a costume with me. Where can I change?

ELMA. Behind the counter. There's a mirror over the sink.

[*Cherie darts behind the counter, digging into her suitcase.*]

BO. [*To Virgil.*] She shines up to *you* like a kitten to milk.

ELMA. Gee, costumes and everything. [*She resumes her study with Dr. Lyman.*]

VIRGIL. [*Trying to make a joke of it.*] Kin *I* help it if I'm so darn attractive to women? [*Unfortunately Bo cannot take this as a joke, as Virgil intended. Virgil perceives he is deeply hurt.*] Shucks, Bo, it don't mean nothin'.

BO. Maybe it don't mean nothin' to *you.*

VIRGIL. She was bein' nice to me cause I was playin' my guitar, Bo. Guitar music's kinda tender and girls seem to like it.

BO. Tender?

VIRGIL. Yah, Bo! Girls like things t'be *tender.*

BO. They do!

VIRGIL. Sure they do, Bo.

BO. A fella gets "tender," then someone comes along and makes a sap outa him.

VIRGIL. Sometimes, Bo, but not always. You just gotta take a chance.

BO. Well . . . I allus tried t'be a *decent* sorta fella, but I don't know if I'm *tender.*

VIRGIL. I think ya are, Bo. You know how ya feel about deer huntin'. Ya never could do it. Ya couldn't any more *shoot* one a them sweet li'l deers with the sad eyes than ya could jump into boilin' oil.

BO. Are you makin' fun of me?

VIRGIL. [*Impatient with him.*] No, I'm not makin' fun of ya, Bo. I'm just tryin' to show ya that *you* got a tender side to your nature, same as anyone else.

BO. I s'pose I do.

VIRGIL. A course ya do.

BO. [*With a sudden feeling of injustice.*] Then how come Cherry don't come over and talk sweet to *me,* like she does to *you?*

VIRGIL. Ya *got* a tender side, Bo, but ya don't know how to *show* it.

BO. [*Weighing the verdict.*] I don't!

VIRGIL. No, ya just don't know how.

BO. How does a person go about showin' his tender side, Virge?

VIRGIL. Well . . . I dunno as I can tell ya.

[*Elma comes over to them ready to start the show.*]

ELMA. Will you go first, Virgil?

VIRGIL. It's all right by me.

ELMA. O.K. Then I'll act as Master of the Ceremonies. [*Centerstage, to her audience.*] Ladies and Gentlemen! Grace's Diner tonight presents its gala floor show of celebrated artists from all over the world! [*Virgil plays an introductory chord.*] The first number on our show tonight is that musical cowboy, Mr. Virgil—[*She pauses and Virgil supplies her with his last name.*] —Virgil Blessing, who will entertain you with his guitar.

[*Applause. Elma retires to the back of the room with Dr. Lyman. Virgil begins to play. During his playing, Bo is drawn over to the counter, where he tries to further himself with Cherie, who is behind the counter, dressing.*]

BO. [*Innocently.*] I think you got me all wrong, Cherry.

CHERIE. Don't you come back here. I'm dressing.

BO. Cherry . . . I think you misjudged me.

CHERIE. Be quiet. The show's started.

BO. Cherry, I'm really a very *tender* person. You jest don't know. I'm so tender-hearted I don't go deer huntin'. 'Cause I jest couldn't kill them "sweet li'l deers with the sad eyes." Ask Virge.

CHERIE. I ain't int'rested.

BO. Ya ain't?

CHERIE. No. And furthermore I think you're a louse fer comin' over here and talkin' while yor friend is tryin' to play the guitar.

BO. Ya talk like ya thought more a Virge than ya do a me.

CHERIE. Would ya go away and lemme alone?

BO. [*A final resort.*] Cherry, did I tell ya 'bout my color-television set with the twenty-four-inch screen?

CHERIE. One million times! Now go 'way.

[*Elma begins to make a shushing noise to quiet Bo. Finally Bo dejectedly returns to the other side of the room, where Virgil is just finishing his number. Bo sits down in the midst of Virgil's applause.*]

CHERIE. That was wonderful, Virge!

DR. LYMAN. Brilliant!   } [*Together.*]

ELMA. Swell! Play us another!

VIRGIL. No more just now. I'm ready to see the rest of ya do somethin'.

BO. [*To Virgil.*] A lot *she* cares how tender I am!

ELMA. [*Coming forth again as Master of Ceremonies.*] That was swell, Virgil. [*Turns back to Dr. Lyman.*] Are you ready?

DR. LYMAN. [*Preening himself.*] I consider myself so.

ELMA. [*Taking the book to Virgil.*] Will you be our prompter?

VIRGIL. It's kinda funny writin', but I'll try.

ELMA. [*Back to Dr. Lyman.*] Gee, what'll we use for a balcony?

DR. LYMAN. That offers a problem.

[*Together they consider whether to use the counter for Elma to stand on or one of the tables.*]

BO. [*To Virgil.*] What is it these folks are gonna do, Virge?

VIRGIL. *Romeo and Juliet* . . . by Shakespeare!

BO. Shakespeare!

VIRGIL. This Romeo was a great lover, Bo. Watch him and pick up a few pointers.

[*Cherie comes running out from behind the counter now, a dressing gown over her costume, and she sits at one of the tables.*]

CHERIE. I'm ready.

BO. [*Reading some of the lines from Virgil's book.*] "But, soft . . . what light through . . . yonder window breaks? It is the east . . . and Juliet is the sun . . . Arise, fair . . ."

[*He has got this far only with difficulty, stumbling over most of the words. Virgil takes the book away from him now.*]

VIRGIL. Shh, Bo!

[*Elma comes forth to introduce the act.*]

ELMA. Ladies and gentlemen! you are about to witness a playing of the Balcony Scene from *Romeo and Juliet.* Dr. Gerald Lyman will portray the part of Romeo, and I'll play Juliet. My name is Elma Duckworth. The scene is the orchard of the Capulets' house in Verona, Italy. This table is supposed to be a balcony. [*Dr. Lyman helps her onto the table, where she stands, waiting for him to begin.*] O.K.? [*Dr. Lyman takes a quick reassuring drink from his bottle, then tucks it in his pocket, and comes forward in the great Romantic tradition. He is enjoying himself tremendously. The performance proves to be pure ham, but there is pathos in the fact that he does not seem to be aware of how bad he is. He is a thoroughly selfish performer, too, who reads all his speeches as though they were grand soliloquies, regarding his Juliet as a prop.*]

DR. LYMAN.

"He jests at scars, that never felt a wound.

But, soft! what light through yonder window breaks?

It is the east, and Juliet is the sun!

[*He tries to continue, but Elma, unmindful of cues and eager to begin her performance, reads her lines with compulsion.*]

Arise . . . fair sun, and . . . kill the envious. . . ."

ELMA. [*At same time as Dr. Lyman.*]

"O Romeo, Romeo! wherefore art thou, Romeo?

Deny thy father and refuse thy name:

Or if thou wilt not, be but sworn my love,

And I'll no longer be a Capulet."

DR. LYMAN.

"She speaks, yet she says nothing: what of that?

Her eye discourses; I will answer it.

I am too bold—"

BO. [*To Virgil.*] Bold? He's drunk.

VIRGIL. Ssssh!

DR. LYMAN.

". . . 'tis not to me she speaks:

Two of the fairest stars in all the heaven,

Having some business, do entreat her eyes

To twinkle in their spheres till they return."

ELMA.

"Ay me!"

DR. LYMAN.

"O! speak again, bright angel; for thou art

As glorious to this night, being o'er

my head,

As is a winged messenger of heaven

Unto the white-upturned . . ."

[*Dr. Lyman continues with this speech, even though Bo talks over him.*]

BO. I don't understand all them words, Virge.

VIRGE. It's *Romeo and Juliet*, for God's sake. Now will you shut up?

DR. LYMAN. [*Continuing uninterrupted.*]

". . . wondering eyes

Of mortals, that fall back to gaze on him

When he bestrides the lazy-pacing clouds,

And sails upon the bosom of the air."

[*He is getting weary but he is not yet ready to give up.*]

ELMA.

"'Tis but thy name that is my enemy;

Thou art thyself though, not a Montague.

What's Montague? it is nor hand, nor foot,

Nor arm, nor face, nor any other part

Belonging to a man. O! be some other name:

What's—"

DR. LYMAN. [*Interrupts. Beginning to falter now.*]

"I take thee at thy word.

Call me but love, and . . . I'll be new baptiz'd;

Henceforth . . . I never . . . will be Romeo."

[*It is as though he were finding suddenly a personal meaning in the lines.*]

ELMA.

"What man art thou, that, thus bescreen'd in night,

So stumblest on my counsel?"

DR. LYMAN. [*Beginning to feel that*

he cannot continue.]

"By a name
I know not how to tell thee . . . who
    I am:
My name, dear saint, is . . . is *hateful* to myself."
[*He stops here. For several moments
there is a wondering silence. Elma
signals Virgil.*]

VIRGIL. [*Prompting.*]
"Because it is an enemy to thee."

DR. LYMAN. [*Leaving the scene of
action, repeating the line dumbly,
making his way stumblingly back to
the counter.*]
"My name . . . is hateful . . . to
    myself . . ."
[*Elma hurries to Dr. Lyman's side.
Virgil grabs hold of Bo, pulls him
back to the floor and shames him.*]

ELMA. Dr. Lyman, what's the matter?

DR. LYMAN. My dear . . . let us
not continue this meaningless little
act!

ELMA. Did I do something wrong?

DR. LYMAN. You couldn't possibly
do anything wrong . . . if you tried.

ELMA. I can try to say the lines
differently.

DR. LYMAN. Don't. Don't. Just tell
your audience that Romeo suddenly
is fraught with remorse.
[*He drops to a stool, Elma remaining by him a few moments, uncertainly. Bo turns to Virgil.*]

BO. Virge, if thass the way to make
love . . . I'm gonna give up.

ELMA. [*To Virgil.*] I'm afraid he
isn't feeling well.

VIRGIL. [*To Elma.*] I tried to prompt
him.

ELMA. [*To herself.*] Well, we've
only got one more number. [*To
Cherie.*] Are you ready?

CHERIE. Sure.

ELMA. Ladies and gentlemen, our
next number is Mademoisell Cherie,
the international *chanteuse,* direct
from the Blue Dragon night club in
Kansas City, *Cherie!*
[*All applaud as Cherie comes forth,
Virgil playing an introduction for her.
Bo puts his fingers through his teeth
and whistles for her.*]

CHERIE. [*Takes off her robe, whispering to Elma.*] Remember, I don't
allow no table service during my
numbers.

ELMA. O.K.
[*In the background now, we can
observe that Dr. Lyman is drinking
heavily from the bottle in his overcoat
pocket. Cherie gets up on one of the
tables and begins singing "That Old
Black Magic" with a chord accompaniment from Virgil. Her rendition
of the song is a most dramatic one,
that would seem to have been created
from Cherie's observations of numerous torch singers. But she has appeal,
and if she is funny, she doesn't seem
to know it. Anyway, she rekindles Bo's
most fervent love, which he cannot
help expressing during her performance.*]

BO. [*About the middle of the song.*]
Ain't she beautiful, Virge?

VIRGIL. [*Trying to keep his mind
on his playing.*] Shh, Bo!

BO. I'm gonna git her, Virge.

VIRGIL. Ssshh!

BO. [*Pause. He pays no attention
to anyone.*] I made up my mind. I
told myself I was gonna git me a gal.
Thass the only reason I entered that
rodeo, and I ain't takin' no fer an
answer.

VIRGIL. Bo, will you hush up and
lemme be!

BO. Anything I ever wanted in this life I went out and got, and I ain't gonna stop now. I'm gonna git her.

[*Cherie is enraged. She jumps down from her table and slaps Bo stingingly on the face.*]

CHERIE. You ain't got the manners God gave a monkey.

BO. [*Stunned.*] Cherry!

CHERIE. . . . and if I was a man, I'd beat the livin' daylights out of ya, and thass what some man's gonna do some day, and when it happens, I hope I'm there to *see*.

[*She flounces back to her dressing room, as Bo gapes. By this time Dr. Lyman has drunk himself almost to insensibility, and we see him weaving back and forth on his stool, mumbling almost incoherently.*]

DR. LYMAN. "Romeo . . . Romeo . . . wherefore art thou? Wherefore art thou . . . Romeo?"

[*He laughs like a loon, falls off the stool and collapses on the floor. Elma and Virgil rush to him. Bo remains rooted, glaring at Cherie with puzzled hurt.*]

ELMA. [*Deeply concerned.*] Dr. Lyman! Dr. Lyman!

VIRGIL. The man's in a purty bad way. Let's get him on the bench.

[*Elma and Virgil manage to get Dr. Lyman to his feet as Bo glides across the room, scales the counter in a leap and takes Cherie in his arms.*]

BO. I was tellin' Virge I love ya. Ya got no right to come over and slap me.

CHERIE. [*Twisting.*] Lemme be.

BO. [*Picking her up.*] We're goin' down and wake up the justice of the peace and you're gonna marry me t'night.

CHERIE. [*As he takes her in his arms and transports her to the door, just as Elma and Virgil are helping Dr. Lyman onto the bench.*] Help! Virgil, help!

BO. Shut up! I'll make ya a good husband. Ya won't never have nothin' to be sorry about.

CHERIE. [*As she is carried to the door.*] Help! Sheriff! Help me, someone! Help me!

[*The action is now like that of a two-ringed circus for Elma and Virgil, whose attention suddenly is diverted from the plight of Dr. Lyman to the much noisier plight of Cherie. Bo gets her, kicking and protesting, as far as the front door when it suddenly opens and Bo finds himself confronted by Will.*]

WILL. Put her down, cowboy!

BO. [*Trying to forge ahead.*] Git outta my way.

WILL. [*Shoving Bo back as Cherie manages to jump loose from his arms.*] Yor gonna do as I say.

BO. I ain't gonna have no one interferin' in my ways.

[*He makes an immediate lunge at Will, which Will is prepared for, coming up with a fist that sends Bo back reeling.*]

VIRGIL. [*Hurrying to Bo's side.*] Bo, ya cain't do this, Bo. Ya cain't pick a fight with the sheriff.

BO. [*Slowly getting back to his feet.*] By God, mister, there ain't no man ever got the best a me, and there ain't no man ever gonna.

WILL. I'm ready and willin' to try, cowboy. Come on.

[*Bo lunges at him again. Will steps aside and lets Bo send his blow into the empty doorway as he propels himself through it, outside. Then Will follows him out, where the fight continues. Virgil immediately follows*]

them, *as Elma and Cherie hurry to
the window to watch.*]

CHERIE. I knowed this was gonna
happen. I knowed it all along.

ELMA. Gee! I'd better call Grace.
[*Starts for the rear door but Grace
comes through it before she gets there.
Grace happens to be wearing a dressing gown.*]

GRACE. Hey, what the hell's goin'
on?

ELMA. Oh, Grace, they're fighting.
Honest! It all happened so suddenly,
I . . .

GRACE. [*Hurrying to window.*] Let's
see.

CHERIE. [*Leaving the window, not
wanting to see any more, going to a
chair by one of the tables.*] Gee, I
never wanted to cause so much trouble t'anyone.

GRACE. Wow! Looks like Will's gettin' the best of him.

ELMA. [*At the window, frightened
by what she sees.*] Oh!

GRACE. Yap, I'll put my money on
Will Masters *any* time. Will's got it up
here. [*Points to her head.*] Lookit
that cowboy. He's green. He just
swings out wild.

ELMA. [*Leaving the window.*] I
. . . I don't want to watch any more.

GRACE. [*A real fight fan, she reports
from the window.*] God, I love a good
fight. C'mon Will—c'mon, Will—give
him the old uppercut. That'll do it
every time. Oh, oh, what'd I tell you,
the cowboy's down. Will's puttin'
handcuffs on him now.

[*Cherie sobs softly. Elma goes to
her.*]

ELMA. Will'll give him first aid. He
always does.

CHERIE. Well . . . you gotta admit. He had it comin'.

GRACE. [*Leaving the window now.*]
I'm glad they got it settled outside.
[*Looks around to see if anything needs
to be straightened up.*] Remember the
last time there was a fight in here, I
had to put in a new window.

[*She goes back up to her apartment,
and we become aware once more of
Dr. Lyman, who gets up from the
bench and weaves his way center.*]

DR. LYMAN. It takes strong men and
women to *love* . . . [*About to fall,
he grabs the back of a chair for support.*] People strong enough inside
themselves to love . . . without humiliation. [*He sighs heavily and looks
about him with blurred eyes.*] People big enough to *grow* with their love
and live inside a whole, wide new dimension. People brave enough to bear
the responsibility of *being* loved and
not fear it as a burden. [*He sighs
again and looks about him wearily.*]
I . . . I never had the generosity to
love, to give my own most private self
to another, for I was *weak*. I thought
the gift would somehow lessen *me*.
Me! [*He laughs wildly and starts for
the rear door.*] Romeo! Romeo! I am
disgusting! [*Elma hurries after him,
stopping him at the door.*]

ELMA. Dr. Lyman! Dr. Lyman!

DR. LYMAN. Don't bother, dear girl.
Don't ever bother with a foolish old
man like me.

ELMA. You're not a foolish old man.
I like you more than anyone I've ever
known.

DR. LYMAN. I'm flattered, my dear,
and pleased, but you're young. In a
few years, you will turn . . . from a
girl into a woman; a kind, thoughtful,
loving, intelligent woman . . . who
could only pity me. For I'm a child, a
drunken, unruly child, and I've noth-

ing in my heart for a true woman. [*Grace returns in time to observe the rest of the scene. She is dressed now.*]

ELMA. Let me get you something to make you feel better.

DR. LYMAN. No . . . no . . . I shall seek the icy comfort of the rest room. [*He rushes out the rear door.*]

GRACE. [*Feeling concern for Elma.*] Elma, honey, what's the matter? What was he sayin' to you, Elma?

[*Goes to her and they have a quiet talk between themselves as the action continues. Grace is quite motherly at these times. Now Virgil comes hurrying through the front door, going to Cherie.*]

VIRGIL. Miss, would ya help us? The sheriff says if you don't hold charges against Bo, he'll let him out to get back on the bus, if it ever goes.

CHERIE. So he can come back here and start maulin' me again?

VIRGIL. He won't do that no more, miss. I promise.

CHERIE. *You promise!* How 'bout him?

VIRGIL. I think you can trust him now.

CHERIE. Thass what I thought before. Nothin' doin'. He grabs ahold of a woman and kisses her . . . like he was Napoleon.

VIRGIL. [*Coming very close, to speak as intimately as possible.*] Miss . . . if he was to know I told ya this, he'd never forgive me, but . . . yor the first woman he ever made love to at all.

CHERIE. Hah! I sure don't b'lieve that.

VIRGIL. It's true, miss. He's allus been as shy as a rabbit.

CHERIE. [*In simple amazement.*] My God!

GRACE. [*To Elma.*] Just take my advice and don't meet him in Topeka or anywhere else.

ELMA. I won't, Grace, but honest! I don't think he meant any harm. He just drinks a little too much. [*Dr. Lyman returns now through the rear door. Elma hurries to him.*] Dr. Lyman, are you all right?

DR. LYMAN. [*On his way to the bench.*] I'm an old man, my dear. I feel very weary.

[*He stretches out on the bench, lying on his stomach. He goes almost immediately to sleep. Elma finds an old jacket and spreads it over his shoulders like a blanket. There is a long silence. Elma sits by Dr. Lyman attentively. Cherie is very preoccupied.*]

GRACE. Let him sleep it off. It's all you can do.

[*Now Carl comes in the rear door. There is a look of impatient disgust on his face, as though he had just witnessed some revolting insult. He casts a suspicious look at Dr. Lyman, now oblivious to everything, and turns to Grace.*]

CARL. Grace, fer Christ sake! who puked all over the backhouse?

GRACE. Oh, God!

[*Dr. Lyman snores serenely.*]

CHERIE. [*Jumps up suddenly and grabs Virgil's jacket off hook.*] Come on, Virge. Let's go.

VIRGIL. [*Enthused.*] I'm awful glad you're gonna help him, miss.

CHERIE. But if you're tellin' me a fib just to get him out of jail, I'll never forgive ya.

VIRGIL. It's no fib, miss. You're the first gal he ever made love to at all.

CHERIE. Well, I sure ain't never had that honor before.

[*They hurry out together.*]

ACT THREE

[SCENE: *By this time, it is early morning, about five o'clock. The storm has cleared, and outside the window we see the slow dawning, creeping above the distant hills, revealing a landscape all in peaceful white.*
Bo, Cherie and Virgil are back now from the sheriff's office. Bo has returned to his corner, where he sits as before, with his back to the others, his head low. We can detect, if we study him, that one eye is blackened and one of his hands is bandaged. Virgil sits close to him like an attendant. Dr. Lyman is still asleep on one of the benches, snoring loudly. Cherie tries to sleep at one of the tables. Elma is clearing the tables and sweeping. The only animated people right now are Carl and Grace. Carl is at the telephone, trying to get the operator, and Grace is behind the counter.]

CARL. [*After jiggling the receiver.*] Still dead. [*He hangs up.*]

GRACE. [*Yawns.*] I'll be glad when you all get out and I can go to bed. I'm tired.

CARL. [*Returning to counter, he sounds a trifle insinuating.*] Had enough of me, baby? [*Grace gives him a look, warning him not to let Elma overhear.*] I'm kinda glad the highway was blocked tonight.

GRACE. [*Coquettishly.*] Y'are?

CARL. Gave us a chance to become kinda acquainted, din it?

GRACE. Kinda!

CARL. Just pullin' in here three times a week, then pullin' out again in twenty minutes, I . . . I allus left . . . just wonderin' what you was like, Grace.

GRACE. I always wondered about *you*, too, Carl!

CARL. Ya did?

GRACE. Yah. But ya needn't go blabbing anything to the other drivers.

CARL. [*His honor offended.*] Why, what makes ya think I'd . . . ?

GRACE. Shoot! I know how you men talk when ya get t'gether. Worse'n women.

CARL. Well, not *me*, Grace.

GRACE. I certainly don't want the other drivers on this route, some of 'em especially, gettin' the idea I'm gonna serve 'em any more'n what they order over the counter.

CARL. Sure. I get ya. [*It occurs to him to feel flattered.*] But ya . . . ya kinda *liked* me . . . din ya, Grace?

GRACE. [*Coquettish again.*] Maybe I did.

CARL. [*Trying to get more of a commitment out of her.*] Yah? Yah?

GRACE. Know what I first liked about ya, Carl? It was your hands. [*She takes one of his hands and plays with it.*] I like a man with big hands.

CARL. You got *every*thing, baby.

[*For just a moment, one senses the animal heat in their fleeting attraction. Now Will comes stalking in through the front door, a man who is completely relaxed with the authority he possesses. He speaks to Grace.*]

WILL. One of the highway trucks just stopped by. They say it won't be very long now.

GRACE. I hope so.

WILL. [*With a look around.*] Everything peaceful?

GRACE. Yes, Will.

WILL. [*He studies Bo for a moment, then goes to him.*] Cowboy, if yor holdin' any grudges against *me*, I think ya oughta ask yourself what you'd a done in my *place*. I couldn't let ya carry off the li'l lady when she din wanta go, could I? [*Bo has no answer. He just avoids Will's eyes. But Will is determined to get an answer.*] Could I?

BO. I don't feel like talkin', mister.

WILL. Well, I couldn't. And I think you might also remember that this li'l lady . . . [*Cherie begins to stir.*] if she wanted to . . . could press charges and get you sent to the penitentiary for violation of the Mann Act.

BO. The *what* act?

WILL. The Mann Act. You took a woman over the state line against her will.

VIRGIL. That'd be a serious charge, Bo.

BO. [*Stands facing Will.*] I loved her.

WILL. That don't make any difference.

BO. A man's gotta right to the things he loves.

WILL. Not unless he deserves 'em, cowboy.

BO. I'm a hard-workin' man, I own me my own ranch, I got six thousand dollars in the bank.

WILL. A man don't deserve the things he loves, unless he kin be a little humble about gettin' 'em.

BO. I ain't gonna get down on my knees and *beg*.

WILL. Bein' humble ain't the same thing as bein' *wretched*. [*Bo doesn't understand.*] I had to learn that once, too, cowboy. I wasn't quite as old as you. I stole horses instead of women because you could *sell* horses. One day, I stole a horse off the wrong man, the Rev. Hezekiah Pearson. I never thought I'd get mine from any preacher, but he was very fair. Gave me every chance to put myself clear. But I wouldn't admit the horse was his. Finally, he did what he had to do. He thrashed me to within a inch of my life. I never forgot. 'Cause it was the first time in my life I had to admit I was wrong. I was miserable. Finally, after a few days, I decided the only thing to do was to admit to the man how I felt. Then I felt different about the whole thing. I joined his church, and we was bosom pals till he died a few years ago. [*He turns to Virgil.*] Has he done what I asked him to?

VIRGIL. Not yet, sheriff.

WILL. [*To Bo.*] Why should ya be so scared?

BO. Who says I'm scared?

WILL. Ya gimme yor word, didn't ya?

BO. [*Somewhat resentful.*] I'm gonna do it, if ya'll jest gimme time.

WILL. But I warn ya, it ain't gonna do no good unless you really mean it.

BO. I'll mean it.

WILL. All right then. Go ahead.

[*Slowly, reluctantly, Bo gets to his feet and awkwardly, like a guilty boy, makes his way over to the counter to Grace.*]

BO. Miss, I . . . I wanna apologize

GRACE. What for?

BO. Fer causin' such a commotion

GRACE. Ya needn't apologize to *me* cowboy. I like a good fight. You're wel come at Grace's Diner *any* time. mean *any* time.

BO. [*With an appreciative grin.* Thanks. [*Now he goes to Elma.*] musta acted like a hoodlum. I apolo gize.

ELMA. Oh, that's all right.

BO. Thank ya, miss.

ELMA. I'm awfully sorry we neve got to see your rope tricks.

BO. They ain't much. [*Pointing to the sleeping Dr. Lyman.*] Have I gotta wake up the perfessor t'apologize t'him?

WILL. You can overlook the perfessor.

[*He nods toward Cherie, whom Bo dreads to confront, most of all. He starts toward her but doesn't get very far.*]

BO. I cain't do it.

VIRGIL. [*Disappointed.*] Aw, Bo!

BO. I jest cain't do it.

WILL. Why not?

BO. She'd have no respeck for me now. She saw me beat.

WILL. You gave me your promise. You owe that girl an apology, whether you got beat or not, and you're going to say it to her or I'm not lettin' you back on the bus.

[*Bo is in a dilemma. He wipes his brow.*]

VIRGIL. G'wan, Bo. G'wan.

BO. Well . . . I . . . I'll try. [*He makes his way to her tortuously and finally gets out her name.*] Cherry!

CHERIE. Yah?

BO. Cherry . . . it wasn't right a me to treat ya the way I did, draggin' ya onto the bus, tryin' to make ya marry me whether ya wanted to or not. Ya think ya could ever forgive me?

CHERIE. [*After some consideration.*] I guess I been treated worse in my life.

BO. [*Taking out his wallet.*] Cherry . . . I *got* ya here and I think I oughta get ya back in good style. So . . . take this. [*He hands her a bill.*]

CHERIE. Did the sheriff make you do this?

BO. [*Angrily.*] No, by God! He din say nothin' 'bout my givin' ya money.

WILL. That's *his* idea, miss. But I think it's a good one.

CHERIE. Ya don't have to gimme this much, Bo.

BO. I want ya to have it.

CHERIE. Thanks. I can sure use it.

BO. And I . . . I wish ya good luck, Cherry . . . Honest I do.

CHERIE. I wish you the same, Bo.

BO. Well . . . I guess I said ev'rything that's to be said, so . . . so long.

CHERIE. [*In a tiny voice.*] So long.

[*Awkward and embarrassed now, Bo returns to his corner, and Cherie sits back down at the table, full of wistful wonder.*]

WILL. Now, that wasn't so bad, was it, son?

BO. I'd ruther break in wild horses than have to do it again. [*Will laughs heartily, then strolls over to the counter in a seemingly casual way.*]

WILL. How's your headache, Grace?

GRACE. Huh?

WILL. A while back, you said you had a headache.

GRACE. Oh, I feel fine now, Will.

WILL. [*He looks at Carl.*] You have a nice walk, Carl?

CARL. Yah. Sure.

WILL. Well, I think ya better go upstairs 'cause someone took your overshoes and left 'em outside the door to Grace's apartment.

[*Will laughs long and heartily, and Elma cannot suppress a grin. Carl looks at his feet and realizes his oversight. Grace is indignant.*]

GRACE. Nosy old snoop!

WILL. I'll have me a cup of coffee, Grace, and one a these sweet rolls. [*He selects a roll from the glass dish on counter.*]

VIRGIL. Come on over to the counter now, Bo, and have a bite a breakfast.

BO. I ain't hungry, Virge.

VIRGIL. Maybe a cup a coffee?

BO. I couldn't get it down.

VIRGIL. Now what's the matter, Bo? Ya oughta feel purty good. The sheriff let ya go and . . .

BO. I might as well a stayed in the jail.

VIRGIL. Now, what kinda talk is that? The bus'll be leavin' purty soon and we'll be back at the ranch in a coupla days.

BO. I don't care if I never see that dang ranch again.

VIRGIL. Why, Bo, you worked half yor life earnin' the money to build it up.

BO. It's the lonesomest damn place I ever did see.

VIRGIL. Well . . . I never thought so.

BO. It'll be like goin' back to a graveyard.

VIRGIL. Bo . . . I heard Hank and Orville talkin' 'bout the new school-marm, lives over to the Stebbins'. They say she's a looker.

BO. I ain't int'rested in no school-marm.

VIRGIL. Give yourself time, Bo. Yor young. You'll find lotsa gals, gals that'll love *you,* too.

BO. I want Cherry. [*And for the first time we observe he is capable of tears.*]

VIRGIL. [*With a futile shrug of his shoulders.*] Aw—Bo—

BO. [*Dismissing him.*] Go git yorself somethin' t'eat, Virge.

[*Bo remains in isolated gloom as Virgil makes his slow way to the counter. Suddenly the telephone rings. Grace jumps to answer it.*]

GRACE. My God! the lines are up. [*Into the telephone.*] Grace's Diner! [*Pause.*] It is? [*Pause.*] O.K. I'll tell

him. [*Hangs up and turns to Carl.*] Road's cleared now but you're gonna have to put on your chains 'cause the road's awful slick.

CARL. God damn! [*Gets up and hustles into his overcoat, going center to make his announcement.*] Road's clear, folks! Bus'll be ready to leave as soon as I get the chains on. That'll take about twenty minutes . . . [*Stops and looks back at them.*] . . . unless someone wants to help me.

[*Exits. Will gets up from the counter.*]

WILL. I'll help ya, Carl.

[*Exits. Cherie makes her way over to Bo.*]

CHERIE. Bo?

BO. Yah?

CHERIE. I just wanted to tell ya somethin', Bo. It's kinda personal and kinda embarrassin', too, but . . . I ain't the kinda gal you thought I was.

BO. What ya mean, Cherry?

CHERIE. Well, I guess some people'd say I led a real wicked life. I guess I have.

BO. What you tryin' to tell me?

CHERIE. Well . . . I figgered since ya found me at the Blue Dragon, ya just took it fer granted I'd had other boy friends 'fore you.

BO. Ya had?

CHERIE. Yes, Bo. Quite a few.

BO. Virge'd told me that, but I wouldn't b'lieve him.

CHERIE. Well, it's true. So ya see . . . I ain't the kinda gal ya want at all.

[*Bo is noncommittal. Cherie slips back to her table. Elma makes her way to the bench to rouse Dr. Lyman.*]

ELMA. Dr. Lyman! Dr. Lyman!

[*He comes to with a jump, staring out wildly about him.*]

DR. LYMAN. Where am I? [*Recognizing Elma.*] Oh, it's *you.* [*A great smile appears.*] Dear girl. What a sweet awakening!

ELMA. How do you feel?

DR. LYMAN. That's not a polite question. How long have I been asleep here?

ELMA. Oh—a couple of hours.

DR. LYMAN. Sometimes Nature blesses me with a total blackout. I seem to remember absolutely nothing after we started our performance. How were we?

ELMA. Marvelous.

DR. LYMAN. Oh, I'm glad. Now I'll have a cup of that coffee you were trying to force on me last night.

ELMA. All right. Can I fix you something to eat?

DR. LYMAN. No. Nothing to eat. [*He makes a face of repugnance.*]

ELMA. Oh, Dr. Lyman, you *must* eat something. Really.

DR. LYMAN. *Must* I?

ELMA. Oh, yes! Please!

DR. LYMAN. Very well, for your sweet sake, I'll have a couple of three-minute eggs, and some toast and orange juice. But I'm doing this for *you,* mind you. Just for you.

[*Elma slips behind the counter to begin his breakfast, as Virgil gets up from the counter and goes to Bo.*]

VIRGIL. I'll go help the driver with his chains, Bo. You stay here and take care a that hand.

[*He goes out. Bo finds his way again to Cherie.*]

BO. Cherry . . . would I be moestin' ya if I said somethin'?

CHERIE. No . . .

BO. Well . . . since you brought the subject up, you *are* the first gal I ever had anything to do with. [*There is a silence.*] By God! I never thought I'd hear m'self sayin' that, but I said it.

CHERIE. I never woulda guessed it, Bo.

BO. Ya see . . . I'd lived all my life on a ranch . . . and I guess I din know much about women . . . 'cause they're *diff'rent* from men.

CHERIE. Well, natur'ly.

BO. Every time I got around one . . . I began to feel kinda scared . . . and I din know how t'act. It was aggravatin'.

CHERIE. Ya wasn't scared with *me,* Bo.

BO. When I come into that night club place, you was singin' . . . and you smiled at me while you was singin', and winked at me a coupla times. Remember?

CHERIE. Yah. I remember.

BO. Well, I guess I'm kinda green, but . . . no gal ever done that to me before, so I thought you was singin' yor songs just fer *me.*

CHERIE. Ya did kinda attrack me, Bo . . .

BO. Anyway, you was so purty, and ya seemed so kinda warm-hearted and sweet. I . . . I felt like I *could* love ya . . . and I did.

CHERIE. Bo—ya think you really did love me?

BO. Why, Cherry! I couldn't be familiar . . . with a gal I din love.

[*Cherie is brought almost to tears. Neither she nor Bo can find any more words for the moment, and drift away from each other back to their respective places. Carl comes back in, followed by Virgil and Will. Carl has got his overshoes on now. He comes center again to make an announcement.*]

CARL. Bus headed west! All aboard! Next stop, Topeka!

[*He rejoins Grace at the counter and, taking a pencil from his pocket, begins making out his report. Will speaks to Bo.*]

WILL. How ya feelin' now, cowboy?

BO. I ain't the happiest critter that was ever born.

WILL. Just 'cause ya ain't happy now don't mean ya ain't gonna be happy t'morrow. Feel like shakin' hands now, cowboy?

BO. [*Hesitant.*] Well . . .

VIRGIL. Go on, Bo. He's only trying to be friends.

BO. [*Offering his hand, still somewhat reluctantly.*] I don't mind. [*They shake.*]

WILL. I just want you to remember there's no hard feelin's. So long.

BO. S'long.

WILL. I'm goin' home now, Grace. See you Monday.

GRACE. S'long, Will.

CARL. Thanks for helpin' me, Will. I'll be pullin' out, soon as I make out the reports.

WILL. [*Stops at the door and gives a final word to Cherie.*] Montana's not a bad place, miss. [*He goes out.*]

VIRGIL. Nice fella, Bo.

BO. [*Concentrating on Cherie.*] Maybe I'll think so some day.

VIRGIL. Well, maybe we better be boardin' the bus, Bo.

[*Without even hearing Virgil, Bo makes his way suddenly over to Cherie.*]

BO. Cherry!

CHERIE. Hi, Bo!

BO. Cherry, I promised not to molest ya, but if you was to give yor permission, it'd be all right. I . . . I'd like to kiss ya g'bye.

CHERIE. Ya would? [*Bo nods.*] I'd like ya to kiss me, Bo. I really would.

[*A wide grin cracks open his face and he becomes all hoodlum boy again, about to take her in his arms roughly as he did before, but she stops him.*] Bo! I think this time when ya kiss me, it oughta be diff'rent.

BO. [*Not sure what she means.*] Oh! [*He looks around at Virgil, who turns quickly away, as though admitting his inability to advise his buddy. Bo then takes her in his arms cautiously, as though holding a precious object that was still a little strange to him.*]

BO. Golly! When ya kiss someone fer serious, it's kinda scary, ain't it!

CHERIE. Yah! It is.

[*Anyway, he kisses her, long and tenderly.*]

GRACE. [*At the counter.*] It don' look like he was molestin' her now.

[*Bo, after the kiss is ended, is dazed. Uncertain of his feelings, he stampedes across the room to Virgil, drawing him to a bench where the two men can confer. The action continues with Dr. Lyman, at the counter, having his breakfast.*]

DR. LYMAN. I could tell you with all honesty that this was the most delicious breakfast I've ever eaten, but it wouldn't be much of a compliment because I have eaten very few breakfasts.

[*They laugh together.*]

ELMA. It's my favorite meal. [*Turns to the refrigerator as he brings bottle out secretly and spikes his coffee.*]

DR. LYMAN. [*When Elma returns.*] Dear girl, let us give up our little spree, shall we? You don't want to go traipsing over the streets of the state capital with an old reprobate like me.

ELMA. Whatever you say.

DR. LYMAN. I shall continue my way to Denver. I'm sure it's best.

ELMA. Anyway, I've certainly enjoyed knowing you.

DR. LYMAN. Thank you. Ah! sometimes it is so gratifying to feel that one is doing the "right" thing, I wonder that I don't choose to always.

ELMA. What do you mean?

DR. LYMAN. Oh, I was just rambling. You know, perhaps while I am in the vicinity of Topeka, I should drop in at that hospital and seek some advice.

ELMA. Sometimes their patients come in here. They look perfectly all right to me.

DR. LYMAN. [To himself.] Friends have been hinting for quite a while that I should get psychoanalyzed. [He chuckles.] I don't know if they had my best interests at heart or their own.

ELMA. Golly. I don't see anything the matter with you.

DR. LYMAN. [A little sadly.] No. Young people never do. [Now with a return of high spirits.] However, I don't think I care to be psychoanalyzed. I rather cherish myself as I am. [The cavalier again, he takes her hand.] Good-bye, my dear! You were the loveliest Juliet since Miss Jane Cowl.

[Kisses her hand gallantly, then goes for his coat. Elma comes from behind counter and follows him.]

ELMA. Thank you, Dr. Lyman. I feel it's been an honor to know you. You're the smartest man I've ever met.

DR. LYMAN. The smartest?

ELMA. Really you are.

DR. LYMAN. Oh, yes. I'm terribly smart. Wouldn't it have been nice . . to be intelligent?

[He chuckles, blows a kiss to her, then hurries out the door. Elma lingers behind, watching him get on the bus.]

CARL. [To Grace.] Hey, know what I heard about the perfessor? The detective at the bus terminal in Kanz City is a buddy of mine. He pointed out the perfessor to me before he got on the bus. Know what he said? He said the p'lice in Kanz City picked the perfessor up for loiterin' round the schools.

GRACE. [Appalled.] Honest?

CARL. Then they checked his record and found he'd been in trouble several times, for gettin' involved with young girls.

GRACE. My God! Did you tell Will?

CARL. Sure, I told him. They ain't got anything on the perfessor now, so there's nothin' Will could do. [Elma makes her way back to the counter now and hears the rest of what Carl has to say.] What gets me is why does he call hisself a doctor? Is he some kinda phony?

ELMA. No, Carl. He's a Doctor of Philosophy.

CARL. What's that?

ELMA. It's the very highest degree there is, for scholarship.

GRACE. Ya'd think he'd have philosophy enough to keep outa trouble.

[ELMA resumes her work behind the counter now.]

CARL. [To Grace.] Sorry to see me go, baby?

GRACE. No . . . I told ya, I'm tired.

CARL. [Good-naturedly.] Ya know, sometimes I get to thinkin', what the hell good is marriage, where ya have to put up with the same broad every day, and lookit her in the morning, and try to get along with her when she's got a bad disposition. This way suits me fine.

GRACE. I got no complaints, either. Incidentally, are you married, Carl?

CARL. Now, who said I was married,

Grace? Who said it? You just tell me and I'll fix him.

GRACE. Relax! Relax! See ya day after tomorrow. [*She winks at him.*]

CARL. [*Winks back.*] You might get surprised . . . what can happen in twenty minutes. [*Slaps Grace on the buttocks as a gesture of farewell.*] All aboard!

[*He hustles out the front door as Bo hurries to Cherie.*]

GRACE. [*To herself.*] He still never said whether he was married.

BO. Cherry?

CHERIE. [*A little expectantly.*] Yah?

BO. I been talkin' with my buddy, and he thinks I'm virgin enough fer the two of us.

CHERIE. [*Snickers, very amused.*] Honest? Did Virgil say that?

BO. Yah . . . and I like ya like ya are, Cherry. So I don't care how ya got that way.

CHERIE. [*Deeply touched.*] Oh God, thass the sweetest, tenderest thing that was ever said to me.

BO. [*Feeling awkward.*] Cherry . . . it's awful hard for a fella, after he's been turned down once, to git up enough guts to try again . . .

CHERIE. Ya don't need guts, Bo.

BO. [*Not quite sure what she means.*] I don't?

CHERIE. It's the last thing in the world ya need.

BO. Well . . . anyway, I jest don't have none now, so I'll . . . just have to say what I feel in my heart.

CHERIE. Yah?

BO. I still wish you was goin' back to the ranch with me, more'n anything I know.

CHERIE. Ya do?

BO. Yah. I do.

CHERIE. Why, I'd go anywhere in the world with ya now, Bo. Anywhere at all.

BO. Ya would? Ya would?

[*They have a fast embrace. All look.*]

GRACE. [*Nudging Elma.*] I knew this was gonna happen all the time.

ELMA. Gee, I didn't.

[*Now Bo and Cherie break apart, both running to opposite sides of the room, Bo to tell Virgil; Cherie, Elma.*]

BO. Hear that, Virge? Yahoo! We're gettin' married after all. Cherry's goin back with me.

CHERIE. [*At counter.*] Ain't it wonderful when someone so awful turns out t'be so nice? We're gettin' married. I'm goin' to Montana.

[*Carl sticks his head through the door and calls impatiently.*]

CARL. Hey! All aboard, fer Christ's sake!

[*Exits. Bo grabs Virgil now by the arm.*]

BO. C'mon, Virge, y'old raccoon!

VIRGIL. [*Demurring.*] Now look, Bo . . . listen t'me for a second.

BO. [*Who can't listen to anything in his high revelry. One arm is around Cherie, the other tugs at Virgil.*] C'mon! Doggone it, we wasted enough time. Let's git goin'.

VIRGIL. Listen, Bo. Now be quiet jest a minute. You gotta hear me, Bo. You don't need me no more. I ain't goin'.

BO. [*Not believing his ears.*] You ain't *what*?

VIRGIL. I . . . I ain't goin' with ya, Bo.

BO. [*Flabbergasted.*] Well, what ya know about that?

VIRGIL. It's best I don't, Bo.

BO. Jest one blame catastrophe after another.

VIRGIL. I . . . I got another job in mind, Bo. Where the feed's mighty good, and I'll be lookin' after the cattle. I meant to tell ya 'bout it 'fore this.

BO. Virge, I can't b'lieve you'd leave yor old sidekick. Yor jokin', man.

VIRGIL. No . . . I ain't jokin', Bo. I ain't.

BO. Well, I'll be a . . .

CHERIE. Virgil—I wish you'd come. I liked *you* . . . 'fore I ever liked Bo.

BO. Ya *know* Cherry likes ya, Virge. It jest don't make sense, yor not comin'.

VIRGIL. Well . . . I'm doin' the right thing. I know I am.

BO. Who's gonna look after the cattle?

VIRGIL. Hank. Every bit as good as *I* ever was.

BO. [*Very disheartened.*] Aw, Virge, I dunno why ya have to pull a stunt like this.

VIRGIL. You better hurry, Bo. That driver's not gonna wait all day.

BO. [*Starting to pull Virgil, to drag him away just as he tried once with Cherie.*] Daggone it, yor my buddy, and I ain't gonna let ya go. Yor goin' *with* Cherry and me cause we want ya . . .

VIRGIL. [*It's getting very hard for him to control his feelings.*] No . . . No . . . lemme be, Bo . . .

CHERIE. [*Holding Bo back.*] Bo . . . ya can't do it that way . . . ya jest can't . . . if he don't wanta go, ya can't make him . . .

BO. But, Cherry, there ain't a reason in the world he shouldn't go. It's plum crazy.

CHERIE. Well, sometimes people have their *own* reasons, Bo.

BO. Oh? [*He reconsiders.*] Well, I just hate to think of gettin' along with-

out old Virge.

VIRGIL. [*Laughing.*] In a couple weeks . . . ya'll never miss me.

BO. [*Disheartened.*] Aw, Virge!

VIRGIL. Get along with ya now.

CHERIE. Virgil—[*Brightly.*] Will ya come and visit us, Virgil?

VIRGIL. I'll be up in the summer.

BO. Where ya gonna be, Virge?

VIRGIL. I'll write ya th' address. Don't have time to give it to ya now. Nice place. Mighty nice. Now hurry and get on your bus.

[*Carl honks the horn.*]

BO. [*Managing a quick embrace.*] So long, old boy. So long!

VIRGIL. 'Bye, Bo! G'bye!

[*Now, to stave off any tears, Bo grabs Cherie's hand.*]

BO. C'mon, Cherry. Let's make it fast.

[*Before they are out the door, a thought occurs to Bo. He stops, takes off his leather jacket and helps Cherie into it. He has been gallant. Then he picks up her suitcase and they go out, calling their farewells behind them.*]

CHERIE. 'Bye—'bye—'bye, everyone! 'Bye!

[*Virgil stands at the door, waving good-bye. His eyes look a little moist. In a moment, the bus's motor is heard to start up. Then the bus leaves.*]

GRACE. [*From behind counter.*] Mister, we gotta close this place up now, if Elma and me're gonna get any rest. We won't be open again till eight o'clock, when the day girl comes on. The next bus through is to Albuquerque, at eight forty-five.

VIRGIL. Albuquerque? I guess that's as good a place as any.

[*He remains by the front entrance, looking out on the frosty morning. Elma and Grace continue their work*] *behind the counter.*]

ELMA. Poor Dr. Lyman!

GRACE. Say, did you hear what Carl told me about that guy?

ELMA. No. What was it, Grace?

GRACE. Well, according to Carl, they run him outa Kanz City.

ELMA. I don't believe it.

GRACE. Honey, Carl got it straight from the detective at the bus terminal.

ELMA. [*Afraid to ask.*] What . . . did Dr. Lyman do?

GRACE. Well, lots of old fogies like him just can't let young girls alone. [*A wondering look comes over Elma's face.*] So, it's a good thing you didn't meet him in Topeka.

ELMA. Do you think . . . he wanted to make *love,* to *me?*

GRACE. I don't think he meant to play hopscotch.

ELMA. [*Very moved.*] Gee!

GRACE. Next time any guy comes in here and starts gettin' fresh, you come tell your Aunt Grace.

ELMA. I guess I'm kinda stupid.

GRACE. Everyone has gotta learn. [*Looking into refrigerator.*] Now Monday, for sure, I gotta order some cheese.

ELMA. I'll remind you.

GRACE. [*Coming to Elma, apologetically.*] Elma, honey?

ELMA. Yes?

GRACE. I could kill Will Masters for sayin' anything about me and Carl. I didn't want you to know.

ELMA. I don't see why I shouldn't know, Grace. I don't wanta be a baby forever.

GRACE. Of course you don't. But still, you're a kid, and I don't wanta set no examples or anything. Do you think you can overlook it and not think bad of me?

ELMA. Sure, Grace.

GRACE. 'Cause I'm a restless sort of woman, and every once in a while, I gotta have me a man, just to keep m'self from gettin' grouchy.

ELMA. It's not my business, Grace. [*She stops a moment to consider herself in the mirror, rather pleased.*] Just think, he wanted to make love to *me.*

GRACE. Now don't start gettin' *stuck* on yourself.

ELMA. I'm not, Grace. But it's nice to know that someone *can* feel that way.

GRACE. You're not gonna have any trouble. Just wait'll you get to college and start meeting all those cute *boys* [*Grace seems to savor this.*]

ELMA. All right. I'll wait.

GRACE. You can run along now, honey. All I gotta do is empty the garbage.

ELMA. [*Getting her coat from closet behind counter.*] O.K.

GRACE. G'night!

ELMA. [*Coming from behind counter, slipping into her coat.*] Good night, Grace. See you Monday. [*Passing Virgil.*] It was very nice knowing you, Virgil, and I just loved your music.

VIRGIL. Thank you, miss. G'night.

[*Elma goes out.*]

GRACE. We're closing now, mister.

VIRGIL. [*Coming center.*] Any place warm I could stay till eight o'clock?

GRACE. Now that the p'lice station's closed, I don't know where you could go, unless ya wanted to take a chance of wakin' up the man that runs the hotel.

VIRGIL. No—I wouldn't wanta be any trouble.

GRACE. There'll be a bus to Kanz City in a few minutes. I'll put the sign out and they'll stop.

VIRGIL. No, thanks. No point a goin' back there.

GRACE. Then I'm sorry, mister, but you're just left out in the cold. [*She carries a can of garbage out the rear door, leaving Virgil for the moment alone.*]

VIRGIL. [*To himself.*] Well . . . that's what happens to some people. [*Quietly, he picks up his guitar and*

goes out. *Grace comes back in, locks the back door, snaps the wall switch, then yawns and stretches, then sees that the front door is locked. The sun outside is just high enough now to bring a dim light into the restaurant. Grace stops at the rear door and casts her eyes tiredly over the establishment. One senses her aloneness. She sighs, then goes out the door. The curtain comes down on an empty stage.*]

DISCUSSION OF *BUS STOP*

Three notable American playwrights emerged in the 1950s: Tennessee Williams, Arthur Miller, and William Inge. Of them, Williams is by far the most prolific, and Miller, mainly on the basis of one play, is probably the best thought of. However, William Inge has a distinction that neither of his contemporaries can boast of, for he has never had a failure on Broadway, and every one of his plays has been made into a highly lucrative film.

Despite commercial success of a high order, Inge has never, in his own mind, bowed down before commercialism. He takes the writing of plays with a high seriousness equaling that of Ibsen and Chekhov, and rather surpassing that of Shakespeare.[1] In the short Foreword to his collected plays, Inge tells us that "a good author insists on being accepted on his own terms" and that each of his four plays "contributed something to the theatre out of my life's experience." To this, add the testimony of Tennessee Williams, in his Preface to Inge's *The Dark at the Top of the Stairs*, that Inge had announced to him even before his first success, *Come Back, Little Sheba*, in fervent and sincere tones, "I want to be a playwright." It is, then, really as impossible to doubt Inge's dedication to his craft as it is to doubt his commercial success in it. Again, however, our problem is to avoid being swayed by either sincerity of intention or volume of bank account. Here we have a play to regard clearly and judiciously, and it is only the worth and integrity of the play itself that we have to pass on.

That does not, of course, mean that we must look only at the play itself. We may look, as we have all the way through this book, at the dramatic theories of people from Aristotle to Inge himself, and we may compare the play with others we have seen and read. As a matter of fact, Inge discusses his dramatic methods at some length in his Foreword. He says there that he is

[1] Shakespeare seems to have taken his playwriting rather casually. He thought his poems were important enough to publish, but he never really bothered about collecting his plays, as Ben Jonson did. His plays were not gathered together and published until two of his friends did it after his death.

against plays "that primarily tell a story." He is against plays that require the "audience to sit through two hours of plot construction . . . just to be rewarded by a big emotional 'pay-off' in the last act." He is against, in other words, the kind of play structure that we have seen earlier in this book, the Aristotelian tragic structure with its beginning, middle, and end, connected by causal and increasingly important incidents. He feels that this kind of structure is not true to life; it is a contrivance.

In place of this kind of structure, Inge is explicit about the kind he wants to use. "I like to keep several stories going at once," he says, and he wants us to see his plays not as narratives but as "compositions." He wants a structure in which all of the characters are equally important and in which each character depends for meaning on his being compared with all of the other characters. This, of course, is the structure of *The Three Sisters* and *The Plough and the Stars*, the structure of tragicomedy. In *Bus Stop*, Inge tells us, he did not think of the individual characters as very meaningful in themselves, but rather intended them to embody "a composite picture of the varying kinds of love." Elma is innocent, Cherie is amoral, the Professor is depraved, and so on. Inge is also proud that he could hold the audience's attention after Bo and Cherie left the stage. Further, Inge is conscious that he is dealing with "surfaces" in his plays. His dialogue is the speech of real life, like the dialogue of Chekhov and O'Casey, and he wants "whatever depths there are in my material" to "emerge unexpectedly," just as in life we discover truth unexpectedly. Inge, in other words, while he does not compare himself with Chekhov and O'Casey, is consciously using all the techniques we have discovered to be characteristic of tragicomedy—equally important characters, ironic juxtapositions of characters and of incidents, a surface realism from which the depth and intensity will emerge as if of their own accord, and a multiple plot structure. Inge's Foreword is helpful because it is a rare instance of a practicing playwright's talking about why he uses a certain structure and what he wants that structure to do.

But structure is only a part of the tragicomic method. The three instances of tragicomic structure that we have seen in brilliant plays are no indication that the structure cannot be misused as badly as either the tragic structure or the comic. The power of the tragicomic structure lies in its complex ironies, in its juxtapositions of tone, language, and characterization, and in its fusion of its diverse elements. Without its ironic complexity, the structure of tragicomedy would be flat and thin indeed.

As an example of the structure used badly, we refer you to the film scenario of *Stagecoach*, which was written by one of the best of screenwriters, Dudley Nichols, and which may be found in an anthology which Nichols edited with John Gassner, *Twenty Best Film Plays* (New York: Crown Publishers, 1943).

Stagecoach, produced in 1939 and directed by John Ford, was an enormously successful film. It is still revived fairly frequently, and is pretty exciting stuff if you like cowboys and Indians. In form, the film is a bad tragicomedy. A number of people of various backgrounds and characters are gathered for a journey by stagecoach. The frame of the film is the dangerous journey, and the inner actions are made up of the stories of the various passengers.

The situation is rather like the situation of *Bus Stop*. A number of people are gathered together for a journey, and we are shown how their characters conflict with and react upon each other. As a matter of fact, there are some close resemblances between some of Inge's characters and some of Nichols'. In both play and film, we have a cowboy and his girl. The girl in both instances is a dance hall girl with a mottled past. In the play we have a drunken, philosophical derelict of a professor, and in the film we have a drunken, philosophical derelict of a doctor. In both we have a wise sidekick, and in both we have a sheriff intent on upholding law and order, a sheriff who is both stern and ultimately human. In both play and film, we have more than one love story, but also in both the love story of the cowboy and the girl comes to take up most of the attention.

On the page, without the helpful distraction of warwhoops, rifle shots, and horses' hooves, the scenario of *Stagecoach* reads like thin stuff, indeed. To indicate just how simple and banal the story is, when compared to either Chekhov or O'Casey, consider the death scene of one of the central characters, Hatfield the gambler. Hatfield has been a particularly sinister individual. He acts with great Southern Chivalry toward the Lady, but he is obviously a man with a lurid past, a man whose real name is not Hatfield, a man who is the black sheep of some noble old Southern family. After the Indian attack, the Ringo Kid sees that Hatfield is wounded:

> [*Hatfield sits slumped, his back against the opposite door. He lifts his head with an effort and tries to smile. He looks up at Lucy and she leans down close to him pityingly. They are seen close together as Lucy bends over his gaunt face. It is an effort for him to speak, but he manages it.*]
>
> HATFIELD. If you ever see Judge Ashburn—[*Fighting for breath.*]—tell him his son died—[*Attempting his old sardonic smile as he whispers.*]—shall we say, better than he lived?
>
> [*And as he slumps forward, the scene fades out.*]

This is an example of the "theatrical death." You may see it better done in Edmond Rostand's *Cyrano de Bergerac*. You may see it more poorly done in the death of Hatfield's twin brother, Oakhurst the gambler, in Bret Harte's story *The Outcasts of Poker Flat*. We are rather foolishly fond of it because it is so bad, but we are not tricked into comparing it with a serious and meaningful representation of death, such as we may see happening to King Lear or to Bessie Burgess.

We have quoted this rather lengthy example from a bad tragicomedy, so that you could compare it with the excellent tragicomedies that you have read, and also so that you would be able to fit William Inge's *Bus Stop* somewhere along this continuum of the excellent to the absurd.

If *Bus Stop* may be compared to the bad tragicomedy *Stagecoach*, you must not forget that it may be compared to the good tragicomedies, *The Three*

Sisters and *The Plough and the Stars.* No matter whether a tragicomedy is good or bad, the same tools of criticism may be applied to determine its worth. This means, then, that your attention may be closely directed to the structure, the characterization, the language, and the use of the chorus, if any, in *Bus Stop.* If you find that Inge has handled these matters as well as Chekhov and O'Casey, then you may be sure that you have read an excellent play.

DISCUSSION QUESTIONS ON *BUS STOP*

1. The storm in *Bus Stop* is the dramatic device by which Inge traps his characters in the little Kansas cafe. When the characters have worked out their separate and joint destinies, then Inge lifts the storm, clears the road, and allows them to leave. The storm is a plausible enough device, for storms do occur, and busses do get held over. We have, however, seen one other storm, in Shakespeare's *King Lear.* Does Shakespeare make a greater dramatic use of his storm than Inge does of his? Does Shakespeare's storm comment upon the action? Does it reflect anything other than bad weather? Is it a symbol? Can the same be said of Inge's storm? Does one storm seem an integral and necessary part of the play, and the other a conventional gimmick? If so, why?

2. Inge says that he is against "two hours of plot construction . . . rewarded by a big emotional 'pay-off' in the last act." Which incidents in *Bus Stop* involve the greatest emotional intensity? Do these occur in an order of increasing intensity, or are they scattered about higgledy-piggledy? Or, is every moment in the play of approximately equal intensity; is the play fairly level, and all of a piece?

3. Is there an over-all mood or tone to the play? Is it mainly light-hearted, gay, and comic? Somber? Serious? Bitter-sweet? Or is it a kaleidoscopic succession of different moods?

4. A merit of both *The Three Sisters* and *The Plough and the Stars* is that a diversity of topics are dramatized in both plays, and that all of these topics are finally harmoniously fused into a central theme. List the various individual actions in both plays, and then in a word or two decide what main topic each action is about. You may find this difficult, for both plays discuss many topics: love, death, religion, politics, economics, idealism, patriotism, duty, and so on.

Now list each of the inner actions in *Bus Stop.* Inge said that he meant the play to give "a composite picture of the varying kinds of love," and he listed some of the different kinds: amorality, earthiness, depravity, innocence. Which actions depict which kinds? Are any of these kinds depicted in *The Three Sisters* and in *The Plough and the Stars?* Is Inge's composite picture all-inclusive? That is, are there any other kinds of love that he might have included? Are any other kinds of love shown in the Chekhov and O'Casey plays? Are Inge's kinds of love—amorality, earthiness, depravity, and innocence—simpler or more complicated than the kinds in the other two tragicomedies?

Are any other topics other than love dramatized in *Bus Stop?* Is the relative simplicity of *Bus Stop* a dramatic virtue or a weakness? Does it, for example, use as much of the tragicomic potentiality as the other two plays?

5. How much connection is there between the three pairs of lovers in the play? Does Bo mainly talk to Cherie, or does he talk significantly with Elma and Grace? Does Dr. Lyman talk significantly with Cherie or with Grace? Does Carl make any meaningful statements about love to either Cherie or to Elma?

Consider how, in *The Plough and the Stars*, Fluther and Bessie Burgess have scenes with practically all of the main characters. Do Bo or Cherie or Virgil or Dr. Lyman have as much to do with the rest of the characters in *Bus Stop* as Fluther and Bessie do with the other characters in *The Plough?*

6. Consider the constant rearrangement of characters in *The Three Sisters*: how they pair off, and then how they all join together in an ensemble scene. Do you find such alignments and realignments in *Bus Stop?*

Do the onstage characters in *Bus Stop* pay as much or as little attention to each other as the onstage characters do in the ensemble scenes of *The Three Sisters?* Are the silent characters in *Bus Stop* given any significant action as are the silent characters in *The Three Sisters?* For example, Dr. Lyman is often seen drinking. Does his drinking develop the whole plot as much as Natasha's crossing the stage with the candle, or Andrey's pushing the baby carriage? Or does Dr. Lyman's drinking only have reference to himself?

Compare Act II of *The Plough* with its constantly shifting alignments of characters to Act II of *Bus Stop*. Which is more intricately constructed? And if intricacy is the essence of tragicomedy, we may then ask the next logical question: which act, O'Casey's or Inge's, is the more dramatically effective?

7. In which of the three pairs of lovers are the partners most ironically contrasted? That is, which partners are the most different from each other? Why is there this difference? What is Inge trying to show?

8. We have seen Chekhov and O'Casey both relying upon literary allusions. In *Bus Stop*, we have one allusion that nobody could miss, the recital of the balcony scene from *Romeo and Juliet*. What does this scene traditionally convey to an audience? Is Inge relying upon the traditional meaning of the scene?

As Dr. Lyman was an English professor, it is plausible that he would remember and might want to recite the scene, but is there any irony in his reciting this particular scene? If there is, is it a simple and obvious irony, or a complex and sneaky one? Is there any way that Inge makes sure that the irony is not lost upon the audience? How about the manner of Dr. Lyman's recital? Is this subtle of Inge, or is it merely underlining the obvious?

9. Are there other literary allusions in the play? Are there as many as in Chekhov and O'Casey? Why, or why not?

10. The Sheriff stands for conventional law and order, and for the standards of society. How much does he approve of the love of Bo and Cherie? How much does he approve of Dr. Lyman and Elma? How much of Grace and Carl? Is the Sheriff's view meant to be the view of the audience? Do we discover any values in these degrees of love that the Sheriff does not? Does Inge

make it clear how much we are to approve of the Sheriff and his views?

11. We have quite noticeably an ensemble scene in the entertainment that the passengers devise for themselves in Act II. Is this scene as integrated as any of the ensemble scenes in Chekhov and O'Casey, or is it only a succession of unconnected episodes?

12. The Grace and Carl story is the one that gets the least attention and development; therefore, it is probably the least important to the audience. Would it have been better if Inge had put them onstage more? What does their story tell us? What does it mean? How important is it? Would a great deal be lost if it were omitted?

The character of Pan, which we have used as a symbol of the tragicomic spirit, seems quite evident in Fluther and Rosie, as they go off at the end of Act II of *The Plough and the Stars*. They go off merrily roistering and boisterously singing. Contrast their love affair with that of Grace and Carl. Is there the same wild, panic spirit in both, or does the Grace and Carl story lack some of the liveliness and joy of Fluther and Rosie?

13. Guarini said that tragicomedy should stop short of the extremes of tragedy and comedy. Does *Bus Stop* satisfy Guarini's dictum? Is there anything in it approaching the tragedy of Bessie Burgess or Baron Toozenbach? Anything approaching the comedy of Fluther or of Vershinin and Masha?

14. Compare Chebutykin with Dr. Lyman. How are they similar in character? How are they similar in what they mean to the play? Which is developed more? Which is the more painful to see? Which is more memorable?

15. One indication of the stock character is that you know immediately what he is like and exactly what he will do. The difference, for instance, between the "adult" western of today and the Saturday matinee western of yesteryear is that the hero of today wears a black hat, rides a black horse, sports a black mustache, drinks, and kisses girls; while the hero of yesteryear wore a white hat, rode a white horse, and eschewed drinks, girls, and mustaches. Perhaps this is an indication of the decline of the race, but at any rate one can still recognize a cattle rustler. He is wicked, and the only other thing that can be said of him is that he is evil.

He never changes from being evil; he is predictably evil. That is, besides rustling cattle, we know that, if given the opportunity, he will kick his dog, spur his horse, and spit. Consider now the characters of *Bus Stop*. Does Will ever act in a way that is out of character with our conception of him as the wise sheriff? Does he ever do anything unpredictable? Does Bo ever act in a way that changes our initial conception of him as the likable, but dumb cowpoke? Does Virgil ever act in a way that changes our conception of him as the wise drifter? Does Virgil, for instance, ever do anything to make us dislike him? Does Elma ever act in a way that shows she is more than a picture of likable innocence? Does she ever do anything to show us that she is different from thousands of other girls of her age?

In other words, are these characters as solid and three-dimensional as most of the characters of Chekhov and O'Casey?

16. We have seen that one of the prime necessities of the tragicomedies of Chekhov and O'Casey was a brilliantly fluent and multileveled irony of language. Can you find many examples of such language in Inge? If you notice a difference, may it be attributed solely to the fact that Inge's people are, for the most part, stupider than Chekhov's and O'Casey's? Is Cherie stupider than Nora? Is Bo stupider than Clitheroe? Is Grace stupider than Mrs. Gogan? Is anybody stupider than the Covey and Peter?

Does the difference, then, lie in a kind of native fluency of speech that Irishmen are born with, and a native tongue-tiedness that all American middle-westerners have? Here it might be well to do some background reading in, for instance, Davy Crockett, Mark Twain, and Will Rogers.

17. Chekhov and O'Casey both used many kinds of music and noise: chuckles, grunts, guffaws, songs, gun shots, offstage voices, and so on. Make a list of similar devices in *Bus Stop*. Are there about as many? Are they used in the same way? Does Inge get as much irony out of them as Chekhov and O'Casey do?

18. *Bus Stop* contains one epigram, and it is said by Dr. Lyman. He says, "Oh, yes. I'm terribly smart. Wouldn't it have been nice . . . to be intelligent?" Is this a well-turned epigram? What is the difference between "smart" and "intelligent"? Would it have been a better epigram if Dr. Lyman had said "wise" instead of "intelligent"?

19. Who are the really "wise" characters in the play? What are the wise speeches in the play? If any of Inge's characters rise, as Chekhov's and O'Casey's frequently do, to eloquence, we might expect them to do so in the "wise" speeches. Let us examine one such speech. At the beginning of Act III, Will has a speech on humility:

> WILL. Bein' humble ain't the same thing as bein' *wretched*. . . . I had to learn that once, too, cowboy. I wasn't quite as old as you. I stole horses instead of women because you could *sell* horses. One day, I stole a horse off the wrong man, the Rev. Hezekiah Pearson. I never thought I'd get mine from any preacher, but he was very fair. Gave me every chance to put myself clear. But I wouldn't admit the horse was his. Finally, he did what he had to do. He thrashed me to within a inch of my life. . . . I had to admit I was wrong. I was miserable. Finally, after a few days, I decided the only thing to do was to admit to the man how I felt. Then I felt different about the whole thing. I joined his church, and we was bosom pals till he died a few years ago.

This should be a convincing speech, for it has some dramatic point in Bo's growth to maturity and humility. Is the speech aptly turned and effectively phrased. Does it contain irony, either intended by Will or by Inge? Is it a straightforward parable? Is its language as simple as that of the best parables in the Bible, in Aesop, or in Bunyan? Is there any eloquent and memorable statement in it? Anything that might find its way into *Bartlett's Familiar Quotations?*

How clear is it? What does "mine" in the sixth sentence refer to? Would an actor, by the inflection of his voice, have to make this sentence clear, or is it clear enough? Why are *wretched* and *sell* italicized? Italics usually infuse more meaning into words than they normally contain. How, then, would the actor have to say these words?

By italicizing *sell*, Inge points up a joke that Will has made. What is the joke? Is it good or bad? Does Will make other jokes? Do you look forward to the jokes in the play? Why or why not?

Do you find hackneyed phrases or clichés in the speech? Many? How much does the speech depend upon them? How effective are clichés, usually? How can they be more effective? (Case in point, O'Casey's "Keep the Home Fires Burning.") Are Inge's clichés effective? Why or why not?

In the last sentence, how strong an ending does "till he died a few years ago" provide? Does it end the speech on a high note or let it dribble off?

20. Will's speech is one of the few long speeches in the play. In fact, it is the only speech of more than two or three lines in the whole third act. Would this overwhelming preponderance of short speeches keep Inge's characters from eloquence?

Notice some of the typical speeches in Act III. For instance, immediately following Will's speech, we get this exchange:

WILL. Has he done what I asked him to?
VIRGIL. Not yet, sheriff.
WILL. [*To Bo.*] Why should ya be so scared?
BO. Who says I'm scared?
WILL. Ya gimme yor word, didn't ya?
BO. [*Somewhat resentful.*] I'm gonna do it, if ya'll jest gimme time.
WILL. But I warn ya, it ain't gonna do no good unless you really mean it.
BO. I'll mean it.
WILL. All right then. Go ahead.

Judge this dialogue by the qualities that Eric Bentley found in Ibsen's realistic dialogue. How many of Bentley's criteria of good realistic dialogue does this fulfill? In other words, how good is Inge's dialogue?

Some Books and Articles About the Drama

As there is no end to making lists, we have limited this one to a few outstanding works.

General

Bentley, Eric. *The Playwright as Thinker*. New York: Reynal and Hitchcock, 1946.

Clark, Barrett H. (ed.). *European Theories of the Drama*, rev. ed. New York: Crown, 1947.

Fergusson, Francis. *The Idea of a Theatre*. Garden City, N.Y.: Doubleday (Anchor Books), 1953.

Gassner, John. *Masters of the Drama*. New York: Dover, 1945.

Hartnoll, Phyllis (ed.). *Oxford Companion to the Theatre*, 2nd ed., rev. London: Oxford University Press, 1957.

Nicoll, Allardyce. *The Theory of the Drama*. New York: Crowell, 1931.

Smith, James Harry, and Edd Winfield Parks. *The Great Critics: An Anthology of Literary Criticism*, 3rd ed., rev. New York: Norton, 1951.

Vowles, Richard B. *Dramatic Theory: A Bibliography*. New York: New York Public Library, 1956.

Tragedy

Henn, Thomas R. *The Harvest of Tragedy*. London: Methuen, 1956.

Lucas, F. L. *Tragedy; Serious Drama in Relation to Aristotle's Poetics*, rev. and enl. ed. London: Hogarth, 1957.

Murray, Gilbert. *The Classical Tradition in Poetry*. New York: Vintage, 1957.

Muller, Herbert J. *The Spirit of Tragedy*. New York: Knopf, 1956.

Steiner, George. *The Death of Tragedy*. New York: Knopf, 1961.

Comedy

Bergson, Henri. "Laughter," in *Comedy*, ed. by Wylie Sypher. Garden City, N. Y.: Doubleday (Anchor Books), 1956.

Freud, Sigmund. "Wit and Its Relation to the Unconscious," trans. by A. A. Brill; in *Basic Writings of Sigmund Freud*. New York: Modern Library, 1938.

Meredith, George. "An Essay on Comedy," in *Comedy,* ed. by Wylie Sypher. Garden City, N. Y.: Doubleday (Anchor Books), 1956.

Potts, L. J. *Comedy.* London: Hutchinson University Library, 1949.

Wimsatt, W. K., Jr. "The Criticism of Comedy," in *English Stage Comedy: English Institute Essays, 1954.* New York: Columbia University Press, 1955.

Tragicomedy

Guarini, Giambattista. *Il Pastor Fido e Il Compendio Della Poesia Tragicomica.* Bari, Italy: Gius. Laterza and Figli, 1914. A partial translation under the title of "The Compendium of Tragicomic Poetry" is made by Allan H. Gilbert in his anthology *Literary Criticism: Plato to Dryden* (New York: American Book Co., 1940).

Herrick, Marvin Theodore. *Tragicomedy: Its Origin and Development in Italy, France and England.* Urbana, Ill.: University of Illinois Press, 1955.

Ristine, F. H. *English Tragicomedy, Its Origin and History.* New York: Columbia University Press, 1910.

Waith, Eugene M. *The Pattern of Tragicomedy in Beaumont and Fletcher.* New Haven: Yale University Press, 1952.

Individual Authors

Chekhov, Anton (1860–1904)

The Selected Letters of Anton Chekhov. ed. by Lillian Hellman, trans. by Sidonie Lederer. New York: Farrar, Straus, 1955.

Hingley, Ronald. *Chekhov; a Biographical and Critical Study.* London: George Allen and Unwin, 1950.

Magarshack, David. *Chekhov the Dramatist.* New York: Auvergne, 1952.

———. *Chekhov: A Life.* New York: Grove, 1953.

Gorky, Maxim, pseud. of Aleksiei Maximovich Pieshkov (1868–1936)

Roskin, Aleksander Iosifovich. *From the Banks of the Volga; the Life of Maxim Gorky.* trans. by D. L. Fromberg. New York: Philosophical Library, 1946.

Inge, William (1913–)

Brustein, Robert. "The Men-taming Women of William Inge." *Harper's Magazine.* 217:1302 (Nov. 1958), 52–57.

James, Henry (1843–1916)

Edel, Leon, ed. *The Complete Plays of Henry James.* Philadelphia and New York: J. B. Lippincott, 1949.

James, Henry. *The Scenic Art: Notes on Acting and the Drama, 1872–1901.* ed. by Allan Wade. New Brunswick: Rutgers University Press, 1948.

Levy, Leo B. *Versions of Melodrama: A Study of the Fiction and Drama of Henry James, 1865–1897.* Berkeley and Los Angeles: University of California Press, 1957.

Jonson, Ben (1573–1637)

Barish, Jonas A. *Ben Jonson and the Language of Prose Comedy.* Cambridge, Mass.: Harvard University Press, 1961.

Chute, Marchette. *Ben Jonson of Westminster*. New York: Dutton, 1953.

Enck, John J. *Jonson and the Comic Truth*. Madison, Wis.: The University of Wisconsin Press, 1957.

Heffner, Ray L. "Unifying Symbols in the Comedy of Ben Jonson." *English Stage Comedy: English Institute Essays, 1954*. New York: Columbia University Press, 1955. Pp. 74–97.

Partridge, Edward B. *The Broken Compass: A Study of the Major Comedies of Ben Jonson*. New York: Columbia University Press, 1958.

Lorca, Federico García (1899–1936)

Barea, Arturo. *Lorca: The Poet and His People*. New York: Harcourt, Brace, 1949.

Campbell, Roy. *Lorca: An Appreciation of His Poetry*. New Haven: Yale University Press, 1959.

Honig, Edwin. *Garcia Lorca*. Norfolk, Conn.: New Directions, 1944.

Molière, pseud. of Jean-Baptiste Poquelin (1622–1673)

Fernandez, Ramon. *Molière: The Man Seen through His Plays*. trans. by Wilson Follett. New York: Hill and Wang, 1958.

Moore, W. G. *Molière: A New Criticism*. Oxford: Clarendon, 1949.

Nelson, Robert J. "The Unreconstructed Heroes of Molière." *Tulane Drama Review*. IV:3 (March 1960), 14–37.

O'Casey, Sean (1880–)

Coston, Herbert. "Sean O'Casey: Prelude to Playwriting." *Tulane Drama Review*. V:1 (Autumn, 1960), 102–112.

Hogan, Robert. *The Experiments of Sean O'Casey*. New York: St. Martin's, 1960.

Krause, David. *Sean O'Casey: The Man and His Work*. New York: Macmillan, 1960.

O'Casey, Sean. *Feathers from the Green Crow*. Columbia, Mo.: University of Missouri Press, 1962.

———. *The Green Crow*. New York: Braziller, 1956.

Shaw, George Bernard (1856–1950)

Bentley, Eric. *Bernard Shaw*, rev. ed. Norfolk, Conn.: New Directions, 1957.

Chesterton, G. K. *George Bernard Shaw*. New York: Hill and Wang, 1956.

Henderson, Archibald. *George Bernard Shaw: Man of the Century*. New York: Appleton-Century-Crofts, 1956.

Shakespeare, William (1564–1616)

Bradley, A. C. *Shakespearean Tragedy*. New York: Macmillan, 1949.

Dean, Leonard, ed. *Shakespeare: Modern Essays in Criticism*. New York: Oxford University Press, 1957.

Granville-Barker, Harley. *Preface to Shakespeare*. Vol. I. Princeton, N. J.: Princeton University Press, 1947.

Heilman, Robert B. *This Great Stage: Image and Structure in "King Lear."* Baton Rouge: Louisiana State University Press, 1948.

Sophocles (ca. 496–406 B.C.)

Bowra, C. M. *Sophoclean Tragedy*. New York: Oxford University Press, 1944.

Goheen, Robert F. *The Imagery of Sophocles' "Antigone."* Princeton, N. J.: Princeton University Press, 1951.

Kitto, H. D. F. *Greek Tragedy.* Garden City, N. Y.: Doubleday, 1955.

Waldock, A. J. A. *Sophocles the Dramatist.* London: Cambridge University Press, 1951.

INDEX

INDEX